ISBN 978-0-260-74595-8
PIBN 10939476

FB &c Ltd, Dalton House, 60 Windsor Avenue, London, SW19 2RR.
Company number 08720141. Registered in England and Wales.

For support please visit www.forgottenbooks.com

HEARINGS

U. S. Congress. House.

HELD BEFORE THE SPECIAL COMMITTEE ON THE

INVESTIGATION OF THE AMERICAN SUGAR REFINING CO. AND OTHERS

ON

DECEMBER 5, 6, 7, 8, 9, 1911, AND
JANUARY 9, 10, 11, 12, 13, 15, 16, 1912

HOUSE OF REPRESENTATIVES

VOL. 4

WASHINGTON
GOVERNMENT PRINTING OFFICE
1912

SPECIAL COMMITTEE ON THE INVESTIGATION OF THE AMERICAN SUGAR REFINING CO. AND OTHERS.

HOUSE OF REPRESENTATIVES.

THOMAS W. HARDWICK, *Chairman*.

FINIS J. GARRETT.
WILLIAM SULZER.
JOHN E. RAKER.
H. M. JACOWAY, Jr.
GEORGE R. MALBY.
J. W. FORDNEY.
A. C. HINDS

AMERICAN SUGAR REFINING CO. AND OTHERS.

SPECIAL COMMITTEE ON THE INVESTIGATION
OF THE AMERICAN SUGAR REFINING CO. AND OTHERS,
HOUSE OF REPRESENTATIVES,
Washington, D. C., December 5, 1911.

The committee met at 10 o'clock a. m., Hon. Thomas W. Hardwick (chairman) presiding.

The CHAIRMAN. Gentlemen, there is a personal matter which the chair wishes to refer to before resuming the work of the committee In this committee we all miss our colleague, Judge Madison, and I am sure that it is a source of great personal bereavement to each member of the committee, as it is to the chair. We were with him here on the most intimate terms. We all knew him and recognized his worth and value, and I consider his death as a great loss to the country, and especially to this committee. It really saddens me to meet in this room again, for the first time since his death, and miss him as I do miss him.

Upon motion of Mr. Hinds a committee of two was appointed to draft suitable resolutions to be spread upon the minutes of the committee.

TESTIMONY OF MR. WALLACE P. WILLETT.

(The witness was duly sworn by the chairman.)

The CHAIRMAN. Mr. Willett, give us your full name, please.

Mr. WILLETT. Wallace P. Willett.

The CHAIRMAN. Your address?

Mr. WILLETT. 82 Wall Street, New York.

The CHAIRMAN. Your business?

Mr. WILLETT. Principally a wire-service news bureau covering the United States and a cable service covering every sugar country in the world, virtually; and also the publishing of a daily and weekly sugar-trade journal, and brokers in raw and refined sugars to a moderate extent.

The CHAIRMAN. Brokers in both raw and refined sugars?

Mr. WILLETT. Yes; to a moderate extent.

The CHAIRMAN. Mr. Willett, are you a member of the firm of Willett & Gray?

Mr. WILLETT. Yes, sir.

The CHAIRMAN. The senior member of that firm?

Mr. WILLETT. Yes, sir.

The CHAIRMAN. How long have you been the senior member of that firm?

Mr. WILLETT. During its entire existence.

The CHAIRMAN. How long is that?

Mr. WILLETT. I have been with that firm and its predecessor since 1853.

The CHAIRMAN. Publishing a sugar-trade journal?

Mr. WILLETT. Since about 1875.

The CHAIRMAN. You have been publishing a weekly sugar journal since about 1875?

Mr. WILLETT. Yes.

The CHAIRMAN. Always under the name of Willett & Gray?

Mr. WILLETT. Oh, no; under the name of Willett & Gray, successors to the former company. The original firm that I went into, when I was 17 years old, was Joseph B. Glover & Co., of Boston.

The CHAIRMAN. Were they publishing a sugar journal?

Mr. WILLETT. No, sir.

The CHAIRMAN. Just start at the time when you went into the sugar trade journal business.

Mr. WILLETT. At the time we started the sugar journal business, the firm was Willett & Hamlin, New York, and Willett, Hamlin & Co., Boston.

The CHAIRMAN. About what time was that?

Mr. WILLETT. I think at the time we began the publication of a sugar trade journal the firm was Joseph B. Glover & Co., in Boston, and Willett, Hamlin & Co., in New York. That is my recollection now.

The CHAIRMAN. How long has Willett & Gray been publishing a weekly sugar journal?

Mr. WILLETT. Since about 1884, I think.

The CHAIRMAN. Since 1884?

Mr. WILLETT. No; previous to that. I could give you the facts exactly at some other time.

The CHAIRMAN. Well, it is not very important. I was simply trying to show how much experience you have had in the business.

Mr. WILLETT. I have been in the business since 1853, and I am now 76 years old.

The CHAIRMAN. You are now 76 years old, and you have been in the sugar business ever since you were 17 years old?

Mr. WILLETT. Yes, sir.

The CHAIRMAN. And you have been publishing or assisting in publishing a sugar trade journal since when?

Mr. WILLETT. I began making sugar figures when I first went into the firm, but we did not publish anything.

The CHAIRMAN. How long have you, in some way or other, been interested in publishing a New York sugar trade journal?

Mr. WILLETT. To the public?

The CHAIRMAN. Yes.

Mr. WILLETT. It must be about 40 years.

The CHAIRMAN. For 40 years you have been publishing sugar statistics?

Mr. WILLETT. Yes; in some shape or other.

The CHAIRMAN. Mr. Willett, I do not wish to strain your modesty, but is not Willett & Gray's considered the leading sugar journal of this continent?

Mr. WILLETT. We try to make it so.

The CHAIRMAN. At any rate, it has a wide circulation among the trade?

Mr. WILLETT. Yes, sir.

The CHAIRMAN. Have you any rivals or competitors in that business?

Mr. WILLETT. We do not consider that we have; no, sir.

The CHAIRMAN. Well, there is the American Beet Gazette, or a name similar to that, is there not?

Mr. WILLETT. Yes; the American Beet Sugar Gazette, published in Chicago.

The CHAIRMAN. That is devoted particularly to the beet interests?

Mr. WILLETT. That is a more modern publication and more scientific.

The CHAIRMAN. You say the modern publications are more scientific?

Mr. WILLETT. No, sir; that is a recent modern publication, of a few years' standing compared with ours.

The CHAIRMAN. Now, Mr. Willett, for the last 40 or 50 years you have been a close observer of sugar conditions throughout the world?

Mr. WILLETT. Yes, sir; I have been in the trade constantly.

The CHAIRMAN. Does that include prices in various foreign countries from year to year?

Mr. WILLETT. Yes, sir.

The CHAIRMAN. It includes, of course, American prices?

Mr. WILLETT. Yes, sir.

The CHAIRMAN. In every section of the country?

Mr. WILLETT. Yes, sir.

The CHAIRMAN. Wholesale and retail?

Mr. WILLETT. Yes, sir.

The CHAIRMAN. Mr. Willett, there was quite a sudden rise in the price of sugar early in the fall. I think it probably began in September, did it not, or possibly a little earlier than that?

Mr. WILLETT. You refer to 1911?

The CHAIRMAN. Yes. There was a sharp advance in price.

Mr. WILLETT. The rise dates back to June or July.

The CHAIRMAN. The movement really started in June or July, 1911?

Mr. WILLETT. Yes.

The CHAIRMAN. But it did not get very much accentuated until the early fall, did it?

Mr. WILLETT. No, sir.

The CHAIRMAN. And then it jumped very suddenly almost 2 cents a pound, did it not?

Mr. WILLETT. Yes, sir.

The CHAIRMAN. Now, will you tell the committee, for its information as well as for the information of the public, what, in your judgment, was the cause of that sudden, sharp rise in the price of sugar, which began, as you say, in the summer of 1911, and was accentuated in the early fall of this year?

Mr. WILLETT. Well, to go back a little to the beginning, the world went over the last sugar campaign with an apparent surplus of some 800,000 tons of sugar beyond requirements for consumption.

Mr. JACOWAY. Mr. Willett, I did not get those figures.

Mr. WILLETT. I say the world went over the last sugar campaign ending September 1, 1910, with an apparent surplus of 800,000 tons of sugar, which surplus caused a very low range of prices throughout the world.

The CHAIRMAN. Now, right there, if it will not interrupt you if we ask you these questions, was this an extra large surplus?

Mr. WILLETT. It was an extra large surplus.

The CHAIRMAN. What is the average stock that they carry over?

Mr. WILLETT. From four to six hundred thousand tons.

The CHAIRMAN. And this last year they carried over 800,000 tons?

Mr. WILLETT. Yes, sir; nearly double. That caused prices to decline to below cost of production in Europe. The cost of production in Europe is considered to be 9 shillings f. o. b. Hamburg, and the sugars went to below 8 shillings 8¼ pence per hundredweight.

Mr. GARRETT. How much would that be?

Mr. WILLETT. Multiply 9 shillings by 218, and that will give it to you in United States currency; that is, for the f. o. b. price in Hamburg.

The CHAIRMAN. Mr. Willett, do you know Mr. George Martineau, the English expert?

Mr. WILLETT. Yes, sir.

The CHAIRMAN. I notice that in the report that he rendered to the British Government he reported that in the sugar crop of 1908–09 the cost of producing a pound of beet sugar averaged from 2.16 to 2.28 cents; in other words, from 9 shillings to 9½ shillings per hundredweight.

Mr. WILLETT. Yes; I might explain that, and say that the cost of production is 9 shillings f. o. b. to the manufacturer, but in order to make his 10 per cent profit for his dividends and his surplus for working capital, he considers his cost of refining 10 shillings.

The CHAIRMAN. But I am simply speaking of this report of Mr. Martineau.

Mr. WILLETT. Yes; that seems to be correct.

The CHAIRMAN. While that was the price for that year and corresponds exactly to the figures you have just given, yet it appears that in the year 1902, after the Brussels convention went into effect, the Hamburg export price—in other words, beet sugar f. o. b. Hamburg—ranged as low as 1.79. Was that under the cost of production?

Mr. WILLETT. What year was that, sir?

The CHAIRMAN. 1902.

Mr. WILLETT. Was that during the cartel year?

The CHAIRMAN. I do not remember the name of the witness who testified to that. I believe, however, it was Mr. Palmer, of the American Beet Sugar Association. I will find out before you conclude.

Mr. WILLETT. Can you tell me if that was the cartel year?

The CHAIRMAN. Yes, sir. The Brussels sugar convention went into effect early in 1902, and after its adoption the export price of raw sugar, beet sugar, f. o. b. Hamburg, was $1.79. That was considered, I believe, the average for the year.

Mr. WILLETT (referring to paper). I want to see what year the cartel was in existence. When the cartel was in existence, the price at Hamburg was far below the cost of manufacture.

The CHAIRMAN. While the cartel was in effect or before the cartel went into effect?

Mr. WILLETT. While the cartel was in effect. While the bounty and the cartel were both in effect.

The CHAIRMAN. The bounty enabled them to sell sometimes under the cost of production?

Mr. WILLETT. Yes.

The CHAIRMAN. But after the cartel went into effect that would not be true any longer, would it?

Mr. WILLETT. No, sir.

The CHAIRMAN. That is the point exactly. I will have to have the printed hearing to direct your specific attention to that testimony; but suppose you go on with your story, and before you conclude I will revert back to that point. You started to explain why sugar went up so suddenly and so sharply this fall.

Mr. WILLETT. Along in March of this year it began to develop by the statistical figures that the 800,000 tons supposed surplus had rapidly disappeared. Nobody knew where, but it was disappearing or had disappeared.

The CHAIRMAN. How could it disappear—by people buying it up in advance to fill advance contracts?

Mr. WILLETT. We can only have a theory on that subject.

The CHAIRMAN. I understand that. Suppose you give us your theory on that subject.

Mr. WILLETT. My theory is that there was a mistake in the crop estimate.

The CHAIRMAN. In other words, that the surplus was not really there?

Mr. WILLETT. Yes.

The CHAIRMAN. It had been reported, but did not exist?

Mr. WILLETT. Yes; and speculators in Europe, who are always looking out for points, began then to make their movement, and as it followed soon after that that bad crop reports for the campaign of the present season began to be made prices began to rise on the speculative sugar exchanges of Europe, and the crop reports going from bad to worse was the immediate cause of the rapid rise which you have called attention to.

The CHAIRMAN. Where were those crop reports from which affected most the sugar market?

Mr. WILLETT. From Germany. Germany produced in 1910, for instance, 2,200,000 tons of sugar. As the reports of damage to the country grew stronger and stronger, the estimate for Germany for this season fell to about 1,200,000 tons.

The CHAIRMAN. In other words, a million tons shortage in Germany?

Mr. WILLETT. One million tons short.

The CHAIRMAN. Can you give us in round figures what the shortage was estimated to be throughout the beet-sugar section of Europe?

Mr. WILLETT. Two million tons.

The CHAIRMAN. A shortage of 2,000,000 in European beet sugar?

Mr. WILLETT. Yes; and Germany was the principal one. Germany above her own consumption sends 774,000 tons to the United Kingdom, and in all her exports sends over a million tons out of the country, while it appears from present estimates that she will have only about 27,000 tons to send out of the country beyond her own requirements for consumption. That leaves the United Kingdom to secure 700,000 tons from other sources during the present campaign, and that is the basis for present prices for sugars in the United Kingdom, and the reason why the British Government is trying to obtain larger concessions on the exportation from Russia this year.

The CHAIRMAN. They are trying to amend the Brussels convention in that respect?

Mr. WILLETT. Yes; in that respect. Russia has 700,000 tons more sugar than she requires, and the world is that much short.

The CHAIRMAN. Russia is not a party to this convention?

Mr. WILLETT. Russia is not a party to the convention except to the extent of exporting 200,000 tons per annum.

The CHAIRMAN. In other words, by agreement between the contracting parties they agree to let Russia export annually 200,000 tons without these duties?

Mr. WILLETT. Yes; so that while the United Kingdom is paying high prices for sugars, the prices in Russia are falling constantly by reason of an oversupply.

The CHAIRMAN. Now, Mr. Willett, you spoke of a shortage estimated at 2,000,000 tons in European beet sugar——

Mr. WILLETT (interposing). I will have to correct those figures later, Mr. Chairman, if I find they are not correct.

The CHAIRMAN. Well, I do not know whether you can do that or not. Are they substantially correct? If we understand that you are giving us figures which are substantially correct, that is near enough.

Mr. WILLETT. The entire deficiency is 2,000,000 tons, as I stated, but I am not quite sure whether it may not be greater than 1,000,000 tons in Germany; that is all.

The CHAIRMAN. In other words, you have approximated it?

Mr. WILLETT. Yes, sir.

The CHAIRMAN. That is all we want.

Mr. WILLETT. I could give you the exact figures if I had a little time.

The CHAIRMAN. Perhaps you can do that later, but all we desire now is to get it substantially accurate. Was there any shortage in the Cuban crop?

Mr. WILLETT. The Cuban crop at the beginning of the season was estimated to reach 1,800,000 tons. As a matter of fact, it reached 1,468,000 tons, a shortage of three or four hundred thousand tons.

The CHAIRMAN. How about the Java crop?

Mr. WILLETT. The Java crop was larger.

The CHAIRMAN. The Java crop was larger?

Mr. WILLETT. Yes; there was no shortage in the Java crop.

The CHAIRMAN. That afforded some little relief?

Mr. WILLETT. Yes.

The CHAIRMAN. Well, what was the total shortage under the estimates?

Mr. WILLETT. Both cane and beet?

The CHAIRMAN. Yes.

Mr. WILLETT. Two million tons.

The CHAIRMAN. About 2,000,000 tons?

Mr. WILLETT. Yes, sir.

The CHAIRMAN. Was that enough to make a great difference in the price?

Mr. WILLET. It was enough to cause high prices and reduce consumption.

The CHAIRMAN. The world's consumption of sugar is between sixteen and seventeen million tons, is it not?

Mr. WILLETT. Yes. Some country will have to go without sugar.

The CHAIRMAN. Or pay more for it?

Mr. WILLETT. Or pay a heap more for it, exactly.

The CHAIRMAN. In accordance with the law of supply and demand?

Mr. WILLETT. Except in this, Mr. Chairman; in all my experience where short crops have been talked of, sugar comes out from some unknown place; we never know where, exactly, but we generally get enough to go around finally, and the latest figures that we have made in the office show us that even with all this shortage there may be enough to go around this year, although the statistics do not show it.

The CHAIRMAN. Now, the price went up about 2 cents, the movement reaching a climax, you might say, in the early fall, and it has recovered now, as I understand, about 1 cent.

Mr. WILLETT. It has reacted a cent and a half.

The CHAIRMAN. In other words, there is only one-half a cent advance really in wholesale prices over what it was before this movement started?

Mr. WILLETT. Sir?

The CHAIRMAN. The wholesale prices are only a half a cent a pound higher than when this movement really got under way?

Mr. MALBY. Mr. Chairman, suppose he gives us the prices.

The CHAIRMAN. Yes; can you give them by months during the period of this extraordinary movement, starting, say, in June?

Mr. WILLETT. For raw or refined sugar?

The CHAIRMAN. Raw or refined, either. They correspond, do they not?

Mr. WILLETT. Suppose we take refined sugar. There is a certain difference between raw and refined. When the movement started along in June or July, refined sugar was then at 5 cents or a little less. At its highest point refined sugar sold at 7.50 less 2 per cent, or 7.35 cents net.

The CHAIRMAN. 7.35 cents net?

Mr. WILLETT. Yes; a difference between 4.75 and 7.35, or between 5.75 and 7.35, represents the entire advance in refined sugar in the United States.

The CHAIRMAN. You mean the difference between 4.75 and 7.35, do you not?

Mr. WILLETT. Yes; between 4.75 and 7.35.

The CHAIRMAN. That is, 2.5 cents?

Mr. WILLETT. 2.5 cents a pound represents the entire advance. From the high price of 7.5 cents it has now declined to 5.88 cents, net.

The CHAIRMAN. 5.88, or a little under 6 cents?

Mr. WILLETT. Yes; 6 cents less 2 per cent.

The CHAIRMAN. About a cent and a half, you say?

Mr. WILLETT. 1.47, or about a cent and a half.

The CHAIRMAN. Now, do you see any reasonable prospect of the decline continuing?

Mr. WILLETT. Yes, sir.

The CHAIRMAN. Resulting in still lower prices for sugar?

Mr. WILLETT. Yes, sir.

The CHAIRMAN. In the near future?

Mr. WILLETT. Yes, sir.

The CHAIRMAN. To what extent?

Mr. Willett. To any extent. It will be stopped at the point where the United Kingdom's wants compel their refiners to enter the Cuban sugar market for a supply of the Cuban crop sugars this season. They would then come into competition with the United States sugar refiners and make the price for Cuban sugars.

The Chairman. Which might, of course, run that price up to some extent?

Mr. Willett. As it stands to-day, the United Kingdom refiners are not in the market for Cuban sugars at present prices.

The Chairman. But their necessities might force them to enter that market?

Mr. Willett. They have already bought speculatively some 140,000 tons of the Cuban crop.

The Chairman. You say we have?

Mr. Willett. No; they have bought that as a matter of speculation.

The Chairman. On future contracts?

Mr. Willett. On future contracts.

The Chairman. Which they might or might not require to be fulfilled?

Mr. Willett. But which they are obliged to take.

The Chairman. Unless they sell them?

Mr. Willett. Yes.

The Chairman. Do they ever do that in the sugar trade?

Mr. Willett. Yes, sir; frequently. That is a speculative movement, in other words.

The Chairman. So that the fact they have bought this 140,000 tons of Cuban sugar does not necessarily mean that they will take it?

Mr. Willett. No, sir.

The Chairman. If they could be supplied elsewhere, where delivery is easier and cheaper, they would probably sell that; is that your idea?

Mr. Willett. Yes, sir.

The Chairman. What did they give for that, do you know?

Mr. Willett. They paid the basis of 3½ cents f. o. b. Habana or f. o. b. Cuba.

The Chairman. Then your judgment is that the conditions are such that there probably will be a still further reduction in the price of sugar, so that it will go back toward where it was before this movement which we have been describing started?

Mr. Willett. The reduction in the price of sugar, as we would consider it, from now forward would be limited to about the difference between the present price of Cuban raw sugars, which is 4.94, and the first deliveries of the Cuban crop, which is 3.50, cost and freight, plus the duty of 1.34, which would be 4.84.

Mr. Malby. At New York?

Mr. Willett. At New York; showing that the present prices in New York are very nearly at the parity of the prices for January and February delivery of Cuban sugars. Now, whether they will go below that parity, as I have said before, depends entirely upon this competition from the United Kingdom.

The Chairman. On the conditions, in other words, which you have just described.

Mr. Willett. And bear in mind that the United Kingdom must have 700,000 tons of sugar from other countries besides Germany or else her consumption must be largely reduced, because last year she got that amount from Germany.

The CHAIRMAN. Then, Mr. Willett, you look for a still further decline? I mean that is your estimate, and of course that is just like any other estimate.

Mr. WILLETT. I look for some further decline.

The CHAIRMAN. As much as a cent?

Mr. WILLETT. Oh, no, sir.

The CHAIRMAN. Half a cent?

Mr. WILLETT. No, sir.

The CHAIRMAN. Just a very slight decline?

Mr. WILLETT. A very slight decline.

The CHAIRMAN. In other words, we are liable to stay during this sugar year at least a cent higher than we were before this movement began last summer?

Mr. WILLETT. Yes, sir; and as the summer approaches, the conditions in the United Kingdom will control that, and prices may be very much higher or very much lower.

The CHAIRMAN. In accordance with the laws of supply and demand?

Mr. WILLETT. It is scarcely likely that prices will be any lower in this campaign. Thus far the United States refiners have not bought a single pound of sugar in Cuba for their January and February requirements.

The CHAIRMAN. Mr. Willett, in your judgment did any American refiner of sugar or any combination of American refiners of sugar have anything to do with putting up the prices of sugar on the American people?

Mr. WILLETT. No, sir; absolutely not.

The CHAIRMAN. When the price advanced in New York, did it advance the same way in London and Hamburg and everywhere else in the world?

Mr. WILLETT. New York followed way behind.

The CHAIRMAN. In other words, the advance did not come as soon in New York?

Mr. WILLETT. It did not come as soon or to as large an extent.

The CHAIRMAN. It did not advance as soon or to as large an extent as it did in these foreign countries?

Mr. WILLETT. It was not as great in New York as in these foreign countries, except at one single period when New York ran absolutely short.

The CHAIRMAN. And had no stock?

Mr. WILLETT. Had no stock, and then we went a little above the world prices, or the Hamburg prices.

The CHAIRMAN. How long did you stay above the Hamburg prices?

Mr. WILLETT. I think not more than two weeks.

The CHAIRMAN. But most of the time you have been under Hamburg prices?

Mr. WILLETT. At all times.

The CHAIRMAN. Does that or not demonstrate, in your opinion, that no local conditions could have caused the advance—that no local conditions or local combination of refiners could have caused the advance?

Mr. WILLETT. Nothing in the United States could have caused it.

The CHAIRMAN. Because if it had been local to the United States, it would not have affected the Hamburg market.

Mr. WILLETT. No, sir.

The CHAIRMAN. Except, probably, in an indirect and a very small way, you think?

Mr. WILLETT. I fancy that the European speculators were influenced in their movement toward higher prices somewhat by that deficiency in the Cuban crop, and by the expectation that the United States refiners would run short of sugar during the end of the season, between crops, and be obliged to go to Europe for sugar.

The CHAIRMAN. Between the crops for what years?

Mr. WILLETT. Between the crop years. European speculators always take note every year of the United States. They watch the United States very closely to see how we are coming out on our tail-end supplies.

The CHAIRMAN. Did any manipulation or combination or agreement or scheme by the American sugar refiners have anything whatever, in your judgment, to do with this recent rise in the price of sugar?

Mr. WILLETT. No, sir; absolutely not.

The CHAIRMAN. You do not think the American Sugar Refining Co. was in anyway responsible for it?

Mr. WILLETT. Not the slightest.

The CHAIRMAN. Or the Federal Sugar Refining Co.?

Mr. WILLETT. No, sir.

The CHAIRMAN. Or the Arbuckle or any other American beet-sugar factory or cane refinery?

Mr. WILLETT. No, sir; absolutely not.

The CHAIRMAN. In other words, the conditions were world-wide?

Mr. WILLETT. Yes, sir.

The CHAIRMAN. And that condition was brought about by crop conditions and in response to the law of supply and demand?

Mr. WILLETT. Yes; and speculation in Europe.

The CHAIRMAN. Well, speculation in Europe was based on what they thought of the crops.

Mr. WILLETT. Certainly. We have no sugar exchanges in the United States, hence we have no speculation. But Europe is a network of sugar exchanges, and they speculate every day.

The CHAIRMAN. Just like we do in cotton and grain?

Mr. WILLETT. Yes.

The CHAIRMAN. We have not that condition in the United States?

Mr. WILLETT. No, sir.

The CHAIRMAN. So that you do not consider any of our American refiners or manufacturers in any way responsible?

Mr. WILLETT. Not in any way, shape, or manner.

The CHAIRMAN. Was it in the interest of any refiner to have this higher price of sugar?

Mr. WILLETT. It was decidedly against their interests.

The CHAIRMAN. Why was it against their interests?

Mr. WILLETT. Because the lower the price of raw sugars the more stable and permanent their profits.

The CHAIRMAN. The less money they would have tied up in raw sugar?

Mr. WILLETT. Yes, sir.

The CHAIRMAN. And the less would be the worth of the sugar lost in refining?

Mr. WILLETT. Yes; and as it happens to-day, after a rise, when the return comes all the refiners are in a position to lose money by the downward movement in the raw-sugar market.

The CHAIRMAN. To the extent of the stock they have on hand?

Mr. WILLETT. To the extent of the stock they carry, which in the case of the Sugar Trust is something like 150,000 tons.

The CHAIRMAN. They might recoup, however, to some extent on advance contracts?

Mr. WILLETT. Oh, yes; they have done that this year.

The CHAIRMAN. If it had not been for that they would all have gone broke on this sort of a movement?

Mr. WILLETT. Yes.

The CHAIRMAN. Now, Mr. Willett, did you ever have any sort of financial connection, outside of what you ordinarily would have in a business way, with the American Sugar Refining Co.?

Mr. WILLETT. No, sir.

The CHAIRMAN. Your journal has always been perfectly independent of that company?

Mr. WILLETT. Perfectly. The American Sugar Refining Co. has been a small item in our business. Our business is world-wide.

The CHAIRMAN. But they are a considerable item in your business so far as this country is concerned?

Mr. WILLETT. Yes; so far as this country is concerned, but our general business, you will notice, is world-wide, and we could not afford to publish such a paper.

The CHAIRMAN. While we do not know whether it is true or not, we have had it stated before us that at one period you made a western trip for Mr. Havemeyer to look into beet sugar.

Mr. WILLETT. Yes, sir.

The CHAIRMAN. You did do that?

Mr. WILLETT. Yes, sir.

The CHAIRMAN. That was in 1901 or 1902?

Mr. WILLETT. That was in November, 1901.

The CHAIRMAN. The trip began in November, 1901?

Mr. WILLETT. Yes; and ended in November, 1901.

The CHAIRMAN. Where did you go?

Mr. WILLETT. May I explain to the committee how that came about?

The CHAIRMAN. Yes; I would be glad if you would do so. We have heard so much talk about that, we would like to know exactly what happened.

Mr. WILLETT. I would like to explain it, too. Mr. McFarland, president of a bank in Grand Junction, southern Colorado, came to New York in October, 1901, with authority to sell the beet-sugar factory located at Grand Junction, Colo. He came to us with his plans, and placed the sale of that factory in our hands. I met Mr. Palmer and talked beet sugars with him, and told him we had such a proposition for the sale of a factory in southern Colorado.

The CHAIRMAN. That was Mr. Lowell M. Palmer?

Mr. WILLETT. Yes, sir; and Mr. Palmer suggested that I place it before Mr. Havemeyer, and he arranged a meeting for me with Mr. Havemeyer.

The CHAIRMAN. Mr. Palmer was then one of Mr. Havemeyer's business associates?

Mr. WILLETT. Yes, sir. I met Mr. Havemeyer and Mr. Palmer, and no one else.

Mr. SULZER. Mr. H. O. Havemeyer?

Mr. WILLETT. Mr. H. O. Havemeyer. I met them at Mr. Havemeyer's office, with all the papers in connection with the sale of that property, and went over the proposition with those two gentlemen, and they appointed an agricultural expert, Mr. Myer, a director of the company, and their chemical expert, Dr. Hooker, to go to Grand Junction with Mr. McFarland and myself and investigate the property. This was on a Tuesday, I think, and we started the following Saturday. After appointing that committee, Mr. Havemeyer said to me: "What are the best States for beet-sugar production and who are the best people in it?" I said that Colorado was one of the best States for beet-sugar production on account of its abundant sunshine, but there was more or less trouble in that State in relation to the farmers producing the beets; that Utah had been more successful because the Mormons could control their farmers.

The CHAIRMAN. Yes; that is exactly what Mr. Palmer told us about that.

Mr. WILLETT. It is? I told him that Mr. Thomas R. Cutler was the best man in the beet-sugar business; that the company of which he was the manager, the Lehi Co., had made the best returns, and Mr. Havemeyer said, "Go out and see him."

The CHAIRMAN. Go out and see Cutler?

Mr. WILLETT. Yes. He said, "You can say to Mr. Cutler that this is not the American Sugar Refining Co., but persons interested in the American Sugar Refining Co." If I may interline that a bit, I will say that at that time Mr. Palmer and Mr. Havemeyer were the people, and that the American Sugar Refining Co. appointed no committee on beet sugars until some time in December.

The CHAIRMAN. That was afterwards?

Mr. WILLETT. Yes. He said, "You can say that this is for parties interested with the American Sugar Refining Co., and we are prepared to purchase a one-half interest in this factory."

The CHAIRMAN. In the Lehi factory?

Mr. WILLETT. In the Lehi factory. "Desiring and wishing to leave one-half interest under the local ownership, and the entire management to be left with the local people. Also, we are prepared to take an interest in other factories in desirable locations to the extent of a one-half interest." With that instruction we went to Grand Junction and looked over the factory and drove around the beet fields.

The CHAIRMAN. Did you meet Mr. Chester S. Morey out there?

Mr. WILLETT. No, sir; he was in Denver.

The CHAIRMAN. You were with Mr. McFarland?

Mr. WILLETT. Yes, sir.

The CHAIRMAN. Was he not identified with Mr. Morey?

Mr. WILLETT. No, sir; Mr. Morey had nothing to do with that factory. The only persons we met were Mr. McFarland and a Mr. Kenney, I think, who was interested in the factory.

The CHAIRMAN. You did not see Mr. Morey at all on that trip?

Mr. WILLETT. Oh, no.

The CHAIRMAN. Now you may continue. I beg your pardon for interrupting you.

Mr. WILLETT. As I say, we drove around the beet fields, and Mr. Hooker had the factory run two or three days, and then those gentlemen returned home. I went on to Salt Lake City, or rather, to Lehi, Mr. Cutler's residence. I found at Lehi that Mr. Cutler was in Salt Lake City. I went down to the Lehi factory and called him up on the telephone. I might say here that I had known Mr. Cutler for several years.

The CHAIRMAN. Prior to this time?

Mr. WILLETT. Yes. I was well acquainted with Mr. Cutler, he having been in New York frequently on business. He replied from Salt Lake City over the telephone that he was just on the point of leaving for San Francisco, and I said I had a business proposition to talk over with him, and that I would like to join him and go to San Francisco with him. He said the train leaving Lehi that morning connected at Ogden with his train, and he would meet me on the platform at Ogden, which he did, and we went together to San Francisco, spending two days in San Francisco. I think it took us two days to go and two days to come and two days there, making six days, and during that time I placed this proposition before Mr. Cutler without specifying who my principals were. I did not mention Mr. Havemeyer or Mr. Palmer.

The CHAIRMAN. He did not ask you those questions?

Mr. WILLETT. He did not ask me my principals, and I did not give them, but I found that Mr. Cutler was favorable to the project; but he said he could not act until he had seen his parties in Salt Lake City interested with him. We returned to Salt Lake City. I might say that I was at Lehi November 16, 1901, and that on the 24th of November we were back in Salt Lake City. From the 24th of November to the 28th of November Mr. Cutler was consulting with his friends, and then advised me on the 28th that he was prepared to go to New York and see my principals about the proposition. I then gave him the names of Mr. Havemeyer and Mr. Palmer and returned to New York myself, leaving Salt Lake City on November 28. In a few days afterwards Mr. Cutler came on. On my return to New York Mr. Havemeyer was sick at his house, and I had no personal communication with him, but received word to bring Mr. Cutler to his house on his arrival. On Mr. Cutler's arrival I took him up to Mr. Havemeyer's house in the morning and introduced him, and Mr. Havemeyer turned to me and said: "Mr. Willett, you can leave. I will talk with Mr. Cutler," and from that day to the day of his death he never mentioned beet sugar to me again.

The CHAIRMAN. That covers all you know about that transaction?

Mr. WILLETT. Yes.

The CHAIRMAN. Of course, you got a brokerage or some sort of compensation?

Mr. WILLETT. I will say that at this conversation between Mr. Havemeyer, Mr. Palmer, and myself, Mr. Havemeyer asked what compensation or what commission we were to have on the sale of the Colorado factory, and I told him, and he said: "Well, we will give you the same commission if anything results from this business. Is that right, Mr. Palmer?" and Mr. Palmer said: "Yes, that is right."

The CHAIRMAN. So, then, they did give you the same commission on the Utah proposition?

Mr. WILLETT. No; they did not.

The CHAIRMAN. They promised it to you?

Mr. WILLETT. They promised it to us.

The CHAIRMAN. What did they pay you?

Mr. WILLETT. About half what was due.

The CHAIRMAN. Would you mind stating the amount they paid you? There is a certain reason why I think it is material.

Mr. WILLETT. If you wish to know, I have no objection. The amount they paid us was $25,000. The commission amounted to $60.000.

The CHAIRMAN. The commission amounted to $60,000?

Mr. WILLETT. Yes; the trade was $1,225 000, according to my recollection, 5 per cent of which would be $62.000. I talked it over with my partner, and Mr. Havemeyer proposed that payment in cash, or we could wait.

The CHAIRMAN. And you decided to take the cash instead of waiting?

Mr. WILLETT. My partner decided to take the cash instead of waiting. I do not know whether he did right or wrong. We were quite satisfied to accept that sum for three weeks' work, anyway.

The CHAIRMAN. Gentlemen, I have concluded all the examination I care to make on every branch of the subject except one. Mr. Willett has been in the employ of the committee recently as an expert to translate, if I may use that word, the reports we have received through the State Department from every country of the world in reference to the wholesale and retail prices of sugars throughout the world for the last five years. I think possibly we had better examine him in reference to that subject in a different way from the way we have been taking the testimony so far, and let him explain his work without much interruption, and I think if you gentlemen want to examine him on any subject other than this expert work, now is perhaps the best time.

Mr. WILLETT. Mr. Chairman, I would like to say regarding that commission, it was 5 per cent, and the amount was just exactly the same as we would have received had we sold the Colorado factory to him, which we did not do. He turned that down.

Mr. MALBY. I think that has been pretty well covered, except as to one thing. You spoke of certain speculators having European exchanges in which they deal in sugar. Will you explain that just a little more fully, Mr. Willett?

Mr. WILLETT. Well, these sugar exchanges——

Mr. MALBY (interposing). Exist where, and what is the course of their operation?

Mr. WILLETT (continuing). Exist in London, Paris, Magdeburg, Germany—these are the principal exchanges. Then there are other minor exchanges in nearly all of the different cities of Europe—Hamburg, Brunswick, Germany; Kief, and St. Petersburg.

Mr. MALBY. What is the course of their operation, or their methods?

Mr. WILLETT. They operate every day in beet sugar, 88 analysis, free on board at Hamburg. They buy and sell that class of sugar for prompt delivery, and delivery in every month in the year, even as far forward as new crops—that is, for 12 months ahead.

Mr. MALBY. Is it purely speculative?

Mr. WILLETT. Absolutely.

Mr. MALBY. Do they actually deliver any sugar at all?

Mr. WILLETT. The contract calls for the actual delivery, and I presume in cases the actual sugar is delivered, but it is not the intention at all.

Mr. MALBY. Well, practically the uniform practice is not to deliver the sugar?

Mr. WILLETT. Yes, sir.

Mr. MALBY. Does that have the effect of lowering or increasing the price of sugar?

Mr. WILLETT. It depends upon whether the bulls are in the ascendant or the bears are in the ascendant. As a rule, the speculation is directed to the bull side of the market.

Mr. MALBY. To increase the price?

Mr. WILLETT. Yes, sir; and there are three or four leading operators there who generally operate on the bull side.

Mr. MALBY. Were they directing the market during four or five months of this year?

Mr. WILLETT. Well, I can not say that they were controlling it. They were in doubt as to the correctness of the report of the shortage, and did not get going until the dealing in September. Then they ruled in November for a short time, and advanced the prices very, very rapidly. Now they have come to a halt on account of this agitation regarding the increase of Russian imports.

Mr. MALBY. Would that fact, in your judgment, have a tendency to increase prices of sugar? The fact that they were operating, would that, in your judgment, have the effect of increasing prices largely?

Mr. WILLETT. Yes, sir. They made the prices at Hamburg.

Mr. MALBY. You think their operations were sufficiently extensive to really make the price of sugar at Hamburg?

Mr. WILLETT. Well, they had the whip hand.

Mr. MALBY. Their operations are practically the same as the operations on the cotton exchange and the wheat exchange?

Mr. WILLETT. Yes, sir. They are very similar.

Mr. MALBY. Then, at present, they have somewhat eased off from their activities?

Mr. WILLETT. Very much; yes, sir. It is like this: For two months to come there is plenty of sugar in the United Kingdom. They have more sugar than they can consume in two months in that country.

Mr. MALBY. Has Russia succeeded in obtaining relief from the condition of supplying to the world's market only 200,000 tons? Have they got relief from that scheme?

Mr. WILLETT. Not yet, and they are not likely to do so until next March, and the governments of Europe have acceded to that in the convention.

Mr. MALBY. How do you fix the 1st of March as being the probable date?

Mr. WILLETT. Well, that is the date for the annual meeting.

Mr. MALBY. The annual meeting of what?

Mr. WILLETT. Of what is known as the Brussels convention proper.

Mr. MALBY. Composed of the representatives of the various countries?

Mr. WILLETT. Yes, sir; but they have a subcommittee that meets every month.

Mr. MALBY. But they have no authority to act?

Mr. WILLETT. No, sir; not without the entire committee representing all the countries.

Mr. MALBY. So, the earliest relief that could be obtained would be at the annual meeting in March?

Mr. WILLETT. Yes, sir.

The CHAIRMAN. There is one thing I omitted to ask you about. You remember that you were speaking about the cost of producing European beet sugar?

Mr. WILLETT. Yes, sir.

The CHAIRMAN. On page 139 of our record is a table which was submitted by Mr. Atkins in which is shown the Hamburg price of sugar for the years 1900 to 1907, inclusive, and you will find by looking at the table, at the top of page 139, that in the year 1902 the price was $1.79, which was considerably under 9 shillings, which you fixed as the cost of producing 100 pounds of beet sugar in Europe.

Mr. WILLETT. If that was a Cartel year, there is an explanation for it.

The CHAIRMAN. I can find that for you here.

Mr. MALBY. Where does the Cartel appear in the record?

The CHAIRMAN. That was furnished for the record by Mr. Palmer—that is, a copy of the Cartel—and it appears at 2642 of the record. March 6, 1902, seems to be the date of the report of the British delegate to the sugar conference. This paper says, "Done at Brussels, the 6th of March, 1902." That is the date of the Brussels convention. That is what you mean, is it not?

Mr. WILLETT. Yes, sir.

The CHAIRMAN. That was the price in the year 1902; the most of it came after March 5.

Mr. WILLETT. That, from January to March, would include the cartel.

The CHAIRMAN. But it is the average price for that year?

Mr. WILLETT. Yes, sir.

The CHAIRMAN. So that would include January, February, and March, and three-fourths of the year was after the adoption of the Brussels convention?

Mr. WILLETT. Yes, sir. But, do you know that in addition to the bounty which the German manufacturers had upon their export business, in addition to the bounty of 38 cents which was repealed by the Brussels convention, there was during the existence of the cartel, up to March, 1902, a cartel bounty of 26 cents, against which the United States never countervailed?

The CHAIRMAN. But after March 5, 1902, that was not in effect. What struck me was the fact that during three-fourths of the first year, after this went into effect, they produced sugar for much less, or they sold it below the cost of production—that is, a half a cent cheaper than the figures you state as the cost of producing European sugar.

Mr. WILLETT. Yes, sir; that is true.

The CHAIRMAN. So that the cost must vary, or the selling price must vary, from year to year?

Mr. WILLETT. Yes, sir.

The CHAIRMAN. And it is hard to tell what the cost is, except from what they sell it for?

Mr. WILLETT. I am satisfied in my own mind that it is decidedly below the cost of production; a half a cent, at least.

The CHAIRMAN. To the extent of half a cent at least?

Mr. WILLETT. Yes, sir; I think the bounty has something to do with it.

I can show you, if you wish, how the German manufacturers and refiners of sugar for from 3 to 4 years, under the cartel, sold all their sugars for export at a loss, and yet made profit.

The CHAIRMAN. On account of these bounties?

Mr. WILLETT. In other words, the cartel gave the manufacturer 26 cents per hundred pounds and the Government gave 38 cents per hundred pounds, and the manufacturers sold their sugar to the domestic consumers for 77 cents per hundred pounds profit, which was returned to them by the cartel. They gave away 26 cents on their exports, which were selling at less than cost, and yet made a profit. I can give you the dollars and cents of the profits made.

Mr. MALBY. I would like to have that go into the record.

The CHAIRMAN. Can you put that into the record without going into the details of the dollars and cents at this time?

Mr. WILLETT. Yes, sir.

The CHAIRMAN. I would like to invite your attention to this extract from Willett & Gray's Statistical Sugar Trade Journal, for June 12, 1901:

> The depression in the sugar markets is world-wide, and is due to the enormous overproduction, especially in Germany, where the combination of manufacturers, known as the "cartel," keeps up the prices so high for home consumption that it is enabled to stand heavy losses on the sugar which is exported.

I will read you again from the same article:

> The heavy protection now granted to beet-sugar producers all goes to the manufacturers, who do not pay the farmers any more than is received by the farmers in Germany for beets. German factories produce refined sugar at a cost of less than 2½ cents per pound, exclusive of bounty, and American factories suitably located and ably managed should be able to do as well. American manufacturers have already demonstrated their ability to produce sugar at 3 cents per pound; therefore the heavy protection now granted is not needed, and the removal of duty on Cuban raw sugar will neither ruin the business of the beet-sugar manufacturers nor injuriously affect the farmer.

That is what you thought in 1901?

Mr. WILLETT. Yes, sir.

The CHAIRMAN. That is true, is it?

Mr. WILLETT. I am wrong on the figures—that is, the 3 cents.

The CHAIRMAN. You are wrong on that?

Mr. WILLETT. I must have been, because beet sugar has never been produced at this price since.

The CHAIRMAN. We have some evidence on that subject.

Mr. WILLETT. Yes, sir.

The CHAIRMAN. The Spreckels produced it at 2.70, according to the evidence.

Mr. MALBY. That was not very clear.

The CHAIRMAN. I thought it was quite clear.

Mr. HINDS. What testimony was that?

The CHAIRMAN. That was the testimony given in their report and furnished to their stockholders, the American Sugar Refining Co.

They testified as to the cost of producing sugar and averaged it, and it averaged 3¾ cents.

Mr. WILLETT. My recollection is that that is the figure of the Lehigh Co., made in 1901.

The CHAIRMAN. The Spreckels plant produced this year at 2.71 cents.

Mr. WILLETT. You mean in 1901?

The CHAIRMAN. No; I mean last year.

Mr. HINDS. Does that include the depreciation?

The CHAIRMAN. I do not know; the record does not show. I do not recall it if it does. That part of the record to which I referred is the statement furnished us by the American Sugar Refining Co., and they received it as stockholders in this plant. That was the lowest figure testified to as to the cost of production.

Mr. WILLETT. That is lower than any I have ever known.

Mr. SULZER. Tell us, Mr. Willett, the effect of the Brussels convention on sugar generally throughout the world.

Mr. WILLETT. The Brussels convention abolished bounties throughout the world. The effect of that was to decrease the production of sugar in Germany and to increase the consumption by reason of the lower price in Germany, and I think the same result would follow naturally throughout the world, and the prices at Hamburg would be increased. The abolition of the bounty by the cartel would increase the f. o. b. prices at Hamburg for the rest of the world. It was only Germany that benefited by the increased consumption. Other parts of the world paid more for sugar after the abolition of the bounties.

The CHAIRMAN. In other words, the nonsugar-producing countries were hurt at the expense of the sugar-producing countries, and that was the real object of the conference?

Mr. WILLETT. Yes, sir.

Mr. SULZER. When you say the convention abolished bounties, you mean export bounties?

Mr. WILLETT. Yes, sir; not internal taxes.

Mr. SULZER. Certain European countries gave a bounty to sugar growers?

Mr. WILLETT. They did at that time; not now.

Mr. SULZER. Does not Russia give a bounty?

Mr. WILLETT. Yes, sir; but that is not called continental Europe; that is outside.

Mr. SULZER. Do you mean it is not bound by the convention?

Mr. WILLETT. It is only bound by the convention as to its limited export of sugar.

Mr. SULZER. Well, that is a very important thing, is it not?

Mr. WILLETT. It is at the present moment.

Mr. SULZER. In other words, this convention restricted Russia to a certain amount of exportations?

Mr. WILLETT. Yes, sir.

Mr. SULZER. Russia is one of the largest sugar-growing countries in the world, is it not?

Mr. WILLETT. Yes, sir.

Mr. SULZER. And this convention limited Russia to how many tons of sugar per year?

Mr. WILLETT. To 200,000 tons per year.

Mr. SULZER. For export?

Mr. WILLETT. Yes, sir.

Mr. SULZER. They can send any amount they want if they pay the tariff?

Mr. WILLETT. No, sir; we will not take their sugar on any tariff.

Mr. SULZER. Is that true of continental Europe generally?

Mr. WILLETT. No, sir; that does not apply to the United Kingdom.

Mr. SULZER. But outside of the United States they will allow as much Russian sugar to come in as they want if they pay the countervailing duties?

Mr. WILLETT. Yes, sir.

Mr. SULZER. When does this convention expire?

Mr. WILLETT. In September, 1913.

Mr. SULZER. What was the object of this convention?

Mr. WILLETT. To do away with bounties and cartels.

Mr. SULZER. Export bounties?

Mr. WILLETT. Yes, sir; and interior cartels.

Mr. SULZER. As a matter of fact, by reason of this convention, this year the European countries like England, France, Germany, Belgium, and others have had to pay more for sugar, so far as the consumers are concerned, than they otherwise would have had to pay if this convention had never been perfected?

Mr. WILLETT. Well, the convention as a regulator of prices had no control of the weather on the crops.

Mr. SULZER. But, if it had not been for this convention, sugar could have been produced cheaper in European countries this year?

Mr. WILLETT. If conditions had prevailed as they were preceding the convention, the price at Hamburg would have been cheaper than it was this year, but Germany would have no sugar to sell. She has not raised any sugar for export this year. There is no other continental country that has any surplus of any account. France has, perhaps, 75,000 tons for export, but no other country has a surplus. Consequently, had the price at Hamburg been higher or lower, it would have had no influence on the quantity exported.

Mr. SULZER. Except from Russia.

Mr. WILLETT. Except Russia, and it is outside of the game.

Mr. SULZER. But for this convention, however, Russia could have exported her surplus sugar, and would have materially cheapened the price to consumers in Europe, if not in the United States?

Mr. WILLETT. Decidedly.

The CHAIRMAN. This convention does not affect the United States at all; we are not a party to it. We could take Russian sugar just as easily as German sugar.

Mr. WILLETT. But Russia can not export more than 200,000 tons of sugar, and in that way the convention reaches us in the United States. If any exported sugar comes to the United States from Russia it must form a part of that 200,000 tons.

The CHAIRMAN. She made that contract with this convention?

Mr. WILLETT. Yes, sir.

Mr. SULZER. Have we no protection against that sort of business?

Mr. WILLETT. We have a countervailing duty.

Mr. SULZER. But we have no defense?

Mr. WILLETT. No, sir. It seems absurd that the United States, having nothing whatever to do with the Brussels convention, should be brought in by these means and really made a party.

Mr. SULZER. That is what I was referring to.

The CHAIRMAN. We are not a party to the Brussels convention, yet under its terms Russia could not furnish us sugar except under those conditions?

Mr. WILLETT. No, sir. At one time Brussels countervailed against our Philippine sugar for two months.

The CHAIRMAN. Why?

Mr. WILLETT. On account of the import duty into the Philippines being more than 5 francs. That was a surtax, as they call it, whenever it exceeds 5 francs.

The CHAIRMAN. Have you the data covering that?

Mr. WILLETT. I have it here somewhere. Philippine sugars went largely into Hongkong, and the governor general of Hongkong issued a circular prohibiting the importation of Philippine sugar into Hongkong.

The CHAIRMAN. For that reason?

Mr. WILLETT. Yes, sir; that the Philippines paid an export bounty, but the Government got on to it pretty quick, and a month or two later the Hongkong governor rescinded it.

The CHAIRMAN. Hongkong is a British possession, is it not?

Mr. WILLETT. It is a free port.

The CHAIRMAN. But it is under British control?

Mr. WILLETT. Yes, sir.

The CHAIRMAN. And Great Britain was really responsible for that?

Mr. WILLETT. Yes, sir; although Great Britain claims that she does not interfere with the workings of her colonies, but she does.

The CHAIRMAN. And if Great Britain was responsible for an act of this kind the native Government, or the Chinese Government, stopped it?

Mr. WILLETT. They have nothing to do with Hongkong. It is a free port.

The CHAIRMAN. Well, how did they get it repealed; that is, this prohibition of the importation of Philippine sugar?

Mr. WILLETT. The governor general of Hongkong prohibited it, and then the governor general of Hongkong rescinded it.

The CHAIRMAN. Because it created so much discontent?

Mr. WILLETT. The United Kingdom is not a producer of sugar, and its interests are all against excluding bounty-paid sugars from the United Kingdom. They want all the sugar they can get, and just as they can get it, and they are now agitating the question of getting outside of or relinquishing their connection with the Brussels convention in 1913, which is the earliest date on which they can get out, and have already so stated.

Mr. SULZER. That was stated recently?

Mr. WILLETT. Yes, sir.

The CHAIRMAN. This seems to be of particular interest.

Mr. WILLETT. These consular reports you gave me to investigate informed me that the French Government is also making certain preparations to put on a bounty after 1913 against any country out of the convention that still pays a bounty.

Mr. SULZER. When was that Hongkong prohibition placed on Philippine sugar?

Mr. WILLETT. The Philippine duty was assessed in October, 1904, and was suspended in 1905. Now, this happens to be the action of the Brussels convention itself upon the Philippine question, and it says that, "Regarding the Philippines, there exists a surtax, and the committee has decided that this surtax can not be construed to mean a bounty on raw or refined sugar." On that action, the governor general of Hongkong rescinded.

The CHAIRMAN. A committee of the Brussels convention decided that?

Mr. WILLETT. Yes, sir; the Brussels convention decided that.

The CHAIRMAN. The governor general of Hongkong first construed the Philippines tax to mean a bounty under the Brussels convention, and for awhile he kept out Philippine sugar on that contention, but when it was decided by the Brussels convention otherwise, he withdrew his proclamation?

Mr. WILLETT. Yes, sir.

Mr. MALBY. Just what were the conditions in the Philippines which induced the British Government to assume that there was a bounty on Philippine sugar? What did the bounty consist of?

Mr. WILLETT. It states here, as I have read, that there exists a surtax.

Mr. MALBY. Well, there was no tax so far as the Philippine sugar was concerned?

Mr. WILLETT. The surtax is the difference between the import duties on the sugar into the Philippines and the export duty out of the Philippines, and inside of a certain amount this Brussels convention held it to be a bounty.

Mr. MALBY. Yes; I see.

Mr. GARRETT. And there has been an export duty on sugar going out of the Philippines?

Mr. WILLETT. Yes, sir.

Mr. GARRETT. When was that?

Mr. WILLETT. This was October 23 to the 30th, 1905. They had been discussing whether there was a Philippine bounty or not for that year, but they decided that there was not any.

Mr. SULZER. The chairman has elicited by his inquiries full information regarding this Brussels conference, and I will take up another line of inquiry. Was the recent increase in the price of sugar to the consumers in the United States brought about by droughts and bad crops in different parts of the world?

Mr. WILLETT. Yes, sir.

Mr. SULZER. And especially in Europe?

Mr. WILLETT. Yes, sir; in Germany and in Europe.

Mr. SULZER. No agency in the United States had anything to do with it——

Mr. WILLETT (interposing). Nothing whatever.

Mr. SULZER (continuing). With the increased price of sugar to the consumer?

Mr. WILLETT. No, sir.

Mr. SULZER. What, in your judgment as an expert, would bring about a permanent reduction of the cost of manufactured sugar to the consumers of the United States?

Mr. WILLETT. By increasing the amount of domestic production and in Porto Rico and Hawaii; that is, by increasing the quantity of sugar within the United States to the extent that we would be required to purchase no sugar whatever at world prices. Last year we bought only 77,000 tons at the world price. We were as near as that to that condition in 1910. We did come within 77,000 tons of being entirely free and independent of the world's prices, whereas a few years before we had been importing 6,700,000 tons.

Mr. SULZER. In other words, you think it advisable for the Government of the United States to do everything within its legitimate scope to encourage the growth of cane and beet sugar in the United States?

Mr. WILLETT. Yes, sir.

Mr. SULZER. And in our insular possessions?

Mr. WILLETT. Yes, sir; in our insular possessions.

Mr. SULZER. And you also would recommend the abolition of all tariff taxes upon the importation of sugar?

Mr. WILLETT. No, sir. Do you mean import duties?

Mr. SULZER. Yes, sir.

Mr. WILLETT. No, sir.

Mr. SULZER. Would not the elimination of import duties on sugar materially reduce the cost to the manufacturers of sugar and the consumers in the United States?

Mr. WILLETT. At times it would, but at other times it would not.

Mr. SULZER. At what times would it not reduce it?

Mr. WILLETT. This year.

Mr. SULZER. Why not this year?

Mr. WILLETT. Well, because we had a very present example that the moment our American beet-sugar production became available on the market the rise stopped, and, owing entirely and totally to this American production, refined sugars were a cent and a half lower than they were at the highest point. But for that American production, we to-day would be buying sugar at the world's prices. We can not get rid of it. There is no other source from which we could get sugar.

Mr. SULZER. But you fail to grasp the point I was suggesting. If the manufacturers of sugar in the United States could get raw sugar free, they would be able to sell the manufactured sugar cheaper to the American consumers just now?

Mr. WILLETT. Yes, sir.

Mr. SULZER. Hence, the elimination of the tariff tax upon importations of sugar would cheapen the price of sugar to the people of the United States?

Mr. WILLETT. Yes, sir; and to the manufacturer.

Mr. SULZER. And that is one way to get cheaper sugar for the people?

Mr. WILLETT. Yes, sir.

Mr. SULZER. And another way to get cheaper sugar for the people of the United States would be to encourage the production of beet and cane sugar in the United States and in her insular possessions?

Mr. WILLETT. Yes, sir.

Mr. SULZER. And these are the only two ways by which sugar can be sold to the consumers more cheaply?

Mr. WILLETT. Yes, sir; and in one of these ways the price of sugar would be dependent on the f. o. b. Hamburg market, but in the other case the price would be entirely independent of the f. o. b. Hamburg market.

Mr. SULZER. England has no tariff duties on sugar?

Mr. WILLETT. No internal tax, but a duty of 40 cents on 100 test sugar, running down through the degrees.

Mr. SULZER. But it has no other tax?

Mr. WILLETT. No, sir.

Mr. SULZER. But manufactured sugar is sold cheaper in England than in almost any other country of the world?

Mr. WILLETT. Yes, sir.

Mr. SULZER. And it would be sold as cheaply in the United States if the United States should remove its restrictions?

Mr. WILLETT. Yes, sir; just as cheap in the United States if the United States should remove its restrictions whenever normal crops existed. In abnormal years like this it would not apply.

Mr. SULZER. Have you considered any method by which the production of cane and beet sugar in the United States and its insular possessions can be encouraged?

Mr. WILLETT. I can not say that I have. I have been, at the request of the chairman, examining the conditions in the different countries of Europe, and I find quite a similarity existing between the United States and the little country of Denmark. They seem to have imposed a duty of $1.22 on foreign sugars and an internal tax of 49 cents per hundred on all consumed in the country, which is rebated on exportation, and under the conditions existing in Denmark for the last 25 years they have increased their domestic production. I have the figures here and will read them later, but it has been increased something like five times, and their consumption has been correspondingly increased. Their per capita has increased from 25 cents a head to 86 cents a head, against 81 cents in the United States.

It is remarkable and astonishing to me what progress a little country like Denmark has made. All of its business is controlled by two refineries, which fix the price for the whole country. They have fixed the price so low that there is no encouragement for competitors to come in. I have found no evidence to show that the Government has given them any monopoly at all. I have made quite a study of that question. Now, that partially answers your question. Denmark has accomplished the very thing you ask about. Now, there is no sugar-producing country in Europe, or elsewhere that I am aware of, that does not collect a revenue upon every pound of sugar that comes in for consumption, either by importation taxes or internal taxes. That has long been an unanswerable problem to me, why Hawaiian and Porto Rican sugar should not pay something for the privilege of coming into this country; but to do so the United States would have to change its entire system of revenue on sugar.

Mr. SULZER. Do you know what is the production of beet sugar in Denmark?

Mr. WILLETT. It was 109,000 tons this last year. Twenty-five years ago it was 25,000 tons.

Mr. GARRETT. You spoke of changing the system?

Mr. WILLETT. Yes, sir; and I am a little surprised that nobody has endeavored to change the entire sugar duty system of the United States, in view of the facts which the gentleman has suggested in regard to increasing the production of beet sugar and domestic sugar.

Mr. GARRETT. In what way?

Mr. WILLETT. Well, Denmark shows the way. They have done it.

Mr. GARRETT. They have a duty of $1.22?

Mr. WILLETT. Yes, sir; on all foreign sugars, and an internal-revenue tax of 49 cents. That is to say, the protection is simply the difference between 49 cents, which is the internal-revenue tax, and $1.22, which is the customhouse duty on foreign sugars. Their protection is 73 cents, or just the same as if our duties were reduced to 73 cents.

Mr. MALBY. Is that exactly true—that is, that their protection is the difference between $1.22 and 49 cents.

Mr. WILLETT. The internal-revenue tax is 49 cents and the tax on foreign sugars is $1.22.

Mr. MALBY. Suppose they import sugar?

Mr. WILLETT. The duty is $1.22.

Mr. MALBY. And not 49 cents also?

Mr. WILLETT. No, sir.

Mr. MALBY. Then, do they pay an internal tax?

Mr. WILLETT. I have it all right here in my record.

Mr. MALBY. Do not spend too much time on it now, but I would like to have you bear that in mind, and indicate it in the record as to whether the importer does not also pay the 49 cents, because if they do not it is different from any other country.

Mr. WILLETT. I will bear that in mind.

Mr. JACOWAY. Do you know the cost of the production of beet sugar in Denmark?

Mr. WILLETT. I think my papers here show it.

Mr. JACOWAY. Do you know the cost of the production of beet sugar in the United States and the cost of production in Denmark?

Mr. WILLETT. I can only give the cost of production from the testimony already had before the committee. I have no personal knowledge of it. The American Sugar Refining Co.'s returns here show what they produced. I think they made 10 per cent on their capitalization last year.

Mr. HINDS. How much beet sugar did they produce in this country this year?

Mr. WILLETT. Five hundred and fifty thousand tons.

Mr. HINDS. How much do you think that they ought to produce in order to maintain a proper equilibrium of prices here?

Mr. WILLETT. Well, just double that amount would do it. I believe that amount, a million tons, would carry us well below any excess in the world's prices.

Mr. HINDS. And would be a great advantage in giving us independence of Europe?

Mr. WILLETT. Yes, sir; and that is a tremendous advantage.

Mr. HINDS. To elaborate a little Mr. Sulzer's question, how would you increase that 500,000 tons of beet sugar to a million tons and still take off the duty? By what method could you do that, and take off the duty?

Mr. WILLETT. Well, I think that is a study for the committee. They have evidence before them as to how much the duty can be reduced without interfering with the American sugar industry. I have not analyzed it sufficiently to be able to answer that question. I have been following casually the returns of the American Sugar Refining Co.'s 36 plants, which are located in every State of the United States, virtually, and my analysis of that statement shows that in 1910 their profits were about $1.10 per hundred pounds.

Mr. HINDS. That is exactly what I was trying to get at. You would not think, then, that free sugar is compatible with the conditions of the beet-sugar industry?

Mr. WILLETT. Decidedly not.

Mr. HINDS. Decidedly not. So that, if you had free sugar, you would have to have some other method of encouraging the beet-sugar industry?

Mr. WILLETT. Well, yes, sir. You mean a bounty?

Mr. HINDS. You would have to have something of that sort, would you not, unless you wished to let the beet-sugar industry go?

Mr. WILLETT. Yes; you would have to have something of that kind. There would be none of the domestic industry that could live under free sugar.

Mr. HINDS. I just wanted to find out exactly what was in your mind on that question, which I thought was a very important question.

Mr. WILLETT. Yes. All the evidence shows that, I think, before the committee or anywhere. As to the exact amount which the duties can be reduced, and the beet-sugar industry not be injured, that is a subject for calculation.

Mr. HINDS. Calculation; yes.

Mr. WILLETT. Yes.

Mr. HINDS. Might not that be a very proper subject for the Tariff Board to take up, with their system of inquiry, by going over the books of the concerns?

Mr. WILLETT. That is what the committee has already done, I understand.

Mr. HINDS. We have had extracts made from the books, but we have not had a real examination, upon our own part, by our own experts.

Mr. WILLETT. I think that is the only way in which you can arrive at just what it costs to produce beet sugar and just what the profits are on its sale. Some of the factories have given you all those facts for the year 1910, which is a normal year.

Mr. HINDS. We got facts as to what it costs to produce a pound of beet sugar.

Mr. WILLETT. I do not think that is of any service to you at all.

Mr. HINDS. That, perhaps, does not give the depreciation. The depreciation would be an essential element, would it not, in keeping an industry?

Mr. WILLETT. The depreciation of a factory is rather a fixed amount. It is generally considered a certain per cent per annum.

Mr. HINDS. It is considered a certain per cent?

Mr. WILLETT. Yes.

Mr. HINDS. That has been arrived at?

Mr. WILLETT. Yes; that has been arrived at, virtually.

Mr. SULZER. On what day of this year did manufactured sugar reach the highest price to the consumer?

Mr. WILLETT. If I had a file of my papers I could give it to you exactly, but I have not.

Mr. SULZER. Will you put that in the record?

Mr. WILLETT. I will put that in. I will make a note of it.

Mr. SULZER. On that day what was the price of manufactured sugar to the people in England? If you have not the figures now, you may put that in.

Mr. WILLETT. No, sir; I have not the figures now.

Mr. SULZER. Will you put those figures in the record?

Mr. WILLETT. Shall I get that for you?

Mr. SULZER. Yes; so that you can put the exact figures in the record. Now tell us, Mr. Willett, why the price on that day was less in England than in the United States.

Mr. WILLETT. I do not think it was, on that day.

Mr. SULZER. I think that on investigation you will find it was.

Mr. WILLETT. It was?

Mr. SULZER. If not——

Mr. WILLETT. I know at that particular time our raw-sugar market had risen above the world's price, for probably two weeks, and during those two weeks we were at the highest point.

Mr. SULZER. I think that is a fact. If it is not so, will you give us your opinion as to why it is not so?

Mr. WILLETT. Yes.

Mr. SULZER. You have said there is a Sugar Trust in Denmark?

Mr. WILLETT. No; two sugar refineries appear to have the entire trade of Denmark. I would not call that a trust.

Mr. SULZER. In your testimony a moment ago you said there was a Sugar Trust in Denmark. You do not mean that?

Mr. WILLETT. No; not precisely.

Mr. SULZER. There is some competition in Denmark?

Mr. WILLETT. No, sir; no competition in Denmark. Two men control the business.

Mr. SULZER. Then those two manufacturers in Denmark have a monopoly?

Mr. WILLETT. Surely; yes, sir; an entire monopoly of the whole country.

Mr. SULZER. You also testified a little while ago that there was a Sugar Trust in the United States. What did you mean by that?

Mr. WILLETT. Why, I meant the so-called Sugar Trust of the United States.

Mr. SULZER. You referred to the American Sugar Refining Co.?

Mr. WILLETT. I referred to the American Sugar Refining Co., the trust, so-called.

Mr. SULZER. As an expert, do you believe that the American Sugar Refining Co. is a trust?

Mr. WILLETT. If you mean by "a trust," a monopoly, no.

Mr. SULZER. What did you mean by "a trust" when you referred to the American Sugar Refining Co. as a trust?

Mr. WILLETT. I was rather taking up the general talk and opinion of the United States; that is all. I simply used the term in the general way in which it is used; that is all.

Mr. SULZER. And not in a legal sense at all?

Mr. WILLETT. No; not in a legal sense at all.

Mr. SULZER. As I understand it, the American Sugar Refining Co. controls about 40 per cent?

Mr. WILLETT. Forty-two per cent.

Mr. SULZER. Forty-two per cent of the manufactured——

Mr. WILLETT. Of the manufacture, yes, sir.

Mr. SULZER (continuing). Of the manufactured product of the United States?

Mr. WILLETT. Of the foreign and domestic trade of the United States.

Mr. SULZER. Yes.

Mr. WILLETT. That is rather larger than the consumption.

Mr. SULZER. And it has, of course, to that extent, material competition?

Mr. WILLETT. Yes, sir.

Mr. SULZER. Do you think it would be a good thing for the consumers of the United States if we could raise in this country enough beet sugar to supply the demands of the people?

Mr. WILLETT. The demands of the people of this country?

Mr. SULZER. Yes.

Mr. WILLETT. I do not think you will ever do that.

Mr. SULZER. Why do you think that can not be done?

Mr. WILLETT. There are several reasons why it can not be done.

Mr. SULZER. Tell us what they are?

Mr. WILLETT. The Sherman law is one.

Mr. SULZER. What has the Sherman law got to do with the production of beet sugar?

Mr. WILLETT. It limits any one interest promoting the beet sugar industry beyond a certain amount. The American Sugar Refining Co., for instance, have reached their limit. They have been the greatest beet-sugar promoters thus far, from 1891 up to recently. Without them the beet-sugar industry to-day would not be half what it is, in all probability, and to-day they are selling out their beet-sugar stocks to bring themselves well within the Sherman law.

This country can not look to them to promote the beet-sugar interests to any further extent.

Mr. SULZER. I think you have misunderstood my question.

Mr. WILLETT. Oh, I beg your pardon.

Mr. SULZER. There is nothing in the so-called antitrust act that limits in any way the production of sugar in this country.

Mr. MALBY. I do not know about that.

Mr. SULZER. You can begin to produce beet sugar. So can I or any other man.

Mr. MALBY. But the extent to which any one person can go——

Mr. SULZER. I am not talking about one person.

Mr. MALBY (continuing). Is clearly within the law.

Mr. WILLETT. The American Sugar Refining Co. have reached the limit to which they can go. They can not promote any more big factories in this country, and it is the Sherman law that prevents it.

Mr. SULZER. I am not talking about that. There is no law that prevents any man in this country from engaging in the production of beet sugar if he wants to engage in the production of beet sugar.

Mr. WILLETT. No, sir; certainly not.

Mr. SULZER. You do not mean to say, as an expert, that the United States can not produce all the beet sugar necessary to meet the requirements of the consumers of the United States? It is simply a question of the cultivation of land, is it not?

Mr. WILLETT. Yes; that is all.

Mr. SULZER. And whether or not it is profitable to the owners of the land to produce sugar beets instead of corn or rye or wheat or barley, or something else?

Mr. WILLETT. Yes.

Mr. SULZER. Now, I ask you again if you think, or if you do not think, that it would be a good thing if the people of the United States could raise all the sugar that they desire?

Mr. WILLETT. A good thing.
Mr. SULZER. Of course it would be a good thing.
Mr. WILLETT. A good thing.
Mr. SULZER. Mr. Hinds suggests that he thinks Sweden does that for itself now. Are you familiar with that?
Mr. WILLETT. I have the Consular Reports on Sweden, but I have not had the time to look them up.
Mr. SULZER. Will you look that up and see whether that is so?
Mr. WILLETT. I will.
Mr. HINDS. I think there has been a Consular Report made within two or three weeks on that subject. I will not be sure of the date.
Mr. WILLETT. I have not had time to examine it. I have the Consular Reports, but lack of time has prevented my examining them all.
Mr. SULZER. If we could produce all the sugar we need for our own consumption, we would be absolutely independent of the world's market, would we not?
Mr. WILLETT. Yes.
Mr. SULZER. And the fixing of prices in Hamburg and other places would have absolutely no effect on the consumers of the United States so far as the price is concerned?
Mr. WILLETT. Not the slightest.
Mr. SULZER. Quite true. Then it is your opinion that it would be a good thing for the Government to encourage the agricultural people of the United States to engage in the production of beet sugar wherever they can do so profitably?
Mr. WILLETT. Decidedly so.
Mr. SULZER. We have vast areas of this country now, have we not, that are peculiarly susceptible to the growth of sugar beets if they were irrigated and properly cultivated?
Mr. WILLETT. Yes.
Mr. SULZER. And with very little effort on the part of the agencies of Government which are not in vogue these vast areas could be brought into production?
Mr. WILLETT. Yes.
Mr. SULZER. And a great increase of beet-sugar production could be brought about?
Mr. WILLETT. Yes.
Mr. SULZER. I think that is all.

(At 12.10 o'clock p. m. the committee took a recess until 2 o'clock p. m.)

AFTER RECESS.

TUESDAY, DECEMBER 5, 1911.

The committee met, pursuant to the taking of recess, at 2 o'clock p. m.

TESTIMONY OF WALLACE P. WILLETT—Continued.

Mr. WILLETT. Mr. Chairman, may I enlarge upon one or two items which were gone over this morning?
The CHAIRMAN. Yes.

Mr. WILLETT. I want to say a word particularly in regard to that low price of 1901. Both the bounty and the cartel were in existence. The treaty was signed March 5, 1902, but it did not go into effect until September 1, 1903.

The CHAIRMAN. We discovered that, by an examination, while you were testifying.

Mr. WILLETT. Yes. In that connection, let me show you what the effect of the postponement of this bounty convention was. You asked what effect that had.

The CHAIRMAN. Yes.

Mr. WILLETT. Take the statistics of those dates. Our Statistical of March 6, 1902, for instance, says:

An agreement to abolish bounties given by the countries represented at this Conference has been reached and was signed March 5.

That was March 5, 1902. Remarking upon that, we say in our paper:

The consensus of opinion seems to be that. as the bounties are not to be abolished until September, 1903, after two crops are marketed, there will be little diminution in the enormous production of beet sugars, in order to take advantage of bounties while they last, and that low prices will continue for a long time to come. Germany may be expected to keep her 400 sugar factories in operation; the beet growers will doubtless accept less for their roots rather than abandon this industry, which they understand so well, and thus the cost of the sugar product will be cheapened while a small advantage will be obtained from the import duty, which is reduced to 6 francs per 100 kilos, equal to about 58 cents per 100 pounds. The German manufacturers will continue to hold the large trade they have built up in England; they are favorably located and will have sufficient advantages to successfully compete with the sugar producers of the West Indies, who must look to the United States for a market.

Mr. Czarnikow, of London, in his report dated London, February 6, 1902, remarked upon this. Shall I read that?

The CHAIRMAN. Yes.

Mr. WILLETT. Under date of February 6, 1902, Czarnikow said:

Should the bounties really be removed—

They were not removed until the 6th of March, and this was one month preceding—

Should the bounties really be removed, the question of date becomes very important; an abolition this autumn would powerfully influence the sowings, as it would raise the cost of production materially. But an abolition in September, 1903, might induce many producers to sow nearly full up, even if they have to pay a little more than present prices of about 80 pfennige=16s. per ton roots. What this price means will become clear from the fact that with less than 7 hundredweight of roots required for 1 hundredweight of sugar, including molasses sugar, and 35 pfennige working expenses, the cost of sugar at factory is 0.80+0.35×7=8s., less official bounty of 1s. 3d., and less the higher cartel bounty. Therefore the contract price of roots could safely be raised, even at present prices of 7s. 4½d. for October–December, of course with the inevitable result that the larger part of the bounties would be frittered away. Owing to the enormous stocks accumulating these would have to be exported or warehoused outside the country before September, 1903. Rumors are current that combined action inside the various associations will be tried to limit sowings, or anyhow, the price of roots, but whether this will succeed remains doubtful, and it partly rests just now with the farmer how much he will sow at present prices. In Germany more than 50 per cent are grown by the factories themselves, and 20 per cent reduction of the balance would only mean 10 per cent of the whole. Elsewhere it is somewhat different. In any case, if bounties are only abolished in 1903, there will be no special inducement to rush permanently into sugar at 7s. 4½d. until a big reduction in sowings has become a certainty.

The CHAIRMAN. The word "roots" is used there by him as synonymous with "sugar beets"?

Mr. WILLETT. Yes; they mean the same thing. That explains the low prices of 1901.

The CHAIRMAN. I notice he gives the cost of production as 8 shillings instead of 9 shillings.

Mr. WILLETT. Yes; that was the extreme low price at that time. Prices ran down extremely low.

Mr. MALBY. What was the effect on the beet-sugar planting and production in the year following 1903, when this agreement did go into effect?

Mr. WILLETT. I have that here. The effect was, in short words, to increase the consumption of sugar in Germany, as I have already explained, and to decrease the production, and to lower the price of sugars to the German consumers very largely and raise the price of sugars for export to the outside world.

Mr. HINDS. That was an export bounty entirely, was it?

Mr. WILLETT. That was an export bounty of 38 cents a hundred which the German Government gave, besides which the manufacturers and the refiners of Germany had a combination which they called a cartel, by which arrangement they sold sugars for export at 26 cents a hundred pounds plus the bounty; bounty 38 and cartel 26.

Mr. HINDS. That bounty applied only to sugars sold abroad?

Mr. WILLETT. That is all.

Mr. HINDS. It did not apply to sugars manufactured and sold in Germany?

Mr. WILLETT. No, sir. The German manufacturers sold sugars to consumers in Germany at 77 cents a hundred profit. They sold sugars for export at 17 cents actual loss.

Mr. HINDS. They sold it under cost?

Mr. WILLETT. Under cost, 17 cents a hundred.

Mr. HINDS. Yes.

Mr. WILLETT. Realizing on the whole business, export and consumption, a profit. I have the cartel here, in detail, which the chairman wished me to put in. Would you like to have me read it?

The CHAIRMAN. No, I think not. I think we already have that cartel in the record.

Mr. MALBY. I was considering, in my own mind, what the cartel was. We have some information about it.

The CHAIRMAN. Are you familiar with it? It is in Mr. Palmer's testimony, I think. Did he not give us the cartel?

Mr. WILLETT. I have not Mr. Palmer's testimony. I think the cartel is in the testimony; but I do not think that the profits which accrued to the German manufacturers and refiners are given.

The CHAIRMAN. Mr. Palmer's Exhibit No. 10, on page 2640 of the record, contains a description of that. Will you look at that and see if that is not the same thing you have, and if it is not, we will try yours.

Mr. WILLETT (after examining p. 2640). It is all there, with the exception that this statement gives, in addition to that, what the syndicate of German sugar refiners make.

The CHAIRMAN. I suppose that is obtained by simply multiplying the number of pounds of consumption by the profits set out here.

Mr. WILLETT. For instance, in brief, during the year ending September 30, 1911, which includes the time of low prices, the German refiners sold 691,000 tons of refined sugar at Magdeburg for home consumption. The profit of 73.6 per hundred pounds on this amount of sugar makes $11,392,102. They sold 547,000 tons at Hamburg, for export, on which they lost 11½ cents a hundred pounds, which on that amount of sugar makes $1,409,072. In other words, the cartel made $11,392,102 for the German refiners on their Magdeburg business and lost them $1,409,072 on their Hamburg business. On all their business they made $9,983,030.

The amount which they threw away or gave away in order to keep out foreign refined sugar under this system was $1,409,072; and after throwing that amount away they had a profit remaining of $9,983,030 on refined sugar.

Mr. RAKER. It pays to throw away a little once in awhile.

The CHAIRMAN. They were doing that to extend their market?

Mr. WILLETT. To make their production larger; to benefit their domestic industry.

Now, there is one other point, and that is with regard to the Philippines. This is under date of November 23, 1904, and was printed in our paper of March 2, 1905. The Brussels convention, in the course of its session, in October, examined the fiscal régime to which sugar is subjected in various countries, including the Philippine Islands. This says:

> In conformity with the stipulations of the Brussels convention, the commission has decided that sugars coming from these countries shall, on importation into the States parties to the sugar union, be subjected to countervailing duties which have been fixed at the rates indicated below:
>
> Philippine Islands, countervailing duties, 11.5 cents per hundred pounds on raw sugars, and on refined sugars, 40.6 cents per hundred pounds.
>
> On an appeal by the Government of Great Britain against the above decision as affecting sugar from all the countries mentioned except Brazil, the Commission agreed to adjourn the fresh discussion of the decision until April next.

That stood in that position, with the countervailing duty on, but not enforced, until, in our paper of December 21, 1905, we say that the Brussels Convention has decided:

> Fifth. Regarding the Philippines there exists a surtax, but the commission has decided that this surtax can not be construed to mean a bounty for raw or refined sugar.

The CHAIRMAN. That was the Philippine matter that we had up this morning?

Mr. WILLETT. The Philippine matter.

The CHAIRMAN. Will any one of you gentlemen supplement the examination any further, or ask any additional questions that have not already been asked, that occur to you?

Mr. MALBY. There is one question that I do not know whether Mr. Willett answered or not—whether the sugar imported into Denmark had to pay an import tax.

Mr. WILLETT. I have not looked that up yet.

Mr. MALBY. That was the only question that I had in mind.

Mr. HINDS. Mr. Willett, you spoke of beet sugar coming onto the market at the time of high prices, this year. At what price did that beet sugar come onto the market?

Mr. WILLETT. The beet-sugar industry this year did not get the advantage of the high prices, to any extent. They did not foresee, evidently, the prices to which sugars would rise, and consequently they began selling their product ahead, and the average price at which the American beet-sugar companies sold their product this year was somewhere about 5¼ cents, whereas the price afterwards rose to 7½ cents.

Mr. HINDS. Seven and a half cents?

Mr. WILLETT. Yes; so that actually they did not get the benefit of the rise.

Mr. HINDS. But they got a little better price than they would get usually, did they?

Mr. WILLETT. Oh, yes.

Mr. HINDS. At about what price do they usually come into the market?

Mr. WILLETT. That is a full cent a pound higher than in 1910.

Mr. HINDS. Then there were two advantages from the beet-sugar crop this year, so far as the public were concerned, the advantage of a slightly lower price because they did not foresee the rise, and the other advantage, of having that store of sugar in the country, I suppose?

Mr. WILLETT. Yes.

Mr. HINDS. That would be the other advantage?

Mr. WILLETT. To supply the country during the intermediate period between crops.

Mr. HINDS. If we had not had that store of sugar in this country, we would have had to do as Europe did, and import sugar?

Mr. WILLETT. We would have had to do as Europe did; import sugar; from Java, principally.

Mr. HINDS. Would that have resulted in slightly further raising the sugar price?

Mr. WILLETT. Undoubtedly; in addition to the demand of Europe, the demand of America would have made the price higher than any other price we have seen.

The CHAIRMAN. Suppose they had not made these future contracts, would not the beet-sugar people have gotten the advantage of this rise?

Mr. WILLETT. Yes.

The CHAIRMAN. So that if they had not sold out to these people in advance, it would not have done the people of the United States any good or been of any advantage to them, excepting so far as it affected the world's supply?

Mr. WILLETT. Yes. The beet-sugar men in Colorado, for instance, and Utah, did at one time make a price for sugars within their States, lower than the current prices outside of the State.

The CHAIRMAN. Since this investigation has been on?

Mr. WILLETT. Since this investigation began.

Mr. HINDS. You think that the 600,000 tons of beet sugar which we produced would not have been a sufficient amount to have tipped the scale of prices this year, in the dearth of this year; that is, if these contracts had not been existing?

Mr. WILLETT. No; 600,000 tons or any other amount less than the actual requirements of the United States, independent of Europe, would not have had any effect.

Mr. HINDS. Yes. In other words, the quantity that you produce is an essential element?

Mr. WILLETT. A very essential element in the prices at one season of the year.

Mr. HINDS. You speak of our being independent of Europe.

Mr. WILLETT. Yes.

Mr. HINDS. Even, although we produced enough to, as you might say, supply ourselves, nevertheless that would not give us sugar any cheaper than they would get it in Europe on that specific year, would it?

Mr. WILLETT. It would give us sugar always cheaper than they would get it in Europe in any year, if I understand your question right.

Mr. HINDS. Yes. You think, then, it would be possible for us to get sugar, by reason of our greater production——

Mr. WILLETT. At all times——

Mr. HINDS (continuing). Under the world's price?

Mr. WILLETT. At all times under the world's price. We get it now at all times except for two or three months in the year.

Mr. HINDS. Would not the sugar prices seek a level? Is it not a fluid enough commodity? If we had a great enough supply in this country, would not that react on Europe and bring the prices down there? Would not that bring prices down there?

Mr. WILLETT. In the distant future, if we ever produce more sugar than we consume, it would have an influence on European prices; that is, under present conditions. But that is in the far distant future, possibly. It looks to me as if this talk about producing all the sugar in this country that we can consume is too large a proposition, and not required. We have got to consider Cuba in this situation, and if you produce 500,000 tons more of beet sugar in this country, the problem will be solved just as readily as if we produced 3,000,000 tons.

Mr. HINDS. Does Germany produce all the beet sugar she uses?

Mr. WILLETT. Yes; and a million tons more, of which 770,000 goes to England.

Mr. HINDS. Does England use much cane sugar?

Mr. WILLETT. Very little.

Mr. HINDS. Very little?

Mr. WILLETT. She uses some, which she gets from her colonies, mainly.

Mr. HINDS. Is there much cane sugar used on the Continent of Europe?

Mr. WILLETT. Very little, comparatively speaking.

Mr. HINDS. Why is that? Cane sugar is produced more cheaply than beet sugar, is it not?

Mr. WILLETT. Well, it depends upon the country where it is produced. Java, for instance, can produce sugars cheaper than Cuban cane sugars.

Mr. HINDS. Can Cuba produce cane sugar cheaper than Germany can produce beet sugar?

Mr. WILLETT. At about the same price.

Mr. HINDS. At about the same price, yes. So that we are in a vastly different situation as regards our sugar supply from that in which European countries are?

Mr. WILLETT. Entirely.

Mr. HINDS. We take largely cane sugar and they take largely beet sugar?

Mr. WILLETT. Yes.

Mr. HINDS. What is the cause of that difference?

Mr. WILLETT. That European countries have promoted their beet industries from nothing to the present size.

Mr. HINDS. That is for the sake of getting the sugar or for the incidental agricultural benefit?

Mr. WILLETT. Well, incidental agricultural benefit. Producing sugar on lands helps the lands for other crops as well. Here is a paper giving the world's production of cane and beet sugars from 1883 to the present time in the principal countries, Europe, Asia, Africa, America, and Australia. In 1883, for instance, the amount of cane sugar produced was 1,277,000 tons, and the amount of beet sugar produced was only 204,000 tons.

Mr. HINDS. How is it to-day, if you have the figures for to-day?

Mr. WILLETT. The year 1905 is the latest that I have on this paper. The cane-sugar production is 4,943,000 tons, and the beet-sugar production is 7,215,000 tons.

Mr. HINDS. Mr. Chairman, I wonder if that table would be worth putting in the record? Have we anything like that in the record?

Mr. LOWRY. You have one like that, which I put in the record.

The CHAIRMAN. Mr. Lowry put in one and also Mr. Foreman put in one.

Mr. WILLETT. I do not think it is possible you could have had this table.

Mr. LOWRY. Mine was taken from Willett & Gray.

Mr. WILLETT. This is the only copy of this in existence. This is not printed.

The CHAIRMAN. Will you look on page 2624 of the record? There you will see, in Exhibit No. 1 of Mr. Palmer, is given the production of cane sugar in the world from 1812 to 1910, inclusive, and also the beet-sugar production of the world. Do you see that statement?

Mr. WILLETT. Yes, sir.

The CHAIRMAN. That seems to be pretty complete, does it not?

Mr. WILLETT. Yes, it is. I think you would probably not need this of mine at all.

The CHAIRMAN. Very well. Take the sugar campaign of 1910 and 1911 and look down there and see whether your figures disagree with his at all. It is about half and half.

Mr. WILLETT (after examination). Yes; that is all correct.

The CHAIRMAN. I thought you gave a different figure on that.

Mr. HINDS. That is for 1905?

The CHAIRMAN. Yes; that is right.

Mr. WILLETT. It is 6,700,000 tons of cane sugar and 7,217,000 tons of beet sugar.

The CHAIRMAN. That is different from his, is it not?

Mr. WILLETT. You see, he does not include Australia.

The CHAIRMAN. He states in a note where he gets his statistics.

Mr. HINDS. I suppose that excess of beet sugar along about 1899 and 1900—for the years along there—was due to the trouble in Cuba, was it?

Mr. WILLETT. The excess of beet sugar?

Mr. HINDS. Yes; in the production.

Mr. WILLETT. No; that was entirely due to the bounty and the cartel.

Mr. HINDS. I say, in Europe.

The CHAIRMAN. The Cuban insurrection might have affected that to some extent, as taking from cane production?

Mr. WILLETT. Yes.

Mr. HINDS. And do you think that with the bounty and cartel abolished the production of cane sugar is going to increase; do you think that the production of cane sugar will go into the ascendancy; that is, that there will be a larger production of cane sugar than beet sugar?

Mr. WILLETT. There is every endeavor making to increase the production of both Cuba and Java, which are the largest cane-producing countries.

Mr. HINDS. I see, apparently, the high tide of beet-sugar production—relative production—was about 1900.

Mr. WILLETT. I think that has been reached.

Mr. HINDS. And since then it has been gravitating around at a little lower proportion.

Mr. WILLETT. From general estimate of the situation, as an expert I should say that beet-sugar production had about reached its highest possible limits.

Mr. HINDS. That is, its highest possible relative limits—relative to cane?

Mr. WILLETT. Yes; relative to cane.

Mr. HINDS. You do not mean its absolute limit as to the amount of production?

Mr. WILLETT. I would almost say that; in Europe, I am speaking of.

Mr. HINDS. In Europe?

Mr. WILLETT. Not here.

Mr. HINDS. Not here?

Mr. WILLETT. Oh, no.

Mr. HINDS. Can beet sugar be produced, for instance, on the seaboard as far north as New England?

Mr. WILLETT. In 1834 the first beet-sugar factory in the country was established at Franklin, Mass. When I was in Boston and located in a country town, Ipswich, the farmers in Ipswich were raising beets for that factory. I do not find my papers on that matter. Did not Mr. Palmer introduce something on that?

The CHAIRMAN. To what do you refer?

Mr. WILLETT. The production of beet sugar from 1830 to 1911?

The CHAIRMAN. Yes.

Mr. WILLETT. You have that?

The CHAIRMAN. Yes; from 1812 to 1910, inclusive.

Mr. WILLETT. From 1830 to 1911, the production of beet sugar in this country?

The CHAIRMAN. Yes; that is there, too, I think, on page 2624.

Mr. WILLETT. I am speaking about the production of American beet sugar.

The CHAIRMAN. Yes; he gives it from 1877 to 1911.

Mr. WILLETT. He does not give it from 1830?

The CHAIRMAN. No, he does not. On page 2627 he gives a table which gives the United States production of beet sugar in long tons, in the second column, from 1877 to 1911. My recollection is that that is the only table of that kind which he gave.

Mr. WILLETT. I have a paper which gives the beet-sugar industry in the United States from its very foundation, in 1830, when it was in an experimental stage. I have not that paper here, but I can send it to you if you wish it, giving the details of the experimental stage of the beet-sugar industry and as far back as 1830; and some years later there was a factory established in Franklin, Mass., and that factory failed. There was a factory in Portland, Me., where they also tried to raise beets, and contracted with the farmers to raise them; but when the time came for delivering the beets at the factory the farmers, on driving their loads of beets to the factory, were met by other farmers, who offered them more money for the beets to feed out to their cattle than the factory was paying them, so that factory failed. It did not get the beets. So that, so far as Massachusetts and Maine are concerned, beet sugar has been tried and has made a failure. In New York State also, although they paid a bounty, it has failed, and they have gone out of business there. So that in answer to your question I can say that the beet-sugar industry would only succeed in the western part of the United States, and particularly in irrigation States or along the Lakes, as on Lake Michigan.

Mr. MALBY. They could not get the farmers in New York to raise the beets?

Mr. WILLETT. No, sir; that was the trouble.

Mr. MALBY. For several years we subsidized them, and regulated the price which they were to receive, not less than $5 a ton; but even then they did not raise them in sufficient quantities to make it possible.

Mr. WILLETT. No; the factories were moved west. One of them is run in California now, by the Warner Sugar Refining Co. It was transported to California by them and is being worked out there now.

Mr. MALBY. There were two in New York—one at Lyons and the other at Binghamton.

Mr. RAKER. The one at Lyons is the one that is now located in California?

Mr. WILLETT. Yes; Warner & Co. bought it and moved it there.

Mr. RAKER. Yes.

Mr. WILLETT. In that connection, why did Warner & Co. choose California in preference to some other State for putting up a beet-sugar factory?

The CHAIRMAN. Why?

Mr. WILLETT. The tariff, I suppose.

The CHAIRMAN. The tariff?

Mr. WILLETT. Yes. If we had free sugar now, the California industry could survive.

The CHAIRMAN. California is best adapted to the cultivation of the sugar beet?

Mr. WILLETT. Yes, it is best adapted; and yet it has a limited market, for less than 100,000 tons, west of the Rocky Mountains. But it could survive and ship its sugar to this side of the Rocky Mountains under free sugar, and that is why Warner & Co. joined the beet-sugar industry.

The CHAIRMAN. Are there any other questions?

Mr. RAKER. This is on a subject you have gone over. Just incidentally, referring to this Warner enterprise in southern California, to show how well they are doing, they offered to their stockholders, those who would go in, 25 per cent dividends, did they not?

Mr. WILLETT. I do not know.

Mr. RAKER. You did not get a record of that?

Mr. WILLETT. No, sir.

Mr. MALBY. They ought not to have had any difficulty in selling that stock.

Mr. RAKER. I really think they did not. Mr. Willett, going back to your trip to the West, for what purpose did you go to California?

Mr. WILLETT. To California?

Mr. RAKER. Yes; on that western trip.

Mr. WILLETT. I went to talk with Mr. Cutler on the way to California and back; that was all.

Mr. RAKER. Did you see any of the sugar people while you were in California?

Mr. WILLETT. Oh, no; nobody.

Mr. RAKER. Did you not discuss the matter there at all?

Mr. WILLETT. No, sir; I left the Golden Gate, and while Mr. Cutler was doing his California business I was seeing the sights. I had never been there before. And it was the same way in Salt Lake City. While Mr. Cutler was fixing deals there I went down in the silver mines, and went to the concert given to Queen Lil in the Tabernacle, and investigated Mormonism from A to Z.

Mr. RAKER. That was interesting; but you did not take in the Idaho matter at all?

Mr. WILLETT. Not at all.

Mr. RAKER. When you returned did you make any report to anyone?

Mr. WILLETT. No, sir.

Mr. RAKER. On the result of that visit?

Mr. WILLETT. No, sir; except that Mr. Cutler was coming on; that was all.

Mr. RAKER. You did not make any observations, in your paper, on the trip, or on the conditions in the beet-sugar industry?

Mr. WILLETT. None at all; no, sir.

Mr. RAKER. Then the statement heretofore made in the record that you were employed by Mr. Havemeyer to make an inspection of the beet-sugar industry of the West for him does not give the facts as they actually existed?

Mr. WILLETT. Oh, no. I have given you the full facts, so far as I am concerned.

The CHAIRMAN. How about Colorado, the factories in Colorado, or the Utah proposition?

Mr. WILLETT. That had nothing to do with it, and the subject was never mentioned afterwards between Mr. Havemeyer and myself.

Mr. RAKER. Did you to any of the other members of the then American Sugar Refinery Co.?

Mr. WILLETT. No, sir.

Mr. RAKER. To any of the other members, stockholders or directors?

Mr. WILLETT. No, sir.

Mr. RAKER. On the supply of sugar, that is the excess over the amount necessary for use, in the year 1910, I understood you to say that it was 400,000 tons; is that it?

Mr. WILLETT. In 1910?

Mr. RAKER. Yes.

Mr. Willett. There was an excess of 800,000 tons over the requirements for consumption. What was left over on September 1 was 800,000 tons.

Mr. Raker. Yes. I want to confine myself to 1910.

Mr. Willett. Yes.

Mr. Raker. What was it in the United States, do you remember?

Mr. Willett. The amount carried over in 1910, in the United States?

Mr. Raker. Yes; can you give it approximately?

Mr. Willett. I can give it to you exactly for 1910.

Mr. Raker. All right.

Mr. Willett. Perhaps this paper will give you what you are aiming at. Here is the total interstate and foreign trade for 1910 of the United States.

Mr. Raker. I wanted to know what was in the United States, or reported in the United States, in excess of the consumption for that year, that was supposed to be held as actual sugar on hand at the end of the year, which you say would be September 1.

Mr. Willett. No; our year would begin the 1st of January.

Mr. Raker. What is that?

Mr. Willett. The first of our year would be January 1.

Mr. Raker. Very well; January 1.

Mr. Willett. About 100,000 tons, approximately. I think it was above that. That would be January 1, 1911.

Mr. Raker. How did you get that information?

Mr. Willett. Of the stock?

Mr. Raker. Yes.

Mr. Willett. We got that from the refineries and importers.

Mr. Raker. That they had that much on hand?

Mr. Willett. Yes; direct.

Mr. Raker. What was the excess on hand January 1, 1911?

Mr. Willett. That is January 1, 1911, which I gave you.

Mr. Raker. No; I said January 1, 1910.

Mr. Willett. Oh, 1910?

Mr. Raker. Yes. This applies, now, to the United States.

Mr. Willett. I will correct those figures which I just gave.

Mr. Raker. All right.

Mr. Willett. The stock, January 1, 1910, was 71,412 tons, and in 1911 it was 50,069 tons, a decrease of 21,343 tons.

Mr. Raker. Between 1910 and 1911?

Mr. Willett. Yes.

Mr. Raker. The rise in the price of sugar commenced some time the latter part of June, did it not, 1911?

Mr. Willett. Of 1911; yes, sir.

Mr. Raker. It was about 10 points, was it not, at that time?

Mr. Willett. This gives 1910, but not 1911. In 1911 the first rise, according to my recollection, was from 4 to 5 cents; for granulated sugar, from 4½, one-half—about half a cent a pound.

Mr. Raker. That was in July?

Mr. Willett. Yes.

Mr. Raker. And it continued along until about the middle of November?

Mr. Willett. Yes.

Mr. Raker. And that was about the highest, some time about the middle of November, was it not?

Mr. WILLETT. I think it was earlier than that; about the first week in November; it went to 7.35.

Mr. RAKER. Have you any statistics showing the amount of foreign sugar imported into the United States between the 1st of July and the 1st of November, 1911?

Mr. WILLETT. I can give you that exactly from my office. I have not the paper here.

Mr. RAKER. Can you give the same data for December 1?

Mr. WILLETT. No; I have no paper with me since January 5, 1911.

Mr. RAKER. You can produce those data?

Mr. WILLETT. Oh, yes; anything you want.

Mr. RAKER. Will you make two tabulated statements, one from January 1, 1911, up to December 1, 1911, and then one from July 1, 1911, to November 1, 1911? I want two tables.

Mr. WILLETT. Imports of foreign sugars?

Mr. RAKER. Yes.

Mr. WILLETT. And from what ports?

Mr. RAKER. And from what ports? I will include in those ports Cuba and Java and Porto Rico.

Mr. WILLETT. And the British West Indies?

Mr. RAKER. Yes.

Mr. WILLETT. They come in. Shall I divide the preferential duty and the full duty?

Mr. RAKER. If you can; if you will.

Mr. WILLETT. I will do that.

Mr. RAKER. Offhand, can you say whether or not there was any more raw sugar sent in during that time, say, from July 1, 1911, until the 1st of November, 1911, than there was during the same time in 1910?

Mr. WILLETT. In 1910 the imports were very much larger than in 1911.

Mr. RAKER. During the same time?

Mr. WILLETT. During the same time; very much larger. Would you like those also?

Mr. RAKER. Yes.

Mr. WILLETT. Compared?

Mr. RAKER. Yes; now, the same way with reference to the prices paid for the imported sugar during the same time. You have not that with you, either, have you?

Mr. WILLETT. Yes; I have that. Prices paid for sugars imported during that period?

Mr. RAKER. Yes.

Mr. WILLETT. Yes, sir; bear in mind that those sugars, the Javas particularly, which were imported in that time, were put on board vessel a month to three months before they arrived, at prices existing sometimes three months before their arrival. Would you rather have the prices when they were put on board ship, or the prices on the days of arrival?

Mr. RAKER. Give the price when they made the contract and also the price on the date of arrival, to show the different prices as they existed on the respective dates.

Do I understand from your analysis of the situation during the months named—June, July, August, September, and October—that the price paid by the importer was correspondingly high as the price he sold his product for?

Mr. WILLETT. Yes.

Mr. RAKER. Did he pay the same, proportionately——

Mr. WILLETT. Yes; the same proportionate prices.

Mr. RAKER (continuing). For the imported sugar as he got for the article sold?

Mr. WILLETT. Yes; no particular variation from normal times. In fact, the refiners' policy always has been, whatever they paid for raw sugar, to add about 87 or 89 cents for cost of refining and profit, and to sell the sugar on that basis, whatever they paid for the raw.

Mr. RAKER. On that question, now, particularly with regard to the months named, have you made an analysis, so as to be able to state that the importers—that is, those who bought the sugar; I do not mean the importers, but I mean those who bought the sugar, the refiners—paid an excess, or an excess equal to the amount for which they sold the refined sugar, giving themselves the same profit as they had done when the sugar was low, during the months named?

Mr. WILLETT. That is my recollection.

Mr. RAKER. Have you statistics to show that fact?

Mr. WILLETT. Yes, sir; I can give you statistics.

Mr. RAKER. And you will do it?

Mr. WILLETT. Yes. What you want is the difference between raw and refined sugar during June, July, August, September, and October?

Mr. RAKER. Yes.

The CHAIRMAN. Let me see if I understand that. He wishes to know whether the refiners' margin increased during that time?

Mr. WILLETT. Yes.

The CHAIRMAN. You say it did not?

Mr. WILLETT. I say my recollection is that it did not vary during that time.

The CHAIRMAN. In other words, that the refiners on their margin got no more?

Mr. WILLETT. They just made the usual average difference above.

Mr. RAKER. Did anybody in the beet-sugar industry make any more during that time?

Mr. WILLETT. No, sir.

Mr. RAKER. Did not the Louisiana sugar refiners send a committee up to New York and sell their crop at an advance? The newspaper reports were that they went home satisfied.

Mr. WILLETT. They went home satisfied.

The CHAIRMAN. We are not weighing anything or passing on anything, or doing anything but taking testimony; but it looks like any fellow wants to get as much as he can for anything he has, cotton or corn or sugar cane.

Mr. WILLETT. That was a very fortunate visit.

The CHAIRMAN. So that they did profit by it?

Mr. WILLETT. It was a fortunate visit that those Louisiana planters made to New York.

The CHAIRMAN. They sent a committee up to New York?

Mr. WILLETT. They sent a committee up and they made a very fortunate contract of sale. To-day those who are not in the contract are not as well off on the present market as those who are in the contract.

The CHAIRMAN. Judge Raker, will you ask him to tell us briefly about that?

Mr. RAKER. Yes.

The CHAIRMAN. Did you notice that in the papers?

Mr. RAKER. Yes. Mr. Willett, what do you know about the recent visit of the Louisiana sugar planters to New York, to the American Sugar Refining Co., and their dealings with them? Just give us the history of it.

Mr. WILLETT. I did not personally see the members, either one of them; and all I know is by——

The CHAIRMAN. General reputation?

Mr. WILLETT. Yes.

The CHAIRMAN. Well, you see, we are not bound by the strict rules of law. Just describe the transaction as you understood it and as you believe it was.

Mr. WILLETT. Why, they came to a conclusion to sell their early production—it is all in our paper, the whole thing.

The CHAIRMAN. It is?

Mr. WILLETT. As I recollect it.

The CHAIRMAN. Well, just state it for us.

Mr. WILLETT. They came to the conclusion to sell their early production at the current price in New York on the day of delivery in New Orleans, for the month of October, which would be very few sugars. For November they sold at the New York price, less——

Mr. LOWRY. Fifteen points.

Mr. WILLETT. Fifteen points; at 12½ points for December, and January and February at 6½ points off the New York price.

The CHAIRMAN. So that they sold for future delivery at the contract price?

Mr. WILLETT. They contracted to sell their entire product, or nearly the entire product, of each planter who was represented by this committee.

The CHAIRMAN. Do you know what percentage of the Louisiana product that committee represented?

Mr. WILLETT. I think they represented 75 per cent of the refining sugar.

The CHAIRMAN. That is about what I read in the paper, that they represented three-fourths, at least, of the Louisiana product.

Mr. WILLETT. Three-fourths of the total production of refining sugars. Of course Louisiana produces sugars for direct consumption.

The CHAIRMAN. I mean outside of the sugars that went into direct consumption.

Mr. RAKER. You made a report on that in your paper?

Mr. WILLETT. It was all in our paper at the time. Would you like a copy of it?

The CHAIRMAN. Yes; you might put that in the record.

Mr. WILLETT. I can vouch for that, because I got that from the American Sugar Refining Co. themselves, and also from New Orleans, so that it is absolutely correct, that statement.

The CHAIRMAN. And it was published in all the journals.

Mr. WILLETT. And it was published all over the East.

Mr. RAKER. Was there any written contract entered into on this matter? Do you know?

Mr. WILLETT. No, sir; I do not know.

The CHAIRMAN. You did not learn?

Mr. WILLETT. No, sir.

The CHAIRMAN. That was the contract, and I guess it was a written contract. That is a mere surmise on my part.

Mr. GARRETT. The jobbers got a lot of profit out of beet sugar, you know.

Mr. WILLETT. The New York quotation is telegraphed to New Orleans every day by the brokers who act as the intermediaries in assigning the New York market price, Nevers & Callahan.

Mr. GARRETT. I understand that the beet-sugar manufacturers did not get any benefit from the increase in price of refined sugar?

Mr. WILLETT. They got some benefit. They did not get all they might have obtained.

Mr. GARRETT. They did not get all they might have, because most of their sugar had been sold on contract?

Mr. WILLETT. Exactly. They got 5½ cents for their sugars, which would be fully 1 cent a pound more than the normal price.

The CHAIRMAN. In other words, they got the advantage of the market price at the time they made the contract, as you would in the sale of cotton.

Mr. GARRETT. But not the full advantage of the increase.

The CHAIRMAN. No.

Mr. WILLETT. Not the advantage which they would have gotten if they had kept the goods until the people wanted them.

The CHAIRMAN. So far as they had not sold their product, they got the benefit?

Mr. WILLETT. Yes.

The CHAIRMAN. And the beet growers got no more, because they had contracted for their crop in advance?

Mr. WILLETT. No, sir.

Mr. GARRETT. The jobbers probably made more out of it than anybody else, so far as beet sugar was concerned.

Mr. WILLETT. The jobbers were the ones who made the money; yes.

Mr. RAKER. Now, going back to the amount of sugar on hand, is it not a fact that these refiners and those interested in the disposing of the sugar keep a plenty on hand to run them two or three months?

Mr. WILLETT. During the crop season, the Cuba crop season, they sometimes have as much as 300,000 tons on hand.

Mr. RAKER. That does not commence until November, does it?

Mr. WILLETT. It begins in January.

Mr. RAKER. January?

Mr. WILLETT. January and February. In February and March, when the Cuba crop is selling at its lowest point in the year, because the Cuban planter wants to sell his crop, a certain portion of it, as fast as he makes it, the price goes to a low level every year. Then the refiner carries a much larger stock or accumulation than at any other season of the year, sometimes as much as 300,000 tons, according to the size of the refinery.

Mr. RAKER. What I want to get at is this. During the months of July and August the refiners had a supply of old sugar on hand, did they not?

Mr. WILLETT. In 1911?

Mr. RAKER. Yes; in 1911.

Mr. WILLETT. Yes, sir; they had a good supply of sugars on hand in 1911.

Mr. RAKER. And they did not have to import any sugar to meet their demand during those months?

Mr. WILLETT. No, sir; they had an abundant supply. Of course, they were buying sugars all that time. They were buying sugars then. Fifty thousand tons of sugar is used a week, you know.

Mr. RAKER. What I am trying to find out from you as an expert, Mr. Willett, who has had a great many years of experience, is whether or not you could tell the committee if these men had on hand a supply of sugar for July and August?

Mr. WILLETT. Undoubtedly.

Mr. RAKER. That they had carried over from May and June?

Mr. WILLETT. Undoubtedly.

Mr. RAKER. Then in raising the price of sugar during that time it was not because they had to pay more for this particular stock of sugar that they sold during the months of June and July?

Mr. WILLETT. No, sir.

Mr. RAKER. Could you say how long that supply, as shown by their records as you have published them, would last them, and did last them, without replenishing it by any new purchases?

Mr. WILLETT. Not over four weeks, at that time of year—about a month.

Mr. RAKER. That would commence in September?

Mr. WILLETT. In September they had less sugar.

Mr. RAKER. The beet sugar would begin to come in, would it not?

Mr. WILLETT. Domestic beet?

Mr. RAKER. Yes.

Mr. WILLETT. Not until October, to any extent. The California beet would come in in August.

Mr. RAKER. That is what I was coming back to.

Mr. WILLETT. California would come in in August; but this side of the Rockies not until October.

Mr. RAKER. Then, they would have in August and September the California beet-sugar supply?

Mr. WILLETT. Yes, sir.

Mr. RAKER. A new supply?

Mr. WILLETT. Yes, sir.

Mr. RAKER. And they paid no more for that because of the raise in sugar, did they?

Mr. WILLETT. The refiners did not buy that. That went direct to the consumers. The California beet-sugar people refine their production at the factory. The refiners do not buy beet sugar.

Mr. RAKER. I understand. But, for the general market, those men had that sugar on hand?

Mr. WILLETT. The California beet-sugar interests got the full price of the sugar for their product, of course.

Mr. RAKER. Themselves?

Mr. WILLETT. Yes.

Mr. RAKER. The man that raised the beets did not get any more?

Mr. WILLETT. No more.

Mr. RAKER. And those that had sold their sugar in advance of course would get the low price that they sold it for if it was sold on future contracts in May and June?

Mr. WILLETT. Your point is that the refiner, on the advancing market, carrying large stocks of sugar, got large profits. That is the fact. On the reverse side, since it turned the high point, carrying stocks he losses money, but carrying small stocks he loses less than he makes.

Mr. RAKER. That is evident to the public; but I want to find out whether you can tell us where we could find out definitely the quantity of sugar that was actually on hand during these months named from their own reports.

Mr. WILLETT. You could get it from their own reports. Our circular of October 1 would give the stock of sugar in the United States.

Mr. RAKER. Yes.

Mr. WILLETT. And that stock on October 1 is corrected from the refiners' stocks. For instance, Mr. Spreckels testified before the committee that we could not possibly know the meltings of sugars because we never asked them. As a matter of fact, our papers all say that our meltings are estimated from week to week and revised at certain periods by favor of the refiners—which is a fact. All the refiners give us their stocks at certain periods—say, January, July, October; about four months in the year—and the Federal Sugar Refiners give us their stocks the same as the others. Mr. Spreckels personally does not give them, but Mr. Smith, the selling agent, does. So that our circular of the 1st of October would answer your question as to the actual stocks on hand held by the refiners and importers—the 1st of October. I might add this: Running from July to August, 1911, on estimates week by week, on the 1st of October we came out within 5,000 tons of the actual meltings. That shows how closely we keep tab. We keep a record of every report that every refiner makes throughout the country for the year. Then all we need, of course, is their stocks from time to time, to see what the meltings were during certain periods; and I think our statistics are correct in that respect.

Mr. RAKER. Then, as a matter of fact, the American Sugar Refining Co. and those who sold during that time made an enormous profit off of the sugar on hand, by virtue of the raising of the price?

Mr. WILLETT. They made a good profit; yes.

Mr. RAKER. Well, above what they stated was a reasonable profit, when sugar was at 4.75 and 5.25. Is not that right?

Mr. WILLETT. Yes; they made a profit of 1 cent a pound there.

Mr. RAKER. The beet-sugar industry in Colorado and Utah begin in September to get their new crop in, too?

Mr. WILLETT. And October. They began to sell it in September before they got it, and selling it in September they took a lower basis than they would have taken if they had waited.

Mr. RAKER. As a matter of fact, taking it all through——

Mr. WILLETT. They derived great benefit from the rise in sugars—both the cane refiners and the beet-sugar men; the cane refiners only on the rise of the raw sugars and not on any difference between the market price of raws and the market price of refined.

Mr. RAKER. It is something peculiar——

Mr. WILLETT. It is an abnormal year, in other words; 1910 was a more normal year.

Mr. RAKER. It is something peculiar to me that the rise of sugar in the East corresponded with the rise in the West. It was just the same, was it not?

Mr. WILLETT. Oh, yes.

Mr. RAKER. It raised 10 points here and raised 10 points all over the United States?

Mr. WILLETT. Well, all the United States prices are based on daily quotations from the New York market.

Mr. RAKER. Irrespective of the quantity of sugar on hand in Colorado, Utah, etc.?

Mr. WILLETT. Irrespective of anything. The price is the New York basis, plus the freight.

Mr. RAKER. And they adopted that, notwithstanding the fact that there was no raw sugar to be imported by them. They raised the price right on up with that placed by the New York market.

Mr. WILLETT. Yes.

Mr. RAKER. And the sugar-beet people—that is, those who were interested in the manufacturing of it—got the benefit, and not the consumer?

Mr. WILLETT. That is right. It was an abnormal year.

Mr. RAKER. The question of the market did not have anything to do with it then, did it? They just raised it because somebody else 3,000 miles away that does not even compete with them did it? Is not that right?

Mr. WILLETT. That is virtually so.

Mr. RAKER. What is that?

Mr. WILLETT. I do not see but that is virtually so. That is virtually so. As someone remarked in California not long ago: "What under the heavens have we to do with the European prices? We are getting sugars in San Francisco without any duty on them. Why under the heavens are we paying the Hamburg price for sugar?"—which they were doing.

Mr. RAKER. Were they not paying the New York price?

Mr. WILLETT. Yes.

Mr. RAKER. New York fixed the price, and raised it, for instance, 10 points in June.

Mr. WILLETT. Yes.

Mr. RAKER. California, Colorado, and Utah immediately raised it 10 points?

Mr. WILLETT. Yes.

Mr. RAKER. And when it got up to 20 points in New York they made it the same?

Mr. WILLETT. Yes.

Mr. RAKER. And when it got up to a dollar and a half and two dollars, they came right up with it?

Mr. WILLETT. Yes.

Mr. RAKER. There was no necessity to do that, was there?

Mr. WILLETT. No. The men in the Hawaiian Islands got the benefit?

Mr. RAKER. The men that are running the institutions, was it not?

Mr. WILLETT. The men in the Hawaiian Islands got that benefit.

The CHAIRMAN. You mean they paid that much more for their raw sugars?

Mr. WILLETT. The Hawaiian Islands contracted for all their crop in 1911, upon a New York basis, delivered in San Francisco. See? Whenever the price in New York raised 10 cents the price in San Francisco raised 10 cents; Hawaiian sugars rose 10 cents, and that 10 cents went to the Hawaiian planter. That is the funny thing about it—that we are paying all this money to Hawaii all these years. They ought to stand a tax on their sugar. Why should we give them all this?

Mr. RAKER. How about the beet-sugar men in California, Colorado, and Utah? Are they not in the same position?

Mr. WILLETT. When they get a crop; yes.

Mr. RAKER. We were not paying all that to California, Colorado, and Utah, were we?

Mr. WILLETT. What is that?

Mr. RAKER. We were not paying all that rise to those people, were we?

Mr. WILLETT. The consumers of the country——

Mr. RAKER. Well, let us see. That is what I want to get at, from your experience in the matter. Suppose it raised 2 cents a pound, or $2 a hundred. The man running the institution, or the sugar-beet factory, got the benefit of it, did he not?

Mr. WILLETT. Yes.

Mr. RAKER. And the consumer did not?

The CHAIRMAN. They would have if they had not sold ahead. He explained that.

Mr. RAKER. Now, I am talking about the consumer.

Mr. WILLETT. You are talking about it without regard to what they did actually give?

Mr. RAKER. Without regard to what they paid at all. That would be the condition, would it not?

Mr. WILLETT. That would be the condition; yes.

Mr. RAKER. The sugar-beet people did not have to pay any more for their beets, did they?

Mr. WILLETT. No, sir.

Mr. RAKER. In all of the four States—Idaho, Utah, California, and Colorado?

Mr. WILLETT. Their profits in 1911 were much larger than they were in 1910, or any other year.

Mr. RAKER. From your observation and from the history of it, the men who owned the factories got this money?

Mr. WILLETT. Certainly.

Mr. RAKER. Because of the rise in sugar; and they followed the New York prices, did they not?

Mr. WILLETT. Certainly.

Mr. RAKER. Is it not a fact that in all of those places that gave a large amount of money to the American Sugar Refining Co. just the same——

Mr. WILLETT. I do not see that that follows.

Mr. RAKER. Let us see if it does not follow.

Mr. WILLETT. The largest business of the American Sugar Refining Co. is refining cane sugars, on which they make 87 cents profit. When it comes into their beet-sugar industry, of course they participate to the same extent as any other factory in the beet-sugar industry.

Mr. RAKER. From the testimony, they own a large percentage of the industry in Idaho and in Utah and in California and in Colorado.

Mr. WILLETT. Yes.

Mr. RAKER. Now, if it raises there $2 a hundred, they get the benefit without any corresponding liability, do they not?

Mr. WILLETT. Certainly.

Mr. RAKER. They raise the prices in New York, and they come up in California; and they sell all their sugar there of that kind, and they get the benefit, do they not?

Mr. WILLETT. You can hardly say "they" raise the price in New York, because they do not.

Mr. RAKER. The price is raised. I will put it that way.

Mr. WILLETT. It is the market. They get the benefit of what the market is.

Mr. RAKER. I will take your statement. The market went up. That is the situation?

Mr. WILLETT. Exactly.

Mr. RAKER. Then, under the actual facts as they exist, no matter who is responsible for it, as a matter of fact the American Sugar Refining Co. did get practically one-half, or say from one-third to one-half, of the benefit that went to these beet-sugar people in the West?

Mr. WILLETT. On the proportion of their business in the beet industry?

Mr. RAKER. Yes.

Mr. WILLETT. Certainly.

Mr. RAKER. And it would be to their interest then to see that sugar went up, would it not, in the West, correspondingly to the price in the East?

Mr. WILLETT. Beet-sugar men, of course, were very glad to see beet sugar go up.

Mr. RAKER. Surely.

Mr. WILLETT. But, as I said before, 1911 does not repeat itself very often. I have not known such a year in all my experience, I might say, and it has covered a great many, many years; 1910 is a much more normal year on which to average estimates.

Mr. RAKER. Then, as a matter of fact, there was not any occasion for the beet-sugar people in the West to raise their prices of sugar as they were raised during the months of July, August, September, October, and November, was there?

Mr. WILLETT. If the beet-sugar men in the West had been satisfied with the same profits they were receiving in 1910, or any other normal year, they need not have raised their prices above the prices of 1910, or other normal years.

Mr. RAKER. Well, now, let us assume that they have testified——

Mr. WILLETT (interrupting). They took advantage of it.

Mr. RAKER (continuing). That during the year 1910, under the conditions as they were, they received a fair profit.

Mr. WILLETT. Exactly.

Mr. RAKER. A good profit, and a good amount of interest on their investment——

Mr. WILLETT. That is correct.

Mr. RAKER. That is their testimony, as I understand it.

Mr. WILLETT. Yes.

Mr. RAKER. Now, taking their profit during the year 1911, $2 a hundred, it is almost 33 per cent, is it not?

Mr. WILLETT. Yes; if they got the full market price.

Mr. RAKER. Yes. They simply took advantage of the public and made the consumer pay it because sugar in New York had gone up that amount?

Mr. WILLETT. Exactly; yes. That is business.

Mr. RAKER. How is that?

Mr. WILLETT. That is business.

Mr. RAKER. Is that what we call "good business"?

Mr. WILLETT. What we call good business, or what they call good business, or anybody. If they had not done it they would have been called fools, would they not?

Mr. RAKER. I do not think so.

Mr. WILLETT. Anybody giving up 2 cents profit?

Mr. RAKER. I do not think so.

Mr. WILLETT. In the business world it would be. As a matter of fact, right there, the Colorado beet-sugar factories did concede to the citizens of their own State, and the factories of Utah also did concede; and had the prices remained high those citizens of those countries where the beet-sugar factories were would have continued to benefit by a reduced price given them locally. The manufacturers of Colorado refused to sell their sugars over the Colorado line at the same price that they would sell them for in the State of Colorado. That shows the benefit of the beet-sugar industry, for instance, in the State of Colorado under an abnormal year like 1911.

Mr. RAKER. What I was trying to get at was this: If there had been twice as much sugar raised in California and Utah and Colorado as there was under the condition as it has been demonstrated in 1911, it would not have made any difference as to the price of sugar to the consumer, would it—if the same conditions applied?

Mr. WILLETT. Raising double the quantity?

Mr. RAKER. Yes.

Mr. WILLETT. Of course.

Mr. RAKER. Why?

Mr. WILLETT. Because increased quantity would knock prices into smithereens.

Mr. RAKER. In California?

Mr. WILLETT. Yes; anywhere. That is the point of the whole thing. To get your prices down, increase your domestic industry in those months.

Mr. RAKER. How does it happen? I have understood that the quantity of sugars in the West has been increased very largely in the last two or three years.

Mr. WILLETT. Yes.

Mr. RAKER. But the price of sugar paid in 1892, 1893, and 1894 is nothing as compared to what it is in 1911—and they raise two or three times as much.

Mr. WILLETT. The beet-sugar industry of the United States has not been and is not progressing as fast as the consumption of the United States.

Mr. RAKER. I know. That is all right; but I wanted the fact, if it could be had——

Mr. WILLETT (interrupting). If you double your production, as you say, naturally you fill that gap.

Mr. RAKER (continuing). If you were to double your production and double the number of people living in the country, that would not affect the question of the price to them, would it? What I am trying to get at, so far as the price of sugar is concerned, is that in those sugar-beet States during 1911 it depended entirely upon the price fixed in New York?

Mr. WILLETT. Yes; which price was fixed by the supply and demand. That is right.

The CHAIRMAN. Just a moment, if you will pardon me.

Mr. RAKER. Yes.

The CHAIRMAN. Each one of those terms, "supply" and "demand," must be considered from the standpoint of the world's supply and demand. Is not that true?

Mr. WILLETT. Yes.

The CHAIRMAN. In other words, the increased production of beet sugar in this country would have just as much effect or just as little effect on the situation, so far as the price of sugar is concerned, as it bears to the total production of the world, correlating with the total consumption?

Mr. WILLETT. Yes, sir.

Mr. RAKER. Then the question of local production does not have anything to do with it. You can raise your sugar right in the locality and if there is a question of shortage or of large crop in some other place——

Mr. WILLETT (interrupting). It does not affect the price.

Mr. RAKER. It does not affect the price at all?

Mr. WILLETT. That is right. The only way it affects the price is to increase your production at home. For instance, we are minus now; we ran down to a minus of 77,000 tons on the refined sugars which we needed to complete our consumption last year; but this year we are running two or three hundred thousand less. If we had two or three hundred thousand tons more this year of local production, then we would be independent of the world's prices. I do not agree with those who maintain that in the course of time the domestic beet-sugar industry will supply the whole needs of this country. I think Cuba has to be considered in that connection, and I do not think the beet-sugar industry will ever amount to any such figure. If it amounts to twice what it is to-day, it will be sufficient to keep the price fixed below the level of the European consumers' prices.

Mr. RAKER. Then I understand that in the Western States there was no more sugar produced this year than was necessary for home consumption?

Mr. WILLETT. Local consumption in the West?

Mr. RAKER. Yes; local consumption in the West.

Mr. WILLETT. They did sell sugars farther east this year than in any former year, to some extent.

Mr. RAKER. You have not any statistics on that, have you?

Mr. WILLETT. Well, I made some up once, on population. The beet-sugar production in the West has now reached and passed beyond the limits of its local consumption.

Mr. RAKER. You have not any idea how much beyond the local consumption there was produced this year, have you?

Mr. WILLETT. They are selling sugars as far east as Pittsburgh.

Mr. RAKER. Did they send any as far east as Pittsburgh during August, September, and October?

Mr. WILLETT. Yes, sir.

Mr. RAKER. Do you know anything about a convention that was held at Chicago during the month of November by the beet-sugar people of the United States?

Mr. WILLETT. No; I knew there was a convention held there, but——

Mr. RAKER. You do not know anything about it?

Mr. WILLETT. No; I know nothing about it.

Mr. RAKER. You have no record in your paper about it?

Mr. WILLETT. No record at all.

Mr. RAKER. That is all, Mr. Chairman.

Mr. MALBY. There are one or two questions that I have in mind.

The CHAIRMAN. Proceed, Mr. Malby.

Mr. MALBY. It is a fact, is it not, that beet sugar was shipped in quite large quantities to the central and eastern portions of the United States this year?

Mr. WILLETT. Not large; no, sir.

Mr. MALBY. Not a large quantity?

Mr. WILLETT. Not large quantities.

Mr. MALBY. Some was shipped as far east as Pittsburgh and Baltimore?

Mr. WILLETT. Yes, sir; I do not know about Baltimore.

Mr. MALBY. Do you know what the average price was that the beet sugar brought wholesale, up to November 1?

Mr. WILLETT. The average price for the year?

Mr. MALBY. The average price of beet sugar, yes, actually sold.

Mr. WILLETT. From January 1?

Mr. MALBY. Up to November; just this year's crop, I mean.

Mr. WILLETT. Oh, the average price from October 1, to November 1? Through October?

Mr. MALBY. Well, whenever it was sold. I do not know. From the time they commenced to sell until they ceased selling the crop. What was the average price?

Mr. WILLETT. The beet-sugar men this year sold their crop largely in anticipation of deliveries along in September.

Mr. MALBY. So that they did not realize large prices?

Mr. WILLETT. I understand they realized about an average of 5¼ cents for their crop.

Mr. MALBY. Which would be much less than the market price at the time of delivery?

Mr. WILLETT. Yes, sir.

Mr. MALBY. Of course the beet sugar coming upon the market at that time undoubtedly did have an effect upon the whole market price of sugar, did it not?

Mr. WILLETT. Yes, sir.

Mr. MALBY. I think we have pretty thoroughly gone over that, so that we understand it pretty well, Mr. Chairman. I do not know of anything more.

The CHAIRMAN. There are one or two questions that I wanted to ask, to verify some conclusions that I have drawn about this evidence. I want to see if they are right or not. It will not take long, and then we will go into this foreign price business, which we have not taken up as yet.

I believe you agree with Mr. Martin's figures, that the average cost of producing a pound of European sugar, year after year, is about a ninth of a shilling, or 2.16 cents a pound?

Mr. WILLETT. Yes.

The CHAIRMAN. I want to call your attention, to see whether you agree with it or not, to the opinion of the Dutch sugar expert, Mr. Prinsen-Geerlings. You know of him?

Mr. WILLETT. Yes.

The CHAIRMAN. He is a world-wide authority on sugar, is he not?

Mr. WILLETT. Yes.

The CHAIRMAN. Please look on page 2797 of the record. You have it before you. You see that quotation at the bottom of the page?

Mr. WILLETT. Yes.

The CHAIRMAN. About the 177 Javan sugar planters?

Mr. WILLETT. Yes.

The CHAIRMAN. He says there, without reading it all—I have made a quotation from it—that Java has repeatedly conquered the sugar markets of the Orient.

Mr. WILLETT. That is correct.

The CHAIRMAN. What is that?

Mr. WILLETT. That is true.

The CHAIRMAN. And is cutting a very wide swath in the sugar industries of the world?

Mr. WILLETT. That is very true.

The CHAIRMAN. And he makes this very remarkable statement: That without tariff aid of any kind she could make 40 per cent profit on sugar at 1½ cents a pound. Further down, and almost at the bottom, he says:

At 1½ cents per pound Java can make 40 per cent profit.

Mr. MALBY. Who makes that statement?

The CHAIRMAN. Mr. Prinsen-Geerlings. That would be nine-tenths of a cent a pound for the cost of production of cane sugar in Java.

Mr. WILLETT. At 9 cents a hundred?

The CHAIRMAN. Yes; or nine-tenths of a cent a pound.

Mr. WILLETT. That is an absurd statement.

The CHAIRMAN. You do not agree with that?

Mr. WILLETT. Oh, no.

The CHAIRMAN. The fact remains, however, that he is considered probably the best authority in the world.

Mr. WILLETT. He is a little off in that statement.

The CHAIRMAN. I understand that you disagree with him?

Mr. WILLETT. My paper gives the cost of Java sugars, from very reliable sources.

The CHAIRMAN. This man Prinsen-Geerlings is considered a pretty good authority himself, is he not?

Mr. WILLETT. All experts sometimes make slips.

The CHAIRMAN. I know that; but the fact is that he is a great world-wide expert, is he not?

Mr. WILLETT. Yes; he is supposed to be.

The CHAIRMAN. Probably one of the greatest in the world?

Mr. WILLETT. Yes. I doubt if he is correctly reported there.

The CHAIRMAN. Well, we have that in two or three different places, I think—that same statement. Corroborating that, I want to call your attention to the fact of this statement from Mr. Palmer. You know of Mr. Truman Palmer?

Mr. WILLETT. Yes.

The CHAIRMAN. He is a pretty careful and accurate man, is he not?

Mr. WILLETT. I consider him so; very—particularly in his Willett & Gray statistics.

The CHAIRMAN. You will notice on page 2798 of the record that Mr. Palmer makes this statement:

I have recently reviewed a book published by the Philippine Government——

Mr. WILLETT. Where are you reading from?

The CHAIRMAN. I am reading from the top of the page.

Mr. WILLETT. What page?

The CHAIRMAN. Page 2798—the next page [continuing reading]:

I have recently reviewed a book published by the Philippine Government, a copy prepared by a sugar expert named Walker, whom the Philippine Government sent down to the island of Negros, with a portable laboratory, to stay on the island all through a sugar campaign, and ascertain what the cost of production was. I am sorry I can not put my hands on it, but I can tell you in a general way.

Mr. Malby was conducting this examination, and at this point of the proceedings he told Mr. Palmer to proceed, and Mr. Palmer said:

Mr. Walker gave the average cost of labor on the sugar estates on the Island of Negros at 12½ cents per day in cash and 7½ cents per day in provender, in food.

Mr. MALBY. They got, then, 19 cents?

Mr. PALMER. Twenty cents.

Analyzing his figures—

A little farther down Mr. Palmer says—

the cost of sugar in the sack at the mill is 55½ cents per 100 pounds.

In other words, it is the least bit over half a cent, averaging one-half as cheap as in Java. You say that is equally unreliable?

Mr. WILLETT. That is right. That is not the same sugar as the Java sugar?

The CHAIRMAN. No——

Mr. WILLETT. It is made in coconut shells. It is sun dried, in the sun. There is no expense in making that sugar at all.

The CHAIRMAN. I understand.

Mr. WILLETT. It is 84 test sugar and the Java is 100 test sugar.

The CHAIRMAN. You are acquainted with the kind of sugar this expert is talking about?

Mr. WILLETT. Yes. That 55½-cent business does not include any machinery at all. In Java they use machinery. Any man can set up a plant in the Philippines for 50 cents.

The CHAIRMAN. That would seem to corroborate Mr. Geerlings, that there is no doubt that sugar can be and is produced very cheaply in Java, would it not?

Mr. WILLETT. Not at all. The conditions are absolutely different, so far as the means and modes of manufacture and everything are concerned.

The CHAIRMAN. Geerlings, the Dutch expert, makes this statement. He says:

Without any tariff favors, Philippines can compete with the world in sugar production.

Mr. WILLETT. Without any what?

The CHAIRMAN. Without any tariff favors. Do you agree with that? Is that true, in your judgment?

Mr. WILLETT. It is true on the sugar that they make; yes.

The CHAIRMAN. If the climate and soil are adapted, they can use machinery and make it cheaper than anyone else?

Mr. WILLETT. No, sir; that changes, because the moment they introduce machinery they put themselves on a level with the world. No, no. We have a very visible example of Philippine sugars in the United States at the present moment. The members of the committee know, undoubtedly, that very little of that grade of sugar can be used in the United States. It is a low-grade sugar, and it can not be used, unless it is mixed with half the amount of centrifugal sugar, to any advantage.

The CHAIRMAN. Do they mix it?

Mr. WILLETT. Yes.

The CHAIRMAN. I notice that we are importing something under 100,000 tons?

Mr. WILLETT. Yes. Several cargoes are awaiting sale in New York now.

The CHAIRMAN. There are several now there, are there?

Mr. WILLETT. Yes. One cargo sold a few days ago at a very materially lower price than the usual difference between the two grades of sugar—the Philippines and the centrifugals.

The CHAIRMAN. Do you know Mr. James H. Post?

Mr. WILLETT. Very well.

The CHAIRMAN. Is he a competent, reliable expert on sugar?

Mr. WILLETT. Very.

The CHAIRMAN. He knows what he is talking about?

Mr. WILLETT. He is a refiner.

The CHAIRMAN. He is interested to some extent in sugar?

Mr. WILLETT. Yes.

The CHAIRMAN. He used to be treasurer of the Cuban-American as well as the National?

Mr. WILLETT. Yes.

The CHAIRMAN. The Cuban-American is the largest in Cuba?

Mr. WILLETT. It controls five estates, I think.

The CHAIRMAN. That is right, I think. Mr. Post gave us the statement—I suppose he gave it from his connection with the Cuban-American Sugar Co.—that the cost of manufacturing a pound of cane sugar in Cuba where they do not use the latest machinery is something like 2 cents a pound. Do you think that is right?

Mr. WILLETT. That is a little high, I should say.

The CHAIRMAN. Well, he did say this——

Mr. WILLETT (interrupting). I think we make it 1.85.

The CHAIRMAN. You do? He did make the statement that it could be produced even at a much lower cost than that, but he said that he supposed the figure I have used there covered it.

Mr. WILLETT. It varies on different estates.

The CHAIRMAN. He so stated.

Mr. WILLETT. From 1 cent and a half to 2 cents.

The CHAIRMAN. That is in Cuba. The Louisiana witnesses whom we have heard have seemed to be unanimous on the proposition. In fact, they admitted that there was a caucus on the subject—I do not use the word offensively—and that their cost of production was about 3¼ cents. Do you think that is somewhere near right?

Mr. WILLETT. I do not know.

The CHAIRMAN. You do not know?

Mr. WILLETT. I do not know.

The CHAIRMAN. You have no opinion on that subject?

Mr. WILLETT. I have no opinion on that subject, really. I think their crop is subject to so many contingencies. Only three days ago our telegrams from New Orleans stated that the frost of the night previous had damaged the 60 per cent cane remaining in the fields. I think it was either 15 or 20 per cent.

The CHAIRMAN. Is it not a fact that Louisiana is almost too far north to be well adapted in climate and soil, or as well adapted as such countries as the Philippines, Java, and Cuba, for the production of cane sugar?

Mr. WILLETT. It is generally considered so.

The CHAIRMAN. Do you agree with the opinion of that expert on the subject of sugar?

Mr. WILLETT. I agree to this extent: That it is impossible to raise sugar in Louisiana as cheaply as in Cuba.

The CHAIRMAN. Or in Java?

Mr. WILLETT. And particularly in Java.

The CHAIRMAN. Do you follow Mr. Geerlings on the propostion that sugar is raised much more cheaply in Java than in Cuba?

Mr. WILLETT. Not very much more cheaply.

The CHAIRMAN. How much more cheaply?

Mr. WILLETT. My statistics show, my recollection is, that it is not over an eighth or a quarter of a cent a pound.

The CHAIRMAN. Not more than that?

Mr. WILLETT. Not more than that.

The CHAIRMAN. In other words, you fix the cost in Java, bearing in mind your testimony, at somewhere under 1½ cents, or a little more?

Mr. WILLETT. Yes.

The CHAIRMAN. So if they are right about it, and it really costs them 3¾ cents a pound to produce cane sugar in Louisiana, it is costing more than double what it is in the most favored countries of the world?

Mr. WILLETT. I do not know, really. It strikes me that that is rather high.

The CHAIRMAN. But they all swear that. I thought so, too, when they were swearing that.

Mr. WILLETT. If they say so, they ought to know.

The CHAIRMAN. Not only that, but in the case of the beet-sugar people, when you average it, and take what their official representative says fixes their cost of production, it is exactly the same in this country as that of the cane people.

Mr. WILLETT. Three and one-quarter cents?

The CHAIRMAN. Three and three-quarter cents.

Mr. WILLETT. You have better testimony than that before the committee.

The CHAIRMAN. What better testimony than that have we?

Mr. WILLETT. The American Sugar Refining Co.'s reports do not show that.

The CHAIRMAN. But if you take those reports and average them, they average 3¾ cents. Take the Spreckels factory in California and it is 2.77, and one of their companies is over 4 cents. When you take the 11 reports that they gave us evidence from, it averages 3¾ cents.

Mr. JACOWAY. Some of them were nearly 5.

The CHAIRMAN. Yes; it went away up. So you have to average them up. That, with Truman Palmer's testimony, in which he fixes

3¾ cents, forces us to the conclusion that they are both claiming about the same thing. I do not know whether it is to show that they are both entitled to the same amount of protection, or what. But to go on—and this is what I have in mind to ask you—is it not true that the world over it is very much cheaper to produce a pound of cane sugar in the most favored cane countries than to produce a pound of beet sugar in the most favored beet countries?

Mr. WILLETT. That is the general understanding. It costs us more to produce a pound of beet than to produce a pound of cane.

The CHAIRMAN. Yes; but even the beet people—I mean the people in Louisiana—do not claim that it costs them any more than it does to produce in this country 1 pound of sugar.

Mr. WILLETT. The less said about Louisiana the better. [Laughter.]

Mr. GARRETT. Why?

Mr. WILLETT. I mean in that connection as to the cost of production.

The CHAIRMAN. He thinks that is rather remarkable.

Mr. WILLETT. As to the cost of production, compared to Cuba and Java.

The CHAIRMAN. It is so much higher than it is in these other countries?

Mr. WILLETT. On account of the relative conditions.

Mr. GARRETT. I was——

The CHAIRMAN. Mr. Willett, just one other question. Did you want to ask a question right there. Mr. Garrett?

Mr. GARRETT. I was particularly interested in that.

The CHAIRMAN. All right. Suppose you ask him.

Mr. GARRETT. Do you mean that in your judgment they can produce in Louisiana cane sugar as cheaply as in Cuba?

Mr. WILLETT. That they can do it?

Mr. GARRETT. Yes.

Mr. WILLETT. Oh, no; they can not do it.

Mr. GARRETT. They can not do it?

Mr. WILLETT. They can not do it. That has been proved over and over again.

The CHAIRMAN. It struck me, though, as really remarkable that they both claimed the cost of production was exactly the same in this country for a pound of beet sugar and a pound of cane sugar. It looks to me as though they are making their interests dovetail.

Mr. WILLETT. That statement is not very far out of the way on the records, if you say it costs the beet people 3¾ cents.

The CHAIRMAN. That is the record before the committee now. There is no doubt about the accuracy of the statement I am making now. That is what they have testified to. That is what makes our record, you know. I have been amazed at it myself, and I just wanted to see how it struck you. You have been in the sugar business for a long time.

Mr. WILLETT. I ran over the American Sugar Refining Co.'s reports. They have 34 or 36 beet factories, scattered in every part of the United States, good, bad, and indifferent, and they ought to certainly show what the average cost of beet sugar is in the United States; and I do not make it as high as you do, in my calculation.

The CHAIRMAN. My calculation, I think, is right.

Mr. WILLETT. I make it about 3.40, instead of 3.75.

The CHAIRMAN. How much?

Mr. WILLETT. 3.44, I think.

The CHAIRMAN. I do not know how you get at that. I made it 3.75 exactly.

Mr. WILLETT. I simply analyzed the statement as it came to me.

The CHAIRMAN. It is in the hearings, at page 2379. Well, that is a mere matter of calculation. I will verify my calculation; but I took the 11 companies that they are interested in and added up the figures and divided by 11. That is the way I got it.

Mr. WILLETT. I took the whole 36, good, bad, and indifferent. You know there are 36 of them.

The CHAIRMAN. Yes; but they did not give us the figures for 36.

Mr. WILLETT. I thought they did.

The CHAIRMAN. Let us see if they did.

Mr. WILLETT. What page are you referring to?

The CHAIRMAN. Page 2379. Here it is. Suppose you take these figures.

Mr. WILLETT. Well, I have the figures here.

The CHAIRMAN. We will not take up your time or the committee's time to make the calculation now. We can verify it. Anyway, that is very close. Your figure is 3.40. It is almost the same.

Mr. WILLETT. I went on further, and showed that in those factories the American Sugar Refining Co. made a profit of $1.10 on their sugars; and that $1.10 on their capitalization, as specified in the record, gave them 10 per cent profit on their capitalization during 1911.

The CHAIRMAN. We are pretty near together on that.

Mr. WILLETT. Considering that they run 100 days in the year, at 10 per cent profit, it does not look like a large remuneration. They are idle 200 days in the year.

The CHAIRMAN. You said something, I believe, while I was out, and I missed it, but some of the members of the committee told me about it, to the effect that we ought to promote the beet-sugar industry, or ought to adopt a legislative policy to promote it. I believe that is your opinion?

Mr. WILLETT. That is my opinion.

The CHAIRMAN. Suppose we had been successful in having Cuban sugar free—as you once advocated, did you not?

Mr. WILLETT. Free Cuban sugar?

The CHAIRMAN. Free Cuban sugar.

Mr. WILLETT. That was before the beet-sugar industry had started or gotten any foundation in the country probably.

The CHAIRMAN. Well——

Mr. WILLETT. The introduction of the beet-sugar industry, of course, changed established conditions in this country.

The CHAIRMAN. In 1901 the beet-sugar industry was established, was it not?

Mr. WILLETT. Oh, no. It did not begin to be promoted to any extent until 1901.

The CHAIRMAN. Until 1901?

Mr. WILLETT. Previous to that there were, perhaps, 36 factories, I think.

The CHAIRMAN. Just leaving out the beet-sugar industry for the moment, and your former position on that question, you think it is a fact that if we had had free sugar with Cuba—if Cuba had had free sugar into this country—that would have tremendously stimulated the production of sugar in Cuba?

Mr. WILLETT. In Cuba?

The CHAIRMAN. Yes. If they had had free entry.

Mr. WILLETT. I consider, as regards Cuba, that the reciprocity treaty, giving them the advantage of 20 per cent, stimulated the production quite as much as free sugar there would. That is sufficient stimulation for Cuba.

The CHAIRMAN. Let me read you this extract from Willett & Gray's statistical sugar journal of December 26, 1901. That was after you made this trip, and probably soon after you made this trip.

Mr. WILLETT. What date in December was it?

The CHAIRMAN. December 26, 1901. It reads:

> The false position occupied by the beet-sugar industry and the "dog in the manger" policy of its action regarding Cuba can not be more forcibly shown than by an examination of our statistical review of the raw and refined sugar markets. A great hue and cry is made against the refining industry or Sugar Trust, and yet the average margin to cover cost of refining and profit for the past 10 years has been but 0.879 cent per pound, while the margin between the cost of producing beet granulated, say, 0.280 cent per pound, by Messrs. Oxnard-Cutting's statement in 1899, and the average price of granulated at the seaboard for 10 years, say, 4.675 cents per pound, shows a net average profit of 1.875 cents per pound, plus the freight from the seaboard. On the average price of granulated in 1901, say, 5.05 cents per pound, the beet-sugar manufacturers' profits on a cost of 2.80 cents per pound, would show 2¼ cents per pound, and even beet-sugar factories, so badly located that they can not produce granulated at less than 4 cents per pound, have had a net profit of 1.05 cents per pound, plus freight from the seaboard, which is at least three times the profit of the Sugar Trust.
>
> We maintain that the industry does not need such enormous protection, and that it is absolutely wrong by such protection to encourage the building of beet-sugar factories in locations where granulated sugar can not be produced at 3 cents per pound.

Exactly what has happened since.

Mr. WILLETT. That was our opinion at that time, based on——

The CHAIRMAN. Wait a minute. There is a little more of it:

> In nearly every irrigation State this can now be done, and in some other States as well. The howl against the Sugar Trust is merely the outward cry made to cover the true inwardness of the beet-sugar conditions, as shown by Messrs. Oxnard & Cutting in their letter, giving the facts of the matter. Take off the duty from Cuban sugars, discourage the building of beet-sugar factories unless upon a solid rock basis with no competition to fear, and the country will be astonished at the wonderful progress this industry will make in the next 10 years.

Mr. WILLETT. Yes.

The CHAIRMAN. That was true then, was it not?

Mr. WILLETT. That was true, on a false basis; do you not see?

The CHAIRMAN. How is that?

Mr. WILLETT. It was based on Oxnard & Cutting's testimony that beet sugar could be produced at 2.80 cents; and the facts since that date have proven that they can not do anything of the kind.

Mr. RAKER. The records of the factories show that they can do it for less than that.

Mr. WILLETT. In California, but not in the rest of the country.

The CHAIRMAN. One or two of Oxnard's factories can do it and have done it—one or two of his favored factories.

Mr. WILLETT. I did know that. You see, if beet sugars could be produced at that price throughout this country those arguments would be absolutely correct.

Mr. MALBY. But experience has shown that it can not be done?

Mr. WILLETT. Experience has shown that it can not be done.

Mr. MALBY. Except in some favored locality?

Mr. WILLETT. Since 1901, since the date of that, the farmers have gone up in their price of beets, labor of all kinds has advanced, and machinery and everything connected with the business has improved; so that that argument, if it was an argument, was based on false information—or rather correct information at the time, which since then has proven incorrect.

Mr. RAKER. There are 1,000,000 acres of land that would produce sugar beets just as good as we have under cultivation, if not better, in California—2,000,000 acres.

Mr. WILLETT. They are occupying it as fast as they can now. Everybody sees that California is the best beet country; and if Congress decides to take the duty off of sugars, California can stand it, and that land will be improved; but the rest of the country can not stand it.

The CHAIRMAN. Let me read again, somewhat on the same line, but a little different, from Willett & Gray's Sugar Journal, a week later, January 2, 1902:

The American beet-sugar industry has made larger progress in the past year than in any other year in its history, both in the increased number of factories built and in the amount of sugar produced, and this industry is now found on such a solid basis that free-duty sugar from Cuba will not retard its progress during the years to come. In fact, we are quite convinced that this industry will astonish its best friends by its increase during the coming 10 years, and the only possible effect that free-duty sugar can make will be to deter the building of beet factories where they ought never to be built by reason of unfavorable conditions, and to throw the industry more largely into such States and locations where 3 cents per pound granulated or less is now being produced and can be considered, as a permanent cost at least in the years to come. There are plenty of such locations awaiting the promoters of the industry and, with the constant fear of free-duty sugar removed, by its actual presence, as far as Cuba is concerned, the incentive to increase beet production in the United States will be wonderfully increased, notwithstanding all talk and predictions to the contrary.

Mr. WILLETT. Do you not see, that was written on——

The CHAIRMAN. January 2, 1902.

Mr. WILLETT. January 2, 1902. That was written on inside information which I had that the American Beet Sugar Co. was going into the beet-sugar industry to promote it——

The CHAIRMAN. The American Sugar Refining Co.?

Mr. WILLETT. The American Sugar Refining Co. was going into the beet-sugar industry, and that people would be astonished by the increase of the industry in 10 years; and the results have proved it.

The CHAIRMAN. What I want the benefit of your opinion on is this——

Mr. WILLETT. The facts show the correctness of that.

The CHAIRMAN. I do not suppose you are recanting either one of the things I have read to you?

Mr. WILLETT. Not at all.

The CHAIRMAN. As a matter of fact, you are probably the greatest sugar expert in the country. Do you not believe we have sugar hot-housed to a considerable extent in this country?

Mr. WILLETT. You have, in certain locations. There is no doubt about it.

The CHAIRMAN. In other words, the tariff is so high that its production, even in unfavorable localities and in unfavorable climates, is encouraged?

Mr. WILLETT. Yes; I think so, too. I modify that by saying it has been encouraged. I think to-day there is much better judgment in the beet-sugar industry than there was 10 years ago.

The CHAIRMAN. Let me continue. See how far you agree with the conclusion I am coming to about this thing. While it might be true that free sugar or anything approximating free sugar would kill the Louisiana sugar industry entirely, and would kill a certain part of the sugar industry of the West, yet there are certain conditions in the West, for instance, like in California, and maybe in some sections of Colorado, and possibly a little in Utah—although I doubt that—where even with free sugar there is no reason on earth why they should not live and make a reasonable profit?

Mr. WILLETT. I think there are some factories that could do that even with free sugar, but very few this side of the Rockies.

The CHAIRMAN. Very few this side of the Rockies?

Mr. WILLETT. Yes. Those factories which under those conditions of free sugar could not exist where they are located, if they wanted to continue business would naturally move.

The CHAIRMAN. To the Pacific slope?

Mr. WILLETT. To where the Pacific slope affords them land. Free sugar would entirely change the conditions.

The CHAIRMAN. That is, the location?

Mr. WILLETT. The location and conditions attending the beet-sugar industry of this country; and it would be extremely difficult, in my opinion, to find people who would be willing to put their money into the business. You can see by your testimony that the American Sugar Refining Co. have been the greatest promoters in this country thus far of beet sugar, and it has been by the money which they had. It takes not only capital to build factories, but it takes a great deal more money to run a factory after it is built. In 1907, during the panic, your evidence shows that the American Sugar Refining Co. had to come to the assistance of every factory in which they were interested. Mr. Cutler testifies that he could not raise money from the banks to carry on his business in his factory, and even the American Sugar Refining Co. had to call upon Havemeyer for $500,000 to help them out.

The CHAIRMAN. They all borrowed money?

Mr. WILLETT. They all borrowed money. With insufficient protection who is going to promote the beet-sugar industry? That is what I can not see clearly. Who is going to put money into it? Personally I would not put my money into it.

The CHAIRMAN. Of course not; but looking at this thing from the standpoint of the consumer, have we not got it hothoused too much for the fellow who pays the bills? Give us your frank opinion about it.

Mr. WILLETT. The position of the committee, I understand, is to ferret out that matter.

The CHAIRMAN. Yes; you are a sugar man, and I just want your opinion, if you do not mind giving it.

Mr. WILLETT. As a sugar expert, I should say, if the question comes as to how much or how little the sugar tariff can be reduced, that you would have to look at it from each man's selfish standpoint in the first instance.

The CHAIRMAN. That is usually the way with tariff questions, I believe.

Mr. WILLETT. And when you do that you have Mr. Spreckels on one side as a free-sugar man—the refiner—and you have the beet-sugar men as the extreme advocates of the present tariff; and you have between the two the American Sugar Refining Co., with both interests, on the fence; neutral, in other words.

The CHAIRMAN. And willing to split the difference?

Mr. WILLETT. Absolutely neutral. It does not matter to them whether you raise or lower the duty one iota. They are in a position to advantage by either move Congress makes, and you can not help it.

Mr. JACOWAY. There is one question that I want to ask.

The CHAIRMAN. Go ahead.

Mr. JACOWAY. You said there were certain localities in the United States—for instance, Colorado and California—that were peculiarly adapted to the growth of beets.

Mr. WILLETT. More than that; Utah and Idaho.

Mr. JACOWAY. And Utah and Idaho.

The CHAIRMAN. And Oregon, maybe, in some parts.

Mr. WILLETT. It is not a good place.

The CHAIRMAN. It is too far north?

Mr. WILLETT. Factories there are a failure, virtually.

Mr. JACOWAY. You further said that the duty could be taken off of sugar and that these factories in these particular localities would thrive.

Mr. WILLETT. In California, I said.

Mr. JACOWAY. Well, say California.

Mr. WILLETT. And some in Colorado.

Mr. JACOWAY. The question I want to ask is this: Is there sufficient land that is peculiarly adapted to the growth of the beet in which the sugar is raised in time to supply the demands of the consumption of the people of the United States?

Mr. WILLETT. Well, there is land enough; but as I said before, there is no such possibility in 100 years, because you have Cuba to consider all the time, right close by us. Cuba has the United States market and is bound to keep it to a certain extent. The moment you increase your domestic sugar industry so that Cuba and the domestic-sugar industry come into conflict in prices, then you lower your price to the consumer; and if your price is lowered sufficiently one or the other of those industries would have to curtail its output.

The CHAIRMAN. The consumers of this country pay as much more for their sugar as the tariff is itself, do they not?

Mr. WILLETT. The consumers of this country paid last year, 1910, $108,000,000 to foreign countries for sugar. In 1901 they paid $70,000,000.

The CHAIRMAN. And besides that, they have paid——

Mr. WILLETT. Besides that they have paid $53,000,000 cash to the Government. In 1901 the consumers of this country paid only $70,000,000 for foreign sugar. The consumption has increased much more rapidly than the sugar has increased.

The CHAIRMAN. And of course that has carried up the total; but we not only pay on sugar that we actually import, but we pay that much more. The tariff is paid on domestic sugars from all our insular possessions, from Louisiana, and from the West.

Mr. WILLETT. Yes. That statement only includes what we actually pay out for sugars which are subject to a duty.

The CHAIRMAN. I understand; but it seems to me the domestic man enhances his price by the amount of the duty.

Mr. WILLETT. What we pay to Porto Rico, the Hawaiian Islands, and the domestic beet interests is additional to that.

The CHAIRMAN. I know; and that is what I wanted to call attention to; because the domestic producer enhances his price every time, because you can not buy it from the foreign people for any less than the tariff is. That is true?

Mr. WILLETT. That is true.

The CHAIRMAN. So we pay this same duty on every pound of Louisiana sugar, on every pound of insular sugar, and on every pound of western beet sugar indirectly.

Mr. WILLETT. Yes; and on Porto Rican and Hawaiian sugar.

The CHAIRMAN. I said insular sugar.

Mr. WILLETT. Of course they get that benefit without any compensating returns.

The CHAIRMAN. Exactly. They add it.

Mr. WILLETT. That is why I do not see why this whole tariff business should not be changed to a different basis.

Mr. MALBY. On that subject, Mr. Chairman, I would like to ask just a question.

The CHAIRMAN. Yes; ask as many as you like.

Mr. WILLETT. I do not say that it ought to be, but it might be. It might be considered and discussed in Congress.

Mr. MALBY. While under present conditions the price of sugar may be enhanced more or less by the tariff, yet the real question which presents itself is as to whether there would be any diminution in the price of sugar to the consumer if the tariff was removed.

Mr. WILLETT. Yes; there would be.

Mr. MALBY. That is the burning question.

Mr. WILLETT. I can tell you how much the reduction was under the McKinley tariff bill, if you wish to know.

Mr. MALBY. Before going into that we would have to make sufficient inquiry to ascertain what the effect on production would be by the removal of the tariff, would we not?

Mr. WILLETT. I have that there as applied to the McKinley bill.

Mr. MALBY. I observe that since Hawaii was permitted to bring sugar into the United States free of duty our production has very largely increased.

Mr. WILLETT. Very largely.

Mr. MALBY. And I think all will concur that the production of sugar increased by reason of the fact that it became very profitable under the new conditions. I likewise observe that the Porto Rican sugar supply since we have admitted their sugar free has greatly increased in amount. I discover by examining the statistics in regard to Cuba, and since we gave Cuba a differential rate of 1.34 plus, that the quantity of sugar produced there has very largely increased. I discover that by the maintenance of our tariff in our own country—at least since that time—the local sugar-beet product has greatly increased in quantity.

So that after all, in determining what the people are going to pay for it all these matters must be taken into consideration. For instance, if the price of sugar be decreased by the whole amount of the tariff, would the Hawaiian planter have increased his product? Would the Porto Rican planter have increased his product? Would the Cuban planter have increased his, and would the American planter have increased his? And if they did not, would the price of sugar be indeed much, if any, less to the consumer than it now is? You have to ask and answer all those questions, do you not, in determining for yourself how much benefit would accrue to the American people by the taking out entirely of the tariff? You have to consider all those steps.

Mr. WILLETT. All those steps; and they are all based on one point.

Mr. MALBY. But it is clearly right to say, I think, that we could not hope, by the wiping out of the tariff so as to admit the world's product, for a reduction which would be equal to the whole amount of the tariff now levied, could we?

Mr. WILLETT. You could not.

Mr. MALBY. Because the entire conditions would be changed.

Mr. WILLETT. The very fact that you state, that those countries have increased their production, has been because the United States has not been open to the whole world on the same basis.

Mr. MALBY. And has been paying them a big price?

Mr. WILLETT. On the same basis.

Mr. MALBY. You see that is the difficulty I have in the matter.

The CHAIRMAN. Those are all considerations, of course.

Mr. MALBY. Those are all considerations.

Mr. WILLETT. What was the actual effect of taking off the 2.24 cent duty under the McKinley bill?

The CHAIRMAN. How did that affect production, you mean?

Mr. WILLETT. How did it affect everything?

The CHAIRMAN. And the price?

Mr. WILLETT. And the price; yes. Would you like to know? I will give that.

The CHAIRMAN. I should like to have it.

Mr. MALBY. I should like to have him give any statistics he has on the effect of the change of the tariff, that actually did take place, if he has anything there that shows it.

The CHAIRMAN. In other words, if it is history instead of prophecy.

Mr. MALBY. Yes; what actually took place when the tariff was changed at any time in the last 20 years. I would like to have you submit it to the committee.

Mr. WILLETT. I have it here.

Mr. MALBY. That will give some little light on the subject.

Mr. WILLETT. This is a statement of free duty versus $2.24 per 100 pounds duty on 96 test raw sugar. During the three years and three months preceding free duty (Jan. 1, 1888, to Apr. 1, 1891) the average cost to refiners of 100 pounds of 96 test centrifugals was $5.849. It requires 107 pounds of 96 test raws to make 100 pounds of granulated of 100 test. One hundred and seven pounds, 96 test, at $5.849, is $6.258. During three years and five months of free duty——

The CHAIRMAN. That is the Wilson bill?

Mr. WILLETT. That is the McKinley bill.

The CHAIRMAN. Yes; they gave a bounty.

Mr. WILLETT. During the 3 years and 5 months of free duty (Apr. 1, 1891, to Aug. 1, 1894) the average cost to refiners for 100 pounds of 96-test raws was $3.390. It requires 107 pounds of 96-test to make 100 pounds of 100-test granulated. That is the Government basis—107 pounds. One hundred and seven pounds raws, at $3.39 per 100 pounds, is $3.67. The refiners' gain by reduction of duty and lower cost of raws is $2.631. That is the difference between $6.258 and $2.631—the cost of the raws.

The CHAIRMAN. Yes.

Mr. MALBY. You say the refiners' gain?

Mr. WILLETT. It cost the sugar refiners $2.631 less for their raw sugars under free duty than it did under the $2.24 duty.

The CHAIRMAN. Yes.

Mr. WILLETT. During the 3 years and 3 months preceding free duty, the refiners sold granulated at an average price per 100 pounds of $6.921; and during the 3 years and 5 months of free duty, at an average price of $4.409; a difference (reduction) of $2.512. Now, the refiner kept the difference between $2.631 and $2.512 per 100 pounds, say $0.119. That was his advantage.

The CHAIRMAN. He made that much more profit by refining, in other words?

Mr. WILLETT. That was his advantage in three years.

The CHAIRMAN. Now, the consumer got sugar how much cheaper per hundred pounds?

Mr. WILLETT. I was going on——

The CHAIRMAN. All right; proceed.

Mr. WILLETT. The refiner kept the difference between $2.631 and $2.512 per 100 pounds—that is, $0.119—he kept that. During the the three years and three months preceding free duty the duty on 96° test raws per 100 pounds was $2.24. The duty on 107 pounds of raws of 96° test required to make 100 pounds of granulated, at $2.24, was $2.397. The refiners' gain from removal of duty and lower cost of raws as above was $2.631, the first price I gave you.

The CHAIRMAN. That would hardly be the refiners' gain, would it?

Mr. WILLETT. No; they gained 11 cents.

The CHAIRMAN. Yes, in a way; you simply say the cost to the refiner on the raw sugar——

Mr. WILLETT. Yes; $2.63 less under free sugar than it was with $2.24 duty; and the duty taken off of 107 pounds was $2.397, leaving the refiners' saving from lower cost of raws and removal of duty $0.234 per 100 pounds.

The refiners kept part of this saving, as before stated, 11.9 cents, and the consumer received the rest of this saving, say, 11.5 cents.

The CHAIRMAN. That is, saving in the refined?

Mr. WILLETT. The saving in the consumers' cost of refined.

The CHAIRMAN. Exactly; but just a moment there——

Mr. WILLETT. The consumer, therefore, received the benefit of the full duty taken off of 107 pounds of raws, $2.397, plus 11.05 cents—$2.512 per pound. That is, during the time of free duty the consumer paid for granulated $4.40; and during the time of $2.24 duty the consumer paid for granulated $6.92. He got the benefit of the full duty taken off.

The CHAIRMAN. And some of the increased profit of the refiner?

Mr. WILLETT. Some of the increased profit, yes. Do you not want the influence on production?

The CHAIRMAN. Yes; but before we go on——

Mr. MALBY. There is one suggestion on that table. What does it cost the Government per hundred pounds for sugar?

Mr. WILLETT. What did the Government receive, you mean?

Mr. MALBY. I mean what the Government paid per hundred pounds. They were paying something for the raising of domestic sugar?

Mr. WILLETT. Two cents a pound.

The CHAIRMAN. Right there, so the thing will be intelligible to the average man. That profit, of which you say the refiner kept part and gave some to the consumer, was the increased profit on refined resulting from lower raw sugar?

Mr. WILLETT. Exactly.

The CHAIRMAN. And that came from two causes, did it not? First, because the sugar itself was worth less——

Mr. WILLETT. Five cents a hundred less.

The CHAIRMAN. Exactly. And they saved that much on the refined; and, secondly, they had less capital locked up, and therefore a less interest account?

Mr. WILLETT. Yes.

The CHAIRMAN. I mean he divided that profit with the consumer besides giving the consumer the full benefit of the duty?

Mr. WILLETT. Yes, sir.

The CHAIRMAN. That is right?

Mr. WILLETT. That is right. Now, the influence on production——

The CHAIRMAN. Yes; that is very interesting.

Mr. WILLETT. I did not have time to write out this matter in regard to the influence on production. It is very simple, however.

Mr. MALBY. You are now going to the question of influence on production?

Mr. WILLETT. Yes, the influence on production, with the duty taken off, and the influence on beet sugar.

Mr. MALBY. The tables which were filed here by Mr. Atkins, I think, covering that period of time and giving the wholesale and retail prices of raw and refined sugar, as I have analyzed them, did not quite agree——

Mr. WILLETT. No; they would not.

The CHAIRMAN. I noticed that, too.

Mr. WILLETT. Because the prices that he gave, which he got from us, were for the full years, those full years.

The CHAIRMAN. The calendar years?

Mr. WILLETT. Yes.

The CHAIRMAN. Instead of the sugar years?

Mr. WILLETT. But I have taken the exact date of the period of free sugar.

The CHAIRMAN. You are sure your tables are reliable?

Mr. WILLETT. The inferences to be drawn from my tables are more reliable than those to be drawn from the others, although the figures in those tables are correct.

The CHAIRMAN. While the table you have just given is pretty strong proof, and I must admit I am somewhat prejudiced, yet it is so contrary to what I thought was true that I will ask this question: Could it be true that the laws of supply and demand were responsible to any extent for that decrease in price in raw, first, which is the main thing, because refined sugar followed it? Have you thought about that? I mean, for instance, say they had a bounteous crop and a large supply compared to demand during those years.

Mr. WILLETT. What influenced the prices during that time more than anything else was that the duty was coming off, and for six months ahead people were getting ready for it.

The CHAIRMAN. Of course, that is a trade condition that follows a contemplated change in legislation?

Mr. WILLETT. Yes.

The CHAIRMAN. But I was wondering—you have given a little over three years in each period.

Mr. WILLETT. I give the exact time, and I took the same period before.

The CHAIRMAN. You took the same period?

Mr. WILLETT. I was going to take the same period afterwards, but I did not have time.

The CHAIRMAN. I was just wondering—and an endeavor to be intellectually honest prompts the question—if it could not be true that to some extent this law of supply and demand had caused these differences in prices, or whether you know about that.

Mr. WILLETT. There was no difference in prices.

The CHAIRMAN. Yes; the tariff difference and a little over.

Mr. WILLETT. Only 5 cents difference in raw-sugar prices in the whole period.

The CHAIRMAN. The in-bond prices?

Mr. WILLETT. Yes; in-bond prices.

The CHAIRMAN. Have you caught my idea?

Mr. WILLETT. I think I have it. I have this sort of thing figured out in another way.

The CHAIRMAN. But I was wondering whether you had considered that thing or not and whether it could be true——

Mr. WILLETT. Certainly; I can give you the same result from an entirely different analysis if you would like to have it.

The CHAIRMAN. I would like it, just to prove the problem.

Mr. WILLETT. I will do it, just to prove the problem. I was under the same impression that you were under before I looked into the matter, and when I analyzed it on the four-year basis, before and after, I was under the impression that the consumer would not get the full benefit. So I went into it particularly to find out whether I was right or wrong, and to do so I took the actual periods and analyzed it in two different ways. I have given it in one way and I will give the other.

The CHAIRMAN. Describe the other without the details.

Mr. WILLETT. I could not do that very well.

The CHAIRMAN. All right; proceed, then.

Mr. WILLETT. It is short and covers the point you raised.

From January 1, 1888, to April 1, 1891, the duty was $2.24 per hundred pounds on 96° test raw sugar. From April 1, 1891, to August 28, 1894, three years and five months, there was free duty. Those were the years of duty and free duty. Now, for analysis, three years and three months before free sugar refined sugars averaged $6.921, the same as in the other statement, and raw sugars $5.849. That covers that point. The difference was $1.072, the difference between raw and refined.

Now, three years and four months of free sugar, refined sugar, $4.409; and raws, average, $3.39. The difference was $1.019 per hundred pounds.

Mr. MALBY. When was that; what year was that?

Mr. WILLETT. These are for the three years and three months preceding—it is odd; it is not even years.

Mr. MALBY. It is 1891 to 1894; for that period?

Mr. WILLETT. From April 1, 1891, to August 28, 1894.

Mr. MALBY. What price do you make it?

Mr. WILLETT. The price of refined sugar was $4.409 and the price of raws was $3.39. It would be different in that other table.

Mr. MALBY. Yes; I was comparing it with this table [indicating another table].

Mr. WILLETT. It does not agree with Mr. Atkins's table exactly. The difference between raws and refined under the $2.24 duty and under free sugar was 5.3 cents per hundred pounds. Before, the refined was $6.921; with the duty taken off it was $2.397. The difference was $4.524, and the difference between the raw and refined was 5.3 cents a hundred, which should be added to the $4.524, making the difference $4.471 to the refiner, between the $2.24 duty and free sugar, and that is the price at which the refiner ought to have sold his sugars to the consumer to give the consumer the full benefit of the duty taken off and the lower cost of raws—$4.471. Now, he did actually sell the sugars to the consumer at $4.409. That is 6.2 cents less than the full advantage of the decrease.

The CHAIRMAN. Have you finished that?

Mr. WILLETT. I will repeat part of that, as I do not think you heard it. You noticed that the difference between raws and refined before free and after free sugar was 5.3 cents per hundred pounds. Now, the refiners sold the raws before at $6.921, and the duty taken off was $2.397, leaving a difference of $4.524, which plus the 5 cents less cost of sugars would make the actual difference between before and after $4.471, which the refiner ought to have sold to the consumer at in order to give the consumer the full benefit of the duty and the 5 cents.

The CHAIRMAN. Now, right there; I do not want to interrupt——

Mr. WILLETT. But he did actually sell at $4.409.

The CHAIRMAN. Then it is a difference of a little over half a cent a pound?

Mr. WILLETT. That is 6 cents a hundred less than he ought to have sold at to give the consumer the full benefit of everything taken off.

The CHAIRMAN. But it is true, is it not, that the McKinley bill carried a duty of one-half a cent a pound on refined?

Mr. WILLETT. That did not enter into this at all. There is no refined imported.

The CHAIRMAN. But did they not take the benefit of that duty?

Mr. WILLETT. Oh, I beg your pardon; that is another subject. Had I not better finish this? I was proving something.

The CHAIRMAN. I was wondering if it were not related to that, though.

Mr. WILLETT. No; that has nothing to do with that.

The CHAIRMAN. Here is the connection it had in my mind. Refined sugar was not entirely free, so that while the duty before the McKinley law was passed was two dollars and some cents on refined sugar, $2.50 maybe, even after the McKinley law passed it remained half a cent a pound, and therefore when it comes to the price of refined sugar, one-half a cent a pound, it seems to me, ought to be added because of the duty. The domestic refiner or producer, taking advantage of the duty, naturally would have added that to his price for refined.

Mr. WILLETT. But he did not.

The CHAIRMAN. He did not. I wonder why he did not.

Mr. WILLETT. Because he could not; if he had, the refined sugars would have come in. As a matter of fact, they did come in, in 1901, did they not?

Mr. JACOWAY. The average margin between raw and refined at that time was 1.7, was it not?

Mr. WILLETT. No; it was 1.1. It was 1.7 before.

Mr. JACOWAY. 1885 shows about the average, does it not?

Mr. WILLETT. Yes; that was about the average. It would give a chance for refined sugars to come in, and they undoubtedly did come in.

The CHAIRMAN. More came in than before?

Mr. WILLETT. Yes, sir. I was proving the problem——

The CHAIRMAN. By working it another way.

Mr. WILLETT. Yes; to get the same result. It shows that the refiner ought to have sold his refined sugar to the consumer under free sugar at $4.471 a hundred pounds, whereas he did actually sell it at $4.409—6.2 cents less than he was entitled to sell it.

The CHAIRMAN. In other words, he did not demand all that he could have demanded according to the rule of trade.

Mr. WILLETT. The difference between raw and refined under the $2.24 duty was $1.072, and the cost of refining was $0.714. The refiners' profit and surplus was $0.358 a hundred pounds.

During free sugar the difference between raw and refined was $1.019 and the cost of refining was $0.548. The refiners' surplus and profit was $0.471. The refiners' profit under free sugar was 11.3 cents more than under free duty. One statement confirms the other.

The CHAIRMAN. Now, having done that—I know the calculation is right, for of course you have proved it mathematically by arriving at the same result in two different ways—here is what I had in mind, and I want to know whether you allowed for this in making these tables. Let me illustrate. For instance, if we had a duty to-day of 2 cents a pound on raw sugar and there was a great, bounteous crop made, as compared to the demand, so that world-wide conditions would give a low price, we might have, even with the duty added, a price, say, of 5 cents on in-bond sugar. Then suppose next year sugar was entirely free, and yet there was a short crop and a tremendous demand, on that account, even in-bond sugar might be worth 6 cents. So, it appears that the fact that you remove the tariff does not necessarily mean that there would be lower sugar at all.

Mr. WILLETT. No, sir.

The CHAIRMAN. Has that been taken into consideration at all in making these tables?

Mr. WILLETT. Yes. I show a difference of 5 cents——

The CHAIRMAN. But the conditions were not different in those two different periods?

Mr. WILLETT. No.

The CHAIRMAN. There were no abnormal conditions that could account for those differences in price?

Mr. WILLETT. No, sir.

The CHAIRMAN. They so nearly corresponded to what the tariff was that it showed that they were practically normal?

Mr. WILLETT. It shows that they were practically normal; yes.

The CHAIRMAN. That is what I wanted to be sure about. That was no abnormal condition independent of the tariff.

Mr. WILLETT. That, you understand, was the average during the three years. There may have been ups and downs.

The CHAIRMAN. But taking in those years altogether there were no abnormal trade conditions that would have affected the prices, according to the law of supply and demand, independent of the tariff?

Mr. WILLETT. No; there were not.

Mr. MALBY. We had a table here.

The CHAIRMAN. Do you refer to the Atkins table?

Mr. MALBY. I think it was submitted by Mr. Atkins. They do not seem to agree. They are so far apart that I wanted to call this witness's attention to it.

Mr. WILLETT. You will bear in mind that the time between January 1 and April 1, 1891, three months, was a very unsettled period, because the $2.24 duty was coming off and everybody was preparing for it.

Mr. MALBY. Of course what I wanted to do was to take a sufficient period of time under one condition and then under the other to see if the whole period of time shows a decrease, and if so, what that decrease would be, and we have a table here——

Mr. WILLETT. We can not take any longer time than either duty actually existed, you know.

Mr. MALBY. Oh, no.

Mr. WILLETT. I have not given the production yet. Do you want that before we forget it?

Mr. MALBY. We want this table. I supposed it was on page 100, but I do not find it there.

The CHAIRMAN. It is in the first hearing.

Mr. WILLETT. Now, take the consumption of sugars——

Mr. MALBY. It was very wide of the present statement.

The CHAIRMAN. He gave the different reasons why there was a shortage.

Mr. WILLETT. That free duty change had a wonderful effect on production and consumption.

The CHAIRMAN. Suppose you go into that a little.

Mr. WILLETT. Well, take the consumption of sugar. It increased 14.32 per cent during the four years preceding free duty, and it increased 30.38 per cent during the four years of free duty in the United States—or about four years.

The CHAIRMAN. It more than doubled.

Mr. WILLETT. When duties were renewed in 1894 the increased consumption in the United States, for the four years following free duty, was only 6.9 per cent.

The CHAIRMAN. Showing that it had a tendency to stop consumption.

Mr. WILLETT. To stop the consumption; yes. Now, the world's production of sugar during the four years preceding free duty was 22,259,258 tons, and during the four years, or about four years, of free duty, the production was 28,988,517 tons, an increase of 6,726,259 tons, or 30.28 per cent. Every year of the four years following the restoration of duties, the world's production of sugar decreased from the crop of the last year of free duty, 1894, or, say, 318,372 tons per year average decrease from 1894.

The effect of free duty on the beet industry. At the beginning of free duty, in 1891, there were 6 beet factories operating in the United States. At the close of free duty, in 1894, there were but 5 beet-sugar factories operating. With the renewal of duties the beet factories increased to 39 in the seven years to 1901, before the American Sugar Refining Co. went into it. That tells the story.

Mr. MALBY. I find here in Mr. Atkins's testimony, and I think he stated he got it from your report——

Mr. WILLETT. It all came from our office.

The CHAIRMAN. Page 176. Have you the first volume there?

Mr. WILLETT. Yes.

The CHAIRMAN. Then you can keep it before you. That is the table that you have been trying to find, is it not?

Mr. MALBY. Yes; this is the one. I see, in 1891——

Mr. WILLETT. Yes; I have it.

Mr. MALBY. Under the head of 1891, "raws, free; refined, one-half cent; bounty on domestics."

Mr. WILLETT. I do not see that.

The CHAIRMAN. In the tariff changes—the column marked "Tariff changes."

Mr. MALBY. Beginning with the year 1885—that is where he begins; but I go to 1891.

Mr. WILLETT. The raw was 4.047.

The CHAIRMAN. No. Look on the left-hand side, 1891. Look in the second column there, headed "Raw, 96° test, centrifugals."

Mr. WILLETT. Yes. "Raws, free."

The CHAIRMAN. Refined, one-half per cent. Bounty on domestics.

Mr. WILLETT. Yes; a bounty on domestics.

Mr. MALBY. From 1885 to 1890, going back to the beginning of his table, there appears to have been a tariff on raw sugar of $2.24. Am I correct about that?

The CHAIRMAN. Yes.

Mr. MALBY. And "refined, 3½." The price for 1885 was $6.441; for 1886, $6.117; 1887, $6.013; 1888, $7.007; 1889, $7.640. From 1891, April 1, "raws, free; refined, one-half cent."

Mr. WILLETT. The price was $4.691, was it not?

Mr. MALBY. Yes; $4.691.

Mr. WILLETT. The year prior it was $6.171. In 1891 it dropped to——

Mr. MALBY. $4.691.

Mr. WILLETT. My figures are the same—$4.409.

Mr. MALBY. Very well. The difference between the tariff on refined sugar was 3½.

Mr. WILLETT. The difference between the tariff?

Mr. MALBY. Yes; the difference of the tariff was 3½ on refined during the period from 1885 to 1890, inclusive.

Mr. WILLETT. Yes.

The CHAIRMAN. And $2.24 on raw.

Mr. MALBY. And $2.24 on raw.

Mr. WILLETT. The difference in duty on refined was $2.397.

Mr. MALBY. From those figures it would not indicate that the average price during the year had equaled the difference in the tariff during that period of time.

Mr. WILLETT. Let us see about it.

Mr. MALBY. You can clearly see that is not so by a glance.

Mr. WILLETT. In 1890 the price of refined was 6.171 cents; in 1891 it was——

Mr. MALBY. 4.691.

Mr. WILLETT. Is that a six or is it a cipher?

Mr. MALBY. 4.691.

Mr. WILLETT. That would be 1.48 difference.

Mr. MALBY. Very well. As a matter of fact, the difference between the tariff is 3 cents.

Mr. JACOWAY. Sugar was not admitted free until April of that year.

Mr. MALBY. I am talking about the refined sugar. Our figures are the refined-sugar figures, the figures we are looking at.

Mr. WILLETT. 2.39 was the difference.

Mr. MALBY. Let us see if it is 2.39. What year are you taking?

Mr. WILLETT. April 1; I take the actual period.

Mr. MALBY. The last year, 1890—you could take any year you wish—it was 6.171.

Mr. WILLETT. Yes; but that year takes in part of the $2.24 duty period and part free duty.

Mr. MALBY. Well, take any other time.

Mr. WILLETT. There is no calendar year that would cover that.

Mr. MALBY. I presume these prices are an average from daily sales, or whatever statistics were at hand——

Mr. WILLETT. Of the year——

Mr. MALBY. And the average prices there found to be what is designated here.

Mr. WILLETT. Yes; that is right.

Mr. MALBY. There is none of those years from 1885 to 1890, inclusive, as compared with 1891 to 1893, inclusive, where the deduction was anywhere near the amount of the difference of the tariff in those periods—no year?

The CHAIRMAN. Oh, yes; some of them were.

Mr. WILLETT. The price was 4.12 in 1894, and I give the average price at 4.40.

Mr. JACOWAY. 7.64 in 1889?

The CHAIRMAN. Yes; you can take the highest year and the lowest.

Mr. WILLETT. But I would not undertake as an expert to compare what will not compare.

The CHAIRMAN. Why will they not compare?

Mr. WILLETT. I can not compare a calendar year with anything else, you know, as an expert; I can not follow that at all.

Mr. MALBY. I think he says these are your figures.

Mr. WILLETT. These are figures for calendar years, but they have nothing whatever to do with actual facts.

Mr. MALBY. Are they not correct as to average price?

Mr. WILLETT. Absolutely correct as to calendar years, but have nothing to do with the intermediate years.

Mr. MALBY. I do not mean the intermediate years. I am talking about the years that he has given there.

Mr. WILLETT. That shows one thing and the other shows the other thing.

Mr. MALBY. I am trying to find out whether I understood you. I am trying to get at the exact facts. Take from 1894 to 1896, inclusive. That seems to have been a period which is not very good for a comparison, because raws are 40 cents ad valorem, I presume, with one-eighth added for refined and one-tenth countervailing duty, and we can not figure that very well, or at least I can not, depending on the price charged for sugar at that time. But we get down to 1897, where the tariff change in refined sugar appears to be 1.95, is it not?

The CHAIRMAN. Yes; that is right. That was the Dingley law.

Mr. MALBY. That is the Dingley law. The price of refined for 1897 was 4.503 cents; for 1896 it was 4.965; for 1899, 4.919; for 1900, without any apparent change in the tariff, 5.32; for 1901 it was 5.05; and then for 1902 it was 4.455; for 1906 it was 4.638. We find Cuban sugar coming in at 1.348, which is a considerable reduction, but we find the price of sugar for 1904 to be 4.772, and for 1905, 5.256, or really a larger price than between 1897 and 1903, inclusive. In other words, I do not follow you that the price is either increased or decreased by so much as the tariff is changed; that is not shown in any of those tables.

Mr. WILLETT. In any of those years?

Mr. MALBY. That is, from 1885 down, that is where it is taken by the year, which I assume is the average price for daily sales, or whatever basis it is estimated upon, I do not find that the price of sugar was increased by the amount of the tariff or decreased by the amount of the tariff, taken by the year. In fact, I find under the head of 1905, for instance, when the Cuban sugar came in, duty 1.348, that the price is 5.256, which is higher than it had been before for 10 years, although the tariff had been reduced. But I see a note here: "Decrease in European supply of a million tons."

The CHAIRMAN. That would account for that year, as you see.

Mr. WILLETT. Where the price for a number of years runs along——

Mr. MALBY. I am trying to get at, if I can, what has actually been the effect of the decrease or increase of the tariff on sugar and from this table, which Mr. Atkins says he took from your reports, by the year, it does not indicate that when the tariff was lowered the price to the consumer was lowered by the amount of the tariff. Neither does it show that when the tariff was increased it was increased to the consumer by the amount of the tariff. That is the way I figure this table. We will carefully go over your statement.

Mr. WILLETT. To analyze all that it would be necessary to take the conditions of supply and demand for each of those years.

Mr. MALBY. I suppose even without any duty——

Mr. WILLETT. The tariff does not have any effect in changing prices as long as the tariff is steady. It is the ups and downs of the supply and demand.

Mr. MALBY. I appreciate that; but taking any one of this group of years——

The CHAIRMAN. Except the one he cites himself which is a different one, and where he says those abnormal conditions did not exist——

Mr. WILLETT. Those figures are correct for what they represent.

Mr. MALBY. So, when we have to consider the question of supply and demand and whether there has been an increase or decrease in the European supply, in order to determine the effect, we are speculating somewhat as to the effect of the increase or decrease of tariff, are we not?

Mr. WILLETT. Oh, yes; those are conditions entirely outside of expert figures. I have only given you the changes in figures, that is all.

Mr. MALBY. I will take great interest in studying your figures and making a comparison with this table.

Mr. WILLETT. I will be very glad if you will write me a line any time, asking just exactly what you will like, and I shall be very glad to enlarge my statement covering that point.

The CHAIRMAN. Mr. Willett, in the morning, when the committee reconvenes we will take up that expert work I have referred to. How long do you think it will take you to go through that and explain it?

Mr. WILLETT. An hour or so.

The CHAIRMAN. In the morning, then, you may do that. We will probably finish this in the course of an hour in the morning.

Mr. RAKER. Just one question before we adjourn. Mr. Willett, for the year which is marked here 1894, the price of refined sugar at that time was 5.256 cents, and they claim that there was 1,000,000 tons shortage in Europe. Now, how does it happen when there was 1,000,000 tons shortage that year that the price of refined sugar to the consumer here was 5.256, and this year it goes up to 7 plus.

Mr. WILLETT. That was not enough. It takes a shortage of 2,000,000 to bring prices where they are to-day.

Mr. MALBY. You might go to 1906 and call attention to the fact that there was an increase in European supply of 2,000,000 and there was only a decrease of three-quarters of a cent in price.

Mr. WILLETT. All those things are governed by local circumstances. The German producers have great financiering ability and great facilities for carrying over their sugars.

Mr. RAKER. I would like to ask one question in that connection. Are not our people in any way allied with the German people in the sugar business?

Mr. WILLETT. Absolutely no connection whatever.

Mr. RAKER. And they have no connection with any foreign branch?

Mr. WILLETT. With no foreign branch; no, sir.

Mr. RAKER. Mr. Chairman, before we adjourn I will say that while in California I met a number of sugar people, and they wanted to know if they could have a hearing before this committee.

The CHAIRMAN. The beet-sugar people?

Mr. RAKER. Yes; I told them that the best thing for them to do would be to get together and select two or three men to represent them and present their evidence before the committee, if they so desired, I putting it to them that it would probably be to their advantage to present their matters before the committee.

The CHAIRMAN. Yes, we will hear them, and if there is any reason why we ought to subpœna them we can subpœna them.

Mr. RAKER. I put it to them this way: That if they wanted to be heard, that the committee would probably be glad to hear them.

The CHAIRMAN. There are some people in Colorado who have insisted that they can give some testimony, the like of which has not been heard, and testimony which they say they are entitled to give. As the resolution contains a specific direction for us to inquire on that precise subject which——

Mr. MALBY. What people are they?

The CHAIRMAN. A committee from the Farmers' Union in Colorado.

Mr. MALBY (addressing Mr. Raker). Are they coming?

Mr. RAKER. I told them that I would see the chairman about it. In the meantime if they were in too big a hurry, I told them they could telegraph Mr. Hardwick; but of course I came right on.

The CHAIRMAN. Let us see what these people from Colorado develop. It may be they will give the evidence that your people will, and it will not be necessary to duplicate.

We will resume at 10.30 in the morning; we will then take up that expert work that Mr. Willett has done.

(Thereupon, at 5 o'clock p. m., the committee adjourned until to-morrow, December 6, 1911, at 10.30 a. m.)

AMERICAN SUGAR REFINING CO. AND OTHERS.

SPECIAL COMMITTEE ON THE INVESTIGATION
OF THE AMERICAN SUGAR REFINING CO. AND OTHERS,
HOUSE OF REPRESENTATIVES,
Washington, D. C., December 6, 1911.

The committee met at 10.30 o'clock a. m., Hon. Thomas W. Hardwick (chairman) presiding.

TESTIMONY OF MR. WALLACE P. WILLETT—Resumed.

The CHAIRMAN. Mr. Willett, when we adjourned yesterday you were discussing some tariff conditions on sugar with Judge Malby and myself. Of course we were asking the questions for the committee. Do you want to make any further statement in reference to that matter before we go into this expert work of yours?

Mr. WILLETT. Yes. I would like to apply Judge Malby's method to my method.

The CHAIRMAN. All right. Suppose you do that in your own way.

Mr. WILLETT. I would like to point out the possible error or the misunderstanding of Judge Malby. I would say that he has not taken into consideration the fact that it takes 107 pounds of raw sugar to make 100 pounds of granulated, consequently the duty on 100 pounds of granulated is not 2.24, but 2.397.

Mr. MALBY. Mr. Willett, I have compared, however, the raw with the raw.

Mr. WILLETT. But not exactly scientifically. I have it here scientifically.

Mr. MALBY. That is to say, I have compared the raw with the raw, and not the refined with the raw. I have compared the refined with the refined, and in each instance I have attempted to arrive at this difference and compare it with the tariff of that year.

Mr. WILLETT. That is true, but in taking the tariff on refined at 2.90, you see there is no such tariff on refined. In actual existence and practice the tariff on refined is only 2.39 instead of 2.90.

Mr. MALBY. You mean 1.90?

Mr. WILLETT. 1.90; yes.

Mr. MALBY. Let us not fall into that error, because so far as my figures are concerned I have made no figures beyond when the differential rate took place in Cuba; so that prior to that time the duty was as I have stated it.

Mr. WILLETT. Yes, sir; that is correct.

The CHAIRMAN. Before you go into that explanation let me suggest this further consideration which is on the mind of the Chair about this very matter. I will not ask you to answer this, but simply to bear it in mind. These figures of Judge Malby, I have noticed, according to my idea, all through this hearing, do not take into consideration crop conditions from year to year. In other words, say the duty was 2 cents, just for the purpose of illustration, this year, and sugar was worth 5 cents a pound; then say next year there was no duty at all, yet if there was a short crop sugar might be worth 9 cents without any duty whatever.

Mr. MALBY. Mr. Chairman, will you permit me to correct that, because I do not wish that to be on the record. I will tell you what I have done.

The CHAIRMAN. Yes; I simply wanted to see whether that is true or not.

Mr. MALBY. The chairman is mistaken about that. On the contrary, I have done this. Instead of picking out one year, I have taken the entire decade, 1885 to 1890, inclusive, which embraces all of the years in which this tariff of 3½ cents on refined and 2.24 on raw was in force.

The CHAIRMAN. I quite understand that; but that is not exactly the point I have in mind.

Mr. MALBY. That is the best we can do.

Mr. WILLETT. What is your final conclusion, Judge, as to how much the consumer did receive of the reduction of the duty? What is the final absolute result of your calculation?

Mr. MALBY. As compared with what?

Mr. WILLETT. Without comparison with anything. How much of the duty did he receive?

Mr. MALBY. Well, you have got to compare with something or else you can not say he got anything. There was a duty between 1891 and 1893.

Mr. WILLETT. What do you consider the duty taken off?

Mr. MALBY. So far as raw sugar was concerned, it was all taken off.

Mr. WILLETT. But so far as refined sugar was concerned?

Mr. MALBY. On refined sugar 1.685 was taken off, because there was no Cuban reciprocity at that time, and there was no other duty except 1.685 on refined.

Mr. WILLETT. We are speaking about the 2.24 duty now.

Mr. MALBY. Do you want to take the 2.24 duty? That was earlier.

Mr. WILLETT. What was the benefit to the consumer from the taking off of the 2.24 cents duty? How much of that duty did the consumer get?

Mr. MALBY. The consumer got the benefit of a little more than 2 cents. I must admit that that was rather a surprise to me, but apparently he did get a reduction of 2 cents.

Mr. WILLETT. Two cents a pound?

Mr. FORDNEY. Was that on account of the duty or on account of crop conditions?

Mr. MALBY. That I do not know; but when you come to take off the 3 cents that followed that, for the same period of time, he did not get so much. The difference was about six-tenths of a cent instead of a quarter of a cent.

Mr. WILLETT. The whole difference in the advantage to the consumer is a pure and simple mathematical calculation.

Mr. MALBY. The consumer got the benefit on raw of 2 cents out of 224, and on the refined he got a reduction of 2.46 out of 3, or about six-tenths of a cent less than the duty; but during the next decade he did not get that for some reason or other.

Mr. WILLETT. I see your position exactly, and if you will permit me, I will compare it with my estimate.

Mr. MALBY. All right.

Mr. WILLETT. The $2.24 duty a hundred on 96° test raws began June 1, 1883, and ended April 1, 1891. If we leave out the first two years, 1884 and 1885, as possibly having been influenced to some extent by the change of tariff or agitation in relation thereto, we have left the years 1886, 1887, 1888, and 1889, during which the conditions were normal, and nothing affected the influence of the 2.24 duty, adversely or otherwise.

Mr. MALBY. You do not take into consideration the entire period.

Mr. WILLETT. I see the difference between yours and mine. I see that difference, Judge, and I will explain mine. Leaving out also the year 1890 as possibly influenced by the agitation of the taking off of the duty, which it undoubtedly was, it leaves the years I have stated. In 1886 the average price of raws was $5.336, and in 1887 the price of raws was—I am quoting now from Mr. Atkins's table—$5.245; in 1888, $5.749; and in 1889, $6.433. Adding those together and dividing by four gives the average for the four years, $5.691. Now for those years, in refined sugar, 1886, the average was $6.117.

Mr. MALBY. That is for the same period?

Mr. WILLETT. The same period. Refined, in 1887, $6.013.

Mr. MALBY. For what year?

Mr. WILLETT. 1887.

Mr. MALBY. You are simply repeating the table.

Mr. WILLETT. Yes; I am repeating the table. In 1888, $7.007, and in 1889, $7.640, added together, $26.777, and divided by four makes $6.694. It requires 107 pounds of raw sugars of 96° test to make 100 pounds of granulated of 100° test. That is the Government basis. One hundred and seven pounds multiplied by 5.69 equals the cost of raws to produce 100 pounds of granulated, $6.08.

Mr. MALBY. They have carried out their margin here between raws and refined as 0.712. Is that figured on the same basis you do, or not; that is, for the first year 0.781, and so on down the list.

Mr. WILLETT. 0.781 was the difference in 1886.

Mr. MALBY. Do they figure the same way you do?

Mr. WILLETT. Yes, sir.

Mr. MALBY. They figure the same way to arrive at the same result?

Mr. WILLETT. Yes, sir; 0.768, 1.258, and 1.207, for the different years, a total of 4.014, divided by 4, is $1.003 for the average difference between raws and refined for the four years. During the four years 1886 to 1889, inclusive, raws cost the refiner 5.69 a hundred pounds, or 6.08 for 107 pounds to make a hundred pounds of granulated. Now during the period of free-duty sugars, which was from April 1, 1891, to August 1, 1894, as I stated yesterday, the cost of 107 pounds of raws to produce 100 pounds of granulated was 3.67. The refiners therefore under free duty had a reduction of 2.41.

Mr. MALBY. How do you arrive at that figure?

Mr. WILLETT. The difference between 6.08 and 3.67 in the case of raw sugar to produce 100 pounds of granulated.

Mr. MALBY. Have you reduced that 3.67 by the process of 107 pounds?

Mr. WILLETT. Yes, sir; by the same process.

Mr. MALBY. I get the average, without any reduction, 3.654.

Mr. WILLETT. Well, you take in the entire years, I presume.

Mr. MALBY. I do; yes.

Mr. WILLETT. That would account for that difference.

Mr. MALBY. There is very little difference.

Mr. WILLETT. Yes; but it accounts for what difference there is.

Mr. MALBY. I was thinking that perhaps yours was a little too small.

Mr. WILLETT. These are exact figures. Now, during the years 1886 to 1889 the refiners sold granulated sugar at 6.694 per hundred pounds.

Mr. MALBY. From 1886 to when?

Mr. WILLETT. During those years, 1886 to 1889, inclusive, the refiners sold sugar at 6.694, while during the period of free sugar they sold granulated at 4.41.

Mr. MALBY. Where do you get that?

Mr. WILLETT. From the average price of refined sugars from April 1, 1891, to August 1, 1894, the exact period of free-duty sugar. That is where you differ from me, in that you take the full year 1891 and the full year 1894, which included, each year, four months full duty.

Mr. MALBY. No; I took from 1891 to 1893, inclusive, and left out 1894, because the agitation was on in 1894, and it did not go through in 1894.

Mr. WILLETT. But you include the four months of 1891 in your calculation?

Mr. MALBY. I do.

Mr. WILLETT. That would account for the slight difference. These are exact figures. What did you make that, do you remember?

Mr. MALBY. Yours was 4.41?

Mr. WILLETT. Yes.

Mr. MALBY. I make it 4.092, that is the average cost of refined sugar between 1891 and 1893, inclusive.

Mr. WILLETT. What I asked was what you made the price at which the refiner sold to the consumer during those years; I make that 4.41.

Mr. MALBY. I make the average price 4.092 for refined granulated.

Mr. WILLETT. For those years?

Mr. MALBY. Yes.

The CHAIRMAN. That is even lower than you make it.

Mr. WILLETT. That is lower than I make it. I make it 4.41. I may be wrong.

The CHAIRMAN. You get it from the Atkins table, do you not, Mr. Malby?

Mr. MALBY. I get it from the table, and I must admit that I figured this a little hurriedly, and I am not vouching for the absolute accuracy of the figures; but what I want to know more particularly is simply the method Mr. Willett is pursuing, and then we can compare his method with the method of the others.

Mr. WILLETT. Yes. Now the refiners kept the difference of 2.41 less the 2.284 which gave the refiners the advantage of 10 cents a hundred pounds.

Mr. MALBY. I do not understand that 10 cents a hundred pounds.

Mr. WILLETT. The difference between 2.41 and 2.284. At the top of the page you will find that the refiners saved in the reduced duty

2.41 cents a hundred pounds, and that they sold granulated during 1886–1889 at 6.694, while under free duty sugar they sold it at 4.41, a difference of 2.284. The difference between 2.284, which they sold at, and 2.41, which they gathered in, shows what the refiners got from the reduced duty. During 1886 to 1889 the duty for 107 pounds of raws with which to make 100 pounds of granulated figures $2.397. The refiners gained, as above, 2.38. The difference between 2.397 and 2.38 is 0.187 per hundred pounds. Of that 18 cents a hundred pounds the refiner, as shown above, gets 13 cents.

The CHAIRMAN. That was the increased profit on account of lower sugar?

Mr. WILLETT. Yes.

The CHAIRMAN. And they kept the bulk of that, namely, 13 cents out of 18 cents?

Mr. WILLETT. Yes; they kept 18 cents and gave 13 cents. They kept 5 cents out of the duty, so that the final result is that the consumer got the entire duty taken off of $2.397 less 5.3 cents. I will put this in proper shape and put it on file here.

Mr. MALBY. Mr. Willett, there is only one other comparison I would like to have you make and put in the record, so that we will have two decades to compare it with, and that is, compare your 1885 to 1890 record—that is, so much of that as you have.

Mr. WILLETT. You mean the record from 1885 to 1889?

Mr. MALBY. Yes; whatever portion of it you have. I take the whole, but that will not make much difference. Compare that with the period of 1898 to 1903, which is the next decade beyond that which you have just figured.

The CHAIRMAN. Mr. Malby, you want him to get those figures up and bring them with him when he comes back after Christmas?

Mr. MALBY. Yes.

Mr. WILLETT. Did you say from 1898 to 1903?

Mr. MALBY. Yes.

Mr. WILLETT. That is under the Dingley bill, a duty of 1.685. That is a different duty.

Mr. MALBY. Yes; that is a different duty.

Mr. WILLETT. I intended to do that before I came here, but I did not have time to do so.

Mr. MALBY. That is the next decade we have.

Mr. WILLETT. Yes, sir; that is an important matter.

Mr. MALBY. I want to see whether this thing holds good.

Mr. WILLETT. Exactly. I will do that.

Mr. MALBY. Make the same figures as to that period and that will furnish us with an example to go by.

The CHAIRMAN. Now, Mr. Willett, will you give us briefly your opinion as to what the effect of the Dutch standard is on American prices of sugar?

Mr. WILLETT. I would rather not go into that problem unless you particularly desire it.

The CHAIRMAN. Can you do so in a very few words?

Mr. WILLETT. Yes, sir.

The CHAIRMAN. I would like to have you do so.

Mr. WILLETT. You want my opinion on that subject?

The CHAIRMAN. We would like to have your opinion on that subject. Let me put it in this way: If the Dutch standard were wiped out completely from our tariff law, what effect, if any, would it have on the price of refined sugar to the American consumer? Would it be considerable or not?

Mr. WILLETT. The position of the Dutch standard in the tariff, in my judgment, is simply a guide to the appraiser for noting the difference between raw and refined sugar. There is no other way to tell. No expert can tell the difference between raws and refined sugar.

The CHAIRMAN. Except by color?

Mr. WILLETT. Except they have a guide to go by in color.

The CHAIRMAN. Is the polariscope a more scientific way of determining that?

Mr. WILLETT. You can not detect raws from refined by the polariscope.

The CHAIRMAN. We have some testimony before us to the effect that the importers can take this ordinary brown sugar and treat it with ultramarine and it can come in and pass the Dutch standard test.

Mr. WILLETT. That is right.

The CHAIRMAN. And therefore the importer can avoid the protection afforded by the Dutch standard on the color test by using ultramarine?

Mr. WILLETT. He can if he knows how to do it and how to avoid the pure-food laws?

The CHAIRMAN. Well, they do that, do they not?

Mr. WILLETT. To-day the refiners put no bluing in their refined sugar.

The CHAIRMAN. How about the importers, do they do that?

Mr. WILLETT. I do not think the Government would allow sugars imported that had bluing in them.

The CHAIRMAN. Is the presence of ultramarine easily detected?

Mr. WILLETT. Oh, yes; it is very easily detected.

The CHAIRMAN. If the Dutch standard were eliminated from our tariff law, is it your judgment that the consumer would get cheaper sugar or not?

Mr. WILLETT. He would not. To eliminate the Dutch standard, you would have to eliminate the differential as well, otherwise you could not tell the difference between raw and refined sugar.

The CHAIRMAN. The polariscope would not afford a sufficient test?

Mr. WILLETT. No, sir. Independent of that one thing, there is no particular advantage in having the Dutch standard.

The CHAIRMAN. Let me direct your attention to this contention made on that precise point——

Mr. WILLETT (interposing). As to that contention, the consumers of the United States do not want anything except refined sugar.

The CHAIRMAN. White sugar?

Mr. WILLETT. White sugar. They can get all the white sugar of No. 20 or No. 24 they want from Porto Rico, the Hawaiian Islands, and Louisiana; but neither of those countries makes those sugars to any extent. The Hawaiian Islands, eight years ago, started one factory making refined sugars, what they called refined sugars; in reality they were not bone-black refined sugars.

The CHAIRMAN. It was like the plantation sugars of Louisiana?

Mr. WILLETT. Yes, sir; sulphur sugars. Eight years ago that factory made 20,000 tons of those sugars and shipped it to the United

States. This last year they are making but 17,000, and no other factory in the Hawaiian Islands has started in to make such sugars.

The CHAIRMAN. Mr. Oxnard testified that Oxnard Bros. were engaged in that industry to a considerable extent or were about to engage in it.

Mr. WILLETT. Yes; they proposed to do that. All the Louisiana planters make a sugar that is above No. 20, but there is very little demand for it in the United States.

The CHAIRMAN. The contention has been made before this committee that if the Dutch standard were eliminated from our tariff laws that brown sugars, sugars that are not as white as our granulated sugar by the bone-black process, but are just as good, just as healthy, and just as useful, would come in and could be sold to the people at a very much cheaper price; and that that is happening everywhere else in the world except here, and for that reason the retention of the Dutch standard is a hardship upon the poor people of this country.

Mr. WILLETT. The class of sugar to which you refer is the Scotch, yellow sugar, testing 83 or thereabouts, but being above No. 16 Dutch standard. Now that class of sugar is not wanted in the United States to any extent. For instance, in 1880——

The CHAIRMAN (interposing). No. 16 is the Dutch standard in the tariff law?

Mr. WILLETT. No. 16 is the Dutch standard in the tariff law.

The CHAIRMAN. What degree would that be? It might be any degree, might it not?

Mr. WILLETT. Yes; any degree.

Mr. MALBY. Any degree below 96?

Mr. WILLETT. It could hardly be any degree of raw, but it could be any degree of refined.

Mr. MALBY. Any degree below 100?

Mr. WILLETT. Yes; any degree below 100. Any degree of Scotch sugar could be from 83 to 100 and yet be above No. 16 Dutch standard. As I was remarking, in 1880——

Mr. MALBY (interposing). What does that 16 stand for—anything in particular?

Mr. WILLETT. That was an ancient custom put out by the Dutch Government years and years ago, before the polariscope was invented.

Mr. MALBY. I know that; but what does the 16 represent; why is it not 14 or 15?

Mr. WILLETT. There is a 14 and a 17, down to No. 10 and up to 24.

Mr. MALBY. What does the 16 represent? Is that a color?

Mr. WILLETT. Sixteen is a color, 15 is a lower color, 14 is a less color.

The CHAIRMAN. Now, if we were to——

Mr. WILLETT (interposing). One moment. I will complete my explanation. In 1880——

The CHAIRMAN (interposing). But you are getting away from what I wanted to know.

Mr. WILLETT. Just one moment. I say that those sugars made in Glasgow or in Scotland would not be used to any extent in this country. In 1880 the consumption of the United States consisted of 60 per cent of such sugars. To-day it consists of about 5 per cent only of those soft sugars.

The CHAIRMAN. Why is that? Is it prejudice?

Mr. WILLETT. The country is demanding better sugar.

The CHAIRMAN. Are the white sugars much better than the brown sugars, much healthier, or anything like that?

Mr. WILLETT. Which white sugars?

The CHAIRMAN. The sugars above the 16 standard.

Mr. WILLETT. They are pure sugars, and raw sugars are not pure sugars. All refined sugars are pure sugars.

The CHAIRMAN. The proposition I particularly want to know about myself is this: The contention is often made, and it is popular throughout the country among a great many people, that the Dutch standard is the real "nigger in the woodpile," as we say down South, and if that were wiped out the sugar consumer of this country could obtain a large quantity of healthy sugar which, while it may not be as white and pretty as the other sugar, would be equally as healthy, at a much lower price; and that the Dutch standard is kept in there to enable the refiner to sell only this high-grade refined sugar. Have I made myself intelligible as to what I am trying to get at?

Mr. MALBY. In other words, that it is a protection to the refiner and not to the consumer.

The CHAIRMAN. Exactly; that it is not to the consumer's benefit to keep it in there, and that it is an antique or archaic way of testing sugar.

Mr. WILLETT. That all depends on whether you can educate the people up to use those sugars instead of what they are using now. They have got accustomed to using the white sugars. Now, if you remove the Dutch standard and bring in a white Java sugar which is as good a color as that [indicating a sample of sugar], then the people might or might not take it. Probably they would take it to a much larger extent.

The CHAIRMAN. Would it be much cheaper?

Mr. WILLETT. It would not be very much cheaper.

The CHAIRMAN. Can you give us an idea of how much cheaper you think it would be sold for? I am not asking you for exact figures, but just an opinion.

Mr. WILLETT. Not exceeding a quarter of a cent a pound.

The CHAIRMAN. And you do not think that would influence the market?

Mr. WILLETT. I do not think that would influence the consumption to any extent.

The CHAIRMAN. Would the elimination of the Dutch standard from our tariff laws hurt the sugar industry of this country?

Mr. WILLETT. I do not see how it would, for the reason, I state, that these sugars would not come in competition with our refiners' sugars.

The CHAIRMAN. Then what is the necessity for its retention if, as a scientific test, it has been superseded by the more scientific test of the polariscope?

Mr. WILLETT. I think any appraiser of the United States Government will tell you that it is a necessity in his business.

The CHAIRMAN. Why?

Mr. WILLETT. Because he can not tell, I can not tell, no expert can tell the difference between raw and refined sugar by the polariscope alone. There must be a standard of color to go by and mark the division between raw and refined to collect the duties. Otherwise there would be no end of litigation in this country.

Mr. MALBY. He could tell the difference, if there was any difference, in the purity of the sugar?

Mr. WILLETT. Yes; but any purity of sugar could be above 16.

Mr. MALBY. Could he tell by the polariscopic test whether there was any difference in the purity of the sugar?

Mr. WILLETT. No, sir.

Mr. MALBY. Why not?

Mr. WILLETT. Because sugars above 16 and sugars below 16 could be of the same purity.

The CHAIRMAN. Then one test is as good as the other?

Mr. MALBY. That is just what I am getting at, that one is refined and one is not, but they possess exactly the same degree of sweetness.

Mr. WILLETT. If at the same time you eliminate the 16 Dutch standard you eliminate the differential on refined, then you are all right. If you will do the two things together, you are all right.

The CHAIRMAN. In other words, the Dutch standard is a protection for the refiner?

Mr. WILLETT. It is not a protection.

The CHAIRMAN. In that it enables them to enforce the differential.

Mr. WILLETT. It enables the refiners to keep out of lawsuits with the Government, because otherwise that is what would happen. The refiner would bring in some sugar, and the Government would say, "That is refined sugar," and the refiner would say, "It is not refined, and you have not got it in the tariff."

Mr. FORDNEY. It protects the consumer in that it insures a pure sugar, does it not?

Mr. WILLETT. Yes, sir.

Mr. FORDNEY. And there is no other way of insuring a pure sugar?

Mr. WILLETT. There is absolutely no other way.

The CHAIRMAN. I have entirely misunderstood you if you answered that question correctly. I thought you said that the purity of the sugar did not depend on color at all; that the polariscope would show the degree of sugar purity in either a brown or white sugar, and therefore the Dutch standard can not possibly protect the consumer when it comes to the question of the purity of the sugar.

Mr. WILLETT. Oh, no. I did not understand that.

The CHAIRMAN. The Dutch standard, however, does protect—I do not use the word "protect" in its narrow sense—the refiner, in that it insures the enforcement of the refiner's margin.

Mr. WILLETT. It insures the keeping out of refined sugars as long as there is a differential on it.

The CHAIRMAN. Now, then, carry this just one step further, and I think the circle is complete. If we wipe out the refiner's margin there would not be the slightest reason for retaining the Dutch standard?

Mr. WILLETT. Not the slightest. The two go together.

The CHAIRMAN. And the Dutch standard is really kept in there to protect the refiner's margin?

Mr. WILLETT. Yes, sir.

The CHAIRMAN. So, if we wipe out one there is no need of keeping the other; and if we wipe out both, some of the refiners have testified they could stand it all right.

Mr. WILLETT. You mean the differential?

The CHAIRMAN. Yes. If we wiped out the differential entirely, and also the Dutch standard. to what extent, in your judgment, would that affect the prices of sugar to the American consumer?

Mr. WILLETT. Under present conditions, it would not affect it.

The CHAIRMAN. Why not?

Mr. WILLETT. Because the differential does not apply at all in actual practice to-day.

The CHAIRMAN. That is just exactly the point. Why not now?

Mr. WILLETT. To make the differential apply you have got to have some country which produces refined sugar on the same basis as the duty now existing on Cuban sugar. In order to make the tariff differential apply, the duties on raw sugars from countries which produce refined sugars would have to be the same as the duty on raw sugars from the island of Cuba. Our present differential is 7.5 cents, and it does not amount to a row of pins, but if the duty on foreign sugars was the same as on Cuban sugars to-day, foreign sugars would be coming into this country by the cartload, or, rather, the shipload. So that the differential is absolutely no protection to the refiner to-day.

The CHAIRMAN. Why is it true that we have no refined sugar imported into this country?

Mr. WILLETT. Because the duty on Cuban raw sugar is $1.34.8, and Cuba makes no refined sugar for export. There is no Cuban-made refined sugar for export. This differential of 7.5 cents would not prevent the refined sugars from coming into this country.

The CHAIRMAN. But if Cuba ever goes into the sugar-refining business we will have that result; that is, the importation of refined sugar?

Mr. WILLETT. Yes, sir; but they will never do that, because it costs so much more to make refined sugar in Cuba. There is no profit in making refined sugar, on account of the cost of bone black, etc.

The CHAIRMAN. In other words, natural conditions are against it?

Mr. WILLETT. Yes, sir.

The CHAIRMAN. Now then, if we should wipe out the refiners' margin and the Dutch standard, your opinion is that it would not affect the refiners at the present time?

Mr. WILLETT. Do you mean refined sugar?

The CHAIRMAN. Under present conditions, you say that that would have no effect upon the refiners?

Mr. WILLETT. Yes, sir.

The CHAIRMAN. And therefore it would not help the consumer?

Mr. WILLETT. It would make no difference.

The CHAIRMAN. Is it your opinion that on account of this differential between raw sugar and refined sugar, amounting to 7.5 cents, which is given to the refiner, that the refiner adds that much to the cost of refined sugar to the wholesale dealer?

Mr. WILLETT. No, sir.

The CHAIRMAN. Why can not the refiner do that?

Mr. WILLETT. As I stated before, he could do that provided Cuba made refined sugar, but when you come to consider the duty on European refined sugar you find instead of the 7.5 cents differential a differential of 7.5 cents plus 34 cents.

The CHAIRMAN. Well, if that differential was wiped out as against Europe—if that were wiped out—what effect would it have?

Mr. Willett. Do you mean if refined sugars were taxed 7.5 cents less than they are now taxed, would that affect the importation of refined sugar?

The Chairman. Yes.

Mr. Willett. No, sir.

The Chairman. But suppose they were all wiped out, the Cuban differential as well as the 7.5 cents?

Mr. Willett. Then refined sugar would come in, because 7.5 cents is no protection in any sense of the word. No refiner could exist on a differential of 7.5 cents.

The Chairman. Then, in your opinion, his real protection lies in the provision relating to Cuban sugars?

Mr. Willett. Yes, sir. If that were wiped out, then the 7.5 differential would bring in refined sugar.

The Chairman. If we had free sugar, that would be wiped out?

Mr. Willett. Yes, sir.

The Chairman. Yet some of the principal refiners of the country contend that they want free sugar. Why is that?

Mr. Willett. Mr. Lowry can explain that.

Mr. Fordney. Mr. Lowry is present——

The Chairman (interposing). Well, he is going on the stand.

Mr. Fordney. Here is an affidavit that I would like to put in the record now.

The Chairman. Not now; it can come in later.

Mr. Fordney. You have asked him what makes up the difference, and I have an affidavit here that I would like to have go into the record.

The Chairman. It can go in in regular order, but not while this witness is on the stand.

Then you do not think that under the Cuban duty the wiping out of the Dutch standard and the differential would have any effect——

Mr. Willett (interposing). On refined sugar; no, sir.

The Chairman. What, in your opinion, would be the effect of free sugar on the prices to the American consumer?

Mr. Willett. That would be a long story.

The Chairman. It would take you some time to go into that?

Mr. Willett. Yes, sir.

The Chairman. Would it reduce the price to any extent? In other words, if we had free sugar, would the American consumer get refined sugar at a lower price than he does now?

Mr. Willett. Yes, sir; because he did get it cheaper under the McKinley tariff.

The Chairman. That brings me to the point I have in mind.

Mr. Willett. We have actual statistics showing that he has got it in the past, leaving out all outside considerations. That is why I took four years for comparison, that is, when the 2.24 duty was in actual nonoperation, without any outside influences affecting it.

The Chairman. If sugar went up after the removal of the tariff—that is, if sugar goes up the next year——

Mr. Willett (interposing). Refined or raw?

The Chairman. Both.

Mr. Willett. Both would have to go up or neither.

The Chairman. Now, we remove the duty on both, and the price goes up, so that the effect is that maybe during the first year of free sugar, sugar is higher in the market, yet, under the same conditions, if there had been a duty, the price would have been that much more, would it not?

Mr. WILLETT. Yes, sir. In addition to the influences which I suggested at the outset as bearing upon this tariff question, I would like to add the sugar speculators of Europe.

The CHAIRMAN. Well, that would apply to any market—on cotton, corn, or wheat?

Mr. WILLETT. Yes, sir; but it is much more active in this case as against the United States.

Mr. FORDNEY. May I ask the witness a question at this point?

The CHAIRMAN. Yes.

Mr. FORDNEY. The witness has stated that under the McKinley law the consumer got his sugar cheaper. Now, under the McKinley law the manufacturers of sugar in this country received a bounty from the Government of 2 cents per pound, did they not?

Mr. WILLETT. Yes, sir; the domestic sugar industry received a bounty of 2 cents per pound.

Mr. FORDNEY. And, in your opinion, did not that cause a lower price for sugar in this country at that time, and not free trade in sugar?

Mr. WILLETT. In answer to that question I would say that the influence of that bounty law did tend to increase the domestic beet-sugar industry.

Mr. FORDNEY. But did not the 2 cents bounty paid by the Government to the domestic manufacturers of sugar have an influence on the sugar market in this country while it lasted? The prices certainly went down.

Mr. WILLETT. I do not see how it could exactly. On consideration I might see it, but not at this moment. As a matter of fact, when the bounty went into operation, there were six beet-sugar factories in operation, and when the bounty was taken off there were but five in operation.

Mr. FORDNEY. Yes, sir; but the manufacture of cane sugar went on just the same.

Mr. WILLETT. Yes, sir; the cane-sugar industry was not influenced by the bounty pro or con.

Mr. FORDNEY. You have stated that the prices went down when the duty was removed. Last year the prices in this country were normal prices, were they not?

Mr. WILLETT. Yes, sir.

Mr. FORDNEY. As compared with years when the duty was removed from sugar, how did last year's prices compare?

Mr. WILLETT. Do you mean 1910?

Mr. FORDNEY. Yes, sir; 1910.

Mr. WILLETT. In 1910 the price of raw sugar was \$4.18$\frac{8}{10}$ and the price of refined sugar was \$4.97$\frac{8}{10}$.

Mr. FORDNEY. Now, compare these prices with the prices in years when sugar was on the free list.

The CHAIRMAN. Take a normal year.

Mr. WILLETT. There is very little difference between these years.

Mr. FORDNEY. There was very little difference in the prices?

Mr. WILLETT. One year it was \$3.86$\frac{7}{10}$, the next year it was \$3.31$\frac{1}{10}$, and the following year it was \$3.81$\frac{8}{10}$.

Mr. FORDNEY. So that the difference between these two periods did not make up the difference in the tariff, did it?

Mr. WILLETT. It would, if you take the 107 pounds required to make 100 pounds of granulated sugar.

Mr. FORDNEY. The price of 107 pounds in 1910 as compared with the price when it was free would make up more. The duty then was $3.24, was it not?

Mr. WILLETT. I propose to make the calculation along these lines. When I get back to my office I can do it.

Mr. FORDNEY. Very well; I am simply trying to make myself clear.

Mr. WILLETT. I understand your point.

Mr. FORDNEY. If I am right, last year's prices were not enough higher than the prices under the free-sugar system to make up the difference in the tariff.

Mr. WILLETT. To answer that question correctly I would have to go into a calculation which would include the cost of raw sugar to the refiner, just the same as I have in other instances; but I will do that for you.

Mr. FORDNEY. Now, if the chairman will permit me, I want to show the price of sugar here this year.

The CHAIRMAN. For 1911?

Mr. FORDNEY. Yes. Mr. Willett, he has asked you about the different prices, and whether the tariff had any effect upon the prices to the consumer. Here is a statement showing the prices of domestic sugar from September 1 to November 20. This is in the State of Michigan.

(The statements above referred to are as follows:)

Summary of net wholesale price at which beet-sugar companies sold this year's output up to Nov. 1, 1911.

Companies.	Number of factories.	Average net wholesale price.
Great Western Sugar Co	11	$5.327
Wisconsin Sugar Co	3	5.55
American Beet Sugar Co	6	5.20
Continental Sugar Co	3	5.55
German-American Sugar Co	2	5.50
Owosso Sugar Co	2	5.55
Western Sugar & Land Co	1	5.45
Sacramento Valley Sugar Co	1	4.80
Carver County Sugar Co	1	5.637
Charles Pope	1	5.70
Los Alamitos Sugar Co	1	4.86
Southern California Sugar Co	1	5.40
National Sugar Manufacturing Co	1	5.60
Holland-St. Louis Sugar Co	2	5.685
Iowa Sugar Co	1	5.73
Michigan Sugar Co	7	5.554
16 companies	44	....

The above is a summary of the data furnished up to December 1, 1911.

The figures are submitted in a general statement by each company, but in each case the company stands ready to furnish an affidavit covering the data.

STATE OF MICHIGAN, *County of Wayne, ss:*

Frederick R. Hathaway, being first duly sworn, deposes and says that he is a resident of the city of Detroit and State of Michigan, and that he is now and has been for several years past secretary of Michigan Sugar Co., having its principal office at Saginaw, Mich., and owning and operating six plants in the State of Michigan for the manufacture of refined sugar from sugar beets; that in addition to his duties as secretary he has charge of the sale of the sugar manufactured by said company; that he is familiar with the prices at which said company has sold its manufactured sugar since it went on the market the present season, and knows of his own knowledge the prices at which all sugar manufactured and sold by Michigan Sugar Co. has been sold the present season.

Deponent further states that the table next following is a statement of the prices per hundred pounds for refined sugar f. o. b. New York, taken from Willett & Gray's Daily Trade Journal from September 1, 1911, to November 20, 1911, both inclusive, such prices being subject to a 2 per cent cash discount for payment within seven days after arrival.

	American Sugar Refining Co.	National Sugar Co.	Warner.	Federal Sugar Co.	Arbuckle Bros.	Remarks.
1911.						
Sept. 1	$6.25	$6.35	$6.35	$6.35	$6.35	
Sept. 5	6.25	6.35	6.35	6.45	6.50	
Sept. 6	6.40	6.50	6.50	6.60	6.50	National and Warner withdraw
Sept. 7	6.50	....	....	6.75	6.60	
Sept. 8	6.60	....	....	6.75	6.75	
Sept. 9	6.70	....	....	7.00	7.00	
Sept. 11	6.75	....	....	7.00	7.00	
Sept. 13	6.75	....	....	7.25	7.25	
Sept. 19	6.75	....	....	7.25	7.50	
Sept. 26	6.75	....	....	7.25	6.75	
Sept. 28	6.75	6.75	....	7.25	6.75	National reenters.
Oct. 2	6.75	6.75	....	6.75	6.75	
Oct. 3	6.75	6.75	6.75	6.75	6.75	Warner reenters.
Oct. 23	6.75	6.75	6.75	6.50	6.75	
Oct. 24	6.70	6.70	6.70	6.50	6.70	
Oct. 25	6.70	6.70	6.70	....	6.70	Federal withdraws.
Oct. 30	6.60	6.60	6.60	....	6.60	
Nov. 2	6.50	6.50	6.50	....	6.50	
Nov. 6	6.40	6.40	6.40	....	6.40	
Nov. 9	6.30	6.30	6.30	....	6.30	
Nov. 13	6.20	6.20	6.20	....	6.20	
Nov. 20	6.10	6.10	6.10	6.10	6.10	Federal reenters.
	6.55$\frac{44}{100}$	6.51$\frac{1}{3}$	6.40	6.78$\frac{1}{8}$	6.66$\frac{81}{100}$	

Deponent further states that said Michigan Sugar Co. began the delivery of this season's sugar October 12, 1911; that up to and including November 18, 1911, it had invoiced 860 cars of sugar (100 barrels or 400 bags to a car).

Deponent further states that the invoice price stated below is the actual basis price per hundred pounds at which the sugar so invoiced has been sold, and that of the 860 cars invoiced up to and including November 18, 1911, 809.2 cars were invoiced at $5.55 New York basis; 14.5 cars were invoiced at $5.65 New York basis; 1 car was invoiced at $5.75 New York basis; 0.3 car was invoiced at $6.10 New York basis; 30 cars were invoiced at $6.20 New York basis; and 5 cars were invoiced at $6.40 New York basis.

Deponent further states that the prices at which the Michigan Sugar Co. has invoiced its sugar, as stated above, are subject to a discount of 2 per cent for payment within seven days after arrival.

Deponent further states that of the total amount of sugar invoiced by Michigan Sugar Co., as above stated, from October 12 to November 18, A. D. 1911, 94.1 per cent was invoiced on the basis of $5.55 per hundred pounds, or 5.55 cents per pound.

FREDERICK R. HATHAWAY.

Subscribed and sworn to before me this 21st day of November, A. D. 1911.

SHERWIN A. HILL,
Notary Public, Wayne County, Mich.

My commission expires August 2, 1915.

I am going to show the prices of beet sugar in the State of Michigan, and give a comparison with the same grade of sugar in New York from September the 1st to November the 20th.

Mr. WILLETT. Michigan had no sugar in September, as I understand.

Mr. FORDNEY. It began in October.

Mr. WILLETT. In September they were selling for future delivery, were they not?

Mr. FORDNEY. No, sir; not until October 12. It began at $5.55. Now, if the witness will take down these figures, I will give them to him. This is a statement of the Michigan Sugar Co., which has six factories in the State of Michigan.

From October 12 to November 20 they sold 809.2 cars, of 100 barrels, at $5.55; they sold 14.5 cars at $5.65; one car at $5.75; three-tenths of a car at $6.10; 30 cars at $6.20, and five cars at $6.40. That is the New York basis. During the same period the American Sugar Refining Co. sold at an average of $\$6.55\frac{45}{100}$—that is the New York basis. Beginning from September 12 the prices range practically the same from that date to November 20.

Mr. WILLETT. What period does that cover?

Mr. FORDNEY. From September 1 to November 20.

The CHAIRMAN. This is from October 12 to November 20.

Mr. FORDNEY. But there will be no difference in the facts. These sales took place at $6.75 on the 11th, 13th, 19th, 26th, and 28th. It did not fall during September. The same price prevailed on October 2, 3, and 23. This table shows the prices on October 2, 3, 23, 24, 25, and 30, and on November 2, 6, 9, 13, and 20.

Mr. WILLETT. Do you happen to have the highest price in New York, $7.50?

Mr. FORDNEY. This is the American Sugar Refining Co.

Mr. WILLETT. They never got up to that.

Mr. FORDNEY. But their average for this period was $\$6.55\frac{45}{100}$.

The CHAIRMAN. What was the highest price of the American Sugar Refining Co.?

Mr. FORDNEY. $6.75. It reached $6.75 on September 11, 13, 19, 26 and 28, and October 2, 3, and 23. On October 2, 3, and 23 it was $6.75, and then dropped to $6.70, and then to $6.60. The highest price in November was on the 2d, when it was $6.50; on the 6th it was $6.40; on the 9th it was $6.30; on the 13th it was $6.20; and on the 20th it was $6.10. During the entire period, the average was $\$6.55\frac{45}{100}$. The National Sugar Co. averaged during that time $\$6.51\frac{1}{3}$; the Warner Sugar Co. averaged during that time $6.40; the Federal Sugar Co. averaged during that time $\$6.78\frac{8}{10}$, and Arbuckle Bros., selling at all times during that period, averaged $\$6.66\frac{81}{100}$.

Mr. WILLETT. But you have not Arbuckle's highest prices?

Mr. FORDNEY. Yes, sir; his highest price was $7.50 on September 19.

Mr. WILLETT. That answers the question. The American Sugar Co.'s highest price was $6.75; the Federal's highest price was $7.25, and the Arbuckle's highest price was $7.50.

Mr. FORDNEY. Yes.

Mr. WILLETT. And Warner was out of the market?

Mr. FORDNEY. Yes.

Mr. WILLETT. They did not help the country out at all.

Mr. FORDNEY. This was while the domestic industry in the State of Michigan was selling at $5.55, $5.65, $5.75, $6.10, $6.20, and $6.40.

Mr. WILLETT. One important point, if you will allow it, is this: Were they selling at that price before they had sugar for delivery or after they had sugar for delivery?

Mr. FORDNEY. No, sir; they began to put sugar on the market on the 12th of October.

Mr. WILLETT. And they did not sell before?

Mr. FORDNEY. No, sir; their first sales were on that date.

Mr. WILLETT. One difference in the western States is that they begin to sell earlier.

Mr. FORDNEY. I will furnish the chairman a copy of their sales books and their invoices. From the first they permitted me to go through the books, and I examined them and have a copy of it.

Mr. WILLETT. Which company is that?

Mr. FORDNEY. The Michigan Sugar Co.

Mr. WILLETT. I was speaking about factories in Colorado and Utah.

Mr. FORDNEY. I do not know about them.

Mr. WILLETT. You see how the Hawaiian people get ahead. They contract for all sugar at New York prices.

Mr. FORDNEY. Whether these contracts were made prior to the 12th of October or not, I do not know; but there is one thing about which I am positive, the consumers got the benefit of the domestic industry, so far as the Michigan Sugar Co. is concerned.

The CHAIRMAN. I do not quite agree with you; I think the middlemen, or jobbers, got the benefit of it, because sugar at home has been selling at about the same price.

Mr. WILLETT. One point is evident, that the beet-sugar industry did not get the advantage of the high prices this year.

The CHAIRMAN. But if they had not sold ahead they would have done it.

Mr. WILLETT. Yes.

Mr. FORDNEY. At the same time, I want this to go into the record: In September and October, while these high prices prevailed in New York, where the most of the refined sugar is imported and refined in this country, I went out on the Pacific coast, and refined sugar was selling for $7.64, where nothing but free sugar is refined. The point is that on the Pacific coast practically all the sugar imported is free sugar—no duty is collected on it at all.

The CHAIRMAN. But, like all domestic favorites of the tariff law, the domestic people charge as much as the foreign people do.

Mr. WILLETT. Yes; the refining companies in New York control the domestic refiners in California and arbitrarily fix the price and control the market.

Mr. RAKER. I would like to ask you whether or not the sales you have reported there were all the sales of the Michigan Sugar Co. during this period, or were they just special sales?

Mr. FORDNEY. It represents all the sales they made from the time they started their factories.

Mr. RAKER. But you were not able to state whether or not they were sales made by prior contract for future delivery, or sales made at the date of delivery.

Mr. FORDNEY. I do not know, but I can get that information for you. The order book shows the first one entered on the 12th of October.

The CHAIRMAN. They would have been entered that way even if the contract had been made for future delivery.

Mr. WILLETT. The figures given by Mr. Fordney show that, with the exception of 809 cars, the sales of the smaller lots were at New York prices.

Mr. FORDNEY. I beg to differ with you; one car was $5.75; three-tenths of a car was $6.10; 30 cars were at $6.20, and five cars at $6.40.

Mr. WILLETT. What was the date of that?

Mr. FORDNEY. This does not give the date; it is the total for the entire period.

Mr. RAKER. Have you any statement showing what was the prevailing price during this time to the consumers in Michigan?

Mr. FORDNEY. I have not, sir. I do not know; that would not interest us in this investigation.

Mr. WILLETT. I can answer that indirectly, unless Mr. Fordney knows, that the Michigan companies anticipated the market. Some of the Michigan companies did anticipate the market, and these sugars sold to jobbers were retailed by the jobbers at lower prices than those at which the factories were selling their sugars probably.

The CHAIRMAN. Why did not the jobbers take advantage of the market.

Mr. WILLETT. They had such a handsome profit that they did not want to lose it.

Mr. FORDNEY. I do not believe that our Michigan factories have ever had any trouble in getting rid of their product.

The CHAIRMAN. But like our cotton people and wheat people they want to get the best price they can for their product. I suppose the Michigan people are not unlike other people in that respect. I presume they are not unlike Georgia people and other people in that particular.

Mr. FORDNEY. I do not know that I would dare to compare them with Georgia people. But the fact is that the prices were less than those that were quoted by the refiners of the country.

Mr. WILLETT. As I understand it, the American beet-sugar people in 1911 did not average over 5½ cents for this crop of sugar.

The CHAIRMAN. Why?

Mr. WILLETT. For the reason that in most of the States the beet-sugar men were satisfied to begin selling when they saw the rise coming on; that is, a month or two months before they had a pound of sugar to deliver. They sold it at the prices prevailing in New York at that time.

Mr. FORDNEY. I do not want it to go into the record that it is positively true that they sold it in advance. You do not know that to be a fact?

Mr. WILLETT. I do not apply that to Michigan, but I know that was the fact in Colorado.

Mr. FORDNEY. I do not want it to go into the record that these prices were due to selling for future delivery.

The CHAIRMAN. Do you want it to go into the record as due to the philanthropy of the Michigan people?

Mr. FORDNEY. No, sir; do not discredit my statement.

Mr. WILLETT. Everything is absolutely correct as to these prices. I can see that plainly.

Mr. FORDNEY. The domestic beet-sugar industry has certainly had a beneficial influence upon the price of sugar.

Mr. WILLETT. Yes, an enormous influence. If it were not for the domestic sugar industry sugars in this country would be to-day very considerably higher. I can not say how much higher, because I can not tell what influence they have had upon the European market, but the refiners would be compelled to purchase a quantity of sugar in foreign ports equal to the production of beet sugar coming into the market from this country. I would not be surprised if it would not be a cent a pound more but for the beet and cane sugar produced in this country.

Mr. HINDS. Mr. Fordney was asking you about the range of prices at the time we had free sugar in this country. Now, while we were having that free sugar, did they have a bounty upon sugar abroad at that time?

Mr. WILLETT. From 1901 to September, 1903, Germany was paying a bounty of 38 cents per hundred pounds on its exportations to the United States, and a combination of German manufacturers—that is, three classes, those that make raw sugar 88 test beet from beet roots, those that make granulated sugar directly from beet juice, and those that refine 88 test and make it 100 granulated—these three different institutions combined in a cartel the result of which was that raw sugars and refined sugars could be sold at a loss. That cartel gave these manufacturers the privilege of deducting 26 cents more per hundred pounds. As a matter of fact they did not deduct as much as that, but they did take off nearly 12 cents per hundred pounds. These quotations in Hamburg show that it was below the cost of manufacture.

Mr. HINDS. So that during that period the world's market was abnormal because of that bounty system? What effect did that have on the world's prices?

Mr. WILLETT. Well, it gave an advantage to the United Kingdom. The consumers of producing countries had to pay that loss.

Mr. HINDS. We countervailed against that, did we not?

Mr. WILLETT. Yes, sir; but not against the cartel scheme. During those years great quantities of sugar came into the United States, and the price was lower than the cost of production in Germany.

Mr. HINDS. Did that have any effect upon the American sugar market?

Mr. WILLETT. Yes, sir; it had this effect, that the refiners could not advance their differences between raw and refined sugars beyond the point at which the foreign sugars would come in.

Mr. HINDS. If we had free sugar to-day, would that same rule be operative?

Mr. WILLETT. No, sir; there is no bounty or cartel to-day, but it is likely there will be after 1913.

Mr. HINDS. Can you, then, reason wholly correctly from the prices of that period as to what we might experience in this country if we should again put sugar on the free list?

Mr. WILLETT. We can not; unless the bounties and cartels were resumed the periods would not be similar.

The CHAIRMAN. You say that this is likely to result again after 1913?

Mr. WILLETT. Great Britain has virtually already given notice that they are to withdraw from the convention in 1913, and France is also taking up the question.

The CHAIRMAN. Will that break it up?

Mr. WILLETT. No, sir; not necessarily.

The CHAIRMAN. Would it be likely to break it up?

Mr. WILLETT. That is a matter of guess. If broken up, it would be replaced by fresh bounties and cartels. The German Government winks at all these things. The German Government is first and last in favor of its beet-sugar industries.

The CHAIRMAN. And it is likely to give bounties again?

Mr. WILLETT. Yes, sir; I read that in Austria they have been talking about a cartel, but can not get any facts about its existence.

The CHAIRMAN. I will ask you now to take up as far as you can the report I expressed to you, and explain the system you used in trying to make them intelligible for the committee and the public.

Mr. WILLETT. I have here an analysis of Abyssinia.

Mr. MALBY. There is one other question. I think Mr. Hinds's question has practically cleared up what I had in mind as to whether conditions now are similar to the conditions existing at the time we were attempting to make comparisons, and it appears that they are not.

Mr. WILLETT. They are not.

Mr. MALBY. Of course, in a general sense, whether we would reap any advantage and, if so, how much from a reduction of the tariff would depend almost entirely upon the present conditions; that is, as to whether the domestic production—and by the domestic production I include the production of our insular possessions as well—would be kept up or not, would it not?

Mr. WILLETT. I can see the bearing of that question.

Mr. MALBY. That is, if domestic production kept up, and the production in Hawaii and Porto Rico kept up, under free sugar, we would undoubtedly get a greater advantage than we would if the result of reduction had a tendency to decrease the supply. The idea I had in mind was that the extent to which we would be benefited by a reduction would depend upon whether the industry in these possessions ceased to increase, or did decrease, as well as whether our domestic industries decreased or increased.

Mr. WILLETT. That is where this new interest would come in—the European speculator.

Mr. MALBY. Of course, it all depends on whether our domestic industry would be or would not be injured?

Mr. WILLETT. Yes, sir.

Mr. MALBY. I desired to ask that in connection with Mr. Hinds's question.

The CHAIRMAN. You may proceed with the analysis you have there, Mr. Willett.

Mr. WILLETT. I have here analyses of Austria, Abyssinia, Belgium, Costa Rica, Cuba, France, the United Kingdom, and several other countries. Which country would the committee prefer to take up first?

The CHAIRMAN. Could you take up the United Kingdom?

Mr. WILLETT. I can give you France very fully.

The CHAIRMAN. Well, suppose you take up France. I suggest that you simply read that paper for the record.

(The matter read by Mr. Willett will be printed as an appendix at the conclusion of the hearings.)

The CHAIRMAN. In the paper you are reading, you have referred to a tax on refiners; what do you mean by that?

Mr. WILLETT. The refiner takes sugar into his refinery, and when he sends it out, as will appear under this French system, he adds to his invoice price two taxes; that is, a tax on refining and an inspection tax.

The CHAIRMAN. And that is a tax the Government charges him for refining?

Mr. WILLETT. The Government charges him that tax for refining, and then reimburses some other people in the country. That is called a tax on distance, so that the refiners who refine sugar in different parts of France, say the north of France, should pay the same price for their raw sugar that the refiners at Paris pay for theirs. The refiners in France obtain their sugar at the same price level, because the Government equalizes it by this tax on refining.

Mr. MALBY. Does the refiner pay that tax?

Mr. WILLETT. The refiner pays the tax of $2.19 to the Government on all sugars going out of the refinery, at the moment of delivery to the customer.

The CHAIRMAN. Your statement shows that in detail?

Mr. WILLETT. Yes, sir.

The CHAIRMAN. Have you the New York prices at the same date with these French prices?

Mr. WILLETT. Yes, sir; the New York quotations appear in this record.

The CHAIRMAN. In other words, I want to know whether your paper shows how much the same sugar would cost in New York if bought on the French basis?

Mr. WILLETT. Yes, sir; the statement I am reading shows that.

The CHAIRMAN. For instance, say sugar is worth so much in Paris on a certain day, do you give the New York price on the same day?

Mr. WILLETT. Yes, sir.

The CHAIRMAN. And you have that all the way through for each country?

Mr. WILLETT. Yes, sir. The final result as between France and the United States is that the French people average 1 cent per pound higher than in the United States.

Mr. FORDNEY. For refined sugar?

Mr. WILLETT. Yes, sir; both wholesale and retail. Now, of course, these reports show that in many of the States they sell refined sugar as a card to draw trade, and in many of these States there are wholesale grocers' associations that govern the price—that is, the wholesale price—in that State and vicinity, and I may say that that seems to apply to Germany and other countries in Europe. In other words, the prices over there are regulated much more closely by trade unions than in this country.

Mr. FORDNEY. But the consumer pays more there than here?

Mr. WILLETT. Yes, sir; 1 cent per pound more for refined sugar.

The CHAIRMAN. But the tax is higher?

Mr. WILLETT. Yes, sir; the tax represents about that difference. The tax is $2.37.

The CHAIRMAN. Then, in other words, the difference is made up by the difference in the tax?

Mr. Willett. Yes, sir; the total tax there is $2.37\frac{2}{10}$ on a hundred pounds of sugar, and the total tax here is $1.34\frac{8}{10}$ plus $2.44.

Mr. Fordney. They are an export nation of sugar and we are not.

Mr. Willett. They export very slightly, however. They import much more than they export. In other words, they have no surplus for exportation that amounts to anything. The only sugars they export are raw sugars brought from their colonies; that is, cane sugars which are refined in France and shipped out. They export very few beet sugars.

The Chairman. Is the difference in the price there and here about the equivalent of the difference in taxation?

Mr. Willett. Yes, sir; the taxes there are $2.37\frac{2}{10}$.

Mr. Malby. That is refined sugar?

Mr. Willett. Yes, sir. Now, the tax here, as based on what we pay for Cuban sugar, is $1.34\frac{8}{10}$, plus the duty on 7 pounds more, which makes $1.44. Now, the difference in the tax explains that 1 cent, which shows that the cost of refining does not vary very materially.

Mr. Fordney. What percentage of their consumption of sugar is produced in France?

Mr. Willett. I think it is all produced there except about 100,000 tons.

Mr. Fordney. They produce at home all but about 100,000 tons?

Mr. Willett. Yes, sir; they bring sugar from their colonies, and that colony sugar is subject to bounty by consent of the Brussels convention, which agreed that France, on going into this arrangement, should charge a less duty on sugars from its colonies than it charges on sugars from other foreign countries.

Mr. Fordney. We import about 75 per cent of the sugar consumed in this country, do we not?

Mr. Willett. We produce at home and in our insular possessions about 1,600,000 tons.

Mr. Fordney. They produce in France and her colonies all they consume?

Mr. Willett. Yes, sir; all they consume at home.

The Chairman. And we produce in this country and in the insular possessions practically half of the sugar we use.

Mr. Willett. The difference between the two systems—that is, between the United States tariff and the customs tariffs of foreign countries—is that every pound of sugar that goes into consumption bears a tax, whereas in the United States, Porto Rican, Hawaiian, and Philippine sugar pays no tax.

Mr. Hinds. That, of course, does not mean that the people of the United States are relieved of paying the equivalent of a tax on sugar from these places.

Mr. Willett. The people of the United States prefer to pay a small tax on sugar to paying an income tax. I believe we would rather pay a small tax on sugar.

Mr. Hinds. Is there any considerable nation that does not raise an income from sugar?

Mr. Willett. None except the United Kingdom.

Mr. Hinds. They raise revenue from it.

Mr. WILLETT. There is no nation that does not assess to the consumer in some shape or other every pound of sugar that goes into consumption.

Mr. HINDS. Why is it that the general consensus of opinion of all mankind seems to be that way?

Mr. WILLETT. I think it is because we had rather pay that little tax on sugar, which amounts to a small sum, than to have an onerous income tax.

Mr. MALBY. In other words, it is a good way to raise revenue?

Mr. WILLETT. Yes, sir.

The CHAIRMAN. That applies to every form of protective tariff; it is a good way to raise revenue.

Mr. WILLETT. It is universally consumed from childhood to the grave. There are nine hundred million spoons going into the sugar bowl every day.

Mr. FORDNEY. Everybody uses sugar and everybody contributes to that revenue, but everybody does not use champagne.

Mr. WILLETT. Yes; everybody uses sugar.

Mr. HINDS. What proportion of the sugar consumed is in the form of luxuries; that is, in the form of candy, and I believe some canned goods are in the nature of luxuries?

Mr. WILLETT. Out of the 81 pounds per capita consumed in the United States not exceeding, I might say, 50 pounds is used in manufactures.

Mr. HINDS. A part of which is in the nature of luxuries?

Mr. WILLETT. Yes, sir.

Mr. HINDS. What proportion of these manufactures would be in the nature of luxuries, meaning candy, tobacco, etc.?

Mr. WILLETT. I think that in such like luxuries as you have mentioned it would be about as 10 pounds is to 30. The other 20 would be in preserving. If you include preserving, it would be half of it, or 15 pounds.

Mr. HINDS. Practically all of that 30 pounds of sugar goes into what would have been considered luxuries 30 or 40 years ago, but to-day only about 10 per cent. Canned goods would have been a luxury 10 years ago.

Mr. WILLETT. Yes, sir. Almost all families do their own preserving. Not until 1911, I think, were any of us heard complaining about the cost of sugar in the United States.

Mr. FORDNEY. I want to know whether I am correct in my premises, that the cost of refining in France appears to be substantially what it is in the United States, but that the price at which the refiner sells to the wholesaler is considerably in advance to that obtained by the refiner in the United States. In other words, the refiners of France really reap a greater benefit from the sale of 100 pounds of sugar than does the refiner in the United States from the sale of 100 pounds of sugar?

Mr. WILLETT. No, sir; the difference is in the tax.

Mr. FORDNEY. Is their margin of profit about the same?

Mr. WILLETT. Yes, sir.

(Thereupon, at 1.15 o'clock p. m., the committee took a recess until 2 o'clock p. m.)

AFTER RECESS.

The committee reconvened, pursuant to the taking of recess, Hon. Thomas W. Hardwick (chairman) presiding.

TESTIMONY OF MR. WALLACE P. WILLETT—Continued.

The CHAIRMAN. Had you finished, Mr. Willett, with your summary of conditions in France? I do not believe you had quite finished. You may have given us a general idea. Do you think you had?

Mr. WILLETT. In a general way I think I have given you all that is necessary.

The CHAIRMAN. That is the plan you are pursuing?

Mr. WILLETT. That is the plan I am pursuing. There are other things, of course, there which I have not given you.

The CHAIRMAN. In detail?

Mr. WILLETT. In detail.

The CHAIRMAN. Let me suggest this to you in completing your work: We would like to know the price, both wholesale and retail, of sugar in these countries in regard to which you are investigating; and we would like to have, as near as you can give it, a comparison with a similar character of sugar in New York at the same date.

Mr. WILLETT. That is exactly what I am doing.

The CHAIRMAN. All right; that is really what we want to get out of this work you are doing.

Mr. WILLETT. And then you want all the customs of the country in selling sugar?

The CHAIRMAN. Yes. Of course it is infinitely important that we should know what the taxes are in each case.

Mr. WILLETT. And for what purpose?

The CHAIRMAN. Yes; and I would like the cost of refining.

Mr. WILLETT. The cost of refining there and here?

The CHAIRMAN. Yes. I think you are doing exactly what we want, and we would like to have you complete that work as soon as possible; and we will ask you, as soon as you get through, to communicate with the chairman or some member of this committee and let us know how soon you can bring your results down here. I think that for to-day you need not go into any further details. I hardly think it is necessary to go into this Denmark proposition.

Mr. WILLETT. Judge Malby asked whether the sugar going into Denmark was subject to an internal-revenue tax in addition, and here is the law. This is in French.

Mr. MALBY. Give us the substance of it, if you can.

Mr. WILLETT. The substance of it is that each kilogram of sugar introduced into the operating establishment or refinery, of polarization of 96, is subject to a tax of 0.498 cent. If the polarization is less than that, the duty is fixed differently. I have figured that all out, showing that the law of May 27, 1908, places an internal tax on the home production of beet sugar and the refining of sugars. The tax on beet sugar polarizing 98 is 0.49 cent a hundred pounds, and the tax or duty on sugar for refining, for each 2.20 pounds of sugar sent to the refinery and not polarizing above 96, is 0.63 cent a hundred pounds.

Mr. MALBY. I wanted to know whether sugar imported into Denmark was dutiable; and, if so, at what rate.

Mr. WILLETT. Refined sugar imported into Denmark is subject to the duty of $1.21 a hundred pounds. Raw sugar imported into Denmark and going to the refinery to be made into refined sugar is subject to a duty of 6½ cents to 69½ cents, according to test; and after it is refined and goes into consumption there is 49 cents added to that, making $1.21 again. Here is the tariff showing that.

Mr. MALBY. Very well. Thank you very much. Is there anything you wanted to elaborate on, or explain, in addition to what is actually contained in your report?

Mr. WILLETT. Everything is in my report.

Mr. MALBY. It illustrates, as you started to explain to us, the similarity of conditions, somewhat?

Mr. WILLETT. That is what I would like to read to the committee regarding Denmark, if you are willing. It will not take long.

Mr. MALBY. So far as I am concerned, I am willing; but the chairman may have a different idea about it.

Mr. WILLETT. Denmark is a little country, and it makes a very interesting study, I have found. It is a country from which much may be learned for the use of the United States. I would like for the committee to have this.

The CHAIRMAN. I do not know whether the committee is going to enter into these questions in their report.

Mr. WILLETT. Shall I read this?

The CHAIRMAN. I do not know; shall he or not?

Mr. MALBY. Read it or file it. Mr. Willett says this has reference to matters somewhat similar to our conditions.

Mr. WILLETT. It is very short.

The CHAIRMAN. Very well; read what you have with regard to Denmark.

Mr. WILLETT. Denmark is a country from which much may be learned for the use of the United States. First, the beet-sugar industry is carried on with two large companies, owning and operating seven factories on near-by islands. One company has six factories, and the other one factory.

The production of sugar in Denmark in 1909 was 62,434 tons, and in 1910-11 it jumped to 109,000 tons.

The consumption in 1909 was 103,862 tons, of which 42,501 tons were imported. You see, they do not produce as much sugar as they require for their consumption—the same as we do. The consumption per capita was 86.42 pounds. Our consumption per capita is 81.6 pounds. It corresponds somewhat to our per capita consumption, also.

Importations have remained unchanged since the sugar factories were started in 1874. Imports in 1909–10 were 33,553 tons. Germany exported to Denmark 24,038 tons of that amount, while in the following years, 1910–11, Germany exported to Denmark only 7,115 tons, showing, as in the United States, that the production is increasing, to the exclusion of the importations, gradually, as here.

The consumption is four times larger than in 1874, when it was 25,065 tons, which was a per capita consumption of about 29 pounds.

Mr. FORDNEY. What is the price to the consumer; have you that?

Mr. WILLETT. I will reach that presently. The exports are not mentioned in the consular reports, but they are given by Otto Licht as, in 1909–10, 5,216 tons. Their exports are small, like those of the United States.

Present prices are as follows: Wholesale, best white granulated sugar, made from cane and beet, is 40 to $4.49 per 100 pounds. Second best white granulated sugar, cane and beet, is $3.90 to $4.40 per 100 pounds. You see they mix their domestic raws and their imported canes together.

Mr. FORDNEY. Is this refined or raw?

Mr. WILLETT. No, sir; this is granulated sugar. Now, those prices at the same date for New York, for similar grades of refined sugars, were $3.29 and $3.20.

Mr. FORDNEY. For raws?

Mr. WILLETT. For raws. The duty-paid price for best white granulated sugars was $5.10 per 100 pounds. In Denmark it was $4.40; in New York $5.10. The price for the second-best white granulated sugars, say, domestic beet sugars, in New York was $4.85, against $4.40 in Denmark.

The in-bond price was $3.20 per 100 pounds.

Raw sugar prices at that time were $3.50 to $3.60 per 100 pounds for part cane and part beet sugars. For all raw cane sugar the price was $3.30 to $4 per 100 pounds for 94 test. The New York price corresponding was $3.86, in bond. Those are wholesale prices. Retail prices vary considerably; usually 30 to 80 cents a hundred pounds, or more, the same as in the United States.

Mr. FORDNEY. The retail price there is about the same as in the United States?

Mr. WILLETT. No. Prices vary about the same as in the United States, from 30 to 80 cents above the wholesale prices. They are irregular, in other words.

Wholesale prices: White granulated sugars, as far back as 1909, are given as $4.70 to $5.20 per 100 pounds; in 1905, $4.50 to $6 per 100 pounds; and in 1910, $4.30 to $5.60 per 100 pounds; a constant decrease in the price of white sugars in Germany.

Granulated sugar in New York during the same years, 1900, $5.32 against $4.70; 1905, New York, $4.27, against $4.50 in Denmark.

Mr. RAKER. $4.27 against $4.50?

Mr. WILLETT. Yes. In 1905, $4.27 in New York, against $4.50 to $6 in Denmark. Denmark was higher than New York then. In 1910 it was $4.18 in New York, against $3.90 in Denmark; very nearly the same.

Without the duty it was $3.42 and $2.378 in 1905, and $2.288 in 1910, in New York.

The import duties are: On refined sugars, polariscopic test above 98 degrees, $1.21 per 100 pounds; refined sugars above 96 degrees and not above 98 degrees test, 79 cents a hundred pounds; raws for refining, no test stated, 72 cents per 100 pounds; and other sugars of 88 degrees test or less, 49 cents per 100 pounds; duties according to the degree of test.

The law of May 27, 1908, places an internal tax on the home production of beet sugar and the refining of sugar. The tax on the production of beet sugar polarizing above 98 degrees is 49 cents per

100 pounds. This grade of sugar is not specially refined, but is semirefined—to some extent. The tax or duty on sugar for refining for each 2.205 pounds of sugar sent to the refineries and not polarizing above 96 degrees is 63 cents a hundred pounds, and it varies from 63 to 69 cents, according to its polarization.

Now, about Denmark's colonies, the internal tax of 49 cents per 100 pounds is on the home production, which evidently includes imported raws which pass through the refineries. Denmark in 25 years has increased its home production of beet sugars largely, under an apparent protection of 72 cents per 100 pounds, and with an excise tax of less than one-half cent. The consumption has risen equally as much in tons as in per capita, until now the latter is much the same as, or a little larger than, that of the United States, the figures being for Denmark 86.42 pounds, and for the United States 81.6 pounds.

The best granulated sugar produced from cane and beet mixed was $4.49 per 100 pounds in Copenhagen, July 8, 1911. Deducting the duty of $1.21 per 100 pounds, theoretical reduction, leaves $3.28 per 100 pounds. Cane granulated sugar in New York, on July 8, 1911, was $4.98 a hundred pounds, duty paid. Deducting the theoretical duty of $1.90 on refined would leave $3.08 per 100 pounds.

Denmark has made great progress in production and consumption under the duty of $1.21 per 100 pounds, on refined sugar above 98 degrees test, and a duty on raws, presumably 96 test, of 62.13 cents per 100 pounds, and an internal tax on home production of 49 cents per 100 pounds.

Only a small part of Denmark appears to be suitable for beet culture, as it is all carried on on a few small islands, and none on the mainland.

The question of labor in Denmark versus the United States would be of interest as related to the remarkable growth of an industry in a small country. The influence of the entire Denmark sugar industry, home and foreign, is in the control of only two companies.

Denmark does not adhere to the Brussels convention. It is a study by itself, different from European countries generally, and not much different in several ways from the United States.

Denmark's methods applied to the United States would mean:

1. A duty of $1.21 per 100 pounds on imported sugar above 98 degrees test, for direct consumption, refined or semirefined.

2. A duty of 72 cents per 100 pounds on imported raw sugar for refining.

3. A government tax on the domestic cane and beet production, Porto Rican, Hawaiian, and Philippine Islands production, brought into the United States, of 49 cents per 100 pounds; about a half a cent per pound.

4. An adjustment of Cuban reciprocity.

A duty on 107 pounds raws to make 100 pounds refined, at $0.72 per 100 pounds for raws equals	$0.77
Internal tax	.49
Per 100 pounds refined	1.26
Present United States duty on 107 pounds Cuban raws (96 test) to make 100 pounds refined, at $1.348 per 100 pounds	1.45
Difference, saving to consumer per 100 pounds	.19

The consumer would save 19 cents upon the present United States basis.

If duty on Cuba 96-test sugar is fixed at $0.72 per 100 pounds and 20 per cent reciprocity continued, the duty on sugar from other countries would be $0.90 per 100 pounds—$0.90 less 20 per cent, 18, equals $0.72; that is, not to put 72 cents against all countries but 72 cents against Cuba; do you see?

Mr. FORDNEY. Yes.

Mr. WILLETT. The revenue to the United States Government from a duty of $0.72 on imported foreign raws and a consumption tax of $0.49 on home production, based on the 1910 consumption, would amount to $18,000,000 on 1,637,780 tons produced in the United States—beet, cane, etc.—Hawaii, Porto Rico, and the Philippines, and $46,000,000 on 1,712,575 tons imported from Cuba and other foreign countries; a total revenue to the United States, on the Denmark basis, of $64,000,000, against the present Government revenue of $53,000,000.

Mr. FORDNEY. Their duty is much higher than ours?

Mr. WILLETT. Yes.

Mr. RAKER. How is that?

Mr. FORDNEY. It is $63,000,000 as against $53,000,000, is it not? Please just repeat that last paragraph you read.

Mr. WILLETT. The United States revenue, to the Government, from a duty of 72 cents on foreign raws imported, and a consumption tax of 49 cents on home production——

Mr. FORDNEY. Which is the Denmark tax?

Mr. WILLETT. Forty-nine cents, which is the Denmark duty—the Denmark basis——

Mr. FORDNEY. Yes.

Mr. WILLETT (continuing). Based on the 1910 consumption, would amount to $18,000,000 on 1,637,780 tons produced in the United States—beet, cane, and so forth—Hawaii, Porto Rico, and the Philippines, and $46,000,000 on 1,712,575 tons imported from Cuba and other foreign countries; a total revenue to the Government of $64,000,000, as against its present revenue of $52,000,000.

Mr. FORDNEY. I see the point.

Mr. WILLETT. And a saving to the consumer, on the Denmark basis, of 19 cents a hundred pounds, the consumer paying 49 cents internal-revenue tax on all the sugar he uses.

Mr. FORDNEY. In other words, if we were collecting on the same basis that Denmark pays, we would collect 19 cents more, and the difference in revenue would be the figures you have given there, $46,000,000, as against $64,000,000. In other words, Denmark collects a higher rate of duty than we do?

Mr. WILLETT. No; Denmark collects lower rate of duty than we do; a much lower rate.

Mr. FORDNEY. Well, taking the two combined——

Mr. WILLETT. The two combined makes $1.21 a hundred.

Mr. FORDNEY. Yes; I see.

Mr. WILLETT. While we collect $1.344 on Cuban raw.

Mr. FORDNEY. Yes; I understand.

Mr. WILLETT. Denmark in 25 years increased its home production of beet sugar largely, under an apparent protection of 72 cents a hundred pounds, and with an excise tax of less than half a cent a hundred pounds. The consumption has risen equally as much in tons, as well as in per capita, until now the latter is much the same as the United States, Denmark being 86.42 pounds and the United States 81.6 pounds.

Denmark has made great progress in production and consumption under a duty of $1.21 a hundred pounds on refined sugars above 98 test, and a duty on raws of 96 test, of 62 cents a hundred pounds, and an internal-revenue home tax of 49 cents per 100 pounds.

Mr. RAKER. How much does that benefit the consumer?

Mr. WILLETT. Nineteen cents a hundred pounds. If Denmark's entire plan was adopted to-day in the United States, the consumer would get his sugars 19 cents a hundred pounds cheaper than he is getting them to-day, and the Government would get $64,000,000 of revenue instead of $53,000,000, and the consumers would pay one quarter of a cent a pound less for their sugars.

Mr. RAKER. How would that affect the beet producers?

Mr. WILLETT. They would pay 49 cents a hundred pounds more on their production.

Mr. RAKER. Would that be to their detriment any?

Mr. WILLETT. Not at all. That would be offset by the other condition. They could well afford to pay 49 cents to have permanency in the tariff, on the Denmark basis. And my idea is that there is no reason why Porto Rico and the Philippines and the Hawaiian Islands should not participate in the revenue of the country to the extent of 49 cents a hundred pounds.

The CHAIRMAN. They get great advantages by being inside of this tariff wall, and they ought to help to pay it.

Mr. WILLETT. They ought to help to pay it; and all these other Consular Reports show that there is not a country in the world excepting the United States that does not collect more or less revenue from sugar from every consumer in the country.

The CHAIRMAN. In other words, if we were to apply the system of Denmark to the United States, we would raise $13,000,000 or $14,000,000 more of revenue, and we would lower sugar something like a quarter of a cent a pound at the same time.

Mr. WILLETT. At the same time.

The CHAIRMAN. That is a very impressive statement.

Mr. FORDNEY. That would be true if their conditions of importation to this country, and the labor conditions and the standard of living were the same here as in Denmark?

Mr. WILLETT. That, I stated, should be investigated, as to labor conditions. That might change the whole thing.

The CHAIRMAN. Those conditions are not entered into in the Consular Reports.

Mr. WILLETT. No; I wish they had been.

The CHAIRMAN. Yes.

Mr. WILLETT. It would be an important study.

Mr. FORDNEY. It might materially change that.

Mr. WILLETT. It might materially change it. I can only give you what I have in the statement before me.

The CHAIRMAN. You mentioned that those things were not considered by you because you had no data from which to draw conclusions.

Mr. WILLETT. Yes.

The CHAIRMAN. If there is nothing further on this Denmark matter, we will excuse Mr. Willett now, with the thanks of the committee for the information he has given us; and we will ask you, Mr. Willett, to pursue the work you are now doing as an employee of the committee, because we want to complete this work as soon after the holidays as possible, and we want to make our report to the House of Representatives as soon after the Christmas holidays as possible.

Mr. WILLETT. I will do it as quickly as possible.

The CHAIRMAN. May I make this suggestion? In your report will the price of sugar to the consumers be summarized and capitulated?

Mr. WILLETT. Yes.

The CHAIRMAN. And compared with New York?

Mr. WILLETT. Yes; and it will be compared with New York on the same dates, as near as possible, by the reports.

Mr. RAKER. There is no method that you have, and there are no data that you have that you could give, with regard to Denmark?

Mr. WILLETT. No; there is nothing in the reports bearing on that.

Mr. RAKER. I mean, outside of the reports?

Mr. WILLETT. No, sir; I have nothing. Mr. Palmer is the man who can give you that, probably. He is making a study of those things.

The CHAIRMAN. I understand that Mr. Palmer has not yet returned from abroad.

Mr. WILLETT. He will return after the holidays, and I think he can give you all those labor conditions in Denmark.

The CHAIRMAN. We are very much obliged to you for your testimony, which is very valuable. We will excuse you now.

TESTIMONY OF MR. JAMES BODKIN.

(The witness was sworn by the chairman.)

The CHAIRMAN. Mr. Bodkin, the opening examination will be conducted by Judge Raker, for the committee.

Mr. RAKER. Mr. Bodkin, how long have you been in Colorado?

Mr. BODKIN. Thirty years, within a few days.

Mr. RAKER. And how long have you been interested in the cultivation of sugar beets?

Mr. BODKIN. About seven or eight or nine years. I laid off. I made six crops out of nine years.

Mr. RAKER. What particular line of the business have you been following?

Mr. BODKIN. General farming.

Mr. RAKER. Beet-sugar farming?

Mr. BODKIN. Yes.

Mr. RAKER. But you have not any experience in the manufacture of beet sugar, have you?

Mr. BODKIN. No, sir.

Mr. RAKER. What part of Colorado have you been interested in and familiar with?

Mr. BODKIN. In Weld County.

Mr. RAKER. What factory is close to your place of raising?

Mr. BODKIN. We ship to the Longmont factory, 10 miles away. It is over in Boulder County.

Mr. RAKER. Have you had any experience in general farming in Colorado, at this same place, before you began to raise sugar beets?

Mr. BODKIN. Yes, sir.

Mr. RAKER. What, and how long?

Mr. BODKIN. This 30 years.

Mr. RAKER. What kind of farming?

Mr. BODKIN. Mostly wheat; some oats and some barley, and hay, and a few spuds.

Mr. RAKER. What has been your experience in irrigation for farming crops in Colorado?

Mr. BODKIN. Yes, we irrigate altogether.

Mr. RAKER. I say, what has been your experience?

Mr. BODKIN. I do not quite understand you.

Mr. RAKER. How long have you been familiar with the modes and methods of irrigating?

Mr. BODKIN. These 30 years.

Mr. RAKER. The same 30 years?

Mr. BODKIN. Yes.

Mr. RAKER. You irrigated these crops you raised before you began to raise sugar beets?

Mr. BODKIN. Yes, always.

Mr. RAKER. And you have used the same land you put sugar beets on to put other crops on, for seven years?

Mr. BODKIN. For nine years.

Mr. RAKER. Then you have been irrigating the beets since you have gone into the raising of beets?

Mr. BODKIN. Yes.

Mr. RAKER. Have you ever acted on a committee appointed by the farmers of northern Colorado to look after their sugar-beet interests relative to the Great Western Sugar Refining Co.?

Mr. BODKIN. Yes.

Mr. RAKER. For how long?

Mr. BODKIN. Since the 13th of September a year ago.

Mr. RAKER. What has been your experience in that matter, and what were your duties in connection with this committee? What was the purpose of it and the object of it, and what did you accomplish, if anything?

Mr. BODKIN. At a farmers' meeting they appointed a committee for the State of Colorado, and there were five of us on that committee. They wanted me then to make a State-wide beet contract, and I soon found that a contract would not apply to the whole State, on account of the different districts being under different conditions; and so, then, I recommended that one man in our district and I take care of the northern district, and these other gentlemen who belonged in the southern district take care of that, and that the man over the slope should handle his district, so that we each would take a district of our own.

Mr. RAKER. You had three districts with unlike conditions; is that it?

Mr. BODKIN. Yes.

Mr. RAKER. You say the farmers wanted to have a beet contract that would apply to the entire State?

Mr. BODKIN. Yes; to the entire State; but although before we went into it we thought that was all right, when we got into it, pretty soon, why, that would not work at all.

Mr. RAKER. Why?

Mr. BODKIN. Down South there were factories where they gave the farmers the beet pulp. Some factories gave them a portion of it. Over the range they did not ask them to silo any beets, where with us we bought our pulp where they would sell it to us; but in a few years they contracted it to feeders, and then we had to silo it.

Mr. RAKER. The purpose of this organization, then, was to get a better and more uniform price for the growing of beets to the farmers?

Mr. BODKIN. Yes.

Mr. RAKER. Did you take this matter up with the various refineries; for instance, with the Great Western Sugar Refining Co.?

Mr. BODKIN. Yes. J. O. B. Wise and myself handled the Great Western territory, and we met with their board.

Mr. RAKER. What was the result of such meetings?

Mr. BODKIN. Well, they came through with as much as we might expect.

Mr. RAKER. What were you getting before?

Mr. BODKIN. $5 flat.

Mr. RAKER. Delivered?

Mr. BODKIN. Yes; we would put them on the cars and they would furnish the dump when they were dumped. When they were not dumped, the people had to shovel them.

Mr. FORDNEY. Was that price at your place or at the factory?

Mr. BODKIN. At the railroad. We had nothing to do with the freight.

Mr. RAKER. Was that price general in the three districts?

Mr. BODKIN. No.

Mr. RAKER. Take the northern district; how much did they get?

Mr. BODKIN. This was the price of the Great Western.

Mr. RAKER. What was the price of the other?

Mr. BODKIN. That was what we could not find out. They would tell us one thing and tell us another, and that is how the organization came about.

Mr. RAKER. Why could you not find out? Did they not deal with the farmers?

Mr. BODKIN. Well, they are quite a distance apart there, and when the newspapers would make reports that they had good things in the South, then of course some of our people would believe them. Then the southern newspapers would report that we had good things in the North, and then they naturally would suppose that that was so. When we came to find out, none of us had those, but we did not find out the truth until after we got our organization.

Mr. RAKER. What was the name of the other sugar company in the North, where the Great Western Co. was?

Mr. BODKIN. That is the Great Western.

Mr. RAKER. I thought you said there was another company there?

Mr. BODKIN. No; we are in the North.

Mr. RAKER. I see.

Mr. BODKIN. Yes; and those other people were in the South.

Mr. RAKER. You could not find out what the other factory was paying?

Mr. BODKIN. Some people might; but, generally, you could not depend on anything as to what was going on. When we would compare notes together we were all mistaken.

Mr. RAKER. This applies to the northern district and the southern district that you have told us about?

Mr. BODKIN. No; this only applies to the northern district. I do not have anything to do with the southern district.

Mr. RAKER. Before the organization, what was the price paid in the other two districts?

Mr. BODKIN. That is what we did not know. We would hear one thing and another thing, but as I say, we did not know.

Mr. RAKER. Did you find out after you had your organization?

Mr. BODKIN. Yes.

Mr. RAKER. What was it after you made this investigation?

Mr. BODKIN. Mr. Wise, our man on our northern district, got a friend down there to send him up a contract for last year, and also one for this year.

Mr. RAKER. Have you got a copy of that with you?

Mr. BODKIN. No; but I can get it. Do you want that?

Mr. RAKER. Yes. It is $5 for a 12 per cent beet, and 33⅓ cents for each 1 per cent thereafter, and with a break on the tenth—pay for each tenth.

Mr. FORDNEY. How is that?

Mr. BODKIN. The polariscope shows a beet $14\frac{1}{10}$ or $14\frac{3}{10}$, and so on; and before we organized it had to reach another point, go the whole per cent; they did not break anywhere short of one whole per cent; but down there they pay for each one-tenth. They pay for a gain of one-tenth.

Mr. FORDNEY. They pay 33⅓ cents on every one-tenth above a certain percentage?

Mr. BODKIN. Yes; they account for each one-tenth, instead of its going a whole per cent before they break—that is, they paid at the rate of 33⅓ cents for 1 whole per cent.

Mr. RAKER. Is that practically the same arrangement that they have in the other districts now?

Mr. BODKIN. No; that is a dollar better than ours in the northern country. Ours is $5 flat for 12 per cent and under 15. When it reaches 15 it is $5.25, and it is 25 cents more for each 1 per cent thereafter, and they break on a half per cent. It has got to reach a half before we get any pay for it.

Mr. RAKER. Even the sixteen?

Mr. BODKIN. Yes; or seventeen or eighteen.

Mr. RAKER. And the others break for one-tenth?

Mr. BODKIN. Yes; whenever it goes to one-tenth they pay for it.

Mr. RAKER. After you made this arrangement and had your own organization, and your committees got busy and began to deal with the sugar people, what did you receive for your beets; what rate? Give it for each district now, as near as you can.

Mr. BODKIN. I can only talk for our district. The other is all hearsay with me.

Mr. RAKER. Your district was what? What is the name of your district, so that it will go in the record? It is the northern district?

Mr. BODKIN. The Great Western Sugar Co.

Mr. RAKER. It is in the territory of the Great Western, of course; but what did you call the district?

Mr. BODKIN. There are nine factories in that system.

Mr. RAKER. Do you not call it by any name?

Mr. BODKIN. The way I happened to use the word "district" is I was speaking of the district that I am looking after in our farmers' organization. That may have gotten me in the way of saying "district."

Mr. RAKER. That is all right. I want to know whether you call it the northern district.

Mr. BODKIN. Our farmers call it the northern district; but the name of the company is the Great Western Sugar Co.

Mr. RAKER. I understand. Now, in the northern district, where the Great Western Sugar Co. is, after you had your organization, what did you get for your beets per 100 pounds?

Mr. BODKIN. Mr. Morey came through with the sliding scale.

Mr. RAKER. What was that?

Mr. BODKIN. That is what I just quoted. Over 12 and under 15 it is $5. When it reaches 15, it is $5.25, and it is 25 cents for each 1 per cent thereafter. That was the first rate. It is for this last year's contract that we had, and have delivered the beets, when we grieved about having to reach a whole per cent before we got any money for that 1 per cent, that he said he would do something for that, and then in a few days he made the contract, and it showed, and he said, that he would break on the half. That one change, breaking on the half, amounted to something like $200,000 to our people. He gave us that. Then they gave us a good deal better treatment in other ways.

Mr. RAKER. In what way?

Mr. BODKIN. One of our big drawbacks was they had a shortage of cars, and people would be hiring men at a big price and going up there and losing time waiting for cars, and the beets would be drying out. This last year they furnished a sufficient number of cars so that you could move your beets and haul them; so that we saved that, and that was a wonderful saving to the people; and other things.

Mr. RAKER. Was there any other change?

Mr. BODKIN. I do not recall anything else just now. The other two districts I am not familiar with.

Mr. RAKER. The other two districts you are not familiar with?

Mr. BODKIN. No.

Mr. RAKER. The other men are here to give testimony as to the prices, are they?

Mr. BODKIN. As to the other two districts, I never knew of them. The manager of our organization of the State does not know anything about anything but our three.

Mr. RAKER. Then you do not know anything about anything except this one district?

Mr. BODKIN. And as to the contract for the southern district.

Mr. RAKER. Which you have just given us?

Mr. BODKIN. Yes.

Mr. RAKER. About how many tons of beets are raised in this district which you represent; say how many were raised last year, and then in 1910.

Mr. BODKIN. 700,000 tons.

Mr. RAKER. 700,000 tons in 1911?

Mr. BODKIN. Yes.

Mr. RAKER. And about how many in 1910?

Mr. BODKIN. As nearly as we can find out, about the same amount.

Mr. RAKER. And how many tons for 1909?

Mr. BODKIN. I just presume that there were 10,000 tons more.

Mr. RAKER. In 1909?

Mr. BODKIN. Yes.

Mr. RAKER. Then the amount is decreasing instead of increasing?

Mr. BODKIN. The last two years, as a whole. I ought not to state about that, because I do not remember. I did not look that up.

Mr. RAKER. Very well. You say there was how much gain on the price to the farmers by virtue of this partial change in the contract; you say it made a difference of about $200,000 to the farmers?

Mr. BODKIN. Yes; last year.

Mr. RAKER. This year, 1911?

Mr. BODKIN. Yes.

Mr. FORDNEY. To how many farmers?

Mr. BODKIN. Something like 5,000 farmers.

Mr. FORDNEY. And what was the total amount of beets; do you remember?

Mr. BODKIN. Something like 700,000 tons.

Mr. FORDNEY. That would be about 30 cents a ton, is that right?

Mr. BODKIN. It averaged something like 6 cents a ton, splitting it in the middle and counting it that way.

Mr. RAKER. Have you people obtained any estimate from the analysis by the Great Western Sugar Refining Co., or by yourselves, or anyone representing you, for the last 10 years or for the last 3 years, as to the percentage of sugar matter in the beets grown in your district?

Mr. BODKIN. The manager at the Longmont factory has wanted me to look at the books, and has thrown them open and showed them; but that did not interest me very much. He told me that for the crop of 1909 it would average, for the Longmont factory, 15.57. He claimed last year it made 16. This year the reports in the newspapers claim that they are richer than ever before.

Mr. RAKER. But the farmers are in no position to find out just exactly about that?

Mr. BODKIN. No, sir.

Mr. RAKER. And they have not been?

Mr. BODKIN. No, sir; there is no way to know.

Mr. RAKER. Why not? Have you ever tried to go into their books or asked for an expert to go in and examine what tests they have made, and the reports of their managers as to the amount of saccharine in the beets?

Mr. BODKIN. I started to look after that, but when I went through the chemist's department I saw that it was not any use to go any further. I told my partner that this was all a joke to us. We did not know anything about what those polariscopes read. We could see what the hands read, but we could not go any further than that.

Mr. RAKER. What I mean is, did you ask them for their books?

Mr. BODKIN. Oh, they insist on us coming and bringing the committee at any and all times to go over them.

Mr. RAKER. The books relating particularly to the amount of sugar in the beets?

Mr. BODKIN. Books of any kind that the company owns.

Mr. RAKER. I see; but you have not done it?

Mr. BODKIN. No use to do it.

Mr. RAKER. Now, why?

Mr. BODKIN. As I say, as soon as I looked at the polariscope I told my partner that that could be changed. One drop of acid in or out, or two or three, whatever the amount needed, and the stuff could be diluted to read a certain per cent, whatever they wanted it to. A little later on we learned that that was a fact; I do not mean to say in that factory, but one drop of acid would make a difference of a certain amount on the polariscope. So there we stopped.

Mr. RAKER. The man who was growing the beets, who was interested in finding out the percentage of sugar in the beets, was left up in the air?

Mr. BODKIN. Yes; and even the chemist that reads the polariscope knows nothing about it. He does not know as to the strength of the drugs he is using. It is all honest work.

Mr. GARRETT. What was that last remark of yours?

Mr. BODKIN. I just said that it is all honest work; up to the people that are working in the chemist's department.

Mr. RAKER. I hoped we would be able to get from you or your organization, by some method you had adopted, the amount of sugar matter in the beets, because that would give us something upon which to work—to see how you were being treated.

Mr. BODKIN. You can not get that from us.

Mr. RAKER. Do you not suppose we could get it?

Mr. BODKIN. You might; but the farmer can not. They simply tell us that they will not do that work for the farmers, because there would be too much of that to do.

The CHAIRMAN. If they pay you by a sliding scale, they have to do it?

Mr. BODKIN. Yes, they do; but I was just explaining——

The CHAIRMAN. You could not tell whether they were treating you fairly, according to the scale, or not?

Mr. BODKIN. We could not tell anything about it.

Mr. RAKER. I was just trying to find out about the amount of sugar matter in the beets which would give the committee some idea how they were being paid for the beets delivered.

Mr. FORDNEY. Can he not tell you that?

Mr. BODKIN. We have tried to get that and could not get it.

Mr. RAKER. And you could not get it?

Mr. BODKIN. No, sir.

Mr. RAKER. How much did the factory pay you for your beets in 1911?

Mr. BODKIN. That would be this year's crop.

Mr. RAKER. Yes.

Mr. BODKIN. I have not received all of it, but my crop has run $5.75.

Mr. RAKER. On the scale of payment you have given us?

Mr. BODKIN. Yes.

Mr. RAKER. What has been the general run?

Mr. BODKIN. Around in our neighborhood they will run pretty close to that; but there are other localities that are down quite a little.

Mr. RAKER. In that same territory?

Mr. BODKIN. Yes.

Mr. RAKER. How much down—how much lower than that?

Mr. BODKIN. I would expect that something like $5.40 would catch several of the factories, just comparing to what the farmers say their beets are running.

Mr. RAKER. How many factories are there in this district you are representing?

Mr. BODKIN. Nine factories.

Mr. RAKER. Are they all owned by one company?

Mr. BODKIN. Yes; the Great Western owns them.

Mr. RAKER. Could you give the names of those companies?

Mr. BODKIN. I think so. They are the Longmont, Loveland, Fort Collins, Windsor, Greely, Eaton, Sterling, Brush, and Fort Morgan. I think that is all, if that is nine.

Mr. RAKER. The American Sugar Refining Co. owns a large block of stock in the Great Western Sugar Co., does it not?

Mr. BODKIN. The reports show that they own more than half of it.

Mr. FORDNEY. More than half of it?

Mr. BODKIN. I think so. Some reports show that, at least, I will say.

Mr. MALBY. Did you ask how much they owned? Was that your question?

Mr. RAKER. I have not asked him that; no.

The CHAIRMAN. There is no need to go into that.

Mr. RAKER. I did not intend to do so. That testimony has been in before, and I just asked him for the names of the factories; that is all. I do not suppose you know, Mr. Bodkin, definitely how much the American Sugar Refining Co. does own?

Mr. BODKIN. No; I do not know.

Mr. RAKER. You are just giving the public reports?

Mr. BODKIN. You mean——

Mr. RAKER. The public rumor; the statements in the public journals.

Mr. BODKIN. You mean about the ownership?

Mr. RAKER. Yes.

Mr. BODKIN. Some say they have half and some say that they have more than half. It does not concern us any.

Mr. RAKER. I understand.

Mr. BODKIN. And we do not know enough to try to find out.

Mr. RAKER. What is the cost of growing beets in this territory that you represent and where these nine factories are where it is done?

Mr. BODKIN. That differs some. I just have it for this year in my own field.

Mr. RAKER. Will you give it, then, for this year, for your own field?

Mr. BODKIN. I just got a copy of it. The field boss asked me to keep it for his experiment man.

Mr. RAKER. We will put it in the record and then return the original to you.

Mr. BODKIN. I was figuring on not giving this report to our field boss, as I thought maybe it would not suit him. It was a little high, and I thought I would look for something a little more moderate. I did a little extra work on mine, to get a little extra crop, as I have a small place. But there is not much extra to it; only a little.

Mr. RAKER. Just give us the statement.

Mr. BODKIN. You mean itemize the work done?

Mr. RAKER. Yes; so that it will show, intelligently, the amount of money invested, and how much it cost; how much you got for your beets and how much you lost or how much you made.

Mr. FORDNEY. Is this per acre or per ton?

Mr. BODKIN. The way I keep it, it is per acre. Of course it would be per ton, according to the ton rate.

Mr. FORDNEY. Yes.

Mr. BODKIN. To start with, you have got to have the land. That rents, in our neighborhood, for $20 cash rent per acre.

Mr. RAKER. You are going now on a cash basis?

Mr. BODKIN. Yes.

Mr. RAKER. What is that land worth?

Mr. BODKIN. For my field I have been offered $250 an acre; but beets would grow on unimproved land just as well, which would be worth only $150 an acre. Of course, that is way out.

Mr. RAKER. On this $250 land would you have a water right?

Mr. BODKIN. Of course, and this cheaper land would, too; but I have other improvements and other things on my land, and it is closer to town. I am saying that sugar beets would grow away out from town, on unimproved ground which could be had for $150 an acre.

Mr. HINDS. By "improvements" you mean buildings?

Mr. BODKIN. Yes.

Mr. HINDS. You mean buildings, and not improvement of the ground itself, as by fertilization?

Mr. BODKIN. Yes, improvements, and a desirable place to live; that is what I refer to.

Mr. RAKER. The $250 land is land that is fenced and has been plowed and has sufficient houses and grounds and all sufficient farm buildings on it to run a place that would make it convenient?

Mr. BODKIN. And close to the dump and elevators, and close to town, with mail and telephone and everything.

Mr. RAKER. That is what I included; and with the water right; and the water right paid goes with that land?

Mr. BODKIN. Yes.

Mr. RAKER. And the land at $150 an acre is land lying farther from the market, farther from the dump, and farther from town, without fencing?

Mr. BODKIN. You might say fenced, but without improvements.

Mr. RAKER. Without houses and barns and without being broken; is that right?

Mr. BODKIN. Yes; it would have to be without being broken, for $150 an acre. When it comes to the rougher land, that would be a little cheaper. This would be good land.

Mr. RAKER. That gives a pretty good idea of that. Now go ahead with your statement.

Mr. BODKIN. That is $20 cash rent for that.

Mr. RAKER. That is cash?

Mr. BODKIN. Yes.

Mr. RAKER. Go ahead. I will not interrupt you any more.

Mr. BODKIN. Well, as we go along if there is anything you think of dig it out. The handwork is $20, our country over.

The CHAIRMAN. In the field; the field work?

Mr. BODKIN. Yes; we call it handwork.

The CHAIRMAN. Do you mean planting the beets or thinning them?

Mr. BODKIN. No, sir; just the handwork.

The CHAIRMAN. "Handwork" does not mean anything to me. Tell me what it means.

Mr. BODKIN. I will as soon as it opens. In the handwork the Russians or other people block and thin the beets, hoe them the second time, hoe them the third time, and in the fall, when you pull them with a puller, then they go over the field and gather them and throw them in bunches with the tops off on the ground, so that you can shovel them up easily.

The CHAIRMAN. All of that is included in that $20?

Mr. BODKIN. Yes; $20 per acre, handwork. Then there is the seed. They require to sow 20 pounds. Most farmers sow what they want to, of course, but I am talking about myself. I sowed 17 pounds, which makes $1.70 for each acre I worked for seed.

Mr. RAKER. That is about an average amount to go on the land?

Mr. BODKIN. Yes; only the contract requires more.

Mr. RAKER. How much more?

Mr. BODKIN. Twenty pounds. They exact everything, so that we break the contract the first day we start to work on it, and then we have no contract.

Then there is the plowing, $2.50 per acre.

Three heavy harrowings; and when I say heavy harrowings I want everybody to understand it is done with a harrow weighted down, with two sections, with two horses. Three heavy harrowings make 80 cents per acre for the three.

Mr. RAKER. 80 cents for the three harrowings?

Mr. BODKIN. Yes.

Mr. RAKER. All right.

Mr. BODKIN. Then three heavy floatings.

Mr. RAKER. Everybody knows what floating is.

Mr. FORDNEY. How much for your floatings?

Mr. BODKIN. Fifty cents for the three per acre.

Planting, 50 cents; that is the drilling of the seed; first cultivating, 60 cents per acre; first ditching, 60 cents per acre; irrigating, $1 per acre.

Mr. RAKER. That is labor?

Mr. BODKIN. Yes.

The next is three cultivatings, at 50 cents per acre each, $1.50 for the three; second ditching, 50 cents per acre; second irrigation, for the labor, $1; cultivating after that, 50 cents per acre; ditching after that, 50 cents per acre; third irrigation, $1 per acre.

Price of the water for this third irrigation, $3.33 per acre. That is, for the labor for the third irrigation, $1, and the price I paid for the water for the third irrigation is $3.33 per acre.

Mr. FORDNEY. The labor was how much?

Mr. BODKIN. $1 per acre. The fourth irrigation, for the labor, $1 per acre, and the price of the water for that fourth irrigation was $3.33 per acre. Pulling or plowing out the beets, $2.50 per acre. Hauling off of the tons that I had, per acre, was $6.37.

Mr. FORDNEY. Are those all the charges?

Mr. BODKIN. Those are all the charges.

Mr. FORDNEY. They amount to how much?

Mr. BODKIN. $69.83.

Mr. RAKER. That is the total cost per acre?

Mr. BODKIN. In this you discover that I have got $6.66 worth of water.

Mr. RAKER. I was going to ask you about that.

Mr. BODKIN. With land rented at $20 per acre, you are mighty lucky on that. Then, for the labor that water should be deducted.

Mr. MALBY. How is that?

Mr. BODKIN. I do not know whether it had been or not. I have got $6.66 of extra water that I ran on these beets. Had I kept that water off, I might have had five or six tons less of beets.

The CHAIRMAN. What we want is just what you did spend.

Mr. BODKIN. I did put a little more of water on this, but I did raise a little more.

The CHAIRMAN. What did you say was the total?

Mr. BODKIN. $69.83 per acre.

The CHAIRMAN. How many tons of beets did you get for it?

Mr. BODKIN. Twelve and three-fourths tons per acre, at $5.75, which makes $73.32.

The CHAIRMAN. At a net gain of how much?

Mr. BODKIN. $3.49.

Mr. RAKER. You have not counted anything for overseeing?

Mr. BODKIN. I did all of that work myself.

Mr. RAKER. You have not included that?

Mr. BODKIN. No; there is no extra charge; only just a regular day's work.

Mr. RAKER. With a net profit of $3.49 per acre?

Mr. BODKIN. Yes.

Mr. RAKER. How is this cultivation that you have given us here, and the price, as compared with the general run of the way they cultivate, plant, and handle beets, in that district where you live?

Mr. BODKIN. They might leave out one or two of these cultivatings.

Mr. RAKER. The more cultivatings, the more beets?

Mr. BODKIN. That was what I was figuring. I put on more, because I have not much land.

Mr. RAKER. That is the actual fact, is it not?

Mr. BODKIN. Yes; it is supposed to be.

Mr. FORDNEY. How many acres did you have?

Mr. BODKIN. Thirteen and one-half acres of beets.

Mr. FORDNEY. Thirteen and one-half acres of beets?

Mr. BODKIN. Yes; but I only farm 40 acres. Then, as to the irrigation; when they have water to give it only two irrigatings, then, of course, you would save $2 per acre there, because you would not have enough water to irrigate as most people in our neighborhood do. Two irrigations is considered a pretty good water right.

Mr. RAKER. What is the average yield from your district, in tons per acre?

Mr. BODKIN. This year, I presume, it would go about 11. We have had a pretty favorable year this year.

Mr. RAKER. Have you any idea of about the average cost of cultivation—I mean of maturing the beet and delivering it—that is, including the rent of the land, stating it as you have now stated it?

Mr. BODKIN. You mean the cost to other people, outside of myself?

Mr. RAKER. Yes; what you have got over that whole country, there. Have you figured on that at all?

Mr. BODKIN. So to speak, if they would farm for all there is in it, it would cost them the same as this. All that they cut then—it would be only cut and slice work.

Mr. RAKER. Does the Great Western Sugar Refining Co., with whom you deal in making your contracts for beets, require this method and mode of planting and cultivating and handling? Is that part of the contract?

Mr. BODKIN. Their contracts provide that we shall do exactly any and all things that their field superintendent shall tell us to do from time to time.

Mr. RAKER. What does he require—these general things?

Mr. BODKIN. It is not often that a farmer cares to have them in the field.

Mr. RAKER. What I want is, to know what he requires.

Mr. BODKIN. No; he might require them to adhere to it..

Mr. RAKER. So far as your knowledge is concerned, did he heretofore make the general requirements as to the method and mode and kind of cultivation and irrigation, plowing and scraping and leveling, as you have done to your land, if you know?

Mr. BODKIN. It depends on who it is. They change the requirements pretty often. Very often we have a superintendent who does not come over in the field to see very many people, because when you pick up such a man—oh, a man who has lived in town all his life and comes out into the country to tell people something, can not tell very many people anything. This year we are getting a nice jolly farmer's boy, and he will come and sit and talk and we will have fun.

Mr. FORDNEY. In other words, a farmer does not want a man of that sort to come and tell him anything about farming?

Mr. BODKIN. No, sir; not if he does not know anything. Of course if he knows anything we are willing to sit and listen.

Mr. RAKER. I knew that would be the result, and you are right on the matter; but what I would like to know, and I would like to have you give us an answer on, the best you can, is this: Are these modes and means and methods of plowing and cultivating and tilling the soil and handling the beet conditions which the company requires?

Mr. BODKIN. Yes; oh, yes; they require it.

Mr. RAKER. I thought you said that the field boss required it?

Mr. BODKIN. No.

Mr. RAKER. Whether he does his duty is one thing, and whether they require it is another thing.

Mr. BODKIN. Yes; they require it.

Mr. RAKER. These are the things necessary to successfully raise beets for a profitable crop?

Mr. BODKIN. Yes; the company requires them.

Mr. RAKER. And the more of these you leave out the poorer crop you get; that is right, is it not?

Mr. BODKIN. Yes.

Mr. FORDNEY. If you do not do it, what is the consequence?

Mr. BODKIN. With whom?

Mr. FORDNEY. With the company.

Mr. BODKIN. Oh, they never say anything, at all.

Mr. FORDNEY. Then they do not make you live up to the contract?

Mr. BODKIN. No, sir; it is broken, as I have said, the first day we start to work.

Mr. FORDNEY. Then the contract does not require anything of you?

Mr. BODKIN. They would soon tell you the contract was broken, and there is nothing to it.

Mr. RAKER. To get away from that contract for just a moment, as to the actual physical facts, are these things necessary to bring a beet crop to a successful crop, I mean to raise a large crop of beets?

Mr. BODKIN. What I have here is necessary.

Mr. RAKER. That is what I am asking you, exactly.

Mr. BODKIN. Yes; but in the contract they will go on and state that we are to protect them from sunlight and frost; and I have yet to see the first blanket thrown over the beets, whether they are in our fields or in the sugar company's fields, to protect them from sunlight. That is one of the conditions in the contract. That is one way that contract is broken.

Mr. HINDS. Do you have to cover the beets?

Mr. BODKIN. The contract requires us to.

Mr. HINDS. To cover them with what?

Mr. BODKIN. I do not know. I have chaffed them about taking them in the house and putting them under the bed. I do not know where else to put them. It says to cover them from the frost, and the temperature is below zero out there.

Mr. FORDNEY. And yet they never enforce the contract?

Mr. BODKIN. No; not any more than to say that the contract is broken if you come back on them for anything.

Mr. FORDNEY. Do you ever find it necessary to come back on them for anything?

Mr. BODKIN. We have. One condition of the contract is that if on the 15th of October there are no cars ready you can shovel your beets off on the ground. One man out there said, when the time came and there were no cars, that he was going to shovel his beets off on the ground, and I said, "No; you are not." The field boss came, and he said, "You know that contract is broken;" and the man did not shovel them on the ground. The contract had been broken long ago.

Mr. RAKER. What effect does the breaking by the farmers of this contract with the Great Western Sugar Refining Co. have as to the farmers getting a legitimate price for their beets?

Mr. BODKIN. It never has had any, because there has never been any fuss made about it.

Mr. RAKER. What have you been getting for your beets, as compared to what you ought to get?

Mr. BODKIN. We had in mind that we ought to have another dollar a ton.

Mr. RAKER. Why?

Mr. BODKIN. Because the farmers want it so bad, and they are just merely playing even, and so many of them are losing money, and the sugar company can afford it so easily.

Mr. RAKER. They have been making money on the deals that they have been having with you, have they?

Mr. BODKIN. Well, in their sugar output we, of course, find that they are making plenty of money.

Mr. RAKER. Have you got any statement to show, for instance, during this last season of 1910 how much they made, those nine factories?

Mr. BODKIN. I think we have another witness who has that information prepared.

Mr. RAKER. All right. From your viewpoint, considering the amount that they have been paying for beets and the amount they have been getting for their sugar on the market, there has been a sufficiently large profit so that they could treat the farmer better and pay him a sufficient price for his beets, and he ought to have it?

Mr. BODKIN. Yes. We can find where, after paying all expenses, they have $8 a ton left.

The CHAIRMAN. $8 a ton profit?

Mr. BODKIN. Yes. $8 a ton profit; and if they would just give us $1 of it it would make us and it would shave them very little.

Mr. RAKER. What per cent would that be on the amount invested in beets?

Mr. BODKIN. Do you mean by the farmers?

Mr. RAKER. No; the factories.

Mr. BODKIN. I could not say. We talk from 50 to 100 per cent. Some of our committee will likely say that they make 100 per cent, and then there is some left.

Mr. RAKER. What was the condition of the price of sugar in Colorado this last year, commencing in July, do you know, running along in various months?

Mr. BODKIN. I never kept posted as to the price. I forget whether it went much above $8 or not.

Mr. RAKER. They kept raising right along, according to the eastern markets did they?

Mr. BODKIN. I could not say as to that. They kept raising.

Mr. RAKER. Are any of you gentlemen prepared here to give us those data?

Mr. BODKIN. I could not say about that price.

Mr. RAKER. If you rotate crops, what is the direct or indirect benefit gained from the cultivation of beets to the grain staples and alfalfa raised upon this land afterwards?

Mr. BODKIN. That depends, again, upon what locality it is. In my field it is quite a gain if something does not happen before I get hold of it.

Mr. RAKER. What do you mean by that?

Mr. BODKIN. I mean when I farm it along and raise beets, I could raise a nice crop of grain on that land, if drought or hail or something like that did not get it. There is a chance for a good indirect benefit. In some localities the potato crop is far ahead of the beet crop in preparing ground for wheat.

Mr. RAKER. That is, to raise potatoes on one tract, and to raise beets on another tract, in the same locality, say right adjoining it?

Mr. BODKIN. Yes.

Mr. RAKER. From land on which the potatoes are raised, you get a better crop of wheat the next year than you do from land on which beets have been raised?

Mr. BODKIN. Far better; but in my particular neighborhood I think it works the other way.

Mr. RAKER. Is it not a fact that when you get down to the direct or indirect benefit to be derived by virtue of the cultivation of the beet, or any vegetable that has roots, and where the ground has to be tilled and plowed, that makes such a crop better for the grain crop?

Mr. BODKIN. I am not certain that it makes any difference what the crop is as long as it is a good cultivated crop, with plenty of water.

Mr. RAKER. I think you have already said, in answer to a question asked by another member of the committee, that you people in your country do not enrich your land by any fertilizer?

Mr. BODKIN. No, we do not; nothing except what comes from the barnyards, and alfalfa.

The CHAIRMAN. You do not use any commercial fertilizer at all?

Mr. BODKIN. No, sir.

Mr. HINDS. What is the relative drain upon the fertility of the soil caused by the beet as compared with the potato—does the potato drain the soil of its virtue as much as the beet? I will say, does it exhaust the soil as much? Perhaps that is a better term.

Mr. BODKIN. I do not know that there is any difference.

Mr. HINDS. Have you ever tested that or tried any experiments in that regard?

Mr. BODKIN. No; experiments are hard to make along those lines on account of seasons and variations of everything.

Mr. RAKER. To go back, before we leave that subject, I asked you in regard to this irrigation question, the use of the water on the land, and you figured the value of the rental at $20 per acre. Are these lands, located as you have described, lands that have a water right of their own?

Mr. BODKIN. They have their own water rights.

Mr. RAKER. Then, why did you pay this $3.333 for this second and third irrigation?

Mr. BODKIN. Because I thought it was profitable to irrigate the second and third times.

Mr. RAKER. Did you have the water of your own?

Mr. BODKIN. No.

Mr. RAKER. You had to buy that of some one else?

Mr. BODKIN. Yes. When you pay $20 an acre for land you are very lucky if you get enough water to irrigate twice.

Mr. RAKER. That explains that, then.

Mr. BODKIN. Nobody will guarantee it.

Mr. RAKER. Then, if you got land upon which there was a water right appurtenant, that would be sufficient to give you four irrigations, as you claim is necessary; it would add that much more to the price originally per acre of the land?

Mr. BODKIN. It would; but on the high ground, where we have good land, nobody has such a water right except it gets to raining—except there is a very rainy time. Last season was a dry year. Very few had water enough for more than one irrigation, and then they had to take it away from all their other crops in order to save the beet crop.

Mr. RAKER. It is more expensive to irrigate the beet crop than any other, is it?

Mr. BODKIN. Yes.

Mr. RAKER. It requires more irrigation; it requires two more irrigations than other ordinary crops. Is that right?

Mr. BODKIN. Yes, sir.

Mr. RAKER. If you keep the beets on the same piece of land do they not injure the soil unless you rotate? You can not have three or four successive beet crops successfully on the same piece of land in your country, can you?

Mr. BODKIN. I do not think beets hurt land very much.

Mr. RAKER. You do not think so?

Mr. BODKIN. No.

Mr. RAKER. A continued crop?

Mr. BODKIN. Of course, it depends on how long—how many years you plant beets on the same land. Three and four years—many times as good a crop has been raised the fourth year as the first year.

Mr. RAKER. Taking it in your part of the country, it is possible to raise beets upon the same tract of land three or four successive years, by reason of irrigation; is not that it?

Mr. BODKIN. I do not think it is the irrigation. We all irrigate, and the irrigation is pretty much alike, if we have the water; but the land varies so much that in some places you dare not irrigate but little, or let it run but a little while, while in our neighborhood water may run two or three days, and there is no difference.

The CHAIRMAN. No difference in the crop, you mean?

Mr. BODKIN. Yes; because there are places where if the water will run 24 hours the leaves will turn yellow: but in our place it will run days before any yellow leaves will appear, and I take it by that that the soil must vary, because the water would be all the same.

Mr. RAKER. Are there any dangers incident to raising beets in your part of the country by virtue of hail and such things as that; does the farmer run any risks?

Mr. BODKIN. Of course some, but if we get the beet crop, that is one of the main holds I guess to the people who raise beets—that the beets stand hail so well. If it were not for that fact I would have quit long ago.

Mr. RAKER. And go to raising other crops, such as potatoes and alfalfa, and so on?

Mr. BODKIN. Yes. It is that insurance that holds them up.

Mr. RAKER. Then taking it all in all you people down there are getting along pretty nicely with the Great Western sugar people, are you not?

Mr. BODKIN. Some of us.

Mr. RAKER. What is the matter with the balance?

Mr. BODKIN. They do not get the tonnage.

Mr. RAKER. What do you mean by that?

Mr. BODKIN. They do not get tons enough to make the money.

Mr. RAKER. Tons enough off of the land?

Mr. BODKIN. Yes. When you come to figure 8, 9, and 10 ons and hire the work done, you have to have a bank account or you can not pay your help.

Mr. RAKER. In other words, you would be running at a loss the time?

Mr. BODKIN. Yes.

Mr. RAKER. For the price you are getting?

Mr. BODKIN. Yes. Anything below 12 tons in my field—it takes right close to 12 tons to pay the cost, the way I work.

Mr. RAKER. How are your farmers there treated by the newspapers as compared with the Great Western Sugar Refining Co., as to giving the facts?

Mr. BODKIN. They give them concerning the farmer, but not concerning the sugar company.

Mr. RAKER. What is the matter?

Mr. BODKIN. Well, they just tell the fellow in plain English that they get their money from the sugar company, and we do not pay them anything only our little $1.50 a year.

Mr. RAKER. In other words, then, the farmer is not in with the newspapers so far as getting the facts is concerned?

Mr. BODKIN. No; they do not dare to do it. I took an item to Mr. Boynton——

The CHAIRMAN. Who is he?

Mr. BODKIN. He is editor of one of the newspapers. He has been there 30 years or more. I asked him if he would run it.

The CHAIRMAN. What did you mean by that?

Mr. BODKIN. I mean I asked him if he would print it in his newspaper, and he at first said he would, and finally he got serious about it, and he told me why he could not do so.

The CHAIRMAN. What was the item?

Mr. BODKIN. Showing how they could afford to give us a dollar a ton more for our beets. It showed that when the Longmont factory slices 80,000 tons of beets, as it did last year, and makes a profit of $1,280,000, if they would give us $1 more a ton, that would be $80,000, and that would only shave their profit down a little bit. That is what I was leading up to in this article—that they had $8 or $9 a ton profit.

Mr. FORDNEY. Where were those figures that you refer to obtained?

Mr. BODKIN. We figured them ourselves from his own quotation.

Mr. FORDNEY. You do not know whether they were correct or not?

Mr. BODKIN. He wanted to show us the book, that they run 16 per cent sugar. He had already said that they had sliced 80,000 tons, and if you figure that up, then he had $1,280,000 worth of sugar, and he had made a sensational brag that he had paid $600,000 for the beets.

Mr. FORDNEY. You are speaking of the superintendent of the factory, are you?

Mr. BODKIN. That was the superintendent that put this item in the newspaper last year, showing what a good thing the sugar factory was, and it was all right, only if we could have had that $80,000 you know it would have helped the Longmont business men that had been opposing us. If we had got that they would have had it the next day, and they would have run double the amount.

Mr. FORDNEY. In other words, if you got it one day they would take it away from you the next day?

Mr. BODKIN. They would not take it away from us; we would give it to them—the business men.

Mr. HINDS. But the factory yields up nothing, as I understand it; the factory does not yield up to the locality?

Mr. BODKIN. No; they beg their way when they give a big feast. They did it this year. They make it off the Longmont merchants.

They took the men away from the dumps and let us sit down there in the cold.

Mr. RAKER. Then this article was leading up to the conditions as the farmer saw them?

Mr. BODKIN. We were getting it up just to that point, showing that they had this amount of money, and if they would give us another dollar a ton how many beets we would raise. But Dr. Bowersock, who is a director in the National Bank——

Mr. FORDNEY. Is he a manufacturer?

Mr. BODKIN. No; he is a banker and a doctor there. I was asking him why the Longmont business men would not stay in with the farmers and get another dollar a ton, showing him that they would get this $160,000 the next day. Mr. Boynton thought anybody ought to see that, and wanted me to take it up. When I got to Dr. Bowersock the first damper he put on it was that he said, "That won't work at all; if we do that, turn against the Great Western and favor the farmers, they will shut down the Longmont factory, and we will be here without any run at all. They will ship the beets somewhere else." So he said they would have to keep still.

Mr. RAKER. Now, to get down to the man who refused to do the publishing, what was his reason for not publishing it, finally?

Mr. BODKIN. One editor ran some stuff, and then when we came back in a couple of weeks he was all mad, and one of our committee asked him what the sugar company said. He swore and said they did not say anything, but that no check came.

Mr. FORDNEY. You farmers pay him a dollar and a half a year for his paper, though?

Mr. BODKIN. Yes.

Mr. FORDNEY. How many farmers are there who pay him that?

Mr. BODKIN. Another committee waited on him—I can get to that this way—and he was showing the other people that came from over the range what was new in our work, and he told this other committee that he was going to side with the farmers now, and why shouldn't he, when there were 7 of the sugar beet manufacturing people who took his newspaper and 2,000 farmers, and why would he not side with the farmers? I told this fellow then to take this man's paper.

Mr. FORDNEY. Two thousand farmers at $1.50 apiece would be $3,000. Then, if he could favor the farmers, the factories must have paid him more than $3,000.

Mr. BODKIN. No; the farmers are there anyhow; and any $5 from the sugar factory would be just that much gain.

Mr. FORDNEY. A small amount of money from the factory then might buy up the paper.

Mr. BODKIN. Because they have the other money, anyhow.

Mr. FORDNEY. Yes.

The CHAIRMAN. Did he say anything about the size of the check that did not come after he published that article?

Mr. BODKIN. No; I did not talk to him any more; I sent somebody else about that check.

The CHAIRMAN. What was that man's name?

Mr. BODKIN. Mr. Beckwith.

The CHAIRMAN. Where does he live?

Mr. BODKIN. In Longmont.

Mr. HINDS. Did you get anything to indicate that he may have taken a part of this money in sugar?

Mr. BODKIN. No; he just said that. I do not know that he got any money, but he said: "No check has come."

Mr. RAKER. What was the policy of the paper after that statement, as to their being in favor of the farmer, to help the farmer along, or was it in favor of the sugar factory?

Mr. BODKIN. I do not think he published anything either way—nothing for the farmer, and the sugar company quit him. I do not take his paper and I could not say, but our committee always remembered that he never did anything for us.

Mr. RAKER. What kind of treatment does the company give the farmers there that raise these beets?

Mr. BODKIN. They get good treatment outside of——

Mr. RAKER. Outside of the money they get?

Mr. BODKIN. Outside of the money treatment; all other conditions are fine, I think.

Mr. RAKER. Now, if you get such a low price for your beets—have to sell them so low that you hardly get a living, from the prices you have given us—why do you not go into some other business?

Mr. BODKIN. I do not know of any other business where I could get in that many days' work; and getting paid for it, and having a small field, I have to buy myself a job.

Mr. RAKER. The farmers generally, I mean.

Mr. BODKIN. They do go into something else. Otherwise the factory would run 175 days instead of 50 days.

Mr. RAKER. That is what I want to get at. In other words, the treatment given the farmers by the sugar factory by reason of the low price, so much lower than they are entitled to, is driving men out of raising beets?

Mr. BODKIN. Yes.

Mr. RAKER. Their production and the amount of beets they handle is much lower than it would be if they were paying the farmers a living wage?

Mr. BODKIN. We would cover them up until they could not commence to take them if they would give us another dollar, but we are just on the nip and tuck edge.

Mr. RAKER. Can you not give us any reason why they are not encouraging the farmer; that is, why they are not paying him more money for his beets, so he can live and prosper and they, in turn, grow and prosper? Give us your view on that question. There must be some reason, you know.

Mr. BODKIN. One thing, Mr. Maury said that they could not tell about the price of sugar; that if they once raised the price to the farmers and they took the tariff off the sugar he could never get the farmers down any, and therefore he had to make some money while he could.

Mr. RAKER. And that is the condition you people find yourselves in?

Mr. BODKIN. Yes. While we would like to see the tariff kept on—for there is no telling what would happen if they would take that off—under the present conditions a statement like that shows that he is simply piling on that tariff right now, paying us the price, as he assumes, that would be kept right on if the tariff were taken off;

but I figure he would wind down on us heavily if they took the tariff off.

Mr. RAKER. I did not exactly understand your answer. Please repeat that.

Mr. BODKIN. If they took the tariff off, they could never get the price down.

Mr. RAKER. You mean the price of beets?

Mr. BODKIN. Yes; the price of beets. He would never grow them for less, and therefore they had to make money while they could. Of course our objection is that this way he is paying us the price as though there were no tariff on.

Mr. RAKER. Not considering the question of tariff at all?

Mr. BODKIN. Not to us.

The CHAIRMAN. In other words, he does not give you your share?

Mr. BODKIN. He does not give us any under his statement. They are making money while they can. We figure that if they do take the tariff off he would wind down on us more and more.

Mr. FORDNEY. You will keep right on raising beets, will you?

Mr. BODKIN. Not unless we find some other crop more profitable so it will tail up the loss.

Mr. FORDNEY. Do you have any other crop now that is more profitable?

Mr. BODKIN. Well, the beet crop varies, so you can not say what you are going to get. We get from 4 to 24 tons, a variation of $100 per acre. Once in a while an acre grows 25 tons, but hundreds of them grow 8 tons for each one of them that grows 25. Therefore, I say we can not tell what we are going to make on beets on account of that variation.

Mr. RAKER. In other words, you are at the mercy of the sugar-beet company there?

Mr. BODKIN. Yes.

The CHAIRMAN. Suppose all these factories were not under the same organization, but were competing. Do you think you would get a better price in that event?

Mr. BODKIN. I could not say.

The CHAIRMAN. But you have but one concern to buy your beets, and that is the Great Western?

Mr. BODKIN. Yes.

The CHAIRMAN. Ordinarily you can get a better price for anything you are producing if there are several people trying to buy it?

Mr. BODKIN. Yes; if you could keep them separate—if there would continue to be several people—but they get so close together so quick.

Mr. RAKER. Is this a sample of the contract that you people have [exhibiting paper].

Mr. DAKAN. I can say that it is.

The CHAIRMAN. This witness had better testify about that.

Mr. BODKIN (after examination). My glasses are so poor that I can not read it very well. Would you please read that?

(Mr. Raker proceeded to read the contract referred to.)

Mr. DAKAN. I can say that that is the 1910 contract.

Mr. BODKIN. For the 1911 crop?

Mr. DAKAN. The 1910 crop.

Mr. BODKIN. But that is not our this year's contract. It is the same with the exception that he pays for each one-half per cent, the price varies with each one-half per cent. I should have noticed that as soon as you started to quote prices. That is the only difference in the contract.

Mr. RAKER. I would like to have this go in the record.

The CHAIRMAN. That may go in.

(The contract referred to is as follows:)

[1910.]

DUPLICATE.

THE GREAT WESTERN SUGAR CO., LONGMONT FACTORY.

Memorandum of agreement between ——, grower, and the Great Western Sugar Co.

1. The grower agrees to prepare the land for, plant, block, thin, cultivate, irrigate, harvest, and deliver during the season 191–, in compliance with directions of The Great Western Sugar Co., as may be given from time to time, —— acres of sugar beets on the following-described lands, to wit: —— quarter, section ——, township ——, range ——, —— County, Colo., but in no event shall the company be held liable in damages for any failure or partial failure of crop or any injury or damage to beets.

2. The seed used shall be only that furnished by the company, for either planting or replanting the acreage herein specified, for which the grower shall pay 10 cents per pound, and not less than 20 pounds per acre shall be used, same to be paid for out of the proceeds of the first beets delivered.

3. The grower agrees that all beets grown by him will be harvested and delivered to the company as directed, at the factory or in cars at designated receiving stations of the company, properly topped at base of bottom leaf, knives or hooks shall not be used for lifting beets, subject to proper deduction for tare, free from dirt, stones, trash, or foreign substance liable to interfere with the work at the factory; and that he will protect the beets from sun and frost after removal from the ground. The company has the option of rejecting any diseased, frozen, or damaged beets, beets of less than 12 per cent sugar or less than 80 per cent purity, or beets that are not suitable for the manufacture of sugar, it being agreed and understood that the company shall not be obliged to receive any beets prior to October 15 containing less than 15 per cent sugar; it also being understood that the company will commence receiving the crop as soon as the beets are thoroughly matured.

4. In the event that any portion of the beets grown under this contract (except that portion of the crop which is to be siloed as herein provided) shall not by the 15th day of October of said year be ordered delivered by the company, then in such case it shall be the duty of the grower to promptly commence and proceed with the harvesting and delivery of such beets as come within the contract requirements after the said 15th day of October without further notice from the company and to fully complete delivery of all of said beets on or before the 1st day of December of said year.

5. The grower agrees to silo, if so directed in writing by the company prior to harvest, any portion of the tonnage produced on the above-contracted acreage not to exceed twenty-five (25) per cent of the entire corp grown hereunder.

6. Beets delivered and accepted will be paid for by the company as follows:

$5 per ton for beets testing not less than 12 per cent sugar and under 15 per cent.

$5.25 per ton for beets testing not less than 15 per cent sugar and under 16 per cent.

$5.50 per ton for beets testing not less than 16 per cent sugar and under 17 per cent.

$5.75 per ton for beets testing not less than 17 per cent sugar and under 18 per cent.

$6 per ton for beets testing not less than 18 per cent sugar and under 19 per cent.

And 25 cents per ton additional for each percentage above 19 per cent.

☞ For all beets siloed 50 cents per ton extra shall be paid. It being distinctly understood, however, than none of such siloed beets shall be delivered until the company sends written instructions to the grower to make delivery of "siloed beets;" also that all of said siloed beets shall be ordered and delivered prior to January 31.

Payment to be made the 15th of each month for beets delivered and received during the previous calendar month.

7. The grower shall have the privilege of selecting, at his expense, a man of reliable character, satisfactory to the company, to check the tares and weights of the beets grown under this contract, at the receiving stations where such beets may be delivered and to check in the tare-room laboratory the polarization of his beets.

8. It is further agreed, in the event of a shortage of cars after October 15, causing serious delay to the grower, said grower shall be allowed to fork his beets into piles, under directions of the company, at the receiving stations, where large elevated dumps are established, and no loose dirt shall be removed from the wagon box until after having been weighed back.

9. To ascertain the quality of said beets, the company shall have the privilege at various times during the growing and harvesting season of causing the beets to be sampled and polarized.

10. The grower agrees not to assign this contract without written consent of the company.

—— —— *Grower.*

THE GREAT WESTERN SUGAR CO.,
By —— ——

—— COLORADO, ——, 191—.

Mr. DAKAN. Here is an actual labor contract which I can identify.

Mr. RAKER. I was just coming to that. This is a contract they make with the foreign labor, or labor generally, is it?

Mr. BODKIN. Yes; the hand labor for the best fields.

Mr. RAKER. I would like to have that go in.

The CHAIRMAN. That may be inserted.

[Duplicate.]

LABOR CONTRACT.

CONTRACT FOR HAND LABOR FOR SEASON OF 1910.

Memorandum of agreement, made and entered into this 6th day of March A. D. 1910, by and between H. G. Slater, of Longmont, hereinafter designated as the grower, and Henry Hessler, of Longmont, hereinafter designated as the contractor.

Witnesseth: Whereas, the grower has entered into a contract with the Great Western Sugar Co., of Longmont, Colo., for the growing of sugar beets, and is desirous of contracting with the contractor for doing the handwork on said crop; now, therefore,

In consideration of the sum of $1, in hand paid by the grower to the contractor, receipt of which is hereby acknowledged, the contractor hereby covenants and agrees with the grower to do the handwork on 40 acres, more or less, of sugar beets planted or to be planted —— —— quarter of section ——, township —— north, range —— west of the sixth P. M., for the season of 1910, in accordance with the rules and regulations printed on the back hereof and made a part of this contract.

The contractor further agrees to receive as full compensation for said work the prices hereinafter specified, and the grower hereby agrees to pay said contractor for said handwork as fast as the respective classes of work have been completed and approved by the agricultural superintendent or field man of The Great Western Sugar Co., Longmont factory, at the prices specified below:

	Per acre.	Per ton.
For bunching and thinning	$6.00	$——
For second hoeing	2.50	——
For third hoeing	1.50	——
For pulling and topping	10.00	——

The grower further agrees to provide reasonable living accommodations for the contractor without expense to him, and to furnish said contractor with water near at hand for drinking and domestic purposes without expense.

This contract shall bind and benefit both parties thereto, and its fulfillment shall be a charge and lien on all the real and personal property of the respective parties.

In witness whereof, the parties hereto have subscribed their names the day and year first written above.

H. G. SLATER, *Grower.*
HENRY HESSLER, *Contractor.*

Rules and Regulations Governing the Handwork on the Within Contract.

BUNCHING AND THINNING.

This work to be commenced by the contractor just as soon as the beets show four leaves and the grower has them cultivated, and must be completed as rapidly as possible in the following manner, to wit: Beets to be thinned from 7 to 10 inches apart, leaving only one plant in each place; no double beets shall be left. This work must be done so that the land will be entirely free from weeds.

SECOND HOEING.

This work must be commenced by the contractor as soon as the thinning is completed and the grower has finished the second cultivation, by hoeing a little deeper than the first hoeing, killing and removing all weeds and removing any double plants that may have been overlooked in the thinning. The grower must keep the crop cultivated so that at least 10 inches of the center of the row remains clear of all weeds and foul growth up to the time of the third hoeing.

THIRD HOEING.

A third hoeing must be given the beets by the contractor, and in addition to such third hoeing any and all further hoeing necessary to keep the beets free from weeds, until harvest of the beets is commenced, must be done by the contractor; and in the event of the beets having grown so large that a third or further hoeing would injure them, then all weeds that grow up to the time of the commencement of harvest must be removed by hand, as the beets must be kept free from weeds at all times until harvested.

PULLING AND TOPPING.

This work must be done just as soon as the grower receives orders from the Great Western Sugar Co. to dig his beets. The plowing out will be done by the grower. The beets must be pulled by the contractor, the dirt knocked off by knocking the beets together as pulled, and throwing them into piles. The ground on which the beets are to be piled must be cleaned off and leveled down by the contractor, so that the grower may fork the beets into the wagon, free from dirt, rocks, leaves, or other trash.

The beets will be topped by the contractor in the following manner, to wit: By cutting off the tops squarely just below the crown at the base of the bottom leaf; knives or hooks will not be used for lifting the beets.

All tools for handwork shall be furnished by the grower.

All cultivating, irrigating, plowing out and loading will be done by the grower unless otherwise agreed upon.

All beets left in the field over night must be properly protected from frost by the contractor by covering the piles with beet tops, and the tops to be removed by the grower.

The grower reserves the right, in the event the handwork is not done properly or with sufficient rapidity by the contractor that the crop would thereby suffer, to engage additional help for doing the work at a price not to exceed the price herein contracted for, and to deduct the expense of the same from this contract; it being agreed and understood, however, that in the event of any dispute arising between the grower and contractor as to the interpretation of the above rules, as to the manner in which the work is being done, or as to the necessity of additional help, the agricultural superintendent or field man of the Great Western Sugar Co., Longmont factory, shall act as referee and his decision shall be final and binding on both the contractor and the grower.

The Chairman. The farmer makes that contract with the contractor, to have the labor done?

Mr. Bodkin. Yes, sir.

Mr. Raker. Let me see if I understand about the labor. What kind and class of labor have you?

Mr. Bodkin. Just about all classes.

Mr. Raker. Japanese?

Mr. Bodkin. Some.

Mr. RAKER. Chinese?

Mr. BODKIN. No; I do not think there are any Chinese.

Mr. RAKER. Hindus?

Mr. BODKIN. I could not say about that. I made a mistake when I said all. I meant all classes of people.

Mr. RAKER. Mexicans?

Mr. BODKIN. Yes, sir.

Mr. RAKER. What per centage of Americans?

The CHAIRMAN. For field labor?

Mr. RAKER. Yes; that is what I am talking about.

Mr. BODKIN. A very small per cent, except those that tend the fields themselves.

Mr. RAKER. Yes, I am coming to that. What does this labor contract apply to?

Mr. BODKIN. What work?

Mr. RAKER. No. Does the company furnish this labor under these contracts?

Mr. BODKIN. If we can't get them. When there was not much labor in the country, they would send a man to the cities, make a deal with the poor people around the slums and sign that contract. I would sign mine and would send it along and he would get them signed up.

Mr. RAKER. That is what I am trying to get at.

Mr. BODKIN. Then, the company would ship them out there and we would pay a dollar an acre to the company to help tail up this expense, in order to get the help——

Mr. RAKER. If I understand you correctly—and I do not want to misunderstand you—you pay very little attention to the kind and class and character of the labor employed?

Mr. BODKIN. You can not have much choice; no sir.

Mr. RAKER. No; that is not the question. Come right to the facts. The question of our labor—whether it is high-priced American labor or not—is not practically considered by the company at all, is it?

Mr. BODKIN. By the company?

Mr. RAKER. Yes.

The CHAIRMAN. By the foreman.

Mr. RAKER. The question is simply whom they can get—the cheapest labor they can get?

Mr. BODKIN. It is all one price, but it is just who they can get. Of course, the farmers are very choice in getting nice people, but they can not choose.

Mr. RAKER. Ordinarily a farmer in employing a man gets the best kind of a man he can and then he takes him right into his home, gives him a good bed, and lets him eat at the same table?

Mr. BODKIN. Yes.

Mr. RAKER. But the method used by the sugar people is to get the cheapest labor they can get?

Mr. BODKIN. Yes.

Mr. RAKER. And there is no difference as to the nationality?

Mr. BODKIN. That is right; yes.

Mr. RAKER. Then, the question that they must pay a large bonus to run their business, because it affects labor, in order to keep up high-priced labor and high character of labor and high-minded men, does not apply in your neck of the woods at all, does it?

Mr. BODKIN. No, sir.

Mr. RAKER. In other words, it is the reverse?

Mr. BODKIN. Yes. They go to the towns that have the greatest slums to hire these people.

The CHAIRMAN. Your company does not furnish that labor?

Mr. BODKIN. No. They run it for us.

The CHAIRMAN. I understand; but you say that is hardly necessary now, and the man who gets this labor that is done under this hand-labor contract is the contractor, who contracts with the foreman?

Mr. BODKIN. Yes.

The CHAIRMAN. And he is the man who brings Hindu and Mexican and other labor to your country?

Mr. BODKIN. He gets them if he can get them, but if he can not get them he is not responsible.

The CHAIRMAN. In other words, he contracts to do the work and has it done any way he can, and it makes no difference how?

Mr. BODKIN. So long as he brings people to do the work, and after the people are in my field if they do not do their work right I object.

The CHAIRMAN. You complain to him?

Mr. BODKIN. Yes, I call on him and of course they pay more attention.

The CHAIRMAN. I was afraid that Mr. Raker was under the impression that the sugar company is responsible for the kind of labor there.

Mr. BODKIN. No——

The CHAIRMAN. That is the contractor that does that?

Mr. BODKIN. Yes.

Mr. RAKER. I want to make this plain and I do not want any misunderstanding in regard to the matter. I understand that they are interested in getting as low-priced labor as possible; that is, the sugar-beet people?

Mr. BODKIN. Yes.

Mr. RAKER. Now, they make an arrangement with the farmers that they will send out their agents to the slums of the cities, wherever they can get cheap, low-priced labor?

Mr. BODKIN. Yes.

Mr. RAKER. You people sign a blank contract with the man's name left out?

Mr. BODKIN. Yes.

Mr. RAKER. And this agent of the sugar-beet people takes this contract to these places, finds the man and writes his name in and has him sign the contract?

Mr. BODKIN. Yes, sir.

The CHAIRMAN. That is different, then.

Mr. RAKER. And that man is shipped to the locality where he is needed?

Mr. BODKIN. Yes.

Mr. RAKER. And if he is not satisfactory, you report to the agent that brought him?

Mr. BODKIN. Yes.

Mr. RAKER. And he then tries to get you another man?

Mr. BODKIN. Yes.

Mr. HINDS. And that agent is an agent of the sugar factory, and not of the farmer?

Mr. BODKIN. He is an agent of the sugar factory; yes.

The CHAIRMAN. In other words, the man that signs as contractor is a man that the sugar factory furnishes?

Mr. BODKIN. He is the farmer himself.

The CHAIRMAN. No; the farmer is called the grower in this contract. The grower is the farmer and the contractor is the man who agrees to have this hand labor done?

Mr. BODKIN. Yes; I got this mixed up, I guess.

The CHAIRMAN. Now, is this contractor an agent of the beet-sugar factory or not?

Mr. BODKIN. Yes.

Mr. HINDS. How much do the men who work in the field make? Take a man who works in your field, how much does he make?

Mr. BODKIN. That kind of work varies so much.

Mr. FORDNEY. Well, about how much does a man get, working in a beet field?

Mr. HINDS. What are the extremes?

Mr. BODKIN. Plenty of men can do as much as five other men do.

Mr. FORDNEY. Then such a man ought to be entitled to five times as much pay. What does he get?

Mr. BODKIN. I have a son who takes out a half acre a day at $10 an acre. He gets $5 a day.

Mr. FORDNEY. For thinning?

Mr. BODKIN. Taking them out and topping them. On the thinning he blocks an acre and a half a day, and that work is classed at $2 an acre.

Mr. FORDNEY. Then he gets $3 for that work?

Mr. BODKIN. Yes.

Mr. RAKER. The trouble is that the witness is giving the earnings of his son as an expert. He is putting up a good, clean white man to work, and such a man, of course, is interested in the work. But what we want is to get at what the labor that is imported gets.

Mr. MALBY. What does the average man make per day? I am not referring to boys or children, but the average man.

Mr. BODKIN. About $2, but he has got to hurry.

Mr. HINDS. Do you have to rake the slums over to get men to work for $2 a day in your country?

Mr. BODKIN. Yes.

Mr. RAKER. For instance, here is a man who has a wife and several children. If his children are over 10 years of age, I suppose they go out and work in the field and help thin the beets? That is right, is it not?

Mr. BODKIN. Yes.

Mr. RAKER. And the wife does the same thing?

Mr. BODKIN. Yes.

Mr. RAKER. Have you figured what the whole family makes in a day?

Mr. BODKIN. It varies so much——

Mr. RAKER. It varies according to the kind and class of man who is doing the work as to how much he would make a day. Is that right?

Mr. BODKIN. Yes.

Mr. RAKER. Can you give us any average that an average man would make in a day for his own labor, excluding his wife and children?

Mr. BODKIN. I am saying that if a man works real good, $2 a day; but you will notice that that is all back-breaking work and there are very few Americans that can do that.

Mr. RAKER. That is what I want you to cut out; I do not want what the exceptional man can do, but what the average man can do; what they do make. These men that come in under these contracts, single men, how much do they make?

Mr. BODKIN. I have averaged it at about $2.

Mr. RAKER. That settles it, then.

Mr. HINDS. You say that it back-breaking work, hard work. Is it harder than ordinary farming work?

Mr. BODKIN. Oh, yes; to certain people. Some people would just as soon work in beets as anywhere. There are kinds of people that can not do it at all.

Mr. HINDS. You mean that they are not trained to it?

Mr. BODKIN. They have not got the back. People that have not got a back so that they can lean over can not do that kind of work.

Mr. HINDS. Can they not do their work by staying on their knees?

Mr. BODKIN. Yes; as long as the hide stays on. But a half a day will take the hide off a man, even tied up in sacks.

Mr. RAKER. You pay them for bunching and thinning $6 per acre?

Mr. BODKIN. Yes.

Mr. RAKER. Now, it may take that man three days or four or five days to do that work. It is wholly immaterial to the employer as long as there are enough of them. Is not that right?

Mr. BODKIN. Yes.

Mr. RAKER. Then for the second hoeing it is $2.50 per acre?

Mr. BODKIN. The prices vary.

Mr. RAKER. Take this contract. The second hoeing, $2.50 per acre. Will this man hoe an acre in a day, the second hoeing?

Mr. BODKIN. It depends on how weedy it is.

Mr. RAKER. Take the ordinary piece of land, with ordinary weed and ordinary conditions and ordinary soil. Can he hoe an acre a day?

Mr. BODKIN. They figure out that by the price.

Mr. RAKER. Do they do it?

Mr. BODKIN. I have seen fellows hoe 10 acres a day and I have seen them hoe only a quarter acre a day.

Mr. RAKER. All right. At the third hoeing they get $1.50 a day an acre, and for pulling and topping, $10 an acre?

Mr. BODKIN. Yes.

Mr. RAKER. So it is pretty hard to figure what they get a day?

Mr. BODKIN. There is more variation in that work than anything else.

Mr. RAKER. It depends upon the strength of a man's back as to how much work he can do in a day?

Mr. BODKIN. And whether he hurries for 14 hours a day.

Mr. RAKER. Do they work 14 hours a day at this work?

Mr. BODKIN. Lots of them; and 15 and 16 hours.

Mr. RAKER. At $2 a day?

Mr. BODKIN. No; I am saying when they are working by the contract. When I say $2 a day, I say that is about the average. It takes a good man to go out and work through the season and have $2 a day through thick and thin. Some years or in some fields the third hoeing lots of times does not have to be performed if the first two are done good and it is a dry year and the weeds do not come on. It is a lottery, the whole work, and that is the trouble. They are afraid they will get stuck and make very small wages, there is such a variation in the work.

Mr. RAKER. Of course I can appreciate that. A weedy patch will take a lot of work and maybe another patch you can go through very rapidly.

Mr. BODKIN. Yes; it differs very much.

Mr. RAKER. Who is to blame for the treatment of the labor there—the farmers or the company?

Mr. BODKIN. I do not think anybody. It is simply disagreeable work and nobody cares to do it.

Mr. RAKER. Why do you not get American labor—this high-class American labor that we are talking about, which is protected by our high tariff? Why do they get this labor from the slums of the cities?

Mr. BODKIN. Americans will not do that work; not 1 in 50.

Mr. RAKER. Then the cry by the beet-sugar people that we must keep up a sort of a bounty, a high tariff, to maintain the high standard of American labor and to enable them to maintain their homes and educate their children does not amount to anything; there is nothing in that, is there? Is that right?

Mr. BODKIN. I think so.

Mr. HINDS. How much does similar labor get in foreign beet fields? Are you acquainted with that?

Mr. BODKIN. No; I do not know.

Mr. MALBY. What you mean to say is that the men who supply the labor get the best help they can to do that particular kind of work?

Mr. BODKIN. There is no doubt of it.

Mr. HINDS. And the reason why the American laborer is not employed is simply because he refuses to do that work?

Mr. BODKIN. He will not do enough to pay to have him. You have not got money enough to pay him for what little he would do.

Mr. MALBY. So you meet conditions by hiring such help as will perform this kind of service?

Mr. BODKIN. That is all we can do, or quit raising beets.

Mr. FORDNEY. You mean to say, then, that all your labor in the beet field is foreign, cheap labor?

Mr. BODKIN. Once in a while there are American boys who work in those fields, if they have to.

Mr. HINDS. Are there women?

Mr. BODKIN. Not American women. This help that comes in consists of men and women and children, all work alike.

Mr. FORDNEY. How much does a woman make a day?

Mr. BODKIN. There are lots of women that do a lot more work than their husbands. The man is usually the boss.

Mr. MALBY. That is part of the foreign custom.

Mr. HINDS. Well, how much will the average smart woman make?

Mr. BODKIN. I would figure that anybody that does a good day's work would make about $2.

Mr. HINDS. A woman?

Mr. BODKIN. Yes.

Mr. HINDS. What would you say of the difficulty of that work, working in the beet fields for a woman, as compared to breaking stone on the roads?

Mr. BODKIN. Breaking stone would be easier than that.

Mr. HINDS. Much easier?

Mr. BODKIN. I should think it would, unless you would supply them with a large, heavy hammer.

Mr. HINDS. About how much easier would you say? What would be the relation between that beet work and breaking stone?

Mr. BODKIN. There might be some people that would prefer one and some the other, but I would take the breaking stone, and I imagine most people would.

Mr. HINDS. As an employer of labor, what would you say would be the difference in the wages you would have to pay as between the labor in the beet field and the labor breaking stone on the road?

Mr. BODKIN. I would not expect that there would be very much difference, for it is to our interest to make them believe that the beet work is very nice.

Mr. HINDS. Would you say $1.50 for the stone-breaking work as compared to $2 for the beet work?

Mr. BODKIN. No; I would not get it down that fine.

Mr. HINDS. I understand that women in Germany work at breaking stones on the roads at 30 cents a day. I have seen that stated. I did not know but that might give you some ratio to compare our labor in the beet fields and in the beet fields of Germany.

Mr. BODKIN. No; I would not catch anything from that, only that they would work in our beet fields for $2 a day well contented if they had been working for that little in Germany.

Mr. RAKER. In the $2 a day work that you have spoken of they work from 10 to 15 hours a day?

Mr. BODKIN. Yes; for 15 hours and more in a busy time. They go out with lanterns after supper and are usually there when I go to bed, and are there when I get up.

Mr. MALBY. That is where they are working upon a contract?

Mr. BODKIN. Yes.

Mr. MALBY. How many hours do they work when they are working by the day?

Mr. BODKIN. Ten hours.

Mr. MALBY. If they have a contract they work as many hours as they please?

Mr. BODKIN. That is their own affair; yes.

Mr. HINDS. Do these men and women work every day?

Mr. BODKIN. They work every day until they get done during the season; yes.

Mr. HINDS. That is, the $2 a day represents continuous work?

Mr. BODKIN. They do not work by the day. Those are the contracts.

Mr. HINDS. Well, are there some days that they do not work at all?

Mr. BODKIN. Not until they get done, unless it is bad weather. About the 1st of June they go over the second hoeing and about the 1st of August the third hoeing, and perhaps it would take them all this time, but if they get done one class of work they may go out and get some other work.

Mr. HINDS. And then they get paid for that in addition to their contract?

Mr. BODKIN. Yes.

Mr. HINDS. Is that outside pay from the farmers in this $2 a day average?

Mr. BODKIN. When they are not busy in the beet fields they work for whoever hires them, for about $2 or $2.50 a day.

Mr. HINDS. Is that in addition to the $2 a day they average in the beet fields?

Mr. BODKIN. That $2 average has nothing to do with the farmer.

Mr. HINDS. So, at the end of the season these men may have made $3 or $4 a day?

Mr. BODKIN. No. For instance, if they made $2 a day in the beet field that only applies to what days they worked in the beet fields. Of course, when they are working outside they are not earning anything in the beet field.

Mr. HINDS. How much would they earn ordinarily outside of the beet fields?

Mr. BODKIN. They would ordinarily have a month in haying, at odd times, and a week or two between hoeing, and then they would follow a thrashing machine; that is, the men and big boys. Usually the women and children do the second and third hoeing, and the men go out in September and October, in that other work.

Mr. FORDNEY. You say they get from $2 to $2.50 a day at farming?

Mr. BODKIN. A day, yes; in harvest or hay work.

Mr. MALBY. And sometimes more than that?

Mr. BODKIN. Some years when help is very scarce and also in spuds picking; that is high-priced work.

Mr. HINDS. Is help hard for you to get?

Mr. BODKIN. It has been easy for the last two years; before that it was very scarce.

Mr. HINDS. Do the Americans like to do that haying and thrashing?

Mr. BODKIN. No.

Mr. HINDS. They have the same repugnance for that work that they have to the work in the beet fields?

Mr. BODKIN. Just about the same.

Mr. RAKER. How is that? Do you say that you can not get Americans to do haying and thrashing?

Mr. BODKIN. He asked me if they liked to do it, and I said no.

Mr. RAKER. Well, I suppose very few men like to work, and if they can get out of work they do so; but you have no trouble in getting Americans to do haying and harvest work, all over the country?

Mr. BODKIN. Up to two years ago they were so scarce you could not get them; but for the last couple of years help has been pretty plenty. But I would say a man is near broke when he goes out haying, except a man who is trying to accumulate something, which is perhaps a very small percentage of our people.

Mr. RAKER. To go back again to this family business, there have not been any statistics that would be reliable to show how much a man would get for two days' work in this locality you have been speaking of, in handling beets?

Mr. BODKIN. No, sir.

Mr. RAKER. The real fact is that the contract is entered into by a man, and he generally has his wife and probably from two to five children?

Mr. BODKIN. Yes.

Mr. RAKER. And the little fellows maybe are only 7 or 8 years of age, and the family goes out as soon as the sun is up and stays out until it is dark or dusk working upon these jobs?

Mr. BODKIN. Yes.

Mr. RAKER. And that is the way the work is handled in cleaning and thinning and hoeing the beets?

Mr. BODKIN. Yes.

Mr. RAKER. That is about the way they work under these contracts?

Mr. BODKIN. Yes.

Mr. RAKER. So it is impossible to give an intelligent answer as to how much a man would get for a day's work in that locality. Is not that right?

Mr. BODKIN. You could not say. It depends on how much help he has got.

Mr. RAKER. That is what I am trying to get at; but the method is as I have described it to you, is it not?

Mr. BODKIN. Yes, sir.

Mr. HINDS. Can the proprietor farmers in your country pay all their taxes and expenses—that is, farm expenses; I would not put in their food and clothing—and average $2.50 a day per year?

Mr. BODKIN. You mean would he have that much to apply on his grocery and store bills?

Mr. HINDS. I mean, take out the interest on the money invested in his farm, the taxes that he pays, the expenses that he pays for labor, everything except his clothes and food and dissipations and dues to the Knights of Pythias and the Masons, can the farmer average $2.50 a day through the year for proprietary farming?

Mr. BODKIN. I would say no. They vary as much as weeds in a beet field.

Mr. HINDS. What I was aiming at was this: If a man was coming into your country, had he better come in and buy a farm or go to the slums and enlist in the beet squad?

Mr. BODKIN. The farmers are just like all other people; some are making money and others are losing it. There is no regularity to it.

Mr. HINDS. But the farmers on an average are not making a great deal?

Mr. BODKIN. No; perhaps 10 per cent are making it.

Mr. FORDNEY. And the others are just living?

Mr. BODKIN. Yes, and some are not living; some are quitting and going to the towns. You might say that there are 7 or 8 per cent of them that are just paying.

Mr. MALBY. Do the farmers generally in your locality regard the raising of beets under present conditions as being a profitable method of farming?

Mr. BODKIN. No.

Mr. MALBY. The profits, if any, are very close?

Mr. BODKIN. Yes.

Mr. MALBY. And returns very slim?

Mr. BODKIN. It is a little like those others; when you get a tonnage crop of 16 or 18 or 20 tons, there is good money in that.

Mr. MALBY. I am speaking of the average conditions.

Mr. BODKIN. The average, of course, shows 11 tons, which barely pays the expense. If you hire it done it will hardly pay the expenses.

Mr. MALBY. In other words, the profits consist of your own labor and the labor of the other members of your family?

Mr. BODKIN. That would take all the profit.

Mr. MALBY. In other words, you simply get good fair pay for your own work?

Mr. BODKIN. Fairly good, taking an average for the State.

Mr. FORDNEY. You have said that you cultivated 40 acres, have you not?

Mr. BODKIN. Yes.

Mr. FORDNEY. Thirteen acres of it in beets?

Mr. BODKIN. About 13½ acres; yes.

Mr. FORDNEY. And you have charged up to those beets $20 an acre rent?

Mr. BODKIN. Yes.

Mr. FORDNEY. Did you make that much on the balance of the 40 acres?

Mr. BODKIN. I did not have any such land in the balance.

Mr. FORDNEY. If you had had that kind of land could you make that much and still make wages yourself?

Mr. BODKIN. And still make the same wages?

Mr. FORDNEY. Yes, sir.

Mr. BODKIN. No, sir.

Mr. FORDNEY. Then the beet crop is the better of the two?

Mr. BODKIN. On account of the amount of days I put in. The other crop would end quicker and I would not have got in so much work.

Mr. FORDNEY. As between the two, even though you lost money on the beets—and you did not lose, because you made $1 or $1.50 an acre—the beet crop was the best?

Mr. BODKIN. It was with me; yes.

Mr. FORDNEY. Is that generally so with the farmers in your State?

Mr. BODKIN. Not generally. We were talking over that, you know. On account of my improvements and location, I have been offered $250 per acre.

Mr. MALBY. Was that for the whole 40 acres?

Mr. BODKIN. Yes. But I say that just as good beets could be grown on $150 an acre land farther out.

Mr. HINDS. What would those people who proposed to pay you $250 an acre for your land grow on that land? How would they use the land?

Mr. BODKIN. They would get it because it is a nice neighborhood and a good place to live.

Mr. FORDNEY. And would they put it into city property?

Mr. BODKIN. No.

Mr. FORDNEY. You said that you adjoined the city, I think?

Mr. BODKIN. No; I said we were near a good little town, and it is a good place to live.

Mr. HINDS. They would not pay that much for farming purposes?

Mr. BODKIN. No.

Mr. HINDS. How much would they pay for land for farming purposes?

Mr. BODKIN. Being close to the town and having the benefit of short hauls, it ought to bring $175 an acre.

Mr. HINDS. Well, that is as much as land in England is worth near large cities, is it not?

Mr. BODKIN. I have no idea.

Mr. MALBY. The crop has got to be a pretty valuable one to justify the payment of $175 an acre, has it not?

Mr. BODKIN. It has; yes.

Mr. MALBY. What other crop could this land be utilized for to justify an investment of $175 an acre?

Mr. BODKIN. I am not sure that there would be any crop year after year, on an average, which would justify that priced land.

Mr. MALBY. Being somewhat of a farmer myself, I do not know of any crop that you could put into the ground in my northern country where you would be justified to pay more than $100 an acre, unless it was near a city and could be used for truck gardening or something of that kind. For the general raising of grains, and so forth, or hay, or anything of that kind, we have no land that our farmers can invest more than $100 an acre in and rely upon the crop giving a remuneration sufficient for a living. But we do not raise beets. Now, if you can pay $175 an acre for the land and raise beets, that is something that the committee would like to know.

Mr. BODKIN. I could not say how many beets they could raise. It is just a chance question.

Mr. MALBY. Could you, one year with another, raise beets enough at the present prices to justify the payment of $175 an acre for the land?

Mr. BODKIN. I have done so all but one year in my field.

Mr. MALBY. My idea about it is that your farmers generally, men who have lands that are worth from $150 to $175 an acre, who hold them at those prices or sell at those prices, must find some method of getting an adequate return to represent such an investment. The question I have in mind is whether the beet crop has been found to justify the farmers either to pay that sum for land, or hold it if they own it to raise beets upon.

Mr. BODKIN. When the business first came into the country they raised a better tonnage, perhaps for three years. Then there were high prices paid for the land on the strength of the beet proposition.

Mr. MALBY. What is the average land in your locality for beet purposes worth per acre now?

Mr. BODKIN. For beet purposes?

Mr. MALBY. Yes.

Mr. BODKIN. They do not talk it for beets any more.

Mr. MALBY. Well, upon which beets could be successfully raised; for what could you buy what might be termed good beet lands in your locality?

Mr. BODKIN. We have good lands for hay and alfalfa—that is what they talk now, but of course they can raise beets on it. They think it is worth about $150 an acre.

Mr. MALBY. Of course alfalfa is a very valuable crop in localities where you can successfully raise it.

Mr. BODKIN. Yes.

Mr. MALBY. Well, would you say your beet land in your locality was worth on an average about $150 an acre?

Mr. BODKIN. I do not quite catch why we should say beet land. If we would say land that would raise beets and other crops, but to just say "beet land"—we do not figure beet land as we used to.

Mr. Malby. Not exclusively beet land, I see.

Mr. HINDS. What proportion of your farm is devoted to beet culture?

Mr. BODKIN. This year?

Mr. HINDS. Yes.

Mr. BODKIN. 13½ acres out of 40 acres.

Mr. HINDS. That is about one-third of your land is devoted to beets?

Mr. BODKIN. Yes.

Mr. HINDS. What proportion of your neighbors' farms are devoted to beets?

Mr. BODKIN. They vary wonderfully.

Mr. HINDS. What would be a fair average as far as your eye can reach?

Mr. BODKIN. About two-thirds of them do not grow any beets at all, and then the others have no telling how much land in beets. Some fellow might feel lucky and make himself believe that he can raise 15 tons or something like that, and he would plant them—I could not give you any idea how much——

Mr. HINDS. And do those that plant beets stay in beet raising year after year or do they just go in and get disgusted and go out?

Mr. BODKIN. That is the way they do.

Mr. HINDS. Not raise beets any more?

Mr. BODKIN. Maybe they will lay off a year or two and then try it again.

Mr. HINDS. Do they lay off a year or two and go back to beet raising because they have gotten back their courage or because they want to rotate the crop?

Mr. BODKIN. Rotation is a good thing and then they change their mind or something or other, and they figure that they might raise a paying crop on account of the rotation, and they try it again, and maybe they will be lucky.

Mr. HINDS. How is it with you? Have you raised beets every year?

Mr. BODKIN. All but one year.

Mr. HINDS. For how many years?

Mr. BODKIN. I first had a contract for three years, and then I raised them one year, and then I laid off, and then I raised them this last year.

Mr. HINDS. Why did you lay off one year?

Mr. BODKIN. Because I had 9 tons to the acre the year before.

Mr. HINDS. That discouraged you?

Mr. BODKIN. I was afraid of it.

Mr. MALBY. What other crops did you raise besides beets?

Mr. BODKIN. This year?

Mr. MALBY. Yes.

Mr. BODKIN. Just wheat.

Mr. MALBY. How many bushels to the acre of wheat did you raise?

Mr. BODKIN. Just about 21.

Mr. MALBY. And what is it worth per bushel?

Mr. BODKIN. $1.20 a hundred.

Mr. MALBY. Do you sell it by the hundred or by the bushel?

Mr. BODKIN. By the hundred; $1.20 a hundred. That is 66 cents a bushel. But I would say that I saved the water off the wheat for the beets until the wheat was nearly burned up, and when we got some more water in the lake I found I would have some for the wheat and the beets, then I irrigated the wheat. That was why it fell down so.

Mr. MALBY. The 21 bushels an acre was not your average crop?

Mr. BODKIN. No, sir.

Mr. MALBY. What would be your average crop of wheat?

Mr. BODKIN. Twenty-one bushels to the acre last year, and other years it ran up to 65. Ordinarily, on good ground, 40 to 50 bushels.

Mr. HINDS. You raise 40 or 50 bushels of wheat to the acre?

Mr. BODKIN. On an average like year, with average like ground.

Mr. HINDS. How much would that net you an acre?

Mr. BODKIN. Depending again on the price.

Mr. HINDS. Well, at 66 cents, which you say you sold yours for?

Mr. BODKIN. That would be four times six is $24. I can not figure it very well.

Mr. HINDS. How much did your beets give you an acre this year?

Mr. BODKIN. I got rent for the land and paid for the work and all that I did, and got $3.50 per acre.

Mr. HINDS. You got paid for your work on the land and $3.50 an acre?

Mr. BODKIN. Yes.

Mr. HINDS. So that, on the whole, it is a better proposition than the wheat?

Mr. BODKIN. This was on my best land. I saved my water for it.

Mr. HINDS. Well, as to this 50 or 60 bushels of wheat an acre that you get, is that on the poorer land?

Mr. BODKIN. No; that is good land. When it is 65 bushels, that is on the best land.

Mr. HINDS. So the wheat and the beets were both on the best land?

Mr. BODKIN. These figures just given were figured on the basis of 40 bushels to the acre. I said I had raised 65 bushels on the acre.

Mr. MALBY. Of course that was extraordinary.

Mr. BODKIN. Which? The 65 bushels?

Mr. MALBY. No; the 40 bushels.

Mr. HINDS. As compared with the greatest wheat-growing nations in Europe, that is a large crop. They do not get over 30 bushels to an acre.

Mr. BODKIN. This is, of course, not an average.

Mr. HINDS. This is an exceptional place.

Mr. BODKIN. You might say a small place.

Mr. RAKER. Is that not the condition all over the West where you can get water on your land? Can you name any place where they do not get from 50 to 80 bushels where they can get water on land, if the land is in the beginning decent land?

Mr. BODKIN. Of course 60 to 80 bushels——

Mr. RAKER. Thoroughly plowed and irrigated, I mean?

Mr. BODKIN. It takes a good season, and then that is just a part of the rop or a part of the choice crop.

Mr. MALBY. I know that the average crop of the Dakotas, according to governmental reports, is about 14 bushels to the acre.

Mr. BODKIN. You have so many cheap acres.

Mr. MALBY. Well, they sow it in wheat. In Kansas and Nebraska, which is supposed to be a pretty good wheat country, it averages about 20 bushels to the acre.

Mr. HINDS. The average for the United States is about 13 or 14 bushels to the acre, is it not?

Mr. MALBY. Yes.

Mr. RAKER. That is where you are figuring wrong. This gentleman is figuring upon land that has been irrigated. Take the land in the Western States where they irrigate, they can raise these crops, and we will find out from him that upon raising wheat in this country right where Mr. Bodkin lives, considering the amount of money spent in irrigation outside of the labor, he will get more than he does in raising beets. Is not that a fact?

Mr. BODKIN. I could not say, on account of the rotation the beets give us. I am not turning down the beet proposition.

Mr. RAKER. I do not want you to turn down the beet proposition; but suppose you raised potatoes one year. That would give you as much as the beets?

Mr. BODKIN. Not quite so much in our neighborhood. In our neighborhood we have a clay soil that is just right for grain, and when you put it into potatoes it makes it a shade too rich, and when you undertake to burn it properly you will have to do some good guessing if you burn it just right.

Mr. RAKER. When you raised alfalfa, how many crops of alfalfa did you raise?

Mr. BODKIN. Three crops.

Mr. RAKER. And that will net you in the neighborhood of $30.

Mr. BODKIN. This year.

Mr. RAKER. Do you raise seed?

Mr. BODKIN. Yes.

Mr. RAKER. The alfalfa crop at $30 per acre was a better crop than the beet crop designated by you to-day, a better crop to the farmer. Taking the figures you gave given, paying $1.50 to cut it and put it in the sack, you can get it done for that, can you not?

Mr. BODKIN. Yes.

Mr. RAKER. You can practically get $20 an acre for your hay?

Mr. BODKIN. $25.

Mr. RAKER. That is not what you have given here. You only get $3.50.

Mr. BODKIN. But I do not buy myself such a long job with the hay.

Mr. RAKER. But, my dear sir, while you are buying yourself a long job with your beets, can not you in the meantime be doing something else?

Mr. BODKIN. I see; you won't give me that money without earning it.

Mr. RAKER. Yes.

Mr. BODKIN. Maybe that would be so; I have not figured it out that way.

Mr. FORDNEY. Do you mean to say that he gets $30 per acre for the alfalfa crop?

Mr. RAKER. Yes; he can clear net $25. That is a small crop.

Mr. FORDNEY. It costs $5 per acre to handle it and harvest it?

The CHAIRMAN. I think you said you made $25 profit out of alfalfa?

Mr. BODKIN. Yes.

Mr. FORDNEY. $5 per acre for the three crops is one and two-thirds dollars for harvesting three crops. Can you do that out there with two and three dollars a day for labor?

Mr. BODKIN. $30 worth of hay, and then, talking $25 profit, leaves $5.

Mr. FORDNEY. For harvesting three crops?

Mr. BODKIN. Yes.

Mr. FORDNEY. Can you harvest three crops per season for $1.66⅔ an acre for each crop?

Mr. BODKIN. No——

Mr. FORDNEY. It costs more than $1.50 an acre, does it not, to cut it and dry it?

Mr. BODKIN. I said it was near that.

Mr. HINDS. I understood that you produced 12¾ tons of beets to the acre?

Mr. BODKIN. Yes.

Mr. HINDS. That is on irrigated land?

Mr. BODKIN. Yes.

Mr. HINDS. And you expected to get how much?

Mr. BODKIN. I expected to get 18 tons.

Mr. HINDS. That would be a good crop, would it not?

Mr. BODKIN. This year 18 tons was what I was looking for.

Mr. HINDS. Why did you not get it this year?

Mr. BODKIN. They did not grow large.

Mr. HINDS. They would in an ordinary year grow large?

Mr. BODKIN. No; I do not say they would. They have such a habit now of not growing large; that is why we do not get the tonnage.

Mr. HINDS. Then for beet culture does that land have the relative superiority that it does for wheat culture? You are producing of wheat three times the average of the United States on your land?

Mr. BODKIN. I presume so.

Mr. HINDS. Are you producing on beets three times the average of the beet fields in Michigan and those places?

Mr. BODKIN. No, sir.

Mr. HINDS. So that your land does not have the relative superiority for beet culture that it does for raising other crops?

Mr. BODKIN. No, no; I did not catch what you stated.

Mr. HINDS. So that you did not get the advantage of irrigation for beets that you do for other crops?

Mr. BODKIN. Not if you lay that to the irrigation.

Mr. HINDS. Well, you have no doubt that it is the irrigation, combined with the soil, that gives you that tremendously large wheat yield?

Mr. BODKIN. The irrigation is only a small part of it.

(Thereupon at 5.15 p. m. the committee adjourned until to-morrow, Thursday, December 7, 1911, at 10.30 a. m.)

18869—11——10

AMERICAN SUGAR REFINING CO. AND OTHERS.

SPECIAL COMMITTEE ON THE INVESTIGATION
OF THE AMERICAN SUGAR REFINING CO. AND OTHERS,
HOUSE OF REPRESENTATIVES,
Washington, D. C., December 7, 1911.

The committee met at 10.30 o'clock a. m., Hon. John E. Raker (acting chairman) presiding.

TESTIMONY OF MR. JAMES BODKIN—Resumed.

Mr. FORDNEY. Mr. Bodkin, in whose interest do you come here to testify? Were you subpœnaed by the committee?

Mr. BODKIN. I have a letter.

Mr. FORDNEY. Were you subpœnaed by the committee?

Mr. BODKIN. I could not say that we were. One of the letters to one of our committee asked if we would come without a subpœna. I do not know whether that letter was considered a subpœna or not, from the chairman, here.

Mr. FORDNEY. The chairman wrote you to come, did he?

Mr. BODKIN. Yes; with that statement along.

Mr. FORDNEY. What sort of statement did he ask you for? I do not know anything about what the committee has said or done in the matter, and I ask for information. What information did the chairman ask you to give when you came here, or what statement?

Mr. BODKIN. He asked that we come to meet this committee on the 5th of December, saying that mileage and witness fees had been allowed. Then he did not say anything about the subpœna in my letter. but in one of the others—in Mr. Combs's letter—it stated or asked if he would come without being subpœnaed.

Mr. FORDNEY. You were asked to bring what kind of a statement—information showing what?

Mr. BODKIN. From this letter of the chairman here?

Mr. FORDNEY. Yes, sir.

Mr. BODKIN. Nothing at all.

Mr. FORDNEY. You were just asked to come here to testify?

Mr. BODKIN. Yes.

Mr. FORDNEY. Without knowing what you were to testify to?

Mr. BODKIN. Yes, sir.

Mr. FORDNEY. Judge Raker, may I ask, do you know why the committee summoned this witness as a grower of beets?

Mr. RAKER. No; not personally, only from the examination I gave him yesterday, and from his testimony I gather that the sugar growers of Colorado would like to have their testimony go into the record here to show their treatment and the amount they are getting for their beets as compared with the amount that the refiners are getting, and to show the cost of production.

Mr. FORDNEY. Then I would like, as a member of the committee, to make the point that I want the committee to also summon some farmers from the State of Michigan who are raising beets. As I understood it when the committee adjourned, it was not intended we should go into this class of information, but I had before requested the chairman of the committee that some farmers might be subpœnaed to give testimony as to the raising of beets for factories; and, therefore, since this witness has been called, I want to call some witnesses from Michigan and from other States that raise beets to testify before us.

Mr. RAKER. Well, no doubt the Chairman will be here in a few minutes and we will take that matter up.

Mr. FORDNEY. Mr. Bodkin, yesterday you evidently complained of the treatment that you were receiving from the manufacturers in tests made of your beets to show the percentage of sugar in the beets, did you not?

Mr. BODKIN. I can't say that it was a complaint. I can say we don't know a thing about it.

Mr. FORDNEY. Well, could you not know all about it if you wanted to? Could you not make your own tests? The people in other States do that. They do in our State.

Mr. BODKIN. I got up a move in our organization to put in laboratories of our own, and we have not accomplished that yet.

Mr. FORDNEY. Mr. Bodkin, any chemist could give you the sugar content of your beets.

Mr. BODKIN. He could; yes.

Mr. FORDNEY. Through a very simple method, and cheap, too. That is frequently done elsewhere.

Mr. BODKIN. Yes, for $5 each, but there are but few of us that have got $5 to have a test made every day or so.

Mr. FORDNEY. Well, I am sorry. You ought to move to Michigan and raise beets, because the farmers in our State consider beets the most valuable crop raised in the State, and it has been contended here time and time again, not before this committee but before the Ways and Means Committee, that the crop of sugar beets raised in arid lands, where sunshine and water is required, where you have sunshine all the time and where you can get water to the beets when they need it, that you get a larger percentage of sugar in the beets and a larger tonnage per acre than is found in the State of Michigan or other States where they depend upon the elements. Now, the amount of beets you raised, as you stated yesterday, is just a little above the average in the State of Michigan, but way below the tonnage raised where a high state of cultivation is given, such as you gave them. You stated yesterday, Mr. Bodkin, that it cost you $69.83 per acre to raise your beets, and you gave that in an itemized manner, giving $20 per acre as a reasonable rent for your land. The cost per acre in the State of Michigan is less than $30, figuring interest on the money invested in the land, team work, labor, everything connected with the raising of beets and marketing them, putting them on the cars ready to send to the factory. That is considerably below $30 per acre in the State of Michigan. You gave your figures as $69.83

per acre. Is that a fair average of cost in the State of Colorado per acre for the raising of beets?

Mr. BODKIN. I said that was what it cost me.

Mr. FORDNEY. I ask you if that is a fair average in the State of Colorado. I know you said that is what it cost you.

Mr. BODKIN. I have applied that $6.66 worth of water. I do not know whether other people irrigated their beets four times in a dry year like last year was or not. They would have to slight the beet crop to do it any cheaper.

Mr. FORDNEY. I ask you now, for this last year's crop, did it cost the average farmer in the State of Colorado $69.83 per acre for raising his beets?

Mr. BODKIN. If he did the work I did it cost him that.

Mr. FORDNEY. Well, that is not the question. Can you not say whether you think that is an average cost? Do other farmers do the same kind of work that you do? That is a matter that we do not know.

Mr. BODKIN. The farmers that farm right do. I don't say that some man might not have cultivated his like mine, and skin plowed it, and done this, that, and the other thing. There are lots of ways to cheapen things.

Mr. FORDNEY. Last year was an exceptionally dry year and an expensive one for beet raising in your State, was it not?

Mr. BODKIN. Not expensive, only in the way of water, all other conditions being the same.

Mr. FORDNEY. Now, you have shown that it cost you about $6 per acre for water, have you not?

Mr. BODKIN. I put that much additional water on mine that I bought outside of my water rights.

Mr. FORDNEY. Now, taking that $6 from that extraordinary cost the average cost would be $63.83, instead of $69.83. Is that a fair average cost for the production of beets in your State?

Mr. BODKIN. That water was at the rate of $3.33, and there would be another 66 cents. There was $6.66 worth of water.

Mr. FORDNEY. Well, take off that 66 cents, then.

Mr. BODKIN. And in one place in my statement I had a 50-cent mistake.

Mr. FORDNEY. Oh, 50 cents would cut but little figure in this estimate. Does it cost the average farmer in your State $60 an acre to raise beets and market them?

Mr. BODKIN. Yes, sir.

Mr. FORDNEY. I want the statement to go into the record that that is twice the cost of the production of beets in the State of Michigan; and the State of Michigan perhaps raises more beets than any other State in the Union.

Mr. BODKIN. I can give you the prices that the Great Western field agents paid in our neighborhood for raising beets one year, if you want it.

Mr. FORDNEY. Well, I want all the information you can give me. You can not give me too much information on this subject.

Mr. BODKIN. C. D. Holmes was field agent in our district for the Great Western. He rented 100 acres of land. I think it was an even hundred acres. It was near my place, and he paid $20 an acre cash rent. He paid the hand labor $20 an acre. He paid Mr. Farr, the owner of it, $20 an acre, and the seed he had to pay the Great Western for, and he had been field boss there in other years and was raised in the neighborhood.

Mr. FORDNEY. And knew what he was doing?

Mr. BODKIN. He must have; and a banker in our town went in partners with him.

Mr. FORDNEY. Did the bank "bust"?

Mr. BODKIN. It did.

Mr. FORDNEY. Beet growing "busted" it?

Mr. BODKIN. I did not say that.

Mr. FORDNEY. I ask you that question. You have said it "busted." Now, did the beet growing "bust" it?

Mr. BODKIN. I might say in a general way it did—the beet business.

Mr. FORDNEY. How many acres did they have, Mr. Bodkin?

Mr. BODKIN. I remember it as 100 acres.

Mr. FORDNEY. One hundred acres then "busted" a bank in your State?

Mr. BODKIN. I did not say that. The failure of the farmers to raise beets profitably——

Mr. FORDNEY (interposing). Mr. Bodkin, pardon me. We are talking about this one contractor. You said the bank went in with him and "busted." Did that one contract "bust" that bank or have anthing to do with its "busting"?

Mr. BODKIN. No, sir.

Mr. FORDNEY. Well, that is all about that matter. You have stated now that for $5 you could get a chemist to give you a test of the saccharine matter in your beets, and you had 13 acres which brought you about $70 an acre, or in the neighborhood of $900 worth of beets. Did you think it worth while to spend that $5 to find out whether or not the company was robbing you, or giving you what belonged to you?

Mr. BODKIN. $5 is not near all that goes along with getting a test made.

Mr. FORDNEY. You said you could get a test made for that amount.

Mr. BODKIN. We did get one for that by making several trips, and waiting until the chemist got permission from the Great Western allowing them to make that test for a beet grower.

Mr. FORDNEY. Do you mean to say the Great Western Co. has such influence over every chemist in the State of Colorado that you can not get a chemist to make an honest test for you?

Mr. BODKIN. I did not say "every chemist."

Mr. FORDNEY. Would you have this committee understand that? You are at liberty to get any chemist you want, are you not? It is your own business, and you are paying for it. You can employ any man you see fit without the dictation of the Great Western Sugar Co.

Mr. BODKIN. I would not know where to find him.

Mr. FORDNEY. Have you not an agricultural department in your State and several chemists connected with it?

Mr. BODKIN. We sent a sample, or Mr. J. O. V. Wise sent a sample, to our Fort Collins agriculturist. He told Wise that he couldn't take it, but he would give him the address of a chemist in Denver that would. Wise went to Denver to have this done. It is a long story, but I can give you the outlines of it.

Mr. FORDNEY. Just give us the substance of it. Did you get the test? That is the point.

Mr. BODKIN. Wise went to Denver, and meanwhile, while he was talking, he picked up a letter lying on his desk, noticing it was from Fort Collins, and he said: "Maybe this may throw some light on the subject." He opened the letter. He had not read it before, but he read it there out loud, and Wise heard it, and the statement in it was he had written the chemist in Denver what we had on hand, and the result was the chemist could not give us anything, and sent us away.

Mr. FORDNEY. Then you would give this committee to understand that you can not get a chemist in the State of Colorado to give you an honest test of your beets; that is, a chemist not influenced by the Great Western Sugar Co.?

Mr. BODKIN. I would not say that.

Mr. FORDNEY. You have practically said so. You said that everybody you have tried has been influenced.

Mr. BODKIN. We have tried three places. That is not all of Colorado.

Mr. FORDNEY. And then you gave it up? You did not try any more than three places?

Mr. BODKIN. No.

Mr. FORDNEY. Did you make an honest effort to get the agricultural department of your State to give you an honest test of the sugar in your beets and fail?

Mr. BODKIN. Yes, sir. He gave us the reason why.

Mr. FORDNEY. He would not tell you the reason why?

Mr. BODKIN. He did.

Mr. FORDNEY. What was his reason? What reason did he give?

Mr. BODKIN. After he showed us what a good fellow he was by taking up tests for the towns that had sent in samples of water, and so forth, then I asked him why he could not make tests for the farmers, and he said: "Well, I will just tell you. If we were to go into that there would be so many come in we could not do it."

Mr. FORDNEY. Well, as the representative of an organization of a certain district, could you not ask to have the tests made on behalf of all the farmers that you represented?

Mr. BODKIN. That I did, as chairman of this organization.

Mr. FORDNEY. Did you get the test?

Mr. BODKIN. No, sir; he said he could not go into that.

Mr. FORDNEY. The State could not give you any such test?

Mr. BODKIN. No.

Mr. FORDNEY. But for a township they could?

Mr. BODKIN. But people living in towns could get a test.

Mr. FORDNEY. People in the city but not the farmers?

Mr. BODKIN. That is correct.

Mr. FORDNEY. Is it possible that such a condition exists in the State of Colorado that a city chap can get favors from the agricultural department of your State when the farmer can not?

Mr. BODKIN. In this case it was.

Mr. FORDNEY. Did you pursue that inquiry any further, and find out whether that man had authority to reject your application? On the other hand, why did you not get some city chap to send your beets there and have them tested—some friend of yours not controlled by the sugar company? Could you not do it in that way?

Mr. BODKIN. Well, there were lots of things we might have done, and we did do lots of things.

Mr. FORDNEY. But you have absolutely failed to have a test made of the sugar content in your beets, except that which was made by the company to whom you sold the beets; is that right?

Mr. BODKIN. No.

Mr. FORDNEY. Then you have had a test made?

Mr. BODKIN. Yes.

Mr. FORDNEY. What did it prove?

Mr. BODKIN. With these same beets we took them to Boulder to the State university, and the chemist said that he would make the test.

Mr. FORDNEY. Did he make it?

Mr. BODKIN. Then he said: "Hold on; I do not know whether I would dare to make that or not." Then he or the president, I would not be certain which, said that they would make the test if they got permission from the Great Western Sugar Co.

Mr. FORDNEY. So the Great Western Sugar Co. controlled that university?

Mr. BODKIN. He said that if he offended them, when he went to ask for an appropriation they would work their influence against his institution.

Mr. FORDNEY. Then you would have the committee understand that that man's opinion is that the Great Western Sugar Co. even controls politics in the State of Colorado?

Mr. BODKIN. I would not say that.

Mr. FORDNEY. That is what he said, was it not?

Mr. BODKIN. If you say controlling politics, it is all right. This is what he said, that if he asked for an appropriation he was afraid they would not get it on account of the sugar company's influence.

Mr. FORDNEY. You said a moment ago that you had had a test of your beets.

Mr. BODKIN. Then the company gave him a permit to test them.

Mr. FORDNEY. The company gave the professor of the University of Colorado permission to make a test of your beets.

Mr. BODKIN. Some member of the company or some man of authority in the Great Western allowed him to give us a test.

Mr. FORDNEY. Who was that man, and what authority have you for making that statement? Do you know that that is true?

Mr. BODKIN. The other member of our committee just told me this. This was a part of his investigation.

Mr. FORDNEY. Do you know that the professor of that university asked for and got permission from the Great Western Sugar Co. to make that test; and if so, who gave that authority?

Mr. BODKIN. J. O. V. Wise just told me that.

Mr. FORDNEY. You do not know whether Wise knew what he was talking about or not, but you believed what he said?

Mr. BODKIN. I do not know that the sun is coming up in the morning, but I believe it.

Mr. FORDNEY. Then you are quite satisfied that he was correct in that statement?

Mr. BODKIN. I am.

Mr. FORDNEY. Then you are of the opinion that you can not get an honest test in your State unless you get permission from the Great Western Co.; is that right?

Mr. BODKIN. No.

Mr. FORDNEY. Then why do you not get it?

Mr. BODKIN. You cover too much territory in your question. We have not tried every place in the State.

Mr. FORDNEY. No; I am simply asking you whether you have had an honest test made of the amount of sugar in the beets you raise and the beets that the people you represent raise; and if so, where did you get it and by whom was it made?

Mr. BODKIN. This one at Boulder is all that we ever got.

Mr. FORDNEY. Well, I would not consider that an honest test, if he could not make the test until he got permission from the sugar company. I would not accept that if I were you.

Mr. BODKIN. I have not accepted any of them.

Mr. FORDNEY. Then you have not had any test made of your beets by any chemist in the State of Colorado, unless permission was obtained from the company to whom you sold your beets?

Mr. BODKIN. No, sir.

Mr. FORDNEY. Do you think you could get such a test made?

Mr. BODKIN. If we could find out where, we certainly would have had it; but, making these two failures, we have not tried any more; and then I proceeded to raise money amongst the farmers to put in a farmers' laboratory.

Mr. FORDNEY. What did the farmers say about that?

Mr. BODKIN. Everybody said all right, but we have not collected the money yet.

Mr. FORDNEY. Then we must understand that you have been unable to get a test made of the sugar content of your beets in the State of Colorado unless permission came from the company for whom you were raising the beets and selling them to?

Mr. BODKIN. That is right.

Mr. FORDNEY. Have you made any effort whatever to have the Federal Government give you an honest test of those beets?

Mr. BODKIN. No.

Mr. FORDNEY. You could do that. All you would have to do would be to request it. Did you know that?

Mr. BODKIN. No, sir.

Mr. FORDNEY. You can do that. Mr. Bodkin, you have testified here about a great many grievances. You say that you have a one-sided contract with the sugar company. Has your land advanced in value since the production of beets began in your State? Have agricultural lands generally advanced in Colorado?

Mr. BODKIN. From the best information we could get on that, we have not advanced as much as most all other places in the United States.

Mr. FORDNEY. Then it is your opinion that farming lands all over the United States have advanced?

Mr. BODKIN. In the last 10 years, a great deal.

Mr. FORDNEY. How long have you been raising beets in Colorado?

Mr. BODKIN. I do not know exactly; something like 10 years.

Mr. FORDNEY. Were average farm lands, such as you can raise beets on, at that time worth $150 an acre?

Mr. BODKIN. No; nor nowhere else that I know of.

Mr. FORDNEY. What was the land worth then?

Mr. BODKIN. Perhaps $80 an acre.

Mr. FORDNEY. You said it is now worth $150, did you not?

Mr. BODKIN. Ordinarily; yes.

Mr. FORDNEY. That is an advance from $80 to $150 an acre for agricultural lands in your State since the growing of beets began; is that right?

Mr. BODKIN. Or since 10 years ago. I would not construe it to the growing of beets.

Mr. FORDNEY. You are not obliged to raise beets for them, are you?

Mr. BODKIN. No, sir.

Mr. FORDNEY. You said yesterday that you were absolutely dependent upon the factory. Now, is it not a fact that the factory is absolutely dependent upon the farmers in your State to raise beets?

Mr. BODKIN. We have gone over that and found out that we are both dependent upon each other.

Mr. FORDNEY. Then when you said yesterday that the farmers were absolutely dependent upon the factory, you want to modify that now and say that one is dependent upon the other?

Mr. BODKIN. I did not know I said that we were not one depending on the other. I did not know I said that.

Mr. FORDNEY. You said yesterday you were absolutely dependent upon the factory.

Mr. RAKER. Mr. Fordney, what I understood him to mean was that when they had grown the beets they were then dependent upon the factory absolutely for the sale of them and for the taking of the beets. Maybe I misunderstood him.

Mr. FORDNEY. He may have meant that. I do not know.

Mr. BODKIN. I certainly did not mean to say we were dependent upon the factory except to sell the beets to them.

Mr. FORDNEY. There is no compulsion on your part to raise the beets?

Mr. BODKIN. No, sir.

Mr. FORDNEY. And when you feel they have mistreated you and that you have not made any money out of your crop, it is reasonable to suppose, then, that you are going to turn your attention to some other crop. Why do you not raise alfalfa? You said yesterday you could make $25 an acre off of alfalfa, and that is more than you made out of your beets. Why do you not raise alfalfa?

Mr. BODKIN. I do not think that is more than I made out of beets.

Mr. FORDNEY. You said yesterday that you only made about $3 an acre off of your beets.

Mr. BODKIN. That is net profit, and did not include the rent and my work by the day. I lived off of that.

Mr. FORDNEY. You said yesterday you could make a net profit of $25 an acre on alfalfa.

Mr. BODKIN. But I would not earn as much money. There would not be as much work for myself on alfalfa. That would be the net profit, of course.

Mr. FORDNEY. Well, you could engage in some other pursuit while you were not raising hay.

Mr. BODKIN. If you would take into account the $20 an acre cash rent, you would notice the difference between the alfalfa and the beet proposition.

Mr. FORDNEY. You have shown that you could make more money out of alfalfa and now you say it only takes you a short time to take care of that crop, and you showed us yesterday that you made from beets only $2 or $3 per acre.

Mr. BODKIN. Three dollars and fifty cents per acre, and I also showed that I got $20 an acre cash rent, making $23.50.

Mr. FORDNEY. Yes; and you were engaged the whole summer in making that.

Mr. BODKIN. And I was getting paid for my work while I was engaged in making that money.

Mr. FORDNEY. In the raising of alfalfa you do the necessary work in a few days and you get $25 an acre and do not have to work all the summer.

Mr. BODKIN. That is the reason I do not raise alfalfa. My days' work then would be only very few.

Mr. FORDNEY. And you would not have anything to do for the balance of the year?

Mr. BODKIN. Not without going away from home; while on the beets I have more employment right at home.

Mr. FORDNEY. Then the beet is the more valuable crop of the two?

Mr. BODKIN. It depends upon how many tons you raise per acre.

Mr. FORDNEY. Well, take your last year's crop. You made more money than you would have made if you had put it in alfalfa and made $25 an acre profit?

Mr. BODKIN. This year; yes, sir.

Mr. FORDNEY. That is what I wanted to know. That is a pretty good crop if you can make more than $25 an acre per year off of your land.

Mr. BODKIN. But I did not make more than $25 per acre. I earned this other money.

Mr. FORDNEY. Yes; I understand that; but you consider that as your profit.

Mr. BODKIN. This money that has been earned?

Mr. FORDNEY. Yes; because you are setting that profit against your profit in alfalfa. You must consider it as profit, then. You would not have earned anything at all if you had not been employed raising beets.

Mr. BODKIN. I would not have worked any at all.

Mr. FORDNEY. Therefore your beet crop is the better crop of the two.

Mr. BODKIN. I would not consider a fellow going out to work for $2 a day that that was a profit. That is wages.

Mr. FORDNEY. Then why do you not raise alfalfa?

Mr. BODKIN. Because there are not many days' work in a season.

Mr. FORDNEY. Then beets are the most profitable crop for you to raise, are they not?

Mr. BODKIN. The crop I raised this year, I said yes.

Mr. FORDNEY. And you have said that you raised below the average crop.

Mr. BODKIN. No; I raised above the average crop.

Mr. FORDNEY. What is the average tonnage per acre of beets raised in the State of Colorado?

Mr. BODKIN. Ten and one-third tons.

Mr. FORDNEY. Ten and one-third tons per acre; but under a very high state of cultivation, such as you gave them, you raised 12¾ tons to the acre?

Mr. BODKIN. Yes, sir.

Mr. FORDNEY. What is the largest amount per acre raised in the State under a high state of cultivation? Do you know?

Mr. BODKIN. Well, those things, you know, are a little like the chemist at Boulder; it is hearsay, you know. I have heard of all the way up to 30 tons.

Mr. FORDNEY. Do you believe that is right?

Mr. BODKIN. I believe it is very easily possible for 30 tons to grow per acre.

Mr. FORDNEY. You said you believed the other statement because you believed it was as much so as that the sun would rise to-morrow. Therefore you must believe all you hear if you are going to believe anything.

Mr. BODKIN. In that particular case I believe it because we went over it so much, and I understand it from start to finish. That is why I believed it when he told me.

Mr. FORDNEY. Mr. Bodkin, you stated yesterday that the sugar company's profit out of the sugar extracted from the beets which you raised was $8 per acre.

Mr. BODKIN. I said $8 per ton.

Mr. FORDNEY. Yes; that is right, $8 per ton. How do you figure that?

Mr. BODKIN. I do not pretend to say that myself, only some of our people have done that figuring, and that is the information I get; and it is not far off, in my opinion.

Mr. FORDNEY. Mr. Bodkin, if your beets tested 15 per cent sugar, that would mean 300 pounds of sugar in the beets per ton. The factory only gets about 85 per cent of the sugar out of the beets, some a little more, some a little less, but 85 per cent of the saccharine matter in the beets is a fair average of extraction. Now, in order for the company to make $8 per ton, they would have to make 3.1 cents per pound profit on their sugar, in order to make $8 per ton in the extraction of 85 per cent of 15 per cent sugar in the beets. Do you think they make that much money? They will have to make a profit of 3.1 cents per pound for 250 pounds of sugar per ton. Do you think they make that much profit?

Mr. BODKIN. I can not see why that statement is right.

Mr. FORDNEY. Well, I want you or some other man to show me that this statement is not right—that when the test shows 15 per cent saccharine matter in beets, if all that saccharine matter were extracted and converted into sugar, it would only make 300 pounds of sugar from 2,000 pounds of beets. Twice 15 is 30. Now, when they extract but 85 per cent of that and convert it into sugar, which is what the average factory in the country does, they get 85 per cent of 300 pounds or 255 pounds.

Mr. BODKIN. Wouldn't you have a right to show me that when they read the polariscope as a beet running 15 per cent that they do not read the polariscope as sugar in the sack and no 85 per cent to it?

Mr. FORDNEY. Oh, no.

Mr. BODKIN. Well, then, we could not say anything.

Mr. FORDNEY. You misunderstand me. It does not mean sugar in the sack.

Mr. BODKIN. Our understanding is that it does, and Mr. Dickson will close up the books mighty quick when you approach him on the subject.

Mr. FORDNEY. You mean he does not want you to know how much sugar is in your beets?

Mr. BODKIN. When you say "Are you not reading sugar in the sack, Mr. Dickson?" he closes up the book and turns red in the face.

Mr. FORDNEY. Do you mean to say that when the chemist extracts the saccharine matter from the beet and shows this 15 per cent sugar of the total content of that beet, that he means sugar in the bag?

Mr. BODKIN. I mean to say that I do not know what he means.

Mr. FORDNEY. I mean to say that I do know that that is not what he means, although I am not a chemist. He means that there is a certain percentage of sugar in that beet; that the beet weighs so much, and that there is enough saccharine matter in that beet to make so many pounds or ounces of sugar. That is all his test could show. They might make molasses out of it, and maybe they are not going to put it into sugar in sacks.

Mr. BODKIN. When it comes to that, I would say that I do not know, but we have some good ideas.

Mr. FORDNEY. I know that those figures are correct. I know enough about the sugar-beet business in my State to know that is right.

Mr. BODKIN. I am speaking of Colorado.

Mr. FORDNEY. Well, they are human and white in Colorado, and you have about the same kind of people that we have in Michigan. They are good people in Michigan. Have you got any better people in Colorado?

Mr. BODKIN. I do not know.

Mr. FORDNEY. Well, neither do I.

Mr. MALBY. Mr. Fordney, is not the test made with the beet itself as a whole?

Mr. FORDNEY. Yes, sir.

Mr. MALBY. And the test is applied to the whole beet.

Mr. FORDNEY. The beet is weighed and the sugar is extracted from that beet by a chemical process.

Mr. MALBY. The beet is sliced and ground up so that the emulsion is tested as to the amount of saccharine matter?

Mr. FORDNEY. The beet is weighed, and the test shows how much sugar is contained in it. For instance, suppose a beet weighed a pound. Fifteen per cent of that pound shows to be sugar, and that is the test; that is, 15 per cent of the total contents of the beet is sugar, and 85 per cent vegetable matter or water or whatever it is.

Mr. MALBY. Is the test made of the beet itself or of the result of the beet when manufactured into sugar?

Mr. FORDNEY. No; the beet is tested by the chemist before it is manufactured.

Mr. MALBY. That was my understanding of it, but I did not know.

Mr. FORDNEY. Now, Mr. Bodkin, taking 15 per cent beets, such as you produced there, 255 pounds of sugar extracted by the company at $5.77 per ton, which is the price paid by the Western Sugar Co., as given to me in a statement furnished me by a gentleman—you say that they paid you $5.75, and that is within 2 cents of the average amount they paid for beets last year.

Mr. BODKIN. You refer to our company last year?

Mr. FORDNEY. This last year; yes.

Mr. BODKIN. Yes.

Mr. FORDNEY. You say you got $5.75 for your crop of beets?

Mr. BODKIN. Yes, sir.

Mr. FORDNEY. The average paid by that company for all the beets they purchased during that season was $5.77, as given to me, so you received very close to the average price. Two hundred and fifty-five pounds of sugar on the basis of $5.77 per ton for those beets is $2.26 per hundred pounds for the sugar in the beets delivered at the factory. That is what the company paid you for the sugar content of your beets. Now, it costs about $1.50 per hundred pounds to manufacture that into sugar, making a total of $3.76. That is very close to the average in the State of Michigan for costs last year. Now then, in order to make 3.1 cents per pound profit, which would give them a profit of $8 per ton on your beets, as you stated yesterday, they would have to make 3.1 cents per pound profit. Do you think they made that much? They would have to have sold their sugar at $7.65 per hundred pounds. Do you think that statement is correct which you made yesterday, that they made $8 per ton profit off of every ton of beets you delivered to them?

Mr. BODKIN. It would not be, according to your figures.

Mr. FORDNEY. Have you any reason to doubt the accuracy of those figures?

Mr. BODKIN. I would say that I have not much to do with them. I am not opposing the sugar company nor the sugar business. I did not come here for that at all.

Mr. FORDNEY. Then what did you come here for?

Mr. BODKIN. I came here because our beet growers of Colorado wanted me to come and see if we could not get a little bit more money from the Great Western.

Mr. FORDNEY. Do you think this committee can get you anything more for your beets from the Great Western people? Do you think this committee can aid you in any way in getting more money out of them by your coming here and testifying that you discredit the correctness of their tests and claim that an honest test can not be obtained by you from any chemist that you have tried on account of the influence of that sugar company; and also exaggerating their profit, as I think you do—not dishonestly, I do not accuse you of that, my friend, because I think you are misguided in your judgment and in your figures. For instance, here is this morning's Washington Post, which says:

PEONAGE IN COLORADO.

Witness says slum derelicts toil in sugar industry—Sensation at House hearing—Men, women, and children labor from 10 to 16 hours a day at "back-breaking work" in beet fields, James Bodkin tells committee—Are kept in state of bondage.

That statement is going out to the people and that will undoubtedly go to the Great Western Sugar Co. as your statement.

Mr. BODKIN. That is old to them. They have heard and know of that.

Mr. FORDNEY. Do you expect to get greater favors from them by making that statement about them than you would if you were to go to them and make an honest appeal to justice?

Mr. BODKIN. Do you think that is not honest? Go out there and take a look.

Mr. FORDNEY. I am talking about an honest appeal to them.

Mr. BODKIN. I did not make these statements except that you people wanted to know what kind of people we had out there. I am not saying anything against those people. This year, when my son had his chums hired in the beet field and was paying them $2.25 a day and they did not want to work for that any longer, I told him not to raise their wages, to let them go, that "there are plenty of Russians getting idle now and we can get some of them who do want to do the work."

Mr. FORDNEY. Mr. Bodkin, I may be misquoting the meaning of your statement here, but I take it for granted that you are exceedingly hostile to that sugar company.

Mr. BODKIN. That is altogether a mistake. I have done that sugar company lots of favors.

Mr. FORDNEY. Well, you are not doing them very much of a favor here.

Mr. BODKIN. I am, if you do not misconstrue it and pick into it and draw out things I do not mean.

Mr. FORDNEY. I would not do that under any circumstances.

Mr. BODKIN. I am so little interested that I am not protecting myself in any way against you sugar people.

Mr. FORDNEY. Do you think that I am hostile to your industry?

Mr. BODKIN. It appears that way.

Mr. FORDNEY. I do not think your industry has a greater friend on the face of the earth than you have in me, sir.

Mr. BODKIN. You mean the sugar end of it?

Mr. FORDNEY. I mean the sugar industry.

Mr. BODKIN. The beet growers is my end of it, if I have any choice.

Mr. FORDNEY. The beet growers' end of it is my end of it. I represent an agricultural district.

Mr. BODKIN. Then I am mistaken.

Mr. FORDNEY. If you misjudge me in that way, you are mistaken. If you judge that I am hostile to the farmers' end of the production of beet sugar in this country, you are greatly mistaken.

Mr. BODKIN. And so are you if you think I am against the Great Western.

Mr. FORDNEY. Well, I would take your statements as being hostile. You have said here, and it has gone into the record in print, that the Great Western Sugar Co. makes $8 per ton profit out of every ton of beets they purchase from you, and that you have practically made no profit, and you have asked them to divide with you by giving you $1 more per ton, which they have refused to do.

Mr. BODKIN. That is exactly what I mean, but by your figures, they do not make that much.

Mr. FORDNEY. No.

Mr. BODKIN. Our figures are different.

Mr. FORDNEY. What are your figures?

Mr. BODKIN. We have got a whole cigar box full of them, but I am not prepared to give them. We have other people here who may go into the figures. I do not expect to do any of that. I just came here to show what I raised this summer and what I did, and these other things—I tried to forget them a year ago. But we have got some other people who perhaps have not forgotten them.

Mr. MALBY. Mr. Bodkin, what the committee wants to know, and what Congressman Fordney is trying to develop, is what are your figures—not what you have been told or what you think or believe, but what is your mathematical calculation? What enables you to arrive at the conclusion that the Great Western Sugar Co. is able to make $8 a ton profit? How do you develop those results? If you can tell us we would be very glad to have you do so.

Mr. BODKIN. I have got another witness along for that. You have got me all off of my line.

Mr. MALBY. If you can not give us that, very well.

Mr. FORDNEY. Mr. Bodkin, what I am trying to find out is what interest you represent; who brought you here; what influence brought you here; what demand brought you here; who gave information to the chairman that you would be a valuable man to bring here, and what sort of testimony you would give or be expected to give?

Mr. BODKIN. You want to know that?

Mr. FORDNEY. Yes, sir; I want to know that.

Mr. BODKIN. Our beet growers heard of this committee coming to Denver, and all around they appointed people to try to get to meet the committee in Denver, and I was one of the appointees who received an appointment along with others, and when we found they could not come to Denver, then they urged that our attorney try to get the committee to allow some of our beet growers to meet this committee, and asked that they send one member of your committee to Denver to take our evidence. Then I think our people sent some of our beet literature to the chairman. I would not be certain about that; but he wrote them a letter along the lines I stated. The growers of our district wanted to be represented, and knew that the Great Western Co. would represent themselves, and have a decoy farmer to represent the farmers and through him criticize. They wanted us to have a man here, and then they picked on me to give the farmers' side of the proposition of what it costs to grow beets. I knew these averages and everything changed so that I told them I would give what it cost me to grow my beets. These other averages are all chopped to pieces because one fellow maybe has nothing and another fellow beside him might have 25 tons on an acre or two, and there is no place to draw an average except by the whole State. Then there is a lot of bad stuff on account of the way beets are harvested and the way beets are planted, and then they strike an average and it runs along about 10 tons per acre.

Mr. FORDNEY. Mr. Bodkin, when you say you have tried through the University of Colorado and through the agricultural department of Colorado to have a chemical analysis made of the sugar content in the beets that you or your associate raised, and you have failed to get it without the consent of the Great Western Sugar Co., there is nothing left for me to understand but that the University of Colorado and the agricultural department of Colorado are corrupted by unjust influences of this Great Western Co. Do you think I can draw any other inference from your statement?

Mr. BODKIN. No; but I don't see that I ought to sanction that again. I have told you just what happened, and then you construe it to suit yourself without my saying anything. Whatever way you construe it, that is right.

Mr. FORDNEY. Then we will have to let that go as it stands. I am sorry I must leave you with the impression on my mind that the Great Western Sugar Co. in Colorado are so strong and have such influence that they absolutely control your university and your agricultural department, and in the three attempts you have made to have a test made of the sugar in your beets you have found their influences at work, which have barred you from getting an independent test. I need not ask you anything further about the manufacturer's profit, because you have stated that in your opinion—I will put it in that way—the Great Western Sugar Co. has made a profit of $8 per ton off the beets delivered by you. I believe Mr. Willett gave it as his opinion day before yesterday, and presented figures for it, that the profit made by the beet-sugar manufacturers of the country was 1.1 cents per pound, the difference between the cost and the price obtained for their sugar. That would make a very great difference, being about one-third of the amount of profit that you claim they have paid. The increased value of land in the State of Colorado you do not believe is due to the beet crop raised in that country, although there has been an increase in the value of agricultural land in the last 10 years from $80 to $150 per acre.

Mr. BODKIN. There and other places as well.

Mr. FORDNEY. All over the United States?

Mr. BODKIN. I learn so. We have it thrown in our faces many times when we bring up the sugar business that we are way behind the times, and when the people go to uphold the sugar business in our country they talk as you do.

Mr. FORDNEY. The farmers or the manufacturers?

Mr. BODKIN. The hired agents, and so forth, of the Great Western Co. According to them all of our benefits grow out of the sugar business.

Mr. FORDNEY. Then you think I talk exactly like a hired agent of the Great Western Sugar Co. of Colorado?

Mr. BODKIN. Quite a good deal, sir.

Mr. FORDNEY. I am glad you put it in that way. You think I am a paid agent or talk like one?

Mr. BODKIN. No; I did not say that.

Mr. FORDNEY. But you think I talk like one?

Mr. BODKIN. I said so.

Mr. FORDNEY. I am paid by the Federal Government to try and get the honest facts in this matter, so that when this question is presented by this committee to Congress and their recommendations are made, I want to have something to present as given by intelligent men that know what they are talking about. Do you know what profit the Great Western Sugar Co. made out of a ton of beets delivered by you to them?

Mr. BODKIN. No. Could I ask you do you know any such thing?

Mr. FORDNEY. I am not engaged in the business and you are. I am not supposed to know that. Ask me something about lumber and I can tell you.

Mr. BODKIN. I am not engaged in the sugar end of it.

Mr. FORDNEY. Oh, yes; you are raising sugar beets.

Mr. BODKIN. That is not the sugar end; that is the grower's end of it.

Mr. FORDNEY. But that is where the sugar starts from, in the grower's end of it. Now, you have told us that you got so much per acre from your beets. Are not the tops worth something to you?

Mr. BODKIN. Yes, sir.

Mr. FORDNEY. How much per acre?

Mr. BODKIN. I sold mine this year for $3.75.

Mr. FORDNEY. Then this profit of $3.50 per acre over and above the cost of production of your beets, was that the total profit you got out of your crop, or did you get an additional $3.75 for the beet tops?

Mr. BODKIN. That is pasture in the field, and of course it is worth a little more than in other crops.

Mr. FORDNEY. Mr. Bodkin, as I understood you yesterday, the sugar company have led you to believe that unless they have adequate protection in the way of a duty on foreign imported sugar they can not run and pay you the prices for sugar beets they now pay you; is that right?

Mr. BODKIN. No. We believe they would not pay us the price, not that they could not.

Mr. FORDNEY. Then how do you feel about the Federal Government maintaining a duty on sugar? Do you want it continued under present conditions?

Mr. BODKIN. I do.

Mr. FORDNEY. You are in favor of a duty on sugar?

Mr. BODKIN. Yes, sir.

Mr. FORDNEY. You and I are getting together now. We are not enemies by any means.

Mr. BODKIN. I could show you why, and then we would be enemies again.

Mr. FORDNEY. Oh, no; we would not. I would not quarrel with you for any reason you might have. Do you want to tell us why you are in favor of a duty on sugar?

Mr. BODKIN. No; I do not want to particularly.

Mr. FORDNEY. You are just in favor of retaining the duty, anyway?

Mr. BODKIN. Yes; I thought maybe you would want to know why I am in favor of it.

Mr. FORDNEY. Yes; I would like to know why. I want all the facts in this case.

Mr. BODKIN. I believe I stated that yesterday. We figure that as it is the Great Western is paying us this price, and if there was no tariff they would not pay up any more money; and he said that if they took off the tariff, then he could never get the farmers to raise the beets, and therefore he had to make money while he could.

Mr. FORDNEY. Who made that statement to you?

Mr. BODKIN. Chester Morey.

Mr. FORDNEY. Chester Morey?

Mr. BODKIN. Chester Morey, the president of the Great Western Sugar Co. Then we figure that if the tariff was taken off he would still tighten down on us, instead of loosening up, but if he would loosen up one of those dollars we would cover him up with beets, and perhaps it would not hurt the welfare of the Nation.

Mr. FORDNEY. But he did not loosen up with that dollar?

Mr. BODKIN. No; but we have got him in a fair way.

Mr. FORDNEY. Well, that is good, and I am glad to hear it. You should have your fair share of profit in the business.

Mr. BODKIN. That is all we have got to say concerning the tariff. If we could get a little of it we would favor the tariff, and we favor the tariff in hopes to get a little of it, because we need it.

Mr. FORDNEY. Mr. Bodkin, are you a Republican or a Democrat in your politics?

Mr. BODKIN. I am nothing.

Mr. FORDNEY. Oh, yes, you are.

Mr. BODKIN. I vote first for one and then for another, always trying to look for something good.

Mr. FORDNEY. You look like an intelligent fellow, and I would take you to be a Republican.

Mr. BODKIN. No; just as good people as you have talked the other way to me, and that keeps me straddling the fence.

Mr. FORDNEY. I will accept that as one on me. You say you are straddling the fence, but you are a protectionist on sugar. You are like the sugar growers of Louisiana. They all vote the Democratic ticket and come up here and pray that their party may fail in their efforts to remove the duty on sugar. Mr. Bodkin, about what percentage of the labor employed in the beet fields are these "degraded laborers" that you spoke of yesterday?

Mr. MALBY. I think, Congressman Fordney, that the designating of the labor being "degraded" is hardly according to the facts.

Mr. FORDNEY. Well, I do not want to put it in that way unless that is what he stated.

Mr. MALBY. We have no degraded labor in the United States. It is all free labor, and all labor is well paid.

Mr. FORDNEY. Then the paper misquotes him, and I understood him just as the newspapers did:

> Witness says slum derelicts toil in sugar industry. Men, women, and children labor from 10 to 16 hours a day at back-breaking work in beet fields.

Mr. BODKIN. That is all right. There is no misquotation about that.

Mr. FORDNEY. It says here that the witness said: "Slum derelicts toil in sugar industry."

Mr. BODKIN. I said that these agents went among the slums to get the poor people. Because a man is poor you consider him a degraded man. We do not consider him such.

Mr. FORDNEY. No; do not put that word in my mouth by any means.

Mr. BODKIN. Where did they get this degraded stuff? I never quoted that. I said they go among the slums and get the poor people.

Mr. FORDNEY. You will have to interview the newspaper reporter. I did not give it to him.

Mr. BODKIN. Did I?

Mr. FORDNEY. He takes it from your testimony given here yesterday, I presume.

Mr. BODKIN. I do not think I ever talked any about a degraded man. I said they go in the slums and get the poor people. Because a man lives in the slums and is poor, the paper then says he is a degraded man, does it?

Mr. FORDNEY. Because a man is poor is no reason he is a slum.

Mr. BODKIN. I said they go in the slums.

Mr. FORDNEY. You mean then that he goes in the districts of the poor people and gets the better class of them?

Mr. BODKIN. He gets any class he can, but when he goes in a district of poor people and gets any class, that is all he can do—get any man that will do this work.

Mr. FORDNEY. I would not say because a man is poor he belongs to the slums. I would infer from the word "slum" that it means the worst class of people we have in the country, not because they are poor at all. Plenty of poor people live right in your community and in every State in the Union, and are good, honest people. Because they are poor is no reason why they are dishonest or slums.

Mr. BODKIN. I might have used the word "slums," but that is what the field agent said, that they go in the slums. That is all I know about that.

Mr. FORDNEY. Do you know about what percentage of that class of people are employed in your fields?

Mr. BODKIN. I could not say.

Mr. FORDNEY. Is it a large or small percentage?

Mr. BODKIN. When they grow lots of beets, then the percentage is more than when they grow a few beets. Some of these people have lived out amongst us until they are not slums, but they still do the work.

Mr. FORDNEY. Mr. Bodkin, in the beet fields of the State of Michigan the farmers and their wives and their children do the heft of the work, and we only have contract labor in that State where a man cultivates a large number of acres of beets. Then he contracts it to some parties, and in some instances, I have been told, that Russians have been brought there from your State to contract for the growing of beets in the State of Michigan, and that they are very efficient labor indeed, and the price paid to those people for doing all the handwork that you spoke of yesterday—in fact doing everything except teamwork—is $20 per acre, in the State of Michigan. Twenty dollars per acre includes the cost of preparing the beets to be loaded onto the wagons to go to the shipping point, and all the cultivating, all the thinning, and all the work of every description except teamwork.

Mr. BODKIN. Would they not use a team to the cultivator? Would not that be considered teamwork?

Mr. FORDNEY. Whatever teamwork is necessary the owner of the land furnishes, and all the handwork is done for $20 per acre.

Mr. BODKIN. I have not any handwork at all in my statement here. It is all teamwork and irrigating.

Mr. MALBY. Is your hoeing teamwork, too?

Mr. BODKIN. No; the handwork is thinning, and they first block them and do the thinning, and then in a month afterwards they go on and hoe them, just chop out the weeds, and so forth; that is the second hoeing. Then there is the third hoeing, and if the beets are big, the labor contract provides that they will pull the weeds out instead of hoeing them. That is the $10 summer work, and then there is the fall work when the farmer plows them out with his beet puller. Then their handwork commences, gathering them and throwing them in place and cutting the tops off and throwing the beets in a pile ready to be loaded.

Mr. FORDNEY. In your statement yesterday you did give handwork, and so described it, and you were asked what you meant by handwork. You said handwork was $20 per acre.

Mr. BODKIN. Yes, sir; that is what I am talking about. That is, topping and thinning and blocking and hoeing. That is what we hire the Russians for. I just told what handwork was. In my statement, itemized, there was no handwork. The handwork was given at the top of the list as $20 per acre, that we pay the Russians, so to speak.

The CHAIRMAN. In other words, he means to say that he did not give an itemized statement of the handwork. The cost of the handwork was included in your statement, Mr. Bodkin?

Mr. BODKIN. Yes.

Mr. FORDNEY. Yes.

Mr. BODKIN. Handwork is $20 per acre, plowing $2.50 per acre, harrowing 80 cents per acre.

Mr. FORDNEY. A portion of each of those is handwork, is it not?

Mr. BODKIN. Harrowing handwork? In harrowing I have four horses. There are no horses used on the handwork.

Mr. FORDNEY. Well, does somebody drive the horses or do they drive themselves?

Mr. BODKIN. Somebody drives them, of course, but that is not handwork.

Mr. FORDNEY. This is what I am talking about. In Michigan all of the work in the field is done for $20 an acre, except what the horses do.

Mr. BODKIN. We have four horses on a harrow, heavy harrowing, as I said yesterday.

Mr. FORDNEY. That is not what I am talking about. You might have six horses, and you would still have to have somebody to drive them.

Mr. BODKIN. Yes; and if you only had one horse you would have to have somebody to drive him. That would be a team.

Mr. FORDNEY. I do not care how many horses you have on that harrow. Three horses might pull it or four horses might pull it or five horses might pull it. I mentioned nothing about that. I am talking about the human labor put upon it, not the horse work. You have said it cost you $20 for handwork, and for plowing, $2.50. Part of that plowing was handwork.

Mr. BODKIN. Part of that plowing handwork?

Mr. FORDNEY. Do you not have somebody to drive the team?

Mr. BODKIN. I never had a team out but what I had somebody to drive it.

Mr. FORDNEY. That is it, exactly.

Mr. BODKIN. Yes; that is team work.

Mr. FORDNEY. Then what is the horse work? Is there not a difference between horse work——

Mr. BODKIN. You are talking about a separate team, without a driver.

Mr. FORDNEY. I am trying to get an intelligent understanding as to what it costs you to raise an acre of beets there, and what kind of work you do on it, horse work or human work.

Mr. BODKIN. We call team work including a driver.

Mr. FORDNEY. Yes.

Mr. BODKIN. We have a driver whenever we take out a team. The work of those Russians has nothing to do with our horses.

Mr. FORDNEY. Besides the $20 handwork, you furnish a team and the man to drive it?

Mr. BODKIN. Yes.

Mr. FORDNEY. You have a team to do the plowing, and a man to drive it?

Mr. BODKIN. Yes.

Mr. FORDNEY. That is so on all those things?

Mr. BODKIN. Yes.

Mr. MALBY. Then the $20 for handwork does not include any work where a team is used?

Mr. BODKIN. No, sir; it is handwork.

Mr. FORDNEY. The planting and cultivating and ditching mentioned two or three times over there in your estimate is all extra work over and above this $20 per acre handwork?

Mr. BODKIN. Yes.

Mr. FORDNEY. If you do not find it profitable to raise beets, there is no power on earth to compel you to raise them, in your State, is there?

Mr. BODKIN. No.

Mr. FORDNEY. That is all. Perhaps some other members have some questions they want to ask.

Mr. MALBY. There is only one thing I want to ask you about. It occurs to me that this item of $20 per acre for handwork, in view of your detailed statement as to the other work, is a little large. Could you give us some of the items that make up that $20 an acre, excluding your seed and plowing and harrowing and planting and cultivating and ditching and irrigation? Twenty dollars would strike me as being a little large for a lump sum.

Mr. BODKIN. For that handwork?

Mr. MALBY. What does that handwork consist of; I mean, in a general way?

Mr. BODKIN. We have got the statement here that contains it. I might misquote it a few cents. I have never looked at one. My son has tended my beets.

Mr. MALBY. Give it in a general way; that is all I want.

Mr. BODKIN. The blocking, I think, is $2 per acre, and the thinning is $4 per acre, which makes $6 for the blocking and thinning; that is, the first time over. Then the second harrowing is $2.50 per acre and the third harrowing $1.50 per acre. I think that is right—the way it is proportioned. That makes $10 for the summer work. The fall work is when the beets are plowed out with a beet puller. The handwork is then to gather all of those beets and throw them in piles. Then they clean away a place of clods and cut the tops off of these beets and throw them on this cleaned-away ground. So far as that being a little high is concerned, the first beets that I ever raised I went out to see if I and my boys could not tend them without hiring it done. I worked something like two hours and then I went to figuring up how much it was going to cost me. I found that it would take $60 an acre on the first time over. I sat right down there and gave my boy a contract for it for $20 an acre to go ahead and I went to the house. If you think that that $20 an acre is too much, I would say that there are only a few people that can do that, and they have got to have a lot of cheap labor in their family.

Mr. MALBY. I thought it was high, without any explanation. What I wanted was the explanation of the matter.

Mr. BODKIN. When you take a lot of beets and think how they have to be fingered over and so on, and come to see where your profit is, you will see how it is; it will not be distributed among Americans, I can tell you that. If they do it, it will be more like $40 an acre.

Mr. FORDNEY. Americans in Michigan do it for $20 an acre and deliver the beets on cars.

Mr. BODKIN. That is the reason that you and I are so far apart.

Mr. FORDNEY. I do not know, Mr. Bodkin, that that is right.

Mr. BODKIN. Well, it certainly is.

Mr. FORDNEY. Mr. Chairman, will you permit me to say just a word at this point?

The CHAIRMAN. Certainly.

Mr. FORDNEY. Before you came in I made a statement which I wish to repeat now. This is the only witness that this committee has called upon to give testimony here who is a beet grower, and his testimony as to the cost per acre of raising beets in Colorado differs so widely from my understanding of the cost—and I have a pretty fair idea of it, I think—in the State of Michigan, and some of the factories in the State of Michigan, it has been stated here before this committee, are owned, or some of the stock in some of the factories in the State of Michigan is owned, by the American Sugar Refining Co. The American Sugar Refining Co., if I am correctly informed, has stock in those companies. I am under the impression that this witness has been brought here to show how unfairly the owners of those factories deal with the farmers, and I would like to have some of the farmers from the State of Michigan who raise beets for the factories in which this same American Sugar Refining Co. is interested in the State of Michigan come here and testify. The testimony of this witness is so different, in my opinion, from what the testimony will be of farmers from Michigan, none of whom I have in mind—but there are 20,000 farmers in our State, or more than that number, raising beets—that I would like to have some of the farmers from our State also give testimony along that line, or find out what this man was brought here for.

The CHAIRMAN. These gentlemen who appear here to testify, who are residents of the State of Colorado, and who are supposed to be, and who I suppose without doubt are, beet-sugar farmers, are here because they applied to the chairman to be heard as farmers.

Mr. FORDNEY. Did this gentleman apply or his organization?

The CHAIRMAN. His organization, as I started to state, if you will allow me to complete the statement——

Mr. FORDNEY. I beg your pardon.

The CHAIRMAN. The Farmers' Union of Colorado applied to the chairman to be heard on the proposition that the beet-sugar factory had not treated fairly the farmers who raised sugar beets; and, as we were specifically directed to inquire as to whether or not the present conditions had caused or tended to cause unfair treatment of the farmers—of the producers, rather—by the beet-sugar factories, the chairman felt that it was his duty to hear evidence, especially when it was represented to him that the evidence would be of a character entirely different from what had been formerly presented to the committee; by Mr. Morey, for instance, from Colorado. Personally, I would say this: Of course it will depend on the committee, and every member of the committee will have just as much voice in it as the chair, and possibly more than the chair.

Mr. FORDNEY. Not at all.

The CHAIRMAN. I am willing, within any reasonable limitations, to hear all the witnesses on any side.

Mr. FORDNEY. Understand me, I do not want to prolong it.

The CHAIRMAN. Yes; I am willing to hear witnesses on any side of any pertinent issue that was raised in the course of these hearings; and while I think that we have got just about enough hearings laid out to last us through this week, and just about enough testimony to last until Saturday night, nevertheless, if after Christmas, when the committee reconvenes, any of the Michigan beet farmers or any of the California sugar-beet farmers, or anybody else wants to be heard by this committee, we will hear them, so far as I am concerned. So far as I am concerned, I will not close my ears to any voice that comes to the committee.

Mr. FORDNEY. With your permission, then, I will ask some of the farmers who raise beets, both for the factories in which the American Sugar Refining Co. have stock and the so-called independent factories, to come here and show what treatment they get.

The CHAIRMAN. All right; we will be very glad to hear them.

Mr. MALBY. And in particular what it costs per acre to produce the beets, and the number of tons produced per acre.

Mr. FORDNEY. Yes.

The CHAIRMAN. We will be very glad to hear them. I am going away.

Mr. MALBY. And also the percentage of sugar in the beets.

Mr. FORDNEY. And how they arrive at that percentage.

Mr. MALBY. Yes.

Mr. FORDNEY. We have had some trouble on that.

The CHAIRMAN. It is my intention to be absent for some time to come, after Saturday; but if the committee, or any three members of the committee, will go on and take the testimony, I will be delighted.

Mr. FORDNEY. You mean after the holidays?

The CHAIRMAN. No; right now.

Mr. FORDNEY. I could not get the men here before the holidays very well.

The CHAIRMAN. That being true, I will say that we will hear any evidence that any member of the committee wants brought before the committee.

Mr. FORDNEY. Thank you very much, Mr. Chairman.

The CHAIRMAN. With this one exception. It will cost to bring witnesses from Michigan probably $200 or $300 apiece, and unless we are satisfied, the same as the committee has been satisfied in other cases, that we are justified in incurring the expense, that these witnesses will testify to facts pertinent to the investigation which will give the committee some new light on matters, we do not want to incur the expense; but if it is something we want to hear, we will hear them, and we will subpœna your witnesses at any time.

Mr. RAKER. May I make this suggestion, which may be applied subsequently to one or two of the other Western States? It seems to me in a matter of that kind that two or three witnesses might be enough.

The CHAIRMAN. Yes; just one moment. For instance, these gentlemen in Colorado wanted me to subpœna six or eight or nine witnesses, and it costs $300 or $400 apiece to bring those witnesses here, so I said, "Just send us two or three."

Mr. FORDNEY. Yes. Let me set myself clear, here. I have no other purpose in view but the one, and that is to lend all the aid in my power for the encouragement of the growth, the increase of the industry, and the production of sugar in the United States. This committee, as I understood it, were appointed to investigate the sugar trusts of the country, and so on. We are making an honest effort to do that, and I think we have some very valuable information. As I before stated, the six factories in the State of Michigan which I have in mind, the Michigan Sugar Co.'s factories, are partly owned—the stock of that company is partly owned— by the American Sugar Refining Co., one of the refining companies which are being investigated here. If this investigation is to reach out to the ends of all the interests belonging to the American Sugar Refining Co., then it affects those six factories in the State of Michigan.

The CHAIRMAN. It undoubtedly will, Mr. Fordney.

Mr. FORDNEY. Yes. Therefore this testimony is quite damaging to the concern in Colorado, I am frank to admit, exceedingly damaging.

The CHAIRMAN. I have not heard the evidence this morning.

Mr. FORDNEY. We heard something very startling, both yesterday and to-day.

The CHAIRMAN. Yes.

Mr. FORDNEY. I want the farmers who furnish beets to those factories in the State of Michigan to come here and testify. I am not interested in the American Sugar Refining Co., not in the least, nor have I a dollar's worth of stock in any of them.

The CHAIRMAN. We know you are disinterested, Mr. Fordney.

Mr. FORDNEY. And I want to get all the information we can get, to enable us to reach a just conclusion.

The CHAIRMAN. So far as the Chair is concerned, I assure you we will afford you all the facilities possible.

Mr. FORDNEY. I will furnish you the names of some of the men who might be called.

The CHAIRMAN. Now I would suggest, as I have many times before, that you should try not to duplicate.

Mr. FORDNEY. I assure you, sir, I will avoid that.

The CHAIRMAN. And try to have your witnesses here as soon after the holidays as possible.

Mr. FORDNEY. Yes.

The CHAIRMAN. I would like to say this: This committee was limited by the resolution of the House to $25,000 for its expenses. The expenses we have so far incurred, independent of these supplemental hearings, which we are holding now, have been about $9,000.

Mr. FORDNEY. That is doing fine.

The CHAIRMAN. I think we have done pretty well.

Mr. FORDNEY. If you need more money, Mr. Chairman, I will join with you in requesting it.

The CHAIRMAN. That includes the printing, I think; so that we have any reasonable amount of money we need for expenses; and it is the purpose of the Chair, and it will be the endeavor of the Chair to treat any gentleman on the committee, regardless of politics or locality or geographical location, with fairness.

Mr. FORDNEY. I believe that is so.

The CHAIRMAN. Thank you. I hope you gentlemen will remember this, that we must avoid duplicating, as much as possible. For instance, the Farmers' Union of Colorado wanted to send us a dozen or a half a dozen or more witnesses. Now, Mr. Fordney, do not send us a whole lot of witnesses from Michigan, every one of whom will follow after the other and testify to the same thing.

Mr. FORDNEY. No; I will aim, Mr. Chairman, to get somebody here from Michigan who is more than the ordinary grower of beets; that is, more than the ordinary farmer.

The CHAIRMAN. You understand the general situation.

Mr. FORDNEY. I mean the ordinary grower who has only 3 or 4 or 5 acres.

The CHAIRMAN. You understand, any witnesses you want called, your desire will receive as much attention as the desire of the chairman. We want to hear anybody you want heard.

Mr. FORDNEY. Yes.

Mr. RAKER. Of course the question of expense is important, and I want to avoid unnecessary expense as much as possible, but I feel that the committee is in duty bound to hear testimony in regard to the conditions of farmers and producers in the Philippines and the Hawaiian Islands. That is a matter we ought not to overlook in this investigation.

(Informal conversation followed, which the stenographer was directed not to take.)

Mr. RAKER. I think I will be able to get a man who is familiar with conditions of labor and of work and contracts, and the whole situation over there, who can testify from the producer's standpoint, so that in addition to Mr. Balleu's testimony we might get both sides of this matter fairly presented before the committee.

The CHAIRMAN. I will say to you just what I have said to Mr. Fordney. I think the purpose of the investigation is to be fair to everybody and every interest, and from every angle; but we do not want to prolong this thing unduly.

Mr. RAKER. I think I know a man who can produce this information without going out of Washington.

The CHAIRMAN. We will now resume the examination of the witness.

Mr. RAKER. Just one question I want to ask, if the other members are through. Mr. Bodkin, what chance has the man who grows beets on his own responsibility, without any contract or any arrangement with the Great Western Sugar Co., to sell his beets to that company without a prior agreement, in advance, with them, before he plants, cultivates, and harvests his crop?

Mr. BODKIN. They would not buy them under any consideration.

Mr. RAKER. Do you intend to tell the committee that that is the condition of the beet-growing industry in Colorado?

Mr. BODKIN. That is only business. It could not be otherwise.

Mr. RAKER. Just a moment. I do not care whether it is business or otherwise. I want the fact.

Mr. BODKIN. Yes.

Mr. RAKER. Do you mean to say it is a fact that a man can not go out and do an honest, open-handed business and grow his beets to suit himself?

Mr. BODKIN. No, sir.

Mr. RAKER. And get his crop ready for delivery, and deliver it to these sugar-beet people?

Mr. BODKIN. No, sir.

Mr. RAKER. In other words, he has got to be bound by contract in advance, before they will even agree to take his beets?

Mr. BODKIN. Yes.

Mr. FORDNEY. Do you know of an instance where a man, independent of a contract, has raised beets, in your State, and the company has refused to take them?

Mr. BODKIN. Yes, sir.

Mr. FORDNEY. What did he do with his beets; were they destroyed?

Mr. BODKIN. No, sir; he is a stock feeder.

Mr. FORDNEY. Why did they refuse to take them, do you know?

Mr. BODKIN. We all know. How could a sugar factory do business on expecting the farmers to grow beets? They have got to have these contracts signed up and keep after the people, until they get sufficient contracts to know what they are going to do.

Mr. FORDNEY. I know this, that in the State of Michigan an independent raiser of beets in that way can find a market if the factory can use his beets unless they are overstocked, and if they are overstocked they always take care of their contracts first.

Mr. BODKIN. The Great Western is too smart to do that loose a business.

Mr. FORDNEY. What do you mean by being "too smart"?

Mr. BODKIN. They are too smart to depend on the farmers. They might not get any contracts, and they would not know what they were doing.

Mr. FORDNEY. I am not talking about their depending on them at all. Some of them have raised beets and could not dispose of them, and you would have us understand that they can not dispose of them without a contract; is that it?

Mr. BODKIN. I would have you to understand that they would not think of taking them.

Mr. HINDS. Is not that the general practice, wherever a factory depends on supplies from the farmers; for instance a corn factory or a tomato factory or any factory that makes its product from the farmers' product, do they not always see, by contract, that they will have supplies enough to keep their factory going?

Mr. BODKIN. Any that I ever heard of did.

Mr. HINDS. Of necessity?

Mr. BODKIN. They always have contracts, to know what they are going to get.

Mr. RAKER. But, in addition to that, the remarkable fact that I wanted to draw out was as to the condition here, which is that if an independent man goes to work, or a man on his own initiative goes to work, and raises beets, he has got to feed his beets to stock, and he can not sell them to the Great Western Co.

The CHAIRMAN. Well, gentlemen, if the fact is established, you can draw your own conclusions. The committee will excuse you from further attendance, Mr. Bodkin, with thanks for your courteous answers to the questions propounded.

TESTIMONY OF MR. E. U. COMBS.

(The witness was sworn by the chairman.)

The CHAIRMAN. Mr. Combs, will you give the stenographer your full name?

Mr. COMBS. E. U. Combs.

The CHAIRMAN. What is your address?

Mr. COMBS. Fort Morgan, Colo.

The CHAIRMAN. The examination in chief for the committee will be conducted by Mr. Fordney; if you please, Mr. Fordney.

Mr. FORDNEY. Mr. Combs, are you a grower of beets in Colorado?

Mr. COMBS. Yes.

Mr. FORDNEY. How many acres of beets did you raise this last year?

Mr. COMBS. I raised only about 10 acres. That is, I harvested only about 10 acres.

Mr. FORDNEY. You have heard Mr. Bodkin's testimony here, have you not?

Mr. COMBS. Yes; part of it.

Mr. FORDNEY. Do you agree with Mr. Bodkin as to the average tonnage per acre of beets raised in Colorado—about 10 tons to the acre—throughout the State?

Mr. COMBS. Statistics give about 10½ tons as the average.

Mr. FORDNEY. What percentage of sugar was shown in your beets? Do you market your beets with the Great Western Sugar Co.?

Mr. COMBS. Yes.

Mr. FORDNEY. What percentage of sugar did you get in your beets?

Mr. COMBS. I have not figured the average percentage as yet, because the returns were not all in when I left; but the average will be about 15 per cent.

Mr. FORDNEY. So that the price per ton will be about how much, to you?

Mr. COMBS. $5.25, that would be.

Mr. FORDNEY. $5.25?

Mr. COMBS. Yes.

Mr. FORDNEY. That is not as high an average as Mr. Bodkin's. He received $5.75 for his, I believe he stated.

Mr. COMBS. Yes; I believe so.

Mr. FORDNEY. Do you know about what is the average price per ton that is paid by that company to the average farmer in your district or in that locality?

Mr. COMBS. I can tell you what Mr. Dixon, the vice president of the Great Western Sugar Co., told me the day before I came away, and he took these figures from his books. He said up to the 19th of November the average test showed 15.57.

Mr. FORDNEY. Then you would get paid on the basis of 16, would you not, according to your contract?

Mr. COMBS. Yes; that would be an average of about $5.50. That is what I have had in my mind all the time.

Mr. FORDNEY. What did you say the yield was per ton?

Mr. COMBS. 15.57 per cent.

Mr. FORDNEY. That would be what price per ton?

Mr. COMBS. That would be $5.50.

Mr. FORDNEY. $5.50?

Mr. COMBS. Yes; under 16 and over 15.50.

Mr. FORDNEY. Have you been satisfied with tests made as to the sugar content in your beets made by this company?

Mr. COMBS. I have had no reason to question them.

Mr. FORDNEY. Then you are satisfied?

Mr. COMBS. I want to say this, if it is admissible.

Mr. FORDNEY. Anything you want to say.

Mr. COMBS. The Great Western Sugar Co. have been perfectly fair. They have lived up to their contract with the farmer as regards the conditions and stipulations of that contract, and in instances I think they have done more than they really agreed to do, so far as the contract goes. As a grower, I have no fault to find with that, but the fault I have to find is that their contract is not liberal enough, the compensation is not great enough, for the grower. I have made these same statements to the officials of the Great Western Sugar Co.

Mr. FORDNEY. Have they at any time given you any encouragement to think that they would change the contract and make better the conditions to the farmer?

Mr. COMBS. They stated within the last week or 10 days that they would consider a proposition that we had made.

The CHAIRMAN. In what period of time do you say?

Mr. COMBS. Within the last two weeks; within 10 days; within the time since they knew we were summoned to Washington.

Mr. FORDNEY. Would you care to state to this committee what your proposition to them is?

Mr. COMBS. I would be glad to.

Mr. FORDNEY. We would be glad to have you do that.

Mr. COMBS. We asked that they pay $5 flat for 12 per cent beets and 25 cents for each unit above 12 per cent, and paying on the tenth of 1 per cent instead of on the half of 1 per cent.

Mr. FORDNEY. I am going to help you a little, if I can, now. Let me tell you under what conditions the farmer in the State of Michigan raises beets for our factory. The factory pays $4.50 per ton for 12 per cent sugar in the beet, and for every 1 per cent above that—I do not think the fraction is considered, but for every 1 per cent above that—the farmer receives 33⅓ cents. He loses 33⅓ cents for each 1 per cent below 12 per cent of sugar in the beet; but the average throughout the State runs, this year, I believe, about 16 per cent.

Mr. COMBS. There is a sliding scale, both ways.

Mr. FORDNEY. The sliding scale goes with it—33⅓ cents for every 1 per cent above 12 per cent and $4.50 flat for 12 per cent beets. The farmers in our State receive upward of $6 a ton for their beets.

Mr. COMBS. I have always contended, and to the sugar people, that by virtue of their contract they have admitted they could pay $5 for 12 per cent beets. That being the case, it figures right near 40 cents a unit. In 12 per cent beets they have paid for the handling of the tonnage, and all of the saccharine extracted from the beet above 12 per cent is really velvet—clear money—except the labor to put the sugar in the bag and a little extra labor in the factory. In view of that fact, they at least ought to be willing to pay the same ratio per cent above 12 per cent that they do up to that point. In fact, the scale should slide the other way—that the greater the per cent the more they should pay for that extra percentage; but we only asked that they pay the same ratio, which would make more money in the end for beets than the farmer was asking.

Mr. FORDNEY. Your proposition to them of $5 per ton flat for 12 per cent and 25 cents for every 1 per cent above is practically the same as $4.50 flat and 33⅓ cents when it gets up to 16 per cent sugar?

Mr. COMBS. I would say yes, without figuring it exactly.

Mr. FORDNEY. So that on 16 per cent beets your proposition would would be almost identical with that now in vogue in the State of Michigan with the farmers, both independent and all others, as I understand it. You are demanding $5 for 12 per cent. That is 50 cents above what is paid in Michigan.

Mr. COMBS. That is 50 cents, exactly, above the price we are being paid now.

Mr. FORDNEY. That is it, exactly.

Mr. COMBS. In other words, we would get $6 for 16 per cent beets.

Mr. FORDNEY. On 16 per cent beets your $5 flat and 25 cents for each per cent is practically equivalent to $4.50 flat and 33⅓ cents for each per cent.

Mr. COMBS. Yes; I presume so, without going into the figures.

Mr. FORDNEY. There would be just a little difference one way or the other. I would be pleased, indeed, to have you make any statement that you see fit to make to this committee, setting forth the conditions as between the farmer and the manufacturer in your State. Have you anything further that you could say without my asking you direct questions?

Mr. COMBS. There is so much to this, and your asking questions refreshes my memory. As I have often said in my talks on this question, I could talk an hour and a half each evening in the week on this subject and not exhaust the subject, and this is a good deal in the same way.

Mr. FORDNEY. What does it cost you per acre to raise your beets? What has it cost you this year? Could you give that in detail or in a lump sum approximately?

Mr. COMBS. I could give some figures. As I have itemized this, the current price for hand labor is $20 per acre in Colorado.

Mr. FORDNEY. Yes.

Mr. COMBS. The plowing of the ground is $3 per acre. Would you like me to itemize this, or shall I give you the sum total? I do not want to be tedious.

Mr. FORDNEY. You can itemize it and then give the sum total, and you can hand that to the stenographer when you get through; but to refresh our memories will you just itemize it as you go along?

Mr. COMBS. Plowing is $3.

Mr. FORDNEY. Yes.

Mr. COMBS. Now, I would like to say that probably some of you gentlemen do not understand about this price for plowing, and it might look high; but when you analyze that you will see that it is not. We plow the ground for beets some 12 inches in depth, and that requires four good horses, and 1¾ acres or 2 acres a day is about all the work you can accomplish. That is why it is worth $3. In fact, you can not hire men to do this work for $3; they will want $4. The harrowing—twice, I figure—is 30 cents for each harrowing, which makes

60 cents per acre. I figure floating the ground close at 30 cents per acre.

Mr. FORDNEY. Floating the ground, 30 cents?

Mr. COMBS. Yes. This all requires four horses. It is heavy work. It is done thoroughly. As to planting, the customary price, and the price the sugar companies used to pay when they drilled the beets for the farmer, at the start, is 50 cents per acre.

The seed is 20 pounds, which we are under contract, I suppose, to plant. That is $2 per acre. Cultivating the beets four times—that is team work—at 40 cents an acre, is $1.60. Some cultivate more and some less. That is about the average.

With us we water the beets twice—some more—and we consider ourselves fortunate to be able to water them twice, and the ditching is, each time, 40 cents, or 80 cents an acre. This is team work.

Mr. FORDNEY. You have just given ditching.

Mr. COMBS. Ditching the beets, ready to run the water in. Then, watering twice at 50 cents an acre each time, is a dollar an acre.

Mr. MALBY. A dollar each time?

Mr. COMBS. $1 for the season, watering twice at 50 cents each time.

Pulling the beets, $2.50 per acre. That is team work.

Hauling the beets, per ton, to the railroad, averages about 50 cents per ton.

The CHAIRMAN. Does that come out of the farmer, or does the factory pay it?

Mr. COMBS. The farmer delivers these beets on the cars.

The CHAIRMAN. That is, he delivers them to the railroad; he does not take them to the factory door?

Mr. COMBS. No, sir; they prepare beet dumps about every 2 or 3 miles along the railroad, and the farthest distance a farmer would have to draw his beets is not to exceed 3 miles, I should judge. The average would probably be 2 miles.

Mr. FORDNEY. In that average per acre for hauling, 10 tons per acre, 60 cents per ton, it would make $6 per acre; is that right?

Mr. COMBS. Yes, sir. I am figuring $6.60, because I am figuring an average of 11 tons.

Mr. FORDNEY. All right.

Mr. COMBS. It ranges from 10½ tons to 11 tons. I think the average for the State is probably nearly 11 tons.

Mr. FORDNEY. All right, sir; thank you.

Mr. COMBS. The cash rent that is customary is, as Mr. Bodkin gave it, $20 per acre for good beet ground. That takes the best land we have, and in the best state of cultivation and the best fertilized.

Mr. FORDNEY. You usually raise beets on the very best land you have?

Mr. COMBS. It is always the best land that is devoted to the beet culture; yes. That makes a total cost of $58.90. I have figured the average at 11 tons per acre, at an average price of $5.50, which would be $60.50.

Now, I will say, in all fairness to everybody concerned, that so far as I am concerned I raised an average of 20 tons of beets to the acre this year on the beets harvested, which shows me a good profit. My yield was the maximum.

Mr. FORDNEY. This was about your cost as well as other people's cost?

Mr. COMBS. Yes. This is the custom of the country. That is what I am trying to give you.

Mr. FORDNEY. But you raised how many tons?

Mr. COMBS. Right at 20 tons. I had not got my last returns.

Mr. FORDNEY. At $5.50 a ton?

Mr. COMBS. No; mine will only run about $5.25. The saccharine matter in the beets was low because of the extensive yield.

The CHAIRMAN. You have given, so far, the figures that you think are average?

Mr. COMBS. Yes.

The CHAIRMAN. Rather than your own individual figures?

Mr. COMBS. Yes. That is not my own individual, but that is the average price paid in the country for this labor; that is what I am giving you. Now, for the hauling some pay 75 cents a ton and some pay 50 cents; but a fair average would be 60 cents.

The CHAIRMAN. Yes.

Mr. FORDNEY. On your land this year your crop yielded you, as you figure it now, $105 per acre, and it cost you $58.90 per acre to produce it?

Mr. COMBS. Yes.

Mr. FORDNEY. Leaving you a profit of $46.10, but you say your crop was the maximum in the State?

Mr. COMBS. Yes. As the sugar people said to me the other day, "We can not see that you have got any kick coming." I said, "I have not, from this year's business; but from my last 20 years' business experience I figure profits. I figure the average profits for a number of years, and when we start out to beat that average we are up against a hard game. And in the same way, in the production of sugar beets, looked at from a business standpoint, we have an average, and that is what we must go by. Now, when we must beat that average to make a profit, we might just as well go out and play a roulette wheel, except that the percentage against us there would not be so large.

Mr. FORDNEY. In your estimate there is $20 per acre for rent of land. If you were renting your land outright and the contractor, or the party renting, were to get as good a crop as you have got he could pay you $20 an acre rent for the land and still make $46.10 profit per acre for the crop. In other words, if you add that $20 rent to your profit you will have $66.10 for your land per acre.

Mr. COMBS. Well, if you added the $20 to the profit, you would have to take the upkeep of your place, including the assessments for the water right and taxes and other expenses.

Mr. FORDNEY. Yes; I say for profit and rent you would have $66.10?

Mr. COMBS. Yes.

Mr. FORDNEY. Now go ahead.

Mr. COMBS. I think of nothing else on that.

Mr. FORDNEY. What class of labor do you get?

Mr. COMBS. The labor we have is principally, in the beet fields in our country, Russians or Belgians or Germans—foreign labor, mostly.

Mr. FORDNEY. About what wages do you pay that labor, where you hire them by the day; or, in other words, if they contract—the handwork—about what wages do they make a day? Can you give us that?

Mr. COMBS. You can not hire those people by the day. In other words, they do not hire by the day, in working the beets.

Mr. FORDNEY. They do it by contract?

Mr. COMBS. They do it by contract; and I will say that one man is supposed to take care of 10 acres of beets, which at $20 an acre would be $200 for handwork on 10 acres. It requires about 90 days in the season to do that handwork.

Mr. FORDNEY. So that for 90 days of work a man earns about $200?

Mr. COMBS. Yes. I do not remember how that would figure, but it would be about $2.25 a day on the average. The man has got then the other nine months of the year to do something else in.

Mr. FORDNEY. Is that a good class of labor, in your State, Russians, at that work?

Mr. COMBS. Do you mean is it efficient labor?

Mr. FORDNEY. Yes.

Mr. COMBS. Yes, very much so; very efficient.

Mr. FORDNEY. One other question. What are your relations, generally, with the Great Western Sugar Co.?

Mr. COMBS. None whatever, except as a grower of beets.

Mr. FORDNEY. Nothing more than the average farmer in the State has?

Mr. COMBS. No, sir.

The CHAIRMAN. If you will excuse me, I want to ask one or two questions now, and I must go away. Mr. Combs, do you know what it costs to produce a pound of beet sugar in these western beet-sugar factories?

Mr. COMBS. Yes.

The CHAIRMAN. Can you give us that?

Mr. COMBS. Now, let me understand what you mean by the cost to produce a pound of sugar. Do you mean the sugar produced and put on the market, or do you mean the factory cost?

The CHAIRMAN. I mean the factory cost, and to put it on the railroad for delivery at the factory door; or, you may put it both ways.

Mr. COMBS. My figures relate to the factory cost.

The CHAIRMAN. At the factory door?

Mr. COMBS. The sugar in the bag at the factory costs $2.591 per hundred pounds.

The CHAIRMAN. Or 2.591 cents per pound?

Mr. COMBS. Yes.

The CHAIRMAN. Are those Colorado figures?

Mr. COMBS. Yes, sir; that is an average cost in the arid States.

The CHAIRMAN. You mean by that, where the sugar beets are irrigated?

Mr. COMBS. Yes. These figures have nothing to do with the production of sugar in any other States except arid States.

The CHAIRMAN. In making those figures, was the depreciation of the plant allowed for?

Mr. COMBS. There is nothing——

The CHAIRMAN. Nothing for that?

Mr. COMBS. That enters in. There is nothing allowed for that. There is nothing allowed for the administration of the business.

Mr. MALBY. Or interest on their investment?

Mr. COMBS. Nothing whatever. That is the actual cost to produce and sack the sugar in the factory.

The CHAIRMAN. Without either depreciation of the plant or interest on the investment?

Mr. COMBS. Nothing of that sort. This is for the labor employed, the fuel, and everything that goes to make a ton of beets.

The CHAIRMAN. Can you give us an itemized statement of what enters into that cost of $2.591?

Mr. COMBS. Yes.

The CHAIRMAN. Will you do that?

Mr. COMBS. In sum and substance, the cost of the fuel per ton for beets, to work them into a sugar, is 51.80 cents.

The CHAIRMAN. That is the cost of the fuel?

Mr. COMBS. Of the fuel to manufacture these beets.

The CHAIRMAN. That is, to manufacture the sugar?

Mr. COMBS. I am talking, now, of everything as based on tons.

Mr. HINDS. That is for the fuel, put into the furnace?

Mr. COMBS. That is the fuel that is used to work a ton of beets into sugar.

Mr. HINDS. Is it the fuel put into the furnace, or do you bring your labor into some other item?

Mr. COMBS. No, sir; that is the straight fuel, the coal and the coke; that is to say. The lime rock used to purify the juice is 30 cents per ton. Now, that is high, because in this average there was much of the sirup worked in Steffens and the sugar extracted. However, in our country they do not do that any more; it does not pay. That requires more. The real average of the sugar, without working that, would be about 16 to 18 cents. I am trying to get averages.

The CHAIRMAN. Yes, averages.

Mr. COMBS. The sacks to sack this sugar would be 29.82 cents per ton. The filter bags, oil, and waste, and things of that sort about the the factory, and running the machinery and things of that sort make about 6½ cents for a ton of beets.

The labor employed is $1.0426. The cost of the beets on the average is estimated as we have given it here, at $5.50 per ton, which makes the total cost $7.7238 for the sugar from a ton of beets in the sacks.

Mr. FORDNEY. How much sugar do you get out of that ton?

Mr. COMBS. 298.20 pounds.

Mr. FORDNEY. In other words, 300 pounds?

Mr. COMBS. Yes.

The CHAIRMAN. You said the cost of producing a pound of beet sugar was 2.951 cents. That is how you got those figures?

Mr. COMBS. Yes; that is how I arrived at those figures.

The CHAIRMAN. By taking it on a ton basis?

Mr. COMBS. Yes.

Mr. FORDNEY. That is on beets that yield a greater percentage than 15 per cent?

Mr. COMBS. I am taking averages.

The CHAIRMAN. You say you are taking averages in this?

Mr. COMBS. Yes.

The CHAIRMAN. On everything?

Mr. COMBS. Yes.

The CHAIRMAN. For how long a period of years?

Mr. COMBS. I am giving you the averages of several factories for one season.

The CHAIRMAN. For one season?

Mr. COMBS. Yes.

The CHAIRMAN. What factories are those whose averages you are giving us?

Mr. COMBS. Well, Mr. Chairman, I would like to ask to be excused from answering that question. I will say that these are factories in the arid States, and the figures I give you are authentic.

The CHAIRMAN. Well, I would like to excuse you, of course, but in order for this testimony to be of any value, it has got to be compared with testimony already given, and it is my judgment, unless some member of the committee thinks otherwise, that you ought to tell where and how you got these figures. Do not you gentlemen think so?

Mr. MALBY. I think so; if it is to be of any value, we ought to know.

The CHAIRMAN. Of course the only reason for excusing you, aside from the obligation that rests upon a gentleman in certain cases, is that you might be about to incriminate yourself in some way by giving the information. With that exception, I think we will require you to answer where you got these figures, and what factories these figures apply to, because the committee, in behalf of the people of the United States, can not determine what this thing means without knowing that, while we regret asking you to testify if you do not want to.

Mr. COMBS. I want to be clearly understood in this, that I am under obligations, confidential, partially, to others, you see.

The CHAIRMAN. You mean by that that somebody gave you this information and made you promise not to tell?

Mr. COMBS. No, not exactly; not all of this information; some of these details.

The CHAIRMAN. Some of these details?

Mr. COMBS. Yes; and the information that the individuals had had not been purloined from the sugar companies in any way. It was legitimately produced.

The CHAIRMAN. It was given to you in confidence?

Mr. COMBS. Yes; that is the position I am in. The party who had this was entitled to the information, and it was not purloined or obtained in any illegitimate way; and I am not a party to that. It is a matter of confidence that is all.

Mr. HINDS. How did you happen to be collecting this information?

Mr. COMBS. That is a long story.

The CHAIRMAN. Tell us how. Answer as shortly as you can. Was it because you are on this beet-sugar committee of the Colorado Farmers' Union?

Mr. COMBS. I have been engaged for years in the grocery business, in a wholesale way. Naturally, I handled the finished product in the sugar business. and there were certain organizations in our State that attempted to maintain a card on sugars and I did not feel that I wanted anybody to dictate to me how I should run my business. Therefore we never agreed. I proposed to buy sugar for the lowest price I could buy it for and to sell it for whatever I pleased. For that reason there was always friction; and from that I commenced the investigation; and at one time I figured, and was identified with some people who expected to start an independent sugar factory, and we were doing this as a small factory, for our own product, that we might market our own product.

The CHAIRMAN. Mr. Combs going back to the question that I left you on the Chair is of the opinion in regard to any information that you have obtained from anybody else whether personally or confidentially or not if you have testified on that basis the committee and the Congress and the people of the United States are entitled to know from what source this testimony is derived; and desiring to personally say to you that I regret very much the personal obligation involved I would like to find out if it would not be possible for you to give us the names of the factories to which these figures apply, and from which they are gathered without naming the individual from whom you acquired the information. Could you do that?

Mr. COMBS. I can say they are in Colorado.

The CHAIRMAN. You know what the factories are?

Mr. COMBS. Yes.

The CHAIRMAN. State what factories they are.

Mr. COMBS. The average of these six factories is the factories of the Great Western Sugar Co.

The CHAIRMAN. Will you give the location of the factories?

Mr. COMBS. I can not do that from this paper.

Mr. FORDNEY. They have only six factories, have they?

The CHAIRMAN. No, they have nine, at least, in Colorado.

Mr. COMBS. They have 10, 9 in Colorado and 1 in Montana.

The CHAIRMAN. One in Montana?

Mr. COMBS. Yes; and they now also have one at Scottsbluff, Nebr. I could not give you those names now.

The CHAIRMAN. But the figures you have given us were taken from six of the factories—the Colorado factories of the Great Western Sugar Co.?

Mr. COMBS. Yes.

The CHAIRMAN. Were they taken from the actual figures in the operation of those factories?

Mr. COMBS. Yes.

The CHAIRMAN. And by a person who you have reason to believe had knowledge whereof he spoke?

Mr. COMBS. There is no question about his knowledge.

The CHAIRMAN. And accurate information?

Mr. COMBS. Yes; no question about it.

The CHAIRMAN. And you have that information in detail?

Mr. COMBS. Yes.

The CHAIRMAN. And the figures you have given us are derived, in part at least, from the information thus obtained by you?

Mr. COMBS. Yes; and these figures corroborate other investigations of my own.

The CHAIRMAN. And they corroborate independent investigations that your committee has made otherwise?

Mr. COMBS. Yes. That is why I feel that I am justified in using these.

The CHAIRMAN. Because you would have arrived at them anyway?

Mr. COMBS. I had arrived at them, and this simply corroborates my figures, that extended over several years of research in this matter.

The CHAIRMAN. Does any member of this committee think that we ought to ask this witness to tell us who this individual was who gave him these figures from the books of the company?

Mr. MALBY. I would like to know the names of the companies. The object of knowing the companies is this: In however good faith the witness may be acting in respect to giving the details, the companies nevertheless may feel as though they disagreed with the results, and they ought to be given an opportunity to file with the committee their statements with respect to this very cost; so that I think the witness should give the factories.

The CHAIRMAN. He said he did not know whether he could identify them from the memorandum before him.

Mr. COMBS. I can furnish you this evidence later. I think I have in my grip, perhaps, the names of the companies.

The CHAIRMAN. You think you can give us the names of the six companies from whose books these figures were taken?

Mr. COMBS. I had them all, but in copying this I left the names off, on purpose.

The CHAIRMAN. You think you can furnish those before you leave the city?

Mr. COMBS. Oh, yes.

(At 1.05 o'clock p. m. the committee took a recess until 2 o'clock p. m.)

AFTERNOON SESSION.

At the expiration of the recess the committee resumed its session.

TESTIMONY OF MR. E. U. COMBS—Continued.

The CHAIRMAN. Mr. Combs, the committee does not like to put you in the attitude of violating a personal confidence. At the same time it feels that its duty to the public is such that it ought to make the most exhaustive examination into the sources of these very startling figures that you have given the committee about the cost of production of a pound of beet sugar in Colorado. So that so far as both the legal and moral responsibility goes for divulging the source of these figures, if there is any confidential feature attached to it, the committee is prepared to assume it. So I believe I will ask you, and in fact require you, to answer the question I propounded to you before the recess, as to where you got the figures as to what it cost to produce a pound of sugar in the six factories of the Great Western Sugar Refining Co., because they have produced voluntarily the figures relating to certain factories before us, which are very different from your figures.

Mr. COMBS. Mr. Keyes, of Colorado, gave me these figures.

The CHAIRMAN. Where does he live?

Mr. COMBS. At Denver, Colo.

The CHAIRMAN. Do you know his initials?

Mr. COMBS. Yes; I do. I know him very well; but there are several of them, and I just get the initials mixed.

The CHAIRMAN. If you are not certain that you remember his initials, tell us, at least, his connection with the sugar business and why his figures were so readily adopted by you and why you contend that they are reliable and accurate and trustworthy figures? You do not think you can give his initials?

Mr. COMBS. I have them, but I do not believe I could give them here. I can give his address.

The CHAIRMAN. Give his address and his business.

Mr. COMBS. I can give his address so that it can be verified.

The CHAIRMAN. You can supply the initials later, if you can do so.

Mr. COMBS. I have known him for years, in the business, and I have always called him "Keyes" and he has always called me "Combs."

The CHAIRMAN. Does he occupy any position with—what is the name of the company?

Mr. COMBS. The Great Western Sugar Refining Co.

The CHAIRMAN. The Great Western Sugar Refining Co.

Mr. COMBS. He does not.

The CHAIRMAN. Give his address.

Mr. COMBS. His address is 1640 Tremont Street. I do not mean his residence. That is his business address.

The CHAIRMAN. Yes; his business address. Denver, Colo.?

Mr. COMBS. Yes.

The CHAIRMAN. What is his business?

Mr. COMBS. He at this time is engaged in the real estate business.

The CHAIRMAN. Has he ever had any connection with the Great Western Sugar Refining Co.?

Mr. COMBS. I think so.

The CHAIRMAN. What connection?

Mr. COMBS. He has been superintendent of their factories, I believe.

The CHAIRMAN. The general superintendent of all their factories?

Mr. COMBS. No; of different factories.

The CHAIRMAN. Do you know how many different factories?

Mr. COMBS. I could not say; more than one, though.

The CHAIRMAN. One that you know of?

Mr. COMBS. More than one, as I understand it.

The CHAIRMAN. More than one, of your own knowledge?

Mr. COMBS. Yes.

The CHAIRMAN. Which one is that?

Mr. COMBS. The Sterling factory, I think.

The CHAIRMAN. Is that in Montana?

Mr. COMBS. That is in Colorado.

The CHAIRMAN. Colorado, I mean.

Mr. COMBS. Yes, sir.

The CHAIRMAN. Speaking from general reputation (because this committee is not held down to the strict rules of law, as in a court of justice) has he been superintendent of that factory?

Mr. COMBS. I think so. I am positive in my own mind that he has.

The CHAIRMAN. Give us your impressions on that subject.

Mr. COMBS. Yes, sir; I think at perhaps two or three different factories.

The CHAIRMAN. At two or three different factories of the Great Western Sugar Refining Co.?

Mr. COMBS. Yes, sir. I will say this: That Mr. Keyes's knowledge probably all did not come from his connection with the Great Western Co., because he operated an independent factory.

The CHAIRMAN. He operated an independent factory?

Mr. COMBS. Yes, sir.

The CHAIRMAN. What factory was that?
Mr. COMBS. That was a little factory at Brighton.
The CHAIRMAN. At Brighton, Colo.?
Mr. COMBS. Yes, sir.
The CHAIRMAN. When was it operated?
Mr. COMBS. That was, to the best of my memory, about 1907 or 1908.
The CHAIRMAN. 1907 or 1908?
Mr. COMBS. Yes, sir.
The CHAIRMAN. Did that become a part of the Great Western Co.?
Mr. COMBS. That little old factory is there yet.
The CHAIRMAN. Has it been abandoned?
Mr. COMBS. It is out of business.
The CHAIRMAN. It does not operate?
Mr. COMBS. No.
The CHAIRMAN. Subsequently he went into the employment of the Great Western?
Mr. COMBS. Yes, sir. I think that his connection with the Great Western was from that time (although I am not right clear on that) until I found he was in this other business.
The CHAIRMAN. Is he a reliable and accurate man in the beet-sugar business in Colorado?
Mr. COMBS. Yes, sir.
The CHAIRMAN. Has he had opportunity for knowing the facts about which he told you?
Mr. COMBS. Yes, sir.
The CHAIRMAN. Are these tables as to which you have testified taken from detailed information that he gave you about this thing?
Mr. COMBS. Yes, sir.
The CHAIRMAN. Did he furnish you with the tables?
Mr. COMBS. Yes, sir.
The CHAIRMAN. Will you tell the committee when he furnished you with these tables?
Mr. COMBS. No; I can not tell the exact date.
The CHAIRMAN. Can you fix it substantially?
Mr. COMBS. Some months back.
The CHAIRMAN. Some months back—during the present year?
Mr. COMBS. Yes.
The CHAIRMAN. What was the occasion of his furnishing these statements? Did you ask him for them?
Mr. COMBS. I went to him for them, to have him tell me what he knew about the sugar business.
The CHAIRMAN. In what capacity did you go? Did you go as a member of the sugar committee?
Mr. COMBS. I went as E. U. Combs, personally.
The CHAIRMAN. And in no representative capacity?
Mr. COMBS. No, sir.
The CHAIRMAN. Did he readily and freely divulge to you the information he had on the subject?
Mr. COMBS. Yes.
The CHAIRMAN. Furnishing you with the tables that you have furnished to the committee on that subject?
Mr. COMBS. Later on.

The CHAIRMAN. Following the conversation he furnished you with these tables?

Mr. COMBS. Yes, sir; but he had given me much information prior to this time many times, as well as other sources of information that I had. And these figures only corroborate the figures and the facts that I had prior to this time.

The CHAIRMAN. Were you ever a member of the beet-sugar committee of the Colorado Division of the Farmers' Union?

Mr. COMBS. I have been a member of that committee at various times.

The CHAIRMAN. But not at present?

Mr. COMBS. Not of that organization. I am connected with other beet growers' associations.

The CHAIRMAN. With other beet growers' associations?

Mr. COMBS. Yes, sir.

The CHAIRMAN. Which are striving for the same purpose?

Mr. COMBS. Yes, sir; the American Beet Growers' League, which is national in its scope.

The CHAIRMAN. Covering all of the growers of sugar beets in those States?

Mr. COMBS. Yes, sir; I am the national lecturer for the National Beet Growers' League.

The CHAIRMAN. What is the object of that organization?

Mr. COMBS. The object of that organization is to encourage, foster, and promote the manufacture of sugar in the United States; to become educated and make this a business, as any other business man makes his business, so that we may better have a knowledge of the production and the refining and everything pertaining to the industry in the United States.

The CHAIRMAN. Yes.

Mr. COMBS. We think that the industry is of so much importance in the United States, and that it is in its mere infancy at this time, that it ought to be promoted.

The CHAIRMAN. The angle from which you view this question is essentially from the standpoint of the farmer producing beets, is it not?

Mr. COMBS. Yes.

The CHAIRMAN. And the members of the organization that you represent are farmers?

Mr. COMBS. Yes; they are growers.

The CHAIRMAN. Growers of the sugar beet?

Mr. COMBS. Yes, sir.

The CHAIRMAN. Did Mr. Key—is his name Key?

Mr. COMBS. Keyes, in the plural.

The CHAIRMAN. Keyes, in the plural. Did Mr. Keyes represent or state to you that these tables and figures that he furnished you, which you have given to this committee, were taken from the actual operations of sugar companies?

Mr. COMBS. Yes, sir.

The CHAIRMAN. They were not mere theories, but actual facts?

Mr. COMBS. Actual facts.

Mr. MALBY. Shown by their books?

The CHAIRMAN. Yes; shown by their books?

Mr. COMBS. Yes.

The CHAIRMAN. In what year?

Mr. COMBS. I asked Mr. Keyes at the time when I left for Washington whether, if he was needed in Washington, he would come, and he said he would.

The CHAIRMAN. I understand that. While we are glad to be advised of that, that is not exactly the question. Do you recall what year he said these were the figures for?

Mr. COMBS. Eight, as I remember it.

The CHAIRMAN. 1908?

Mr. COMBS. Yes.

Mr. FORDNEY. That was the average price?

The CHAIRMAN. That was the average for the six factories of the Great Western?

Mr. COMBS. Yes.

Mr. FORDNEY. Just for that year, or the average of the years?

Mr. COMBS. That year.

The CHAIRMAN. The average for that year?

Mr. COMBS. Yes.

The CHAIRMAN. Was that an abnormal year in any way?

Mr. COMBS. I think not. I think the tonnage was greater, however. That was the time before the farmers had become disgusted with the sugar-beet business. They raised more acreage at that time than they do now. I think their tonnage was better in those days for some reason, but why I do not know.

The CHAIRMAN. Anyhow, it was better?

Mr. COMBS. Yes.

Mr. MALBY. Were the prices the same?

Mr. COMBS. The prices of beets?

Mr. MALBY. Yes.

Mr. COMBS. No; they got less. They were paid at this time on a flat rate of $5 regardless of percentage.

The CHAIRMAN. The farmers got somewhat less for the beets?

Mr. COMBS. Yes; they got $5 regardless of percentage.

The CHAIRMAN. Therefore the factories paid somewhat less at that time, when these figures were given, for their beets?

Mr. COMBS. Yes.

The CHAIRMAN. And, of course, to the extent, at least, which they have increased the price they have paid for sugar beets, to that extent they have increased the cost of production of a pound of beet sugar since that time, have they?

Mr. COMBS. They have; but the figures I have given you, I notice, show the total cost to produce a sack of sugar based on a cost of the raw material at $5.50, which we are paying, while at this time they only paid $5. So the actual cost at that time was just that difference less, you see.

The CHAIRMAN. Now, Mr. Combs, have you prepared any other figures except these in reference to what the farmers get or have gotten out of a pound of beet sugar, or any of those cognate questions?

Mr. COMBS. What the farmers realize?

The CHAIRMAN. Yes. You appear to have some tables there, and I want to see what you can tell us about that.

Mr. COMBS. In this connection, if you want these different factories separated I will give it to you in detail.

The CHAIRMAN. Yes. We want them. It is very important that we should have that, and we will ask you before you leave the city to supply the names of those factories with the tables to the reporter.

Mr. COMBS. I will endeavor to do that. I looked in my grips a few moments ago, and I think I can give these from memory. It may not be accurate.

The CHAIRMAN. Suppose you make it up subject to revision if you should discover that there is any mistake.

Mr. COMBS. The average price—I have not got those figures here, but I have figured it a great many times—as I remember it, is about $1.85 for a sack of sugar that the grower gets for the sugar content of his beet; that is in the beet, $1.85. That is what has caused all this discontent with the grower—that he puts a sack of sugar in the back part of the factory, in the beet, for $1.85, and he drives around in front and takes one out at $8; and the difference between the two figures is too great.

Mr. FORDNEY. How much sugar is there in the sack for $1.85?

Mr. COMBS. He delivers 100 hundred pounds of sugar in the beet for about $1.85.

Mr. FORDNEY. $1.85 for 100 pounds?

Mr. COMBS. Yes.

The CHAIRMAN. There is 100 pounds of sugar product in the beets furnished?

Mr. COMBS. Yes; and when he buys it back he pays anywhere from $7 to $8 or $9, as it has been recently, for this sack of sugar. That difference between those sacks of sugar is what has caused the dissatisfaction of the grower, because he is not getting any of this profit.

Mr. MALBY. Your factories do not get $8 or $9. What did they get, or what do they get?

Mr. COMBS. On an average—I am trying to figure this—they are getting $5.

Mr. FORDNEY. Five cents a pound for sugar?

Mr. COMBS. Yes.

Mr. MALBY. They did not get that prior to a very recent date, did they?

Mr. COMBS. In Colorado they did.

Mr. MALBY. Sugar was selling here at wholesale during the forepart of the year at a much lower figure. That is, cane sugar.

Mr. COMBS. We have the protection in our country of the seaboard. I think that is always added.

Mr. FORDNEY. Where is your sugar principally marketed that is manufactured in Colorado?

Mr. COMBS. It should be marketed within a radius that would give the 25-cent freight rate between Denver and the Missouri River points. The product of the State is protected by a 55-cent rate from the coast to Denver or to the Missouri River.

Mr. FORDNEY. But when you get back to the Missouri River, who takes advantage of that difference?

Mr. COMBS. They still have 25 cents the best of it.

Mr. FORDNEY. Thirty cents; the differences between 25 and 55.

Mr. COMBS. Yes; 30 cents difference. They still have the best of that. Naturally, as business men, they do, just as you or I would do.

We would take advantage of that. That is what they are in business for.

The CHAIRMAN. They get the market, in other words, for their sugar?

Mr. COMBS. Certainly. There is no reason for us to say mean things about these people. That is good business.

The CHAIRMAN. In other words, they sell their sugars only as cheaply as they have to sell them in competition?

Mr. COMBS. Exactly. They are going to pay the growers just what they have to pay. If we agree to a price of $4, do not blame them for giving $4.

The CHAIRMAN. If they can buy cheaply, of course they buy as cheaply as they can.

Mr. COMBS. Certainly; without any feeling about the matter.

The CHAIRMAN. That is common sense. It is so the world over. Do you know anything about what the capitalization of these beet-sugar factories is and what they are making on their capitalization? Do you know anything about what percentage they are realizing on their investment? Have you ever investigated that question?

Mr. COMBS. I know the capitalization.

The CHAIRMAN. Of each one of them?

Mr. COMBS. No; they all come under the Great Western.

The CHAIRMAN. Take the Great Western.

Mr. COMBS. It is capitalized for $30,000,000.

The CHAIRMAN. Have you ever made any inquiry or investigation as to the value of the properties in the organization or owned by that company?

Mr. COMBS. No. I could only draw conclusions as to that from their assessed valuation.

The CHAIRMAN. From the assessed valuation? What is the assessed valuation of the properties of the Great Western?

Mr. COMBS. I believe I can not give you exact evidence on that.

The CHAIRMAN. Give it substantially.

Mr. COMBS. It is about two and a half million dollars.

The CHAIRMAN. Two and a half million dollars?

Mr. COMBS. Yes, sir.

The CHAIRMAN. That is what they pay taxes on?

Mr. COMBS. Yes, sir; and they pay dividends on $30,000,000.

The CHAIRMAN. They pay dividends on $30,000,000 and taxes on $2,500,000?

Mr. COMBS. Those are the facts. Other witnesses have the exact figures; but I have these figures. Some of these I got myself the day before I left from Morgan County and from Logan County. I got them from the treasurer. I got the actual taxes that they pay.

The CHAIRMAN. Suppose you give them to us.

Mr. COMBS. I prefer to leave that. Mr. Dakan has those figures; and he has brought the figures from each county treasurer.

The CHAIRMAN. But you say, in round numbers, in a general way, that this company is capitalized at about $30,000,000, and pays dividends on that amount, and that it pays taxes on what?

Mr. COMBS. It pays taxes on $2,754,410; but in this is included the Great Western Railroad Co., $260,920, and land, $1,470. That should properly be deducted from the Great Western.

The CHAIRMAN. $1,000 worth of land?

Mr. COMBS. $1,470 worth. I presume that includes the land where the little railroad station is.

The CHAIRMAN. In the factories and on the railroad?

Mr. COMBS. No; on the railroad. This is in connection with the railroad; of course, that is owned by the Great Western Sugar Co.

The CHAIRMAN. The railroad itself is owned by them?

Mr. COMBS. Yes. I did not go into this, but it is given to me, and is supposed to be reliable information. I can not testify as to this being a fact, you understand, but I understand that they own their limekilns and quarries. Of course, the officials of the Great Western Sugar Co. own that, and, as I understand it, it costs $1.70 a ton to quarry and deliver this lime rock to the different factories that they own. The average is $1.70, and they charge the factory $3. In that way it is possible to take money out of one pocket and put it in the other one, and it does not show profits on the sugar. but on the lime.

The CHAIRMAN. That is a bookkeeping plan that they adopt?

Mr. COMBS. Yes. I intended to get the rate they pay themselves for hauling their beets on the railroad, but I just did not have time. My time was too short.

Mr. FORDNEY. Mr. Chairman, while the gentleman is on that question, I would like to ask him if he can tell the committee what proportion of the real value of the property is fixed in the assessment on property in his State?

Mr. COMBS. As I understand it, it is about 25 per cent.

The CHAIRMAN. In other words, they assess property at 25 per cent of its actual value.

Mr. COMBS. Yes.

The CHAIRMAN. So that, applying the general rule that prevails in Colorado generally, this two and one-half millions of valuation that they are assessed would mean really about ten millions of actual value?

Mr. COMBS. Yes; nine or ten millions, as I understand.

The CHAIRMAN. As against thirty millions of stock?

Mr. COMBS. Yes.

Mr. MALBY. Is there not also another consideration in your State, and that is that there was a sort of a quasi understanding with the beet-sugar men that if they would erect these factories they would be assessed with considerable liberality?

Mr. COMBS. There is no such arrangement that I ever knew of. I never heard of it.

Mr. MALBY. You think they are assessed as other property is assessed?

Mr. COMBS. Yes, sir.

Mr. MALBY. And about in the same proportion?

Mr. COMBS. Yes.

Mr. MALBY. That is all.

The CHAIRMAN. Have you made any investigations as to what dividends this Great Western Sugar Co. has paid, or has been able to pay, on its capitalization, and as to the relation that bears to the profit which it actually makes on its real investment?

Mr. COMBS. No; I have not. The only thing I can figure is the possible net profit in the business from the figures that I actually have.

The CHAIRMAN. What are those figures that you actually have?

Mr. COMBS. You understand, I am not going into the matter of the administration of this business—the salaried officers, the deterioration of the plant, their taxes, and the insurance, and the things that naturally go to make up the expense account for conducting this business from the administration end of it.

The CHAIRMAN. That is, the expense account of the general administration?

Mr. COMBS. Yes; I am figuring on the sugar as it is.

The CHAIRMAN. And leaving out those considerations to which you have just adverted?

Mr. COMBS. Yes.

The CHAIRMAN. Leaving out those, what do your figures show on that proposition?

Mr. COMBS. I will give it as it is condensed here.

The CHAIRMAN. Suppose you do that.

Mr. JACOWAY. Right there, what per cent does the Great Western Co. pay on this $30,000,000? What per cent of dividends does it pay? Do you know that?

Mr. COMBS. No; I have never gone into that. I have left that to the other parties.

Mr. MALBY. That is in the record anyway.

Mr. FORDNEY. Does that $30,000,000 include any other factories except those nine in Colorado?

Mr. COMBS. Except the Billings, in Montana.

Mr. FORDNEY. The Billings and another that they have at Scottsbluff, Nebr.?

Mr. COMBS. My figures do not include the one at Billings. That is outside of the State. I am talking about the State.

Mr. FORDNEY. Well, they have a capitalization of $30,000,000. Have they two organizations and two capitalizations?

Mr. COMBS. No; I think not. That must cover them.

Mr. FORDNEY. The other two factories, one at Billings, Mont., and another at Scottsbluff, Nebr.?

Mr. COMBS. Yes. I have not gone into that as closely as I might, from the fact that I knew other members of this committee that came down here had gone into that more fully. But if you gentlemen want this I will give you the itemized statement as I got these figures.

The CHAIRMAN. Where did you get these figures?

Mr. COMBS. These are the figures that I have been referring to—the six factories. The average days that these factories run here was 101. The total tons they sliced was 695,425. The average daily slicing for each plant was 993.46 tons. The average test of these beets was 17.50—17½ per cent. The average purity of these beets was 85.43.

Mr. FORDNEY. Per cent?

Mr. COMBS. Yes, sir. The percentage of raw sugar left in the factories from the year previous was 0.16. The percentage of sugar put in the bag was 14.91—just under 15. The average tons of sirup refuse left from each factory was 5,265. The average percentage of this sirup on the beets was 5.33. The percentage of coal averaged on a ton of beets—this was all based on tons, you understand—is 23.43 for the coal. The percentage of coke on a ton of beets is 0.69.

Mr. FORDNEY. Twenty-five cents for the fuel, did you say?

Mr. COMBS. I beg your pardon.

Mr. FORDNEY. Twenty-five cents per ton for fuel, for coal?

Mr. COMBS. Fifty-one cents, I believe—51,80.

Mr. FORDNEY. Did you not say the coal was 25 cents, on an average?

Mr. COMBS. No; you misunderstood me. The percentage of coal on a ton of beets, to work it, is 23.43. In other words, it would take about 465 pounds of coal to work a ton of beets into sugar, you understand.

Mr. FORDNEY. I understand.

Mr. COMBS. That is the percentage of coal on a ton of beets.

Mr. FORDNEY. Yes.

Mr. COMBS. In round numbers. I have taken all my figures from this, to make my total figures as to the profits from the factory end.

Mr. FORDNEY. Will you pardon me, Mr. Chairman——

The CHAIRMAN. Yes.

Mr. FORDNEY. In making up that cost, $2.59, you have not given any cost for interest on the investment, for taxes on the property, for depreciation of property, for field work, campaign, management, or anything of this kind?

Mr. COMBS. The field work is included in this. No; as I have stated before, I am showing the cost to produce a sack of sugar in the factory, and to leave it in the factory.

Mr. FORDNEY. Just in the factory?

Mr. COMBS. Without any cartage or cost of selling. I am showing what it would cost to produce a sack of sugar in the sack.

Mr. FORDNEY. That does not include what is termed overhead expenses—management, etc.?

Mr. COMBS. No. The administration of the business is not included.

Mr. FORDNEY. That is, repairs, depreciation, insurance, interest on the investment, etc.?

Mr. COMBS. Yes.

Mr. MALBY. Do you include railroad transportation?

Mr. COMBS. Nothing, except the sugar, as they buy the beet and condense it and put it in the sack and leave it in the factory. I have left the sugar in the factory. There is nothing beyond that.

Mr. MALBY. They haul it to the factory. There is some expense in that. Does it cover that?

Mr. COMBS. I will give you in detail my deductions from this.

Mr. FORDNEY. Mr. Combs, can you come somewhere near to the cost per ton, or per 100 pounds, for the other items I have mentioned? Have you any idea as to that?

Mr. COMBS. Well, from my past business experience I would be able to arrive at a pretty close approximate cost.

Mr. FORDNEY. Figuring the interest upon the investment, and figuring everything that would be a proper charge, what in your estimation is a fair estimate?

Mr. COMBS. I could not give it offhand, but I think I have the figures in my grip. I would have to look that up before I could talk intelligently on the subject. I would not want to make an estimate.

Mr. FORDNEY. All right.

Mr. COMBS. I want to be fair to everybody concerned in this matter. What I am telling is just what I know, to the best of my knowledge, and I do not want to misquote or misrepresent.

Mr. Fordney. Do not understand that I question your fairness in the least.

Mr. Combs. No, sir; I do not question your intentions.

Mr. Fordney. I had no such intention.

Mr. Combs. They made 2,073,750 sacks of sugar.

Mr. Garrett. Two million seven hundred thousand?

Mr. Combs. No. Now I have it. Two million seventy-three thousand seven hundred and fifty-seven sacks.

Mr. Fordney. Why do you take the year 1908 particularly?

Mr. Combs. Because these figures happen to cover that year.

Mr. Fordney. In that year the percentage of sugar in the beets was above the average, or above normal, was it not?

Mr. Combs. I do not think so, though I could not state positively.

Mr. Fordney. This gentleman, Mr. Bodkin, has stated that the percentage was 15 per cent in your part of the country, and I took it for granted that that might be a fair average—I think he said it was a fair average of the sugar content in the beets throughout the State.

Mr. Combs. I am not prepared to state, but I have always been under the impression that it was higher than that.

Mr. Fordney. That it was higher that year than this year?

Mr. Combs. Oh, no; that each year there was a higher percentage than 15.

Mr. Fordney. Oh, yes. I interrupted some one. I did not intend to.

Mr. Garrett. Go ahead, Mr. Fordney. The chairman has gone out. Continue your examination.

Mr. Fordney. Mr. Combs, your price given as $2.59 includes these items—namely, fuel, lime rock, sacks, oil, and so forth, labor—labor in the factories—and the beets, making up $2.59 as you have stated there?

Mr. Combs. Yes, sir.

Mr. Fordney. I have here from a number of factories in the State of Michigan their cost for the past five years—each year in detail—which does not include interest on the capital invested, taxes, insurance, and such things, given by affidavit. Here is an independent factory. I would like to have this go into the record at this point as an illustration of what the additional cost might be, and the additional cost given by you of $2.59, as you gave it, for other expenses. If the chairman will permit me, as this is very brief, I will state it:

The secretary and treasurer of the Owosso Sugar Co., a corporation owning and operating a beet-sugar factory in the city of Owosso, Mich., and one in the city of Lansing, in the State of Michigan, says under oath that he knows the cost of making sugar at each of the said plants for the last five years, and that the following is a true and correct statement of the cost of making 100 pounds of sugar at each of said factories during the year as stated.

Then he gives the cost per 100 pounds, etc.

Mr. Malby. What does he give it at?

Mr. Fordney (reading):

Said items of cost do not include any interest charges or cost of selling or overhead expenses.

Those are the expenses I have named here. He gives it for the year 1906——

Mr. Garrett. Does it include depreciation?

Mr. FORDNEY. No; that is an overhead expense. That is part of our overhead expense. It does not include taxes, insurance, depreciation, superintendence. All that might be considered as overhead expenses. This is the actual labor employed.

Mr. MALBY. Together with the cost of the beets?

Mr. FORDNEY. Yes; together with the cost of the beets—3.274 cents; cost of labor and materials, .665 cent, or a total of 3.939 cents for the year 1906; 1907, 3.365; 1908, 3.417; 1909, 3.899; 1910, 4.0728. Those are five years. I have all the rest of them here, which run along about the same. So you are not prepared to say that if all the expenses which should be a proper charge were added to the price you have given—$2.59—it might not bring up the price to average the same as the figures I have given—$3.75, $3.80, or $3.90?

Mr. COMBS. No, sir; I think not.

Mr. FORDNEY. You think it would not bring it up to that price?

Mr. FORDNEY. Could you give us those figures, to show exactly what the cost per pound is?

Mr. COMBS. I could, but I could not just now. I could give you this later if I was called again, but I can not do it now.

Mr. FORDNEY. I wish you would do so.

Mr. COMBS. I will make estimates. They will only be estimates from my past business experience along that and other lines. That is all I can get it from.

Mr. FORDNEY. I wish you would give it.

Mr. COMBS. And I could only give it as an estimate.

Mr. FORDNEY. Yes.

Mr. COMBS. Do you care for these figures?

Mr. GARRETT. Yes; you were in the midst of giving some figures.

Mr. COMBS. I gave the number of sacks, and my average price for this sugar is $5. That is $10,368,785. The pulp, 25 per cent of this tonnage on the beets, is 173,856 tons. That is 35 cents a ton. These are the by-products. That is $60,839.60. The sirup refuse, at 5.33 per cent, is 33,783 tons, at half a cent per pound—$337,830, making a total production of $10,767,454.60. Now, we come to the cost of this production. Six hundred and ninety-five thousand four hundred and twenty-five tons of beets, at $5.50—that is the probable average cost this year, but not at that time; it was $5 flat—makes $3,824,837. They used 162,938 tons of coal, at $2, or $325,876. They used 4,298 tons of coke, at $8, which is $34,384. They used 49,375 tons of lime rock, at $3, which is $148,125. Two million seventy-three thousand seven hundred and fifty-seven sugar bags, at 10 cents, $207,375.70. Filter bags, oil, waste, etc., about the factory, $45,202.62. Two thousand four hundred and sixty-six men, 101 days, at an average wage of $2.60 a day, is $647,571.60. Salaries of superintendent, field men, managers, etc., for the year, is $76,496.75, making a total expenditure of $5,309,869.17, leaving a factory profit of $5,457,585.43.

Mr. MALBY. What was their total income?

Mr. COMBS. $10,767,454.60.

Mr. GARRETT. Mr. Combs, just there, while it is on my mind, I want to call your attention to a statement which appears on page 2894 of our record. It is an affidavit of Mr. W. A. Dixon, vice president and general manager of the Great Western Sugar Co., I suppose, purporting to give the cost prices of producing sugar.

Mr. JACOWAY. That is in Michigan, Mr. Garrett.

Mr. GARRETT. In the several factories in Colorado. You note that that statement says:

Includes credits from by-products, pulp, molasses, sheep and cattle feeding, company farming operations, and all other outside revenues. Does not include charges to improvements nor depreciation, nor does it include freight, brokerage, insurance, and miscellaneous charges after sugar has left the factory.

I want to ask you about whether or not there is included in the tables that you have given us and excluded therefrom substantially the same things that are stated here as being included and excluded, if you know.

Mr. COMBS. I do not know. I have not gone over this. This that I have given you is a factory report from the superintendent to the head office of the campaign.

Mr. GARRETT. Do you know, for instance, whether it includes credits from by-products, pulp, molasses, sheep and cattle feeding, company farming operations, and all other outside revenues?

Mr. COMBS. No. There are no credits in these figures. In this I have taken into account, though, the by-products, you see, in the total production.

Mr. GARRETT. Yes.

Mr. COMBS. I have included the by-products, which amount to practically half a million dollars, in their income—the production.

Mr. FORDNEY. Will you pardon me just a minute?

Mr. GARRETT. Certainly.

Mr. FORDNEY. Mr. Combs, in order to get a correct comparison of your figures with those given by Mr. Morey, we should have the names of the six factories to which you refer. From Mr. Morey's statement I take the average for the campaign of 1910–11, and the ten different factories given there average 3.487, as given by him. That is at page 2894 of our record. One factory is left out there—Fort Morgan—but from the ten factories given his average is 3.487.

Mr. GARRETT. 3.33, is it not?

Mr. FORDNEY (continuing). Or about three-quarters of a cent, or a little below eight-tenths of a cent above the cost given by you, of $2.59. Add three-quarters of a cent to that and it would make $3.34.

Mr. COMBS. I will give you the average for all 10 factories if you want it.

Mr. FORDNEY. That is what we would like to have in order to get it so that we might compare it with the figures given by Mr. Morey.

Mr. COMBS. Without stopping to figure this out I could not give you the actual——

Mr. FORDNEY. You are using 1908 and Mr. Morey used 1910. I will give you the figures for 1908 if you will bear with me for a minute.

Mr. COMBS. I have it right before me. I have the same figures.

Mr. FORDNEY. But I will give you the total average for those factories for that year if you will bear with me for a minute.

Mr. MALBY. Mr. Morey's statement for 1907–8 here is considerably more advantageous than any other. They manufactured there in one factory as low as $2.87—in the Longmont factory. It cost $3.45 this year—the same factory. There was at least a difference of 20 per cent, I notice here. I do not know that you and Mr. Morey are so much apart. I do not think you are so much apart, if you add the other figures which made up the complete cost. You might not be much apart, if any. I can not see how the limited amount of figures which he has given us would be found beneficial unless we have them all, because we have no means of knowing about this unless we inquire further into it.

Mr. GARRETT. He was just saying that he would give us the average of the 10 factories. You might give that, Mr. Combs.

Mr. COMBS. I have not figured this out, as yet. I can do it, though, in a moment, I think.

Mr. FORDNEY. I find the figures for 1908 as given by Mr. Morey are identical with the cost for the campaign of 1910–11, $3.487. So if the gentleman will add to his figures three-quarters of a cent for overhead expenses it would bring it right up to those figures exactly.

Mr. GARRETT. I do not understand that Mr. Morey's total included overhead expenses. In fact it expressly states that it does not. He says:

> Does not include charges to improvements nor depreciation, nor does it include freight, brokerage, insurance, and miscellaneous charges after sugar has left the factory.

It did not include, as I understand, the overhead expenses. It did not purport to do so.

Mr. MALBY. It includes a portion of them, because while improvements and depreciation come within overhead expenses, yet there are other overhead expenses, such as insurance, manufacturing, etc.

Mr. FORDNEY. He says:

> The yearly average for the Colorado factories for the past eight campaigns is $3.42, and adding to it as a fair average of 35 cents per bag for depreciation, would bring it to $3.77 per hundredweight.

Mr. GARRETT. Yes.

Mr. FORDNEY. That is what I am contending.

Mr. GARRETT. Whereas, if you add that same amount to Mr. Combs's figures, 35 cents for depreciation, it would bring it from $2.51 to——

Mr. FORDNEY. From $2.59 to $3.34, adding three-quarters of a cent for overhead expenses.

Mr. MALBY. Mr. Fordney, by casting your eye on the campaign of 1907–8 as given here in this table, you see it is 20 per cent less than the campaign of 1910–11, or about that.

Mr. FORDNEY. The average cost of the years 1907–8, and 1910–11 is identical, $3.487. Adding them up and dividing by the number of factories you will get at it. Mr. Willett divided one and handed it to me, which shows $3.487. I added the whole together and divided by the number of factories, which makes $3.487 for 1910–11, which is exactly the same as for the year 1908.

Mr. MALBY. He must be mistaken about that. I would like to know whether he figures 1907–8 or 1908–9, just to carry out your suggestion. The campaign of 1907–8 is certainly the cheapest one reported here, and it does not average $3.

Mr. FORDNEY. Do your figures include the year 1907–8 or 1908–9?

Mr. COMBS. 1908–9, as I understand it.

Mr. FORDNEY. 1908–9.

Mr. COMBS. 1908–9. That is right.

Mr. MALBY. It makes all the difference in the world which one it is.

Mr. FORDNEY. Are you sure it is 1908–9, Mr. Combs?

Mr. COMBS. I am positive; yes, sir.

Mr. MALBY. What year would you call this, in the sugar year?

Mr. COOMBS. I would call it 1911.

Mr. MALBY. It is 1911-12?

Mr. COMBS. Yes; we speak of it as 1911-12, but it is the campaign of 1911.

Mr. MALBY. According to his statement it would be 1908-9. He says it was the campaign of 1908. That would be the fall of 1908 and the spring of 1909.

Mr. FORDNEY. Taking the gentleman's calculation as he has it there; that is, $3.768—the average given by Mr. Morey——

Mr. COMBS. Wait, and I will count that up in a moment. Without figuring as to the parts of cents, you take the 10 factories, and it produces $2.82 instead of $2.59.

Mr. FORDNEY. $2.82?

Mr. COMBS. Yes.

Mr. FORDNEY. For that year?

Mr. COMBS. $2.82.

Mr. FORDNEY. Yes.

Mr. COMBS. Leaving off the fractions.

Mr. FORDNEY. Or, in other words, 94 cents below the figures given by Mr. Morey.

Mr. COMBS. I will tell you why.

Mr. FORDNEY. He includes everything there but the 35 cents for depreciation.

Mr. COMBS. Gentlemen, let me tell you, if you care to hear it, why I left off three factories. I left off three factories, but I had a reason for doing it. As you understand, I did not start out to do the Great Western Sugar Co. any injury in this.

Mr. FORDNEY. I understand.

Mr. COMBS. That was not the idea. I am in possession of these figures; you ask for the facts as I know them, and I am giving them to you.

Mr. FORDNEY. That is right.

Mr. COMBS. There is no use in causing any feeling between the Great Western Sugar Co. and myself if it can be avoided. That is why I asked that I be not asked this question. Not but that I am entitled to these figures and all that, but if I said there were 10 factories you would know in a minute who owns 10 factories in Colorado. That is one reason why I gave six. Another reason is that at this time the Brush factory was not working successfully, so that it would hardly be fair to the Brush factory, and the Morgan factory in the same way. These figures prove this assertion. At Brush at that time they had 16.67 test, and they only put 12.52 sugar in the sack. You see that shows that this factory was not a success, which I knew at that time.

Mr. MALBY. The factories that you refer to are the Greeley, the Windsor, and the Fort Collins, the Loveland, and Longmont?

Mr. COMBS. No; Eaton, Longmont, and Billings. That is out of the State, you see. Billings in that year, you see, ran away beyond. It showed 18.56 per cent in beet average.

Mr. MALBY. According to this report Billings was——

Mr. FORDNEY. That is away above the normal, or average.

Mr. COMBS. They put in the sack 321 pounds of sugar per ton.

Mr. FORDNEY. That would make a very great difference in the average.

Mr. COMBS. I am giving you the average in 10 factories; but the point is that I did not think, in justice, that the average in a factory which was not a success should be charged up to the other factories. Another thing to be considered in this cost is that if you study this table carefully you will see that the factory that sliced the greatest number of tons of beets during the campaign and produced the most sugar gave better results than the factories slicing a less capacity. Factories running 1,300 and 1,400 tons daily and producing sugar are more fortunate, in other words, than factories slicing in less capacity.

Mr. GARRETT. What is the table you are now reading from?

Mr. COMBS. 1908.

Mr. GARRETT. Will you put that in the record?

Mr. COMBS. That is what I am giving you—the 10 factories: that is $2.82 average.

Mr. FORDNEY. You left out the Brush factory in your statement because you said it was not a success. However, Mr. Morey shows that it produced sugar nine-tenths of a cent cheaper that year than the Fort Morgan factory did, and that it only cost three-hundredths of a cent more than the Eaton factory—$4.12 as against $4.15; and $4.15 for the Brush factory as against $4.24 for the Fort Morgan factory that year.

Mr. COMBS. I can not tell what other conditions might have prevailed locally at that time. I am giving my figures from the results of the campaign, which showed that they lost better than 4 per cent of the sugar content in that factory, while some of these other factories lost less than 3 per cent—2.65 and 2.75. That is why I say this factory was not a success, and it was generally so understood at that time. The cause was that the battery end of the factory was too small for the sugar, and the juice deteriorated before they could get it through their sugar end. That was discovered to be the trouble with this factory, as I understand it. That is why I left that out. But here is an average of $2.82 for the 10 factories. While you might say Billings had a better average, it would, perhaps, be fair for one to offset the other. But you will notice that those averages in the test of sugar in the different places ran almost alike, as I have got them here: 17.18, 16.31, 17.34, 18.56—which is exceptionally high—17.62, 17.64, 17.57, 16.55, and 16.67. It shows an average of 17.37—average test.

Mr. GARRETT. Is there some other question, Mr. Fordney?

Mr. FORDNEY. No; I understood that you were questioning him.

Mr. COMBS. Mr. Fordney, I beg you pardon for asking you this question, but you say this practically corroborates the statement there?

Mr. FORDNEY. If you were to add——

Mr. COMBS. I understand that——

Mr. FORDNEY (continuing). The additional cost of overhead expense of about three-quarters of a cent per pound, it would bring out the total cost as given by Mr. Morey, practically.

Mr. GARRETT. But I do not understand that is included in Mr. Morey's statement, however.

Mr. FORDNEY. How is that?

Mr. GARRETT. I do not understand that the three-quarters of a cent is supposed to be included in Mr. Morey's statement.

Mr. FORDNEY. Why, Mr. Morey has not given us any figures for the following charges. I have it here: Interest on capital invested, taxes, depreciation of property, insurance, field work for men——

Mr. GARRETT. No.

Mr. FORDNEY (continuing). Management, superintendence, and nothing of that kind.

Mr. GARRETT. No; he has not. Neither has Mr. Combs.

Mr. FORDNEY. I mean Mr. Combs has not. Mr. Morey did give it.

Mr. GARRETT. No; it expressly says:

Does not include charges to improvements nor depreciation, nor does it include freight, brokerage, insurance, and miscellaneous charges after sugar has left the factory.

Mr. FORDNEY. Where do you get that?

Mr. GARRETT. Right at the beginning of the letter.

Mr. FORDNEY. The second paragraph says:

The yearly average for the Colorado factories for the past eight campaigns is $3.42, and adding to it as a fair average of 35 cents per bag for depreciation, would bring it to $3.77 per hundredweight.

Mr. GARRETT. Yes. There is that item there, but I call attention to——

Mr. FORDNEY (interrupting). That is 35 cents per bag on 300 pounds, and you have $1.05. I am only asking that you add three-quarters of a cent, instead of $1.05.

Mr. GARRETT. I call attention to the first part of the letter.

Mr. FORDNEY. At the top?

Mr. GARRETT. At the top.

Mr. FORDNEY (reading):

Net cost of manufacturing 100 pounds of sugar at factory doors—includes credits from by-products, pulp, molasses, sheep and cattle feeding, company farming operations, and all other outside revenues. Does not include charges to improvements nor depreciation, nor does it include freight, brokerage, insurance, and miscellaneous charges after sugar has left the factory.

We were not trying to include the latter part.

Mr. GARRETT. I understand that these statements purport to include substantially the same thing.

Mr. FORDNEY. Well, we ought, really to know.

Mr. GARRETT. Yes; we ought to know about that.

Mr. FORDNEY. That is very important.

Mr. GARRETT. He goes on in the body of the letter to say what would be a fair amount to allow for depreciation, down there.

Mr. RAKER. What do you figure their factory has depreciated every year—43 per cent. as he has it here?

Mr. FORDNEY. Oh no. I do not know what they figure.

Mr. RAKER. He says here:

The amount of depreciation charged off each fiscal year would be from 28 to 43 cents per 100 pounds sugar.

Mr. FORDNEY. I had not figured it that way. That would complicate the matter for me. I am only judging from the general manner of keeping books in an industry—not of sugar. But 10 per cent. or about 10 per cent, depreciation is very fair.

Mr. HANLON. I think the Great Western charge 3 per cent depreciation. That is my impression.

Mr. COMBS. That is my understanding.

Mr. FORDNEY. This number of cents per bag, figured on the output of the factory, then, measured by the investment, would bring it out 3 per cent?

Mr. HANLON. I am sure it is 3 per cent depreciation.

Mr. COMBS. As I understand it, that corroborates the figures. I think the Great Western people claim that the Brush factory is a million-dollar factory. If they allowed 3 per cent on that, that would allow $30.000 for depreciation each year.

Mr. RAKER. On what?

Mr. COMBS. On the Brush factory. They have allowed for next year, as I understand it, $28,000 to the superintendent for depreciation at this factory to put it back in condition, and that would be practically the gentleman's statement of 3 per cent on a million-dollar factory.

Mr. FORDNEY. No doubt that is correct, because, as you know, the work is carried on through the entire year. After the running season is over——

Mr. COMBS. I understand.

Mr. FORDNEY (continuing). In putting in new machinery and repairing there is an enormous expense. It should be charged somewhere along the line. It is not charged in the depreciation, but there is a depreciation in your plant each year. There is an end to it somewhere, and it must be charged in, in proportion to the number of years of the life of the plant.

Mr. RAKER. Is it not something peculiar, on this question of depreciation, that after a factory runs 5 or 6 years and then stands for 8 or 10 years they will take that old plant and move it 3,000 miles and put it in a new factory rather than buy new machinery, if it depreciates so?

Mr. FORDNEY. Judge, that may be true, but here is a principle that you must lay down, and that can not be departed from without making an error. The life of your plant depends upon the number of years you are going to run it.

Mr. RAKER. I think so.

Mr. FORDNEY. If the life of the plant is 10 years, then the depreciation at 10 per cent is correct. If it is 33⅓ years, 3 per cent is the proper depreciation. Whatever the life of the plant is is the amount of depreciation you must figure on. But you sell your factory when you have done with it for scrap generally, and if you figure 3 per cent, the life of that factory being 33⅓ years, then you must figure that the present machinery will not be modern at that time and will be worth nothing more nor less than scrap, and you will obtain for it about what it costs you to dispose of it.

Mr. COMBS. I can not see where they get the 35 cents a sack that they charge off for depreciation, or $30,000 for the factory, taking the case we have just mentioned.

Mr. FORDNEY. Three cents on the percentage you gave, 300 pounds, practically, would be $1.05 per ton.

Mr. COMBS. But 35 cents a sack, you see, which would be $1.05 a ton for beets at 300 pounds of sugar——

Mr. FORDNEY. That would give you $50,000.

Mr. COMBS. No. Oh, yes—the tonnage. It would give about $50,000, which is double what they really allow for this depreciation, which they give the superintendent. Perhaps in that figure he has charged some of these repairs, or something. It might be there would be a difference in the way different men would figure this depreciation. Some men put in the actual new machinery added to the plant as depreciation.

Mr. FORDNEY. That should be done, should it not?

Mr. COMBS. But some men put that in as part of the overhead expense. It depends on the way you keep the books. The depreciation would be the cost to keep the factory in the same state of repair for the next campaign that it was in when they started in with the present one.

Mr. FORDNEY. Mr. Garrett, if you will permit me just at this moment, and if Mr. Combs will wait a minute, to show the point I am trying to get out in connection with his total cost, I will give for the purpose of comparison the figures of three other factories in the State of Michigan. This is an affidavit which is sworn to by the secretary and treasurer of the St. Louis Sugar Co.—Mr. B. C. Hubbard. He gives the cost per hundred pounds of sugar for the campaign of 1906–7 and for four succeeding years, as follows:

Campaign of 1906–7	$3.88
Campaign of 1907–8	3.62
Campaign of 1908–9	3.34
Campaign of 1909–10	3.66
Campaign of 1910–11	3.90

He adds:

Statement of cost of making sugar for years shown at plant of the St. Louis Sugar Co. This does not include cost of selling, freight, or storage on the finished product, but does include cost of the raw material and the converting of it into sugar.

Now, then, here is the statement of the West Bay City Sugar Co. by Mr. M. J. Bialy, its secretary. It gives the cost of beets per ton the cost of beets per 100 pounds of sugar, the cost of manufacturing 100 pounds of sugar, and the total cost of 100 pounds of sugar. The average is $3.63; but for the year 1906 it was $3.62; for 1907, $3.50; for 1908, $3.42; for 1909, $3.55; and for 1910, $4.09.

He says:

The manufacturing cost is derived from payment for account of labor, supplies, insurance, interest paid, taxes and repairs.

Now I have the statement of the German-American Sugar Co., certified to by E. Wilson Cressey. It states:

E. Wilson Cressey, of Bay City, Mich., being duly sworn, says he is secretary of the German-American Sugar Co., a corporation organized under the laws of the State of Michigan, is familiar with the books of the company, that the figures given below are taken from the books of the company, are correct, and that they show the cost, per 100 pounds, of producing sugar during the last five years, exclusive of the selling cost and interest on the capital invested.

	Cost per 100 pounds.
1906	$3.679

Mr. GARRETT. That includes it.

Mr. FORDNEY. It does not include the selling cost and the interest on the capital invested. [Continuing:]

	Cost per 100 pounds.
1907	$3.774
1908	3.568
1909	3.614
1910, Bay City (Mich) plant	4.018
1910, Paulding (Ohio) plant	4.354

That is subscribed and sworn to before a notary public.

Mr. RAKER. Would it not be a good idea to have Mr. Fordney's statement in the record, and then let those three statements follow just as they occur?

Mr. FORDNEY. Yes, if you please, because there it shows the affidavits attached, and all that.

The statements above referred to are as follows:

ST. LOUIS SUGAR CO.,
St. Louis, Mich., September 2, 1911.

Hon. JOS. W. FORDNEY,
Saginaw, W. S., Mich.

DEAR SIR: Attached is a statement showing the cost of making sugar, not including the cost of selling, freight outbound, or interest on capital invested. The cost of selling is from 20 cents to 25 cents per hundred pounds, which includes freight, brokerage, storage, etc.

If there is anything further that you would desire in the way of statistics, would be pleased to furnish.

Yours, truly,

B. C. HUBBARD,
Secretary and Treasurer.

Statement of cost of making sugar for years shown at plant of the St. Louis Sugar Co.

[This does not include cost of selling, freight, or storage, on the finished product, but does include cost of the raw material and the converting of it into sugar.]

	Per hundred pounds.
Campaign of 1906–7	$3.88
Campaign of 1907–8	3.62
Campaign of 1908–9	3.34
Campaign of 1909–10	3.66
Campaign of 1910–11	3.90

STATE OF MICHIGAN, *County of Gratiot, ss:*

B. C. Hubbard, secretary and treasurer of St. Louis Sugar Co., being duly sworn, states that the above amounts represent the cost of making sugar, including the price of beets per 100 pounds of product, exclusive of the cost of selling, storage, freight, etc., on the finished article.

B. C. HUBBARD.

Sworn to before me this 2d day of September, 1911.

[SEAL.]

CARRIE CHAPPELL,
Notary Public.

My commission expires July 17, 1915.

BAY CITY, W. S., MICH., *August 31, 1911.*

Hon. J. W. FORDNEY, M. C.,
Saginaw, Mich.

DEAR SIR: In reply to your request for the statement of the cost of production of sugar for the past five years, we give you the following for the years 1906 to 1910, inclusive:

Cost of beets per ton	$7.01
Cost of beets per 100 pounds sugar	2.64
Cost of manufacturing 100 pounds sugar	.99
Cost of 100 pounds sugar	3.63

These figures are derived from the following years:

Years.	Cost of beets per 100 pounds sugar.	Manufacturing cost.	Cost of 100 pounds sugar.
1906	$2.70	$0.92	$3.62
1907	2.46	1.04	3.50
1908	2.44	.98	3.42
1909	2.70	.85	3.55
1910	2.90	1.19	4.09

The manufacturing cost is derived from payment for account of labor, supplies, insurance, interest paid, taxes, and repairs.

Yours, very truly,

WEST BAY CITY SUGAR CO.,
M. J. BIALY, *Secretary.*

STATE OF MICHIGAN, *County of Bay, ss:*

Personally appeared before me, a notary public in and for Bay County, Mich., M. J. Bialy, secretary of the West Bay City Sugar Co., who acknowledged the foregoing statement to be true to the best of his knowledge and belief.

GILBERT J. DUROCHER,
Notary Public.

My commission expires January 5, 1913.

BAY CITY, MICH., *September 1, 1911.*

Hon. JOSEPH W. FORDNEY,
Saginaw, W. S., Mich.

DEAR SIR: Replying to your favor of August 26, we inclose herewith sworn statement of the secretary of this company as to the cost, per 100 pounds, of manufacturing sugar during the last five years, exclusive of selling cost and interest on capital invested.

If this is not just what you want, please write us, giving further details.

Yours, very truly,

GERMAN-AMERICAN SUGAR CO.
E. WILSON CRESSEY,
Secretary and General Manager.

E. Wilson Cressey, of Bay City, Mich., being duly sworn, says he is secretary of the German-American Sugar Co., a corporation organized under the laws of the State of Michigan, is familiar with the books of the company, that the figures given below are taken from the books of the company, are correct, and that they show the cost, per 100 pounds, of producing sugar during the last five years, exclusive of the selling cost and interest on the capital invested.

	Cost per 100 pounds.
1906	3.679
1907	3.774
1908	3.568
1909	3.614
1910, Bay City, Mich., plant	4.018
1910, Paulding, Ohio, plant	4.354

E. WILSON CRESSEY, *Secretary.*

Subscribed and sworn to before me, a notary public in and for the county of Bay, State of Michigan, this 1st day of September, A. D. 1911.

JAMES A. SCOTT,
Notary Public in and for Bay County, Mich.

My commission expires November 18, 1911.

Mr. GARRETT. Mr. Combs, I think it is quite important, if possible for the purpose of comparing your table with the tables here of others, that we get clearly just what is included in your table. I want to call your attention to page 2893 of our record, to the letter of Mr. Chester S. Morey, which precedes the letter addressed to Mr. Morey by Mr. Dixon, which is the real affidavit giving that table. Mr. Morey makes a little more elaborate explanation, however, than is made in the letter of Mr. Dixon to him. He says:

You will note that we have included all credits from by-products—pulp, molasses, sheep and cattle feeding, as well as company farming operations—in fact, all outside revenues have been credited to the cost of producing a bag of sugar. The pulp and molasses rightly belong, but sheep and cattle feeding and farming operations could just as well have been kept separately; but unfortunately, our books have been kept in that way, and our cost of making sugar is reduced thereby, and we could not very well separate them at this time.

Do you know whether any of that is included in your table?

Mr. COMBS. No, sir.

Mr. GARRETT. Do you know that it is not?

Mr. COMBS. It is not. Oh! What do you mean?

Mr. GARRETT. The cost of the pulp and by-products.

Mr. COMBS. They are credited with that.

Mr. GARRETT. They are credited with that in the table which you present, are they?

Mr. COMBS. Yes, sir; we credit them with $525,000 in round numbers, in by-products—half a million dollars. We credited them with that.

Mr. FORDNEY. There is just one more thing, if you will permit me to interrupt you at this point.

Mr. GARRETT. Yes, certainly.

Mr. FORDNEY. To get a comparison of the cost of the production of sugar in Colorado and in Michigan, the average sugar content in the beets in Colorado should be given with the average content of the beets in Michigan.

Mr. COMBS. Certainly.

Mr. FORDNEY. Last year in Michigan it is my recollection that the sugar content in the beets was 16.1, or thereabouts.

Mr. COMBS. That is practically a 2 per cent difference, which makes a vast difference when you get down to it.

Mr. FORDNEY. A vast difference; yes.

Mr. COMBS. It will cost you a little more to handle the product of a 17-per-cent beet than of a 15-per-cent beet in the factory.

Mr. GARRETT. Is that all in that table? If so, what is the next one?

Mr. COMBS. In this table I have an itemized statement of the 10 factories, and in that I have included freight on this sugar to the distributing warehouse, which is an item of $247,658.50.

Mr. GARRETT. You may insert that, too.

Mr. COMBS. Now, if you want this sum total of the entire 10 factories, I can give you that. I think that would be well. For fuel, it is 45.50 cents per ton of beets. The lime rock is 21 cents; sacks, 28.75 cents; filter bags, oil, waste, etc., 6.50 cents; labor per ton of beets, $1.03; interest per ton of beets for the campaign, at 6 per cent, 30 cents; freight on sugar to warehouse, 26 cents a ton; cost of beets, $5.50. That makes a total of $8.1075.

Mr. FORDNEY. Per ton?

Mr. COMBS. Factory production; yes, sir. The receipts from a ton of beets are as follows: Sugar, 287.5 pounds at $5.50 in this case—and I think probably that price is too high. I have figured the other at $5, and I have figured this at an average of $5.50. I think that is not justice to the sugar people. I think it would not average $5.50. It might last year, but that was exceptional. But, anyway, I will give the figures as I have them. At $5.50 it amounts to $15.82 for the sugar. The pulp from a ton, 500 pounds, is worth 9 cents, and the sirup from a ton, 102 pounds, at a half cent, is 51 cents, making the total receipts $16.42, against $8.1075.

Mr. RAKER. Against what?

Mr. COMBS. $8.1075; leaving a factory profit, after we have allowed 6 per cent and the freight to the warehouse, of $8.32 a ton. That is not for any of your overhead charges, so far as the salaries and the thousand and one incidentals that go with the business are concerned. Mr. Morey's $25,000 a year salary, and all the other officials, in the same proportion, come out of this yet.

Mr. FORDNEY. Mr. Morey gets a salary of $25,000 a year, does he?

Mr. COMBS. That is what I have always understood; and I see by the record, in his own testimony here, that he gets $25,000 a year.

Mr. FORDNEY. That is better than being a Congressman.

Mr. RAKER. Right in this connection, have you any statement or data from which you can tell the committee what this overhead charge is, or would be, per ton?

Mr. COMBS. I have not right here, but I will be in town to-morrow and will be here, and I will be glad to prepare an estimate. I can only give you this as an estimate from my past business experience along other lines.

Mr. RAKER. You will do it, will you?

Mr. COMBS. Yes.

Mr. JACOWAY. That is, insurance, interest on capital, and depreciation on plant, cost of administration——

Mr. COMBS. I know the things that go with a business of this kind, and I will make it up as I understand it and give it to you as an estimate.

Mr. RAKER. Very well.

Mr. GARRETT. Have you any other table there?

Mr. COMBS. I have nothing that would be of importance to you gentlemen. I have the assessed valuation. I gave you that, did I not? However, I did not give that as authentic.

Mr. GARRETT. You said you preferred not to go into that question.

Mr. COMBS. Mr. Dakan will go into that in detail, I think.

(The statements presented by Mr. Combs to the committee in connection with the foregoing testimony are as follows:)

Days run	101
Total tons	695,425
Average daily slicing	993.46
Average test of beets	17.50
Average purity	85.43
Per cent of raw sugar from last year	0.16
Per cent of sugar in the bag	14.91
Average tons molasses made	5,265
Average per cent on beets	5.33
Per cent, coal on beets	23.43
Per cent, coke on beets	0.69

Production:		
2,073,757 sacks sugar, at $5		$10,368,785.00
Pulp, 25 per cent on beets, 173,856 tons, at 35 cents		60,839.60
Sirup refuse, 5.33 per cent, 33,783 tons, at $10		337,830.00
		10,767,454.60
Cost of production:		
695,425 tons of beets, at $5.50	$3,824,837.00	
162,938 tons of coal, at $2	325,876.00	
4,298 tons of coke, at $8	34,384.00	
49,375 tons of lime rock, at $3	148,125.00	
2,073,757 sugar bags, at 10 cents	207,375.70	
Filter bags, oil, waste, etc	45,202.62	
2,466 men, 101 days, average wages, $2.60	647,571.60	
Salaries, superintendent, field men, managers, etc.	76,496.75	
		5,309,869.17
Factory profit		5,457,585.43

Cost of fuel per ton of beets	$0.5180
Cost of lime rock per ton of beets	.3000
Cost of sacks per ton of beets	.2982
Cost of filter bags, oil, waste, etc., per ton of beets	.0650
Cost of labor per ton of beets	1.0426
Cost of beets	5.5000
	7.7238
Receipts from a ton of beets:	
Sugar, 298.20 pounds, at $5	14.9100
Pulp, 25 per cent, 500 pounds	.0875
Sirup refuse, 106.60 pounds, at 50 cents	.5330
	15.5305
Factory profit	7.8067
Cost per 100 pounds	2.5901
Cost per pound	.0259
Number days run	95.7
Tons sliced	862,321
Average tons daily	862.37
Per cent beets test	17.87
Average purity	85.39
Per cent raw sugar	0.21
Per cent sugar in bag	14.36
Tons molasses refuse	44,951
Per cent molasses on beets	5.13
Per cent coal on beets	22.83
Per cent coke on beets	0.67
Per cent lime on beets	7.01

Production:		
2,476,585 sacks sugar, at $5.50		$13,621,217.50
Pulp, 25 per cent on beets, or 215,580 tons, at 35 cents		75,453.00
Sirup refuse, 5.13 per cent, 44,957 tons, at $10		449,570.00
		14,146,240.50
Expense account:		
862,321 tons beets, at $5.50	$4,742,765.50	
Coal, 22.83 per cent on beets, or 196,609 tons, at $2	393,218.00	
Coke, 67 per cent on beets, 5,777 tons, at $8	46,216.00	
Lime, 7.1 per cent on beets, 61,224 tons, at $3	183,672.00	
2,476,585 sugar bags, at $100 per thousand	247,658.50	
Filter bags, oil, waste, etc., 6½ per cent	56,050.86	
3,050 men, for 95.7 days, at $2.60	758,901.00	
Superintendent, field men, managers, etc., salaries	87,094.21	
Freight on 2,476,585 bags sugar to warehouse, at 10 cents	247,658.50	
		6,763,234.57
Total profit		7,383,005.93

These figures and percentages are based on the average of 10 sugar factories and the result of one campaign.

Estimates:	
Fuel per ton of beets	$0.4550
Lime rock per ton of beets	.21
Sacks per ton of beets	.2875
Filter bags, oil, waste, etc	.0650
Labor per ton of beets	1.03
Interest per ton of beets	.30
Freight on sugar to warehouse	.26
Cost of beets	5.50
Total cost	8.1075

Receipts from a ton of beets:	
Sugar from a ton, 2.875 pounds, at $5.50	$15.82
Pulp from a ton, 500 pounds	.09
Sirup from a ton, 102 pounds, at ½ cent	.51
Total receipts	16.42
Net profit to the factory per ton of beets	8.32
One factory, handling 75,000 tons of beets in one campaign, earns a net profit of	624,000.00
The cost to build and equip a factory of 600 tons capacity is about	400,000.00
The factory therefore pays for itself in one campaign and leaves for the company	224,000.00

or 56 per cent on the investment.

Mr. GARRETT. Are there any further questions?

Mr. FORDNEY. Do you handle, as a merchant, any other sugar except beet sugar?

Mr. COMBS. Yes, sir.

Mr. FORDNEY. Where do you buy that sugar and from whom?

Mr. COMBS. At this time, while I am interested in the grocery business, I give it no attention, and have not for two years or better. Prior to that I was in business 16 or 17 years, and at one time, when I was in business in Denver, which covered a period of 10 years, we bought it all from the Great Western people—that is, practically all. I say "we." I mean the jobbers did. As I said here before, there was a friction between myself and the sugar companies. I was a kind of a thorn in the flesh all the time because I reserved the right to run my business as I saw fit, without having anybody dictating to me; and if I bought sugar at a given price I reserved the right to sell it at whatever price I pleased. That brought about friction of course. Therefore we attempted to buy sugar outside. We would go to some little factory down in Texas and the South, where we would find a small amount of sugar, and could get a car of sugar occasionally, but it appeared by the time it was rolling the information was in Denver, and when we went back to get more they did not have any. So it was a matter of buying it there or going without.

Mr. FORDNEY. Does your firm purchase sugar from the New York refiners?

Mr. COMBS. What is that?

Mr. FORDNEY. Have you or has your firm in recent years purchased from the New York refiners?

Mr. COMBS. No, sir.

Mr. FORDNEY. Directly or indirectly, have you purchased any sugar?

Mr. COMBS. No, sir.

Mr. FORDNEY. So you have purchased from the Great Western people except what you purchased down in Texas?

Mr. COMBS. Yes; but during this friction, in trying to get sugar outside, the jobbers that did an extensive business could not afford to take that chance, because people using two or three cars of sugar a week had to go where they could get the sugar. Of course they could not go outside to try to get it.

Mr. FORDNEY. Concerning this statement sent out from the Federal Sugar Co. by Mr. Lowry, who sits at the end of the table, did your firm ever get any requests to send out those circulars, demanding of your constituents free trade on sugar?

Mr. COMBS. Not to my knowledge.

Mr. FORDNEY. Well, I suppose the money paid by Mr. Spreckels would not reach everybody. Mr. Combs, how did you happen to come here as a witness to testify? Were you subpœnaed by the chairman of the committee?

Mr. COMBS. Yes, sir.

Mr. FORDNEY. Do you know anything about how your name was given or by whom your name was given to the committee?

Mr. COMBS. I could not quite say who furnished these names, but I believe Mr. Dakan conducted the correspondence principally with the chairman of this committee; and when he was asked for a number of names he gave some six or eight names, I think, and I happened to be one of the number that was chosen. That was all. I do not know who had the selection of these names, but they appeared to select men who knew as much as possible about the sugar business. Why they selected me I do not know, unless it was because of the fact that I was supposed to know some things, at least, being the national lecturer for this association. That is all I can say.

Mr. FORDNEY. You say you purchase practically all the sugar that your firm handles from the beet-sugar factories of your State. What proportion of the sugar consumed in Colorado is made in Colorado, or what proportion of the sugar made in Colorado is consumed in the State of Colorado? Do you know?

Mr. COMBS. Well, I should say nine-tenths of it. There is no sugar, to my knowledge, in the history of my business—that is, beet sugar—that ever came from outside. Of course, there is the cane sugar, which is probably one-tenth. Now, I am only making an estimate of this, but that would be, to the best of my knowledge, about one-tenth.

Mr. GARRETT. Cane sugar?

Mr. COMBS. Yes; one-tenth cane sugars and nine-tenths beet sugar. I believe nine sacks of beet sugar are sold to one sack of cane sugar.

Mr. FORDNEY. By your firm?

Mr. COMBS. I believe that is the average of the jobbers in Denver.

Mr. FORDNEY. Then nine-tenths of the sugar that is consumed in the State is made in the State. That is what you mean?

Mr. COMBS. Yes, sir.

Mr. GARRETT. You spoke awhile ago of there being friction at one time between your firm and the Great Western, was it?

Mr. COMBS. Well, I will say the sugar interests.

Mr. GARRETT. The sugar interests?

Mr. COMBS. Yes.

Mr. GARRETT. Over your desire to sell sugar at whatever price you chose?

Mr. COMBS. Yes.

Mr. GARRETT. When was that?

Mr. COMBS. That covered a number of years. Let me see. This is 1911. That was along about the years of 1903 to 1907 or 1908, or along there.

Mr. GARRETT. Do I understand that in those years the manufacturers of the sugar undertook to control the price at which the jobber should sell?

Mr. Combs. Well, the broker did. I can not say as to the sugar refiners, but the sugar broker was the man. It is only presumable that he was acting under the instructions of the sugar people. We had no way of knowing then.

Mr. Malby. Was he the broker for the refiners or the broker for the wholesale dealer?

Mr. Combs. He was the broker for the refiners.

Mr. Malby. Does not the refinery sell to the wholesaler and the wholesaler sell to the trade?

Mr. Combs. The refiners sell to the wholesaler through the broker. The broker transacts all of that business.

Mr. Malby. You buy from the wholesaler?

Mr. Combs. What is that?

Mr. Malby. You buy from the wholesaler, do you not?

Mr. Combs. Well, at times I did and at times I did not. The jobbers bought from the refiner, and I was supposed to be in the wholesale business.

Mr. Malby. Oh. That I did not hear.

Mr. Combs. I will say this, however——

Mr. Malby. What I want to know is as to whether the direction given by the broker was given to the wholesaler or whether it was given to the retailer, and who the broker represented.

Mr. Combs. He represents the sugar refiners and is the sales agent for them to the jobber.

Mr. Malby. By the jobber you mean the wholesale dealer?

Mr. Combs. Yes.

Mr. Malby. Was it in your capacity as a wholesale purchaser that you had the unpleasantness, if I might so designate it?

Mr. Combs. Not exactly; no. At that time I owned the Midland Grocery Co. My especial business was to sell to large contractors and Government contractors, and extensive stockmen, such as Senator Warren, for instance, who would buy $5,000 or $6,000 worth of stuff a year, in carload lots, for his stock industries. I catered particularly to that line of business. It was always a wholesale business, but in that instance I was not on the jobbers' list, you see. Then I had to get my sugar through the wholesaler. I could not buy it direct from the refiner.

Mr. Malby. What was the particular friction over? Was it over the fact that you were going to buy it direct?

Mr. Combs. There was in the State a retail grocers' association that was composed of practically all of the retailers in the State. That was one wheel. The broker had the wholesalers organized, and through them he manipulated both of these associations. Now the jobber says, "We want to get thus and so for sugar, and we have an agreement among ourselves." Mr. Morey is a wholesale grocer, you understand. The price is fixed, and we are notified every day what this price is, and we sell it for that price. If the price is $5.25 he will say, "We bill this to you at $5.25 for the sugar." The jobber says, "Now you sell it at a price that shows a certain profit, say 15 cents a bag. If you have kept the sugar card at the end of 30 days we will rebate you 10 cents a sack on the business done for that 30 days."

Mr. Malby. That is, if you did not cut the price?

Mr. Combs. Yes. "If you live up to the sugar card." If the retailer did not live up to the sugar card that was sent out by the secretary of their association once a week governing that and other commodities, he was reported, and the jobber from whom he bought the goods—and in fact all the jobbers—were notified that Brother So-and-so had fallen from grace and had broken the sugar card "and we notify you that if you sell this man any more sugar we will boycott your house."

That state of affairs put me in a bad position. In fact the jobbers notified me that they had been notified that if they sold me any more sugar they would be boycotted.

Mr. MALBY. Who did the boycott come from—the retailers?

Mr. COMBS. That boycott came from the retailers on the wholesaler, you see.

Mr. MALBY. In other words, this boycott was by the retail dealers, and your rebate came from the wholesaler?

Mr. COMBS. It extends all down the line. One was a wheel inside of another wheel.

Mr. MALBY. Your association was an association of retail dealers, and the person who was to pay you the 10 cents was the wholesaler, was he not?

Mr. COMBS. What is that? I did not quite catch that.

Mr. MALBY. I say the fellows who had the organization were the retail dealers, and the man who was to pay you the 10 cents rebate was the wholesaler?

Mr. COMBS. No, sir.

Mr. MALBY. Who was to pay you the 10 cents?

Mr. COMBS. The broker.

Mr. MALBY. He represented the wholesaler?

Mr. COMBS. Whether he had that in the sugar refiners' hands or otherwise, I am not able to state.

Mr. MALBY. It is quite important to us to know whether this was a matter in which the sugar refiners were interested.

Mr. COMBS. It is a matter of importance to us. We arrived at certain conclusions, but we could not prove anything.

Mr. MALBY. Who was to pay to you the 10 cents, or who did?

Mr. COMBS. The broker.

Mr. MALBY. And he is the representative of the wholesaler?

Mr. COMBS. No, sir; he is the sales agent for the Great Western Sugar Co.

Mr. MALBY. You did not pay anything to the Great Northern Sugar Co. direct, did you?

Mr. COMBS. No; but I am talking about the jobber. He did at this time. Later——

Mr. MALBY. Before we leave that I want this other matter cleaned up. Whether this money goes back by direction of the refiners or not is a matter that we are interested in.

Mr. COMBS. I understand.

Mr. MALBY. We are not interested in what the wholesalers or retailers do in the State of Colorado, but we are interested in the matter as to what the manufacturer himself does. Whether he assumes by any system of coercion to compel sugar to be sold to the consumers through any arrangement as to price is a matter that we are interested in.

Mr. COMBS. I understand.

Mr. MALBY. Now, what I want to know is whether the manufacturers of sugar, through their agents or servants, direct, paid to you or to anyone a rebate on condition of your living up to or observing any rules or regulations propounded by them as to what the price of sugar should be at retail?

Mr. COMBS. Not to me.

Mr. MALBY. Well, to anyone?

Mr. COMBS. Not in the capacity that I was in at that time, because I bought from the wholesaler.

Mr. MALBY. The broker is the agent of the wholesaler?

Mr. COMBS. No; I beg your pardon. The broker is the sales agent for the sugar refiners. He is the man that markets all their sugar.

Mr. MALBY. Does he agree to pay 10 cents back to anybody, or did he at any time?

Mr. COMBS. He always did it, as I understand it. If you will let me go a little farther I will explain that, so that it will be a little more clear to you. The time I refer to, of my own transactions in sugar, was the time I was buying this sugar from the wholesaler. Then I was in such shape, boycotted, you might say, that with my capital I could not conduct my business.

Mr. FORDNEY. You were boycotted by the wholesalers?

Mr. COMBS. It came about through the retailers, you understand. Then I went to a man who was in the wholesale grocery business, and I said, "How about this? They have got me in a pretty sharp corner. I have not got capital to conduct my business because I must buy goods in such large quantities that I can not do it with the capital I have. How would you like to go into this proposition with me?" Anyway, we made an arrangement, and we incorporated the Midland Grocery Co. He and I owned it. He was already in the wholesale grocery business. He built a large wholesale grocery house, and built it to accommodate the two concerns, with my offices on the one side and his on the other. The buyer for that wholesale grocery concern bought all the goods for both concerns. The goods were turned into my department at the actual cost of the purchase, and we kept the books for the other concern. However, we carried no stock. It all came out of the other stock. There was nobody to account to for the profits except this individual and myself. We conducted it in that way. I became familiar with it. While I did not do this buying, I got the benefit of all this buying, you see, in the other association, and there were no bones about it. All the jobbers and everybody talked of this rebate and all this business. That is exactly the way the business was done; and, while I did not do the buying, of course everything was taken for granted, and it was not necessary that I should go into the details of it. But it was always my understanding that they charged about 25 cents, and generally a cent for selling the sugar—that is the way we got it—and they rebated 10 cents if you did not break the sugar card.

Mr. MALBY. That was allowed by the refining company?

Mr. COMBS. I do not know anything about the refineries. We never had anything to do with them. We did the business with their agent, their broker.

Mr. FORDNEY. It came directly from the broker to your firm?

Mr. COMBS. That was always my understanding.

Mr. MALBY. What company was that?

Mr. COMBS. I do not understand who you mean.

Mr. FORDNEY. Was that the Great Western Sugar Co.?

Mr. COMBS. Yes. This person, so far as I know, I think represented nobody else but them. Possibly he did represent other factories. He was always supposed to control the sugar situation in Colorado.

Mr. MALBY. What year was that?

Mr. COMBS. It extended over the years 1903 to 1907, I think.

Mr. RAKER. 1903 to 1907?

Mr. COMBS. Yes.

Mr. MALBY. Has that all been done away with now?

Mr. COMBS. Well, yes. I had the satisfaction of knowing that the sugar card, as they all termed it, was broken in Colorado about the time I quit business, and everybody was going wild. They were selling sugar the way they wanted to, so far as the retailer is concerned. This is only hearsay, and I do not give it as a fact, but I understand there is still a card there among the jobbers and the brokers. They get 30 cents a sack now for selling the sugar. The wholesaler gets 30 cents a sack.

Mr. MALBY. I think there was at a certain period—and I thought it was prior to that time—a general contract that was entered into between the wholesalers and the refinery companies throughout the United States, including the American Sugar Refining Co., by which they agreed to sell to certain brokers or wholesalers only upon certain terms and conditions; and they, in turn dealt with the retail dealers; that they should not sell except to certain persons who observed certain rules and regulations prescribed by them. But that, however, as the testimony appears, has all been broken up, and nothing of that kind exists now, so far as they are concerned. But I was wondering whether it had been continued by any separate concern since that time. The testimony is that, so far as the American Sugar Refining Co. is concerned, it has not existed for several years.

Mr. JACOWAY. Relatively speaking, Mr. Combs, what is the price of sugar from January to June? Is it high or low?

Mr. COMBS. It is low as a rule.

Mr. JACOWAY. What is the price from October to December—high or low?

Mr. COMBS. Well, generally about an average price during those months.

Mr. JACOWAY. What is it from June to October?

Mr. COMBS. Well, it is generally high.

Mr. JACOWAY. Now, taking those three periods of time, when is there the greatest consumption of sugar—between January and June, or October and December, or from June until October?

Mr. COMBS. From June 1 to November.

Mr. JACOWAY. That is when your berries and fruits and everything else are ripe there and the canning season is on, is it not?

Mr. COMBS. Yes, sir.

Mr. JACOWAY. As a general rule do those prices become higher from June to October every year?

Mr. COMBS. Yes, sir.

Mr. JACOWAY. Can you explain to the committee why that is, when the consumption is the greatest?

Mr. COMBS. I can give you my idea of it.

Mr. JACOWAY. Give it, please.

Mr. COMBS. This is the way we have always understood it among ourselves: That that is the time when there is a demand for sugar, and the greatest quantities are used during these months. During the months of February, March, and April, and along there—spring months—there is but little demand for sugar, as compared with those other months, and if there was a reduction in sugar it appeared to be in those months when there is the lightest consumption; and we used to try to take advantage of those times when sugar was low. But we never were able to purchase any quantity.

Mr. JACOWAY. You could not get sufficient quantities in order to meet the advanced price from June to October. Is that it?

Mr. COMBS. No. What we wanted, naturally, was to speculate. We knew that past experience had shown us that within the next few months or weeks sugar would be back again; and we at one time, with my associates, as I have explained, got hold of about 8,000 sacks of sugar, as I remember, at a little better than $4, or $4.50.

Mr. JACOWAY. I infer that the high price from June to November is not governed by the law of supply and demand, but is strictly a sugar speculation.

Mr. COMBS. That is the way it has always seemed to us. If we could have bought the amount of sugar that we wanted, at the low terms, we would have bought it. Perhaps there might have been a scarcity, or some other reason. We rather thought there would be a surplus; but when we found we could not buy the sugar except just to meet our immediate needs, then we thought probably this price was to fool all of us people and you gentlemen; that "there is a war on, and we can not help this thing. Somebody has cut the price and we have to meet it." That was always our general impression that this was done for that purpose.

Mr. JACOWAY. Another thing, we would like to have you state to the committee what is the attitude of the farmers to the factory.

Mr. COMBS. Well, generally pretty bitter.

Mr. JACOWAY. Do all the farmers entertain hostile feelings toward the factory?

Mr. COMBS. Apparently so. You could go out and talk to a hundred men that grow beets, and while they might not be hostile individually they express no personal hostile sentiment or anything of that kind, still they all feel like they were working for the sugar refiners without any profit to themselves. That is the way they feel.

Mr. JACOWAY. If I get your idea correctly, you say that the Great Western Sugar Co. lives up absolutely to their contract; that when they make a contract they even go a little better than the contract calls for?

Mr. COMBS. I think so; yes.

Mr. JACOWAY. But your grievance is that the man who plants the beets and tills them and brings them to fruitage and sells to the factory, gets far too little for his labor and that his profit is far too little as compared with what the factory gets after the factory takes his beets and produces the sugar and sells the sugar to the consumer?

Mr. COMBS. That is where the whole trouble arises.

Mr. JACOWAY. That is your only grievance, judging from your testimony, I believe?

Mr. COMBS. That is all.

Mr. JACOWAY. You say that the farmer just about breaks even on the average from one crop to another?

Mr. COMBS. Practically so; that is the way the figures show. That is the way they all seem to talk, too. Of course some of us make money, just as I did, but we have to break the average to do it and have to be lucky.

Mr. JACOWAY. Mr. Combs, take a family of four people—a man and his wife and a boy 10 years of age and a girl 8 years of age. What would be their combined earnings for a period of 90 days—that is, from the time the beet is planted until it is sold to the factory?

Mr. COMBS. About $800 earning capacity for the four of them. They would earn about that amount.

Mr. JACOWAY. Do you consider that a fair wage for labor?

Mr. COMBS. Yes, I do. I think it is good wages. While it is hard work, yet it is contract work and they make harder work of it than they would if they were working by the day. But they are thrifty people; generally speaking they are foreigners, and their demands are not what ours are. They will live on one-quarter, perhaps, of what it is necessary for Americans to live on, and therefore they can and do save money.

Mr. JACOWAY. Would it be a good wage for an American?

Mr. COMBS. Yes, good wages, I think.

Mr. JACOWAY. Do you know of any instances in your part of the country, or anywhere else, where any factory or factories have divided up territory and one says to the other, "You may sell up to this point," and "You may sell up to that point," or, in other words, establish selling zones?

Mr. COMBS. No; I would not state positively that I know that, although that is the general impression.

Mr. JACOWAY. Well, give us the general impression, hearsay, in regard to that.

Mr. COMBS. The general impression is that the different sugar companies say: "This is my territory, and don't you invade my territory, and we will not invade your territory" and it appears that way.

Mr. JACOWAY. I will ask you if you have any evidence of that fact along that line. For instance, have you any evidence that drummers or brokers, representing, we will say, one factory, will travel to a certain point and go no farther, and others representing another factory will come up to that point and go no farther, and in that way have you any physical evidence of the fact that the territory is divided?

Mr. COMBS. No, I could not say that, to be authentic.

Mr. JACOWAY. But that is the general impression?

Mr. COMBS. Yes, sir.

Mr. JACOWAY. Do you know of any rebates that have been given to any railroads or corporations of any kind?

Mr. COMBS. I do not.

Mr. MALBY. There are one or two more questions that I would like to ask. I take it that the farmers who raise beets for the factory and complain that they have not a fair division of profits really have no monopoly of that complaint, but rather that that sort of a complaint is quite universal, whether it applies to the raising of beets or the canning of tomatoes or corn or peas or beans, or anything else relating to the operation of any factory operated with reference to the natural products of the soil; that the conditions between the raiser and the manufacturer are substantially the same whatever the product may be and in whatever part of the country a man may be operating. That is about so, is it not?

Mr. COMBS. I did not catch the first part of that statement or question.

Mr. MALBY. I say that the farmer who raises beets for the factory has not any particular monopoly of finding fault with the manufacturer, because that custom exists wherever there is the producer and the manufacturer, whether it is in the manufacture of sugar or the manufacture and canning of tomatoes or peas or beans, and so forth; the same feeling exists between the grower and the manufacturer in the one case that does in the other?

Mr. COMBS. I could not say as to that because I never had any experience or occasion to know about it.

Mr. MALBY. And another thing. You suggested that the growing of beets for the factory is quite advantageous to those who exceed the average and not very profitable to those who do not exceed the average; but really is not that a universal rule which is correct with reference to all who are engaged in agriculture or, in fact, almost any other business; it is not the average man, in other words, who makes a large sum of money, but it is the man who exceeds the average?

Mr. COMBS. Well, but that is a hazardous business to engage in, when you must beat the average in order to be successful.

Mr. MALBY. But is it not true that the average farmer who does not beat the average does not get anything more than a living?

Mr. COMBS. That may be true. It is a bad state of affairs, however, that we people, particularly in our own legislative halls, have to admit that our people only make a bare living. It does not sound good.

Mr. MALBY. Well, the average man may make more than a living, but what I mean is this: If you are going to be really progressive and have a constant feeling and realization of the fact that you are making progress, you must always beat the average.

Mr. COMBS. Well, it is not true in other businesses.

Mr. MALBY. I do not know. My observation is that it is true in other businesses. A man who raises the average cotton crop is not succeeding very well; a man who raises the average tobacco crop is not getting rich; a man up in my country who has the average dairy on the farm is just getting along; if he has an average orchard he is just getting along; but if he beats the average he is acquiring success, and nobody is successful in turning out the natural products of the soil unless he beats the average; he gets along, but he does not succeed, so to speak, unless he beats the average. That is the only suggestion I have in mind.

Mr. COMBS. In my instance I made some money off the acreage of beets I planted this year, or that I harvested this year rather, for I planted 18 acres of beets and I harvested only 10 acres. As to the others, I lost the use of those 8 acres of land for that season. We find those things often, that we lose a certain percentage of the beets that we plant. So if you count the land of mine that lay idle on account of not having a stand of beets you will see that I made no money this year.

Mr. FORDNEY. But you lost it because of the drought or lack of water.

Mr. COMBS. No; because of the high winds and the fact that with this delicate beet the dirt and gravel and sand blows it and cuts it right off to the earth.

Mr. MALBY. Of course that is the chance you are taking in that, as well as in other things.

Mr. COMBS. Yes. I am not charging up that to the beet crop, but I say that I lost the use of that land this year.

Mr. MALBY. And next year you might plant 20 acres and get a crop on the 20 acres; and so the average for a certain period of time would be good.

Mr. COMBS. But we have to take all those things into consideration, and that is why I say on the average the grower gets no profit. We are looking to the indirect profits that Mr. Palmer tells us about. We have not seen them yet, but they may come. I believe in the duty we have on sugar. I believe it ought to be kept there as it is, for the protection of the industry, and I do not believe we can overestimate the importance of this industry in the United States. But I do object to one class of individuals getting the benefit of all this duty.

Mr. MALBY. Now, we have got down to the exact point that we want to talk about for just a minute. What authority has Congress, and how can we in any wise help the farmer who grows the beets? How can we help you? Can you point out some way or some plan, which, if carried into law, would help the farmer to better his condition?

Mr. FORDNEY. Other than to maintain the duty?

Mr. MALBY. Other than to maintain the duty. Is there anything else that we can do?

Mr. COMBS. No, I think not, unless it can be proven absolutely that the industry is hampered on account of the interests. The only solution I could see to this problem is that the duty should be kept on sugar and that cooperation or independent factories be encouraged. I mean by cooperation that capital will come in and interest itself with us; that men with capital will come in and interest themselves with us as growers and let us purchase an interest in the business, and that we bind ourselves to the factory that we will grow beets for so many years; that we will own a certain percentage of this stock and have cooperation in the matter, and keep down this friction.

Mr. MALBY. Of course, there is no objection to your doing that.

Mr. COMBS. No; but I say that if we can do this in a few years we will produce all the sugars that we consume. There is no question about that.

Mr. FORDNEY. You would have no trouble about doing that, if you were satisfied that the tariff on sugar was not going to be tampered with?

Mr. COMBS. Yes, naturally we would. People are afraid of what is termed the Sugar Trust. We know of some factories that have been started and put out of business; they are out of business, at least to-day, and capital is about the most timid thing we have. They will say "We do not want to go against the trust proposition."

Mr. FORDNEY. Those two elements, then, are the real elements of danger to any capital that might possibly go into this business?

Mr. COMBS. If we can be assured that we can run a factory in an independent way, in a cooperative way, I will agree that I will put double the number of factories in Colorado that are there to-day. The farmers are ready to do that, and there have been overtures made to me by people who have the money, and they will fix it so the farmers are able to do this; but they must know that the duty is going to be left where it is, and that they can do this and be strong enough to do it without being affected by the interests.

Mr. MALBY. How would the consolidated interests, say of the Great Western Sugar Co., affect you? I mean, what power have they to affect you in such an organization?

Mr. COMBS. In a great many ways. I will give you one instance: In the case of this Brighton factory, the party made an arrangement with a man. "I will operate this factory, but when I commence to put this finished product in the warehouse I have not got the money to conduct this campaign, and will you furnish me the amount of $3 per bag on this sugar as I put it in the warehouse and take warehouse receipts for it?" He answered that he would; he agreed to it. Well, he started in, and on his first five carloads he asked for the money, and the man said: "Well, I do not know; you are not running this factory right or it does not look just right to me, and there is some danger perhaps, and I believe I can not furnish you this money." Well, he was out of the race, of course. He had no funds, and on investigating, he found out that this individual was a director in the Great Western Sugar Co. So there he was, broke.

Mr. GARRETT. When did this occur?

Mr. COMBS. This occurred—oh, I can not give you the year, but I should say, offhand, about four years ago.

Mr. GARRETT. Who was this man?

Mr. COMBS. This was Mr. Keyes. He has recited to me as a fact, given it to me as a fact, many instances wherein the concealed hand operated apparently to defeat him, and did defeat him and broke him.

Mr. FORDNEY. Undoubtedly when that man promised to furnish that money he intended to lead him into a trap?

Mr. COMBS. It is self-evident that he did, and he accomplished it. Now, it is just such things as that that the people are afraid of.

Mr. MALBY. Of course, there are independent bankers and moneyed men who would be willing to lend money under usual trade conditions in Colorado as well as elsewhere?

Mr. COMBS. Yes; but if they could be shown before the time comes that it would be more to their interest not to do it, the money would probably not be available. I have said to people who have made overtures to me along those lines, "Have you money enough to build this factory and a half million dollars in cash to conduct the campaign? If you have, I am interested, and my people will be interested, and I can give you the balance of the money and the people necessary to carry it through in a short space of time; but if you have not got that much money, count me out, because I do not want to have to count on somebody else for it." My experience in 20 years of business has taught me something, and I know the rules and tricks, and how those things come about, and whether you can prove them or disprove them does not matter. You know they exist, and Mr. Keyes has not much show.

Mr. FORDNEY. Was Mr. Keyes's factory a sugar factory in every sense, or a sirup factory? I think somebody has suggested that it was a sirup factory.

Mr. COMBS. A sugar factory. It was on quite a small scale, though. He manufactured sirup afterwards for years—the Keyes sirup.

Mr. MALBY. He simply lacked the capital or the ability to get it?

Mr. COMBS. Yes.

Mr. FORDNEY. Is the beet sugar manufactured in Colorado on the market all the year around?

Mr. COMBS. Yes.

Mr. FORDNEY. With us it is not; it is marketed during their campaign and as quick as they can get rid of it they sell it off.

Mr. COMBS. No; we have handled it the year around, except that I can not say that we did the last year. I think there was a scarcity of Colorado sugar last year.

Mr. FORDNEY. Especially during those months when the high prices prevailed?

Mr. COMBS. Yes; I think that was the condition.

Mr. FORDNEY. Is there any competition among the sugar factories of your State or of the southern part of the State, for beets, with the various farmers?

Mr. COMBS. None.

Mr. FORDNEY. You have only the one concern to sell to?

Mr. COMBS. There is no competition whatever in that respect.

Mr. FORDNEY. In the whole State?

Mr. COMBS. No; in our northern district if you want a market for your beets it must be with the Great Western Sugar Co. There is no competition.

Mr. MALBY. That is not an extraordinary condition, is it? If you were going to build a factory of your own and accept the management of it, you would not build it in a district, so to speak, where one of the Great Western sugar refineries is now located, but you would rather seek that section where the territory is unoccupied?

Mr. COMBS. Certainly.

Mr. MALBY. Where you would not be obliged to enter into competition with each other?

Mr. COMBS. Just the same as any other competitive business.

Mr. MALBY. Exactly, you would seek to get away from competition?

Mr. COMBS. I would, unless I had the acreage in that particular locality contracted for a number of years. If I had, then the other people would have to move.

Mr. MALBY. Then it would not make much difference.

Mr. FORDNEY. You say there is no competition in the purchase of beets or the growing of beets in Colorado. Is that the only concern in the State—the Great Western Sugar Co.?

Mr. COMBS. Oh, no; there are other companies down in the Arkansas Valley.

Mr. FORDNEY. That is away from your territory?

Mr. COMBS. That is away from our territory, yes. We could not market beets there.

Mr. MALBY. The only security you have got in the sale of beets, in other words, is the one of necessity to pay you such a price that you will continue to grow them?

Mr. COMBS. That is all; it is just a matter of consideration.

Mr. MALBY. Of course they might get it down so low that you would stop.

Mr. COMBS. Yes. Well, they are stopping. The tonnage in Colorado is far lighter than it used to be. In the several talks that I have made through northeastern Colorado in the last three of four weeks, I have distributed slips of paper among the audience, the beet growers, and asked them to state on there "I grew so many acres of beets this year; I would grow so many next year providing the price was equivalent to $6." And it shows an increase of about 33⅓ per cent in the acreage, if they could get that advance of 50 cents. We realize that the beet crop is one of the surest crops that we have in the State and if we could grow them so as to be assured of a profit we would grow more of them.

Mr. MALBY. What argument do they present to your request? When they pay you $5 a ton for 12 per cent sugar in beets, what argument do they present for not allowing you a similar percentage for every degree in advance of that which you produce?

Mr. COMBS. There is no argument; there is simply——

Mr. MALBY. An arrangement?

Mr. COMBS. They reserve the right to run their own business, which they have a right to do.

Mr. MALBY. But they pay you a certain sum for one percentage of sugar, up to 12 per cent?

Mr. COMBS. Yes.

Mr. MALBY. They pay you a certain amount for 12 per cent beets. Now, if they get 13 or 14 or 15 per cent, they pay you no more. And besides that, they have the advantage of not handling an additional quantity of beets. In other words, every per cent that you produce in excess of 12 per cent is more advantageous than any one of the percentages below that quantity?

Mr. COMBS. Yes. That is what looks strange to me, and I have always contended, and I made that argument with the sugar people at one time, just as I stated to-day, on the basis of 12 per cent and pay the same ratio above that. They said immediately that they could not afford to do this on 12 per cent beets. We have a leeway, you see, between 12 and 15, and I expected them to say that, and that is what I wanted them to say. "Now we will start at 13½ per cent," I said. "Now pay us 38 cents from there up." And what would we have? We would have more money than we are asking for. I said to them: "You have admitted you could pay us that." "Well," they said, "we do not care to discuss the subject." There was nothing to discuss. They had admitted it. I believe the only just way to buy or sell sugar beets is on the sugar content, absolutely, for both sides.

Mr. RAKER. It is just like testing milk.

Mr. COMBS. Just the same. That is the only business way to conduct it, I think. The sugar company gets pay for what they give and we would get paid for what we delivered. It will come to that some day, I think.

Mr. MALBY. I think that is a fair way to do it.

Mr. FORDNEY. When you refuse to raise beets unless they comply with your requests, then they have either got to come to your price or go out of business, have they not?

Mr. COMBS. Yes; if the farmers would stand together.

Mr. FORDNEY. That is what I mean.

Mr. COMBS. But they will not do that. They go out to that fellow and this fellow and, for instance, at Fort Morgan they have got a man—we call them "decoys"—and he grows a couple of hundred acres of beets each year, and he apparently is satisfied. Well, they go to him in the spring, the first one, and he signs up for 200 acres. They go to the next one and say: "Mr. Chase has signed up; he is willing to take this," and that is the way they get started. Then they go to the next man and they say: "Here are two men who have signed up; why are you fellows standing out?" And in some of these instances, where the men have signed up for 200 acres, they will plant only 50 or 60 acres, but it shows apparently that they are so anxious to make a contract for their beets that they will put in 200 acres, and that is the way they get them.

Mr. GARRETT. The Great Western, as I remember, grows on its own land about 36 per cent of the beets it uses. Is that correct?

Mr. COMBS. Oh, no; I could tell by the reports, but what they grow is not a drop in the bucket.

Mr. MALBY. Do they grow all they can; is all their land under cultivation?

Mr. COMBS. Oh, yes; and they rent lands.

Mr. MALBY. Then they must find it profitable themselves?

Mr. COMBS. Well, they want the beets and they will pay $60 or $70 an acre to grow these beets. There must be a profit in them or they would not want them.

Mr. MALBY. I should think they would rather pay you $60 than to spend $70 in growing them.

Mr. COMBS. It is a question of getting the beets.

Mr. MALBY. But you will furnish them if they will pay you more?

Mr. COMBS. Well, that is the point. They fought just as hard against the raise from $4.75 to $5 as they are fighting to-day.

Mr. FORDNEY. In the State of Michigan the farmers are getting much better conditions to-day than they were getting in the early stages in the beet-sugar industry.

Mr. COMBS. Yes, sir; but I see by the average of the beets grown in 1909, in Michigan—you say the cost is $30 per acre?

Mr. FORDNEY. Less than $30 an acre.

Mr. COMBS. They had an average tonnage of 7.31.

Mr. FORDNEY. In Michigan?

Mr. COMBS. Yes.

Mr. FORDNEY. Where did you see that?

Mr. COMBS. It is in the Government report.

Mr. FORDNEY. I think that is wrong. It is nearer 10 tons per acre than it is 9. It is nearer 10 tons and has been nearer 10 tons than 9 for the past several years. That must be an error, Mr. Combs. The highest average cost I have heard of was $30 per acre.

Mr. COMBS. In 1909, Michigan, 7.31; Colorado, 10.33—according to these figures.

Mr. FORDNEY. That must be an error. Is that a Government report?

Mr. COMBS. Yes.

Mr. FORDNEY. Then that is a mistake. It was upward of 9 tons. I do not know when it has gone below 10 tons.

Mr. COMBS. But I think the main restraint, offering my opinion without being asked for it, in the sugar industry to-day, is just the facts I stated awhile ago, that the people fear they can not get protection to cooperate in the sugar manufacturing end of the business.

If they could be assured of that—if there is any way that they could be assured that the growers would participate, like a great many of them in Germany are able to participate, in the dividends coming from the refining of sugar—it would get away from all this friction, and they would not be so particular about the price per ton, because they would get their dividends from the other end. If that state of affairs could be brought about, it would not be five years until the United States could export sugar. If they could do that under a protective tariff, when it reached that stage we could take off at least a part of the tariff and the Government could fix a duty for an internal revenue of a certain amount that would amount probably to what they get now. That looks to me like a solution of the problem.

All the grower wants is protection and he will grow the beet. There is no question about that. We have the territory, we have the land—in the arid States particularly—thousands of acres that are adapted to beet growing; and sugar factories would spring up all over if they knew they could be protected. But, as you say, there is no way that I see that Congress can regulate those things.

Mr. GARRETT. I want to correct what might be a wrong impression from the question I asked as to the Great Western Sugar Co. growing 36 per cent of the beets it uses. I got the testimony of Mr. Maury and Mr. Spreckels confused on that question. It is the California Co., of which Mr. John D. Spreckels is the head, that raises about 36 per cent of the beets the company uses, and not the other company.

Mr. FORDNEY. What you want is protection from foreign importation and protection from corporate interference.

Mr. COMBS. Yes. I am a standpatter on protection.

Mr. FORDNEY. That is, oppression by great combinations of capital and wealth?

Mr. COMBS. After we have grown large enough in this industry so that we can stand alone, I would be in favor of the duty being practically taken off and having an internal revenue established. Of course, that is what is the matter with the sugar companies to-day. "We do not know what is going to be done with the tariff, and we do not believe we can do as well by you as we did last year." That is what they say. It is the uncertainty, do you not see?

Mr. GARRETT. You say when the industry reaches the point where it can stand alone. That is, of course, assuming it does not stand alone now. How long do you suppose it would take, and what elements are there that would enter into the production of beets in the future that would give it any stronger standing, without a tariff, say, 15 years from now, than it has to-day?

Mr. COMBS. Well, if we produced our own sugar equal to our consumption at home, we need not fear imported sugar, because we would have the market at home. It probably, however, would be necessary to have a protection to a certain degree; but not to this extent, is what I mean. And then let the Government get an internal revenue from this production in the United States.

Mr. MALBY. To make up for the revenue which they would lose?

Mr. COMBS. Yes. They get some $5,000,000 I understand now. A small tax on the amount of sugar we consume would make that amount much more, and it would be so small that the consumer would not notice it.

Mr. RAKER. You were asked how you came here, and you explained. Now I want to ask if you anyone talked with you when anyone found out that you were coming here as a witness?

Mr. COMBS. Well, that is a pretty broad question. A great many came to me; yes.

Mr. RAKER. Did anyone discuss with you about your coming here and discuss the conditions of the farmers in Colorado and the sugar conditions there related to the Great Western Sugar Co.?

Mr. COMBS. Yes, sir; the Great Western Sugar people did.

Mr. RAKER. What was the purport of the conversation?

Mr. COMBS. Well, they were very much concerned about what we were going to say down here, and the principal thing that they seemed to be most concerned about was my attitude in regard to the tariff. At least, they asked me a great many questions about that, and I told them just where I stood on the tariff question, and I also said that I was coming down here and for what purpose I scarcely knew; that I did not know what this committee would ask me, but that I wanted to represent the industry in all fairness to everybody concerned, and I had a right to my own views, and there was nothing personal in this, no sentiment, and that I was going to give the facts as I understood them and knew them, and that if there was anything they could set me right in in regard to figures I would appreciate it, because I wanted to represent everybody in fairness.

Mr. FORDNEY. Did they come to you or did you go to them first?

Mr. COMBS. I went to them first. I went to them to talk to them about a contract for next year.

Mr. FORDNEY. And took this matter up?

Mr. COMBS. Yes; and then later they asked us about this trip. They brought that up themselves.

Mr. RAKER. They broached that subject themselves?

Mr. COMBS. Yes. They said, "I see by the papers that several of you have been summoned to Washington." I said, "Yes." Then the next day I asked Mr. Dickson if they would give me the average price of sugars per year and per month and for a number of years, from their books. I said that I could get these figures from the office, but I did not have the time to do so. He declined to accede to my request.

Mr. RAKER. Did you ask him for their cost in manufacturing sugar?

Mr. COMBS. No. I would not be guilty of asking a man in his own business that kind of a question. I asked him if he would mind giving me the average selling price that the refineries got for sugar in Colorado covering these periods, taking it from his books, but he said he could only give it to me in an offhand way, approximately. Well, I paid little attention to it, but I think he said it was 5.50. Whether he meant that to apply to the last year or an average I do not know, because I did not give it any thought after he evaded my question, because my own figures were that it was an average of about $5.

Mr. RAKER. Did you have any further conversation on that subject in relation to your coming here?

Mr. COMBS. No. Only in a general way. He seemed very anxious in the matter, as he had a right to be, to know about how they would be represented here, as to whether it would be in a spirit of fairness or from an antagonistic standpoint, he knowing that the growers, as a rule, are bitter toward them. Mr. Boettcher came in then. He called for him and he introduced me. He said, "I have had a talk with Mr. Combs, and I feel that he is a fair minded business man and that he looks at these things in a business way." He said, "This matter, so far as he is concerned, is purely a business proposition, and he looks at it in that way, and as long as he does that we feel if he only understands it right that he will represent everybody correctly."

Mr. GARRETT. Did you want to leave to-night, Mr. Bodkin?

Mr. BODKIN. No.

Mr. GARRETT. You can make your supplemental statement to-morrow, then.

Mr. COMBS. You asked me to prepare a statement as to the overhead charges, in my opinion.

Mr. RAKER. He has to come back to-morrow with that statement, and so I suggest that we adjourn now.

Mr. GARRETT. Very well, the committee will stand adjourned until to-morrow morning at 10.30.

(Thereupon at 4.40 p. m. the committee adjourned until to-morrow, Friday, December 8, 1911, at 10.30 a. m.)

AMERICAN SUGAR REFINING CO. AND OTHERS.

SPECIAL COMMITTEE ON THE INVESTIGATION OF THE AMERICAN SUGAR REFINING CO. AND OTHERS,
HOUSE OF REPRESENTATIVES,
Washington, D. C, December 8, 1911.

The committee met at 10.30 o'clock a. m., Hon. Thomas W. Hardwick (chairman) presiding.

TESTIMONY OF MR. E. U. COMBS—Resumed.

Mr. COMBS. Mr. Chairman, I was asked to make an estimate of the overhead charges in a beet factory and add it to the figures I gave yesterday. I have gone into that but I gave the reporter the papers last night and I can not get them back until this morning, so I can not get the number of sacks to figure the number of cents per sack. I presume I can do that just as well later.

The CHAIRMAN. Yes, sir.

Mr. FORDNEY. Do you get those figures from the same man that you got the other figures from?

Mr. COMBS. No; as I said last night, these estimates that I make are only estimates, and I give them as estimates.

Mr. RAKER. Mr. Combs, I understood from your testimony yesterday that the quantity of land which was in sugar beets was only about one-third of the land which is within reasonable distance of the factories; for instance, in the vicinity of the Longmont factory; is that right?

Mr. COMBS. No; I do not remember that I said anything whereby you could construe that meaning.

Mr. RAKER. Then perhaps it was the other witness who stated that.

Mr. COMBS. I remember I said that there was probably only one-third of the acreage now compared with what they had at one time.

Mr. RAKER. How is it now?

Mr. COMBS. I have reference to the past year.

Mr. RAKER. About one-third of the acreage?

Mr. COMBS. That would just be my judgment.

Mr. RAKER. Would the other two-thirds of the acreage be land on which sugar beets could grow?

Mr. COMBS. Yes; practically the whole area of the country is adapted to the growing of sugar beets.

Mr. RAKER. Does that same statement apply to the other localities where the factories are situated? I understand there are nine in the territory you speak of.

Mr. COMBS. No; not exactly. In northeastern Colorado, what we call the northeastern district, there are three factories, and while the acreage there is not what it has been in the past, yet the percentage with reference to former years is greater than it is in part of the northern district. Around Collins and up through that country, in a good many places, they have almost quit raising beets.

Mr. RAKER. Are there not large tracts of land in the same vicinity where these factories are which are susceptible of raising beets just as well as where the beets are now raised?

Mr. COMBS. Oh, yes, indeed.

Mr. RAKER. Are there large quantities of it?

Mr. COMBS. Yes, sir.

Mr. RAKER. Now, upon what did you make your statement yesterday that it would not pay to put up another factory?

Mr. COMBS. I meant in the same vicinity. These factories, for instance, the one at Brush—they have a daily slicing capacity of about 1,000 tons. The campaign ought to extend over 120 days' time, and they should slice 120,000 tons of beets. They are capable of doing that. However, they will slice only about 75,000 tons, perhaps, this year, because they have not got the tonnage. In other words, they could take care of twice the amount of beets if they had them. Therefore another factory could not operate in that particular vicinity unless they could get a greater acreage, which they could get; yet that greater acreage could be taken care of by this one factory.

Mr. RAKER. But there are other localities, and many of them, where factories could be located, where the ground is susceptible, where the climate is proper, and where you have irrigation, where many other factories could be established?

Mr. COMBS. Oh, yes; there is plenty of territory in Colorado for probably 30 or 40 factories instead of 16.

Mr. RAKER. Is there any reason why they have not been established, if the factories that are now established are making large returns; in other words, making from $6 to $8 per ton off of the beets?

Mr. COMBS. As I stated yesterday, the reason is that capital is a very timid thing, and it is not going into an investment that looks as though the other interests combined can defeat it; and I believe that if we could have some cooperative factories in which the grower could be interested—if we had some way to assure these people that their capital was protected and that their interests could not be jeopardized by other interests, there would be no trouble about getting plenty of sugar factories. There would be no trouble about getting all the farmers to invest money and cooperate and stop this friction, because what they did not get as a profit on their tonnage they would get in dividends from the factory.

Mr. RAKER. In other words, if the matter was so arranged between the men who owned the factories and the beet growers that the man who owned the factory would get fair returns and the beet growers would get fair returns for the amount of money invested, and they could harmonize, and if one was not trying to get an advantage of the other—assuming that—there is plenty of land and plenty of opportunity to raise three or four or five times as many beets and produce that much more sugar in these Western States than is being done to-day.

Mr. COMBS. Oh, yes, indeed. As I stated yesterday——

Mr. RAKER (interposing). With a good profit to the factory as well as to the farmers?

Mr. COMBS. Yes, sir. As I stated yesterday, if that protection could be assured in a cooperative way I believe that in five years the United States could produce all the sugar we consume.

Mr. RAKER. And still at the present time the beet grower, as you understand it, has not been given any benefit from this large tariff that is upon sugar at the present time?

Mr. COMBS. No, sir.

Mr. RAKER. But if the matter could be so adjusted that the beet manufacturer was compelled to deal in a business way and to give the grower the same interest that he ought to have, then the business would flourish; if that right?

Mr. COMBS. Yes, sir; if there was a more equitable division, as we see it, of the profits that are made.

Mr. RAKER. And you have not devised any methed by which that equitable division could be brought about by law for the protection of the factory, the grower, and the consumer?

Mr. COMBS. No.

Mr. RAKER. Except what you have already stated?

Mr. COMBS. There is no way I can see. We have laws all along those lines now which lead just up to what you gentlemen are trying to do now—to get rid of this difficulty; but I can see no way whereby there could be any protection extended to the people. These facts exist, and while we know them of a certainty, yet there are many reasons why we can not prove these things.

Mr. RAKER. As a matter of fact, the way it is now arranged, with a fewer number of factories and the way they have been doing business, it gives them a better advantage, a better opportunity to make more money, than if there were more sugar factories?

Mr. COMBS. Oh, yes; I think so.

Mr. FORDNEY. Mr. Combs, you stated just now that this one factory at Brush this year, which would be an average, will grind about 75,000 tons of beets?

Mr. COMBS. That is an estimate.

Mr. FORDNEY. It has been stated here—I do not know whether by you, but by Mr. Bodkin who preceded you—that the profit of the factory is $8 per ton of beets delivered by the farmers; that the profit to the factory is $8 per ton.

Mr. COMBS. My figures are $8.32 factory profit without any overhead charges.

Mr. FORDNEY. Now, Mr. Combs, 75,000 tons of beets, at $8 per ton, would be $600,000 profit?

Mr. COMBS. Yes.

Mr. FORDNEY. Mr. Willett, of Willett & Gray, states that the average profit is $1.10 per hundred pounds, which would be $250,000 profit to that factory on 22,500,000 pounds of sugar made, or 300 pounds per ton on 75,000 tons. Those are the figures you gave. You would have to have at least 17½ per cent sugar in your beets in order to get 300 pounds of sugar per ton. You can not get 300 pounds of sugar per ton from 15 per cent beets.

Mr. COMBS. I understand that. I gave you the facts just as I had them. It was not guesswork.

Mr. FORDNEY. According to your figures 17½ per cent is the average?

Mr. COMBS. Yes; that was the average, too, for all these factories.

Mr. FORDNEY. Is that about the average percentage you get out of beets in Colorado, 17½ per cent?

Mr. COMBS. We have never known exactly.

Mr. FORDNEY. Now, take the year 1908 which, according to Mr. Morey's report, is shown to be a good year—some years the beets run higher in percentage than in others, do they not?

Mr. COMBS. Yes; but, as a rule, our beets run high.

Mr. FORDNEY. Now, on 75,000 tons ground out by that factory and 300 pounds of sugar per ton you would get 22,500,000 pounds of sugar; and a cent a pound would be $225,000 profit and a cent and one-tenth would be $250,000, but on a profit of $8 per ton that factory would make $600,000.

Mr. COMBS. On that basis. On the basis of my figures, they made $635,000.

Mr. FORDNEY. On 75,000 tons of beets?

Mr. COMBS. Yes, sir; a 600-ton-capacity factory. If they ground 75,000 tons per year in a campaign, they would earn $625,000 factory profit. In other words, the factory would practically pay for itself and pay a dividend of 50 per cent out of the factory profit.

Mr. FORDNEY. You think those figures are correct, do you, Mr. Combs?

Mr. COMBS. I know they are, to the best of my knowledge and belief, and that is what I am testifying to.

Mr. FORDNEY. Mr. Combs, you come here and testify not as a farmer but as a merchant?

Mr. COMBS. No; I am testifying from my experience as both.

Mr. FORDNEY. Your principal business has been that of a grocery merchant?

Mr. COMBS. I am a farmer now.

Mr. FORDNEY. You have no interest in the grocery business any more?

Mr. COMBS. I have a slight interest now in it; yes.

Mr. FORDNEY. But your business is that of farming?

Mr. COMBS. Yes, sir; I live on a farm with my family.

Mr. FORDNEY. And you raised 17 acres of beets this year?

Mr. COMBS. Yes; I planted that much.

The CHAIRMAN. Mr. Combs, there is one matter the Chair wishes to direct your attention to. I think you said in the early part of your testimony that you were prepared to give us some figures as to the cost of a beet factory. Correct me if I am wrong about that. Did you not say you could do that?

Mr. COMBS. Yes. I have had some estimates made on this subject. I have thought somewhat about interesting myself in some factories in the West, and I got some estimates. However, I never got those from manufacturers, but I have got them from other people; in fact, Mr. Keyes had some estimates which he had had prepared.

The CHAIRMAN. Mr. Keyes, the same gentleman you were speaking of before?

Mr. COMBS. Yes, sir.

The CHAIRMAN. Have you those estimates at hand?

Mr. COMBS. No; I have not. I have not them in figures, but I can give them to you as I remember them.

The CHAIRMAN. Well, give them to us as you remember it. What did it cost you to construct a beet factory?

Mr. COMBS. A 600 daily capacity factory——

The CHAIRMAN (interposing). A slicing capacity of 600 tons?

Mr. COMBS. Yes, sir. That figures $367,000, as I remember it, the actual figures. However, in speaking of it we always spoke of it as $400,000.

The CHAIRMAN. $400,000 for a 600-ton factory?

Mr. COMBS. Yes, sir.

Mr. FORDNEY. About $600 per ton of capacity?

Mr. COMBS. Something like that.

The CHAIRMAN. Just on that point, Mr. Oxnard estimated for this committee that the cost of equipping a first-class beet factory was $1.000 per ton of slicing capacity. He finally increased his estimate by 25 per cent to include the latest improvements and processes. Mr. Hathaway, of the Michigan Sugar Co., seems to have estimated it at one time in a hearing before a congressional committee at $1,000. Mr. Warren, the president of the Michigan Sugar Co., figures it at $1,500 per ton. Mr. Morey, the president of the Great Western Sugar Co., at $1,500 per ton; Mr. Nibley, who seems to be interested in the business in Utah, at $1,000 per ton. We asked them the cost to build and equip and get ready for operation a first-class factory, with all the latest improvements; in other words, a good beet factory, such as a man ought to have.

Mr. COMBS. That is my understanding, too.

The CHAIRMAN. You say according to the estimates you got when you were actually seeking to build one it was $600 per ton of capacity, or something near that amount?

Mr. COMBS. Something like that.

The CHAIRMAN. Did those figures contemplate a factory of the latest kind, with all the latest improvements, the Steffens process, and with everything up-to-date?

Mr. COMBS. Yes. The Steffens process they do not use in our country any more. We do not consider that because it does not pay to work it.

The CHAIRMAN. In other words, did the sort of factory you were getting the bids made on include all the latest improvements and processes used in your country?

Mr. COMBS. Yes, sir.

The CHAIRMAN. And those are the actual figures—what you could have had it put up for?

Mr. COMBS. Yes, sir; that is, as I remember it.

The CHAIRMAN. I mean substantially.

Mr. COMBS. Yes; substantially. The variation between my statement and $1,000 you will perceive is not as great as the variation in the statements of the other gentlemen here. It is a difference of $500.

The CHAIRMAN. They vary a great deal among themselves. The reason I call your attention to those figures is that the lowest estimate we have had submitted yet was $1,000 a ton and the highest was the one submitted by Mr. Morey, from your State, who placed it at "$1,500 per ton or even more," is the way he put it.

Mr. FORDNEY. If the chairman will permit me, however, I will say that Mr. Warren's statement of the cost of $1,500 per ton included the latest improvements and a new process—the Steffens process—and also their latest improved methods of drying pulp, and everything that went into a first-class, complete factory.

Mr. COMBS. I will say that my estimate did not include the drying process. That is a rather expensive process, and is not employed in our country at all.

The CHAIRMAN. You say that process is not employed in your country, yet Mr. Morey's figures must have been given for exactly the sort of plant you were thinking of putting up.

Mr. COMBS. They must have been, because that is the kind of plant they operate, and there was a time when they used the Steffens process in some of those factories, but it proved unprofitable, so they have quit it.

The CHAIRMAN. So that if you had unlimited capital you would not put that up?

Mr. COMBS. No, sir.

The CHAIRMAN. You think $600 per ton or the figures you gave are correct, and that you could have built the factory for that?

Mr. COMBS. Yes, sir; as I remember it.

The CHAIRMAN. When was it that you got those figures; what year?

Mr. COMBS. That was last year.

The CHAIRMAN. Do you know from whom this gentleman, Mr. Keyes, got them?

Mr. COMBS. No; I do not; but he is a man who is posted on such things, and he is not only a sugar refiner, and can go into a mill and refine sugar, but he can put the machinery in place. He understands that part of it, so I feel quite sure that he would be a reliable man to get up such figures. He had the specifications drawn, and there were other parties at that time who talked about taking over this little factory at Brighton and making it a 500-ton capacity factory, and these figures came from those investigations, as I understand it. But, from the statement given, the variation between those gentlemen who are supposed to be——

The CHAIRMAN (interposing). This is a matter of opinion, more or less. Of course, I am not trying to impeach anybody.

Mr. COMBS. I understand that exactly; but, understand, I would not put up my judgment against such gentlemen as those in the business who have spent years at it, and they are in a position and should know more about this than I know. I am only giving you the facts as I understand them and know them.

The CHAIRMAN. But the important part about this is that you are giving us not an estimate but an actual fact, if you are right about it, that you went out to put up just this sort of factory.

Mr. COMBS. Yes, sir; and from a disinterested standpoint.

Mr. FORDNEY. Do I understand that the chairman says that you went out and put up such a factory?

Mr. COMBS. No; I was making investigations with that in view.

The CHAIRMAN. That is what I meant—that he was looking into it.

Mr. MALBY. Did you receive any bona fide offer from any responsible people to construct a complete factory at $600?

Mr. COMBS. I did not. We did not go that far. I did not, at least.

Mr. MALBY. Did anybody, to your knowledge, receive such an offer that they would build and completely equip a factory for $600 per ton?

Mr. COMBS. I could not say positively whether these people had made a proposition on his specifications or not. I can not state that. I saw those specifications, and he told me that.

The CHAIRMAN. That was his estimate?

Mr. COMBS. Yes, sir; whether he had actual figures on this—I presume he did, and I think he said so, but I would not say positively that he did say so.

The CHAIRMAN. What is that gentleman's name? Have you been able to remember his initials?

Mr. COMBS. I could not find it in my book, but I will supply that later. I will be glad to do it. There are a number of other Keyes there, and I get their initials mixed.

Mr. MALBY. The only difficulty I see about the testimony is that the manufacturers from Michigan and Colorado and Utah and California have testified that their actual cost of construction was not in any case lower than $1,000, and from that amount to $1,500.

The CHAIRMAN. I do not remember the testimony in exactly that way. As I understand it, that was their estimate based upon their knowledge.

Mr. FORDNEY. I think, Mr. Chairman, we have it in evidence here over and over again that the contract price is $1,000 per ton.

TESTIMONY OF MR. JAMES BODKIN—Recalled.

Mr. GARRETT. Mr. Bodkin, I understood that you desired to supplement your statement along certain lines. Just make the statement in your own way.

Mr. BODKIN. On the line that Mr. Fordney led me. Some of his testimony that he brought out for me to sanction may have been so long I did not catch all of it, and anything that I sanctioned that he said I would not want it to go as my testimony without I thoroughly understood it.

Mr. FORDNEY. I do not understand that I put anything in the witness's mouth. He was speaking for himself, and I asked him certain questions, and anything he has answered in the record is no answer of mine at all.

The CHAIRMAN. Not at all. Of course, you are not testifying.

Mr. Bodkin, do you want to change any statement you made in answer to any question?

Mr. BODKIN. Yes; one thing.

Mr. FORDNEY. If I misled you in the slightest, you can correct me.

Mr. BODKIN. One thing the committee thought I said, and I did say, that they went in the slums, and then he did not ask me to give where I got my information. I was quoting the information that the agent told. I just used his words. I do not mean that it is me who says they got slum help.

The CHAIRMAN. They told you that themselves?

Mr. BODKIN. I heard that talked around, and that I led the committee to think that these people were under bondage to the Great Western, and I was throwing that insinuation against the Great

Western. These people are not under bondage. They are hired just the same as all the people in this house. They can quit any time they want to, and they are not under bondage at all; and the way I came to say that they went to the slums and got them, that was the quotation that the agent used, that he went to the slums.

The CHAIRMAN. The agent of whom?

Mr. BODKIN. Of the Great Western Sugar Co. Then, also, along the lines of raising beets cheaply, I quoted what I did do, and that it cost me $69, or in the neighborhood of that, to raise beets. They do not quote anything about $9 of that was for water and extras above the average price. Taking that out, I did not pay no more for my beet raising than the average of the country, which is $60, without the seed. Then, to compete with the Michigan prices, next year I expect to raise beets for less than $30 an acre. That might seem strange, but it is mighty easy. The land I expect to use is worth nothing. I will have to summer fallow it. I would not get a cent out of it if I didn't put it in beets. Then there are only 4 acres, and I can do that little work myself when I am resting and when my horses have no work.

Mr. FORDNEY. But if you work it on the same basis you worked the other land it will not pay you.

Mr. BODKIN. I am saying I can do that because I have nothing else to do like the Michigan people may have; and then the horses would not cost me anything, because I own them and I would not need to charge for them, and I expect to only irrigate it once with the water that comes with my water rights, and I would save that expense. So I figure that I can raise beets on this particular patch next year for less than $30.

Mr. FORDNEY. If you do not charge anything for your land or your labor?

Mr. BODKIN. My land would be worthless next year.

Mr. FORDNEY. Did I lead you to believe that that is the way the Michigan people raise beets?

Mr. BODKIN. It has got to be something along that line or it would cost them more money.

Mr. FORDNEY. Well, the Michigan people will be here to testify for themselves.

Mr. BODKIN. Yes; we can bring you decoys from Colorado to testify, too.

Mr. FORDNEY. We do not raise beets with decoys in Michigan.

Mr. MALBY. I feel, Mr. Chairman, I ought to object to the attitude of the witness toward a member of our committee.

The CHAIRMAN. Yes.

Mr. MALBY. Yesterday the witness referred to Mr. Fordney as talking like a representative of the Sugar Trust.

Mr. FORDNEY. Like one of their hirelings, is the way he put it.

Mr. MALBY. To-day he is charging him with producing decoy farmers, and the committee is not here for the purpose of hearing that sort of testimony.

The CHAIRMAN. I will say this, in justice to our colleague and as bearing on the question raised by Mr. Malby, the chair will not permit, of course, any witness to reflect on any member of the committee or to use any improper language in giving his testimony. I presume this witness did not intend anything he said to reflect personally on Mr. Fordney or on any other member of the committee, but I wish to caution this witness. Of course, each member of the committee will be polite to the witnesses and I trust we will not have any misunderstandings like this. I am sure the witness in what he says to-day or in what he said yesterday did not mean any personal reflection upon our colleague, whom we all esteem very highly. We will try to proceed in order.

Mr. FORDNEY. Mr. Chairman, I wish to ask the witness a question. He has now stated that he was quoting the saying of an agent of the sugar company when he spoke about the employing of slums. What is the name of that agent, if you please? Give us the name and address of the agent who made that statement to you.

Mr. BODKIN. I do not know where he is now. His name is Land.

The CHAIRMAN. Can you give us his initials?

Mr. BODKIN. No; it has been some four or five years ago.

The CHAIRMAN. What was his position then and where did he live at that time?

Mr. BODKIN. He was a labor contractor among the farmers.

The CHAIRMAN. Was he an agent or did he have anything to do with the Great Western Sugar Co.?

Mr. BODKIN. He pretended to be acquainted with the slums, and on account of his acquaintance with the slums of some of the various towns they employed him to go amongst the slums.

Mr. FORDNEY. Who employed him?

Mr. BODKIN. The Great Western paid him.

The CHAIRMAN. The Great Western paid him for doing this work?

Mr. BODKIN. Yes, sir.

The CHAIRMAN. Which he professed was done because he was acquainted among the slums and knew how to get this labor?

Mr. BODKIN. Yes, sir.

The CHAIRMAN. Where was his residence at that time?

Mr. BODKIN. He lived at Highland Lake.

The CHAIRMAN. Highland Lake, Colo.?

Mr. BODKIN. Yes, sir.

The CHAIRMAN. Do you know where he is now?

Mr. BODKIN. No; I do not. He has been gone three or four years.

The CHAIRMAN. Is he in Colorado now?

Mr. BODKIN. I couldn't say. I have heard he has a daughter there. But Hastings, Nebr., is one of his main places. He moves around a great deal.

The CHAIRMAN. Hastings, Nebr., was one of the places where he makes his headquarters?

Mr. BODKIN. Yes, sir; he lives there sometimes.

The CHAIRMAN. After he left Colorado?

Mr. BODKIN. Well, before that, sometimes.

The CHAIRMAN. Before he came to Colorado, sometimes he was at Hastings?

Mr. BODKIN. Yes, sir.

The CHAIRMAN. Is there anything else that you wish to add by way of correction or explanation of the testimony you gave yesterday?

Mr. BODKIN. No; I think not.

TESTIMONY OF MR. ALBERT DAKAN.

(The witness was duly sworn by the chairman.)

The CHAIRMAN. Give us your full name, please?

Mr. DAKAN. Albert Dakan.

The CHAIRMAN. Your residence?

Mr. DAKAN. Longmont, Colo.

The CHAIRMAN. Your business?

Mr. DAKAN. Attorney at law.

The CHAIRMAN. Are you engaged in the practice of law in Colorado?

Mr. DAKAN. I am.

The CHAIRMAN. Have you any official or professional connection with the Sugar Beet Growers' Association of Colorado?

Mr. DAKAN. I am attorney for the sugar-beet committee of the district board of northern Colorado of the Farmers' Union—the Farmers' Educational and Cooperative Union.

The CHAIRMAN. You are attorney for their sugar-beet committee for the northern district of Colorado?

Mr. DAKAN. Yes.

The CHAIRMAN. How long have you held that position?

Mr. DAKAN. About a year and a half.

The CHAIRMAN. Do you know of your own knowledge about the sugar industry out in Colorado? I mean, have you any personal knowledge of the conditions there? You live near the beet fields?

Mr. DAKAN. Yes, sir; I have been among the beet fields, you might say, since the inception of the industry at Longmont. I have been agent for farmers who have raised beets, and I have stood in the landlord's shoes for a number of acres around Longmont, and was attorney for a company that rented 300 acres of beet land to secure the factory at Longmont, and have the papers here regarding that and the report showing the experience of the first beet crop; and since that time I have been more or less connected with the industry in the way of standing in the landlord's shoes.

The CHAIRMAN. Now, Mr. Dakan, since you are a lawyer, we will not have to lead you very much, and I will just ask you to begin and tell in your own way, and according to your own plan, what you have to submit to the committee.

Mr. DAKAN. The first proposition would be the assessed valuation of the Great Western Sugar Co.

The CHAIRMAN. I had just started to make a general statement explanatory of the evidence we want you to give. We want you to give this committee all the information you have as to the price of beets and the treatment of the beet growers by these sugar companies, the cost of producing sugar beets, and the cost, if you know, of producing a pound of beet sugar at the factory, and labor conditions generally in the beet-sugar industry of Colorado, and all questions connected with this matter. You have heard some of the testimony, and you have observed the line we are pursuing. You can just take up those points one by one and go over them and tell us what you know about them, and from time to time we will ask you such questions as occur to us.

Mr. DAKAN. The assessed valuation of the property of the Great Western sugar factory in northern Colorado by companies was obtained partly by personal investigation of the records and partly by letters received from the assessor or treasurer of each county. Beginning with Denver County, the assessed valuation for 1910 of the Great Western Sugar Co. was $75,000. I asked the treasurer to give me the total assessed valuation of the property of the Great Western Sugar Co., and those are the figures given me. The assessed valuation, from my own examination in Boulder County, Colo., of the total property on which the company paid taxes in Boulder County, Colo., for 1910, was $438,500. The assessed valuation of that company for Larimer County, Colo., is taken from a letter from Frank W. Moore, treasurer of Larimer County:

I, Frank W. Moore, treasurer of Larimer County and State of Colorado, do hereby certify that the amount of taxes paid by the Great Western Sugar Co. in the said county amounted to $30,524.05 for the year 1910.

FRANK W. MOORE,
Treasurer of Larimer County.

Mr. FORDNEY. How many factories are in that county?

Mr. DAKAN. Two factories, rated at 1,200 tons.

The CHAIRMAN. How many factories are in the other county you mention?

Mr. DAKAN. In Boulder County, one factory rated at 1,200 tons capacity.

The CHAIRMAN. According to that, they are upon what valuation?

Mr. DAKAN. I have this letter from the county assessor:

FORT COLLINS, COLO., *November 21, 1911.*

I hereby certify that the assessed valuation of the Great Western Sugar Co. for the year 1910 was $676,400.

That is for Larimer County.

Mr. FORDNEY. That is the county where the taxes were $30,000?

Mr. DAKAN. Yes; $30,524.

Mr. FORDNEY. About 6 per cent; is that right?

Mr. DAKAN. Yes; on the assessed valuation.

Mr. FORDNEY. About 6 per cent on the assessed valuation?

Mr. DAKAN. Yes, sir.

Mr. FORDNEY. Do you know what those factories cost?

Mr. DAKAN. No, sir.

The CHAIRMAN. Have you summarized those taxes, assessments, and valuations for the entire State?

Mr. DAKAN. No, sir. I have just gotten a lot of these; in fact, some of them have come while I have been here. It is awful hard to get them by letter.

The CHAIRMAN. They are matters of public record, are they not?

Mr. DAKAN. But when you write to an official for this kind of material you may get an answer or you may not. The assessed valuation of property of the Great Western Sugar Co. for Weld County, Colo., for 1910, and the taxes for each factory, are as follows—this is from a personal examination of the records.

The CHAIRMAN. There are how many factories in that county?

Mr. DAKAN. Three; Eaton factory, $193,030; total tax. $7,525.58.

The CHAIRMAN. What is the capacity of that factory?

Mr. DAKAN. It is rated a 600-ton factory. The Greeley factory, assessed valuation for 1910, $191,740.10.

The CHAIRMAN. What is the capacity of that factory?

Mr. DAKAN. It is rated at 600 tons. The taxes were $8,287.58. The Windsor factory is rated a 600-ton capacity; assessed valuation for 1910, $211,330; taxes, $8,230.35.

Mr. FORDNEY. Mr. Dakan, do you know what the assessed valuation of property is in those counties compared with actual value?

Mr. DAKAN. The farmers are supposed to pay on about 35 per cent valuation.

Mr. FORDNEY. How about city property—all other property except farm property?

Mr. DAKAN. That is the general scheme. The general scheme is from 25 to 35 per cent, from one-fourth to one-third.

Mr. FORDNEY. They are assessed from 25 to 35 per cent of their real value?

Mr. DAKAN. Yes.

Mr. FORDNEY. Now, if these factories cost what Mr. Morey claims they did—$1,500 per ton—then those two factories cost $3,600,000, on which they paid $30,000 taxes.

Mr. DAKAN. I think you misunderstand me, Mr. Fordney. The two factories in Weld County are rated as 600-ton.

Mr. FORDNEY. Mr. Dakan, I do not think I misunderstand you. You perhaps misunderstand me. What I want to get at is the average assessment they are paying taxes on; for instance, whether the assessed valuation of property ranges from 25 to 35 per cent of its real value in those counties.

Mr. DAKAN. That is the scheme of taxation in northern Colorado.

Mr. FORDNEY. If the assessed valuation ranges from 25 to 35 per cent, then the assessed valuation was $600,000, while they cost $3,600,000; am I right about that?

Mr. DAKAN. Each would cost $600,000 if the cost to build the factory was $100,000 per 100 tons.

Mr. FORDNEY. No; $1,500 per ton was the cost.

Mr. DAKAN. I am figuring on a basis of 100 tons, and I think that is where our trouble has come.

The CHAIRMAN. Taking Mr. Morey's estimate, the cost of them would be greater than that, if he is correct in his view.

Mr. FORDNEY. According to Mr. Morey's estimate of the cost, those two factories, with 1,200 tons capacity daily, would cost $3,600,000, at $1,500 per ton, on which they paid $30,000 taxes.

Mr. DAKAN. Or $9,000 on each factory, depending on whether you use $100,000 for each 100 tons or $150,000 for each 100 tons.

The CHAIRMAN. Mr. Fordney is applying now Mr. Morey's figures.

Mr. DAKAN. But we must understand each other before I can answer him.

Mr. FORDNEY. I am trying to get at the percentage of assessed value compared with its real value.

Mr. DAKAN. Yes, sir.

Mr. FORDNEY. Did I understand you to say that the assessed valuation of those two factories was $600,000?

Mr. DAKAN. You mean the assessed valuation of the three factories?

Mr. FORDNEY. No; of the two factories in the first county you mentioned.

Mr. DAKAN. Oh, I beg your pardon; I have been thinking of Weld County and you have been talking of Larimer County.

Mr. FORDNEY. I mean the two factories in the first county you mentioned.

Mr. DAKAN. In Larimer County, the two factories, of 2,400 tons capacity, are assessed at $667,400.

The CHAIRMAN. What is the basis, about 1 to 3 or 3 to 4?

Mr. DAKAN. From 2 to 5 or 4 to 5.

The CHAIRMAN. Which is it?

Mr. DAKAN. It varies; one-third is the general scheme.

The CHAIRMAN. That is the scheme applying to these people?

Mr. DAKAN. Yes, sir; in these counties in northern Colorado, they aim to assess the property at about one-third its value.

The CHAIRMAN. Do you think that was done in this case?

Mr. DAKAN. The Great Western Sugar Co. has its dealings with the State board of equalization, and it is not under the jurisdiction of the county authorities altogether, but where there is an assessor who has knowledge, of course, he has some influence with the State board of equalization. For instance, in Boulder County, the assessed valuation in round numbers is $440,000 on one 1,200-ton factory, and two 1,200-ton factories in Larimer County are assessed at $676,400.

The CHAIRMAN. Well, it varies a little?

Mr. DAKAN. There is a variation of about $325,000. Of course, you gentlemen are familiar with the possible reasons for variation in these matters.

The CHAIRMAN. It would depend on how rigid the county authorities are on the companies.

Mr. FORDNEY. It might be necessary to raise more money in one county than in another.

Mr. DAKAN. There are a number of reasons.

The CHAIRMAN. That would affect the rate of taxation, but not the assessment.

Mr. FORDNEY. That would affect the assessment of the property as compared with its true value.

Mr. DAKAN. In so far as any accounting was made on the valuation of the actual physical property——

Mr. FORDNEY (interposing). It may have been fixed higher once and then cut down.

Mr. DAKAN. We all understand the tax assessor's troubles.

For Weld County the assessed valuation of the Great Western Railroad Co. is $260,970, and its taxes are $8,478.65.

Mr. FORDNEY. Do you know the true value of that property?

Mr. DAKAN. There are 48.13 miles of railroad in Weld County belonging to the Great Western Railroad Co.

It is assessed at $5,421 per mile by the State board of equalization in conjunction with all the other assessors of the State.

Mr. FORDNEY. If you assess that on the basis of one-third of its true value, the value would be over $15,000 per mile.

Mr. DAKAN. Yes, sir; but I do not know anything about railway assessment values, but that is the rate there for that class of railroads.

Mr. FORDNEY. Does that include the rolling stock and all the property?

Mr. DAKAN. I understand so; that is the assessed valuation. I wish the committee to understand and to distinguish that as the Great Western Railroad Co.

Mr. FORDNEY. I understood you.

Mr. DAKAN. It is a subsidiary corporation of the Great Western Sugar Co., as we understand.

Mr. FORDNEY. They own their own railroad?

Mr. DAKAN. That is as we understand it. I think that is in the record. Mr. Morey, I think, explained something about that.

Mr. MALBY. He explained all about that.

Mr. DAKAN. We understand that it is the practice of the sugar company to ship its sugar from Eaton down to Longmont over its line for delivery to the C. & S. Road instead of transferring it to the Union Pacific. They ship it the 40 miles over their road from Eaton to Longmont instead of delivering it to the Union Pacific, and then they ship their sugar from Longmont to Eaton, the same distance, instead of transferring it to the C. & S. or C., B. & Q. Railroad.

Mr. FORDNEY. Is it a difficult country in which to build a railroad? Is it a rough or hilly country?

Mr. DAKAN. Well, it is not heavy work. It is just average construction work for a road not intended to be a through line. It is not an especially hilly country.

Mr. FORDNEY. And no heavy work?

Mr. DAKAN. No, sir.

Mr. MALBY. It is probably of cheap construction, but is it not also used to accommodate the local communities?

Mr. DAKAN. Yes, sir; for local freight. They touch the towns of Eaton, Windsor, Johnstown, and Longmont. They zigzag through the country to gather beets from the territory west of the Platte River and between the C. & S. lines.

Mr. MALBY. Do they carry passengers?

Mr. DAKAN. Yes, sir; they carry combination trains once or twice a day between these towns. I think they carry mail also.

The assessed valuation of the Fort Morgan factory at Fort Morgan, Colo., belonging to the Great Western Sugar Co., for the year 1911 was $182,160.

The CHAIRMAN. What is its capacity?

Mr. DAKAN. Six hundred tons capacity. The taxes are $7,559.64. The assessed valuation of the Brush factory in Morgan County, Colo., is $210,090, and the taxes are $9,349. The total assessed valuation of these two 600-ton factories in Morgan County, Colo., is $392,250. That is for 1911, and in order that you may have a basis for comparison in Morgan County I will say the assessed valuation in 1910 for the Fort Morgan factory was $205,545; for the Brush factory, $240,495. That was the 1910 assessed valuation. The 1909 assessed valuation for the Fort Morgan factory was $92,580, and for the Brush factory, $192,145. These are the total assessed valuations for three years for Morgan County, Colo.

Mr. JACOWAY. Have you given the total valuations?

Mr. DAKAN. No, sir. The assessed valuation for the factory at Sterling, Colo., in Logan County, was $241,820 for the year 1910.

I will now read a letter from the county assessor of Logan County, dated October 4, 1910, containing a table:

STERLING, COLO., *October 4, 1910.*

ALBERT DAKAN, *Longmont, Colo.*

DEAR SIR: In reply to your inquiry concerning the assessed valuation of the Great Western Sugar Co. in Logan County, I give you these figures:

	1908	1909	1910
Land and improvements	$10,270	$13,530	$11,305
6 beet dumps	1,500	2,100	2,100
Sugar in stock	20,000	10,000	15,000
Capital in manufactures	180,000	180,000	180,000
Machinery and live stock	1,100	1,100	8,415
Steffens plant	....	25,000	25,000

B. J. RAGATZ, *Assessor.*
By F. L. KRAUSE, *Deputy.*

That totals up $241,820. I have not the total of all these figures, as some of them have just come in, but it amounts, in round numbers, outside of the Great Western Railroad Co., to about $2,300,000; that is the total assessed valuation of the Great Western Sugar Co. in northern Colorado, for the factories and the sugar building in Denver; that is, the head office building, which, as is shown here, was assessed in 1910 for $75,000.

Mr. JACOWAY. What sort of system do they have for assessing property in those counties? You spoke of a State board of equalization working in conjunction with county assessors.

Mr. DAKAN. Yes, sir.

Mr. JACOWAY. State what the system is out there. How do you arrive at the assessment?

Mr. DAKAN. Ordinarily the county assessors visit each property owner, and he then gives in his property or lists his property. The taxpayer then swears to the schedule, as it is called; that is, that the schedule contains an itemized list of the property. In the case of large corporations, there is a board, called the State board of equalization, that meets at certain seasons of the year and establishes these assessed valuations of the property of the corporations owning a large amount of property. I am not familiar with the details of the matter.

Mr. JACOWAY. You stated that there are 40 miles of railroad out there owned by this company. What is the character of country through which this railroad runs?

Mr. DAKAN. It is a rolling prairie country.

Mr. JACOWAY. That is all at present. Just continue your statement.

Mr. DAKAN. Mr. Chairman, I have here a copy of the first contract that was put out in the Longmont district. This is the contract for the first farmers raising beets.

The CHAIRMAN. Do you mean the contract between the grower and the beet-sugar companies?

Mr. DAKAN. Yes, sir; and, if you care, that might go in, so that it may be compared with the present contract.

The CHAIRMAN. Just hand it to the reporter for insertion in the record.

(The paper referred to is as follows:)

THE LONGMONT BEET SUGAR CO.—SUGAR-BEET CONTRACT.

This agreement, made and entered into this 7th day of April, A. D. 1903, by and between Boulder Weld Sugar Beet Co., residing at or near ———, party of the first part, and The Longmont Beet Sugar Co., party of the second part.

Witnesseth, That in consideration of the covenants and agreements of the party of the second part, hereinafter set forth, the party of the first part covenants and agrees with the party of the second part, its successors and assigns:

1. That for three (3) consecutive years, beginning with 1903, he will plant or cause to be planted, cultivated, and harvested, on lands suitable for beet culture, on W. ½ NW. ¼ of sec. 35, T. 3, R. 69 W., 6 P. M., 50 acres of sugar beets, from seed furnished by party of the second part, its successors or assigns.

2. That he will prepare the said 50 acres of ground in a thorough and proper manner, and that the seed will be planted, and the beets grown, harvested, and delivered, according to the instructions and under the general supervision of the duly authorized agents or field superintendents of the party of the second part, its successors or assigns.

3. That he will commence and proceed with the harvesting and gathering of the crop (which must be completed before freezing weather) at such times as the duly authorized agents or field superintendents of the party of the second part, its successors or assigns, shall direct.

4. That he will make delivery of said beets to the factory, or the nearest receiving station of the party of the second part, its successors or assigns, at such times and in such quantities as the agents or field superintendents of said party of the second part, its successors or assigns, may direct.

5. That all beets delivered at any receiving station of the party of the second part, or its assigns, other than the factory, shall be delivered f. o. b. cars in full carload lots.

6. That he will protect said beets, as far as possible, from frost and sun at the time of harvest and delivery, and deliver the same in first-class condition, properly topped, with all of the leaves (and any portion of the beet that may have grown above the surface of the ground) squarely cut off.

7. That he will plant or cause to be planted not less than fifteen (15) pounds of seed per acre.

The party of the second part covenants and agrees with the party of the first part:

1. That it, its successors or assigns, will furnish the seed for planting the acreage herein specified, for which said party of the first part shall pay not to exceed fifteen cents (15c.) per pound, and, when so requested, after the ground has been thoroughly and properly prepared, will plant said seed as fast as circumstances will permit, and said party of the first part shall pay for such planting the sum of fifty cents (50c.) per acre.

2. That it, its successors or assigns, will purchase all beets suitable for sugar-making purposes, grown, harvested, and delivered in accordance with the terms, specifications, and requirements of this contract, and pay therefor at the rates hereinafter specified (less the usual deductions for dirt, leaves, and improperly topped or damaged beets), to wit:

For all beets in good condition of eighty per cent (80 per cent) purity or better, and containing fifteen per cent (15 per cent) or more sugar, four dollars and fifty cents ($4.50) per ton.

For all beets in good condition of eighty per cent (80 per cent) purity, containing not less than twelve per cent (12 per cent) and under fifteen per cent (15 per cent) sugar, four dollars and twenty-five cents ($4.25) per ton.

In case any part of the beets grown on said land shall not be ordered to be delivered by the agents or field superintendents of the party of the second part, or its assigns, before November 15th of any year, then it, or its assigns, shall purchase all such beets delivered at the factory or receiving stations, as aforesaid, on and after the fifteenth (15th) day of November and up to the first (1st) day of December, in that year, of the kind and quality agreed to be purchased as aforesaid, and at the prices aforesaid. But, it or its assigns, shall not be bound to receive or purchase any damaged or injured beets, or beets of less than eighty per cent (80 per cent) purity, or containing less than twelve per cent (12 per cent) sugar. The purity and sugar content to be determined by the usual tests employed at the factory of the party of the second part, or its assigns.

3. That it, its successors or assigns, will make settlement on or about the fifteenth day of each month for all beets delivered and received during the previous calendar month.

4. That to ascertain the quality of said beets, the second party, or its assigns, shall, at various times during the growing and harvesting season, and also at the time of delivery at the factory, cause the beets to be sampled and polarized in the manner usually employed by first-class sugar factories.

It is further agreed the party of the first part will not assign or transfer this contract without the written consent of the party of the second part, its successors or assigns.

In witness whereof, the parties hereto have set their hands and seals the day and year first above written.

THE BOULDER WELD SUGAR BEET COMPANY,
By H. M. MINOR, *President.* [SEAL.]
LONGMONT BEET SUGAR CO.,
By F. M. DOWNER, V. P. [SEAL.]

Attest:
J. W. DANIELS. *Secretary.*

REMARKS AND INSTRUCTIONS.

Nothing less than five acres in one piece will be contracted for, planted, or sampled.

Always select the very best land for sugar beets. Avoid poor land, land where sheep have recently pastured, sandy land that will drift, cold, wet, late land, and above all alkali or mineral land.

Do not put a heavy coat of coarse manure on your land previous to planting beets. It is very apt to hurt the quality of the beets so they will not reach the requirements of this contract; and do not plant beets on lucerne land that has not been planted with other crops for two previous seasons.

Get your soil in the very best possible condition; put the beets in early and work them early, thinning out carefully to only one in a place, then cultivate the soil often. This always pays well.

In thinning, always select the strongest, healthiest, and most uniform-sized plants. Great care should be taken to leave the young plant in as good condition as possible by placing a little earth around the root so that it can not fall down and get sunburned.

We do not advise planting seed more than three-fourths to one and one-fourth inches deep, nor in rows more than sixteen to eighteen inches apart, nor less than fifteen to twenty pounds of seed per acre. The soil should be in the very best condition to receive it, pulverized fine and worked down, but not packed.

It is the salts, mineral, and water in the beet that reduces its purity.

Every part of salts in a beet prevents four parts of sugar from crystallizing. A large portion of the salts lie in the top of the beets at the base of the leaves. It is important, therefore, when topping to cut the tops off squarely under the bottom leaf, otherwise they are apt to show low purity.

All land that is going to be planted into sugar beets should be plowed the previous fall, if possible.

Undesirable beets as well as small tonnage per acre is usually due to one of the following causes: 1st, poor stand; 2nd, too much manure; 3rd, not sufficient moisture to keep the crop growing during July and August; 4th, September irrigation; 5th, thinning the beets out too far apart in the rows.

Mr. DAKAN. Mr. Fordney, I have here the Michigan Sugar Co.'s contract.

Mr. FORDNEY. Yes.

Mr. DAKAN. I ask that that go into the record also.

Mr. FORDNEY. I do not know anything about that contract, except what has been testified to.

(The contract referred to is as follows:)

MICHIGAN SUGAR COMPANY (BAY CITY PLANT). MEMORANDUM OF AGREEMENT CONCERNING RAISING AND DELIVERY OF SUGAR BEETS FOR CAMPAIGN OF 1910.

The undersigned hereby agrees to plant, cultivate, and harvest and deliver during the year, commencing with the spring of 1910, to the Michigan Sugar Company (Bay City Plant), at its factory in Essexville, Michigan, ten acres of sugar beets on the following-described lands, to wit: In sectoin 30, township of Hampton, in the county of Bay, State of Michigan.

About 15 pounds of seed per acre shall be planted, which seed shall be furnished by the Michigan Sugar Company at 10 cents per pound, and the cost of same is to be deducted from the first payment made for beets delivered.

The beets are to be given due care and, as far as practicable, the undersigned will follow instructions in regard to preparing the soil, seeding, caring for, and harvesting the crop. For beets delivered at the factory under this contract the company will pay at the rate of four dollars and fifty cents ($4.50) per ton for beets testing 12 per cent sugar, and 33⅓ cents per ton additional for each per cent above 12 per cent, and 33⅓ cents less per ton for each per cent below 12 per cent sugar in the beets.

It is agreed that the freight to be paid on beets delivered to the company shall not exceed the freight to be paid on beets delivered to any other sugar factory.

Said beets shall be harvested and loaded by the grower for the company on cars or delivered at factory sheds at such times and in such quantities as may be directed by the company, allowing each grower his pro rata amount. The company will not be liable to receive or pay for beets which are rotten or otherwise unfit or undesirable for making sugar.

An additional price of 50 cents per ton will be paid by the company for pitted beets delivered after December 1st, free from frost or rot when unloaded from grower's wagon.

Payment to be made on the 15th of the month following the delivery of the beets.

If necessary, the growers must join together to fully load all the cars.

This contract not valid until signed by an officer of the company or its agriculturist, and no agent of the company has any authority to change or alter the terms and conditions of this contract.

(Signature of grower) ——— ———.
MICHIGAN SUGAR COPANY (Bay City Plant),
Per T. H. BURTON.

FEBRUARY 1, 1910.

(On back:) Contract No. —; No. acres, 10. Michigan Sugar Company (Bay City Plant). Sugar-beet contract with Peter King; P. O., Bay City; R. 2; county, Bay; loading station, factory; sec. 30; township, Hampton. Pounds of seed wanted, 150. Seed to be shipped to factory. Date, February 1, 1910. Agent, T. H. Burton.

Always select the best land for sugar beets.

Plow your land in the fall, if possible; get down deep with your plow, and put your land in the best condition possible.

A little extra work in preparing the land will save lots of time and money when it comes to thinning and weeding.

At least 20 pounds of seed per acre is recommended by the company.

Sow the seed as soon as the soil is warm and moist enough to germinate it.

Better have too many plants than not enough.

Cultivate at least once a week; keep the ground loose and mellow.

Keep your beets clean and free from weeds.

Block out to at least 8 to 10 inches in the row.

Thin to one beet in a place.

Do not harvest until the beets are ripe.

Beets should be topped square below lowest leaf growth.

Mr. FORDNEY. For what year is that contract?

Mr. DAKAN. Last year.

Mr. Chairman, there is one of the first actual accounting sheets rendered by the Longmont factory to the grower, and one rendered this fall in the Longmont district.

The CHAIRMAN. Do you wish these to go into the record also?
Mr. DAKAN. Yes, sir.
(The papers referred to are as follows:)

L. F. 10. V. C. No. 277.

Statement of beets delivered to the Longmont Sugar Co. during November under contract No. 26, of I. L. Beasley, contractor, Longmont.

Load or car No.	First net weight of beets.	Per cent tare.	Net weight of beets.	Rate per ton.	Amount.
FORD FACTORY.					
1008	6,395	32	4,349		
1009	6,190	32	4,209		
1081	5,315	28	3,827		
1087	8,255	28	5,944		
1105	7,780	28	5,401		
1181	4,750	28	5,420		
1190	7,975	28	5,742		
1215	8,085	13	7,034		
1320	7,495	13	6,746		
1411	4,905	13	4,267		
1523	5,525	13	4,807		
1524	8,110	13	7,056		
1639	5,210	13	4,533		
1657	8,460	13	7,360		
1706	8,120	13	7,064		
1708	4,960	13	4,315		
1880	4,825	13	4,198		
2178	7,850	8	7,222		
972	5,220	18	4,280		
985	7,120	18	5,838		
1032	6,680	8	6,145		
1067	7,840	6	7,370		
1083	4,890	6	4,597		
1112	7,310	6	6,871		
1182	8,000	6	7,520		
1224	7,650	6	7,191		
1263	7,910	6	7,435		
1264	8,550	6	8,037		
1294	7,920	6	7,445		
1296	8,150	6	7,661		
1311	8,310	6	7,811		
1354	8,170	6	7,680		
1383	8,520	6	8,009		
1418	3,970	6	3,732		
1561	9,100	6	8,554		
1611	8,070	6	7,586		
1640	8,370	6	7,868		
1664	8,250	6	7,755		
1692	9,250	6	8,695		
			245,774	$4.50	$552.99

Total		552.99
Less deductions, as follows:		
Amount due for seed		
Amount due for planting		
Amount due order (Farmers National Bank)	$150.00	150.00
Balance due as per voucher		402.99

Grower retains this statement.

18869—11——16

Grower's delivery record, the Great Western Sugar Co., Longmont factory.

Grower's No. 56. Month of October, 1911. Delivered at factory. W. E. Milner, grower.
This grower had 10½ acres rented at 4/5.

Date.	Number of loads.	First net weight.	Tare.		Final net weight.	Sugar content (per cent).	Distribution of final net weight (pounds).							
			Per cent.	Pounds.			12 per cent and under 15 per cent, $5.	15 per cent and under 15.5 per cent, $5.25.	15.5 per cent and under 16 per cent, $5.375.	16 per cent and under 16.5 per cent, $5.50.	16.5 per cent and under 17 per cent, $5.625.	17 per cent and under 17.5 per cent, $5.75.	17.5 per cent and under 18 per cent, $5.875.	18 per cent and under 18.5 per cent, $6.
3	3	16.780	7	1,175	15,605	16.5					15,605			
4	3	20,300	2	406	19,894	16.8					19,894			
5	2	12,935	4	517	12,418	15.4		12,418						
6	1	7,305	3	219	7,086	16.4				7,086				
7	2	13.555	4	542	13,013	14.0	13,013							
9	2	14,150	3	425	131725	16.0				13,725				
10	2	15.055	3	452	14,603	15.9			14.603					
11	2	14.405	4	576	13,829	15.7			13,829					
12	2	15.255	3	458	14,797	18.1								14.797
13	2	15,225	3	457	14,768	16.6					14,768			
14	2	15.575	3	467	15,108	17.1						15.108		
16	2	15,595	3	468	15,127	17.9							15,127	
17	2	15,035	2	301	14,734	16.7					14,734			
18	2	13,320	4	533	12.787	15.4		12.787						
23	1	7,125	2	143	6,982	15.4		6,982						
24	2	15,085	3	453	14,632	15.9			14,632					
25	1	6,080	2	122	5,958	17.6							5,958	
26	1	4,795	1	48	4,747	16.8					4,747			
	34				229,813		13,013	32,187	43,064	20,811	69,748	15,108	21,085	14,797

RECAPITULATION OF NET WEIGHTS.

Tons.		Price.	Amount.
13,012		$5.00	$32.53
32,187		5.25	84.49
43,064		5.375	115.73
20,811		5.50	57.23
69,749		5.625	196.17
15,108		5.75	43.44
21,085		5.875	61.94
14,797		6.00	44.39
229,813	Total		635.92
	Less account as rendered		16.00
	Balance due		619.92

Mr. DAKAN. I would like to state, concerning the inception of the industry at Longmont, Colo., that the town or the community was promised a factory if the farmers and others would subscribe or contract for 4,000 acres for the years 1903, 1904, and 1905; that after the utmost efforts of solicitors, local and imported, for acreage, the solicitors failed to secure the required acreage, so two companies—small corporations—were organized for the purpose of allowing the stockholders of this company, or the subscribers to the stock of this company, to subscribe a certain amount of money sufficient to rent outright from the farmers, at $10 per acre, land on which the companies could raise beets for the factories to bring up the contract acreage to 4,000 acres; and if you care for anything of that kind, there is the original of that sort of agreement.

The CHAIRMAN. I do not see how this would serve any particular purpose. You have already stated the facts about it.

Mr. DAKAN. The Boulder & Weld Sugar Co. was organized in this manner, and rented some 300 acres of land adjacent to Longmont and attempted to grow beets for the company. They signed up contracts with the owners of farm land at $10 per acre and hired all the work done, of course, just as the Great Western Sugar Co. is doing now. In the first year of the operation of this Boulder & Weld Sugar Co. the annual report shows that, under the fourth section, the proportion of capital stock in said company actually paid in is as $3,984.75 is to $10,000. That is the amount paid in, $3,894.75, or about 38.94 per cent.

The CHAIRMAN. That was the amount paid in?

Mr. DAKAN. Yes, sir. The indebtedness of the said corporation at this time was $2,937.27, and the company lost on these 300 acres, on this first year of raising beets, about $3,000. The company had visions of profit in beet growing that was given rise to by glowing statements about growing sugar beets, but these visions faded into a deficit of about $3,000 the first year. The next year they cut out all but about 140 acres, and they managed to pay up about 80 per cent of this debt, in addition to the subscriptions that they collected that had not been paid up before to the company's stock. The third year the company absolved them from the contract, and did not require them to grow beets on the contract any longer, for the reason that the farmers around subscribed sufficient acreage to run the factory, and the factory has continued each year from that time, and is running at the present time.

Mr. FORDNEY. About what is their acreage annually for a factory of 600 tons per day capacity?

Mr. DAKAN. The Longmont factory is a 1,200-ton factory, and their normal capacity is 170,000 tons annually of beets.

Mr. FORDNEY. They run about 120 days?

Mr. DAKAN. Yes, sir; they are qualified to run 120 days—and this factory was running at the rate of 1,200 tons per day of 12 hours. I think this year their rate is 1,700 tons per day. They have gone up to nearly 1,900 tons.

Mr. FORDNEY. Have they increased their slicing capacity?

Mr. DAKAN. They have made some increase and they have also increased the efficiency of their operations. As we understand it, there is a rivalry among the factories to obtain the best efficiency, and a prize of some thousands of dollars is offered to the head officials of each factory for the man who shows the best efficiency in the operation of his factory.

The CHAIRMAN. Does that about cover the papers you have there to put in the record?

Mr. DAKAN. Not quite all. I understood from the information I had concerning the object of this committee that its investigation should cover the question of whether the combination of the refiners reduces or tends to reduce the price of beets and cane to the growers.

The CHAIRMAN. That is true. We were directed by the House to inquire into that question, and if you will give us some facts on that subject we will be obliged to you.

Mr. DAKAN. Well, I have been working among the growers, and my duties have taken me among the growers of northern Colorado.

Mr. FORDNEY. As their attorney?

Mr. DAKAN. Yes, sir.

The CHAIRMAN. Did you have any litigation for these sugar people or this sugar committee?

Mr. DAKAN. No, sir.

The CHAIRMAN. What do they want an attorney for?

Mr. DAKAN. They first employed me—and that was the inception of my connection with this committee—to draft a growers' contract from the point of view of the grower.

The CHAIRMAN. The growers' contract for labor?

Mr. DAKAN. No, sir; to grow beets.

The CHAIRMAN. You mean with the sugar companies?

Mr. DAKAN. Yes, sir.

The CHAIRMAN. You mean that you were employed to look after their interests in drafting contracts with the sugar companies?

Mr. DAKAN. Yes, sir.

The CHAIRMAN. Did you have any trouble about that?

Mr. DAKAN. I found on perusing the contract they brought to me that terms were used that involved a technical knowledge of the subject. For instance, they used the term "80 per cent purity."

Mr. FORDNEY. That was in the contract prepared by the sugar companies?

Mr. DAKAN. Yes, sir; it provided that beets must test 80 per cent purity, and that 12 per cent sugar should be received by the company. I asked the committee if they understood these terms, that is, 80 per cent purity and 12 per cent sugar. Up to that time the farmers had been paid what was called a flat rate.

The CHAIRMAN. How much per ton?

Mr. DAKAN. $5 at that particular time.

The CHAIRMAN. How long ago was that?

Mr. DAKAN. A year ago last September. The refiners' contract was a rate of $4.50. The company had been paying $5. None of the farmers knew the technical significance of these terms I have mentioned.

Mr. FORDNEY. The 80 per cent purity, then, was the "nigger in the fence"?

Mr. DAKAN. Do you quote me as saying that?

Mr. FORDNEY. You intimated that it was, as I understood you. You stated that they did not understand it, and it was put in there by the company. That is what you stated.

Mr. DAKAN. Let us understand each other, if you please.

Mr. FORDNEY. Yes, of course; I am not hostile to you.

Mr. DAKAN. I do not want to be hostile to you, but I am trying to get it right. The farmers did not understand what 80 per cent purity meant; they did not understand that, and they did not understand what 12 per cent sugar meant. When they referred the matter to me, that is, to draw the contract, I was not familiar with these terms, and I said to them, "I can not draw this contract and use these terms intelligently unless I understand their technical significance." It was necessary, apparently, to use these terms in the contract. There is no imputation there. They were terms that in my profession I had never met up with, and these terms implied a knowledge of chemistry as applied to the sugar business.

Mr. FORDNEY. Well, what did it mean—80 per cent purity? Did it mean that the beets should be 20 per cent pure? If so, pure what?

Mr. DAKAN. Saccharin matter. I could only give my idea of the matter because I only had a general knowledge of chemistry. I told them that I had some general knowledge of chemistry obtained at college, and they asked what to do about the matter. I explained to them that if they cared to wait, I would brush up and learn the meaning of these terms.

Mr. FORDNEY. Do I understand you to say that 80 per cent purity means saccharin matter? Do you not mean that the 12 per cent meant saccharin and not the 80 per cent?

Mr. DAKAN. I am coming to that.

Mr. FORDNEY. Thank you.

Mr. DAKAN. As I understood it, after some investigation, the juice of the beet contains impurities that interfere with the extraction of the sugar from the juice, and the richness of that juice, with reference to the purity or impurity of the juice, is indicated in that way; that is, 80 per cent or 85 per cent purity. You read something yesterday about saccharin in beets, 85 per cent.

Mr. FORDNEY. That is the loss in extraction. For instance, if beets tested 15 per cent saccharine matter, there was a loss of 15 per cent——

Mr. DAKAN (interposing). I do not know what relation 80 per cent purity has to 80 per cent extraction, but, as I gather, there are certain impurities in the juice that will not allow the sugar to crystallize, and that amount of purity or impurity, whichever way you look at it, is defined by percentage in that manner. It is 80 per cent purity or 92 per cent purity, and the greater the purity the greater the amount of sugar extracted from the beet. For instance, in the pulp, in getting all the sugar out of the pulp a few years ago—three, four, or five years ago—the operators must leave at least about 35 per cent of the 100 per cent of sugar in the pulp. If they extracted more from the pulp than that amount they could not get the impurity out of it, and that would prevent the sugar from crystallizing. The efficiency of operation has now increased to the point where they range down to 14 per cent extracted, leaving only fourteen one-hundredths of 1 per cent sugar in the pulp. They go down that low before they get this impurity that interferes with crystallization; and 12 per cent sugar is by weight, as we understand that. That is, the beets must carry at least 12 per cent sugar by weight. Then, after I had gone into that subject somewhat, I prepared a contract for the growers' benefit to present to the corporation.

The CHAIRMAN. What does the grower now get in Colorado for his sugar beets?

Mr. DAKAN. That has been testified to. He is paid $5 per ton for beets testing from 12 to 14 per cent; for beets that test 15 per cent, $5.25, and 25 cents for each 1 per cent, splitting on the half per cent.

Mr. FORDNEY. Above 15 per cent?

Mr. DAKAN. Yes, sir. The company accounts to the farmer for each five-tenths of 1 per cent. Here is the table [indicating]; this is an accounting sheet to Longmont farmers this fall.

The CHAIRMAN. How much does the farmer get? How many pounds of sugar does a ton of beets make?

Mr. DAKAN. One hundred pounds of beets, 15 per cent sugar, would produce 15 pounds of sugar. That would be 15 pounds of sugar to 100 pounds of beets if they could get that 15 per cent of sugar out of the beets.

The CHAIRMAN. But they can not do that, can they?

Mr. DAKAN. We understand that not all the sugar companies extract that. There are losses in the pulp, in the filter cloth, in the sweet waters, and in the liming.

The CHAIRMAN. What does the farmer get for his 15 per cent beets?

Mr. DAKAN. By the ton?

The CHAIRMAN. What does the farmer get for the raw material from which a pound of beet sugar is made, and then I want to see what the company gets? Can you go into that question with us?

Mr. DAKAN. Well, say the beets average 16 per cent.

The CHAIRMAN. You can take that for purposes of illustration.

Mr. DAKAN. That would amount to 320 pounds of sugar per ton of beets, on that basis. I think the farmers at Longmont are paid more than at this rate of 16 per cent. Now, 320 pounds of sugar would come from a ton of beets, and the farmer receives $5.50 a ton. Now, if you divide $5.50 by 320 you have $1.72. One and three-quarters cents is what they pay for the raw material. Of course the figures would vary according to the amount of sugar extracted, but this is a fair average.

The CHAIRMAN. Now, that was for 16 per cent sugar. Using that for illustration, they paid 1¾ cents per pound for the raw material?

Mr. DAKAN. Yes, sir; if they averaged 16 per cent sugar. Some beets run as high as 19 and 20 per cent.

The CHAIRMAN. And they pay more for it?

Mr. DAKAN. Yes, sir.

The CHAIRMAN. Now, it appears from your calculations that they pay 1¾ cents per pound for their raw material. Now, how much did they get for that sugar this year?

Mr. FORDNEY. Is the gentleman giving the total cost of manufacture now?

The CHAIRMAN. No, sir; I am trying to show what they pay for their raw material.

Mr. FORDNEY. You want to find out what the farmers get for beets.

Mr. DAKAN. And what he pays per pound when it comes out.

Mr. MALBY. Do you estimate, in making your estimates there, that all of the sugar in the beet is extracted, or do you make allowances?

Mr. DAKAN. Yes, sir; for the purpose of the estimates, about 3 per cent. I think it goes below that.

Mr. MALBY. Do they extract all the sugar in a beet except about 3 per cent by your method of calculation?

Mr. DAKAN. Yes, sir.

Mr. FORDNEY. The figures in Michigan differ very materially from those. I believe about 15 per cent is the lowest figure with us.

Mr. DAKAN. The maximum retail price in 1911 to a jobber who lives in Boulder County, so he told me two weeks ago last Wednesday, when I had a talk with him, was $7.60. That was the retail price, and it was billed to jobbers at $7.30, less 2 per cent for cash. It was billed to the jobbers by the factory or by the selling agent, he did not know which, at $7.30. That was the maximum price.

The CHAIRMAN. That was what the factory got?

Mr. DAKAN. Yes, sir. Two weeks ago last Wednesday he said the price of sugar billed to jobbers was $6.20, less 2 per cent for cash.

The CHAIRMAN. I thought you stated $7.30?

Mr. DAKAN. The maximum price in 1911 was $7.30 billed to jobbers, and the jobbers sold it to the retailers at $7.60. He said the day I was talked with him, two weeks ago, that sugar was billed to him at $6.20, less 2 per cent for cash.

The CHAIRMAN. In other words, that is what he was paying for it?

Mr. DAKAN. Yes, sir.

Mr. MALBY. Have you any figures to show the average price at which the manufacturer sold his product?

Mr. DAKAN. He told me that the lowest he knew was $4.95, and only once he knew of that. I went into the question of the relative consumption of sugar with him during the months of June, July, August, and September.

The CHAIRMAN. But before the sharp rise in price and afterwards, to see how it affected consumption?

Mr. DAKAN. Yes, sir. His estimate was that it was one and one-half times greater than during the other period.

The CHAIRMAN. Do you mean one and one-half times greater while it was low than when it went up?

Mr. DAKAN. No, sir; during June, July, August, and September. The housewives are then putting up preserves and the canneries are using sugar, and the demand is heavier in those months. There is a sharp rise during the canning and preserving season. The factories take advantage of that, and the price then makes a sharp rise, and it continues high until that season of demand is over.

Mr. FORDNEY. Do you say that that was the custom each year in the past, or only during the past year?

Mr. DAKAN. It is the custom each year.

Mr. MALBY. Have you anything with you from which you can tell the committee what was the average price received by the refiners during the season of 1911?

Mr. DAKAN. We have been trying for some four weeks to get that.

Mr. MALBY. And you have not got it?

Mr. DAKAN. No, sir; it seems to be a delicate point.

Mr. MALBY. You have also told us about the increased consumption during the months of June, July, August, and September. Will you tell us when Colorado sugar first goes upon the market? When do they have anything to sell?

Mr. DAKAN. About the 1st of October. Pardon me a moment; they have immense warehouses at each factory and they are able to store the product of each factory, as we understand the situation. In that way they feed the market according to the market demand, and a jobber or retailer who might have some money and who wanted to speculate in sugar is unable to buy sugar from them during the season of slack consumption.

Mr. MALBY. Our information has been along the line that there was what has been termed a "sugar campaign," which opens, say, on the 1st of October and continues through into January, when the crop of beet sugar was marketed, and that after that time there was not very much beet sugar on the market. How does that information accord with the practice in Colorado?

Mr. DAKAN. Ordinarily, I think the warehouses are full of sugar after the factory closes down.

Mr. MALBY. At all seasons of the year?

Mr. DAKAN. No, sir; it is slowly shipped out.

Mr. MALBY. Do you agree with the statement that there is a campaign, so called, for the sale of beet sugar during the months I have mentioned—October, November, December, and January? Is that the season during which the beet-sugar manufacturers attempt to get rid of their product?

Mr. DAKAN. I can only give you this season's observations.

Mr. MALBY. Of course, this season would not quite answer my question, because we are still in the month of December, which is during what is termed "the campaign period."

Mr. DAKAN. Most of the western sugar factories are closed now.

Mr. MALBY. But are they getting rid of their product? What I want to know is whether or not the beet-sugar manufacturers do sell substantially all their product during what is called their campaign—that is, during the months of October, November, December, and January? Has that been their practice in former years?

Mr. DAKAN. I take it this way: As soon as sugar is made, it begins going in the sack in October—that is, it begins with the beginning of the slicing of the beets. Within 24 hours after slicing the first beet, I think the sugar begins to flow, and we begin to notice reports of this kind in the local newspapers: "The company shipped so many cars of warm sugar."

Mr. MALBY. Do they attempt to dispose of it all during the season, or do they store it and hold it for distribution during the year?

Mr. DAKAN. My opinion, from observation, is that they sell it as fast as they can at the beginning of the campaign, when the market is high, before it goes down to the minimum.

Mr. MALBY. Of course, it is important for the committee to know whether the manufacturers of beet sugar, even this year, had an opportunity to take advantage of the really high prices in sugar, which existed from August to September, or whether they sold their products on the decline which has taken place since that time.

Mr. DAKAN. In answer to that, I will say, the experience of the purchasers of sugar is that they can not get sugar in big quantities when it is cheap, so the inference is that the company is holding it to speculate upon when the price of sugar is high during the preserving and canning season.

Mr. MALBY. Of course, it would be common information as to whether there is a campaign or not. It should be common information as to whether they store it up and sell it next summer, or whether they sell it as rapidly as possible.

Mr. DAKAN. I only know from common information that the buyers of sugar say that they can not get it when it is cheap.

Mr. MALBY. Perhaps I can put it this way: After the 1st of January, and from January to next October are the refiners able to furnish plenty of sugar which they had stored up for the market? Have they been able in the past to do so?

Mr. DAKAN. You say a plenty of sugar?

Mr. MALBY. That is, sufficient to supply the market.

Mr. DAKAN. Well, day after day, at Longmont, the reports go this way: Three cars shipped out, four cars shipped out, five cars shipped out, and that continues through the season. That continues almost during the year. You would not notice from the reports of the shipments any difference.

Mr. MALBY. Do you know whether any cane sugars from Louisiana are shipped into your territory during this time?

Mr. DAKAN. Yes, sir.

Mr. MALBY. Is any shipped from San Francisco?

Mr. DAKAN. I know it is on the market.

Mr. MALBY. At all seasons of the year?

Mr. DAKAN. Yes, sir.

Mr. MALBY. But whence it comes, you do not know?

Mr. DAKAN. No, sir.

(Thereupon, at 12 o'clock noon, the committee took a recess until 2 o'clock p. m.)

AFTER RECESS.

The committee met, pursuant to the taking of recess, at 2.30 o'clock p. m., Hon. Thomas W. Hardwick (chairman) presiding.

TESTIMONY OF MR. ALBERT DAKAN—Continued.

Mr. DAKAN. I was asked to total the assessed valuation of the Great Western Sugar Co. in northern Colorado.

The CHAIRMAN. Yes.

Mr. DAKAN. I find that in the counties in which the nine factories are located, and in Denver County, the assessed valuation is $2,414,-210, according to the figures obtained from the various county officials of the counties wherein property is located.

Mr. RAKER. And their capitalization is how much?

Mr. DAKAN. The capitalization is $30,000,000. From the farmer's point of view, the company pays taxes on $2,500,000 in round numbers, and collects dividends on $30,000,000.

Mr. RAKER. What is the dividend they pay?

Mr. DAKAN. Five per cent on common stock and 7 per cent on preferred stock.

Mr. RAKER. Do you know how much surplus they have on hand, these various factories? Have you anything to show that?

Mr. DAKAN. We have attempted to get at the surplus, and a collection of our information shows from three to four million dollars.

That is just an estimate. Now, the farmer pays taxes on an assessed valuation of about one-third of the market value of his property. That is the general scheme. If it varied to one-fourth, and they gave the company the advantage of this one-fourth proportion of the value of the property, the physical value of the company's property would then be something like $10,000,000 in northern Colorado for the nine factories.

Mr. RAKER. Does this $30,000,000 with a surplus of $4,000,000, with the dividends paid, include these subsidiary companies as well as the railroad and the lime company?

Mr. DAKAN. I do not understand it does. I understand they are subsidiary companies incorporated by the officials and parties interested in the Great Western Sugar Co.

Mr. RAKER. How does their assessment compare with their capitalization and the dividends paid on the common and preferred as compared with the statement you have given in regard to the Great Western Sugar Co.?

Mr. DAKAN. We have never gone into the dividends or relative assessed valuation of the lime company, the railroad company, or the feeding company. They have subsidiary feeding companies. I might say in this connection that the Great Western Sugar Co. or the officials through a subsidiary corporation are engaged in building what is called a chain of alfalfa-meal mills, with the purpose of using the sirup, mixing the refuse sirup of all of the plants in northern Colorado with alfalfa meal, making stock food. Heretofore the farmers have bought sirup and mixed it with alfalfa or pulp to feed stock. Within the last year or so some independent alfalfa-meal mills have attempted to buy the sirup to mix with their alfalfa meal to make stock food for sale. The company this year notified them that they could not sell stock food compounded of alfalfa meal and sirup. They could feed it themselves. If the alfalfa-meal mill companies desired to feed on their own responsibility, they would sell them sirup for that, but they would not sell sirup to an independent meal mill to make stock food for the market. They are going into that business themselves. And further, in this relation, the company or its officials feed large numbers of cattle at various yards, especially at Longmont.

I do not know just what interest the company has in the cattle or in the feeding business, but the farmers are unable to get pulp to feed to any extent. They used to be able to get the pulp to feed stock, and they would feed stock on a small scale on the pulp obtained from the company, but the company has taken over that business itself. In that connection I would say that Mr. Truman G. Palmer recently caused a bulletin to be issued—at the expense of the Government, I presume—wherein he details his investigation of the beet-sugar industry in foreign countries, and is especially interested in giving the method of management of foreign manufacturers of large estates, where they use all of the by-products, are not only manufacturers of sugar but are stock feeders and the manufacturers of various products from the by-products of the factory, to a degree that these companies own a business that comprehends the entire profit to be gained by the maintenance of a sugar factory, and using the land and the products of the factory all for its own benefit; and I take it from that—from the observation of the company's exploitation of northern Colorado—that the Great Western Sugar Co. would like to make a grand baronial estate of the sugar-beet region of northern Colorado, having the farmers work for them there as the peasants do in Germany and Austria, and make all of the money that is to be made out of the lime that they get from the hills of that very region, out of the beets that the farmers raise for them, out of the stock feeding industry incident to pulp and molasses, out of the alfalfa-meal business—for there is a great deal of alfalfa raised there, and it must be raised to fertilize the soil—and out of all the varied subsidiary industries that can be grown or established in connection with the operation of a beet-sugar plant.

Mr. RAKER. And still these subsidiary companies and the profit made by them are not included in any way with the general statement they here make in regard to their profit on the handling and the manufacturing of the beets alone?

Mr. DAKAN. No, sir.

Mr. RAKER. That is all kept back?

Mr. DAKAN. These men who run the sugar companies have these other companies, too.

Mr. FORDNEY. In Colorado?

Mr. DAKAN. In northern Colorado.

Mr. FORDNEY. In the territory where you live?

Mr. DAKAN. Yes. There is a corps of officials for each one of these subsidiary corporations, and the commonalty of names in the various corporations makes interesting reading. We see them in newspaper reports only. We can not get at the inwardness of the subsidiary companies.

The CHAIRMAN. You mean they have the same officers in these various companies?

Mr. DAKAN. The same man will be an officer of several companies.

The CHAIRMAN. And will get a salary for each office?

Mr. DAKAN. I do not know about that.

The CHAIRMAN. You do not know that?

Mr. DAKAN. I do not know whether they do or not.

The CHAIRMAN. You do not know whether those salaries add largely to the cost of producing beet sugar or not; or have you gone into that?

Mr. DAKAN. We have attempted to go into that, and the result of that is—this is only an opinion——

The CHAIRMAN. You may give it.

Mr. DAKAN. Our opinion is that each of these corporations is a separate entity and does not have anything to do with the reports of the cost of production of beet sugar; that is, the operation of a beet-sugar factory is a separate business from feeding stock for the market——

The CHAIRMAN. Yes.

Mr. DAKAN. And from transporting the beets, and from securing lime from the quarries in northern Colorado, to the factories.

Mr. RAKER. In other words, part of the same men who own the stock and are interested, for instance, in the Great Western Sugar Co. organize a company to manufacture alfalfa meal? Those men, then, who organize the company that manufactures the alfalfa meal are the same men who are interested in the Great Western Sugar Co., and the Great Western Sugar Co. has refused to sell the by-products of sirup to the general community—to the farmers?

Mr. DAKAN. To the independent meal mills.

Mr. RAKER. To the farmer, or even to the independent alfalfa-plant man, but they sell it to these men who have organized a subsidiary company of their same men?

Mr. DAKAN. That is what we understand.

Mr. RAKER. Yes.

Mr. DAKAN. As to how far that goes we can not state.

Mr. FORDNEY. You do not know who owns the stock in these various companies?

Mr. DAKAN. No, sir.

Mr. FORDNEY. You only surmise that the others do?

Mr. DAKAN. How is that?

Mr. FORDNEY. You only surmise that the stockholders of the Great Western Sugar Co. own the stock of those subsidiary companies?

Mr. DAKAN. As subsidiary companies.

Mr. FORDNEY. You do not know whether that is true? You do not know who the stockholders are? You think that is right?

Mr. DAKAN. No, sir; there is no way of getting at the business of a corporation in this country or in Colorado. That is one trouble with the management of corporations in the United States, I think.

Mr. FORDNEY. Getting at those alfalfa-meal companies, and so on, they are generally beneficial to the agricultural interests of the State, are they not? They encourage them and make more valuable your lands and give greater advantages for the farmers to raise alfalfa? Or do those companies purchase alfalfa? Do they handle nothing but what they raise themselves?

Mr. DAKAN. No; they purchase alfalfa from the farmers.

Mr. FORDNEY. Yes.

Mr. DAKAN. At the present time I think alfalfa is about $10 a ton in the stack.

Mr. FORDNEY. Is that scheme of theirs, then, and are those companies of theirs, beneficial to the farmers or not by making a market for their alfalfa?

Mr. DAKAN. Yes; it helps to make a market. Everything that increases the demand does that.

Mr. FORDNEY. Yes; so that that is beneficial to the farmers of your State, then; these subsidiary companies that you have mentioned are beneficial to the farmers?

Mr. DAKAN. There is this difference in the benefit. The farmers before had independent alfalfa-meal companies who would get the sirup to make this stock food, which makes very valuable stock food.

Mr. FORDNEY. Yes.

Mr. DAKAN. But the company informs them that they will not sell the sirup.

Mr. FORDNEY. Because they want it themselves?

Mr. DAKAN. Yes; they want it themselves.

Mr. FORDNEY. But it does make a market for the farmers' alfalfa?

Mr. DAKAN. Yes; it helps to increase the demand for alfalfa.

Mr. FORDNEY. Yes.

The CHAIRMAN. Have you been able to compare, Mr. Dakan, the price that is paid for beets in Colorado with the price paid for alfalfa in Colorado?

Mr. DAKAN. I have here a report, in the American Sugar Industry, of which Mr. Willett spoke, the technical sugar journal published in Chicago.

The CHAIRMAN. Published for the beet people?

Mr. DAKAN. Ostensibly for the beet people and sugar people.

The CHAIRMAN. I say, for the beet-sugar people.

Mr. DAKAN. That is better. There is a distinction always to be made between beet people and beet-sugar people.

The CHAIRMAN. Yes.

Mr. DAKAN. On page 423 in the issue for September, 1911, of the American Sugar Industry, is a paragraph which I will read:

The British consul in Spain gives, in his annual report which has just been issued by the foreign office, an interesting account of the industry in that country. The industry was introduced into Spain in 1882, and the price of beets has undergone wide variations since then. The cultivation of the root is only profitable when the average price of the raw material is £1 2s. per ton.

The CHAIRMAN. £1 2s. per ton?

Mr. FORDNEY. How much is that in our money?

The CHAIRMAN. You mean a pound sterling, do you not?

Mr. DAKAN. Yes.

The CHAIRMAN. Are the figures there in metric tons or long tons?

Mr. DAKAN. I do not see here.

Mr. FORDNEY. A pound is $4.87, and 2 shillings is 48 cents.

The CHAIRMAN. That makes the amount $5.35 or $5.36.

Mr. MALBY. Does that have any regard to the percentage of sugar that is in the beets?

Mr. DAKAN. Something on that will come in later, I think.

The CHAIRMAN. Do you find anything there which will clear up whether they use the metric ton or the long ton?

Mr. DAKAN. I do not see that stated here. I do not know whether it appears. I want to repeat that last sentence which I read:

The cultivation of the root is only profitable when the average price of the raw material is £1 2s. per ton. Before 1890, however, the price fell as low as 16s. per ton. In the year last named the construction of seven new factories, and consequent competition, brought the price to £1 2s. per ton, and since the tendency has been upward, the price at Grenada has, owing to competition between the Sugar Trust and the independent factories, touched £2 14s.

The CHAIRMAN. That is pretty high.

Mr. DAKAN (continuing reading):

The present price is fairly steady, at £1 10s.

The CHAIRMAN. £1 10s.?

Mr. DAKAN. That is this year.

The CHAIRMAN. Yes; that would be $7.32 in our money.

Mr. DAKAN. Now I want you to notice this:

The present price is fairly steady at £1 10s., and the position of the beet producer is moderately satisfactory at that.

The CHAIRMAN. You all would feel pretty well satisfied if you got that, would you not; $7.32?

Mr. DAKAN. We are only asking this year what amounts to about $6.

The CHAIRMAN. These people get $7.32?

Mr. DAKAN. According to this report published by the British consul.

Mr. MALBY. Where is that; in Spain?

The CHAIRMAN. In Spain.

Mr. MALBY. Is there anything there to indicate what they pay for sugar?

Mr. DAKAN. No.

The CHAIRMAN. We have that in the record.

Mr. MALBY. I wanted it right in this connection. I think we have it in the record.

The CHAIRMAN. Is there anything in that article, Mr. Dakan, about what refined sugar sells for over there?

Mr. DAKAN. No.

Mr. MALBY. Will you let me look at the article, if you are through with it?

Mr. DAKAN (handing paper to Mr. Malby). There are conditions there which go into the duty, and so on, which you will probably understand from the reports that you have.

The CHAIRMAN. Do you know what farmers generally get for their beets in France?

Mr. DAKAN. One of the reports that we had for 1909 gave the average as $4.90 per ton, but said that the price per ton was somewhat fictitious because the growers benefited by the dividends; they were cooperative owners of factories to a large degree, and had an interest in the factories, and they received money from both ends of the business—the beet end and the sugar end—so that, to compare German conditions with American conditions would be hardly fair or be an intelligent basis of comparison, because American conditions did not exist there.

The CHAIRMAN. Is the same thing true of France?

Mr. DAKAN. I have not any information or records from the French sugar industry.

The CHAIRMAN. This Spanish report which you have given us is very interesting.

Mr. RAKER. That German proposition is an important thing. If those growers are interested cooperatively with the manufacture of it, and they get a percentage out of that, we can readily see why they get a lower price for their beets.

The CHAIRMAN. This committee was directed to inquire whether or not combination existed between these beet factories or between refineries or factories.

Mr. MALBY. There is something more in connection with this Spanish matter, and perhaps if the article was to go in it might be important.

Mr. FORDNEY. You had a scale of prices paid by the factories which you presented this morning. Have you that now?

Mr. DAKAN. Yes; it was an actual accounting to one of the farmers near Longmont this fall, just as it was paid to the farmer. That is in the record.

Mr. MALBY. After giving the price of beet sugar this article says:

The sugar manufacturer is worse off than the cultivator. The existing situation in the industry is due in part to the action of the combination known as the Sugar Trust and in part to the action of the Government. Up to 1899 home-grown sugar, while protected by a heavy import duty, was not subject to any internal taxes. In 1902 the Sugar Trust was formed, with the avowed object of preventing overproduction and in the secret hope of being able to buy up all the sugar interests and create a monopoly. In 1907 the industry was going through a crisis. A law was passed increasing the excise duty to 75 pesetas—

One peseta is equal to about 17 cents—

prohibiting the establishment of new factories for a period of three years, and also prohibiting for an additional term of three years the establishment of any new factories within a radius of 50 miles of those already existing.

That creates quite a different situation.

The CHAIRMAN. That is exactly in the line of the question that I wanted to ask you: Whether or not your beet people there, the people who raise the beets, have more than one customer to whom they can sell, or whether all these different factories are under the same management, and how that affects the farmer?

Mr. DAKAN. The farmer believes that that is exactly the situation that he is laboring under; that this organization prevents competition.

The CHAIRMAN. Exactly.

Mr. DAKAN. And prevents overproduction; and that that is one of the chief objects of the combination of the sugar companies.

The CHAIRMAN. In other words, these nine different companies do not bid for the farmer's beets, but if they are all under the same management they all work together?

Mr. DAKAN. The contract was to be made on the 7th of December, Wednesday, for next year, by the Great Western directors, calling in all the field men to Denver. Mr. Dixon told me that himself, two days before we left there, that on the 7th of this month Mr. Morey would be in Denver and that they would take up the contract for the year 1912 with all of the field men and factory managers of northern Colorado; that those managers were acquainted with the disposition of the farmers, and they called them in to the Sugar Building in Denver, in the head offices there, and grouped all the Great Western directors and its agents from northern Colorado to make a contract to present to the farmers next year; and the business of the field men was to advise the directors of the company in regard to the farmers, and to get in that way the scale that they thought the farmers would stand for. This contract was made for all northern Colorado.

The CHAIRMAN. I understand in regard to the beet-sugar industry in Colorado that every single beet-sugar concern there belongs to the Great Western Sugar Co.

Mr. DAKAN. In northern Colorado.

The CHAIRMAN. In northern Colorado?

Mr. DAKAN. Yes.

The CHAIRMAN. There are nine of those factories in northern Colorado?

Mr. DAKAN. Yes.

The CHAIRMAN. But for the organization of this company they would have been possible competitors of each other for the beets that the farmers raise, to some extent, would they not; and instead of one big strong customer with nobody to bid against him, you would have had nine customers bidding against each other, to a certain extent at least?

Mr. DAKAN. Yes.

The CHAIRMAN. These factories were some of them built, and some of them purchased, by the Great Western Sugar Co., were they not?

Mr. DAKAN. There was so much horseplay in the landing of a factory in each community that it would be impossible to tell the details of each factory.

The CHAIRMAN. Mr. Morey, particularly, virtually said that, too. They bought some that were already built when they went into the business, and promoted and built others, developing the business.

Mr. DAKAN. The perfection of the organization did not then exist that exists now, and there were independent capitalists, as we understood, attempting to get a foothold in this rich beet region; and the water facilities and the irrigation there, the character of the soil, and the absence of clouds made it a particularly desirable location for this business; and when it was discovered, after experimentation with the sugar beet, that this region excelled almost any other region in America for this purpose, there was then some competition in landing independent capital for a sugar factory; and by manipulation, in one way or another, all of these companies were combined and gathered together—we know not how—in the Great Western Sugar Co., until now there is a perfect organization on the part of the sugar company.

The CHAIRMAN. They have a practical monopoly, then, of the beet-sugar market?

Mr. DAKAN. An absolute monopoly.

The CHAIRMAN. There is nobody else to buy beets except them?

Mr. DAKAN. No, sir; we all sign this contract. No other contract can be made.

The CHAIRMAN. But if this combination did not exist, the conditions would be different?

Mr. DAKAN. I refer you to the Spanish experience.

The CHAIRMAN. And you think that would be locally the situation in this country?

Mr. DAKAN. That was the condition of business before.

The CHAIRMAN. That is exactly the point. Before these factories were combined, did the farmers get any better prices, and did they have conditions that were any fairer than they have now?

Mr. DAKAN. I was only familiar with the Longmont factory, when they were first built. I do not think there was any difference in the prices paid, but I do not know what the treatment about the community was. That was 8 or 10 years ago. I have never gone into that.

The CHAIRMAN. You farmers contend that if you had more than one customer you would get along better?

Mr. DAKAN. If there was actual competition.

The CHAIRMAN. Actual competition for the beets?

Mr. DAKAN. And if they could deal freely with the different men. Here they are not consulted in any way concerning the contract.

The CHAIRMAN. You mean as to how much they shall be paid?

Mr. DAKAN. Yes, sir.

The CHAIRMAN. This big concern, that has got all these nine plants in your region, just gets its agents there together and fixes a figure and notifies the farmers, "We will pay you so much for sugar beets," and it is either take it or leave it; is that right?

Mr. DAKAN. Yes. There has been a rise in the price since the farmers' organization got to work.

The CHAIRMAN. The Farmers' Union attempts to meet that situation, and that is one of the objects of the organization?

Mr. DAKAN. That is just one of the numerous objects.

The CHAIRMAN. I say it is one of the objects?

Mr. DAKAN. Yes.

The CHAIRMAN. They have got a committee that handles that?

Mr. DAKAN. Yes; they have also the American Beet Growers' League out there.

The CHAIRMAN. And their officers undertake to do the best they can with this company and to get as much of a price as possible for the farmers for their beets?

Mr. DAKAN. Yes; make it a cooperative business, as far as is possible with a business of that kind.

The CHAIRMAN. They want the Great Western Sugar Co. to kind of divide up profits with them; is that the idea?

Mr. DAKAN. Yes. The farmer, on the average yield and price of beets paid, just breaks even. The company, according to their own reports, make a profit of $1.10 a sack. The farmer, on the average, does not make a profit. He gets his wages. He is not allowed to count any profit or any salary for himself.

The CHAIRMAN. Does the farmer get the benefit of any of this protection we have on beet sugar?

Mr. DAKAN. Only in the way indicated here.

Mr. FORDNEY. Mr. Combs testified yesterday that he got a profit. You say the farmers are not allowed a profit. He showed a profit of $46.10 an acre in his testimony yesterday.

Mr. DAKAN. Mr. Fordney, I was speaking of the average man, the average of the business, if you please. The average of Colorado just about lets the farmer break even. That takes in Mr. Combs and Mr. Bodkin and any other man.

The CHAIRMAN. And every other man, averaging them up?

Mr. DAKAN. The average of the business on the side of the farmer does not allow him to make a profit; and, according to your figures, the company makes $1.10 a sack; so that the farmer sees the company making $1.10 a bag profit——

Mr. FORDNEY. No; I beg to differ with you; I gave you Mr. Willett's estimate of 1.10 cents a pound.

Mr. DAKAN. And there are 100 pounds in a bag.

Mr. FORDNEY. Yes; that is $1.10 a bag.

The CHAIRMAN. That is right; that is what he said.

Mr. DAKAN. Now I will give you another illustration. The profit is $1.10 a bag. The average percentage of extraction is 15 per cent, or three bags per ton.

Mr. FORDNEY. That is the estimate given by Mr. Combs, not by me.

Mr. DAKAN. Well, for illustration——

Mr. FORDNEY. In other words, 15 per cent beets will not yield 300 pounds of sugar per ton; it will take 17½ per cent beets to yield that much.

Mr. DAKAN. But we have factories that do yield that.

Mr. FORDNEY. There are some beets that do that; yes, sir.

Mr. DAKAN. Now, I want to illustrate that.

Mr. FORDNEY. Yes.

Mr. DAKAN. Suppose they extract 15 per cent of sugar; that is three bags of sugar per ton extracted from the beets. If the average yield is 10 tons per acre for the State, there is 30 bags of sugar per acre that the company gets out of the soil in Colorado. They make on that $1.10 per bag, according to the figures given.

Mr. FORDNEY. Is that your average? Do your beets in Colorado average 17½ per cent?

Mr. RAKER. He is figuring it on a 15 per cent basis.

Mr. DAKAN. I am just illustrating it.

Mr. FORDNEY. No; but pardon me. I am not quarreling with you; I am trying to get this right. You do not get three bags of sugar out of a ton of 15 per cent beets, and you have shown that 15 per cent is the average.

Mr. DAKAN. Pardon me. Wait until I get through and I will get to that.

Mr. FORDNEY. Pardon me.

Mr. DAKAN. This is an illustration on a 15 per cent basis.

Mr. FORDNEY. That is right.

Mr. DAKAN. The company makes $33 per acre, on the average, on this basis.

Mr. FORDNEY. From the lands of the Colorado farmer?

Mr. DAKAN. Yes.

Mr. FORDNEY. And on 15 per cent beets?

Mr. DAKAN. On the extraction of 15 per cent sugar.

Mr. FORDNEY. On the extraction?

Mr. DAKAN. That is what I am saying.

Mr. FORDNEY. That means 17½ per cent beets on the test.

Mr. DAKAN. Some factories run up that way. I am not very far wrong, when I get to the point.

Mr. FORDNEY. Yes.

Mr. DAKAN. This, then, means that the company makes $33 an acre profit after paying its officials enormous salaries and charging that out of that. In addition to these enormous salaries it makes $33 an acre off the farmer's land in Colorado. The farmer just breaks even on the business basis of management by the company. The farmer has made no profit, and the company has made $33 an acre off the land of the farmer on that basis.

Mr. FORDNEY. Do you know that the factory makes that? That is the point I want to get at. And if so how do you arive at your figures showing their profit?

Mr. DAKAN. I am taking Mr. Willett's estimate of the profit. I as taking your estimate.

Mr. FORDNEY. Oh, well, Mr. Willett is a New York man, and this firm is in Colorado. The average I gave, as given by him, gives a profit of 1.10 cents per pound, which is, as I understand it, throughout the whole United States—the entire beet-sugar industry of the United States.

Mr. DAKAN. And we understand that the efficiency of the factories in Colorado is such that they excel in the extraction of sugar.

Mr. FORDNEY. do not so understand that. I do not know why. If so, why? Tell me why your factories there can get any more sugar out of beets than other factories? I am not quarrelling with you, but I want to know these things.

Mr. DAKAN. I do not know why, because we are not allowed to go into that with the company.

Mr. FORDNEY. I think you are mistaken in that. Perhaps you are right and I am wrong.

Mr. DAKAN. Mr. Fordney.

Mr. FORDNEY. Yes.

Mr. DAKAN. When we asked Mr. Dixon whether the figures he read were not the extraction, when he said 15.57 per cent sugar, he was very much embarrassed, closed up his records, and would not answer the question—would not speak to us concerning that any more

Mr. MALBY. Let me ask you on that point: Are these companies all organized under the laws of the State of Colorado, or elsewhere?

Mr. DAKAN. Some of the subsidiary companies are organized in Colorado.

Mr MALBY. I mean the sugar companies. Is the Great Western Sugar Co. a Colorado corporation, or not?

Mr. DAKAN. I could not say. My impression is that it is a New Jersey corporation.

Mr. MALBY. Do they make reports to the secretary of state or other officials of the State of Colorado under your taxing system? Do they make any report?

Mr. DAKAN. Not that is of any value from a taxation point of view.

Mr. MALBY. Do they make any report at all as to their receipts and income and disbursements and capital stock?

Mr. DAKAN. They make a report of the capital stock of the company—I may not be altogether corect in this, but that is the general scheme—of the stock outstanding and the debts of the company.

Mr. MALBY. And their income?

Mr. DAKAN. I think not.

Mr. MALBY. Are there any laws in the State of Colorado taxing the income, gross or net?

Mr. DAKAN. Not that I know of. I am not familiar enough with the corporation law to go into that.

Mr. MALBY. You see, unless we have all of the details that go in to make up a company's income, as well as their outgo, we are apt to come to an erroneous conclusion.

I notice on page 2729 of our hearings that Mr. Palmer, in response to a question put by our chairman with reference to the Great Western Sugar Co. at Denver, testified as follows:

The CHAIRMAN. * * * Then we go to Colorado. The concerns about which I have been reading are the very biggest in the business, are they not?

Mr. PALMER. Yes, sir.

The CHAIRMAN. I will read again from the Beet Sugar Gazette, which is a standard publication and reliable?

Mr. PALMER. Yes, sir.

The CHAIRMAN. And published in the interest of the beet-sugar industry?

Mr. PALMER. Yes, sir.

The CHAIRMAN (reading):

"Great Western Sugar Co. dividend. The Great Western Sugar Co., of Denver, Colo., has declared two quarterly dividends of 1½ per cent each on the common stock. The first is payable July 2. to stock of record June 15; the second is payable October 3, to stock of record September 15. The company has declared quarterly dividends on the preferred stock for a year to come. The first is payable July 2, to stock of record June 15; the second, October 3, to stock of record September 15; the third, January 2, 1911, to stock of record December 15, and the fourth, April 3, 1911, to stock of record March 15, 1911. There is

$13,130,000 preferred and $10,544,000 common outstanding. The company has paid dividends on the preferred stock since 1905 at the rate of 7 per cent. The first dividend on the common stock was paid in January of this year at rate of 5 per cent."

Would you say that is a true statement of the conditions so far as the Great Western is concerned?

Mr. PALMER. I should judge so. They did not commence to pay dividends on the common stock until just recently, as I recollect. The last quotation I have heard on their common stock was 89.

Now, it would appear from the reading of this document that while there may be a capitalization in excess of that outstanding, the outstanding stock is something like $23,700,000, instead of $30,000,000. It would appear that they had paid dividends only on $13,130,000 since 1905, and that no dividend had been paid on any other portion of it until about a half a year ago. The point that occurs to me is that, if you are correct about the company making such vast sums of money, it certainly is not indicated by the payment of any dividends to the stockholders who own the company. I am wondering—and that is why I asked you whether there is any report made to your secretary of state or any other officer—whether their receipts and disbursements, if such a statement was filed, would not show that you must be mistaken with reference to your deductions as to the excessive revenue in proportion to the amount of business that was done. You see, there has been no dividend on the common stock, except two quarterly dividends, recently declared. The first common stock dividend was payable on July 2, and the second was payable on October 3. I take it that that must be 1910.

Mr. RAKER. What was the amount of that dividend, 40 per cent?

Mr. MALBY. It was 1¼ per cent; a quarterly dividend, at the rate of 5 per cent per annum.

Mr. DAKAN. That is on the common stock; and the dividend on the preferred stock is 7 per cent.

Mr. MALBY. Yes; but that is only $13,000,000 instead of $30,000,000. How do you account for the payment simply on $13,000,000 of the preferred stock, and none on the common stock except for about a year, now, if they are in receipt of such a vast amount of money?

Mr. DAKAN. I can only suppose that it is put in the surplus and undivided profit.

Mr. MALBY. I think they report on that.

Mr. FORDNEY. If you will permit me, here is the testimony of Mr. Morey, which explains the stock question. Mr. Malby was examining him. I read from page 874 of the record:

Mr. MALBY. The Great Western Sugar Co. was incorporated in the State of New Jersey?

Mr. MOREY. Yes, sir.

Mr. MALBY. With a capital stock of how much?

Mr. MOREY. Originally, $20,000,000. That was the authorized capital, $10,000,000 of preferred and $10,000,000 of common, and then afterwards it was increased, making $30,000,000 of capital, $15,000,000 of each, but it is not all issued.

Mr. MALBY. How much of it has been issued?

Mr. MOREY. Of the preferred, there has been issued 136,300 shares.

Mr. MALBY. Thirteen and some odd million dollars?

Mr. MOREY. Yes; and of the common, 105,440 shares, or $10,500,000.

That makes $23,130,000.

Mr. MALBY. That is substantially this statement. All that I wanted was to insert here their own records, as being a sort of an appropriate place for a comparison between that and the other. The full statement may go in at any time, when I find it. Figuring upon the basis that Mr. Dakan has given, of course it would be difficult to ascertain what they were doing with their money, because it certainly has not gone to the stockholders of the company.

The CHAIRMAN. You want a statement from the Great Western Sugar Co.?

Mr. MALBY. From the Great Western.

Mr. FORDNEY. While you are finding that, may I ask a few questions?

The CHAIRMAN. Certainly.

Mr. FORDNEY. I have made some comparison here of the prices paid by independents and the Michigan Co.'s factories in the State of Michigan, under their contract which you gave me a copy of a little while ago, which I understood to be exactly as it is stated there, with the prices obtained by the Colorado farmers. From the testimony given by Mr. Bodkin and Mr. Combs and yourself—I do not know whether you have yet given that—I am quite satisfied that it costs you considerably more per acre to produce your beets in Colorado than it costs to produce beets in the State of Michigan. In Colorado you must pay for water and you must dig ditches to distribute that water over the fields, whereas in Michigan we get water from the elements without cost. You, by being able to give the beets water when they need it most, and having sunshine practically all the time during the growing season of beets, have an advantage over a State that depends upon the elements, because beets need sunshine all the time, and water——

Mr. DAKAN. When they need it.

Mr. FORDNEY (continuing). When they need it. Sometimes we get too much of it, in Michigan, and sometimes not enough. I have made a comparison of the prices paid, with the various percentages of sugar content in the beets, and I wanted to give them to you; and you correct me if I am wrong. I want them to go in the record. For 12 per cent beets your Colorado farmers, as I remember from the statement you made here, get $5 per ton, flat?

Mr. DAKAN. Yes.

Mr. FORDNEY. The Michigan farmer gets $4.50 per ton.

Mr. DAKAN. Yes.

Mr FORDNEY. For 13 per cent beets you get $5, flat.

Mr. DAKAN. Yes.

Mr. FORDNEY. The Michigan farmer gets $4.83⅓. For 14 per cent beets you get $5, flat. The Michigan farmer gets $5.16⅔ per ton. On 15 per cent beets you get $5.25. The Michigan farmer gets $5.50. For 16 per cent beets the Colorado farmer receives $5.50 per ton, and the Michigan farmer $5.83⅓. For 17 per cent beets the Colorado farmer gets $5.75 per ton, and the Michigan farmer gets $6.16⅔ per ton. For 18 per cent beets the Colorado farmer gets $6 per ton, and the Michigan farmer gets $6.50 per ton. Is not that about right, so far as Colorado is concerned?

Mr. DAKAN. That is correct.

Mr. FORDNEY. That was my understanding in Michigan, and that is according to the Michigan contract which you gave me a few moments ago.

Mr. DAKAN. Yes.

Mr. FORDNEY. That is not such a very great difference in the price paid per ton; it ranges from 50 cents. The higher the percentage the greater the difference between your prices and the Michigan prices.

Mr. DAKAN. But the difference in the cost of producing the beets is nearly double.

Mr. FORDNEY. It is much more, as I said. But it has always been contended before the Committee on Ways and Means—I do not know that that information has been presented here—that you were getting a higher per cent of sugar in your beets in irrigated land districts, and a higher tonnage per acre. But Mr. Bodkin stated yesterday, I think—or Mr. Combs stated—that your average tonnage per acre there was about 10 tons. That does not vary very much from the tonnage harvested in the State of Michigan.

Mr. DAKAN. May I give you there a record which I have here, something concerning those things?

Mr. FORDNEY. Yes; we will be glad to have that.

Mr. DAKAN. In 1908 the total acreage in Colorado was 119,475. The yield was 9.28 tons.

Mr. FORDNEY. May I ask you who made up those statistics? Are those Government reports or your State reports, do you know?

Mr. DAKAN. I think I got these figures from the American Sugar Industry, this sugar-beet journal.

Mr. FORDNEY. That is the Government estimate?

Mr. DAKAN. I am not sure about that.

Mr. FORDNEY. Yes. I want to say that yesterday or this morning an estimate was given on the crop of Michigan taken from some Government report here, which widely differs from the real results in the State, showing but a fraction over 7 tons per acre there.

Mr. DAKAN. I beg your pardon; this is for 1908. I am going on three years.

Mr. FORDNEY. Yes; but you do not know whether this is from a Government report or from State reports?

Mr. DAKAN. I think it is taken from the American Sugar Industry, this technical journal.

Mr. FORDNEY. The figures being, perhaps, taken from Government reports?

Mr. DAKAN. Yes. I will just give this table, so that the stenographer may have it compact.

Mr. FORDNEY. Yes.

Mr. DAKAN. Total acreage, Colorado, 1908, 119,475; yield per acre, 9.28 tons; per cent of sugar, 13.85; 1909, total acreage, 141,600; yield per acre, 10.33 tons; per cent of sugar, 14.24.

Mr. FORDNEY. That is below the general average of Michigan. You can not get 300 pounds of sugar out of a ton of beets of that percentage, can you?

Mr. DAKAN. No, sir.

Mr. FORDNEY. Then your figures of 300 pounds per ton must be for some other years or on some other basis.

Mr. DAKAN. I took the basis of 17, for the sake of illustration. If that illustration is objectionable, I would reduce it to 12 per cent.

Mr. FORDNEY. It is not objectionable at all.

Mr. MALBY. It is not objectionable, if it is based on the actual conditions.

Mr. FORDNEY. The illustration should be taken by this committee as dealing with actual results, in showing excessive profits, as you claim, by the sugar factories, and such poverty-stricken profits by the farmers for their crops.

Mr. DAKAN. Well, suppose we get at this year, for an illustration.

Mr. FORDNEY. If you can, do that. For instance, you take——

Mr. DAKAN. The crop of 1911.

Mr. FORDNEY. Of 1910–11?

Mr. DAKAN. No; the 1911 crop.

Mr. FORDNEY. Your 1911 crop has not been ground out yet.

Mr. DAKAN. Up to last Wednesday Mr. Dixon informed us that the average was 15.57 per cent.

Mr. FORDNEY. For the State?

Mr. DAKAN. For the State.

Mr. FORDNEY. 15.57?

Mr. DAKAN. Yes, for the State; that is as we understood it. Now, I do not know what the per cent of extraction is there, but I will ask you to give me that.

Mr. FORDNEY. I know, from statements that are general in the business, that it is about 85 per cent of the extraction, with the Steffens process, which is the most modern process. In other words, if you extract 100 pounds you save only 85 pounds of it. I think that is about correct.

Mr. DAKAN. That would make three sacks and 11.4 pounds.

Mr. FORDNEY. Yes; but you do not get three sacks out of those percentages.

Mr. DAKAN. Now, take 85 per cent of that.

Mr. FORDNEY. Eighty-five per cent of 15.57?

Mr. DAKAN. Yes. That figures out 2.6469.

Mr. FORDNEY. Mr. Hamlin figures here that with 15 per cent sugar, 85 per cent of 15.57 extraction would give 264⅛ pounds, by the Steffens process, which is used; and he says that under other methods considerably less than that much sugar would be saved. You know that they have the Steffens process?

Mr. DAKAN. I know that they have it in some of the factories, and the sirup is shipped to those factories. Some of the factories have the Steffens, and some do not, but from those that do not the sirup is shipped in tanks to those that have the Steffens, so that they use all the sirup they manufacture in that way. That is, they get all of the sugar that they can get out of the sirup. Of course there is some sirup left then.

Mr. FORDNEY. Yes, refuse; that is bitter sirup. They extract alcohol from that in our country.

Mr. DAKAN. Yes, and they also use it for stock food, mixing it with alfalfa and straw?

Mr. FORDNEY. Yes, it is used so with us, too.

Mr. DAKAN. In northern Colorado the extraction, as nearly as we can get at the actual conditions, this year is 264⅛ pounds from a ton, and they make $1.10 profit per bag.

Mr. FORDNEY. Per 100 pounds, yes.

Mr. DAKAN. Per 100 pounds.

Mr. MALBY. How many bags do you figure?

Mr. DAKAN. 2.64 bags.

Mr. MALBY. I mean, what was the output of Colorado?

Mr. DAKAN. This year?

Mr. MALBY. Any year—take any year. Each year has its own, of course. That would be less than 3 cents a pound profit at $1.10.

Mr. DAKAN. The average tonnage for 1909 was 10⅓.

Mr. MALBY. I mean what was the output in bags of the factories of Colorado. You give the profit on each bag. You are figuring the profit on each bag. On what number of bags do you figure? How many bags was the output?

Mr. DAKAN. Our estimate for the Great Western Sugar Co. in tonnage this year is 700,000 tons for northern Colorado.

Mr. FORDNEY. I will help you, if you will permit me, Mr. Malby. We were figuring on saving 85 per cent of sugar in the beets, on 15.57 per cent in the beets, which means 264⅓ pounds from a ton of sugar, and if Mr. Willett's estimate of 1.10 cents a pound is correct, the profit to the factory is $2.91 profit per ton of beets worked.

Mr. DAKAN. Now we are getting at the comparison that I wish to state that causes the farmer to ask for a larger price for his beets. At the average cost to the farmer of raising beets, he just about breaks even. He sees the company making about $30 per acre on this basis off of the land that he does not make anything from as a profit.

Mr. FORDNEY. Or a very small one, if he makes any?

Mr. DAKAN. A comparatively small one, I mean compared with the profit of the company.

Mr. FORDNEY. His investment is, of course, much less in proportion than that of the factory. However——

Mr. DAKAN. But he gets no salary. He sees the officials of the company getting millions of dollars in salaries, and that is not included in these profits.

Mr. FORDNEY. Oh, yes.

Mr. MALBY. If they get millions of dollars in salary, what are the salaries? You have referred to excessive salaries several times. Have you any figures on what salaries they get?

Mr. DAKAN. We do not know what the officials of the American Sugar Refining Co. get.

Mr. FORDNEY. No; but the officials of your company?

Mr. MALBY. We know about that.

Mr. DAKAN. We do not know, but they own a large proportion of the stock.

Mr. MALBY. What do the officials of your local company get?

Mr. DAKAN. Mr. Morey probably gets $20,000 or $25,000 a year.

Mr. FORDNEY. He superintends the 11 factories, does he?

Mr. DAKAN. I presume so. I do not know. I have not heard of Mr. Dixon.

Mr. FORDNEY. They have nine factories in your State?

Mr. DAKAN. Nine in our State, and one at Scottsbluff, Nebr.

Mr. FORDNEY. Is not Mr. Morey superintendent over all of those factories?

Mr. DAKAN. I do not know.

Mr. FORDNEY. That would be a little more than $2,000 a year for each factory, for his salary?

Mr. DAKAN. If you care to figure it that way.

Mr. FORDNEY. I do not want to figure it that way unless it is right. Is he superintendent of the entire eleven factories, do you know?

Mr. DAKAN. I do not know just what his official connection is.

Mr. MALBY. The evidence shows that.

Mr. FORDNEY. The information given me by Mr. Hamlin, who is present, is that Mr. Morey is at this time president of the eleven factories owned by the Great Western Sugar Co.

Mr. MALBY. Mr. Morey's own testimony shows that to be a fact.

Mr. FORDNEY. And I am informed that he gets $25,000 a year, which is a little more than $2,000 to be charged to each factory, if it is equally proportioned. We are trying to get at the salaries paid to the officers, that is all, Mr. Dakan. I am not disputing you. I do not know anything about the matter.

Mr. DAKAN. There are numerous salaries of $10,000 which are reported, and some $5,000 and $7,000 salaries, but we do not know.

Mr. FORDNEY. You do not know how many in each factory receive a salary of $10,000?

Mr. DAKAN. No; nor in any factory, how much any receive. But, for instance, take the chemist in chief; I do not know what his official title is, but the man who has charge of and is responsible for the chemical management of the industry for the Great Western Sugar Co.; he is a high-salaried official. Then, the general superintendent, the general field man, and the general agriculturalists. They have experts from Germany who are engaged in the conduct of agricultural experiments.

Mr. FORDNEY. Mr. Morey gave all the salaries of the officers and high-priced men connected with the company, and that is already in the record. Have you examined that?

Mr. DAKAN. No, sir.

Mr. FORDNEY. I believe that is in the record.

Mr. DAKAN. I have examined the record, but I did not see the list of salaries. I did not see the record until we got here on Tuesday.

Mr. COMBS. Mr. Morey did give them. I read them.

Mr. DAKAN. Did it purport to be the salaries of all of the officials?

Mr. FORDNEY. I do not know. We can find that in the record.

Mr. MALBY. While we are stopping on that, for a moment, let me ask another question. The witness was testifying as to the output of their concerns in bags of 100 pounds each, and the method of ascertaining what the output is, and so forth. You have been dealing somewhat in acreages, but I desire to call your attention to some statistics offered by Mr. Morey as to the output of his united factories. How much per bag of 100 pounds do you figure the profit would be, under the method you have described? How much would be the profit on 100 pounds of sugar?

Mr. DAKAN. $1.10

Mr. MALBY. How many bags do you figure?

Mr. DAKAN. On the average yield per acre it would be 29⅜, at 10 tons per acre.

Mr. MALBY. But what would be the aggregate, I mean; what would be the aggregate output? You must have something to go by to ascertain what their entire income would be?

Mr. DAKAN. I mean in northern Colorado.

Mr. MALBY. I mean the Great Western Sugar Co., if that is where they are located.

Mr. DAKAN. There are two factories, you know, that are not in northern Colorado, which belong to the Great Western Sugar Co., so that we can only estimate their output in northern Colorado.

Mr. MALBY. What would you estimate that to be?

Mr. DAKAN. We estimate it this year at 700,000 tons of beets.

Mr. MALBY. Reduce that to sugar in bags, and tell me what it would be.

Mr. DAKAN. It is 2.9 bags per ton.

Mr. MALBY. You and Mr. Fordney have gone over that. Get it down to bags of sugar, so that we can make a comparison of estimates between your figures and Mr. Morey's figures.

Mr. DAKAN. This would be for this year.

Mr. MALBY. All right; any year.

Mr. DAKAN. For the present campaign.

Mr. MALBY. All right. So long as we get the price per bag, we can easily enough ascertain as to the balance.

Mr. DAKAN. On the basis of a yield of beets in northern Colorado for the campaign of 1911 of 700,000 tons, and an extraction of 2.9 bags per ton, the number of bags produced on that estimate for the present campaign would be 2,030,000 bags of sugar of 100 pounds each.

Mr. MALBY. Upon which you calculate there is a profit of $1.10 a bag?

Mr. DAKAN. If that profit is correct.

Mr. MALBY. That would yield you about $2,233,000.

Mr. FORDNEY. Those are the nine factories you are figuring on, Mr. Dakan?

Mr. DAKAN. Yes.

Mr. FORDNEY. They would yield 2,030,000 bags?

Mr. DAKAN. Yes.

Mr. MALBY. Now, I call attention to Mr. Morey's statement as to what their actual output was for the campaign of 1909–10, 2,146,828 bags. For the campaign of 1910–11 it was 1,462,798 bags.

Mr. DAKAN. When did he give that testimony?

Mr. MALBY. It was given on June 24, 1911.

Mr. DAKAN. He was dealing in futures, then, for 1910–11.

Mr. MALBY. This is the campaign of 1911–12, so that there would not be any futures about that testimony.

Mr. DAKAN. I am estimating for the campaign now of 1911–12.

Mr. MALBY. What we are trying to find out is not what the profits were for a given year, but in a certain period of time which would represent the fair and uniform income of the company. You can not tell what the income of a man or a corporation is by selecting one year, but you can by taking a period of years.

Mr. DAKAN. But last year there was a very short acreage for the Great Western Sugar Co.

Mr. MALBY. Yes; I know; but apparently they have their ups and downs the same as everybody else does. They have the same expenses; their fixed charges are just the same. Now, they would make money, I suppose, during the campaign of 1909–10. There might not be much profit on 1,462,798 bags, while there might be a profit on 2,146,828 bags.

I will now turn to page 900, and I find, according to Mr. Morey's statement, the following. He was under cross-examination by Mr. Jacoway. They quoted the selling price for the years 1908–9, 1909–10, and 1910–11, which averaged $4.485, and the cost was stated at $3.712, making a net profit of 78.5 cents per bag, instead of $1.10 per bag.

Mr. DAKAN. Whose testimony is that?

Mr. MALBY. Mr. Morey's.

Mr. DAKAN. Shall I do some estimating, now, on his own statement?

Mr. MALBY. Why, if there is anything which you can add to that, we would be very glad to have you do so. Apparently, however, he figures his profits considerably less than we have been figuring them.

Mr. DAKAN. Let us take him at his own figures, then.

Mr. MALBY. Well, that would answer.

Mr. DAKAN. 78.5 cents profit, per bag, and 2.9 bags per ton.

Mr. MALBY. I have not said he quoted 2.9 bags per ton. I have not read that. Now, if he says that, all right. I am not aware that he did say that. He gives the number of bags that they did actually produce, the number of bags in their actual output.

The CHAIRMAN. Do you know how many bags there were?

Mr. MALBY. I take it the number of bags given here that the company sent out was an actual tabulation from the books, as to what the output was. It would be foolish for us to speculate on it.

The CHAIRMAN. Yes; and we know how much sugar is in a bag.

Mr. MALBY. Yes; 100 pounds. He says there is 100 pounds in a bag, and they sent out so many bags. I was fearing that Mr. Dakan was taking, as a basis for calculation, something that did not exist.

Mr. DAKAN. Mr. Malby, I should like very much for you to give me a basis of Mr. Morey's own figures, with which I may compare our own, for you, on the matter.

Mr. MALBY. I can give you only this, and this is in the testimony. I read from page 899:

> Mr. JACOWAY. Now, Mr. Morey, you said that the output of the concern in which you are interested, for the year 1908–9, was 1,808,834 bags, a 100 pounds to the bag?
>
> Mr. MOREY. Yes.
>
> Mr. JACOWAY. And in 1909–10 it was 2,146,828?
>
> Mr. MOREY. Yes.
>
> Mr. JACOWAY. And in 1910–11 it was 1,462,798 bags?
>
> Mr. MOREY. Yes.

So that you see there has been given to us the exact number of bags which he swears the corporation turned out.

Mr. DAKAN. Did he give the number of acres under cultivation during those years?

Mr. MALBY. He did not. He gave some acreages here, but the acreages have reference to what the company itself is interested in, rather than the entire acreage.

Now, I turn to the following page, which is page 900, and I find that Mr. Jacoway has tabulated the three years 1908–9, 1909–10, and 1910–11 at 100 pounds of sugar to the bag, and I read as follows:

Mr. JACOWAY. I am just interested in some figures here. You produced 5,418,460 bags of sugar, at 100 pounds to the bag, in the period of time mentioned awhile ago, to wit, 1908–9, 1909–10, and 1910–11. As I understand you to say, your average selling price for those periods was 4.485?

Mr. MOREY. No; I did not say for those periods. I said the average, but it did not refer to those three or four years' average.

That is the general average, I suppose. Then he continues:

Mr. JACOWAY. Can you approximate that?

Mr. MOREY. I do not believe it would be very different. That other happened to be here.

Mr. JACOWAY. Approximately, are your selling prices for this period of time and your cost prices for this period of time about the same as for the period of time you gave and for which you quote the selling price at 4.485 and the cost at 3.70?

Mr. MOREY. I do not think there would be much change.

Mr. JACOWAY. It would be approximately and substantially correct?

Mr. MOREY. Yes; I think so.

Mr. JACOWAY. That being true, and on that assumption, and looking at it on that basis, then your profit for that period of time would be the difference between the selling price of 4.485 and the cost price of 3.712, which would net you 78.5 cents on each bag of sugar. Is that correct?

Mr. MOREY. I have not gone over your figures, but I presume so.

Mr. JACOWAY. That is, it would be the total number of bags multiplied by 78½ cents—78½ cents multiplied by the number of bags of sugar you produced?

Mr. MOREY. Yes.

Mr. JACOWAY. As I figure it, that would be $4,253,491.10. Can you verify those figures?

Mr. MOREY. I can not verify them. I can get all the figures you want later.

That is the testimony we have on that matter. That is, it comes to us in the total output of the concern, with the statement of Mr. Morey as to what he received for his sugar and what his profits were per bag. If you have any other deductions in any other form that might be permissible.

Mr. DAKAN. I just want to make an illustration and use his own figures, and make the illustration safe.

Mr. MALBY. All right.

Mr. DAKAN. It will be 78.5 cents profit per bag?

The CHAIRMAN. Yes; that is what he says.

Mr. DAKAN. And an extraction of 2.5 bags of sugar per ton, which is within what is actually extracted. Now, we have a yield this year of 11 tons per acre.

Mr. MALBY. Yes.

Mr. DAKAN. I am very sure that is within all calculations and actual results as well.

Mr. MALBY. Yes; I think that is safe.

Mr. FORDNEY. Mr. Malby, here are the salaries given by Mr. Morey.

Mr. MALBY. Just a minute, please, before we go into that.

Mr. FORDNEY. All right, sir.

Mr. DAKAN. I would like to get this into the record. At that yield the farmer just about breaks even; that is, without a profit on his acreage. He sees the company making $21.58 profit off his land. So he is working his land at a big profit for this company and at no profit for himself, and that is why he is asking for a small increase in the price of beets.

Mr. MALBY. That is quite a fair statement, is it; that is to say, it gets $21 per acre; that is true——

Mr. DAKAN. That is a profit out of the farmer's land.

Mr. MALBY. That is the profit; but let us see what the company has to do with that profit. According to the statement here they have stock outstanding in the sum of $23,000,000, and without going into the question of whether that is overcapitalization or not, they must pay out of that income the dividends on that stock. If it is an honest capitalization, of course all of us will concede that they would be entitled to a fair return on it, and perhaps 7 per cent on the preferred stock and 5 per cent on the common stock in the State of Colorado would not be regarded as excessive. Is that true?

Mr. DAKAN. The way we view that is that the capitalization is manipulated so that the profit will appear small.

Mr. MALBY. Without going into that question, which would be quite lengthy, perhaps, 7 per cent profit would not be regarded as excessive—7 per cent interest on money would not generally be regarded as excessive in Colorado?

Mr. DAKAN. On an honest investment——

Mr. MALBY. On an honest investment; yes.

Mr. DAKAN. No, sir; that would be a fair return.

Mr. MALBY. You see for the three years which I have taken here, according to his statement, their income would be, on an average, on the investment which they have, $1,417,000. Whether it is $21 an acre or more than that, that is their aggregate average.

Mr. DAKAN. About $1,417,000; but they average this profit and the farmer does not. Besides, the farmer sees a few men getting all this enormous sum in salaries. May I go into that?

Mr. MALBY. In the aggregate that is large, but when distributed among the stockholders it would not amount to a very large sum.

Mr. DAKAN. If one stockholder holds more than a million dollars' worth of stock, he would notice that he had an income at 7 per cent.

Mr. MALBY. You see, if that capitalization was but $20,000,000, at 7 per cent it would take $1,400,000 to pay the interest on it alone.

Mr. FORDNEY. He could get that much interest on his money by loaning it in other ways in the State of Colorado, could he not?

Mr. DAKAN. That is why the capitalization is put the way it is.

Mr. FORDNEY. Well, he could do that, could he not?

Mr. DAKAN. Yes.

Mr. FORDNEY. So he does not make any more money by investing his money and taking this great chance of loss that he takes than he would make if he loaned his money out at 7 per cent interest?

Mr. DAKAN. He has not invested his money in this business; he gets stock dividends. For instance, he pays taxes on $2,500,000. But this would indicate that the physical value of his property is somewhere between $10,000,000 and $12,000,000.

Mr. FORDNEY. No; not exactly. You intimated that some folks "see" the assessor occasionally.

Mr. MALBY. I think in all fairness to Mr. Dakan I should say that Mr. Morey's testimony was that this property was carried on the books of the company at $15,000,000.

Mr. DAKAN. Then there is that difference to be accounted for otherwise.

Mr. MALBY. The original investment, if I remember rightly, was $10,000,000 of preferred and $10,000,000 of common, and I do not know whether it would be fair to assume that they organized their company in the same way that many other companies are organized, the preferred stock representing real value and common stock representing speculation.

Mr. DAKAN. Here is something, perhaps, that will have some bearing on the Great Western Sugar Co. management. It is a clipping from a Denver paper, I think about June. [Reading.]

G. W. SUGAR CO. TO ASK LISTING OF ITS STOCKS ON 'CHANGE—PRICE JUMPS IN NEW YORK FROM 63 TO 70 IN THREE DAYS.

The Great Western Sugar Co., the largest manufacturers of beet sugar in the Western States, is about to apply to the governors of the New York Stock Exchange to have both its preferred and common stock listed. There are $15,000,000 of each class, of a par value of $100 a share. The formal request will be made, according to an authoritative source, after the meeting of the directors, about the end of this month.

Knowledge of the intention of the board to make an effort to have the stock placed upon the list of the New York Stock Exchange is responsible for a sharp rise in the price of the stock, which on Saturday last was offered in large quantities at $63 a share by Boettcher & Porter, acting for the controlling interests in the company.

The offer was formally withdrawn yesterday when the price per share had advanced to $70 bid. It was then announced that no more shares would come out, and the presumption among bond dealers is that a sufficient quantity had been taken up to warrant the company in seeking the listing privilege.

This year, according to W. A. Dixon, vice president of the company, promises to be the best in the history of the beet-sugar industry in Colorado. He says:

"Reports from our field agents indicate that the acreage in the district which supplies our nine factories in northern Colorado will be from 35 to 40 per cent larger than last year, when it was 48,000. That would make it from 65,000 to 67,000 acres in 1911.

"The soil is in prime condition, we are advised, and, barring the elements, we have every reason to hope for a record-breaking campaign. We are now in the midst of the planting season, and while it has been a dry winter there is the best of reasons to expect that the growth will be equal to, if not better than, any previous year. A good rain or a heavy snowfall would help a great deal.

"All the farmers have signed the contracts and are apparently well satisfied with the company's offer, which was the best we could make under all the circumstances. So we expect that again Colorado will be the banner State in sugar production, as it has been for several years."

Mr. MALBY. You see, the question which you raise with us is one exceedingly difficult of solution, and that is to say, that the Great Western Sugar Co. is reaping an unjust profit in a joint venture in which the stockholders of the company have invested capital and the farmers have invested their farms. I do not know what remedy we would apply, even if that state of affairs existed. If you have any suggestions as to in what way we could be of service, we would be glad to hear it; because I think if there is a disproportion of distribution of profits, and if there is any way by which they could be equalized, that that course should be adopted.

Mr. DAKAN. That is just what we want to get at; that is why we are here.

Mr. MALBY. But, of course, the nature of the testimony taken heretofore has been to the effect that the beet-sugar manufacturers, as well as the growers, have not had altogether an easy time; that neither of them has reaped very great profits, until very recent years. During the past half a dozen years it may be said that the manufacturers of sugar from beets have made a fair profit, but up to that time the profits were not large, and in many cases no dividends whatsoever had been paid. I recall that the Colorado Co., for instance, until 1905, did not pay any dividends at all, either on the preferred or on the common stock. In 1905, and down to the present time, they have paid 7 per cent interest on the preferred stock and 5 per cent, for about a year, on the common stock. Of course, to the stockholders that does not appear to be, on the face of it, a very large sum. Now, if there is any other method of profit which they have participated in in any way——

Mr. DAKAN. That is just what I would like to go into.

Mr. MALBY. I would like to have that expounded if we can get some intelligent basis for an accurate calculation, but up to the present time we have not been able to get very much of anything excepting this statement that they organized some years prior to that and that they were without dividends, and that since 1905 they have received the dividends which I have mentioned. Now, what proof have you that they have gotten any more than appears from their dividends? We have a fairly accurate statement, if Mr. Morey is to be believed, and I suppose he is, when he gives us the exact number of bags his company has put out. I suppose those figures are taken from the books of the company and are subject to verification. He seemed to give the exact number of bags each year, which I have given to you. He tells us what his profits are. That may be correct or not.

Mr. RAKER. Mr. Malby——

Mr. MALBY. Yes.

Mr. RAKER. Did not Mr. Morey agree to furnish a statement from the books of the company?

Mr. MALBY. I am not quite sure, Judge, about that. I have been looking over his testimony for just that statement.

Mr. RAKER. Do you remember, Mr. Chairman?

The CHAIRMAN. I think he did.

Mr. RAKER. I was looking for it.

Mr. MALBY. I was looking for his financial statement.

Mr. DAKAN. I have tried to take from your reading of Mr. Morey's statement his own profits, and I find them to be, as nearly as I can estimate from his own figures, $21.58 on the farmer's land. The farmer works that land without a profit and without the salaries. Now, then, as to the failure to pay dividends up to a short time ago, the farmer believes that the stockholders of the company are principally the officials of the company, or, in other words, that the officials of the company own practically all of the stock; that a few officials in the company own great blocks of the stock; that these men get salaries and dissipate the profit in the salaries they pay themselves and their superintendents.

Mr. MALBY. I do not think we have any testimony on that subject which quite authorizes that subject.

Mr. DAKAN. Have you a list of the stockholders of the company?

Mr. MALBY. No; we have not.

Mr. DAKAN. Could you get a list of the stockholders of the company?

Mr. MALBY. I presume we could; but is your statement quite correct when you say that the farmer gets nothing and the company gets $21? In all the estimates furnished here the farmer starts out with allowing himself $20 an acre for the use of his farm, and they still show some profit beyond that.

Mr. DAKAN. Mr. Malby, we can not discuss profits on that basis. I thought we were discussing profits on the basis of the financial management of the Great Western Sugar Co.

Mr. MALBY. I know; but on the one hand the farmer has his farm as an investment, and, on the other hand, the sugar company has its property as an investment. Now, the farmer claims $20 an acre for his farm, and very properly. Of course he claims it because he has an investment in his farm which justifies him in charging $20 an acre, which he must be paid back before he gets what he calls profit. Now, likewise, you must concede——

Mr. DAKAN. That was the high-priced land that brought $20 an acre.

Mr. MALBY. Well, the two witnesses testified yesterday, as I recall it, that in making up their expenses in management of lands $20 an acre was allowed.

Mr. DAKAN. It was in those instances, but that is not the average rental.

Mr. MALBY. I understood they were figuring the average.

Mr. DAKAN. No; they were not.

Mr. MALBY. Well, whether it should be $20 or some lesser sum, they take that out for their investment. Now, clearly, if they take that out as their investment before they count profits the company will have to take something out for their dividends before they can say they have like profits which ought to be shared between you. In other words, each party ought to be paid a reasonable sum for his money actually invested before there is a quarrel about the surplus. Our inquiry is to find out whether there is a surplus after allowing each a fair amount of income for the property invested.

Mr. DAKAN. But, as I said, when income is dissipated in salaries the farmer is not satisfied with that sort of a situation.

Mr. MALBY. Of course, we would not think so, either. But let me suggest this to you. What did Mr. Morey say he got as a salary?

Mr. FORDNEY. It gives it briefly here.

The CHAIRMAN. He said $25,000 a year, did he not?

Mr. FORDNEY. Yes; he received $20,000 up to a certain time, and now he gets $25,000 a year. The treasurer receives $3,000; the secretary-treasurer receives $7,500 per year; the general counsel receives $10,000 a year, and the second vice president receives $10,000 a year. He says those are the principal salaries. Then, on the other side, you asked him a question about imported sugar brought into competition with his sugar, which cost $3.65 and $3.75.

Mr. MALBY. Of course, a salary of $25,000 a year for an expert who has devoted his life to the business, devoting his time to the affairs of a company with $23,000,000 capital, might or might not be regarded as excessive. I do not know what you in Colorado would say about it. Mr. Havemeyer receives $100,000.

Mr. DAKAN. That came out of the Colorado farmer in a small way.

Mr. MALBY. In some proportion——

Mr. FORDNEY. That would be about one-tenth of 1 per cent on the stock issued, for the president's salary.

Mr. MALBY. As I say, I did not know whether that would be regarded in Colorado as an excessive salary or not—for a man of that kind who has spent his life in the business and built up the business.

Mr. DAKAN. But the duties they perform are to keep the farmers down, keeping them from getting more for their beets, preventing competition.

Mr. MALBY. If you will tell this committee how they can get more, I think you can get help.

Mr. DAKAN. That is a pretty big question, but we have ideas. Congress makes, or probably will make in the future, Federal corporation laws for the control of corporations. Laws exist whereby a corporation is given life, either by the legislature or by the Congress, and then both legislature and Congress immediately lose control of that corporation and it exploits the people. For instance, the capitalization of the Great Western Sugar Co. is based not only upon the physical property necessary to the business but upon its ability to control the market, the same basis that a traction company is capitalized on—on the value of a franchise. That franchise is valuable by reason of the patronage of the car riders of a city. The basis of the capitalization is its ability to exploit a given community of people.

Mr. MALBY. On its ability to do business.

Mr. DAKAN. I said to exploit a given community of people.

Mr. MALBY. Well, to do business; that is what it is.

Mr. DAKAN. Well, in the traction company, if it cuts out competition it capitalizes the value of a franchise and manipulates the capitalization in such a way that dividends appear small. Now, then, if the State legislature were forbidden by Congress, or if the power were taken away from the State legislature to create a corporation that could do an interstate business without supervision by the Federal Government, such supervision as would enable the Federal Government to go to the books of the company and get these figures without drumming and drumming away, as this committee has evidently done, judging by questions asked the sugar men in the 3,000 pages of the reports already published, and publicity were given to the operations of these corporations, that publicity would be a feature that would aid in controlling the corporation and in preventing the imposition of a corporation upon a people, as the Great Western imposes upon us in northern Colorado. That is, this control compelling this creature of the law to show up its books to the Government, or to a Government official, would be a measure that would tend to assist in the control of the impositions, or the prevention of impositions, that are rife in the United States at the present time.

In other words, the legislative bodies of the United States give life to legal beings called corporations, and immediately lose control of those beings, and they run around over the country exploiting humanity.

Mr. MALBY. Of course, you are not quite correct about that. That is to say, the Government of the United States does not do any such thing. We do not give life to any corporation; we do not incorporate corporations. Those things are done by the various States, and not by the Government of the United States.

The CHAIRMAN. You possibly both misunderstand each other a little. As I understand, Mr. Dakan says that it ought to be done.

Mr. DAKAN. Yes.

The CHAIRMAN. So that the Government could control them.

Mr. DAKAN. Speaking correctly, I should say that the legislature of a State gives life to a being that then imposes not only upon the government of the State but the United States Government—the Federal Government. Now, you take the instance of the Great Western Sugar Co.

The CHAIRMAN. That is a New Jersey corporation, is it not?

Mr. DAKAN. I think so. It comes out in Colorado, and we are helpless. There is, as we understand it, very poor control exercised by the Government over such corporations at the present time; but the Government receives absolutely no revenue from the sugar made in Colorado. That institution, the Great Western Sugar Co., pockets the tariff and the farmer pays it, and there is no benefit from it in the way of revenue to the Government, while the man who consumes the sugar that is imported pays a revenue to the Government. The Government gets a revenue from that sugar, but we of Colorado pay our money into the coffers of the Great Western Sugar Co. and they pocket that tariff——

The CHAIRMAN. Just a moment there. By adding to the price of the sugar the amount of the tariff?

Mr. DAKAN. Yes; by adding the amount of the tariff. They not only add to the price of sugar the tariff, but they add the freight.

Mr. FORDNEY. Are you in favor of free trade on sugar?

Mr. DAKAN. Practically no.

Mr. FORDNEY. Are you in favor of the tariff or the duty on sugar as it now is?

Mr. DAKAN. Not as it is now—not a scheme, as it is now. I am in favor of a scheme by which the sugar manufactured by the Great Western Sugar Co. would pay an internal revenue to the Government.

Mr. FORDNEY. You are in favor, then, of putting sugar on the free list and putting on an internal-revenue tax?

Mr. DAKAN. I do not know how that could be manipulated.

Mr. FORDNEY. The same as on whisky.

Mr. DAKAN. As I say, we now pay the freight as well as the tariff.

Mr. FORDNEY. Whom would you pay it to if sugar were on the free list and the refining companies crushed out your local industry and you would have to buy it from New Orleans or New York—to whom would you pay it then? Whom did you pay the big price to in September and October and August?

Mr. DAKAN. To the Great Western Sugar Co.

Mr. FORDNEY. No; they were not the ones that put up the price. The refiners of foreign sugars, companies that imported sugars, put up the price.

Mr. DAKAN. But the Great Western Sugar Co. got our money.

Mr. FORDNEY. Do they furnish sugar all the year round or do you have to buy cane sugar?

Mr. DAKAN. We buy sugar all the year round.

Mr. FORDNEY. The Great Western Sugar Co. furnishes you sugar all the year round?

Mr. DAKAN. Every bag of sugar and every neighbor I have in my town that gets sugar buys sugar that is marked "Great Western Sugar Co."

Mr. FORDNEY. Then you do not consume any other sugar in your town but Great Western sugar?

Mr. DAKAN. I did not say that. There is a small quantity of cane sugar consumed.

Mr. FORDNEY. Do you know about how much?

Mr. DAKAN. No. In this connection I would like to make this statement: There are about 7,000,000 bags of sugar made in Michigan, Montana, Colorado, and Nebraska. I am giving this as an illustration. In the States bordering that community there are about 20,000,000 inhabitants, so that the manufacturers of that sugar have a market home. Yet they add the freight from seaboard points to the price of sugar we pay. That is, the local freight. So we pay an excessive amount that they pocket. There is no return for it.

Mr. FORDNEY. Let me say this to you: That we have in the record here a statement from Mr. Warren, who represents the Michigan Sugar Co., and whose firm has six factories in the State of Michigan. He stated that they manufactured last year 124,000,000 pounds of sugar, and marketed 18,000,000 pounds, in round numbers, in the State of Michigan, and the balance of it went to other States.

Mr. RAKER. You mean that many bags, do you not?

Mr. FORDNEY. No, sir; that many pounds, 124,000,000 pounds.

Mr. DAKAN. What other States did he market it in?

Mr. FORDNEY. He named a great many States. Maryland, Pennsylvania, Ohio, Indiana, Missouri, Illinois, some in Kentucky, I remember, and some in Wisconsin.

Mr. DAKAN. Did he say how much?

Mr. MALBY. Yes; he did.

Mr. FORDNEY. He gave the various amounts and the markets, but they only marketed 18,000,000 pounds in Michigan out of 124,000,000 pounds.

Mr. DAKIN. I desire to repeat, again, that in these States I have mentioned, the chief sugar producing inland States, about 7,000,000 bags are produced annually, and there is a population of about 20,000,000 people. Now, then, of the actual consumption, as stated in the testimony, somewhere about 54 pounds per capita of sugar, or we will say a half a bag——

Mr. RAKER. He means 54 pounds excluding the amount that is used in manufacture. The manufacturers take up 80 pounds.

Mr. DAKAN. To make it certain we will say 50 pounds per capita. Fourteen million inhabitants would consume the product of all these factories in this inland territory that is affected by seaboard freights. In other words, the product of the inland sugar factories is consumed—that is, there is population enough to consume it at home and still leave about 6,000,000 inhabitants over that must be fed sugar.

Mr. FORDNEY. Yes; but your figures do not give the exact conditions. Michigan, for instance, last year produced about $13,000,000 worth of sugar. We consume in the State but little over one-half of that amount. Eighty per cent of the sugar, I may say, as a fair estimate, was marketed outside of the State.

Mr. DAKAN. What is the population of Michigan?

Mr. FORDNEY. 2,700,000 or 2,800,000.

Mr. MALBY. I have a table here, think, submitted by Mr. Morey, in which he states where he sold the sugar.

The CHAIRMAN. Mr. Morey or Mr. Warren?

Mr. MALBY. Mr. Morey. It is to be found at page 895. I think that is what that table means.

The CHAIRMAN. Yes.

Mr. MALBY. Very much to my surprise, Colorado shows only 265,295 bags, while Illinois was 259,666 bags; Iowa, 247,826 bags; and Missouri, 383,468 bags. In other words, out of 2,146,939 bags manufactured in 1909 and 1910 only 265,000 was consumed in Colorado all told.

Mr. DAKAN. Just a moment. There are 799,000 inhabitants in Colorado in round numbers.

The CHAIRMAN. Say 800,000.

Mr. DAKAN Say 800,000 inhabitants in Colorado. At one-half a bag per person; that is, I mean to say, one bag to two persons——

Mr. FORDNEY. Why do you not put in the total consumption for manufacture and table use, both?

The CHAIRMAN. You manufacture there.

Mr. FORDNEY. You are only figuring the amount consumed on the table and not that which you use in manufacturing.

The CHAIRMAN. Say 81.6.

Mr. DAKAN. You will see at a glance that the consumption of 265,000 bags with that population is evidence of the consumption of beet sugar becoming popular in Colorado. If each person consumes one-half of a bag the 800,000 would consume 400,000 bags.

Mr. FORDNEY. But you must figure more than that; you must figure the total consumption, the amount used in manufacture, because we each use our proportion of sugar in tobacco, condensed milk, medicines, and other things that require sugar in their manufacture. I presume that it would be fair to say that the people of Colorado are about the same as other people.

Mr. DAKAN. That would be about 640,000 bags we would consume if we consumed up to our quota. We only consumed about 50 per cent of it. That shows that the consumption of beet sugar in Colorado is comparatively high as compared with Michigan, for instance.

Mr. MALBY. That would illustrate, however, that a large quantity of sugar at some time of the year is shipped into Colorado, would it not?

Mr. DAKAN. Yes, sir.

Mr. MALBY. Mr. Morey testified that there is a large quantity shipped in from Louisiana and some from Utah and some from California.

Mr. DAKAN. Now, if the committee please, I might go into the method of controlling farmers in northern Colorado.

Mr. RAKER. Mr. Morey claims that none gets in from the Utah factories, Mr. Malby.

Mr. MALBY. I think I have it before me.

Mr. RAKER. I have it, at page 896. [Reading:]

Mr. MOREY. They can not get out so far. It would be too much for them.

Mr. MALBY. How about the Utah factories?

Mr. MOREY. They do not get into our territories much. They could not get anything by it. They could not get any better price than they get at the Missouri River.

That is his testimony.

Mr. MALBY. Yes; but subsequent to that you will find this:

Is there any competition outside of the local factories in the State of Colorado?

Mr. MOREY. Oh, yes; the main competition is outside.

Mr. MALBY. What is the population of Colorado; do you recall?

Mr. MOREY. About 800,000, I should say.

Mr. MALBY. Nine hundred thousand, I understand, nearly. How about California granulated sugars? Do they come into your territory?

Mr. MOREY. Yes, sir.

Mr. MALBY. And you sell in competition with them?

Mr. MOREY. Yes.

Mr. MALBY. And you sell also in competition with Michigan factories?

Mr. MOREY. They can not get out so far. Utah factories do not get into our territory much.

Mr. RAKER. I think you will find that the only competition they had at all in Colorado was what little came in from Texas.

Mr. MALBY. No; he gives it here somewhere.

Mr. DAKEN. Here is another view to take of those States——

Mr. MALBY (reading, p. 898):

Mr. MALBY. Where is your chief competitor located?

Mr. MOREY. It is a different people in the different markets. In Colorado territory, we will say, it is the California & Hawaiian Co., and the Western in San Francisco.

Here is Mr. Spreckles's statement, I think, at page 2881, showing that in Colorado there were sold, in 1906, 15,232,611 pounds.

Mr. FORDNEY. Cane sugar?

Mr. MALBY. Of cane sugar; and 1,931,800 beet sugar. That is 1906. It runs along until, say, 1909, where it is 16,655,515 of cane sugar; and, beet sugar, 1,649,000 in round numbers; and for 1910 it is 13,235,000 cane sugar and 2,090,000 of beet sugar, indicating two things; one is that you do not sell all your sugar in Colorado, and the other is that other companies do sell in Colorado in competition with your own.

Mr. DAKAN. Does Mr. Morey state how much he sells in Kansas?

The CHAIRMAN. Yes; he gives that figure, too.

Mr. MALBY. Yes.

Mr. DAKAN. Let us have those States bordering, please?

The CHAIRMAN. Kansas, 277,810 bags.

Mr. DAKAN. And Nebraska?

Mr. MALBY. 139,908 bags.

Mr. DAKAN. Oklahoma?

Mr. MALBY. 96,770 bags.

Mr. DAKAN. Wyoming?

Mr. MALBY. 20,930 bags.

Mr. FORDNEY. Does he give Colorado?

Mr. MALBY. Yes.

Mr. DAKAN. What is Colorado?

Mr. MALBY. 265,295.

Mr. DAKAN. What is Illinois?

Mr. MALBY. 259,666.

Mr. DAKAN. What is Indiana?

Mr. MALBY. Indiana is very small—8,611.

Mr. DAKAN. What is Iowa?

Mr. MALBY. 247,826 bags.

Mr. DAKAN. Then he sells almost all his product close to home. He is selling his product practically all in the neighboring States.

Mr. MALBY. Naturally he sells it as close to his factory as he can.

Mr. DAKAN. And he charges the consumer the freight from the seaboard—the farmers pay that.

Mr. FORDNEY. Do not put it all on the farmer. The people in the cities have to pay it.

Mr. DAKAN. I said the consumers pay it; I did not intend to put it on the farmer.

Mr. FORDNEY. I am not here pegging for the Great Western Sugar Co. or any other sugar company, but this thing is going to be discussed in the House of Representatives, and go to the country, and we want it right, and we want to show that while there are 35 per cent in rural districts the other 65 per cent of the people are in the cities, and they use sugar, and the farmers alone do not pay these things.

Mr. DAKAN. And these figures show that the sugar company takes advantage of the local market.

Mr. FORDNEY. It can not do otherwise; they can not market their sugar in Hawaii.

Mr. DAKAN. I am not saying so; I simply call attention to the fact that they do.

Mr. FORDNEY. That is the consequence of trade anywhere; you must market your goods where you can get the best price, and you have the advantage of home markets?

Mr. DAKAN. Yes.

Mr. RAKER. What the witness complains about is that they charge the freight rate from the seaboard.

Mr. FORDNEY. I believe it is done by every sugar factory.

Mr. RAKER. Well, is it right?

Mr. FORDNEY. Whether right or not, how can we change that situation? We can not change the laws of the State of Colorado. The Colorado State Legislature can pass a law that will prevent that company from doing business in the State unless they incorporate under the laws of the State if they so choose.

Mr. DAKAN. I beg your pardon, but can you not control the interstate business.

Mr. FORDNEY. We have a law for that, and we have officers to enforce those laws. Congress can not do it.

Mr. DAKAN. Congress makes that law.

Mr. FORDNEY. The law is made and is upon the statute books.

Mr. DAKAN. And it does not control?

Mr. FORDNEY. What right has Congress to go out and sue you, or any other man or any other corporation? The Judiciary Department of this Government has that right.

Mr. DAKAN. Does not Congress give the judiciary the club to do that?

Mr. FORDNEY. They have the club and they have the law.

Mr. DAKAN. And they are not doing it.

Mr. FORDNEY. I do not say that they are not doing it.

The CHAIRMAN. There is no law that has ever been passed by our States yet regulating that, though.

Mr. FORDNEY. No; and there is no way of regulating the price of any commodity on the market. There is no way of regulating the price of your services, that you demand from your clients.

Mr. DAKAN. You are getting away from the subject.

Mr. FORDNEY. Oh, no, I am not. You are getting all for your services that you can, are you not?

Mr. DAKAN. We are discussing the control of interstate business by corporations. We were discussing the control of interstate business by corporations, and Congress has that power. Congress has the power to make laws for interstate business.

Mr. FORDNEY. Yes. I say we have a law now. I say that we have the so-called Sherman antitrust law, and another antitrust law called the Hepburn Act, and we have a Judiciary Department in the Federal Government to enforce those laws. Congress has nothing to do with the enforcement of those laws. If I am wrong about it I want to be corrected. Judge, you are a lawyer; I am simply a layman. I will ask you whether I am right about it?

Mr. RAKER. You are pretty nearly right; yes.

Mr. DAKAN. I am not disputing that statement, that the judiciary has the business of enforcing the laws; but Congress is clothed with power to make a law that is effective. Now, there is a question whether this law is effective. It does not control the interstate business of the corporations that the States create.

Mr. FORDNEY. We have in power in the House of Representatives good people. I do not agree with them politically, but they are good men, just as honest as any other poliitical party. I am going to say that much for the Democrats, because I believe that. The Democratic Party is in power. If they believe that our present antitrust laws are not sufficient they are in power and they alone can give us some other law.

The CHAIRMAN. I suppose that is the reason the witness is giving his ideas about what that law is. One of the things that this committee is authorized and instructed to do is to make certain recommendations.

Mr. FORDNEY. I know that, and I am not complaining with him at all except in reference to his statement that the farmer paid all this. That is what started me.

The CHAIRMAN. Well, he meant to say the consumer.

Mr. FORDNEY. Well, the consumer——

Mr. DAKAN. There is one more point. The effect of the combination of the sugar company and factories in the control of the farmers.

The CHAIRMAN. Yes; that is directly in point.

Mr. DAKAN. The business men of each town are threatened that if they do not assist the company in making beet growing popular they will close the factory down at that particular town, and when the farmer asks the business man to consider his side of the case for a moment the business man seems to get into a panic of fear; he seems to think that the company will shut the factory down, and that this particular town will lose the revenue obtained if we do anything of that kind.

Mr. FORDNEY. Your condition is very unfortunate under such circumstances. The factory, if you only knew it, is absolutely dependent on you farmers to raise beets. If you refuse to raise beets, their property is valueless. They will be obliged to come to your terms if you refuse to raise beets at the price that you are obtaining. The farmers in Michigan have bettered their condition by fighting as you are. I want to see the farmers well paid for their services, and I want to see you helped, if I can. They have done it in our State and they get better prices than you do.

Mr. DAKAN. Then, do I understand correctly that you compliment your farmers for the fight that they have made?

Mr. FORDNEY. Yes, sir; and I am with them every day in the year.

Mr. DAKAN. And if we have gained in the last few years a 50-cent raise, you are glad?

Mr. FORDNEY. Yes; and I would aid you every minute I could.

Mr. DAKAN. That is why we are here. We are here to show the treatment we have received.

The CHAIRMAN. You claim that you do not receive a large enough share of the profits?

Mr. DAKAN. Does not the average yield show that we do not receive a profit? We are asking for a bare profit.

Mr. FORDNEY. I want to see you get a profit, but if the sugar company is only making a fair profit to-day, whatever you add to the price the farmer will get for his beets will come out of the consumer. What have the refiners done in the city of New York in the last six months? Every penny more they paid for their foreign raw sugar came out of the consumer, and came mighty quick, too. It ran from 5 cents up to 7½ cents a pound.

Mr. DAKAN. There are from 3,000 to 5,000 farmers in northern Colorado that are asking for a profit.

Mr. FORDNEY. I want to see them get it. I would like to help you if I can.

Mr. DAKAN. They have families; each one of those represent four or five persons. There are from 12,000 to 20,000 people of the agricultural inhabitants in northern Colorado dependent on agriculture and raising beets, and wanting to raise beets, for the company. Do you blame them for wanting to raise them for a profit?

Mr. FORDNEY. Do I blame them? I would like to aid them.

Mr. DAKAN. We are coming here to show you by evidence that can not be disputed that we do not get a profit. The evidence has shown that the company gets $21.58 at least on each acre of that land.

Mr. FORDNEY. Yes. While not doubting the correctness of those figures, yet Mr. Morey's statement differs very materially as to their profit, as to the profit you seem to think they get.

Mr. DAKAN. But that is out of our land, each acre of our land.

Mr. FORDNEY. And their capital invested.

Mr. DAKAN. And our capital invested; we make no profit on our capital; we only get wages.

The CHAIRMAN. You say they do not divide up fairly with you?

Mr. DAKAN. Now, we want to raise beets, I say.

Mr. FORDNEY. It was in you power to make them come to time for this next year's contract; and why did not you do it?

Mr. DAKAN. I will go further; we even tried to get the editors——

Mr. FORDNEY. If you refuse to raise beets you will accomplish the whole thing in a short time.

Mr. DAKAN. We want to raise beets.

Mr. FORDNEY. But if you refuse to enter into a contract until they come to your terms you will have accomplished everything, you will have won the day.

Mr. DAKAN. Fifty per cent of the acreage fell off, or there was a fall of 50 per cent of acreage for the crop of 1910, due to this fight.

Mr. FORDNEY. And that must have cost the sugar companies a great deal of money?

Mr. DAKAN. Yes; and they came up last year 12 per cent on our demands.

Mr. FORDNEY. That is good.

Mr. DAKAN. Now, then, we are asking for another small raise.

Mr. FORDNEY. That is right. You have the matter in your own hands.

Mr. DAKAN. We are showing why we do not get it. I want to show a little further why we do not get it. We asked the editors whose papers we support to help us. If they did not have the farmers' subscriptions they could not run their papers. We asked those papers to print the farmers' side of the story, and they refused to print a line.

Mr. FORDNEY. Then boycott the papers; they can not get along without you. You do not need the paper. We used to get along without papers when I was a boy.

Mr. DAKAN. That is good advice. Now I want to tell you what the papers are doing. The Denver Republican seems to be the mouthpiece of the Sugar Trust. They seem to have a press agent. I do not know who he is. They quote Mr. Hamlin right along—from Chicago, from Washington, from everywhere. They set that up with headlines on the front page, week after week; that material is lifted by each of the local papers in each town in northern Colorado, and that is all that is printed—that material that is censored by some representative of the Great Western Sugar Co., and that is all that the local papers in northern Colorado will print in reference to the subject; so that the press of northern Colorado is subsidized, in effect, by the Great Western Sugar Co. That is the condition that we find in this fertile region.

Mr. FORDNEY. Do you know that the sugar company controls that paper—as you say, subsidized by them—so that you can not have published in the paper such information as the farmers desire to have published?

Mr. DAKAN. I have tried, Mr. Fordney, in a great many instances, to get material printed; for instance, to get these assessed valuations in the various counties printed, and showing the difference in the assessed valuation of the company and the stock issued, outstanding, and compare that. Not a line will be printed.

Mr. FORDNEY. Taking your testimony as to the control of the newspapers by this company, and taking the testimony given by Mr. Bodkin that that company controls your State university, or the professor there, and also the chemical department of the agricultural college of the State, so he could get no tests made of his beets, either by the University of Colorado or the agricultural department of the State, without the consent of the Great Western Sugar Co., and the reason given by one of the institutions—I do not remember which—as given by Mr. Bodkin, was that he was afraid that the Great

Western Sugar Co. would interfere with the appropriation for the institution if they published anything of that kind, you are in bad shape in Colorado. That sugar company controls the entire community, practically?

Mr. RAKER. That has been the condition, from the testimony here, of a great many communities.

Mr. FORDNEY. That is not so in the State of Michigan, I am happy to say; at least I do not believe that is the condition.

Mr. DAKAN. The Great Western Sugar Co., allied with the light and power companies and the traction companies and the railroad companies——

Mr. FORDNEY. And the assessor and the State university, and the department of agriculture of the State, and the newspapers, all together, put the average farmer in Colorado in mighty bad shape.

Mr. DAKAN. I agree with you, and I would put it even stronger than that. That is the way we express it, only we speak of it even stronger than you have expressed it.

The CHAIRMAN. I think you have pretty well covered the ground. You can supplement your testimony.

Mr. DAKAN. One more on the newspapers.

Mr. MALBY. Well, we understand them pretty well.

Mr. DAKAN. I can give you something new.

Mr. FORDNEY. If it will add any flavor, let us have it.

Mr. DAKAN. The Evening Courier, of Fort Collins, for Monday November 6, 1911, a daily paper—this is the way we get our information. This is an editorial in this issue:

Horace Havemeyer, the only son of the late H. O. Havemeyer who was the head of the American Sugar Refining Co., recently spent a few days in Colorado, visiting Fort Collins and other sugar manufacturing points. While in Denver he gave out an interview to the Republican in which he said: "That the production of beet sugar throughout the United States has become a great basic industry, especially in Colorado and the West, has been fully proven during the present shortage of sugar beets in Europe. In Colorado the agricultural output has been maintained in the face of failures in other crops because of the steady demand for sugar beets. Were it not for the fact that 500,000 tons of beet sugar are refined annually in this country from grown beets the price of sugar would be 10 to 12 cents a pound instead of 6 to 8 cents at present. Potatoes, hay and grain, and other products of the farm have suffered failures over large areas of the country while the sugar-beet crops have increased to keep pace with a growing demand."

The point is that Mr. Havemeyer did not submit to interviews to the local papers at the factories where he stopped. He simply gave one interview to the Denver Republican, knowing that that would be lifted and commented upon in his favor by each paper in northern Colorado. So, statements are made to the press agent, to the Denver Republican or to the reporter of that paper, and in that way they are carried through northern Colorado, they knowing that those statements will in that way be given to the readers of northern Colorado. [Reading further from the editorial referred to:]

No other industry in Colorado and the West is more intimately associated with the farmer than the sugar refining industry, and no other product of the soil is more immune from speculative influences than the sugar beet.

Mr. RAKER. That makes you laugh?

Mr. DAKAN. They control the output. Their capitalization is big enough to control the sugar output of their factories. He says it is "immune from speculative influences."

Mr. FORDNEY. What do you think he means by that? I do not know.

Mr. DAKAN. That a man who wanted to buy a stock of sugar during the low prices could not buy it.

Mr. FORDNEY. Is that what he means by that?

Mr. DAKAN. That is what I think he means. That they hold the sugar and sell it on the high price, and only feed the market slowly during the low prices of sugar.

Mr. FORDNEY. Our people have testified over and over again before the Ways and Means Committee, and I am not sure that they have not testified before this committee, that they can not long hold refined sugar made from beets; that it hardens in the sack and they must sell it shortly after it is manufactured, and within about 90 days from the close of their season their sugar is generally all gone and they have none for the summer months at all.

Mr. DAKAN. I will go on [reading]:

Your agricultural output has more than recouped your temporary losses in mining and the sugar-beet crops have had a predominating effect in sustaining Colorado's increase in wealth year by year. Without the development of the beet fields the farmers would not have fared well anywhere in the West and a general business stagnation would have been the inevitable result. The tariff on importation of raw sugar has enabled Colorado and the entire sugar-beet producing area of the United States to keep busy while other sections have lagged; and it has enabled the Great Western Sugar Co. to reduce the price of sugar while sugar interests on the seaboard are effected by the European crop failure, which has forced the price up. The raising of sugar beets offers a constant demand for labor, it brings about the settlement of the public domain, multiplies the farmers, presents the solution of the problem of congested cities, and gives employment to thousands in the refineries and on the railroads. I know of no other industry more typically a home industry and an American industry than the business of producing and refining sugar. We do not have to prove the efficiency of the present tariff on sugar by a citation of figures. All one has to do is to traverse the great stretches of cultivated farms that were wastes a few years ago and to see the communities that have sprung up around the sugar refineries. Here is your real, visible evidence of the benefits of a protective tariff on sugar. It has contributed more than any other agency, outside of reclamation, to the settlement of the public lands, and through this industry the reclamation of the public lands has received a decided impetus. The interest of sugar men in maintaining the tariff is identical with the interest of the farmer, the laborer, and the entire country, because we are able, through the tariff, to produce our own sugar beets, refine our own sugar from them, and to meet the foreign shortage with our home-grown product at prices lower than on the seaboard

Mr. FORDNEY. That is a good statement, is it not? I would like to ask one more question. What did you pay in Colorado for sugar before the beet-sugar industry was inaugurated there? Do you remember about what price it was; was it more or less than you have paid generally?

Mr. DAKAN. I think the average is about the same.

Mr. FORDNEY. About the same price?

Mr. DAKAN. Yes; that is my recollection.

Mr. FORDNEY. Have you raised any beets yourself?

Mr. DAKAN. No; I have stood in the landlord's shoes and taken charge of the farm.

Mr. FORDNEY. I meant off your own land?

Mr. DAKAN. No.

There is one more statement I want to make in regard to the building of competitive factories. The proposition was made to the committee of which I am a member, about a month ago, that if the farmers would subscribe acreage of beets or capital, say a third of the capital necessary to build a 600-ton factory, or 50 per cent—or they could take the long end, as it was put—that the money could be secured to build a factory in northern Colorado and on a competitive basis, and take these big profits. The promotor who made that proposition said he was in touch with capital which, with the assistance of the farmers, could build a 600-ton factory, and he assured us that the profits would be as we have been quarreling about.

Mr. FORDNEY. The man who offered to build the factory told you your profits would be great?

Mr. DAKAN. Would be great.

Mr. FORDNEY. Was he a sugar manufacturer?

Mr. DAKAN. No.

Mr. FORDNEY. Or a builder of factories?

Mr. DAKAN. I would say he was a builder of factories, but perhaps a promoter. He said he would get the capital if the farmers would put up a third or one-half the money—either the money or raise the beets and give notes and apply the acreage to the payment of the notes.

Mr. FORDNEY. Do you know where that man was from?

Mr. DAKAN. I think he is in Denver. I think his name is W. R. Terry.

Mr. FORDNEY. Do you know what machinery he proposed to put in—whether it was Cleveland or otherwise?

Mr. DAKAN. A modern plant.

Mr. FORDNEY. And he did not specify any machinery?

Mr. DAKAN. I want now to get at the result of this conference. I asked him why it was, if the profits were as great as he said they were, 30 to 40 per cent on the investment required, that he could not get independent capital to build a factory, and he did not know. He said capital was too timid to go in alone, and that the farmers would have to join.

Mr. FORDNEY. He did not tell you that the agitation of the tariff was the biggest stumbling block?

Mr. DAKAN. No.

Mr. FORDNEY. That is true, though, is it not?

Mr. DAKAN. No.

Mr. FORDNEY. Would you put your money in if you knew the tariff was going to be taken off of sugar?

Mr. DAKAN. I would not put my money up against the Great Western Sugar Co.——

Mr. FORDNEY. I did not say against the Great Western Sugar Co.

Mr. DAKAN. In Colorado?

Mr. FORDNEY. Anywhere—on Pikes Peak.

The CHAIRMAN. The question was, Would you put your money in northern Colorado if you thought the tariff would be taken off sugar.

Mr. DAKAN. Yes; I think the beet-sugar industry in northern Colorado is so favored by conditions—climate, soil and water, and other conditions—that sugar can be produced there cheaper than in many other sections.

Mr. Fordney. Could be produced in competition with free foreign imported sugar, and you would not hesitate to put in your money?

Mr. Dakan. As far as I can determine, I think that is true.

Mr. Fordney. When you acted as a landlord and represented the real raiser, did you make a profit or salary? You said you represented the real landlord.

Mr. Dakan. I was paid so much for taking care of his interests. I want to get to this promoter's stand. I told him that we could get from 4,000 to 8,000 acres of land, first-class beet land, subscribed if his men would put up the money. He said it was impossible to get capital to go into the business unless the farmer took, say, a third or a half. Now, in the experience of the farmer of the West, undertakings of that kind go until the farmers' money is used up. The independent money does not come. So that the promoters and the fellows who do the work on the factory to get it built get the money.

Mr. Fordney. Have you had that experience in Colorado; is that a surmise on your part, or do you know that that would be the result?

Mr. Dakan. That was about the result in the Brighton factory.

Mr. Fordney. You are only guessing at that, are you not, as to what that would be in another case? You are only making an estimate, are you not?

Mr. Dakan. Yes. I am surmising that from observation. I used to track rabbits into a hole, and when I found a track leading to a certain hole and none coming out I was pretty sure that there was a rabbit in the hole.

Mr. Fordney. And you thought when you scared up another rabbit he was going to that same hole?

Mr. Dakan. I was not talking about another rabbit.

Mr. Fordney. But you are now; you are comparing the future factory with the one in the past.

Mr. Dakan. I am saying if we watch the hole long enough we will catch the Great Western, the rabbit, in the hole.

Mr. Fordney. I have watched the sugar hole business, the industry started, and I want to say this—and I want it to go into the record— that when Cuban reciprocity was brought about, reducing the duty on imported sugar 20 per cent, there were 32 factories under construction, or that many companies formed to construct factories, all of which immediately went out of business because of that reduction. It intimidated capital; it immediately withdrew; and I think I am right in saying that since that time, 1903, and December was the month, I think, that that bill became a law, there have not been more than 10 or 12 factories built in the United States in addition to those existing at that time. Something stopped it. Capital was intimidated. I think that was the general result all over the country. Agitation of the tariff intimidates capital, and it is afraid to invest. I am sorry to have to leave you.

Mr. Dakan. Just one moment. I desire to call the attention of the committee to the publication of Mr. Palmer, especial attention to the baronial estates which Mr. Palmer describes in such glee, and to say that the farmers of northern Colorado object to being made a baronial estate by the Great Western Sugar Co., and ask that the committee consider the difference between the farmers of Colorado owning their homes as they do——

Mr. FORDNEY. Tell me how to do that——

Mr. DAKAN. And the peasants of Germany and Austria and Russia who grow beats for these baronial estates.

The CHAIRMAN. You have everything in the record that you want to put in, have you?

Mr. DAKAN. May I ask a question of my associates?

The CHAIRMAN. Certainly.

Mr. DAKAN (after a conference with his associates). No; I do not think there is anything else.

(Thereupon, at 5.15, the committee adjourned until to-morrow, December 9, 1911, at 10.30 o'clock a. m.)

AMERICAN SUGAR REFINING CO. AND OTHERS.

SPECIAL COMMITTEE ON THE INVESTIGATION
OF THE AMERICAN SUGAR REFINING CO. AND OTHERS,
HOUSE OF REPRESENTATIVES,
Washington, D. C., December 9, 1911.

TESTIMONY OF MR. ALBERT DAKAN—Recalled.

The CHAIRMAN. Mr. Dakan, is there anything further you desire to add to the testimony you gave yesterday?

Mr. DAKAN. If the committee please, I indicated yesterday the attitude of the local press of northern Colorado in the beet-growing district toward the farmer with respect to the beet-sugar industry, and I desire now to place in the record an editorial printed in the Fort Collins Daily Review.

The CHAIRMAN. Of what date?

Mr. DAKAN. Of date Tuesday evening, November 28, 1911. This is the first instance that has come to my attention, in an investigation and observation covering some three years of the sugar-beet industry and the beet-sugar industry in the northern Colorado district, wherein a local paper has given editorial support to the beet growers' side of the industry.

The CHAIRMAN. If it is not too long you may read it.

Mr. DAKAN. It is not very long, and is as follows:

NO GAME FOR A PIKER.

A visitor at the sugar factory last Saturday took advantage of the occasion to inspect the warerooms, where enormous quantities of sacked sugar, ready for the market, are kept on hand during the season awaiting shipment. Astounded by the large piles of sugar which he saw, he and a friend took occasion to count the number of sacks in the length, width, and height of the various piles, and found that the total number of sacks of sugar now on hand at the factory, compiled from these dimensions, amounted to 463,090, each sack weighing 100 pounds.

At the present price of sugar to the retailer—$6.50 per 100—the little piles amounted to approximately $3,010,085, delivered at the door to the retailer. This may or may not include more sugar than has been manufactured at the local factory this year. Certainly it is more than the product from beets raised in this immediate district during the campaign, and probably it includes practically all the product from beets shipped in from outside poi its.

In any event, counting a product of 300 pounds of sugar from each ton of 15 per cent beets, the total sugar stacked at the factory represents the product from approximately 154,363 tons of beets. If the beets were paid for at the rate of $5.50 per ton, the total amount paid out for beets was $848,996, nearly twice that paid out to growers under the local factory. Add to the sum paid out for beets $60,000, representing 6 per cent on an investment of $1,000,000, and $72,000, representing the wages of employees during the campaign (400 men at $3 per day for 60 days), and the total outlay is $980,996, as against $3,010,085 in sugar now on hand, leaving a net sum of $2,029,089.

Of this sum probably not all is profit, so deduct another even million for expenses and incidentals and there is left $1,029,089, a large part of which must represent the profit on the Fort Collins factory.

The original investment may have been more than a million on which interest was allowed, but it is doubtful if such is the case. In any event, the net profit seems to be in the neighborhood of 100 per cent per annum, and in rather a bad annum at that.

Does it prove that we need a tariff on sugar to protect an infant industry?

Does it prove that the factory is paying a fair price to the grower for his beets?

What does it prove? We don't know, unless it proves that the manufacture of sugar is absolutely no game for the piker to play.

Mr. FORDNEY. Mr. Chairman, I want to ask the gentleman one or two questions. Mr. Dakan, yesterday you stated at one time you represented a farmer as manager of a beet field, if I remember correctly.

Mr. DAKAN. Yes, sir.

Mr. FORDNEY. What profit per acre did you make, if any? What did it cost you per acre to raise beets under your management, and what did you get per acre for your crop?

Mr. DAKAN. We estimated at that time, without the rent, that it cost $45.

Mr. FORDNEY. To produce an acre of beets?

Mr. DAKAN. That was on that farm.

Mr. FORDNEY. What did you get per acre for that crop?

Mr. DAKAN. I think the yield was 12 tons.

Mr. FORDNEY. What did you get for the 12 tons?

Mr. DAKAN. $5.

Mr. FORDNEY. $60.

Mr. DAKAN. That was before the sliding scale.

Mr. FORDNEY. So at $60 per acre for your crop you made $15 profit. How much did you charge up for the rent of your land?

Mr. DAKAN. There is no rent charge in that. I might say that the landlord got one-fourth of the total crop. He got three tons per acre.

The CHAIRMAN. $15.

Mr. DAKAN. Yes; the landlord received $15. I would like to say, however, that that varies. Sometimes the landlord receives one-fourth and sometimes one-fifth, depending on conditions, as you will find from those agreements between renters and landlords. Sometimes it is one-fourth and sometimes one-fifth of the crop.

Mr. FORDNEY. You have stated that you were attorney for the beet growers and represented them?

Mr. DAKAN. Yes, sir.

Mr. FORDNEY. Not only in preparing their contracts but otherwise. You come here as a witness who is really hostile to the Great Western Sugar Co., do you not?

Mr. DAKAN. I do not like for you to put it that way. I come here to tell the facts concerning our treatment.

Mr. FORDNEY. Well, you have said you did not believe they were just fair—I will not put it just that way, because I do not know whether you used that language; but your testimony has led me to believe you are not satisfied with the treatment the farmers are getting in that country from this company.

Mr. Dakan. If our farmers do not make a profit and they do, our farmers feel that the farmers should make a profit along with the company.

Mr. Fordney. But the profits you show the company to make and the profits the company show they make by Mr. Morey's statement differ very widely.

Mr. Dakan. Yes, sir; we feel that it is a method of bookkeeping.

Mr. Fordney. Have you taken from their books the cost that you have given this committee as to what it costs them to produce sugar?

Mr. Dakan. I beg your pardon.

Mr. Fordney. Mr. Morey undoubtedly took from their books the items of cost as given to this committee. Did you take your estimates or figures from their books also, or are they simply estimates?

Mr. Dakan. They are estimates from the various investigations that we have made. They are such reports as the Sugar Co. sees fit to put in the newspapers. Under the sliding scale they have to give their estimates. On the accounting sheet for this year, which you have in the record now, you will find detailed statements to the farmer for his beets load by load. Now, then, in doing that they must give away certain things concerning their business.

Mr. Fordney. You heard Mr. Bodkin testify that he had not been able to get a chemist in your State who would make a test of beets for the farmers. Have you had that same experience? That is, he stated that he had not been able to get a chemist either in the agricultural department of the State, the State university, or individual chemists that were not under the influence of the management of the Great Western Sugar Co. Has that been your experience?

Mr. Dakan. My experience has only been their experience in that line. But I would like to supplement that a little further and say that it costs some $5 to make a test outside of the Agricultural College, and in order to make the testing of any value to the farmer there must be a number of tests made—that is, from week to week and from plat to plat of the beets. The same beet field varies in its test of sugar, and in order to intelligently study the growing of beets the tests must be taken from week to week and made systematically, so that you have a chart from which to judge of the growth of sugar in the beets. Now, that is impractical——

Mr. Fordney. No; I beg your pardon.

Mr. Dakan. I would like to finish this statement, if you please.

Mr. Fordney. All right, sir.

Mr. Dakan. It is impractical, then, for the agricultural college, which is the only place which could be used to carry on tests that would be of benefit to the farmer in the growing of beets—it is wholly impracticable for the college to do that, and then, as Mr. Bodkin said, the colleges are tender about taking up these matters when there is chance of a difference between their chemist and the factory chemists.

Mr. Fordney. Is it not true that, under your contract, you are permitted, as a representative of the farmers, to put a chemist in the company's office and see whether or not that test is correct?

Mr. Dakan. Yes, sir.

Mr. Fordney. The cost of that would be very reasonable to the farmers, would it not?

Mr. DAKAN. It would.

Mr. FORDNEY. You have not done that?

Mr. DAKAN. No; because it is useless.

Mr. FORDNEY. Why is it useless?

Mr. DAKAN. Chemists have privately told us so.

Mr. FORDNEY. Has any chemist told you that he is not competent to go in there and get the correct information for you, or that he would be under the influence of the company, or what reason is it that you can not put an honest man in there and get an honest test; do you know of any?

Mr. DAKAN. Oh, I should have to carry in my answer an implication that I would not care to stand for and could not prove.

Mr. FORDNEY. That is all, Mr. Dakan.

TESTIMONY OF MR. E. U. COMBS—Recalled.

The CHAIRMAN. Mr. Combs, the committee asked you, I believe, to make an estimate of the overhead charges and add that in and see what the cost of production is?

Mr. COMBS. Yes, sir.

Mr. FORDNEY. This is to be added to your estimate of 2.59?

Mr. COMBS. No; to 2.80; 2.80 was the last figure I gave. If you remember, I gave you two figures. The average of 6 factories showed a less cost than the average of 10, but in the average of the 10 I included the freight to the distributing warehouse and 6 per cent interest on the estimated value of the property or of the investment; that was included in the 2.80. Now, this is the overhead expense outside of the freight and 6 per cent estimate.

Mr. FORDNEY. Will you give it in detail?

Mr. COMBS. Yes, sir. The taxes on the assessed valuation of $2,500,000—I am not positive that these are the exact figures, but they are practically so—at 6 per cent is $150,000. The upkeep of equipment is 3 per cent——

Mr. FORDNEY. Mr. Combs, do you figure that out and show the cost per pounds of sugar produced so as to add that to the 2.80?

Mr. COMBS. Yes; I do, finally. I will give you that at the end. The upkeep of equipment is 3 per cent. I believe you have the record that they do add 3 per cent. That would be $300,000 on $10,000,000 invested. I allowed for brokerage 5 cents per sack, or $123,738; the insurance, $50,000; official salaries, including attorneys, $70,500——

Mr. FORDNEY (interposing). This is for the 11 factories?

Mr. COMBS. This is for the Great Western Sugar Co. Expert work, $25,000; office force at head office and incidental expenses, $75,000, which makes a total of $794,238, or 32 cents per bag.

Mr. FORDNEY. In those figures you estimated on 300 pounds, which would make 96 cents.

Mr. COMBS. I am not figuring on pounds, Mr. Fordney. I am figuring 32 cents per bag overhead charges added to $2.80. and $2.80 includes, as I said, 6 per cent on the investment.

Mr. FORDNEY. That makes it $3.12?

Mr. COMBS. That makes my cost for this sugar sold, brokerage paid, $3.12.

The CHAIRMAN. With the brokerage paid?

Mr. COMBS. Yes, sir.

The CHAIRMAN. In other words, that is the cost of producing a pound of beet sugar at these factories?

Mr. COMBS. Yes, sir; I have added 5 cents a bag for selling the sugar, but I have learned that it is only 3 cents.

Mr. FORDNEY. Does that include all expense for employees not included in your figure of $2.80?

Mr. COMBS. In that expense is included the field managers and the superintendents covering the season at each factory.

Mr. FORDNEY. And also the bookkeepers and the annual employees who are employed all the time by the company?

Mr. COMBS. Yes, sir; 3,050 men employed at this time; and, then, also is included the superintendent and the field men. and so forth.

Mr. MALBY. In other words, it includes every expense which the sugar manufacturers incur except charges for depreciation?

Mr. COMBS. That is allowed for.

Mr. MALBY. Then it includes every charge except dividends on their stock or a fair return on the capital invested?

Mr. COMBS. I have allowed 6 per cent on the investment.

Mr. MALBY. So that it includes everything?

Mr. COMBS. Yes, sir; 6 per cent on the investment is allowed in this estimate.

Mr. MALBY. Is there any expense or charge which you can recall, which they are subjected to, which is not included in your estimate?

Mr. COMBS. There is nothing, unless it would be of an incidental nature. I have tried not to overlook anything.

Mr. FORDNEY. Your figures are $3.12 per hundred pounds, and Mr. Morey's figures, as given in his testimony, which I noticed yesterday, are $3.65 to $3.75.

Mr. COMBS. I do not know how Mr. Morey figures it. I am just giving my own figures as I understand it.

Mr. FORDNEY. That is the figure he gave. Have you any means of comparing the two in order to see where the difference comes in?

Mr. COMBS. I expect to take his testimony which you have here and compare it and see where the difference is, but I have not compared the figures as yet.

The CHAIRMAN. Mr. Combs, is there anything else you wish to present to the committee?

Mr. COMBS. Mr. Chairman, I see Mr. Fordney, in his explanation of my testimony, when I said under our new schedule we got for beets $5 flat for 12 per cent and 25 cents a unit, in his figures all the way through he has figured it at 21 cents.

Mr. FORDNEY. I just gave the units, but I did not give the fractions. It was one-half per cent.

Mr. COMBS. But I said we were to get 25 cents a unit for everything over a certain amount, and in your figures you computed it at 21 cents a unit, and it has gone in the record that way.

Mr. FORDNEY. I thank you for the correction. It should be 25 cents, Mr. Combs?

Mr. COMBS. Yes, sir.

TESTIMONY OF MR. FRANK C. LOWRY—Recalled.

(The witness was duly sworn by the chairman.)

The CHAIRMAN. Mr. Lowry, there are one or two matters supplementary to your previous testimony to which I wish to direct your attention. First, what percentage of the total customs revenue does sugar produce, and how much should the duty be reduced?

Mr. LOWRY. The Government figures show that for the year 1910 the duty collected on sugar was $52,810,995.31, and that figures out just about 17 per cent of the total customs revenue.

The CHAIRMAN. How much?

Mr. LOWRY. Seventeen per cent of the total customs revenue.

The CHAIRMAN. In other words, we get 17 per cent of all of our revenue from sugar, or did that year?

Mr. LOWRY. Yes; from imported sugar, which is a little over 50 per cent of the sugar we use, the balance coming from domestic production and from our insular possessions.

The CHAIRMAN. The bulk of that coming from Cuba?

Mr. LOWRY. The bulk of the duty sugars coming from Cuba.

The CHAIRMAN. Now, how much reduction could be made and still produce a revenue?

Mr. LOWRY. Taking the Government figures from 1900 to 1910, inclusive, they show that the average in bond cost of sugar imported was 2.443.

The CHAIRMAN. For what period?

Mr. LOWRY. For the period from 1900 to 1910.

The CHAIRMAN. Inclusive?

Mr. LOWRY. Inclusive.

The CHAIRMAN. Eleven years, then?

Mr. LOWRY. Yes. Of course, that is all sugar, low-grade sugar and high-grade sugar and Cuban sugar, on which there is a 20 per cent preferential tariff; and I figure that the full duty rate of 1.685 on that basis would be 69 per cent.

Mr. FORDNEY. You mention low-grade sugar; how much of that is low-grade sugar?

Mr. LOWRY. I can not find any report that gives that.

Mr. FORDNEY. It is exceedingly small compared with the total imports of sugar, is it not?

Mr. LOWRY. Yes. I should think it might raise that average 10 points. In other words, instead of making the average price—which is what the domestic factory would have to figure on for the value of foreign sugars—2.44, it might be 2.54.

Mr. FORDNEY. What percentage of the total would have to be of low grade to raise that 10 points, or are you simply jumping at a conclusion or have you figured it?

Mr. LOWRY. In reaching that conclusion I included not only the low grade, but I included the amounts which come from Cuba at the preferential rate. That is just a guess; yes. I have no way of getting at it accurately.

The CHAIRMAN. You have given us the in-bond values for the last 10 years?

Mr. LOWRY. Yes. Now, then, if you are figuring at the price that the domestic factory would have to figure on foreign sugars if the duty was reduced, if we add that figure of 2.44, which, as I say, is a little too low, but we will take that figure, and we add 47 cents duty on 96° test, which is the rate of duty charged by Germany, Austria, and France——

Mr. FORDNEY (interposing). Forty-seven cents for refined?

Mr. LOWRY. No; raw sugar.

Mr. FORDNEY. That would be 2.91?

Mr. LOWRY. That would be 2.91; yes. Then the average price between raw and refined sugars has been 89 points. With a reduction in the duty there would be some saving. I have added that in as 85 points. That would be 3.763. Then I have taken the average advantage which the domestic beet-sugar factory has in the way of freight as 25 points. I think that is probably too low, because most of them are in the West, where their protection is larger than that—65 points, and so on.

Mr. FORDNEY. In Michigan it is way in excess of the freight.

Mr. LOWRY. Well, I think you will find that Michigan sells a good deal of its sugar in Michigan, Indiana, Illinois, Wisconsin; and they have an advantage there of perhaps 15 or 18 cents.

The CHAIRMAN. It is not quite as large in Michigan as elsewhere?

Mr. LOWRY. It is not quite as large in Michigan; but I have taken an average of 25 points, which seems to be most conservative. That would make the price which the beet men would have to figure on 4.01; that is, not adding, of course, any expenses for administrative expense, selling expense, and so on. So it would be somewhat higher than that. If they can produce sugar around 3 cents a pound, as some of this evidence seems to show, it would show them a cent a pound profit, roughly.

The CHAIRMAN. If we reduced the duty to what the duties are in these foreign countries, it would still leave them that profit?

Mr. LOWRY. Yes, sir.

The CHAIRMAN. What are those countries?

Mr. LOWRY. The rates of duty now charged on imported sugars in Germany are 47 cents on raw and 52 cents on refined; in France, 48 cents on raw and 53 cents on refined; Austria, 47 cents on raw and 52 cents on refined: Belgium, 48 cents on raw and 53 cents on refined.

The CHAIRMAN. So that we could reduce the duty about 1 cent a pound and still be in the neighborhood of where they are?

Mr. LOWRY. More than a cent a pound.

Mr. FORDNEY. In the figures you gave a few minutes ago of 69 cents, did you mean that the duty collected on all sugars imported, duty paid or free, would average 69 cents per hundred pounds?

Mr. LOWRY. That is a question I have not quite been able to satisfy my mind on from this Treasury report.

Mr. FORDNEY. Then what did you mean by 69 cents?

Mr. LOWRY. It is under the heading here "Dutiable sugar," and it shows the amount collected. Now, in the next column it says "Free and dutiable," and I notice, for example, under the dutiable column in 1906 it shows the number of pounds imported was 3,979,331,430, and then under the column "Free and dutiable" it shows 3,979,331,430 pounds; so, you see, the figure is the same in each column. So I have taken it on the basis that it includes everything, both free and dutiable.

Mr. FORDNEY. It must, because we produced in the United States about 900,000 tons of beet and cane sugar last year.

Mr. LOWRY. Yes.

Mr. FORDNEY. And we consumed 3,350,000 tons.

Mr. LOWRY. Yes.

Mr. FORDNEY. So we imported, in round numbers, two and one-half million tons.

Mr. LOWRY. Yes.

Mr. FORDNEY. Now, about how much—600,000 tons of that came from Hawaii and Porto Rico——

The CHAIRMAN. Oh no; over 833,000.

Mr. FORDNEY. Eight hundred and thirty-three thousand from——

The CHAIRMAN (interposing). Hawaii, Porto Rico, and the Philippine Islands.

Mr. FORDNEY. That would leave 1,700,000 tons of dutiable sugar.

The CHAIRMAN. Yes.

Mr. LOWRY. You see if those importations from Porto Rico and Hawaii and the Philippines are included in these figures we should deduct them, and that would make the percentage rate of duty paid higher.

Mr. FORDNEY. Very much. It would be above 1.35, because Cuban sugar is the lowest duty-paid sugar that comes into our market. Instead of being 69——

Mr. LOWRY. Sixty-nine per cent imported——

Mr. FORDNEY. Sixty-nine per cent of all the imported sugar is dutiable sugar; is that what you mean by that?

The CHAIRMAN. The duty amounts to 69 per cent reduced to the percentage basis; that is what he means. In other words, the duty is equivalent to a 69 per cent ad valorem duty.

Mr. FORDNEY. That is not correct in my opinion.

Mr. MALBY. That is based on the full duty of 1.96 per pound.

Mr. LOWRY. No; I say the full rate of duty—1.685—is equal to 69 per cent, but that is too small, because those free sugars are included in there apparently.

Mr. FORDNEY. Sugar paying a duty of 1.685, which is the maximum under the present law, you say that 69 per cent of the imported sugar paid that rate of duty?

Mr. LOWRY. Oh, no.

The CHAIRMAN. Only 72,000 tons paid it.

Mr. LOWRY. To make it clear, I will repeat. I say that if we had the total amount of sugar imported and divide it by the total amount of revenue derived from importations of sugar and figure that out as so much per pound and then took the average in-bond price of foreign sugars for the same years, we will find——no; I should say take that and the average in-bond price of foreign sugars for a period of years was 2.443. That was the price of the sugars. Then, if we took the full rate of duty, 1.685——

Mr. FORDNEY. For this whole number of years?

Mr. LOWRY. Yes. It has been the same for all those years. We will find that it is 69 per cent of the total— at the rate of 69 per cent. I noticed that Mr. Willett said that the bounties paid by the European countries were 0.31 points. I did not understand that, because our Government regulations provided that when a country pays a bounty a countervailing duty equal to the bounty in addition to the regular rates of duty will be assessed: and I find that in the old bounty days the Government only assessed a countervailing duty from Germany of 0.259 per pound on raw sugars and 0.313 per pound on refined; in Austria, 0.203 on raw sugar and 0.293 on refined; in Holland, 0.211 on raw sugar and 0.239 on refined; Belgium, 0.341 on raw and 0.385 on refined. That led me to believe that those amounts equalled the bounties paid by those foreign countries.

Mr. FORDNEY. I wish you would give the committee the rate of duty collected on Cuban sugar, showing the time and the amount of sugar imported.

Mr. LOWRY. The rate of duty?

Mr. FORDNEY. Yes; the average. That is, before you get through. It will take some time, perhaps.

Mr. LOWRY. I have not the figures here to do that. I have figures here that might be interesting; that show the average rate of duties collected on all importations——

The CHAIRMAN. Well, what is that?

Mr. FORDNEY. Free and dutiable included?

Mr. LOWRY. No; just dutiable. In 1910, 41.52 per cent.

The CHAIRMAN. In other words, that was the average duty we collected in 1910 on articles the Government did collect a duty on.

Mr. LOWRY. Yes.

The CHAIRMAN. And the sugar duty figured what?

Mr. LOWRY. Fifty-nine per cent.

The CHAIRMAN. Figured from the Cuban rate, what would it have figured?

Mr. FORDNEY. Sixty-nine per cent ad valorem?

Mr. LOWRY. That is what these figures seem to show.

Mr. FORDNEY. And last year the duty was 41 per cent ad valorem on the duty-paid sugar. Is that what you mean?

Mr. LOWRY. No, no; on all importations—the average ad valorem rate of duty on all importations.

Mr. FORDNEY. Free and dutiable?

Mr. LOWRY. On everything—silks and everything else.

Mr. FORDNEY. Oh, I understand now; I thought you were talking sugar.

The CHAIRMAN. No. In other words, his proposition is that, while the average duty collected was 41 per cent on all articles, the average sugar duty was 65 per cent. I believe that is what he means.

Mr. LOWRY. Yes; that is correct. The point I wanted to bring out and to call to your attention was that if Germany, for example, with their present rate of duty on raw sugar of 47 cents, was still granting a bounty equal to 2.59—and I might mention that whether or not that or Mr. Willett's rate of 36 cents is the correct rate can be confirmed by the Treasury Department—they will know why they charge this countervailing duty. That will make a total protection, direct bounty and indirect, through their duty of 7.29, against our full rate at present of 1.685. So it will be seen that we have almost two and one-third times as much protection or bounty for the domestic industry as the German factories have.

The CHAIRMAN. As the German factories had under the old bounty system.

Mr. LOWRY. That is it; as the German factories would have if the bounties were continued to-day.

The CHAIRMAN. Or if they were renewed.

Mr. LOWRY. Yes; and we now have 3½ times as much as the German factories have.

The CHAIRMAN. We now have 3½ times as much protection for our domestic producers as the Germans?

Mr. LOWRY. Yes; and Germany is one of the largest beet-sugar producing countries in the world.

The CHAIRMAN. How do we compare with France?

Mr. FORDNEY. What is the duty on sugar imported into Germany. You say it is 3½ times as much in this country as in Germany.

Mr. LOWRY. I said it was 47 points on raw sugar.

Mr. FORDNEY. What do you mean by points?

Mr. LOWRY. 0.47 a hundred.

The CHAIRMAN. Now, compare it with France, and see how much more protection we have got than they have got.

Mr. LOWRY. France and Germany and Austria and Belgium, which are the principal convention countries, are all charging the same rates of duty, practically 0.47 or 0.48 in the case of France.

The CHAIRMAN. So we have about 3½ times as much protection as those countries?

Mr. LOWRY. Yes.

Mr. MALBY. I do not notice that he has included Russia, which is a very large sugar-growing country.

Mr. LOWRY. I was very anxious to review the Russia situation a little later.

Mr. MALBY. If we are to have an average of anything like the European production, Russia ought to be figured in.

Mr. LOWRY. I am not giving that now.

Mr. MALBY. They have a tariff there.

Mr. LOWRY. Yes; I was going to do that a little later.

The CHAIRMAN. Can you do that now?

Mr. LOWRY. Yes; I could do that now.

The CHAIRMAN. A roll call summons us to the House, and therefore we will adjourn until 2 o'clock.

(Thereupon, at 12.05 o'clock p. m., the committee took a recess until 2 o'clock p. m.)

AFTER RECESS.

The committee met, pursuant to the taking of recess, at 2.15 o'clock p. m., Hon. Thomas W. Hardwick (chairman) presiding.

TESTIMONY OF MR. FRANK C. LOWRY—Continued.

The CHAIRMAN. Mr. Lowry, you were about to explain the Russian situation. I will ask you to give us your idea of what would be the result of this proposition. Would European countries, in dealing with us, look on our sugar tariff as a bounty if we were to undertake to export our domestic sugars?

Mr. LOWRY. I understand your question to mean, if we attempted to ship any American beet sugar to Germany?

The CHAIRMAN. To Germany or Austria or any other country.

Mr. LOWRY. I do not think there is any question but what they would.

The CHAIRMAN. Why do you think that?

Mr. LOWRY. I say that, first, because that is the light in which our own Government regards a protective tariff on foreign sugars. They regard that tariff as a bounty.

The CHAIRMAN. How do you know that?

Mr. LOWRY. I will refer you to the Supreme Court's decision in the October term, 1902, 187 U. S., 496, in the case of Downs *v.* The United States. In rendering that decision the court stated that Russian sugars were to be excluded unless they paid a countervailing duty.

The CHAIRMAN. In other words, holding that under our tariff laws the tariff duty ought to be higher on our sugars?

Mr. LOWRY. Yes.

The CHAIRMAN. That was held in that case?

Mr. LOWRY. Yes.

Mr. FORDNEY. That was because Russia paid a bounty to her manufacturers.

Mr. LOWRY. That is what we are going to get to.

Mr. FORDNEY. Do you consider our tariff as the same thing?

Mr. LOWRY. Yes.

Mr. FORDNEY. Well, I can very quickly show you that it is not at all.

Mr. LOWRY. Well, shall I give my testimony or will you give yours?

Mr. FORDNEY. Do not be too sarcastic.

Mr. LOWRY. No; I do not mean to be sarcastic.

The CHAIRMAN. Gentlemen, do not let us have this.

Mr. LOWRY. The Supreme Court said, at page 513:

> Conversely, a bounty upon production operates to a certain extent as a bounty upon exportation, since it opens to the manufacturer a foreign market for his merchandise produced in excess of the demand at home. A protective tariff is the most familiar instance of this, since it enables the manufacturer to export the surplus for which there is no demand at home. * * * If the additional bounty paid by Russia upon exported sugar were the result of a high protective tariff upon foreign sugar, and a further enhancement of prices by a limitation of the amount of free sugar put upon the market, we should regard the effect of such regulations as being simply a bounty upon production.

At page 515, the court says:

> The mere imposition of an import duty of 3 rubles per pood, paid upon foreign sugar is, like all protective duties, a bounty, but is a bounty upon production and not upon exportation.

The CHAIRMAN. They said there that the Russian duty was really a bounty upon production.

Mr. LOWRY. I consider this subject is particularly interesting at the present time, when the tariff is under discussion.

Mr. FORDNEY. Is that a decision of our Supreme Court?

Mr. LOWRY. Yes; a decision of our Supreme Court. The Constitution, Article I, section 8, provides that Congress may levy taxes to "provide for the common defense and general welfare of the United States," and in Field *v.* Clark (143 U. S., 649), it was claimed that this provision was not broad enough to allow for the payment of a bounty to the Louisiana planters, as provided in the McKinley bill. The same point was raised in United States *v.* Realty Company (163 U. S., 427).

The CHAIRMAN. That was the Louisiana sugar case, when they did make a bounty, and the constitutionality of that was questioned.

Mr. LOWRY. As I see it, the Supreme Court first decides that a protective duty is a bounty, and then that it is unconstitutional.

Mr. FORDNEY. Under that we can impose a countervailing duty upon German sugar or Cuban sugar or sugar from any country in the world coming here, except from England. Every country that has a duty upon sugar then should be considered, under your construction of that duty, as being a bounty-paid country, and therefore we would be entitled to put a countervailing duty upon sugar coming from every country.

Mr. LOWRY. I suppose the court would be called upon to decide the difference between a revenue tariff and a high protective tariff. It says that a high protective tariff is a bounty.

Mr. FORDNEY. It does not make any difference whether it is high or low, so long as it is a protective tariff. Germany has a protective tariff, and so has Cuba.

Mr. LOWRY. Yes; that is the point. So has every other country that makes sugar, except Great Britain.

Mr. FORDNEY. Then you think that we should impose, under law, according to our——

Mr. LOWRY. I do not know. I only cite these rulings.

Mr. FORDNEY. That has no bearing upon it at all, in my opinion. I would not think so. That relates absolutely to a bounty paid over there.

Mr. LOWRY. I beg your pardon. There is no bounty paid in Russia.

Mr. FORDNEY. Yes; there is.

Mr. LOWRY. There is no bounty there.

Mr. FORDNEY. I had occasion to go to the Secretary of the Treasury and ask him to impose a countervailing duty because of the bounty paid in Russia.

Mr. LOWRY. You did that?

Mr. FORDNEY. Yes.

Mr. LOWRY. It was some Russian sugars that the case came up on. As commission merchants in New York, we had been selling, as representatives of a man in Hamburg, Max Muller, Russian crystals, and they had been coming in under the regular rate of duty; 1.95 was the tariff on them. We had begun to build up quite a nice business with the manufacturing trade, or at least with the merchants who sold to the manufacturing trade, and that was causing more or less disturbance in refined sugar circles, and one day the Treasury Department made a ruling that thereafter all Russian sugars imported must pay a countervailing duty of about three-fourths of a cent a pound. They did not even give the merchants who had purchased the sugar—and as a matter of fact a great deal of it was afloat at the time—a chance to turn around. They clapped it on right away, and those men lost very heavily. One company lost enough so that it crippled them so that they afterwards went out of business. The case was tried, and it finally reached the Supreme Court.

The CHAIRMAN. That is the case you cited?

Mr. LOWRY. Yes; that is the case I cited.

Mr. FORDNEY. You asked me if I did that. Do not understand me to say that I was the man who influenced the Treasury Department to impose that countervailing duty. I did not say that. I was one of several who did go to the Secretary of the Treasury and ask that it be done, and the Treasury did do it because of the bounty paid by the Russian Government to the domestic manufacturer in Russia.

Mr. LOWRY. Yes.

The CHAIRMAN. Did the Russian Government at that time pay a bounty in any other way except by the protective tariff?

Mr. FORDNEY. Oh, yes.

The CHAIRMAN. Do you know about that, Mr. Lowry?

Mr. LOWRY. Yes.

The CHAIRMAN. All right.

Mr. LOWRY. If the committee will go to the record of that case they will get the whole thing, but I have here a letter outlining the situation from the counsel who tried the case. Shall I read that?

The CHAIRMAN. Yes; I would be very glad if you would.

Mr. LOWRY (reading):

The Russian sugar case provided that the ministry should estimate annually the probable consumption of sugar and the possible production; apportion to each manufacturer his proportionate share of the domestic market; impose an excise tax on the allotted amount and a double excise tax on sugar produced in excess of the allotment. A high protective tariff insured the home market and the consumer was protected by a maximum price fixed by the Government. All excise taxes were remitted on exportation. The refiner located in a populous district far from the seacoast wanted to sell more than his allotment and was willing to pay for the privilege. The refiner located at the seaport was willing to sell his privilege of placing his allotment on the home market, which in his case might be a less active market than in the interior. The interior refiner could afford to pay an amount approximating the difference between his cost of production, plus the excise tax, and the price prevailing on his local market. The exporter could afford to accept a price which, added to the foreign market price of his exportation, would insure him a profit. On these two factors was based the value and price of the transferable export certificate issued by the Government, shifting from the exporter to the interior merchant the right to put on the local interior market an amount of sugar equal to the amount originally allotted to the seaport merchant and by him exported.

Under section 5 of the Dingley Act a countervailing duty was imposed on foreign products benefited by a bounty on exportation. The Treasury Department concluded that the price received by the exporter for his certificate was in effect a bounty on exportation, and this was the subject of the Russian sugar case. (Downs v. U. S., 187 U. S., 496, October term, 1902.)

The fact was that the man in the interior of Russia was allotted first by the Government the privilege of selling on the home market so many pounds of sugar. If he produced and tried to sell on the home market more than his allotment, he had to pay a double tax, so that that absolutely prevented his doing so. He got the full price, because of the high protective tariff, for his product.

The CHAIRMAN. Yes.

Mr. FORDNEY. What was the high protective tariff; do you remember?

The CHAIRMAN. In Russia, at that time?

Mr. FORDNEY. Yes.

Mr. LOWRY. You will get that in your consular reports.

Mr. FORDNEY. No; I want to know where you got it. You call it a high protective tariff, and I want to know whether it is high or low.

Mr. LOWRY. The customs duty was 8.58 cents per pound, and the excise duty 2½ cents a pound.

Mr. FORDNEY. At that time?

Mr. LOWRY. This was in 1905. I think it was the same at the time I refer to. In fact, I do not think it has been changed now.

Mr. MALBY. Eight cents a pound?

Mr. LOWRY. Yes; 8.58 cents; and sugar was selling in Russia at that time at 15 cents a pound.

The CHAIRMAN. It was practically prohibitive.

Mr. LOWRY. Yes; they wanted to keep everything out.

Mr. FORDNEY. Yes; I agree with you; it was pretty high. That is just a little above ours.

Mr. LOWRY. You see, in that case the protection rendered the Russian producer was the difference between the customs duty of 8 cents a pound and the excise tax, which would be about 6 cents a pound.

Mr. FORDNEY. What did sugar sell for in Russia at that time?

Mr. LOWRY. 9.15 cents a pound.

Mr. FORDNEY. With a duty of how much?

Mr. LOWRY. 8.58 cents.

Mr. FORDNEY. 8.58 cents?

Mr. LOWRY. Yes.

The CHAIRMAN. Because the Russian Government passed a law regulating the price of sugar, and they would not allow them to charge more than a certain price. That is what we will have to do here.

Mr. FORDNEY. The difference was 57 cents a hundred pounds; 9.15 against 8.58 for the tariff. That gives 57 cents for manufacturing and refining in Russia, if they could manufacture for the difference between the tariff and the price it sold at.

Mr. LOWRY. No. The point, as I see it, was that a Russian refinery had their cost of production, whatever that might be, and the excise tax to be added to that. If their cost of production was 3 cents and the excise tax was 2½ cents, before they could begin to get a profit they would have to pay 5½ cents. Then, if this was the retail price, 9.15 cents, I suppose the factory price might be 8 cents, under those conditions. So that it gave them a very handsome profit, and they could afford to make more than their allotment for the domestic market and sell the surplus for export at cost, or even under cost.

Mr. FORDNEY. The agreement entered into by all the principal nations of the world at the so-called Brussels conference, about that time or shortly after that time, abolished all bounties and cartels, by whatever name they were called, in practically every country, did it not?

Mr. LOWRY. Russia for a number of years was not a party to that conference.

Mr. FORDNEY. The Brussels conference?

Mr. LOWRY. No.

The CHAIRMAN. Russia is not a party to it yet.

Mr. FORDNEY. Germany became a party?

Mr. LOWRY. Germany did.

Mr. FORDNEY. She was the last to come in, I think.

Mr. LOWRY. But, you see, to bring that to our own market here, if the present tariff, for example, remained, and if the average price in our local market was 5 cents a pound for sugar, and the domestic beet-sugar producers produced all the sugar we consumed in our local market and got 5 cents a pound for it, if their cost was 3 cents, they would make 2 cents a pound profit.

The CHAIRMAN. Yes.

Mr. LOWRY. Now, they could well afford to make more sugar and sell it at 2 cents a pound profit, and do a bigger business, and keep their plants running, and when that sugar was exported, it would certainly be ruled against by those nations which are parties to the Brussels conference.

Mr. FORDNEY. Where in the world do you get any such inference from any law on our statute books, that if, as I understand it, the domestic producers were to produce all the sugar we consumed in this country, and we still retained the same rate of duty against foreign sugar, if our domestic industry were to produce more than we could consume and then export some, a countervailing duty would be imposed it? Is that it?

Mr. LOWRY. Yes.

Mr. FORDNEY. What for? We pay no bounty.

Mr. LOWRY. I believe you would find that foreign countries construed our high protective tariff as a bounty, and they would make a ruling against it.

Mr. FORDNEY. Then why do they not do it now?

Mr. LOWRY. None of our sugar is exported.

Mr. FORDNEY. Germany is an exporting country.

Mr. LOWRY. None of our sugars are ever exported.

Mr. FORDNEY. But the same conditions prevail in Germany. She has an import duty. Cuba has an import duty.

Mr. LOWRY. Yes.

Mr. FORDNEY. Every country in the world that exports sugar has an import duty, except Great Britain.

Mr. LOWRY. Yes.

Mr. FORDNEY. Why, then, do not these other countries impose a countervailing duty now? The same condition would exist then as exists to-day, only it does not exist against this country because we are not exporters. All other countries are. It is suggested to me by Mr. Balleu, who is an attorney and is well posted in the sugar business, and represents Hawaiian sugar manufacturers, that that was tried against Philippine sugar, and it was held not to be a bounty.

Mr. LOWRY. In the first place, at the time that was tried, I think you will find that Philippine sugars were not admitted to this country free. They paid a duty. In the second place, I think you will find, too, that the case was so small that other governments did not want to take issue with us at that time.

Mr. FORDNEY. Whether they came here to an important amount cut no figure, so long as they had an import duty on their sugar; that is the case you are arguing with us, against our domestic industry. The Philippines do have an import duty now on sugar. Why?

Mr. LOWRY. I did not know any sugar was imported into the Philippines.

Mr. FORDNEY. Oh, yes.

Mr. LOWRY. It must be a very small amount.

Mr. FORDNEY. Well, whatever it is, they have a duty on imported sugar, put on it by the Congress of the United States.

Mr. LOWRY. Well, I still think that you will find that what I said is correct, and if you want to test it you can easily do so. But, of course, if the amount to be exported and dumped into these other countries was not large, they probably would not take issue with us until it was large. I am not alone in that opinion, as you will find.

Mr. FORDNEY. Perhaps you are right; but you are focusing your views at a very long range when you talk of our exporting sugar.

Mr. LOWRY. Well, that was not the point I wanted to make. I have referred many times to the high protective tariff as a bounty, and I wanted to substantiate the fact that it was a bounty; and I think this does substantiate it. Now, if it is the opinion of the committee that it does not, that is all right.

Mr. FORDNEY. It has never been imposed by any government in the world, has it, under circumstances such as exist here?

Mr. LOWRY. I do not know of its ever being tried out; but, as you say, we are not exporters of domestic sugar, and are not likely to be for some years.

Mr. FORDNEY. I would like to see it. I would like to see the time come when we would produce more sugar in this country than we consume. Then we certainly would have cheap sugar.

Mr. LOWRY. Russia does not.

Mr. FORDNEY. Why?

Mr. LOWRY. Partly because of their excise tax.

Mr. FORDNEY. That is it, exactly.

Mr. LOWRY. And that is just the point. If we produced all the sugar we consumed, we would have to have an excise tax, would we not?

Mr. FORDNEY. Why?

Mr. LOWRY. Where are we going to get all of this revenue we need? That is one of the points that the sugar men make—that we have got to have a duty to get revenue.

Mr. FORDNEY. You are in favor of free trade on sugar, and where do you propose to get it? That is for you, and not me.

Mr. LOWRY. When I was here in August I said I thought that the rates of duty should be cut in half. That would bring them down to 80 points on raw sugar and 20 per cent less on Cuban sugars, and it would give us $26,000,000. Now, I also said that I thought all domestic sugars—not Cuba, but Porto Rico, Hawaii, Philippine, Louisiana, and domestic beet—should pay an internal tax of 25 cents a hundred pounds.

Mr. FORDNEY. If you change our protective system or policy from protection to the industry and impose a tax upon them——

Mr. LOWRY. We are talking revenue, are we not?

Mr. FORDNEY. But that is a double dose of free trade for the sugar industry. Taking off the protective tariff would put them out of business.

Mr. LOWRY. If you will allow me to continue——

Mr. FORDNEY. I will be glad to.

Mr. LOWRY. Roughly, taking 2,000 pounds to the ton, we have 1,500,000 tons, practically; and that, at 25 cents per 100 pounds, would be $7,500,000 added to your $26,000,000.

Mr. FORDNEY. Yes.

Mr. LOWRY. That is $33,500,000. Now, when the duties were removed in 1891 consumption increased in one year 23 per cent, so that it would be reasonable to suppose that consumption under this ruling would increase 10 per cent. That would mean that 10 per cent more sugar would be imported. That would bring us up $2,600,000. That would give us from sugar $36,000,000. It would give the domestic industry a protection of about a half a cent a pound, which is the same protection granted by Germany, France, and Austria, and it would reduce the price of sugar to the consumer.

Mr. FORDNEY. But at that time our Government offered a bounty to the domestic industry of 2 cents a pound. You have not taken that into consideration.

Mr. LOWRY. Why should we?

Mr. FORDNEY. That is principally what lowered the price of sugar.

Mr. MALBY. Not a tax, but a bounty.

Mr. FORDNEY. Yes; a bounty of 2 cents. That had a tendency to lower the price of sugar, certainly, and did.

Mr. LOWRY. Why?

Mr. FORDNEY. Do you ask me why? A sugar manufacturer, as you are, ask me why. I can tell you why. It costs the Louisiana planter to-day 3.75 cents, or the beet-sugar industry, to make sugar.

Mr. LOWRY. Yes.

Mr. FORDNEY. The manufacturer would get 2 cents. That would leave him 1.75 cents cost of production, less the bounty. Could he not afford to sell sugars cheaper than he is selling them to-day?

Mr. LOWRY. Louisiana sugars did not fix the market. The market was fixed by the value of imported sugars plus the duty, and the Government conceded that that price would be so low that Louisiana could not live. We will say it was 4 cents a pound. So they said to Louisiana, "You only get 4 cents a pound. Under this you would quite starve to death," and they gave them 2 cents a pound, and the Louisiana people put it in their pockets.

Mr. FORDNEY. Did they not sell the sugar for less than they were selling it for?

Mr. LOWRY. Louisiana at that time was producing perhaps 300,000 tons.

Mr. MALBY. Mr. Fordney, you have not gotten an answer to your question as to whether the price was reduced.

Mr. LOWRY. Well——

Mr. FORDNEY. I bought sugar then for 3.70.

Mr. LOWRY. They were happy days for the consumer.

Mr. FORDNEY. They had a bounty and got 5.70 cents.

Mr. LOWRY. I do not agree that Louisiana fixed the price of sugar at that time.

Mr. FORDNEY. Well, I never knew you to agree with me on anything. What was it that fixed the value of sugar two or three months ago—the value of foreign sugars or the domestic industry?

Mr. LOWRY. I think the domestic industry did their share.

Mr. FORDNEY. Here is what your boss says—your organization, your committee, and so on. Mr. Spreckels said in an interview recently:

> I believe that the peak of the upward movement has been passed for good, and the tendency now will be toward lower levels. This is due to the fact that the domestic beet and cane sugar is now coming on the market.

Mr. LOWRY. Yes.

Mr. FORDNEY. That is a confession from your side.

Mr. LOWRY. The high price in any commodity always comes between seasons.

Mr. FORDNEY. What justified you—your firm—in selling September sugar at 7.25 cents a pound, when the domestic industry shortly after, as soon as their sugar began to go on the market, sold for 5.55? What caused you to come down on the price?

Mr. LOWRY. They sold for what?

Mr. FORDNEY. 5.55.

Mr. LOWRY. Do you not know that the domestic industry was at that time quoting 6.5 cents a pound?

Mr. FORDNEY. No.

Mr. LOWRY. I know that it was.

Mr. FORDNEY. I put an affidavit in the record on that.

Mr. LOWRY. I am sorry, because I know that they were then quoting 6.5.

Mr. FORDNEY. You had no sugar on the market in September; you had none until their season opened, on October 12, and they began selling at 5.55 f. o. b. factory.

Mr. LOWRY. And when did they begin selling at 5.55?

Mr. FORDNEY. As soon as the season opened.

Mr. LOWRY. Not at all. They began when cane sugars were selling at 5.65.

Mr. FORDNEY. I beg you pardon. I looked up the records themselves, the bill books and the invoices, and on October 12, when the season opened, they quoted sugar at 5.55, and sold it at that, and continued to sell. They sold 809 carloads out of about 850 carloads at that price, 5.55, while your firm was selling at 7.25.

Mr. LOWRY. Now, Mr. Fordney, you are a business man, and do you not know that our firm could not sell at 7.25 if another competitor was selling at 5.55?

Mr. FORDNEY. I am taking Willett & Gray's report.

Mr. LOWRY. That information you have there is not correct.

Mr. FORDNEY. Then you want to get Willett & Gray to correct their trade journal, because I took this from their journal.

Mr. LOWRY. I am selling sugars every day, except when I am in Washington, and I know something about the market, and I know that the domestic beet-sugar interests this year sold the same as they have sold in all other years; they based their price at the time they sold on the cane-sugar price, which, in turn, was based on the value of imported sugars, plus the duty. There is no question about it.

Mr. FORDNEY. What are you selling for to-day?

Mr. LOWRY. The beet-sugar people?

Mr. FORDNEY. No; you.

Mr. LOWRY. We began to sell in California beet in July for future delivery, and the price July 1 was 4.95. On July 6 the refiners advanced their price from 5 cents to 5.1. Then the shortage——

Mr. FORDNEY. Mr. Lowry, you are not answering my question. I asked you what you sold sugar for in September, October, and November and what you are selling for now.

Mr. LOWRY. I am going back clear to August and coming right up.

Mr. FORDNEY. No; you have been talking about California sugar. I want to know what the Federal Sugar Refining Co. sold sugars for.

Mr. LOWRY. The Federal Sugar Refining Co. and other refineries on July 6 advanced their price from 5 to 5.1. Shortly after that the market advanced rapidly because of the drought in Europe doing serious injury to the beet crop. The market advanced 10 points, 15 points, and so on, and about the 1st of August it reached 5.75. These dates are not absolutely correct, but they are approximately correct.

Mr. FORDNEY. I understand.

Mr. LOWRY. The beet-sugar men saw that price and it looked awful good to them, and they commenced to sell for future delivery right along; they commenced to sell for delivery in October.

Mr. FORDNEY. What beet-sugar men do you refer to?

Mr. LOWRY. I refer to the general beet-sugar situation.

Mr. FORDNEY. Do you know that the Michigan Beet Sugar Co. sold at that time for future delivery?

Mr. LOWRY. I believe so; yes. That is, whether the Michigan Sugar Co. did or not, I do not know. I only know that as a competitor, and I just know what they do, because it is my business to keep track of what competitors are doing. Now, the market advanced right on up to 6.75 and the trade kept buying on each successive advance. When the market reached 6.75——

Mr. FORDNEY. When was that?

Mr. LOWRY. In the latter part of September—somewhere around the 25th of September, I think.

Mr. FORDNEY. Yes.

Mr. LOWRY. The American Sugar Refining Co. was over 30 days oversold—could not deliver. The price might as well have been 10 cents, as far as prompt delivery was concerned. They could not make it. Howe was out of the market for the same reason. The Warner Sugar Refining Co. was out of the market for the same reason. The Federal Sugar Refining Co. had been selling on a graded scale all the way up, and they still had some sugar, but were about a week oversold. The demand came on to us so fast we could not take care of it and we went to 7 cents. Arbuckle & Co. were delivering promptly and they went to 7 cents. We were about 10 days oversold at the time and Arbuckle was the only refiner prepared to give immediate delivery, and he jumped his price to 7.5 cents. We had, as I remember it, somewhere in the neighborhood of enough raw sugar on hand to make 60,000 or 75,000 barrels of sugar, and the trade was coming to us so fast that it soon cleaned us up. We did not want to be cleaned out. We wanted to keep in the market and supply our customers right along, and we put the price at 7.25, and at 7.25 the market stopped, and from that time on, whether we talk about beet sugars or cane sugars, the market became absolutely a jobber's market. The beet-sugar price was 6.5 cents.

Mr. FORDNEY. Please let me interrupt you. What caused you to put your price up to 7.25? Was it because of the high price of imported raws or just because you could get it?

Mr. LOWRY. It was partly the high price of imported raws, but mostly because we did not want to be cleaned up. We wanted to keep on doing business every day.

Mr. FORDNEY. And you put the price up so high that they could not reach you?

Mr. LOWRY. No; it lasted, I think, perhaps 10 days or so.

Mr. FORDNEY. What are you selling for now?

Mr. LOWRY. We have been cutting the market this last week and got down to 5.65.

Mr. FORDNEY. 5.65. Now, why?

Mr. LOWRY. The same price made by the Michigan beet-sugar companies.

Mr. FORDNEY. What is the difference between the price of raws to-day and the price of raws when you charged 7.25?

Mr. LOWRY. I do not know what the raw market is to-day. I imagine that it is somewhere between 4.86 and 4.90.

Mr. FORDNEY. The newspapers stated, as coming from the refineries in New York, that the high price of sugar for September, October, and November was due to the high price of raws, because of the shortage in the world's supply of sugar. I want to know what change has taken place in the shortage in the world's supply between September and to-day.

Mr. LOWRY. Raw sold sometime in January as low as $2\frac{1}{16}$. Add 1.35 and that would give 3.41, duty paid, for raw sugar.

Mr. FORDNEY. Did you add the Cuban rate?

Mr. LOWRY. Yes. If you will let me continue there I will show you what happened. That was 3.41 for raw sugars testing 96. Cuban sugars sold as high as 5.96, duty paid. That made an advance in raw sugar from the lowest price to the top price of 2.55 cents a pound. Now, the Federal Sugar Refining Co. sold sugar at the begining of the year at 4.55. The other refiners were quoting 4.60, and the Federal Sugar Refining Co. sold sugar as high as 7.25, which would be an advance of 2.70 cents a pound.

Mr. FORDNEY. Then, taking the highest market price for Cuban sugar, duty paid, 5.96, as given by you, and adding 40 cents for refining—is that a fair price for refining?

Mr. LOWRY. Do you mean just for the bare refining cost?

Mr. FORDNEY. Yes.

Mr. LOWRY. I could not tell. I think Mr. Post testified something to that effect.

Mr. FORDNEY. I think that is it, about.

Mr. LOWRY. The average margin between raw and refined sugar is 89 points.

Mr. FORDNEY. I want to show what your company did.

Mr. LOWRY. Yes.

Mr. FORDNEY. Take $5.96 and add 40 cents for refining, making $6.36, and you sold sugar for $7.25 a hundred pounds at one time.

Mr. LOWRY. You know, we have to put the sugar in bags or barrels, and the cost of a barrel is about 15 cents a hundred pounds. Then we have the same overhead charges that these domestic beet-sugar manufacturers talk about.

Mr. FORDNEY. There has been no change in the situation as to the world's supply of sugar between the 1st of September and now, has there?

Mr. LOWRY. No change?

Mr. FORDNEY. Yes.

Mr. LOWRY. The difficulty in September was due to the fact that the Cuba crop was over. Practically all of it had been used up.

Mr. FORDNEY. Do you mean manufactured?

Mr. LOWRY. And there was no supply of raw sugar.

Mr. FORDNEY. Do you mean Cuban sugar is manufactured and off the market in September?

Mr. LOWRY. The Cuban crop, which as been, roughly, 500,000 tons as against the expectation of 1,008,000 tons. It had been to a great extent used up.

Mr. FORDNEY. This year's crop?

Mr. LOWRY. Yes; in September.

Mr. FORDNEY. They do not egin to grind until December.

Mr. LOWRY. You are talking about the crop of 1911–12 and I am am talking about the crop of 1910–11.

Mr. FORDNEY. Last year's crop?

Mr. LOWRY. Yes; last year's crop. That is the crop that we imported this last summer.

The CHAIRMAN. Mr. Fordney, let us finish these other things first and then you can take Mr. Lowry all through that.

Mr. FORDNEY. Very well.

The CHAIRMAN. Is there anything else about this Russian business?

Mr. LOWRY. No, sir.

The CHAIRMAN. I wanted to know whether you could furnish the committee with any additional information on the subject, as to what the farmer or grower in Europe gets for the beets, in addition to the statement you made when you were here before.

Mr. LOWRY. Messrs. Czarnikow, of London, are an unquestioned authority in London, accepted generally by the sugar trade, and I have noticed that what they have said has been referred to by others.

The CHAIRMAN. Yes.

Mr. MALBY. Mr. Chairman, have we not those Czarnikow reports, or can we not get them, so that we can look at them for ourselves? I would like to have them, so that we could compare them and not have the information just picked out in little pieces in this way.

The CHAIRMAN. This committee not being sugar experts, it would take them probably a month to look these things through. Mr. Lowry has picked out these things which he is giving us. Of course, he does not know these facts of his own knowledge, but he gives us the place where he gets them from. He is doing just what others have done before the committee.

Mr. FORDNEY. In other words, he picks out the sore spots in the whole report.

Mr. LOWRY. We will see if he does.

The CHAIRMAN. I think we should let the witness testify and then judge of the matter for ourselves, unless you make that objection, Judge Malby. We have been doing that all through the hearings.

Mr. FORDNEY. I do not think we ought to take extracts from that report without having the whole report.

The CHAIRMAN. That has been done by every witness, from Mr. Atkin on down. A man can not testify in any other way. Of course that may be a very good point, only it goes to the probative value of the testimony as to how far we ought to rely on what the witness says.

Mr. LOWRY. If you will ask your consuls to confirm this information you will find they will do it, I am satisfied.

Mr. MALBY. I do not object to any quotations from Willett & Gray or from Czarnikow, because they are supposed to be authorities on those points; but I think we have quite uniformly had the documents before us. We have had Willett & Gray's published journals. My only point about it is that we want to avoid, I would imagine, as much as possible having any special plea made.

The CHAIRMAN. Oh, yes.

Mr. MALBY. And in order to avoid that, if Mr. Lowry is quoting from Czarnikow's reports, he probably has them, and we should have the reports. Then, if he calls our attention to a report and cites certain statements, I can not see any objection to it.

Mr. LOWRY. Czarnikow has never made a report, so far as I know, on this matter. I wrote to these various people in Europe to find out what the factories of Europe were paying the farmers for the beets, in the belief that they were not paying any more than the farmers were receiving in this country. They have written me these letters. When I wrote these letters I did not expect to use them before this committee. I was just getting this information for myself. Here it is. If you want it, and want to confirm it through your consuls, you can do it. You can pass on it and ask your own consuls to furnish you with the information. It seems to me important, if you are considering our domestic manufacturers' relations with the foreign manufacturers. If you show that the domestic manufacturer's first cost—the cost of his beets—is the same as the foreign manufacturer's first cost, and then proceed to show, as you can show, that manufacturing of beets into sugar is a mechanical process—the manufacturers themselves say that their sugar must be very pure, because it is not touched by a human hand from the time that the beets enter at one side until the sugar is turned out at the other side—you can see that the labor cost in the manufacture is not very expensive.

Mr. MALBY. The only point about it is this: I regard the information as valuable, but it ought to come from such a source that there will be no doubt in the mind of any member of the committee as to its accuracy; and also, it should be sufficiently comprehensive to cover the entire situation. This is information which comes to a refiner, which I do not desire to designate as hostile to the industry, except to the extent of saying that the testimony of Mr. Spreckels himself was to the effect that he wanted to have all duties on sugar wiped out; and he has issued different documents containing an analysis of what purports to be the sugar situation in this country. I would hardly regard a mere correspondence with unknown people—unknown, at least, to us—as being testimony of such a character as would furnish us with information which ought to serve as a guide. We ought to be able, I think, to secure something more tangible than the result of a correspondence with individuals. If Mr. Lowry has any of Czarnikow's reports on that subject, if they are produced before the committee, we will concede that Czarnikow is an authority; but not the private correspondence of a refiner. I hardly think that the committee has received that testimony. However, I am simply expressing my views in relation to it, which I desire to have made a matter of record, that the mere correspondence by anyone, whether he be a refiner or not, with residents and citizens of a foreign country, in response to a communication written by himself, is not evidence of such reliability that it should be received and considered by this committee. Now, having said so much, I desire to abide by whatever disposition the chairman may make of the matter.

The CHAIRMAN. I want to be fair about all these matters—I try to be—but it strikes me that we have allowed testimony to be given here that would not be allowed in any court of justice, such as a man's tariff views, whether he favors high duty or low duty, and letting a man come in and say that he knows a certain thing because a certain man told him that. We have permitted that sort of evidence before this committee, because we were all men experienced in the weighing of evidence, all of us lawyers enough not to let the testimony sway us for more than its probative value. We can not subpoena these witnesses from foreign countries, and bring them here. They are not subject to any process of the United States, that I know of, and there is no way to get that evidence at first-hand.

Mr. MALBY. Do not our consular reports cover this subject?

The CHAIRMAN. No; they do not. I would be very glad if they did. In reply to a memorandum to the State Department which Mr. Hinds and Judge Madison and myself prepared they did not put that in; I do not know why.

Mr. MALBY. My point is that if this is to be used by the committee as a basis for calculation and report and recommendation, such testimony, such information, would not rise to the dignity of information that the committee should have. It was a very good rule to follow, and I thought it was a very sensible one, when we said we would not even receive the statement of the secretary of the American Sugar Refining Co. as to the fact that they had disposed of their California holdings, because that was not the character of testimony which we thought the committee should have. It was not under oath and not certified to.

The CHAIRMAN. And not subject to cross-examination.

Mr. MALBY. And we ought to have what the fact was.

The CHAIRMAN. How would that apply to this question? How could you procure the testimony of a witness who was not accessible or subject to the jurisdiction of the committee? We can not go into Germany and elsewhere for these people, and make them testify.

Mr. MALBY. Of course it is highly important not to receive testimony that would not be received anywhere as evidence of the fact.

The CHAIRMAN. No; but you will recall that during this investigation we have allowed witnesses to testify in a similar way. When Mr. Truman Palmer, particularly, was on the stand, we let him testify, and when Mr. Atkin was on the stand we let him testify, as we have done time after time with experts, to facts that they had no knowledge of at all.

Mr. MALBY. I do not recall that.

The CHAIRMAN. It is a fact.

Mr. MALBY. Mr. Truman Palmer, as the evidence shows, is a very high expert, so far as the beet-sugar manufacture is concerned. Mr. Palmer had traveled extensively in Europe, and had personally examined the fields and the growing crops and made diligent inquiry of all persons who would have knowledge of the facts, and he gave us as accurate information as any person could.

The CHAIRMAN. Let me call your attention to an exactly parallel incident in Mr. Palmer's testimony. Mr. Palmer submitted evidence as to labor conditions in western beet-sugar factories, which he got by correspondence, and he specified the people that he got the letters from and their replies.

Mr. MALBY. I do not think that was very satisfactory.

The CHAIRMAN. We let that go in for what it was worth; and if evidence of that character was contradicted by evidence of a direct character, of course we would disregard it.

Mr. MALBY. But this information on the cost of sugar in foreign countries, and what it costs to produce it, or what the farmer is paid, I regard really as a matter of very great importance to the members of the committee, if we can obtain it something near first-hand.

The CHAIRMAN. Of course, the chairman will put the objection, if it is made as an objection, to his going into the letters he has gotten on this subject.

Mr. MALBY. Am I to understand that the information which Mr. Lowry has received is the result of a correspondence between himself and people residing abroad?

The CHAIRMAN. I think that is it.

Mr. MALBY. And their answers thereto?

The CHAIRMAN. Mr. Lowry, did you not get this information by letters which you wrote to people abroad?

Mr. LOWRY. Yes; the condition is that I wrote letters to them instead of going to see them; that is all.

The CHAIRMAN. In one case a man goes over and talks to them and comes back and tells us what they have said, and in the other case Mr. Lowry has written letters to people and has their replies. I do not see any difference myself.

Mr. MALBY. I do. When I see a thing, I have some idea of its value.

Mr. LOWRY. I would suggest that I am quite sure; if you want to confirm this, you can easily do it.

Mr. MALBY. I am not entering a general objection; I am simply calling the attention of the committee to the character of the evidence which it is proposed to put in the record.

The CHAIRMAN. Yes.

Mr. MALBY. And I want to express, personally and individually, my disapproval of such testimony as being unreliable, and such as ought not to be offered as proof of the facts to which it refers.

The CHAIRMAN. That may be. You may be right about that. I admit that it is not as satisfactory as direct evidence, but I do not know of any way to get these people from there to come over here. I would rather see what this is, anyhow, and each one of us can judge what it is worth.

Mr. MALBY. Well, I do not know. I have had some experience with the witness along those lines.

Mr. FORDNEY. If the chairman is going to accept these letters, I would like Mr. Lowry to also file with the committee the letters which he has gotten, from which he takes his information.

The CHAIRMAN. Yes. We do not accept them. We will hear them. I say we do not accept them; we do not necessarily say that that is the only evidence, or very good evidence, or express any opinion on that point. We take it for what it is worth.

Mr. Lowry, please tell us what information you have been able to get up about what the farmer gets for his beets in other countries?

Mr. LOWRY. Czarnikow of London advised that the price paid by the establishment—that is, the factory—to the farmer for sugar beets in convention countries, during the present year, varies considerably.

The CHAIRMAN. What is the date of this letter?

Mr. LOWRY. October 12, 1911. Contracts have been made from 20 shillings to 24 shillings per ton, delivered at the factory, cleaned and topped, and half the pulp to be returned to the farmer for cattle food.

Mr. MALBY. What is the American equivalent of that?

Mr. LOWRY. Twenty shillings and 24 shillings is equal to from $4.85 to $5.85 per ton in our currency; and, of course, half of the pulp to be returned to the farmer means that there is some increase in value to the farmer—that pulp that is returned has some value to him. I do not know what that value is.

The CHAIRMAN. Twenty to twenty-four shillings is how much?

Mr. LOWRY. Twenty to twenty-four shillings is equal to $4.87 to $5.85. And he goes on to say that the leading price has been 21 shillings to 22 shillings 6 pence per ton in Europe. Twenty-one shillings to 22 shillings 6 pence per ton, which he says is the leading price, is equal to $5.11 to $5.48 per ton.

The CHAIRMAN. What does he mean by "the leading price"?

Mr. LOWRY. He means that most of the contracts have been made on that basis.

The CHAIRMAN. Oh, yes.

Mr. LOWRY. That is the basis on which most of the business has been done.

The CHAIRMAN. Who is it that says that?

Mr. LOWRY. Czarnikow.

The CHAIRMAN. The great London statistician?

Mr. LOWRY. Yes.

The CHAIRMAN. All right.

Mr. LOWRY. L. Behrens & Son, of Hamburg, say that prices have been made between marks 1.1 and marks 1.4 for 50 kilos. That is equal to $5.32 to $6.76 per ton of 2,240 pounds.

H. J. Merck & Co., of Hamburg, say that for the district of Stettin the average price has been marks 1.2 for 50 kilos. That is $5.78 per ton.

In Posen the prices vary from marks 1.16 to marks 1.35. That is from $5.59 to $6.49 per ton. The average has been marks 1.3, or $6.27, per ton.

In Belgium and Holland the average has been 30 francs, which is equal to $5.79 per ton. On that point it is apparent that a rather different situation exists in Europe from what exists here. Mr. Willett called our attention particularly to Denmark; and I thought possibly the Danish Government might own the sugar factories, but I find that is not so—that the entire industry has for many years been carried on by a private, independent concern, the Danish Sugar Factories. Apparently one concern does the whole business. This concern has built and owns all the present factories all over the country, and has to pay taxes the same as any other concern. The Government taxes imported sugar at the rate of 10 ore per kilo, with a polarization of 98° or over, and on a graduated scale downward for lower sugar.

There is an internal-revenue tax which is equal to about 0.7 cents a pound on all Danish-grown sugar of 98 per cent or over, and pro rated downward. That is the point I thought would be of interest in connection with the Colorado situation. The company makes contracts running several years with the farmers for the growing of the beets, paying the farmers a fixed price at the end of the company's fiscal year, and also a pro rata share of the company's earnings.

Mr. RAKER. That is in what country?

Mr. LOWRY. In Denmark.

The CHAIRMAN. From whom is that information?

Mr. LOWRY. That is from a friend of mine in New York, Mr. C. F. Hage, a Dane. When Mr. Willett brought this question up the other day I conferred with Mr. Hage. His father has estates in Denmark and grows sugar beets.

The CHAIRMAN. These communications which you have just read, and which you say you will file with the reporter, are they from gentlemen who are recognized sugar experts?

Mr. LOWRY. Beyond question.

The CHAIRMAN. Are they the highest experts in those places?

Mr. LOWRY. They are the highest I know. Certainly Czarnikow is, if not the leading, one of the leading, sugar brokers in London, and the others are all reputable men.

The CHAIRMAN. The ones in Hamburg are?

Mr. LOWRY. Yes; and with no interest in the matter at all. They had no idea what the information was going to be used for. I simply wrote them and asked them to tell me the prices paid farmers in the country for sugar beets.

Mr. FORDNEY. The witness must admit that everything would depend on the sugar contents of the beet.

Mr. LOWRY. Mr. Oxnard has testified that the sugar contents average the same as here.

Mr. FORDNEY. Yes; but we do not know whether that gentleman gave you the average of one month or one year.

Mr. LOWRY. Yes; he says the average, and I asked for the averages. The letters will show that.

The CHAIRMAN. The letters show that they have given the average for this year?

Mr. LOWRY. Yes.

The CHAIRMAN. And they show the length of time you take, and it is the average price for that length of time?

Mr. LOWRY. Yes; during the year 1911. In fact, the figures state that. They say they range from a certain price up to a certain other price. Some of these figures run away, away up. It is apparent that over there, when a man has not sold his beets in advance and sells them later, he often gets a very high price. For instance, there is a record here of the equivalent of $10.47 to $11.90 having been paid; but I did not put that in, because it is not fair. It is an unusual condition, and perhaps happens once in 20 years.

The CHAIRMAN. That big figure which you gave, of over $10, was where the beet farmer got the advantage of this great rise recently?

Mr. LOWRY. Yes.

The CHAIRMAN. And that might not come again in a long period of time?

Mr. LOWRY. Once in 20 years would be as often as it would happen.

The CHAIRMAN. And you did not cite that?

Mr. LOWRY. No; because it is misleading and should not be considered. It simply shows that over there, if a man takes the risk of the market, he might once in 20 years get a big rise.

Mr. RAKER. On the question of high prices stated in the letter you read, supposing that the sugar factories in the West should enter into a contract with these farmers, for from two to five years, to pay them so much for their beets at a certain percentage, and then the payment to rise according to the percentage of the beet, and should give them a certain percentage of the net earnings of the factory, that would practically wipe out this difficulty between the people and give both the grower and the manufacturer fair treatment, and the consumer also, would it not?

Mr. LOWRY. That is the way I see it.

The CHAIRMAN. That is the way they do in Denmark?

Mr. LOWRY. In Denmark; yes. They do the same in other countries.

Mr. FORDNEY. Do those figures cover short tons or long tons?

Mr. LOWRY. Long tons.

The CHAIRMAN. The Chair has completed the examination he had in mind, and any other member of the committee might take this witness up on any point that has not been brought up.

Mr. LOWRY. I have been thinking over this matter which was discussed this morning, of the refiners furnishing the committee with their cost of production. It seems to me that every beet-sugar refiner in the country should be required to show the average price which they paid for their beets, and their average test of their beets, and the cost of working those beets into sugar, in the same way, so that you can get an idea of the real cost of production. The reason I say that is this: Take Mr. Oxnard's figures, for example. He has taken all his factories and averaged them up, and he says, "Our cost of production and marketing," I think he calls it marketing, "is so much"; and in his figures for the cost of marketing he says that he has added the freight, which in many cases is 60 points. You can see that those figures are, in many cases, very misleading. He should have given the figures for each factory. The averaging process is very bad. Take two of his factories, and one produces at a cost of 4 cents, a small amount, and another produces a large amount at 3 cents, and yet he could say, if he gave those two factories, "My average cost is 3.5 cents." He could say the cost of one is so much, and the cost of the other is so much, and divide by two. The number of pounds of sugar produced should be considered.

Mr. FORDNEY. You say that if he produced a small amount at 4 cents and a large amount in another factory at 3 cents, he could say, "My average is 3.5 cents." That is not a fair average. You must consider the number of pounds made, and the average would be much higher than 3.5 cents.

Mr. LOWRY. That is the point I make, and I think Mr. Oxnard does that, and I think if he, and the other beet-sugar manufacturers as well, will show that, there will be a different result.

Mr. FORDNEY. We have that, so far as Michigan is concerned. Mr. Warren gave those figures for Michigan.

The CHAIRMAN. And Mr. Cutler gave us that for Utah.

Mr. FORDNEY. Yes.

Mr. LOWRY. I looked over the Utah and Idaho figures, and I could not analyze them. The best I could make out was that the cost of working the beets into sugar would be a little less than a cent a pound, and if they paid an average of 2.08 for the beets, that would make a total cost of turning those beets into sugar of 3.08. That was as close as I could get.

Mr. FORDNEY. Mr. Warren gave the cost per ton of beets to their factories, and the cost of working them, making a total cost ranging in the six factories from 3.65 to 3.75. He gave the price paid by the company for beets.

Mr. LOWRY. Did he analyze that statement?

Mr. FORDNEY. He gave it in great detail.

Mr. LOWRY. When did he do that, recently?

Mr. FORDNEY. He gave that testimony when he was here.

The CHAIRMAN. He gave it during the summer. Suppose you analyze those figures, at your leisure, and if there is anything obscure about it, you can clear it up.

Mr. LOWRY. I should think they could say, "We paid so much for our beets, and it cost so much to work them into sugar, and our executive work was so much," and then show it for each factory, and not average it up. For instance, Mr. Oxnard admitted to me that he wanted to make it very high, and that is the reason he did it that way. His object was to cloud the issues.

Mr. FORDNEY. And his testimony given under oath?

Mr. LOWRY. No; we were in the hotel at lunch.

Mr. FORDNEY. No; but he was under oath here. He testified before this committee under oath. You say he said that he wanted to make it high?

Mr .LOWRY. I say that is the way we did it; and the fact itself shows.

Mr. FORDNEY. The point I make is that his testimony was under oath; and after he gave his testimony under oath you say he admitted to you that he had given the price high, or tried to make it high. Is that right?

Mr. LOWRY. He said that when he was right here. He stood right here and said this about the freights, and it was apparent that he wanted to make it high. He might just as well have gone on and said, "The cost to the jobber to sell the sugar is so much, one-fourth, and the retailer ought to have a half a cent a pound, and therefore our total cost of putting beet sugars on the market is three-quarters of a cent higher than I have given." It is just as logical to do that as to add in the freight from the factory to point of destination.

The CHAIRMAN. Now, Judge Malby, will you proceed with this witness?

Mr. LOWRY. While we are on the prices, Mr. Fordney, I would like to call your attention to the fact that beet sugars, f. o. b. Hamburg, sold up as high this year as 18 shillings and 9 pence.

Mr. FORDNEY. How much is that in our money?

Mr. LOWRY. I have not the calculation here.

Mr. FORDNEY. That is all Greek to me.

Mr. LOWRY. I think as I go on I can make it clear. The quotation was 16 shillings when I came down here on Monday, so that the beet-sugar market in Hamburg had declined 2 shillings 9 pence, equal to 66 points—66 cents a hundred pounds. The American beets sold off to the basis of 6.50 New York, and when I came down here were selling down to 5.90 New York, a decline of 60 points.

Mr. MALBY. There are only one or two questions I desire to call your attention to. While we are talking about cheap sugar, I want to call your attention to a quotation from Willett & Gray's Weekly Statistical Sugar Trade Journal, under date of October 19, 1911, in which they say:

Cane granulated is steady and firm by all refiners at 6.75 cents, less 2 per cent.

Beet granulated in Michigan, 6.50 cents to 6.40 cents, less 2 per cent New York basis, and Colorado 6.80 cents, less 2 per cent f. o. b. Denver.

Mr. Lowry. Then I did not go high enough on the American beet. Yes; that is so. That is Denver.

Mr. Malby. This is f. o. b. Denver. This article continues:

This latter gives consumers there, near the beet factories, their supply at 0.58 cent per pound less than the consumers of cane granulated made from foreign raws.

Are those figures correct, as you recall the market price at that time?

Mr. Lowry. The situation this year was uncommon——

Mr. Malby. Now, Mr. Lowry, you are going off on something else. If you will just answer one or two questions I will be obliged to you. I am simply asking whether those prices are as you recall them to have been at that time?

Mr. Lowry. I am not familiar with the prices in Denver. I would take Willett & Gray's statement.

Mr. Malby. Was the price of cane granulated at that time 6.75, less 2 per cent, in New York? You will remember that, probably.

Mr. Lowry. When was this?

Mr. Malby. October 19, 1911.

Mr. Lowry. I think that is correct. If Willett & Gray say it is, I will accept it. I know that about that time it was 6.75.

Mr. Malby. It appears from the remaining quotations which you did not verify that granulated in Michigan was selling at 6.50 to 6.40, less 2 per cent; that they were selling granulated sugar at that time from 25 to 35 cents a hundred pounds less than the refineries were selling granulated sugar for in New York.

Mr. Lowry. Does that say whether the sugars were being sold in first or second hands? For instance, at that time, when the Federal's price was 6.75, jobbers in Chicago were selling our own sugars at 6.50 a pound. Beet sugars were the same way. The market advanced rapidly, and they bought all the way up and at a nice profit, and they wanted to take it.

Mr. Malby. Let us see if we can not keep within the scope of my questions. I am giving you Willett & Gray, and I suppose you are familiar with the methods of making quotations?

Mr. Lowry. Yes.

Mr. Malby. They say:

Cane granulated is steady and firm by all refiners at 6.75 cents, less 2 per cent.

Beet granulated in Michigan, 6.50 cents to 6.40 cents, less 2 per cent, New York basis.

If that is a correct statement, it would indicate that the beet sugar was being sold at from 25 to 35 cents a hundred pounds less than granulated.

Mr. Lowry. Yes; but the point is that they do not say whether it is being sold by the factory or by the jobber.

Mr. Malby. It says "f. o. b." What does that mean—"free on board"?

Mr. LOWRY. Yes.

Mr. MALBY. That means sold to the consumer or the retailer or wholesaler free on board, does it not?

Mr. LOWRY. Yes; but the jobber who bought sugar at 6 cents might sell sugar at that price f. o. b.

Mr. MALBY. Why not stick to something that is before us. They say that the price in Michigan was 6.40 to 6.50 cents f. o. b.

Mr. LOWRY. But they do not say that it was sold by the factory.

Mr. MALBY. Yes; it says, "Beet granulated in Michigan."

Mr. LOWRY. It is true that those sugars were sold by the jobbers, who had bought them on the way up.

Mr. MALBY. The quotations were from 25 to 35 cents different per 100 pounds.

Mr. LOWRY. I do not know of any time this year when the factories made more than the normal difference between cane and beet sugars.

Mr. MALBY. I am quoting the figures.

Mr. FORDNEY. The jobber does not sell sugar at the factory in the State of Michigan; it is the manufacturer that sells it there.

Mr. LOWRY. I beg your pardon; the Chicago jobbers sold a great deal of Michigan sugar right down into Pittsburgh and Buffalo and shipped it from the factory.

Mr. FORDNEY. That may be true, but it does not give the price at the factory.

Mr. MALBY. These quotations are given f. o. b. I take it that means that sugar was on the road to somewhere; it was out of the hands of the factory. At least, they were putting it on the cars to go some place.

Mr. LOWRY. I will answer that question as I did a moment ago—that I do not know of any period this year when the factories made more than the normal difference between beet and cane, which is 20 points.

Mr. MALBY. I do not know; I have got the report here. There is only one other matter here that I can see. Under date of October 26, 1911, Willett & Gray report as follows:

The Federal closed their refinery for annual clean up, and in order to dispose of their product remaining on hand they reduced prices 0.25 cent, to the basis of 6.50 cents less 2 per cent; they now announce having practically no stock at their refinery and that their price applies on unsold sugar at consignment points.

Does that correctly state the condition of the Federal Sugar Refining Co. at that time?

Mr. LOWRY. Yes; we did that

Mr. MALBY (continuing reading):

The other refineries in the East and at New Orleans made a reduction of 0.05 cent in their list to basis of 6.70 cents less 2 per cent, or 6.566 cents net each. * * *

Beet granulated remains unchanged on New York basis of 6.40 cents less 2 per cent for deliveries west of Buffalo and Pittsburgh.

Did I understand you correctly to say that the lowest price of the year for raws was 3.41?

Mr. LOWRY. 2-1/16 for Cuba's would be 3.41; yes; that is what it was.

Mr. MALBY. 3.41; and the lowest price at which sugar was sold was 4.55?

Mr. LOWRY. That is right; less 1 per cent.

Mr. MALBY. Less 1 per cent; yes. So that the margin of profit to the factories, to the refiners, was $1.04 at the lowest prices; is that the correct situation?

Mr. LOWRY. That is the correct situation; yes. There was very little sugar bought at 2-1/16. The average at that time was higher. I was quoting the extreme.

Mr. MALBY. The extreme low price at which sugar was bought and the extreme low price at which sugar was sold showed a profit to the refinery of $1.04 per 100 pounds, or more than 1 cent a pound?

Mr. LOWRY. That seems to be right.

Mr. MALBY. I also notice, if I have taken the figures correctly, here——

Mr. LOWRY. That should not be called a profit of $1.04; it is a margin of $1.04.

Mr. MALBY. Yes; it is a margin of $1.04; and the highest price paid, as I understood you, was $5.96. Am I correct about that?

Mr. LOWRY. On raw sugars.

Mr. MALBY. On raw sugars, yes; $5.96. So that the difference between the highest and lowest price would be $2.55. The difference between $3.41 and $5.96 would be $2.55?

Mr. LOWRY. Yes. I figured that all out a moment ago, when I put it in.

Mr. MALBY. It does not require very much figuring. Now, the highest price at which you sold was 7.25?

Mr. LOWRY. Yes; that is right.

Mr. MALBY. And the lowest was 6.55?

Mr. LOWRY. That is right. We should deduct the percentages. 7.25 was less 2 per cent. That would bring it down to 7.105, I make it, as compared with the 4.55 price less 1 per cent, which would be 4.50.

Mr. MALBY. The rise without the deductions would be about 2.70?

Mr. LOWRY. 2.70; yes; and with the deductions 2.60.

Mr. MALBY. So that the rise about kept pace with the increased price of raws?

Mr. LOWRY. Just about.

Mr. MALBY. I think that this testimony is already in. Your business is that of refining sugar from sugar cane, is it not?

Mr. LOWRY. Yes.

Mr. MALBY. And have you had any experience whatever in the manufacture of sugar from sugar beets?

Mr. LOWRY. No.

Mr. MALBY. This is just for the purpose of the record. I simply desire the facts and ask the questions in no spirit of criticism whatever. You have never attempted to cultivate beets, and you personally have no knowledge of what it costs to raise beets, have you?

Mr. LOWRY. No; except what I see in the record.

Mr. MALBY. That is your research and investigation?

Mr. LOWRY. Yes.

Mr. MALBY. Neither have you been connected with one of the refineries which manufacture sugar from the beets?

Mr. LOWRY. No.

Mr. MALBY. So that, personally, you would not have knowledge of that expense?

Mr. Lowry. No; except as I have made more or less of a study of the general situation.

Mr. Malby. Except as you have made it a matter of study. Of course the price of beets varies somewhat with the seasons, does it not? For instance, the Colorado company reported one year that they had something more than 2,000,000 tons of beets and next year about 1,475,000 tons.

Mr. Lowry. Pounds, I guess that is.

Mr. Malby. Well, perhaps that was bags.

Mr. Lowry. Yes; bags of 100 pounds each.

Mr. Malby. Of course that would indicate to your mind, would it not, that what it cost to raise beets would depend a great deal upon the abundance of the crops in different years, would it not?

Mr. Lowry. And the number of beets sliced and the percentage of sugar contents.

Mr. Malby. I am, of course, speaking now of the farmer and not of the sugar company. I am speaking now of the cost to the farmer. I say the cost to the farmer to raise beets would depend upon the abundance of his crop, to some extent, and on the amount of sugar in the beet itself.

Mr. Lowry. Yes.

Mr. Malby. If he had an abundant crop, say from 15 to 20 tons to the acre, he could afford to raise them for a much less price than if they ran from 5 to 10 tons per acre?

Mr. Lowry. Yes.

Mr. Malby. So that in determining the cost to the farmer to raise beets, for commercial purposes, it would be quite necessary, would it not, to take a period of years rather than one year, because the one year would be apt to be misleading, as the price might be high or low?

Mr. Lowry. I think that always, in any figures, you should take a period of years.

Mr. Malby. I agree with you. Now, do your foreign records there refer to any other year than this one, or is it confined to this year.

Mr. Lowry. No. In the first instance it referred to last year, and the other is all this year.

Mr. Malby. The rest of it is all this year?

Mr. Lowry. Yes. To get it properly, the committee should ask the consuls to furnish them the information for five years.

Mr. Malby. I think it would be very much better if you had it so.

Mr. Lowry. I think the result will not be very different from what I learned from the other side.

Mr. Malby. That is all I have to ask.

Mr. Fordney. Mr. Lowry, I will not be more than a few minutes. I will be as brief as I can. In giving your cost, I would like to have the Federal Sugar Refining Co. give the purchases of raw sugar as much in detail as possible during the months of August, September, October, and November of this year. You gave, a little while ago, your estimate of the ad valorem duty on sugar. Was not that what you were figuring on this morning when you were talking?

Mr. LOWRY. Yes. If you will pardon me, I suggested to the chairman when I came here that I put these figures, which are the Government figures, right in the record.

Mr. FORDNEY. I received from the Bureau of Statistics, an hour or two ago, the figures showing importations for the fiscal year ending June 30.

Mr. LOWRY. Last year?

Mr. FORDNEY. This year.

Mr. LOWRY. You see, I took the averages for 10 years previous, and not any one year. The figures are deceptive, because as the price goes up, the percentage itself goes down.

Mr. FORDNEY. There is given here the ad valorem, and this is under present rates of duty. Of course, high rates of duty were charged a few years ago, before we reduced the rate on Cuban sugar or on Philippine sugar, and so on. The average rates were higher. But on all importations, molasses included—free sugar not given—it is 53.96.

Mr. LOWRY. Is that for this year?

Mr. FORDNEY. Yes.

Mr. LOWRY. You see, the figures are deceptive when you take one year. That is why I took 10 years.

Mr. FORDNEY. Why do you say the figures are deceptive?

Mr. LOWRY. Because the prices are high that year, and you have a specific duty, and it makes your percentage lower. On the other hand, it is unfair to take a year when the price is very low. But you have gone back over the period before there was reciprocity with Cuba. Cuban reciprocity was not adopted until 1904 or 1903, I think, so that that would not be a fair average.

Mr. MALBY. I do not think it would make very much difference with Mr. Lowry's figures, because, as I understood him, he figured the higher duty all the time.

Mr. FORDNEY. That is what I say; it would make a vast difference between his figures and the figures given on the duty now collected.

Mr. LOWRY. What did you say were the Government figures?

Mr. FORDNEY. On molasses and everything, 53.96. That is, however, on a rate of 1.65—20 per cent less 1.65—and this is 95 test instead of 96 test. When you go on that test the rate of duty is higher, because there is less sugar contents. If it was 96 it would be less, but being 95 it is only 53.13 per cent; so that I think your figures are high.

Mr. LOWRY. You know, I think it would be very wrong in considering this question to arrive at a conclusion that the American consumer was likely to get sugar cheaper because Cuba had a preferential tariff of 20 per cent. Hawaii is a striking example of where the planters have banded together; and as soon as they do that, and hold back their sugars, they get the benefit of the whole height of the tariff wall. Hawaii is 20 per cent from the top that wall, and as soon as she can hold back her sugars she will get the advantage of that whole 20 per cent and the American will not get it.

Mr. FORDNEY. That is not true of sugar alone. That was done with hides and leather. As soon as the duty was lowered, up went the price.

Mr. LOWRY. We can say, in all fairness, if Cuba sugars were to-day selling at 25 points under the world's value and the preferential rate which Cuba receives is 34 points, the committee would argue—or at least it might be argued—that Cuba was only getting the advantage of the preferential tariff to the extent of 9 points; but we must not overlook the fact that before Cuba had any preferential tariff, when she paid the same rates of duty as any other country, Cuba sugars frequently sold at anywhere from 10 to 25 points under the world's market.

Mr. FORDNEY. Why?

Mr. LOWRY. Because of the pressure to sell and because of the disorganization in Cuba.

Mr. FORDNEY. Was it not because she had no other customer in the world except the refiners in New York and New Orleans?

Mr. LOWRY. When Cuba did not have a preferential tariff? No; she had the world for a customer.

Mr. FORDNEY. She had not any other customer. She has not to-day since we gave her that treaty.

Mr. LOWRY. They do, at times, sell sugar to Europe. Mr. Willett testified to that the other day—that they sold some this year and last year they sold about 102,000 tons.

Mr. FORDNEY. Cuba has not sold 2 per cent of her sugar there.

Mr. MALBY. I was recently in Cuba, in Habana, talking with a prominent gentlemen, a banker there. He told me that the Cuban exporter did not get 34 cents, the real differential, because he sold his sugar in the New York market for about 15 cents less than the world's market. How is that?

Mr. LOWRY. That the Cubans sold their sugars 15 cents less than the world's market, on the average?

Mr. MALBY. Yes.

Mr. LOWRY. The preferential tariff is 34 points, and if the statement is correct that Cuba has sold her sugars at 15 points less than the world's market, then it would indicate that the American consumer had gotten the advantage of 20 points, or 19 points, of that preferential tariff. But you see the point is that Cuba, before she had any preferential tariff, used to sell her sugars at from 10 to 25 points less than the world's market values, so that Cuba is, under those conditions, getting the full advantage of reciprocity. But they do not figure that way down there. I understand why they said that to you.

Mr. FORDNEY. Would the consumer get the benefit of it, or would the refiner in New York get it?

Mr. LOWRY. The margin shows that he got the benefit of it.

Mr. FORDNEY. You take Willett & Gray, and I figured it out at great length, and it showed that the refiner got it all.

Mr. MALBY. The refiners have always said that Cuban raw is, say, 2 cents plus 1.348. As a matter of fact, they did not pay 1.348, but they paid 15 cents less than that to the Cuban; and in all of our calculations it is made a duty of 1.348, whereas, as a matter of fact, the Cuban says he pays 15 cents of that 1.348.

Mr. LOWRY. That man did not mean you to construe it that way, because otherwise it would be a fraud.

Mr. MALBY. What he says is that he gets 15 cents a hundred pounds less than the quotations on the New York market.

Mr. GARRETT. That is, less than the New York market, but that does not necessarily mean 15 cents less than the duty, less than the 1.34, because the world's market is not fixed by the 1.34; it is fixed by the 1.68.

Mr. MALBY. You will remember that the custom in New York was to purchase sugar at the docks in New York at the price that sugar was bringing on that day.

Mr. GARRETT. Yes.

Mr. MALBY. The Cuban says he does not get that price, of the New York market on that day, but that he does get 15 cents less.

Mr. LOWRY. Who pays him that?

Mr. MALBY. All the refineries.

Mr. LOWRY. No; not at all.

Mr. MALBY. I did ask the Federal Sugar Refining Co. to furnish a statement to the committee of what they had actually paid.

Mr. LOWRY. That is in the record.

Mr. FORDNEY. You are still the secretary of this committee of the wholesale grocers' organization?

Mr. LOWRY. So far; yes, sir.

Mr. FORDNEY. You testified here last spring that you were "it"—the whole thing?

Mr. LOWRY. No: I did not mean for you to construe it that way. I do not construe it that way.

Mr. FORDNEY. Well, have conditions changed as to finances, and initiation fees, and dues, and all those things, since the time when you were here last spring?

Mr. LOWRY. No.

Mr. FORDNEY. Does Mr. Spreckles donate all the expenses, pay all the expenses of sending out this literature? That is what you told us before.

Mr. LOWRY. He has been the only subscriber so far.

Mr. FORDNEY. He donates the money and you do the business?

Mr. LOWRY. Yes. It is similar to the association just formed of the beet-sugar men in Chicago, the American Beet Sugar Association. I think that assessed the factories $300 to $400 apiece, and the purpose of the organization, they said, was to prevent the reduction of duties on sugar.

Mr. RAKER. Have you any record of their resolutions?

Mr. FORDNEY. The secretary of that association is in the room.

Mr. RAKER (addressing Mr. Hamlin). You are the secretary of this association organized at Chicago?

Mr. HAMLIN. Yes; and I can give full information on that. I intended, at the close of this hearing, to volunteer that information, in view of Mr. Raker's question to Mr. Willett the other day.

Mr. RAKER. I have been very anxious to get that.

Mr. FORDNEY. Right on that point, Mr. Hamlin, what assessment was made on each factory——

Mr. GARRETT. I beg your pardon, Mr. Fordney; you hardly want to begin taking this gentleman's testimony without his being sworn, do you?

Mr. FORDNEY. Well, I wish you would swear Mr. Hamlin and let him answer my question.

Mr. HAMLIN. I will give you full information on that.

Mr. FORDNEY. Well, let that go at that, then. Mr. Lowry, you have been very industrious—perhaps wisely so—in sending out those circulars in the State of Michigan, and here one of your letters was sent to a factory in that State and the gentleman who received it, who is at the head of the farmers' organization, sent this to me, and he says: "This was sent to our farmers' club. Thought it would interest you. Perhaps you will get signers to the petition—nit. W. C. Mallory." You are still carrying on that campaign, trying to induce the farmers to appeal to their Congressmen to vote for lower rates of duty on sugar? That is the object of the association, is it?

Mr. LOWRY. Yes, sir.

Mr. FORDNEY. You are strongly in favor of a substantial reduction of duty on sugar?

Mr. LOWRY. Strongly.

Mr. FORDNEY. And it was said to-day you are in favor of taking half of it off now, are you?

Mr. LOWRY. Yes.

Mr. FORDNEY. Do you believe that would in any way affect the domestic industry, the cane and beet-sugar industry of the country?

Mr. LOWRY. I do not think it would—materially. It might affect a few factories that are in unfavorable locations, where the costs are very high. I think that it will not materially affect the industry. One gentleman who was on the stand yesterday said he would be willing to put his money into sugar beets in Colorado under free trade.

Mr. FORDNEY. Oh, he was a lawyer representing a lot of farmers, and he came here hostile to the company to which his farmers were selling beets.

Mr. RAKER. Let me ask the witness whether he has talked with any sugar-beet growers in the West who feel that the tariff ought to be reduced half or more, or with any refiners?

Mr. LOWRY. I have talked to the sugar-beet growers who were here, and with some refiners——

Mr. FORDNEY. There is every evidence, Mr. Chairman, that the same snake bit this witness that bit all three of those gentlemen who testified here the other day.

Mr. RAKER. I think that is common all over the country, when it comes to sugar. We find here the same dope that is going out from the organization, getting into the farmers' papers, and then the local papers copy it as coming from the farmers, when it is originated by the organization.

Mr. MALBY. We understand that.

Mr. RAKER. Yes; but the great public do not understand it; that is the trouble.

Mr. FORDNEY. I want this to go into the record at this point, because there is such a volume of the testimony given here that it may be lost in the shuffle—it is in the record already—that during the high prices for sugar this year, when the price was abnormally high, Mr. Spreckels, in an interview, said in so many words that the beet-sugar crop coming onto the market was a godsend to the consumer; that it had a tendency to lower the price. And yet the price of refined sugar manufactured from imported raws fluctuated like wildfire.

Mr. RAKER. That same matter is added to a statement furnished by the organization of the beet-sugar industry. Whether Mr. Spreckels made that statement or not. I do not know. He has been on the stand, and it is contrary to all his statements heretofore made.

Mr. Fordney. No; he testified that sugar was sold for 7.25. And then, when they were closed down and had no sugar to sell, they advertised that they had reduced the price of sugar. But they had none to sell.

Mr. Lowry. Yes; we had in the neighborhood of 32,000 barrels to sell.

Mr. Fordney. You sanctioned Willett & Gray's statement.

Mr. Lowry. They went on to say that we had sugar at consignment points, and it was in the neighborhood of 30,000 barrels. And I might add, about the sugar crop, the farmers' having a scarcity of any crop would have a tendency to raise prices, and the coming in of the Cuban crop would have a tendency to put prices down.

Mr. Fordney. Here we have had this great scarecrow of scarcity of the world's supply of sugar, of failure of the crop in those places from which we get the majority of our sugar, of scarcity and failure in Cuba, reports that the crop is ruined; and the price of sugar has gone away up. Now it is going down. Why? Because our beet-sugar crop is in the market forcing it down.

Mr. Lowry. With an average crop of 400,000 tons.

Mr. Fordney. And all this time Michigan sugar was sold by the Michigan Sugar Co. and all other factories in that State at 5.55.

Mr. Lowry. Is not that because they used bad judgment?

Mr. Fordney. Well, they may be a pack of fools, but they are generally intelligent enough, there in New York.

Mr. Lowry. They sold out at that price because they thought it was a good figure; and I will tell you that they were blamed sorry, when the market got up to 6.50, that they had sold out.

Mr. Fordney. No; it was when sugar was at 6.50 that they were selling it at that.

Mr. Lowry. No; you are wrong on that.

Mr. Fordney. How do you know I am wrong on that? I saw their books.

Mr. Lowry. My business, Mr. Fordney, is to sell sugar, and I keep pretty good track of what is going on.

Mr. Fordney. But you do not know anything about what the Michigan man's mind is, and what his contracts are, or anything about it.

Mr. Lowry. The Michigan man is the same as a man anywhere; he wants to get the highest price he can. He sells his sugar at the highest price he can get for it, and he sells it when the market is right; and if he has misjudged the market he is very sorry.

Mr. Fordney. I have been in the lumber business all my life, and I know something about my own business, but I do not know anything at all about the other man's business. I have got all I can do to look after my own. I do not know why any man fixes prices or how, or what he gets for his product. I can surmise, but I do not know anything about it.

Mr. Fordney. Then I lose my custom.

Mr. Lowry. I tell you in sugar the prices are illustrated, and I can show many market reports reporting Michigan sugars at over 6 cents a pound.

Mr. Fordney. This paper states over 6 cents.

Mr. LOWRY. But they sold out at 5.35, and therefore showed bad judgment.

Mr. FORDNEY. I do not think so; I think it showed good judgment and their heart on the right side.

Mr. LOWRY. The heart did not enter into it at all.

Mr. FORDNEY. They were satisfied with a reasonable profit.

Mr. LOWRY. No; they thought it was not going any higher.

Mr. FORDNEY. Wait a minute. You people in New York do not seem to have that opinion. You force it up to any point you can force it to.

Mr. LOWRY. No——

Mr. FORDNEY. You have said it.

Mr. LOWRY. Do you do that with lumber?

Mr. FORDNEY. Certainly we do, we would be big fools if we did not.

Mr. LOWRY. Then the people in New York are not such fools——

Mr. FORDNEY. But the conditions there are entirely different from the conditions in the sugar business. There is no monopoly in the manufacture of lumber and there is monopoly in the manufacture of refined sugar.

Mr. LOWRY. Do you think that is a fair statement?

Mr. FORDNEY. Absolutely fair.

Mr. LOWRY. Do you not know that the Federal Sugar Refining Co. is an independent company? If you do not, I will tell you so.

Mr. FORDNEY. Oh, yes; but wait a minute. This committee is showing that monopoly controls the majority of the refined sugar put on the market.

Mr. LOWRY. And that same monopoly is heavily interested in beet sugar.

Mr. FORDNEY. Oh, no; it is not heavily interested.

Mr. LOWRY. The record shows it.

Mr. FORDNEY. Oh, no——

Mr. LOWRY. But the point is this——

Mr. FORDNEY. Wait a minute. This committee is going to show, I think, from the testimony presented here, that the Arbuckles and the American Sugar Refining Co. have controlled the market from time to time, and that the Federal Sugar Refining Co. has kept pace with them all the time on prices.

Mr. LOWRY. Then let it also show that the Federal Sugar Co. as recently as Monday of this week, cut the market from 6 cents to 5.65 cents.

Mr. FORDNEY. Without being sarcastic, perhaps they shut down again for repairs.

Mr. LOWRY. You are mistaken about that. I want to say, about prices, that the Federal Sugar Refining Co. has come before this committee and has said: "Take all the duty off of sugar. If you give us free raw sugar, make refined free, make us compete with the world's market, with the foreign refiner, and that will insure the American consumer getting sugar at all times at the world's value."

Mr. FORDNEY. Your company is an independent company and if I am correct, Mr. Lowry, from all the great volume of testimony taken here, there is more watered stock in the Federal Sugar Co.'s organization than any other organization that has been presented here, from any testimony taken. If I am not right on that I want to know it.

Mr. Lowry. As the Federal Sugar Refining Co.'s position on the tariff is to take the duty off, it is not asking the Federal Government to protect it, so it can pay dividends on watered stock which the beet-sugar companies are doing; but I want to call the attention of the committee to this: When I was here last August you said that the Federal Sugar Co., with a capitalization of $3,300,000, produced over 300,000 tons of refined sugar. I want to make the point clear. Take that fact in connection with the statement I made that a cane-sugar factory with $10,000,000 capitalization could produce as much as the total beet-sugar production. If your premises are correct, then a cane-sugar refinery with $10,000,000 real capital at the start should produce three times as much as the Federal Sugar Refining Co., or between 900,000 tons and 1,000,000 tons of sugar as compared with 450,000 as produced by the domestic beet manufacturers in 1910.

Mr. Fordney. I do not remember that argument between you and me.

Mr. Lowry. You will find it in the record.

Mr. Fordney. But your factory runs 12 months in the year and the other fellows run three or four months.

Mr. Raker. You have explained what occasioned the high prices of sugar during July, August, September, and October, up to the middle of November. Now, will you explain to the committee what caused the decline of the prices from the 1st of November?

Mr. Lowry. The freer supply of sugar.

Mr. Raker. From where?

Mr. Lowry. From Louisiana, principally.

Mr. Raker. And from any other place?

Mr. Lowry. No; the supply from Louisiana mainly. There have been more Java sugars arriving, of course; but the main reason——

Mr. Raker. Before you go on, let me ask this: Then the supply that came from Louisiana supplied the market and put sugar on the market immediately and thereby reduced the price. Is that correct?

Mr. Lowry. That is correct. You see the refiners, we will say, in May and June, in estimating on their requirements, say "After a certain period we will have Louisiana sugar." So they only purchased up to that period. If there were not any Louisiana sugars they would purchase in the early months heavily of Java sugars to come in in the fall.

Mr. Raker. I understood from your statement that these men, for instance the American Sugar Refining Co., the Federal Co., as you explained it, and Arbuckle, did not have any sugar on hand; they were behind. The American Sugar Refining Co. was behind a month; you say you were behind 10 days, and Arbuckle was behind 15 or 20 days in their sales, and still they were selling sugar high, and the only sugar they got was that which came——

Mr. Lowry. Not the only sugar.

Mr. Raker. Where else did they get sugars?

Mr. Lowry. Java sugars had been arriving, and Cerrulean, since October.

Mr. RAKER. During November did the Java sugars arrive at the port?

Mr. LOWRY. Yes.

Mr. RAKER. Ready to be refined and delivered?

Mr. LOWRY. Yes.

Mr. RAKER. Was there any from any other place that could be had or was delivered at the ports of New York and Philadelphia and Boston?

Mr. LOWRY. Oh, yes.

Mr. RAKER. During the months of June, July, August, September, and October?

Mr. LOWRY. Yes.

Mr. RAKER. From where?

Mr. LOWRY. There have been Cerrulean and Brazils and, of course, the Hawaiians, coming in all the time to the American Sugar Refining Co.

Mr. RAKER. And the East?

Mr. LOWRY. Yes; and the Philippine sugars have come in. And then, of course, you must also take into consideration that the demand after the 1st of——

Mr. RAKER. I do not care about the demand. I want to get at the actual stuff on hand. There has been testimony about future contracts—the estimates by the jobbers and the brokers—and I would like to get the facts—the physical facts.

Mr. LOWRY. Would you like a statement of the arrivals of all sugars during September and October?

Mr. RAKER. During July, August, September, and October; yes.

Mr. LOWRY. I can furnish such a statement.

Mr. RAKER. Will you do that, please?

Mr. LOWRY. Yes.

Mr. RAKER. During the month of July the sugars began to be put on the market from the beets in California?

Mr. LOWRY. Yes.

Mr. RAKER. And during the months of August and September those shipments were quite heavy?

Mr. LOWRY. Yes.

Mr. RAKER. That was their heaviest run?

Mr. LOWRY. Yes.

Mr. RAKER. And that was the time when the sugars were actually being placed on the market new—practically their whole crop, to say nothing about the crop that had been held over—the sugar in the West was the highest at any time during the year?

Mr. LOWRY. Yes; and here is a statement of a California company showing they got 6½ cents for its output.

Mr. RAKER. Yes. Now, how can you explain the fact that the beet-sugar people reduced the cost of sugar to the consumer?

Mr. LOWRY. I do not explain it, and I do not believe it. They followed the market; that was all.

Mr. RAKER. They were also getting during the same time, during the months named, commencing July up until the middle of November, the cane sugar from the Hawaiian Islands?

Mr. LOWRY. Yes.

Mr. RAKER. Is that right?

Mr. LOWRY. Yes.

Mr. RAKER. Can you give an estimate now of the quantity of cane sugar that came from the Hawaiian Islands to the United States during that time? Just give us a rough estimate.

Mr. LOWRY. My understanding is that about every 10 days a cargo comes in from Hawaii, and those cargoes are about 79,000 tons' capacity, I think.

Mr. RAKER. That is to New York?

Mr. LOWRY. Yes, sir.

Mr. RAKER. And how about the amount that went to the Pacific coast during the same time?

Mr. LOWRY. I am not familiar with that; I presume they shipped a regular amount to both ports, according to the requirements of the refineries that they make a contract with the American Sugar Refining Co.

Mr. RAKER. Did the consumers in the East, or in the West, get any benefit from this large quantity of sugar coming from the Philippines or the Hawaiian Islands or the beet-sugar industry in the West during this high price of sugar?

Mr. LOWRY. No; the producer got all the advantage. The men in Hawaii that sell sugar to the American Sugar Refining Co. got the advantage.

Mr. RAKER. You mean the man that produced the raw sugar?

Mr. LOWRY. Yes.

Mr. RAKER. Not the grower of the product?

Mr. LOWRY. I think in Hawaii——

Mr. RAKER. In Hawaii it would be the grower of the product?

Mr. LOWRY. Yes.

Mr. RAKER. In California, if the grower had made his contract in advance as it has been testified most of them do, he would get no benefit of the raise in price?

Mr. LOWRY. No; the factory would get the benefit of the raise.

Mr. RAKER. The factory would get the benefit of the raise?

Mr. LOWRY. Yes.

Mr. RAKER. And they simply raise their price from 5 to 7½ cents or even 8 cents to the consumer?

Mr. LOWRY. And if the market had gone to 10 they would have come along with it.

Mr. RAKER. That sugar from the West could have been brought into the East by the American Sugar Refining Co. and others by boat, one way being via Panama and another way being by Tehauntepec, and have reduced the price of sugar in the East?

Mr. LOWRY. Did the Hawaiians want to reduce the price of sugar?

Mr. RAKER. No; the American Sugar Refining Co.

Mr. LOWRY. The American Sugar Refining Co. contracts with the Hawaiian planter that they shall pay for the Hawaiian sugars on the basis or close to the basis of the prevailing market price the day of arrival. So the Hawaiian planter as the market advanced kept getting a higher price for the sugars that arrived in New York or San Francisco.

Mr. RAKER. Can you say from your experience as an expert, and from your investigation, that the supply of beet sugar in any way affected the reduction of the price of sugar during the last five months, and if so, what?

Mr. LOWRY. The price of beet sugar at all times was based on the value of foreign sugars, plus the duty and cost of refining, and, of course, it was a supply of sugar and it meant that if that supply had not been there that that much more sugar would have had to come from some other country. But, on the other hand, if that supply had never been there the other countries would have been supplying us with more sugar. So it is the world's value that counts.

Mr. RAKER. Well, not only the world's value; but does it not depend entirely upon the condition of these people having control of the situation, and do they not naturally act just as the situation appears to them; if they can raise it they do it, and they lower it accordingly?

Mr. LOWRY. By these people you mean——

Mr. RAKER. All of them. I take you in, too.

Mr. LOWRY. As we have to take the Federal Sugar Refining Co., as our price of raw sugar advances, of course we want to advance the price of refined. Otherwise we would lose money.

Mr. RAKER. But you had a large supply on hand during July and August and September.

Mr. LOWRY. And if by our foresight we had a large supply on hand we would profit by the advance.

Mr. RAKER. But you have not answered my question. You did have a large supply on hand?

Mr. LOWRY. We did not have as large a supply as we would have liked to have. We profited by the advance.

Mr. RAKER. About how much?

Mr. LOWRY. The Federal Sugar Refining Co., and I think all refining companies, aims to carry or to have bought in advance a stock of in the neighborhood of a month's supply, which we say would be about 30,000 tons.

Mr. RAKER. And how much did you have?

Mr. LOWRY. And we had a little more than that; somewhere between that and 40,000 tons. I am stating it from memory. Then we had a stock of refined sugar which might have amounted to 100,000 barrels.

Mr. RAKER. Now, as a matter of fact, not throwing any aspersion on any one, you folks had a large quantity of sugar on hand during this high price of sugar to commence with, that you bought at low price?

Mr. LOWRY. We had a very fair stock; yes.

Mr. RAKER. Now, you folks did not make any attempt or pretense to lower the price of sugar when it was going up, did you?

Mr. LOWRY. No. We went along with the market and made the extra profit, and were glad to do it. In fact we bought the sugar in advance because we thought the market was going up and wanted to take advantage of it, just as when we thought the market was going to break, when it was near the top, we closed down and saved about half a cent a pound on our raw sugars. The raw sugar went down about half a cent, and then we came in again. We think that is good business.

Mr. RAKER. In other words, you mean by "good business" that the large interests, as the sugar interests appear, and in a few hands, raise and lower the price of sugar so that it will give the manufacturer and refiner of beet sugar all that the public will stand. That is about it, is it not, in rough words?

Mr. LOWRY. Have it bear all the traffic will bear?

Mr. RAKER. Yes; that is about the situation, is it not?

Mr. LOWRY. That is about the situation. In asking to have the duties removed we say we are willing for you to see that the traffic will not bear too much for the consumer. That would protect him absolutely.

Mr. RAKER. Have you in your own mind any plan by which the situation could be changed from the way it has been for the last 10 years in the sugar markets? Have you studied out any plan that would bring a more equal price of sugar to the consumer?

Mr. LOWRY. My opinion is that that would be entirely regulated by the duty, absolutely.

Mr. RAKER. And no other method?

Mr. LOWRY. No other method. I believe if you remove the duty from raw and refined sugar, have no duty at all on either, that this entire industry of the United States could be combined, put under one head, have one man at the head of it, and the consumer would never have to pay for his sugar more than the world's value; because as soon as they attempted to put the price up we would come into competition with the foreign refiners and down would go the market.

Mr. RAKER. Well, that would not be quite fair under present conditions to the Government. Proceeding on the idea that we would have to have some revenue, have you any plan?

Mr. LOWRY. The best plan is the one I stated a while ago. I think that is very sound.

Mr. FORDNEY. May I interrupt?

Mr. RAKER. Yes; at any time.

Mr. FORDNEY. Mr. Chairman, I would have this information put into the record here at this point, and I read from page 2521 of the proceedings a statement made by Mr. Spreckles on July 29, 1911. He states that the Federal Sugar Refining Co., incorporated June 18, 1902, in the State of New Jersey; that it was organized with a capital of $100,000. On July 2, 1902, the certificate of incorporation was amended to make the capital stock $50,000,000, of which $25,000,000 was preferred and $25,000,000 common stock. That capital was again changed to $20,000,000 preferred and $30,000,000 common. On February 18, 1905, the certificate of incorporation was again amended to reduce the preferred stock to $10,000,000 and the common stock to $15,000,000.

On May 3, 1907, the Federal Sugar Refining Co. was incorporated under the laws of the State of New York, with the consent of the Jersey corporation of the same name. The capital stock of this corporation was $10,000,000, consisting of $3,322,800 preferred stock, and $6,677,200 of common stock, showing that this company never had more than $3,322,800 capital paid in, but was organized with a capital stock of $25,000,000 preferred and $25,000,000 common.

Mr. LOWRY. Might I state right there that when we organized the company the plans were very different from those finally carried out, the original plan being to work under a new process and to establish small refineries throughout the country.

Mr. FORDNEY. So far as the public knew, so far as the facts show, there never was a time when the capital consisted of more than $3,322,800—$25,000,000 of it preferred and nearly $25,000,000 of it water, and all of the common stock, $25,000,000, water. That is a pretty good-sized bundle of water. It beats anything in history, I believe.

Mr. LOWRY. Oh, no.

Mr. FORDNEY. Anything that ever came to my notice.

Mr. LOWRY. The stock of the American Federal Sugar Refining Co., I might mention, has always been very closely held. The few people that went into the company originally own by far the majority of the stock, and always have, and the public has never dealt in it generally. So, so far as this is concerned, it seems to me that the capital could have been continued at $100,000,000 and the public could have bought that stock if it wanted to, and the Federal Sugar Refining Co. is not asking the United States Government to arrange a tariff law which will enable them to pay dividends on any excessive stock.

Mr. FORDNEY. That is just what you are asking for when you are asking for a reduction of the duty on sugar, and nothing else, my friend.

Mr. LOWRY. I do not agree with you.

Mr. FORDNEY. What do you want it for if it is not to benefit you? Are you doing all this work and spending $12,000,000 advertising for the benefit of the consumers? Answer that question. Are you doing it all for the consumer and nothing for the Spreckles family or youself?

Mr. LOWRY. The Federal Sugar Refining Co. wants a reduction of the duties on sugar for the same reason that the consumer and grocer want the reduction. They want to do a larger business at a reduced expense.

Mr. FORDNEY. In other words, you want to make greater profit with less capital?

Mr. LOWRY. And if we refer to the American Sugar Refining Co.'s last statement—and the American Sugar Refining Co. is the Federal Sugar Refining Co.'s largest competitor—we will see that the American Sugar Refining Co. made out of operation $3,077,143.03. They require, to pay dividends, $6,299,958.

Mr. FORDNEY. When and where and how much?

Mr. LOWRY. That was the year 1910. That shows that the American Sugar Refining Co., from operation in competition with the Federal Sugar Refining Co., in operation did not make its dividends; but from outside investments which the American Sugar Refining Co. had, and which are generally understood to be largely in beet-sugar factories, the American Sugar Refining Co. made $2,273,473.22. That money was not made by superior management. It was made because the Government has a high tariff on sugar and practically put that bounty or subsidy into their laps.

Mr. FORDNEY. Let me ask you this: Do you mean to say by that statement now that the American Sugar Refining Co. made a profit in the beet-sugar factories and paid dividends on their stock in refineries that refined foreign imported sugar?

Mr. LOWRY. That is what it shows.

Mr. FORDNEY. Now, do you not know from the statements of the beet-sugar factories of the dividends paid by them, if they are right—and they testified under oath—that no such thing exists at all?

Mr. LOWRY. No such thing as the American Sugar Refining Co. getting dividends from the——

Mr. FORDNEY. No; but taking their profits out that they make from the beet-sugar companies and paying dividends on the stock in the refineries in New York, that they did not make it out of the refineries, but made it out of the beet-sugar factories and paid a dividend on the stock held in the refining companies?

Mr. LOWRY. If the American Sugar Refining Co. receives a dividend from the Great Western Sugar Co. and the Michigan Sugar Co., for example, they would naturally apply that dividend to the stockholders of the American Sugar Refining Co.

Mr. FORDNEY. Oh, I beg to differ with you.

Mr. LOWRY. What would they do?

Mr. FORDNEY. Oh, I see your point. They would apply it to the people who held the stock in those various factories.

Mr. LOWRY. If the American Sugar Refining Co. held the stock, then this dividend would come to the stockholders of the American Sugar Refining Co.

Mr. MALBY. Of course the American Sugar Refining Co. owns stock in the subsidiary companies, and they simply receive dividends on that.

Mr. FORDNEY. But what he said is that the profits made on the real, genuine mother company of the American Sugar Refining Co. were not sufficient to pay dividends on that capital invested, but that they have made money out of their investments in the beet-sugar factories and paid dividends on stock in the mother company—the old original American Sugar Refining Co.

Mr. LOWRY. That is what the statement shows.

Mr. FORDNEY. Is that correct?

Mr. LOWRY. Yes.

Mr. FORDNEY. Who made the statement?

Mr. LOWRY. The American Sugar Refining Co. You have it in the record.

Mr. FORDNEY. Do you not know that the testimony given before this committee—and you have listened to it or read it all in detail no doubt more than once—that the testimony shows that they have not received more than about a 6 per cent dividend on their investment in those beet-sugar factories?

Mr. LOWRY. Well, was not that distributed among the stockholders of the American Sugar Refining Co.?

Mr. FORDNEY. I do not want to argue that any longer. You will not see that point.

Mr. MALBY. Well, that is not quite a correct statement, I think you will admit. Your statement in substance is that out of the surplus which the American Sugar Refining Co. has heretofore made in the years gone by, that they purchased their interest in the various beet-sugar factories, and that hence they are looking to these former investments to now pay dividends on the American Sugar Refining Co.'s stock. That is not quite according to the exact testimony which we have, which is that the American Sugar Refining Co. increased its capital stock from $75,000,000 to $90,000,000, and out of that $15,000,000 increase of capital stock they have purchased interests in various beet-sugar companies. So that really they were receiving interest, so to speak, on simply an investment which accrued in an industry which they had purchased by issuing stock of their own company. In other words, it was paying interest simply on their increased capitalization, and scarcely that, because the amount received was about 6 per cent——

Mr. LOWRY. The point I want to make is that the American Sugar Refining Co. has $90,000,000 of stock and that they themselves will tell you, as they have told others, that they would have been badly in the hole last year had it not been for their earnings from beet-sugar factories on the Pacific coast.

Mr. MALBY. I know that has a bearing, but at the same time it must be remembered that they acquired beet-sugar factories by the issuing of stock of their own companies. Otherwise they would not have that obligation to-day.

Mr. FORDNEY. How could 6 per cent, which is about the amount they receive on the $15,000,000 invested in beet-sugar factories, aid materially in the $75,000,000 capital in the old company?

Mr. MALBY. Well, the answer to that is, Mr. Fordney, that the beet-sugar companies all told, as I recall it, are carried on the books of the American Sugar Refining Co. at about $16,000,000—their increase in capital stock was $15,000,000; so that when they got their interest at 6 per cent they did not get enough out of the $16,000,000, they did not get enough, quite, at 6 per cent, to pay the 7 per cent on the stock which they took over from these other companies.

Mr. FORDNEY. I want to beg the pardon of the committee for trespassing on the time of the committee so long.

Mr. GARRETT (acting chairman). That is all right, I am sure. Have you finished, Mr. Fordney?

Mr. FORDNEY. Yes; I am though, and ready to quit.

Mr. MALBY. There is one question here that we asked Mr. Spreckels when he was on the stand which perhaps Mr. Lowry can give us some light on. He was requested to furnish the price of raw and refined sugar in London and Hamburg from 1895 to 1910.

Mr. LOWRY. Yes; I furnished that. I was asked the same thing. I believe Mr. Spreckels did not furnish it.

Mr. MALBY. Is it in the record?

Mr. LOWRY. Yes it is all in the record. You will find all of that in volume No. 3 of the testimony.

Mr. MALBY. Under date of July 19, Mr. Spreckels says that he has been unable to get that information, but that he would do it later.

Mr. LOWRY. Well, I did not confer with Mr. Spreckels about it; but you asked me to supply it, and you will find it in the record as I have stated.

Mr. MALBY. You are sure that has been furnished?

Mr. LOWRY. Yes; it is in volume No. 3.

Mr. MALBY. Look at page 2896 and see if that is your exhibit.

Mr. LOWRY. Yes; that is it.

Mr. MALBY. That is the one?

Mr. LOWRY. That is the one; yes.

Mr. MALBY. All right. That is all.

Mr. GARRETT (acting chairman). The committee will excuse you, Mr. Lowry.

Mr. LOWRY. Just a moment. There was a question that came up about freight rates from the beet-sugar factories to distributing centers, and I had that table made up; and I understood the chairman wanted it to go into the record. I perhaps should have spoken to him.

Mr. MALBY. The freight rates from the sugar-beet factory——

Mr. LOWRY. Yes; it gives freight rates from the various sugar-beet factories to various distributing centers. Whether it is important or not I do not know.

Mr. GARRETT. You understood the chairman desired it?

Mr. LOWRY. Yes.

Mr. MALBY. Is it correct as you have it there?

Mr. LOWRY. Yes; I believe it to be correct.

Mr. GARRETT. Did you have this prepared by your freight man?

Mr. LOWRY. It was prepared by our traffic manager. There was some question as to whether we should put him on the stand, and the chairman said that that would not be necessary if we would have it made up and if I would state that it was correct.

Mr. GARRETT. All right. Is there anything further, Mr. Lowry?

Mr. LOWRY. That is all.

Mr. GARRETT. Very well, we will excuse you, then.

(The table submitted by Mr. Lowry is as follows:)

Freight rates on granulated sugar (carloads).

From—	To—													
	Louisville, Ky.	Detroit, Mich.	Buffalo, N. Y.	Pittsburgh, Pa.	Chicago, Ill.	St. Louis, Mo.	Missouri River points.	Denver, Colo.	Salt Lake City, Utah.	Spokane, Wash.	Billings, Mont.	Phoenix, Ariz.	Portland, Oreg.	San Francisco, Cal.
Caro, Mich.	$0.16	$0.09½	$0.15	$0.15	$0.11	$0.16	$0.38	$0.78	$1.44	.....	.....	.....	.....	.....
Carrollton, Mich.	.16	.10	.15	.15	.11	.16	.38	.78	1.44	.....	.....	.....	.....	.....
Bay City, Mich.	.16	.10	.15	.15	.11	.16	.38	.78	1.44	.....	.....	.....	.....	.....
Alma, Mich.	.16	.10	.15	.15	.11	.16	.38	.78	1.44	.....	.....	.....	.....	.....
Crosswell, Mich.	.16	.10	.13	.15	.11	.16	.38	.78	1.44	.....	.....	.....	.....	.....
Holland, Mich.	.16	.10	.15½	.15½	.11	.16	.38	.78	1.44	.....	.....	.....	.....	.....
St. Louis, Mich.	.16	.10	.15	.15	.11	.16	.38	.78	1.44	.....	.....	.....	.....	.....
Charlevoix, Mich.	.25	.15½	.18	.25	.11	.26	.38	.78	1.44	.....	.....	.....	.....	.....
Swink, Colo.	.....	[1] .48 [2] .38	.....	[1] .52½ [2] .43	[1] .35 [2] .25	[1] .30 [2] .25	.25	.15	.94½	$1.35	$1.05	$1.12	$1.60	$0.85
Rocky Ford, Colo.	.....	[1] .48 [2] .38	.....	[1] .52½ [2] .43	[1] .35 [2] .25	[1] .30 [2] .25	.25	.15	.94½	1.35	1.05	1.12	1.60	.85
Loveland, Colo. Longmont, Colo.	.....	.....	.....	.....	[1] .35 [2] .25	[1] .30 [2] .25	.25	.10	.79½	1.20	.90	1.12	1.60	.85
Logan, Utah	.....	.....	.....	.....	.....	.....	.....	.....	[1] .15	1.20	1.24	1.84½	1.09	1.01½
Ogden, Utah	.....	[1] .73 [2] .63	.....	[1] .78 [2] .68	[1] .60 [2] .50	[1] .55 [2] .50	[1] .55 [2] .50	[1] .55 [2] .50	[1] .15 [2] .12	1.09	1.24	1.69½	.94	.79½
Garland, Utah	.....	.....	.....	.....	.....	.....	.....	.....	[1] .15	1.10	1.24	1.84½	1.10	.97½
Alvarado, Cal.	.....	.....	.....	.....	.....	.....	.....	.....	.79½	.78	.....	1.00	.20	.05
Betteravia, Cal.	.....	.....	.....	.....	.....	.....	.....	.....	.....	.88	.....	1.00	.30	.15
Oxnard, Cal.	.....	[1] .65	.....	.....	[1] .65	[1] .65	[1] .60	[1] .60	[1] .60	1.02½	[1] .93	.96	.47½	.25
Spreckels, Cal.	.....	[2] .55	.....	.....	[2] .55	[2] .55	[2] .55	[2] .55	[2] .55	.85½	[2] .85	1.00	.27½	.07
San Francisco, Cal.	.....	.....	.....	.....	.....	.....	.....	.....	.79½	.75	.....	1.00	.20	.....
New York, N. Y.	.21	.18	.14	.16	.23	.23	.38	.71	1.27	1.64	1.29	1.67	[3] 1.88	[3] 1.08 [4] .75
Philadelphia, Pa.	.19	.16	.14	.14	.21	.21	.36	.71	1.27	1.62	1.27	1.67	[3] 1.86	[3] 1.06
New Orleans, La.	.17	.23	.....	.....	.23	.17	.32	.62	1.45	1.63	.....	1.43	1.65	.85

[1] 33,000 pounds. [2] 60,000 pounds. [3] Rail. [4] Water.

TESTIMONY OF MR. C. C. HAMLIN.

(The witness was sworn by the acting chairman.)

Mr. FORDNEY. Mr. Hamlin, will you please state to the committee whether or not you are secretary of this beet-sugar association that was recently organized in Chicago?

Mr. HAMLIN. As a manufacturer and one of the executive officers of a beet-sugar company, I am chairman and a member of the executive committee. I am vice president of the United States Sugar & Land Co. in western Kansas, an entirely independent company.

Mr. FORDNEY. What is the name of this organization?

Mr. HAMLIN. The United States Beet-Sugar Industry. Our meeting, which Mr. Raker referred to and asked about the other day, was held in Chicago on November 15.

Mr. FORDNEY. What assessment for the maintenance of your organization is made?

Mr. HAMLIN. I would like to go fully into the purposes of the organization.

Mr. FORDNEY. I was going to ask you further about it, but I would like to know what initiation fees and so on are paid. I do not want to prolong this, Mr. Chairman, in the slightest.

Mr. GARRETT. Well, the witness says that he would like to go into it fully.

Mr. HAMLIN. If you only have a few minutes to hear me now, I would prefer to come back some other time.

Mr. GARRETT. After the holidays?

Mr. HAMLIN. Yes; but I can probably state the purposes briefly. I want to say that this inquiry for the last two days here, going into matters surrounding the agricultural end of the business, and then the refiners coming in and being heard on the tariff end of it, opens up a very broad field of inquiry, and I feel, as an independent operator, that if these matters are going to be considered by this committee, that there ought to be a full hearing upon them.

Mr. FORDNEY. Perhaps you had better come back at another time, and I would suggest in the meantime you prepare a statement of the purposes and object of that association, to have it ready at that time.

Mr. MALBY. He can, no doubt, give it offhand when he appears before the committee again.

Mr. GARRETT. We will hear you right after the holidays, then.

Mr. HAMLIN. I would be glad to make a full statement at that time. We have nothing to conceal, and I would like to make a perfectly open and complete statement.

Mr. GARRETT. The committee will stand adjourned, subject to the call of the chairman.

(Thereupon, at 4.40 p. m., the committee adjourned.)

AMERICAN SUGAR REFINING CO. AND OTHERS.

SPECIAL COMMITTEE ON THE INVESTIGATION
OF THE AMERICAN SUGAR REFINING CO. AND OTHERS,
HOUSE OF REPRESENTATIVES,
Washington, D. C., January 9, 1912.

The committee met at 10 o'clock a. m., Hon. Thomas W. Hardwick (chairman) presiding.

The CHAIRMAN. Gentlemen, I want to put in the record at this time certain letters which, by direction of the committee, were sent during my absence to the different sugar refining companies and to the different beet-sugar factories to obtain certain information.

WASHINGTON, D. C., *December 13, 1911.*

AMERICAN SUGAR REFINING CO.,
New York City, N. Y.

GENTLEMEN: The special committee appointed under House resolution 157, to investigate violations of the antitrust act of July 2, 1890, desire the following information, for the use of the committee, not later than January 1, 1912, which shall be sworn to before an officer authorized to administer oaths by some person of your company who has actual knowledge of the facts desired, and respectfully request that this information be given by said time:

(*a*) A sworn statement showing the actual cost of refining sugar during each of the past five years, such cost of refining to show each and every item of cost exclusive of all charges for depreciation of the refineries and interest on investment.

(*b*) Date of each purchase of raw; name of country or State in which raw sugar thus purchased was produced; number of pounds covered by each purchased; actual dates of deliveries of each purchase, with the number of pounds delivered at each date of delivery; price paid by buyer per hundred pounds, delivered at the refinery, for each such purchase, said price to include actual duty paid.

(*c*) Stock of raw sugar on hand on July 1, 1911, together with the cost of same per hundred pounds.

(*d*) Entire amount of raw sugar bought or contracted for but not actually delivered, on July 1, 1911, said amount to include all raw sugars bought or contracted for and in transit on July 1, 1911, together with the cost of same per hundred pounds; also the actual dates of delivery of all such sugar.

(*e*) Number of pounds of refined sugar in stock owned by deponent on July 1, 1911, such amount of refined sugar to include the total refined stocks of deponent wherever stored, provided the same was not actually invoiced to the buyer on July 1, 1911.

(*f*) Number of pounds of refined sugar actually sold to bona fide purchasers, but not invoiced, on July 1, 1911.

Please let it appear in the body of the affidavit that the person making the same has full knowledge of the facts testified to, and in such combined form as to cover all your various refineries, and shall state the name and location of each.

Trusting that the committee may be favored with the above information by the time suggested, I am,

Respectfully,

FINIS J. GARRETT,
Acting Chairman.

WASHINGTON, D. C., *December 14, 1911.*

Mr. C. S. MOREY,
President Great Western Sugar Refining Co.,
Denver, Colo.

DEAR SIR: The special committee appointed under House resolution 157, to investigate violations of the antitrust act of July 2, 1890, desire the following information for the use of the committee not later than January 1, 1912, which shall be sworn to before some officer authorized to administer oaths by some person of your company who has the actual knowledge of the facts desired, and I respectfully ask that you have the same furnished the committee on or before said time: (1) Tons of beets sliced; (2) average sugar test; (3) sugar extraction per ton of beets sliced; (4) average price paid for beets; (5) cost of manufacture, subdivided as follows: (*a*) Cost of raw material; (*b*) factory cost; (*c*) overhead administration charges; (*d*) taxes and insurance.

Second. A statement showing the actual cost of refining sugar for each of your factories during the past five years in consolidated form, except interest on investment, depreciation of plant, and cost of selling.

Third. (*a*) Number of pounds of refined sugar in stock owned by your company on July 1, 1911, such amount of refined sugar to include the total refined stock of your company wherever stored, provided the same were not actually invoiced to the buyer on July 1, 1911.

(*b*) Number of pounds of refined sugar actually sold to bona fide purchasers but not invoiced on July 1, 1911.

In this connection I wish to ask that you let it appear in the body of the affidavit that the person making the same has full knowledge of the facts testified to, and that the same be in such combined form as to cover all your various refineries, together with the name and location of each.

I shall thank you to furnish this information to the committee not later than January 1, 1912.

Very truly, yours,

FINIS J. GARRETT,
Acting Chairman.

DECEMBER 14, 1911.

MICHIGAN SUGAR REFINING CO.,
Detroit, Mich.

GENTLEMEN: The special committee appointed under House resolution 157, to investigate violations of the antitrust act of July 2, 1890, desire the following information for the use of the committee not later than January 1, 1912, which shall be sworn to, before some officer authorized to administer oaths, by some person of your company who has actual knowledge of the facts desired, and I respectfully ask that you have the same furnished the committee on or before said time: (1) Tons of beets sliced; (2) average sugar test; (3) sugar extraction per ton of beets sliced; (4) average price paid for beets; (5) cost of manufacture, subdivided as follows: (*a*) Cost of raw material; (*b*) factory cost; (*c*) overhead or administration charges; (*d*) taxes and insurance.

Second. A statement showing the actual cost of refining sugar for each of your factories during the pass five years in consolidated form, except interest on investment, depreciation of plant, and cost of selling.

Third. (*a*) Number of pounds of refined sugar in stock owned by your company on July 1, 1911, such amount of refined sugar to include the total refined stock of your company, wherever stored, provided the same were not actually invoiced to the buyer on July 1, 1911.

(*b*) Number of pounds of refined sugar actually sold to bona fide purchasers but not invoiced on July 1, 1911.

(*c*) The number of tons of sugar beets imported from Canada by each and all of your factories from January 1, 1911, to September 1, 1911, the dates of each importation, and the number of tons imported each time.

In this connection I wish to ask that you have it appear in the body of the affidavit that the person making the same has full knowledge of the facts testified to, that the same be in such combined form as to cover all your various refineries, together with name and location of each.

I shall thank you to furnish this information to the committee not later than January 1, 1912.

Respectfully,

FINIS J. GARRETT,
Acting Chairman.

VARIOUS LETTERS WITHOUT STATEMENTS.

MOUNT CLEMENS SUGAR CO.,
Mount Clemens, Mich., December 26, 1911.

Mr. FINIS J. GARRETT,
Acting Chairman Special Committee,
House of Representatives, Washington, D. C.

DEAR SIR: We acknowledge due receipt of your valued favor of the 14th instant. Your letter has also been referred to Capt. James Davidson, president of this company, who has looked into the matter very carefully, and beg to advise we are now in the middle of our campaign and will be very busy until about March 1, and before that time it would be impracticable to furnish the information you desire. Later on, however, we would be very glad indeed to take this matter up, gather the data, and make a five-year statement for you as requested. This is an independent company, operated by James Davidson, of Bay City, Mich., has very few stockholders, the stock being owned principally by James and James E. Davidson, and we are very glad indeed to note that a committee has been appointed under House resolution to investigate the violations of the antitrust act.

Trusting this will meet with your requirements, we remain,

Yours, very truly,

GEO. ELSEY, Jr.,
General Manager.

NEW YORK, *December 27, 1911.*

Hon. FINIS J. GARRETT,
Acting Chairman Special Committee on the
Investigation of the American Sugar Refining Co. and Others.

DEAR SIR: Your letter of December 14, asking for the information mentioned therein, has been received.

We apprehend that you are aware of the extent of the work required to furnish this information. We hope to give you answers to the inquiries under the subheads *b, c, d, e,* and *f* within a few weeks. As to the information under the subhead *a*, this will take quite some time to prepare and tabulate.

You are probably aware that this is a very busy period of the fiscal year for us, but notwithstanding this we are giving your request careful attention.

Very respectfully, yours,

THE NATIONAL SUGAR REFINING CO. OF NEW JERSEY,
By JAMES H. POST, *President.*

AMALGAMATED SUGAR CO.,
Ogden, Utah, December 20, 1911.

Hon. FINIS J. GARRETT,
Acting Chairman, House of Representatives, Washington, D. C.

MY DEAR SIR: Replying to yours of December 14, just received, requesting certain information on behalf of a special committee appointed under House resolution 157, to investigate the violation of the antitrust act, desire to say that during the night of November 15–16, 1911, the office building of the Amalgamated Sugar Co. and Lewiston Sugar Co., at Ogden City, Utah, had a very disastrous fire, resulting in the utter destruction of the building and its contents. We saved nothing, excepting the current books, and consequently are in no position to give you the information requested. It is possible, however, that by gathering data from the different factories, printed reports, etc., we might be able to get together a great deal of the information you desire, and I shall immediately take steps to secure the same, but it will be wholly impossible to furnish it to the committee on the date named, and when furnished, of course, it will be based on the best hearsay evidence we can get.

Trusting that this will excuse my noncompliance, I remain,

Yours, very truly,

HENRY H. ROLOFF, *Secretary.*

NEW YORK, *December 19, 1911.*

Hon. F. J. GARRETT,
Acting Chairman, Washington, D. C.

DEAR SIR: We beg to acknowledge receipt of your favor of the 13th instant and have noted your request carefully. The letter in question has been submitted to our counsel and we will communicate with you as soon as we hear from him on the subject.

The data required, if given as requested, could not be furnished by January 1.

We beg to remain,

Yours, very truly,

ARBUCKLE BROS.

NATIONAL SUGAR MANUFACTURING CO.,
Baltimore, Md., January 2, 1912.

Mr. FINIS J. GARRETT,
Acting Chairman Special Committee, House of Representatives.

DEAR SIR: Your letter of the 14th ultimo asking for certain information was duly received.

The advent of the holidays in the meantime have prevented close application to the preparation of the figures you desire, but the same are nearing completion and will be mailed to you so that you will receive them about the 4th or 5th instant.

Yours, very truly,

JOHN H. WINDFELDER,
President and General Manager.

CONTINENTAL SUGAR CO.,
Cleveland, Ohio, December 19, 1911.

Hon. FINIS J. GARRETT,
Acting Chairman Special Committee, House of Representatives.

SIR: Acknowledging yours of the 14th instant addressed to our Blissfield office, we shall be very glad to place any information before your committee that may be of value, but suggest that your very comprehensive specifications are extremely difficult and even impossible to prepare at the present time. We are in the height of our campaign, but have not received all of our beets. Our tests are not yet an average for sugar content, extraction, or average price. The cost of manufacture is necessarily incomplete and the factory costs require inventory to arrive at the total consumption and average cost. We have not yet completed our total production, and, altogether, it is physically impossible to give you results for the current campaign.

We have been subpœnaed to appear before the United States district court in New York on January 2 covering the early years of our operations, and it would seem as if the records of that court should furnish your committee all of the information you desire. We shall, however, be very glad to be of any assistance possible to you at any time when it is possibly practicable to furnish it.

Very truly, yours,

CONTINENTAL SUGAR CO.,
By FRED T. SHOLES, *Secretary.*

WASHINGTON, D. C., *January 5, 1912.*

Hon. THOMAS W. HARDWICK,
Chairman Special Committee, House of Representatives.

DEAR SIR: I beg to inclose herewith letter from the Speckels Sugar Co., explaining their delay in submitting statement of cost of production. The letter is addressed to Mr. Garrett, but he has requested me to forward it to you, as he informs me you are in town.

Very truly, yours,

HARRY A. AUSTIN,
Private Secretary.

SAN FRANCISCO, CAL., *December 30, 1911.*

Hon. FINIS J. GARRETT,
Acting Chairman Special Committee, Washington, D. C.

DEAR SIR: Owing to the limited amount of time available, we have been unable to prepare the statement asked for in your letter of December 14 in time to have it reach you by January 1, the time specified in your letter It will be mailed, however, not later than next Tuesday, January 2.

We regret very much that the statement will not be in your hands earlier, but under the circumstances it could not be avoided.

Yours, truly,

Spreckels Sugar Co.,
By H. E. Jones, *Office Manager.*

American Sugar Refining Co.,
New York, January 2, 1912.

Hon. Finis J. Garrett,
Acting Chairman Sugar Investigating Committee, Washington, D. C.

Dear Sir: Replying to your valued favor of December 13, the company takes pleasure in sending an affidavit as requested, covering in detail the information sought, so far as has been possible to secure the same within the time provided in your letter.

Very truly, yours,

J. E. Freeman.

The United States of America. In the House of Representatives. In the matter of the investigation of the American Sugar Refining Co. and others by a select committee of the House of Representatives, appointed under House resolution No. 157.

State of New York,
County of New York, ss:

W. Edward Foster, being duly sworn, deposes and says: That he resides in Hackensack, N. J., and is the comptroller of the American Sugar Refining Co. above named; that he has read the letter addressed to said company under date of December 13, 1911, by Hon. Finis J. Garrett, acting chairman of the said committee, and requesting certain information for the use of said committee; that the statements herein contained are within the personal knowledge of deponent in the sense that they are based upon, or compiled from, facts and figures returned to the comptroller's department from different branches of the business of said company.

Referring to the paragraphs of said letter marked (*c*), (*d*), (*e*), and (*f*), the stock of raw sugar owned by said company and actually on hand on July 1, 1911, was 137,382 tons, of which the average cost was 3.85 cents net per pound for 96° centrifugals. This amount of raw sugar was equivalent when melted to 125,000 tons of refined sugar. On said date of July 1, 1911, the company had also bought to arrive 168,972 tons of raw sugar at an average cost of 3.94 cents net per pound for 96° centrifugals, which last-mentioned raw sugar so bought arrived at various dates during the months of July and August last, and when melted produced about 150,000 tons of refined sugar. On July 1, 1911, the company also had on hand at all points 51,273 tons of refined sugar not already invoiced to purchasers. To the foregoing should be added the Hawaiian raw sugar hereinafter referred to. It thus appears that, excluding said Hawaiian sugar, the total stock of raw and refined sugar on hand or to arrive July 1, 1911, was the equivalent of 326,273 tons of refined sugar. Inasmuch as the meltings of the company during July were 156,000 tons of raw, and during August were 135,000 tons of raw, it appears that the entire raw stock on hand and to arrive on July 1, 1911 (excluding as aforesaid Hawaiian sugars), was slightly in excess of two months' melting.

The office of the company was closed July 1 to July 4, 1911, inclusive. Including July 5 and 6, the total sales of refined sugar up to July 6, 1911, not previously invoiced were 1,473,975 barrels, or 230,000 tons, of which 482,362 barrels had been sold for future delivery at an average of 4.81 cents per pound net, and the balance, 991,613, at an average of 4.90 cents net. It is thus apparent that by July 6, 1911, there had been sold for future delivery an amount of refined sugar equivalent to about two-thirds of the entire stock of raw and refined sugar which said company had on hand or to arrive on July 1, as aforesaid (except Hawaiian sugars). Such refined sugar had been sold from time to time at the market prices prevailing before the setting in of the advance due to the partial failure of the European beet sugar crop. The remainder of the sugar on hand or to arrive on July 1, 1911, as aforesaid (excluding Hawaiian sugars), or, say, 96,273 tons, was sold for future deliveries at various dates during the following months at the prices fixed by the company for its own sales on the said dates.

In addition to the supply of raw sugar on hand or to arrive which the company had on July 1 last, as above specified, the company was on that date under contract to receive shipment of Hawaiian raw sugars which were to be, and which were, paid for at a price based on the current price prevailing at New York for 96° centrifugal sugars, duty paid, on the day before the arrival of the vessel carrying the cargo. The following list shows the amounts of such sugars received, together with the price of the same to the American Sugar Refining Co.:

	Tons.	Price (cents per pound).
1911.		
July	22,950	4.14
August	40,158	4.77
September	27,962	5.59
October	36,399	5.75
November	10,485	5.11
December	3,578	4.96
Total	141,532	[1] 5.11

[1] Average price.

These Hawaiian raw sugars were for the most part melted gradually in the regular course of business, during the months ensuing their arrival, but some of them are still on hand. The refined sugar resulting from their melting was sold from time to time as the prices fixed by the company for its own sales.

W. EDWARD FOSTER.

Subscribed and sworn to before me this 2d day of January, 1912.

[SEAL.]

JNO. H. THOMPSON,
Notary Public, Kings County, N. Y.

Certificate filed in New York County.

SACRAMENTO VALLEY SUGAR CO.,
Hamilton City, Cal., December 29, 1911.

Mr. THOMAS W. HARDWICK,
Washington, D. C.

HONORABLE SIR: In reply to letter of December 14 by Mr. Gorsett, acting chairman, I herewith inclose the requested answers.

I am sorry that this will not reach you by January 1, 1912, as requested, but it was impossible for me to get this off sooner owing to my having been absent from here and only receiving your letter a few days since.

Yours, very truly,

E. B. HAMILTUS, *Manager.*

Report Sacramento Valley Sugar Co.'s factory, located at Hamilton, Glenn County, Cal.

	1907	1908	1909	1910	1911
(1) Tons (2,000 pounds) of beets sliced	19,821	23,513	34,064	36,005	55,499
(2) Average sugar test (sugar and purity):					
Sugar	16.7	16.4	16.4	19.5	17.3
Purity	82.2	81.5	81.8	83.4	82.5
(3) Pounds granulated sugar extraction per ton of sliced beets	261.6	266.7	275.9	338.8	280.7
(4) Average price paid for beets per ton (2,000 pounds)	$5.03	$5.51	$5.75	$5.88	$5.92
COST OF MANUFACTURE.					
(a) Cost of raw material per ton of beets	$5.81	$6.21	$6.34	$6.50	$6.98
(b) Factory cost do	$6.03	$5.44	$4.77	$5.73	$4.27
(c) Overhead and administration charges do	$0.89	$0.73	$0 53	$0.78	$0.69
(d) Taxes and insurance do	$0.19	$0.20	$0.14	$0.20	$0.06
Actual cost of refining sugar, not including any interest on investment, depreciation of plant, or cost of selling (per ton of beets)	$4.68	$5 04	$4.26	$4.87	$3.30
(A) Pounds refined sugar stored (not invoiced), July 1, 1911					None.
(B) Pounds refined sugar sold (not invoiced), July 1, 1911					4,110,000

STATE OF CALIFORNIA, *County of Glenn:*

Ernest C. Hamilton, being first duly sworn, deposes and says that he is a resident of Hamilton, Glenn County, State of California, and that he is now and has been for six years general manager of the Sacramento Valley Sugar Co., having its principal office at Los Angeles, Cal., and owning and operating a plant at Hamilton, Glenn County, State of California, for the manufacture of refined sugar from sugar beets; that he is thoroughly conversant with the business and accountings of the Sacramento Valley Sugar Co., and to his best knowledge and belief the figures given above are true and correct.

ERNEST C. HAMILTON.

Subscribed and sworn to before me this 29th day of December, A. D. 1911.

[SEAL.]

ARTHUR M. GELSLOR,
Notary Public, Glenn County, Cal.

UTAH-IDAHO SUGAR CO.,
Salt Lake City, Utah, December 28, 1911.

Hon. THOMAS W. HARDWICK,
Chairman Special Committee on Sugar Refining Co.,
House of Representatives, Washington, D. C.

DEAR SIR: Inclosed please find information asked for by Mr. F. J. Garrett, acting chairman, as per his letter of December 14.

Very truly, yours,

UTAH-IDAHO SUGAR CO.
THOMAS R. CUTLER,
General Manager.

SALT LAKE CITY, UTAH, *December 27, 1911.*

Mr. THOMAS R. CUTLER,
Vice President and General Manager,
Utah-Idaho Sugar Co., City.

DEAR SIR: Beg to advise that on July 1, 1911, we had actually sold to bona fide purchasers 7,740,000 pounds of refined sugar, not invoiced on that date.

Yours truly,

JOSEPH GEOGHEGAN, *Broker.*

Subscribed and sworn to before me this 27th day of December, 1911.

[SEAL.]

L. T. WHITNEY,
Notary Public.

(My commission expires September 9, 1912.)

Information submitted to special House Committee investigating violations of antitrust act.

[Utah-Idaho Sugar Co., Salt Lake City, Utah.]

	Name of factory and location.					
	Lehi, Lehi, Utah.	Garland, Garland, Utah.	Idaho Falls, Idaho, Falls, Idaho.	Sugar City, Sugar City, Idaho.	Blackfoot, Blackfoot, Idaho.	Nampa, Nampa, Idaho.
Year 1906-7.						
Tons beets sliced	133,440	82,055	64,305	76,216	37,937	40,867
Average sugar test:						
Sugar content.....per cent..	13.11	16.66	16.06	16.37	17.01	16.62
Purity.....do....	78.88	84.50	85.27	85.64	85.00	85.10
Extraction beets sliced.....do....	9.66	12.64	12.43	13.07	13.44	12.67
Average price paid grower for beets	$4.6584	$4.6452	$4.4853	$4.5158	$4.9286	$4.5153
Average price beets delivered at factory	$5.1390	$5.1127	$4.9477	$4.8874	$5.4828	$5.6551

Information submitted to special House Committee investigating violations of antitrust act—Continued.

[Utah-Idaho Sugar Co., Salt Lake City, Utah.]

	Name of factory and location.					
	Lehi, Lehi, Utah.	Garland, Garland, Utah.	Idaho Falls, Idaho, Falls, Idaho.	Sugar City, Sugar City, Idaho.	Blackfoot, Blackfoot, Idaho.	Nampa, Nampa, Idaho.
Year 1907-8.						
Tons beets sliced	109,699	60,749	65,587	70,333	45,635	42,754
Average sugar test:						
Sugar content, per cent	16.22	17.66	17.31	17.27	17.61	17.16
Purity, do	86.35	87.02	86.85	87.90	87.34	87.50
Extraction beets sliced, do	13.20	14.06	13.18	13.87	14.01	13.76
Average price paid grower for beets	$4.6343	$4.6221	$4.4107	$4.5499	$4.9174	$4.5110
Average price beets delivered at factory	$5.1714	$5.0208	$4.8583	$5.0281	$5.5400	$5.7498
Year 1908-9.						
Tons beets sliced	124,214	74,279	58,884	72,655	35,077	35,187
Average sugar test:						
Sugar content, per cent	14.07	15.43	15.85	15.75	15.88	15.95
Purity, do	84.47	86.46	86.86	86.34	87.60	86.84
Extraction beets sliced, do	11.20	11.82	12.16	13.16	12.09	12.65
Average price paid grower for beets	$4.6420	$4.6360	$4.5664	$4.6339	$4.6450	$4.5247
Average price beets delivered at factory	$5.1651	$5.1345	$5.0463	$5.1056	$5.3045	$5.8094
Year 1909-10.						
Tons beets sliced	128,260	81,666	59,721	70,536	28,132	None.
Average sugar test:						
Sugar content, per cent	15.45	15.31	16.27	15.37	16.50	None.
Purity, do	85.00	85.60	86.54	85.37	86.91	None.
Extraction beets sliced, do	12.10	11.43	12.44	12.00	13.11	None.
Average price paid grower for beets	$4.6961	$4.6250	$4.5451	$4.6370	$4.2956	None.
Average price beets delivered at factory	$5.2488	$5.1375	$5.1134	$5.1151	$5.4916	None.
Year 1910-11.						
Tons beets sliced	100,947	58,261	50,839	48,638	None.	4,595
Average sugar test:						
Sugar content, per cent	15.85	16.85	17.68	15.65	....	16.96
Purity, do	86.32	87.23	88.50	85.92	....	86.96
Extraction beets sliced, do	12.84	13.12	14.09	13.46	....	10.90
Average price paid grower for beets	$4.6085	$4.5830	$4.8076	$4.8471	....	$4.9055
Average price beets delivered at factory	$5.2622	$5.1264	$5.5524	$5.4650	....	$9.3110

Sugar on hand July 1, 1911, unsold, 14,559,500 pounds.

STATE OF UTAH, *County of Salt Lake, ss:*

Walter T. Pyper, first being duly sworn, says that he is the assistant secretary and treasurer of the Utah-Idaho Sugar Co., and as such is in charge of all of the books, records, and statements of the said corporation; that the foregoing statement is in all respects true, full, and correct as it appears by the records of the said company in his possession.

WALTER T. PYPER.

Subscribed and sworn to before me this 27th day of December, 1911.

[SEAL.] L. T. WHITNEY, *Notary Public.*

(My commission expires September 9, 1912.)

Statement showing cost of sugar furnished special House committee investigating violations of antitrust laws.

[Utah-Idaho Sugar Co., Salt Lake City, Utah.]

[Per 100 pounds granulated.]

	Factory.					
	Lehi.	Garland.	Idaho Falls.	Sugar City.	Black-foot.[1]	Nampa.[2]
Year 1906-7.						
Cost of beets	$2.0966	$2.0742	$2.1158	$1.9694	$2.3031	$2.2867
Operating and maintenance expenses	1.0536	.8138	1.0167	1.0891	1.1842	.9428
General expenses	.0862	.0779	.1203	.1024	.0879	.1471
Taxes and insurance	.1009	.0800	.0949	.0812	.0970	.0346
Total	3.9373	3.0459	3.3477	3.2421	3.6722	3.4112
By-products, Dr. or Cr	.0485	.0318	.0361	.0659	.0550	.2186
Total	3.9858	3.0141	3.3116	3.3080	3.6172	3.1926
Miscellaneous revenue and expenditures, Dr. or Cr	.0399	.0313	.0454	.1654	.0216	.0165
Total, exclusive of interest	3.9459	2.9828	3.3570	3.4734	3.5956	3.1761
Interest and interest on bonds	.2006	.1430	.1250	.1005	.1572	.0456
Total as per yearly reports	4.1465	3.1258	3.4820	3.5739	3.7528	3.2217
Year 1907-8.						
Cost of beets	2.0663	1.8346	1.9181	1.9642	2.2000	2.2309
Cost of sugar and molasses purchased			.0087			
Operating and maintenance expenses	.9950	.9478	1.0942	1.2707	1.2675	1.2508
General expenses	.1113	.1675	.1279	.1274	.1295	.2008
Taxes and insurance	.0743	.0938	.0825	.0939	.0907	.1205
Total	3.2469	3.0437	3.2314	3.4622	3.6877	3.8030
By-products, Dr. or Cr	.0322	.0979	.0799	.0484	.1093	.0097
Total	3.2147	2.9458	3.1515	3.4138	3.5784	3.8127
Miscellaneous revenue and expenditures, Dr. or Cr	.0920	.1512	.1284	.3040	.3230	.2459
Total, exclusive of interest	3.3067	3.0970	3.2799	3.7178	3.9014	4.0586
Interest and interest on bonds	.1897	.1897	.1897	.1897	.1897	.1897
Total as per yearly reports	3.4964	3.2867	3.4696	3.9075	4.0911	4.2483
Year 1908-9.						
Cost of beets	2.4443	2.1601	2.1120	2.0362	2.1393	2.4280
Operating and maintenance expenses	1.0968	.9745	1.1907	1.2088	1.4651	1.4187
General expenses	.1051	.1538	.1532	.1324	.1651	.2267
Taxes and insurance	.0799	.0891	.0952	.0976	.1029	.1253
Total	3.7261	3.3775	3.5511	3.4750	3.8724	4.1987
By-products, Dr. or Cr	.0745	.0858	.2209	.0738	.0312	.0392
Total	3.6516	3.2917	3.3302	3.4012	3.8412	4.1595
Miscellaneous revenue and expenditures, Dr. or Cr	.0023	.0174	.0317	.1023	.0754	.1648
Total, exclusive of interest	3.6493	3.3091	3.3619	3.5035	3.9166	4.3243
Interest and interest on bonds	.1760	.1760	.1760	.1760	.1760	.1760
Total as per yearly reports	3.8253	3.4851	3.5379	3.6795	4.0926	4.5003
Year 1909-10.						
Cost of beets	2.2534	2.1556	2.0875	2.2163	2.1970	....
Cost of sugar and molasses purchased				.0100		....
Operating and maintenance expenses	1.0381	.8637	.9468	1.1262	1.2081	....
General expenses	.1201	.1604	.1565	.1619	.1863	....
Taxes and insurance	.0690	.0795	.0852	.0939	.1294	....
Total	3.4806	3.2592	3.2760	3.6083	3.7208	....
By-products, Dr. or Cr	.1228	.1425	.0179	.1401	.2346	....
Total	3.3578	3.1167	3.2581	3.4682	3.4862	....

[1] Not operated in 1910-11. Losses $48,138 19, not included in cost of production of any other factory.
[2] Not operated in 1909-10. Losses $120,300 45, not included in cost of production of any other factory.

Statement showing cost of sugar furnished special House committee investigating violations of antitrust laws.

	Factory.					
	Lehi.	Garland.	Idaho Falls.	Sugar City.	Black-foot.[1]	Nampa.[2]
Year 1909-10—Continued.						
Miscellaneous revenues and expenditures, Dr. or Cr.	$0.0116	$0.0152	$0.0239	$0.1306	$0.1659	....
Total, exclusive of interest	3.3462	3.1319	3.2820	3.5988	3.6521	....
Interest and interest on bonds	.1210	.1210	.1210	.1210	.1210	....
Total as per yearly reports	3.4672	3.2529	3.4030	3.7198	3.7731	....
Year 1910-11.						
Cost of beets	2.1703	1.8681	2.1544	2.1039	....	$03.7930
Cost of sugar and molasses purchased	....	....	....	.0223	....	....
Operating and maintenance expenses	1.0237	.8629	.9230	1.0091	....	3.0736
General expenses	.1633	.2066	.1825	.2133	....	.6503
Taxes and insurance	.0856	.0997	.0941	.1323	....	.8681
Total	3.4429	3.0373	3.3540	3.4809	....	8.3859
By-products, Dr. or Cr.	.0899	.1931	.3122	.1174	....	.3544
Total	3.3530	2.8442	3.0418	3.3635	....	8.7403
Miscellaneous revenue and expenditures, Dr. or Cr.	.0064	.0284	.0587	.2606	....	6.3420
Total, exclusive of interest	3.3466	2.8726	3.1005	3.6241	....	15.0823
Interest and interest on bonds	.1263	.1263	.1263	.1263	....	.1263
Total as per yearly reports	3.4729	2.9989	3.2268	3.7504	....	15.2086

The above figures do not include dividends paid, depreciation of plant, nor cost of selling.

STATE OF UTAH, *County of Salt Lake, ss:*

Walter T. Pyper, first being duly sworn, says that he is the assistant secretary and treasurer of the Utah-Idaho Sugar Co., and as such is in charge of all the books, records, and statements of the said corporation; that the foregoing statement is in all respects true, full, and correct as it appears by the records of the said company in his possession.

WALTER T. PYPER.

Subscribed and sworn to before me this 27th day of December, 1911.

[SEAL.] L. T. WHITNEY, *Notary Public.*

(My commission expires September 9, 1912.)

SOUTHERN CALIFORNIA SUGAR CO.,
Santa Ana, Cal., December 26, 1911.

Mr. THOMAS W. HARDWICK,
Chairman Special Committee, House Resolution No. 157,
Washington, D. C.

DEAR SIR: Replying to your letter of the 14th instant, we inclose you herewith statements and information requested. We beg to advise you that this company owns and operates but one factory, and it has been in operation for only three campaigns.

Yours, truly,

SOUTHERN CALIFORNIA SUGAR CO.,
By F. B. CASE, *Manager.*

STATE OF CALIFORNIA, *County of Orange, ss:*

Denton Fritz, being duly sworn, on oath states that he is now and since August 1, 1909, has been the bookkeeper in charge of the books of the Southern California Sugar Co., and that the attached statement covering cost of manufacture of sugar at the factory of said company for the years 1909, 1910, and 1911 was prepared by him, and that he knows same to be correct as appears on the books of the said sugar company under his charge.

DENTON FRITZ.

Subscribed and sworn to before me the 26th day of December, 1911.

[SEAL.]

F. O. DANIEL,
Notary Public, Orange County, Cal.

FIRST.—*Southern California Sugar Co.*

(1) Tons of beets sliced:

	Tons.
1909	42,015
1910	52,261
1911	50,488.7

(2) Average sugar test:

	Per cent.
1909	17.91
1910	17.75
1911	17.24

(3) Average extraction per ton of beets sliced:

	Per cent.	Pounds.
1909	14.04	280.8
1910	13.45	269.0
1911	13.09	261.8

(4) Average price paid for beets:

	Per ton.	Freight.
1909	$5.20	$0.343
1910	5.49	.344
1911	5.52	.345
Average	5.40	.344

(5) Cost of manufacture subdivided as follows:

	1909.	1910.	1911.
(a) Cost of raw material	$250,819.77	$304,523.28	$295,582.99
(b) Factory cost	122,248.21	155,738.69	135,373.16
(c) Overhead or administration charges	29,674.93	34,717.09	33,456.64
(d) Taxes and insurance	355.80	6,769.65	7,268.02
	403,098.71	501,748.71	471,680.81

United States tax 1911 not as yet assessed

SECOND.—*Southern California Sugar Co.—Cost of manufacture of sugar, 1909, 1910, 1911.*

	Cost per 100 pounds.		
	1909	1910	1911
Labor	$0.40664	$0.2865	$0.2606
Factory salaries [1]		.1152	.1264
Coke	.04118	.0444	.0346
Chemicals	.00855	.0058	.0114
Filter cloth	.01265	.0100	.0222
Fuel oil	.30736	.2727	.2651
Lime rock	.09431	.0946	.0930
Tools and equipment [2]		.0158	.0069
Factory supplies	.03105	.0306	.0285
Laboratory supplies	.00352	.0046	.0026
Repairs and replacements	.01065	.0846	.0632
Hospital fees		.0024	.0005
Beets	2.12593	2.158	2.2424
Beet dumps, expense	.05902	.0301	.0287
Field salaries and expense	.02647	.0206	.0245
Factory sheds and yard expense [3]		.0607	.0586
Wells and water supply expense	.03476		
Pipe line		.0249	
Sugar bags	.11293	.1115	.1228
Freight and drayage		.0023	.0041
General expense	.03235	.0227	.0152
Insurance	.00302	.0101	.0126
Interest on loans not on investment	.01292	.0479	.0419
Office expense and supplies	.01374	.0065	.0089
Office salaries	.07958	.0532	.0566
Storage		.0020	.0041
Taxes		.0379	.0425
	3.41663	3.5556	3.5783

[1] Factory salaries 1909 included in labor.
[2] Tools and equipment 1909 included in repairs and replacements and factory supplies.
[3] Factory sheds and yard expense 1909 included in beet dumps.

THIRD.—*Southern California Sugar Co.*

(*a*) No refined sugar in stock or in storage on July 1, 1911.
(*b*) No refined sugar sold but not invoiced on July 1, 1911.

THE NATIONAL SUGAR MANUFACTURING Co.,
Baltimore, Md., January 4, 1912.

Hon. FINIS J. GARRETT,
Acting Chairman Special Committee,
House of Representatives, United States, Washington, D. C.

DEAR SIR: Please find inclosed a statement prepared in conformity with our understanding of your request of December 14, 1911.

We regret that we found it impossible to furnish you this information by January 1, 1912, as you desired, and hope the delay has not caused your committee any inconvenience.

Respectfully, yours,

J. H. WINDFELDER,
President and General Manager.

The National Sugar Manufacturing Co., Sugar City, Colo.

This statement is submitted in compliance with the written request of Finis J. Garrett, acting chairman of the special committee, House resolution No. 157.]

[This company operates one 500-ton plant at Sugar City.]

	1907	1908	1909	1910	1911
(1) Beets sliced, tons of 2,000 pounds	56,386	32,259	37,831	26,796	24,519
(2) Average sugar content of beets, per cent	15.6	13.2	13.4	14.5	16.1
Average purity content of beets, per cent	85.1	80.9	80.1	81.5	83.4
(3) Sugar extracted per ton sliced. pounds	248.2	224.5	208	224.4	272.4
(4) Price paid growers per ton	$5.00	$5.00	$5.00	$5.00	$5.50
Average cost delivered to factory per ton	$5.65	$5.69	$5.58	$5.46	$5.91
(5) Total cost of manufacture	$531,113.62	$335,756.90	$347,340.27	$252,229.59	$250,295.29
Total cost of manufacture, subdivided as follows:					
(a) Raw material delivered to factory	$318,580.90	$183,667.91	$211,094.96	$146,382.11	$144,907.29
(b) Factory cost	$165,397.44	$106,920.94	$100,056.81	$67,536.59	$68,412.29
(c) Administration expenses	$38,798.60	$35,435.41	$28,054.75	$30,628.46	$30,192.74
(d) Taxes and insurance	$8,336.68	$9,732.62	$8,133.75	$7,682.43	$6,782.97
Total cost of operations, interest on investment and depreciation not included	$531,113.62	$335,756.90	$347,340.27	$252,229.59	$250,295.29
Total sugar manufactured........pounds	13,995,000	7,242,800	7,862,700	6,013,800	6,678,400
Cost per pound, sacked, in factory warehouse, interest on investment and plant depreciation not included, cents	3.8	4.6	4.4	4.2	3.8

Number of pounds of refined sugar in stock owned by the National Sugar Manufacturing Co. on July 1, 1911, 14,273 bags=1,427,300 pounds.

Number of pounds of refined sugar actually sold to bona fide purchasers, but not invoiced on July 1, 1911, 8,480 bags=848,000 pounds.

BALTIMORE, MD., *January 4, 1912.*

John H. Windfelder, being first duly sworn, deposes and says that he is president and general manager of the National Sugar Manufacturing Co.; that he is familiar with all the matters set out in the aforegoing statements; that these statements were prepared by him in compliance with the request of Finis J. Garrett, acting chairman of the special committee on the investigation of the American Sugar Refining Co. and others; and that the information given is true according to the best of his knowledge, information, and belief.

J. H. WINDFELDER.

Subscribed and sworn to before me this 4th day of January, 1912.

[SEAL.]

HOWARD, D. ADAMS,
Notary Public, Baltimore, Md.

(My commission expires May 1, 1912.)

OWOSSO SUGAR CO., OF OWOSSO, MICH.,
Bay City, Mich., December 30, 1911.

Mr. FINIS J. GARRET, *Acting Chairman Special Committee*
Appointed under House Resolution No. 157,
House of Representatives, Washington, D. C.

DEAR SIR: In response to your request of December 14, we inclose herein statement covering the operations of the Owosso Sugar Co. for five years last past, which we trust you will find satisfactory.

Very truly, yours,

OWOSSO SUGAR CO.
C. N. SMITH,
Secretary and Treasurer.

(1) *Statement made by the Owosso Sugar Co. for use before the special committee appointed under House resolution No. 157.*

[This statement covers the operations of the beet-sugar factories owned by said Owosso Sugar Co. located at Owosso, Mich., and at Lansing, Mich., for the term of five years.]

	Owosso.	Lansing.
1906.		
(1) Tons of beets sliced	92,000	41,000
(2) Average sugar test ... per cent	13.9	13.39
(3) Sugar extraction per ton of beets sliced ... do	10.97	10.97
(4) Average price paid for beets	$6.27	$7.10
(5) Cost of manufacture per 100 pounds sugar:		
(a) Cost of raw material	$3.0073	$3.27
(b) Factory cost	.6509	.67
(c) Overhead or administration charges	.2900	.14
(d) Taxes and insurance	.0600	.05
	4.0082	4.13
1907.		
(1) Tons of beets sliced	61,000	32,000
(2) Average sugar test ... per cent	14.18	14.62
(3) Sugar extraction per ton of beets sliced ... do	11.71	11.99
(4) Average price paid for beets	$6.66	$6.99
(5) Cost of manufacture per 100 pounds sugar:		
(a) Cost of raw material	$2.915	$2.865
(b) Factory cost	.511	.805
(c) Overhead or administration charges	.481	.400
(d) Taxes and insurance	.080	.080
	3.987	4.150
1908.		
(1) Tons of beets sliced	44,000	19,000
(2) Average sugar test ... per cent	16.5	16.5
(3) Sugar extraction per ton of beets sliced ... do	13.3	13.64
(4) Average price paid for beets	$6.14	$8.41
(5) Cost of manufacture per 100 pounds sugar:		
(a) Cost of raw material	$2.75	$2.85
(b) Factory cost	.65	.56
(c) Overhead or administration charges	.60	.88
(d) Taxes and insurance	.10	.17
	4.10	4.46
1909.		
(1) Tons of beets sliced	66,000	27,000
(2) Average sugar test ... per cent	16.2	15.70
(3) Sugar extraction per ton of beets sliced ... do	12.8	12.00
(4) Average price paid for beets	$6.32	$8.06
(5) Cost of manufacture per 100 pounds sugar:		
(a) Cost of raw material	$3.14	$3.314
(b) Factory cost	.45	.585
(c) Overhead or administration charges	.50	.50
(d) Taxes and insurance	.06	.12
	4.15	4.619
1910.		
(1) Tons of beets sliced	106,000	58,000
(2) Average sugar test ... per cent	15.69	15.19
(3) Sugar extraction per ton of beets sliced ... do	12.03	12.22
(4) Average price paid for beets	$6.47	$7.96
(5) Cost of manufacture per 100 pounds sugar:		
(a) Cost of raw material	$3.77	$3.51
(b) Factory cost	.71	.56
(c) Overhead or administration charges	.40	.27
(d) Taxes and insurance	.05	.07
	4.93	4.41

(2) Cost per 100 pounds of sugar.

	Owosso.	Lansing.
1906.		
Cost of beets	$3.0073	$3.274
Cost of labor and materials	.6509	.665
	3.6582	3.939
1907.		
Cost of beets	2.9156	2.860
Cost of labor and materials	.5117	.805
	3.4273	3.665
1908.		
Cost of beets	2.7526	2.852
Cost of labor and materials	.5551	.565
	3.3077	3.417
1909.		
Cost of beets	3.1492	3.314
Cost of labor and materials	.4581	.585
	3.6073	3.899
1910.		
Cost of beets	3.7718	3.5095
Cost of labor and materials	.7124	.5633
	4.4842	4.0728

Said items of cost do not include any interest charges, cost of selling, overhead expenses, or depreciation.

(3) (*a*) This company owned no refined sugar on July 1, 1911. (*b*) This company had not sold any refined on July 1, 1911. (*c*) This company imported from Canada during the month of January, 1911, for its Owosso factory 448 tons of sugar beets and for its Lansing factory 358 tons.

STATE OF MICHIGAN, *County of Bay, ss:*

Carman N. Smith, being first duly sworn says that he is the secretary and treasurer of the Owosso Sugar Co., a corporation owning and operating a beet-sugar factory at the city of Owosso and one at the city of Lansing, in the State of Michigan, that he has full knowledge of all the statements of cost and operation of the said two factories during the five years specified in the foregoing statement, and that the statements and figures set forth in the foregoing attached statement are true and correct of affiant's own knowledge.

CARMAN N. SMITH.

Sworn to and subscribed before me this 30th day of December, 1911.

[SEAL.] EVA L. KELLEY,
Notary Public.

My commission expires November 5, 1912.

THE GREAT WESTERN SUGAR CO.,
Denver, Colo., December 28, 1911.

Hon. FINIS J. GARRETT,
Acting Chairman, House of Representatives, Washington, D. C.

DEAR SIR: Replying to yours December 14, I beg to inclose herewith sworn statement of our present auditor, Mr. R. K. Marsh.

Mr. Marsh has been connected with our company for the past eight years, commencing at one of our factories as cashier, then came to the general office as assistant to the secretary, afterwards appointed manager of our Brush and Fort Morgan factories, which position he held for two and one-half years, and was then recalled to the general office and elected auditor on July 1, 1910.

Mr. Marsh is personally familiar with our records from the beginning of this report. He has been very thorough in his replies and I trust the information furnished, when taken in connection with that already supplied and sworn to by Mr. Dixon (see pp. 2893–2894 of hearings), will place before your committee the facts required. We have held nothing back. I am anxious that you should know the facts, and all the facts, regarding the affairs of this company.

If there is anything further you wish to have from us, a request from any member of your committee will be complied with cheerfully and promptly.

Respectfully, yours,

C. S. MOREY, *President.*

THE GREAT WESTERN SUGAR CO.,
Denver, Colo., December 26, 1911.

Mr. C. S. MOREY,
President The Great Western Sugar Co., Denver, Colo.

DEAR SIR: As requested, I herewith give you certain information asked for by the special committee, Hon. Finis J. Garrett, acting chairman, in his letter of December 14, 1911, addressed to you.

1. *Tons of beets sliced.*

	1903–4	1904–5	1905–6	1906–7	1907–8	1908–9	1909–10	1910–11
Eaton, Colo	53,153	32,900	66,783	90,962	72,162	63,655	71,648	47,026
Greeley, Colo	51,340	42,564	69,743	100,182	68,435	57,435	49,324	44,758
Windsor, Colo	38,702	27,380	63,676	93,705	82,185	60,987	67,223	49,001
Fort Collins, Colo	35,882	76,002	128,780	180,263	171,171	138,465	167,668	96,523
Loveland, Colo	115,799	105,274	130,195	152,476	143,594	120,272	146,278	88,590
Longmont, Colo	28,402	48,648	106,796	166,600	171,260	133,868	151,560	78,971
Sterling, Colo			35,800	82,409	78,430	84,147	81,457	70,716
Brush, Colo				52,942	47,651	68,502	68,304	59,106
Fort Morgan, Colo				16,998	63,887	59,311	71,812	
Billings, Mont				55,200	88,874	108,138	107,560	112,296
Scottsbluff, Nebr								46,817
Total	323,278	332,768	001,773	991,737	987,649	894,790	982,824	693,800

Where tons are spoken of in this letter, 2,000 pounds has been used.

2. *Average sugar test.*

[Beets sliced.]

	1903–4		1904–5		1905–6		1906–7	
	Sugar.	Purity.	Sugar.	Purity.	Sugar.	Purity.	Sugar.	Purity.
	Per cent.		*Per cent.*		*Per cent.*		*Per cent.*	
Eaton Colo	15.06	80.68	15.56	83.98	14.68	82.86	14.97	82.22
Greeley, Colo	15.88	82.16	16.94	85.50	14.80	83.60	15.15	83.10
Windsor, Colo	16.87	82.90	16.60	85.90	15.05	84.50	15.45	84.73
Fort Collins, Colo	16.43	76.56	16.44	84.21	15.10	82.10	15.70	81.40
Loveland, Colo	16.46	83.63	16.34	83.38	15.49	82.31	16.65	81.30
Longmont, Colo	16.91	80.00	16.90	84.50	15.54	83.96	15.99	83.30
Sterling, Colo					14.73	81.40	15.69	82.20
Brush, Colo							14.27	79.45
Fort Morgan, Colo							13.89	75.52
Billings, Mont							18.14	82.60
Scottsbluff Nebr								
Grand average	16.27	80.99	16.46	84.58	15.05	82.96	15.64	82.21

2. *Average sugar test*—Continued.

	1907-8		1908-9		1909-10		1910-11	
	Per cent sugar.	Purity.	Per cent sugar.	Purity.	Per cent sugar.	Purity.	Per cent sugar.	Purity.
Eaton, Colo	17.64	87.50	14.15	83.30	14.98	83.80	15.93	85.3
Greeley, Colo	17.76	86.10	15.25	84.60	15.77	84.90	16.62	86.1
Windsor, Colo	17.69	87.30	14.28	84.40	14.82	83.60	15.89	84.9
Fort Collins, Colo	17.40	84.94	13.64	82.63	14.31	82.09	15.33	83.1
Loveland, Colo	16.84	84.30	14.37	83.56	14.27	81.90	15.89	85.4
Longmont, Colo	17.49	84.58	14.80	83.50	14.84	82.49	15.92	84.4
Sterling, Colo	17.38	84.75	13.54	82.60	15.57	83.55	16.21	83.3
Brush, Colo	16.65	83.95	13.18	81.58	16.08	84.02	15.67	82.4
Fort Morgan, Colo	17.00	84.17	13.63	81.59	15.92	83.74		
Billings, Mont	18.63	84.90	16.04	85.00	16.76	84.30	17.27	85.3
Scottsbluff, Nebr							15.50	82.8
Grand average	17.45	85.14	14.34	83.31	15.15	83.11	16.08	84.3

3. *Sugar extraction per ton of beets sliced* (*pounds*).

	1903-4	1904-5	1905-6	1906-7	1907-8	1908-9	1909-10	1910-11
Eaton, Colo	226	245	229	211	279	210	221	245
Greeley, Colo	232	273	226	222	282	222	239	261
Windsor, Colo	259	264	229	235	290	210	222	248
Fort Collins, Colo	220	297	258	280	313	243	249	282
Loveland, Colo	253	273	253	262	302	251	245	289
Longmont, Colo	261	307	266	280	313	262	256	299
Sterling, Colo			201	258	301	224	266	291
Brush, Colo				124	251	188	249	247
Fort Morgan, Colo				89	259	193	239	
Billings, Mont				291	333	285	282	313
Scottsbluff, Nebr								222
Average	243	280	245	248	299	237	249	276

4. *Average price paid for beets* (*to growers*).

[This is price for beets delivered at company's receiving stations. Does not include any freight, as the company assumes this.]

	1903-4	1904-5	1905-6	1906-7	1907-8	1908-9	1909-10	1910-11
Eaton, Colo	$5.05	$5.00	$5.00	$5.00	$5.09	$5.07	$5.08	$5.47
Greeley, Colo	4.56	5.00	5.00	5.00	5.04	5.08	5.08	5.56
Windsor, Colo	4.90	5.00	5.00	5.00	5.08	5.06	5.09	5.44
Fort Collins, Colo	4.15	5.00	5.00	5.00	5.08	5.04	5.11	5.37
Loveland, Colo	4.53	5.00	5.00	5.00	5.04	5.06	5.07	5.47
Longmont, Colo	4.40	4.95	5.00	5.00	5.02	5.04	5.07	5.47
Sterling, Colo			4.75	4.97	5.06	4.98	5.02	5.31
Brush, Colo				5.00	5.01	5.01	4.91	5.36
Fort Morgan, Colo				5.00	5.03	5.03	5.06	
Billings, Mont				4.99	4.96	4.93	4.93	5.88
Scottsbluff, Nebr								5.10

In the foregoing tables, where no figures are shown, factories were not built at that time, except in the case of Fort Morgan factory, 1910-11; it did not operate that year on account of lack of sufficient supply of beets.

Assuming that it is not the intention of the committee to burden themselves with figures which they already have, I respectfully refer you to pamphlet No. 36, pages 2893-2894, of the testimony taken by the committee, where a table is shown which gives the cost of manufacturing 100 pounds of sugar at each of our factories from the campaign of 1903-4 to and including the campaign of 1910-11. I think this table, together with the information that follows, will give not only as much but more information than they ask for in division No. 5 of first question and second question.

I will attempt to explain in detail what elements enter into the costs shown in pamphlet No. 36, on pages above referred to, so that the committee may, by reason of the fact that the information is given in detail, be in a better position to compare those figures with figures submitted by other persons.

Take, for instance, the first figure on the table, that of the Eaton factory, for 1903–4, $4.42, as well as the figure shown opposite the Eaton factory at a later date, 1910–11, $3.56. These two figures, as well as all the other figures in the table, are made up with a few slight, but no substantial, variations from year to year, as follows:

	1903–4	1910–11
No. 1. Cost of beets	$2.72	$2.59
No. 2. Factory labor (operating period)	.52	.27
No. 3. Coal, coke, lime rock, and burnt lime	.45	.24
No. 4. Miscellaneous factory supplies	.29	.14
No. 5. Intercampaign (osmose)	.07	....
No. 6. General expense	.16	.11
No. 7. Taxes and insurance	.07	.08
No. 8. Maintenance	.20	.29
No. 9 Miscellaneous revenues and raw sugar and molasses adjustments	.06	.16
	4.42	3.56

Explaining the foregoing figures further, I will say that—

No. 1. *Cost of beets* includes such expenses as money paid growers for beets, freight on beets, as well as the cost of receiving beets from growers; piling and reloading them at receiving stations; securing acreage, transportation of beet laborers, tare room and laboratory tests, salaries and expenses of agricultural superintendents and field men; donations or subscriptions, county roads, bridges, beet laborers' churches, etc.

No. 2. *Factory labor (operating period)*.—Money paid superintendents and assistants, factory clerks, chemists, firemen, coal passers, engineers, oilers, beet-shed laborers, sugar boilers, as well as all other station and other factory men during the operating period.

No. 3. *Coal, coke, lime rock, and burnt lime*. Mine, oven, quarry, and kiln cost on coal, coke, and lime rock, as well as the freight charges and cost of unloading.

No. 4. *Miscellaneous factory supplies*.—Cost of sulphur, muriatic acid, sal soda, soda ash, lubricating oils, and waste; cutter knives, twine, filter cloth, osmose paper, sugar bags, etc.

No. 5. *Intercampaign (osmose)*. Cost of labor and material during intercampaign period, working brown sugar out of molasses.

No. 6. *General expenses*.—Administration salaries, such as president, vice president, general manager, secretary, auditor, etc.; office clerks, telegrams, telephones, printing and advertising; stationery and postage; traveling expenses, legal expenses, stable expenses, etc.

No. 7. *Taxes and insurance*.—Includes all taxes, whether Federal, State, or county, on real estate and personal property, as well as incorporation, Federal income tax, etc.; also insurance on all material, supplies, real estate, boilers, employers' liability; in fact, insurance on everything except sugar.

No. 8. *Maintenance*.—Cost of labor and material during intercampaign period; repairing all factory machinery, tanks, buildings, etc.

No. 9. *Miscellaneous revenues and raw sugar and molasses adjustments*.—This is miscellaneous revenues, expenses on account of sale of by-products, such as pulp, molasses, lime cake, as well as money made or lost on account of sheep and cattle feeding operations, beet seed, boarding-house operations, and other side operations; adjustments on account of different quantities of brown sugar and molasses being left over from year to year.

While the foregoing figures include those items mentioned, they do not include such expenses—a fact brought out plainly by you and Mr. Dixon in your letters shown on pages 2893–2894—as charges to improvements and depreciation; nor do they include freight, brokerage, insurance, or miscellaneous charges after sugar has left the factory. Neither do they include interest on capital invested nor dividends on preferred and common stock.

Wrong conclusions may easily be drawn from the above figures unless they are thoroughly understood; for instance, while the cost of making 100 pounds of sugar, under the heading, "Cost of beets," shows a smaller amount in 1910–11 than it does in 1903–4, the difference is not explained by saying that we paid less per ton for beets in 1910–11 than in 1903–4; we really paid considerable more. (See No. 4, p. 4 of this letter.) It is explained by the fact that the factories are more efficient to-day than they were a few years ago; and this reason, more than any other, is the real reason for the difference. The same may be said of the factory labor, as well as miscellaneous factory supplies. Supplies and labor both cost more to-day than they did several years ago, though the cost per 100 pounds of sugar produced is less.

I also call attention to the fact that though the committee's letter of December 14 asks for figures for only five years, I have given figures for eight years, as they will then cover the same period that you and Mr. Dixon reported on.

(A) Number of pounds of refined sugar in stock owned by your company on July 1, 1911, such amount of refined sugar to include the total refined stock of your company wherever stored, provided the same were not actually invoiced to the buyer on July 1, 1911—18,170,200 pounds.

(B) Number of pounds of refined sugar actually sold to bona fide purchasers, but not invoiced on July 1, 1911—9,687,300 pounds.

We therefore had on hand July 1, sugar to sell to the extent of 8,482,900 pounds, or 84,829 100-pound sacks, about 5¼ per cent of our production for that year.

Although the information is not asked for, I wish to state for your information, in connection with first question, divisions No. 1 and No. 3, that although the total tons of beets sliced, as shown on statement No. 1, amounts to 5,808,619 tons, during the same period the company actually paid the beet growers for 6,119,690 tons. It will be apparent to the committee from these figures that during the eight campaigns we paid the growers for 311,071 tons more than we have actually sliced in the factories; this is due principally to shrinkage, which the company stands.

In connection with division No. 3, first question, the average extraction per ton of beets sliced for the eight years amounts to 259.8 pounds. A similar figure based on per ton of beets paid for, is 246.6 pounds, making a difference of 13.2 pounds, or about 5 per cent.

Mr. Dixon, in pamphlet No. 36, page 2894, states: "The yearly average for the Colorado factories for the past eight campaigns is $3.42, and adding to it as a fair average of 35 cents per bag for depreciation, would bring it to $3.77 per hundredweight." I find the average cost of manufacturing 100 pounds of sugar, Colorado factories, for the eight years has been $3.35 (Mr. Dixon's figure, $3.42, is a yearly average; that is, the aggregate of the eight years' averages divided by eight; whereas the figure $3.35 mentioned above is arrived at by dividing the total cost of manufacture for the eight years by the number of bags produced during the same period; this latter basis is also used in obtaining the average net selling price per 100 pounds); if to this is added $0.41 per 100 pounds as a fair average for plant depreciation (the $3.35 includes no depreciation), for the eight years, which is based on annual charge of 5 per cent (our books show that less than an average of 5 per cent has been deducted, owing principally to the fact that in the earlier years no charges were made for depreciation), we have a total of $3.76.

During these same years the average net selling price we received for sugar was $4.54 per hundredweight. (You, in pamphlet No. 11, page 889, stated that our average selling price for sugar for five years was $4.485. The difference between that figure and the $4.54 mentioned above is explained by saying that the figure $4.54 is for eight years.)

The cost, $3.76 per hundredweight, deducted from the average net selling price, $4.54 per hundredweight, shows a profit per hundredweight of $0.78.

Our books show that during the eight years our net profit per ton of beets paid for has been $2.31, but this figure includes only the actual depreciation charge. (Some of the factories in the earlier years did not make any depreciation charges.) If a 5 per cent annual depreciation, which we consider a fairer basis, had been charged off, our net profit per ton of beets paid for would have been $1.90.

I hereby state that I have full knowledge regarding the foregoing statements, and that from my own knowledge and belief I believe them to be truthful.

Respectfully, yours,

R. K. Marsh, *Auditor.*

State of Colorado,
City and County of Denver, ss:

I, Earl F. Shepard, a notary public within and for the county and State aforesaid, do hereby certify that R. K. Marsh, who is personally known to me, being duly sworn, deposes and says that the foregoing facts and figures shown on pages 1, 2, 3, 4, 5, 6, 7, and 8, hereto attached, are true to his best knowledge and belief.

Given under my hand and notarial seal this 28th day of December, A. D. 1911.

[seal.] Earl F. Shepard, *Notary Public*

My commission expires November 24, 1913.

GERMAN-AMERICAN SUGAR CO.,
Bay City, Mich., December 23, 1911.

Hon. FINIS J. GARRETT,
Acting Chairman Special Committee,
House of Representatives, Washington, D. C.

DEAR SIR: In response to your request of the 14th instant, we hand you herewith our reply, giving information as we understand you want it. Should this not conform with your wishes we will be pleased to give you anything in our power additional that you may deem necessary.

Yours, very truly,

GERMAN-AMERICAN SUGAR CO.,
E. WILSON CRESSEY,
Secretary and General Manager.

The German-American Sugar Co. owns and operates two factories for the manufacture of sugar from beets, one situated in Monitor Township, Bay County, Mich., and one in Paulding Township, Paulding County, Ohio.

No. 1.—*Factory in Monitor Township, Bay County, Mich.*

	1906-7	1907-8	1908-9	1909-10	1910-11
1. Tons of beets sliced	55,868	58,693	52.439	73,582	102.475
2. Average sugar test ... per cent	15.3	15	17.2	17.2	16.1
3. Sugar extraction per ton of beets ... do	12.38	11.907	13.717	13.078	11.477
4. Average price paid for beets	$5.60	$5.50	$6.23½	$6.23½	$5.86⅜
Cost of manufacture:[1]					
a. Cost of raw material	$2.503	$2.514	$2.513	$2.607	$2.903
b. Factory cost	.950	.978	.840	.863	.962
c. Overhead or administration	.169	.224	.155	.102	.126
d. Taxes and insurance	.057	.058	.060	.042	.027
Total	3.679	3.774	3.568	3.614	4.018

[1] Exclusive of interest on investment, depreciation of plant, and cost of selling, per 100 pounds of sugar.

Factory in Paulding Township, Paulding County, Ohio, 1910-11.

[Factory built during 1909 and 1910.]

1. Tons of beets sliced	70,876
2. Average sugar test ... per cent	15
3. Sugar extraction per ton of beets ... do	10.32
4. Average price paid for beets	$5.50
Cost of manufacture, exclusive of interest on investment, depreciation of plant, and cost of selling, per 100 pounds of sugar:	
a. Cost of raw material	$3.098
b. Factory cost	1.052
c. Overhead or administration	.197
d. Taxes and insurance	.007
Total	4.354

No. 2 This company has never refined sugar from raws. It produces refined sugar direct from the beet, the cost to manufacture which is shown in No. 1.

No. 3. (*a*) This company owned no refined sugar on July 1, 1911.

(*b*) This company had no sugar sold but not invoiced of July 1, 1911.

(*c*) This company has never imported beets from Canada.

E. Wilson Cressey, being duly sworn, states that he is the secretary of the German-American Sugar Co., a corporation, of Monitor Township, Bay County, Mich., and as such has actual knowledge of the facts herein set forth; that the figures herein given are given in such form as to cover the two factories owned and operated by this company, with the name and location of each, and that such figures are true and correct.

E. WILSON CRESSEY.

Subscribed and sworn to before me, a notary public in and for Bay County, Mich., on the 23d day of December, A. D. 1911.

[SEAL.]

JAS. E. DUFFY,
Notary Public, Bay County, Mich.

My commission expires March 10, 1913.

MENOMINEE RIVER SUGAR CO.,
Menominee, Mich., December 27, 1911.

Hon. F. J. GARRETT,
Acting Chairman Special Committee, Washington, D. C.

DEAR SIR: In compliance with your request of the 14th instant, we are inclosing herewith statement covering the cost of manufacture of sugar in our factory for the years 1906 to 1910, inclusive, as shown by the books of the company, and also statement as to paragraphs 2 and 3. Paragraph 2 seems to be covered by the "Cost of manufacture," but if this is not what you want, we will be pleased to furnish you any additional information that may be desired.

Very truly, yours,

MENOMINEE RIVER SUGAR CO.,
F. L. BROWN, *Secretary.*

Cost or production of granulated sugar at the Menominee River Sugar Co.'s factory, at Menominee, Mich., from 1906 to 1910, inclusive.

1906.

1. Tons of beets sliced	40,375
2. Average sugar test ... per cent	14.4
3. Sugar extraction per tons of beets sliced ... pounds	234.2
4. Average price paid for beets	$6.6395
5. Cost of manufacture per 100 pounds granulated sugar:	
a. Cost of raw material	$2.8337
b. Factory cost	.9238
c. Overhead or administration charges	.3440
d. Taxes, insurance, and interest other than on capital	.2549
	4.3564
Less credit for by-products	.0731
Total	4.2933

1907.

1. Tons of beets sliced	34,567
2. Average sugar test ... per cent	16.16
3. Sugar extraction per ton of beets sliced ... pounds	253.4
4. Average price paid for beets	$6.5466
5. Cost of manufacture per 100 pounds granulated sugar:	
a. Cost of raw material	$2.3711
b. Factory cost	1.0068
c. Overhead or administrative charges	.2621
d. Taxes, insurance, and interest other than on capital	.3290
	3.9690
Less credit for by-products	.0715
Total	3.8975

1908.

1. Tons of beets sliced	19,608
2. Average sugar test ... per cent	17.66
3. Sugar extraction per ton of beets sliced ... pounds	285.4
4. Average price paid for beets	$7.0562

5. Cost of manufacture per 100 pounds granulated sugar:

a. Cost of raw material	$2.5546
b. Factory cost	1.0201
c. Overhead or administration charges	.5595
d. Taxes, insurance, and interest other than on capital	.3754
	4.5096
Less credit for by-products	.1150
Total	4.3946

1909.

1. Tons of beets sliced	28,452
2. Average sugar test ... per cent	17.30
3. Sugar extraction per ton of beets sliced ... pounds	284.4
4. Average price paid for beets	$7.2705

5. Cost of manufacture per 100 pounds granulated sugar:

a. Cost of raw material	$2.6159
b. Factory cost	.7468
c. Overhead or administration charges	.3561
d Taxes, insurance, and interest other than on capital	.2261
	3.9449
Less credit for by-products	.2580
Total	3.6869

1910.

1. Tons of beets sliced	23,672
2. Average sugar test ... per cent	16.144
3. Sugar extraction per ton of beets sliced ... pounds	261.76
4. Average price paid for beets	$7.4858

5. Cost of manufacture, per 100 pounds, granulated sugar:

a. Cost of raw material	$3.0010
b. Factory cost	.7897
c. Overhead or administration charges	.5184
d. Taxes, insurance, and interest other than on capital	.2466
	4.5557
Less credit for by-products	.1406
Total	4.4151

Inquiry No. 2. Shown by a, b, c, d in "Cost of manufacture."

Inquiry No. 3. (*a*) Number of pounds of refined sugar in stock owned by this company on July 1, 1911.

Answer. None.

(*b*) Number of pounds of refined sugar actually sold to bona fide purchasers but not invoiced on July 1, 1911.

Answer. None.

(*c*) Number of tons of beets imported from Canada.

Answer. None.

MENOMINEE RIVER SUGAR CO.,
By F. L. BROWN, *Secretary*.

F. L. Brown, secretary of the Menominee River Sugar Co., of Menominee, Mich., being first duly sworn, states that the foregoing statements are as shown by the books of the company, are correct, he being familiar with the books. The cost of production, as shown by the statements, for the five years, 1906 to 1910, inclusive, is exclusive of the cost of selling, storing, or interest on the capital invested.

Subscribed and sworn to before me, a notary public, in and for the county of Menominee, State of Michigan, this 27th day of December, 1911.

[SEAL.]

V. B. DE MORAINVILLE,
Notary Public.

My commission expires January 10, 1914.

AMERICAN BEET SUGAR CO.,
SECRETARY'S OFFICE.
New York, December 20, 1911.

DEAR SIR: I am in receipt of your valued favor of December 19, concerning the statements requested by you, and note that their submission by mail will be sufficient, but as you doubtless wish to arrive at the cost of making sugar, and as it is impossible to obtain that cost, with the exclusion of the cost of depreciation, it seems most advisable that the auditor should personally attend your committee and present to the inadequate statement, which you call for, an addenda, including depreciation and other costs, which are as essential and as much a part of the cost of making sugar as the cost of beets and their slicing.

Yours, very truly,

CHARLES C. DUPRAT,
Assistant Secretary.

Hon. FINIS J. GARRETT,
Acting Chairman Special Committee
Investigating American Sugar Refining Co.,
House of Representatives, Washington, D. C.

AMERICAN BEET SUGAR CO.,
OFFICE OF THE CHAIRMAN OF THE BOARD OF DIRECTORS.
New York, January 5, 1912.

DEAR SIR: Herewith is respectfully presented, in accordance with your request of December 14, 1911, statement of the cost of the sugar production of the American Beet Sugar Co. for five years ending March 31, 1911, together with the auditor's affidavit as to the correctness of the statements, and the amount of sugar on hand July 1, 1911, and the amount of sugar sold at that date.

In explanation of the 398,007 bags of sugar sold July 1, 1911, please note that there was on hand 52,095 bags, leaving to be made to complete that sale 345,912 bags, which the Oxnard and Chino factories would make at the rate of 11,000 bags per day from the start of operations, usually July 15 to 25.

It is the practice of the company to sell its sugars as fast as the market will take them, and in doing so it anticipates the production when it can be safely estimated.

I have the honor to be, dear sir, your obedient servant,

H. RIEMAN DUVAL, *President.*

Hon. FINIS J. GARRETT,
Acting Chairman Special Committee
Investigating American Sugar Refining Co.,
House of Representatives, Washington, D. C.

STATE OF NEW YORK, *County of New York*:

On this 5th day of January, 1912, personally appeared before me, a notary public in and for the county of New York, Elisha Gee, auditor of the American Beet Sugar Co., who, being duly sworn, did depose and say, that the tons of beets sliced; the average sugar test; the sugar extraction per ton of beets sliced; the average price paid for beets; the cost of manufacture, and the total cost to produce and sell sugar, for all factories in consolidated form, and for each factory, for the five years ending March 31, 1911, was as per statements attached hereto and marked Exhibits "A," "B," "C," "D," "E," "F," and "G"; that the number of pounds of refined sugar owned by the company on July 1, 1911, was 5,209,500 pounds, and that the number of pounds of refined sugar actually sold to bona fide purchasers, but not invoiced, on July 1, 1911, was 39,800,700 pounds; that he has full knowledge of the facts testified to and that the above and foregoing statements are true and correct to the best of his knowledge and belief.

ELISHA GEE

Sworn to and subscribed before me the day and year aforesaid.

[SEAL.]

CHARLES C. DUPRAT,
Notary Public No. 131, for New York County.

EXHIBIT A.

American Beet Sugar Co., cost of sugar.

ALL FACTORIES.

[From Apr. 1, 1906, to Mar. 31, 1911.]

	1906-7	1907-8	1908-9	1909-10	1910-11	Total.
Tons of beets sliced	549,947	470,081	374,629	472,106	498,955	2,365,718
Average sugar test	15.54	15.83	16.64	16.62	17.60	16.42
Sugar extraction per ton of beets	263.74	276.37	290.09	292.04	315.76	287.04
Average price of beets	$5.50	$5.56	$5.66	$5.83	$6.25	$5.76
Cost of manufacture:						
Cost of raw material	$3,026,977.83	$2,615,542.18	$2,118,905.76	$2,754,461.71	$3,117,972.82	$13,633,860.30
Factory cost	1,935,572.05	1,687,862.54	1,356,252.62	1,743,734.80	1,716,642.27	8,440,064.28
Overhead or administrative charges	138,265.54	158,981.45	175,951.66	177,266.36	187,269.72	837,734.73
Taxes and insurance	54,324.28	58,514.38	65,154.27	59,843.98	64,746.99	302,583.90
Total	5,155,139.70	4,520,900.55	3,716,264.31	4,735,306.85	5,086,631.80	23,214,243.21
Bags of sugar produced	1,450,411	1,299,182	1,086,777	1,378,739	1,575,480	6,790,589
Cost per bag	$3.55	$3.48	$3.42	$3.43	$3.23	$3.42
Other expenses:						
Selling	$569,696.05	$824,053.15	$828,835.84	$739,502.47	$934,159.68	$3,896,247.19
Interest paid on borrowed money	314,441.16	301,430.88	189,617.60	100,203.56	46,158.98	951,852.18
Depreciation	326,642.71	330,588.14	335,495.64	347,509.79	358,125.59	1,698,361.87
Total cost to produce and sell sugar	6,365,919.62	5,976,972.72	5,070,213.39	5,922,522.67	6,425,076.05	29,760,704.45
Total cost per bag to produce and sell sugar	4.39	4.60	4.67	4.30	4.08	4.38

EXHIBIT B.

American Beet Sugar Co., cost of sugar.

OXNARD FACTORY.

[From Apr. 1, 1906, to Mar. 31, 1911.]

	1906-7	1907-8	1908-9	1909-10	1910-11	Total.
Tons of beets sliced	201,333	134,722	174,444	235,668	286,908	1,033,075
Average sugar test	17.25	17.74	18.56	18.03	18.90	18.17
Sugar extraction per ton of beets	298.71	321.82	332.73	323.46	341.34	324.95
Average price of beets	$5.49	$5.78	$6.01	$6.11	$6.51	$6.04
Cost of manufacture:						
Cost of raw material	$1,106,073.59	$779,090.78	$1,049,272.07	$1,440,745.04	$1,868,338.29	$6,243,519.77
Factory cost	698,400.86	533,544.16	558,913.26	772,997.94	800,845.02	3,364,701.24
Overhead, or administrative charges	62,219.49	60,412.95	66,861.63	67,361.22	71,162.49	328,017.78
Taxes and insurance	19,443.27	20,295.34	17,580.24	14,090.16	16,331.46	87,740.47
Total	1,886,137.21	1,393,343.23	1,692,627.20	2,295,194.36	2,756,677.26	10,023,979.26
Bags of sugar produced	601,410	433,570	580,420	762,296	979,320	3,357,015
Cost per bag	$3.14	$3.21	$2.92	$3.01	$2.81	$2.99
Other expenses:						
Selling	$275,826.42	$376,029.54	$483,231.39	$468,931.54	$631,620.81	$2,235,638.70
Interest paid on borrowed money	141,498.52	114,543.73	72,054.69	38,077.35	17,540.41	383,714.70
Depreciation	138,343.75	138,289.75	139,275.92	146,670.95	152,050.94	714,631.31
Total cost to produce and sell sugar	2,441,804.90	2,022,206.25	2,387,189.20	2,948,874.20	3,557,889.42	13,357,963.97
Total cost per bag to produce and sell sugar	4.06	4.66	4.11	3.87	3.63	3.98

EXHIBIT C.

American Beet Sugar Co., cost of sugar.

CHINO FACTORY.

[From Apr. 1, 1906, to Mar. 31, 1911.]

	1906–7	1907–8	1908–9	1909–10	1910–11	Total.
Tons of beets sliced	69,975	39,355	65,096	79,562	87,241	341,229
Average sugar test	14.60	16.14	16.75	17.17	17.54	16.54
Sugar extraction per ton of beets	217.23	267.00	284.24	294.15	310.29	277.57
Average price of beets	$5.04	$5.43	$5.66	$5.62	$5.97	$5.58
Cost of manufacture.						
Cost of raw material	$352,381.41	$213,549.10	$368,766.72	$447,401.28	$520,629.39	$1,902,727.90
Factory cost	269,395.49	192,529.85	222,520.36	309,149.36	344,656.63	1,338,251.69
Overhead or administrative charges	22,122.49	20,667.59	22,873.72	23,044.63	24,345.06	113,053.49
Taxes and insurance	11,681.87	10,957.78	13,025.11	11,102.87	12,773.20	59,540.83
Total	655,581.26	437,704.32	627,185.91	790,698.14	902,404.28	3,413,573.91
Bags of sugar produced	152,005	105,382	185,029	234,036	270,702	947,154
Cost per bag	$4.31	$4.15	$3.39	$3.38	$3.33	$3.60
Other expenses:						
Selling	$91,536.43	$65,825.06	$89,898.03	$118,185.95	$132,435.14	$497,880.61
Interest paid on borrowed money	50,310.59	39,188.02	24,650.29	13,026.46	6,000.67	133,174.03
Depreciation	55,403.25	56,510.13	57,376.46	61,521.17	65,989.02	296,800.03
Total cost to produce and sell sugar	852,831.53	599,225.53	799,110.69	983,431.72	1,106,829.11	4,341,428.58
Total cost per bag to produce and sell sugar	5.61	5.69	4.32	4.20	4.09	4.58

Exhibit D.

American Beet Sugar Co., cost of sugar.

ROCKY FORD FACTORY.

[From Apr. 1, 1906, to Mar. 31, 1911.]

	1906-7	1907-8	1908-9	1909-10	1910-11	Total.
Tons of beets sliced	174,436	160,777	83,883	97,441	101,152	617,689
Average sugar test	14.99	15.24	14.09	14.49	14.29	14.74
Sugar extraction per ton of beets	266.03	280.00	258.88	264.19	265.66	268.36
Average price of beets	$5.58	$5.52	$5.11	$5.57	$5.78	$5.53
Cost of manufacture:						
Cost of raw material	$973,967.86	$886,971.84	$428,487.31	$543,002.51	$584,281.57	$3,416,711.09
Factory cost	551,724.88	500,046.04	285,714.30	333,386.07	328,494.63	1,999,365.92
Overhead or administrative charges	31,801.07	30,206.48	33,430.82	33,680.60	35,581.25	164,700.22
Taxes and insurance	14,161.82	15,212.89	15,815.04	16,398.70	16,934.19	78,522.64
Total	1,571,655.63	1,432,437.25	763,447.47	926,467.88	965,291.64	5,659,299.87
Bags of sugar produced	464,048	450,277	217,160	257,432	268,723	1,657,640
Cost per bag	$3.39	$3.18	$3.52	$3.59	$3.59	$3.41
Other expenses:						
Selling	$138,427.35	$247,401.08	$147,822.78	$93,837.29	$148,347.87	$775,836.37
Interest paid on borrowed money	72,321.47	57,271.87	36,027.34	19,038.68	8,770.20	193,429.56
Depreciation	76,624.22	78,606.33	80,755.20	80,994.29	81,856.18	398,836.22
Total cost to produce and sell sugar	1,859,028.67	1,815,716.53	1,028,052.79	1,120,338.14	1,204,265.89	7,027,402.02
Total cost per bag to produce and sell sugar	4.01	4.03	4.73	4.35	4.48	4.24

EXHIBIT E.

American Beet Sugar Co., cost of sugar.

LAS ANIMAS FACTORY.

[From Apr. 1, 19 , to Mar. 31, 1911.]

	1906-7	1907-8	1908-9	1909-10	1910-11	Total.
Tons of beets, sliced		67,238	24,726	25,335		117,299
Average sugar test		14.49	13.95	14.00		14.27
Sugar extraction per ton of beets		213.70	208.73	204.39		211.01
Average price of beets		$5.44	$5.31	$5.40		$5.40
Cost of manufacture:						
Cost of raw material		$365,545.23	$131,242.47	$136,904.77		$633,692.47
Factory cost		173,700.85	150,952.28	145,483.86	$101,470.95	571,607.94
Overhead or administrative charges		25,437.03	28,152.26	28,362.62	29,963.16	111,915.07
Taxes and insurance		1,377.60	8,065.50	8,152.77	9,165.33	26,761.20
Total		566,060.71	318,412.51	318,904.02	140,599.44	1,343,976.68
Bags of sugar produced		143,710	51,612	52,193		247,515
Cost per bag		$3.94	$6.17	$6.11		$5.43
Other expenses:						
Selling		$21,130.52	$64,988.26	$34,869.70	$8,945.92	$129,934.40
Interest paid on borrowed money		48,228.94	30,338.82	16,032.57	7,385.44	101,985.77
Depreciation						
Total cost to produce and sell sugar		635,420.17	413,739.59	369,806.29	156,930.80	1,575,896.85
Total cost per bag to produce and sell sugar		4.42	8.02	7.09		6.37

Exhibit F.

American Beet Sugar Co., cost of sugar.

LAMAR FACTORY.

[From Apr. 1, 1906, to Mar. 31, 1911.]

	1906-7	1907-8	1908-9	1909-10	1910-11	Total.
Tons of beets sliced	60,211	49,486		20,221		129,918
Average sugar test	13.70	13.97		13.50		13.77
Sugar extraction per ton of beets	225.56	242.46		236.15		233.65
Average price of beets	$5.56	$5.47		$5.45		$5.52
Cost of manufacture:						
Cost of raw material	$335,017.48	$271,512.98		$110,194.85		$716,725.31
Factory cost	245,419.80	199,845.30	$44,170.02	117,174.51	$34,447.99	641,057.62
Overhead or administrative charges	12,443.90	12,718.51	14,076.13	14,181.31	14,981.58	68,401.43
Taxes and insurance	5,298.32	6,554.33	6,347.59	6,193.44	5,704.89	30,098.57
Total	598,179.50	490,631.12	64,593.74	247,744.11	55,134.46	1,456,282.93
Bags of sugar produced	135,813	119,986		47,752		303,551
Cost per bag	$4.40	$4.09		$5.19		$4.80
Other expenses:						
Selling	$37,851.49	$86,188.68	$23,452.07	$15,062.30	$4,574.35	$167,128.89
Interest paid on borrowed money	28,299.70	24,114.47	15,169.41	8,016.29	3,692.72	79,292.59
Depreciation	35,116.04	36,044.18	36,932.72	36,724.39	36,026.95	181,444.28
Total cost to produce and sell sugar	699,446.73	636,978.45	140,147.94	307,547.09	100,028.48	1,884,148.69
Total cost per bag to produce and sell sugar	5.15	5.31		6.44		6.21

EXHIBIT G.

American Beet Sugar Co., cost of sugar.

GRAND ISLAND FACTORY.

[From Apr. 1, 1906, to Mar. 31, 1911.]

	1906-7	1907-8	1908-9	1909-10	1910-11	Total.
Tons of beets sliced	43,992	18,503	26,480	13,870	23,654	126,508
Average sugar test	13.93	16.29	14.33	13.88	16.19	14.78
Sugar extraction per ton of beets	220.80	246.00	198.47	180.35	239.85	219.52
Average price of beets	$5.89	$5.34	$5.33	$5.40	$6.12	$5.69
Cost of manufacture:						
Cost of raw material	$259,537.49	$98,872.25	$141,137.19	$76,213.26	$144,723.57	$720,483.76
Factory cost	170,631.02	88,196.34	93,982.40	65,543.06	106,727.05	525,079.87
Overhead or administrative charges	9,678.59	9,538.89	10,557.10	10,635.98	11,236.18	51,646.74
Taxes and insurance	3,739.00	4,116.44	4,320.79	3,906.04	3,837.92	19,920.19
Total	443,586.10	200,723.92	249,997.48	156,298.34	266,524.72	1,317,130.56
Bags of sugar produced	97,135	46,257	52,556	25,031	56,735	277,714
Cost per bag	$4.57	$4 34	$4.76	$6.24	$4.70	$4.74
Other expenses:						
Selling	$26,055.36	$27,478.27	$19,443.31	$8,615.09	$8,235.59	$89,828.22
Interest on borrowed money	22,010.88	18,085.85	11,377.05	6,012.21	2,769.54	60,255.53
Depreciation	21,155.45	21,137.75	21,155.34	21,598.99	21,602.50	106,650.03
Total cost to produce and sell sugar	512,807.79	267,425.79	301,973.18	192,525.23	299,132.35	1,573,864.34
Total cost per bag to produce and sell sugar	5.30	5.78	5.75	7.69	5.27	5.67

HOLLAND-ST. LOUIS SUGAR CO.—*Statement of costs to manufacture sugar, not including selling expense, interest on investment, and depreciation of plant.*

	1906-7, factories at—		1907-8, factories at—		1908-9, factories at—		1909-10, factories at—		1910-11, factories at—	
	Holland, Mich.	St. Louis, Mich.	Holland, Mich.	St. Louis, Mich.	Holland, Mich.	St. Louis, Mich.	Holland, Mich.	St. Louis, Mich.	Holland, Mich.	St. Louis, Mich.
Tons of beets sliced, factory weights	27,578	50,232	20,775	40,049	18,148	32,606	21,338	35,692	27,330	56,371
Average test ... per cent	13.8	13.9	15.5	15.1	16.4	17.2	15.8	17.6	14.5	16.4
Pounds of sugar in ton of beets	272	278	310	302	328	354	316	352	290	328
Pounds of sugar extracted per ton of beets	220	214	261	244	280	280	256	260	238	235
Average price paid for beets per ton	$5.91	$5.67	$6.34	$5.91	$6.67	$6.51	$7.53	$7.01	$7.31	$6.80
Cost of manufacture per 100 pounds sugar:										
Cost of beets	$2.67	$2.65	$2.42	$2.45	$2.37	$2.32	$2.93	$2.69	$3.08	$2.89
Cost of raw sugar purchased		.08								
Factory cost	.89	.95	.86	.89	.81	.83	.89	.74	.76	.80
Overhead expense	.13	.134	.13	.14	.155	.105	.143	.11	.135	.10
Taxes and insurance	.09	.076	.12	.09	.125	.095	.137	.11	.105	.08
Cost of manufacture per 100 pounds sugar in consolidated form, not including selling expense, interest on investment, and depreciation of plant	$3.85		$3.55		$3.39		$3.81		$3.94	

Number of pounds of refined sugar in stock owned by this company on July 1, 1911, not invoiced, none.

Number of pounds of refined sugar actually sold to bona fide purchasers, but not invoiced, on July 1, 1911, none.

Number of tons of sugar beets imported from Canada from January 1, 1911, none.

B. C. Hubbard, of Holland, Mich., being sworn, says that he is the secretary and treasurer of the Holland-St. Louis Sugar Co., a corporation organized under the laws of the State of Michigan; that this company operates refineries at Holland and St. Louis, Mich.; that he is familiar with the books and records of the company; and that the figures shown herein are taken from the records and are true to the best of his knowledge and belief.

B. C. HUBBARD,
Secretary and Treasurer.

Subscribed and sworn to before me, a notary public in and for the county of Ottawa, State of Michigan, this 3d day of January, A. D. 1912.

[SEAL.]

W. J. GARROD,
Notary Public, Ottawa County, Mich.

My commission expires September 15, 1915.

STATEMENT OF DR. H. W. WILEY, CHIEF OF THE BUREAU OF CHEMISTRY, DEPARTMENT OF AGRICULTURE.

(The witness was duly sworn by the chairman.)

The CHAIRMAN. Doctor, state to the committee your name.

Dr. WILEY. Dr. H. W. Wiley.

The CHAIRMAN. Your official position?

Dr. WILEY. Chief of the Bureau of Chemistry, Department of Agriculture.

The CHAIRMAN. How long have you held that position, Doctor?

Dr. WILEY. Almost 29 years.

The CHAIRMAN. Doctor, are you tolerably familiar with what is known as the Dutch standard, as the term is used in our tariff laws?

Dr. WILEY. I think I understand it pretty well.

The CHAIRMAN. There has been a great deal of loose and, the chairman thinks, inaccurate information or misinformation on that subject throughout the country, and to some extent even in Congress, and as we have had some testimony on that subject we thought we would ask you to explain what the Dutch standard is, its effect on the sugar industry and on sugar importations to this country, and whether or not it is of value in protecting the people of the United States from impure sugar, sugar that is unhealthy or contains an unsatisfactory amount of saccharine matter. From what the Chair has outlined to you I presume you will understand exactly the idea we have in mind.

Dr. WILEY. It is hardly necessary to go into the history of the Dutch standard, as it has been well presented, I think. But it originated in early times in Holland, particularly, as the means of judging their colonial sugars, especially those produced in Java; and it came into general use at a time when the methods of analyses of sugar were slow and tedious to a certain extent and inaccurate. The Dutch standard is based on the idea that the color of a sugar is an index of its purity and saccharine strength; that the deeper-colored sugars are less pure and the lighter-colored sugars are more nearly pure. That was a perfectly legitimate idea at the time the Dutch standard was inaugurated. You will understand that when the Dutch standard was inaugurated the modern methods of manufacturing sugar had not come into vogue. In those days all sugars, or practically all sugars, were boiled in what we call the open kettle, and as they were concentrated they acquired more or less a brownish-red color, due to caramelization of sugar in the pan, and due also to the concentration of impurities in the sugar. At the time when the sugar was about ready to be finished the temperature was very high, and naturally, as open fires were mostly used in those days and not much steam, there was great danger of caramelization; and even when steam was used there was danger. So that the mush sugar which was made was rather deeply colored. The old-fashioned method of purifying the sugar also was to place it in vessels with perforated bottoms, and allow the molasses to run out as much as possible. They had no centrifugal machines, and, of course, the separation of the molasses was imperfect; each crystal would still have some of the molasses adhering to it, giving to the crystal a deeper color than it would have had otherwise; and the Dutch standard was put up to match the general run of sugars. They were all at that time cane sugars.

The CHAIRMAN. It was supposed to be a test by which it could be determined to some extent, and to the best extent known at the time it was begun, the sugar purity.

Dr. WILEY. Yes; the sugar purity; the percentage of sugar.

The CHAIRMAN. Is that still true in the development of the sugar industry?

Dr. WILEY. Well, as the sugars are put out to-day, it will be found, as a rule, the lighter-colored standards have a higher percentage of sugars than the darker. That is still true as far as the standard is concerned itself.

The CHAIRMAN. But has not the application of the polariscopic test superseded to some extent the necessity or usefulness of the Dutch standard?

Dr. WILEY. So far as I know, no sugars are bought and sold on the Dutch standard anywhere.

The CHAIRMAN. Then what is the object and what is the use of retaining the Dutch standard in our tariff law?

Dr. WILEY. It has no scientific or commercial use, so far as I know.

The CHAIRMAN. You know Mr. Willett, at least by reputation?

Dr. WILEY. Yes.

The CHAIRMAN. He is considered, I believe, to be the great sugar expert in this country?

Dr. WILEY. Yes.

The CHAIRMAN. Mr. Willett testified in effect before this committee that the only useful purpose he could see for retaining the Dutch standard in our tariff laws was to protect the refiners who make the white sugars; and in substance he said this: That if the differential, for instance, between raw and refined sugars were wiped out of the tariff law, there would be no earthly sense in keeping the Dutch standard on the statute books, because, as I understood him, as far as the test of sugar purity is concerned, the polariscope is much more nearly accurate and has entirely superseded the other test, except on the one proposition of color.

Dr. WILEY. Of course, I would not be prepared to state what the object of the Dutch standard is in the law, but many years ago, when

I was before a committee on this same subject, I testified just as I am testifying now, and I had my box of Dutch standards, which I had polarized, showing as the standards are put up they still represent an increasing purity, with perhaps one or two exceptions.

The CHAIRMAN. Of the lighter colors?

Dr. WILEY. Yes; but their value for grading the purity of sugar has wholly disappeared because of the modern methods of making sugar.

Mr. MALBY. Doctor, will you please explain that method?

Dr. WILEY. The present methods of making sugar are, first, if it is sugar cane, the expression of the juice in some way, or in the case of beets, either by means of pressure or by a process of diffusion extracting the juice with water. With beet sugar the diffusion process is universally used, and with sugar cane the mill is almost universally used with scarcely any exception, the pressure method. These juices, after purification by heat and the use of lime and sometimes sulphur to lighten the color, are placed in a vacuum, the air being exhausted so that they boil at a low temperature, a much lower temperature than boiling water. In that way not only is the evaporation accelerated and made less expensive, but the danger of burning is entirely removed, so that the juice can be concentrated to a great density without getting hot and without danger of caromelization. The result of that is that it makes a much lighter product for the same degree of purity than it did before, and hence the application of the Dutch standard to that kind of sugar would let in a much lower grade, because it was lighter, than it would otherwise with the old method. Then there are the methods of bleaching sugar which have come into use. I have already mentioned the use of sulphur. There is also the use of bone black, so that white sugar can be made from the lowest grades of material, and hence the Dutch standard would be of no value whatever.

The CHAIRMAN. It would not keep that low-grade white sugar out at all?

Dr. WILEY. No; it would be of no value whatever in trade and is not used. I have never known in the 25 years of my experience—and I have been with the brokers a great deal and the men who value the sugar for tariff purposes—I was superintendent for 12 years of all the laboratories that fix the tariff on sugar, and I have never known, except for tariff purposes, a tariff to be fixed, except in those above 16 Dutch standard, nor have I ever known a duty to be assessed, except in that particular case, nor a transaction in trade, except by polariscopic test, in all that time.

The CHAIRMAN. The polariscopic test superseded it?

Dr. WILEY. The polariscope superseded it for all commercial purposes; yes.

The CHAIRMAN. Now, Doctor, to put a plain, direct question to you, in your opinion does the retention of the Dutch standard in our tariff law protect the people against impure sugar, considering the other tests we have, to any extent, and does the Dutch standard serve any useful purpose in our tariff laws in getting for the people a better and a purer sugar than they would get if the Dutch standard was not there?

Dr. WILEY. I do not think it has anything to do with it at all.

The CHAIRMAN. In other words, it is no safeguard to the public health in the way of getting better sugar?

Dr. WILEY. No; nor to the public purse. So far as I know, it is no safeguard to either.

The CHAIRMAN. It does not do them any good?

Dr. WILEY. No; it is a tariff measure pure and simple, in my opinion.

Mr. MALBY. How does it apply?

Dr. WILEY. It is a tariff measure which places a higher duty on a certain colored sugar.

The CHAIRMAN. Regardless of its sugar purity?

Dr. WILEY. Regardless of its saccharine strength. Any sugar above 16 Dutch standard pays a higher duty, no matter what its polarization is. It may polarize as low as 90 and still have to pay a duty.

Mr. HINDS. In a rough way I understood you to say that the Dutch standard went along with the saccharine test by the polariscope, and that the lighter sugars would be stronger in saccharine strength. Did I understand you to say that?

Dr. WILEY. Yes; because I understand the Dutch standards are made by the same kind of sugars they were originally made by. They try to match them. Every year they make a new set of standards, but they matched the old standard as near as possible in some way.

Mr. HINDS. So your polariscope is a little more scientific and exact than your Dutch standard? That is the distinction between the two, is it?

Dr. WILEY. Well, it is not a little more; it is entirely more.

Mr. HINDS. Considerably more?

Dr. WILEY. Yes; entirely more. For instance, the Dutch brokers who make these standards, if they wanted to could make an almost perfectly white sugar, say, as high as No. 20 Dutch standard, polarize as low as 95 or lower. If they wanted to do so it would be perfectly possible to do that with modern methods of making sugar. I have seen sugars of a low grade above 16 Dutch standard many a time.

The CHAIRMAN. Are they made to appear that way by the use of ultramarine or something like that?

Dr. WILEY. No; it is by bleaching with bone black, mostly.

The CHAIRMAN. I think in the evidence this committee has taken it has been suggested that on some occasions it has been suspected, at least, that these people put ultramarine or whitening in the sugar.

Dr. WILEY. It is not a suspicion, it is a certainty.

The CHAIRMAN. Well, what about that? While you are here I would like to have you state what you know about that.

Dr. WILEY. Well, color, you know, is a complex impression, and while black may not appear white, it may almost do so at times; and if you put a bluish tint into a partially white material you make it look whiter than it looked before. For instance, they will put sugar up, you will notice, in boxes with blue paper in them, and the contrast between the blue and the white makes the white look whiter. So they put a blue substance into the sugar which is not actually white, or perfectly white, and to the eye it looks perfectly white by the contrast.

The CHAIRMAN. Who does that now?

Dr. WILEY. The refiner.

The CHAIRMAN. Do you think the refiners do that generally in this country?

Dr. WILEY. They only do it with the low grade of sugars.

The CHAIRMAN. But they do do that with the low grade of sugars?

Dr. WILEY. I do not think they put it in the higher grades of sugar. It would not be necessary.

The CHAIRMAN. But when they have a low grade of white sugar, which will not show up as white as the higher grades, they put this ultramarine in it, and that makes the sugar look as white as the other?

Dr. WILEY. Yes, sir.

The CHAIRMAN. Is there any doubt about the fact that the refiners generally do that?

Dr. WILEY. I think they generally do that with the low-grade white sugars only.

The CHAIRMAN. I mean in that kind of sugar.

Dr. WILEY. Yes; I have seen sugars that when you melt them the blue scum would come to the top and you could see it with the eye.

The CHAIRMAN. That is a fraud on the purchaser, is it not?

Dr. WILEY. That is a fraud covered by the pure-food law.

The CHAIRMAN. And you gentlemen are trying to stop that?

Dr. WILEY. We are after it; yes.

The CHAIRMAN. Doctor, Mr. Hinds asks me to ask you whether or not there has been very much of that; whether you have had much experience of that kind?

Dr. WILEY. Well, I could not say just what percentage of the sugars on the market are of that kind. I have never had any opportunity of ascertaining.

The CHAIRMAN. Have you had any cases like that?

Dr. WILEY. We have never brought any cases under the law, so far as I know.

The CHAIRMAN. But you are investigating that subject?

Dr. WILEY. We are investigating the subject; yes. We have had applications made to us by refiners as to whether they could use this or that bluing, and we have always replied to them that in our opinion the use of any kind of bluing would be a violation of the law.

The CHAIRMAN. Because it would indicate to the purchaser of sugar that he was getting a very different grade and strength of sugar from what he was really buying?

Dr. WILEY. It would indicate that he was getting a whiter sugar and probably a sugar of a higher grade than he thought, and the food law provides that if an article is powdered, colored, or stained, whereby inferiority is concealed, it is an adulterated article.

The CHAIRMAN. This practice clearly comes within that language?

Dr. WILEY. Yes; the word "stained" covers it. I could not tell you gentlemen what proportion of that sugar is on the market, because practically everybody in this country tries to get what we call a granulated sugar. The people of the country have been taught—and I do not know but what with some degree of benefit to them—to ask for a white and dry sugar, so that they buy nothing but sugar; and I must say that the granulated sugars on the market in this country are of a very high grade. I will give the refiners that credit. They are making a splendid article of sugar, undoubtedly, and yet the refining of sugar takes away from it any characteristic of the source from which it is derived. To that extent refining may be an injury. For instance, you gentlemen know the value of maple sugar. If you refined maple sugar it would be just like the granulated sugar of commerce. You could not tell them apart. Therefore, the value of maple sugar is in what we call the impurities in the sugar that go with it and give it its flavor.

The CHAIRMAN. Doctor, right in that connection, that suggests to me this question: It has been suggested here by various witnesses that there are throughout the world, in the West Indies and such places particularly, a number of really healthful brown sugars that are darker in color than the ordinary white granulated we have just been discussing—cheaper in price and really just as healthy and just as safe in every way as white sugars; and if this Dutch standard were taken out of the tariff laws those sugars would be admitted to this country at a cheaper price and could be sold at a cheaper price, and the people would get equally as good and equally as healthy sugar. Have you any opinions on that subject you would care to give the committee the benefit of?

Dr. WILEY. I have very decided opinions.

The CHAIRMAN. I would like to hear them, if you do not mind voicing them.

Dr. WILEY. I think an unrefined cane sugar is the best sugar in the world, best for the health and best for the purse, the old-fashioned crystal sugar which they made in Louisiana before the war. In my opinion, that was the best sugar ever made.

The CHAIRMAN. The Louisiana plantation sugar?

Mr. FORDNEY. It was called then the New Orleans sugar.

Dr. WILEY. Yes; it was called that in those days.

The CHAIRMAN. They call it now Louisiana plantation sugar, I think.

Dr. WILEY. Yes.

The CHAIRMAN. We had some samples of those sugars.

Dr. WILEY. If you have them I would like to see them, because they are pretty well out of the market now. There may be a few places, small farmers, making a small quantity by the old method.

The CHAIRMAN. But it is a comparatively trifling percentage, is it not?

Dr. WILEY. It is an impossible method to practice commercially with the present prices. The modern methods have driven the old-fashioned method out, but so far as the sugar itself was concerned it was the most palatable and, in my opinion, the most wholesome. When you take that sugar and refine it, you do the same thing you would do if you took maple sugar and refined it. You make a pure white sugar. There is no question of that; but you take away from it its natural flavor and aroma which add so much to its value. But with the beet sugar just the opposite is the case. The raw beet sugar is of bad odor and bad taste, and therefore raw beet sugar could not be used and would not be used. It is absolutely necessary to refine beet sugar. If you gentlemen were ever in a cane-sugar factory, you will recall that the whole factory was full of the most pleasant odors and aromas. When you go into it it is almost like going into a perfumery store; but go into a beet-sugar factory, and it smells like an old passé packing house. It has a bad odor and a bad flavor, but of course the beet sugar when refined is identical with refined cane sugar.

The CHAIRMAN. Do you happen to know, or have you any opinion on the subject, whether or not there is any considerable supply of sugars of the kind you have been mentioning, the old Louisiana plantation sugars, in the West Indies which we could get?

Dr. WILEY. Well, I do not know anything about the West Indies, but I imagine they have changed their methods of making sugar there.

The CHAIRMAN. In other wors, the difficulty about the proposition is that when it comes down to a commercial standpoint that kind of sugar is manufactured by such an antiquated and expensive process they have had to quit treating the sugar in that way?

Dr. WILEY. Yes. I do not think there is any commercial quantity of it on the market anywhere. There may be places in the West Indies where they still make sugar that way, and also in the Philippines, but if they do so they can not do it and compete with the other sugars.

The CHAIRMAN. You mean they could not do it on any considerable scale in competition?

Dr. WILEY. No, sir.

The CHAIRMAN. I would be gald if you would tell us what that process is and how much refining is involved in it.

Dr. WILEY. In making sugar?

The CHAIRMAN. No; the difference between the old method and the way they refine it now.

Dr. WILEY. The old-fashioned way was to boil it in an open kettle, and when the density was right, they would pour it off into a box to crystallize, and it would stay in that box until it was a solid mass of crystals. Then they would put those crysrals in hogsheads with perforated bottoms, with a little straw or cane trash on the bottom, and let it drain as long as any molasses would drop out of it. Then the residue was the old-fashioned sugar.

Mr. HINDS. That is what you call the plantation sugar?

Dr. WILEY. Yes.

Mr. HINDS. Did they strain it in any way?

Dr. WILEY. Not the sugar, only in that way.

Mr. HINDS. The difference between that method and modern refining is the bone-black straining?

Dr. WILEY. No. The difference is this: The sugar is now crystallized while it boils. It is crystallized in the boiling pan, and when it has finished boiling the crystals are all formed, and then they pass it directly to a centrifugal machine and by centrifugal force throw the molasses out and leave the crystals of sugar on the lining of the centrifugal. In five minutes after the strike was dragged out of the pan I have seen one centrifugal full of sugar, finished ready to barrel, you might say, unless it is granulated which they want to water first.

Mr. HINDS. They put water in it first?

Dr. WILEY. They wash it in the centrifugal with water, and sometimes with bluing, as I have just said. It is not an unusual thing to wash the crystals in the pan with a little of this bluing material. To what extent that is done, I do not know. I think pretty largely.

The CHAIRMAN. Is the plantation sugar of such color that the retention of the Dutch standard in our tariff laws would affect the duty it pays?

Dr. WILEY. The plantation sugars that are made of what we call the first jet can be made very readily, with a little care, above 16 Dutch standard, so that the Dutch standard would be a protection to that kind of sugar; but usually they do not do that. They make it at a lower grade because they sell it to the refiner. The fact of the case is that the people of this country won't buy an off-colored sugar. It has got to go to the refiner anyway.

The CHAIRMAN. Doctor, you will remember that the people used to buy it before the war, this brown sugar, you know?

Dr. WILEY. That was the only kind they had then. You can not put an off-colored sugar on the market and sell it to-day, because nobody will have it.

The CHAIRMAN. The people demand a white sugar?

Dr. WILEY. Yes. They will not buy a 16 Dutch standard, or even above that, a 17 Dutch standard. They want a white sugar. Everybody wants it. The poorest man wants a white sugar, and there are certain advantages about that, because the white sugar has no water in it.

Mr. HINDS. You can not sell an off-colored flour, can you, Doctor?

Dr. WILEY. Oh, yes.

Mr. HINDS. I mean to the average run of customers. Do they not demand the whitest and best flour?

Dr. WILEY. Of course, the so-called patent flours are of a lighter color than flours of a lower grade, but the people of this country are not so anxious to buy white flours as they were a few years ago, since they have learned that they whiten low-grade flours by bleaching them and sell them for white flour. People have learned that the old-fashioned with its little yellow tint is the best flour, and they are buying that flour now by preference, and the bread that has a little yellow tint is now in much more vogue than the dead-white bread we had a few years ago, due to bleaching. And I may add that in some parts of the world the yellow sugar is still the fashionable sugar. That is so in London. They make a yellow crystal sugar which is the fashionable sugar in London to-day.

The CHAIRMAN. Is this prejudice, if you want to call it that, or this preference of the American people for the whiter sugar a reasonable one; and is it one that will preserve and promote the health of the country, or would it be just as well to use the brown sugar?

Dr. WILEY. I think it is an unreasonable prejudice myself. I would like to see the people of this country taught to use a naturally tinted sugar again, and in that way we could get rid of the refiners altogether.

The CHAIRMAN. We could?

Dr. WILEY. Yes.

Mr. HINDS. Could they produce this naturally tinted sugar as cheaply?

Dr. WILEY. Yes; the beet-sugar makers of this country do not send their sugars to the refiner. They sell direct to the people, and the cane-sugar makers, if the pe ple would take the old-fashioned yellow-tinted sugar, they could do it, too.

The CHAIRMAN. In other words, the refining process is really not a necessary one at all.

Dr. WILEY. It is unnecessary, and the people would be better off without it, in my opinion.

Mr. HINDS. If the refiners were out of the way, the sugar growers could not go back to the old Louisiana plantation method and still sell sugar as cheaply?

Dr. WILEY. No; but they could sell a yellow clarified as cheaply. They make a grade of sugar called yellow clarified, which is a fine sugar.

Mr. HINDS. Who makes that?

Dr. WILEY. The sugar-cane growers. They make it right on their plantation.

Mr. HINDS. What is their process?

Dr. WILEY. They use the sulphur methods. They boil it in the pans as I described, in vacuums, and then centrifugal it and make a light-colored sugar, which is excellent. They call that "yellow clarified."

Mr. HINDS. Can they put that on the market as cheap——

Dr. WILEY (interposing). They could; yes.

Mr. HINDS (continuing). As cheap as the refiners put their sugars on the market?

Dr. WILEY. Yes; a good deal cheaper.

Mr. HINDS. That is, they would get rid of the bone-black process, which is an expensive one?

Dr. WILEY. They get rid of the bone-black process, and make an excellent sugar which tastes well and has as good sweetening power; but because it is off-colored the people will not buy it, and they have to sell that yellow clarified to the refiners. They do sell some of it on their local markets, but I doubt if you can find any yellow clarified sugar in Washington to-day.

The CHAIRMAN. Doctor, we had a committee of Louisiana sugar planters appear before us with a number of samples of what they called Louisiana plantation sugar, and from your description I am satisfied that it was exactly what you are now talking about, and they said it had a considerable sale locally.

Dr. WILEY. The people would like it here if they could get it.

The CHAIRMAN. And Mr. Oxnard tells us that he has gone into the business of making that sort of sugar on quite a considerable scale.

Dr. WILEY. Yes. The refiners by making this white sugar—and I am not saying anything against their white sugar, because it is excellent—they have taught the people of this country to eat nothing else, and hence you can not sell this yellow clarified sugar, although in my opinion it is better sugar. I would rather have it myself.

Mr. FORDNEY. So far as the healthfulness of the sugar is concerned if the consumer could be educated to know that the sugar, before being put through a process of refining, is as good, if not better, than the real granulated refined sugar; if they could be educated to understand that we could save this 40 or 50 cents per hundred pounds for refining and the refiner's profit in addition thereto?

Dr. WILEY. Let me explain that. The sugar I speak of is what I call the first jet, but then there remains in the molasses large quantities of sugar which also can be obtained. Those sugars are of so low grade that nobody, perhaps, wants to use them. So the refiner is necessary. It is a necessary business. But I believe that so far as sugar cane is concerned, we could have just the same condition to-day we have now from the sugar-beet factory. I believe if people would take a little off-colored sugar, the sugar-cane grower could sell the most of this sugar right to the consumer, just as the beet-sugar factory does to-day. But of course there is some sugar at a beet-sugar factory which they can not sell.

The CHAIRMAN. They would have to equip their plantations with certain classes of modern machinery which they do not have now?

Dr. WILEY. No; that is the advantage which the sugar cane has over the sugar beet. The sugar-cane maker can make this sugar by his present process, without any bone black.

The CHAIRMAN. He can?

Dr. WILEY. Yes.

The CHAIRMAN. And without any machinery?

Dr. WILEY. Without any further machinery than he has now, and it is a good, merchantable sugar.

The CHAIRMAN. I got the idea from Mr. Oxnard's testimony they could do it, but it would require a good deal of tolerably expensive machinery which they did not now have, and they would be thrown in competition with a tremendous company like the American Sugar Refining Co. and other large refiners, and for that reason they hesitated to embark their capital in such an enterprise.

Mr. FORDNEY. Mr. Chairman, if you will permit me, I think you misunderstood Mr. Oxnard, if I am correct.

The CHAIRMAN. Maybe I did.

Mr. FORDNEY. I do not know whether I am correct or not, but I think Mr. Oxnard contended that they were installing machinery to make a refined granulated sugar from cane.

The CHAIRMAN. May be so; I am not sure about it.

Mr. FORDNEY. And this extra expense was for extra machinery for making the granulated sugar. The sugar as it comes now from the Louisiana planters as 96° sugar—is that the sugar you are speaking about as being a healthful sugar, Doctor?

Dr. WILEY. Ninety-six and of higher polarization—98 and 98½.

Mr. FORDNEY. They can make it higher?

Dr. WILEY. If you wanted to make a sugar out of sugar cane that would polarize 99.9, which the white granulated sugar does do at times, then you would have to put in this expensive machinery to get that polarization; but I am speaking of the yellow clarified sugar, which is an excellent product, well suited to our consumption and of which they make a considerable portion now.

The CHAIRMAN. With their present machinery?

Dr. WILEY. Yes.

Mr. MALBY. Tell us what that polarizes, Doctor.

Dr. WILEY. 97 to 98½.

Mr. MALBY. And what is the balance up to 100?

Dr. WILEY. There is a little ash and a little reducing sugar; that is, sugar that is inverted. However, it is sweet—that invert sugar is sweeter than the cane sugar.

Mr. MALBY. It is not dirt?

Dr. WILEY. No; it is not dirt at all. It is a little ash, which does not hurt you. You have got to eat a little ash, anyway. You have got to eat a little phosphorus and lime, otherwise you would not have any bones or teeth. It is just as much food as sugar. The reducing sugar that is there is not only sugar, but it is a sweeter sugar by about one-half per cent.

Mr. MALBY. There are no deleterious substances at all?

Dr. WILEY. No. The first thing done to cane sugar by nature is to invert it, when you eat it. You can not digest it in its present state. It has to be inverted first, and there is a little invert sugar which comes naturally in the cane and makes the molasses, which is wholesome. Molasses is a wholesome product. There is nothing unwholesome about a sugar of that kind. On the contrary, I think it is more wholesome than the refined sugar, and it is a better food.

Mr. RAKER. Then the contention which has been going on for the last 20 years that in this sugar which is not refined there is a living microbe—there is nothing in that, is there, Doctor?

Dr. WILEY If sugar is wet enough, sugar lice will grow in it; but you do not need to have them in it unless you want to. The sugar louse is not a microbe. It is a big louse, and you get it in your imported figs and dates, if you want to eat them. You can find millions of them in those figs and dates, and nobody objects to them, because they are good food. But we do not need to have lice in sugar. Lice do not grow in yellow clarified sugar. They only grow in the low-grade sugar, which has plenty of moisture in it.

Mr. MALBY. Doctor, the name "louse" is not suggestive of wholesome diet.

Dr. WILEY. It may not sound well, but it tastes good.

Mr. HINDS. Doctor, is this yellow clarified sugar as good for canning and for condensed milk and such purposes?

Dr. WILEY. It is better, in my opinion. It makes a better tasting candy than white sugar does. If we want the best candy we take the old-fashioned New Orleans molasses and make candy out of that.

Mr. HINDS. Do they use it much commercially?

Dr. WILEY. I do not know what trade it has. It is used locally to a large extent, but they have difficulty in selling it in the North here, because we want perfectly white sugar.

Mr. HINDS. Doctor, the polariscopic test is much more scientific than the Dutch standard is, you say?

Dr. WILEY. The Dutch standard is no longer scientific at all. It was at the time it was made, but not now.

Mr. HINDS. But as sugars go commercially, as the general practice of the trade is, does it not in a rough way indicate what kind of sugars may come in through the customhouse?

Dr. WILEY. Yes; in a rough way.

Mr. HINDS. Now, in the use of the polariscope, is there not a great possibility of partiallty and fraud if the operator is not strictly conscientious or exceedingly well balanced in his judgment?

Dr. WILEY. Well, there is no more danger of fraud in using a polariscope than in counting money; not a bit.

Mr. HINDS. It is a positive machine, is it?

Dr. WILEY. It is a positive machine. You can count money fraudulently. People in this northern country won't buy the No. 16 Dutch standard sugar, or sugar of that color. Yellow clarified sugar is a much lighter color than No. 16.

I have here before the committee a polariscope, which I shall be glad to explain to you gentlemen; also a number of bottles containing sugars of different kinds, and will be glad to explain what each represents. Here is No. 16, and here is another. Now, yellow clarified is much lighter in color than either of these.

The CHAIRMAN. That is 98 polarization?

Dr. WILEY. Yes; there is about yellow clarified No. 24. Here is another sugar, which is gray. Yellow clarified is more yellow than that.

Mr. RAKER. Can you tell blue with the polariscope?

Dr. WILEY. Let me explain this instrument for a moment. I now hold in my hand what we call a sugar flask. It has indicated on the stem by little marks, after careful measurement, its content capacity. Up to the mark to which I now point it will hold 100 cubic centimeters. These instruments are graduated to polarize at a certain temperature, which is 20° C. or 68° F. If you raise or lower the temperature from that point, you get different polarizations, which different polarizations we can easily calculate, for that matter, but we are now building rooms for the purpose of maintaining that temperature. In fact, we have in our laboratory at this time such a room, which room keeps the temperature at 20° C. all the year round, so that we have to make no calculations for differences of temperature, the reading being the exact sugar strength—of course, if we have pure sugar.

We measure out a given weight of sugar, say 26 grams, or a little less than an ounce, and put it into this flask, add water, and shake it until it dissolves, the water being at 68° Fahrenheit. If it all dissolves, it is clear, as this would be [holding up bottle containing sugar], and we make it up to that mark [indicating on flask]. If it is a low-grade sugar, it will not be clear and we have to pulverize it. Then we have to add a clearing agency, which is acetate of lead. We put that in before it is filled up to the mark. We stir it until everything is precipitated and then fill it up to the mark, filling it before we polarize it. We then put that solution in this glass tube, having at the top ground edges and covered with a glass cap, and and screw down the glass cap or cover. There is a column of sugar solution 200 millimeters, or 20 centimeters, in length, absolutely accurate measurement as to length. This is then put into the trough of the polariscope and a lamp or electric light, a lamp being preferable, is held here at the point I indicate. We have in this instrument lenses to make the rays parallel, so that they run straight through. Then we have here a crystal of crystalline limestone, Iceland spar. This crystal has the property of separating the ray of light into two rays, so that instead of seeing one object you see two objects. For instance, if you hold the crystal of Iceland spar over a letter, you will see two letters instead of one. The ray of light goes through there and is polarized into two rays, an extraordinary ray and an ordinary ray. This crystal is cut before it is put in the instrument, and, together with a film of Iceland spar cut to a certain angle, is then put in, and one of the rays is so deflected that when it strikes this Iceland spar it goes straight through it and the other ray goes through this way. This gives you the polarized ray. I can not explain about the polarized light—what it is—because I do not know; but it is different from the ordinary light as to luminosity. If I could represent a ray of light vibrating in a cylinder, like the stem of this flask—a ray of light vibrating in cylindrical form—it might explain what I mean. That is one ray; if you compress that ray so that it would vibrate in a plane, like a plank cut from a sawlog—that is the best illustration I can give of a polarized ray—this would be just as though you would take a plank out of a tree.

The results of the test will be according to the amount of sugar in the solution and the length of the tube through which it passes. If this tube would deflect the ray 40°, then a tube twice its length would deflect it 80°, having a ray of the same strength. The polariscope is an instrument that measures the degree of that test with great accuracy. This measuring apparatus is incased in this box so as to keep it dry. This is the polarizing angle, and it is set with screws so that it may be turned; or, if it is fixed, so that the wedge or quartz, ordinary rock crystal, may be at the proper place. You can then read on this scale the number of degrees this has been moved, showing the percentage of sugar in the solution. If that scale reads 40, it is 40 per cent sugar; if it reads 100, it is 100 per cent, or pure sugar.

The CHAIRMAN. Right there. A very large refiner testifying before this committee gave me this impression of the polariscopic test: He said that it was liable to vary just as the human eye varied. Do you gentlemen of the committee remember that?

Mr. HINDS. That is the reason I was going to ask about it; yes.

The CHAIRMAN. He said the polariscopic test was subject to the imperfections of the human eye. Is that statement right or wrong?

Dr. WILEY. Oh, when the polariscope had a colored field, one-half blue and one-half red, if you were color blind you had great difficulty in reading it. But we have remedied that by having one-half the disk, about the size of a nickel, yellow and the other half black, and anybody, no matter how color blind, can tell the difference between light and darkness.

The CHAIRMAN. That is the way you have removed the trouble he spoke of?

Dr. WILEY. Yes.

The CHAIRMAN. And that is now, as a matter of fact, removed?

Dr. WILEY. Yes. Anyone now who can see the colors in the instrument can tell; and before, any man who was a good judge of colors could tell just as accurately as with this. The difference in favor of this instrument is simplification. With this instrument all one has to do is to read between the shadow and the light. As you move this screw on here you come to the neutral point, and the shadow will leap from side to side, just like a boy jumping over a fence, and you stop it just like a boy standing on the middle of the fence, and then you have an accurate measurement.

The CHAIRMAN. I suppose he referred to the conditions before the polariscope had been brought to its present state of perfection, if we may so term it?

Dr. WILEY. Probably so. For instance, you might read this shadow instrument and I might read it and there might be a difference of five-hundredths per cent between our judgment, just as the judgment of two men might vary about when the boy was on the top of the fence. I might think he was on the middle of the fence while you might think he was close to the middle of the fence. But what is five-hundredths of 1 per cent compared with one of those things making a mistake of 2 or 3 degrees; in fact, you might quite easily make a mistake of 5 degrees, or even possibly 10 degrees, with the color test.

The CHAIRMAN. This polariscopic test is a scientific means of testing sugars?

Dr. WILEY. It is the most accurate measurement of sugar there is.

Mr. HINDS. Suppose you were to put a little salt water into the mixture that you put into the polariscope, what would it do as to eliminating it. Are there any substances that it will throw out?

Dr. WILEY. Yes; a good many optical substances, but salt is not one of them. There are substances that you could put in there that would have polarized properties and they have to be got out. Then there are substances which come in sugar. Take invert sugar that I have just spoken of; that has a different polarizing power from sucrose. When beets have been injured by frost, by freezing, a condition is produced sometimes that gives a higher polarizing power. We have methods, by the use of the polariscope, to remedy even these faults.

Mr. HINDS. What I was trying to get at was this: Of course all tests at customhouses and other places are for the purpose of safety against frauds, and the use of the polariscope would make tests as obvious as possible to the eyes of many people?

Dr. WILEY. Yes.

Mr. HINDS. That is, whether with the polariscope, with its great delicacy and the possibility of chemical miztures being put in, there is not need of something more obvious, something more feasible to the eyes of all? That is the question I had in mind in connection with the Dutch standard.

Dr. WILEY. Of course with the Dutch standard you may make a personal error of $500 or $1,000 much more readily than by the use of the polariscope, the former being just by judging the color.

Mr. HINDS. Isn't the chemist who runs that machine, the polariscope, something in the position of the medicine man; may he not do about as he will and little be known about it?

Dr. WILEY. Oh, yes; a man could change the polariscope if he wanted to. In that connection I might refer to a most remarkable thing. When it was claimed that the polarizations, for instance at the port of New York, were lower than at any other ports, I was appointed one of a committee to investigate the matter, and we found that such was the case, that the polarizations at New York were lower than those at Boston, Philadelphia, and so on. But I did not find that the chemists who were making those polarizations were to blame, because they had set their instruments with the quartz plate, which was very commonly used for the purpose, as the same should be set, but the quartz plate was in error. The person who furnished the quartz plate may have done it for that very purpose, and as a result the Government was losing a very large amount of money.

Mr. HINDS. What was the Government losing, and how did it come about?

Dr. WILEY. My recollection is that it read about one-half degree too low, and that was costing the Government a good deal of money. That was about 20 years ago. Then I was put in charge of these laboratories on request from the Secretary of the Treasury to the Secretary of Agriculture, being detailed to look into and see about this matter. In other words, I had a commission from the Secretary of the Treasury to supervise all laboratories, and I instituted a system of control by means of which there might be absolutely eliminated any possibility of error or fraud.

Mr. FORDNEY. Could that fraud be overcome by the use of the Dutch standard test?

Dr. WILEY. Not at all.

Mr. HINDS. The use of the Dutch standard test would not act as a corrective?

Dr. WILEY. Not at all. The possibility of fraud with the Dutch standard test is infinitely greater than with the polariscopic test.

Mr. MALBY. I think the gentleman the chairman referred to awhile ago as being connected with a large sugar refinery said he was in favor of abolishing the polariscope as not being a correct method of determining the saccharine matter in sugar and therefore at the present time serving no useful purpose. Dr. Wiley, you do not agree with that gentleman in that view?

Dr. WILEY. No; I could not understand any such statement as that being true.

Mr. HINDS. Mr. Malby, did you mean the polariscope or the Dutch standard?

Mr. MALBY. I meant the polariscope, or at least that is my recollection of what he stated to us.

Mr. HINDS. Who was that?

Mr. MALBY. Mr. Spreckles, of Yonkers.

The CHAIRMAN. Well, if Mr. Malby is mistaken about what Mr. Spreckles said the record will show.

Dr. WILEY. I do not think you gentlemen understand me as saying that the reading as shown by the polariscope is absolutely correct, but so far as I know there is no better method of determining this matter.

Mr. MALBY. It is substantially correct, as I understand from you, Dr. Wiley, and the only method now employed by the general public to find impurities in sugar?

Dr. WILEY. What I mean is, that while there may be an error in reading we have means which are easily applied of correcting those errors by the polariscopic test so that it may be shown correctly. For instance, if you take a very low-grade sugar or molasses and take 26 grams of that low grade sugar or molasses and make it up to this standard and polarize it the reading of the polariscope does not indicate the quantity of sucrose which that body contains, because this body may contain 5 per cent, 8 per cent, or even 10 per cent invert sugar, maybe, and the optical properties of invert sugar are very different from the optical properties contained in this body of sugar which I now hold in my hand. This body is right-handed rotation. This turns the plane of the light to the left, while polarized sugar is in the other direction. It turns it the same as the quartz test at ordinary temperatures. If you heat this cylinder to 88° F., almost to boiling point of water, then at that point invert sugar has no optical properties at all. That is, the invert sugar being made up of two bodies, one a right-handed body and the other a left-handed body, this polarization is the algebraic sum of those two polarizations, but the left handed rotation is greater than the right handed rotation, and hence the algebraic sum is a minus quantity. If you have a lot of that in molasses the optical reading if taken directly does not give you the true percentage of sucrose.

But by a simple repetition of polarization, making it up in a different way, you can eliminate it; or by inverting the whole sugar and making it all into invert sugar and polarizing it you can get the exact proportion of cane sugar which it contains.

Mr. HINDS. Can you tell what makes this invert sugar; that is, as to whether it is owing to any peculiarity in the cane?

Dr. WILEY. No: it is natural to sugar cane. It does not exist in bodies, but all sugar cane has invert sugar. That condition changes with the growth and ripening of the cane, in the early stages there being more of it, although in perfectly ripe sugar cane there is some of it.

Mr. HINDS. Invert sugar is grown?

Dr. WILEY. It is natural in cane, even in ripe cane, but in less quantity. In Louisiana invert sugar averages about 1¼ per cent, or from 1$\frac{1}{10}$ per cent to 1½ per cent. In Hawaii and in Cuba, where the cane is riper, I have seen it as low as two-tenths of 1 per cent, but it never disappears altogether.

Mr. HINDS. This invert sugar is a much lower grade?

Dr. WILEY. It is a much better sugar than sucrose, sweeter, but it does not crystallize; makes more molasses instead of sugar. The more invert sugar you have the larger your output of molasses.

Mr. HINDS. So that as the cane ripens it loses some of it?

Dr. WILEY. Loses its invert sugar to a certain extent and makes more sucrose.

Mr. HINDS. And therefore loses some of its sweetness?

Dr. WILEY. Invert sugar is sweeter than sucrose, so that it does lose some of its sweetness, taking that point of view.

Mr. FORDNEY. I wish to ask if the German-grown beet does not contain a greater amount of sugar and purity than the American-grown beet?

Dr. WILEY. No; I think just the opposite is the rule. They do not grow in Germany any such beets as we grow in our so-called arid regions.

Mr. FORDNEY. It has been claimed that on account of our lands being newer—cultivated for a shorter period of time than is true of the German lands—the purity of the sugar was less in this country than in Germany. I understand that that has been claimed as a fact by some of the beet-sugar men and would like to have you explain to us what the situation in that respect really is.

Dr. WILEY. It may be possible of some localities that that is true, because we have found out all round just where our beets grow best. If you were to try to bring the beet-sugar industry south you would have beets more and more impure the farther South you proceeded. That is, the purity would be reduced, the less the sugar you would have in them. On the other hand, the farther north you can get them and grow them at all the better your beets. Beets that grow in the high plateaus of our western region where irrigation is practiced seem to be best. Such locations seem to be ideal for the sugar beet. Beets grown in California are good.

Mr. FORDNEY. They are rich in sugar?

Dr. WILEY. Yes; but so far as purity is concerned I imagine probably our beets are a little less in power; that is, with a given amount of sugar we might get a slightly less yield than is had in

Germany. On the other hand, I believe that our beets, as a rule at least, contain more sugar than the German beets.

Mr. FORDNEY. I saw a report gotten out by the Agricultural Department and which just came to my office on Saturday as I recall, being for 1909-10, in which it was stated that the sugar in beets in Germany showed 17 per cent, while in this country it was much lower than that. What about that?

Dr. WILEY. I do not recall seeing any such figures, but if that is true they are growing great deal better sugar beets in Germany now than they were growing when I was studying and keeping in closer touch with their work. At that time you never saw a yield of 17 per cent in a whole crop.

Mr. FORDNEY. There have been figures at 17 per cent?

Dr. WILEY. Oh, yes; individual figures as high as 17 per cent; but I referred there in my answer to the whole crop. The crop ran a little lower than that; I think about 14 per cent, or probably about 15 per cent. Whole crops in this country have been higher than 15 per cent this past year.

Mr. FORDNEY. August, 1911, is the report to which I refer, but it gives the 1909-10 crop. It is now up in my office, and while I am not trying to prove that 17 per cent is the figure, my recollection of it is that 17 per cent is the figure stated for the German beet, and even that may be lower than the beets raised in this country, is why I asked the question.

Dr. WILEY. I should be rather surprised to see a whole crop in Germany average 17 per cent. However, I confess that for the past 10 years I have not kept up with the German beet industry.

Mr. HINDS. Is it not true that in Germany they give greater attention to breeding the beet in order to bring up its standard, and that being done, and probably having been done for years past, may it not well be that their beets would be better than our own?

Dr. WILEY. The whole value of the sugar beet is due to breeding. The natural sugar beet, from which the present sugar beet has been evolved, probably did not have more than 6 per cent or 7 per cent of sugar in it.

Mr. HINDS. Germany being its breeding place, might they not have a better beet?

Dr. WILEY. They have no more skill, I take it, and so far as the seeds are concerned ours were largely imported from Germany originally, though they may not be now.

Mr. MALBY. They are imported now, I believe.

Dr. WILEY. Then we get as good seed as they do.

Mr. HINDS. Do we get as good seed as they use?

Dr. WILEY. I imagine that they sell us as good seed as they use themselves. Of course there is this about the German industry and the French industry, it is 70 years old.

The CHAIRMAN. And they have therefore had more experience?

Dr. WILEY. Yes; they have had more experience and know where good beets grow. The first thing we had to do in this country, when I had charge of the official sugar-beet investigation, was to continue the work Dr. McMerkle started in 1878 and determine where the beets would grow.

Mr. HINDS. What did you find about the northeastern portion of this country—say, in New England, New York, and that region—what sort of territory would that be, naturally, for the sugar beet?

Dr. Wiley. Well, they grow good beets there; but somehow or other they never could grow them with profit.

Mr. Hinds. They are very near to the refineries, of course; but so far as the soil is concerned, is what I mean, and the climate.

Dr. Wiley. Soil is not much of a factor in producing the sugar beet. It is climate that makes the beet. It is just like the orange. You can not grow oranges in the open out here; but you can grow them in the sand in Florida. The sugar beet needs the climate; any good farmer can make the soil.

Mr. Hinds. What climate is required—combined sunshine and rain?

Dr. Wiley. Combined sunshine and low temperature during the summer. The sugar beet needs hours of sunshine and low temperature, and provided you have plenty of water you can make the soil all right. The soil, so far as sugar content is concerned, has nothing to do with it, though the soil determines the yield of crop. A poorer soil is apt to produce a smaller sugar beet, and the smaller the beet the sweeter it is.

Mr. Hinds. Where does the sugar that is in the beet come from?

Dr. Wiley. It comes from the sunshine and carbon dioxid and water; the Lord makes it. Not a particle of it comes from the soil. It is a pure gift from heaven.

Mr. Hinds. In other words,, it is more a pure gift from heaven than the result of the efforts of our people?

Dr. Wiley. Just as much, and not a particle of the sugar in the crop comes from the soil.

Mr. Hinds. If you could raise beets, extract the sugar, and put the pulp back on the land, your land would stand just as well as ever in the sum of its content, it only being the Lord who is drawn on?

Dr. Wiley. Yes; you could sell the sugar so gotten without impoverishing the land at all. If all of the beet except the sugar were put back on the soil the soil would be just as rich as before the beet was planted and grown.

The Chairman. Might that be kept up from year to year? In other words, if you had a yield of 15 tons of sugar-beets from a given field and you put back everything, but the sugar could you indefinitely maintain the fertility of the soil of that field?

Dr. Wiley. Yes.

Mr. Fordney. Plant food does not go into the sugar but into the other structure of the beet?

Dr. Wiley. The things that go into the beet do so to make up its structure, and if you put everything but the sugar back on the soil you thereby put back all potash, nitrogen, and so on.

The Chairman. Then there is no necessity for rotating the crops?

Dr. Wiley. Well, I would not say that. There is such a thing as making the soil tired of the crop. I think it might probably be better to rotate the crops. The beet attracts a huge army of enemies, bacterial and insectorial, and the longer you grow them the more danger you will have from that source. You should put in another crop in order to kill out enemies of a bacterial and insect nature which infest the land where beets are grown. But so far as nourishment in the soil is concerned you might grow beets forever without injury thereto.

The Chairman. The reason you have just given is the reason that seems to make for rotation of crops?

Dr. WILEY. That is one of the great principles of rotation, is that fact. And, furthermore, we never put back on a field all that we take off in the case of any crop, unless it be in the form of manure, because there is some waste.

Mr. MALBY. The matter of rotation is not peculiar to the sugar-beet crop but is applicable to all crops on a farm?

Dr. WILEY. Yes; the same principle of rotation seems to apply. Wheat is the only crop we seem to be able to grow year after year on the same field.

Mr. HINDS. Is that peculiarity of taking a great deal from the heavens above especially applicable to the beet?

Dr. WILEY. Oh, no; every crop that makes sugar or cellulose, those are the two great crops.

Mr. HINDS. Is it peculiar to turnips, corn, and those things?

Dr. WILEY. Every bit of sugar in turnips and corn and so on comes from the atmosphere and water and sunshine, and all cellulose and wood fiber. They contain nitrogenous matter besides. Cotton is almost purely a gift from heaven. The farmer who sells butter and fat of every kind is selling what is a gift of God, that does not come from the soil. The farmer who sells lard, butter, or sugar does not impoverish his soil in the production thereof.

Mr. HINDS. Provided he sees that the waste goes back?

Dr. WILEY. Yes. The man that makes butter and keeps his cattle and puts the manure back on the soil enriches it, and the soil thereby gets richer and richer every year.

Mr. HINDS. Is that true also of the starch of the potato?

Dr. WILEY. Starch is the same thing. Starch is a gift from heaven, just as sugar is. Not a particle of starch comes from the soil; in fact, there is not much that comes from the soil because the nitrogenous and phosphorus bodies that are useful to man are to build the crop. The phosphorus and nitrogen that we have largely comes from the soil.

The CHAIRMAN. Are there any further questions which the members of the committee wish to ask?

Dr. WILEY. There is one thing that I thought would be useful to this committee. My assistant and I have calculated, from a scientific point of view, as nearly as we can how much tax sugar ought to pay on the basis of 1 cent per pound for pure sugar, from which basis any amount of revenue that you gentlemen might place on sugar may be worked out from that simple factor.

The CHAIRMAN. In other words, taking 100 per cent sugar, you may figure out by comparison what would be fair for other sugars?

Dr. WILEY. Yes.

The CHAIRMAN. All right, we will be glad to have that information.

Dr. WILEY. We have gone over all the authorities we can find to get at what sugar may yield. If you have 100 pounds of pure sugar, that is your yield, and the tax on that is 1 cent. The first column refers to polarization, starting at 99 and goes down to 75.5.

The CHAIRMAN. That will be interesting.

Dr. WILEY. The tables do not include any extra cost of manufacture. They only include what sugar has averaged if you are going to get it of a certain grade polarization. For instance, you go down to 75 per cent, which is the basic polarization for the present tariff, you would only get 53 pounds of sugar out of 100 pounds of 75 per cent polarization. We say if the tax is 1 cent per pound it should be fifty-three one hundredths of 1 cent on that to give it a fair show.

Mr. FORDNEY. Is the other 47 per cent sirup?

Dr. WILEY. It is ash and waste which comes in to pull down the yield. For instance, 100 pounds of 99 per cent polarization ought to yield 98 pounds refined sugar; 100 pounds of 98 per cent polarization ought to yield 97 pounds refined sugar, and so on all the way down, one by one. I furnish two tables here, one cane sugar and the other beet sugar.

Table giving figures for direct polarization, percentage of ash, percentage of reducing sugars, and rendement or "net analysis."

The rendement is obtained by subtracting five times the ash, also the percentage of reducing sugars, from the polarization.

In calculating the values which are given in the last column, the average rendement for the different degrees polarization is given.

CANE SUGAR.

Country and kind of sugar.	Polarization.	Ash.	Reducing sugars.	Rendement.	Value.
Sucrose	100.0	......	......	100.00	1.0000
Java, whites	99.0	0.13	0.20	98.15	.9815
Java, crystals	98.8	.13	.30	97.85	.9745
Do	98.6	.22	.40	97.10	
Egypt, first sugar	97.9	.31	50	95.85	
Peru, crystals	97.6	.47	.90	94.35	
Trinidad, centrifugals	97.5	.45	.67	94.08	
Java:					
Crystals	97.5	.35	.60	95.15	.9421
Seconds	97.2	.38	1.01	94.29	
Crystals	97.0	.23	.76	95.09	
Seconds	97.0	1.10	.85	90.65	
Surinam, first sugar	96.8	.23	1.28	93.37	
Hawaii, crystals	96.6	.54	.83	93.07	
Java, crystals	96.5	.47	.84	93.41	
Trinidad, crystals	96.5	.38	.99	93.61	
Cuba, crystals	96.4	.54	.67	93.03	.929
Brazil, crystals	96.3	.18	1.67	93.73	
Louisiana, crystals	96.1	.50	1.47	92.13	
Hawaii, crystals	96.0	.77	1.32	90.83	
Porto Rico, crystals	95.8	.43	1.40	92.25	
Demerara, crystals	95.8	.38	1.42	92.48	
Java, crystals	95.5	.95	1.40	89.35	
Hawaii, crystals	95.4	.74	.77	90.93	.9125
Peru, crystals	95.3	.32	1.87	91.83	
Demerara, crystals	95.0	.59	1.40	90.65	
Mexico, crystals	94.7	.63	1.57	89.97	.8832
Java, seconds	94.0	1.11	1.78	86.67	
Mexico	92.6	1.19	1.47	85.18	.8518
Jamaica, grocery	90.3	.97	3.08	82.33	.8176
Philippine, mat sugar	90.1	1.08	3.51	81.19	
Barbados, muscovado	88.6	.47	5.30	80.95	.7685
Demerara, grocery	88.5	2.54	3.06	72.74	
Guatemala, grocery	86.4	.50	7.32	76.58	.7254
Barbados, grocery	86.2	2.66	4.40	68.50	
Java, concrete sugar	84.8	2.25	2.74	74.81	
Philippine, mat sugar	84.0	1.62	7.02	68.88	.6764
Peru, sirup sugar	84.5	4.70	1.76	59.24	
Demerara, sugar	82.9	3.58	3.84	61.26	.6325
Java, molasses	82.4	2.27	5.81	65.24	
Brazil, molasses	80.5	1.85	6.83	63.43	
Egypt, second sugar	80.4	5.52	3.40	49.40	.5615
Philippine, mat sugar	80.5	3.06	9.56	55.64	
Java. concrete sugar	75.5	2.50	9.60	53.40	.5340

This table has been prepared from the figures given in Gredinger's "Die Raffination des Zuckers."

BEET SUGAR.

Table giving figures for direct polarization, rendement or "net analysis," and value.

Polarization.	Rendement.	Value.
100.0	100.00	1.0000
99.0	96.62	.9662
98.0	95.6	.956
97.0	94.2	.942
96.0	92.2	.922
95.0	90.2	.902

The rendement of a beet sugar is generally determined by subtracting five times the ash from the direct polarization, although of late some authorities calculate it by subtracting two and a quarter times the total nonsugars from the direct polarization.

Mr. HINDS. How does that run with the present classification, with the present law?

Dr. WILEY. I think it is pretty close, but I have not made any calculation.

Mr. HINDS. Did they take your advice when they were framing the present law?

Dr. WILEY. I don't think they did in all cases. I advised them strongly to leave out the Dutch standard as long ago as 1897.

Mr. HINDS. But they did have apparently some scientific information?

Dr. WILEY. The tariff was based on some computation such as this, but we did not make it. This is based solely on the yield as established by the best authorities on the supposition that the tax ought to be in keeping with the yield of refined sugar.

Mr. HINDS. What was your reason for recommending that they leave out the Dutch standard, to rehabilitate the old brown sugar?

Dr. WILEY. The reason I urged it before was because I thought it was a protection to the refiners.

Mr. HINDS. That is, the cane refiners?

Dr. WILEY. Well, the sugar refiners.

Mr. HINDS. That means the cane refiners in this country?

Dr. WILEY. In this country largely, because we do not use much but cane sugar except what we grow ourselves. I did not see reason for doing any other way is the reason I urged it, and always have urged it before the committees because it was only just.

The CHAIRMAN. It is just as much protection to people who sell beet sugar?

Dr. WILEY. Yes; the basic tariff on the amount of sugar brought into this country is a protection to the beet-sugar men the same as to anybody else.

Mr. HINDS. Just how does that work out for the refiner?

Dr. WILEY. It enables the refiner by having produced this taste for white sugar—and I am not complaining of that—absolutely to control the whole sugar supply in this country. That is, we have no chance to get any sugar in this country to-day except as we get it through the refiner in this country.

Mr. HINDS. Are there stores of sugar that would not come through the refiners that would come in here from the world at large?

Dr. WILEY. That might be, but they would only get in according to the protection. The refiner in England can sell it here just the same as the refiner in this country can, and then we would have the same chance of getting sugar, if we did not want to buy from our own refiners. Now, we can not do that; they do not bring any refined sugar into this country now at all of any consequence.

The CHAIRMAN. Why not?

Dr. WILEY. Because of this differential.

The CHAIRMAN. And if the Dutch standard could be wiped out it could all come in?

Dr. WILEY. Yes; if we could import as much refined sugar as raw sugar; but it wouldn't do any good in the world and would hurt the beet-sugar industry, and I have been encouraging it. I believe it to be one of the best things for the agriculture of this country that could possibly exist, because if one raises beets he must use scientific methods. Every beet-sugar field is practically an experimental station, which teaches every farmer in the neighborhood. I am in favor of protecting the sugar crop in Louisiana and all along the coast. I am not making a plea for taking the tariff off of sugar at all; I am only trying to tell you what the Dutch standard does.

The CHAIRMAN. You say you are in favor of protecting sugar. Do you believe there will ever be any chance for our competing with the world without protection?

Dr. WILEY. Maybe so in the future.

The CHAIRMAN. Although you see reasonable prospects of that I ask do you see any chance of it?

Dr. WILEY. I would protect them even if I thought there would never be any chance of it. I want to purchase our own sugar at home.

Mr. FORDNEY. You are now with me way down in the bottom of my heart. Dr. Wiley, you and I are together on that proposition.

Dr. WILEY. Very well, are you going to join me in getting rid of this differential?

Mr. FORDNEY. Anything that is best and that will help the situation. It has been said that the Dutch standard does not meet the situation?

Dr. WILEY. I think that is it.

Mr. FORDNEY. Dr. Wiley, I will say that I am with you heart and soul in the sentiment you just expressed, and if this will be the proper thing and prevent any injustice all right.

Dr. WILEY. I think that is true.

The CHAIRMAN. The same thing is true of the differential.

Dr. WILEY. That is the differential that I am talking about. The differential is fixed on the Dutch-standard plan. I would be opposed to it if it were the polarization differential, just the same.

Mr. FORDNEY. Maybe I did not make myself plain just now. The abolishment of the Dutch standard and resort altogether to the polariscope would be no advantage whatever to the refiner; to use the Dutch standard instead of the polariscope as a test, that is an advantage to the refiner. Is that so?

Dr. WILEY. Well, of course the differential is based on the Dutch standard, but you can base it on the polariscope. It would be just as bad if you were to say that all sugar polarizing over 97 should pay a differential; you would have the same bad condition as you have to-day.

Mr. HINDS. When you use 16 Dutch standard?

Dr. WILEY. Yes; I would be opposed to that.

Mr. FORDNEY. The differential being the same as 190 to 21½. Is that 21½ on pure sugar?

Dr. WILEY. I have not looked at that.

Mr. HINDS. It is 195, isn't it?

Dr. WILEY. No; the Payne law reduced it from 195 to 190.

Mr. HINDS. Do you mean by abolishing the differential that the refiner shall take the raw sugar, paying the tariff on that, but that the refined-sugar tariff shall be so adjusted as to leave him no protection on his refining process?

Dr. WILEY. Our refiners can beat the world without any differential if they want to. They have more skill and more ingenuity than the foreign refiners. They can compete with them without any trouble.

Mr. HINDS. How much does the labor of refining enter into the cost of refined sugar?

Dr. WILEY. Well, that is not very much, because one man can handle 100 tons per day.

Mr. FORDNEY. You say the labor cost of refining sugar is very small?

Dr. WILEY. Yes.

Mr. FORDNEY. In the 40 cents per 100 pounds which it costs to refine sugar there enters any loss or shrinkage between raw and refined sugar, labor, capital invested, wear and tear on machinery, interest, taxes, and everything, I suppose?

Dr. WILEY. I have not gone into that point at all. I imagine it is that way, however.

Mr. HINDS. Can you refer us to any authorities on that point?

Dr. WILEY. Well, the only authorities that I know of would be the books of the refiners, which would show just what the cost is.

Mr. HINDS. Do you not think that a question of that sort would have to be examined into quite scientifically by the tariff board or some body of that sort?

Dr. WILEY. I think it ought to be.

Mr. HINDS. I should imagine so myself.

Dr. WILEY. But the point I am giving is this, that under the present system we are absolutely dependent upon the refiners of this country for our sugar. They have taught us to use white sugar and we will not take any other kind, and therefore they can fix any price thereon they please. I will say, on the question of price, that I think they are very reasonable about it and do not try to squeeze us very much. At the same time, whenever the Louisiana sugar comes in the price of sugar drops, and whenever the crop of beet sugar comes in the price of sugar drops. Again, as soon as the Louisiana and beet sugar men sell all they have to sell the price of sugar goes up again.

Mr. FORDNEY. That is true of last summer, I believe.

Dr. WILEY. Yes; and when the price of sugar went up to 7 cents retail I said, "Watch out; when the sugar crop comes in it will go down," and it did, and there was no sugar in the country even then.

Mr. FORDNEY. Was there any difference in the world supply?

Dr. WILEY. No; we know just about as much about the world supply now as then. I do not think it right to make it possible to manipulate prices that way.

Mr. HINDS. The London Economist has kept an index number for many years, and I was reading an article in that paper which gave an index number in the United States and in England for quite a considerable range of food products, and also a range of what they call materials, such as cotton, wool, and things of that sort. They compared a 10-year period, 10 years back, with the present; that is, not exactly the present cost, because their table did not include this recent rise in sugar, but what was called their present price was last year's price. As I say, they issued an index number on all those commodities, the prices rising greatly with the exception of one commodity, and that was sugar. It showed sugar had risen very little in the United States, I think four points, while it had actually decrease a little in England. Can you tell me why it is or what conditions caused sugar to be so unique among the products showing a rise in prices in the last 10 or 15 years?

Dr. WILEY. Well, of course I do not have those figures before me, but I know that a few years ago the price of raw sugar, under the bounty system which was in vogue in Europe, fell almost or entirely below the possible cost of production.

Mr. HINDS. That is, the stimulation of that bounty system affected the production?

Dr. WILEY. Yes; the Germans were paying for all of the sugar that the English ate, and that depressed the markets of the world; 10 or 15 years ago the Cuban could not get one-twelfth cent for his raw sugar hardly. Sugar raisers are getting more for their sugar to-day than ever.

Mr. HINDS. The stimulation of that beet-sugar crop in Europe and the increase in the world's crop may affect the price of sugar phenomenally?

Dr. WILEY. I look at this matter as I do everything else in which the farmers are interested; I want the farmers to have a fair chance in the markets, governed by supply and demand as to rise and fall, and not have everything they grow and everything they buy manipulated as to price by somebody that has nobody's interests at heart but their own. I can not sell a steer to-day, or a bushel of wheat, or a bushel of corn at a price governed by supply and demand, nor can you. The price of a steer, or of a bushel of wheat, or of a bushel of corn is set by a set of gamblers in Chicago or elsewhere.

Mr. HINDS. Is sugar affected in the same way; have they been able to get hold of sugar?

Dr. WILEY. Sugar is right in the hands of the refiners of this country, and they can do anything they please with it.

Mr. FORDNEY. Is that price of sugar fixed by the beet-sugar manufacturers or by some fellows over in New York?

Dr. WILEY. Somebody fixes it—it is not left to supply and demand.

Mr. HINDS. Why have the refiners been very much more reasonable during the past 10 years than others, then?

Dr. WILEY. The business man who manipulates prices now must keep it close to the margin or else the people will rise in rebellion. I am not complaining about the price they put on sugar, but am complaining of the principle of the thing.

Mr. FORDNEY. Can you imagine why the refiners of foreign sugars with their factories located in Philadelphia, Boston, and elsewhere are so anxious to have the duty on imported sugar removed?

Dr. WILEY. I beg pardon, but I did not catch your question.

Mr. FORDNEY. Can you imagine why the refiners of foreign sugars are so anxious to have the duty removed from that foreign raw sugar, except it be to compete with the domestic industry and control the market?

Dr. WILEY. My idea of a tariff—whether it be called a protective tariff, a revenue-producing tariff, or by any other name—is that it should be what may be necessary under the circumstances, but that it should not permit of manipulation or make it possible for somebody to corner the market by some differential or other way that we do not see plainly.

Mr. FORDNEY. The fact is that the refiner in New York does not control the market while our domestic sugar crop is on the market?

Dr. WILEY. As soon as the domestic sugar crop comes on they let the price drop, for they are then buyers themselves. They buy the most of the domestic crop except the beet sugar—buy almost all of the Louisiana crop.

Mr. FORDNEY. That is because it is raw sugar?

Dr. WILEY. Yes. They then want to buy and put the price down.

Mr. FORDNEY. And as soon as the crop is purchased they increase the price, do you mean?

Dr. WILEY. Yes; as high as they think the people will stand for. They do not put the price out of sight, because that would not be good business.

Mr. FORDNEY. Last year they put the price at 7½ cents per pound?

Dr. WILEY. Yes.

Mr. FORDNEY. The people had to have it during the canning season?

Dr. WILEY. Yes.

Mr. FORDNEY. That is when they were making the most profit?

Dr. WILEY. Yes. I was asked the other day about refined Scotch sugar. Being a Scotchman myself and knowing the canny nature of our people, I wondered if a Scotchman could make Scotch sugar perfectly dry polarize 85. I didn't think that he could do it. There was a sample of Scotch sugar claimed to have very low polarization, but we found it ordinary 96 per cent sugar. There is no way by which a Scotchman can make sugar, which is surcose, polarize 85 per cent and have it dry unless he mixes some mineral substance with it, which is adulteration.

Mr. HINDS. Don't they make a cake in Scotland that polarizes near 100?

Dr. WILEY. Ordinary loaf sugar, do you mean?

Mr. HINDS. No; shortcake, I think they call it.

Dr. WILEY. I haven't seen it.

Mr. HINDS. I have had some brought to me.

Dr. WILEY. There is a conical mass of dry sugar that is sold all over Europe, but I haven't seen it in Scotland. Now, gentlemen of the committee, what I am submitting to you is simply this special difference between the methods of grading sugar by the Dutch standard, which are totally unreliable, and the accurate method secured by the use of the polariscope, which is reliable, and submitting a set of yield records from different polarizations taken from the best authorities we can get.

Mr. FORDNEY. A minute ago you said something about the duty——

Dr. WILEY. I say that the consumer pays the duty.

Mr. FORDNEY. In the report of the Tariff Board, submitted a few days ago, they contradict that idea as to one grade of cloth, saying that the consumer here does not pay the duty fixed by law.

Dr. WILEY. Who does pay it?

Mr. FORDNEY. The competition here has brought the price of cost of production down way below the amount of the duty. As an illustration, I will tell you that they found from 16 different kinds of cloth, which they put together, cost in England $41.84, the duty on which was $76 and some cents. If the duty were added to the $41.84 that cloth would cost $118 and some cents—we will say $118.80. The Tariff Board says that the cost of production here is double what it is over there, which would make these articles cost $83.68. Yet with this cost in England of $41.84 and duty of $76, making a total of $118, this same cloth is being sold here for $69.90. That is the Tariff Board's report on those 16 articles of cloth.

The CHAIRMAN. That is a funny report and at variance with every principle of common sense.

Mr. RAKER. Is that just one article?

Mr. FORDNEY. No; 16 different kinds of cloth. In this case it would seem that the consumer does not pay the duty.

The CHAIRMAN. That is just a remarkable exception which proves the rule.

Mr. HINDS. I will say that I bought 4½ yards of cloth at a Maine mill, in the district where I live, and paid $3.75 for the cloth, the price which the mill asked for it. I took it to the Portland customhouse and the appraiser of customs took it to his room, measured it, weighed it, went through it according to his method, and told me the duty on that cloth if I were bringing it in from England would be $3.65. Yet I paid $3.75 for it at the mill.

Mr. FORDNEY. If you paid the duty on that cloth the cost of production was practically nothing.

Mr. HINDS. There was 10 cents difference between the duty and what I paid for the cloth.

Mr. FORDNEY. Yes; the difference between the cost you paid and the duty was 10 cents, leaving 10 cents for the real cost of production.

Mr. HINDS. Dr. Wiley, do you not wish to qualify your statement that the consumer pays the whole duty, the amount of duty that is on the article, and say depending upon the amount of the commodity that is in the country at the time? For instance, our farmers in Maine tell us that the potato duty—they say that three years out of four or five the potato duty does not amount to anything, but if there does come a year of excessive production in this country that year it does help them. In other words, is not that addition of the duty to price a variable thing, depending upon the ratio of duty to consumption in the country at the time?

Dr. WILEY. Of course I am not a business man, but if I were in business and would bring in an object to this country and pay a duty on it I would expect to sell it for enough to pay me for that duty and make some profit besides. That is the only way I would know how to do business.

Mr. MALBY. You see that that principle does not apply in the case that Mr. Hinds refers to. This year we are importing potatoes from

Scotland. There were 100,000 bushels unloaded in New York during the past month, coming from Scotland. They paid 25 cents per bushel duty on them. At the same time that shipment had no particular relation to the tariff. There is a very great scarcity in this country, and that condition controlled the price.

Dr. WILEY. If the man who brought in those 100,000 bushels had not paid that 25-cent duty could he not have sold them 25 cents cheaper to the people of this country?

Mr. FORDNEY. I doubt whether he would.

Dr. WILEY. He could have done it, whether he would have done it or not.

Mr. MALBY. He would get all that he could probably?

Dr. WILEY. Yes.

Mr. MALBY. There is a question always in my mind when we talk about the consumer paying the duty. While technically he may pay a portion or in some instances all of the duty, yet that is not very useful in determining exactly what he would have to pay were we entirely dependent on the foreign producer to supply us with the needful article. That is to say, if we import granulated sugars under present conditions the consumer might have to pay nearly the amount of the tariff, but that does not indicate at all to my mind what the consumer would have to pay if we did not have any sugar manufacturers in New Orleans, or the beet-sugar industry were entirely wiped out, as it probably would be if we did not have any tariff. So that when we are considering what is wise and best to do with the tariff on sugars, applying it to this case, we can not very well console ourselves with the thought that if the tariff were entirely removed we would get sugars for so much less. Because, forsooth, we might have nothing to come in competition with it at all, and then the price might be very much higher than with a tariff.

Dr. WILEY. That is the very reason why I am a protectionist. But my idea of protection is to raise the price so that the man in this country can make a living.

Mr. MALBY. That is my idea, too.

The CHAIRMAN. If the duty did not raise the price, there would be no protection?

Dr. WILEY. Undoubtedly. If the tariff does not raise the price to the consumer, it isn't any protection at all.

Mr. MALBY. It certainly does raise the price under the then existing condition, but it doesn't solve the question at all.

Dr. WILEY. I quite agree with you that under a temporary increase in price we might establish an industry in this country which will eventually decrease the price to our people.

Mr. MALBY. Take the case at hand; we know that when the cane sugar and the beet sugar came upon the market the price of refined sugar went down. What would have been the result if we had none at all?

Dr. WILEY. It probably would have been the same thing.

Mr. MALBY. Do you think it would have gone down?

Dr. WILEY. The minute they begin to market the crop the price falls.

Mr. MALBY. I do not quite agree with you on that.

Mr. FORDNEY. Very well, we paid 7½ cents per pound for sugar in September without any domestic crop on the market. Now, if we had had no domestic crop at all there is no reason to suppose the price of refined sugar would be any lower to-day than it was in September, because then there would be no crop conditions to change that price?

Dr. WILEY. No; but crop conditions are even worse than in September. The crop of sugar is going to be less in this country on account of the great freeze in Louisiana, which cut off 100,000 pounds in one night.

Mr. FORDNEY. That is the answer to the whole subject in a nutshell.

Mr. RAKER. Still sugar went down instead of going up?

Dr. WILEY. Yes.

Mr. HINDS. Isn't it a fact that the amount of sugar in the world is of more importance than the tariff or anything else?

Dr. WILEY. Sir?

Mr. HINDS. Isn't it reasonable to suppose that the great stimulation in the production of sugar in the world, due to certain arrangement in European countries, is what makes sugar to-day so exceptional a commodity, and that it has grown, if anything, cheaper instead of dearer amid a general rise in prices?

Dr. WILEY. That is the reason I am a protectionist, just to establish such industries.

Mr. HINDS. The increase in the amount of the commodity is more vital than the tariff?

Dr. WILEY. Yes; but I can not see any benefit in giving a differential on sugar.

Mr. MALBY. Of course sugar hasn't got a monopoly upon the question of the tariff. That is, the woolen goods, cotton goods, and boot and shoe manufacturers, and so on, could not continue their business in this country without a protective tariff; so that the tariff on sugar is not special with reference to that?

Dr. WILEY. They might have a tariff called a tariff for revenue.

Mr. MALBY. I do not care what you call it.

Dr. WILEY. If you lay the same duties and say they are for revenue, of course you get the same effect. That is true.

Mr. MALBY. I do not care what you call them.

Mr. HINDS. If we require the sugar refiners to put out an immense amount of money for paying duty on raw sugar—and that is one of the burdens they complain of, Mr. Spreckels and other refiners, and that is to continue if we are to keep that duty on raw sugar—of course they would be at considerable disadvantage if all of the differential were taken off, wouldn't they, in that they would lose that amount of capital continually?

Dr. WILEY. Well, I can not see it that way, because they would be brought into competition then. Sugar is a manufactured article, whether raw or refined. The duty on sugar is a duty on a manufactured article. Sugar cane is brought in at a much lower rate of duty than sugar. We already recognize sugar as a manufactured article. Let us lay a duty on all of it as a manufactured article; don't make a separation between grades except as to weight, and that is already fixed by the scale of the tariff—a higher polarization, a higher duty. If you want to manufacture it completely it is a higher rate, and if you want to manufacture it lower it is a lower rate.

Mr. MALBY. I have been wondering what the producer of raw sugar would do to comply with your suggestion and bring in sugar in the State where it could be used. We find millions of pounds of sugar in the raw state from all parts of the world, sugar enough for human consumption, we will say, but some process would have to be adopted to make it fit for use here. It occurred to me that it was a question whether your small sugar producer, say in Java, the Philippines, and some other places, could have his raw sugar in such shape as it could be sold to the consumer; it did not appear to me that that is possible except through a great deal of labor. In other words, I wonder if they have or could obtain the facilities with moderate expense, so that the man who produced sugar from a small place, say a small plot of ground in Java, could put it on the market in America direct without going through some other hands?

Dr. WILEY. My only impression is that we are finding the industry necessary. In a small way some are trying to make the other sugar popular, but it could not bear the test of commercial competition here now. In this country and in other countries we have come to manufacture on a large scale raw sugar that is edible; cane sugar of course in every way can be used. But, I say, if our people would learn to use the yellow sugar it would be very much cheaper and better.

Mr. MALBY. I think it would be all right if they could produce it in such shape as you have it exhibited here, but I apprehend that if you took the Java planter, who perhaps has half an acre, or maybe as low as a quarter acre, whatever little plot of ground he could afford to handle, he would hardly be able to put the sugar on the market in any form that it could be used, and if he had to sell it to somebody he would do it through the refiner.

Dr. WILEY. It would probably have to be sold to the refiner. The same thing is true of maple sugar, if you send out in Canada.

Mr. MALBY. We manufacture a good deal of maple sugar in northern New York. I used to manufacture it myself when I was a boy on the farm, and it is not difficult to produce maple sugar that is edible.

Dr. WILEY. Yes, the Indians do it to-day in Canada.

Mr. MALBY. I do not know why the Canadians produce some maple sugar that is so black.

Dr. WILEY. If our people could be taught to use yellow cane sugar all of these people would try to make better sugar; and just see what we would save in freights. Lots of this sugar comes over here 50 per cent water and dirt, and we have to pay the freight on it. It would be cheaper to bring it over here in a higher state.

Mr. HINDS. Dr. Wiley, as a scientist, would you not think, in view of the many delicate questions of chemistry and production and habit and predisposition of the public and everything of that sort, that the only way we could get at what adjustments of duties ought to be made, what the adjustments of differential ought to be, would be to have this whole question gone into by the Tariff Board as a matter of business, as they have gone into wool? Do you believe that by investigating the subject in a desultory way, like this committee is and must do it, it is possible for us to go into these adjustments any better than the Ways and Means Committee have done it?

Dr. Wiley. I could not express an opinion on that. To go into this in a scientific way you would have to supplement what my assistant and I have done—to go into the actual production of sugar. It may cost more to take raw sugar and make good sugar; that is a matter we did not consider in these tables. We can tell you from the point of view covered here what sugar will yield of different grades, based on the experience of many years of practice. Now, the additional cost of making white sugar out of low-grade sugar must come into consideration. But then you must remember that they get more by-products out of the low-grade sugar.

The Chairman. Those matters are easily ascertainable.

Dr. Wiley. Yes; but the point I am making is as to this refining industry. The fingers of my two hands [holding up hands] are about all there are in this country.

Mr. Fordney. Your fingers are too many to express them.

Dr. Wiley. Yes, and to put the control of the business in those few hands, we come here and put a differential on sugar and it practically puts the supply of sugar in this country into those hands. I do not think that is right.

The Chairman. Let me ask you one or two questions. Do you believe that the sugar refiners had anything to do with raising sugar 2 cents in price?

Dr. Wiley. Well, I would not like to say. I have been so lambasted for saying just incidentally things of this kind that I am very thin skinned about it.

The Chairman. All right; I won't embarrass you. I am not thin skinned, although I have been lambasted I am taking up for them on this proposition. In the first place, if the rise in sugar was not confined to this country, but was greater at Hamburg and at London and in other markets, it would seem to acquit our American refiners of any particular guilt about it?

Dr. Wiley. Well, it would seem so; yes.

The Chairman. If it also is true that they have to pay more money, lock up more capital—in other words, if raw sugar went up just the same as refined sugar, it was not to the refiners' interest to run the price up except to correspond?

Dr. Wiley. It is not to their interest to make the price too high, as I said awhile ago.

The Chairman. I can not see how it would be to the interest of the refiners, but I will not press the question, as I do not care about embarrassing you. I will add, that if the price of refined sugar was run up without running the price of raw sugar up, of course it would be to the interest of the refiners. We can all see that. But if when the price of refined sugar goes up the price of raw sugar goes up correspondingly, I do not see anything that the refiners make out of it.

Dr. Wiley. Why does the price go up?

The Chairman. They would put it up because they buy the raw sugar at a higher price?

Dr. Wiley. Somewhere it is put up.

The Chairman. The people who sell the raw sugar put it up.

Dr. Wiley. Do they put it down, too?

The Chairman. It is just like anything else, I take it, supply and demand, I think.

Dr. WILEY. If you will notice since the wheat harvest wielded an influence in this country, the magnitude of it, the price of wheat varies at different times; the price of wheat has varied 10 cents per bushel in the past two months.

The CHAIRMAN. I knew there had been some little change.

Dr. WILEY. The extremes in price have varied as much as 10 cents per bushel in the past two months; why is that?

The CHAIRMAN. Because the crop of wheat is larger than they gambled on?

Dr. WILEY. I don't know why.

Mr. HINDS. The explanation given in the London Economist as to price of sugar was that in Europe when the price went up it was because of reports of shortage in the European crop instead of sugar speculators.

The CHAIRMAN. Yes; you will find that the American refiners actually paid as much more for their raw sugar as they got out of their refined.

Dr. WILEY. So they didn't make any more.

The CHAIRMAN. They made less, because their raw sugar cost them more, and in my opinion they actually lost money.

Mr. FORDNEY. I want to say that I have a statement in my possession, which I will produce when we come to make up our report, showing the importation of sugar at every port of entry in the United States for the last fiscal year, or for July, August, September, and October, 1911, and the prices taken from the invoices on those entries shows that sugar purchased for delivery in July, August, September, and October, 1911, were on contracts made when the price of sugar was low, and that there were no sugars being imported in August and September, 1911, or practically none at all, on the quotations given for those months.

The CHAIRMAN. That does not make any difference.

Mr. FORDNEY. It makes a whole lot of difference.

The CHAIRMAN. It shows that the refiners took advantage of their opportunities, the same as do the beet-sugar men.

Mr. FORDNEY. It shows the difference in the propositions, because when the beet-sugar crop came on the market it brought the price down from 7½ cents to 5.55 cents.

Mr. RAKER. You answered a question a moment ago that I want a little explanation on. You said you had not investigated the matter of sugar refiners raising the price and did not want to express an opinion thereon, and in that connection using the expression "thin skinned." In anything you have made an investigation of and understand, there is nothing thin skinned about you and about what you have to state on subjects of that kind, is there?

Dr. WILEY. Not a bit. I want to say this: That all these questions on political economy and prices are beyond the scope of my investigation. I will not say anything on a thing I have not investigated, and did not come here to speak on them at all.

The CHAIRMAN. There is one more question I want to ask, and this would not be asked but for the statement you made. You said you were a protectionist and believed in encouraging this sugar industry as well as all other industries in the United States, I believe?

Dr. WILEY. I believe in establishing the sugar industry in the United States.

The CHAIRMAN. Let us see how far you go in this matter of protection. Suppose the truth is that it cost about 4 cents per pound to produce every pound of beet and cane sugar in the United States, while other countries may on account of their conditions, method of production, labor, or other causes, produce cane sugar for 1 cent per pound and beet sugar for 2 cents per pound, do you still think the American consumer ought to pay the difference in price?

Dr. WILEY. That is a pretty difficult proposition; you are asking me to consider a good many things.

The CHAIRMAN. I just want to see how far you are a protectionist.

Dr. WILEY. I will tell you very frankly how far I will go. I will go this far as a protectionist: When I consider the beneficial effect of this sugar industry on other agricultural industries I would go as far as it would be profitable to the farmers of the United States to maintain that industry.

The CHAIRMAN. No matter how much it cost the people who consumed that sugar?

Dr. WILEY. Yes; no matter how much it cost. If it were a benefit to the agricultural interests of this country as a whole, then I am for it. If I looked at it simply from the standpoint of the interest of the man making the sugar, as I stated before, I would not want to tax myself as a consumer too much; but if I see that by paying a little more for my sugar the great agricultural industry in this country is benefited, I am willing to pay it. I would go just that far.

Mr. HINDS. Would you also not be governed by the fact of the general prosperity which has come in this country, giving a present income to workers of from two to two and one-half times what it is elsewhere? Isn't that a problem to be considered in that connection also?

Dr. WILEY. I do not know just what the difference is.

Mr. HINDS. Well, it is close to that, isn't it?

Dr. WILEY. I do not know that labor in this country is more highly paid than similar labor in other countries.

The CHAIRMAN. And you know that it costs a good deal more to live here than in England?

Dr. WILEY. Yes; it costs more.

Mr. MALBY. But not in that proportion.

Mr. RAKER. If two-thirds of this labor, or maybe three-fourths of it, were foreign labor, used in producing cane and beets?

Dr. WILEY. Yes; with foreign labor.

Mr. RAKER. Wouldn't you make a difference there also?

Dr. WILEY. Yes; but because the labor is performed in the United States. I think that is a benefit to the United States. I think it is a benefit to me that my shoemaker lives in this country, even if I pay a little more for my shoes, because he is a citizen and he contributes to the general welfare.

Mr. RAKER. If these men have protection for the purpose of producing their sugar beets and cane ought they not to pay good, high American wages for their labor instead of foreign labor?

Dr. WILEY. Do you mean that he imports foreign labor?

Mr. RAKER. Yes.

Dr. WILEY. Well, that is contrary to law.

Mr. RAKER. I mean that he has here.

Dr. WILEY. He probably hires labor as low as he can, but do you think you can get foreign labor in this country at less than you have to pay home labor?

Mr. RAKER. Oh, yes. It has been testified here that sugar-beet and sugar-cane people do that.

Dr. WILEY. Then I wish they would send some up to my farm in Loudoun County, Va.

Mr. RAKER. You would employ your neighbors or low-price labor?

Dr. WILEY. I pay pretty good wages.

The CHAIRMAN. Have the members of the committee any other questions to ask Dr. Wiley?

Dr. WILEY. Gentlemen of the committee, this discussion of political economy by me I hope you will not take too seriously, because that is not my specialty. I have my own views about it, but would not like to say they are perfectly safe.

Mr. MALBY. You can do as well as the rest of us on that score, for the rest of us are more or less guessing at it.

The CHAIRMAN. If there are no other questions we will excuse Dr. Wiley, with the thanks of the committee for his attendance.

(The committee took a recess until 2 o'clock p. m.)

AFTER RECESS.

The committee met, pursuant to the taking of a recess, at 2 o'clock p. m.

Mr. FORDNEY. Mr. Chairman, before we resume, will you allow me to correct a statement I had in mind when Dr. Wiley was on the stand? It was a matter I wanted to ask him about, but I could not ask it until I looked it up a little later. I asked him about the differential, which was the difference between 168½ and 190. It is really only 7½ cents, because on each one of the degrees above 96 degrees it is 3½ cents per hundred pounds, which runs it up to 82½, and the real differential, instead of being 21½, as we had it, is but 7½ cents, because on 96-degree sugar it is 168½; on 97-degree it is 172, or 3½ cents per hundred pounds difference; 98-degree, 175½; 99-degree, 179; and 100-degree sugar, 182½. Now, the differential is 190, making a difference of 7½ cents.

TESTIMONY OF MR. THOMAS DOYLE.

(The witness was duly sworn by the chairman.)

Mr. FORDNEY. Mr. Doyle, give the stenographer your residence.

Mr. DOYLE. I live in Saginaw County, village of Merrill, Mich.

Mr. FORDNEY. Mr. Doyle, you are a farmer?

Mr. DOYLE. Yes, sir.

Mr. FORDNEY. And you raise some sugar beets. Will you tell the committee, in your own way, about how long you have raised sugar beets, and what it costs you per acre to raise those beets, and what you get for your crop, and about what your profit is.

Mr. DOYLE. Well, I never raised them but once. They put in beets on my farm of 160 acres. The Saginaw Valley sugar people rented the land, and then I put in some the next year. I put in 66½ acres, and they rented the land the next year.

Mr. FORDNEY. This year you rented the land to them, and they raised the crop?

Mr. DOYLE. Yes, sir. That one year I raised them myself. My son has raised them ever since. Altogether, six years we have been engaged in the beet business. The lowest our crop ever ran was 10 tons to the acre, and from that up to 20; probably an average of about 15 tons to the acre, or near that.

Mr. FORDNEY. Mr. Doyle, how far is your farm from the railroad?

Mr. DOYLE. Two miles and a half to the first edge of it.

Mr. FORDNEY. Now, Mr. Doyle, can you give us the cost of production? What does it cost you to produce an acre of beets?

Mr. DOYLE. Yes, sir.

Mr. FORDNEY. To plow the land and seed it and cultivate it, and your hand labor, and to pull the beets, and so on. Give that in detail, if you can.

Mr. DOYLE. It costs about $2 to plow the land. It costs about 50 cents an acre to get it ready for beets.

Mr. FORDNEY. That is $2.50 for plowing and harrowing and preparing the ground to seed?

Mr. DOYLE. Yes. It costs about 40 cents to seed and 50 cents an acre to cultivate them. You cultivate them four times.

Mr. FORDNEY. Mr. Doyle, it costs you about 40 cents to seed?

Mr. DOYLE. To sow the seed.

Mr. FORDNEY. And it costs you about 50 cents an acre to cultivate them?

Mr. DOYLE. Yes, sir.

Mr. FORDNEY. And you cultivate how many times during the year?

Mr. DOYLE. Four times.

Mr. FORDNEY. That would be $2 per acre for cultivating?

Mr. DOYLE. Yes; and the seed costs me $2.

Mr. FORDNEY. You planted $2 worth of seed per acre?

Mr. DOYLE. Yes; I put on 20 pounds to the acre; but that is not the rule. They put on about 10 or 15 pounds usually.

Mr. FORDNEY. At 10 cents per pound?

Mr. DOYLE. At 10 cents per pound.

Mr. FORDNEY But you planted 20 pounds?

Mr DOYLE Yes; it was my first experience, and I wanted to put on lots of it.

Mr FORDNEY. Now, Mr. Doyle, in addition to that, what else does it cost you to raise that crop?

Mr. DOYLE. Well, the handwork costs me $20 an acre; that is, what the foreigners do.

Mr. FORDNEY. You pay the foreigners $20 an acre for thinning and hoeing, and so on?

Mr. DOYLE. Yes; and topping the beets in the field and putting them in place, and it costs me about $1.50 an acre for lifting them with my own teams, and so on.

Mr. FORDNEY. Is that all the cost of production besides hauling?

Mr. DOYLE. That is all.

Mr. FORDNEY. That puts them in piles ready to load and be hauled?

Mr. DOYLE. Yes; they get them loaded cheaper now than they did then, about $2 per acre less for labor.

Mr. FORDNEY. Now, that makes $2.50 per acre for preparing the land for seeding, 40 cents an acre for seeding, 50 cents per acre for cultivating, $2 per acre for seed, $20 for hand labor, and $1.50 for lifting the beets?

Mr. DOYLE. Yes, sir.

Mr. FORDNEY. That is $28.40 per acre. Now, Mr. Doyle, what does it cost you to deliver those beets to the railroad?

Mr. DOYLE. Well, it is pretty hard to get at that unless you hire it done. You could hire it done for about 75 cents an acre on my place. A little farther back it would cost more.

Mr. FORDNEY. Seventy-five cents per ton, you mean?

Mr. DOYLE. Yes, sir.

Mr. FORDNEY. But you haul with your own teams?

Mr. DOYLE. Yes; and I averaged that fall 3 tons to the load and hauled two loads a day.

Mr. FORDNEY. And if you were compelled to have that done, you say about 75 cents per ton would be a fair price?

Mr. DOYLE. Yes, sir; for that distance.

Mr. FORDNEY. About how many tons do you raise to the acre on an average, Mr. Doyle?

Mr. DOYLE. About 15 tons.

Mr. FORDNEY. That would make the cost of hauling about $11.25, and you would add that to your total cost?

Mr. DOYLE. Yes.

Mr. FORDNEY. Making $39.65 for raising the beets and delivering them on board the cars, or at the cars?

Mr. DOYLE. Yes.

Mr. FORDNEY. And you raise 15 tons to the acre, Mr. Doyle?

Mr. DOYLE. On an average about that. I have raised more.

Mr. FORDNEY. You have raised as high as 20 tons?

Mr. DOYLE. I had a little over 20 tons one year. It runs all the way from 10 to 20 tons.

Mr. FORDNEY. But on an average for a period of years it would be about 15 tons?

Mr. DOYLE. 15 tons would be about the average.

Mr. FORDNEY. About what price, Mr. Doyle, do you get these beets delivered at the railroad?

Mr. DOYLE. About $5.50 on an average. Sometimes there is about $1.30 difference, according to the richness of the beets. Some years they are richer than others. They average about $5.50 right through the six years.

Mr. FORDNEY. That would leave you $42.65 an acre profit, not counting anything for rent for your land. What did you rent your land per acre for when you rented it to the St. Louis Sugar Co.?

Mr. DOYLE. I rented them 160 acres the first year for $1,600. I rented it to them the next year for $1,200.

Mr. FORDNEY. $10 an acre would be a fair price for rent for your land?

Mr. DOYLE. Yes, sir.

Mr. FORDNEY. Deducting that as interest upon the investment in your land would leave you $32.85 per acre profit. Is that about a fair average?

Mr. DOYLE. That is about a fair average for our country.

Mr. FORDNEY. Did I ask you, Mr. Doyle, how many acres you planted each year, on an average?

Mr. DOYLE. One year the St. Louis Co. had in over 200 acres. They had in 160 acres and I had 66½ acres. We vary from 50 to 80 acres each year, and 30 acres sometimes.

Mr. FORDNEY. Mr. Doyle, may I ask you whether or not in your opinion the growing of beets in your country, being a profitable crop as it is and being intense cultivation, whether it fits your land better for other crops? Does it make it more valuable for other crops after you have raised beets?

Mr. DOYLE. A great deal more so, more than any crop I have ever raised, for this reason: If you grow any beets, you have got to keep your land clean all the summer. They hoe it twice, and you have got to keep your land clean. You can take a field full of Canada thistles, and our country is quite a Canada thistle country, and by keeping the beets clean it kills the thistle. You have to cut them so many different times that it leaves the land clean and nice. We never think of plowing for the next crop. We put the ground in oats, usually, the next time.

Mr. FORDNEY. Is there any other crop raised on your farm that yields you the profit per acre that beets do?

Mr. DOYLE. I do not think any other corp yields us half as much. We have done well since we raised beets. We have all done tolerably well.

Mr. FORDNEY. Mr. Doyle, do you make any use of the tops?

Mr. DOYLE. Yes, sir.

Mr. FORDNEY. Do you sell them or feed them?

Mr. DOYLE. We feed them. Last year we fed 51 steers and this year we are feeding 50. We commence about the time we commence pulling the beets in the fall and drawing them out, and they feed cattle faster than anything I ever used. But we have to feed some dry feed with them, like hay or corn or stalks, or something like that, because the beets alone would fix the cattle so they would not thrive so well.

Mr. FORDNEY. What do you figure your beet tops worth per acre as fodder for your cattle?

Mr. DOYLE. Well, it would be hard to tell. If the beets are put in late there are a great deal more tops on them, and if they are put in early and get ripe quick there are not so many tops on them. I would say from $3 to $5.

Mr. FORDNEY. Per acre?

Mr. DOYLE. Yes.

Mr. FORDNEY. They are worth about $3 per acre for food?

Mr. DOYLE. Yes, sir.

Mr. FORDNEY. That amount should be added to the figures already given here as your profit?

Mr. DOYLE. Yes. They are not only good for cattle; they are good for sheep. They are good things to feed any animal of that nature. either sheep or cattle.

Mr. FORDNEY. You spoke of foreign labor. What kind of labor is that foreign labor? Is it of the same average efficiency as the labor you could employ in the neighborhood?

Mr. DOYLE. We get Bohemians mostly in there. They are good people, most of them. They buy lots of grub and work hard, and buy some whisky and beer.

Mr. FORDNEY. Their money, then, is spent in the neighborhood?

Mr. DOYLE. You bet it is. There are a few of them who have bought farms around there, quite a few, perhaps a dozen within my scope of knowledge, in the last four or five years.

Mr. FORDNEY. You told me, Mr. Doyle, about a young man, an Austrian, who came to work on your farm six years ago, 18 years of age. I would like for you to tell the gentlemen of the committee what success the young man has made in those six years.

Mr. DOYLE. Well, he has got $5,000 in our bank, and he has gone back to Austria to get himself a wife and then come back and buy a farm.

Mr. FORDNEY. He started as a boy 18 years of age six years ago?

Mr. DOYLE. Yes.

Mr. FORDNEY. And worked for you each year, but raised some beets last year?

Mr. DOYLE. For the last two years he has raised some beets for himself, renting a piece of land near a corner of our farm.

Mr. FORDNEY. And in six years' time he had $5,000 in the bank?

Mr. DOYLE. He had $5,000 in the bank at the last bank meeting. We were talking there about it. He had got enough then and gone to the old country for a wife and left the money in the bank until he got back.

Mr. FORDNEY. You say the labor there is good?

Mr. DOYLE. Yes.

Mr. FORDNEY. As good as the average labor you can pick up at home?

Mr. DOYLE. A great deal better. These people work very hard. They commence as soon as they can see and work as long as they can see, and after they get through with the beets the farmers use them in other ways.

Mr. FORDNEY. Organized labor does not affect them in their day's work?

Mr. DOYLE. No. They work hard for us. When I left home there were four of them drawing beets.

Mr. FORDNEY. In your opinion has the growing of beets added value to the general wealth of the country and the price of land in your neighborhood?

Mr. DOYLE. Well, our land has gone up 75 per cent. In other words, I have got a farm I bought at $10 per acre about 25 years ago, in a raw state, you know, and cleared it up, and I can get to-day $100 an acre for it any time. Then we have a little bank there. I am interested in it. Before this beet industry came in we had $60,000, the highest we ever got, and now it amounts to almost $300,000. We started another one 5 miles east of there two years ago, and the cashier said if he could get it up to $100,000 he would be tickled. He is a boy we had with us who thought he could do well. He now has $212,000, and the bank is only three years old next spring.

Mr. FORDNEY. How far apart are those banks?

Mr. DOYLE. Five miles.

Mr. FORDNEY. So your bank covers a territory, say, of two miles and a half each way?

Mr. DOYLE. Yes. Well, north and south it would cover more of a territory, probably 9 miles north, but not so far south. It is a good farming country.

Mr. FORDNEY. Is the heft of that money deposited by the farmers, or people in the village?

Mr. DOYLE. By the farmers. The merchants have a little money there, but they borrow more than they ever have on deposit.

Mr. FORDNEY. Then, in your opinion, the beet industry has added much to the value of the land?

Mr. DOYLE. It is the grandest thing that ever struck our country for everybody, not only for the man that grows the beets, but by bringing these people in there we can use them for other purposes, on the farm and everywhere. We are all happy, and we are all getting along good, and everybody has got a few dollars in money.

Mr. FORDNEY. Mr. Doyle, are there many mortgages on the farms in your vicinity?

Mr. DOYLE. We have to hunt around quite a bit to find a place to put money. Now, you see about all the mortgages left are when some Ohio man or Indiana man comes in there to buy one of our farms, he has perhaps about half enough to buy it, and he borrows the rest of it. They are about all the mortgages left. Mr. Hansey told you that, you will remember, coming along on the train. I said to him: "You used to be quite a lender of money in our country, how many mortgages have you got now?" He said: "I haven't got any."

Mr. FORDNEY. Mr. Doyle, you are evidently pleased with the industry?

Mr. DOYLE. Sure.

Mr. FORDNEY. I want to ask you if there are any men in your neighborhood who raise beets and have complaints to make, and who are not satisfied?

Mr. DOYLE. Mr. Fordney, you will find that everywhere. The general tone of the people is that they are satisfied and willing to raise the beets, and I can prove it to you. Now, last year there was some fellow went around and was going to get them $6 sure per ton, and a lot of them held off. They don't get that. They get about $5.50. Now, there is always some fellow, you know, who won't work, and who would not have any money unless the price of washing went up, or something like that, but the tone of affairs, as a rule, they are all happy and contented.

Mr. FORDNEY. And if the price of washing went up, that fellow's wife would do the work?

Mr. DOYLE. Yes.

Mr. FORDNEY. Mr. Doyle, is there any division of territory in the vicinity in which you live; that is to say, do the different sugar companies compete in that territory?

Mr. DOYLE. There are three of them there, the Owosso, the St. Louis, and the Michigan Sugar Co.

Mr. FORDNEY. Have you raised beets for more than one firm?

Mr. DOYLE. I have raised beets for the whole of them. We have raised them for the Saginaw Sugar Co., and my boy was a little slow contracting last winter, and when it came contracting time they had all they wanted, so he couldn't get a contract, and the Owosso people gave him a contract.

Mr. FORDNEY. So you are raising beets this year for the Owosso Co., which is an independent company, and the Saginaw Co. is one of the Michigan Sugar Co.'s factories?

Mr. DOYLE. Yes; I guess it is.

Mr. FORDNEY. And you say you have also raised beets for the St. Louis Sugar Co.?

Mr. DOYLE. Yes.

Mr. FORDNEY. That is an independent company?

Mr. DOYLE. Yes.

Mr. FORDNEY. Do you find any great difference in the treatment you receive?

Mr. DOYLE. There is no difference. The men are on the ground all the time, and if you like one better than the other you deal with him. So far as the result is concerned I would just as leave work for one as the other.

Mr. FORDNEY. The chairman wants to know whether you are a Democrat. I told him you are a dyed-in-the-wool Democrat, and he said you must be a Fordney Democrat.

Mr. DOYLE. If he will go to my country he will find more of them.

The CHAIRMAN. I can very well understand that.

Mr. DOYLE. Mr. Fordney has always stood by us, and I don't know why us Democrats should go back on him.

Mr. FORDNEY. Mr. Doyle, I ask this question because some testimony has been given here that the sugar factories held the sugar-beet farmers up strictly to the terms stated in their contracts. Do the sugar companies in the vicinity of your home, or those for whom you raise beets, hold you strictly to the terms of your contract?

Mr. DOYLE. I will bet any man in Washington or who will come here that if I get a contract from any one of the contractors for five acres that I will be allowed to raise 100 acres if I care to.

Mr. FORDNEY. Will they permit you sometimes to raise more beets, plant more acreage, than you contract for?

Mr. DOYLE. They will give me a contract for 5 acres if I ask for it and yet give me all the seed I need for 100 acres if I wish it, and even then, if I am not satisfied with their treatment, I can go to the next man with my beets. They have offered me these things.

Mr. FORDNEY. Are the conditions any better now for the average farmer raising sugar beets than they were when you first began?

Mr. DOYLE. Oh, yes; a good deal better. Well, when they first commenced raising beets they had to put them on the car. They would say they would have a car there like to-day— and, of course, they didn't own the railroads—but the car would'nt get there until to-morrow. You would come out with a load of beets expecting the car, and might get there with two or three loads and no car, and there you would be. Now they have weigh stations and they weigh the beets right there, each and every wagonload, and give you a bill for what beets you weigh, and your wagon can go back for another load, and they give you a bill for what beets you bring, right along. If they don't have the car right there they now let you put your beets on the ground and they load them on the car at their own expense.

Another thing that they do to help the farmer: You can pile your beets up in a pile in half ton or ton piles and cover them up and keep them until December in good shape, and they will give you half a dollar extra—above the price paid in the fall. In that way a fellow is liable to do a little more than he has to, rather than otherwise. For instance, that will allow you to go ahead in the fall and do your fall plowing, and get up with your work, and then, when you could not do anything else, you can haul those beets, and even then get half a dollar a ton extra in price.

Mr. FORDNEY. You can haul them in December or in January?

Mr. DOYLE. You can commence any time after the 1st of December, and then they will give you half a dollar per ton extra price.

Mr. FORDNEY. Have you delivered your beets this year?

Mr. DOYLE. Oh, no; or at least they hadn't hauled them away when I left on the 14th.

Mr. FORDNEY. They give you 50 cents per ton extra to cover the work of covering the beets and holding them?

Mr. DOYLE. To hold them until December, yes, sir.

Mr. FORDNEY. The object of that is that when the season first opens they have a great rush in delivery of beets, and they wish to have some held back?

Mr. DOYLE. I will tell you, Joe, how that is. You can not haul your beets in a great pile, and sometimes they pile them too big and don't have proper stuff to cover them over with, and rainy warm weather comes, but the sugar companies have already paid for them, or has already bought them and given you your ticket, and the beets go into the sugar companies, and every night in 15 minutes you get your pay. If they are out in the field where they grew and are put up in proper shape they are in just as good shape as when you pull them. If you put them in good big piles and throw all of the leaves over them they don't freeze, and the leaves come off easy. If you put them in a little small square, leaves out and not properly covered they may freeze, but if you put them in a good big pile I have had them to keep until February just as good as in the fall.

Mr. FORDNEY. Mr. Doyle, you spoke of freezing and thawing causing them to ferment. If you store them that way do they depreciate any as to sugar content?

Mr. DOYLE. I couldn't tell you a thing about that. You will have to ask the sugar people about that.

Mr. FORDNEY. They pay you the same price?

Mr. DOYLE. We are paid just the same, because they were all right when we let go of them.

Mr. FORDNEY. The sugar factories would have to lose if there was any loss?

Mr. DOYLE. Yes, sir.

Mr. FORDNEY. They do not deduct any loss from your price?

Mr. DOYLE. No, no.

Mr. FORDNEY. What price do you pay for seed?

Mr. DOYLE. Ten cents per pound.

Mr. FORDNEY. I think you told me once when coming down on the train that while you had used $2 worth of seed, or 20 pounds to the acre, yet you found that 10 pounds or 10½ pounds to the acre was a plenty?

Mr. DOYLE. Yes, yes; 10 is enough. Since that time a fellow learns a little you know.

Mr. FORDNEY. You thought if there was any virtue in 1 pound there was more virtue in 2 pounds?

Mr. DOYLE. I thought I would do my best. It was my first effort with beets. I had been watching beets for years, but was scared when I started in.

Mr. FORDNEY. You thought it to be a good crop and that you would plant some in an experimental way?

Mr. DOYLE. Yes, yes; I had good land.

Mr. HINDS. For the sake of satisfying my curiosity I will ask how large are the piles in which you pile the beets?

Mr. DOYLE. Well, my friend, about 12 rows and about 3 rods apart is the way I pile them.

Mr. HINDS. Twelve rows in a pile?

Mr. DOYLE. Yes. That would be 12 rows in length, about the length of this table, and sometimes 20 and sometimes 24 and sometimes 28 inches apart. We raise beets about 24 inches apart, and we put in 12 rows, and that is about as far as you can throw the beets; a rod and a half each way to throw them.

Mr. HINDS. That would make a pile, say, about 6 feet high?

Mr. DOYLE. About 4 feet high and sometimes about 6 or 8 feet across.

Mr. HINDS. That would conical, or like a haycock?

Mr. DOYLE. Yes, sir.

Mr. HINDS. You just put the beet leaves on them?

Mr. DOYLE. That is all.

Mr. HINDS. How cold weather will that stand?

Mr. DOYLE. With the beet leaves put on it will stand zero weather, and a good deal more for a good while.

Mr. HINDS. Without snow covering the pile up?

Mr. DOYLE. Oh yes, yes.

Mr. HINDS. Doesn't the rain get in?

Mr. DOYLE. Not with the beet leaves on them.

Mr. HINDS. You just throw them on?

Mr. DOYLE. Yes; throw the leaves right on. The beet leaves are around on the outside of the pile in the first place. We throw the beets in a pile, leaving a place in the middle, and then we commence on top and throw beets in the space, with the beet leaves on the front of the pile, and all you have to do is just to throw them on.

Mr. HINDS. How cold weather do you have?

Mr. DOYLE. Oh, we have it down below zero once in a while.

Mr. HINDS. And still the beets will not freeze?

Mr. DOYLE. Not if the beet leaves are properly put on, the beets won't freeze at all.

Mr. HINDS. You could not pile potatoes or pumpkins or anything of that sort in that way, could you?

Mr. DOYLE. Oh, no; you couldn't keep potatoes or pumpkins or anything else like that.

Mr. MALBY. Not without covering them up?

Mr. DOYLE. No; you couldn't keep them in that way anyhow.

Mr. FORDNEY. Beets seem to stand freezes better than the other things?

Mr. DOYLE. They put these piles of beets 12 feet wide and 8 or 10 feet high sometimes, but that is too high.

Mr. HINDS. Do these beets freeze sometimes in the pile?

Mr. DOYLE. Yes.

Mr. HINDS. That doesn't hurt them?

Mr. DOYLE. Yes: they are not hurt so long as they don't freeze and thaw and keep on doing that. They have had a little before this year; that is, as I overheard of it. We are having a terrible winter up there now; that is, freezing and thawing, until I came away from home. Where beets were in those big piles they claim they were damaged a little.

The CHAIRMAN. Have the beet growers of your section of Michigan any sort of association or organization?

Mr. DOYLE. Oh, no; every man is on his own hook. Do you mean the farmers?

The CHAIRMAN. Yes. Is there any organization among them?

Mr. DOYLE. Oh, no; not in my country.

The CHAIRMAN. You will excuse me if I ask you these questions, but we ought to find out about these things.

Mr. DOYLE. Sure. That is what we are here for, to tell you all we know.

The CHAIRMAN. Do you know of any such association around you?

Mr. DOYLE. No, sir.

The CHAIRMAN. Do you own any interest in any beet-sugar company or factory?

Mr. DOYLE. No, sir.

The CHAIRMAN. Do you own any stock in any such company?

Mr. DOYLE. Not a dollar.

The CHAIRMAN. Do any of your people own any stock in any beet-sugar company or factory?

Mr. DOYLE. None of my people own any.

The CHAIRMAN. You are simply a plain Michigan farmer?

Mr. DOYLE. Yes; that is all.

The CHAIRMAN. Do you live in town?

Mr. DOYLE. I live in a village.

The CHAIRMAN. How large is the village?

Mr. DOYLE. About 500 or 600 people.

The CHAIRMAN. How much of a farm have you?

Mr. DOYLE. 640 acres.

The CHAIRMAN. That is considerable of a farm in Michigan, I take it?

Mr. DOYLE. Yes; some farm.

The CHAIRMAN. And you do not raise any beets at all now?

Mr. DOYLE. No, sir; my son looks after the business now.

The CHAIRMAN. Does he raise any beets?

Mr. DOYLE. Oh, yes; right along, every year.

The CHAIRMAN. I thought he rented his land to the company?

Mr. DOYLE. No; it was me that done that when I first commenced.

The CHAIRMAN. Now you raise all of the beets yourself?

Mr. DOYLE. Yes, sir.

The CHAIRMAN. You found out that it was about the most profitable crop that you could raise?

Mr. DOYLE. Altogether so.

The CHAIRMAN. It beats wheat?

Mr. DOYLE. Yes, sir.

The CHAIRMAN. It is a better crop than wheat?

Mr. DOYLE. Oh, Lord; yes. You can get $1,000 any time out of 10 acres of land put in beets. How many acres of wheat would you have to raise to get $1,000?

The CHAIRMAN. A good many more acres than that.

Mr. DOYLE. Sure, you would. We haven't any crop that will stand the trouble beets do.

The CHAIRMAN. Can you plant beets year after year without alternating your crop, or do you alternate your crops?

Mr. DOYLE. No; we don't do it, but I done it once. I rented 160 acres to these beet-sugar people, and had a horse pasture in the corner of the 160-acre field. They put in beets the second time, while I raised beets right across the fence from them. In order to get the full amount of 160 acres they had to go over a couple of yards beyond the fence; and, as I said, they had the land twice, and then the next year I put those two rods along the fence they had had to make up their 160 acres into beets again. Their beets all blighted, and mine blighted as far as those two rods of land went.

The CHAIRMAN. That experience seemed to prove that you ought not to plant beets in the same land in two successive years?

Mr. DOYLE. Yes, sir.

The CHAIRMAN. When you do plant beets as your crop on a piece of land, do you put all of the by-products back on the land?

Mr. DOYLE. No, sir; none of it.

The CHAIRMAN. Is there any by-product that the farmer gets after selling his beets to the sugar factory?

Mr. DOYLE. Yes; those leaves.

The CHAIRMAN. What is that?

Mr. DOYLE. He gets his leaves.

The CHAIRMAN. What do you do with them?

Mr. DOYLE. Feed them to the cattle or to sheep.

The CHAIRMAN. Are they good for them?

Mr. DOYLE. Dandy.

The CHAIRMAN. Is there any other by-product that you get back?

Mr. DOYLE. No.

The CHAIRMAN. The balance goes with the beets to the factory?

Mr. DOYLE. Yes, sir.

The CHAIRMAN. Is there any part of the beet that would make a good improving fertilizer if turned in on the land?

Mr. DOYLE. It might be that the pulp would.

The CHAIRMAN. But the factory has that?

Mr. DOYLE. Yes, sir.

The CHAIRMAN. Is there anything else but leaves, and they are too valuable to be used as fertilizer?

Mr. DOYLE. Yes, sir. We then sow oats on the land, and seed it down and raise hay, and pasture it, and go on again with the beets.

The CHAIRMAN. You are quite firm in your opinion that it is not profitable to plant beets successively in the same land?

Mr. DOYLE. It was not profitable in our locality. Maybe somewhere else it is, but I don't know of it.

The CHAIRMAN. In your part of Michigan it would not do?

Mr. DOYLE. No, sir; I don't think it would be profitable to do that.

The CHAIRMAN. I can not think of any other questions I wish to ask Mr. Doyle at this time.

Mr. FORDNEY. A gentleman just tells me that the only thing left at the factory is the lime cake, and that that is thrown away, and that the factories will give same to the farmers if they will haul it away.

The CHAIRMAN. Mr. Doyle, did you know about that?

Mr. DOYLE. No, sir; I didn't know, but it is too far away for me to haul it.

The CHAIRMAN. How far is the factory from your farm?

Mr. DOYLE. The closest one is 14 miles.

The CHAIRMAN. Which factory is that?

Mr. DOYLE. The St. Louis factory.

The CHAIRMAN. What company owns that factory, the Michigan Sugar Co.?

Mr. DOYLE. No, sir; the St. Louis Sugar Co.

The CHAIRMAN. Do you sell anything to the Michigan Sugar Co.?

Mr. DOYLE. Yes, sir; I sold them beets three years.

The CHAIRMAN. Which one of their plants do you sell to?

Mr. DOYLE. I mostly take beets to Bay City, but if they get too many there I ship them to their other factory?

The CHAIRMAN. Do you deliver your beets to these sugar factories or are they shipped from stations?

Mr. DOYLE. They have stations. One of their factories is 19 miles and the other 22 miles from me.

The CHAIRMAN. They run a car up to the station at your place, and you dump the beets down there?

Mr. DOYLE. We dump them into the car, if they have one there; if not, we dump the beets on the ground and they put them into the car.

The CHAIRMAN. They consider that a delivery to them?

Mr. DOYLE. Yes, sir; a delivery to them just as much as if put into the car. They go out and have men to load the beets into cars.

The CHAIRMAN. Do they weigh the beets?

Mr. DOYLE. Yes, sir.

The CHAIRMAN. Where?

Mr. DOYLE. Right at your station.

The CHAIRMAN. You can go and look at the weighing?

Mr. DOYLE. Oh, yes; they have a man there to see to that.

The CHAIRMAN. Your belief about it is that they treat you pretty square?

Mr. DOYLE. I do not believe anything about it; I know they do. I am an old man and have had considerable experience with people and would be pretty apt to know what sort of treatment I get.

The CHAIRMAN. You have no complaint to make?

Mr. DOYLE. No, sir; their treatment of me has been good; their treatment of me and everybody else.

The CHAIRMAN. I am very glad to hear it. I am a pessimist on that.

Mr. FORDNEY. Do all of the sugar companies treat you alike?

Mr. DOYLE. All treat me alike, and everybody else. The only difference we have is to change sometimes. We think sometimes, after we have sold beets a certain number of years to one fellow, that we would like to change, and we will go to the other fellow. The reason we changed last year was because we could not help ourselves.

The CHAIRMAN. I wonder if your farmers are like ours. They think they never get enough for cotton, even if they are getting 20 cents per pound. Do you people think that about the sale of your sugar beets?

Mr. DOYLE. Well, we may have some extreme fellows like that, but as a rule our people are satisfied.

The CHAIRMAN. Don't the majority of them think they ought to have a little more for beets?

Mr. DOYLE. If they hadn't they wouldn't have held out last fall and would have contracted in time.

The CHAIRMAN. So some farmers even in Michigan wish to get a bigger price for beets?

Mr. DOYLE. Oh, yes; that is human nature.

The CHAIRMAN. I thought so, but didn't know whether it was the same up there or not. Do you gentlemen of the committee wish to ask any other questions?

Mr. HINDS. I would like to ask one or two. Did I understand you to say, Mr. Doyle, that you figured out to Mr. Fordney the profit on an acre of beets was $32.85?

Mr. DOYLE. I don't know how it figured out; Mr. Fordney can tell.

Mr. FORDNEY. I will repeat it so as to get it correct. Mr. Doyle gave me the cost—and see if I am correct, Mr. Doyle, and if not, correct me—as follows:

	Per acre.
Plowing land	$2.50
Labor seeding	.40
Seed	2.00
Four cultivations of land, at 50 cents each	2.00
Hand labor	20.00
Lifting	1.50
Total	28.40

Mr. MALBY. Is that the complete list of expenses?

Mr. FORDNEY. All except hauling, which was $11.25 per acre, or 75 cents per ton for hauling 15 tons. Adding the hauling, $11.25, to the $28.40 gives us $39.65.

Mr. DOYLE. Mr. Fordney, that $20 per acre is too high for hand labor. We get it done now for $16 and $18. Isn't that so [turning to one of the Michigan growers behind him]?

Mr. RUST. Yes.

Mr. DOYLE. That $20 per acre is based on 20-inch rows of beets.

Mr. FORDNEY. The cost of hand labor per acre varies according to the width of the rows of beets?

Mr. DOYLE. Yes, sir. We don't raise any more less than 24 and 28 inches, and the 28-inch rows are $16 per acre for hand labor, and the 24-inch rows are $18.

Mr. FORDNEY. You paid $20 per acre for hand labor for the beets you raised?

Mr. DOYLE. Yes; I paid that, exactly.

Mr. FORDNEY. And you raised 15 tons per acre, for which you received $5.50 per ton, or $82.50 per acre, that figure being your gross receipts?

Mr. DOYLE. Yes, sir.

Mr. FORDNEY. Deducting $39.65 from $82.50 leaves $42.85. Now, deducting from that $42.85 $10 for rent of your land leaves $32.85 besides what profit there is in the tops, which you say is from $3 to $5 per acre. Adding the smaller amount named for value of tops, $3 per acre, to the $32.85, which we had, makes $35.85 after allowing $10 for the rent of your land?

Mr. DOYLE. Yes, sir.

Mr. HINDS. The gross income from beets per acre is $82.50?

Mr. DOYLE. That would be for the beets alone.

Mr. HINDS. And then you had the tops?

Mr. DOYLE. Yes, sir.

Mr. HINDS. That would be on toward $90 per acre gross receipts?

Mr. DOYLE. Yes, sir; $85.50 to $88.50 per acre, according to the value of the tops.

Mr. HINDS. How would that compare with the gross receipts from potatoes?

Mr. DOYLE. I never raised a potato in my life.

Mr. HINDS. That is not in the potato region?

Mr. DOYLE. No; you have to go 40 miles west of us. Half of our potatoes that we eat there where I live we get from that country west of us.

Mr. HINDS. Do you raise any corn?

Mr. DOYLE. Yes, sir.

Mr. HINDS. For the canning factories?

Mr. DOYLE. No, sir; just for our own use.

Mr. FORDNEY. You have that to feed your stock, and you have sheep and cattle?

Mr. DOYLE. Yes, sir; we always have 50 or 100 steers to sell in the fall.

Mr. HINDS. So that aside from the cattle business the only article you sell at all raised on your farm in its first form is beets?

Mr. DOYLE. Yes, sir.

Mr. HINDS. You transform your other products into cattle?

Mr. DOYLE. Yes, sir.

Mr. MALBY. Another thing, gentlemen, while Mr. Doyle has only about 65 acres in beets——

Mr. DOYLE (interrupting). No; I have 640 acres.

Mr. MALBY. I mean in beets.

Mr. DOYLE. Oh, yes.

Mr. MALBY. While you have about 65 acres in beets, they are grown on a farm consisting of 640 acres, and the inquiry I would like to make is as to whether that is about as much land as it would be profitable for you to have in beets as compared with a farm of that size?

Mr. DOYLE. Yes, sir.

Mr. MALBY. Owing to your rotation system of crops?

Mr. DOYLE. Yes, sir.

Mr. MALBY. So that it would not be possible or profitable to have a much greater acreage than you do have in beets on a farm of that size?

Mr. DOYLE. No; it wouldn't.

Mr. MALBY. Let me ask you what crop immediately succeeds the beets?

Mr. DOYLE. Oats.

Mr. MALBY. Does that come next, oats?

Mr. DOYLE. Yes, sir.

Mr. MALBY. How long would it be before you would go back to beets again? What do you have after your oat crop?

Mr. DOYLE. We don't go back to beets again for four or five years. We have so much land that we usually sow the beet land to oats next year, and the next year we have hay on it, and maybe we get hay twice, and then feed the cattle on it.

Mr. MALBY. Is that about the way the average farmer in that locality uses his land?

Mr. DOYLE. Yes, sir.

Mr. MALBY. Do they raise as much beets per acre as you do?

Mr. DOYLE. Oh, some of them do, and some of them more.

Mr. MALBY. I am trying to get at the average crop in your locality. Would the average be as much as 15 tons per acre?

Mr. DOYLE. I think it would be right around our country. It is very much adapted to beets. When you get to the more rolling country, it is not so good. Our country is black-ash swamp land and is rich. Black ash, elm, oak, and basswood grows there.

Mr. MALBY. A good soil?

Mr. DOYLE. Yes, sir.

Mr. MALBY. What kind of soil is it?

Mr. DOYLE. Alluvial clay.

Mr. MALBY. What would be the average, would you imagine, beet crop in that part of Michigan, and particularly in that locality and, say, for 15 or 20 miles around, what number of tons would they raise per acre?

Mr. DOYLE. Well, I couldn't say. I never saw them except when growing. When you get on the rolling land, which is higher and nicer land to raise grain on, the beets don't look as thrifty as down with us. The tops don't look as good, and they seem to die down.

Mr. MALBY. How about the cost per acre with your neighbors; does it correspond with your own?

Mr. DOYLE. Yes, anybody where he hires it done. Sometimes a man with his own family works 5 acres, or 2 acres, or something like that; and then, of course, you have his own time to consider.

Mr. MALBY. I think you have stated that the factory men did not seek to take any advantage of the growers of beets through any technicality of any kind?

Mr. DOYLE. No; they don't.

Mr. MALBY. They do not seek to enforce a mere technical part of their agreement against the beet grower so as to embarrass him or prevent his getting a fair price for his product?

Mr. DOYLE. They are the best about that of any set of people at all. They will come and advance you m ney with which to take care of your crop if you can't do it yourself.[o] They have local men, and they have a certain territory to look after. Sometimes a man will think he can take care of himself; well, he can't do it. Harvest comes on, and he can't get help, and they will furnish him money to get help to get his beets in shape.

Mr. MALBY. That soil of yours is fairly easy to cultivate, is it not?

Mr. DOYLE. Yes, sir.

Mr. HINDS. Mr. Doyle, when you put in your crop of oats after you have raised beets on the land, how many bushels of oats will you get per acre that year?

Mr. DOYLE. Well, let's see. After that crop, the oats I think I got was 48 bushels per acre. It was a few years ago, when the blight went all over the country, and then I got 10 or 15 bushels more than my neighbors because I got them in early. One year I got my oats sowed before the freeze was out of the ground; just threw my oats on the ground and dug them in. That year I was lucky because I was ahead of my neighbors, and they came along after it came on.

Mr. HINDS. How much was that, 48 bushels to the acre?

Mr. DOYLE. Yes, sir. Usually we get 60 bushels of oats to the acre.

Mr. HINDS. Suppose you hadn't had beets on that land the year before, but had been doing general farming with it, how many bushels of oats per acre would you have got?

Mr. DOYLE. I might have got just the same thing if I had had them in as early.

Mr. HINDS. Then you do not think the fact of your putting beets on the land increased the crop of oats you got the next year?

Mr. DOYLE. It increases it in this way. It gets the land clean. There are no weeds or thistles in your crop the next year. That is the only advantage I know of.

Mr. HINDS. It does not help the land any?

Mr. DOYLE. I don't understand that it enriches or impoverishes the land, not either one.

Mr. HINDS. It makes it cleaner?

Mr. DOYLE. Yes, sir; keeps foul stuff off.

Mr. HINDS. Do you employ Bohemians?

Mr. DOYLE. Austrians, and sometimes Belgians, and sometimes Bohemians.

Mr. HINDS. Do they do the work by contract?

Mr. DOYLE. Yes, sir.

Mr. HINDS. Can you give me any idea as to how much the Austrian men earn per day?

Mr. DOYLE. Well, he works about three days in one. In the summer, say in June, he works as soon as he can see in the morning and as long as he can see at night. I have seen them in my field—and your hands and feet are both on the ground when at that work, and say the rows half a mile long—never straighten up from one side of the field to the other. They just go out into the field and work very hard, early and late. They eat four or five times a day. They fetch their grub out in the field in the morning, and if they get hungry they go and eat. And those men, working that way, make from $3 to $5 per day.

Mr. HINDS. Working that length of time?

Mr. DOYLE. Yes, sir.

Mr. HINDS. That is, while they work?

Mr. DOYLE. Yes, sir.

Mr. HINDS. They earn from $3 to $5 per day each?

Mr. DOYLE. Yes, sir.

Mr. HINDS. Can you translate that labor into tons, or, say, the labor of the ordinary farm hand? Suppose those Austrians worked only as long as your ordinary farm hand works, about how much would they get?

Mr. DOYLE. $3 per day.

Mr. HINDS. That is, from 7 o'clock in the morning until 5 o'clock in the afternoon?

Mr. DOYLE. If they worked from 7 to 6 they would get from $3 to $3.50 per day by working as they do.

Mr. HINDS. But I mean if you could reduce their work to the terms of the work performed by the ordinary American farm hand, what would they get?

Mr. DOYLE. Well, I think you would have to sell the sugar for about 10 cents per pound to pay them. You can not find any Americans up there working in beets.

Mr. HINDS. Suppose you yourself were working at the gait at which you work, reducing their work to those terms, about what compensation would they get?

Mr. DOYLE. They would get $2.50 per day.

Mr. HINDS. $2.50 per day?

Mr. DOYLE. From $2 to $2.50 per day.

Mr. HINDS. I wanted to get at the normal wages paid when working in a normal way in the beet field, and you think it would be $2.50 per day?

Mr. DOYLE. Yes, sir.

Mr. HINDS. How much do you pay farm hands up there, say, working in haying time if you raise any hay?

Mr. DOYLE. We pay them $2 and $2.50.

Mr. HINDS. So that this Austrian in the sugar-beet field gets the regular wage scale?

Mr. DOYLE. Oh, yes; when we get through with the beets we hire them by the day or month.

Mr. HINDS. What do you pay them then?

Mr. DOYLE. $1.50 or $2 a day.

Mr. HINDS. That is for the ordinary farm work?

Mr. DOYLE. Yes, sir.

Mr. HINDS. On the stress work, like harvesting?

Mr. DOYLE. Yes, sir.

Mr. HINDS. You mean that beet culture is like harvesting some other crops?

Mr. DOYLE. Yes, sir; it is hurry-up while it lasts.

Mr. HINDS. Do you have any knowledge of how much these men got in the beet fields of Austria?

Mr. DOYLE. Only by what they say.

Mr. HINDS. What do they say?

Mr. DOYLE. About 30 cents a day in Belgium and France.

Mr. HINDS. For working how long?

Mr. DOYLE. I asked that question and they said they didn't work quite as long as they do here, but that was all I got.

Mr. HINDS. They got 30 cents per day over there for that work?

Mr. DOYLE. Yes, sir.

Mr. HINDS. You think that by 30 cents they meant it was fair compensation there for a fair sort of day's work?

Mr. DOYLE. Yes, sir.

Mr. HINDS. Such as you think they would get $2.50 a day here for?

Mr. DOYLE. Yes. sir.

Mr. HINDS. Well, did they say anything to you about the relative advantage of the two kinds of wages to them? That is, did they have more left at $2.50 per day paid in this country?

Mr. DOYLE. Oh, yes; they soon pile up money here. Some of them spend it, and others hang on to it and make homes for themselves. Half a dozen or perhaps a dozen in the vicinity of our country have farms there now.

Mr. HINDS. What did you gather was their condition in their native country?

Mr. DOYLE. I think about the same as in my native country. I am a foreigner.

Mr. HINDS. What countryman are you?

Mr. DOYLE. I am an Irishman.

Mr. HINDS. How was that?

Mr. DOYLE. Well, we got small wages over there, too. My father got small wages; I was only a boy 12 years old when I left there.

Mr. HINDS. Considering the cost of living, were you as well off there as here?

Mr. DOYLE. No. If you would live there like you do here, you couldn't exist a week on a month's wages. You would have to get a bit ahead to live. You Americans don't understand it and you can't learn it.

The CHAIRMAN. Are there any other questions, gentlemen?

Mr. SULZER. You are a beet-sugar grower here now?

Mr. DOYLE. Yes, sir.

Mr. SULZER. And making money out of the business?

Mr. DOYLE. Yes, sir.

Mr. SULZER. Do you know of others in the business that are making money?

Mr. DOYLE. I don't know of anybody that don't make it up our way.

Mr. SULZER. They all make money, then?

Mr. DOYLE. Yes, sir. Well, now, I wouldn't say all. There is always an exception, and there may be a few men that don't make money at it, but the majority of them are satisfied and doing well.

Mr. SULZER. If they do not, it is due very much to themselves?

Mr. DOYLE. It is due very much to themselves, yes, sir; for they have a chance to do it. We have been there before there were sugar factories, but we are making money now faster than ever before.

Mr. SULZER. What is your opinion as to growing sufficient sugar beets in the United States to supply the demand here?

Mr. DOYLE. Let me get nearer to you. I am a little hard of hearing.

Mr. SULZER. What is your opinion about growing enough sugar beets in the United States to supply all the sugar the people of the United States want?

Mr. DOYLE. I wouldn't be any authority on that at all. I never was around the country and don't know how much land is adapted to it, and don't know how many factories you need at all, and never thought of it. I merely know what comes under my own observation in my own little burg. I have been across the United States on the railroad once or twice, and that is all. I am an uneducated man.

Mr. SULZER. You don't want the Government to help you, do you?

Mr. DOYLE. Why, sure. I help the Government and I want the Government to help me.

Mr. SULZER. What do you want the Government to do for you?

Mr. DOYLE. Nothing but what it has done—give me a chance to earn a living, and it has always done that.

Mr. SULZER. Do you mean to say by that that you would like to have the Government pay you for raising beets?

Mr. DOYLE. Well, I don't know that the Government pays me for raising beets. The sugar people are paying me for raising beets. I don't know whether the Government makes anything out of it or how.

Mr. SULZER. You don't want any subsidy as a beet-sugar grower, do you?

Mr. DOYLE. I don't understand your language.

Mr. SULZER. Well, you don't want any aid from the Government?

Mr. DOYLE. No; I am able to aid myself.

Mr. SULZER. All you want to do is to be left alone?

Mr. DOYLE. Yes, that is all I want, for the Government to leave us and the sugar factories alone, and let us work it out amongst ourselves. We have been happy ever since they came in there.

Mr. SULZER. And all of you are making money?

Mr. DOYLE. I don't know anything about them; we are.

Mr. SULZER. You are entirely satisfied?

Mr. DOYLE. Entirely satisfied; yes, sir. I never was more satisfied in farming in my life than I have been since the sugar beets came in.

Mr. HINDS. Do you think that you can hold up your end if the man over in Belgium paying 30 cents per day for his labor while you pay $2.50 is allowed to ship his beets into this country, or the sugar made from those beets, considering the very cheap ocean rates? I mean do you think that you could hold up your end under any such conditions as those?

Mr. DOYLE. I want the man in Belgium to come over here if he wants any help from me. Let him come over here and help to build up this country as I did. I came here as a boy and have helped to build up this country while building up myself. Just invite him to come over here if he wants to have the chances here.

Mr. HINDS. You do not want him to stay at home and have certain advantages of low cost of production and compete with you here when you are paying something like 10 times the wages he is paying there?

Mr. DOYLE. No, sir. Let him come over here. I don't want to help him while he is over on the other side of the pond. All I have done for them has been to pay them when they get here; I never sent a dollar there.

Mr. SULZER. There is nothing to stop them from coming if they want to come, is there?

Mr. DOYLE. Not that I know of; and let them come over here if they want to share our prosperity and advantages.

The CHAIRMAN. Are there any further questions?

Mr. FORDNEY. When I saw Mr. Doyle—and I have known him since I was a boy, and knew that I would get through him just such information as is contained in his statement given here before us; a full, frank, open, straightforward statement—I asked him if he would consult some of his neighbors in that part of the country as to the number of beets they raised, the prices they got for them, etc. The result of that inquiry which he made brings me a whole lot of letters with affidavits, or the most of them accompanied by affidavits, from various people, giving the number of acres of beets they raised and what they got for them. I would like to have this data go into the record if it is not objectionable.

The CHAIRMAN. I have no earthly objection to that, and the only objection that could be suggested would be the cost of printing.

Mr. FORDNEY. I do not think that would add much, and this is most interesting and valuable because it comes from various counties. Men heard of it and, I will say, asked some others throughout their neighborhood to send letters.

The CHAIRMAN. All right; they may be put in here at the end of Mr. Doyle's statement as an exhibit.

ASHLEY, MICH., *December, 1911.*

I do hereby certify to the following:

I have raised beets about 12 years for the Alma factory. I raised 35 acres this year. The price I have received has been all the way from $90 to $95 per acre, and my land is in better condition than before. I think this sugar-beet industry has been one of the best that ever struck Gratiot County. It has made better farmers and put our farms in better shape than anything that ever struck us, and I for one would rather see this sugar-beet industry keep up just the way it has been. I can get labor more plentiful now than I could before. The companies have made every effort possible to supply labor for taking care of the beets. This beet industry has paid me better than anything that I have ever tried before. I have put my attention to the raising of sugar beets. It is way ahead of raising corn and oats, and for myself I would rather raise beets than anything else.

There are three different companies in my vicinity that I can raise beets for, and the competition between the three companies is very strong. I am not under obligations to raise beets for any one company. If one proves unsatisfactory, I can easily change to another.

DARNE STINE.

Subscribed and sworn to before me this 28th day of December, A. D. 1911.

I. W. KNOERTZER,
Notary Public in and for Gratiot County, Mich.

My commission expires March 16, 1914.

ALMA, MICH., *January 2, 1912.*

I do hereby certify to the following:

I commenced raising sugar beets the first year the beet business started in Gratiot County, which was in 1899. I raised 10 acres the first year for the Alma factory, and a sand storm came along and shortened the crop until I got only 7 tons to the acre, but the next year I had 12 acres and they went 12 tons to the acre. The next year I had 6 acres, which yielded 11 tons to the acre, and the next year I raised 8 acres, which yielded 16 tons to the acre. After the second year's beet crop I raised 50 bushels of oats to the acre and got the finest kind of a clover seeding. After the third year I had 60 bushels of oats to the acre and a fine clover seeding, and I have never missed a good clover seeding after a beet crop, which I think is very essential in keeping up our farms. I have never raised less than 11 tons of beets to the acre since the third year, and I think the beet crop helps to make better farmers and puts our farms in a higher and better state of productivity than any crop that is grown, unless it is red clover. I think my farm is producing better every year.

The general cost of raising beets is about $30 per acre, which would leave a net profit to the farmer of about $30 to $35 per acre, where other crops would only net the farmer from $12 to $25.

In our territory we have three sugar factories, and there is a strong competition between them, and we are not obliged to continue raising beets for any one factory if they prove unsatisfactory, as there will be plenty of agents from the different companies after you.

The sugar companies spare no pains in assisting to procure laborers for taking care of the beet crop. We have mostly foreign laborers, and I think the foreign laborers are much better for taking care of this crop.

BIRTON I. GEE,
Alma, Rural Free Delivery 4, Mich.

Subscribed and sworn to before me this 4th day of January, A. D. 1912.

[SEAL.]

R. L. ANDERSON,
Notary Public in and for Gratiot County, Mich.

My commission expires November 16, 1912.

FOSTERS, MICH., *January 5, 1912.*

MICHIGAN SUGAR CO., *Saginaw, Mich.*

GENTLEMEN: In regard to the raising of sugar beets, I have heard quite a discussion pro and con of the subject, whether the same is beneficial to the farmer, his land, etc. I desire to say that in my opinion I consider the raising of sugar beets to be one of the best crops that a farmer can raise from a financial standpoint. I consider and I know that the growing of beets is not injurious to the land if properly taken care of—that is, if the several crops are grown in rotation along with the beet crop, then beet growing is not in the least hurtful to the land any more than any other crop, for the reason that beet cultivation is one of the best crops for the working of the land that a farmer can grow. From the time he commences to work his land until the beets are lifted, the land is undergoing a complete renovation of the soil that in any other crop would never see daylight, which in the culture of beets is brought to the surface, and the owner of the farm is thereby benefited by increasing the fertility of the farm. I have raised beets a number of years, and the average amount per acre has been from $80 to $100, and I have failed to realize anything like that amount per acre on any other crop. Then, again, the amount of labor involved brings into the community an immense amount of money, which is expended, and the farmer is thereby benefited in more ways than one. Take the sugar industry out of the country, do away with the sugar factories, and you will find the acreage of sugar beets converted into the raising of oats, corn, potatoes, etc., thereby bringing the prices of these commodities down so low that the farmer will be placed on the same plane that we were a number of years ago, when oats were bringing 20 and 25 cents per bushel, corn 15 and 20 cents, potatoes 15 cents. Now these cereals bring: Oats, 50 cents; corn in the ear, 35 cents; potatoes, 90 cents; hay, $18 per ton, and everything else in proportion. But why all this discussion? The farmer knows what is right. He is no longer a back number. He has his telephone, rural delivery, and is in complete touch with the outside world as well as the man who walks the streets of the city. He knows what he wants, and if you will let him alone he will tell you every time to raise beets, keep the sugar factories, and make things hum in general. Three factories contracting here.

Yours, respectfully, JOSEPH LEACH.

Subscribed and sworn to before me this 5th day of January, 1912.

[SEAL.] JAMES C. MCNALLEY,
Notary Public in and for Saginaw County, Mich.

My commission expires December 9, 1913.

CLIO, MICH., *January 4, 1912.*

MICHIGAN SUGAR CO., *Saginaw, Mich.*

GENTLEMEN: Three years ago I purchased 80 acres of land 2½ miles east of Clio; at that time it was a solid Canada thistle patch. In 1909 we grew 60 acres of beets, with an average of 7 tons per acre. In 1910 we grew 30 acres, with an average of 10 tons per acre. In 1911 we grew 15 acres, with an average of 12 tons per acre. I have never failed to get a seeding of clover with oats, following a beet crop. I consider sugar beets, planted in rotation, the best money crop the farmer can raise. It has taken three crops of beets to rid the farm of thistles. While my first year's crop was light, I figure I have been well repaid in clearing up the farm. Three sugar companies contracting here.

Respectfully, yours, L. B. FULLER.

STATE OF MICHIGAN, *County of Saginaw, ss:*

Personally appeared before me, this 4th day of January, A. D. 1912, the subscriber, L. B. Fuller, who, upon being sworn, deposes and says that the foregoing is true to the best of his knowledge and belief.

[SEAL.] MARK W. BEARINGER,
Notary Public in and for Saginaw County, Mich.

My commission expires September 8, 1914.

SAGINAW, MICH., *January 4, 1912.*

DEAR SIR: My experience in raising sugar beets is of great value to this vicinity. I have raised from 20 to 25 acres every year and have made more profit from them than from any other crop. From $65 to $76 has been my net proceeds; and my farm has been kept free from weeds and I can raise more grain per acre than ever before. The farms in my vicinity have raised 50 per cent in value since sugar beets have been raised.

Sugar beets are of great value to Michigan. There are three companies contracting here.

Yours, very truly, JAMES HAYES.

STATE OF MICHIGAN, *County of Saginaw, ss:*

Personally appeared before me, this 4th day of January, A. D. 1912, the subrer, James Hayes, who upon being sworn, deposes and says the foregoing statement is true to the best of his knowledge and belief.

[SEAL.] MARK W. BEARINGER,
Notary Public in and for Saginaw County, Mich.

My commission expires September 8, 1914.

SAGINAW, WEST SIDE, MICH., *January 4, 1912.*

DEAR SIR: In regard to raising beets in this vicinity, I must say that the beet industry is one of the best things that ever happened in Michigan. The farmers that have raised beets are paying off their mortgages. It makes the farmers prosperous. I have raised beets for nine years; 5 acres each year, and have done my own work on them and received as high as $400 each year. I have had a mortgage on my place, and I know what it is. I think it is no more than right to protect the American beet industry.

Yours, respectfully,

GEORGE C. SCHERZER.
WM. G. SCHERZER.

STATE OF MICHIGAN,
County of Saginaw.

Personally appeared before me this 5th day of January, A. D. 1912, William G. Scherzer, one of the above subscribed, who upon being sworn said that the foregoing is true to the best of his knowledge and belief.

[SEAL.] MARK W. BEARINGER,
Notary Public in and for Saginaw County, Mich.

My commission expires September 8, 1914.

ROGERSVILLE, MICH., *January 2, 1912.*

MICHIGAN SUGAR CO.

DEAR SIRS: I take the pleasure to write you in regard to what the growing of sugar beets and what they have done for me as a moneyed crop and building up the soil condition. I experimented on a portion of a field, growing six crops in succession, from 9 tons to 17 tons per acre. I commenced with spring 1903 and continued the season of 1908, following with oats, getting about 15 bushels more per acre than on balance of field, and have cut two crops of hay, cutting about one-third more than after other crops. I did not try to build up my land, as I wanted to see if I could ruin my land by growing beets. I find that it is one of the best crops to sow that can be raised in Michigan to build up soil condition.

I have grown beets for 12 years, with average yield of 13 tons per acre. I find it the best paying crop to grow. Two sugar companies contracting here.

Yours truly,

A. E. BACHE.

SAGINAW, MICH., *January 4, 1912.*

GENTLEMEN: As an old and experienced beet grower, I wish to say this in regard to growing sugar beets: The sugar-beet industry has been a boon to the farmer in general. In the first place it helps to keep the land clean, and the beet crop also improves the ground for crops of all kinds, especially grain. As a rule I clear a net profit of $30 per acre. Four sugar companies contracting here.

JOHN D. HAYES.

CARROLLTON, *January 4, 1912.*

MICHIGAN SUGAR CO.:

My experience in raising sugar beets has been quite satisfactory. With land in proper condition I don't think one would be out of the way to expect $75 per acre from beets. I have never had a piece I considered right for beets and I have realized from $63 to $73 per acre. Will say in regards the officials of the Carrollton plant, they treat the farmers the very best.

In regards to the beets as a crop rotation I consider it one of the very best.

OSCAR COOK.

STATE OF MICHIGAN, *County of Saginaw, ss:*

Personally appeared before me this 4th day of January, A. D. 1912, the subscriber, Oscar Cook, who upon being sworn, deposes and says that the foregoing statement is true to the best of his knowledge and belief.

[SEAL.] MARK W. BEARINGER,
Notary Public in and for Saginaw County, Mich.

My commission expires September 8, 1914.

MICHIGAN SUGAR CO., SAGINAW PLANT.

DEAR SIRS: In regard to your request as to my experience of raising sugar beets, would say that I have raised beets for the past eight or nine years, and have found them the best paying crop on the farm, and have found them very good to have in the rotation of farm crops. Receive larger crops of oats, barley, and clover after beets than any other crop grown. Beets average from $60 to $70 per acre, and after all labor, both hand and team labor, rent for land, leaves a balance of about $20 per acre to the good.

Yours, FRANK LENT.

STATE OF MICHIGAN, *County of Saginaw, ss.:*

Personally appeared before me this 4th day of January, A. D. 1912, the subscriber, Frank Lent, who upon being sworn deposes and says the foregoing statement is true to the best of his knowledge and belief.

[SEAL.] MARK W. BEARINGER,
Notary Public in and for Saginaw County, Mich.

My commission expires September 8, 1914.

BUENA VISTA, *January 8, 1912.*

MICHIGAN SUGAR CO.

DEAR SIRS: My experience in raising beets is the best paying crop on a farm. I have raised beets for six years and find it does not rob the soil. The following year I have seen better oats on beet ground than ever was raised on the same ground before.

Yours, truly,

THOMAS GREEN.

STATE OF MICHIGAN, *County of Saginaw, ss:*

Personally appeared before me this 4th day of January, A. D. 1912, the subscriber, Thomas Green, who upon being sworn deposes and says the foregoing statement is true to the best of his knowledge and belief.

[SEAL.] MARK W. BEARINGER,
Notary Public in and for Saginaw County, Mich.

My commission expires September 8, 1914.

LAWNDALE, MICH., *January 4, 1912.*

MICHIGAN SUGAR CO.,
Saginaw.

GENTLEMEN: Referring to your inquiry regarding my experience in raising sugar beets, I have been growing beets since first factory was started, some 10 or 12 years, from 4 to 14 acres each year. I figure my net profit during entire period to be about $20 per acre. I don't think it robs the soil, but on the contrary know it improves the soil; and have better crops of clover and oats after beets than after any other crop.

Very truly,

WM. ULRICH.

STATE OF MICHIGAN, *County of Saginaw, ss:*

Personally appeared before me this 4th day of January, A. D. 1912, the subscribed Wm. Ulrich, who, upon being sworn, deposes and says that the foregoing is true to the best of his knowledge and belief.

[SEAL.] MARK W. BEARINGER,
Notary Public in and for Saginaw County, Mich.

My commission expires September 8, 1914.

ZILWAUKEE, *January 4, 1912.*

MICHIGAN SUGAR CO.

DEAR SIR: I have been raising beets for the last eight years. Not only find that it pays to grow them, it puts my land in better shape for next year's crop. I received for last year's crop for 4½ acres of beets $401.25.

Yours truly,

FRED OTTO.

STATE OF MICHIGAN, *County of Saginaw, ss:*

Personally appeared before me this 4th day of January, A. D. 1912, the subscribed Fred Otto, who, upon being sworn, deposes and says that the foregoing statement is true to the best of his knowledge and belief.

[SEAL.]

MARK W. BEARINGER,
Notary Public in and for Saginaw County, Mich.

My commission expires September 8, 1914.

FLUSHING, MICH., *January 4, 1912.*

MICHIGAN SUGAR CO., SAGINAW PLANT.

DEAR SIR: I find that the beet crop is a good one and good payer. My father and I have grown beets the last six years and the crop has paid $40 per acre for the six years.

Yours, truly,

ELLIS BRADLEY.

STATE OF MICHIGAN, *County of Saginaw, ss:*

Personally appeared before me this 4th day of January, A. D. 1912, the subscribed Ellis Bradley, who, upon being sworn, deposes and says the foregoing statement is true to the best of his knowledge and belief.

[SEAL.]

MARK W. BEARINGER,
Notary Public in and for Saginaw County, Mich.

My commission expires September 8, 1914.

FERGUS, MICH., *January 4, 1912.*

MICHIGAN SUGAR CO., SAGINAW PLANT.

DEAR SIRS: In reply to your request would say that I have raised beets for the past five years and have found them the best paying crop that I have raised. I think that the beet-sugar industry is a good thing for the State. My average is about $77 per acre, and after all labor, both hand and team labor and seed, leaves a balance of $42 per acre for the good.

Yours, truly,

DAVID RUSHER.

STATE OF MICHIGAN, *County of Saginaw, ss:*

Personally appeared before me this 4th day of January, A. D. 1912, the subscribed David Rusher, who, upon being sworn, deposes and says the foregoing statement is true to the best of his knowledge and belief.

[SEAL.]

MARK W. BEARINGER,
Notary Public in and for Saginaw County, Mich.

My commission expires September 8, 1914.

I, C. D. Histed, of section 19, Merritt Township, Bay County, Mich., am pleased to make the following statement regarding the growing of sugar beets.

I have grown beets upon my farm for the last eight years, and am pleased to state that it gives me better returns than any other crop I can grow upon the farm. I also note that it has increased the value of land from 25 to 50 per cent. I believe it has increased the price of all farm produce in this vicinity, and I know of no other crop equal to it if we can secure the price of $4.50 for 12½ per cent beets, and an increase of 31¼ cents for each additional per cent.

C. D. HISTED.

Subscribed and sworn to before me this 30th day of December, 1911.

P. P. BITTNER,
Notary Public in and for Bay County, Mich.

My commission expires September 25, 1913.

I, Jos. McInerney, of section 18, Merritt Township, Bay County, Mich., depose and say that it gives me great pleasure to state that I have grown sugar beets every year since 1898, and I consider it far the best crop of all that I can grow upon my farm. It is a mortgage lifter and brings money in at a time just before taxes are due; it helps out with ready cash, as payments are made every month and we always know that we can receive money for beets much more readily than any other crop.

If I desired to dispose of my farm now I could sell it for more than double the price I would have received for it prior to the sugar industry being located in our vicinity.

Jos. McInerney.

Subscribed and sworn to before me this 30th day of December, 1911.

P. P. Bittner,
Notary Public in and for Bay County, Mich.

My commission expires September 25, 1913.

I, G. W. Tennant, of section 16, township of Merritt, county of Bay, State of Michigan, depose and say that I have grown beets continually every year since the first factory in Michigan was built in 1898. I have found the growing of beets is one of the best paying crops that I have ever grown upon my farm. I have cleared a net profit of from $20 to $40 per acre. The crop (the same as all others) depends largely upon the season, rainfall, etc. I also find that there is as much competition for our beets among the different factories as there is among the different grain buyers. I have grown beets for different companies. I have noticed an increase in the value of land since the beet industry was commenced in this community of from 33 to 50 per cent. I have also found that the beet crop is one of the best that a farmer can grow upon his farm. If he has any foul land, such as Canada thistles or milk weeds, it being a hoe crop it gives the farmers a chance to get rid of all foul weeds, and prepares his land for the future crops so that it increases the tonnage.

G. W. Tennant.

Subscribed and sworn to before me this 30th day of December, 1911.

P. P. Bittner,
Notary Public in and for Bay County, Mich.

My commission expires September 25, 1913.

I, Charles Guinup, of Portsmouth Township, Bay County, Mich., depose and say that I am a farmer and have grown beets for several years and dislike very much to see the industry hampered and the factories closed down, as there is no crop that the farmer can grow that brings him like returns. I know when I put the seed into the ground what I am going to receive for it—I have received as high as $80 per acre for beets grown upon my farm. I think it has advanced the price of all farm produce, and I think one of the greatest benefits to the farmer is the condition it leaves his land in after he has one or two crops of beets. If the land is foul, after two seasons growing beets it is free and clear—if the beets are properly taken care of—of all foul weeds.

Charles Guinup.

Subscribed and sworn to before me this 30th day of December, 1911.

O. F. Muselbach,
Notary Public in and for Bay County, Mich.

My commission expires July, 1912.

I, J. M. Halstead, of section 31, Portsmouth Township, Bay County, Mich., wish to state that it gives me great pleasure to say a good word for the sugar-beet industry.

I have grown beets continually ever since the second factory was built in Michigan, in 1899. I have had solicitors from the different factories every year, and I find the competition among the factories for the growing of beets has been as great if not greater than the competition on balance of the farm produce that I grow upon my farm. In my territory it has advanced the price of land from 30 to 50 per cent.

I believe the sugar factories being located in our vicinity not only helps us in the growing of beets, but advances the price of all other farm products, as the thousands of acres of land now used in Michigan for the growing of beets takes that much land away from the growing of other crops.

J. M. HALSTEAD.

Subscribed and sworn to before me this 30th day of December, 1911.

O. F. MUSELBACH,
Notary Public in and for Bay County, Mich.

My commission expires July, 1912.

I, O. F. Meiselbach, of section 35, Portsmouth Township, Bay County, Mich., depose and say that I am a farmer, and am very much elated over the growing of sugar beets. I am quite heavily engaged in the dairy business, and find the beet tops are excellent for the feeding of cows, and the price obtained for the growing of beets is greater than for any other crops that I have grown on my farm since this industry started. It has advanced the value of farm lands from 35 to 40 per cent in my locality. Many farms have changed hands near me since the beet industry started that were a drug upon the market before the erection of the sugar factories in this vicinity.

O. F. MEISELBACH.

Subscribed and sworn to before me this 30th day of December, 1911.

J. E. MACDONALD,
Notary Public in and for Bay County, Mich.

My commission expires June 9, 1915.

THE PLYMOUTH TOMATO GROWERS' ASSOCIATION,
PLYMOUTH, MICH., *December 29, 1911.*

MICHIGAN SUGAR CO.,
Saginaw Plant, Saginaw, Mich.

SIRS: Do I want the tariff taken off sugar? I, as a farmer and grower, say no. Beets are my best cash crop, for my price is guaranteed before my seed is sown. Beets are an ideal crop to work in with a four-year rotation, via corn, beets, oats or wheat, and clover. By raising beets I eradicate all noxious weeds, get my land in better condition, because of the hand labor, than is possible with any other crop. And since raising beets have had an increase in the cereal crops following by at least 10 per cent, and have yet to have a failure in a catch of clover. The labor sent by the companies to care for beets has solved the labor problem, as the beets do not require their attention through haying and harvesting; we are able to secure crops in the best of condition. Competition is very keen for our business, as there are three companies in this territory, each hustling for our acreage.

Yours, for better land and more money for the American farmer via of sugar beets.

I remain,

PAUL T. BENNETT.

ALLENTON, *January 1, 1912.*

I have grown sugar beets for eight years for different companies and the crop nets me, one year with another, $50 per acre; that is, I have this amount per acre left after deducting from the gross receipts the entire expense of growing and handling the crop. I consider the growing of sugar beets very profitable for other reasons than large returns received for the crop, in that it cleans uf the land of weeds and greatly improves the condition of the soil for any grain crop which may follow the beets. From my experience I know that sugar beets do not rob the soil, but greatly improves the land in every way. There are four sugar companies soliciting sugar-beet acreage in this section of the country.

FRED KORTH,
JACOB POWERS,
Allenton.

STATE OF MICHIGAN, *County of St. Clair:*

On this 1st day of January, 1912, personally appeared before me the above-named Fred Korth, who swears that the above statement is true to the best of his knowledge and belief.

C. B. TALLMADGE, *Notary Public.*

St. Johns, Mich., *December 30, 1911.*

Michigan Sugar Co., *Saginaw, Mich.*

Gentlemen: In reply to your request that I state my experience in beet growing will say that I grew my first crop of beets in 1908. The field was well covered with milkweeds. This first crop brought me $68 per acre. In 1909, wishing to grow a larger acreage, I again planted this same field to sugar beets. I received $76.50 per acre from this second crop. These were the first beets grown in this neighborhood. Some of my neighbors really believed that I had ruined this field; that the two crops of beets had taken every particle of plant food from the soil, and that it would be many years before I could grow another crop of any kind on this field. In the following spring I sowed the field to oats. The field had been accurately measured and the oats were carefully weighed. Result, 68 bushels 7 pounds of oats per acre, while the next best crop that I heard of was less than 65 bushels per acre. I followed the oats with wheat and had 26 bushels per acre. Seeded to June clover and have a fine catch, and not a milkweed to be seen. Practically every farmer is growing beets here now, and they all agree that beets are the most profitable crop they can grow.

First. As a money-making crop they are sure, as they will stand dry weather well and wet weather does not injure them.

Second. They improve the soil; we get better crops of oats, barley, wheat, or grass following a beet crop.

Third. For ridding the soil of all noxious weeds by thorough cultivation.

We rotate our crops here: First corn, then beets, then oats or barley, and seed.

Yours, truly,

H. V. Hostetter.

St. Johns, Mich., *December 23, 1911.*

Michigan Sugar Co.

Dear Sirs: I have been requested to write you my experience in growing sugar beets, and will say I have grown them for the last nine years and never have had a failure. I think they are the best-paying crop we have, and where grown in rotation with other crops, such as corn, oats, and clover, I think they will improve our land each year. They are a crop that will stand more wet weather, spring or fall, and more drought than any other crop grown. If you want to make money at farming, and at the same time improve your land (and of course we all do), then tie to sugar beets.

Yours, truly, John Hiller, *St. Johns.*

P. S.—If this isn't put together right, then fix it to suit. I have tried to make my idea in regard to growing beets as plain as I could.

Allenton, *January 1, 1912.*

I have grown sugar beets for eight years for different companies, and the crop nets me one year with another, $50 per acre—that is, I have this amount per acre left after deducting from the gross receipts the entire expense of growing and handling the crop. I consider the growing of sugar beets very profitable for other reasons than large returns received for the crop, in that it cleans up the land of weeds and greatly improves the condition of the soil for any grain crop which may follow the beets. From my experience I know that sugar beets do not rob the soil, but greatly improves the land in every way. There are four sugar companies soliciting sugar-beet acreage in this section of the country.

David Graham,
Herbert Howell,
Allenton.

State of Michigan, *County of St. Clair:*

On this 1st day of January, 1912, personally appeared before me the above-named David Graham, who swears that the above statement is true to the best of his knowledge and belief.

C. B. Zallmadge,
Notary Public.

SAGINAW, MICH., *January 1, 1912.*

SAGINAW SUGAR CO.

DEAR SIR: Your request for a statement of our success raising sugar beets, I would say that we have found them to be the most profitable crop we raise, averaging $65 per acre, and I am satisfied they greatly improve the soil. We always get a fine crop of oats after beets without plowing.

I have heard people say they exhaust the soil, but that is a great mistake. Beets improve the soil every time. It is the greatest industry this country has ever known, and will be still greater if Congress will stop tinkering with the tariff. It is a great shame that an industry that is destined to benefit so many should be sacrificed to the interest of a few greedy refiners. I wish the beet success.

Very truly, yours, GEO. TARRANT, Sr.

SAGINAW, MICH., *January 2, 1912.*

DEAR SIR: In regard to the raising of sugar beets, I have raised sugar beets for the past nine years and have found them one of the best paying crops on the farm.

I figure on from $60 to $70 per acre, and after the hand labor, team work, and rent of land taken from same, which amounts to about $43 per acre, leaving a balance of $21.50 per acre.

As to improving the soil, we raise the best oats or barley, and receive the best results in getting stand of clover than we can from any other crop.

At present I am renting my farm, and the man who rents it is compelled to put in 15 acres a year to sugar beets. Then I am sure that my farm is free from all foul weeds, and the farm is better for it.

FRANK LENT, *Saginaw, Mich.*

DECKERVILLE, MICH., *December 29, 1911.*

I have grown sugar beets 11 years for different companies and the crop nets me, one year with another, $25 per acre; that is, I have this amount per acre left after deducting from the gross receipts the entire expense of growing and handling the crop. I consider growing sugar beets very profitable for other reasons than large returns received for the crop, in that it cleans up the land of weeds and greatly improves the condition of the soil for any grain crop which may follow the beets. From my experience I know that sugar beets do not rob the soil, but greatly improves the land in every way. There are two sugar companies soliciting sugar-beet acreage in this section of the country.

RICHARD M. GOUGH.

STATE OF MICHIGAN, *County of Sanilac:*

On this 29th day of December, 1911, personally appeared before me the above-named Richard M. Gough, who swears that the above statement is true to the best of his knowledge and belief.

[SEAL.] R. A. WEST,
Notary Public, Sanilac County, Mich.

My commission expires January 13, 1913.

CAPAC, MICH., *January 1, 1912.*

I have grown sugar beets for four years for different companies and the crop nets me, one year with another, $45 per acre; that is, I have this amount per acre left after deducting from the gross receipts the entire expense of growing and handling the crop. I consider the growing of sugar beets very profitable for other reasons than large returns received for the crop, in that it cleans up the land of weeds and greatly improves the condition of the soil for any grain crop which may follow the beets. From my experience I know that sugar beets do not rob the soil, but greatly improves the land in every way. There are four sugar companies soliciting sugar-beet acreage in this section of the country

STEPHEN GOULD.

STATE OF MICHIGAN, *County of St. Clair:*

On this 1st day of January, 1912, personally appeared before me the above-named Stephen Gould, who swears that the above statement is true to the best of his knowledge and belief.

[SEAL.] GEO. C. WATSON,
Notary Public, St. Clair County, Mich.

My commission expires March 22, 1913.

CAPAC, MICH., *January 1, 1912.*

I have grown sugar beets for four years for different companies and the crop nets me, one year with another, $40 per acre; that is, I have this amount per acre left after deducting from the gross receipts the entire expense of growing and handling the crop. I consider the growing of sugar beets very profitable for other reasons than large returns received for the crop, in that it cleans up the land of weeds and greatly improves the condition of the soil for any grain crop which may follow the beets. From my experience I know that sugar beets do not rob the soil but greatly improve the land in every way. There are four sugar companies soliciting sugar-beet acreage in this section of the country.

HENRY SHARRARD.

STATE OF MICHIGAN, *County of St. Clair:*

On this 1st day of January, 1912, personally appeared before me the above-named Henry Sharrard, who swears that the above statement is true to the best of his knowledge and belief.

[SEAL.]

GEO. C. WATSON,
Notary Public, St. Clair County, Mich.

My commission expires March 22, 1913.

CAPAC, MICH., *January 1, 1912.*

I have grown sugar beets for three years for different companies, and the crop nets me, one year with another, $30 per acre; that is, I have this amount per acre left after deducting from the gross receipts the entire expense of growing and handling the crop. I consider the growing of sugar beets very profitable for other reasons than large returns received for the crop, in that it cleans up the land of weeds and greatly improves the condition of the soil for any grain crop which may follow the beets. From my experience I know that sugar beets do not rob the soil but greatly improve the land in every way. There are four sugar companies soliciting sugar-beet acreage in this section of the country.

JOSHUA (his x mark) HILL.

Witness to mark:
S. E. BISSONETH.

STATE OF MICHIGAN, *County of St. Clair:*

On this 1st day of January, 1912, personally appeared before me the above-named Joshua Hill, who swears that the above statement is true to the best of his knowledge and belief.

[SEAL.]

GEO. C. WATSON,
Notary Public, St. Clair County, Mich.

My commission expires March 22, 1913.

STATE OF MICHIGAN, *County of Huron, ss:*

John C. Hornbacher, being duly sworn, deposes and says that he resides in Fairhaven Township, in Huron County, State of Michigan, and that he is an experienced beet grower and has grown beets for 12 years; that upon his own experience he bases the following statement of his average expense and gross and net profits per acre, as follows:

Gross profit per acre		$95.00
Preparing the land	$3.50	
Sowing beets	.50	
Cultivating	3.00	
Harvesting and working beets	20.00	
Hauling	12.00	
Total expense		39.00
Net profit per acre		56.00

Deponent further states that as a result of his raising beets the land used for this purpose is now in a better condition than it was previous to the sowing of said beets and is in a higher state of cultivation than it ever showed before; that the results of following crops show a net increase of 10 per cent over previous crops, and that since beet industry has been promoted in this section of the country land has increased in value 100 per cent.

Further deponent saith not.

JOHN C. HORNBACHER.

Subscribed and sworn to before me this 30th day of December, A. D. 1911.

ELLERY C. PENGRA,
Notary Public, Huron County, Mich.

My commission expires June 28, 1915.

STATE OF MICHIGAN, *County of Huron, ss:*

Fred Erbisch, being duly sworn, deposes and says that he resides in Sebewaing Township, in Huron County, State of Michigan, and that he is an experienced beet grower and has grown beets for five years; that upon his own experience he bases the following statement of his average expense and gross and net profit per acre, as follows:

Gross profit per acre		$80.00
Preparing the land	$3.50	
Sowing beets	.50	
Cultivating	3.50	
Harvesting and working beets	20.00	
Hauling	7.20	
Total expense		34.70
Net profit per acre		45.30

Deponent further states that as a result of his raising beets the land used for this purpose is now in a better condition than it was previous to the sowing of said beets and is in a higher state of cultivation than it ever showed before; that the results of following crops show a net increase of 10 per cent over previous crops, and that since the beet industry has been promoted in this section of the country land has increased in value 100 per cent.

Further deponent saith not.

FRED ERBISCH.

Subscribed and sworn to before me this 30th day of December, A. D. 1911.

RICHARD MARTINI,
Notary Public, Huron County, Mich.

My commission expires October 25, 1914.

CAPAC, MICH., *January 1, 1912.*

I have grown sugar beets for three years for different companies and the crop nets me, one year with another, $30 per acre; that is, I have this amount per acre left after deducting from the gross receipts the entire expense of growing and handling the crop. I consider the growing of sugar beets very profitable for other reasons than large returns received for the crop, in that it cleans up the land of weeds and greatly improves the condition of the soil for any grain crop which may follow the beets. From my experience I know that sugar beets do not rob the soil, but greatly improve the land in every way. There are four sugar companies soliciting sugar-beet acreage in this section of the country.

PHILIP F. MORLEY, *Emmett, Mich.*

STATE OF MICHIGAN, *County of St. Clair:*

On this 1st day of January, 1912, personally appeared before me the above-named Philip F. Morley, who swears that the above statement is true to the best of his knowledge and belief.

GEO. T. WATSON,
Notary Public, St. Clair County, Mich.

My commission expires March 22, 1913.

STATE OF MICHIGAN, *County of Huron, ss:*

David Rothfuss, being duly sworn, deposes and says that he resides in Winroe Township, in Huron County, State of Michigan, and that he is an experienced beet grower and has grown beets for nine years; that upon his own experience he bases the following statement of his average expense and gross and net profits per acre:

Gross profits per acre		$65.00
Preparing the land	$3.50	
Sowing beets	.50	
Cultivation	2.50	
Harvesting and working beets	20.00	
Hauling	15.00	
Total expense		41.50
Net profit per acre		23.50

Deponent further states that as a result of his raising beets the land used for this purpose is now in a better condition than it was previous to the sowing of said beets and is in a higher state of cultivation than it ever showed before; that the results of following crops show a net increase of 10 per cent over previous crops, and that since the beet industry has been promoted in this section of the country land has increased in value 100 per cent.

Further deponent saith not.

DAVID ROTHFUSS.

Subscribed and sworn to before me this 30th day of December, A. D. 1911.

J. T. HADWIN,
Notary Public, Huron County, Mich.

My commission expires January 7, 1914.

ALLENTON, *January 1, 1912.*

I have grown sugar beets for three years for different companies, and the crop nets me, one year with another, $75 per acre; that is, I have this amount per acre left after deducting from the gross receipts the entire expense of growing and handling the crop. I consider the growing of sugar beets very profitable for other reasons than large returns received for the crop, in that it cleans up the land of weeds and greatly improves the condition of the soil for any grain crop which may follow the beets. From my experience I know that sugar beets do not rob the soil, but greatly improve the land in every way. There are four sugar companies soliciting sugar-beet acreage in this section of the country.

J. B. CURRY,
WM. POWEN,

STATE OF MICHIGAN, *County of St. Clair:*

On this 1st day of January, 1912, personally appeared before me the above-named J. B. Curry, who swears that the above statement is true to the best of his knowledge and belief.

C. B. TALLMADGE,
Notary Public.

STATE OF MICHIGAN, *County of Huron, ss:*

George Collison, being duly sworn, deposes and says that he resides in Fairhaven Township, in Huron County, State of Michigan, and that he is an experienced beet grower and has grown beets for 10 years; that upon his own experience he bases the following statement of his average expense and gross and net profits per acre, as follows:

Gross profit per acre		$75.00
Preparing the land	$3.50	
Sowing beets	.50	
Cultivating	3.50	
Harvesting and working beets	20.00	
Hauling	12.00	
Total expense		39.50
Net profit per acre		35.50

Deponent further states that as a result of his raising beets the land used for this purpose is now in a better condition than it was previous to the sowing of said beets and is in a higher state of cultivation than it ever showed before; that the results of following crops show a net increase of 10 per cent over previous crops, and that since the beet industry has been promoted in this section of the country land has increased in value 100 per cent.

Further deponent saith not.

GEORGE COLLISON.

Subscribed and sworn to before me this 30th day of December, A. D. 1911.

[SEAL.] R. C. RANKE, Jr.,
Notary Public, Huron County, Mich.

My commission expires July 27, 1911.

STATE OF MICHIGAN, *County of Huron, ss:*

Jacob Binder, beind duly sworn, deposes and says that he resides in Fairhaven Township in Huron County, State of Michigan, and that he is an experienced beet grower and has grown beets for 10 years; that upon his own experience he bases the following statement of his average expense and gross and net profits per acre, as follows:

Gross profit per acre		$90.00
Preparing the land	$3.50	
Sowing beets	.50	
Cultivating	3.00	
Harvesting and working beets	20.00	
Hauling	12.00	
Total expense		39.00
Net profit per acre		51.00

Deponent further states that as a result of his raising beets the land used for this purpose is now in a better condition than it was previous to the sowing of said beets and is in a higher state of cultivation than it ever showed before; that the results of following crops show a net increase of 10 per cent over previous crops; and that since beet industry has been promoted in this section of the country land has increased in value 100 per cent.

Further deponent saith not.

JACOB BINDER.

Subscribed and sworn to before me this 30th day of December, A. D. 1911.

ELLERY C. PENGRA,
Notary Public, Huron County, Mich.

My commission expires June 28, 1915.

STATE OF MICHIGAN, *County of Huron, ss:*

Christ Winter, being duly sworn, deposes and says that he resides in Sebewaing Township in Huron County, State of Michigan, and that he is an experienced beet grower and has grown beets for 14 years; that upon his own experience he bases the following statement of his average expense and gross and net profits per acre, as follows:

Gross profit per acre		$80.00
Preparing the land	$3.50	
Sowing beets	.50	
Cultivating	2.00	
Harvesting and working beets	20.00	
Hauling	7.50	
Total expense		33.50
Net profit per acre		46.50

Deponent further states that as a result of his raising beets the land used for this purpose is now in a better condition than it was previous to the sowing of said beets and is in a higher state of cultivation than it ever showed before; that the results of following crops show a net increase of 10 per cent over previous crops; and that since the beet industry has been promoted in this section of the country land has increased in value 100 per cent.

Further deponent saith not.

CHRIST WINTER.

Subscribed and sworn to before me this 30th day of December, A. D. 1911.

J. V. HADWIN,
Notary Public, Huron County, Mich.

My commission expires January 7, 1914.

ALLENTON, *January 1, 1912.*

I have grown sugar beets for four years for different companies, and the crop nets me, one year with another, $90 per acre; that is, I have this amount per acre left after deducting from the gross receipts the entire expense of growing and handling the crop. I consider the growing of sugar beets very profitable for other reasons than large returns received for the crop, in that it cleans up the land of weeds and greatly improves the condition of the soil for any grain crop which may follow the beets. From my experience I know that sugar beets do not rob the soil, but greatly improves the land in every way. There are four sugar companies soliciting sugar-beet acreage in this section of the country.

CHAS. SCHOOK, *Allenton.*

STATE OF MICHIGAN, *County of St. Clair, ss:*

On this 1st day of January, 1912, personally appeared before me the above-named Charles Schook, who swears that the above statement is true to the best of his knowledge and belief.

C. B. TALLMADGE, *Notary Public.*

STATE OF MICHIGAN, *County of Huron, ss:*

Thomas W. Moody, being duly sworn, deposes and says that he resides in Brookfield Township, in Huron County, State of Michigan, and that he is an experienced beet grower and has grown beets for nine years; that upon his own experience he bases the following statement of his average expense and gross and net profit per acre, as follows:

Gross profit per acre		$75.00
Preparing the land	$3.50	
Sowing beets	.50	
Cultivating	3.50	
Harvesting and working beets	20.00	
Hauling	7.50	
Total expense		35.00
Net profit per acre		40.00

Deponent further states that as a result of his raising beets the land used for this purpose is now in a better condition than it was previous to the sowing of said beets and is in a higher state of cultivation than it has ever shown before; that the results of following crops show a net increase of 10 per cent over previous crops; and that since the beet industry has been promoted in this section of the country land has increased in value 100 per cent.

Further deponent saith not.

THOMAS W. MOODY.

Subscribed and sworn to before me this 30th day of December, A. D. 1911.

ELLERY C. PENGRA,
Notary Public, Huron County, Mich.

My commission expires June 28, 1915.

I hereby certify that the following is a true report of the acreage, tonnage, and amount each grower received for his beets for the years specified, as taken from the books of the St. Louis plant.

Dated this 5th day of January, 1912.

HOLLAND-ST. LOUIS SUGAR CO.,
J. H. WHITING, *Vice President.*

Name.	Year.	Cont. No.	Acreage.	Tonnage.	Amount.
Richard Method	1907	1445	6	81	$438.47
	1908	1458	6	48	241.10
	1909	1406	9	59	406.10
Sylvester Frost	1907	1447	5	46	267.89
	1908	1354	5	51	332.17
	1909	1382	5	39	262.13
	1910	1520	6	66	404.72
John Fleming	1907	1659	10	71	353.36
	1908	1533	10	64	319.90
	1909	1483	16	104	663.98
	1910	1473	20	276	1,702.13
Michael Fleming	1907	....	....	....	....
	1909	1373 1374½ 1374	12	55	339.15
	1910	1376	7	55	316.22
Daniel Miles	1907	1602	3	30	150.51
	1909	1403	4	11	73.09
	1910	1403	5	52	321.01
Frank Levi	1907	1503	4	49	262.26
	1908	1324	2.5	17	114.36
	1909	1413	4.5	34	218.53
	1910	1399	3	27	169.39
Thomas Mayer	1907	....	....	....	....
	1910	1365	16	98	596.00
F Doehring	1907	....	....	....	....
	1909	1368	4	24	151.09
	1910	1459	11	69	426.94
Wm. Elson	1907	1446	6A	38F	196.18
	1908	1344-1355	7.5	66	420.21
	1909	1400-1404	30	99	632.14
	1910	1368	4	96	569.19
L. Cornwell Est	1910	1439	84	905	5,394.17
	1911	1148	57	844	4,729.21
August Schmidt	1907	1870	3	31	156.79
	1909	1651	2	25	170.52
John Ranchhols	1907	1736	2.5	18	93.76
	1908	1619	2	29	184.68
	1909	1677	3	26	173.28
	1910	1629	2	30	183.47
Wm. Phelps	1907	1705-1705½	8	72	376.69
	1908	1617	7	75	493.74
	1910	1678	8	116	712.46
Charles Cusick	1907	....	....	....	....
	1909	1750	8	52	355.06
Michael Blank	1908	1651	2A	20F	127.79
	1909	1684	2.5	13	84.73
	1910	1610	3	28	167.44
Andrew Doyle	1907	1900	1	6	33.00
	1909	1690	7	50	321.33
	1910	1689	12	55	319.06
Albert Kube	1907	1740	4	48	265.55
	1908	1610	3	52	337.17
	1909	1694	3.5	26	175.48
	1910	1652	4	53	333.99
Fred Fiting	1910	1628	3	25	155.10
August Frederick	1910	1637	4	33	198.61
Wm. Dungey	1907	1714	2	13	65.33
	1908	1689	2	20	99.30
	1909	1759	2	10	50.60
	1910	1611	2	25	145.92
Freeman Dungey	1907	1741	9	82	449.53
	1908	1691	9.5	85	425.88
	1910	1633	2	15	92.26

Acres	458.5
Tons	4,607
Average tons	10½
Price per acre	$61.95

SAGINAW PLANT, JANUARY 2, 1912.

DEAR SIR: In reply to yours of December 30, I will say I have raised sugar beets for about 10 years, I raise about 4 acres each year and they average about 15 tons per acre, and the average price I received for them is about $5 per ton, clear of freight. Sugar beets are certainly a good thing for the Michigan farmers to raise, especially the small farmer with large families, because the beets are a sure cash crop for us to raise. They will stand more rain or more dry weather than any other crop. I hope that sugar-beet raising will be continued in Michigan, as it is a good thing for the laboring people, as well as the farmer.

Yours, very truly,
N. WILLING.

ST. CHARLES, MICH., *January 3, 1912.*

Mr. DOYLE.

DEAR SIR: Yours of the 30th instant at hand. In reply would say we have raised sugar beets for a number of years with success. We raise from 5 to 10 acres each year, although I am unable to give you the average tonnage or the net proceeds of same only for the last two years. In 1910 we raised 7½ acres with an average of 18 tons per acre, with net profit of $60 per acre. In 1911 we raised 10½ acres with an average of 14 tons per acre, with net profit of $30 per acre. I consider beet raising has been a great help to the farmers of Michigan.

Yours truly,
H. H. SANDERSON.

Sugar beets raised in and near Merrill for the Saginaw plant of the Michigan Sugar Co., and delivered at the Merrill weigh station.

1910 campaign:	
Tons raised	6,819.15
Paid farmers	$39,413.98
Average tare	2.84
1911 campaign, up to and including the 23d of December, 1911:	
Tons raised and hauled up to above date	2,971.15
Paid farmers to date	$15,479.71
Average tare	5.24
Raised and hauled to Hemlock, Mich., for same company as above:	
1910 campaign—	
Tons raised	3,438.43
Paid farmers	$20,481.48
Average tare	3.58
1911 campaign, up to and including Dec. 23, 1911—	
Tons raised	2,308.44
Paid farmers	$13,107.01
Average tare	5.97

Ben O'Toole (near Merrill), 1910, had 13 acres, $1,008.54; 1911, had 11 acres. $1,150.50.

Phil Potvin (near Merrill), has raised beets five years; 12 to 15 acres per year, 10 to 20 tons per acre; averaged about $5.50 per ton.

Chas. Griffith (near Merrill), manager Cornwell estate farms, has raised beets five years; 50 to 80 acres per year, 12 to 18 tons per acre; averaged $6 per ton.

Wm. Elson (near Merrill), in 1910 raised beets on 4 acres and realized $636 from them alone, or an average of $159 per acre.

Dan McLeod has raised beets six years; first year raised 10 tons to the acre, and since has raised as high as 20 tons per acre, and has averaged about 16 tons to the acre. Received an average of $5.50 per ton. Had from 5 to 10 acres each year, and cared for them all with his own family.

TESTIMONY OF MR. E. G. RUST.

(The witness was duly sworn by the chairman.)

Mr. FORDNEY. Give your place of residence.

Mr. RUST. Bay City, Mich.

Mr. FORDNEY. What is your business?

Mr. RUST. Farming now.

Mr. FORDNEY. Do you raise some sugar beets?

Mr. RUST. Yes, sir.

Mr. FORDNEY. How much farm have you?

Mr. RUST. Three hundred and thirty three acres.

Mr. FORDNEY. How many acres of beets do you raise?

Mr. RUST. I raised 53¾ acres this year.

Mr. FORDNEY. What sugar company did you sell your beets to, or raise them for, rather?

Mr. RUST. The Michigan.

Mr. FORDNEY. The Michigan Sugar Co.?

Mr. RUST. Yes, sir.

Mr. FORDNEY. Located where?

Mr. RUST. At Bay City.

Mr. FORDNEY. Is that one of the Michigan Sugar Co.'s factories, or do you know?

Mr. RUST. The one is.

Mr. FORDNEY. Is it one of the Michigan Sugar Co.'s factories?

Mr. RUST. Yes, sir.

Mr. FORDNEY. Did you raise those beets under contract?

Mr. RUST. Yes, sir.

Mr. FORDNEY. Through this so-called Michigan Sugar Co.?

Mr. RUST. Yes, sir.

Mr. FORDNEY. Which is one of the Michigan Sugar Co.'s six factories in the State?

Mr. RUST. Yes, sir.

Mr. FORDNEY. Will you give us the cost per acre of production of your crop; for raising your crop what has it cost you per acre? Give the different items if you can. You heard Mr. Doyle's statement; can you give the different items of cost of production of your beets?

Mr. RUST. Yes, sir.

Mr. FORDNEY. Give it in your own way.

Mr. RUST. I kept a correct account of mine right through, and the cost of mine per acre was $35.80.

Mr. FORDNEY. $35.80 per acre. That included everything outside of what?

Mr. RUST. Everything.

Mr. FORDNEY. Outside of the delivery of the beets to the factory?

Mr. RUST. That included everything, delivery, freight, and all.

Mr. FORDNEY. That is your total cost?

Mr. RUST. Yes, sir.

Mr. FORDNEY. What did you pay for your hand labor?

Mr. RUST. $18 per acre, 24-inch rows.

Mr. FORDNEY. I think it was stated by Mr. Doyle that the price paid for hand labor depends upon the width of your rows, did he not?

Mr. RUST. Yes, sir; and it does.

Mr. FORDNEY. How does that range?

Mr. RUST. 20-inch rows cost $20 per acre, 24-inch rows $18 per acre, and 28-inch rows $16 per acre. That is the rule. The difference is, the farther apart the rows the less rows there are on an acre

Mr. FORDNEY. Certainly, and the less hand labor required?

Mr. RUST. Yes, sir.

Mr. FORDNEY. You planted your beets in 24-inch rows?

Mr. RUST. Yes, sir.

Mr. FORDNEY. Because you paid $18 per acre for that hand labor?

Mr. RUST. Yes, sir.

Mr. FORDNEY. How many tons of beets per acre did you raise on those 53¾ acres?

Mr. RUST. Mine yielded 10 tons per acre.

Mr. FORDNEY. Ten tons per acre?

Mr. RUST. Yes, sir; on an average, right through.

Mr. FORDNEY. How much did you receive per ton for your beets?

Mr. RUST. They brought me, gross weight—that is, dirt and all from the field—$5.57 per ton.

Mr. FORDNEY. Now, how much was deducted from that for so-called tare? You say that included dirt, so that there was tare to be deducted from that.

Mr. RUST. The average tare was 7.12 of the whole.

Mr. FORDNEY. In other words, about $5.50 per ton you got for them after deducting tare?

Mr. RUST. After deducting tare, they brought me just a trifle over $6 per ton.

Mr. FORDNEY. Yes; $6 per ton.

Mr. RUST. Yes, sir.

Mr. FORDNEY. Now, deducting 7.12 per cent from 10 tons per acre, what do you get? I am a little dull on figures, so about what did that average you per acre, if you have figured it out? In other words, what were your total receipts for the 53¾ acres of land; can you tell, or give it per acre?

Mr. RUST. That is, the gross, do you mean?

Mr. FORDNEY. No; the net. You figure it out and tell it in your own way.

Mr. RUST. $19.20 per acre.

The CHAIRMAN. That is, net profit?

Mr. RUST. Yes, sir.

The CHAIRMAN. Not allowing anything for the land?

Mr. RUST. No, sir.

The CHAIRMAN. That $19.20 did not allow anything for the rent of the land, which you owned individually?

Mr. RUST. In my account it would.

Mr. FORDNEY. $19.20 per acre added to $35.80 would be exactly $55 per acre. It cost you $35.80 per acre to deliver them, and you got $19.20 net, so adding them together would be the gross receipts, which would be exactly $55 per acre for that crop?

Mr. RUST. Yes, sir.

Mr. FORDNEY. Does more than one company compete for beets in the territory where you live and raise beets?

Mr. RUST. Yes, sir. There are the German-American, the Michigan, and the West Bay City.

Mr. FORDNEY. The West Bay City factory and the German-American factory are independent factories, so called, are they not?

Mr. RUST. Yes, sir.

Mr. FORDNEY. And the factory of the Michigan Sugar Co. is the one that belongs to the company that has six factories in the State?

Mr. RUST. Yes, sir.

Mr. FORDNEY. Do you get any advantages by reason of these different factories? Do you raise beets for either one of them?

Mr. RUST. Yes, sir; for either one of them.

Mr. FORDNEY. It is about the same distance for delivery, as you live close to town?

Mr. Rust. I live about a mile, or less than a mile, from the weigh station. All three of the factories have weigh stations right there.

Mr. Fordney. You only have to haul your beets about a mile to town to the weigh station?

Mr. Rust. Yes, sir.

Mr. Fordney. What value do you think, if any, beet raising has added to the land in that vicinity?

Mr. Rust. Why I should think it had added from 40 per cent to 50 per cent.

Mr. Fordney. Your land is worth that much more per acre because of the privilege of raising beets?

Mr. Rust. Yes, sir; take land that was worth $50 per acre before and it is worth $90 to $100 per acre now.

The Chairman. How about land generally enhancing in value during that time independent of beet raising; isn't that a fact?

Mr. Rust. Yes, sir.

The Chairman. How much of that enhancement in value do you credit to the sugar-beet proposition and how much to independent enhancement?

Mr. Rust. I would be unable to state that; it would be an estimate.

The Chairman. I know. Of course it is only a matter of opinion.

Mr. Rust. In that immediate locality, where there is a sugar-beet belt, the majority of it is due to beet raising.

The Chairman. Have other lands in neighboring counties where there is no sugar-beet belt enhanced as much as this sugar-beet belt land has enhanced, or if not, what it the difference?

Mr. Rust. I don't think they have in some of the counties, such as western portion of Genesee, but we have been raising sugar beets in and about Swartz Creek, and land has gone up to $100 an acre.

The Chairman. How much of that enhancement would probably have occurred but for the beets, and the only way to judge that is to take some section around in that section, land about as good but where the beets are not grown, and compare the enhancement of the sugar-beet belt there with the enhancement of the other territory?

Mr. Fordney. Where it is handy to the railroad?

The Chairman. Where the conditions are about the same and as near as you can come to the sugar-beet section, or what is known as the sugar-beet section. Can you do that?

Mr. Rust. I couldn't positively do it; it would be an estimate.

The Chairman. Can you give an estimate of that kind?

Mr. Rust. I should think that in the sugar-beet belt, where it has increased 40 to 50 per cent, the other land has increased probably 25 per cent.

The Chairman. That is during the same period of time in Michigan?

Mr. Rust. Yes, sir.

The Chairman. I was asking you awhile ago something about whether you considered interest on your land in the cost of growing beets, and I am not sure I clearly understood your answer.

Mr. Rust. I am not sure that in my own account I charged up $6 more as interest.

The Chairman. Is that included in the $35.80?

Mr. Rust. No, sir.

The Chairman. In addition to the $35.80 per acre cost of producing beets if you charge up interest upon the money invested in your land you would have to add $6 per acre?

Mr. RUST. Yes, sir.

The CHAIRMAN. That is, as interest upon the value of your land used for the purpose?

Mr. RUST. Yes, sir.

The CHAIRMAN. That is 6 per cent upon the valuation of $100 per acre for that part of your farm used for growing sugar beets?

Mr. RUST. Yes, sir.

The CHAIRMAN. Deducting that from the $19.20, you would then have a net profit of $13.20 per acre—that is, after receiving interest upon your money invested in that land?

Mr. RUST. Yes, sir.

The CHAIRMAN. Do you get satisfactory treatment from the sugar companies in the weighing of your beets, or do you weigh your beets yourself, or check them up, or how do you do that?

Mr. RUST. I weigh a load once in a while—run them over my own scales to see if they correspond—and they are correct every time. I only now and then would weigh a load to keep tab to see if their weighing was correct.

The CHAIRMAN. To see whether they were giving you correct weight?

Mr. RUST. Yes, sir.

The CHAIRMAN. Or, to see if their weight agreed with yours?

Mr. RUST. Yes, sir. I never asked them about the tare until I got through, and it was always very satisfactory.

The CHAIRMAN. Of course, in order to get a good crop you must keep the weeds out?

Mr. RUST. Yes, sir.

The CHAIRMAN. And this $18 per acre for hand labor keeps the weeds out of the crop?

Mr. RUST. Yes, sir.

The CHAIRMAN. They hoe the land?

Mr. RUST. Yes, sir.

The CHAIRMAN. That leaves the land in better shape for the crops that follow?

Mr. RUST. A great deal.

The CHAIRMAN. Do you rotate the crops after raising beets by putting in oats, and so on?

Mr. RUST. Oats after beets, the following year, and seed it down after oats.

The CHAIRMAN. By seeding you mean hay?

Mr. RUST. Yes, sir; grass seed.

The CHAIRMAN. Seed it down to clover or timothy?

Mr. RUST. I might state here that I had one 22-acre lot that I had put into beets, that before was covered with Canada thistles in a solid mass, and we had three very heavy rains and it came up a solid green mat all over.

The CHAIRMAN. The thistles came up?

Mr. RUST. Yes, sir; there were 4 acres drowned out entirely, but we had to take care of them, hoe all of them out. But I am now rid of all those thistles, and it is clean and nice.

The CHAIRMAN. Those 4 acres were in your 53¾ acres?

Mr. RUST. Yes, sir.

The CHAIRMAN. So really you had 49 acres of beets to harvest, on account of the 4 acres drowning out?

Mr. RUST. Yes, sir.

Mr. FORDNEY. You started to tell what shape that left the land in, where the thistles were in the 22 acres.

Mr. RUST. It left the land perfectly clean. I don't think there were any at the time of lifting.

Mr. FORDNEY. No thistles at all?

Mr. RUST. No. The ground is in better shape on account of the lifting every 24 inches, too—going down so deep and opening up the pores of the soil. We figure that our oats will yield anywhere from 5 to 10 bushels more per acre after beets than from fall plowing.

Mr. FORDNEY. What kind of labor did you have to do this work?

Mr. RUST. They were Polacks, but residents of Detroit.

Mr. FORDNEY. They came up there for the work during the beet harvest?

Mr. RUST. Yes, sir.

Mr. FORDNEY. Is it efficient labor, good labor?

Mr. RUST. Real good. I furnished them two houses. Two families came and lived in the houses. They were 90 days in doing this work, six of them.

Mr. FORDNEY. Six men?

Mr. RUST. Four men and two women.

Mr. FORDNEY. Did the women work in the field, too?

Mr. RUST. Yes, sir.

Mr. FORDNEY. How much money did you pay them for those 90 days' work?

Mr. RUST. I think it was $967.50.

Mr. FORDNEY. For 90 days work by four men and two women?

Mr. RUST. Yes, sir.

Mr. FORDNEY. Did they do any other work during those 90 days?

Mr. RUST. Yes, sir; they went and worked in different beet fields by the day. They also hoed my corn at $1.50 per day.

Mr. FORDNEY. They worked in your corn for $1.50 per day?

Mr. RUST. Yes, sir; and in my beans.

Mr. FORDNEY. How much time during those 90 days did they spend in your cornfield, or how much did you pay them for that work?

Mr. RUST. $56 for my corn, though I can not tell you the exact number of days; and $25, I think it was, that I paid them for hoeing my beans.

Mr. FORDNEY. Then, $56 for work in corn and $25 for work in beans should be added to the $967.50 as the amount they earned from you?

Mr. RUST. Yes, sir.

Mr. FORDNEY. Did they work for anybody else during that time?

Mr. RUST. Yes, sir; they went out and worked in other beets at $1.50 per day. They also went down to the sugar factory and helped them there, but I couldn't tell you exactly the number of days they put in down there. They had the opportunity of working topping beets for neighbors, but they went back to Detroit to work in the automobile works on account of the weather getting bad.

Mr. FORDNEY. Did any of this foreign help that worked in the beet fields live in or about Bay City, where you live?

Mr. RUST. A great many.

Mr. FORDNEY. Live right there in the city?

Mr. RUST. Yes, sir; they work out by the day all through beet harvest.

Mr. FORDNEY. And go home at night or live on the farm where they do the work?

Mr. RUST. A good many live on the farms and others the farmers take back and forth.

Mr. FORDNEY. To their homes?

Mr. RUST. Yes, sir. I think the rule is to go and get them and take them back home and feed them dinner and pay $1.25 per day.

Mr. FORDNEY. And they live in their own homes and furnish themselves with their breakfast and supper, as we would call it on the farm?

Mr. RUST. Yes, sir.

Mr. FORDNEY. And the farmer takes them to and from their work and gives them their dinner and pays them $1.25 per day?

Mr. RUST. Yes, sir.

Mr. FORDNEY. Do you ever raise beets for more than one firm?

Mr. RUST. No, sir.

Mr. FORDNEY. Is your treatment by the factory satisfactory?

Mr. RUST. Yes, sir; it is.

Mr. FORDNEY. About what is the sugar content of your beets? Do you remember about that?

Mr. RUST. They ran from 14.8 to 19; but they averaged right through, say, 16.5.

Mr. FORDNEY. 16.5?

Mr. RUST. Yes, sir; if I am right.

Mr. FORDNEY. Which brought you for 53¾ acres $55 per acre gross, about $5.50 per ton?

Mr. RUST. Yes, sir; it was $5.57 per ton on gross weight, which was after I had charged up for my freight taken out.

Mr. FORDNEY. You have to pay the freight from the weigh station to the factory there where you live?

Mr. RUST. Yes, sir; everybody does, according to the contract.

Mr. FORDNEY. How far is it from your farm to the factory?

Mr. RUST. Well, it isn't quite 3 miles.

Mr. FORDNEY. So if you were to deliver your beets to the factory you would have no freight to be charged up, of course?

Mr. RUST. No, sir.

Mr. FORDNEY. What is the freight charge from that station?

Mr. RUST. 25 cents per ton.

Mr. FORDNEY. It pays you better to deliver them on cars and deduct the 25 cents per ton freight charge than it would to haul them directly to the factory for that 25 cents?

Mr. RUST. Yes; at that particular time our time was worth more than the extra 25 cents per ton. I did not cover them up, but had three teams and hauled them as fast as they were lifted. I lifted them myself and the three teams drew them, foreigners topping the beets, so that there was no waste.

Mr. FORDNEY. Do you think that your crop is a fair average crop and that your treatment by the sugar factory is the average treatment accorded the average farmer in that vicinity?

Mr. RUST. I think my crop is an average crop for this year, although it is below other years. Everybody is below the average crop this year in that vicinity.

Mr. FORDNEY. Why is that?

Mr. RUST. Well, a good many of these beets were planted early, and very heavy, packing rains seemed to kind of stunt the early beets; they did not do as well. The treatment was good. I do not hear any complaints, and I have asked as to that of a good many farmers. Once in a great while some farmer wants to get more than what belongs to him; he is, of course, never satisfied.

Mr. FORDNEY. I do not believe there is anything more I wish to ask.

Mr. MALBY. There is one thing I forgot in this inquiry: Did you say that you sowed this land to oats after the beat crop is taken off?

Mr. RUST. Yes; the following spring.

Mr. MALBY. Do you plow the land for that purpose?

Mr. RUST. No, sir.

Mr. MALBY. So there would be the additional benefit which you really get the following year, and that is that you do not have to plow the land. How do you handle it; cultivate it?

Mr. RUST. We usually spring-tooth it once, which is on the principle of the cultivator. If you fall-plowed this land you would have to spring-tooth it a couple of times more to get it in as good condition.

Mr. MALBY. How many oats to the acre do you raise?

Mr. RUST. Well, I raised 35 bushels to the acre this year.

The CHAIRMAN. You have no interest or stock in the sugar factories?

Mr. RUST. No, sir; I wish I had.

The CHAIRMAN. None of your people have any?

Mr. RUST. No, sir.

The CHAIRMAN. You have no connection direct or indirect or in any way with the sugar companies?

Mr. RUST. No, sir.

Mr. FORDNEY. I would like to say that my meeting with this gentleman here is the first time I ever met him. I never knew Mr. Rust before.

The CHAIRMAN. That is all right. It would make no difference if you had known him all your life.

Mr. FORDNEY. I just wished it shown that these are not picked men.

The CHAIRMAN. If there are no other questions, we will excuse Mr. Rust with the thanks of the committee for his attendance.

TESTIMONY OF CARL VOLC.

(The witness is sworn by the chairman.)

Mr. FORDNEY. Mr. Volc, where do you live?

Mr. VOLC. In Sebewaing, Huron County, Mich.

Mr. FORDNEY. What is your business?

Mr. VOLC. Farmer.

Mr. FORDNEY. How long have you lived in the vicinity of Sebewaing?

Mr. VOLC. Fifty-six years.

Mr. FORDNEY. Fifty-six years?

Mr. VOLC. Yes; I was born there.

Mr. FORDNEY. You were born at Sebewaing?

Mr. VOLC. Yes, sir.

Mr. FORDNEY. How much of a farm have you, how many acres of land?

Mr. VOLC. Two hundred and forty acres.

Mr. FORDNEY. Two hundred acres of land?

Mr. VOLC. Yes, sir; 160 acres where I live, and I have another 80 acres.

Mr. FORDNEY. All improved farm land?

Mr. VOLC. It is improved, yes.

Mr. FORDNEY. Do you raise beets?

Mr. VOLC. Yes; I have raised beets for 12 years now.

Mr. FORDNEY. Have you during that time raised beets for more than one company?

Mr. VOLC. Well, the first two years I raised and shipped beets to the Bay City, Mich., factory, and since we have a factory in Sebewaing I always raise beets for that same factory. It is the same company, I suppose.

Mr. FORDNEY. Tell, in your own way, about how many beets—and if you have a memorandum of it refer to that—you have raised every year and about what price you got for them. You can state how many tons of beets per acre, or the total amount, any way you want to put it.

Mr. VOLC. The first beets I raised was in 1900, and I had 2 acres and got $148 for them.

Mr. FORDNEY. $148 off of 2 acres of land?

Mr. VOLC. Yes, sir; $148. In 1901 I had 5 acres and got $396. In 1902 I had 24 acres and they fetched me $1,846. The next two years I did not put them down.

Mr. FORDNEY. You mean that you did not keep an account of the yield during the next two years; that is, during the years 1903 and 1904?

Mr. VOLC. No, sir. In 1905 I had 26 acres and they came to $1,457. In 1906 I had 14 acres and received $820 for them.

Mr. FORDNEY. You received $820 for 14 acres in 1906?

Mr. VOLC. Yes, sir; $820. In 1907 I had 17 acres and they brought me $900. In 1908 I had 20 acres and they brought me $1,250. In 1909 I had 20 acres and they brought me $1,613. In 1910 I had 34 acres and they brought me $2,638.45. In 1911 I had 43 acres and they came up to $3,612.

Mr. FORDNEY. Now, can you give us about the average price per acre that you received for that beet crop during all those years you have named, or what your profit was above the cost, and what that cost was?

Mr. VOLC. The whole amount received for those years I have named came up to $14,674.45.

Mr. FORDNEY. How many years is that?

Mr. VOLC. That is for 10 years. That shows an average per year of $65.21.

Mr. FORDNEY. Per acre?

Mr. VOLC. Yes, sir.

Mr. FORDNEY. What did it cost you to produce those beets?

Mr. VOLC. The expense to grow 1 acre is—

Plowing the ground twice	$3.00
Harrow it twice; that is, to pulverize it twice and roll it	2.00
Sow seed	.50
Cultivate it four times during the summer	2.50
Fifteen pounds seed	1.50
Lifting the beets	1.00
Haul beets to factory	6.00
Hand labor	20.00
Total	36.50

Mr. FORDNEY. That is the total cost per acre to raise and market the beets?

Mr. VOLC. Yes, sir. Take this expense off from the price of $65.21 leaves me $28.71 per acre profit.

Mr. FORDNEY. That is your average profit for 10 years?

Mr. VOLC. Yes, sir.

Mr. FORDNEY. From that if you were to deduct anything for rent of your land it would still make a further reduction? You have not included anything for rent of your land.

Mr. VOLC. No, I didn't deduct anything as rent for the land.

Mr. FORDNEY. How much do you figure the rent of your land should be worth per acre per year? What do you figure your land to be worth per acre?

Mr. VOLC. About $140.

Mr. FORDNEY. So that if you deducted 6 per cent on $140 per acre that would leave you the net profit from your beet crop after paying all expenses and allowing interest on your investment, would it not?

Mr. VOLC. Yes, sir.

Mr. FORDNEY. The rental value of your land at 6 per cent on a valuation of $140 per acre would mean $8.40 per acre?

Mr. VOLC. Yes, sir.

Mr. FORDNEY. That would mean a still further deduction from the profit of $28.71 of $8.40, leaving a net profit of $20.31 after giving you 6 per cent interest on the money invested in your land?

Mr. VOLC. Yes, sir.

Mr. FORDNEY. That is your net return?

Mr. VOLC. Yes, sir.

Mr. FORDNEY. Over and above the interest on your investment in the land used?

Mr. VOLC. Yes, sir.

Mr. FORDNEY. Do you have any trouble with the sugar factories in the matter of settlement or treatment?

Mr. VOLC. Not yet.

Mr. FORDNEY. About how much per ton do you get for your beets? What percentage of sugar is there in your beets; do you remember that? What is the test?

Mr. VOLC. Well, the average test was 16 per cent last year.

Mr. FORDNEY. That is, this last year, 1911?

Mr. VOLC. Yes, sir. I have had it above 18 per cent and 18½ per cent, and a couple of loads came down to 14½ per cent.

Mr. FORDNEY. You got around $6 per ton for your beets?

Mr. VOLC. Something like that; some over that and some less than that.

Mr. FORDNEY. When you began growing beets on your land 12 years ago, what was a fair valuation for your land per acre?

Mr. VOLC. The value has increased about 50 per cent. Ten years ago 80 acres sold for $5,000 in my neighborhood.

Mr. FORDNEY. That would be $62.50 per acre?

Mr. VOLC. Yes, sir. That same land sold last spring for $11,000. A few years ago 40 acres were sold for $2,400, and that same tract was sold last winter for $6,000. Here is the deed to another piece that was sold in 1893 for $800, and a few years later, in 1900, it was sold for $1,500, and in 1910 I bought the same piece of land and paid $6,500 for it. These are the deeds right here from 1893 down to date.

Mr. FORDNEY. What do you consider that land to be worth now?

Mr. VOLC. $9,000.

Mr. FORDNEY. That is a pretty fair increase?

Mr. VOLC. Yes, sir.

Mr. FORDNEY. Do you attribute the increase in value largely to the introduction of the beet crop in that vicinity?

Mr. VOLC. Yes; if it wouldn't have been for the beets the land wouldn't be up at that price.

Mr. FORDNEY. Are there a good many beets raised in the vicinity of your home?

Mr. VOLC. That is the main crop, what we are raising all the way down as far as 40 miles.

Mr. FORDNEY. Do you raise more than one crop off the same land without rotating your crops and putting some other crop on that particular piece of land?

Mr. VOLC. Do you mean beets?

Mr. FORDNEY. Yes.

Mr. VOLC. I have tried it for several years with beets, but it didn't do very good.

Mr. FORDNEY. You should rotate your crops?

Mr. VOLC. Yes, sir; have only one crop of beets and the second year have a failure probably. Once in a while you may get fair beets the second time, but it is doubtful.

Mr. FORDNEY. What crop do you follow on the land after having beets planted?

Mr. VOLC. What we have followed beets with so far is barley and oats.

Mr. FORDNEY. And then you follow with what?

Mr. VOLC. With barley or oats the first year, and then we put on wheat, and then seed it down to clover and take off a crop of hay. After that we pasture the land or turn the clover under and put corn in.

Mr. FORDNEY. And then follow again with beets?

Mr. VOLC. Yes, sir; after that.

Mr. FORDNEY. Corn does best on sod land?

Mr. VOLC. Yes, sir.

Mr. FORDNEY. I used to be a farmer myself and remember that much of it.

Mr. VOLC. Yes, sir.

Mr. FORDNEY. How far is your farm from the railroad? Or, in other words, how far do you have to haul your beets?

Mr. VOLC. Just 3 miles from the factory.

Mr. FORDNEY. You deliver them right to the factory?

Mr. VOLC. I deliver to the factory.

Mr. FORDNEY. How far do they generally raise beets from a factory or from a weigh station; or, how many miles off the railroad?

Mr. VOLC. Before they had a weigh station on the Michigan Central line they hauled them 10, 12, or 15 miles.

Mr. FORDNEY. They did?

Mr. VOLC. Yes, sir. Now they have a weigh station every 2½ miles.

Mr. FORDNEY. It is quite expensive to haul beets 10 or 15 miles?

Mr. VOLC. Yes; but they raise beets all the same.

Mr. FORDNEY. Do you get a better crop, do you think, when you rotate your beets, barley, or oats, sow grass seed, and so on, than when you didn't put in beets at all?

Mr. VOLC. Yes, sir.

Mr. FORDNEY. It puts the land in better shape for the other crops?

Mr. VOLC. Yes, sir; in far better shape, and you don't need to plow it in the following spring. The ground has just settled down good, and it is kept clean, and you can follow with a good crop. So that in addition to the profit that you get out of your beet crop it adds value to the other crops on account of the improved state of cultivation and absence of weeds, and so on.

Mr. FORDNEY. If farm values in that vicinity have advanced to the prices you have given us since beets began to be raised in that vicinity, that has affected other farms as well as yours?

Mr. VOLC. Just as well.

Mr. FORDNEY. You think that farm lands have advanced how much per acre, or what has been the percentage of advance since they began raising beets there generally in that vicinity, and what portion of it has been due to the raising of beets?

Mr. VOLC. Well, I would think 50 per cent is the increase on the value of the land.

Mr. FORDNEY. Do you think that that is largely due to the raising of beets rather than other crops?

Mr. VOLC. Mostly all of it is on account of raising beets.

Mr. FORDNEY. After planting to beets it leaves just that many acres of land less in the neighborhood to be planted to oats and other crops, and consequently curtails other crops and makes them more valuable, does it not?

Mr. VOLC. Yes, sir.

Mr. FORDNEY. You have a lesser number of acres in oats, wheat, corn, and so on, than you would have had before you raised beets, with a consequent scarcity of those other articles and advance in price for them, isn't that so?

Mr. VOLC. The price of grain has increased over 50 per cent.

Mr. FORDNEY. In that same time?

Mr. VOLC. Yes, sir; on account of raising beets, so many acres of land being devoted to beet raising and less grain being raised, the price has advanced.

Mr. FORDNEY. Have you ever had any unsatisfactory dealings with the sugar factories, or have they always treated you well?

Mr. VOLC. Always treated me well.

Mr. FORDNEY. You never had any trouble with them at all?

Mr. VOLC. I never had any trouble at all.

Mr. FORDNEY. You have always had them to give you what you were entitled to?

Mr. VOLC. Yes, sir; always.

Mr. FORDNEY. Pay you promptly, do they?

Mr. VOLC. Yes, sir; promptly.

Mr. FORDNEY. Do they aid you in getting farm labor if it is scarce?

Mr. VOLC. Yes; they do.

Mr. FORDNEY. They will send you men if you ask for them?

Mr. VOLC. Yes, sir; they will hunt them up and send them out.

Mr. FORDNEY. Do they advance money to any farmers in your part of the country in case they need money to take care of their beet crop?

Mr. VOLC. Yes; they will advance you money if you need it.

Mr. FORDNEY. And they charge you what rate of interest on that money while it is loaned to you?

Mr. VOLC. They did charge 5 per cent up to this last year, when they took 6 per cent.

Mr. FORDNEY. They charged you 6 per cent from the time you got your money until you delivered your beets?

Mr. VOLC. Yes, sir.

Mr. FORDNEY. And they deduct that money they advanced, with 6 per cent interest?

Mr. VOLC. Yes, sir.

Mr. FORDNEY. Is that about the same rate of interest at which you get money from the banks?

Mr. VOLC. Well, we don't get it for 6 per cent from the banks.

Mr. FORDNEY. You don't?

Mr. VOLC. No.

Mr. FORDNEY. What rate of interest do the banks charge you?

Mr. VOLC. I don't know exactly what they charge now. I don't get any there.

Mr. FORDNEY. Well, I didn't know. I am very glad to hear that you don't have to get it; that you don't have to borrow money. Do you make any use of the beet tops?

Mr. VOLC. We feed them to the cattle.

Mr. FORDNEY. Do you figure that they are of some value?

Mr. VOLC. Oh, yes.

Mr. FORDNEY. About how much per acre are they worth to you for feed?

Mr. VOLC. About $4 or $5. If you drive the cattle into the beet field after the betts have been hauled out it does not take them long to fatten up.

Mr. FORDNEY. You turn them into the field and allow them to pick up the beet leaves?

Mr. VOLC. Yes, sir.

Mr. FORDNEY. How long do the beet leaves lay in the fall before they become unfit for food for stock?

Mr. VOLC. Beet tops?

Mr. FORDNEY. Yes. How long can they lay in the field and feed cattle on them after they are cut off from the beets?

Mr. VOLC. I don't understand your question.

Mr. FORDNEY. Do they spoil in a little while?

Mr. VOLC. No; cattle can run in there all winter.

Mr. FORDNEY. And live on the beet tops?

Mr. VOLC. Yes, sir.

Mr. FORDNEY. Unless they get covered up with snow, of course?

Mr. VOLC. Yes, sir.

Mr. FORDNEY. If they get covered up with snow and you turn your cattle into the beet field in the spring will they then eat the beet tops?

Mr. VOLC. No.

Mr. FORDNEY. They are spoilt by spring?

Mr. VOLC. Yes, sir; they have to be covered by spring.

Mr. FORDNEY. Do you know of anybody in your neighborhood seeling beet tops; and if so, how much do they get for them per acre?

Mr. VOLC. No, nobody sells; they all want them for themselves.

Mr. FORDNEY. They have cattle, sheep, and so on?

Mr. VOLC. Yes, sir.

The CHAIRMAN. What nationality do you belong to, Mr. Volc? Or, where were you born, did you say in this country?

Mr. VOLC. In Sebewaing, Huron County, Mich. Yes, sir, in this country.

The CHAIRMAN. What nationality are you, or to what race do you belong?

Mr. VOLC. German.

The CHAIRMAN. Your people were Germans?

Mr. VOLC. Yes, sir; came from Wurttemburg.

The CHAIRMAN. You have no interest in any of these beet-sugar factories?

Mr. VOLC. No.

The CHAIRMAN. Do you own any stock in them?

Mr. VOLC. No stock.

The CHAIRMAN. Did they ever lend you any money?

Mr. VOLC. Sometimes; when I got a family and would be short of money?

The CHAIRMAN. You would then get it from the sugar factory?

Mr. VOLC. Yes, sir.

The CHAIRMAN. You do not want any more money for your beets than they pay you?

Mr. VOLC. Well [the witness hesitates].

The CHAIRMAN. In other words, you are getting enough for your beets?

Mr. VOLC. Yes; I am getting enough.

The CHAIRMAN. You don't want any more for them?

Mr. VOLC. That is a pretty hard question.

The CHAIRMAN. Well, you need not answer it. I realize that it is human nature to want all one can get.

Mr. FORDNEY. You are satisfied as conditions now are if you are let alone?

Mr. VOLC. Yes, sir.

The CHAIRMAN. You would not like to have any less money for your beets?

Mr. VOLC. No, sir.

The CHAIRMAN. If there are no other questions, we will now excuse Mr. Volc, with the thanks of the committee for his attendance.

It is now about time to take a recess, and before doing so I wish to call the attention of the committee to a telegram received by me to-day from Brush, Colo., signed by a committee on resolutions of the beet growers of that district.

BRUSH, COLO., *January 8.*

CHAIRMAN CONGRESSIONAL COMMITTEE INVESTIGATING SUGAR TRUST,
Washington, D. C.:

The attitude of the beet growers in this district relative to the Coumbs testimony before your committee is expressed in the following resolutions, which we ask to be made a part of your record:

Resolutions adopted by the beet growers of the Brush district in mass meeting assembled:

Whereas the Hardwick committee has seen fit to summons a committee representing the beet growers of Colorado before the congressional committee; and

Whereas said committee, consisting of E. U. Coumbs, Albert Dakan, and James Bodkin, did appear before the said congressional committee; and

Whereas the press attempted to and did garble and make sensational reports concerning said testimony; and

Whereas we, the beet growers of the Brush district in mass meeting assembled, believe the committee, and Mr. Coumbs especially, has rendered all the beet growers a great, honest, and fearless service in presenting the facts as they existed relative to the sugar beet and the beet-sugar industry: Therefore be it

Resolved, That we, the beet growers of the Brush district, condemn the action of all newspapers, real-estate exchanges, commercial clubs, or individuals who attempt to refute, weaken, or belittle the committee or the evidence produced as unjust, unwarranted, and a direct slap in the face of the farmer and the growers of beets, who create the major part of the wealth of this State and Nation upon which they subsist; and be it further

Resolved, That we recognize in Mr. Coumbs the peerless champion of our cause, a man of sterling ability and integrity, the one man who could render so valuable service; and be it further

Resolved, That we congratulate, commend, and accord to him our highest appreciation for his efforts in behalf of the beet growers.

H. W. Twomley.
James Bolinger,
L. A. Matteson,
Resolution Committee.

(Thereupon, at 4.45 p. m., the committee adjourned until to-morrow, Jan. 10, 1912, at 10.30 a. m.)

AMERICAN SUGAR REFINING CO. AND OTHERS.

SPECIAL COMMITTEE ON THE INVESTIGATION
OF THE AMERICAN SUGAR REFINING CO. AND OTHERS,
HOUSE OF REPRESENTATIVES,
Washington, D. C., January 10, 1912.

The committee met at 10 o'clock a. m., Hon. Thomas W. Hardwick (chairman) presiding.

TESTIMONY OF MR. JOHN H. RILEY.

(The witness was duly sworn by the chairman.)

Mr. MALBY. Mr. Riley, where do you reside?

Mr. RILEY. At Fowler, Colo.

Mr. MALBY. What is your occupation?

Mr. RILEY. I am a farmer, and I feed cattle and hogs.

Mr. MALBY. Are you engaged in the raising of sugar beets for the market?

Mr. RILEY. I am; yes, sir.

Mr. MALBY. How long have you been engaged in that business?

Mr. RILEY. About 10 years; ever since the first factory started in the Arkansas Valley.

Mr. MALBY. At the same place?

Mr. RILEY. Yes, sir.

Mr. MALBY. What quantity of ground do you cultivate?

Mr. RILEY. In beets, do you mean?

Mr. MALBY. Yes.

Mr. RILEY. About 150 acres.

Mr. MALBY. And has that been your general average for some years past, or has it been more or less?

Mr. RILEY. Between 100 and 162 acres.

Mr. MALBY. To whom do you sell your beets?

Mr. RILEY. To the American Beet Sugar Co. at Rocky Ford.

Mr. MALBY. Is that the name of the company doing business there?

Mr. RILEY. Yes, sir; the American Beet Sugar Co.

Mr. MALBY. I did not know but what it might be one of their subsidiary companies?

Mr. RILEY. No.

Mr. MALBY. That is the Oxnard company, is it?

Mr. RILEY. Yes, sir. Pardon me just a moment. As to this 160 acres, I have some renters. I have never raised over 12 acres on the part I have myself.

Mr. MALBY: You cultivate directly about 12 acres and rent the balance?

Mr. RILEY. Yes, sir.

Mr. MALBY. What is your cost in production in detail of beets?

Mr. RILEY. To the man who owns the land it will approximate $35; to the renter about $10 more—that is, including the rent he pays.

Mr. MALBY. Can you give the committee a detailed statement of what the $35 is made up of?

Mr. RILEY. In my own case, I can.

Mr. MALBY. Well, perhaps that will answer.

Mr. RILEY. We have always kept approximately a correct tabulated statement of it. We could not keep it exactly correct.

Mr. MALBY. Well, substantially.

Mr. RILEY. It costs $31 to do the farming of ourselves where we let the thinning.

Mr. MALBY. Let us get at it in this way, so we will have a detailed statement of it. What does it cost you to plow the land?

Mr. RILEY. Well, I never have kept it in that way. I have kept the time of my men and my teams when they have been at work, and approximated that.

Mr. MALBY. You hire a given number of men and they do all of the work and you keep track of the amount you pay them; is that the idea?

Mr. RILEY. Yes, sir.

Mr. MALBY. You keep track of every expense connected with the tilling of the land by way of wages which you pay to them?

Mr. RILEY. Yes; the thinning and topping we let out by contract always, and the $31 an acre, approximately, is what it costs me for the work I do myself.

Mr. MALBY. $31 an acre?

Mr. RILEY. Yes, sir.

Mr. MALBY. And how much for the thinning? You say you let that out?

Mr. RILEY. $7, more or less. Sometimes it is a little less and sometimes a little more.

Mr. MALBY. How much do you pay for the topping?

Mr. RILEY. We pay the same for that, $7 approximately.

Mr. MALBY. Then it would be $31 plus $14?

Mr. RILEY. Yes; that is, including the work.

Mr. MALBY. What I want to get at is, you say it costs you $31 an acre, and then you let the thinning and topping?

Mr. RILEY. Yes, sir.

Mr. MALBY. Does that amount include the thinning and topping?

Mr. RILEY. No; the thinning and topping is outside of the $31.

Mr. MALBY. Then let us add that to the $31. How much do you pay for thinning?

Mr. RILEY. $7.

Mr. MALBY. How much do you pay for the topping per acre?

Mr. RILEY. The topping is also $7.

Mr. MALBY. That would be $45?

Mr. RILEY. Yes. I want to say to you, if you will pardon me, that that amount should have been $21 instead of $31. I added the $10 for rent when I stated that amount.

Mr. MALBY. How many tons of beets are you able to raise to the acre?

Mr. RILEY. Well, that is a good deal owing to the land and a good deal owing to the intelligence and energy of the farmers. I raised on this 12 acres of mine about 11½ tons to the acre.

Mr. MALBY. Was that an average crop?

Mr. RILEY. I regard it as being a very good average; yes, sir.

Mr. MALBY. What would be the general average in the neighborhood in which you live?

Mr. RILEY. I should think it would be 11 or 11½ tons. I think about 11½ tons per acre.

Mr. MALBY. How much do you get a ton for your beets?

Mr. RILEY. We have two contracts. The one I was turning my beets in under was under the sliding scale, and they average $5.85 a ton.

Mr. MALBY. Delivered where?

Mr. RILEY. Delivered on the dump. I have a dump right there, and a railroad siding, and we deliver them on the cars to the sugar factory, who pay all expenses after that.

Mr. MALBY. That is, you deliver them at the dump?

Mr. RILEY. On the cars; yes, sir.

Mr. MALBY. On the cars?

Mr. RILEY. Yes, sir.

Mr. MALBY. And the amount you received under the sliding scale was how much?

Mr. RILEY. $5.85 a ton.

Mr. MALBY. How far did you draw them?

Mr. RILEY. Not very far, because the dump was right on my place; the siding was.

Mr. MALBY. Now, Mr. Riley, I suppose you received the same price that others received for similar beets?

Mr. RILEY. Oh, yes, sir; the beets went nearly 15 per cent sugar.

Mr. MALBY. Can you give us the scale paid for beets?

Mr. RILEY. I have it at the hotel and forgot to bring it down with me. I have both scales and will be glad to put them in.

Mr. MALBY. I wish you would file them with the committee.

Mr. RILEY. I will. I have both scales.

Mr. MALBY. Your beets ran 15 per cent plus?

Mr. RILEY. A little bit less than 15 per cent.

Mr. MALBY. So you got the 14½ per cent plus rate, whatever that rate was?

Mr. RILEY. Yes.

Mr. MALBY. How about the other producers of beets in your neighborhood? Would that be a fair statement as to what their beets contained?

Mr. RILEY. I think so. I think if there is any change at all it is not over half a ton to the acre, and it would be against me, because the renters did a little better than I did with my hired men.

Mr MALBY. I asked would the percentage of sugar in the beets be about the same—15 per cent on an average?

Mr. RILEY. Yes; that is regarded as being about the average for the ground around the factory, and mine was about the same.

Mr. MALBY. And among your tenants you say the tonnage would perhaps be a little more?

Mr. RILEY. Yes: the tonnage is a little more.

Mr. MALBY. Do you receive prompt payment?

Mr. RILEY. We get our payment on the 15th of every month—a check for the beets turned in the preceding month.

Mr. MALBY. Is there anything to which you desire to call the committee's attention with reference to the treatment which you receive or your neighbors receive at the hands of the manufacturers, which you regard as improper?

Mr. RILEY. Well, for three years preceding this year there was some friction between the growers and the factories.

Mr. MALBY. Growing out of what?

Mr. RILEY. Growing out of the price paid for beets.

Mr. MALBY. Have those differences been settled and adjusted?

Mr. RILEY. In the last year they have been. Everyone is satisfied there now. I do not know that the factories themselves are, but I know the beet growers are, and the superintendent of the factory told me that they have given us the same scale for the coming year, and told me they felt satisfied, unless there was a change made by you gentlemen present, or by Congress, they could continue to pay us that price.

Mr. MALBY. What is the rental value of beet land in your locality?

Mr. RILEY. I get one-fourth of the gross amount of the beets, put on the cars, free to me of all cost. That is the general rule in our section.

Mr. MALBY. Have you figured in your mind what you got per acre for your beets at $5.85 a ton? Can you tell me how much you really got or the aggregate sum you realized off of the 12 acres?

Mr. RILEY. I have not got that data with me. Twelve times 6 is 72, and it costs say $37—about $25 an acre.

Mr. MALBY. About $25 an acre?

Mr. RILEY. Yes, sir. I think that is correct. I have just figured it in my mind.

Mr. MALBY. Do you and the other farmers located in that locality regard that as a fair return for your efforts and investment, and so forth?

Mr. RILEY. Yes, sir; but there were years I did not get that. I am speaking of this last year, when we had an increase, approximately the best price we have ever received, and we had a very fair year. We irrigate there entirely, and the amount of waterfall that we have in the ditches that we have our land under has a great deal to do with the amount we raise on the land.

Mr. MALBY. The $35 which you represent as being the total cost includes your irrigation, I suppose?

Mr. RILEY. Yes, sir; everything.

Mr. MALBY. It includes everything?

Mr. RILEY. Everything except it does not include taxes or anything of that kind.

Mr. MALBY. What is a fair average farm worth per acre in that locality?

Mr. RILEY. Well, may I state about my own? I have lived there for some time. I can state what I paid for it.

Mr. MALBY. Yes; that is some evidence of value.

Mr. RILEY. I went in there in 1893, and we bought 1,100 acres of land, a gentleman named Col. Lockhart and myself. I was equally interested. We bought it at $19. That was the price set, and then we got a pretty good price for our cows, which we traded for it. We have sold off that place only 40 acres, and we sold that last year. We got $150 for it, and we would refuse $150 for a great deal of our land.

The man who bought this land was a tenant who was working for us. I can not recall names, but I know the man very well.

Mr. MALBY. Well, the name is not material.

Mr. RILEY. He was working for us, and stayed right on there as a tenant, and he paid for his land $150 an acre for the 40 acres, and paid cash for it. He made a little money outside of that, just working around, he and his boys, but he made nearly all of the money right off of the land.

Mr. MALBY. In how long a time?

Mr. RILEY. Well, he worked for us when we first went there in 1893, but he did not rent from us for about 2 years, and he did not make any money until the factory started about 10 years ago. He made all of that money after the factory was put up at Rocky Ford.

Mr. MALBY. And paid you $150 an acre for the land?

Mr. RILEY. Yes, sir.

Mr. MALBY. Did he make it out of beet culture?

Mr. RILEY. Yes, sir.

Mr. MALBY. Do you regard the cultivation of beets in your locality as being a profitable crop for the farmers to raise?

Mr. RILEY. At the present prices we think it is the best crop we have got. It helps put our land in fine shape for any other crop. It rotates well with other crops we have there, and the farmer feels better knowing he can change to beets better than he can with any other crop we can think of. We have found that out by experience.

Mr. MALBY. Do you rotate your beet crop with something else?

Mr. RILEY. Yes.

Mr. MALBY. How often do you plant the beets?

Mr. RILEY. We aim to keep land in beets four or five years.

Mr. MALBY. Without a change?

Mr. RILEY. Yes, sir; without a change.

Mr. MALBY. And then you rotate to what crop?

Mr. RILEY. We prefer alfalfa, because it has protein in it, and it enriches the ground quicker than anything else we can plant.

Mr. MALBY. So that in your judgment you receive some other benefits besides the immediate profits arising from your beet crop?

Mr. RILEY. Yes, sir. We feed it. Our country has got to be a great feeding section. The by-product, the pulp, is being fed all over the country there.

Mr. MALBY. Being fed to cattle?

Mr. RILEY. To cattle and hogs. Well, not fed much to hogs, nor to sheep much; some all ewes are fed it, but it is fed to cattle principally.

Mr. MALBY. What do you do with your tops?

Mr. RILEY. They are regarded as being worth about $2.50 an acre after we take the beets off.

Mr. MALBY. Do you get your beet pulp back?

Mr. RILEY. We got one-fifth of it back, 20 per cent; yes, sir.

Mr. MALBY. And what do you have to pay for it if you buy it?

Mr. RILEY. I paid 45 cents last year; and the factory was very fair this year past, knowing we lost money as a rule feeding cattle last year, and they have put the pulp to me and to others, those whom I know, at 25 cents a ton at the factory; that is, they have cut it nearly in two.

Mr. MALBY. You do your own drawing?

Mr. RILEY. Yes, sir; we pay the freight on it. To my place the freight is 30 cents a ton, or 1½ cents a hundred.

Mr. MALBY. Have you much country in your locality which can be used for beet culture?

Mr. RILEY. Yes, sir. This is data I got from the agriculturist representing the beet-sugar factories. He said that this last year there were 23,000 acres, approximately, in the valley there between Pueblo and the State line; that is, between Colorado and Kansas.

Mr. MALBY. Your beets, being sold on the sliding scale, necessitates an analysis of the beets to ascertain the amount of sugar they contain?

Mr. RILEY. Yes, sir; that is done at the sugar factory.

Mr. MALBY. Are you satisfied with the honesty of the sugar factories in making an analysis of your beets?

Mr. RILEY. The people are satisfied now, sir. There was for years quite a friction on that question, but the factories are getting the confidence of the people to a greater extent every year. This last year, of course, we have made money, and that makes us better jurors, I presume, in the case.

Mr. MALBY. I think that is a good way to put it. Are you and your neighbors now satisfied you are getting a fair deal?

Mr. RILEY. Yes, sir, we are; and not only that, but when I left there the people generally came into the little town, and there is not a business man nor any other person who does not look on the beet-sugar industry as being the mainstay of the valley. We are learning that business, and our farmers are getting to have more confidence in the factories in the raising of beets, and the results have been better than they expected, and it would be a very, very great blow to the valley if we were not permitted, at least until we got ourselves into a condition wherein we could intelligently handle it through experience, of which we have already had a great deal, to let it go as it is now.

Mr. MALBY. In other words, present conditions are satisfactory to you?

Mr. RILEY. They are satisfactory to me and to every beet grower in the valley. They were not last year or the year before. As proof of that there was quite a friction, as I said, between the growers and the factory or the gentlemen who were representing the factories. We felt, and I think it is admitted now, that those gentlemen had very little tact, although they were good men. There was a German in charge of them there, and we did not get together. As a result we refused to raise beets, and they closed three of their factories and kept them closed. This year they changed that manager, and the man who came there went out amongst the beet growers and got them interested, and he raised the price after looking into it, until we are getting approximately $6 a ton for our beets, and as a result I am told by this same manager the factories will open this year—that is, the three that have not been doing anything. There are three different managements of the factories there. The American Beet Sugar Co. have three factories, one at Rocky Ford, one at Las Animas, and one at Lamar, and then the Holly and Swink have two, one at Holly and one at Swink, and the National have one at Sugar City on the north side of the river.

Mr. MALBY. Those are separate business concerns, are they?

Mr. RILEY. Yes, sir; but this man told me these factories would be set to work this year, the men who were raising beets having made promises to him that they would break more land and put more beets in; and there is the very best of feeling now between the factories and the farmers in that valley. The fact of the matter is in this question you can not divide the interests; they are both identical. You can not hurt the factories without hurting us, because they can not pay, as they say, and they have ample proof of their explanation—they say if they have to pay any more they will have to shut their factories up, and we have not found others who would pay us more, and we are satisfied with the present situation.

Mr. MALBY. I think that is about all I have in mind unless you have something else you wish to state to the committee. Is there anything else you have in mind you desire to state?

Mr. RILEY. I would like to state about one matter, and that is the men who work on the beets and take contracts. I am only speaking for our own valley. Dry farming has taken hold in Colorado, and they are having quite a hard time there. When we are topping our beets these people, as a rule, come in and help us. We also have the sons of the best farmers in the valley. They make from two to three dollars a day, and those youngsters go out there, four or five of them together, and they do a great deal of our thinning. We have some Mexicans from New Mexico. They came up there and they all made money. A man will probably come up with 10 or 15 men. Several men came that way, and would take the contracts around, and we get rid of that portion of the work in that way very quickly, and also take care of our other interests there. I am very certain that all testimony you will find on that question from our valley is that the laborers, like ourselves, are satisfied that they get good pay.

Mr. MALBY. You are a little differently situated, I judge, from some other places. You have some local labor assistance?

Mr. RILEY. Yes, sir; Our valley has grown wonderfully and is growing to-day.

Mr. MALBY. You get some of your labor from the citizens who live there?

Mr. RILEY. Yes, sir; the best boys in the community. I say the "best boys," because they are the hardest working boys. For instance, I had two sons of the agriculturist of the beet-sugar factory. who helped to do this work for me this year.

Mr. MALBY. You might state what price you pay for this labor.

Mr. RILEY. They get $7 an acre for thinning and $7 an acre for topping. And they go in groups of 15. We pay them by the acre. I should think they made $3.50, probably—the expert toppers and thinners.

Mr. MALBY. Do you have any others employed besides the boys and men; any women?

Mr. RILEY. No, sir; although the women do some of the work. We have a great deal of this work done by the farmers themselves—the poor farmers.

Mr. MALBY. I mean outside of the immediate family of the man who cultivates the land?

Mr. RILEY. No; I have never seen women so employed.

Mr. MALBY. I mean, do you hire any women?

Mr. Riley. No, sir; I never have. I have never seen any around the section I live. I understand it is done in Colorado, but I haven't seen it.

Mr. Hinds. These men work very hard and very long hours in the beet fields, do they not?

Mr. Riley. Well, they work very hard while they are at it, but not long hours.

Mr. Hinds. Not longer than the ordinary hours for farm work?

Mr. Riley. Not as long, because it is harder work, and it is contract work, and they can quit whenever they want to.

Mr. Hinds. So that in your beet fields the labor condition is not conspicuous for unusual effort for an unusual length of time each day?

Mr. Riley. No, sir; it is controlled by just what they feel they can do and make the most money out of it. That controls the length of time.

Mr. Hinds. That is, the man works at the ordinary pace that an ordinary farm worker would work at?

Mr. Riley. No; a great deal faster, because it is contract work, and contract work is generally done much faster than when you are paying men by the month.

Mr. Hinds. How much would a man make in the beet fields under the conditions under which you hire men, working at the ordinary pace of an ordinary farm laborer?

Mr. Riley. I do not know. They make about $3.50, and I pay my men for ordinary farm work $35 a month and board.

Mr. Hinds. For harvesting you pay more?

Mr. Riley. No, sir.

Mr. Hinds. You pay that right straight through the year?

Mr. Riley. Yes, sir. I may have to employ a few extra men during the harvest time, but as a rule my men stay with me all the time.

Mr. Hinds. What do you pay if you employ a man in the harvest time?

Mr. Riley. We pay him $1.50 a day and board.

Mr. Hinds. For haying?

Mr. Riley. Yes, sir.

Mr. Hinds. A man would make as much as that in the beet fields.

Mr. Riley. A good deal more; double that, I should think.

Mr. Hinds. Working at the same rate of effort?

Mr. Riley. Oh, no, sir. He works harder in the beet fields.

Mr. Hinds. But, working at the same rate of effort, about how much would you think a man would get in the beet fields?

Mr. Riley. I prefer not to answer that question. You see, I have told you just about what they get. They get so much an acre, and that work never comes under our supervision at all. It is done by contract.

Mr. Hinds. I did not know but what you had some idea about it.

Mr. Riley. Not any I could intelligently give you now. By thinking over it I could probably figure it out.

Mr. Malby. I will ask you whether you are interested in any manufacturing establishment there?

Mr. Riley. Not a bit, sir.

Mr. Malby. Have you been interested in any of the manufacturing establishments, owning stock, or having any financial interest in any of the factories?

Mr. RILEY. None at all, except buying and paying for what I got. I came here because our people got stirred up and I pay my own expenses and I am doing it with pleasure, because I have got a farm there and the value of my land has enhanced so I should not like to see anything done that would throw us back.

Mr. MALBY. Do the factories make it a custom in case of necessity to advance money to the growers in your locality?

Mr. RILEY. Yes, sir; they do. I do not think they make a custom of it, but I know of several instances where the growers got in a position where they had to have money, and they made a little advance.

The CHAIRMAN. Mr. Riley, you live at what place?

Mr. RILEY. I live at Fowler. During the winter I feed cattle there.

The CHAIRMAN. Where is this beet region you speak of?

Mr. RILEY. Right in the Arkansas Valley.

The CHAIRMAN. What is the name of the place?

Mr. RILEY. Fowler.

The CHAIRMAN. That is where your beet crop is located?

Mr. RILEY. Yes, sir; my farm is three-quarters of a mile from Fowler.

The CHAIRMAN. How far is that from Longmont?

Mr. RILEY. I should judge probably 150 miles or maybe 200 miles.

The CHAIRMAN. That is a different section of the State?

Mr. RILEY. A different section of the State entirely.

The CHAIRMAN. Do you know personally Mr. James Bodkin?

Mr. RILEY. No, sir.

The CHAIRMAN. Do you know Mr. E. U. Combs?

Mr. RILEY. No; I know none of the gentlemen who have been before you here.

The CHAIRMAN. They have both testified before this committee.

Mr. RILEY. There are some others coming from that same section, but I do not know any of the people up there at all.

The CHAIRMAN. Have you any other business besides that of farming?

Mr. RILEY. I am a cattle raiser. I live in the summer time in Colorado Springs, and I have pastures rented there, and have about from 1,000 to 2,000 head of cattle, which I keep there. I bring about 1,000 of them to Fowler on the 1st of December every year. As I testified, I have been living at Fowler, and interested there since 1893. I bring the cattle down, and feed them on the feed lots of Fowler, and stay there during the entire time of the feeding, unless I should go on some little business to Colorado Springs.

The CHAIRMAN. I do not know whether I understood you correctly or not, but I thought you said something about a paper called the Agriculturist. You are not a publisher in any way, are you?

Mr. RILEY. No, sir.

The CHAIRMAN. You are engaged in no business except agriculture, in some form or other?

Mr. RILEY. No, sir; that is all.

The CHAIRMAN. You came here entirely on your own motion?

Mr. RILEY. Not only that, but I am trying to stir the farmers and everybody up on this question.

The CHAIRMAN. On what question?

Mr. RILEY. On the question of reducing the tariff. As we understand it, reducing the tariff on beets would injure our business.

The CHAIRMAN. As I understand it, you are opposed to any reduction of the tariff?

Mr. RILEY. I do not care to go into that matter, except to give you the facts, and leave that question to Congress.

The CHAIRMAN. Of course, I understand that. You would have to leave that matter with Congress in any event; but, personally, you are opposed to any reduction of the duties; and is that what you mean the issue is that brought you down here?

Mr. RILEY. I came down here for the reasons I have stated clearly before this committee.

The CHAIRMAN. I want you to repeat them, though.

Mr. RILEY. To repeat those reasons?

The CHAIRMAN. Yes.

Mr. RILEY. I came down here because I have lived in that valley since 1893, when I bought land there. Until the factory started it was worth about $20 an acre. As soon as the factory started it began to go up, until my land to-day is worth $150 an acre, at least, and I was averse to seeing anything done by Congress that would hurt us. Also, if you will pardon me, I saw at that time a valley that had only a few people in it. I came to Colorado first in 1868, although I have lived in New Mexico part of the time out of that period. I know Colorado pretty well. I have seen it grow, I have benefited by the growth of that valley, and I feel sure in my own mind that the beet-sugar industry has tended to enhance the value of our property and brought into the valley the homes and the little houses you see on every 40 acres, and I feel that in my own interest solely I ought to do everything I can to try and keep that progress going on, and I feel that with a reduction of the tariff that progress would not go on.

The CHAIRMAN. In other words, that is the reason you thought it was proper to come down here, on account of this talk about reducing the tariff on sugar?

Mr. RILEY. Yes; that is true.

The CHAIRMAN. That is exactly what I wanted to get at. You must understand this, however, and I want this to go in the record, it was not the purpose of the chairman to criticize you or anyone else who may entertain your views about this matter.

Mr. RILEY. I am here to tell you the truth about it.

The CHAIRMAN. Even if I differed from you as far as one pole from another, I would not criticize you for coming here and stating your views. We are not hidebound at all. We want to hear you, whether we may agree with you or not. And now you say you do not know Mr. Bodkin?

Mr. RILEY. No, sir.

The CHAIRMAN. Or Mr. Combs?

Mr. RILEY. No, sir.

The CHAIRMAN. Or Mr. Dakin?

Mr. RILEY. I think not.

The CHAIRMAN. Are you a member of the Farmers' Union of Colorado?

Mr. RILEY. No, sir.

The CHAIRMAN. You do not belong to that organization at all?

Mr. RILEY. No, sir.

The CHAIRMAN. You do not belong to the beet growers' division of that association?

Mr. RILEY. No, sir.

The CHAIRMAN. You belong to no organization of the beet growers of Colorado?

Mr. RILEY. No, sir.

The CHAIRMAN. Is the organization I have mentioned the only one in Colorado, or do you know about that?

Mr. RILEY. I do not know about that. I never attended but one of their meetings, and I went there and didn't like the way they talked, and quit it.

The CHAIRMAN. What was the trouble?

Mr. RILEY. They wanted to run up the price on everybody, laborers and factories, and everybody else, and I felt it was unfair, and I did not want to belong to it.

The CHAIRMAN. And your proposition is that the beet-sugar factories are giving you as much as they can afford to give for the beets, in your judgment?

Mr. RILEY. If I thought they were making more money, I would probably want more for the beets, but I believe this price is fair, and when I say I believe it, everybody who is raising beets seems to be satisfied with the present prices.

The CHAIRMAN. Everybody you know of; that would be a better way of stating it, would it not?

Mr. RILEY. I didn't say that? I meant that.

The CHAIRMAN. Of course you meant that. You could not mean those you do not know of?

Mr. RILEY. No, sir.

The CHAIRMAN. We have some evidence of people who are not satisfied. Is there plenty of competition among the beet-sugar factories in your part of the country; that is, can you sell to more than one company?

Mr. RILEY. I never tried.

The CHAIRMAN. You have more than one customer for your beets?

Mr. RILEY. Naturally there is a tariff there; that is, the railroad.

The CHAIRMAN. The railroad rate is the tariff?

Mr. RILEY. I suppose that is it; I don't know that to be so. I sell mine to a factory 16 miles away.

The CHAIRMAN. How close is the nearest other factory?

Mr. RILEY. About 24 miles, just on a line right along.

The CHAIRMAN. How far away is the next factory?

Mr. RILEY. The next one is, I guess, 65 miles away.

The CHAIRMAN. So really you only have two factories that you can very well sell to?

Mr. RILEY. Oh, yes; I have a factory about 12 miles away, on the other side of the river.

The CHAIRMAN. You do not patronize the one nearest to you?

Mr. RILEY. No, sir.

The CHAIRMAN. Why not?

Mr. RILEY. There is a great big river there.

The CHAIRMAN. There is a natural barrier between you and that factory—a river?

Mr. RILEY. Yes, sir.

The CHAIRMAN. The factory that you do patrionize, as I understand, is one of the factories of the American Beet Sugar Co.?

Mr. RILEY. Yes, sir.

The CHAIRMAN. These other factories around you are not of the American Beet Sugar Co.; or, are they or not?

Mr. RILEY. No, sir; two others belong to the American Beet.

The CHAIRMAN. Two others of those you have mentioned?

Mr. RILEY. Well, I have mentioned all of them at some time.

The CHAIRMAN. Two of those you mentioned as being nearest to you?

Mr. RILEY. No, sir; neither one except the Rocky Ford factory. That is the one I mentioned that belongs to the American Beet Sugar Co. The next one, 8 miles beyond, belongs to another party; and the other one, across the river, about 12 miles, belongs to the National Co.

The CHAIRMAN. They belong to three separate corporations?

Mr. RILEY. Yes, sir.

The CHAIRMAN. If one plant in your particular section paid too low a price for beets the other fellows would be liable to pay a little higher price and get the beets?

Mr. RILEY. Now, Mr. Chairman, I don't know really anything about that. I will tell you all that I do know, but I came here as a farmer and don't know about that point.

The CHAIRMAN. That is your position?

Mr. RILEY. Yes, sir; and I don't know about those things.

The CHAIRMAN. You never inquired about prices except at one factory?

Mr. RILEY. Oh, yes; we know about that.

The CHAIRMAN. That is the point. Don't you get the prices from the sugar factories closest to you?

Mr. RILEY. No, sir; I don't think so. I never have.

The CHAIRMAN. You sell to one without knowing what the one closest to you would pay for beets?

Mr. RILEY. There is a general feeling, and while I do not know it to be true, I believe it to be true, that the factories are all paying about the same price. Well, now, I know they are not, because Garden City pays less. I haven't mentioned that factory, which is located in Kansas.

The CHAIRMAN. The ones you have mentioned, about your neighborhood, you believe generally pay about the same price?

Mr. RILEY. I believe that is true.

The CHAIRMAN. Don't you, as a prudent business man, investigate that price proposition before selling your sugar-beet product?

Mr. RILEY. There is one thing sure and that is I know I would find it out if one was paying more than the others, because I would hear about it and would give them the business.

The CHAIRMAN. But if you give your business to one factory without knowing what the others pay, how could you do it?

Mr. RILEY. We are a community and everyone knows what the others know.

The CHAIRMAN. That is exactly what I am getting at. In other words, is there any competition between those three people? Do they acquaint you with the prices they pay; give you that information in any way, so as to give you fair competition according to what each fellow thinks he can get?

Mr. RILEY. I think we have been treated very fairly. Whenever a sugar factory stops work, and especially three of their factories, where they have an investment of one or two millions of dollars, rather than pay a higher price, it is very strong proof in my opinion that they are not making very much money out of the refining.

The CHAIRMAN. Yes; but that is not the case with the most of these big factories.

Mr. RILEY. They have done this in the valley.

The CHAIRMAN. In your particular section?

Mr. RILEY. Yes, sir; and that is the only place that I am giving testimony about. I am not conversant with any other part of Colorado.

The CHAIRMAN. You are just telling what you know, and that is a very good thing to do. Now, let us go back to where we were, because that is the very kernel of this particular matter. We were talking about how you and your neighbors in that immediate vicinity regard these factories whom you could patronize, any one of which you could sell to. Do you regard them as actual competitors with each other, not engaged in any combination to keep prices uniform, and as giving the farmer a fair market price for his sugar beets according to the law of supply and demand, and what they can afford to pay him and make a reasonable profit for themselves or not? What is the truth about that proposition? Tell us about that particular phase of the situation if you know it.

Mr. RILEY. Well, sir, I think of all combinations in the country to-day—and we read in the newspapers about many different combinations—there is no combination with so much wealth behind it that is so much at the mercy of the beet growers.

The CHAIRMAN. That is what we want to know about.

Mr. RILEY. For instance, when we sugar-beet farmers can not raise beets at a price at which we can make money we can go at something else, and which we can and will do. Perhaps we may not make quite so much money, but we can go at something else. If we feel that the factories are making a fair amount and will not pay us what we should have we can easily turn to something else until we are paid what is fair and right.

The CHAIRMAN. In other words, if you feel that the factories are not paying you sugar-beet farmers a fair price for your product you can turn your attention to some other crop?

Mr. RILEY. That is our proposition.

The CHAIRMAN. You think that fact tends to hold the sugar factories in check?

Mr. RILEY. Yes, sir.

The CHAIRMAN. In your immediate section it would appear that conditions were peculiarly favorable to growing the sugar beet; and, further, it would seem that price conditions are also peculiarly favorable, because there seem to be three distinct independent sugar corporations that take your crop, and therefore if one factory tried to pull the price down too low probably the others would pay what they could afford to pay?

Mr. RILEY. I do not know about that feature of it. However, I rather disagree with you about it.

The CHAIRMAN. Well, now, that is what I want to know about, and tell me if I am wrong in that assumption.

Mr. RILEY. Really, I don't know about that.

The CHAIRMAN. Why are you inclined to disagree with me on that proposition? I am anxious to know.

Mr. RILEY. Because I think, as a matter of fact, they pay about the same price.

The CHAIRMAN. Why do they pay about the same price?

Mr. RILEY. I don't know.

The CHAIRMAN. In other words, you think those three factories pay the farmers exactly the same price?

Mr. RILEY. I think that is so, but do not know positively about it.

The CHAIRMAN. In other words, that there is no competition?

Mr. RILEY. I do not say that. I have never tried it, and don't know. However, upon reflection, I will add that I think you may be right about that, rather think you are, although I do not know.

The CHAIRMAN. The situation existing in your vicinity, at any rate, is that there are three factories independent of each other?

Mr. RILEY. Of course I want to correct what you said awhile ago about that other factory. The situation there is this, that there is a railroad on the north side of the river and a railroad on the south side. The south-side sugar growers are cut off entirely from the sugar factory on the other side of the river.

The CHAIRMAN. There is no way of getting over to that factory 12 miles distant?

Mr. RILEY. No; not very well.

The CHAIRMAN. They can not get across the river?

Mr. RILEY. Oh, yes; they can get across the river.

The CHAIRMAN. They can not get there in a cheap way?

Mr. RILEY. No, sir.

The CHAIRMAN. That would make the difference?

Mr. RILEY. Yes, sir.

The CHAIRMAN. That would leave you two possible competitors, whether it is really so or not?

Mr. RILEY. Yes, sir.

The CHAIRMAN. The farmers make no complaint that these two concerns are in league with each other, or in a combination with each other, or have a gentlemen's agreement, or anything like that, do they?

Mr. RILEY. No, sir; we feel that for the reasons I have stated that that is not so.

The CHAIRMAN. On account of the natural conditions you have you sugar-beet growers can take care of yourselves?

Mr. RILEY. Yes; if we did not grow the beets for them they would have to buy up all our farms in order to grow sugar beets for themselves, and they don't want to do that. We are not anxious to sell either, but would do so if they would pay our prices. Yes; if they would pay our prices we would be very willing to sell our farms to the sugar factories.

The CHAIRMAN. All right; I believe that is all I wish to ask.

Mr. MALBY. You would sell your farms to the sugar factories at those prices?

Mr. RILEY. Yes, sir.

The CHAIRMAN. Is this land of yours irrigated?

Mr. RILEY. Yes, sir; every foot of it; 1,000 or 1,200 acres.

The CHAIRMAN. This cost of $35 which you gave us as covering an acre of beets covered everything pertaining to cultivation, inclusive of irrigation?

Mr. RILEY. Yes, sir.

The CHAIRMAN. That runs higher according to whether they irrigate the land or not?

Mr. RILEY. You can't raise beets without irrigating.

The CHAIRMAN. In Colorado?

Mr. RILEY. No, sir.

The CHAIRMAN. They can in other States.

Mr. RILEY. I don't know about that. I have been there since I was a boy.

The CHAIRMAN. You haven't been in other States?

Mr. RILEY. No, sir.

The CHAIRMAN. In Colorado they have to irrigate?

Mr. RILEY. Yes, sir.

The CHAIRMAN. In all estimates of cost given there the cost of irrigation is included?

Mr. RILEY. Yes, sir.

Mr. FORDNEY. Mr. Riley, you stated that there are three distinct sugar companies in that valley to whom you can ship your beets, but that you shipped to the one whose factory was nearest to your locality. Do farmers in your vicinity raise beets for any other factory or factories than that one that you sell your beets to?

Mr. RILEY. Yes, sir; the farmers from Rocky Ford—and that is the one that I do business with, and this factory which is farthest north or west, close to Denver—all around that territory, sell to this place and other places. The Swink factory gets beets at Fountain and some other little stations there. They don't all ship to the same factory in this section to my knowing.

Mr. FORDNEY. They do in that particular territory, then, raise beets for more than one company?

Mr. RILEY. Yes, sir.

Mr. FORDNEY. I wanted to ask you, to illustrate the point of the question I am asking you, that in Michigan, my home State, there are several factories contracting for beets in one immediate neighborhood or locality and ship from the one station; but it is true also with them that they all give the same contract to the farmer, at the same price, identically the same price, as I will explain to you, Mr. Riley. For 12 per cent sugar in the beets the factories give $4.50 per ton, and for each 1 per cent above that percentage of sugar they pay 33⅓ cents additional. So that a 15 per cent beet would bring $5.50, and an 18 per cent beet would bring $6.50 per ton, and so on. Yet all of the sugar factories give exactly the same conditions to the farmers, the same price is named in their contracts, with the same advantages on the railroad, and so on. Yet it does not appear that there is any combination among them, but in order to get the farmers to raise beets one must pay the farmer the same as the other. I presume the same condition exists with you in Colorado?

Mr. RILEY. That is my information. I suppose they do have an understanding about it, because they pay the same price as near as I know. I have never done business with but one factory, but they pay about the same price. We get 50 cents more on a 12 per cent beet than what they pay up your way.

Mr. FORDNEY. You don't get 33⅓ cents for every 1 per cent above the 12 per cent?

Mr. RILEY. Yes, sir; but a 15 per cent beet brings us about $6 per ton.

Mr. FORDNEY. Mr. Bodkin testified that their price was $5 for 12 per cent beets and 25 cents for each 1 per cent above that?

Mr. RILEY. It is 33⅓ cents.

Mr. FORDNEY. That is all I wish to ask.

Mr. RILEY. At what time may I leave the contracts?

The CHAIRMAN. Any time you wish.

Mr. RILEY. I will bring them up this afternoon.

The CHAIRMAN. Just leave them with the secretary of the committee in case we should not be here when you bring them up. We will now excuse you, Mr. Riley, with the thanks of the committee for your attendance.

Representative KINKAID. Mr. Chairman, the witness whom I was arranging to come here from my district, at the request of our sugar-beet growers, I infer is not coming, because the organization, the Scottsbluff Club, Scottsbluff, Nebr., has sent me some papers to file with your honorable committee. Therefore at this time I wish to file these papers, and wish to repeat in my own behalf the request made of me that the committee do these people the kindness to examine them carefully. They have sworn to their papers and wish them to be taken as sworn testimony in the case. They have sworn to each separate petition, and there are several pages of them here fastened together.

What I want to emphasize is that the president of the commercial club says they are very much in earnest about this matter. I can add that I know personally that they are in earnest, because I have visited them several times since they commenced growing sugar beets and since they have had sugar factories there in their midst. If the committee will be kind enough to give consideration to these papers, that is all that our people ask.

The CHAIRMAN. Gentlemen of the committee, this appears to be a letter from Charles Morrill, president of the Scottsbluff Club, Scottsbluff, Nebr., accompanied by a number of petitions signed by numerous citizens of the State of Nebraska in Mr. Kinkaid's district.

Representative KINKAID. Yes; and they run over into the edge of Wyoming, but in the same sugar belt.

The CHAIRMAN. The signatures to these petitions are genuine, are they?

Representative KINKAID. Yes, sir.

The CHAIRMAN. If it is the pleasure of the committee, we will be glad to have them printed with to-day's testimony. Inasmuch as there are several petitions, all upon the same printed form, I take it all that is necessary is to have one heading included in our printed report and follow with the entire list of names.

PETITIONS FROM NEBRASKA.

[Presented by Representative Kinkaid.]

THE SCOTTSBLUFF CLUB,
Scottsbluff, Nebr., January 6, 1912.

Hon. M. P. KINKAID,
House of Representatives, Washington, D. C.

DEAR SIR: We are forwarding herewith a protest signed by beet growers of this section, addressed to the Hon. Thomas W. Hardwick, chairman of the Special Committee on Sugar Investigation. We request that you deliver this document to Mr. Hardwick and that you will also see to it that the same is brought to the attention of the whole committee. The signatures are sworn to by the men who circulated the papers, and we desire that the whole document be introduced as sworn testimony and entered upon the records.

In connection with the number of signers, we wish to make it clear to you, and through you to make it plain to the committee, that every beet grower approached by the canvassers willingly and gladly signed the same.

This petition represents the growers of 6,150 acres of the 10,100 acres planted to sugar beets.

It was the intention to secure the signature of every beet grower in this valley, but owing to the fact that the weather has been extremely cold and our petition was not circulated until January 2, 1912, it has been impossible to canvass the outlying district. Not knowing how soon the committee may discontinue its hearing, we consider it important that this petition, though incomplete, reach you not later than the first of the week.

We would like to have it impressed upon the investigating committee that practically every inhabitant of this valley, no matter what his vocation may be, is directly interested in seeing a further development of sugar production throughout this section.

It is the agricultural development of this irrigated valley, approximately 100 miles long and ranging from 3 to 20 miles wide, which we consider of paramount importance. We recognize that the location of our local sugar factory makes the town of Scottsbluff and its immediate vicinity the principal beneficiaries of such advantage as accompany the operation of that large manufacturing industry. However, without minimizing these benefits, we desire to make it clear that in undertaking to present the sentiments of this community we have in mind, primarily, the positive improvement of social and economic conditions which has been realized through those rural sections which constitute the beet-growing territory.

We take it that the report of said committee may, to a certain extent, become a basis for future legislation affecting the domestic sugar industry, and therefore we deem it most essential that the true conditions be correctly represented and that such representation be incorporated into the committee's record.

You will greatly oblige this community by presenting its interests and its wishes with all the vigor you can command. It is a matter which we consider worthy of your strongest efforts.

Yours, very truly,

THE SCOTTSBLUFF CLUB,
By CHAS. A. MORRILL,
President.

SCOTTSBLUFF, NEBR., *December 29, 1911.*

Hon. THOS. W. HARDWICK,
Chairman Special Committee on Sugar Investigation,
House of Representatives, Washington, D. C.

DEAR SIR: We, the undersigned farmers and beet growers of the North Platte Valley, residing in the counties of Morrill and Scotts Bluff, State of Nebraska, and the county of Goshen, State of Wyoming, knowing from personal experience in the growing of sugar beets that the testimony given before your committee purporting to reflect the sentiment and condition of the farmers and beet growers of the West is false, misleading, and malicious in character, and in no sense a just or true statement of real conditions of either the beet growers or their field labor; and knowing that such misinformation will mislead your committee, and will poison public opinion in regard to the industry, which should be fostered, we desire to present the following statement of facts:

First. The sugar-beet crop is the most remunerative crop raised in this valley, yielding, where conditions are favorable, a net profit of from $20 to $50 per acre.

Second. It is the hardiest and most reliable crop we raise, being the most immune from hail and other destructive storms.

Third. The labor employed in the beet fields, contrary to the testimony given before your committee, is well paid and housed, thrifty and law-abiding; is largely of German and German-Russian origin, frugal in habits, honest and industrious, and in no sense composed of "slum derelicts."

Fourth. The presence of this labor on our farms throughout the growing season affords us the additional farm help we require for the production of diversified crops.

Fifth. Our experience demonstrates that intensive cultivation as practiced by us in beet culture renders our soil more highly productive of other crops.

Sixth. The beet tops constitute a valuable forage, and, together with the pulp and molasses from the factory, form an important part in the upbuilding of our stock-feeding industry which, in turn, produces a large increase in the amount of manure available for fertilizing our lands.

Seventh. Beet growing promotes the subdivision of our large farms; it both directly and indirectly increases our population and furnishes employment for the same; it brings about a condition of better highways; it increases the number of rural mail routes and multiplies our telephone facilities; all of which constitute a distinct advancement in the conditions surrounding farm life.

We believe that the problem of increasing our soil production is one of the great problems confronting the American people. We believe that in the solution of this problem the greatest advance will be accomplished by intensive cultivation under a systematic rotation of diversified crops. With the conditions prevailing throughout this section we have found the beet crop to be a valuable factor. We are in full accord with that national policy of protection which has brought the sugar industry into our valley, and thus enable us to become producers of sugar. We desire to continue and to increase this production, to see additional sugar factories built in this section, and accordingly we protest against the admission of false testimony and the injuries it unjustly entails. We urge that your committee obtain the whole truth, particularly in reference to the economic features which are involved.

Beet grower.	Post-office address.	Beet acreage, season 1911.
R. S. Hunt	Scottsbluff	$48\frac{1}{3}$
H. C. Brashear	do	29
Harvey Beche	Mitchell	11
Nidy Christianson	do	$11\frac{4}{16}$
Barney Smith	do	32
John Engstrom	do	67
Geo. Monunok	do	71
Nakayama & Iwata	do	80
N. Nikoido	do	66
Wm. Ledingham	do	28
Sved Eckhardt	do	8
T. R. Evirett	do	92
H. E. Brown	Scottsbluff	15
W. M. Barbour	do	150
Geo. Hettinger	do	5
Henry Negelin		90
Roy Konkle	Scottsbluff	60
J. L. Shiri	do	$29\frac{84}{100}$
F. H. Kaenig	do	32
A. F. Goos	do	30

State of Nebraska, *County of Scotts Bluff, ss:*

I, A. H. Hamilton, being first duly sworn, on oath, depose and say I presented the foregoing petition to the beet growers whose names appear thereon; that they signed the same in my presence as their voluntary act and deed.

A. H. Hamilton.

Witness:
H. T. Bowen.

Subscribed and sworn to before me this 5th day of January, A. D. 1912.

[seal.] H. T. Bowen,
Notary Public.

(My commission expires Mar. 12, 1915.)

Beet grower.	Post-office address.	Beet acreage, season 1911.
Wm. H. Gable	Scottsbluff, Nebr	124
Orr & Howard	do	130
Wm. Schleisher	do	45
Heinrich Heimlich	do	90
T. C. Halley	do	32
William Yost	do	46
Howard Raymond	do	27
Phillip Hartwig	do	10

Beet grower.	Post-office address.	Beet acreage, season 1911.
W. E. Fairbrother	Scottsbluff, Nebr	60
Geo. L. Helzer	do	30
J. S. Rosenfelt	do	32
T. V. Adams	do	26
Tony Tanaka	do	63
John Ross	do	50
Jay Raymond	do	25
F. R. Sylvester	do	40
F. Hisatoni	do	65
G. T. Ohsumi	do	152¼
W. H. Stalnaker	do	24⅝
Ben Weber Levi Schwoortzkopf	do	85

STATE OF NEBRASKA, *Scotts Bluff County, ss.:*

I, E. M. Sawyer, on oath, say that I presented the above petition to the beet growers whose names are signed thereon, that they signed same in my presence as their voluntary act.

[SEAL.] E. M. SAWYER.

Subscribed and sworn to before me this 5th day of January, 1912.

N. T. BOWEN,
Notary Public.

(My commission expires Mar. 12, 1915.)

Beet grower.	Post-office address.	Beet acreage, season 1911.
E. A. Chorn	Morrill	10
Franklin Lane	Mitchell, Nebr	20
L. J. Wyman	Henry, Nebr	24
S. Hashiba	do	43
A. C. Ray (per son)	do	25
Paul Harvel	do	17
E. E. Cluck	Morrill, Nebr	7
A. L. Kilstrup	do	7
Gerb. Gompert	do	11
Geo. W. Bowen	Mitchell	15
John W. Parton	Morrill	10
W. H. Johnson	do	4
Valentine Thomas	do	10
Martin Hawkins	do	5

I hereby certify that the above signatures were made in my presence this 4th day of January, 1912.

J. E. FENTON.

Subscribed and sworn to before me this 4th day of January, 1912.

[SEAL.] JOHN BOATSMAN,
Notary public.

Beet grower.	Post-office address.	Beet acreage, season 1911.
Robt. F. Neeley	Gering, Nebr	17½
C. C. Hampton	do	40
J. W. Kirmamon		20
M. J. Hoffman	Gering, Nebr	40
H. B. Brown	do	26
Fred Reuble		35
P. H. Pope		15
Arthur Marsh	Gering, Nebr	14
Geo. W. Lawyer	do	15
J. A. Butler	do	25
W. V. Kinsey	do	20
A. E. Leonard	do	25
C. L. and F. D. Turner	do	19
John Bensel	do	40
Vernon Spunir	do	12
F. M. Sands	do	18
J. C. Allison		20
J. W. Bickmarter		15
A. Thurman		9
E. C. Foss		12½

STATE OF NEBRASKA,
Scotts Bluff County, ss:

I, C. H. Irion, on oath say that the 20 names signed to the petition on the opposite side of this paper were signed in my presence and were the voluntary acts of the parties signing.

CHARLES H. IRION.

Subscribed and sworn to before me this 5th day of January, A. D. 1912.

[SEAL.] H. T. BOWEN,
Notary Public.

(My commission expires Mar. 12, 1915.)

Beet grower.	Post-office address.	Beet acreage, season 1911.
Alex Brandt		26
C. D. Cooper		27
P. Hall		20
Daniel C. Hopson	Gering	8
O. O. McHenry	do	40
Wm. Lamm		50
W. T. Beck		20
Thos. W. Bracken		5
G. Harry Hawley		8½
Samuel Barton		32
O. P. Olsen		20
A. S. Bracken		5
Jas. McKinley		25
W. H. White		20
E. McClenahan	Scottsbluff	34
The Imperial Land Co., S. Stark Cashin	do	141
L. A. Everett	do	80
Mehling Bros., by Geo	do	62½
John Schumacher		12

STATE OF NEBRASKA,
Scotts Bluff County, ss:

I, C. H. Irion, on oath say that the signatures to the foregoing petition were signed in my presence. That said signers signed as their voluntary act and deed.

CHARLES H. IRION.

Subscribed and sworn to before me this 5th day of January, A. D. 1912.

[SEAL.] H. T. BOWM,
Notary Public.

(My commission expires Mar. 12, 1915.)

Beet grower.	Post-office address.	Beet acreage, season 1911.
D. T. Skinner	Torrington	85
E. McConnell	do	55
P. B. Scott	do	85
E. O. Smith	do	9
Fred Greenwald	Lingle, Wyo	55
Joe Rief	do	25
August Aschenbrenner	do	27
Geo. Mitsui	do	2.80
Fred W. Frevert	do	25
Otto Tärgens	Minatare	30
C. H. Flower	do	24
G. M. Crabill	do	34.5
J. Lawrence	do	16
B. F. Hobbeck	do	40
Robert M. Lee	do	24
J. P. Wood	do	23
T. F. Breene	do	20
F. Skelledy	Scottsbluff, Nebr	88
Henry Safford	do	20

STATE OF NEBRASKA,
Scotts Bluff County, ss:

I, E. M. Sawyer, on oath say I presented the above petition to the beet growers whose names appear above; that they signed said petition in my presence as their voluntary act.

E. M. SAWYER.

Subscribed and sworn to before me this 5th day of January, 1912.

[SEAL.] H. T. BOWEN,
Notary Public.

(My commission expires Mar. 12, 1915.)

Beet grower.	Post-office address.	Beet acreage, season 1911.
O. B. Brown & Son (by Harley)	Morrill, Nebr	10
S. E. Roberts	do	15
Geo. H. Garrard	do	16
James R. Russell	Mitchell, Nebr	21
T. Erwin Powell	Morrill, Nebr	5
J. N. Hudson		4
Christ Dietz	Morrill, Nebr	45
H. T. Craig	do	3

I hereby certify that the above signatures were made in my presence this 4th day of January, 1912.

W. A. STOCKWELL.

Subscribed and sworn to before me this 4thday of January, 1912.

[SEAL.] JOHN BOATSMAN,
Notary Public.

Beet grower.	Post-office address.	Beet acreage, season 1911.
A. C. Davis	Scottsbluff	120
Heinrich Köhler	do	
Geo. W. Claus	do	28
Nick Adam		100
H. N. Crow	Scottsbluff	6
R. W. Pattison	Gering	66
Ludwig Koch	Scottsbluff	75
Heywood G. Leavitt	do	[1]
Thomas Hall		100

STATE OF NEBRASKA,
Scotts Bluff County, ss:

I, H. S. Stark, on oath say I presented the above petition to the beet growers whose names are signed thereon; that they signed same in my presence as their voluntary act.

H. S. STARK.

Subscribed and sworn to before me this 5th day of January, 1912.

[SEAL.] H. T. BOWM,
Notary Public.

(My commission expires Mar. 12, 1915.)

Beet grower.	Post-office address.	Beet acreage, season 1911.
George Laucamer	Scottsbluff	26
C. H. Irion	do	120
Philip Flohr	do	60
Marten Nelson	do	5½
Martin Schumacher	do	23
Carlen Lobic	do	30
Heinrich Burbach	do	35
W. W. Henderson	do	30
Ira Blaiß	do	30
Geo. Schinck	do	20
Frank Long	do	25
G. C. Bottom	Mitchell	14
T. M. Raymond	Scottsbluff	30
Chas. Raymond	do	50
John Hohnstein	do	60
Fred Knaub	do	28
A. Simonian	do	80
Adam Papep	do	52
E. A. Walker	do	55
F. F. Everett	do	80
Henry Heagel	do	22

STATE OF NEBRASKA,
Scotts Bluff County, ss:

I, H. T. Bowm, on oath say that the 20 names appearing on the petition on the opposite side of this paper was signed in my presence and was signed as their voluntary act. I further swear that they are the names and signatures of the beet growers growing beets in the valley for year 1911 and that the number of acres indicated opposite their names represents the number of acres grown as indicated by their contract.

H. T. BOWM.

Subscribed and sworn to before me this 5th day of January, 1912.

[SEAL.] E. M. SAWYER,
Notary Public.

(My commission expires Mar. 26, 1916.)

Beet grower.	Post-office address.	Beet acreage, season 1911.
Martin Draker	Scottsbluff	20
Will Otte	do	47
R. C. McDowell		12
—— – ——		35
Jacob Muth		40
D. T. Wright	Scottsbluff	90
Fred Martin		40

STATE OF NEBRASKA,
County of Scotts Bluff, ss.

I, Charles H. Irion, on oath, say the seven names signed to the above petition were signed in my presence and were signed as their voluntary act.

CHARLES H. IRION.

Subscribed and sworn to before me this 5th day of January, A. D. 1912.

[SEAL.] H. T. BOWM,
Notary Public.

(My commission expires Mar. 12, 1915.)

[1] 16,000 acres in last 21 years.

The CHAIRMAN. Before we call the next witness I wish to bring to the attention of the committee a letter received by Mr. Garrett, who was acting chairman of the committee at the time his letter was written to which this is a reply. I take it this had better go in our minutes, because attached to the letter is a sworn statement.

WESTERN SUGAR REFINING CO.,
Marine City, Mich., January 5, 1912.

Hon. FERRIS J. GARRETT,
House of Representatives, Washington, D. C.

DEAR SIR: Your favor of the 14th ultimo has been handed to me, and I regret to advise that reply to same has been unavoidably delayed. For your information we have drawn up statement, herewith inclosed, which we trust will fill your requirements. Kindly note that our factory was not in actual operation until beginning of season 1910, and we are therefore unable to go back earlier than this time. We might say our season of 1911 has not yet closed, and at present are not able to determine the figures you require. However, if you will want same at end of season, we will be pleased to send them to you.

Yours, very truly,

WESTERN SUGAR REFINING CO.,
Per R. E. CORDON, *Superintendent.*

STATE OF MICHIGAN, *County of St. Clair, ss:*

Robert E. Gorden, being first duly sworn, deposes and states that he is superintendent of the Western Sugar Refining Co., a corporation organized and existing under the laws of the State of Ohio, and doing business at Marine City, Mich. Deponent further states that he makes this affidavit for and on behalf of the said Western Sugar Refining Co., having full knowledge of all the facts hereinafter stated.

Deponent further states that said Western Sugar Refining Co. has only been actively engaged in business during the past two years; that the figures hereinafter given refer to the business done during the season of 1910–11.

Deponent further states that during that season there were 15,361 tons of beets sliced; that the average sugar test was 15.79 per cent; that the sugar extractions per ton of beets sliced amounted to 260.08 pounds; that the average price paid for the beets was $7.98; that the cost of manufacture was as follows: Cost of raw material $3.570 per hundredweight; factory cost, $1.115 per hundredweight; overhead and administration charges, $0.016 per hundredweight; taxation and insurance, $0.057.

Deponent further states that the said Western Sugar Refining Co. has no factories other than the one located at Marine City, Mich.

Deponent further states that the number of pounds of refined sugar in stock, owned by the Western Sugar Refining Co., July 1, 1911, was XX, which included the total refined stock of the Western Sugar Refining Co., wherever stored, and that was not actually invoiced to the buyer on July 1, 1911; that XX number of pounds of refined sugar was actually sold to the bona fide purchasers, but not invoiced on July 1, 1911; that XX number of tons sugar beets were imported from Canada by the factory of the said Western Sugar Refining Co. from January 1, 1911, to date; that the dates of importation of such sugar beets, with the number of tons thereof, are as follows:

Importation began October 11, 1910. Importation ended December 3, 1910. Total tons imported, 10,307.

R. E. GORDON.

Subscribed and sworn to before me this 5th day of January, A. D. 1912.

C. L. DOYLE,
Notary Public, St. Clair County, Mich.

My commission expires December 7, 1912.

TESTIMONY OF JOHN W. EDGAR.

(The witness is sworn by the chairman.)

The CHAIRMAN. Give the committee your full name.

Mr. EDGAR. John W. Edgar.

The CHAIRMAN. Where do you live?

Mr. EDGAR. Two miles and a half south of Rocky Ford, on a farm.

The CHAIRMAN. Rocky Ford, Colo.?

Mr. EDGAR. Yes, sir; on a farm.

The CHAIRMAN. How long have you lived there?

Mr. EDGAR. I have been there for about 13 years.

The CHAIRMAN. And you have lived there for about 13 years?

Mr. EDGAR. Yes, sir.

The CHAIRMAN. Have you been engaged in farming during all of that time?

Mr. EDGAR. All my life.

The CHAIRMAN. Where did you come from before you moved there?

Mr. EDGAR. I was an Iowa farmer.

The CHAIRMAN. Are you engaged in the cultivation of sugar beets?

Mr. EDGAR. I am.

The CHAIRMAN. To what extent?

Mr. EDGAR. Well, I have cultivated beets—I signed one of the first 10-acre sugar-beet contracts ever signed in the State of Colorado, when this factory was built there, the first factory in the State. I have grown sugar beets from that time to this year. For the next coming year I have 100 acres contracted for with the sugar company, to raise sugar beets.

The CHAIRMAN. You have 100 acres contracted for with the company to raise beets 2 miles from Rocky Ford, Colo.?

Mr. EDGAR. Yes, sir.

The CHAIRMAN. Contract with what company?

Mr. EDGAR. The American Beet Sugar Co.

The CHAIRMAN. That is the same company?

Mr. EDGAR. Yes, sir; I suppose so. It is the American Beet Sugar Co., but we usually refer to it as the American Beet. I am just a farmer and use the farmer's language.

The CHAIRMAN. That is all right. You need not try to be technical.

Mr. EDGAR. That is all I know.

The CHAIRMAN. Have you any sort of interest in or connection in any way with the American Beet Sugar Co. except as a farmer to sell them beets?

Mr. EDGAR. No, sir; no interest in them whatever.

The CHAIRMAN. You are not coming here at their instance?

Mr. EDGAR. Oh, no; not at all.

The CHAIRMAN. Have you had any consultation with them or any of their officers?

Mr. EDGAR. I have some credentials from our farmers' club at Rocky Ford. A few other farmers chipped in with their means and we all together pay our expenses here.

The CHAIRMAN. I am glad that you put that into the record.

Mr. EDGAR. Yes, sir; that is the fact.

The CHAIRMAN. In other words, your expenses are paid by the farmers of your section who want to be heard by our committee on this question?

Mr. EDGAR. Yes, sir; by them and myself.

The CHAIRMAN. Do you know Mr. James Bodkin?

Mr. EDGAR. No, sir.

The CHAIRMAN. Do you know Mr. E. U. Combs, who seems to be a lecturer for the beet growers' association in Colorado?

Mr. EDGAR. No, sir.

The CHAIRMAN. Do you know Mr. Albert Dakan, who seems to be the counsel there of the beet growers' association?

Mr. EDGAR. No, sir. I don't belong to any farmers' union at all.

The CHAIRMAN. You are not a member?

Mr. EDGAR. No, sir.

The CHAIRMAN. Are those gentlemen you spoke of, who are your neighbors, that chipped in to pay your expenses here, members of any farmers' union?

Mr. EDGAR. No, sir; not to my knowledge. We have no farmers' union there that I know of. There was at one time one organized, but there is none there that I know of now.

The CHAIRMAN. You say that you are now under contract to cultivate 100 acres of sugar beets for this company?

Mr. EDGAR. Yes, sir.

The CHAIRMAN. What do they agree to pay you for the beets?

Mr. EDGAR. Our contract this last year has been better than we have had with them, and for next year it is the same.

The CHAIRMAN. What is that?

Mr. EDGAR. They promise $5 per ton for 12 per cent beets, with 33⅓ per cent additional for every 1 per cent or fraction thereof above 12 per cent.

The CHAIRMAN. Is that 33⅓ per cent or 33⅓ cents?

Mr. EDGAR. Thirty-three and one-third cents. And if there are any fractions of 1 per cent, say, one or more tenths, they give us the benefit of it.

The CHAIRMAN. But what I asked was, do they give you 33⅓ cents or 33⅓ per cent for each 1 per cent above the 12 per cent?

Mr. EDGAR. Thirty-three and one-third cents.

The CHAIRMAN. You said first "per cent," and as I thought you meant "cents," I wanted to get it straight in the record.

Mr. EDGAR. Yes, sir; I meant "cents" and did not understand you, because I thought I had said "cents."

Mr. FORDNEY. It is 33⅓ cents increase for every 1 per cent increase of sugar content?

Mr. EDGAR. Yes, sir: that is a term that might slip a plain farmer like myself, but I meant 33⅓ cents, because that is our contract.

Mr. FORDNEY. I just want it right.

Mr. EDGAR. Yes, sir.

Mr. FORDNEY. That is the same as the Michigan factory contracts?

Mr. EDGAR. Yes, sir; I suppose so, except that our contract is 50 cents better than yours for the 12 per cent beet.

Mr. FORDNEY. Yes; you get $5 for the 12 per cent beet, whereas our Michigan farmers get $4.50 for 12 per cent.

Mr. EDGAR. Yes, sir.

Mr. FORDNEY. Your contract reads $5 for 12 per cent beets?

Mr. EDGAR. Well, whereas our contract reads $4.50, there is a guarantee in the contract that the price shall not be less than $5 for 12 per cent.

The CHAIRMAN. We will proceed now with your line of examination. Last year how many acres of beets did you cultivate?

Mr. EDGAR. About 70 acres.

The CHAIRMAN. What was your yield—how many tons of beets per acre on those 70 acres?

Mr. EDGAR. I think our beets may have averaged a little better than the average in that country.

The CHAIRMAN. What was your average?

Mr. EDGAR. Mine were 12 or a fraction better.

The CHAIRMAN. Twelve and a fraction tons per acre?

Mr. EDGAR. Yes, sir.

The CHAIRMAN. That is a little better than the average?

Mr. EDGAR. Yes, sir; I believe so.

The CHAIRMAN. What did they average?

Mr. EDGAR. About 11 tons per acre.

The CHAIRMAN. How far are you from Mr. Riley—or, first, do you know him?

Mr. EDGAR. Yes, sir; I know of him. I met him only about a week ago for the first time, though he has lived in that county many years, and I may have met him before.

The CHAIRMAN. How far apart are you?

Mr. EDGAR. Oh, 25 miles, I suppose. He is in one part of the county and I am in another.

The CHAIRMAN. What did you say was your average for beet yield in your neighborhood?

Mr. EDGAR. About 11 tons per acre.

The CHAIRMAN. You did a little better than 12 tons per acre?

Mr. EDGAR. Yes, sir.

The CHAIRMAN. What did your beets average you in price per ton; I mean those that you raised?

Mr. EDGAR. My beets have averaged, I think, a little better than 15 per cent.

The CHAIRMAN. A little better than 15 per cent of sugar content?

Mr. EDGAR. Yes, sir.

The CHAIRMAN. According to the scale which you just gave me, what price did you get per ton for those beets?

Mr. EDGAR. $6.

The CHAIRMAN. And you raised a little more than 12 tons per acre?

Mr. EDGAR. Yes, sir.

The CHAIRMAN. Can you give it to me exactly?

Mr. EDGAR. I will give it as 12 tons per acre, because I did not get any fraction. I did not get this exactly in figures, gentlemen of the committee, as I doubtless should have done.

The CHAIRMAN. That will do. That gives a gross result of $72 per acre?

Mr. EDGAR. Yes, sir; about that.

The CHAIRMAN. What is that land worth per acre?

Mr. EDGAR. At present the farms I cultivate are worth about $200 per acre.

The CHAIRMAN. Is it irrigated land?

Mr. EDGAR. Oh, yes, sir; all of it.

The CHAIRMAN. How many irrigations do you give it in order to produce those beets you speak of?

Mr. EDGAR. About two irrigations to raise a good crop of beets.

The CHAIRMAN. Now, let us see what it cost you to produce those beets. We will leave out the rental value of the land for the moment. Tell us what it actually costs you to produce those beets—and you can just figure it out on that pad of paper if you wish to do it that way.

Mr. EDGAR. I will give it to you, and you can take the figures.

The CHAIRMAN. I will try to do that.

Mr. EDGAR. As near as I can, I will give you what it cost, although I do a great deal of work myself, or myself and sons. The price for plowing is $2.50 per acre; that is, for plowing the land at first.

The CHAIRMAN. Well, now, give me the next item.

Mr. EDGAR. Leveling and harrowing means about $2 per acre.

The CHAIRMAN. That is leveling and harrowing?

Mr. EDGAR. Yes, sir; I did not hire these things done, gentlemen of the committee, and therefore this is an estimate, in which I may be a few cents wrong.

The CHAIRMAN. You hired the handwork done?

Mr. EDGAR. Yes, sir; I hired the handwork done. My own teams do the teamwork, and my own men do some of this work.

The CHAIRMAN. That is all right. What is the next item?

Mr. EDGAR. The next item would be seeds, $2.

The CHAIRMAN. $2 per acre for seed?

Mr. EDGAR. Yes, sir. That is what they charge us for the seed, 20 pounds, at 10 cents per pound.

The CHAIRMAN. The next item will be what?

Mr. EDGAR. Planting, about 50 cents per acre.

The CHAIRMAN. All right. Give us the next item.

Mr. EDGAR. It takes three irrigations, and that is worth $3 per acre.

The CHAIRMAN. Three cultivations means $3 per acre?

Mr. EDGAR. No; I said irrigations. It costs about $1 per acre for an irrigation and requires about three irrigations.

The CHAIRMAN. All right. Three irrigations means $3 per acre.

Mr. EDGAR. Yes, sir.

The CHAIRMAN. The next is handwork—or does anything else come in before the handwork?

Mr. EDGAR. Well, there is cultivation that comes in, either before or after.

The CHAIRMAN. Give us the cost of cultivation.

Mr. EDGAR. I will give you $2.50 per acre for cultivation.

Mr. FORDNEY. Right there, how many times do you cultivate?

Mr. EDGAR. Sometimes more than others.

The CHAIRMAN. It depends upon the season, I suppose?

Mr. EDGAR. Yes, sir. Sometimes it requires four cultivations and sometimes one or two cultivations are enough, just according to conditions.

The CHAIRMAN. All right; we have $2.50 per acre for cultivation.

Mr. EDGAR. Yes, sir. We plow four rows at a time.

The CHAIRMAN. Now, how about the handwork?

Mr. EDGAR. $7 for handwork. I have hired it done for less and for more.

The CHAIRMAN. What is next?

Mr. EDGAR. $2 for weeding out—that is, for hoeing and weeding.

The CHAIRMAN. What is the next item?

Mr. EDGAR. There is a division that should be made in that. It costs $7 per acre to get that topping done and it is worth $2 per acre for the pulling.

The CHAIRMAN. All right, $7 per acre for topping and $2 per acre for pulling.

Mr. EDGAR. Yes, sir.

The CHAIRMAN. Is there anything else?

Mr. EDGAR. Yes, sir; delivery. The cost for delivery may differ with some other people; some may deliver their beets cheaper than I can. From my place I have to haul those beets to the factory, on the other side of town, and with me it is a distance of about 3 miles, which is worth 75 cents per ton.

The CHAIRMAN. All right; $9 per acre for delivery of the beets to the factory. The word "delivery" will cover that matter, will it not?

Mr. EDGAR. Yes, sir.

Mr. GARRETT. Is that $9 per ton for delivery?

Mr. EDGAR. Oh, no; 75 cents per ton, and with 12 tons to the acre means $9 per acre for delivery.

The CHAIRMAN. Is that all?

Mr. EDGAR. Yes, sir.

The CHAIRMAN. I figure that up as $39.50 per acre?

Mr. EDGAR. Yes, sir; I suppose that is right.

The CHAIRMAN. The figures I took down as you gave them are as follows, per acre:

Plowing	$2.50
Leveling and harrowing	2.00
Seed	2.00
Planting	.50
Three irrigations, at $1	3.00
Cultivation	2.50
Handwork	7.00
Hoeing and weeding	2.00
Topping	7.00
Pulling	2.00
Delivery, 12 tons, at 75 cents	9.00
Total	39.50

That is a little high in your case for delivery?

Mr. EDGAR. Yes, sir. Some men don't have to haul their beets more than a mile or a half mile.

The CHAIRMAN. The average cost will not be anything like that for delivery?

Mr. EDGAR. No, sir.

The CHAIRMAN. You say that your average is a little better on production and you have higher-price land than some other people?

Mr. EDGAR. Yes, sir.

The CHAIRMAN. We will take for rental value of your land 6 per cent on what you say is the value of the land.

Mr. EDGAR. You mean 6 per cent interest on the value of the land?

The CHAIRMAN. Yes. At a valuation of $200 per acre what does it make?

Mr. EDGAR. I don't know what it makes; but if I were renting out my land I would get one-fourth of the beets.

Mr. FORDNEY. Yes; but you want a profit on your land, and about 6 per cent would be the profit?

Mr. EDGAR. Yes, sir.

The CHAIRMAN. Six per cent on $200 would be $12 per acre for rental value of your land. That added to the $39.50 gives a total expense, counting interest on your land investment, of $51.50. You get $72 per acre for your beet crop?

Mr. EDGAR. Yes, sir.

The CHAIRMAN. So, according to these figures, you would make $20.50 besides your 6 per cent investment in land?

Mr. EDGAR. Yes, sir; and that is the sweet part of it, and the part that makes me want to raise beets.

The CHAIRMAN. And gives you a profit of $32.50 per acre, exclusive of your land investment?

Mr. EDGAR. Yes, sir.

The CHAIRMAN. Does that profit compare favorably with what you can do with any other farm crop?

Mr. EDGAR. That is better than I can do with any other crop. I want to say to you gentlemen further that the cultivation of sugar beets has brought our soil up and thereby helped us in other ways.

The CHAIRMAN. You rotate beets with other crops, do you not?

Mr. EDGAR. Yes, sir. I can raise more oats to the acre following beets. As big a crop of oats as was ever raised in our State was raised on a piece of land after it had had beets on it, after five years the yield being 105 bushels of oats. That was the first time such an oat yield was ever secured.

The CHAIRMAN. After you had raised five successive crops?

Mr. EDGAR. Yes, sir; but I generally have difficulty raising beets five years in succession.

The CHAIRMAN. About how long do you raise them?

Mr. EDGAR. Three successive years.

The CHAIRMAN. Do you think that condition generally true of Colorado?

Mr. EDGAR. Well, I don't know anything about northern Colorado.

The CHAIRMAN. In southern Colorado you do that?

Mr. EDGAR. Yes, sir; I am satisfied that that is all right.

The CHAIRMAN. And after three years then you rotate to something else?

Mr. EDGAR. Yes, sir; sow to oats, or probably wheat, and sow alfalfa with either one of the small grains.

The CHAIRMAN. How long before you come back to beets?

Mr. EDGAR. Three years again.

The CHAIRMAN. You take a piece of land and run it for three years in sugar beets, and then rest it for three years so far as beets are concerned, and then come back to beets again?

Mr. EDGAR. Yes, sir; come back all right.

The CHAIRMAN. So that according to that plan you can so cut off your arable land as to continue beet culture?

Mr. EDGAR. Yes, sir; I can do that very well, raising a good crop of beets every year.

The CHAIRMAN. You sell to the American Beet Sugar Co.?

Mr. EDGAR. Yes, sir; I do.

The CHAIRMAN. Have you ever gotten anybody else's prices or does anybody in your community sell to them?

Mr. EDGAR. No; they don't.

The CHAIRMAN. Who else do they sell to?

Mr. EDGAR. Well, I don't believe I can give you the correct names of the firms, but we call them the Swink & Holly factory; that is one firm, and——

The CHAIRMAN (interrupting). The Holly factory buys in that section?

Mr. EDGAR. Yes, sir. It is called Holly, but it goes to Swink, of course. And the Sugar City factory; as I heard it called to-day, the National. I didn't know their name until to-day. They don't buy over in our district, as it is not handy for them.

The CHAIRMAN. Then the American Beet and Holly factories?

Mr. EDGAR. Yes, sir.

The CHAIRMAN. Are the tops of those beets worth anything?

Mr. EDGAR. Yes, sir.

The CHAIRMAN. Have they any money value?

Mr. EDGAR. Oh, yes.

The CHAIRMAN. What are they worth per acre?

Mr. EDGAR. Well, I will tell you, they brought as high by tons as $15 per acre this year, or $5 per ton converted into cattle.

The CHAIRMAN. If you were going to turn them into stock what are they worth?

Mr. EDGAR. The amount of stock fed on these beets would bring $15.

The CHAIRMAN. It would mean three tons of tops to the acre at $5 per ton?

Mr. EDGAR. Yes, sir.

Mr. FORDNEY. Is there anything received in the way of pulp?

Mr. EDGAR. We get 20 per cent, that is, one-fifth.

The CHAIRMAN. What is that?

Mr. EDGAR. We get 20 per cent of the gross weight of the beet back.

The CHAIRMAN. What do you do with that? Do you use it?

Mr. EDGAR. Yes, sir; a great many years I have fed it, and this year I will not feed it and sold it for 50 cents per ton.

The CHAIRMAN. What will an acre of beets produce of that?

Mr. EDGAR. It means 20 per cent of my 12 tons of beets.

The CHAIRMAN. That is 2½ tons?

Mr. EDGAR. Not quite 2½ tons.

The CHAIRMAN. And you sold it at 50 cents per ton?

Mr. EDGAR. Yes, sir; 50 cents per ton, and I never touched it.

The CHAIRMAN. That would be 2.4 tons?

Mr. EDGAR. Yes, sir.

The CHAIRMAN. And you sold it for how much, 50 cents per ton?

Mr. EDGAR. Yes, sir. I am telling you what I did.

The CHAIRMAN. That is $1.20 per acre more to be added to cover this pulp?

Mr. EDGAR. Yes, sir.

The CHAIRMAN. So that would represent a total profit from your land, after paying 6 per cent interest on the investment, of $26.70, now that we include the tops, instead of the $20.50 we had figured out?

Mr. EDGAR. Yes, sir.

Mr. MALBY. Right on that point, about the tops, let me ask Mr. Edgar if he had to haul the tops.

Mr. EDGAR. Yes, sir; I did.

Mr. MALBY. Then you must deduct something for that hauling of 3 tons of tops?

Mr. EDGAR. Yes; we would have to take off about $1 per ton for hauling the tops.

The CHAIRMAN. They wouldn't be worth anything at all?

Mr. EDGAR. Oh, yes; I can get $5 a ton for them, but hauling them would mean about $1 per ton, which would leave about $4 per ton for the tops.

The CHAIRMAN. So it would take $3 off that amount we had, $26.70, leaving $23.70 as the net profit, after paying 6 per cent interest on the investment, per acre?

Mr. EDGAR. Yes, sir.

The CHAIRMAN. You are pretty well satisfied with that result?

Mr. EDGAR. Well, I will say that I went there with nothing and have done pretty well since I have been there.

The CHAIRMAN. You think the sugar beet the best crop that you know of?

Mr. EDGAR. Yes, sir. And, further, the cultivation of sugar beets has brought the land up to a standard where we are raising a great deal better crops than we did before. When I went there the farm I now live on—and I did not have sense enough to buy it, or didn't have the money if I had had sense enough to buy it—was offered to me for $20 per acre with 10 years in which to pay for it.

The CHAIRMAN. How long ago was that?

Mr. EDGAR. Thirteen years.

The CHAIRMAN. As a matter of fact land throughout that section and the entire country has enhanced tremendously in value in that time, that land whether beets are on it or not?

Mr. EDGAR. A great deal of it I attribute to the effect of the beet industry; that the beet industry brought it about.

The CHAIRMAN. Do you know how that compares with the enhancement in value of southern lands, where there are no beets at all?

Mr. EDGAR. No, sir; but they may have something else down there.

The CHAIRMAN. That is exactly it. I want to know how much of that enhancement—and of course it is great and gratifying—is due to the beets and how much to general conditions all over the country?

Mr. EDGAR. I believe that land everywhere has gone up to some extent. But to say how much of this enhancement has been brought about just by the growing of beets would be hard to say. We know that an additional advantage has come with the growing of beets, and that is, for one thing, that we can raise better crops of other things; and another thing, it has attracted lots of cattle feeders, the by-products being utilized. It has brought in these other things and that has increased the demand for other crops, so that our crop of hay this year brought $8, while when I went there I couldn't get more than $1.50 or $2 per ton for it and then couldn't get a buyer. While it may have been fortunate for me then, if I had had to buy hay, because if I had needed a ton I couldn't have bought it at $8, but conditions have changed very much. These cattle feeders give us a market for our hay, oats, and straw; they want all this stuff, and are willing to pay you for it. Everything that you grow they want.

The CHAIRMAN. Which fellows?

Mr. EDGAR. The stock feeders. They can not raise all the stuff they want out on the range. Eleven thousand sheep and lambs from one farm have needed extra stuff for feeding, and these feeders have come in and bought stuff from me to feed their stock.

The CHAIRMAN. That has nothing to do with this inquiry.

Mr. EDGAR. No, sir, probably not; but in answer to your question I was trying to tell you how and why the value of our land had gone up. Many of these things are directly or indirectly attributable to the sugar-beet industry.

The CHAIRMAN. You are satisfied with the treatment the factories give you?

Mr. EDGAR. I am at present. I wasn't at one time.

The CHAIRMAN. Were you ever dissatisfied?

Mr. EDGAR. Yes, sir.

The CHAIRMAN. What about?

Mr. EDGAR. Almost anything that I could mention.

The CHAIRMAN. You were dissatisfied about everything?

Mr. EDGAR. I was awfully dissatisfied at one time, and my home was mortgaged, and I didn't know whether I would pay for it because I couldn't raise beets.

The CHAIRMAN. They didn't pay you enough?

Mr. EDGAR. They didn't pay us enough, and didn't treat us right.

The CHAIRMAN. Didn't treat you right in what respect?

Mr. EDGAR. Oh, we had a management there that was very unsatisfactory to every man, or, at least, to every American man.

The CHAIRMAN. In what respect was it unsatisfactory?

Mr. EDGAR. In the first place he was born a German, and he thought we were just the same as those Russian women, and we thought we wasn't.

The CHAIRMAN. How do they treat those Russian women?

Mr. EDGAR. Well, I have read of and seen how they treated them in the beet fields there, and we wasn't that kind.

The CHAIRMAN. Who does your thinning work in your section?

Mr. EDGAR. That is a very important thing, and I am glad you asked me that question. We have a great many dry farmers in Colorado—farms above the ditches—that have taken claims from your Government and are making homes, and they are very much dependent upon us for their support until they find a better way of making a living than they have found so far. I have had numbers of them working for me, probably with their families on claims 40 or 50 miles from us, and they draw their salaries and send to them to keep them alive. If the beet business were not there I couldn't use them, and I don't know what on earth they would do.

The CHAIRMAN. Do you use them?

Mr. EDGAR. Yes, sir; for pulling beets, and hauling, and everything.

The CHAIRMAN. To get at the kernel of the matter, is the hand work in your part of the beet-growing region of Colorado performed by foreigners or by American citizens?

Mr. EDGAR. A great deal of it by Americans. Then we have a great many of your Indian-school boys doing thinning. They come out and do a good deal of it.

The CHAIRMAN. What would you estimate is done by American labor and what by foreign labor?

Mr. EDGAR. Would you call those from out of the neighborhood foreign?

The CHAIRMAN. We will say, first, what part is done by American citizens and call the balance of them all foreign.

Mr. EDGAR. Well, I think one-third.

The CHAIRMAN. One-third of the work done by Americans?

Mr. EDGAR. Yes, sir; home people.

The CHAIRMAN. Who does the other two-thirds?

Mr. EDGAR. Well, the Indian-school boys and others.

The CHAIRMAN. How much do the boys from Indian schools do; any considerable extent of it?

Mr. EDGAR. Yes, sir; they are good thinners.

The CHAIRMAN. Are there many of them, relatively?

Mr. EDGAR. A good many are brought in for the season for thinning purposes.

The CHAIRMAN. Are there any considerable number of them as compared with the number of foreigners?

Mr. EDGAR. Well, the New Mexicans are up there a good deal, and they run along with the Indians in about equal parts of the two-thirds.

The CHAIRMAN. About equal parts of the two-thirds?

Mr. EDGAR. Yes, sir; in my neighborhood.

The CHAIRMAN. Do you have any Polacks or other foreigners?

Mr. EDGAR. We have Russian families that raise beets and do their own thinning principally.

The CHAIRMAN. I mean that are hired to do this thinning?

Mr. EDGAR. No, sir; not to my knowledge.

The CHAIRMAN. No Polacks or Russians?

Mr. EDGAR. Oh, those Russian families rent some lands sometimes and farm them.

The CHAIRMAN. I mean, do they do contract work?

Mr. EDGAR. Not very much that I know of at all. There may be once in a while some cases.

The CHAIRMAN. There are some cases?

Mr. EDGAR. It may be possible.

The CHAIRMAN. What makes you say "it may be possible"? What is the fact about it?

Mr. EDGAR. About six years ago some did, but I don't know of any since.

The CHAIRMAN. Your labor for field work, what we term hand-work in this investigation, is done partly, and you think about one-third, by American farmers who have what you call dry farms and have to do other work?

Mr. EDGAR. Yes, sir.

The CHAIRMAN. The balance, about two-thirds, is done by Mexicans from New Mexico?

Mr. EDGAR. Yes, sir.

The CHAIRMAN. And the other part of the two-thirds is done by boys from Indian schools?

Mr. EDGAR. Yes, sir. That is about the estimate that I want to put on that.

The CHAIRMAN. Going back for a moment to the time when you were so dissatisfied with the way the beet-sugar factories were treating you, when did that end?

Mr. EDGAR. About five years ago.

The CHAIRMAN. Were you selling then to the same company you sell to now?

Mr. EDGAR. Yes, sir.

The CHAIRMAN. But they had a different management then?

Mr. EDGAR. Yes, sir; and different prices.

The CHAIRMAN. Did they pay you the same prices then that they pay you now?

Mr. EDGAR. No, sir. It was so you couldn't get more than $4.50 per ton.

The CHAIRMAN. Regardless of the sugar content?

Mr. EDGAR. Part of the time they did have a sliding scale but we hardly ever got up to it.

The CHAIRMAN. That is what you got out of it, $4.50 per ton?

Mr. EDGAR. Yes, sir; and finally they made a flat rate of $5 per ton.

The CHAIRMAN. And then they came to this scale you now tell us about?

Mr. EDGAR. Yes, sir.

The CHAIRMAN. And you have been better satisfied with this scale than ever before?

Mr. EDGAR. Yes, sir; much better satisfied.

The CHAIRMAN. During the time that you were dissatisfied with the way the American Beet Sugar Co. was treating you, did you make any effort to do business with any other company?

Mr. EDGAR. I think the other company at that time was paying about the same price. They were newer in the country.

The CHAIRMAN. They were following the lead of the American Beet Sugar Co.?

Mr. EDGAR. Yes, sir; I suppose so.

The CHAIRMAN. You say they were a new company?

Mr. EDGAR. Yes, sir; a little newer company and paying the same prices.

The CHAIRMAN. They wouldn't pay any more than the other fellows did?

Mr. EDGAR. I never knowed of it if they did.

The CHAIRMAN. You looked into it as you were dissatisfied?

Mr. EDGAR. I didn't hear any such news.

The CHAIRMAN. You must have looked into it?

Mr. EDGAR. Yes, sir.

The CHAIRMAN. How about this other treatment that you were dissatisfied with. Were they giving as bad treatment to you in that way as in other respects?

Mr. EDGAR. Oh, it ran about the same.

The CHAIRMAN. So the faults in management were just about as bad in one management as it was in the other?

Mr. EDGAR. It was with me.

The CHAIRMAN. You didn't try the other people?

Mr. EDGAR. Yes, sir; I sold the other company about five or six years ago one small contract I had with them.

The CHAIRMAN. Did you have any trouble with them?

Mr. EDGAR. There was no use to fuss with them, and I took what they gave me.

The CHAIRMAN. In other words, the point of the trouble was that they didn't give you enough?

Mr. EDGAR. We were not getting enough at that time.

The CHAIRMAN. You feel better satisfied at this time?

Mr. EDGAR. Yes, sir.

The CHAIRMAN. And you would be still better satisfied if you got a little more?

Mr. EDGAR. If it is justly coming to us, we would.

The CHAIRMAN. That is right. Every man that has anything to sell wants as much as he can get.

Mr. EDGAR. He ought to have what it is worth.

The CHAIRMAN. You feel like at the present you are getting all you ought to have for beets?

Mr. EDGAR. Well, I can make a living at it and pay my expenses.

The CHAIRMAN. That is not the question.

Mr. EDGAR. There is a question that no ordinary farmer can answer intelligently. He doesn't know what the sugar factories can pay.

The CHAIRMAN. I will give you a theoretical case. Suppose——

Mr. EDGAR (interrupting). Well, I don't know what they are making.

The CHAIRMAN. Suppose they are making 150 per cent on their investment, would you think then that you were getting enough for your sugar beets?

Mr. EDGAR. Well, I can't get that much out of my investment.

The CHAIRMAN. Do you think that you ought to have as much as they do?

Mr. EDGAR. Well, maybe we haven't as much invested as they have.

The CHAIRMAN. I mean, proportionately, as far as the rate goes?

Mr. EDGAR. Well, I wouldn't like to see the beet-sugar industry turned down.

The CHAIRMAN. I know that, because you fear that you might go with it.

Mr. EDGAR. We would go with it sure.

The CHAIRMAN. But you do want a fair division of whatever profits the whole thing pays?

Mr. EDGAR. Yes, sir; I would like to ask that.

The CHAIRMAN. You would like to have the same rate of profit?

Mr. EDGAR. I would like to have justice.

The CHAIRMAN. How would you like to have a proposition for them to pay you a certain per cent of interest in their earnings for your beets instead of a given price for the beets?

Mr. EDGAR. Oh, I don't know about that. I never like to get in partnership very much, especially about things I don't know about, and I don't know that I would like that.

The CHAIRMAN. You don't think that you would like that because if there were no earnings you wouldn't get anything?

Mr. EDGAR. Yes, sir. They might figure me out of it.

The CHAIRMAN. Is there anything else you gentlemen wish to ask Mr. Edgar about?

Mr. EDGAR. Anything I know I am willing to answer, and as far as I know.

Mr. FORDNEY. The general conditions in your neighborhood; do you represent them in your statement here? In other words, do the farmers feel about as you do, as far as you know?

Mr. EDGAR. Yes, sir; I am in quite good shape to know that, or they wouldn't have helped me to come. They came to me and asked me to come before you.

Mr. FORDNEY. You think the sugar beet one of your best farm crops?

Mr. EDGAR. Yes, sir.

Mr. FORDNEY. If that industry were to close to-day, how much less do you believe your lands would be worth, if any less?

Mr. EDGAR. It would grow so much worse that I really don't know what would happen to us. It would fetch on an awful calamity in our community. It would do the whole thing up. And this labor would go down with us because we couldn't hire them.

Mr. FORDNEY. There is no other crop that you raise that after you plant it doesn't fluctuate in price except the beet; the price of all other crops fluctuates?

Mr. EDGAR. Yes, sir.

Mr. FORDNEY. So that when you raise a good crop of oats you don't know what you are going to get for it until you sell it?

Mr. EDGAR. No, sir; and that is one thing I would like to lay stress upon, about the payments. Even as long as we did not like that company they always paid us on the 15th. They always paid us when they promised; I give them credit for that, whether they liked it or not. And I do not believe that the company was to blame; it was the management. Now, we have one of the finest managers that ever was with any firm, a man who walked into the factory and shoveled beets for his start.

The CHAIRMAN. You don't believe that the manager fixed the price, do you?

Mr. EDGAR. No, sir; but he was the means of getting the beets. If he treats the farmers right, he gets their beets.

The CHAIRMAN. When you were so awfully dissatisfied awhile ago, when their man tried to treat you as if you were Russian women, you didn't blame him then for the low prices paid for beets; but that was the general policy of the company, I suppose?

Mr. EDGAR. I suppose so.

The CHAIRMAN. You do not think that he fixed the price?

Mr. EDGAR. I don't suppose so.

Mr. FORDNEY. How much less price did you get for your beets then than now?

Mr. EDGAR. We started at $4.50.

Mr. FORDNEY. And then got a 33⅓-cent increase?

Mr. EDGAR. I won't say how much we were getting then. It hardly ever went up to it, so that we didn't know what it was.

Mr. FORDNEY. It didn't work for you?

Mr. EDGAR. No, sir; and we got $5 per ton afterwards.

Mr. FORDNEY. Under the new management it has been beneficial to you?

Mr. EDGAR. Yes, sir.

Mr. HINDS. Who was this manager that treated you like Russian women?

Mr. EDGAR. Frederick Rucher.

Mr. HINDS. Was he a German?

Mr. EDGAR. Yes, sir; he couldn't be anything else.

Mr. HINDS. Had he managed for beet-sugar factories in Germany?

Mr. EDGAR. I don't know, but he had in Nebraska.

Mr. HINDS. He came from Germany?

Mr. EDGAR. He came there from Nebraska, to our place.

Mr. HINDS. In that connection, you spoke of the condition of labor and production in Germany and abroad; do you have some knowledge of that?

Mr. EDGAR. Oh, I have been told by parties who have been in that country, and I have talked to some of these Russians that live in our country and raised beets in the old country.

Mr. HINDS. What did they say about the condition of labor and compensation over there?

Mr. EDGAR. Very poor, very poor indeed as compared with ours here.

Mr. HINDS. Did they specify any amounts?

Mr. EDGAR. Well, I was acquainted with one German at one time who told me he had worked as a sugar boiler in Germany, and he seemed not to work here at all for some reason, but I didn't know why, and he said he got 60 cents per day there.

Mr. HINDS. As a sugar boiler?

Mr. EDGAR. Yes, sir; that is what he told me.

Mr. HINDS. How much would a sugar boiler get in this country?

Mr. EDGAR. He told me he could get $5 per day here if he worked at it.

Mr. HINDS. $5 per day here instead of 60 cents per day there?

Mr. EDGAR. Yes, sir; that is what he said.

Mr. HINDS. Is $5 per day the regular compensation for sugar boilers in your country, or was that an exceptional time?

Mr. EDGAR. No, sir; I believe they paid that. I have a son who, while not a sugar boiler, told me that that was the amount they were paying at this factory this year.

Mr. HINDS. Did you learn anything about the price of labor in beet fields over in Europe?

Mr. EDGAR. No, sir; not particularly.

The CHAIRMAN. You don't know anything about the truth of that statement the German gave you?

Mr. EDGAR. Oh, no. I am not putting this in as a fact. I only want to testify to what I personally know in my own experience.

The CHAIRMAN. You don't know anything about that at all?

Mr. EDGAR. No, sir; I never worked in a factory a minute in my life, more than to dump my beets. I have driven many hundreds of tons of beets into the factory and dumped them.

Mr. FORDNEY. Do some of the men go to work in the factory in the winter time when there is no work on the farm, and does it benefit the community in that way?

Mr. EDGAR. That is another point. I think that two-thirds of the labor in our factory this winter came from these dry farms, farmers who came there to earn money with which to support their families. That is a fact. Lots of them work for us on our farms.

Mr. FORDNEY. When you say "dry farmers" you mean men who are trying to farm without irrigation?

Mr. EDGAR. Yes, sir; who have filed on a homestead and are holding it down until times get better or they can make a living; they are not making a living at it to-day.

The CHAIRMAN. That is all we wish to ask you, Mr. Edgar. You are excused, with the thanks of the committee for your attendance.

TESTIMONY OF MR. WALLACE P. WILLETT.

(The witness duly sworn by the chairman.)

The CHAIRMAN. Mr. Willett, when you were on the stand last just before the holidays I understood that at the request of certain members of the committee you would prepare certain tabulated statements and present them at a later hearing. Are you now prepared to do that?

Mr. WILLETT. Yes; I am now prepared to do that.

Mr. MALBY. In order to correct the record, Mr. Chairman, before you begin, let me ask Mr. Willett one or two questions.

The CHAIRMAN. Very well; go ahead.

Mr. MALBY. Mr. Willett, I call your attention to a statement on page 3152 of the printed record of our hearings, under date of December 6, 1911, being pamphlet No. 38, in which it is made to appear the following:

> The CHAIRMAN. But, like all other domestic favorites of the tariff law, the domestic people charge as much as foreign people do?
>
> Mr. WILLETT. Yes. The refining companies in New York control the domestic refiners in California and arbitrarily fix the price and control the market.

What have you to say with reference to the correctness of that record, or is it correct as printed?

Mr. WILLETT. Mr. Fordney tells me that he made the remark instead of myself.

Mr. MALBY. Is that correct, as you now remember it?

Mr. WILLETT. It is.

Mr. MALBY. That answer was Mr. Fordney's instead of your own?

Mr. WILLETT. Yes, sir.

Mr. FORDNEY. That is correct.

Mr. MALBY. And you did not want to be put in the position of making such a reply to such a question?

Mr. WILLETT. No, sir.

Mr. MALBY. That is all, Mr. Chairman.

The CHAIRMAN. You will now please furnish the tables you were requested to furnish at our hearings before the holidays.

Mr. WILLETT. Mr. Chairman, I have prepared several tables intended to answer questions asked by the committee at my former hearing. If convenient, I will enter them now.

Hearings No. 37, page 3067, I said: "My theory is that there was a mistake in the crop estimate." On investigation I find there was no mistake in the crop estimate and Table No. 1 (WPW), which I submit herewith, explains what became of the large surplus of 800,000 tons and also gives the exact figures relating to deficiencies mentioned by myself on page 3068, when I said, "I will give you the exact figures if I have a little time."

I suggest here that if these several tables could be put in print to-night, so they could be before the committee, or while I am here, it might be of service. I have not had time to have them typewritten, but the printer will have no difficulty in copying them as I present them.

European statistics of the six principal countries signatory to the Brussels convention—namely, Germany, Austria, France, Holland, Belgium, and United Kingdom—are very completely kept, but are, as a rule, corrected considerably during, perhaps, 12 months following their date of first issue.

Russian statistics are less completely kept, but are improving considerably. The Government keeps a very close check upon the industry and advances a program for the distribution of each year's production.

Little or no attempt is made to keep statistics of the other and smaller countries of Europe, some of which belong to the Brussels convention while others do not. About the only statistics of these countries are those of production and the exports from the principal countries of Europe, whose exports are reported in detail.

TABLE No. 1A.

Comparison of authorities for 1910–11, six principal countries, proving that the estimates of crops were practically correct, and their disposition.

(See Hearings, p. 3066.)

	Year Sept. 1–Aug. 31.					
	1 1910–11, Licht, September figures.	2 1910–11, Czarnikow.	3 1910–11, from other data	4 1910–11, Licht, Dec. 15 figures.	1909–10, Licht.	1908–9, Licht.
	Tons.	*Tons.*	*Tons.*	*Tons.*	*Tons.*	*Tons.*
Stock Sept. 1	538,568	670,000	671,000	641,320	579,491	654,204
Imports	2,536,536	2,203,000	2,251,513	[1] 2,536,536	2,358,699	2,363,933
Production	5,354,425	5,264,000	5,323,934	5,378,125	4,545,058	4,761,178
Total supplies	8,429,529	8,146,000	8,246,447	8,552,982	7,483,248	7,779,315
Stock Aug. 31	576,249	666,000	688,690	644,895	538,568	579,491
Deliveries	7,853,280	7,480,000	7,557,757	7,908,087	6,944,680	7,199,824
Export	2,755,502	2,576,000	2,481,509	[1] 2,755,502	2,262,645	2,490,852
Consumption:						
Calculated	5,097,778	4,904,000	5,076,148	5,252,585	4,682,035	4,708,972
Given	5,094,669	4,895,000	4,826,809 4,898,291	5,117,489	4,674,674	4,712,317
Molasses, calculated, imports over exports			67,163			
Consumption, less molasses			5,008,985			

[1] Figures of September.

Countries.—Germany, Austria, France, Belgium, Holland, United Kingdom.

TABLE No. 1B

COMPARISON OF AUTHORITIES TO SHOW GENERAL AGREEMENT IN THE DISTRIBUTION OF THE 1910–11 BEET CROP.

Column 1, F. O. Licht's figures from Monthly, September, 1911. (W. & G., Oct. 11, 1911.)

Column 2, Czarnikow figures from September 21, 1911, using all figures from main-table, taking October to August, adding last September (1910), and allowance for conversion to raw value.

Column 3 made up from other data.

Stock, W. & G., page 404, found from total stock by deducting sum of Cuba and United States.

Production, latest factory estimate using F. O. Licht for countries not covered by factories. (See W. & G., Jan. 11, 1912.)

Imports, sum of figures for United Kingdom from International Sugar Journal, September, 1911, and January, 1910; Germany, W. & G., page 451; France, W. & G., page 464; Austria, none; Holland, W. & G., page 451; Belgium, Deutsche Zuckerindustrie, October 6, 1911. All figures reduced to raw value by adding 11 per cent to refined and deducting one-half weight of molasses.

Exports, same as imports and Austria. (W. & G., p. 421.)

TABLE No. 1E

Russia.

CROP YEAR SEPT. 1-AUG. 31.

[See pp. 3067-3081.]

[Figures, F. O. Licht and official. Valued as raw. Tons of 2,204 pounds.]

Results.	1910-11	1909-10	Difference, 1910-11 and 1909-10.	1908-9	Difference, 1910-11 and 1909-10.
1. Production	2,140,000	853	+1,013,147	1,243,533	+896,467
2. Stock, Sept. 1, 1910, 1909, 1908	57,993	344,653	− 286,660	504,813	−446,820
3. Imports		1,126,			
4. Supplies	2,197,993	1,471,506	+ 726,487	1,748,346	+449,647
5. Consumption	1,302,270	1,315,269	− 13,399	1,108,653	+193,617
6. Exports	359,181	98,244	+ 261,337	295,040	+ 64,141
7. Deliveries	1,661,451	1,418,513	+ 247,938	1,403,693	+257,758
8. Stock, Aug. 31, 1911, 1910, 1909	536,542	57,993	+ 478,549	344,653	+191,889

PROSPECTS, 1911-12.

	1911-12	1910-11	Difference, 1911-12 and 1910-11.	1909-10	Difference, 1911-12 and 1909-10.
9. Estimated production	2,050,000	2,140,000	− 90,000	1,126,853	+ 923,147
Stock, Sept. 1	536,542	57,993	+478,549	344,653	+ 191,889
Production and stock	2,586,542	2,197,993	388,549	1,471,506	+1,115,036

POSSIBLE SURPLUS, BASED ON EXPECTED CROP, AND OFFICIAL PROGRAM.

	1911-12		1910-11	Difference, 1911-12 and 1910-11.	
10. Consumption allowed for	1,296,480	Actual.	1,302,270	− 5,790	....
11. Export contingent west	222,000	Actual.	221,227	+ 773	....
12. Allowance Finland exports	53,502	Actual.	49,229	+ 4,273	....
13. Allowance Persia exports	89,244	Actual.	88,725	+ 519	....
Deliveries allowed	1,661,226	....	1,661,451	− 225	....
Excess, 1912	925,316	....	536,542	+388,774	....
16. Inviolable reserve	142,080	....	145,385	− 3,305	....
Surplus stock (tied up)	783,236	....	391,157	+392,079	....

TABLE No. 1F.

SUPPLIES—SOURCES OF DATA AND EXPLANATIONS—RUSSIA.

1. Production, 1909-10, 1908-9, from table in F. O. Licht's Monthly, April 21, 1911. Production, 1910-11, from F. O. Licht's latest estimate, December 15, 1911. (W. & G., Jan. 4, 1912.)

2. Stock, September 1, 1909, 1908, F. O. Licht, April 21, 1911.
Stock, September 1, 1910, F. O. Licht, November 17, 1911.

3. Imports, F. O. Licht, April 21, 1911.

5. Consumption, calculated.

6. Exports, 1909-10, 1908-9, F. O. Licht, April 21, 1911.

11-13. Exports, 1910-11, Circulaire Hebdomadaire, November 14, 1911.

8. Stock, August 31, 1909, F. O. Licht, April 21, 1911.
Stock, August 31, 1910 and 1911, F. O. Licht, November 17, 1911.

9. Production, 1911-12, from F. O. Licht's latest estimate, December 15, 1911. (W. & G., Jan. 4, 1912.)

10. Consumption, 1911-12, allowance according to the official program for 1911-12, as printed in W. & G., October 5, 1911, plus 11 per cent to convert into raw.

12-13. Exports, 1911-12, to Persia and Finland, same source. The exports given for 1910-11 in same article are not usable, as they are the official allowance for such purpose last year and not the actual. Owing to high prices and trouble in Persia these are liable to be smaller, if anything.

11. Exports, 1911-12, to convention countries, full 200,000 tons allowed valued as raw, the allowance given on authority being valued as refine.

16. Inviolable reserve, 1910-11, F. O. Licht, November 17, 1911.

Inviolable reserve, 1911-12, same source as consumption, 1911-12.

17. Surplus stocks; from these may be deducted later any amount over 200,000 tons which Russia may later be allowed by the Brussels convention to export during 1911-12.

Table No. 1G.

All Europe.

CROP YEAR SEPT. 1-AUG. 31.

[See pp. 3067-3068, 3081.]

[Figures calculated. Valued as raws. Tons, 2,204 pounds.]

	1910-11	1909-10	Difference, 1910-11 and 1909-10.	1908-9	Difference, 1910-11 and 1908-9.
1. Production	8,095,000	6,136,911	+1,958,089	6,543,865	+1,551,135
2. Stock, Sept. 1	596,561	924,144	− 327,583	1,159,017	− 562,456
3. Imports	3,035,091	2,696,442	+ 338,649	2,894,092	+ 140,999
4. Supplies	11,726,652	9,757,497	+1,969,155	10,596,974	+1,129,678
5. Consumption	7,499,178	6,800,657	+ 698,521	6,886,938	+ 612,240
6. Exports	3,114,683	2,360,279	+ 754,404	2,785,892	+ 328,791
7. Deliveries	10,613,861	9,160,936	+1,452,925	9,672,830	+ 941,031
Stock, Aug. 31, 1911, 1910, 1909.	1,112,791	596,561	+ 516,230	924,144	+ 188,647

PROSPECTS 1911-12.

	1911-12	1910-11	Difference, 1911-12 and 1910-11.	1909-10	Difference, 1911-12 and 1909-10.
9. Estimated production	6,250,000	8,095,000	−1,845,000	6,136,911	+113,089
Stock, Sept. 1	1,112,791	596,561	+ 516,230	924,144	+188,647
Production and stock	7,362,791	8,691,561	−1,328,770	7,061,055	+301,736

STATISTICS BASED ON PREVIOUS YEARS.

	1910-11		1910-11 and 1909-10.		1909-10
Production and stock, 1911-12.	7,362,791	....	....	....	7,362,791
Imports, 1910-11	3,035,041	....	....	1909-10	2,696,442
Supplies	10,397,882	....	10,397,882	....	10,059,233
Consumption, 1910-11	7,499,178	1909-10	6,800,657	1909-10	6,886,938
Surplus stock	2,898,704	....	3,597,225	....	3,172,295
Exports	3,114,683	1909-10	2,360,279	1909-10	2,360,279
Deficit	−215,979	Excess.	+1,236,946	Excess.	+812,016
16. Tied up in Russia	783,236	....	783,236	....	783,236
Artificial deficit	−999,215	....	+453,710	....	+ 28,780

Table No. 1H.

SUPPLIES—SOURCES OF DATA AND EXPLANATIONS—ALL EUROPE.

1. Production, 1910-11, 1909-10, 1908-9, F. O. Licht's estimate, November 17, 1911. (W. & G., Dec. 7, 1911.)

2. Stock, six principal countries and Russia. Stock in other smaller countries is small, anyway, as they are either importers of sugar or simply supply themselves, and is also considered to change but little from year to year.

3. Imports, six countries and Russia and +498,555, 337,743, and 530,159 tons in the three years, respectively, which is the total exports to the lesser countries of Europe,

valued as raws, from Germany, France, Austria, Holland, and Russia, as reported by the best authorities and, except Russia, printed in W. & G. of November 9, 1911; November 16, 1911; and October 19, 1911. Russia is from Circulaire Hebdomandaire November 14, 1911. A few thousand tons exported from United Kingdom are disregarded, as they and the small amount of cane sugar imported into these countries, figures for which are unobtainable, are considered to about equal the small exports made by several of them.

5. Consumption calculated, all other figures being obtained from authority.

6. Exports, six countries and Russia, see imports for reason for not considering other countries.

9. Estimated production, 1911-12, F. O. Licht's latest estimate, December 17, 1911. (W. & G., Jan. 4, 1912.)

16. Stocks "tied up in Russia," surplus stocks remaining there which can only be freed by action of the Brussels convention.

In considering prospects for 1911-12, figures based on imports of 1910-11 and deliveries of 1909-10 would seem to most nearly approximate conditions as given in second column.

Table No. 1J.

All Europe—Imports.

[See pp. 3067-3081.]

[Used in all-Europe data. Valued as raw. See W. & G., Oct. 16, 1911, Nov. 9, 16, 1911, and Circulaire Hebdomandaire, Nov. 14, 1911. Tons=2,204.6 pounds.]

To—	From—	1910-11	1909-10	1908-9
Switzerland	France	8,000	14,000	20,000
	Germany	34,000	26,000	25,000
	Austria	86,686	55,000	57,000
Turkey	Russia	83,757	2,400	80,000
	Austria	106,000	83,600	72,000
	France	7,000	7,000	11,000
Denmark	Germany	7,500	25,000	26,000
Norway	do	42,100	41,000	35,000
Portugal	do	9,000	4,500	17,000
Balkan States	Austria	21,460	15,000	23,000
Greece	do	22,323	30,000	23,000
Italy	do	5,500	2,200	5,000
Finland	Russia	49,229	23,843	127,159
Other countries	France	4,000	4,000	4,000
	Germany	12,000	4,200	5,000
Total		498,555	337,743	530,159
Imports to 6 countries		2,536,536	2,358,699	2,363,933
Total imports, all Europe		3,035,091	2,696,442	2,894,092

Table No. 1c.

Supplies, six principal countries, showing where large crop of 1910-11 went.

CROP YEARS SEPT. 1-AUG. 31.

[See pp. 3067-3081.]

[All figures from F. O. Licht. Valued as raws. Tons, 2,204 pounds.]

Results.	1910-11	1909-10	Difference, 1910-11 and 1909-10.	1908-9	Difference, 1910-11 and 1908-9.
Production	5,354,425	4,545,058	+709,367	4,761,178	+593,247
Stock, Sept. 1	538,568	579,491	− 40,923	654,204	−115,636
Imports	2,536,536	2,358,699	+177,837	2,363,933	+172,603
Supplies	8,429,529	7,483,248	+946,281	7,779,315	+650,214
Consumption	5,097,778	4,682,035	+305,233	4,708,972	+384,322
Exports	2,755,502	2,262,035	+493,467	2,490,852	+264,650
Deliveries	7,853,280	6,944,680	+798,700	7,199,824	+655,456
Stock, Aug. 31	576,249	538,568	+ 47,681	579,491	− 3,242

TABLE No. 1c—Continued.

Supplies, six principal countries, showing where large crop of 1910–11 went—Continued.

ESTIMATES.

	1911–12	1910–11	Difference, 1911–12 and 1910–11.	1909–10	Difference, 1911–12 and 1909–10.
Estimate, Dec. 17, production	3,670,000	5,354,425	−1,684,425	4,545,058	−875,658
Stock, Sept. 1	576,249	538,568	+ 37,681	579,491	− 3,242
	4,246,249	5,892,993	−1,646,744	5,124,549	−878,300

PROSPECTS, 1911–12.

[Statistics showing possible deficit based on figures of two preceding years.]

	1910–11		1910–11 and 1909–10		1909–10
Production and stock, 1911–12	4,246,249				4,246,249
Imports, 1910–11	2,536,536				2,358,699
Supplies	6,782,785		6,782,785		6,604,948
Consumption, 1910–11	5,097,778	1909–10	4,682,035	1909–10	4,682,035
Surplus	1,685,007		2,100,750		2,022,913
Exports, 1910–11	2,755,502	1909–10	2,262,033	1909–10	2,262,033
Deficit	1,069,495		161,283		139,120

TABLE No. 1D.

SUPPLIES—EXPLANATORY.

Six principal countries, which are Germany, Austria-Hungary, France, Belgium, Holland, United Kingdom.

All figures from F. O. Licht. All those for 1910–11, 1909–10, 1908–9 from Monthly, September, 1911—W. & G., October 11, 1911.

(a) This gives production 1910–11, 5,354,425 tons, which was increased on December 15, 1911, to 5,375,126 tons (W. & G., Dec. 28, 1911).

(b) This gives stocks, September 1, 1911, 538,568; 1910, 579,491; 1909, 654,204, which on December 15, 1911, were changed to 644,895; 1910, 641,320; 1909, 665,301.

F. O. Licht, December 15, 1911, gives no other changes, for instance, for imports and exports, and consequently does not balance. Therefore, as the changes are either slight or counterbalanced by similar changes in other years, it seemed better to use the table which did balance than to estimate for differences.

It will be noted that these new stock figures compare more closely with Czarnikaw than did the others.

Figures of production for 1911–12 are from Licht's latest estimate of December 17, 1911 (W. & G., Jan. 4, 1912).

In considering the prospects for 1911–12, the second (middle) column would seem to most nearly approximate the conditions of this year, although, of course, exports will probably show even greater reductions.

Mr. GARRETT. What do these tables refer to, stating it as briefly as you can?

Mr. WILLETT. They refer to the European statistics, a comparison of authorities for 1910–11, proving that the estimates of crops were practically correct and what became of them. Another table shows the statistics for Russia, which is outside of the European countries, so called convention countries. Another table shows crop year 1910–11 compared with crop year 1909–10, all of Europe, including Russia. Another table shows the exports to other countries, from all Europe, convention countries, into nonconvention countries. Those countries into which exports from Europe were made were: Switzerland, Turkey, Denmark, Norway, Portugal, Balkan States,

Greece, Italy, Finland, and other nonproducing countries. Another table shows the supplies of the six principal countries of Europe, showing where the large crop of 1910–11 went. These tables answer the question you have just asked.

The CHAIRMAN. Does the compilation of this information cause you to modify your opinion expressed to the committee before the holidays as to what caused this sharp advance in price of sugar during August and September, 1911?

Mr. WILLETT. No, they simply explain what became of the 800,000 tons. This information changes my explanation of what became of the 800,000 tons from a possible error in crop estimates to what these tables show the exports and consumption were. In other words, there was an excess of 800,000 tons of sugar, and we now see that it disappeared into consumption and exports to other countries.

The CHAIRMAN. I will ask you this one general question along that line. Have you modified in any way the opinion you expressed before the holidays as to why sugar went up so sharply?

Mr. WILLETT. Not at all.

The CHAIRMAN. You do not regard the American refiners as responsible in any way for the increase?

Mr. WILLETT. Absolutely not. These tables simply explain what became of the 800,000 tons of sugar which, according to my statement then made, I attributed to an error in the crop estimate, but which, in the light of this subsequent information, we find went to exports and consumption.

The CHAIRMAN. All right. You may go ahead with your next statement.

Mr. WILLETT. The chairman remarked (p. 3072, at bottom of page), "and the less will be the worth of the sugar lost in refining." All the analyses of changing from duty to free sugar show that whenever duty is taken off the cost of refining decreases and when duty is added the cost of refining increases, but these analyses also show that whenever duty is taken off the consumer gets the full benefit of the amount of duty taken off and also a part of the lower cost of refining, and whenever the duty is increased the refiners bear a certain portion of the increase and the consumer does not pay the full addition of the duty. The following tables show this clearly:

Refiners gave consumers the full benefit of the lower cost of raws under free duty. This result is so exact to a cent that it would seem to have been the policy of refiners to do this.

Pages 3139 to 3141: The calculation done before the committee, as printed in the hearings, has several inaccuracies in the details and the final result should read that the consumers got the entire duty taken off plus $0.115 instead of minus $0.053. I submit a corrected statement simplified and showing this result.

TABLE NO. 3B.

METHOD NO. 1.—*Effect of reduction of $2.24 per 100 pounds duty on 96° sugar to free sugar.*

[See Table No. 8B for Method No. 2.]

[See pp. 3071–3081.]

	100 pounds.	107 pounds.
During 3 years and 3 months preceding free duty (Jan. 1, 1888, to Apr. 1, 1891), the average cost to refiners of 100 pounds of 96° test centrifugals was	$5.849	
It requires 107 pounds of 96° test raws to make 100 pounds of granualted of 100° test; 107 pounds 96° test, at $5.849 is		$6.258
During 3 years and 5 months of free duty (Apr. 1, 1891, to Aug. 1, 1894), the average cost to refiners for 100 pounds of 96° test raws was	3.390	
It requires 107 pounds of 96° test to make 100 pounds of 100° test granulated; 107 pounds raws, at $3.39 per 100 pounds is		3.627
Refiners gain by reduction of duty and lower cost of raws		2.631
During the 3 years and 3 months preceding free duty refiners sold granulated at average price per 100 pounds of	6.921	
During 3 years 5 months of free duty at average price of	4.409	
A difference (reduction) of		2.512
Refiner kept the difference between $2.631 and $2.512 per 100 pounds		.119
During the 3 years 3 months preceding free duty the duty on 96° test raws per 100 pounds was	2.24	
Duty on 107 pounds raws 96° test (to make 100 pounds granulated), at $2.24, was	2.397	
Refiners gain from removal of duty and lower cost of raws as above		2.631
Duty taken off of 107 pounds 96° test raws		2.397
Leaving refiners saving from lower cost raws		.234
Refiners kept part of this saving, as above stated		.119
The consumer received the rest of this saving per 100 pounds		.115
The consumer therefore received the benefit of the full duty taken off of 107 pounds raws, $2.397 plus the $0.115		2.512
During the time of free duty the consumer paid for granulated		4.409
During the time of $2.24 duty the consumer paid for granulated		6.921

TABLE NO. 4.

Effect of difference between 40 per cent ad valorem and free sugar.

[See pp. 3071–3081.]

	100 pounds.	107 pounds.
The 40 per cent ad valorem duty equaled average of	$0.915	
Free duty	.000	
Difference in duty	.915	
The duty on 107 pounds 96° test raws, at $0.915		$0.979
The duty on 107 pounds 96° test raws, free		.000
The difference in duty on 100 pounds refined was		.979
The period of 40 per cent ad valorem duty from Aug. 28, 1894, to July 24, 1897, was 155 weeks.		
The period of free duty from Apr. 1, 1891, to Aug. 28, 1894, was 179 weeks.		
The average price of 96° test centrifugals for 155 weeks of 40 per cent duty was	3.434	
And for 179 weeks of free duty	3.390	
Reduction in raws under free duty	.044	
It requires 107 pounds of 96° to make 100 pounds 100° test.		
Under 40 per cent duty 107 pounds raws, at $3.434, cost		3.674
Under free duty 107 pounds raws, at $3.39, cost		3.627
Under free duty refiners paid less for raws		.047
Under 40 per cent duty refiners sold granulated at	4.311	
Under free duty refiners sold granulated at	4.409	
Under free duty refiners sold granulated at more by	.098	
Under free duty refiners saved in price of raws	.047	
Under free duty refiners were better off (than under 40 per cent duty) by	.145	

Or to reverse it, refiners lost $0.145 per 100 pounds by the change from free to $0.979 duty and the consumer paid $0.834 per 100 pounds of the increased duty.

In other words, the refiner paid $0.145 of the increased duty and the consumer the balance, $0.834.

TABLE No. 5.

Effect of difference between 40 per cent ad valorem duty and the Dingley law of $1.685 per 100 pounds duty on 96° test sugar before reciprocity.

[See pp. 3071-3081.]

	100 pounds.	107 pounds.
The Dingley duty on 96° centrifugals was	$1.685	
The 40 per cent ad valorem duty	.915	
Difference in duty	.770	
Duty on 107 pounds 96° test raws, at $1.685, equals		$1.803
Duty on 107 pounds 96° test raws, at $0.915, equals		.979
		.824
The period of the Dingley law $1.685 duty was from July 24, 1897, to Dec. 27, 1903, when reciprocity began, 340 weeks, and the period of 40 per cent duty from Aug. 28, 1894, to July 24, 1897, 155 weeks.		
The average price of 96° centrifugals for 340 weeks of Dingley bill was $4.075 per 100 pounds	4.075	
And for 155 weeks of 40 per cent duty	3.434	
Less under 40 per cent duty	.641	
It requires 107 pounds 96° test to make 100 pounds 100° test.		
Under Dingley bill 107 pounds 96° cost, at	4.075	4.360
Under 40 per cent bill 107 pounds 96° cost, at	3.434	3.674
Under 40 per cent duty refiners paid less for raws		.686
Under Dingley bill refiners sold granulated at	4.897	
Under 40 per cent bill refiners sold granulated at	4.311	
Under 40 per cent refiners sold granulated at less by	.586	
Under 40 per cent refiners paid less for raws	.686	
Refiners were better off under 40 per cent duty	.100	

To reverse, refiners lost $0.10 per 100 pounds by the change from 40 per cent to $1.685 duty and consumers paid $0.720 per 100 pounds of the increased duty. The difference between $0.724 of duty paid by consumers and only $0.586 increase in the price of granulated was because of the lower range of prices for raws, owing to overproduction of supplies. From 1897 to 1903 beet sugar increased about 1,000,000 tons; cane sugar increased about 1,300,000 tons.

TABLE No. 6A.

[See pp. 3071-3081.]

Effect of reduction of 20 per cent reciprocity with Cuba under Dingley law.

The full duty on 96° test centrifugals, per 100 pounds	$1.685
20 per cent less allowed to Cuba, per 100 pounds	1.348
The reduction in duty, per 100 pounds	.337
The full duty on 107 pounds raws to make 100 pounds granulated was	1.803
The 20 per cent less duty on 107 pounds raws to make 100 pounds granulated was	1.442
The reduction in duty on 100 pounds refined was	.361

The period of the Dingley law without reciprocity was from July 24, 1897, to December 27, 1903, 340 weeks.

The period of the Dingley law with reciprocity was from December 27, 1903, to August 6, 1909 (date of the Payne bill), comprising 298 weeks.

The average price of 96° centrifugals for 340 weeks without reciprocity was, per 100 pounds	$4.075
And for 298 weeks with reciprocity, per 100 pounds	3.940
Reduction in raw quotations, per 100 pounds	.135

It requires 107 pounds of centrifugals of 96° test to make 100 pounds of refined of 100° test.

Without reciprocity raws, at $4.075 per 100 pounds, cost refiners, per 107 pounds	$4.360
With reciprocity raws, at $3.940 per 100 pounds, cost refiners, per 107 pounds.	4.209
With reciprocity refiners paid less price for raws, per 107 pounds	.151
Without reciprocity refined granulated sold by refiners, per 100 pounds, at	4.897
With reciprocity refined granulated sold by refiners, per 100 pounds, at	4.809
With reciprocity refiners sold less price for granulated, per 100 pounds.	.088
Result, refiners saved in price of raws, per 107 pounds	.151
Refiners lost in price of refined, per 100 pounds	.088
Net gain of refiners by Cuban reciprocity	.063
Amount of duty taken off 100 pounds granulated	.361
Of which the refiners kept	.063
Leaving for division between Cuba and United States consumers	.298

In order to obtain the correct division of the $0.292 per 100 pounds gained by Cuba and United States consumers separately, the following analysis must be made.

The average difference between centrifugal sugars of 96° polariscope in New York and raw beet sugar 88° analysis f. o. b. Hamburg, reduced to the parity of 96° centrifugals in New York, for six years under Dingley bill preceding reciprocity, compared with eight years of reciprocity, is shown in this table:

TABLE NO. 6B.

[See pp. 3071-3081.]

Year.	Number of weeks.	Beets at New York, duty paid.	Centrifugals at New York, duty paid.	Centrifugals.	
				Higher.	Lower.
1898	52	$4.271	$4.235		$0.036
1899	52	4.393	4.419	$0.026	
1900	52	4.454	4.566	.112	
1901	52	4.088	4.047		.041
1902	52	3.645	3.542		.103
1903	52	3.940	3.720		.220
Average		4.132	4.088	.138	.400
					.138
					6) .262
For 6 years preceding reciprocity centrifugals lower					[1].044
1904		4.141	3.974		.167
1905		4.420	4.278		.142
1906		3.800	3.686		.114
1907		3.990	3.756		.234
1908		4.208	4.073		.135
1909		4.311	4.007		.304
1910		4.722	4.188		.534
1911		4.749	4.453		.295
Average 8 years of reciprocity		4.291	4.051		[1].240

[1] Per 100 pounds.

Of the $0.337 reciprocity Cuba received $0.097, refiners received $0.063, and consumers received $0.177 per 100 pounds.

These tables show that during the six years of Dingley law preceding reciprocity, Cuba sold her crop within $0.044 per 100 pounds of the world's price as fixed by the Hamburg market, notwithstanding it included countervailing duty of $0.27, was assessed by the United States, while during the eight years of reciprocity Cuba has sold her crop at an average per year of $0.240 per 100 pounds below the world's price.

The reciprocity duty allowance to Cuba is $0.337 per 100 pounds, of which amount Cuba received $0.097 per 100 pounds. Our first analysis shows that refiners received of the $0.337 allowance $0.063; total, $0.160, leaving the gain to consumers by reciprocity $0.177 per 100 pounds.

Cuba received $0.097; consumer received $0.177; Cuba and consumer received $0.274 per 100 pounds, which virtually confirm our first table, that Cuba and consumer received together $0.298 per 100 pounds.

TABLE NO. 7B.

Effect of changes in tariff.

[See pp. 3071–3081.]

	A. Commission bill, 1883.	B. Free duty, Apr. 1, 1891.	Difference, A and B.	C. 40 per cent advance, Aug. 28, 1893.	Difference, B and C.	D. July 24, 1897, Dingley without reciprocity.	Difference, C and D.	E. Dec. 27, 1903, Dingley with reciprocity.	Difference, D and E.
Duty on raws, 107 pounds	$2.397	....	−$2.397	$0.979	+$0.979	$1.803	+$0.824	$1.442	−$0.361
Raws, without duty, 107 pounds	3.861	$3.627	− .234	2.695	− .932	2.557	− .138	2.767	+ .210
Raws, duty paid, 107 pounds	6.258	3.627	− 2.631	3.674	+ .047	4.360	+ .686	4.209	− .151
Refined, 100 pounds	6.921	4.409	− 2.512	4.311	− .098	4.897	+ .586	4.809	− .088
Refiners' margin	.663	.782	+ .119	.637	− .145	.537	− .100	.600	+ .063
Consumer's benefit	....	....	+ .115	....	+ 1.077	....	+ .238	....	+ .030
Decline in raws	....	....	.115	....	.932	....	.138	....	....
Absorption by refiners	....	....	....	....	.145	....	.100	....	....
Portion of tariff paid by consumers	....	....	....	....	.834	....	.724	....	.063
Duty on refined, 100 pounds	3.50	.50	− 3.00	1.104	+ .604	1.95	+ 8.46	1.95	....

Page 3141: Mr. Malby asks for comparisons of 1885–1889 with the period of 1898–1903. I have done this in table below:

TABLE NO. 8A.

Comparison of 1885–1889 with 1898–1903.

[See pp 3071–3081.]

	100 pounds.	107 pounds.
1885–1889, $2 24 duty, 96° test raws were	$2.24	$2.397
1898–1903, $1.685 duty ($1.348 on cubes), cost	1.685	1.803
Difference in duty	.555	.594
1885–1889, average price of 96° test raws	5.698	6.099
1898–1903, average price of 96° test raws	4.088	4.374
Less under $1.685 duty	1.610	1.725
1885–1889, granulated sold at	6.644	....
1898–1903, granulated sold at	4.891	....
1898–1903, granulated sold less	1.753	....
1898–1903, refiners paid less for raws	....	1.725
Refiner gained by reduced duty	.028	....
Consumers gained the balance	.466	....
Portion of reduction in refined cost by reducing of duty	.566	....
Portion of reduction by raw sugar decline	1.159	....
	1.725	....
1885–1889, granulated sold at	6.644	....
Duty taken off	.594	....
Should have sold at	6.050	....
Did sell at	4.891	....
Less price owing to raw fluctuations	1.159	....
Less price owing to reduced duty	.566	....
	1.725	....

TABLE No. 8B.

METHOD No. 2.—*Effect of reduction of $2.24 per 100 pounds duty on 96° test sugar to free duty sugar.*

[See pp. 3071-3081.]

	100 pounds.	107 pounds.
From Jan. 1, 1888, to Apr. 1, 1891 (3 years and 3 months preceding reciprocity), the duty on raw sugar of 96° test was, per 100 pounds	$2.24	....
From Apr. 1, 1891, to Aug. 1, 1894, 3 years and 5 months of free duty	0.00	....
Before free duty refined granulated averaged	6.921	....
Before free duty raw 96° averaged	5.849	....
Difference between raw and refined	1.072	....
During free duty refined averaged	4.409	....
During free duty raws averaged	3.390	....
	1.019	....
Difference between the above differences was	.053	....
Duty on 100 pounds 96° raws at $2.24 equals duty on 107 pounds raws required to make 100 pounds of granulated	....	$2.397
Refined before free duty sold at, per 100 pounds	6.921	....
Duty taken off price 100 pounds refined was	2.397	....
Leaving free duty value with duty off	4.524	....
Difference between raws and refined, less, under free duty	.053	....
Under free duty refiners should sell refined at	4.471	....
During free duty refiners sold refined at	4.409	....
Benefit to consumer from low cost of raws	.062	....
Giving the consumer the benefit of the full duty on 100 pounds refined	2.397	....
Total benefit to consumer	= 2.459	....
Before free duty the difference between raw and refined was	1.072	....
Cost of refining under $2.24 duty was	.714	....
Refiners' profit and surplus was	.358	....
During free sugar the difference between raw and refined was	1.019	....
Cost of refining under free duty was	.548	....
Refiners' profit and surplus under free duty was	.471	....
Refiners' profit and surplus under $2.24 duty was	.358	....
Refiners saved under free duty	.113	....

The first method gave refiners increased profit under free sugar of $0.119 and consumers a total benefit of $2.512 per 100 pounds.

(See Table No. 3B for first method.)

I would like to have the committee satisfied that any reduction of duty goes to the consumer and any addition of duty is paid by the consumer in any year under any duty which differs from any other duty, making necessary allowances for market fluctuation effected by supply and demand. (See Table No. 5.)

Page 3149: Mr. Fordney asked if prices last year, 1910, were enough higher than the prices under free duty to make up the difference in the tariff. An analysis will show.

TABLE No. 8c.

Year 1910 compared with free duty.

[See pp. 3071-3081.]

	100 pounds.	107 pounds.
1910, duty on raws	$1.348	$1.432
1891-1894, free sugar	0.000	0.000
Reduction of duty	1.348	1.432
1910, average of raws (Atkin's table)	4.188	4.472
1891-1894, free raws	3.390	3.627
1910, higher cost of raws	....	.845
1910, granulated sold at (Atkin's table)	4.972	....
1891-1894, granulated sold at	4.410	....
1910, consumers paid more for granulated	.562	....
1910, refiners paid more for raws	.845	....
Refiners' smaller profit in 1910	.283	....
Consumer paid more for granulated	.562	....
Refiner made less profit	.283	....
Producer of raws accepted less for his product	.587	....
	1.432	....

NOTE.—The general in-bond market price of raw sugar in 1910 was $0.40 to $0.50 lower than in 1891-1894; otherwise the consumer would have been obliged to pay a larger proportion of the addition of duty.

The CHAIRMAN. If that concludes your explanation of that matter, you may now proceed to the next.

Mr. WILLETT. On page 3071 I say the advance was not as great in New York as in foreign countries, except at one single period when New York ran absolutely short. The table following will show this in detail:

TABLE No. 2.

Comparison of prices, American and German granulated in New York and Tate's granulated in London.

[See p. 3071.]

[In cents per pound.]

Date.	American granulated.	German granulated.	Difference.	Date.	London granulated.	Difference from American granulated.	Same less difference in duty of $1.04 per 100 pounds.
1911.				1911.			
June 29	4.900	4.83	+0.070	June 28	3.611	1.289	0.249
July 6	4.900	5.03	− .130	July 5	3.692	1.208	.168
July 13	5.047	5.14	− .093	July 12	3.938	1.109	.069
July 20	5.047	5.16	− .113	July 19	3.938	1.109	.069
July 27	5.341	5.33	+ .011	July 26	4.047	1.294	.254
Aug. 3	5.537	5.45	+ .087				
Aug. 10	5.537	5.61	− .073	Aug. 9	4.257	1.276	.236
Aug. 17	5.635	5.77	− .135	Aug. 16	4.415	1.220	.180
Aug. 24	5.831	5.80	+ .031				
Aug. 31	6.125	6.02	+ .105	Aug. 30	4.742	1.383	.343
Sept. 7	6.370	6.39	− .020	Sept. 6	4.742	1.528	.488
Sept. 14	H 6.615	6.39	+ .225	Sept. 13	H 5.396	1.219	.179
Sept. 21	6.615	6.39	+ .225				
Sept. 28	6.615	6.39	+ .225	Sept. 27	5.178	1.437	.397
Oct. 5	6.615	6.45	+ .165				
Oct. 11	6.615	6.45	+ .165				
Oct. 19	H 6.615	H 6.53	+ .085	Oct. 18	5.123	1.392	.352
Oct. 26	6.566	6.37	+ .196	Oct. 25	4.919	1.657	.617
Nov. 2	6.370	6.28	+ .090	Nov. 1	4.919	1.451	.411
Nov. 9	6.174	6.12	+ .054	Nov. 8	4.810	1.364	.324
Nov. 16	6.076	6.20	− .124				
Nov. 23	5.978	6.10	− .122				
Nov. 29	5.880	6.10	− .220	Nov. 29	4.701	1.179	.139
Dec. 7	5.537	6.07	− .533	Dec. 6	4.636	.901	.139
Dec. 14	5.635	5.87	− .235	Dec. 13	4.636	.999	.041
Dec. 21	5.635	5.69	− .055				
Dec. 28	5.635	5.66	− .025	Dec. 26	4.442	1.193	.153
Jan. 4	5.537	5.74	− .203				
Average	5.892	5.904	−0.012		4.533	1.359	

German granulated is parity of quotations f. o. b. Hamburg. H = high point.

The CHAIRMAN. In other words, it is demonstrated that this advance in the price of sugar was not an American advance, but was a world-wide advance, and not as great here as in other countries with one exception?

Mr. WILLETT. Yes, sir.

The CHAIRMAN. All right. Go ahead.

Mr. WILLETT. On page 3079, request for details of profits of cartel in Germany. This was answered on page 3092, so I will not repeat it here.

On page 3079, regarding extract from Willett & Gray's paper of June 12, 1901. That should be December 12, 1901. I thought the chairman was at the time reading from our paper and not from a memorandum handed up by Mr. Lowry, otherwise I would have asked for the paper, which concludes the ex-manipulated extract, quoted as follows:

> No one is seeking to crush the beet-sugar or the Louisiana sugar industry. That which is asked for is justice to all branches of our sugar industry and to the people, which everyone, who looks at the matter broadly, will admit that our Government is under moral obligations to grant.

The CHAIRMAN. That was not in the article I quoted.

Mr. WILLETT. No, sir.

The CHAIRMAN. Was this other a correct quotation, as far as it went?

Mr. WILLETT. Yes, sir.

The CHAIRMAN. Your complaint is that I did not quote all of it?

Mr. WILLETT. Yes, sir.

The CHAIRMAN. I just wanted to see whether he sent me anything that you did not publish. You are now adding the balance of the article which was not in the extract Mr. Lowry furnished me?

Mr. WILLETT. Yes.

The CHAIRMAN. All right.

Mr. WILLETT. I would like to make some other remarks in that connection.

I would add that all the extracts quoted from our paper in favor of reduction of duties were based upon the evidence given at the time by Messrs. Cuttings, Oxnard, and by some others engaged in promoting the beet-sugar industry by alluring prospectuses of low cost of manufacture below 3 cents per pound, and I say now that whenever it is satisfactorily proved that the majority of beet-sugar factories now built can produce granulated sugar and place it on the market at 3 cents per pound or below, the duties on sugar can be cut from present cost of such majority of factories down to the basis of 3 cents per pound without material injury to the industry.

During the existence of the present tariff the cost of manufacture has undoubtedly been reduced at least one-half cent per pound to 3¼ cents to 3½ cents per pound, by the evidence before the committee, and a similar reduction in duties might be made if such reduction would not tend to discourage the promotion of the home industries up to the point of increased supplies of free and partially free duty sugar equal to and, say, 100,000 to 200,000 tons in excess of our requirements to cover contingencies of short crops in some instances.

This promotion of our industry is a much more vital point (from the consumers' standpoint included) than is a reduction of tariff to a point that lets in foreign sugar and thereby diminishes the home production. Whenever we reach the condition indicated, competition between our free and partially free duty producers will begin and the consumers will benefit thereby and the United States will be entirely free from the speculative and other influences which control the world's price, and it is not unreasonable to expect that under the conditions indicated the United States will become a considerable exporter of its surplus production to the foreign countries which may be short of supplies as under present conditions abroad.

As showing the ultimate effect of home production equal to or surpassing home consumption, I call attention specially for earnest consideration to the fact that in 1910 we reached this desired consummation within 74,000 tons, and as a result we were almost independent of Europe; so much so in fact that we got our supplies from Cuba at over one-half cent per pound under world's prices, during which time one man (Santa Maria) was carrying on a big bull speculation in Europe in which we would certainly have been involved but for this limited amount we required that year. In 1911 the Cuban crop fell short of 1910 by 320,898 tons, and we required 212,182 tons from abroad to complete our supplies; hence we were involved in the world's prices in 1911, and the result was a hue and cry against the high prices of sugar. I am not making an argument, but am simply pointing to the facts that appear to me to make the consideration of the increase in our local supplies of greater importance in legislation than a reduction of duties beyond certain limits, those limits to be such as will positively exclude all sugars outside those of our States and dependencies.

The CHAIRMAN. Let me ask you a question about the 74,000 tons. You say we reached a point in 1910 within 74,000 tons of the desired amount of sugar. In making that statement do you not include the Cuban sugar?

Mr. WILLETT. Oh, yes. I count Cuban sugar as a part of our home production. Independent of Europe is my statement. In all my statements I am figuring on the amount of production of domestic sugar as including Cuba, the Philippines, Hawaii, which are subject to preference over foreign countries. In these estimates of total requirements in the United States as a against consumption I include Cuban sugar.

Mr. MALBY. Before you pass from that point, let me ask, am I correct in understanding that you have repeated the suggestion that the American sugar producer can profitably, in your judgment, raise sugar and put it on the market for 3 cents per pound, and that it would be safe to reduce the tariff to such a point that he would receive only 3 cents per pound?

Mr. WILLETT. What I say is, that whenever it is proved, to the satisfaction of this committee for instance, that the majority of the beet factories in this country are so located that they can produce sugar at 3 cents per pound or less, then you may reduce your duties accordingly. But as long as the majority of the factories can not do that it is more important to increase production until they can do it. They have made great progress in 10 years in the matter of cost of production; that is, in lowering the cost of production.

Mr. MALBY. I catch your meaning now.

Mr. HINDS. Do you think it would be an easy thing to ascertain exactly those facts?

Mr. WILLETT. Certainly.

Mr. HINDS. You think it would be easy?

Mr. WILLETT. I think it would be extremely easy. A committee appointed to do that and making that its special object could easily do it.

Mr. HINDS. Don't you think the existing Tariff Board would perhaps be the better agency to go through the books of the companies, study the practice here and abroad, and make a report? Don't you think that they could do it with better facility than this committee?

Mr. WILLETT. This committee has already so much information bearing on that subject that it seems to me the supplemental information required is not so great that it might not get it. On the other hand, the Ways and Means Committee would have to go over the whole ground that this committee has gone over.

Mr. HINDS. No; I was asking more with the idea of putting accountants on the books of the companies, and going into the subject thoroughly. Would that not bring out the information desired in a more thorough and satisfactory manner?

Mr. WILLETT. It is really the only way in which the facts can be brought out.

Mr. HINDS. That is, an inquiry of that sort?

Mr. WILLETT. Yes, sir. You see that my statement involves considerable besides what I say. You see that I limit the retention of duties entirely to the time when the majority of the factories—there are a few of them to-day that can do it, but if the tariff were reduced to-day to that extreme more than half of the beet-sugar factories would be closed or have to move to other localities where they could do business to advantage. Then would come the question of whether a multiplication of factories in certain favorable locations would not bring about another condition of things.

Mr. HINDS. In other words, that is a pretty large question?

Mr. WILLETT. A very large question indeed. What I mean to say is, that I believe all legislation to-day should be directed toward promotion of the increase of our preserves, where we get our supply from, independent of Europe, to a point from 200,000 to 500,000 tons in excess of our actual yearly requirements.

The CHAIRMAN. Do you think that doctrine ought to be carried out to the extent that it would keep up the tariff simply because in certain localities they do not seem to be able, whether by reason of conditions of climate or soil or other reasons, to produce sugar as it is produced in many other sections? In other words, to keep the duties up to protect them, whereas in southern California or Colorado or elsewhere that is not true of the conditions at all?

Mr. WILLETT. That indicates that the whole duty is to be taken off. You can make a reduction in this duty to a certain amount and it will not affect any beet factory in this country, or at least very few of them. I mean to say by that that while a few factories can produce sugar at 3 cents per pound in other sections they can produce it at 3½ cents or 3¾ cents, and the conditions are such that to meet what the few can do you would cripple the others. In the next few years every factory produ ing sugar now at 3½ cents or 3¾ cents per pound will bring the cost of production down to 3 cents.

The CHAIRMAN. They do not encourage us to believe that they can do it?

Mr. WILLETT. Others have done it, and I believe they can.

The CHAIRMAN. Spreckles has done it at 2.70 cents.

Mr. WILLETT. Well, the others can do it, I think.

The CHAIRMAN. Suppose we found it to be true that in Louisiana, taking the testimony of people who have appeared before us on this question, that they can not produce sugar cane for less than nearer 4 cents per pound, whereas we know that in Java it is being produced at 1 cent per pound, and at a goodly profit—that is, if we take the testimony of the greatest experts in the world. Now, ought we to keep the tariff up to let those people produce cane sugar in Louisiana when they can not pr uce it except at about 4 cents per pound, while the balance of theoworld is producing it at about one-quarter of that cost?

Mr. WILLETT. I don't want to say anything about Louisiana.

The CHAIRMAN. I know you don't, and neither do I, as I am a heap closer to them than you are; but what about the fairness and justice of that proposition?

Mt. WILLETT. I can say this, that a gentleman from New Orleans was in my office after he came from an appearance before this committee, and he said Louisiana could not live on free sugar, but that if Congress decided to have free sugar he hoped they would give them five years' notice, in which they might have time to see what they could do, and not put it on all at once. If they gave them five years' notice, they would see about changing their manufactories to Cuba or other countries.

The CHAIRMAN. In other words, when the scales of justice are held in balance between the consumer and the producer isn't there some point where legislation ought not to hot-house industry?

Mr. WILLETT. Certainly. But don't you see where Louisiana would be crowded out in case of a reduction in the tariff? Of course Louisiana will be crowded out anyhow sooner or later by the increase in production of sugar. For when we get a production of from 200,000 to 500,000 tons above our consumption requirements they must meet the new conditions which will then arise to confront them.

Mr. FORDNEY. Mr. Willett, it has been shown here repeatedly, if I am correct, and I think I am, that the cost of production of beet sugar to-day in the United States is somewhere, on an average, from 3.60 cents to 3.70 cents?

Mr. WILLETT. I agree with that, Mr. Fordney. That is my estimate of cost of production in the United States during the last 10 years. It has been reduced to that point from a half cent higher than that.

Mr. FORDNEY. And of that cost, say, 3¾ cents per pound, the farmer receives about 2½ cents per pound for the sugar contained in his beet extracted by the factory, leaving the factory cost, all expenses of the factory, about 1¼ cents. One way of reducing the cost, and probably the most striking way, would be to pay the farmer less for his beets?

Mr. WILLETT. Yes.

Mr. FORDNEY. If the farmer would raise his beets for less price than he receives for them to-day the cost of production of beet sugar could be materially lowered at once, but it will take the greatest economy all along the line, which is being accomplished every day and has been accomplished during the past 10 years, to reduce this cost. The cost to-day over and above the sugar in the beet paid to the farmer is 1¼ cents per pound, to reach which point the factories have been working incessantly for the past 10 years, the Michigan Sugar Co. showing their cost of production having been lowered 68.2 cents per 100 pounds.

Mr. WILLETT. That confirms what I have said.

Mr. FORDNEY. If the time comes when the farmer can afford to raise beets at a less price than is paid him to-day we can then materially reduce the cost of production?

Mr. WILLETT. Yes, and why should not the farmer make the same improvements in cultivation of beets that the factories make?

Mr. FORDNEY. There isn't any reason that I know of, as I said on yesterday, and perhaps you can bear me out. I asked Dr. Wiley on yesterday about sugar content and purity as to beets, and he differed with me. When I reached home I got that statement again that was sent out on January 5, 1912, by the Agricultural Department, which shows that the percentage of sugar in the German beets this last year was 17.63 per cent, and in Michigan it is 12.56 per cent. The purity of the sugar in those beets raised in Germany is about 4 per cent or 5 per cent greater than in ours?

Mr. WILLETT. Not higher than in Colorado.

Mr. FORDNEY. When the industry first started in Germany they only secured 9 per cent sugar in their beets; in 1910, 17.63 per cent.

Mr. WILLETT. Quite an advance.

The CHAIRMAN. Does not the evidence we have been taking recently seem to indicate to you that the beet farmers have a tremendously profitable thing in this matter like it is, and also indicate that they could stand a little reduction?

Mr. FORDNEY. That is an argument. After the expeirence of a number of years, becoming more competent, better qualified, and their lands brought up to a higher state of efficiency, as they have been brought up in Germany, we will probably have improved both in the beets raised and the amount of saccharine matter contained therein, when possibly the farmers can raise beets at a lower price, or, by producing a better beet whereby the factory may extract more sugar, make more money, and yet lower the cost, as the factories have lowered their cost. That is a matter of development.

Mr. HINDS. Will it not also be true that as you get this industry more diffused, get more farmers interested in raising beets, that possibly they will take less profit as their methods progress? When working up a business and before it becomes diffused, if you press them are they not apt to throw up the whole thing for something else?

Mr. WILLETT. On that line I will say that we have letters recently from Wisconsin, and I remember the remark in one of those letters that the farmers are getting crazy to raise beets. Now, a few years ago the farmers were not crazy to raise beets; they were anything but crazy to raise beets.

Mr HINDS. In the corn-canning business, if you will pardon the suggestion, a farmer will raise this year for the corn-canning factory and if he gets a little bit dissatisfied he will not grow corn next year for the factory, but the business of raising corn for the factories is so well understood that there are always others who will do it and do it so that the factories do not have to stop. Along that line I take it the idea is to diffuse the raising of beets so that they will always have reserves to call upon. The beet is a new industry and not so well understood as is the matter of raising corn.

Mr. WILLETT. It is becoming so.

(The committee took a recess until 2.30 p. m.)

AFTER RECESS.

(The committee met at 2.30 o'clock p. m., pursuant to the taking of the recess.)

STATEMENT OF MR. WALLACE P. WILLETT—Resumed.

Mr. WILLETT. Mr. Chairman, I would like to add this to what I answered regarding Louisiana: To refer again to Louisiana, it may be possible that conditions there are not so very different from the beet-sugar conditions; that is, there may be factories in Louisiana that can make sugar more cheaply than other factories, and if duties are reduced so that a minority of the beet factories can not exist, then also those factories similarly placed in Louisiana would be obliged to do as the beet-sugar factories must do, improve their process and make refined sugars direct for consumption, as I understand Mr. Henry Oxnard is about to do. If this is correct, then the same problem applies as to whether the tariff should be kept high enough to protect all the beet and cane factories, or reduce it to a point that protects the best factories and obliges the poorer factories to either improve their process or change their location.

The CHAIRMAN. Now, Mr. Willett, you may submit the next table.

Mr. WILLETT. Page 3081 of the record, surplus of sugar available for export by European countries is shown in detail in Table No. 9A, as follows:

TABLE No. 9A.

Surplus for export, in detail, from latest statistics obtainable.

	A	B	C	D	E	F	G	H	I
	Stock, Sept. 1, 1911.	Production, 1911–12, estimated Dec. 15, 1911.	Supplies.	Consumption, 1910–11.	Excess of supplies.	Net exports, 1910–11.[1]	Consumption, 1909–10.	Excess of supplies.	Net exports, 1909–10.[1]
Germany	175,120	1,480,000	1,655,120	1,422,776	232,344	1,121,955	1,280,218	374,902	788,145
Austria	110,359	1,150,000	1,260,359	679,182	581,177	811,535	596,138	664,221	704,045
France	132,896	550,000	682,896	788,895	−105,999	11,556	683,513	−617	128,015
Belgium	39,126	235,000	274,126	130,180	143,946	148,298	112,933	161,193	123,824
Holland	9,357	255,000	264,357	119,755	144,602	106,668	113,189	151,168	76,917
Total	466,858	3,670,000	4,136,858	3,140,788	996,070	2,200,012	2,785,991	1,350,867	1,820,946
Russia	536,542	2,050,000	2,586,542	1,302,270	1,284,272	359,181	1,315,269	1,271,273	98,244
Total	1,003,400	5,720,000	6,723,400	4,443,058	2,280,342	2,559,193	4,101,260	2,622,140	1,919,190
Other countries		530,000	530,000	1,099,130	−569,130	−428,555	903,353	−373,353	−337,743
United Kingdom	178,037		178,037	1,976,701	−1,798,654	−1,981,046	1,896,147	−1,718,110	−1,918,314
Grand total	1,181,437	6,250,000	7,431,437	7,518,889	−87,442	79,592	6,900,760	530,677	−336,867
Tied up in Russia			783,236		783,236			783,236	
Accessible			6,658,201		−870,678			−252,559	

[1] Net exports are the amount which the exports from a given country exceed the imports.

Columns A, B, F. O. Licht's latest figures, Dec. 15, 1911, are used, except for Russia. Russian stock from F. O. Licht, Nov. 17, 1911. C=A+B. E=C−D. H=C−G. D, F, except Russia and other countries, from F. O. Licht's Monthly, December, 1910, and Dec. 15, 1911, made up for 12 months. D, F, G, I, Russia and other countries, from Tables 1E and 1G. G, I, except Russia and other countries, from F. O. Licht's Monthly, Sept. 16. 1910.

On page 3082 I refer to the import duty into the Philippines as a surtax. The question asked there is answered on page 3093.

The CHAIRMAN. That is, the ruling of the Brussels convention on that point?

Mr. WILLETT. Yes; that is covered already in the record here.

The CHAIRMAN. You do not care to add anything to that answer except to direct attention to your subsequent answer?

Mr. WILLETT. No.

On page 3086 Mr. Malby says: "Indicate in the record as to whether the importer in Denmark does not also pay the 49 cents." The importers of refined sugar into Denmark pay $1.21 per hundred pounds, and pay no further tax. The importer of raw sugar into Denmark pays 72 cents per hundred pounds customs duty, and when refined it pays 49 cents per hundred pounds Government tax more if it goes into consumption, say 72 plus 49 cents, making $1.21 per hundred pounds, or the same as the duty on refined; but if exported as refined it does not pay the 49 cents, and apparently does not get the 72 cents duty refunded, according to consular reports; but according to French authorities, there is a drawback on exportation of 66 cents per hundredweight.

The CHAIRMAN. But they get what is equivalent to a 49-cent drawback by being relieved of the revenue tax in that case?

Mr. WILLETT. Exactly.

Mr. MALBY. They pay 72 cents going in and do not pay anything if it is exported?

Mr. WILLETT. That is it. But if they refine it and it goes into consumption they pay the 49 cents.

On page 3087 Mr. Sulzer asked: "On what day did manufactured sugar reach the highest price to the consumer in the United States, and on that day what was the price of manufactured sugar to the people of England?" Table No. 2 gives prices in New York and parity of Hamburg price during whole period in 1911 compared. The United Kingdom parity would be freight and duty added to Hamburg quotations, say, duty $0.399 per 100 pounds plus freight charge of $0.12, or $0.519 per 100 pounds. So that having the Hamburg quotations, they can be easily compared with New York quotations or with United Kingdom quotations.

On page 3090, Mr. Sulzer: "Will you look up and see if Sweden raises all the sugar that they desire?" The analysis of Sweden will show that.

The CHAIRMAN. What does it show about that?

Mr. WILLETT. I do not remember.

The CHAIRMAN. But the analysis you have in your other report will show that?

Mr. WILLETT. Yes, sir.

On page 3100 Mr. Raker asked for prices from June, 1911, onward. They are given in Table No. 2 and on page 8 of Willett & Gray's Statistical of January 4, 1912.

Mr. MALBY. Have you put that table in, Mr. Willett?

Mr. WILLETT. Not yet. Shall I put the table in?

The CHAIRMAN. Yes; unless the exact figures have been already covered.

Mr. WILLETT. This table covers the whole subject.

Net cash quotations for 96° centrifugal sugar.

[Cents per pound.]

Date.		1911	1910	1909	1908	1907	1906	1905	1904	1903	1902
Jan.	5	3.86	4.02	3.73	3.85	3.56	3.625	4.875	3.47	3.875	3.625
	12	3.675	4.02	3.73	3.94	3.56	3.625	4.875	3.47	3.875	3.56
	19	3.515	4.17	3.73	3.92	3.56	3.75	5.06	3.35	3.875	3.375
	26	3.42	4.08	3.67	3.80	3.50	3.625	5.24	3.31	3.81	3.50
Feb.	2	3.45	4.08	3.67	3.75	3.48	3.56	5.25	3.31	3.69	3.69
	9	3.48	4.17	3.64	3.75	3.48	3.50	5.25	3.35	3.625	3.69
	16	3.545	4.11	3.61	3.67	3.42	3.36	4.94	3.35	3.69	3.625
	23	3.67	4.20	3.61	3.67	3.42	3.36	4.94	3.35	3.75	3.625
Mar.	2	3.78	4.36	3.735	3.885	3.38	3.36	5.06	3.375	3.75	3.625
	9	3.76	4.39	3.735	3.89	3.42	3.39	5.125	3.44	3.78	3.375
	16	3.83	4.36	3.80	4.05	3.51	3.44	5.06	3.44	3.75	3.40
	23	3.92	4.36	3.92	4.125	3.50	3.52	4.88	3.50	3.72	3.44
	30	3.86	4.36	3.92	4.36	3.51	3.56	4.84	3.60	3.625	3.625
Apr.	6	3.86	4.36	3.985	4.36	3.58	3.50	4.81	3.67	3.56	3.625
	12	3.86	4.36	3.955	4.36	3.61	3.55	4.94	3.67	3.50	3.375
	20	3.92	4.30	3.92	4.36	3.735	3.48	4.88	3.61	3.59	3.375
	27	3.92	4.30	3.86	4.49	3.765	3.42	4.72	3.54	3.69	3.44
May	4	3.795	4.30	3.92	4.42	3.73	3.375	4.625	3.70	3.69	3.50
	11	3.86	4.30	3.86	4.36	3.765	3.48	4.625	3.73	3.69	3.50
	18	3.86	4.24	3.92	4.36	3.83	3.48	4.50	3.75	3.69	3.50
	25	3.86	4.24	3.95	4.24	3.86	3.42	4.34	3.88	3.69	3.44
June	1	3.86	4.27	3.92	4.27	3.92	3.42	4.375	3.95	3.625	3.44
	8	3.86	4.24	3.89	4.36	3.90	3.45	4.375	3.95	3.59	3.44
	15	3.89	4.24	3.86	4.40	3.84	3.47	4.375	3.875	3.59	3.50
	22	3.98	4.17	3.92	4.31	3.73	3.50	4.25	3.84	3.59	3.50
	29	3.98	4.24	3.92	4.25	3.71	3.50	4.31	3.94	3.56	3.31
July	6	4.05	4.30	3.92	4.39	3.875	3.61	4.25	3.94	3.56	3.375
	13	4.23	4.33	3.92	4.39	3.835	3.75	4.19	3.94	3.56	3.31
	20	4.36	4.30	3.92	4.36	3.835	3.72	4.00	3.94	3.69	3.31
	27	4.61	4.36	3.95	4.25	3.835	3.72	4.00	3.94	3.69	3.375
Aug.	3	4.61	4.36	3.985	4.25	3.94	3.75	4.06	3.94	3.66	3.375
	10	4.8675	4.36	4.05	4.125	3.94	3.80	4.06	4.06	3.72	3.40
	17	4.92	4.39	4.08	4.08	3.94	3.875	4.125	4.125	3.72	3.40
	24	5.00	4.45	4.11	4.08	3.89	3.875	4.125	4.25	3.81	3.375
	31	5.25	4.15	4.11	3.90	3.89	3.94	4.00	4.25	3.875	3.375
Sept.	7	5.75	4.425	4.17	3.96	3.92	4.00	4.00	4.31	3.875	3.41
	14	5.75	4.36	4.20	3.90	3.92	4.00	4.00	4.31	3.875	3.50
	21	5.92	4.36	4.21	3.95	3.95	4.09	3.875	4.31	3.875	3.47
	28	5.965	4.24	4.235	3.98	3.95	4.125	3.625	4.25	3.91	3.50
Oct.	5	5.80	4.05	4.235	3.98	3.95	4.06	3.69	4.31	3.91	3.50
	11	5.96	3.95	4.235	3.98	3.95	4.00	3.61	4.29	3.85	3.50
	19	5.96	3.90	4.27	3.96	3.95	4.00	3.625	4.25	3.875	3.56
	26	5.735	3.86	4.30	4.04	3.90	4.00	3.58	4.25	3.875	3.625
Nov.	2	5.30	3.80	4.30	3.98	3.90	4.00	3.50	4.22	3.875	3.625
	9	5.12	3.80	4.30	3.95	3.90	3.88	3.50	4.41	3.81	3.625
	16	5.12	3.86	4.45	3.94	3.90	3.81	3.44	4.41	3.81	3.69
	23	5.0625	3.90	4.42	3.94	3.80	3.81	3.44	4.625	3.75	3.81
	29	5.0625	3.93	4.36	3.94	3.70	3.81	3.55	4.75	3.75	3.875
Dec.	7	4.9375	3.93	4.33	3.92	3.625	3.84	3.56	4.75	3.69	3.94
	14	4.875	4.05	4.315	3.86	3.625	3.84	3.56	4.75	3.625	3.94
	21	4.715	4.00	4.17	3.77	3.85	3.875	3.625	4.875	3.625	3.94
	28	4.65	3.985	4.02	3.67	3.85	3.875	3.625	4.875	3.56	3.94

Centrifugals.—Average price per pound for 1911, 4.453 cents. 1910, 4.188 cents; 1909, 4.007 cents; 1908, 4.073 cents; 1907, 3.756 cents; 1906, 3.686 cents; 1905, 4.278 cents; 1904, 3.974 cents; 1903, 3.72 cents; 1902, 3.542 cents.

Net cash quotations for granulated sugar.

[Quotations for sugar in barrels. Cents per pound.]

Date.	1911	1910	1909	1908	1907	1906	1905	1904	1903	1902
Jan. 5	4.75	4.80	4.50	4.55	4.62	4.45	5.70	4.36	4.55	4.46–4.52
12	4.75	4.80	4.45	4.75	4.62	4.45	5.70	4.36	4.55	4.46–4.50
19	4.60	4.90	4.50	4.75	4.50	4.55	5.80	4.36	4.68	4.37–4.41
26	4.60	4.90	4.50	4.75	4.62	4.35	5.90	4.36	4.68	4.46–4.51
Feb. 2	4.55	4.90	4.50	4.75	4.60	4.35	6.00	4.26	4.68	4.46–4.51
9	4.55	4.90	4.50	4.75	4.65	4.35	6.00	4.26	4.55	4.46–4.51
16	4.55	4.90	4.50	4.65	4.50	4.35	5.90	4.26	4.55	4.46–4.51
23	4.55	4.90	4.30	4.55	4.55	4.30	5.90	4.26	4.55–4.61	4.51–4.56
Mar. 2	4.55	5.00	4.45	4.65	4.55	4.30	5.90	4.26	4.60–4.65	4.51–4.56
9	4.65	5.10	4.45	4.75	4.55	4.35	5.90	4.31	4.65–4.70	4.46–4.51
16	4.75	5.20	4.55	4.85	4.55	4.45	5.90	4.41	4.65–4.70	4.46–4.51
23	4.75	5.20	4.70	5.05	4.55	4.45	5.90	4.50	4.60–4.65	4.46–4.51
30	4.75	5.20	4.70	5.25	4.55	4.45	5.90	4.50	4.60–4.65	4.51–4.56
Apr. 6	4.655	5.10	4.80	5.25	4.55	4.45	5.90	4.50	4.50–4.60	4.51
12	4.606	5.10	4.80	5.25	4.55	4.55	5.90	4.40	4.50–4.60	4.51
20	4.802	5.05	4.80	5.35	4.65	4.45	5.90	4.40	4.65–4.70	4.51
27	4.802	5.10	4.80	5.35	4.65	4.40	5.90	4.40	4.75	4.51
May 4	4.802	5.10	4.90	5.35	4.60	4.30	5.90	4.55	4.75	4.46
11	4.802	5.05	4.90	5.15	4.60	4.40	5.90	4.55	4.75	4.46
18	4.802	5.20	4.75	5.35	4.70	4.45	5.70	4.55	4.70–4.75	4.41
25	4.802	5.20	4.70	5.35	4.85	4.35	5.50	4.75	4.70–4.75	4.41
June 1	4.802	5.20	4.80	5.20	4.85	4.35	5.60	4.80	4.65–4.75	4.41
8	4.90	4.95	4.80	5.20	4.85	4.35	5.60	4.80	4.65–4.75	4.41
15	4.90	5.10	4.60	5.20	4.85	4.45	5.60	4.75	4.70–4.75	4.45
22	4.90	5.10	4.70	5.25	4.85	4.45	5.60	4.75	4.70–4.75	4.41
29	4.90	5.10	4.75	5.25	4.85	4.45	5.35	4.75	4.70–4.75	4.41
July 6	4.90	5.00	4.70	5.25	4.85	4.45	5.25	4.75	4.65–4.70	4.41
13	5.047	5.05	4.66	5.25	4.85	4.55	5.25	4.80	4.65–4.70	4.41
20	5.047	5.05	4.70	5.25	4.75	4.55	5.15	4.85	4.75–4.80	4.41
27	5.341	5.10	4.70	5.25	4.75	4.45	5.05	4.85	4.85–4.90	4.41
Aug. 3	5.537	5.10	4.80	5.15	4.70	4.65	4.90	4.95	4.85–4.90	4.41
10	5.537	5.05	4.80	5.05	4.65	4.65	5.05	5.00	4.85–4.90	4.41
17	5.635	5.10	4.80	5.05	4.65	4.75	5.10	5.00	4.75–4.80	4.41
24	5.831	5.10	4.80	5.05	4.65	4.75	5.10	4.95	4.75–4.90	4.41
31	6.125	5.20	4.90	4.75	4.65	4.65	5.10	4.95	4.75–4.90	4.41
Sept. 7	6.37	5.20	4.90	4.95	4.65	4.65	5.00	5.00	4.75–4.90	4.41
14	6.615	5.00	4.90	4.95	4.66	4.65	5.00	5.00	4.75–4.90	4.41
21	6.615	5.00	5.00	4.95	4.65	4.75	4.90	4.95	4.75–4.80	4.45
28	6.615	5.00	4.85	4.95	4.65	4.75	4.65	4.95	4.75–4.80	4.45
Oct. 5	6.615	5.00	4.85	4.95	4.65	4.75	4.55	5.00	4.75–4.80	4.41
11	6.615	5.00	4.85	4.85	4.65	4.55	4.55	4.90	4.55	4.41
19	6.615	4.85	4.90	4.85	4.65	4.65	4.55	4.90	4.55	4.41
26	6.566	4.75	4.90	4.75	4.65	4.65	4.45	4.80	4.55	4.41
Nov. 2	6.37	4.70	4.90	4.85	4.65	4.65	4.45	4.80	4.50	4.41
9	6.174	4.55	4.95	4.75	4.65	4.55	4.35	5.00	4.50	4.31
16	6.076	4.55	5.00	4.60	4.65	4.55	4.35	5.20	4.50	4.21
23	5.978	4.55	5.00	4.55	4.60	4.55	4.35	5.30	4.45	4.41
29	5.88	4.55	5.00	4.55	4.60	4.55	4.45	5.30	4.36	4.50
Dec. 7	5.587	4.55	5.00	4.55	4.60	4.55	4.45	5.30	4.36	4.60
14	5.635	4.55	5.00	4.55	4.55	4.62	4.45	5.40	4.36	4.70
21	5.635	4.75	5.00	4.60	4.55	4.62	4.45	5.50	4.36	4.60
28	5.685	4.75	4.80	4.50	4.55	4.62	4.45	5.50	4.36	4.55

Granulated.—Average price per pound for 1911, 5.345 cents; 1910, 4.972 cents; 1909, 4.765 cents; 1908, 4.957 cents; 1907, 4.649 cents; 1906, 4.515 cents; 1905, 5.256 cents; 1904, 4.772 cents; 1903, 4.638 cents; 1902, 4.455 cents.

On page 3101 Mr. Raker asked for a statement of imports, one from January 1, 1911, to December 1, 1911, and one from July 1, 1911, to November 1, 1911. Table No. 11, which I have already submitted, gives this in detail of countries from January 1, 1911, to December 31, 1911, and gives the amount of preferential; that is, Cuban sugars, 1,218,152 tons, and the amount of full-duty sugar 212,182 tons. Page 5 of Willett & Gray's Statistical, January 4, 1912, compares 1911 imports with 1910 imports by countries, as follows:

Receipts at the four ports (in tons).

From—	Jan.	Feb.	Mar.	Apr.	May.	June.
Cuba	69,559	150,389	226,588	181,500	219,334	108,273
Porto Rico	8,096	14,818	25,268	36,640	34,811	16,357
Surinam	855	45		184		231
San Domingo	4,146				3,041	134
Peru	692	401				
Europe	11,012	97	125	5	4	
Philippine Islands	2,100				7,500	15,500
Hawaii	13,165	19,191	25,649	21,261	32,202	34,537
Sundries	13			19	403	268
Foreign	109,638	184,941	277,630	239,609	297,295	175,300
Domestic (Louisiana)	17,000	386	607	390	282	436
Total	126,638	185,327	278,237	239,999	297,577	175,736

From—	July.	Aug.	Sept.	Oct.	Nov.	Dec.
Cuba	132,363	99,150	24,732	5,509	317	438
British W. I. Islands			1,923	1,244	126	
Trinidad, P. S				553		
Porto Rico	14,880	13,906	7,065	271	174	2,658
St. Croix	1,071	2,833	3,482		15	
Demerara				2,166	9,286	507
Surinam	904	1,056	516	433	696	1,016
Mexico				578		
San Domingo	1,355	604	2,115	115	98	553
Brazil				2,489	7,812	675
Peru	240		472	2,563	699	713
Europe					2,903	
Philippine Islands	26,300	18,975	9,400	41,150	35,090	8,160
Java		7,000	23,300	61,570	34,200	12,400
Hawaii	23,027	31,313	32,458	33,304	14,055	5,184
Mauritius			125	80		
Sundries				38		33
Foreign	200,140	174,837	105,538	152,063	105,471	32,337
Domestic (Louisiana)	323	240	47	352	27,979	45,766
Total	200,463	175,077	105,585	152,415	133,450	78,103

From—	Entire year—				
	1911	1910	1909	1908	1907
Cuba	1,218,152	1,452,467	1,330,595	884,486	1,211,239
British W. I. Islands	3,293	51	363	15,888	2,169
Trinidad, P. S	553				
Porto Rico	174,944	192,619	*172,846	141,425	121,921
St. Croix	7,351	953	7,257	7,095	8,074
Demerara	11,959	6,311	11,235	14,291	121
Central America				229	
Surinam	5,936	2,330	3,791	5,291	6,639
Mexico	578	1,500		465	1,402
San Domingo	12,161	1,161	19,110	48,416	27,220
Brazil	10,976	256	5,301	9,927	7,479
Peru	5,780	4,157	7,508	6,776	9,658
Europe	14,146	149	403	77,633	6,780
Philippine Islands	164,175	82,715	41,370	45,069	8,700
Java	138,470	90,579	145,356	417,352	254,916
Hawaii	285,346	252,389	267,374	200,013	238,404
Mauritius	205				
Sundries	774	58	83	194	296
Foreign	2,054,799	2,087,695	2,012,592	1,934,570	1,905,618
Domestic (Louisiana)	93,808	72,235	39,731	35,628	29,650
Total	2,148,607	2,159,930	2,052,323	1,070,198	1,935,268

Receipts at the four ports (in tons)—Continued.

From—	Entire year—				
	1906	1905	1904	1903	1902
Cuba	1,081,102	1,002,882	972,902	737,938	682,024
British W. I Islands	11,600	22,785	32,079	47,583	86,016
Trinidad, P. S.	70	....	698	27,866	11,992
Porto Rico	166,044	94,594	82,748	71,651	82,827
St. Croix	15,053	4,002	11,963	15,184	11,696
Demerara	26,444	16,954	26,093	57,947	95,971
Central America	....	....	....	964	....
Surinam	7,210	5,118	3,770	6,506	8,155
Mexico	1,145	4,556	....	....	....
San Domingo	47,922	47,616	43,852	45,783	50,660
Brazil	23,606	21,333	2,948	32,143	102,475
Peru	6,625	13,904	22,756	32,301	39,364
Europe	147,847	3,671	62,524	10,392	86,362
Philippine Islands	....	44,841	22,100	29,947	2,550
Java	162,617	353,916	401,930	262,920	340,356
Hawaii	212,939	227,428	219,877	230,171	167,339
Egypt	....	....	....	7,977	27,102
Sundries	....	1,159	3,594	136	....
Foreign	1,910,224	1,864,759	1,909,834	1,617,409	1,794,889
Domestic (Louisiana)	24,954	29,484	13,728	8,122	11,677
Total	1,935,178	1,894,243	1,923,562	1,625,531	1,806,566

1910 receipts from Cuba include 17,816 tons reshipped from Europe.

Mr. RAKER. That shows a comparison of the two years in detail?

Mr. WILLETT. It does; yes, sir. Page 8 gives the prices paid for sugar during those periods for both years, already submitted.

On page 3102 Mr. Raker asked for a statement showing the difference between the actual cost of raws in advance of melting and the price the refined was sold at, produced from such melting.

Table No. 12 gives this clearly or as closely as can be calculated for each month, July, August, September, October, November, 1911, compared with the same months of 1910, as follows:

Supplies in United States and approximate cost, etc., 1911 and 1910.

Raws, basis 96° centrifugals; refined, basis 100° granulated. All prices net cash. Comparison is between 100 pounds raws and 100 pounds granulated.

[Cost in cents per pound.]

JULY.

	1911				1910			
	Tons (2,240 pounds).	Cost.	Date.		Tons (2,240 pounds).	Cost.	Date.	
Stock July 1, importers	52,871				64,732			
Raws, July 1, 1911, 3.980; raws, July 1, 1910, 4.30. Net cash.								
Refiners left from May receipts	32,773	3.86	June 1		101,701	4.24	June 1	
Refiners left from June purchase					1,757	4.26	Importers' average	
Refiners left from June receipts	164,302	3.911	June A		220,833	4.234	June A	
Stock, July 1, refiners	197,075				324,291			
Purchases from importers in July	28,640	4.570	July A					
Receipts to refiners in July	200,463	4.285	do		187,419	4.336	July A	
Supplies of refiners for July	426,178				511,710			
Meltings of refiners for July	229,000				206,000			
Of which were—								
May receipts	32,773	3.86	June 1	4.90, July 6.	101,701	4.24	June 1	5.071, July A.
June purchases					1,757	4.26	Imp. A	Do.
June receipts	164,302	3.911	June A	5.125, July A				
July purchases	28,640	4.570	Actual	do	102,542	4.234	June A	Do.
July receipts	3,285	4.050	July 6	5.125				
Stock, Aug. 1:								
Refiners	197,178				305,710			
Importers	24,231				71,903			
Receipts in July to importers					7,171			
Sales in July importers to refiners	28,640							
Stock, total Aug. 1	221,409				377,613			

AUGUST.

Stock Aug. 1, total	221,409				327,613			
Raws Aug. 1, 1911, 461 c. net; raws Aug. 1, 1910, 436 c. net.								
Importers	24,231				71,903			
Refineries left from June receipts					118,291	4.234	June A	
Refineries left from July receipts	197,178	4.285	July A		187,419	4.336	July A	
Stock Aug. 1, refiners	197,178				305,710			
Purchases from importers in August	24,231	5.070	Average		1,512	4.425	Actual	
Receipts to refiners in August (total)	175,077	4.880	Aug. A		140,172	4.408	Aug. A	
Supplies of refiners for August	396,486				447,394			
Meltings of refiners for August	237,000				215,000			
Of which were—								
June receipts					118,291	4.234	June A	5.128, Aug. A.
July receipts	197,178	4.285	July A	5.686, Aug. A	96,709	4.336	July A	Do.
August purchases	24,231	5.070	Average	do				
August receipts	15,591	4.610	Aug. 3	6.000, estimated				
Stock Sept. 1:								
Refiners	159,486				232,394			
Importers					70,391			
Stock Sept. 1, total	159,486				302,785			

Supplies in United States and approximate cost, etc., 1911 and 1910—Continued.

Raws, basis 96° centrifugals; refined, basis 100° granulated. All prices net cash. Comparison is between 100 pounds raws and 100 pounds granulated.

[Cost in cents per pound.]

SEPTEMBER.

	1911				1910			
	Tons (2,240 pounds).	Cost.	Date.		Tons (2,240 pounds).	Cost.	Date.	
Stock, Sept. 1, total	159,486				302,785			
Stock, Sept. 1, importer's	None.				70,391			
Raws, Sept. 1, 1911, 5.25; raws, Sept. 1, 1910, 4.425.								
Refiner's, left from July receipts	None.				90,710	4.336	July A	
Refiner's, left from August purchases					1,512	4.425	Actual	
Refiner's, left from August receipts	159,486	4.88	Aug. A		140,172	4.408	Aug. A	
Refiner's, Sept. 1	159,486				232,394			
Purchases from importers in September					24,311	4.263	Average	
Receipts to refiners for September	105,585	5.794	Sept. A		113,280	4.272	Sept. A	
Supplies of refiners for September	265,071				369,994			
Meltings of refiners for September	152,000				224,000			
Of which were:								
July receipts					90,710	4.336	July A	5.013, Sept. A.
August purchases					1,512	4.408	Aug. A	5.000, Sept. 8-29.
August receipts	152,000	4.88	Aug. A	6.542, Sept. A	131,778	4.408	do	Do.
Stock Oct. 1:								
Refiners	113,071				145,994			
Importer's					46,080			
Total	113,071				145,994			

OCTOBER.

Stock Oct. 1, total	113,071				145,994			
Stock Oct. 1, importers					46,080			
Oct. 1, 1911, 5.965 c. net; Oct. 1, 1910, 3.950 c. net.								
Refiners, left from August receipts	7,486	5.25	Sept. 1		8,394	4.425	Sept. 1	
Refiners, left from September purchases					24,311	4.263	Averaged	
Refiners, left from September receipts	105,585	5.794	Sept. A		113,289	4.272	Sept. A	
Stock Oct. 1, refiners	113,071				145,994			
Purchases from importers in October					27,017	3.889	Actual average	
Receipts to refiners in October	150,638	5.896	Oct. A		115,320	3.882	Oct. A	
Supplies of refiners in October	263,709				288,331			
Meltings of refiners in October	154,000				168,000			
Of which were—								
August receipts	7,486	5.250	Sept. 1	6.615, Oct. 5	8,394	4.425	Sept. 1	5.000, Oct. 6.
September purchases					24,311	4.263	Sept. A	1.850, Oct. 13.
September receipts	105,585	5.794	Sept. A	6.584, Oct. A	113,289	4.272	Sept. A	4.808, Oct. A.
October purchases					22,006	3.901	Actual averages last ½.	4.700, Oct. 27.
October receipts	40,929	5.80	Oct. 5	6.566, Oct. 26				
Stock Nov. 1:								
Refiners	109,709				120,331			
Importers	1,777				19,063			
Receipts in October to importers	1,777							
Sales in October, importers to refiners					27,017			
Stock Nov. 1, total	111,486				139,394			

Supplies in United States and approximate cost, etc., 1911 and 1910—Continued.

Raws basis 96° centrifugals; refined, basis 100° granulated. All prices net cash. Comparison is between 100 pounds raws and 100 pounds granulated.

[Cost in cents per pound.]

NOVEMBER.

	1911				1910			
	Tons (2,240 pounds).	Cost.	Date.		Tons (2,240 pounds).	Cost.	Date.	
Stock Nov. 1, total	111,486				139,394			
Raws, Nov. 1, 1911, 5.735 c. net; raws, Nov. 1, 1910, 3.8 c. net.								
Importers	1,777				19,063			
Refiners, left from October purchase					5,011	3.833	Actual last sales	
Refiners, left from October receipts	109,709	5.896	Oct. A		115,320	3.882	Oct. A	
Stock Nov. 1, refiners	109,709				120,331			
Purchases from importers in November					15,506	3.853	Average	
Receipts to refiners in November	122,687	5.127	Nov. A		77,058	3.881	Nov. A	
Supplies of refiners for November	232,396				212,895			
Meltings of refiners for November	113,000				115,000			
Of which were—								
October purchases					5,011	3.838	Actual last 3 sales.	4.55, Nov. A.
October receipts	109,709	5.896	Oct. A	6.117, Nov. A	109,989	3.882	Oct. A	Do.
November receipts	3,291	5.300	Nov. 1	5.880, Nov. 29				
Stock Dec. 1:								
Refiners	119,396				97,895			
Importers	12,540				3,557			
Receipts in November to importers	10,763							
Sales in November, importers to refiners					15,506			
Stock, Dec. 1, total	131,936				101,452			

DECEMBER.

Stock Dec. 1, total	131,936				101,452			
Stock Dec. 1, importers	12,540				3,557			
Raws Dec. 1, 1911, 4.9875; raws Dec. 1, 1910, 3.8800 net.								
Refiners left from—								
October receipts					5,331	3.80	Nov. 1	
November purchases					15,506	3.853	Nov. A	
November receipts	119,396	5.127	Nov. A		77,058	3.881	do	
Stock Dec. 1, refiners	119,396				97,895			
Purchases from importers in December	400	4.65	Sale		3,557			
Receipts to refiners in December	67,340				65,980			
Supplies of refiners for December	186,736				167,432			
Meltings by refiners for December	125,000				117,000			
Of which were—								
October receipts					5,331	3.80	Nov. 1	4.55, Dec. 1.
November purchases					15,506	3.853	Nov. A	4.55, Dec. 8.
November receipts	119,396	5.127	Nov. A	5.669	77,058	3.881	do	4.70, Dec. A.
December purchases	400	4.65	Sale	5.635	3,557	4.050	Actual	4.75, Dec. 22.
December receipts	5,204	4.94	Dec. 7	5.635	15,548	3.930	Dec. 1	4.75, Dec. 24.
Stock Jan. 1, refiners	61,736				50,432			
Sales in December, importers to refiners	400				3,557			
Stock Jan. 1, importers	12,190							
Stock Jan. 1, total					50,432			

Table showing refiners' supplies and costs, June to December, 1911.

[Tons, 2,240 pounds. Prices in cents per pound.]

Melted.	1911				1910			
	Amount.	Raw price.	Refined price.	Difference.	Amount.	Raw price.	Refined price.	Difference.
Received, May	32,773	3.86	4.90	1.04	101,701	4.24	5.071	0.831
Purchased, June					1,757	4.260	5.071	.811
Received, June	164,302	3.911	5.125	1.214	102,542	4.234	5.071	.837
Purchased, July	28,640	4.570	5.125	.555				
Received, July	3,285	4.060	5.125	1.075				
July	229,000	3.984	5.093	1.109	206,000	4.237	5.074	.837
Received, June					118,291	4.234	5.128	.894
Received, July	197,178	4.285	5.686	1.401	96,709	4.336	5.128	.792
Purchased, August	24,231	5.070	5.686	.616				
Received, August	15,591	4.61	6.000	1.390				
August	237,000	4.344	5.706	1.362	215,000	4.280	5.128	.848
Received, July					90,710	4.336	5.013	.677
Purchased, August					1,512	4.408	5.000	.592
Received, August	152,000	4.88	6.542	1.662	131,778	4.408	5.000	.592
September	152,000	4.88	6.542	1.662	224,000	4.379	5.005	.626
Received, August	7,486	5.250	6.615	1.365	8,394	4.425	5.000	.575
Purchased, September					24,311	4.263	4.850	.587
Received, September	105,585	5.794	6,584	.790	113,289	4.272	4.808	.636
Purchased, October					22,006	3.901	4.700	.799
Received, October	40,929	5.800	6.566	.766				
October	154,000	5.768	6.579	.811	168,000	4.218	4.809	.591
Purchased, October					5,011	3.833	4.550	.717
Received, October	109,709	5.896	6.117	.221	109,989	3.882	4.550	.668
Received, November	3,291	5.300	5.380	.580				
November	113,000	5.874	6.110	.236	115,000	3.880	4.550	.670
Purchased, November					15,506	3.853	4.550	.697
Received, October					5,331	3.800	4.550	.050
Received, November	119,396	5.127	5.669	.542	77,058	3.881	4.700	.819
Purchased, December	400	4.650	5.635	.985	3,557	4.050	4.750	.700
Received, December	5,204	4.940	5.635	.685	15,548	3.930	4.750	.820
December	125,000	5.117	5.668	.551	117,000	3.885	4.682	.797

Mr. RAKER. The table will give it for each month separate and distinct and make it perfectly plain?

Mr. WILLETT. Yes; I will show you it does, if you wish.

Mr. RAKER. Yes; I would be glad if you would.

Mr. WILLETT. For instance, July 1, 1911, the importers' stock in the ports of the United States was 52,871 tons. The refiners had left over from their May receipts 32,773 tons, the value of which on the 1st of June was $3.86 per 100 pounds, and on the 1st of July they had left over from their June purchases nothing. Left over from June receipts they had 164,302 tons, making their total supplies on the 1st day of July 197,075 tons. Now, this statement shows that those sugars left over from June receipts were valued at $3.91, a little higher than those which were left over from May receipts.

Mr. RAKER. Why did they value those sugars higher, because of the higher price paid for them?

Mr. WILLETT. Yes, sir; because of the advanced price paid for them. This is my estimate of the price they paid for those sugars. That gave them a stock at the 1st of July of 197,075 tons. Now, during the month of July they purchased from importers 28,640 tons, at $4.57 per 100 pounds. There is an advance from the June purchases of over half a cent a pound.

The CHAIRMAN. Mr. Willett, will it disturb you if I interrupt you to ask you about something right at this point?

Mr. WILLETT. Not at all.

The CHAIRMAN. Mr. Fordney has advanced the idea, and he may be right about it—I want to know from you whether he is or not—that the customhouse receipts will show in reference to raw sugar imported during the period of this recent rise that the American Sugar Refining Co. and the various refiners of the country got a considerable advantage because of this recent increase in the price of sugar. Is not this the case, that the only way that could be true is they probably took advantage of the rise so far as the stock they had on hand was concerned? Was that the way of it, or what was the fact as to that?

Mr. WILLETT. Before I am through with this statement you will have that very clearly before you.

Mr. RAKER. These statements you have are intended to cover the point which the chairman has asked you about?

Mr. WILLETT. Yes; it covers that point entirely. You will learn from these statements just what the refiners paid for their sugars, and if you choose to question as to what they sold their refined at, I can give you that, if it does not appear in the statement.

The CHAIRMAN. That is the reason I asked you about it. I was not sure whether it appeared or not.

Mr. WILLETT. After we get through with what they pay for the raw sugar, then if you ask me what they got for the refined I can tell you.

The CHAIRMAN. Very well; suppose you cover that point in your own way before you finish this branch of the matter.

Mr. FORDNEY. Mr. Chairman, if you will permit me, before Mr. Willett explains that matter, I would like to tell you just what I did say. I said that I have a statement in my possession giving the importation of sugar from every country at every port of entry in the United States for the last fiscal year, in months, and for July, August, September, and October of 1911.

Mr. WILLETT. Probably taken from our Statistical, undoubtedly.

Mr. FORDNEY. No.

Mr. WILLETT. There is no other source.

Mr. FORDNEY. I got it here from the Government.

Mr. WILLETT. Oh, yes.

Mr. FORDNEY. And the invoice price or value of each month's importations.

Mr. WILLETT. What is that based on?—the price in the country of export or the price in the United States?

Mr. FORDNEY. The invoice price at which it is entered.

Mr. WILLETT. That is the country of export.

Mr. FORDNEY. I presume whoever sold the sugar sent with it an invoice showing the price he received for it; that is what the State Department informs me.

Mr. WILLETT. The point is whether that is the price received in New York or in Cuba or Java. I am giving you the values in New York.

Mr. FORDNEY. The only difference would be the freight.

Mr. WILLETT. Suppose they were Java sugars and three months on the way, and the market had gone up in the meantime 2 cents?

Mr. FORDNEY. Suppose it was six months on the way; I refer to whatever price the man paid for it here on the contract. The point is he contracted for this sugar long before it was entered at New York at a price much lower than the prevailing price the day it was entered.

The CHAIRMAN. That is the point, exactly.

Mr. WILLETT. I have covered it as well as I can in these papers. That would apply to Java sugars. It would not apply to Cuban sugars.

Mr. MALBY. In other words, the Government reports would have to do with and show only the valuation put upon it by the importer when he paid the duty?

Mr. WILLETT. No; when he shipped the goods.

Mr. MALBY. Oh, no; I beg your pardon, they haven't anything to do with that. They levy a duty upon the value of the goods when they are entered.

Mr. FORDNEY. No; there is a specific duty on sugar.

Mr. WILLETT. There is no ad valorem duty on sugar, and it does not make any difference what the invoice shows.

Mr. MALBY. Yes; that is correct.

Mr. FORDNEY. For instance, suppose a man in Cuba sold sugar on contract in February, to be delivered when they called for it in August or September. The invoice would show the contract price in February, delivered at New York. The point I make is that they were not paying the call prices or the European prices as quoted in October, but were paying the prices they contracted to pay, we will say, in February.

Mr. WILLETT. The actual method of business, not theoretical, is that the refiner buys his sugar, cost and freight, delivered in New York, and that includes the f. o. b. invoice price in Cuba plus the cost of the freight, making it equivalent to the price in New York

The CHAIRMAN. Mr. Willett, let me put the question to you in a little different way. Mr. Fordney's idea is this, that while sugar did go up all over the world, raw and refined, very rapidly in July and August and the early fall, that the American refiners had bought ahead largely; that they had bought under contract for future delivery, and the greater part of the sugar they used in filling their contract was of that character; and when they did fill their contract they took advantage, of course, of the market price for raw at the time they filled the contract. Now, the question is, Do you know whether that is true in point of fact or not?

Mr. WILLETT. No; it is not true in point of fact. Part of it is true and part of it is not. The first part is true as to the purchases of sugar, but the last part is not true, that after the sugar came in they sold it at the higher market price to the consumers of the country. That is not true.

The CHAIRMAN. Why did they not do that?

Mr. FORDNEY. They did sell sugar at that price.

Mr. WILLETT. When they bought a supply of raw sugars 30 days ahead they contracted on their books for enough refined sugar against those purchases. They sold ahead, too. That is the way they carried the business on. There was no time during the six months of June to December when the American Sugar Refining Co. was not sold ahead 30 days against previous purchases.

Mr. FORDNEY. That report I referred to shows there was some sugar imported during that time—I do not remember what month, July, August, September, or October—at a value as low as $1.88, but during that time your Statistical Trade Journal shows refined sugar selling at from 6½ to 7½ cents a pound.

Mr. WILLETT. That price of $1.88 was Philippine sugar, I take it.

Mr. FORDNEY. You may be right, but I do not think it was. I think it was West Indian sugar.

Mr. WILLETT. Sugar subject to 1.685 duty?

Mr. FORDNEY. Yes.

Mr. WILLETT. I cover your point here perhaps a little plainer. Your point is covered in this table. This is the final compilation of those months. This table shows, and agrees with Mr. Fordney's position, that at one time the difference between raw and refined, in the month of July, averaged $1.10.

The CHAIRMAN. That is the refiner's margin, as it is commonly called?

Mr. WILLETT. That is the difference between what the refiner actually paid for the raw sugar, as closely as I can calculate, and the price of refined on the market; not what he got for it, because he did not sell then. He had sold ahead. In the month of August the difference between what the refiner paid on his sugars bought before arrival and the quotation for refined sugars was 1.36 per hundred pounds; and during the month of September that difference increased to 1.60 per hundred pounds. Now the natural presumption would be that the refiner was getting $1.60 per hundred pounds profit. That is your idea, is it not?

Mr. FORDNEY. Yes, sir; the difference between what he paid for the raw, no matter when he bought it or contracted for it, and the price he sold his refined at.

Mr. WILLETT. No; you are wrong; the price of the New York market for refined.

Mr. FORDNEY. I stand corrected; that is what I meant to say. Your quotation on refined sugar.

Mr. WILLETT. Yes. Taking our quotations on refined sugar and taking what he actually paid for his raws, there was a difference of $1.66 in September, but the refiner having sold ahead constantly during those months against his purchases of raw, took no more than the usual difference of parity between raw and refined.

The CHAIRMAN. In other words, he did not take it because he couldn't. He had contracted short, too.

Mr. WILLETT. He was of the same opinion that these sugar men were. Nobody saw this rise coming all over the world. It came out of a clear sky, and nobody was prepared for it. Nobody kept back their sugars to get their profit.

Mr. FORDNEY. But, Mr. Willett, taking these importations for July, August, September, and October, compared with the consumption of sugar during that time, the importations are only about half the amount of consumption?

Mr. WILLETT. Yes; that is shown here. On the first day of any month they did not have enough sugar for their meltings that month.

Mr. FORDNEY. For instance, take the last week in August, the amount of importation during that week and the amount of consumption during that week and see how they compare. The evidence I get is they had a large amount of sugar on hand and took advantage of the market. Mr. Willett, I do not want to betray a confidence, but I will say this much, a gentleman connected with one of the firms stated that one of those concerns could have sold out their raws and made $7,000,000, and would not do it. That came to me very straight.

Mr. WILLETT. That is a moonshine story.

Mr. FORDNEY. It came from a man connected with one of the concerns.

Mr. WILLETT. I am beginning to think I do not know anything about this business.

The CHAIRMAN. You think that is utterly unreasonable?

Mr. WILLETT. Yes. I must hunt up some of these people who know something about this business.

Mr. FORDNEY. As I understand it, the conditions surrounding the situation during this year was an inducement not to bleed for all the blood you could get?

Mr. WILLETT. Let me instance one refiner, the Warner Co. The Warner Co. sold so many sugars ahead, booked so many orders ahead, at 5 cents a pound, or close to it, that they were unable to sell any sugars during the latter part of those months and were actually delivering refined sugar at a loss on their cost of raws—a heavy loss. Against sales made at 5 cents for refined they had to buy raws at over 5 cents.

The CHAIRMAN. They had not bought ahead as fast as they had sold ahead?

Mr. WILLETT. No, sir.

Mr. FORDNEY. I was informed they went out and purchased other sugars at a loss of a cent a pound to make good their contract.

Mr. WILLETT. Yes; they bought back contracts which they had sold at 5 cents at a cent a pound loss, too. That was Warner's position.

The CHAIRMAN. All those things happen in accordance with the laws of trade which are fixed and certain. For instance, a man does not sell at a loss unless he is under a contract which makes him do it, and the reason he does not take advantage of a rise in the market is because he is under contract?

Mr. WILLETT. It is the same old story, foresight first is backsight last.

Mr. FORDNEY. We can not get away from this fact, however, that the very minute our domestic crop came on the market down went sugar a cent and a half a pound.

The CHAIRMAN. Now, why?

Mr. WILLETT. I answered that in the other hearing.

The CHAIRMAN. Would you mind repeating it?

Mr. FORDNEY. Mr. Willett answered that question this morning.

The CHAIRMAN. Well, I do not want to duplicate.

Mr. FORDNEY. He said the domestic crop forced the price down.

Mr. WILLETT. But in answer to Mr. Fordney's suggestion as to what he has obtained from the Government, that these refiners had such an enormous amount of sugar during all these months, the facts were otherwise, as taken from our books, and we keep tab on every pound of sugar that arrives, and the Government very kindly favors us with all the customhouse returns throughout the United States, so that our records of import sugars are exactly like the Government's, or they ought to be, as they are made up from Government returns.

Mr. FORDNEY. I will take the matter up again with them to see where we differ, if we do differ. I am not disputing your records at all.

Mr. WILLETT. All our figures of imports come from the Government directly.

The CHAIRMAN. Mr. Willett, what was your statement about the proposition that the beet sugar coming on the market lowered the price of sugar? Did it have that effect?

Mr. WILLETT. This last year, 1911?

The CHAIRMAN. Yes, sir. Were the beet-sugar people sold ahead or not, or do you know?

Mr. WILLETT. All the beet-sugar people except Michigan were sold ahead. Mr. Fordney says Michigan was not sold ahead.

Mr. FORDNEY. Thirty days and 45 days, I was informed, were the furthest sales ahead.

The CHAIRMAN. In other words, they were sold ahead to that extent?

Mr. FORDNEY. All sugar is sold on 30 days' delivery.

The CHAIRMAN. My idea in having this matter repeated, if it is repetition, was to understand, Mr. Willett, who is probably the greatest living American authority on sugar prices, whether or not in point of fact the market and trade reports seemed to indicate that the beet-sugar people were sold ahead nor not. You say they were sold ahead?

Mr. WILLETT. They were sold ahead.

Mr. FORDNEY. How far did they sell ahead?

Mr. WILLETT. From 30 to 60 days.

Mr. RAKER. If that is a fact can not Mr. Willett give us his view, from his thorough examination and knowledge of the matter, what was the prime inducement that brought down the price of sugar?

Mr. WILLETT. It was the coming on to the market of the American beet-sugar crop; but not put on the market by the refiners but by the jobbers who had bought it at the lower refined price and sold it at the market price. The jobbers made the money and the beet-sugar men did not.

Mr. FORDNEY. You say they were sold ahead from 30 to 60 days. The beet sugar came on the market in Michigan in October?

Mr. WILLETT. Yes, sir.

Mr. FORDNEY. The highest price it reached was in August. Why should they sell ahead at a cent and a half or 2 cents below the market price of August, unless they felt pretty sure the market was going to drop, and they were just as well aware of the world's supply of sugar as anyone else.

Mr. WILLETT. It was sold two months previous to October.

Mr. FORDNEY. Our crop came on the market on the 12th of October.

Mr. WILLETT. I do not know about your crop.

Mr. FORDNEY. And that being true, if they were sold ahead 60 days they then would have sold in the middle of August, when very high prices were prevailing, and they knew at that time as well as they know now what the condition of this year's crop was going to be.

Mr. WILLETT. My records show they sold that sugar between 5 and 6 cents per pound, and if they sold it between 5 and 6 cents then they must have made their contracts before the 1st day of August.

Mr. FORDNEY. Our men say the longest contract was 45 days, and only a few sales at that.

Mr. WILLETT. They might have made contracts in July.

Mr. FORDNEY. No; they did not grind out until the middle of October, and they could not make delivery before that.

Mr. WILLETT. The western factories sold sugar long before they had a pound to deliver.

Mr. FORDNEY. I am speaking of Michigan.

Mr. WILLETT. I know nothing about the Michigan people. You know more about them than I do.

Mr. FORDNEY. I know nothing about the western people at all.

Mr. WILLETT. I have records of Michigan, just like the other States; but I do not like to make any statement about them, because you know about certain of the factories in Michigan; but there were some factories in Michigan that did the same thing the western factories did; but they may not have been your factories.

Mr. FORDNEY. I do not know. I only have it from a man whom I believe to be truthful that the Michigan Sugar Co. and the St. Louis and the Owosso Sugar Co.——

Mr. WILLETT (interposing). Then there was the German American Co., which is independent, and they might have sold ahead.

Mr. FORDNEY. They may have sold ahead, for all I know; but these three concerns are very large concerns, one of them having a large factory with a slicing capacity of 1,200 tons a day, the St. Louis Co. owning 2 factories, and the Michigan Sugar Co. owning 6 factories, making 9 out of the 17 factories in the State; and a gentleman connected with those concerns told me the longest sales they had made ahead were 45 days, and those contracts were only for a large quantity; that the heft of their sales were 30 days in advance.

Mr. WILLETT. The prices which you reported before when I was here go to show that fact, because otherwise if they were selling in September they would have got $6.54 a hundred instead of $5.54, which you reported they got.

Mr. FORDNEY. We have it in the record here that out of nearly 900 cars less than 50 cars were sold at above $5.55 up to the 30th of November.

Mr. WILLETT. There was no New York quotation for granulated sugar below 6 cents after the 1st day of August.

Mr. FORDNEY. They are selling yet in our State at $5.55. They started in at $5.55 and kept it up.

Mr. WILLETT. From 6 cents the market advanced to 6.615. During all that advance from 6 cents to 6.615 your Michigan factories were selling at 5½ cents and upward.

Mr. FORDNEY. The 12th of October was the first sugar turned out in the State and was sold at 5.55.

Mr. WILLETT. The price at that time was 6.11.

Mr. FORDNEY. In New York.

Mr. WILLETT. In New York it was $6.11 per 100 pounds.

Mr. FORDNEY. Whether they were sold ahead or were not sold ahead, the fact is that the domestic crop, no matter when it was sold, went to the consumer at 5.55, and brought down the price of granulated sugar in the United States.

The CHAIRMAN. And they could have bought the foreign crop in Java if they had bought ahead, and it would have had the same effect?

Mr. WILLETT. There is no question whatever, Mr. Chairman, that the coming on to the market in October of the Michigan sugars and other domestic sugars dropped the price from 6.57 in October down to 6.11 in November, and December 5.63.

The CHAIRMAN. And if the same amount of sugar had come in from Java or from Cuba or any other part of the world that had been bought on future delivery at a cheaper price, it would have had the same effect on the market, would it not?

Mr. WILLETT. I do not think it would at all.

The CHAIRMAN. Why not?

Mr. WILLETT. In the first place, not speaking theoretically but actually, the cost of Java sugars at 1.685 duty was so far above the value of the domestic because of demand elsewhere, principally in England, that they could hardly have been bought at a competitive price.

The CHAIRMAN. I am just illustrating the principle.

Mr. WILLETT. Theoretically you are right, but practically you are wrong.

The CHAIRMAN. Of course there may have been practical reasons why they could not have bought it or brought it in.

Mr. WILLETT. I like to deal in facts rather than theories, if I can.

The CHAIRMAN. I do not like to have reasons given that are utterly unsound.

Mr. WILLETT. That is right.

The CHAIRMAN. As a matter of fact, it was not because the sugar was raised in this country?

Mr. WILLETT. If you will change that and say, instead of Java, if Cuba had had 500,000 tons more sugar to send us, that would have caused the same result, exactly, because that is one of the points from which we could have gotten sugars, but Java is not a point from which we are accustomed to get sugars.

The CHAIRMAN. I will have to change my ideas of common sense if it is not true that the fact that this sugar was raised in the United States was not what brought the market down, but the fact that it was sold in the United States.

Mr. WILLETT. Yes; and we might go a little further and say if we had received 224,000 tons of sugar from Cuba and our domestic possessions we never would have had these high prices at all in the United States.

Mr. MALBY. And to go a little further, carrying out the chairman's suggestion, there was one other reason why the price went down, and that was that we did actually have the sugar, and we did not actually have any other. We did actually have the beet sugar here, and we did not have any other.

Mr. WILLETT. That is another point.

Mr. MALBY. So that the practical fact is that the beet sugar was here and was sold at a price which brought the prices down. Now, I rather agree with the chairman that if we had had other sugar it might have produced the same effect, but the value of the inquiry does not seem very important because we did not have it.

The CHAIRMAN. We could have gotten it, possibly.

Mr. MALBY. The witness says we could not because they did not have it to sell at that price.

Mr. WILLETT. In other words, if the beet-sugar crop matured in June or July instead of October, that would have filled the gap, or if Cuba had had that 200,000 tons.

Mr. RAKER. If two months ahead these importers had bought sugar on a prior contract from Cuba which was cheap sugar and had it to bring in on the market at that time just as the beet sugar came in, would it not have had the same effect upon the market as the beet sugar coming in had if it had been contracted two months in advance?

Mr. WILLETT. Yes; if they had bought enough of it.

Mr. RAKER. I am assuming that.

Mr. WILLETT. But the fact is they did not buy enough.

Mr. RAKER. But I am assuming they had bought enough.

Mr. WILLETT. Yes.

Mr. RAKER. And having the sugar, having bought it in advance at a lower price, it of necessity would have reduced the price and brought the market down?

Mr. WILLETT. Yes.

Mr. RAKER. And it did not make any difference where the sugar came from or the kind of sugar, if it was bought in advance at a low price, when sugar was high, by reason of having this sugar bought at a low price, putting it on the market would bring the high prices down; is not that right?

Mr. WILLETT. That is right.

Mr. HINDS. Mr. Willett, was the price at which the suger had been contracted for the controlling factor? Was not the fact that there was such a supply of sugar available for the country the main factor and not the contract price?

Mr. WILLETT. I do not quite understand that.

Mr. HINDS. When the sugar prices came down and when the beet sugar went onto the market, was not the fact that there were 500,000 tons of beet sugar coming into our market the dominant factor in price, and not the price at which that sugar had been contracted for earlier?

Mr. WILLETT. Of course.

Mr. HINDS. In other words, the contract price is a mere arrangement of men that the supply of the product may knock into a cocked hat, to use a modern expression?

Mr. WILLETT. When supplies are short and any new crop comes onto the market, prices always go down.

Mr. HINDS. And if there had been a million tons instead of 500,000 tons of beet sugar, might not the prices have even gone below the contract prices?

Mr. WILLETT. Not if that million tons did not come in until October and the shortage was in September. The shortage, understand, was from July to September, and there was no crop in the world that could meet that shortage at prices available. When it came in in October, then there was plenty of sugar available, and down went the price.

Mr. HINDS. But did the price go down before the sugar was actually on the market?

Mr. WILLETT. No, sir; not to any extent.

Mr. HINDS. Not until the actual sugar was put on the market?

Mr. WILLETT. Not until the sugar was put on the market by the jobbers who had bought it.

Mr. HINDS. This fact of contracting at a lower price did not of itself, irrespective of the material presence of the sugar, have any lowering effect on prices?

Mr. WILLETT. Except to the extent that the jobber who bought cheap wanted to realize his profit before the market went down.

Mr. HINDS. And clean out his own stock?

Mr. WILLETT. Resell the stock he had contracted for with the factories.

Mr. HINDS. So, to some extent, coming events cast their shadows before them?

Mr. WILLETT. To some extent; and yet a jobber could not deliver his sugar until he got it.

Mr. FORDNEY. Mr. Willett, on October 12, when Michigan sugar came on the market—October 12 was the first day's grind in the State, if I remember correctly—from Willett & Gray's report refined sugar was quoted in New York that day at $6.75 by the American Sugar Refining Co., $7.25 by the Federal Sugar Co., and $7.50 by Arbuckle's.

Mr. WILLETT. They are the gross prices without the discount.

Mr. FORDNEY. Yes; without the discount of 2 per cent.

Mr. WILLETT. The American Sugar Co.'s price was 6.615; Arbuckle's 7.35.

Mr. FORDNEY. That is, after taking off the discount?

Mr. WILLETT. Yes.

Mr. FORDNEY. Now, the reason for those high prices at that time was because the coming crop of 1911 and 1912 was short?

Mr. WILLETT. Oh, no. The reason was there was no supply here to be sold.

Mr. FORDNEY. Were they not anticipating a short crop? The papers were full of that, at any rate.

Mr. WILLETT. The whole rise of the year was because of the expected short crops of Europe.

Mr. FORDNEY. Now, between the 1st or 12th of October and the 20th of November nothing had transpired to change in the mind of any man what the world's supply of sugar was, outside of that produced in the United States, and we knew what it was here; there was no particular change as to the world's supply of sugar?

Mr. WILLETT. Oh, yes.

The CHAIRMAN. That is exactly the point we want to get at.

Mr. WILLETT. Oh, yes. The European speculator had found out, when he ran his sugars up to 19 shillings at Hamburg, the highest point reached there, soon after that——

Mr. FORDNEY (interposing). When was that, Mr. Willett?

Mr. WILLETT. That was when we were at 6.61, our highest point.

Mr. FORDNEY. October 12?

Mr. WILLETT. Along in September or October. A little earlier than October, late in September—September 11 to October 23.

Mr. FORDNEY. There was practically nothing happened——

The CHAIRMAN (interposing). Allow him to finish his statement, please.

Mr. FORDNEY. Pardon me.

The CHAIRMAN. You say the European speculator discovered something at that time?

Mr. WILLETT. Mr. Licht, the great expert on beet sugars, was inclined to change his estimates of the coming beet crop, and to think there was not going to be as much shortage——

The CHAIRMAN (interposing). In other words, the shortage had been overestimated?

Mr. WILLETT. Yes; the shortage had been overestimated; and also at that time he discovered the Brussels convention was inclined to admit three or four hundred thousand tons of sugar from Russia to eke out the supply. Those two things combined changed the speculative situation in Europe, so that the prices declined rapidly from 19 shillings to 15 shillings and something.

Mr. FORDNEY. But as to Cuba, where we get the heft of our sugars, there was no change?

Mr. WILLETT. Cuba did not enter into conditions in that month.

Mr. FORDNEY. I mean the prospective crop for us was to come from Cuba?

Mr. WILLETT. We were not calculating on the Cuban crop until November or December. The Cuban crop at that time was non est, or not considered.

Mr. FORDNEY. Was this mistake discovered just at the time our beet sugar came onto the market in this country? Was the mistake in the world's supply discovered just at that time?

Mr. WILLETT. A little previous to that time.

Mr. FORDNEY. But, Mr. Willett, immediately after our beet sugar came onto the market in October down went the price of sugar to about 5.75.

Mr. WILLETT. That was because of the coming on of the beet crop filling up the gap of known supply.

Mr. FORDNEY. That is it exactly. That is what I wanted to know.

Mr. WILLETT. These statements show that. At each month of the year, beginning with the several months, the refiner did not have sufficient supplies of sugar on the first day of the month to meet his requirements for that month.

Mr. RAKER. Mr. Chairman, the witness has a statement as to when these various sugar crops come in, and I would like to have it put in the record.

Mr. WILLETT. This is right up to date, January 4, 1912, and shows that in the United States the Louisiana crop begins in September, Texas in September; the crop in Porto Rico begins in January, the Hawaiian Islands in November.

The table is as follows:

Sugar crops of the world.

[Willett & Gray's estimates of cane crops, Jan. 4, 1912. Figures include local consumption of home production wherever known.]

	Crop begins.	1911-12	1910-11	1909-10
		Tons.	*Tons.*	*Tons.*
United States:				
Louisiana	September	300,000	300,000	325,000
Texas	do	8,000	11,000	10,000
Porto Rico	January	350,000	295,000	308,000
Hawaiian Islands	November	500,000	506,096	402,613
Cuba, crop	December	1,800,000	1,483,451	1,804,349
British West Indies:				
Trinidad, exports	January	40,000	36,000	44,139
Barbados, exports	do	40,000	35,000	36,389
Jamaica, exports	do	20,000	22,000	12,000
Antigua and St. Kitts	do	18,000	18,000	20,000
French West Indies:				
Martinique, exports	do	40,000	35,438	39,950
Guadeloupe	do	40,000	39,000	48,000
Danish West Indies: St. Croix	do	15,000	15,000	15,000
San Domingo and Haiti	do	100,000	89,979	93,003
Lesser Antilles, not named above	do	8,000	6,000	6,000
Mexico, crop	December	140,000	120,000	147,905
Central America	January	22,000	21,000	19,161
South America:				
Demerara, exports	October and May	110,000	108,297	101,843
Surinam, crop	October	13,000	13,000	12,055
Venezuela	do	3,000	3,000	3,000
Peru, crop	do	150,000	150,000	150,000
Argentina, crop	June	170,000	147,678	123,674
Brazil, crop	October	260,000	287,000	253,000
Total in America		4,147,000	3,741,939	4,035,081
Asia:				
British India, crop (consumed locally)	December	2,100,000	2,226,400	2,127,100
Java, crop	May	1,395,000	1,229,100	1,200,618
Formosa, Japan, crop	November	220,000	267,000	205,000
Philippine Islands, exports	December	225,000	205,000	116,114
China (consumption large, mostly imported).				
Total in Asia		3,940,000	3,927,500	3,648,832
Australia and Fiji:				
Queensland	June	180,000	210,756	134,584
New South Wales	do	17,000	18,828	14,750
Fiji Islands, exports	do	75,000	69,000	68,900
Total in Australia and Polynesia		272,000	298,584	218,234
Africa:				
Egypt, crop (consumed locally)	January	55,000	55,000	52,525
Mozambique, crop	do	40,000	26,000	15,000
Mauritius, crop	August	160,000	217,757	244,597
Reunion, exports	September	40,000	43,128	39,319
Natal, crop	May	90,000	82,000	66,000
Total in Africa		385,000	423,885	417,441
Europe: Spain	December	21,000	21,000	20,300
Total cane sugar crops (W. & G.)		8,765,000	8,412,908	8,339,888
Europe: Beet-sugar crops (F. O. Licht)	September	6,250,000	8,105,126	6,136,911
United States: Beet-sugar crops (W. & G.)	July and October	540,000	455,220	450,595
Grand total cane and beet sugar		15,555,000	16,973,254	14,927,394
Estimated decrease in the world's production		1,418,254		

Mr. RAKER. Mr. Willett, right in this same connection, are the sugar people in the habit of preparing a statement in advance which will show the prospective crop for the coming year?

Mr. WILLETT. They do not, but we do.

Mr. RAKER. And is that published?

Mr. WILLETT. Yes; the prospects for 1911 and 1912 are stated in these papers.

Mr. RAKER. And that has been used and is used to some extent to sort of figure on the price, is it?

Mr. WILLETT. Yes; and it is very funny, because it shows you how far Willett & Gray can get astray sometimes on these estimates of future supplies depending largely on crop weather.

Mr. RAKER. Mr. Willett, ought there not to be some method or some means by which that could be controlled by law, this matter of preparing statements of crops, and let it apply to sugar as well as to other crops upon which the people have to rely? These statements go broadcast, and there is no denial and there is no way to know what it will really be, and unintentionally it may work a hardship a great many times upon the consumer. Could you suggest any method by which that could be regulated?

Mr. WILLETT. The Government of Russia does that.

Mr. RAKER. What do you think about that?

Mr. WILLETT. When you get to Russia you will find out all about it.

Mr. RAKER. I do not know whether they will permit me to come over there now.

Mr. WILLETT. I will tell you, Mr. Raker, All European Governments—France, Great Britain, Belgium, Germany—have their methods of keeping tab on the stocks, production, exports, etc., of sugar, but it is not like our Government. We are more up to date. Those Governments are always 30 or 60 days, or any amount of time, behind in the data. We, you see, with our statistics of the United States, are right up to date every moment, while the European countries are always 30 days behind, at least.

Mr. RAKER. But would it not be a wise thing if there was provision by which you could get from the department, coming out each week, the amount of sugar actually on hand in the various refineries and factories, and then also a statement from the Government as to the condition of the crops, and some regulation by which we could know the actual conditions; and then the public would be in a position to deal intelligently. Do you not think we could get some remedy for that which would be better than it is now?

Mr. WILLETT. I do not think so, no. I do not think anything could be better than what I am giving you. It is up to date in every respect, and what you speak about the Government doing the Government already does. They give us the figures and we compile them. The only difference would be the Government would do the work instead of us.

The CHAIRMAN. Mr. Raker's idea is, why should the Government employ your concern?

Mr. WILLETT. They are kind enough to give us the figures, and they accept our figures. We have just given them these January, 1912, figures for their annual statement. We reciprocate. If we want something sometimes from the Government and we ask for it, they very kindly give it to us, and if they want some information they ask us for it and we give it to them.

Mr. RAKER. What I mean——

Mr. WILLETT (interposing). I know what you mean. You will find it in Russia. If you want to adopt the Russian system, you could do it.

Mr. RAKER. I am asking for your opinion.

Mr. WILLETT. In fact, the Russian Government does everything. For instance, on the 1st day of September of each year the Government of Russia sets down exactly—the first thing they set down is how many sugars shall be manufactured into refined by each factory in Russia. They also dictate how many tons of sugar shall be manufactured by those refineries for the consumption of Russia. They also dictate how many tons of sugar shall be manufactured above what they think will be required for consumption, to be held as a reserve. In case the consumption increases they allow a certain part of that reserve to go into consumption. If the consumption of the country decreases so that those reserves are not required, they oblige the people to send them out of the country on export. They allow each factory to produce as much sugar as it pleases up to its capacity, but the surplus which every factory produces above what the Government specifies, if it goes into consumption, has to pay two taxes, 4.98 a hundred pounds including the ordinary tax of 2.49. Now, there are lots of other things about their production of sugar which you will notice when I get to that table, regulating the production, consumption, and export. Now as to prices, they specify the limit of price at which sugars can be sold in Russia. They fix a limit of price for granulated sugar at the ports of Kief and Odessa. If granulated sugar rises one-fourth of a cent a pound above the Government price at Kief, then the Government turns on to the market a sufficient portion of this reserve stock to bring the price back to where it was before. So that the prices in Russia to the consumer can never advance above a certain price. They have a duty on sugar in Russia, I think it is $5 and something per hundred pounds, but if the country is running short of supply, the Government temporarily reduces that duty from $5.50 to $2.89, as they did recently, in order to let refined sugars into Russia from other countries, to bring down the price again. From A to Z the Government and the sugar people run hand in hand, and the Government controls it.

Mr. HINDS. On the other hand, do the people of Russia get sugar any cheaper than we do?

Mr. WILLETT. Oh, yes. While we were paying 6½ cents for sugar in this country, the people of Russia were getting it at 5 cents and something.

Mr. HINDS. But I mean year in and year out, do the people of Russia get sugar any cheaper than we do?

Mr. WILLETT. I do not think they do, because their tax is 2.49.

Mr. RAKER. Of course, that tax goes toward maintaining the Government?

Mr. WILLETT. Yes,; it is an internal-revenue tax.

Mr. RAKER. And that situation practically eliminates any monopoly in the sugar business?

Mr. WILLETT. Yes; it eliminates any monopoly. They go so far as to limit the number of beet-sugar factories. They can not be located within certain distances of each other in Russia, and the transportation is all regulated.

Mr. FORDNEY. That eliminates competition among those factories, does it not?

Mr. WILLETT. Yes. Then there is another thing which came up lately, when some of the factories in Russia which had been making raw sugars arranged their machinery so as to make granulated sugar directly from the juice, just as we do in this country, the Government put a stop to that, or fixed regulations so they could not make any profit out of it any more than the other people were making.

Mr. RAKER. Why does not Russia allow her factories to run at full capacity and export more?

Mr. WILLETT. For the simple reason she is not free to export. The Brussels convention limits her export to all convention countries of Europe to 200,000 tons, and their exports can only go to Finland and the other nonconvention countries, and those countries do not want as much sugar as Russia could give them.

Mr. RAKER. What is the object of that convention?

Mr. WILLETT. The Brussels convention?

Mr. RAKER. I mean the object of that restriction, to keep the price of sugar from going too low in Europe?

Mr. WILLETT. No; it does not have that effect. The object of the Brussels convention was to do away with bounties, and they have done away with bounties. No country that gives a bounty on sugar can send a pound of sugar into a convention country without paying a countervailing duty. Russia can not export into the United States.

Mr. FORDNEY. Russia pays a bounty, does she not?

Mr. WILLETT. They interpret that Russia pays a bounty, but Russia says they do not. The United States countervails against a bounty of 72 cents in Russia, while Great Britain says the Russian bounty is 23 cents a hundred pounds. The Brussels convention does not specify at all what the bounty is. It is not a bounty; it is an advantage which the exporter gets if he sends his sugar abroad. For instance, following out what I have said about the division of the production of sugar in Russia, and the amount set apart for export, now all these internal-revenue taxes in Russia are paid at certain dates, June, September, and January or December, so that the refined sugar which is on hand in the factory on the 1st of June has to pay the Government tax on that date. The Government gets its tax ahead of its consumption. Now the amount which is allowed for export has already paid a tax. When a request is made to export a portion of that sugar, the Government releases it at the port of exportation and gives an export certificate, that so many tons of sugar have gone out of the country, which have paid a tax of $2.49. Now the exporter can not go to the Government and get that $2.49 back in money, but out of this surplus sugar which he has made, on which he has to pay two taxes if it goes into consumption, with this permit he can put that into consumption without paying but a single tax on it. Now those certificates have a market value. There is another certificate besides that which is a permit certificate which applies directly to the export of these 200,000 tons to convention countries. Each factory has its pro rata and receives a certificate that it is allowed to export to convention countries so many tons. Now, these factories pool those certificates, and the manager of the pool puts the certificates on the market. Sometimes they are worth 23 cents a hundred pounds, sometimes they are worth 72 cents a hundred pounds, and just recently they drew very high prices. They were worth $1.14 a hundred. Now, that 23 cents, or $1.14, is interpreted as a bounty. At the time we countervailed the certificates were worth 72 cents. To-day they are worth 79 cents, I think.

Mr. HINDS. We still countervail, do we?

Mr. WILLETT. We still countervail, and to be exact we should countervail at 79 cents instead of 72 cents. Great Britain said they were paying a bounty of 23 cents, but then Great Britain does not countervail at all. They simply exclude sugars that pay a bounty. No sugar can go into the United Kingdom that pays a bounty at any rate of duty. It is excluded.

Mr. HINDS. Then, Mr. Willett, the world's price for sugar is not a supply and demand price entirely, is it?

Mr. WILLETT. What reference has that to Russia?

Mr. HINDS. With all these arrangements of bounty and these other arrangements, it results that the supply and demand of sugar——

Mr. WILLETT (interposing). You mean it is not free to seek a proper level?

Mr. HINDS. Yes.

Mr. WILLETT. No; it is not free throughout the world to seek a proper level of price.

Mr. HINDS. And the world price is an artificial price?

Mr. WILLETT. To the extent that the trade of the world is not free and open and clear, and it is subject to bounties and restrictions and conditions. What we want to do is to get independent of all that, and we can do it.

Mr. HINDS. Suppose we increase considerably in the Philippines and Cuba increases considerably and the beet-sugar supply in this country doubles, will not that make a revolution in sugar?

Mr. WILLETT. Most decidedly. That is what I say, increase the Cuban, Porto Rican, Hawaiian, Philippine, and domestic cane and beet sugar industry to a point above our requirements for consumption up to 500,000 tons, so that if Cuba should give out some year and not produce much sugar, we would still have enough for our consumption. Then we would be indipendent of the world and we would make our own (world's) price.

Mr. HINDS. And what ought that price to be in the United States?

Mr. WILLETT. That price, after equalizing the production to consumption, will depend upon the competition between the different interests—between Cuba, Porto Rico, Hawaii, and the domestic beet and cane industry. They will all be working to get our market, and the consumer then will get the advantage.

Mr. HINDS. And probably we would get the cheapest sugar on earth?

Mr. WILLETT. We would get the cheapest sugar on earth under those conditions. There is no doubt about that.

Mr. HINDS. And is that situation reasonably in sight, do you think?

Mr. WILLETT. We came within 74,000 tons of it in 1910, and this year, according to the outlook of the Cuban crop at the present moment, we will come—I should say that we might meet it, provided that the shortage in Europe does not infringe upon our Cuban reserve. Already the United Kingdom has bought 140,000 tons away from our supply in Cuba, but they are reselling it or trying to.

The CHAIRMAN. While that situation would be ideal and I thoroughly agree with you, yet its ideal beauty is somewhat affected, so far as the consumer is concerned, by whatever duty we lay against Cuban sugar, is it not?

Mr. WILLETT. Not as long as you make the Cuban sugar duty lower than you make the foreign sugars.

The CHAIRMAN. But this is the effect of that, is it not, that whatever you lay the Cuban duty at, the Hawaiian, the Porto Rican, the beet-sugar men in the West, and the cane-sugar men in the South all levy that tax on the consumer?

Mr. WILLETT. The prices of all of them go to that level. When we get to Great Britain, I will show you how you can give our people cheap sugar. There is a great deal of talk about the people of Great Britain getting their sugar cheaper than the rest of the world; but if you will change our system of taxing sugar in the United States, you can give our consumers sugar at the same price the people of the United Kingdom get sugar, and at the same time get $50,000,000 revenue, the same as you do now, and, furthermore, you will increase your revenue every year as consumption increases, instead of decreasing it as consumption increases.

The CHAIRMAN. Have you already explained the method the sugar refiners adopted or used last year in July and August and September and October and November in selling their product?

Mr. WILLETT. No, sir.

The CHAIRMAN. I would like to have you explain that, following the table you have already introduced.

Mr. WILLETT. I have touched upon that informally in this discussion.

The CHAIRMAN. Could you not give us that information just at this place?

Mr. WILLETT. I think I have covered that pretty well, have I not, by saying these tables will show that the refiners never at any time from June to October had more than a supply of 30 days of raw sugar, and they were sold ahead that much on their refined. Consequently, the level of difference between raw and refined did not vary in practice, as is shown by the variations in the quotations.

I was asked on page 3103 to give the Louisiana contract. That was given in Table No. 13. I do not seem to have it before me at the moment, unless it has already gone in the evidence; but at any rate I covered that point fully in my former hearing, and what I said then covers that matter.

On page 3113 I was asked about Prinsen-Geerligs. Mr. Palmer claimed that Prinsen-Geerligs made the statement to him that at 1¼ cents per pound Java can make 40 per cent profit. I said that that was an absurd statement. I will show you that Mr. Palmer was mistaken, and that he did not understand German. Mr. Prinsen-Geerligs is a great sugar man who prints books, and has printed three volumes of sugar statistics, and one volume is on the production of sugar on the island of Java. I have those books in my office. They are in Dutch, so I did not bring them down, but I translated them far enough to show you he was mistaken.

The CHAIRMAN. I find on page 2797 of the record this language in extenso, which I quote from. Mr. Palmer says:

> I am quoting from the notes which I made after my interview and which notes have been passed upon by Mr. Geerligs as being correct.

Mr. MALBY. What is your statement about it, Mr. Willett?

Mr. WILLETT. My statement is that Mr. Prinsen-Geerligs's book states—and he gives the details of the cost of refining sugar in Java as applied to three of the most prominent factories in Java, and ends by saying—that the average cost of manufacture of sugars in Java, according to these reports from these three large factories, is $1.49 a hundred.

Mr. FORDNEY. What grade of sugar, refined or raw?

Mr. WILLETT. They do not make any refined sugars in Java. It is semirefined. In India they call it refined sugar.

The CHAIRMAN. About 96°.

Mr. WILLETT. 98½ or 99. Rub out your number 16 and they would be asking whether that is refined or raw sugar.

Mr. HINDS. What kind of labor do they employ in Java in the production of sugar? What are the conditions of its production?

Mr. WILLETT. The natives do the producing of sugar. The production of sugar is done under the direction of the Dutch Government.

Mr. HINDS. Is it free labor, semicontract, or slave?

Mr. WILLETT. I think it is free labor. The Dutch Government controls the labor. The natives have a native prince, but the native prince is subject to the Dutch Government at home.

Mr. FORDNEY. Is it peonage?

Mr. WILLETT. Virtually so, I should think. You can not do anything on the island of Java unless you get the consent of the Government. They tax anybody and everybody.

Mr. HINDS. While they are doing all those things, do you suppose they keep their hands off entirely from the day's work of the native, and that he is under some peonage system?

Mr. WILLETT. I do not think he is. A young man from our office went to Java and lived there a number of years, and I never heard anything of that kind from him.

Mr. HINDS. The reason I ask is, such systems are common in that latitude, and I had the impression there was something of that sort in Java.

Mr. WILLETT. I do not think so.

Mr. MALBY. We have had a good many references in our hearings to Java, one way and another, but the fact about the business is that Java has probably reached its limit of production, has it not?

Mr. WILLETT. Oh, no; not at all.

Mr. MALBY. I supposed it had.

Mr. WILLETT. No; it increased 100,000 tons last year, I think.

Mr. MALBY. I thought we had had some testimony to the effect that Java had reached its limit.

Mr. WILLETT. Oh, no. I will tell you what it is doing—it is turning its production into these high-grade white sugars more than ever. It is producing two or three hundred thousand tons of these 99-test sugars which are supposed to come in here as raw sugars if you eliminate the Dutch standard.

The CHAIRMAN. And it would cheapen sugar a good deal to do that?

Mr. WILLETT. It would not under the present duty.

The CHAIRMAN. I mean to eliminate the Dutch standard and let those sugars come in?

Mr. WILLETT. No; it would not. I stated the other day it would not make a difference of over a quarter of a cent a pound. I have the calculation here, which I will put in later, that with our present duty those sugars would be about 17 cents a hundred pounds less than the price of granulated sugar. I take the consul's report, and add the cost, freight, and duties, and it is 19 cents less than the price of granulated in New York at the same time. At the present date, if you eliminate the Dutch standard and pay the duty scale up to 99, the difference between New York granulated and that Java sugar is 26 cents a hundred pounds.

The CHAIRMAN. That would be about a quarter of a cent a pound?

Mr. WILLETT. The consumers will not buy that sugar at that difference. The manufacturers might; probably would.

Mr. MALBY. If they can manufacture that sugar so cheap in Java and there is such a tremendous demand for it, I do not see why they do not do it.

Mr. WILLETT. They do do it. I say they have increased very much.

Mr. MALBY. But these prices have been pretty good here for several years, and they could get into Great Britain without paying much, if any, duty.

Mr. WILLETT. That is where it goes—to Great Britain. Great Britain relies on Java for its sugar supply, largely.

Mr. MALBY. They could get in here in this country if they can manufacture so cheaply.

Mr. WILLETT. They can not come in here with our present rate of duty.

Mr. MALBY. If they can manufacture for about a cent a pound, they could afford to pay that duty.

Mr. WILLETT. They can not do that. To go back to that point, Mr. Prinsen-Geerligs, in his book, says that the cost of producing sugars in the island of Java is 1.49.

The CHAIRMAN. Do you know what the date of that book is?

Mr. WILLETT. It is a recent publication.

The CHAIRMAN. Can you give us the date it was printed?

Mr. WILLETT. It is volume 4 of a series of handbooks of Java, by Prinsen-Geerligs, published in the service of the sugar culture and sugar factories of Java, and on page 145 are given the costs of production by a number of Java factories. This gives an average cost of about 5 florins a pound, or $1.49 per hundred pounds. The date does not seem to be given.

The CHAIRMAN. Will you supply the date for us later?

Mr. WILLETT. Yes, sir. Mr. Prinsen-Geerligs says that the cost of producing sugar in the island of Java is 1.49 or 1.50, in round numbers. Another statement by Mr. Geerligs is this: At 1.50 cost in Java those factories can make 40 per cent profit by selling their sugars at 2.10 a pound, instead of making 60 cents a hundred out of the cost of production, which is an absurdity, of course. They could not make any profit below the cost of production.

The CHAIRMAN. It has been testified here that he told Mr. Palmer that at 1½ cents a pound Java can make 40 per cent profit.

Mr. WILLETT. If the sugar sells at 2.10.

The CHAIRMAN. He did not say that.

Mr. WILLETT. That is the natural inference. He could not sell below the cost of production and make 40 per cent.

The CHAIRMAN. I do not know what his cost of production is.

Mr. WILLETT. Doesn't it say there?

The CHAIRMAN. He says that at 1.49 cents he can make 40 per cent profit.

Mr. WILLETT. That is a mistake. Prinsen-Geerligs says in his book it costs 1.50 to produce sugar in Java. That is the cost of production, and that gives 40 per cent profit on the price which Java is selling her sugars at. That is confirmed by the consular reports as to the price Java is getting for her sugars. Now, Mr. Palmer did not understand Dutch sufficiently to get that straight.

The CHAIRMAN. Your idea is that at a cost of 1.5 cents a pound they would have 40 per cent profit in it at the present price?

Mr. WILLETT. Yes; that is the explanation. There can not be any other.

Mr. HINDS. Mr. Palmer says it was in 1908 when he had this interview.

Mr. WILLETT. No matter what year it was, he never could have done that.

Mr. HINDS. Does the Government of Java intervene to fix the selling price of sugar?

Mr. WILLETT. No; not on sugar. They do on coffee, but not on sugar.

Mr. HINDS. They do on coffee?

Mr. WILLETT. They put up their coffees at auction. Anybody can buy sugar, but all their coffee production is sold at auction every year and limited within certain prices. If it does not bring a certain amount they do not sell it.

Mr. HINDS. Is this profit of 40 per cent a natural profit?

Mr. WILLETT. Yes; that is a bona fide profit over and above the cost of production, the cost of production being a cent and a half, and they are selling their sugar at 2.10.

Mr. HINDS. That is a reasonable profit?

Mr. WILLETT. That is a reasonable profit; yes, sir. I have that all figured out for you in the tables.

Mr. HINDS. So that the sugar leaving Java sells at 2.10?

Mr. WILLETT. Yes; it is worth that in the markets of the world.

Mr. HINDS. What is the freight on it to the western world a hundred? It must be about 20 or 30 cents?

Mr. WILLETT. I think it is 39 cents. I have that information in my papers here.

Mr. HINDS. So that Java sugar afloat, ready to be disembarked in this country, would be something like 2.40 or 2.50 a hundred?

Mr. WILLETT. Java sugars sold in this country on July 27 at 12 shillings 10 pence halfpenny, or $4.54 a hundred pounds, including the duty. If you take the duty of 1.685 off of that it would be 2.855.

The CHAIRMAN. Then take off 25 cents more for freight.

Mr. HINDS. I was trying to find out the cost landed here without the duty.

Mr. WILLETT. 2.85.

Mr. HINDS. That is for raw sugar?

Mr. WILLETT. Yes; raw sugar. That is under No. 16. That would not be the same as their white sugar if you took No. 16 out: that is a different sugar and costs 2 shillings more.

Mr. HINDS. Is that white sugar an unrefined sugar?

Mr. WILLETT. It is mighty close to refined sugar. India calls it refined sugar. They use it in India and call it refined sugar.

Mr. HINDS. What is the process by which it is made—a draining process?

Mr. WILLETT. It is made the same way all semirefined sugars are made, out of cane. For instance, the way Cuba makes its 16 sugar to come into this market, they pass through a centrifugal, and at a certain point in the revolution of the centrifugal they stop it, leaving on the surface of the sugar a sirup, which discolors the crystal and brings it below No. 16. Now in Java or in Cuba, if they were making the high-colored sugars, No. 24 Dutch standard, at that point they would take an ordinary garden watering pot with very fine spray, and would hold that pot inside of the centrifugal while it is revolving rapidly, and just enough water would go in there to wash off this sirup which is on the crystal, and that would leave the crystals white. That is the process.

Mr. HINDS. Has that Java sugar been boiled?

Mr. WILLETT. Oh, yes, sir; it has been boiled and has reached the centrifugal.

Mr. HINDS. But it has not been filtered through bone black?

Mr. WILLETT. No; it has not been filtered through bone black, and that is the only difference.

Mr. HINDS. And they produce in Java a very fine grade of sugar that differs——

Mr. WILLETT. I will show it to you. [Exhibiting samples of sugar to the committee.]

Mr. HINDS. Mr. Willett, how much did you say that Java sugar would cost laid down at New York duty free?

Mr. WILLETT. The modus operandi of estimating that is in my Java papers and will come up to-morrow; but, offhand, I remember it is 26 cents exactly below the value of the American granulated with the No. 16 eliminated. With the present arrangement it would cost about 19 cents a hundred less than the American granulated.

(Thereupon, at 5 o'clock p. m., the committee adjourned until Thursday, January 11, 1912, at 10.30 o'clock a. m.)

AMERICAN SUGAR REFINING CO. AND OTHERS.

Special Committee on the Investigation
of the American Sugar Refining Co. and Others,
House of Representatives,
Washington, D. C., Thursday, January 11, 1912.

The committee met at 10.30 o'clock a. m., Hon. William Sulzer (acting chairman) presiding.

TESTIMONY OF MR. WILLIAM P. WILLETT—Resumed.

Mr. Fordney. Mr. Chairman, on day before yesterday while Dr. Wiley was before the committee, I asked the doctor whether or not the sugar content and the purity of the sugar in German beets was not considerably more than the sugar content and the purity thereof in beets raised in this country. Dr. Wiley stated he did not think there was any greater amount or that the difference did not amount to very much. I had before me then and have now a report from the United States Department of Agriculture, Farmers' Bulletin No. 52, issued September 29, 1910, which gives a table showing the number of acres of land planted to beets at that time in Germany, Austria, France, Russia, Belgium, Holland, Sweden, Denmark, and the United States, showing that the number of tons of beets raised per acre for all lands planted in Germany averaged 10.99 tons to the acre; it is somewhat larger in some of the other countries and much less in some of the others, but in the United States it is 9.71 tons. The sugar content of the beets in Germany is 17.63, while in Austria it is 17.52; France, 13.35; Russia, 14.97; Belgium, 15.14; Holland, 15.67; Sweden, 15.13; Denmark, 14.98: and in the United States, 12.56. The number of pounds of sugar raised per acre in Germany is 4,200 pounds, the highest amount in any country named, while in the United States we produced 2,439 pounds of sugar per acre.

I also have before me a statement which I obtained from the Bureau of Statistics, Department of Commerce and Labor, dated December 15, 1911. I asked for and obtained the import values of all sugars in all principal ports of entry in the United States. I asked for the quantity of sugar, in pounds, imported with the imported value for the months of July, August, September, and October, 1911, and I find as follows:

At the port of Boston there was entered in the month of July 14,432,791 pounds of sugar, and the value taken from the invoices, which are certified to as being correct, is $2.43 per hundred pounds; and at the port of New York (I will not give the odd numbers), 248,000,000 pounds, import value $2.43; at the port of Philadelphia, 30,000,000 pounds, import value $2.47; and at New Orleans, 83,800,000 pounds, import value $2.56. These are all Cuban sugars.

Now, for August, at Boston, 26,000,000 pounds, import value $2.53; at New York, 187,000,000 pounds, import value $2.62; at Philadelphia 7,500,000 pounds, import value $2.58; and at Galveston, 6,325,000 pounds, import price $2.52; at New Orleans, 43,000,000 pounds, price $2.90.

Now, for the month of September, sugar entered at Boston from Cuba, 7,500,000 pounds, price $3.31; at New York, 63,000,000 pounds, price $3.25; at Philadelphia, 12,400,000 pounds, price $1.88; at Galveston, 6,500,000 pounds, price $3.74; at New Orleans, 7,500,000 pounds, price $2.68.

Now, for the month of October there was no sugar entered at Boston from Cuba, but at New York, in round numbers, 12,000,000 pounds, price $4.12; at Philadelphia only 27,000 pounds, price $3.45. There was none at Galveston and none at New Orleans.

Then, for the same month, July, all sugars paying full duty of 1.685 entered at New York, $2.20; and at San Francisco, full-duty paying sugars, $2.33. For August, all full-duty paying sugars entering the port of New York, price $2.14.

Mr. WILLETT. Of course, you understand those are not Cuban sugars.

Mr. FORDNEY. No: they are full-duty paying sugars, Mr. Willett, and are practically all West India Island sugars.

Mr. WILLETT. Then, would you not infer from those prices that the sugars entering Philadelphia at 1.88 were also full-duty sugars instead of Cuban sugars?

Mr. FODRNEY. No; I asked the man who prepared this statement that question and he said they were Cuban sugars.

Now, all full-duty paying sugars entered at the port of San Fancisco during the month of August, the price was $2.66.

For September, those entering the port of Boston 2.03, and at the port of New York 2.93, and at San Francisco 2.17, and for the month of October all sugars entering the port of Boston 2.51, and those entered at New York 2.78, and at New Orleans 1.93. These were Dutch East Indies sugars, entering the port of New Orleans; and those entering the port of San Francisco for October, 1911, full-duty bearing sugars, $2.30 per hundred pounds. Now, then, for all sugars entering all those ports for the month of July averaged 2.44, and for the month of August 2.56, and for September 2.74, and for August 2.59.

Mr. SULZER. Mr. Fordney, is that an official table?

Mr. FORDNEY. Yes, sir; it is certified to and comes from Mr. Austin's office.

Mr. SULZER. You have no objection to having the statement incorporated in the record?

Mr. FORDNEY. No, sir; I would like to have it put in the record. This is furnished by Mr. O. P. Austin from the bureau, prepared for me on December 15, 1911.

Mr. SULZER. There being no objection, the statement will be incorporated in the record.

The statement referred to is as follows:

Imports of sugar, not above No. 16 Dutch standard in color, into the United States from foreign countries during the four months ending Oct. 31, 1911.

Customs districts and countries.	July, 1911.		August, 1911.		September, 1911.		October, 1911.	
	Pounds.	*Dollars.*	*Pounds.*	*Dollars.*	*Pounds.*	*Dollars.*	*Pounds.*	*Dollars.*
Boston:								
Cuba	14,432,791	351,246	25,877,846	654,406	7,550,698	249,996		
British Guiana							3,596,749	142,835
Dutch East Indies					26,324,635	534,712	12,258,227	255,441
Philippine Islands			6,797,326	147,600				
Total	14,432,791	351,246	32,675,172	802,006	33,875,333	784,708	15,854,976	398,276
New York:								
England					1,036,100	32,065	3,157,346	116,491
Canada					642,046	21,780	2,259,642	71,450
Barbados					659,736	18,923	1,109,046	39,123
Jamaica					816,905	30,169	515,387	16,617
Trinidad							1,278,958	53,777
Other British West Indies					220	8	777,161	36,297
Cuba	248,371,230	6,022,649	187,164,096	4,908,557	62,801,904	2,039,455	11,929,903	491,750
Danish West Indies	1,455,000	30,846	8,752,189	208,051	7,770,376	217,711	29,265	1,567
Santo Domingo	4,307,813	93,202	2,299,620	66,445	4,328,415	146,529	214,669	8,762
Brazil							6,133,953	252,717
Colombia							128	7
British Guiana							644,935	26,391
Dutch Guiana	1,785,720	42,316	2,094,370	55,375	1,018,305	26,984	155,424	5,810
Peru			558,703	11,127	989,809	28,415	4,830,547	131,725
Venezuela							188,241	6,758
Dutch East Indies			15,679,878	287,500	13,440,090	377,811	67,934,414	1,711,847
Hongkong	4,050	62						
Philippine Islands	47,479,423	1,144,096	30,163,430	651,305	16,212,768	402,573	74,391,898	1,984,354
Total	303,403,236	7,333,171	246,712,286	6,188,369	109,716,584	3,342,423	175,550,917	4,955,443
Philadelphia:								
Cuba	29,936,346	738,580	7,509,849	194,010	12,422,930	232,994	27,740	956
Dutch East Indies							42,005,372	824,550
Philippine Islands	11,330,341	261,000			9,070,996	212,239	12,688,630	290,320
Total	41,266,687	999,580	7,509,849	194,010	21,493,926	445,233	54,721,742	1,115,826
Galveston: Cuba			6,325,056	159,305	6,439,160	208,392		
New Orleans:								
Cuba	83,807,746	2,144,358	43,375,829	1,258,948	7,596,149	204,000		
Dutch East Indies							12,676,648	244,181
Total	83,807,743	2,144,358	43,375,829	1,258,948	7,596,149	204,000	12,676,648	244,181

Imports of sugar, not above No. 16 Dutch standard in color, into the United States from foreign countries during the four months ending Oct. 31, 1911—Continued.

Customs districts and countries.	July, 1911.		August, 1911.		September, 1911.		October, 1911.	
	Pounds.	*Dollars.*	*Pounds.*	*Dollars.*	*Pounds.*	*Dollars.*	*Pounds.*	*Dollars.*
San Francisco:								
Canada	947,608	21,241						
Guatemala	85,750	2,735						
Mexico	3,196	94						
Chinese Empire	30,266	788	40,700	1,081	350,000	11,304	40,000	1,315
Dutch East Indies					13,302,490	284,779	4,129,025	94,762
Philippine Islands			4,144,000	116,050			488,343	22,800
Total	1,066,820	24,858	4,184,700	117,131	13,652,490	296,083	4,657.368	118,877
All other districts	65,866	2,690	49,846	1,515	47,415	1,293	36,867	1,048
Grand total	444,043,143	10,855,903	340,832,738	8,721,284	192,823,057	5,282,132	263,498,518	6,833,651

Mr. FORDNEY. I also have here the following statement which was published in the Inter-Ocean of Chicago, Saturday morning, September 30, 1911, as an advertisement from the American Sugar Refining Co., as follows:

THE FACTS IN THE SUGAR SITUATION.

The American Sugar Refining Co., which refines 42 per cent of the sugar used in the United States, realizes that the advance in the price of sugar is of deep concern to every consumer. Pursuant to the policy of its present management, as announced in its annual report of January 12, 1910, it recognizes "the legitimate interest which the public has in a business organization which deals in a necessity of life," and desires to state the facts which have caused the advance and its own policy in connection therewith.

WORLD'S RAW SUGARS SHORT.

The crop just harvested in Cuba shows a shortage of about 300,000 tons from the previous crop, a direct loss in our supplies, as these sugars come to the United States almost exclusively.

Long-continued heat and drought in Europe, corresponding closely to the untoward summer weather conditions in this country, have so seriously impaired the growing beet-sugar crops of France, Germany, and Austria that estimates indicate a reduction of 1,500,000 tons or more—over one-fifth—in the supplies of Europe.

This threatened scarcity has caused excessive speculation in Europe and has advanced the sugar prices at London and Hamburg—the leading sugar markets of the world—1¾ cents per pound since June 15, while growers of cane sugar, in the face of an anxious demand and a sudden shortage in the beet product, have similarly advanced the price of their product over 2 cents per pound in the same period.

WE PRODUCE NO RAW SUGAR.

The American Sugar Refining Co. does not own an acre of cane-sugar land, nor does it produce a pound of raw sugar; it depends for its supplies of raw sugar upon the growers of Cuba, Porto Rico, the Philippines, Hawaii, Java, and other sugar countries.

It has, in common with all other refiners at home and abroad, been compelled to secure its supplies from these sources at constantly advancing prices.

On June 15 raw sugar could be secured at 3.89 cents per pound. The corresponding price now is 5.96 cents per pound. On the June date this company was selling granulated sugar at 4.90 cents per pound net, while our price since September 11 has been 6.62 cents per pound net.

As regards our policy, it will be seen from these prices that our margin between the raw and the refined sugar has at no time been excessive. We believe it only just to add that the grocery trade of the country has likewise maintained a fair parity to the consumer.

OUR PRICES UNDER COMPETITORS'.

During the rise our prices have ruled lower than our competitors', having been from one-quarter to three-quarters cent per pound below the quotations of other refiners.

We share the hope that every consumer undoubtedly entertains that the loss in Europe has been exaggerated (the actual figures can not be known before December or January), and that the calls upon what are almost exclusively American supplies of raw sugar will gradually diminish.

Happily, the domestic sugar crops promise good yields, and with their harvesting, which has already commenced and which will be in full progress in October, the present tension should disappear.

In the meantime our policy as regards a reasonable margin over raw-sugar prices will be continued. It is dictated not only by a recognition of our peculiar relationship to the welfare of the country's households, but also by good business, for any decided check in consumption with a profit margin as narrow as that in sugar refining could only occasion heavy losses to all refiners.

THE AMERICAN SUGAR REFINING CO.,
Makers of Crystal Domino and Other Quality Sugars.

SEPTEMBER 27, 1911.

Now, then, on Sunday, September 28, 1911, the same article appeared in the World, of New York.

Mr. WILLETT. I can identify that statement, Mr. Fordney, signed by the American Sugar Refining Co., as being their original statement.

Mr. HINDS. I would like to submit at this point the following table taken from the London Economist:

[From the London Economist of Dec. 23, 1911.]

Comparison of English and American price-index numbers, average for 1891–1900=100.

Articles.	United Kingdom.			United States.		
	1894–1898	1906–1910	Percentage increase or decrease.	1894–1898	1906–1910	Percentage increase or decrease.
Food:						
Wheat	94.8	110.9	+ 13½	95.8	132.8	+ 38
Oats	93.0	103.3	+ 11	96.1	168.3	+ 85
Maize	98.4	127.8	+ 31½	87.9	152.7	+ 77
Potatoes	98.6	103.4	+ 5	83.3	114.8	+ 38
Beef	96.2	117.4	+ 22	98.8	129.4	+ 31
Sugar	87.8	84.0	− 4	94.2	102.0	+ 8
Pork	94.6	113.6	+ 20	90.1	156.9	+ 74
Butter	95.6	111.6	+ 16½	89.9	126.8	+ 41
Materials:						
Coal	91.0	102.6	+ 13	91.5	126.8	+ 38
Iron	96.0	123.0	+ 28	85.0	132.0	+ 55
Copper	92.4	140.4	+ 52	86.1	127.2	+ 48
Tin	80.2	191.2	+139	81.2	186.5	+130
Cotton	90.8	154.0	+ 70	91.1	156.1	+ 71½
Wool	103.8	106.2	+ 2½	83.4	120.6	+ 44½
Flax	97.0	109.2	+ 12½	....	....	....
Petroleum	97.8	124.0	+ 26½	111.15	178.4	+ 60

Mr. HINDS. You will notice that table, Mr. Willett, of index numbers, compares the prices of sugar at two periods, 10 years apart, the present period and 10 years ago.

Mr. WILLETT. No; not 10 years apart—1891 to 1903 and 1896 to 1910.

Mr. HINDS. It may be more than 10 years.

Mr. WILLETT. It is less than 10 years; 1891 to 1893 compared with 1906 to 1910.

Mr. HINDS. Now, you will notice there are columns of percentages showing the increase or decrease of prices of England and the United States in that table.

Mr. WILLETT. Yes, sir.

Mr. HINDS. You will notice, for instance, that wheat in both countries has had a large percentage of increase, not so large in the United Kingdom as in the United States, but a very large increase.

Mr. WILLETT. Three times as large in the United States as in the United Kingdom.

Mr. HINDS. But relatively large in both countries. And also oats, a large increase.

Mr. WILLETT. Eight times as large in the United States as in Europe.

Mr. HINDS. And maize, a large increase.

Mr. WILLETT. Double the increase.

Mr. HINDS. I am not particular to get the comparison between the two countries, but to show there has been a large increase in both countries. In the United States it is somewhat larger.

Mr. WILLETT. Yes, sir; all the way through.

Mr. HINDS. And also a large increase in potatoes, especially in the United States.

Mr. WILLETT. Seven times as large.

Mr. HINDS. Now, when you come to the item of sugar, do you notice there is an actual decrease in the price of sugar in England?

Mr. WILLETT. Four per cent.

Mr. HINDS. And in America a relatively small increase.

Mr. WILLETT. Eight per cent. The difference between the two would be 12 per cent.

Mr. HINDS. And you will notice in going through the table that sugar is differentiated from every other commodity, both of food or material.

Mr. WILLETT. In what way?

Mr. HINDS. In that the percentage of increase is much less.

Mr. WILLETT. Yes, sir; much less.

Mr. HINDS. In England it is even a decrease, while everything else has been increasing?

Mr. WILLETT. Yes.

Mr. HINDS. And with us it is only 8 per cent, whereas in other things it runs as high as 88, 77, 31, 41, and 131.

Mr. WILLETT. Yes, sir.

Mr. HINDS. You will notice from that statement that sugar seems to occupy an absolutely exceptional position to any other commodity.

Mr. WILLETT. Entirely so.

Mr. HINDS. Now, how do you explain that?

Mr. WILLETT. Well, I know nothing about anything except sugar. I am not an expert on any of those other articles, consequently I could not explain it.

Mr. HINDS. Are you aware of any exceptional conditions relating to the production of sugar that would account for that?

Mr. WILLETT. In its relation to wheat and oats and other things?

Mr. HINDS. Are there any exceptional influences governing the production of sugar which possibly do not exist as to wheat or oats?

Mr. WILLETT. The United Kingdom produces no sugar at all, and depends entirely upon its imports of sugar; consequently all that affects the price of sugar in the United Kingdom is the import duty of 40 cents a hundred. That is what would apply as to sugar. As to what would apply to the other articles, I do not know.

Mr. HINDS. Of course, wheat is a world product, produced all over the world, and wheat goes into England free, without any duty, and yet the increase in the price of wheat has been 13½ per cent and sugar has decreased 4 per cent in that period.

Mr. WILLETT. That would rather indicate that the production of sugar had largely increased during that period?

Mr. HINDS. Let me ask you if this is a fair inference—that the production of sugar in the world is fostered in every country by protective arrangements; that is, it may be said to be hothouse in every country, except England, of course, and England is governed by the world's price. Is it not a fact that sugar, you might say, is hothouse?

Mr. WILLETT. Why, as to that I will say this: That sugar throughout the world is not free of duty. That is to say, there are duties upon sugar, and bounties upon it, or were, and restrictions upon it. The convention countries restrict the importation of sugar into their countries and it is not free, whether it is by means of countervailing duties or not. We do the same in the United States. So that looking at it in the United States sugar never seeks its level on an absolutely free-of-duty basis in all countries.

The CHAIRMAN. The sugar industry is very highly protected everywhere, isn't it, except in England? That is, Germany has high protection for sugar, and France has high protection, Austria, and all other countries, have they not?

Mr. WILLETT. With the exception of the United Kingdom and Denmark.

The CHAIRMAN. There is artificial stimulation of the industry almost everywhere; in the United States, on the Continent of Europe, etc.?

Mr. WILLETT. Yes, sir.

The CHAIRMAN. Evidently that is so.

Mr. WILLETT. Yes, sir.

The CHAIRMAN. More artificial stimulation than there is for wheat, oats, or any of those things. Isn't that so?

Mr. WILLETT. I should say so.

The CHAIRMAN. And in spite of that sugar in the last 10 years has advanced less than other articles?

Mr. WILLETT. That is a notable feature.

The CHAIRMAN. Isn't that a most amazing phenomena?

Mr. WILLETT. It is a notable feature.

The CHAIRMAN. Did it ever occur to you that the price of what you may call natural labor, the labor of the man as disassociated from the machine, that is the man standing out like the man who trundles the wheelbarrow, or carries the hod, or handles freight on a railroad, or stands behind the counter and sells goods, that is, the man unassisted by the invented machine, that that man in the United States gets two or two and one-half times as much as in these other countries; had you ever thought that that would go into the price?

Mr. WILLETT. That is offset to some extent by the cost of living in the different countries.

The CHAIRMAN. And that may account for the slight increase that sugar has made in the United States over what it has in England, because we had the same tariff 10 years ago and now on sugar in the United States?

Mr. WILLETT. I should trace all advances in the price of sugar to the law of supply and demand directly.

The CHAIRMAN. To supply and demand and not to the handling of it by unskilled labor?

Mr. WILLETT. And not to the handling of it by unskilled labor?

The CHAIRMAN. Well, that may be so. I am just searching around for a reason for what would seem to be an amazing phenomena. Then these bounties, which, by the way, are not being given now, but this hot housing of the sugar industry, as you may call it, and they do in Europe, has apparently so stimulated production as to keep down the price. That seems to be so, doesn't it?

Mr. WILLETT. Well, not exactly. When Germany gave a bounty and cartel that stimulated production, but when they did away with the bounty and cartel there was no stimulation of production beyond natural causes, and, in fact, the doing away of these two bounties, as it were, decreased instead of increased consumption.

The CHAIRMAN. When did Germany do away with these bounties and cartels?

Mr. WILLETT. In 1903.

The CHAIRMAN. Yes; and that was in the middle of this period?

Mr. WILLETT. Yes, sir.

Mr. HINDS. May this exceptional slowness of sugar in rising in price, together with all this question, be due somewhat to the fact that a large part of the sugar supply is produced in tropical countries, where labor is very cheap? I want to be very fair about this and get at the reasons that bear on it. Do you think that that would have some effect?

Mr. WILLETT. You wouldn't call the countries of Europe tropical countries.

Mr. HINDS. No; but I would call Java, and Cuba to some extent, and possibly Hawaii may have some tropical conditions. I don't know what the wages are there, but the Philippines certainly come in.

Mr. WILLETT. The Philippines produce an inferior sugar. The world's sugar is 96 test and the Philippines sugar is 84. You have to count out the Philippines in that question and apply it only to Cuba and other strictly tropical countries.

The CHAIRMAN. If the labor were cheap or high, that would not affect fluctuations in price unless the labor cost fluctuated?

Mr. WILLETT. No. Of course, tropical labor is cheaper than labor in temperate climate; but where tropical labor is cheaper, whether it is as profitable as temperate-climate labor is a question to consider. Can a man do as much in a tropical climate as in a temperate climate?

Mr. HINDS. Probably not.

Mr. WILLETT. And are the natives of tropical countries as energetic as are the natives of the north? Consequently the labor question, as to cheapness in producing sugar in tropical countries, is offset by the disadvantages of that labor.

Mr. HINDS. That may be. Of course labor in the United States and in England has increased in price in the last 10 years; in the United States especially?

Mr. WILLETT. Yes, sir.

Mr. HINDS. In England it oscillates according to whether times are good or bad, but just now it is increased somewhat?

Mr. WILLETT. Yes, sir.

Mr. HINDS. So that, on the whole, your conclusion would be that this exceptional condition as to sugar is due to artificial encouragement the industry had in Europe?

Mr. WILLETT. Do you mean the conditions in 1911?

Mr. HINDS. I mean the fact that sugar has advanced so little in price relatively to other products and materials.

Mr. WILLETT. Is owing to what?

Mr. HINDS. Owing to the artificial conditions put around its production.

Mr. WILLETT. Do you mean that these artificial conditions are in favor of a smaller increase in price?

Mr. HINDS. They are in favor of increasing the volume of the product, are they not?

Mr. WILLETT. Yes.

Mr. HINDS. And there being a large volume of the product it would follow, would it not, that the price would have more difficulty in advancing?

Mr. WILLETT. I think so.

Mr. HINDS. I believe that is all I wish to ask now.

The CHAIRMAN. I believe that Mr. Willett has already given as best he can come at it his idea of this matter of price, and while there are a number of theories connected with the question I do not know that we need ask him anything more on that subject. What is the next line of inquiry you wish to give us?

Mr. WILLETT. Shall I complete my criticism on the hearings before we take up the other matters?

The CHAIRMAN. Yes; I think so.

Mr. WILLETT. Page 3124 of the record, Mr. Malby asks what actually took place when the tariff was changed at any time in the last 20 years. Tables Nos. 3 to 8, inclusive, which I gave with my testimony on yesterday (see pp. 3395 to 3407) show this in several changes of tariff, up and down.

The CHAIRMAN. Where are they?

Mr. WILLETT. It comprises practically the whole of pamphlet No 42, which includes pages 3394 to 3412.

The CHAIRMAN. I was afraid we might have difficulty in understanding your answer unless attention were here directed where to find the tables.

Mr. WILLETT. Yes; inasmuch as the tables have headings showing what they contain I think the information may easily be found.

The CHAIRMAN. All right, go ahead.

Mr. WILLETT. There are so many errors of punctuation in these statements on pages 3124 to 3129 that I will present two tables, Nos. 3–A and 3–B, to take the place of those pages. The tables show the same results as those given, with corrections of typographical errors only.

The CHAIRMAN. On what pages of pamphlet No. 42 do those tables occur?

Mr. WILLETT. One of these tables is from January 1, 1888, to April 1, 1891, found toward the bottom of page 3127, and compared with April 1, 1891, to August 28, 1894. You will find corresponding table at page 3405 of temporary pamphlet No. 42.

The CHAIRMAN. All right. You may proceed.

Mr. WILLETT. The table on page 3405 is to take the place of the two statements appearing on pages 3127 to 3128, inclusive.

The CHAIRMAN. That is the question discussed on pages 3127 to 3129, inclusive?

Mr. WILLETT. Yes, sir.

The CHAIRMAN. Does that complete your corrections or supplemental statements?

Mr. WILLETT. Just one thing more. This is for the special benefit of Judge Malby, and I am sorry to see that he is not present at this time.

The CHAIRMAN. That is all right. He does not happen to be here at this moment, but he reads this all over very carefully and therefore will have the benefit of it.

Mr. WILLETT. As shown on pages 3132–3133 of the record, Judge Malby wished to make the figures of Mr. Atkins show a difference between the raw and refined quotations of the amount of duty called for by the tariff, say 3½ cents per pound, against $2.24 on raws, which it could not possibly do, because, while the tariff places the duty on refined at 3½ cents per pound, such a rate is purely theoretical, inasmuch as no refined sugar came into the country and paid that rate of duty into the customs. The over 1,500,000 tons of refined sugar which went into consumption was manufactured from raw sugar of 96° test which paid $2.24 per 100 pounds duty, and every 100 pounds of refined consumed consisted of 107 pounds of raws which had paid an actual duty of $2.40 per 100 pounds instead of the theoretical duty mentioned in the tariff of 3½ cents per pound, so that the Atkins table could not possibly show any larger difference between raw and refined than $2.40 per 100 pounds; and inasmuch as production of sugar in the world, speculation in large or short crop conditions, supply, and demand make constant changes in the prices of raw sugar, the Atkins tables would include these changes, and no practical deduction can be had from those tables as to the actual effect to the consumer of a reduction or increase of duties. This can only be done by an analysis such as I give in Tables Nos. 3–8.

These explanations will tell why the Atkins tables show the difference in prices caused by the changes in tariff and the changes in market conditions combined and do not show the effect of either condition separately.

The Tables Nos. 3–8 show the effect of each of these conditions separately.

The CHAIRMAN. Is there anything else in the way of supplemental testimony which you wish to put in?

Mr. WILLETT. Simply this: On page 3149 of the hearings Mr. Fordney asked for the prices in 1910, whether they were enough higher than the prices under the free-sugar system to make up the difference in the tariff. I have answered that question in the table to be found on page 3406.

Mr. FORDNEY. Was it before the holidays that that question was asked?

Mr. WILLETT. Yes, sir. You wanted at that time a comparison of something like a new decade with an old decade, which I have furnished at page 3406, and it is a rather remarkable comparison.

Mr. FORDNEY. All right; I thank you very much for it.

The CHAIRMAN. Is there anything else before we take up the consular reports?

Mr. WILLETT. I will at this point introduce one more table, No. 11.

TABLE No. 11.—*Receipts, 1911, by months and sources, four ports.*

	January.	February.	March.	April.	May.	June.	July.	August.	September.	October.	November.	December.	Total.
Louisiana	17,000	386	607	390	282	436	323	240	47	352	27,979	45,766	93,808
Porto Rico	8,096	14,818	25,268	36,640	34,811	16,357	14,880	18,906	7,065	271	174	2,658	174,944
Hawaii	13,165	19,191	25,649	21,261	32,202	34,537	23,027	31,313	32,458	33,304	14,065	5,184	285,346
Philippines	2,100	....	....	....	7,500	15,500	26,300	18,975	9,400	41,150	35,090	8,160	164,175
Total free	40,361	34,395	51,524	58,291	74,795	66,830	64,530	64,434	48,970	75,077	77,298	61,768	718,273
Cuba	69,559	150,389	226,588	181,500	219,334	108,273	132,363	99,150	24,732	5,509	317	438	1,218,152
Total preferential	109,920	184,784	278,112	239,791	294,129	175,103	196,893	163,584	73,702	80,586	77,615	62,206	1,936,425
West Indies	....	....	....	....	....	....	1,071	2,833	5,355	1,797	141	....	11,197
Demerara	....	....	....	....	....	....	....	....	....	2,166	9,286	507	11,959
Surinam	855	45	....	184	....	231	904	1,056	516	433	696	1,016	5,936
Mexico	....	....	....	....	....	....	....	....	....	578	....	....	578
Santo Domingo	4,146	....	....	....	3,041	134	1,355	604	2,115	115	98	553	12,161
Brazil	....	....	....	....	....	....	....	....	....	2,489	7,812	675	10,976
Peru	692	401	....	....	....	....	240	....	472	2,563	699	713	5,780
Mauritius	....	....	....	....	....	....	....	....	125	80	....	....	205
Java	....	....	....	....	....	....	....	7,000	23,300	61,570	34,200	12,400	138,470
Europe	11,012	97	125	5	4	....	....	....	....	....	2,903	....	14,146
Sundries	13	....	....	19	403	268	....	....	....	38	....	33	774
Total full duty	16,718	543	125	208	3,448	633	3,570	11,493	31,883	71,829	55,835	15,897	212,182
Total four ports	126,638	185,327	278,237	239,999	297,577	175,736	200,463	175,077	105,585	152,415	133,450	78,103	2,148,607
New Orleans:													
Domestic (domestic includes exports to four ports)	17,390	2,795	2,519	1,841	2,660	2,980	3,843	3,823	861	13,990	79,701	77,377	209,780
Porto Rico	2,328	9,171	16,961	13,194	28,678	9,685	16,849	11,348	2,464	....	....	....	105,678
Hawaii	....	....	....	....	....	....	....	9,208	....	....	....	....	9,208
Cuba	....	9,072	32,524	37,109	28,128	22,567	28,826	19,452	3,429	....	....	....	181,107
Java and Europe	....	....	....	E 25	....	....	....	....	J 5,660	....	....	E 3	5,688
Total	19,718	21,038	52,004	52,169	54,466	35,232	49,518	43,826	12,414	13,990	79,701	77,380	511,496
To San Francisco	15,211	10,914	36,804	28,651	31,402	36,188	30,357	21,102	21,597	8,866	2,193	3,839	242,123
From—													
Philippines	....	....	....	....	6,325	....	6,208	....	475	....	....	....	13,008
Java	....	....	....	....	....	....	....	....	9,235	....	....	....	....

Most of rest was from Hawaii.

The CHAIRMAN. What is that table?

Mr. WILLETT. Receipts of sugar by months and from what sources, in the four ports of the United States, as called for by Mr. Raker.

The CHAIRMAN. During what period?

Mr. WILLETT. During the entire year 1911 by months. It separates the free sugars and the preferential sugars and the full-duty sugars. It also includes a statement of receipts at New Orleans of domestic, Porto Rican, Hawaiian, Cuban, Java, and European sugars. It also includes the receipts during 1911 at San Francisco from the Philippines and Java as well as from Hawaii.

I also have here a table which I consider very important and which I will put in, showing tariff comparisons. This table I will number 12.

TABLE No. 12.—*Tariff comparisons.*

[See hearings, p. 3141. Amounts are tons of 2,240 pounds.]

	Number of weeks.	Prices.					Tariff.			Refined.		Production. (For crop year preceding date, for example, 1909 is crop 1909–10.)				
		Average refined, 100 pounds.	Average raws, 100 pounds.	Raw and refined, difference, 100 pounds.	Average raws, 107 pounds.	Raw and refined, difference, 107 pounds.	Refined, 100 pounds.	Raws, 100 pounds.	Raws, 107 pounds.	Exports.	Imports.	Cuba.	Total cane (without India).	Total beet.	Total.	United States beet.
Apr. 3, before	....	$6.921	$5.849	$1.072	$6.249	$0.672	$3.50	$2.24	$2.397	....	....	....	....	....	....	....
1891	40	4.241	3.400	.841	3.638	.603	....	....	....	25,591	4,453	819,760	2,668,900	3,695,567	6,353,467	3,459
1892	52	4.346	3.311	1.035	3.543	.803	....	....	....	4,454	5,586	976,789	3,232,061	3,501,920	6,733,981	5,356
1893	52	4.842	3.689	1.153	3.947	.895	....	....	....	3,633	14,277	815,894	3,033,486	3,454,198	6,487,684	12,018
1894	35	4.053	3.055	.998	3.269	.784	....	....	....	3,965	14,524	1,054,214	3,531,921	3,909,988	7,441,909	19,850
Free	179	4.409	3.390	1.019	3.627	.782	.50	....	....	....	....	....	....	....	....	....
Aug. 28: 1894	19	4.225	3.553	.672	3.802	.423	....	.970	1.0379	3,965	14,524	1,054,214	3,531,921	3,909,988	7,441,909	19,850
1895	53	4.152	3.270	.882	3.499	.653	....	.866	.927	3,937	28,036	1,004,264	3,510,970	4,810,973	8,321,943	20,092
1896	53	4.532	3.624	.908	3.878	.654	....	.955	1.022	3,100	77,362	225,221	2,809,477	4,314,649	8,124,126	38,220
July 24, 1897	30	4.257	3.315	.942	3.547	.710	....	.852	.912	2,516	77,288	212,051	2,941,857	4,954,032	7,895,889	37,536
Wilson	156	4.311	3.434	.877	3.674	.637	1.1022	.915	.979	....	....	....	....	....	....	....
July 24: 1897	23	4.777	3.872	.895	4.143	.634	....	1.685	....	....	....	212,051	2,871,857	4,924,032	7,795,889	37,536
1898	53	4.965	4.235	.730	4.531	.434	....	1.685	....	4,192	26,625	305,543	2,864,255	4,872,173	7,736,428	40,399
1899	53	4.919	4.419	.500	4.728	.191	....	1.685	....	14,984	5,935	345,266	2,995,438	5,024,572	8,020,010	32,471
1900	53	5.320	4.566	.754	4.886	.434	....	1.685	....	6,042	17,743	308,543	3,056,294	5,590,992	8,647,286	72,944
1901	53	5.05	4.047	1.003	4.330	.720	....	1.685	....	6,434	42,515	639,856	3,646,059	6,066,939	9,712,998	76,859
1902	53	4.455	3.542	.913	3.790	.665	....	1.685	....	5,576	24,506	855,181	4,079,742	6,913,604	10,993,346	163,126
Dec. 24, 1903	52	4.645	3.722	.923	3.983	.662	....	1.685	....	3,754	5,457	998,878	4,163,941	5,756,720	9,920,661	195,463
1897–1903	340	4.897	4.075	.822	4.360	.537	1.950	1.685	1.803	....	....	....	....	....	....	....

Dec. 24:																
1903	1	4.260	3.470	0.790	3.713	0.447	....	1.348	....	10,833	6,590	1,640,228	4,234,298	6,089,468	10,823,671	308,135
1904	53	4.772	3.974	.795	4.262	.520	....	1.348	....	4,464	3,662	1,163,258	4,594,782	4,918,480	9,512,262	309,722
1905	53	5.256	4.278	.978	4.577	.679	....	1.348	....	4,540	2,986	1,178,749	5,005,665	7,216,060	12,221,726	283,717
1906	53	4.515	3.686	.829	3.944	.571	....	1.348	....	5,420	1,098	1,427,673	5,124,017	7,143,818	12,367,835	433,010
1907	53	4.689	3.758	.898	4.619	.680	....	1.348	....	7,975	1,774	861,958	4,870,763	7,002,474	11,873,287	440,200
1908	53	4.957	4.078	.884	4.358	.599	....	1.348	....	....	....	....	....	....	....	....
1909	32	4.658	3.845	.818	4.114	.544	....	1.348	....	34,565	766	1,513,582	5,762,938	6,927,875	12,690,818	384,010
1904–1909	298	4.809	3.949	.869	4.209	.600	1.986	1.348	1.442	....	....	....	....	....	....	....

The CHAIRMAN. Explain Table No. 12.

Mr. WILLETT. It is headed "Tariff comparisons," being a comparison of all the tariffs and the time they were in operation; average price of refined sugar, average price of raws, difference between raw and refined per 100 pounds, average cost of 107 pounds, or raws to make 100 pounds granulated.

The CHAIRMAN. Seven pounds being lost in the refining?

Mr. WILLETT. Yes, sir. It gives the difference between the raws and the refined on the basis of 107 pounds; the tariff rates of duty per 100 pounds and also per 107 pounds—that is, reduced to that equivalent; the refined exports and refined imports for each year; the production for crop years, total cane and total beet, with total of both cane and beet; the United States beet crops; in a separate column for the years 1891 to 1894, which covered one rate of duty—that is, free sugar during that period—and from August, 1894, to July 24, 1897, which covers the Wilson bill, and for the years from July 24, 1897, to December 24, 1903, covering the Dingley bill, and the period from December 24, 1903, up to and including 1909, covering the period of Cuban reciprocity; the calculation made on the basis of number of weeks during which each of these tariffs was in operation, so as to make the periods exact.

The CHAIRMAN. That ought to be very interesting.

Mr. WILLETT. Mr. Raker asked about prices paid for Hawaiian and Java sugars, and these prices appear in detail in the tables I have put in. In addition to that it has been quite difficult to ascertain the exact prices at which Java sugars were sold—that is, as to the exact day on which purchased; but I have a memorandum of sales of Java sugars in July and August—there were no sales preceding those dates—and will give them to you:

Sales July 27 of cargo at 12s. 10½d., equal to $4.54 per 100 pounds.

The next are July, August, and September shipments from Java, and they arrived in September and October, when the price was $5.75 market value.

August 3 there was a sale of Java for August shipment at 13 shillings, equal to $4.58 per 100 pounds, which cargo arrived in October, at a time when the price was $5.96, the highest point we touched during the year.

There was another sale in August, on the 31st, of Javas, at $4.94 per 100 pounds, which arrived in November, when the value was $5.12 per 100 pounds. I think that answers your question, Mr. Raker.

Mr. RAKER. Yes, sir; that covers the question of value.

Mr. WILLETT. Now, referring to Hawaiian sugars—which, you understand, are sold upon the basis of New York price on day before arrival less 10 cents per 100 pounds—all these Hawaiian sugars are given, as follows:

Date.	Tons.	At—	Approximate market value.
1911.			
June 6	7,483	Philadelphia	$3.76
12	3,079	New York	3.76
14	4,749	Philadelphia	3.79
19	7,852	do	3.79
24	3,284	New York	3.88
29	8,090	Philadelphia	3.88
	34,537		
July 11	9,061	do	3.95
15	2,075	do	4.13
21	7,752	do	4.26
27	2,342	do	4.41
3	1,797	New York	3.88
	23,027		
Aug. 2	7,719	Philadelphia	4.51
10	3,332	do	4.51
16	8,102	do	4.82
24	4,894	do	4.90
26	4,306	do	4.90
23	2,960	New York	4.90
Sept. 8	7,742	Philadelphia	5.65
20	10,357	do	5.65
4	1,369	New York	5.15
15	1,696	do	5.65
20	8,169	do	5.65
30	3,125	do	5.865
Oct. 3	7,785	Philadelphia	5.865
17	5,489	do	5.86
28	7,963	do	5.625
9	1,643	New York	5.85
14	7,998	do	5.86
23	2,426	do	5.86
Nov. 8	7,896	Philadelphia	5.05
30	3,593	do	4.96
4	2,567	New York	5.15
Dec. 16	5,184	do	4.775

Mr. FORDNEY. Where did you get those values?

Mr. WILLETT. As I stated, they are the market values on the day preceding the arrival of the sugars, and 10 cents per 100 pounds should be deducted from those prices to make their price.

Mr. FORDNEY. Do you mean quotations on European sugars?

Mr. WILLETT. Oh, no; quotation on 96 centrifugals on New York market.

Mr. FORDNEY. No matter where they came from?

Mr. WILLETT. This is all raw Hawaiian sugar sold under contract to the American Sugar Refining Co. on the basis of 96 centrifugals New York market on the day preceding arrival, less 10 cents per 100 pounds.

Mr. RAKER. On contract made some time before for the shipment of the entire year?

Mr. WILLETT. Oh, yes; contracts made for three or four years. These contracts have been renewed last October. This statement shows the actual prices on Hawaiian sugars which the American Sugar Refining Co. paid less 10 cents.

Mr. RAKER. And each shipment as designated in the statement and as given by you should have deducted 10 cents per 100 pounds?

Mr. WILLETT. Under that contract. That is all on this.

Mr. RAKER. Just one question before you leave that point, and which may give us a little information. Dr. Wiley, of the Department of Agriculture, gave us a table in regard to the amount of pure sugar that would be actually extracted from each 100 pounds——

Mr. WILLETT. That is, according to the polariscope test?

Mr. RAKER. Yes. Have you gone over that table?

Mr. WILLETT. I have not seen it.

Mr. RAKER. I believe it is now being printed—we have gotten a little behind this week owing to existing conditions—and I would like for you before you leave to go over his table and explain it to us from your knowledge as a sugar man.

Mr. WILLETT. Certainly, I will do it with pleasure.

Mr. RAKER. I understand that that testimony will be available in printed form to-morrow morning.

Mr. WILLETT. Very well, as soon as I may have it.

(And at 1 o'clock the committee took a recess until 2.30 o'clock p. m.)

AFTER RECESS.

The committee met, pursuant to the taking of recess, at 2.30 o'clock p. m.

The CHAIRMAN. Now, Mr. Willett, you may resume.

Mr. WILLETT. I will put in a table of the progress in 24 years of the beet-sugar industry in this country, which brings it up to date, which I will mark "Table No. 13:"

Progress in twenty-four years.

[We have prepared the following statistics to show the progress made by the beet-sugar industry in the United States during the past 24 years. The production stated for the present season (1911-12) is necessarily estimated, as some factories have not yet completed their run.]

	Sugar produced (tons of 2,240 pounds).	Factories operated.		Sugar produced (tons of 2,240 pounds).	Factories operated.
1911-12	[1] 540,000	63	1899-1900	72,944	31
1910-11	455,220	64	1898-99	32,471	15
1909-10	450,495	65	1897-98	40,399	9
1908-9	384,010	63	1896-97	37,536	7
1907-8	440,200	63	1895-96	29,220	6
1906-7	433,010	63	1894-95	20,092	5
1905-6	283,717	53	1893-94	19,550	6
1904-5	209,722	51	1892-93	12,018	6
1903-4	208,135	53	1891-92	5,356	6
1902-3	195,463	44	1890-91	3,459	3
1901-2	163,126	39	1889-90	2,203	2
1900-1901	76,859	34	1888-89	1,861	2

[1] Estimated.

This is Table No. 14. Reference to it is made in the hearings on page 2624, as follows:

TABLE No. 14.—*Crops of the world.*

[Tons of 2,240 pounds.]

	Total.	Beet.	Cane.	India.	Cane, less India.	United States beet.
1911-12	15,545,000	6,780,000	8,765,000	2,100,000	6,665,000	540,000
1910-11	16,963,128	8,550,220	8,412,908	2,226,400	6,186,508	455,220
1909-10	14,927,394	6,587,506	8,339,888	2,127,100	6,212,788	450,495
1908-9	14,563,713	6,927,875	7,635,838	1,872,900	5,762,938	384,010
1907-8	13,920,137	7,002,474	6,917,663	2,046,900	4,870,763	440,200
1906-7	14,473,135	7,143,818	7,329,317	2,205,300	5,124,017	433,010
1905-6	13,947,225	7,216,060	6,731,165	1,725,500	5,005,665	283,717
1904-5	11,513,262	4,918,380	6,594,782	[1] 2,000,000	4,594,782	209,722
1903-4	12,323,671	6,089,468	6,234,203	[1] 2,000,000	4,234,203	208,135
1902-3	12,020,661	5,756,720	6,263,941	[1] 2,100,000	4,163,941	195,463
1901-2	13,193,346	6,913,604	6,279,742	[1] 2,200,000	4,079,742	163,126
1900-1901	12,250,592	6,066,939	6,183,653	[2] 2,537,594	3,646,059	76,859
1899-1900	10,499,087	5,590,992	4,908,095	[2] 1,852,801	3,055,294	72,944
1898-99	10,096,244	5,024,572	5,071,672	[2] 2,076,234	2,995,438	32,471
1897-98	9,986,428	4,872,173	5,114,255	[1] 2,250,000	2,864,255	40,399
1896-97	10,045,889	4,954,032	5,091,857	[1] 2,250,000	2,841,857	37,536
1895-96	9,624,126	4,314,649	5,309,477	[1] 2,500,000	2,809,477	29,220
1894-95	10,821,943	4,810,973	6,010,970	[1] 2,500,000	3,510,970	20,092
1893-94	9,941,909	3,909,988	6,031,921	[1] 2,500,000	3,531,921	19,550
1892-93	8,987,684	3,454,198	5,533,486	[1] 2,500,000	3,033,486	12,018
1891-92	9,233,081	3,501,920	5,732,061	[1] 2,500,000	3,232,061	5,356
1890-91	8,861,467	3,695,567	5,168,900	[1] 2,500,000	2,668,900	3,459
1889-90	7,895,478	3,619,678	4,275,800	[3] 2,000,000	2,275,800	2,203
1888-89	7,066,544	2,785,844	4,280,700	[3] 2,000,000	2,280,700	1,861
1887-88	6,923,950	2,481,950	4,442,000	[3] 2,000,000	2,442,000	....
1886-87	7,062,106	2,750,206	4,311,900	[3] 2,000,000	2,311,906	....
1885-86	6,519,273	2,229,973	4,289,300	[3] 2,000,000	2,289,300	....

[1] Estimate based upon Handbooks of Java, vol. 4, by Gerligs, p. 44.
[2] Production as given in World's Sugar Production and Consumption.
[3] Pure estimate.

Figures all from Willett & Gray's latest estimates of the crops of the world, except a few of the smaller United States beet crops, which are from "Progress in 24 years" (see Jan. 4, 1912), and India before 1904-5.

These figures differ slightly from those printed in the hearings on page 1571, submitted by Mr. Lowry, and on page 2624, submitted by Mr. Palmer.

This is largely because the others have not taken all these figures from our very latest estimates, which applies especially to the last two or three years.

The admission of India prior to 1905-6 in these tables leads to a very erroneous impression regarding the comparative size of the cane and beet crops before and after that date.

This table gives the crops of the world up to and including the estimates of 1911-12 from 1885-86, and differs slightly from those printed in the hearings at page 1671, as submitted by Mr. Lowry. This is largely because these others have not taken all these figures from our very latest estimates, which applies especially to the last two or three years. The admission of India prior to 1905-6 in these tables leads to very erroneous impressions regarding the comparative size of the cane and beet crops before and after that date.

I also present Statement No. 15, giving the progress of the beet-root sugar industry in America from 1830 to 1890. From 1890 on you already have in the record, as follows:

STATEMENT No. 25.

[Willet & Gray's Weekly Statistical Position of Sugar, Dec. 18, 1890.]

BEET ROOT SUGAR IN AMERICA, 1830 TO 1890.

For the purpose of making a record of this industry to the present time, we will briefly review the attempts which have been made to introduce sugar-beet culture into the United States.

1830—*Pennsylvania.*—Two Philadelphians made the first experiment, but from lack of knowledge of the culture of the roots and the extraction of the sugar it did not succeed and a second trial has not since been made in this State, although the subject received some attention around Chester in 1879. (France produced about 5,000 tons of beet-root sugar in 1830.)

1838–39—*Massachusetts.*—Mr. David Lee Child experimented in a small way at Northampton, making 1,300 pounds sugar, at an estimated cost of 11 cents per pound. He obtained from the roots 6 per cent of sugar and 2½ per cent of molasses. He made the cost of culture at the rate of $42 per acre, with an average yield of 13 to 15 tons of beet roots. No further efforts were made in this State until 1879. (France produced 26,930 tons beet-root sugar in 1840 and 76,151 tons in 1850.)

In 1870 the Massachusetts Legislature exempted from taxation for 10 years all capital and property engaged in the beet-sugar industry, and later gave a bounty of 1 cent per pound on all sugar produced. The Franklin Sugar Refining Co. was organized in 1879, with $75,000 capital, at Franklin, Mass., and furnished seed to farmers under contract for a certain number of acres cultivation. The writer visited some of the beet fields and found that the farmers as a rule paid very little extra attention to the culture, and the roots they did raise were worth more for feeding to cattle than the factory could afford to pay. The company therefore failed in a very short time, and the industry has not started again in this State.

1863-1871—*Illinois.*—The third experiment, and really the first of any magnitude in the United States, began in 1863, at Chatsworth, Ill., by the Germania Beet Sugar Co., under the management of Genert Bros., experts from Braunschweig, Germany. The machinery was imported from Europe and paid a heavy duty. About 1,000 acres of land were under cultivation. During the early years 3½ per cent of sugar was obtained, which was increased later to 5½ per cent, under a change of management. The small percentage of sugar obtained from the beets during the early years, bad culture in 1868, deluging rains in 1869, drought in 1870, and generally a lack of sufficient labor at the right time led to a disastrous ending. About $300,000 were said to have been lost in this enterprise. Serious difficulty was experienced from the large amount of niter and potash in the soil and the scarcity of water. There being no stream at Chatsworth, all the water had to be pumped from a well, the level of which was 50 feet under ground, the depth of the well being 1,327 feet. It required 15 cubic feet of water per minute to run the factory of 100 tons of beets per day. In 1871 the Germania Beet Sugar Co. removed its machinery to Freeport, Ill., where the soil was better but the climate unchanged, and the company went out of existence at the end of the year. The industry has not yet started again in this State. (France produced 100,876 tons beet sugar in 1860 and 272,109 tons in 1870.)

1868-1871—*Wisconsin.*—A company with $12,000 capital was started in 1868 at Fond du Lac, Wis., by two German experts, Messrs. Bonesteel and Otto, who made a good success for two years on a small scale, but receiving an offer to take charge of the Alvarado Sugar Co., California, they abandoned their works at Fond du Lac. A cooperative enterprise was started in 1870 at Black Hawk, Wis. The crop partially failed through drought; only a portion of the roots were worked for lack of water and the rest were fed to cattle. Additional machinery was brought from Freeport and Fond du Lac in 1871, but the enterprise did not succeed, and beet culture for sugar in Wisconsin has not yet been resumed.

1870–1890—*New Jersey.*—This State exempted from taxation for 10 years all capital and property engaged in the beet-sugar industry. Nothing but the smallest kind of experiments in beet-sugar manufacture have been made in this State. These experiments still continue in connection with the sorghum factory at Rio Grande, but the industry has made no progress beyond experiments to the present time.

1876—*Maine.*—The State legislature in session in 1876–77 offered a bounty of 1 cent per pound for the manufacture of sugar from beets grown in the State, the amount so paid not to exceed $7,000 in any one year and not to extend beyond a term of 10 years. This action was brought about by a series of experiments which showed that the soil and climate of Maine were capable of producing beets of a high sugar-yielding quality. The Forest City Sugar Refining Works in Portland were adapted to beet-sugar making by the addition of machinery brought from Germany, and the "Maine Beet Sugar Co." was incorporated in 1877, with Mr. Ernest Th. Gennert as superintendent for the first year and Mr. Joseph A. Barker afterwards. The first year was largely experimental, the company making 180,000 pounds of sugar and melada. German and French sugar-beet seed was distributed to the farmers, who were paid during the second year $5 per ton for roots delivered at the railroads and $6 per ton delivered at the factory. About 1,700 farmers entered upon the culture, and about 1,200 acres were planted with varying success, according to the care taken to follow the instructions given out with the seed. Many farmers could not make it profitable even at the high prices paid for the roots. One farmer planted 2 acres and raised 23 tons of beets, using on the land 40 cartloads of manure and $20 worth of superphosphates. Other farmers raised as high as 40 tons the acre, and in one instance 49½ tons. The roots yielded variously, but an average of about 10 per cent of sugar. The factory used 120 to 150 tons of beets per day and produced beet melada and refining sugar of good quality, which was sold to sugar refineries. The year 1879 showed a small profit in the business but no dividends. Nine thousand tons of beets were worked into 900 tons of sugar and melada in 65 working days and sold for over $100,000. The difficulty of obtaining a supply of beets led to an early abandonment of the industry, and it has not since been renewed in this State.

1877—*Delaware.*—The Delaware Legislature in 1877 appointed a State commission and gave it $1,500 to be expended in seed and in premiums, etc., to stimulate sugar-beet culture. In 1879 the Delaware Beet Sugar Co. built a 3-story brick factory at Edgemoor, 3 miles north of Wilmington. Having at the outset no refining machinery, they produced beet melada or sirup, and obtained 4 per cent to 6 per cent of saccharine from the roots. They paid the farmers $4 per ton for the roots. Only short crops resulted from the ignorant cultivaiton. No profits were made, and the industry was soon abandoned and has not been renewed in this State.

1879—Maryland.—The Beet Sugar Co. of Hartford, Md. (R. B. McCoy, president), produced a few beets, which averaged within a fraction of 10 per cent of sugar, but for some reason the industry was soon abandoned and has not since been renewed in this State. (France produced 333.614 tons of beet-root sugar in 1880.)

1890—Kansas.—This State, while principally engaged in sorghum culture, is also experimenting in beet-root culture to a small extent. There are eight sugar companies in the State. This year the Parkinson Sugar Co. at Fort Scott raised 1,000 acres of sorghum and 10 acres of sugar beets. The latter are an experiment, as sugar beets have never been raised in this section of the State. The Topeka Sugar Co., of Topeka, also raised 1,200 acres of sorghum and 10 acres of beets. The Medicine Lodge Sugar Works & Refining Co., at Medicine Lodge, planted 4.7 acres of sugar beets in 1889, producing 63.23 tons of beets, from which there were made 10,158 pounds sugar, of which 2,800 pounds were seconds or molasses sugar. In 1890 they have 160 acres in beets and 2,400 in sorghum. The Ness County Sugar Co., of Ness City, planted 800 acres in sorghum and 15 acres in beets (besides contracts for 1,200 acres sorghum outside). We believe their factory was burned down before manufacture began. The Kansas State Sugar Co., of Attica, had 1,200 acres of sorghum and no beets. The Southwestern Sugar Co., of Liberal, Arkalon, and Meade, had 900 acres of sorghum and 6 acres of beets at Liberal and 790 acres of sorghum at Arkalon. Their factory at Meade remains idle. The Conway Springs Sugar & Sirup Co., of Conway Springs, is a new company which has leased the plant of the Southwestern Kansas Sugar Co. They had 300 acres of cane and no beets. In 1889 there were less than 5 acres of beets planted in Kansas, while in 1890 there are 200 acres planted. A careful record is being taken of the results of the beet-root culture, which will be given out later. Kansas pays a bounty of 2 cents per pound on all sugar produced.

1889—Nebraska.—To Mr. Henry T. Oxnard, the son of one of New York's best sugar refiners and especially educated to the business himself, is due the first grand experiment of sugar-beet culture in the United States east of the Rocky Mountains, which promises to result in unbounded success. Before deciding to locate his factory in Nebraska, he distributed beet seeds throughout the State in 1889, and as a result obtained from 385 analyses of different beets produced an average of 16.1 per cent of saccharine against an average in Europe of a little over 14 per cent, which show apparently that the soil and climate are better adapted to the growth and development of sugar beets than that of Europe. The Oxnard Beet Sugar Co. was organized at Grand Island, Nebr., and has built a factory with a capacity of 350 tons of beets per day, equipping it with the latest and best machinery from Germany, imported free of duty. The factory was completed during the present autumn and has now been running for some time. The results for 1890 are being carefully noted by Government officials and will be given out later. If as satisfactory as was anticipated, many new enterprises will be entered upon for the coming year in this and other States. Nebraska pays a bounty of 1 cent a pound on all sugar produced. (France produced 770,000 tons of beet-root sugar in 1890.)

Besides the foregoing private enterprises, the Government in 1889 tested beets at its experiment stations in the States of Indiana, Michigan, Wisconsin, Iowa, Nebraska, South Dakota, Kansas, and the published reports are very interesting and encouraging. The report says that the exceptionally high percentages of sucrose found in some samples show very conclusively that there are many parts of this country where sugar beets of the highest grade can be produced.

1869—California.—The first attempt to manufacture beet-root sugar in California was made at Alvarado in 1869. Messrs. Bonesteel, Otto & Co., from Fond du Lac, Wis., with others, organized the California Beet Sugar Co., with a capital of $250,000. The factory was built in 1870 on the farm of E. H. Dyer, on the east side of the bay,

24 miles from San Francisco. After running four years it proved a financial failure. A new company bought the machinery and removed it to Soquel, Santa Cruz County, where after operating a few years at a loss the enterprise was abandoned. The quantity of beet sugar produced in California was 500,000 pounds in 1870, 800,000 pounds in 1871, 1,125,000 pounds in 1872, 1,500,000 pounds in 1873. Mr. E. H. Dyer bought the buildings and a portion of the lands of the old company at Alvarado, and in 1879 the Standard Sugar Manufacturing Co. was organized, with a capital of $100,000, which was soon increased to $200,000 and the name changed to the Standard Sugar Refinery. This company made a success of the business from the start, and in 1884 had enlarged to a capacity of about 100 tons per day, employing 125 men, and 1,000 to 1,570 acres of land were under cultivation, producing 20,358 tons (2,000 pounds), from which 2,134,273 pounds of refined sugars were made. In 1885, 1,343,148 pounds was produced; in 1886, 1,688,258 pounds; in 1887, 572,466 pounds. The factory at Alameda was again reorganized and supplied with new machinery and is now known as the Alameda Sugar Co. It produced in 1888 about 1,000,000 pounds sugar, and in 1889 about 2,000,000 pounds sugar. Its present capacity is about 150 tons beets a day, which will be increased to 250 tons. The Western Beet Sugar Factory, established in 1887 at Watsonville, began manufacture in 1888, producing in that year 1,640 tons (2,000 pounds) from 14,077 tons beets (2,000 pounds). The average polarization of beets was 14.60 and the average sugar recovered 11.65 per cent. Five dollars and four cents was paid for beets per ton, and 5.64 cents per pound obtained for the sugar, which averaged 95.40 polarization. The factory run 61 days and employed 135 men. The company produced 1,585 tons (2,000 pounds) in 1889 out of about 16,000 tons beets cultivated. Its present capacity is 300 tons beets a day. The farmers made considerable money in 1889 and put in larger crops in 1890. A movement was also made to establish the industry in Los Angeles and other places during the year.

The production of beet-root sugar in California has been as follows: 1870, 225 tons; 1871, 357 tons; 1872, 500 tons; 1873, 670 tons, 1874 to 1879, little if any; 1880 to 1882, small; 1883, 535 tons; 1884, 953 tons; 1885, 600 tons; 1886, 800 tons; 1887, 255 tons; 1888, 1,910 tons; 1889, 2,308 tons; 1890, estimated, 4,000 tons.

The production of beet-root sugar in the United States may be given in figures as follows: 1830, a few hundred pounds; 1831 to 1837, none; 1838 and 1839, 1,300 pounds; 1839 to 1862, none; 1863 to 1871, 300 and 500 tons per annum; 1872, 500 tons; 1873, 700 tons; 1874 to 1877, under 100 tons per annum; 1878, 200 tons; 1879, 1,200 tons; 1880, 500 tons; 1881 to 1882, less than 500 tons; 1883, 535 tons; 1884, 953 tons; 1885, 600 tons; 1886, 800 tons; 1887, 255 tons; 1888, 1,910 tons; 1889, 2,600 tons; 1890, estimated, 10,000 tons. At the close of 1890 there are three beet-root sugar factories in the United States, one at Grand Island, Nebr., with a capacity of working 350 tons of beets a day; one at Alvarado, Cal., with a capacity of working 150 tons of beets a day, and one at Watsonville, Cal., with a capacity of working 300 tons beets a day. The United States Government will pay a bounty of 2 cents a pound on all sugar produced in 1891 and until 1905.

This record completes the history of sugar-beet culture in the United States east and west of the Rocky Mountains up to the present time. It is not a satisfactory record, particularly when compared with the parallel column showing how the beet-sugar industry in France has grown under the fostering care of the Government. With the advantage now of the knowledge acquired by Europe in growing beets and extracting all the sugar by the best machinery and methods, and with a Government bounty of 2 cents per pound, the United States may yet astonish the world by the rapid increase in the production of home-grown sugar.

TESTIMONY OF MR. BRUCE G. EATON.

The witness was duly sworn by the chairman.

The CHAIRMAN. Mr. Eaton, give us your full name.

Mr. EATON. Bruce G. Eaton.

The CHAIRMAN. Your residence.

Mr. EATON. Eaton, Colo.

The CHAIRMAN. How long have you resided at Eaton, Colo., Mr. Eaton?

Mr. EATON. I have been there thirty-odd years.

The CHAIRMAN. How far is Eaton from Longmont?

Mr. EATON. About 42 miles.

The CHAIRMAN. And how far from Fort Morgan?

Mr. Eaton. About 70 miles.

The Chairman. Are you now engaged in the culture of sugar beets?

Mr. Eaton. Yes, sir; as a landlord.

The Chairman. Explain to the committee what you mean by "as a landlord." You do not cultivate the beets yourself, but you rent out your land to other people?

Mr. Eaton. We rent our land to the farmers in that community for a share of the crops.

The Chairman. What percentage of the crop do you get?

Mr. Eaton. We get one-fourth of the beets delivered at the factory free of all expense to us.

The Chairman. You get one-fourth of the gross receipts from the sugar beets when they are delivered to the factory?

Mr. Eaton. Yes, sir.

The Chairman. Instead of paying all of it to the farmer, they give you one-fourth of it as rent?

Mr. Eaton. Yes, sir.

The Chairman. How many acres of land which you owned last year were planted in beets?

Mr. Eaton. We had planted six hundred and odd acres, but we had high winds in the spring which blew out a little over half of them, so we had about 300 acres to harvest last fall.

The Chairman. How much rent did you get for that 300 acres? Can you take some year when that did not happen, because I want to know how much rent you get ordinarily for your land under the system you have just described.

Mr. Eaton. It just depends on the season and the climatic conditions. I have run over here some figures, and it is very easy for a man to figure out just exactly how the proposition would run. I have an average for the nine years we have raised beets. I will say that you might in a way consider me as unfriendly to the beet-sugar industry to a certain extent.

The Chairman. Why?

Mr. Eaton. For the simple reason I have bucked them more or less, and one year I refused to raise any beets or have any raised on my land at all.

The Chairman. What was the trouble between you?

Mr. Eaton. They wanted me to silo the beets in the fall, and to pay us 50 cents a ton for siloing. So I stopped the renters from raising beets that year. It has run with us for the 9 years—we have had a factory in our midst 10 years, and we have raised beets 9 years—and our average has run from 12 to 14 tons.

The Chairman. Per acre?

Mr. Eaton. Per acre.

The Chairman. And you would get one-fourth of that?

Mr. Eaton. Yes, sir.

The Chairman. What has the rental of an acre of ground averaged during that period with you?

Mr. Eaton. As a beet proposition?

The Chairman. Yes.

Mr. Eaton. For a number of years we got $5 flat, and since then we have been getting a sliding scale which has run it up to about $5.625 on an average.

The CHAIRMAN. Since you have had this 5.625 scale what has been the average rental of an acre of land adapted to beet culture, rented on the basis you have just described?

Mr. EATON. It would run about $15 to $18 per acre.

The CHAIRMAN. That is what you get out of it by making this contract?

Mr. EATON. Yes, and we would have to pay our water assessment, our taxes, out of that.

The CHAIRMAN. When you rent your land to the farmer to raise beets on, and get one-fourth of the crop as rent, do you agree to furnish the water?

Mr. EATON. We furnish the improvements and the water.

The CHAIRMAN. You furnish the water for the culture of the beets?

Mr. EATON. The water for the crop; yes.

The CHAIRMAN. How much does the water cost you?

Mr. EATON. This water we have there is perpetual water, but some of the propositions are new and the building of new reservoirs to get water to raise beets is necessary. We were raising potatoes entirely before. We had to build new reservoirs, and consequently we had to pay our assessments to build those reservoirs.

The CHAIRMAN. But that improved the value of your land independent of the beets, did it not?

Mr. EATON. It makes the whole price of the land more valuable, and we have to pay more taxes accordingly.

The CHAIRMAN. Of course, you would have to pay taxes. You would have to pay taxes if you had any money, would you not?

Mr. EATON. Some of them do.

The CHAIRMAN. And they may not pay full value on the land at that. What do you consider the land worth that you speak of?

Mr. FORDNEY. Mr. Chairman, he has not answered the question as to what the water costs per acre.

The CHAIRMAN. What did the water you furnished cost per acre—not the investment for putting it in? Do you pay the irrigation charges after the system is in?

Mr. EATON. Yes, sir; that is, we pay an assessment to run that water each year.

The CHAIRMAN. I thought the farmers, who have been testifying before this committee and who have told us about this, have counted as a part of their expense for raising beets the water for three irrigations, and sometimes four, I believe.

Mr. FORDNEY. That is where they purchase the water. This gentleman evidently owns an interest in an irrigation plant, and does not have to pay that.

Mr. EATON. These are perpetual rights which we have.

The CHAIRMAN. And you get as many irrigations as you want without paying for it?

Mr. EATON. We do some years. Last year and this year were dry years, and we did not get enough water. We pay so much for a right in the ditch, then each year we have to pay an assessment for the maintenance and the running of that water.

The CHAIRMAN. Suppose you did not own irrigation rights, but had to pay for the water as some of these farmers who have testified before us did, what would the water be worth to irrigate an acre of beets in an average year?

Mr. EATON. We figure a right of way will take and irrigate from 15 to 20 acres of row crops, and that all depends upon the climatic conditions, whether it is a dry or a wet year. An ordinary year it would irrigate pretty close to 20 acres, one right would, and that right, if we were to take and rent it, depends again on whether it is a wet or dry year, if it was a wet year you can get your water for $1.50 an acre a year, or you can take a dry year and you might have to pay $3.

The CHAIRMAN. Could you not strike an average on that proposition?

Mr. EATON. I do not know that I can.

Mr. FORDNEY. Does it cost you $3, or $10, or $5 an acre, as an average?

The CHAIRMAN. For an average year.

Mr. EATON. I should say about $6.

The CHAIRMAN. So that from the $15 to $18 rental you get, you really think about $6 ought to be deducted for the water you furnish?

Mr. EATON. Yes, sir.

The CHAIRMAN. Now, what is that character of land worth?

Mr. EATON. That land will bring anywhere from $80 to $150 right on the market.

The CHAIRMAN. Can you approximate an average for that character of land?

Mr. EATON. No; I can not, because it just depends on the location and on how much love a man has for the land. In certain locations it will bring more on account of schools and one thing and another.

The CHAIRMAN. Tell us what your land is worth where it is located?

Mr. EATON. The land we have there would probably sell for an average of $100 to $125 an acre.

The CHAIRMAN. Do you have to pay taxes on it at any such rate as that?

Mr. EATON. No; I do not think we do.

The CHAIRMAN. What do you pay taxes on?

Mr. EATON. I think the taxes are put on an average valuation of about $55 or $60.

The CHAIRMAN. In other words, 50 per cent less?

Mr. EATON. No; I think they figure a little less than that, about 40 per cent.

The CHAIRMAN. Is that the general average throughout that community?

Mr. EATON. I do not know about that.

The CHAIRMAN. You know that is what you pay on that land, which you say is worth from $100 to $125?

Mr. EATON. Yes, sir.

The CHAIRMAN. They do not charge you but $55 or $60 for taxes. They value it in that way for taxation?

Mr. EATON. Yes, sir.

The CHAIRMAN. You said just now you had some disagreements with the sugar factories. Have you ever raised sugar beets yourself for the sugar factories?

Mr. EATON. No, sir.

The CHAIRMAN. How have you been fighting the sugar-beet factories, then?

Mr. EATON. Just from the standpoint of getting a higher price for the rentors so we would make more. We figure on the beet sugar as an industry there that we want it fostered for the simple reason that it is the surest crop we have. This year we had a failure absolutely on potatoes.

The CHAIRMAN. Whatever disagreement you have had with the beet-sugar factories has been because you did not think they gave you enough for the beets; was that the real reason?

Mr. EATON. Yes, sir.

The CHAIRMAN. You have had those sort of disagreements with them?

Mr. EATON. Yes, sir.

The CHAIRMAN. More than one year?

Mr. EATON. Well, when they first started, the silo proposition was the first time the matter came up, and then I have tried to get the price raised to a $6 flat rate.

The CHAIRMAN. You think they have given you enough now?

Mr. EATON. The farmers are satisfied. They are satisfied this way—they had such a failure on potatoes and made good on their beets this year, and that was the only money we did get.

The CHAIRMAN. Do they ever fail on beets and make good on potatoes?

Mr. EATON. This is the first year we have had an absolute failure on potatoes. We always make a success of our beets; that is, we never have a total failure.

The CHAIRMAN. But they have failed partially in some years?

Mr. EATON. In some localities they have been bothered with hailstorms. We have had hailstorms hail out our potatoes, but the beets, while it does not do them any good to have them hailed out, we have had them hailed out almost every month in the year and still they would come on and make a fair crop, so we would get some money out of them. While this year with the potatoes, which we have always banked on, and our immediate community is a potato country, this is the first year we have ever had what we call an absolute failure, and this year we did have an absolute failure.

The CHAIRMAN. And you think that has made the farmers a little better satisfied with the beet proposition?

Mr. EATON. Yes; and they have raised now on the silo proposition from 50 cents to 75 cents, and the sliding scale. If the farmers will get to farming as they should and manure the ground and get the percentage of sugar a little bit higher by taking better care of their beets, they will get pretty close to the $6 flat rate, which I have always tried to get the factories to give us.

The CHAIRMAN. Are you acquainted to any extent, of your own knowledge, with the amount of profits the beet-sugar factories are making?

Mr. EATON. No, sir.

The CHAIRMAN. You do not know anything about that?

Mr. EATON. No, sir.

The CHAIRMAN. You have no stock in those companies?

Mr. EATON. No, sir; I have been offered stock if I wanted to buy it.

The CHAIRMAN. I suppose the stock is on the market like any other stock?

Mr. EATON. Yes, sir.

The CHAIRMAN. And you do not happen to own any?

Mr. EATON. No, sir.

The CHAIRMAN. What organization do you represent, Mr. Eaton, in appearing before this committee and making your statement?

Mr. EATON. The Commercial Club of Eaton, Colo.

The CHAIRMAN. That is a business man's organization?

Mr. EATON. It is a business man's organization, a town organization.

The CHAIRMAN. How large a town is Eaton?

Mr. EATON. The census gives it 1,100, and that does not include the east side, where the factory help are, which would make it about 1,800 people, I should judge.

The CHAIRMAN. And they sent you on here to tell the committee what the situation is in your section?

Mr. EATON. Yes, sir.

The CHAIRMAN. Do you know Mr. James Bodkin, of Longmont?

Mr. EATON. No, sir.

The CHAIRMAN. Do you know Mr. E. U. Combs, of Fort Morgan?

Mr. EATON. No, sir.

The CHAIRMAN. Do you know Mr. Albert Dakin, of Longmont?

Mr. EATON. No, sir. I have just heard of them, and then I read pieces of their testimony.

The CHAIRMAN. Did you read all of their testimony?

Mr. EATON. No, sir.

The CHAIRMAN. You just read extracts?

Mr. EATON. I just read pieces of it that was kind of laughable to me; that was all.

The CHAIRMAN. Did you know anything about the facts concerning which they testified?

Mr. EATON. That was why the commercial club sent me back here, because that literature was there at the club and they took it up there.

The CHAIRMAN. You mean their testimony?

Mr. EATON. Yes.

The CHAIRMAN. As reported in these hearings?

Mr. EATON. Yes, sir; and they did not figure the testimony as right, and they wanted to have a representative here.

The CHAIRMAN. In what respect is it wrong?

Mr. EATON. In the price of land; also in the way the help is taken care of. He says they are the scum of the civilized world.

The CHAIRMAN. Who was it said that?

Mr. EATON. I think it was Bodkin, if I remember rightly.

The CHAIRMAN. Are you sure you are quoting his language? Do you not think it is a rather unsafe proposition to criticize a man's evidence without reading it over?

Mr. EATON. I think I can refer in that pamphlet to where he said it was the scum—may be not of the civilized world, but of a big city.

The CHAIRMAN. I do not think that is exactly correct.

Mr. EATON. I would not say exactly what his language was.

The CHAIRMAN. The proposition is simply this: Do you know the conditions at Longmont?

Mr. EATON. No, sir; I do not.

The CHAIRMAN. Do you know the conditions at Fort Morgan?

Mr. EATON. No, sir.

The CHAIRMAN. Do you know that what these gentlemen testified to is not true in that locality?

Mr. EATON. I know in regard to the land.

The CHAIRMAN. Then I will ask you some questions to see whether you do or not. His testimony begins on page 3165, and he swears he is an actual beet farmer himself and has been engaged in the cultivation of sugar beets for about eight or nine years. You can not dispute that statement, can you?

Mr. EATON. No, sir.

The CHAIRMAN. He says he lives in Weld County. You know where that is, do you?

Mr. EATON. Yes, sir; I live in Weld County.

The CHAIRMAN. How close do you live to where he lives?

Mr. EATON. I should judge about 40 miles.

The CHAIRMAN. Mr. Bodkin says he ships to the Longmont Co. over in Boulder County. Your people ship to that factory also?

Mr. EATON. No, sir; to the Eaton factory.

The CHAIRMAN. So you do not patronize the same factory. What particular statement of his is it you want to dispute?

Mr. EATON. About the $250.

The CHAIRMAN. The value of his land?

Mr. EATON. If you will let me suggest something, we have a party here from that locality who is well versed in that question, and as I look at it I am simply killing time by trying to figure on that, because we have a party here from Longmont who can tell you about land in that country.

The CHAIRMAN. Then your evidence about that would simply be hearsay?

Mr. EATON. I have a brother who lives at Longmont, and all I get is from what he has told me, what he could buy land for and what land is worth there.

The CHAIRMAN. You would prefer not to contradict his evidence yourself?

Mr. EATON. I just figure on it that his land is not worth that much, because he is buying water there to irrigate his beets, and land is not worth that much in that country. I can buy all the land there is in that country for less money. We have men here that have hired the help to work in these beet fields strictly as farmers, and I am a landlord and all I get is what I pick up from the renters.

The CHAIRMAN. I guess that is a very good point you are making on that proposition, that you do not personally know about it. This man swears that for his field he has been offered $250 an acre; that the beets would grow on unimproved land just as well, which would be worth only $150 an acre.

Mr. EATON. I will say that another thing which has raised the price of land considerably in that locality, what we call "around the Horn," at Collins and Longmont and Loveland, all the way through in there, they are raising alfalfa mostly, and grain. With us we have raised nothing practically but potatoes. That has been our leader right straight through, and we make more money out of our potatoes than we ever did out of our beets, but the beets are our sure crop.

The CHAIRMAN. As a matter of fact, it seems to me you have done this gentleman a little injustice as to what his statement was. He testified that while he allowed for all this water as part of the cost.

that this was highly irrigated land which he owns, and right near a little town, and he went on to explain why it was worth more than the average land, because it was so close to town and to schools and churches, and so on.

Mr. EATON. I have 2,000 acres of land and every foot of it lies against the town of Eaton, which is larger than Meade; we have more water than they have over there, because we don't rent any water. We have plenty of water for our land, and I could not sell it to-day for $200 an acre, and I have the finest kind of improvements, big barns and everything like that.

The CHAIRMAN. But here is a man who says he has been offered that for his land.

Mr. EATON. I would not believe him.

The CHAIRMAN. And he might not believe you if you said your land was worth $150 an acre.

Mr. EATON. I think he would if he saw the ground.

The CHAIRMAN. Have you ever seen his land?

Mr. EATON. No, sir; but I was offered ground next to Longmont, a town of 8,000 people, and they said I could buy land there for less than $250 under the old ditch and better water than at Meade.

The CHAIRMAN. And I presume, probably, if people wanted to buy land in your section they could buy it at a less figure than you have named. You know value is a pretty elastic thing; and as far as land goes, people don't value their land alike.

Mr. EATON. As I said, it depends on how much love you have for your land, the same as for an old family driving horse.

The CHAIRMAN. Now, let us see what else there was about Mr. Bodkin's statement that you did not think was fair?

Mr. EATON. About the help the factories furnished being the scum.

The CHAIRMAN. Do you know anything about the help they furnished in your community?

Mr. EATON. We have to furnish the material to build their houses, and I see a good deal of them.

The CHAIRMAN. It is foreign labor?

Mr. EATON. We have different classes.

The CHAIRMAN. I mean the help he is talking about—the people who do the handwork. It is foreign labor?

Mr. EATON. Yes, sir; most of it.

The CHAIRMAN. And most of it is brought from the city?

Mr. EATON. It was in the first place, but now they stay with us the year round.

The CHAIRMAN. To what nationality do they belong?

Mr. EATON. Germans, Russian-Germans, Japs, Mexicans, and Negroes.

The CHAIRMAN. Does that about cover the help?

Mr. EATON. One year they said there were some Koreans in there, but the Japs and Koreans all look alike to me.

The CHAIRMAN. Then, so far as his statement sought to impress the committee with the idea that they were foreign labor and were brought out from cities in a large measure, you do not dispute that?

Mr. EATON. No, sir.

The CHAIRMAN. That is true?

Mr. EATON. I think it is.

The CHAIRMAN. Then let us see where else he so badly misrepresented things.

Mr. EATON. In regard to what he has made on his ground. He charges up there $20 an acre which he could rent his land for as a cash rent, and then at the end, after figuring all his expenses, he figures that he only made about $3, or something like that.

The CHAIRMAN. You think he allowed too much for rent?

Mr. EATON. Yes.

The CHAIRMAN. Of course that would depend on whether he allowed too much as the value of his land.

Mr. EATON. Yes, sir.

The CHAIRMAN. So after all it goes back to the question you first raised?

Mr. EATON. Yes, sir.

The CHAIRMAN. Was there anything else, now?

Mr. EATON. No, sir.

The CHAIRMAN. Is it your idea, then, that beet growing is a very profitable thing in Colorado; more profitable than he painted it? Is that where you want to take issue with him?

Mr. EATON. No; I do not know as it is. I do not know what they make in his locality.

The CHAIRMAN. You were complaining about the way he figured in allowing too much as rent, and you said the amount he made out of it did not look right to you. Is it your idea that the farmers make more than he represented to this committee?

Mr. EATON. Well, it just depends on how you figure that statement he has made.

The CHAIRMAN. I am asking you to figure it correctly. You say he figured it wrong.

Mr. EATON. It figures out wrong to me in reading that whole thing over.

The CHAIRMAN. I thought you said you did not read it all over.

Mr. EATON. I did not. I think I read every bit of his testimony over.

The CHAIRMAN. Then I did you an injustice. I thought you said you read only extracts from his testimony, and I assumed you meant extracts printed in some of the newspapers out there.

Mr. EATON. No; there were three testimonies—Combs, Dakin, and his. I think I read all of his. I would not be sure.

The CHAIRMAN. As I understood you, you said this was the most profitable business the farmers had out there?

Mr. EATON. Not with us. I think it is with them, because they do not raise the potatoes we do. Our main industry is the potatoes.

The CHAIRMAN. You live in the same county that Mr. Bodkin does?

Mr. EATON. But they do not raise potatoes like we do.

The CHAIRMAN: Generally, throughout the beet-raising section of Colorado, do you regard sugar-beet culture as the most profitable crop?

Mr. EATON. Taken as a whole I think it would be.

The CHAIRMAN. And you think the farmer is getting a fair price?

Mr. EATON. I do, now.

The CHAIRMAN. And they have not quite gotten up to $6 a ton yet; $5.62, I believe?

Mr. EATON. Not quite $6. Five dollars and sixty-two cents is about what we got last year. I think they will get up to $6. The industry is young. We haven't got started out there yet.

The CHAIRMAN. You are getting started pretty well if in a young industry you are making more now than in any other branch of farming.

Mr. EATON. I said potatoes were more profitable, but the beet is the surest crop.

The CHAIRMAN. Is the beet crop which they raise in the beet-growing section of Colorado the most remunerative and the most profitable crop for the farmers?

Mr. EATON. In our country potatoes have always been the most profitable.

The CHAIRMAN. I asked you to strike an average, and I understood you to say you thought, taking the beet-growing section of Colorado as a whole and averaging things, that beet culture was the most profitable thing the farmer could engage in.

Mr. EATON. Yes; I think it is.

The CHAIRMAN. Then, why could he not stand a little reduction in the tariff in behalf of the American consumer?

Mr. EATON. I do not know a thing as regards to that, because I do not know their business.

The CHAIRMAN. You mean you do not know anything about the beet farmers?

Mr. EATON. No; the sugar companies' business. I do not know what it costs them.

The CHAIRMAN. In other words, you do not know whether they are giving the farmer a fair percentage of the profit or not, do you?

Mr. EATON. I do not know, as a man would testify he did know.

The CHAIRMAN. You have no figures on that question. You have not figured it out, like Mr. Combs?

Mr. EATON. No, sir.

The CHAIRMAN. You have not figured what a farmer got out of a pound of sugar beets and what the factory got out of a pound of sugar beets after it was converted into sugar, and the percentage of profit each gets. You have not done that?

Mr. EATON. No, sir.

The CHAIRMAN. And you are not prepared to dispute his figures on that point?

Mr. EATON. I do not think it would do any good to dispute his figures.

The CHAIRMAN. No; I do not think it would if you have not looked into the question. Can you add anything to what I have asked you? Is there any point I have overlooked? As I understand it, you gentlemen have come here to give this testimony, and if there is anything about the situation in your section that you have not been asked about, the committee would like to hear it.

Mr. EATON. The only thing—you asked me in regard to lowering the tariff, if it could not be lowered and still they pay us the same amount. Was that the question?

The CHAIRMAN. I said if beet culture was the most profitable agricultural pursuit in the beet-growing region of Colorado, why could not the farmer, even if he had to take a little lower price, stand some reduction in the interests of the American consumer? That was the question, and I think you said you did not want to express an opinion or did not have an opinion. However, I would be glad to have any opinion you may have on that question.

Mr. EATON. The only proposition is this: The people that I represent there figure it this way, that at the present time we have a fair chance to make a good thing out of raising beets, but if the tariff is lowered, so that the sugar factories are not making what they figure on they should make for the amount they have invested, it would necessarily mean they would make a cut on our beets, and if they did we would have to go back to a lower price.

The CHAIRMAN. Suppose the sugar factories are making 30 or 40 per cent or even more on an honest capitalization, would it be your opinion they could still pay the farmer as much as they are paying for beets at the present moment, take a smaller profit themselves, and still put sugar to the American consumer a little cheaper? In other words, why could they not stand some tariff reduction without reducing the price of beets to the farmer, if that is true?

Mr. EATON. Probably they could.

The CHAIRMAN. If that is true in point of fact?

Mr. EATON. If that is true.

The CHAIRMAN. Of course, I do not ask you to express any opinion on that, and I am not expressing any myself, and you have not figured it out along that line to see whether they could stand any reduction or not?

Mr. EATON. No, sir.

The CHAIRMAN. I understand your position, and it is a perfectly natural point of view, and you must not understand that I am criticizing you for any opinion you may entertain. As I understand it, what you want is not to have anything done that would cause the farmer to get a smaller price for his sugar beets; is that the truth about the matter?

Mr. EATON. Yes, sir; I think that is really the truth. This business started 10 years ago. When they started the first factory in that country at Loveland, my father had this big acreage of land, he was living at that time, and he figured on a sugar factory, and he told them flatly unless they would pay $5 flat instead of $4.50 they need not figure on building a factory there, because he had the ground and they could not get the acreage.

The CHAIRMAN. He would not give them the beets?

Mr. EATON. No. We started in and got $5 flat. Then all the factories came to $5 flat; and there have been several little differences come up in regard to the siloing, and that has been raised this year. What I have told their field men who have come to me is that I just wish they would light somewhere and quit this everlasting changing, so we would have a little peace and harmony and could get together, and then we would try to swamp their factories with beets instead of having them run, like this year, only 60 days.

The CHAIRMAN. Now, your proposition is that your people who own land which you rent to people who grow these sugar beets are very averse to seeing anything done that will lower the price of the beets?

Mr. EATON. Yes, sir.

The CHAIRMAN. And their fear that something in the testimony of these three gentlemen might have that effect was what caused you to come on here?

Mr. EATON. Yes, sir.

The CHAIRMAN. I think that is a very candid statement, and I want to compliment you for making it.

Mr. EATON. And what we figured on is, we have the commercial clubs at the different towns that these five gentlemen come from, and they have been sent just the same way I was sent by our commercial club, and while we figure that they represented only a few acres, we represented a large number of acres, and while we do not wish to appear swelled up, we feel that we were sent here as the pick from our community.

The CHAIRMAN. And isn't it a fact that the future idea that brought you here was that if you all got to quarreling with the beet factories about a division of the spoils—I do not mean to use that term in an offensive sense—or about a division of the profits, and kept up a quarrel with them, the result would be the whole business would suffer, the farmers, the beet factories, and everyone else. Is not that one of the ideas back of this thing?

Mr. EATON. Yes, sir; so far as I am concerned, I would just as leave pay $30 a sack for sugar or $100 a sack for potatoes, if everything was in proportion. That is where I stand on that.

The CHAIRMAN. Of course you look at it from the standpoint of the producer.

Mr. EATON. Yes, sir.

Mr. FORDNEY. Mr. Eaton, you say you get one-fourth of the tonnage?

Mr. EATON. Yes, sir.

Mr. FORDNEY. What do you get per ton for the beets?

Mr. EATON. About $5.625, I think it was last year.

Mr. FORDNEY. Mr. Eaton, you come here principally because you and your farmers were riled by a statement made by Mr. Bodkin and the other gentlemen, Mr. Combs and Mr. Dakin?

Mr. EATON. Yes, sir.

The CHAIRMAN. Mr. Fordney, permit me to ask just one other question, which I overlooked. Mr. Eaton, do you belong to the Farmers' Union of Colorado?

Mr. EATON. No, sir.

The CHAIRMAN. Or to the beet growers' division of the Farmers' Union of Colorado?

Mr. EATON. No, sir.

The CHAIRMAN. Do you know anything about the strength and respectability and standing of the Farmers' Union of Colorado in point of numbers and character of membership, and so on?

Mr. EATON. It is only hearsay as far as Mr. Bodkin is concerned, but in our own community the leader and president of the farmers' union there is a man that is working every end he can to run for State representative, and he is using it for his own individual aims, and I have found out, so that I know just what I am talking about, that that is his one ambition to be a representative.

The CHAIRMAN. In the legislature?

Mr. EATON. In the legislature of the State; and he works that as a drawing card, and he was defeated two years ago by—I do not know, but I guess he and his wife voted for him, and that was about all.

The CHAIRMAN. In other words, I gather from what you say you regard it as principally a political organization?

Mr. EATON. No. sir; he is a Republican and so am I.

The CHAIRMAN. I did not mean a partisan organization, but an organization that bound its members together for political purposes, whether partisan or nonpartisan.

Mr. EATON. No, sir; they are not supposed to be that way, but he is kind of the father of the organization. In other words, the general run of those organizations you will find out in that country are put in by what we would call rather cranks in a way. They are fellows that own a very small proportion and yet do a whole lot of talking.

The CHAIRMAN. Are there many of them?

Mr. EATON. Not so very many of them.

The CHAIRMAN. Do you know what their membership is in the State of Colorado?

Mr. EATON. No, sir; I do not.

Mr. FORDNEY. Mr. Eaton, you have stated about what class of labor you employ. You employ some farmers who have begun to settle in the vicinity of your territory, and so on. Do they become good citizens?

Mr. EATON. Yes, sir. There are a lot of Russians who have come in there who are buying land.

Mr. FORDNEY. What do they get per day for working in the beet fields? About how much; do you know?

Mr. EATON. I only get it from hearsay from the renters, but we have men here who know just exactly what they have paid them.

Mr. FORDNEY. On page 3188 of the record, Mr. Raker was asking Mr. Bodkin about the kind of labor they had and this is what he said:

> If we can not get them. When there was not much labor in the country they would send a man to the cities—

He is speaking now of the company—

> make a deal with the poor people around the slums and sign that contract. I would sign mine and send it along and he would get them signed up.

And on the next page Mr. Malby said to him:

> What does the average man make per day? I am not referring to boys or children, but the average man.
>
> Mr. BODKIN. About $2, but he has got to hurry.
>
> Mr. HINDS. Do you have to rake the slums over to get men to work for $2 a day in your country?
>
> Mr. BODKIN. Yes.

Do you agree with that statement?

Mr. EATON. No, sir; I do not.

Mr. FORDNEY. You are satisfied with present conditions, if you can only be let alone?

Mr. EATON. Yes, sir.

Mr. FORDNEY. Is that the general opinion of the farmers in your territory?

Mr. EATON. That was the opinion expressed at this commercial club meeting.

Mr. FORDNEY. You feel you are getting fair treatment from the factories?

Mr. EATON. Yes, sir.

Mr. FORDNEY. Have you any trouble with the company about the test of the purity or the amount of sugar in your beets?

Mr. EATON. There has been no objection raised at all at the Eaton factory by anybody I have ever heard of.

TESTIMONY OF MR. R. A. CHACE.

The witness was duly sworn by the chairman.

The CHAIRMAN. Mr. Chace, give us your full name.

Mr. CHACE. R. A. Chace.

The CHAIRMAN. Your residence, Mr. Chace.

Mr. CHACE. Fort Morgan, Colo.

The CHAIRMAN. How long have you resided there?

Mr. CHACE. Twenty-four years.

The CHAIRMAN. Do you know Mr. E. U. Combs?

Mr. CHACE. Yes, sir.

The CHAIRMAN. How long have you known him?

Mr. CHACE. About a year or 18 months.

The CHAIRMAN. How well do you know him?

Mr. CHACE. I have met him at meetings and I have been at his house with him.

The CHAIRMAN. What business are you engaged in?

Mr. CHACE. Stockman and ranchman and farmer.

The CHAIRMAN. And no other business except that?

Mr. CHACE. No, sir.

The CHAIRMAN. Are you engaged in any way in the culture of sugar beets?

Mr. CHACE. Yes, sir.

The CHAIRMAN. In what way?

Mr. CHACE. I plant from 80 to 200 acres.

The CHAIRMAN. Of your own land or rented land?

Mr. CHACE. On my own land.

The CHAIRMAN. How long have you been engaged in the culture of sugar beets, Mr. Chace?

Mr. CHACE. Six years.

The CHAIRMAN. Is that about the average size of the farm you have devoted to the culture of sugar beets, or have you had varying amounts in beets?

Mr. CHACE. Well, from 80 acres to 200 acres during the six years.

The CHAIRMAN. You have always been engaged in the culture of beets on a fairly good scale there?

Mr. CHACE. Yes; ever since the factory was located at our town, and in fact one year before.

The CHAIRMAN. To what factories do you sell your beets?

Mr. CHACE. The Fort Morgan factory.

The CHAIRMAN. Is that the Great Western?

Mr. CHACE. Yes, sir.

The CHAIRMAN. Is that the only factory the people in your neighborhood sell to?

Mr. CHACE. No, sir; some sell to the Brush factory. They are only 10 miles apart.

The CHAIRMAN. Have you always sold to the Fort Morgan factory?

Mr. CHACE. No, sir; we shipped to the Longmont factory one year.

The CHAIRMAN. How far is that away from you?

Mr. CHACE. About 80 miles, I should judge.

The CHAIRMAN. That was before this other factory was built?

Mr. CHACE. Yes, sir.

The CHAIRMAN. But since the Fort Morgan factory has been built, you have sold to them always?

Mr. CHACE. We shipped to the Brush factory last year.

The CHAIRMAN. Do you get prices and quotations from both of the factories accessible to you?

Mr. CHACE. Yes, sir.

The CHAIRMAN. In other words, are they competitors of each other?

Mr. CHACE. No, sir; it is all the same company.

The CHAIRMAN. They both belong to the same company?

Mr. CHACE. Yes, sir.

The CHAIRMAN. The Great Western owns them both?

Mr. CHACE. Yes, sir.

The CHAIRMAN. Then, after all, your customer is the Great Western Sugar Co., and they buy your stuff?

Mr. CHACE. Yes, sir.

The CHAIRMAN. Does anybody else compete with them?

Mr. CHACE. No, sir; not in that part of the State.

The CHAIRMAN. In other words, you have only one buyer for your crop?

Mr. CHACE. That is all.

The CHAIRMAN. In your judgment, does that particular situation put the farmer at any disadvantage?

Mr. CHACE. No, sir; it does not.

The CHAIRMAN. In other words, you think the Great Western Sugar Co. treats you fairly?

Mr. CHACE. I do.

The CHAIRMAN. You think the farmer receives a fair division and a fair price, considering the profit made?

Mr. CHACE. Yes, sir; I do.

The CHAIRMAN. Have you ever considered what the factories make?

Mr. CHACE. No, sir.

The CHAIRMAN. But they give you, at any rate, a price which you regard as fair remuneration for the product you give them?

Mr. CHACE. Yes, sir; I do.

The CHAIRMAN. Of course, you are not interested in any way in the Great Western Sugar Co.?

Mr. CHACE. No, sir.

The CHAIRMAN. Have no stock and no interest, direct or indirect, in that company?

Mr. CHACE. No, sir; none whatever.

The CHAIRMAN. Do you represent any particular organization in your community?

Mr. CHACE. No, sir; I do not. Here I represent the Fort Morgan Chamber of Commerce.

The CHAIRMAN. That is exactly what I mean. You come here at their instance?

Mr. CHACE. Yes, sir.

The CHAIRMAN. Why?

Mr. CHACE. To represent the beet growers of our section.

The CHAIRMAN. On what proposition, Mr. Chace?

Mr. CHACE. To contribute my mite, if possible, to the benefit of the beet growers, as I look at it.

The CHAIRMAN. In what way?

Mr. CHACE. To aid, if possible, in letting the duty remain on sugar and not lessening the price of our beets.

The CHAIRMAN. The reasons that caused you to appear here are about the same as described by the last gentleman, Mr. Eaton?

Mr. CHACE. Yes; I suppose so.

The CHAIRMAN. That if you get into a row about whether the factories are giving you enough, the result might be that the whole thing would suffer?

Mr. CHACE. Yes, sir; that is just my idea, exactly.

The CHAIRMAN. And even if you are not getting quite as much as you would like to have, you think you had better take as much as you have and swing to it, rather than risk losing the whole thing by getting into a row about it? Is that your idea?

Mr. CHACE. Yes, sir.

The CHAIRMAN. And is that the idea of the people who sent you here?

Mr. CHACE. Yes, sir.

The CHAIRMAN. You have not made any study about what percentage of profits the Great Western Sugar Co. gets for their sugar in order to compare it with what the farmers get, and in order to determine whether there is a fair division of profits between them?

Mr. CHACE. Not to any extent that would aid me in forming an opinion on that question. I did have access, as a representative of the beet growers, two or three years ago, to their books in our factory there. Two other men and myself were appointed a committee to meet with the officials and see if we could not have the contract modified to our advantage.

The CHAIRMAN. You wanted a little better price?

Mr. CHACE. Yes, sir.

The CHAIRMAN. Did you get a concession from them?

Mr. CHACE. I think we did, in the way of payments and delivery or something of that kind. I think we did not get any advance in price at that time.

The CHAIRMAN. How many tons of beets did you produce last year to the acre?

Mr. CHACE. About 12 tons on an average.

The CHAIRMAN. Is that a fair average for your neighborhood?

Mr. CHACE. It is probably a little above the average, I should say.

The CHAIRMAN. Did you have irrigated ground?

Mr. CHACE. Yes, sir.

The CHAIRMAN. Would you mind running over a sum for us as to what it costs you to farm an acre of this beet land and how much profit you got out of it, considering how many tons of beets you raised per acre; or have you worked that sum out?

Mr. CHACE. I have made several computations along that line.

The CHAIRMAN. Have you a memorandum accessible which we could use?

Mr. CHACE. No; I have not with me. I have it in my mind. I think I could give it to you. I have four farms, and there are such varying conditions——

The CHAIRMAN (interposing). That is interesting. Are there varying conditions between those farms?

Mr. CHACE. Yes, sir.

The CHAIRMAN. Is there a wide variation?

Mr. CHACE. Yes, sir.

The CHAIRMAN. What causes that?

Mr. CHACE. Many things, the distance from the dump, the condition of your soil, the amount of water you have to apply when you are irrigating, and the plowing. I have land that three horses might plow easily, and other lands I use five horses on, and some of my land I can get it in fairly good shape with two or three harrowings, and other lands I have harrowed five or six times, and those conditions are so varied I haven't any exact figures.

The CHAIRMAN. Is there any way to give us a statement of what would be a reasonable average?

Mr. CHACE. I can give you a table showing each item, if necessary. I have figured it often enough.

The CHAIRMAN. The proposition in my mind is, I do not care for the figures unless they will constitute an average for the surrounding territory.

Mr. FORDNEY. By taking his total acreage, some of his land being expensive and some otherwise, you would get an average.

The CHAIRMAN. I do not know whether we would or not; that is just the point.

Mr. CHACE. I think you would.

The CHAIRMAN. You think that would give us the average for the surrounding territory if we take it all together?

Mr. CHACE. Yes, sir. Some of my land lies just across the road from the dump.

The CHAIRMAN. Is your land highly irrigated?

Mr. CHACE. Yes, sir.

The CHAIRMAN. What is it worth an acre?

Mr. CHACE. From $100 to $160 or $175 and $200, along there.

The CHAIRMAN. You are giving us a pretty broad range. Can you average that?

Mr. CHACE. Just my land or for the district?

The CHAIRMAN. We will take your land first. Tell us what that is worth.

Mr. CHACE. About $100.

The CHAIRMAN. $100 an acre would be a fair average, you think, for your land?

Mr. CHACE. Yes, sir.

The CHAIRMAN. What do you pay taxes on?

Mr. CHACE. On one-third value, I think.

The CHAIRMAN. Now give us the figures applying to your own land. As I understand it, you think that when you do that, and take the total, that would be a fair average for the neighborhood. Leave out the rent to start with, and start just with the farm work, the seeding and harvesting and plowing and handwork and everything else.

Mr. CHACE. Plowing about $3, I should think; and harrowing 30 cents.

The CHAIRMAN. This is on an acreage basis?

Mr. CHACE. Yes, sir; and that is for each harrowing.

The CHAIRMAN. How many harrowings?

Mr. CHACE. Well, make it three.

The CHAIRMAN. That makes 90 cents.

Mr. CHACE. Yes, sir; leveling, 30 cents for each leveling.

The CHAIRMAN. And three levelings?

Mr. CHACE. Yes, sir; 90 cents. Planting, about 50 cents.

The CHAIRMAN. And for seed?

Mr. CHACE. $1.75; cultivating, 50 cents an acre for each cultivating, three times, $1.50; irrigating, three times, about $1.50; and lifting, $2.50; and handwork, $20 an acre; and delivering——

The CHAIRMAN. How far do you deliver?

Mr. CHACE. As I say, one of my places is just across the road and some places are 3 miles away.

The CHAIRMAN. Then the average would be a mile and a half?

Mr. CHACE. Yes; 50 cents a ton for delivering it.

Mr. FORDNEY. How many tons to the acre?

Mr. CHACE. Twelve tons to the acre.

Mr. FORDNEY. That is $6, and that delivers it ready for delivery to the factory?

Mr. CHACE. Yes, sir; I think so.

The CHAIRMAN. Now $100 an acre land, figuring it at 6 per cent, that would be $6 more for rent?

Mr. CHACE. Yes, sir.

The CHAIRMAN. That makes $54.50.

Mr. FORDNEY. Perhaps, Mr. Chairman, the land planted to beets would be worth a little more than his average land; is that right, Mr. Chace?

Mr. CHACE. No, sir; I think not.

The CHAIRMAN. Now that makes a total of $54.50. You say you get from an acre of that land 12 tons of beets?

Mr. CHACE. Yes, sir.

The CHAIRMAN. What will they average?

Mr. CHACE. I can not answer positively. I did not look over my test checks, but about $5.50, probably.

The CHAIRMAN. I thought you said just now $5.625.

Mr. CHACE. That was the other witness. That is just an estimate, gentlemen.

The CHAIRMAN. That will be $66. Take $54.55 from that and you would have $11.45 net profit per acre?

Mr. CHACE. Yes, sir.

The CHAIRMAN. Do you get these tops that others feed to their cattle?

Mr. CHACE. Yes, sir.

The CHAIRMAN. What are they worth?

Mr. CHACE. $5.

The CHAIRMAN. $5 per acre?

Mr. CHACE. Yes, sir.

The CHAIRMAN. Did they cost you anything for delivery?

Mr. CHACE. No, sir.

The CHAIRMAN. So you will say net $5 per acre?

Mr. CHACE. Yes, sir; they put them right on the ground.

The CHAIRMAN. At $5 per acre?

Mr. CHACE. Yes, sir.

The CHAIRMAN. Adding the $5 per acre for tops to the $11.45 per acre we had without tops, makes $16.45 net profit per acre after paying for irrigation and every other expense, such as rent of land and so on?

Mr. CHACE. Yes, sir; that is my sum as near as I can get at it.

The CHAIRMAN. Do you know Mr. Combs?

Mr. CHACE. Yes, sir.

The CHAIRMAN. He is an official of the Farmers' Union of Colorado?

Mr. CHACE. Yes, sir; State organizer.

The CHAIRMAN. A pretty intelligent man, is he?

Mr. CHACE. Why, in some lines, yes, sir.

The CHAIRMAN. Well, in his line?

Mr. CHACE. Well, yes, I think he is.

The CHAIRMAN. What is his line?

Mr. CHACE. Organizer of the beet growers.

The CHAIRMAN. He knows the beet business pretty well, does he or not, I mean to ask?

Mr. CHACE. Well, he hasn't had much experience in our county. But I haven't talked with the gentleman since last spring, about a year ago. During the meetings of the beet growers I met him and have heard of him.

The CHAIRMAN. Did he make the impression on you as being a man of brightness or not, at those meetings?

Mr. CHACE. I have had better impressions made on me.

The CHAIRMAN. I mean, from the standpoint of quick perception and shrewd ability?

Mr. CHACE. Well, yes, sir.

The CHAIRMAN. You would regard him as an able man and a smart fellow?

Mr. CHACE. Reasonably so.

The CHAIRMAN. Do you know Mr. Dakan?

Mr. CHACE. No, sir.

The CHAIRMAN. Do you know Mr. Bodkin?

Mr. CHACE. No, sir; I don't know him.

The CHAIRMAN. Is there any particular point in this evidence of these gentlemen I have named whose position caused you all to come here?

Mr. CHACE. I would like to refer to page 3274.

The CHAIRMAN. What particular point or statement of Mr. Combs do you wish to give us additional light on?

Mr. CHACE. It begins at the bottom of page 3273, where his answer to your question is as follows:

> Mr. COMBS. But they will not do that. They go out to that fellow, and this fellow, and, for instance, at Fort Morgan they have got a man—we call them "decoys"—and he grows a couple of hundred acres of beets each year, and he apparently is satisfied. Well, they go to him in the spring, the first one, and he signs up for 200 acres. They go to the next one and say: "Mr. Chace has signed up, he is willing to take this," and that is the way they get started. Then they go to the next man and they say: "Here are two men who have signed up; why are you fellows standing out?" And in some of these instances, where the men have signed up for 200 acres, they will plant only 50 or 60 acres, but it shows apparently that they are so anxious to make a contract for their beets that they will put in 200 acres, and that is the way they get them.

I wish to unqualifiedly deny that that statement is true.

The CHAIRMAN. I don't suppose that Mr. Combs intended to embarrass you, did he?

Mr. CHACE. Undoubtedly he did.

The CHAIRMAN. Is there no other man there by the name of Chace?

Mr. CHACE. No, sir.

The CHAIRMAN. I will say very frankly here now that so far as I am concerned I never thought at the time Mr. Combs was testifying that he was referring to any particular individual, but thought he was speaking by way of illustration.

Mr. CHACE. I deny his charge as false, and say that there is no ground for it whatever as far as I am concerned, and so far as the sugar company is concerned, judged by my connection with the sugar company.

The CHAIRMAN. You think that he meant to refer to you directly rather than to illustrate by the use of the first name that came to his mind?

Mr. CHACE. Yes, sir.

The CHAIRMAN. Why?

Mr. CHASE. Because that is my name, and I plant 200 acres of beets.

The CHAIRMAN. Well, the cap does seem to fit——

Mr. CHACE (interrupting). But I deny that it is true.

The CHAIRMAN. Well, do not misunderstand me as meaning any criticism of you at all, but I meant that what he said in using your name and mentioning 200 acres of beets seems to fit your name and that number of acres, and therefore that he might have meant to refer to you. However, at the time it did not make any impression on the committee, or at least it did not on my mind, that Mr. Combs used the name and number of acres other than to illustrate his point.

Mr. CHACE. He charges further on in his answer, after mentioning me by name, that after promising to plant 200 acres I only planted 50 or 60 acres; or, at least, while not later on again mentioning my name he says "they," and I take it the proper inference to be drawn therefrom, judging by the mention of my name and 200 acres just preceding, is that he meant to refer to me. I wish to unqualifiedly state that that is also untrue. There has not been a season since we commenced putting in beets that I have not put in more than I contracted for. This year that Mr. Combs speaks of I put in 10 or 15 acres more than I signed up for. Furthermore, I was nearly the last man that signed up, because I did not know how many acres I would put in, and then finally I did sign up. So that I also deny that portion of his assertion about signing up first and that fact being used with other farmers.

Mr. RAKER. So that while the name he used applies to you the facts stated by him do not apply to you—that is, as to the question of number of acres put in and time of signing up? Is that it?

Mr. CHACE. It looks that way.

Mr. RAKER. Do you live in the same neighborhood with Mr. Combs?

Mr. CHACE. About 5 or 6 miles from him.

Mr. RAKER. You live about 5 or 6 miles from Mr. Combs?

Mr. CHACE. Yes, sir.

The CHAIRMAN. Well, Mr. Chace, on that subject I will say for the committee that if Mr. Combs was referring to you we did not know it at the time, and really thought he was using the name and number of acres merely in an illustrative way.

Mr. CHACE. I think not.

Mr. FORDNEY. I would remark that you are a rather respectable looking decoy.

Mr. CHACE. Thank you.

Mr. RAKER. I would add that that is generally the case with decoys, though I do not mean for one moment to intimate that Mr. Chace is a decoy.

Mr. CHACE. Certainly not.

The CHAIRMAN. I repeat that I had no idea at the time that Mr. Combs referred to any particular individual. I thought he was merely illustrating his point, and think even yet that maybe that was the case and that he just happened to hit upon your name.

Mr. CHACE. It seems hardly probable.

The CHAIRMAN. I do not know that, of course.

Mr. CHACE. Well, I have come all the way here to deny that statement.

The CHAIRMAN. Yes, sir; we understand, and we are glad to hear you and anyone else who has any information to give us. Now, let me ask, was there some other particular point in his testimony, outside of this reference that you think was meant for yourself personally, that you wish to correct?

Mr. CHACE. I do not recall any very specific statements that he made outside of that, but he intimated in a general way that the farmers were dissatisfied and that he was organizing them in order to dictate terms to the sugar company. I will say that I consider that detrimental to the best interests of Morgan County.

The CHAIRMAN. Your idea is that you better not get into a row with the sugar companies?

Mr. CHACE. Yes, sir.

The CHAIRMAN. That the farmers and sugar companies better stick together?

Mr. CHACE. I will say that I am not here to fight the sugar companies or get into a row with anybody, but am here in the interest of R. A. Chace and others like him. But I will add that I do think such an organization as he is trying to form would be a detriment to the farmers.

Mr. RAKER. According to that reply I take it that you do not belong to the organization Mr. Combs referred to?

Mr. CHACE. No, sir.

Mr. RAKER. Are there two factions of farmers there?

Mr. CHACE. I do not know what you would call "two factions," but there is no organization there. I do not belong to it, and when I left home there was no man in the Morgan district that did belong to it. There are some in that vicinity, Fort Morgan beet growers, and they affiliated.

The CHAIRMAN. You never took any particular stock in that matter?

Mr. CHACE. No, sir.

The CHAIRMAN. Of course you only know that these beet growers are satisfied that you know about. You haven't been over the State of Colorado as widely as Mr. Combs has; or, I will ask, have you?

Mr. CHACE. I think I have been around the Sterling, Greeley, Fort Morgan, Loveland, Eaton districts as much as he has. I have been over all these places.

The CHAIRMAN. Does that cover the entire sugar-beet district of the State of Colorado?

Mr. CHACE. I think so.

The CHAIRMAN. Of both northern and southern Colorado?

Mr. CHACE. No, sir; that is of northern Colorado.

The CHAIRMAN. You do not represent any organization but just happened to be going around, and were not going particularly with reference to this sugar-beet industry?

Mr. CHACE. No, sir.

The CHAIRMAN. Did you make it your special business to make inquiry?

Mr. CHACE. I have talked to a good many beet growers of those sections, as farmers usually do when they meet.

The CHAIRMAN. Do you know how many beet growers belong to this beet-growers' union in Colorado?

Mr. CHACE. No, sir. There was a meeting of beet growers advertised for last Saturday at Brush; but what they accomplished I haven't heard.

The CHAIRMAN. Was that a farmers' union meeting?

Mr. CHACE. Yes, sir.

The CHAIRMAN. I do not know myself, but would like to know how many beet growers there are in Colorado and how many of them belong to the farmers' union. You could not give me that information?

Mr. CHACE. No, sir.

Mr. FORDNEY. Mr. Chace, what percentage of farmers in your vicinity belong to that organization?

Mr. CHACE. None, to my knowledge, when I left home.

Mr. FORDNEY. Mr. Combs stated while here before our committee that he was a beet raiser; also, at one time, a grocery merchant, and had trouble with the sales agent of the sugar company; but that as a beet raiser his transactions with the beet-sugar company was entirely satisfactory. That was his statement, and I believe you may have seen it?

Mr. CHACE. Yes, sir; I have seen it.

Mr. FORDNEY. He was only complaining of the trouble he had had while handling their sugar, having had some misunderstanding with them. Is it your understanding and information that the average farmer in that vicinity is pleased with conditions in raising beets now?

Mr. CHACE. Yes, sir; I do, under present conditions.

Mr. FORDNEY. You think they have fair treatment from the sugar factory?

Mr. CHACE. If he does not it is through his own fault. I have done business for 54 years, and—while, as I stated before, I am not fighting the battles of the sugar companies, yet I want to state the facts—I fail to come in contact with any company that I thought was willing to be more fair and square with their customers than the Great Western Sugar Co. I have been delegated a great many times to represent the farmers and appear before or confer with the sugar companies on various matters, and I have always received the very best treatment, and I will say for whatever it is worth that I think they are treating the farmers very fairly. They may be able to pay the farmers $6 or $8 or $10 per ton for their beets, but I don't know about that. However, when I sign my name to a contract, if they make more that is all right; I must stick to my price and they must stick to it.

Mr. FORDNEY. You are satisfied for them to comply with the conditions of the contract that you sign and you intend to live up to those conditions?

Mr. CHACE. Yes, sir.

Mr. FORDNEY. Do they generally do that?

Mr. CHACE. Yes, sir; that has been my experience.

Mr. FORDNEY. Do the sugar factories, by restoring to technicalities hammer you and discredit you after you have signed your contract by making you live up strictly to the technical requirements of the contract?

Mr. CHACE. I never dealt with a firm that was more liberal. I have never heard of their penalizing anybody for nonfulfillment of contract, not anybody in our neighborhood. There has been a little dissatisfaction with some of their employees about test, delivery of beets, and such as that, but I happen to be in a position to know the situation as to that. I was elected by the beet growers to hire a chemist to check up the factory chemist in their laboratory last winter. I hired a competent chemist from Pennsylvania, and took him down to Brush and introduced him to the manager of the company——

Mr. FORDNEY (interrupting). Was that Pennsylvania, Colo., some town in your State named "Pennsylvania" or from the State of Pennsylvania?

Mr. CHACE. No, sir; from the State of Pennsylvania. If you wish to hear this, all right?

Mr. FORDNEY. Yes, I wish to hear that, but wanted to understand as we went along just where he was from. You have opened up on just what I wanted to ask you. I wanted to ask you what percentage of sweetness or sugar in the beets the sugar factory credited you with and what percentage your own chemist found in your beets.

Mr. CHACE. I can not answer that definitely because I haven't looked over my test checks.

Mr. FORDNEY. Give it, about.

Mr. CHACE. I think I have told the committee my beets would average about $5.50 per ton. They tested this year so as to bring me about $5.50 per ton.

Mr. FORDNEY. What percentage of sugar would you have to have to get that? In other words, you would get $5 per ton for 12 per cent beets and 25 cents for each per cent above 12 per cent.

Mr. CHACE. Yes, sir.

Mr. FORDNEY. So that your beets, then, tested about 14 per cent if you got $5.50 per ton?

Mr. CHACE. Yes, sir; I think it would figure out about that.

Mr. FORDNEY. Mr. Chace, as to the amount of money that the sugar company is making out of the beets which you deliver to them, do you know how much sugar is extracted from a ton of beets that tests 14 per cent?

Mr. CHACE. I do not.

Mr. FORDNEY. For the sake of getting clearly before you what I want I will say that they estimate in the State of Michigan that 16 per cent beets turn out from 240 to 250 pounds of sugar. There is a loss in the process of extraction, of course. If they could extract from 16 per cent beets the entire 16 per cent they would make more sugar than 250 pounds to the ton of beets, of course, but they do not get it all, losing 1 per cent or 2 per cent or 3 per cent in the process of extraction. Now, if they pay you $5.50 per ton and save 250 pounds of sugar from a ton of beets they are paying you 2 cents per pound for the sugar content of your beets.

Mr. CHACE. I have not figured that out.

Mr. FORDNEY. I am not trying to make you say that, but merely making the statement that that is my understanding. Have you had any trouble in having a test made yourself of your beets to see whether or not the factory gave you the correct percentage of sugar content of your beets?

Mr. CHACE. Well, if it is agreeable to the committee, I will go on with what I started to tell about the chemist I hired.

Mr. FORDNEY. Do that, please, and in your own way.

Mr. CHACE. In our contract for the past two years the factory has given us the privilege of a checkman to check the tare and also the sugar content, in their laboratory. We have—

Mr. FORDNEY (interrupting). A checkman is a weighman?

Mr. CHACE. No, sir; a checkman is a man to check up their own man, to see whether he gives us the right tare and test.

Mr. FORDNEY. That is, to check their man as to the dirt sticking to the beets?

Mr. CHACE. Yes, that is the tare part of it. Now the test is as to the sugar content of the beets as shown in the laboratory.

Mr. RAKER. Is that at Fort Morgan?

Mr. CHACE. Yes, sir.

Mr. FORDNEY. All right, Mr. Chace, go ahead with your explanation of the check man as to tare and test, or more particularly now as to the test, because you have practically explained about the tare.

Mr. CHACE. So the sugar-beet growers authorized me to hire a chemist to appear in their laboratory and check up the factory's chemist at Brush, last year, as our factory did not run. I corresponded with the agricultural college and got into touch with a man in Pennsylvania, an excellent young man, or so recommended to me, and I hired him. When he arrived I took him down to Brush and introduced him to the general manager of the sugar company, Mr. Lawson, who happened to be there at the time. When I went in and introduced him, he said, "Mr. Chace, with your permission I want to examine your man to see whether he is competent to fill this position, and will do it in your presence." He said he would do it only in my presence. So we went into his office, and he questioned the young man in regard to his qualifications, as to where he had received his education, what experience he had had, and satisfied himself that he was a competent man to have in the laboratory——

Mr. BAKER (interrupting). Mr. Chace, do I understand aright from your testimony that you permitted the general manager of the sugar company to test the competency of a qualified chemist whom you had employed and who was to report to you as a check on their tests? Is that what you mean to convey here?

Mr. CHACE. We had passed upon him ourselves.

Mr. RAKER. But is that what you intend to convey to this committee?

Mr. CHACE. Yes, sir.

Mr. RAKER. That they were to determine the competency of your chemist, of the expert you had employed to deal for you people?

Mr. CHACE. That is what they did. We passed upon him and considered him competent.

Mr. RAKER. Isn't that action contrary to every other known method of doing business? That is, when you are trying to find out whether you are getting a square deal to go to the man you are going to investigate and have him pass upon the competency of the man you are employing to get that information? Wouldn't it strike you that way, no matter whether that man be a lawyer, or a doctor, or whatever his business, if he is to determine your business for you why should you let the man he is investigating say whether or not your specialist is competent? Isn't that an unusual method?

Mr. CHACE. It may be.

Mr. RAKER. Did they demand that privilege of you?

Mr. CHACE. No, sir; they did not.

Mr. FORDNEY. I will say, Mr. Chace, that Judge Raker and I do not understand this matter quite in the same way. As I look at it, instead of the general manager of that sugar company dictating to you who should make that test he merely wanted to examine the man you brought there, and do it in your own presence, to satisfy himself as to the competency of the man who was going to decide between the company's test and your own test?

Mr. CHACE. Yes, sir.

Mr. RAKER. I would like to make the observation, How can a man who does not claim to be a chemist determine by an oral examination whether or not the man this witness had employed was a competent chemist? Such a proposition is so far beyond any method of doing business that I know of that I do not see how those sugar-beet growers could get any result therefrom.

Mr. FORDNEY. I think that would be entirely in keeping with gaining a correct and fair understanding between the interested parties before the test was to be made. The parties had one aim in view, securing a correct test.

Mr. RAKER. If I should go to a competent engineer and surveyor and employ him to make some measurement or do some engineering work for me as against a company I was dealing with and that was trying to handle my business, I would consider they had nothing to do with determining the competency of my employee.

Mr. FORDNEY. There is where you and I disagree. It seems to me that the competency of the man who was to help decide a point is of the greatest importance to both parties interested, and I can see no impropriety in the action of the witness in permitting the general manager to inquiry as to the study and experience of the chemist he brought there.

The CHAIRMAN. Very well, gentlemen, that is a matter of argument upon a question as to which men may differ, and I think we better proceed with the examination of the witness now.

Mr. FORDNEY. Certainly. The general manager of the sugar factory, when you presented your representative, satisfied himself as to his competency as a chemist?

Mr. CHACE. Yes, sir; and then he turned around, in my presence, and authorized his own chemist to allow this man the courtesy of the laboratory, or you might say, gave him the freedom of the office. And later on my chemist reported to me that the sugar factory's head chemist got instructions that where there was a dispute as to any test the judgment of my man must be considered, and he generally had his way. In looking through the polariscope sometimes they differed in regard to the registration.

Mr. FORDNEY. Was your man's test of the beets satisfactory to you; and did it compare favorably with the test made by the factory's chemists?

Mr. CHACE. Yes, sir; they differed very little. Sometimes there would be a little variation, so he informed me.

Mr. FORDNEY. You were satisfied with it?

Mr. CHACE. Yes, sir; the growers seemed to be all satisfied, perfectly satisfied.

Mr. FORDNEY. So that you feel now that you got from the company a fair test and what belonged to you?

Mr. CHACE. I do; yes, sir.

Mr. FORDNEY. Mr. Chace, Mr. Bodkin made a statement here that the sugar company practically controlled the press of the State of Colorado; that the sugar company controlled the assessor and that the assessor fixed the valuations on the company's properties, I think he said in so many words, to the satisfaction of the sugar company; that he had gone to the agricultural department of the State of Colorado and the chief chemist had said that he was afraid to make a test for the farmers for fear the sugar company would influence the legislature and the legislature would fail to make appropriations to carry on the agricultural department of the State; that he had gone further, to the University of the State of Colorado, and met exactly the same conditions there, the professor of chemistry in the university stating that he could not make a test for him for fear the sugar company would influence the legislature and the legislature would fail to make the necessary appropriation for the maintenance of the university of the State of Colorado. Thereupon I said to him that if that is true the politics of Colorado is in mighty bad shape indeed. What do you say as to the correctness of Mr. Bodkin's statement as I have given it to you?

Mr. CHACE. Well, I will simply say that I can not conceive of any ground for such an assertion.

Mr. FORDNEY. In order to be absolutely free from any influence you got an outside chemist, and his test was very satisfactory to you?

Mr. CHACE. Yes, sir.

Mr. FORDNEY. You therefore believe that the farmers of Colorado are getting what belongs to them in the way of tests, at least from the sugar companies?

Mr. CHACE. Yes, sir; I do.

Mr. FORDNEY. I do not believe, Mr. Chairman, there is anything further I wish to ask.

Mr. RAKER. Did I understand you, Mr. Chace, that you had not participated with the farmers' organizations?

Mr. CHACE. No, sir.

Mr. RAKER. You never had?

Mr. CHACE. No, sir.

Mr. RAKER. What was this organization that you represented?

Mr. CHACE. That was a kind of local affair. There was no permanent organization. The beet growers simply met and told me to hire a chemist.

Mr. RAKER. What did you hire a chemist for?

Mr. CHACE. To comply with the terms that were granted us in our contract. They granted us permission to have a test made of our beets by our own man.

Mr. RAKER. What induced you to hire a chemist? What was the incentive to do that, if the company was giving you good returns?

Mr. CHACE. I will say that there is always some that are suspicious that they are not getting a square deal, and the object of that action was to satisfy those that were suspicious and prove whether we were getting a square deal or not.

Mr. RAKER. Taking the whole community of sugar-beet growers, how did the number that selected you to do this compare with the number that did not participate therein—I mean how did the number that did not participate in this local organization or gathering compare with those that did?

Mr. CHACE. I do not know that I caught your question.

Mr. RAKER. How many men participated in this local gathering?

Mr. CHACE. Every man that delivered beets at the factory contributed toward the payment of the chemist. We levied an assessment.

Mr. RAKER. And they did that because they thought they were not getting the full sugar content of their beets?

Mr. CHACE. Some of them did.

Mr. RAKER. Enough of them thought so well of that idea that they all contributed to it?

Mr. CHACE. Yes, sir.

Mr. RAKER. Did they have meetings to discuss this matter?

Mr. CHACE. Yes, sir.

Mr. RAKER. Where was the meeting held?

Mr. CHACE. It was held at Fort Morgan.

Mr. RAKER. Pretty nearly everybody attended the meeting?

Mr. CHACE. Pretty nearly all of the beet growers.

Mr. RAKER. How many of the beet growers that delivered beets at the Morgan factory attended?

Mr. CHACE. Well, I can not recall. A good deal of the understanding was had over the phone. We called up and wanted to know if they were willing to contribute toward hiring a chemist.

Mr. RAKER. Approximately how many attended?

Mr. CHACE. Well, I should say a dozen or fifteen.

Mr. RAKER. You organized a little gathering, had a chairman and secretary?

Mr. CHACE. I think we did, but won't be positive about that.

Mr. RAKER. And those that did not attend you communicated with over the phone after this little organization was had, and they all contributed, and you proceeded then to employ a chemist to do the work?

Mr. CHACE. Yes, sir; of course the contributions were made.

Mr. RAKER. Did you discuss any other subject in regard to beet growing?

Mr. CHACE. Yes, sir.

Mr. RAKER. The amount of money that you were getting for your beets?

Mr. CHACE. Yes, sir.

Mr. RAKER. A number of them thought that they were not getting sufficient money for their beets?

Mr. CHACE. Yes, sir; a great many wanted to demand $6 flat.

Mr. RAKER. About what proportion of the farmers made that demand?

Mr. CHACE. I couldn't say. That meeting where it was talked over most was held at Brush, and I was not present then.

Mr. RAKER. I only want to know of the meeting that you participated in.

Mr. CHACE. They discussed a modification of the contract. Some wanted $6 flat. Of course we were all anxious to get all we could, and it was talked over whether we thought that could be done.

Mr. RAKER. Were any other subjects discussed?

Mr. CHACE. I think the subject of pay day was discussed—to have two pay days instead of one.

Mr. RAKER. Well, wasn't the general modus operandi of the conduct of the business between the beet-factory people and the farmers discussed by the farmers from the standpoint of the farmers?

Mr. CHACE. Yes, sir.

Mr. RAKER. They were doing that for the purpose of bettering their condition?

Mr. CHACE. Yes, sir.

Mr. RAKER. And getting better prices?

Mr. CHACE. Yes, sir.

Mr. RAKER. And getting more sugar out of their beets?

Mr. CHACE. Yes, sir.

Mr. RAKER. They did not think that they were getting enough sugar from their beets?

Mr. CHACE. Yes, sir; some of them did not think so.

Mr. RAKER. Well, give us an idea as to the proportion of the sugar-beet farmers around this factory that believed they were not getting the full amount of sugar they were entitled to out of their beets.

Mr. CHACE. Well, probably at that organization there may have been 50 per cent of them at that time. That was before we had had the chemist, or the checkman, as we call him.

Mr. RAKER. Who was this chemist?

Mr. CHACE. His name was Henry; and I have forgotten his first name.

Mr. RAKER. I would like to have his full name, if you can remember it.

Mr. CHACE. I don't believe I can recall it.

Mr. RAKER. He made a scientific report of his analyses and investigation to you farmers, did he not?

Mr. CHACE. No, sir; when they made a test they had a test sheet——

Mr. RAKER (interrupting). Just make your answer quick and short so that we may get through.

Mr. CHACE. No, sir; he did not. He just O. K'd. their test.

Mr. RAKER. Of course, I did not want that just there, but we will get at it. There was no written report made by your chemist to the farmers who employed him?

Mr. CHACE. No, sir.

Mr. RAKER. No report in writing made by this chemist of yours at all?

Mr. CHACE. No, sir; I think not.

Mr. RAKER. You do not remember his name?

Mr. CHACE. Not his first name.

Mr. RAKER. How long did he remain in the sugar factory?

Mr. CHACE. During one campaign.

Mr. RAKER. How much did you pay him?

Mr. CHACE. $100 per month.

Mr. RAKER. All of the information that you had from him was when he came out of the factory, without making a written report week by week or month by month or for each individual's crop that had been sent in, simply to state that the report of the chemist for the company as made to you was all right?

Mr. CHACE. Yes, sir.

Mr. RAKER. Well, now, did all of the farmers think that was all right?

Mr. CHACE. I don't know. I never heard any complaint.

Mr. RAKER. You never discussed it with them?

Mr. CHACE. No, sir.

Mr. RAKER. How old was this man?

Mr. CHACE. He was about 25, I should guess.

Mr. RAKER. And where did you say he was teaching chemistry before you employed him?

Mr. CHACE. I can not remember.

Mr. RAKER. He had been a teacher in chemistry?

Mr. CHACE. He attended school and got his education, I think, in the University of Michigan.

Mr. RAKER. I am not talking about his schooling, but where did he teach chemistry?

Mr. CHACE. I think not.

Mr. RAKER. You got him just as a graduate from one of our colleges?

Mr. CHACE. Yes, sir; and he was employed by a large iron firm in Pennsylvania—a manufacturing concern of some kind.

Mr. RAKER. For what purpose?

Mr. CHACE. I don't know.

Mr. RAKER. You went and got a man that was in the iron mines, acting as chemist for a coal and iron mining company, to come to Colorado and make a thorough investigation of the beet conditions—chemical tests as to the conditions attending the manufacture of beets. Is that right?

Mr. CHACE. We had a friend of his that lived there that gave us a strong recommendation. I can not tell you about his experience.

Mr. RAKER. Just answer that question. Is that a fact as I have outlined it in my question?

Mr. CHACE. That we employed him from some large company in Pennsylvania?

Mr. RAKER. From some iron or mining company, yes.

Mr. CHACE. Yes, sir; I think so.

Mr. RAKER. And he came down there to take up the subject of analyzing beets in the factory, didn't he?

Mr. CHACE. Yes, sir.

Mr. RAKER. Without any prior knowledge or information on the subject, so far as you know?

Mr. CHACE. Not so far as I know.

Mr. RAKER. And the chemist of the sugar-beet factory, after finding out that he had been interested in some mining or coal company, had been a chemist in one of their places or had worked there, of course, so far as he and his company were concerned, was entirely willing to let him remain in the laboratory as representing you people. That is the situation, is it?

Mr. CHACE. Yes, sir.

Mr. RAKER. Did you ever meet with Mr. Combs in any of these farmers' meetings?

Mr. CHACE. Yes, sir.

Mr. RAKER. You have participated together in them?

Mr. CHACE. We talked the matter over, as to the beet-growing industry. The first time I met him was in a beet-growers' meeting 'sh.

Mr. RAKER. Well, he attended the organization meeting?

Mr. CHACE. Yes, sir.

Mr. RAKER. And you attended the organization meeting?

Mr. CHACE. Yes, sir.

Mr. RAKER. You both belonged to the organization?

Mr. CHACE. No, sir; I was not a member. There was no organization at that time, I believe.

Mr. RAKER. Did they have a public meeting?

Mr. CHACE. Yes, sir.

Mr. RAKER. And had a chairman and secretary?

Mr. CHACE. Yes, sir.

Mr. RAKER. Well, they had what they call this general organization?

Mr. CHACE. Yes, sir; they had.

Mr. RAKER. You did not belong to it?

Mr. CHACE. Yes, sir; I belonged to that little local organization. I thought you had reference to this farmers' union.

Mr. RAKER. I am not particular as to what you call it. These unions generally grow out of a primary organization. Did Mr. Combs belong to this?

Mr. CHACE. I think he did. He contributed toward the chemist.

Mr. RAKER. Well, did you and he attend any other meeting or meetings?

Mr. CHACE. I do not remember ever meeting with him in any meet except at that time.

Mr. RAKER. Is there any little feeling existing between you and Mr. Combs?

Mr. CHACE. Not in the least.

Mr. RAKER. When you saw this little book here, containing a reference, as you thought, to your name, did you kinder feel a little piqued about it?

Mr. CHACE. I did.

Mr. RAKER. Then, as a matter of fact, there is existing all of the conditions and complaints testified to by Messrs. Combs, Dakan, and Bodkin upon the part of the farmers of Colorado as to the treatment of them and conditions existing between them and the beet-sugar factories?

Mr. CHACE. I think not to the extent that they claimed.

Mr. RAKER. I am not figuring out as to any particular extent. I will wind that up in a minute, if you will give me a categorical answer to my question. Generally speaking, all the conditions as complaints by the beet growers, as stated by these men, did actually exist at one time or other in Colorado on the part of the sugar-beet farmers against the Geat Western Sugar Co.?

Mr. CHACE. I think not.

Mr. RAKER. Did the majority of them exist?

Mr. CHACE. Yes; I would say probably they did. But I want to say——

Mr. RAKER (interrupting). I can wind this up in a very few minutes by a general question. What particular condition did not exist among those testified to by these men, taking them down as one, two, three and four. Now for the first exception, what is it?

Mr. CHACE. I would have to know what all they testified to.

Mr. RAKER. You have read their testimony over?

Mr. CHACE. I did two or three days ago but I can not recall all of them at this time.

Mr. RAKER. If there were any material or vital question they set out with which you disagree it would occur to you, would it not?

Mr. CHACE. It might not.

The CHAIRMAN. Can you think of any more besides those you have already outlined? If so, state them.

Mr. CHACE. No, sir; I do not at this time.

Mr. RAKER. Now, with the exception of those you have named, the conditions as represented by these three men have practically heretofore existed in that part of the country?

Mr. CHACE. Yes, sir; I suppose so, to a certain extent. But I want to say——

Mr. RAKER (interrupting). That is all.

Mr. FORDNEY. Mr. Chace, in the first place, as to the testimony that you referred to, given by Mr. Combs, as found on page 3273 of the record, in which your name appeared and in which certain charges were made, as you construed coupling your name with them, you wished to answer that, as you have done?

Mr. CHACE. Yes, sir.

Mr. FORDNEY. And, in the second place, you wished to tell about this chemist that you employed?

Mr. CHACE. Yes, sir.

The CHAIRMAN. That has all been gone over.

Mr. FORDNEY. Maybe so, in a way, but please let me finish this short inquiry. You were satisfied with the chemist's tests as he made them?

Mr. CHACE. Yes, sir.

Mr. FORDNEY. You heard the question asked the other gentlemen who have appeared here before this committee about the labor employed being secured from the "slums." Do you agree with Mr. Bodkin on that point?

Mr. CHACE. I do not.

Mr. FORDNEY. Is that one of the reasons why you wanted to answer his testimony, too?

Mr. CHACE. Yes, sir.

Mr. FORDNEY. Do you have a pretty good class of labor?

Mr. CHACE. We do. They have built two new churches, and, as president of the school board, we allowed them to hold services in our schoolhouses around.

Mr. FORDNEY. Are you permitted by the sugar factories to employ check men at the weigh stations to see to the weighing of your beets?

Mr. CHACE. Yes, sir.

Mr. FORDNEY. In Michigan they do permit that.

The CHAIRMAN. I think he said they did in Colorado, too.

Mr. FORDNEY. Did you say that?

Mr. CHACE. No; I think I said a tare checker. I do not know as that is embodied in the contract, either.

Mr. FORDNEY. It is not in the contract anywhere, but they permit that to be done?

Mr. CHACE. It is for the tare-check man and for the chemist; it is embodied in the contract.

Mr. FORDNEY. Do you know whether you would be permitted to have a check weighman to see about the weighing of your beets?

Mr. CHACE. Well, I don't know.

Mr. FORDNEY. Do you weigh your beets either on your own scales or on anybody else's scales?

Mr. CHACE. Yes, sir.

Mr. FORDNEY. Do you find that your weights agree with their weights, generally?

Mr. CHACE. Sometimes one way and sometimes the other. I have found some loads weighed more than they gave it and sometimes less than they gave it.

Mr. FORDNEY. Generally you are satisfied with their weights?

Mr. CHACE. Yes, sir.

Mr. FORDNEY. That is all I wish to ask.

The CHAIRMAN. If there are no other questions we will excuse Mr. Chace, with the thanks of the committee for his attendance.

STATEMENT SUBMITTED BY ARBUCKLE BROS.

The CHAIRMAN. I now have the answer of Arbuckle Bros. in answer to questions propounded by Mr. Fordney, and if it is agreeable the same will be put into the record at this point.

Mr. FORDNEY. I will be very glad to have that done.

NEW YORK, *January 8, 1912.*

Hon. F. J. GARRETT,
Acting Chairman Special Committee Under House Resolution No. 157.

SIR: Complying with your favor of December 13, we transmit herewith a schedule which shows the following: The date of every purchase of raw sugar made by us on and after January 1, 1911, to July 1, 1911; the name of the country in which the sugar was produced; the number of pounds covered by each purchase; the dates and number of pounds of every delivery thereof; the stock of raw sugar on hand July 1, 1911, and the duty-paid price thereof per hundred pounds; the amount of raw sugar bought at July 1, 1911. but then not yet delivered; the dates and number of pounds of every delivery thereof; the name of the country where produced; the duty-paid price thereof.

We beg to report also as follows:

That on July 1, 1911, our total stock of refined sugar wherever situate was approximately 13,930,000 pounds, or say, 39,800 barrels. The exact weight can not be stated because our refined product is usually weighed only as shipped.

That on July 1, 1911, our actual bona fide sales of refined sugar not yet invoiced were 85,100 barrels—say, the equivalent of 29,785,000 pounds, averaged at 350 pounds to the barrel.

It may be pertinent to add that, in addition to the sales last mentioned, our actual bona fide sales of refined sugar the first three business days of July were 214,300 barrels, which virtually closed out our entire interest in raw sugar at that time. These sales were made in the belief that the then current price was high and that it was well to sell our limit. Our observations, we think, warrant the belief that the other refiners entertained the same opinion and generally sold against their stocks of raw as largely as they dared.

In the list of sugars purchased but not yet delivered at July 1 may be noted a purchase of Philippine sugars for which the price has not been stated. This is because the transaction is still incomplete and final cost not yet fixed.

Very respectfully, yours,

ARBUCKLE BROS.

STATE OF NEW YORK, *County of New York, ss:*

Wm. A. Jamison, being duly sworn, deposes and says that he is one of the partners in the above-named firm of Arbuckle Bros. and signed the foregoing statement; that said statement was prepared at his direction and under his supervision from the books and records of said firm, and is true and correct to the best of his knowledge and belief.

WM. A. JAMISON.

Subscribed and sworn to before me this 9th day of January, 1912.

FRED K. A. DELATOUR,
Notary Public, 151, Kings County, N. Y.

Schedule of sugar purchased and delivered.

SUGAR PURCHASED FROM JAN. 1, 1911, TO JULY 1, 1911.

Date of purchase.	Where produced.	Amount purchased.	Date of delivery.	Amount delivered.	Price delivered at refinery, including actual duty.	Remarks.
		Pounds.		*Pounds.*		
Jan. 10	Cuba	3,458,467	Feb. 7	3,449,558	3.5987	
18	do	1,751,198	do	1,723,549	3.4816	
18	do	3,162,148	Feb. 24	3,121,128	3.4905	
18	do	3,148,589	Feb. 14	3,168,800	3.4572	
20	Porto Rico	474,300	Jan. 28	472,481	3.3136	
26	Cuba	3,137,209	Feb. 28	3,090,684	3.4115	
28	do	7,584,498	Feb. 21	7,537,577	3.[illegible]	
31	do	4,881,427	Feb. 28	4,867,461	3.[illegible]	
Feb. 7	do	950,693	do	940,310	3.4558	
7	do	3,302,325	Feb. 23	3,278,860	3.4387	7 bags short.
17	do	1,650,033	Feb. 27	1,646,012		
17	do	1,553,020	Mar. 1	1,644,652	3.5689	
17	do	3,281,800	Mar. 24	3,254,784		
17	Porto Rico	4,416,700	Mar. 17	4,441,721	3.5473	
17	do	333,250	Apr. 12	340,912		
20	Cuba	956,718	Mar. 1	947,377	3.6488	
20	do	1,327,316	Feb. 28	1,305,703		
20	do	1,635,921	do	1,610,769	3.6742	78 bags short.
20	do	1,975,143	Mar. 22	1,941,200		
20	do	3,148,589	Mar. 13	3,164,841		
20	do	1,574,295	Mar. 27	1,574,822	3.6472	
20	do	1,574,295	Apr. 10	1,582,426		
20	do	3,478,060	Mar. 29	3,446,918	3.5606	18 bags short.
20	do	1,524,150	Mar. 16	1,514,992	3.6384	
23	do	1,982,465	Mar. 15	1,972,431	3.6914	
23	do	6,517,579	Mar. 22	6,482,759	3.6852	5 bags short.
27	Porto Rico	6,820,000	Mar. 17	6,811,068	3.8058	9 bags over.
27	Cuba	3,490,830	Apr. 3	3,438,444	3.7878	
28	Porto Rico	1,092,725	Mar. 29	1,097,447	3.7908	15 bags over.
28	do	1,565,660	Apr. 12	1,557,677		
Mar. 9	Cuba	7,949,626	Mar. 20	7,954,865	3.7423	
9	do	3,294,450	Mar. 29	3,279,796	3.7050	
13	do	3,261,505	do	3,248,289	3.7243	
13	do	8,200,976	Mar. 23	8,294,159	3.7058	
13	Porto Rico	4,061,000	Apr. 1	4,025,026	3.8480	60 bags short.
13	do	2,500,000	Mar. 21	2,453,916	3.8258	177 bags short.
21	Cuba	1,648,734	Apr. 6	1,645,654	3.8288	
21	do	1,647,740	Apr. 17	1,644,676	3.8876	3 bags short.
21	do	1,651,163	May 2	1,649,167		
21	do	7,753,039	do	7,729,930	3.9379	
21	do	7,418,620	Apr. 11	7,274,622	3 9084	
21	do	1,647,225	Apr. 22	1,642,112	3.8986	
21	do	1,651,163	Apr. 4	1,612,250	3.7903	
21	Porto Rico	1,250,000	Apr. 18	1,247,468	3.8805	
21	Cuba	1,961,581	Apr. 15	1,936,659	3.8907	
21	do	3,417,296	Apr. 18	3,404,144	3.9198	
Apr. 18	Porto Rico	6,789,000	May 7	6,803,574	3.9460	
18	Cuba	2,534,657	Apr. 26	2,508,185		
18	do	1,598,924	Apr. 29	1,584,373	3.9485	8 bags short.
18	do	2,267,104	May 4	2,245,824		
18	do	2,050,177	May 19	2,027,580		
18	do	5,399,299	May 9	5,332,315	3.9656	
18	do	3,155,458	May 19	3,122,551		
18	do	6,096,600	May 12	6,048,476	3.7449	
18	do	1,651,163	June 16	1,622,574	3.9216	
24	do	1,653,513	May 6	1,641,692	3.9098	
24	do	1,524,150	May 1	1,519,232	3.8654	
24	do	3,253,939	May 18	3,254,203	3.8299	2 bags short.
25	Porto Rico	1,250,000	May 4	1,253,406	3.9489	
May 31	Cuba	3,794,402	June 13	3,737,581	3.8121	
June 1	Porto Rico	4,898,000	do	4,947,364	3.8755	
7	Cuba	6,499,103	June 8	6,435,296	3.7817	
13	do	2,625,683	June 13	2,610,992	3.7325	
13	do	1,003,600	do	995,173	3.7855	
21	Porto Rico	4,103,540	June 27	4,068,529	3.8840	
21	Cuba	1,651,068	do	1,644,436	3.8961	
22	Porto Rico	4,662,710	do	4,634,703	3.9798	

Schedule of sugar purchased and delivered—Continued.

SUGARS DELIVERED AT REFINERY AFTER JULY 1.

Date of purchase.	Where produced.	Amount purchased.	Date of delivery.	Amount delivered.	Price delivered at refinery, including actual duty.	Remarks.
		Pounds.		*Pounds.*		
June 22	Cuba	2,451,595	Aug. 10	2,416,583		
22	....do	1,619,110	Aug. 14	1,608,520	3.7958	1 bag short.
22	....do	3,623,641	Aug. 22	3,561,403		41 bags short.
22	....do	2,361,837	..do	2,327,304		
22	....do	5,404,305	Aug. 24	5,350,438	3.9332	14 bags short.
22	....do	8,147,472	July 31	8,063,132	3.9329	72 bags short.
22	....do	1,629,217	July 15	1,604,157	3.7946	
22	....do	6,461,187	July 20	6,445,275	3.9189	
22	Porto Rico	2,380,000	Aug. 21	2,371,192	3.9565	
22	....do	1,827,750	July 13	1,831,469	3.9690	
22	....do	723,000	July 17	717,788		
22	Cuba	8,247,433	July 20	8,096,364	3.9707	
22	....do	1,662,616	July 25	1,631,736		
24	Philippine	6,585,600	Oct. 24	6,589,540		
27	....do	1,097,000	...do	1,081,587	(1)	
27	....do	965,978	Oct. 23	945,595		
27	....do	131,712	Nov. 9	134,240		
29	Cuba	2,529,937	Aug. 9	2,512,394		
29	....do	1,582,342	Aug. 4	1,572,606	3.8370	1 bag short.
29	....do	1,582,342	July 31	1,575,528		
29	....do	1,816,223	Aug. 2	1,813,748		
		62,890,897				

[1] Not completed.

Stock of raw sugar on hand July 1 .... pounds.. 21,044,800
Cost of same 3.957

Sugar purchased before and delivered after July 1 .... pounds.. 62,890,897
Sugar on hand July 1 .... do.... 21,044,800

Total interest in raw sugar July 1 .... do.... 83,935,697

TESTIMONY OF MR. W. A. HOEL.

Witness is sworn by the chairman.

The CHAIRMAN. Give the committee your full name?

Mr. HOEL. W. A. Hoel.

The CHAIRMAN. And your residence?

Mr. HOEL. Stirling, Colo.

The CHAIRMAN. How long have you lived there?

Mr. HOEL. Twelve years.

The CHAIRMAN. How far are you from Fort Morgan?

Mr. HOEL. I think about 48 miles.

The CHAIRMAN. How far from Longmont?

Mr. HOEL. Well, I don't know exactly, but something like 100 or 120 miles, I guess. I wouldn't say for sure.

The CHAIRMAN. What business are you engaged in?

Mr. HOEL. Engaged in farming now.

The CHAIRMAN. In farming?

Mr. HOEL. Yes, sir.

The CHAIRMAN. Are you engaged in anything else but farming?

Mr. HOEL. No, sir.

The CHAIRMAN. Have you any other line of business?

Mr. HOEL. No, sir.

The CHAIRMAN. Are you engaged in the culture of sugar beets?

Mr. HOEL. Yes, sir.

The CHAIRMAN. How long have you been so engaged?

Mr. HOEL. Ten years.

The CHAIRMAN. Do you rent land or use your own land?

Mr. HOEL. I tend my own land.

The CHAIRMAN. This last year you had how many acres in sugar beets?

Mr. HOEL. Twenty-nine acres.

The CHAIRMAN. Is that about a fair average?

Mr. HOEL. That is the heaviest I have ever had.

The CHAIRMAN. How many acres of land do you own?

Mr. HOEL. I own 160 acres, but there is only 100 acres of it under irrigation.

The CHAIRMAN. How many beets do you raise per acre?

Mr. HOEL. Fifteen tons per acre this year.

The CHAIRMAN. That is a good deal above the average, isn't it?

Mr. HOEL. That is above the average of the whole district.

The CHAIRMAN. It is above the average for the whole district?

Mr. HOEL. Yes, sir.

The CHAIRMAN. What do you figure your land as worth; the value of it?

Mr. HOEL. Well, I could have sold it lots of times for $125 per acre and didn't do it. That is a fair valuation.

The CHAIRMAN. That is a fair valuation?

Mr. HOEL. It might not be to take the whole 160 acres, but it would be worth $100 per acre clear through, with the dry land on it.

The CHAIRMAN. It is worth $100 per acre?

Mr. HOEL. Yes, sir; that would be a fair average.

The CHAIRMAN. What is the land worth which you have devoted to beet culture?

Mr. HOEL. $125 per acre.

The CHAIRMAN. Which is irrigated land?

Mr. HOEL. Yes, sir; that is irrigated land.

The CHAIRMAN. What price did you get per acre for these 15 tons of beets, or what did you average last year?

Mr. HOEL. $5.03 per ton.

The CHAIRMAN. So that the sugar content of your beets is rather lower than the average?

Mr. HOEL. Yes, sir; we had along a few days after we began the harvesting of our beets a large rain which started our beets to growing again, and the sugar content pushed down a little.

The CHAIRMAN. That is a gross return per acre of $75.45?

Mr. HOEL. I have it $75.88, but may have made a slight mistake in calculation.

The CHAIRMAN. Did you say $5.03 per ton?

Mr. HOEL. Yes, sir.

The CHAIRMAN. And 15 tons exactly per acre is the amount you gave me. Isn't there a fraction over 15 tons?

Mr. HOEL. Yes, sir; a right small fraction, maybe.

The CHAIRMAN. Well, I will take your figures.

Mr. HOEL. $75.88 per acre gross is what I have made it.

The CHAIRMAN. What did it cost you to raise an acre of those beets?

Mr. HOEL. Well, I figured the amount of hand labor, teamwork, and all, $38.90.

The CHAIRMAN. $38.90 per acre cost to you?

Mr. HOEL. It varies considerably, according to the distance a man lives from the dump.

The CHAIRMAN. But they are your figures of cost to you?

Mr. HOEL. Yes, sir.

The CHAIRMAN. Well, without going into all of the details, that leaves an apparent profit of $36.98 per acre. Take from that 6 per cent on a valuation of $125 for your land, which is $7.50 per acre rental value, and it still leaves you $29.48 net per acre. What were beet tops worth?

Mr. HOEL. $5 per acre.

The CHAIRMAN. Adding the $5 per acre for tops, gives us $34.48 profit per acre?

Mr. HOEL. I think that a little bit out of the way. Either you or I have made a mistake. I have down here $75.88, as what my beets brought me an acre. The tops were worth $5 an acre, and that makes a total of $80.88. Deducting $38.90 for my own labor and the hand labor, leaves me $41.98. I counted my taxes and interest on my land at about $10 per acre.

The CHAIRMAN. Well, the difference between you and me seems to be that you counted the interest on your land at a different percentage?

Mr. HOEL. Yes, sir; a little bit higher than you did, and then, too, I didn't figure down to the fraction. I just added these amounts up on this memorandum, not taking care of the fractions, and it made this.

The CHAIRMAN. You had to pay taxes, of course, as all good people must do, especially if they take the interest in their Government that they should take and want to do the fair thing.

Mr. HOEL. Yes, sir.

The CHAIRMAN. And you have to take out your taxes if you have your crops or not?

Mr. HOEL. Yes, sir.

The CHAIRMAN. A man must pay his taxes on the assessed value of his land, regardless of whether he raises crops or not?

Mr. HOEL. Yes, sir.

The CHAIRMAN. And, exclusive of taxes, my figures are right?

Mr. HOEL. Yes, sir; something like that.

The CHAIRMAN. And you figured that after paying taxes and allowing interest at 6 per cent on the value of your land you had a net profit of how much?

Mr. HOEL. About $31.98.

The CHAIRMAN. That is, after paying interest on your investment in land devoted to beet culture, and taxes on the assessed valuation of your land, hand labor and all other labor, water rent, and so on, you had a net return of $31.98 per acre?

Mr. HOEL. Yes, sir. It gave me about $18.90 per acre, counting my own labor for myself for cultivating these beets and hauling them off, but for the hand labor I paid that out in money.

The CHAIRMAN. That would give you $18.90 for your own labor?

Mr. HOEL. Yes, sir.

The CHAIRMAN. That is what you think fair?

Mr. HOEL. Yes, sir.

The CHAIRMAN. That is a pretty fair return on the money invested, isn't it?

Mr. HOEL. Yes, sir.

The CHAIRMAN. On the labor, capital, and everything involved?

Mr. HOEL. Yes, sir.

The CHAIRMAN. Now, isn't that a pretty fair profit, Mr. Hoel?

Mr. HOEL. Well, I would call it, when I get that much out of cultivating an acre of beets, that it is good pay for doing the work myself. I had the team labor.

The CHAIRMAN. Do you know of any other farm product that will pay that well per acre?

Mr. HOEL. Well, it hasn't been my experience there in Colorado or anywhere else.

The CHAIRMAN. At present prices beet growing is about the most profitable crop in the pursuit of farming?

Mr. HOEL. Yes, sir; taking the hail and freezes and everything that we have to contend with. I had my beets hailed out one day on the 12th day of June, all ruined, and I planted them again on the 19th or 20th of June, and I got——

The CHAIRMAN (interrupting). You need not go into all those details: You think you are getting a fair price for your beets?

Mr. HOEL. Well, we are perfectly satisfied with it.

The CHAIRMAN. You would like to have more?

Mr. HOEL. Oh, of course, it is quite natural for us in this world to want all we can get, but——

The CHAIRMAN (interrupting). You sell for as much as you can get?

Mr. HOEL. But the way things are now I am satisfied.

The CHAIRMAN. Let us see about that point. Have you figured on the percentage that the sugar factory makes?

Mr. HOEL. No, sir.

The CHAIRMAN. When you say you are satisfied with things the way they are now is it not because you feel that if you got into a wrangle, to use a plain everyday expression, like two dogs fighting over a bone, a third one might come along and take it all away? Did that thought have anything to do with your satisfaction?

Mr. HOEL. No, I don't know as it has. This is a pretty good profit for a crop of any kind, whosoever it is or whatever it is, and I am satisfied. And when one is satisfied I think the best thing that can be done is to let well enough alone.

The CHAIRMAN. Does this idea I have stated influence you, or does it in any manner account for your satisfaction, that probably if you get into a row, so far as the farmers are concerned, with the sugar-beet factories, the whole thing may have a bad effect upon the tariff and hurt all of you?

Mr. HOEL. Well, I would like to see things remain just as they are now. We are satisfied with present conditions.

The CHAIRMAN. Well, just answer my question that I asked you, please. Has that idea entered into your calculations; is that one of the arguments being made to the sugar-beet farmers in Colorado?

Mr. HOEL. Well, really it is; yes, sir. But we haven't argued anything about that.

The CHAIRMAN. That is the sentiment?

Mr. HOEL. Yes, sir.

The CHAIRMAN. That is, if you got to fussing about this division of profits between the sugar-beet growers and the sugar factories the tariff might be lowered and hurt all of you?

Mr. HOEL. Yes, sir.

The CHAIRMAN. All right; I thought you would tell me frankly about that. Do you represent any organization in coming here?

Mr. HOEL. Well, the Stirling Real Estate Exchange sent me here to tell the truth about this sugar-beet matter as I understand it.

The CHAIRMAN. And is paying your expenses?

Mr. HOEL. Yes, sir.

The CHAIRMAN. What is the Stirling Real Estate Exchange?

Mr. HOEL. It is an organization of the real estate men there, practically.

The CHAIRMAN. Is it an association of the real estate dealers?

Mr. HOEL. Yes, sir; that is my understanding.

The CHAIRMAN. Who belongs to it?

Mr. HOEL. Well, I couldn't give you but a few of their names. They are——

The CHAIRMAN (interrupting). I don't care anything about their names. How many people are in it?

Mr. HOEL. Quite a few.

The CHAIRMAN. How big a town is Sterling?

Mr. HOEL. Something over 4,000 inhabitants.

The CHAIRMAN. Is it an organization of real estate dealers or merchants or what?

Mr. HOEL. Real estate dealers, as I understand it.

The CHAIRMAN. Real estate dealers only?

Mr. HOEL. Yes, sir.

The CHAIRMAN. There are not more than 12 or 15 real estate dealers in a town of that size?

Mr. HOEL. I wouldn't be surprised if there are more than that number.

The CHAIRMAN. About 20, then?

Mr. HOEL. Yes, sir; I would say that.

The CHAIRMAN. Is that a fair guess at the number?

Mr. HOEL. Yes, sir; I would think so.

The CHAIRMAN. Those 20 men, who are real estate dealers in Sterling, sent you here to Washington to present the farmers' view?

Mr. HOEL. Yes, sir.

The CHAIRMAN. Who picked you out to come?

Mr. HOEL. Well, the real estate exchange asked me if I would go as a representative farmer.

The CHAIRMAN. Did they have a meeting of the farmers to consult over that matter?

Mr. HOEL. Well, they called one and wanted the farmers to come in but it was so snowy and bad that the farmers did not come in.

The CHAIRMAN. What was the particular occasion for the real estate exchange doing this?

Mr. HOEL. I don't know.

The CHAIRMAN. They are not beet growers?

Mr. HOEL. No, sir.

The CHAIRMAN. And are not farmers?

Mr. HOEL. No, sir.

The CHAIRMAN. What is their interest in this beet-sugar investigation?

Mr. HOEL. Well, I suppose they were interested in seeing things remain just as they are—this matter left alone.

The CHAIRMAN. Their idea was to keep everything smooth and lovely?

Mr. HOEL. Yes, sir; I suppose so.

The CHAIRMAN. And in agreement and accord?

Mr. HOEL. Yes, sir.

The CHAIRMAN. Harmonious, etc.?

Mr. HOEL. Yes, sir.

The CHAIRMAN. Was there any particular testimony given before this committee that had anything to do with your coming here to Washington to testify before us?

Mr. HOEL. I suppose the testimony of some of those others did.

The CHAIRMAN. Those representatives of the farmers' union stirred your people up?

Mr. HOEL. Yes, sir; I suppose so.

The CHAIRMAN. Have you studied their testimony?

Mr. HOEL. I have read some of it.

The CHAIRMAN. Did you read it all?

Mr. HOEL. No, sir.

The CHAIRMAN. Outside of the facts which you have given us about what it cost you to produce a ton of beets, or, that is, what it cost you to farm an acre of beets, and what you got out of them, and about the general satisfaction of the people out there in Colorado, and their interest in seeing nothing done about the tariff to disturb them, is there anything you would like to say?

Mr. HOEL. I would like to say that I have had American labor tend my beets for two years.

The CHAIRMAN. The hand labor?

Mr. HOEL. Yes, sir.

The CHAIRMAN. That is not the rule, is it?

Mr. HOEL. Yes, sir. And I want to add that the same American labor will tend mine another year.

The CHAIRMAN. You are the exception rather than the rule?

Mr. HOEL. Yes, sir; generally.

The CHAIRMAN. Usually the bulk of the handwork performed in the State of Colorado in sugar-beet culture is by foreigners?

Mr. HOEL. Yes, sir.

The CHAIRMAN. Foreigners brought out to the farms under contract from the large cities?

Mr. HOEL. Well, they may have come from the large cities in the first place; yes, sir; but in our place we have no trouble at all. All the farmers generally get their own help, and there are plenty of help live right around there.

The CHAIRMAN. Where do they get the help?

Mr. HOEL. Plenty live right there, and in the summer time they go out and live on a man's farm.

The CHAIRMAN. Are they Pollocks, Mexicans, negroes——

Mr. HOEL (interrupting). We have no negroes at all. They are mostly Russians, Japs, or German people.

The CHAIRMAN. Are they American citizens, those people you refer to?

Mr. HOEL. Well, of course a good many of them, I suppose, are not naturalized yet. I mean that their naturalization papers have not been taken out.

The CHAIRMAN. They are all foreigners?

Mr. HOEL. The most of them.

The CHAIRMAN. They do the bulk of the handwork in the sugar-beet culture?

Mr. HOEL. Yes, sir.

The CHAIRMAN. The conditions on your farm are the exception to the general rule?

Mr. HOEL. Yes, sir; it is an exception.

The CHAIRMAN. Is there anything else that you care to add?

Mr. HOEL. Well, I don't know that there is.

The CHAIRMAN. Is there any particular part of the testimony of any one of those three witnesses, viz, Messrs. Combs, Dakan, or Bodkin, of which complaint is made by you that you want to correct except what you have done already?

Mr. HOEL. No more than what I have done already.

The CHAIRMAN. Do any of the members of the committee wish to ask any questions?

Mr. RAKER. I would like to ask a few questions. Mr. Hoel, these figures as to the amounts that you got for your beets of course you got from your reports received from the sugar factory?

Mr. HOEL. Yes, sir.

Mr. RAKER. And you averaged it at $75.88?

Mr. HOEL. Yes, sir; not counting $5 per acre for the tops.

Mr. RAKER. You had a statement from each load you took to the factory?

Mr. HOEL. For every load we take there we get a statement. We keep the weight ticket for every load, and every month the factory sends us a statement for the number of loads of beets we hauled.

Mr. RAKER. You get your weigh ticket at the time the load is delivered and at the end of the month you get a statement showing the sugar content of your beets?

Mr. HOEL. Yes, sir.

Mr. RAKER. This statement as to the cost of plowing, seed, planting, cultivating, handwork, and harvesting you have made up since you were asked to come here as a witness?

Mr. HOEL. Yes, sir; but I always had it in my mind and knew what it was, generally, just as it is on this little memorandum.

Mr. RAKER. I understand; we always have these things in our mind, but sometimes do not definitely fix them there. You people got together and came on here and while coming on here you figured up about what it cost to raise these beets. You have never taken your farm and figured out as you went along what it cost you to do this work?

Mr. HOEL. I do not keep a record of every day's work as I go along, but I know what it costs me to plow an acre of land, and what I can plant in a day, and what beets I can cultivate in a day.

Mr. RAKER. Do you keep an account of how much money you have made each year from the growing of sugar beets?

Mr. HOEL. I don't keep any record of it.

Mr. RAKER. You are just like the rest of the farmers who are not hiring a great many men—you put in so much money and take out so much for the work, and then when you get to talking about it you figure it out?

Mr. HOEL. Yes, sir.

Mr. RAKER. That is what you did here?

Mr. HOEL. Yes, sir.

Mr. RAKER. All right, that is all I wish to ask.

Mr. FORDNEY. So far as the question of whether or not your labor is naturalized, the men that work on your place, you don't know anything about that?

Mr. HOEL. Yes, sir; I do.

Mr. FORDNEY. You have seen their naturalization papers?

Mr. HOEL. I have not seen them, but they are American citizens.

Mr. FORDNEY. Well, I mean the Japs that you spoke of more specially.

Mr. HOEL. Oh, no, sir. I thought you had reference to my hand labor this year.

Mr. FORDNEY. No; I meant your own hand labor and that of the average man in the beet fields as well.

The CHAIRMAN. He testified that his people were Americans, while the others were mostly foreigners.

Mr. FORDNEY. Oh, I didn't understand that. I suppose that the interest the real estate men have in sending you here is to see that the value of the farm lands in that vicinity keep up to the present standard, or increased if possible, because they are in that business, and believe that the growing of sugar beets enhances the value of all that property in the farming districts, and if that is true, it also enhances the value of city property as well?

Mr. HOEL. I suppose so.

Mr. FORDNEY. I would naturally suppose that the real estate men were interested in that direction?

Mr. HOEL. Yes, sir; and there was no organization of the farmers to get together and do anything.

Mr. FORDNEY. What did you say about Mr. Bodkin's statement as to the labor employed in the beet fields of Colorado? Do you think he is right or wrong?

Mr. HOEL. Well, I don't know what is the situation up there where Mr. Bodkin lives, but I know what is the case down where I live.

Mr. FORDNEY. He said when the farmers needed labor to raise beets they went to the sugar company and the company sent men to the slums and there employed help and sent the help to the farmers.

Mr. HOEL. I can only answer for myself and our country at Stirling, and I haven't had to have help once from the sugar company.

Mr. FORDNEY. Is the labor in your sugar fields the average class of farm labor?

Mr. HOEL. Not always. A good many are Russians that have only been here a few years, and you couldn't put them up to the standard of Americans.

Mr. FORDNEY. When they become citizens do they make good citizens?

Mr. HOEL. They are good. I have two Russian neighbors who have been over here I don't know how long, and both bought farms adjoining me this spring; one of 240 acres and one of 160 acres that adjoins me. They were beet hoers at one time.

Mr. FORDNEY. You farmers in your vicinity are generally satisfied with the treatment you receive, and the price you get for your beets, and you want to be left alone?

Mr. HOEL. Yes, sir; as a rule.

Mr. FORDNEY. If any legislation here were to injure the industry so as to lower the value of your product you wish to protest?

Mr. HOEL. Yes, sir. We would like to see things remain so we may have a fair price for our beets; that is all.

Mr. FORDNEY. I believe that is all I care to ask.

Mr. RAKER. It would be wholly immaterial to you farmers how much the sugar factory made under present conditions so long as they let you alone to make as much as is designated in your testimony?

Mr. HOEL. Yes, sir.

Mr. RAKER. That is all.

The CHAIRMAN. If there are no other questions we will excuse Mr. Hoel, with the thanks of the committee for his attendance.

TESTIMONY OF MR. A. L. GIBSON.

Witness is sworn by the chairman.

The CHAIRMAN. What is your full name?

Mr. GIBSON. A. L. Gibson, and I might say, Abraham Lincoln Gibson.

The CHAIRMAN. What is your residence?

Mr. GIBSON. Longmont, Colo.

The CHAIRMAN. How long have you lived there?

Mr. GIBSON. Since 1886.

The CHAIRMAN. Do you know James Bodkin?

Mr. GIBSON. I know the gentleman.

The CHAIRMAN. How long have you known him?

Mr. GIBSON. Well, I should think it would be five or six years.

The CHAIRMAN. Do you know Mr. E. U. Combs?

Mr. GIBSON. No, sir.

The CHAIRMAN. Do you know Mr. Albert Dakan?

Mr. GIBSON. Yes, sir; I saw him the morning I left Longmont.

The CHAIRMAN. What business are you engaged in?

Mr. GIBSON. I am a farmer. That is my business entirely, I would say.

The CHAIRMAN. Have you any outside line at all?

Mr. GIBSON. No, sir. I might have some interests in stock or something like that in some concerns, but I have no other business.

The CHAIRMAN. Have you any sugar stock?

Mr. GIBSON. Oh, no; no, sir.

The CHAIRMAN. Do you cultivate beets yourself?

Mr. GIBSON. No, sir; I don't have time to cultivate them.

The CHAIRMAN. Do you cultivate them on your land?

Mr. GIBSON. Yes, sir.

The CHAIRMAN. Do you have it done?

Mr. GIBSON. Yes, sir.

The CHAIRMAN. Do you rent land?

Mr. GIBSON. I go in partnership with my tenant. I have three different places where I raise beets.

The CHAIRMAN. What system do you adopt?

Mr. GIBSON. I have a place right near Longmont, practically adjoining Longmont. That is, the acreage of small tracts of land adjoin my place, and that is the particular place I will give you information about, and then tell you about the rest of them.

The CHAIRMAN. All right; go ahead.

Mr. GIBSON. The others I rent and they take care of their own beets. At this particular place I furnished the land, the water, the seed, and pay $10 on the hand labor. The tenant has got to furnish all the teams and all the machinery with which to do the work. He prepares the ground, getting it into shape, plants the beets, cultivates them, irrigates them, pulls them, and delivers them.

The CHAIRMAN. How do you divide?

Mr. GIBSON. One-half.

The CHAIRMAN. Under that system what do you realize per acre net on the land, not allowing for taxes?

Mr. GIBSON. That makes a great deal of difference. I have raised as high as something like 17 tons per acre, and as low as 10 tons; some 800 pounds per acre.

The CHAIRMAN. What would it average?

Mr. GIBSON. As to the average I couldn't tell you.

The CHAIRMAN. Give me the figures for last year.

Mr. GIBSON. I can give you in detail right up to the cent, if that is what you want.

The CHAIRMAN. For last year?

Mr. GIBSON. Yes, sir.

The CHAIRMAN. All right, suppose you do.

Mr. GIBSON If you will let me refer to my notes?

The CHAIRMAN. Do you mean this year?

Mr. GIBSON. I mean 1911.

The CHAIRMAN. Go ahead. Refresh your memory from that memorandum and tell us about it.

Mr. GIBSON. I will take mine as the first part of it. That is, the taxes were $1.07 per acre.

The CHAIRMAN. The taxes?

Mr. GIBSON. Yes, sir; that is, the taxes on my property. I divide the taxes on the whole place.

The CHAIRMAN. All right.

Mr. GIBSON. The expense for my part is as follows:

	Per acre.
Taxes	$1.07
Water	.53
Seed	2.00
Hand labor (my portion)	10.00
Total	13.60

The CHAIRMAN. What did you realize from those beets, per acre?

Mr. GIBSON. I got for them $3,157.28.

The CHAIRMAN. For how many acres?

Mr. GIBSON. For 50 acres.

The CHAIRMAN. That is, for your part of the beets?

Mr. GIBSON. No; I got half of the beets.

The CHAIRMAN. Do you get half of the tops?

Mr. GIBSON. The tops are left on the place and we feed them.

The CHAIRMAN. Well, do you get half of the tops in that way, or how is it?

Mr. GIBSON. Well, we just feed them to the cattle.

The CHAIRMAN. Do you and your tenant own the cattle together, or are they your cattle?

Mr. GIBSON. Yes, sir; we own the cattle together.

The CHAIRMAN. And in that way you get half of the tops?

Mr. GIBSON. Yes, sir. Or, I might go back of that and say that I furnish the beet tops and he does the work, and we divide half of the profits in the cattle. We may go in a hole on the cattle, but I can not tell you about that.

The CHAIRMAN. But you have a one-half interest in the cattle?

Mr. GIBSON. Yes, sir.

The CHAIRMAN. So therefore you get half of the beet tops in their being fed to the cattle?

Mr. GIBSON. Yes, sir.

Mr. FORDNEY. That is $63.14 per acre?

Mr. GIBSON. Yes, sir.

The CHAIRMAN. What are half of the beet tops worth?

Mr. GIBSON. They said $5 per acre, but that is a question——

The CHAIRMAN (interrupting). Do you think that a fair estimate?

Mr. GIBSON. I would think that a fair price. I would say that is all right. I don't know that anybody got $5 per acre for them, however.

The CHAIRMAN. They say that is what they are worth to feed?

Mr. GIBSON. Yes, sir; I think that is right.

The CHAIRMAN. That would make a total of $65.64 if you add $2.50 for your half of the beet tops?

Mr. GIBSON. Yes, sir.

The CHAIRMAN. That is what you got for your investment and use of the land?

Mr. GIBSON. Yes, sir.

The CHAIRMAN. What is that land worth?

Mr. GIBSON. I couldn't tell you. I can tell you what I paid for it in 1899, and I can tell you what land adjoining me sold for in blocks of 5 and 10 acres.

The CHAIRMAN. You may take all those things into consideration and give me your opinion, because all values are matters of opinion. Just give me your estimate.

Mr. GIBSON. I can give it to you in this way: I know one piece of land that sold for $15,000, 80 acres. And 20 acres adjoining me sold for $4,500.

The CHAIRMAN. That is pretty nearly as fine land as Bodkin's. I understood one of you gentlemen to say that he utterly disputed there being any such land.

Mr. GIBSON. Those are 5 and 10 acre tracts that I am talking about.

Mr. FORDNEY. Your land adjoins the city?

Mr. GIBSON. Yes, sir.

The CHAIRMAN. Bodkin's did, too?

Mr. GIBSON. Well, I can tell you about Bodkin, if you want me to.

The CHAIRMAN. Your land is worth about what Bodkin put as a value on his land?

Mr. GIBSON. I don't know about that.

The CHAIRMAN. Well, the figures show that.

Mr. GIBSON. I presume so, but don't know.

The CHAIRMAN. What would you say was the value of your land per acre?

Mr. GIBSON. If this man sold his place of 80 acres near me for $15,000, and mine being right at it, it ought to be worth a price of $200 per acre.

The CHAIRMAN. How far are you from town?

Mr. GIBSON. I am a mile from the city.

The CHAIRMAN. How far is Bodkin?

Mr. GIBSON. From my town, 10 miles.

The CHAIRMAN. Yours from town is about how far?

Mr. GIBSON. The little city is on the corner and there is a quarter section of land between me and the city.

Mr. RAKER. Just a quarter is my understanding.

Mr. GIBSON. Yes, sir; and his 40 acres come next.

The CHAIRMAN. He is a quarter of a mile out of town?

Mr. GIBSON. That is just a little burg.

The CHAIRMAN. That is a town?

Mr. GIBSON. Yes, sir; I presume so.

The CHAIRMAN. You are a mile from your city?

Mr. GIBSON. Yes, sir; from this little city.

The CHAIRMAN. You say your land in your opinion is worth about $200 per acre, and Bodkin said his land was worth $250 per acre?

Mr. GIBSON. I believe that was his testimony.

The CHAIRMAN. Well now, that showed a gross proceeds of $65.64 per acre per year from your land?

Mr. GIBSON. Yes, sir.

The CHAIRMAN. And you didn't invest but how much?

Mr. GIBSON. $13.60, but I have to furnish the land in addition.

The CHAIRMAN. For that $65.64 you put out $13.60?

Mr. GIBSON. $13.60 and the land.

The CHAIRMAN. This $63.14 is your one-half interest in the whole thing?

Mr. GIBSON. No, sir; the whole amount of money received from the 50 acres was $3,157.28, and my half of it would be what?

The CHAIRMAN. Oh, I thought that was your half, but that is the whole business?

Mr. GIBSON. Yes, sir. Take one-half of that and you will get my part.

The CHAIRMAN. That is $31.57 per acre that you get?

Mr. GIBSON. Yes, sir.

The CHAIRMAN. I thought that $3,157.28 was your half of the gross proceeds from the 50 acres?

Mr. GIBSON. Oh, no; that is the whole amount received.

The CHAIRMAN. We will take that $31.57 and add the $2.50 for one-half the tops, and it makes $34.07. Then deduct the $13.60, which you expended, and you have $20.47 net?

Mr. GIBSON. Yes, sir.

The CHAIRMAN. You have already counted your taxes into that proposition?

Mr. GIBSON. Yes, sir.

The CHAIRMAN. And if you figure your land as worth $200 per acre, 6 per cent on that would be $12 to come off from that $20.47?

Mr. GIBSON. Yes, sir; leaving $8.47.

The CHAIRMAN. So that without doing anything but furnish a little money, you didn't do any work?

Mr. GIBSON. No, sir; but there was hardly a day but what I oversaw it.

The CHAIRMAN. You got $20.47 for your land without doing anything?

Mr. GIBSON. Yes, sir.

The CHAIRMAN. Now, how does the tenant come out?

Mr. GIBSON. I will tell you about that. He charges up—

	Per acre.
Plowing	$2.50
Harrowing	.25
Leveling	.25
Drilling	.50
Cultivating	1.55
Ditching	1.05
Irrigating	1.50
Plowing out	2.50
Delivery, at 30 cents per ton	3.24
Hand labor	9.00
Total	22.34

The CHAIRMAN. Back there about the delivery; how many tons to the acre were there of beets?

Mr. GIBSON. Ten tons and 817 pounds, I think.

The CHAIRMAN. And the next item was?

Mr. GIBSON. He has to pay for the topping and pulling.

The CHAIRMAN. I thought that was hand labor?

Mr. GIBSON. That was hand labor, but I paid the first part and he pays the next. It is $9 that he pays.

The CHAIRMAN. I thought you paid one-half of that?

Mr. GIBSON. That was the original contract, but this year we had two different contracts. The Russians or Germans left and went to Denver, and we had another contractor to take the topping and pulling.

The CHAIRMAN. Did the foreigners come out from Denver to do the hand work?

Mr. GIBSON. Yes, sir; that is where they came from to do our hand work.

The CHAIRMAN. Is that every item?

Mr. GIBSON. Unless you are going to put in $2.50 for his one-half of the tops.

The CHAIRMAN. Well, we want to understand his expenses first.

Mr. GIBSON. That makes $22.34.

The CHAIRMAN. What are his one-half of the proceeds?

Mr. GIBSON. The same as mine.

The CHAIRMAN. $31.57 per acre plus $2.50 for tops makes $34.07, and deducting the tenant's expenses leaves him $11.73?

Mr. GIBSON. Yes, sir. Now, the difference between the $11.73 per acre which the tenant gets and the $20.47 which I get is what I am allowed for the land; or, taking off $12 for the land, leaves me $8.47. Wouldn't that be it?

The CHAIRMAN. No; that is not a fair way of figuring it, I don't think; because this is this tenant's business all the time, and you come only once in a while.

Mr. GIBSON. Well, I am there quite often.

Mr. RAKER. That is a clear gain to you while the tneant has to keep his family on his part.

Mr. GIBSON. Every item of work he has performed he has been paid for.

The CHAIRMAN. Very well; we will draw our own deductions from the figures.

Mr. GIBSON. All right.

Mr. FORDNEY. These figures that you have given figure the tenant's wages as so much, and in addition he gets $11.73 per acre profit, over and above his labor?

Mr. GIBSON. Yes, sir.

The CHAIRMAN. The tenant charges in his own labor?

Mr. GIBSON. Yes, sir; just as I told you.

The CHAIRMAN. And still he makes this profit of $11.73 per acre?

Mr. GIBSON. Yes, sir. Perhaps you want to know what my percentage is this year?

The CHAIRMAN. Well, we can figure that for ourselves, though we may not figure it as you do.

Mr. GIBSON. I mean the sugar content of my beets, how much per ton I get?

The CHAIRMAN. I thought you gave us that just now?

Mr. GIBSON. I averaged $6.31 per ton of beets.

The CHAIRMAN. What percentage of saccharine matter or sugar purity was there in your beets?

Mr. GIBSON. I will give you the sugar company's sheet.

The CHAIRMAN. We have the schedule all right.

Mr. GIBSON. I can show it to you if you wish.

The CHAIRMAN. No; it is already in.

Mr. FORDNEY. Are your figures so much for 12 per cent and an increase of 33⅓ cents or 25 cents for each 1 per cent above that?

Mr. GIBSON. Mine is 25 cents.

The CHAIRMAN. We have the contracts.

Mr. GIBSON. They sent me a slip for the different percentages of sugar.

The CHAIRMAN. That is what you got for all of the beets on that tract of 50 acres?

Mr. GIBSON. Yes, sir; $6.31 per ton.

The CHAIRMAN. And it amounted to the figure which you gave, $3,157.28?

Mr. GIBSON. Yes, sir.

Mr. FORDNEY. That is a little better than 17 per cent beets?

Mr. GIBSON. Yes, sir.

The CHAIRMAN. Is there any other particular matter that you wanted to go into that I haven't asked you about?

Mr. GIBSON. Yes, sir; there is something that I either want you to ask me about or let me ask you about, and I don't know which it should be.

The CHAIRMAN. Well, you better tell us about it as we are trying to find out.

Mr. GIBSON. These are my credentials:

LONGMONT COMMERCIAL ASSOCIATION,
Longmont, Colo., January 6, 1912.

CHAIRMAN OF THE SPECIAL COMMITTEE INVESTIGATION OF THE AMERICAN SUGAR REFINING CO. AND OTHERS:

DEAR SIR: At a special meeting of the board of directors of the Longmont Commercial Association held January 5, 1912, the board appointed Mr. A. L. Gibson to represent this association before your honorable body.

As Mr. Gibson is a farmer of great experience and a man highly thought of in this community, we believe that he is amply able to give testimony which will be of great value to your committee, and all courtesy extended to him will be greatly appreciated by this association.

Yours, very respectfully,

V. R. PENNOCK, *President.*
CLIFFORD DAVIS, *Secretary.*

The CHAIRMAN. I did overlook that. What interest did you come here to represent?

Mr. GIBSON. It shows there, the Longmont Commercial Association.

The CHAIRMAN. What is that, a business men's organization?

Mr. GIBSON. Yes, sir; it is composed of the business men and farmers.

The CHAIRMAN. Composed of business men and farmers?

Mr. GIBSON. Yes, sir; the farmers are interested just as much as others in the conditions existing there.

The CHAIRMAN. Has Longmont about 8,000 or 10,000 inhabitants?

Mr. GIBSON. No, sir; they have about 5,000 inhabitants.

The CHAIRMAN. And they selected you to come out and make these representations to the committee?

Mr. GIBSON. Yes, sir.

The CHAIRMAN. And they pay your expenses?

Mr. GIBSON. Yes, sir; they pay my expenses.

The CHAIRMAN. They do that?

Mr. GIBSON. Yes, sir.

The CHAIRMAN. What is their particular interest in this matter?

Mr. GIBSON. To show the conditions there. They think the beet industry a good industry, one of the best they have.

The CHAIRMAN. To show their interest in that industry and their support of it?

Mr. GIBSON. Yes, sir.

The CHAIRMAN. Was there any particular occasion why they wanted you to come here?

Mr. GIBSON. They had a meeting, and I think they read that night some evidence from Mr. Bodkin and Mr. Dakan.

The CHAIRMAN. And they wanted you to come and contradict some parts of their testimony?

Mr. GIBSON. Yes, sir.

The CHAIRMAN. Have you contradicted all parts of the testimony of Mr. Combs, Mr. Bodkin, and Mr. Dakan that you wanted to contradict, or is there anything further that you can think of that you specially want to talk to us about that I have not asked you about?

Mr. GIBSON. I don't know that there is.

The CHAIRMAN. Have you read their evidence?

Mr. GIBSON. Part of it, but not all of it. I saw some of it in the newspaper.

The CHAIRMAN. Extracts were published in your papers?

Mr. GIBSON. Yes, sir.

The CHAIRMAN. Have you read all of their evidence given at our hearings?

Mr. GIBSON. No, sir; not all of it.

The CHAIRMAN. Have you read some of it?

Mr. GIBSON. Yes, sir; part of it.

The CHAIRMAN. Is there now any particular part of it that you want to tell us about; any specific thing they said that you do not agree with them about; if so, what is it?

Mr. GIBSON. Well, yes; I want to contradict Mr. Bodkin's evidence so far as our beet help is concerned.

The CHAIRMAN. About the labor?

Mr. GIBSON. Yes, sir.

The CHAIRMAN. Are you contradicting him in terms or just on substantial facts stated by him to this committee that the labor that performed the handwork were brought out on contracts from the big cities. Is that true or false?

Mr. GIBSON. He said from the slums.

The CHAIRMAN. Well, they were just terms used.

Mr. FORDNEY. Excuse me, Mr. Chairman, but my recollection is that he was very positive and explicit in his statement on that subject.

The CHAIRMAN. Well, I will change my question. Is it true that the bulk of the people that do this farm handwork are foreigners that are brought from the poorer quarters, to use a less offensive term; is that true or false?

Mr. GIBSON. I don't say that it is false, and I will give you my reasons for my view. My understanding is that the labor that came there came from Nebraska, and——

The CHAIRMAN (interrupting). Didn't you say something just now about bringing people from Denver, or your own people going back to Denver?

Mr. GIBSON. The ones that we hired.

The CHAIRMAN. Is that a great city?

Mr. GIBSON. I would call it a fairly good sized city.

The CHAIRMAN. It is one of the great western cities?

Mr. GIBSON. Yes, sir.

The CHAIRMAN. Therefore your experience corroborates what he said about that?

Mr. GIBSON. That they go to the slums for them; no.

The CHAIRMAN. Well, you are confining your fault-finding to the use of the word "slums" more than to anything else. That may have been oratorical; I don't know. What else are you finding fault with except the use of the word "slums"? Those people are the poorer people?

Mr. GIBSON. Yes, sir; they are a laboring class of people.

The CHAIRMAN. They live in the poorer parts of the city when they go back to the city?

Mr. GIBSON. Yes, sir.

The CHAIRMAN. They wouldn't live on Fifth Avenue in New York if they went to New York?

Mr. GIBSON. No, sir.

The CHAIRMAN. They live in what is, in common vernacular, called the "slums"?

Mr. GIBSON. I suppose that may be true.

The CHAIRMAN. Then why is Mr. Bodkin's statement such an outrageous lie, if that is true?

Mr. GIBSON. I do not know that it is such an outrageous lie.

The CHAIRMAN. Why is it false then? You say that it is false, and yet in your own testimony you admit that it is true; why is his statement false?

Mr. GIBSON. Why, I don't think that they all come from Denver.

The CHAIRMAN. He didn't say that they all came from Denver, as I remember his evidence.

Mr. GIBSON. I wish to say, as for my help, I never went outside of the city, or outside of my place to get any help that came there.

The CHAIRMAN. They came from Denver?

Mr. GIBSON. Yes, sir; they came from Denver.

The CHAIRMAN. How did they come there?

Mr. GIBSON. Usually in the spring, when we got out our contracts, they come and look over the ground.

The CHAIRMAN. They came out from Denver?

Mr. GIBSON. Yes, sir; I suppose that is right.

The CHAIRMAN. And work in the beet fields under contract?

Mr. GIBSON. Yes, sir.

The CHAIRMAN. And go back to Denver when the work is over?

Mr. GIBSON. They did in my case.

The CHAIRMAN. Then in what respect has Mr. Bodkin falsely represented the situation to this committee? Do you just object to his use of the word "slums"?

Mr. GIBSON. Yes.

The CHAIRMAN. You wouldn't say that these people live in the finer quarters of the city?

Mr. GIBSON. Oh, no; they are the working classes.

The CHAIRMAN. They are living in what is commonly called "the slums" in New York, Chicago, Denver, and other large cities?

Mr. GIBSON. Perhaps so, but the ones that took our contract last were Mexicans.

The CHAIRMAN. What was that?

Mr. GIBSON. The ones that took the contract to pull our beets last were Mexicans.

The CHAIRMAN. Where did they come from?

Mr. GIBSON. Longmont.

The CHAIRMAN. Do you regard them as white American citizens?

Mr. GIBSON. Well, I don't know about that.

The CHAIRMAN. I don't know what they are myself and am simply trying to find out.

Mr. GIBSON. They came from New Mexico.

The CHAIRMAN. Are they people of our blood and color?

Mr. GIBSON. No; they are as dark as Mexicans.

The CHAIRMAN. They are a different race?

Mr. GIBSON. Yes, sir.

Mr. RAKER. They live in the poorer quarters?

Mr. GIBSON. Yes, sir.

The CHAIRMAN. They have a quarter of their own down in the south?

Mr. GIBSON. I don't know about that.

The CHAIRMAN. You have never been there?

Mr. GIBSON. No, sir.

The CHAIRMAN. I suppose they are people something like that?

Mr. GIBSON. I suppose so.

The CHAIRMAN. Is there anything further that you wish to say to this committee?

Mr. GIBSON. I also have a letter from the University of Colorado, which possibly may be of interest.

The CHAIRMAN. Yes; that is on the proposition stated by Mr. Bodkin that he could not get the University of Colorado to analyze his beets?

Mr. GIBSON. Yes, sir.

The CHAIRMAN. Explain that.

Mr. Gibson. I will just read the letter, which is as follows:

University of Colorado,
Boulder, Colo., January 5, 1911.

Mr. Clifford Davis,
Secretary Longmont Commercial Association,
Longmont, Colo.

Dear Sir: I have your letter regarding the attitude of the University of Colorado in the matter of chemical analyses. The university, as such, does not make chemical analyses for the public; it has not extra funds and teaching force necessary for the purpose. But the regents do allow certain departments to do expert work on their own account to a limited extent, provided this work does not interfere with the efficiency of the departments. In accord with this general practice, Dr. Ekeley, professor of chemistry, made an analysis of beets for certain parties, and offered to make further tests, of course, under the conditions, at a certain cost for the service. Any charges or implications that may have been made not in accord with this statement I believe to be incorrect.

Very truly, yours, James H. Baker.

The Chairman. You don't know anything about whether Mr. Bodkin went there and tried to get that analysis made or not, do you?

Mr. Gibson. No, sir.

The Chairman. Then you can not contradict his evidence in that respect?

Mr. Gibson. No, sir; no further than this letter does it.

The Chairman. That you do not know about. You are only stating what you know about these things?

Mr. Gibson. Yes, sir. This evidence was gotten by the Longmont Commercial Association, as you will see the letter from the president of the University of Colorado is addressed to the secretary of the Longmont Commercial Association.

The Chairman. They do not say anything in that letter about Mr. Bodkin?

Mr. Gibson. No, sir; not directly, but say anybody,

The Chairman. We will now have to adjourn, as the hour has arrived, but will conclude with your testimony to-morrow morning.

And, at 5 o'clock p. m., an adjournment was taken to 10.30 o'clock a. m., Friday, January 12, 1912.

AMERICAN SUGAR REFINING CO. AND OTHERS.

SPECIAL COMMITTEE ON THE INVESTIGATION
OF THE AMERICAN SUGAR REFINING CO. AND OTHERS,
HOUSE OF REPRESENTATIVES,
Washington, D. C., Friday, January 12, 1912.

The committee met at 10 o'clock a. m., Hon. Thomas W. Hardwick (chairman) presiding.

TESTIMONY OF MR. A. L. GIBSON—Resumed.

The CHAIRMAN. Mr. Gibson, I believe yesterday, when the committee adjourned, we were discussing the labor question, and the chairman had asked you to point out specifically not so much the conclusions, as about which you differed from Mr. Bodkin and the other witnesses about whose testimony you complain, but the precise facts which you say they have not fairly represented to the committee. Can you give us anything further on that line?

Mr. GIBSON. Yes. I took his testimony home and looked it over as well as I could last evening, and I want to deny some of the charges which he makes—that is, I want to deny the charge made against the University of Colorado as not being true about making those tests.

The CHAIRMAN. In reference to the tests by the University of Colorado—that they had refused to make the tests?

Mr. GIBSON. Yes; as shown by the letter I left with you yesterday.

The CHAIRMAN. That letter has gone into the record?

Mr. GIBSON. Yes, sir.

The CHAIRMAN. You are familiar with its contents?

Mr. GIBSON. I read it over.

The CHAIRMAN. That letter did not deny that Mr. Bodkin had made an application to them and had been refused?

Mr. GIBSON. No, sir.

The CHAIRMAN. It simply undertook to state the policy of the university in general terms?

Mr. GIBSON. That they would make the tests.

The CHAIRMAN. And of your own knowledge you know nothing whatever about the truth of that statement?

Mr. GIBSON. No, sir; this evidence was got for me by the Commercial Club.

The CHAIRMAN. It is simply a letter which the university has written in defense of its own policy and practices? You know nothing of your own knowledge about the facts stated therein?

Mr. GIBSON. No, sir.

The CHAIRMAN. Now, what is the next point you wish to refer to?

Mr. GIBSON. I wish to deny the testimony about our cheap labor.

The CHAIRMAN. Do you remember on what page of the record that is?

Mr. GIBSON. No, sir; I do not remember. Twenty dollars an acre is a pretty good price for labor when a whole family can make from $1.75 to $2 a day.

The CHAIRMAN. Did those witnesses say anything about cheap labor?

Mr. GIBSON. Yes; that they got the cheap labor from the slums.

The CHAIRMAN. We went over that before.

Mr. GIBSON. Yes, sir.

The CHAIRMAN. I do not think he said it was cheap labor.

Mr. FORDNEY. He stated it was $2-a-day labor, and that you had to "go some" to get labor as cheap as that.

The CHAIRMAN. Mr. Gibson, is that cheap labor?

Mr. GIBSON. No; I wouldn't consider it so.

The CHAIRMAN. What other language of his do you take exception to? We went over the slums matter fully yesterday.

Mr. GIBSON. That is all.

The CHAIRMAN. You have not told me what it is about the labor situation you take exception to.

Mr. GIBSON. That he thought——

The CHAIRMAN. I am not asking you about what he thought, but what he testified to.

Mr. GIBSON. That the help was gotten from the slums. I do not consider them slums.

The CHAIRMAN. We went over that fully. You stated you brought your people from Denver and that they lived in the poorer quarters of the larger cities, and that you did not consider them slums. I do not care anything at all about the difference.

Mr. GIBSON. All right, sir.

The CHAIRMAN. Is there any other specific statement he made you want to give us further light on?

Mr. GIBSON. I want to say I do not think his land is worth $250 an acre, for the reason that land in Colorado has got to have a good water right before it is worth $250 an acre.

The CHAIRMAN. Did you examine his testimony on that subject?

Mr. GIBSON. Yes.

The CHAIRMAN. Do you know whether he said his land was good irrigated land?

Mr. GIBSON. It ought to be if he values it at $250, and he had to hire water to irrigate his beets.

The CHAIRMAN. He did not hire water, did he?

Mr. GIBSON. Yes, sir; that is what he said.

The CHAIRMAN. I thought he simply charged up what the water would have cost him if he hired it.

Mr. GIBSON. I think you will find he hired it.

Mr. MALBY. I had the impression there was not any beet land in the State of Colorado except irrigated land.

Mr. GIBSON. There may be some dry lands above ditches.

Mr. MALBY. Is that beet land?

Mr. GIBSON. No, sir.

Mr. MALBY. I am talking about beet land. I said my understanding was that there was not any beet culture except in irrigated districts.

Mr. GIBSON. Yes.

The CHAIRMAN. Let me call your attention to Mr. Bodkin's statement on that subject:

> Mr. BODKIN. To start with, you have got to have the land. That rents, in our neighborhood, for $20 cash rent per acre.
>
> Mr. RAKER. You are going now on a cash basis?
>
> Mr. BODKIN. Yes.
>
> Mr. RAKER. What is that land worth?
>
> Mr. BODKIN. For my field I have been offered $250 an acre.

You do not deny that statement?

Mr. GIBSON. I do not deny he was offered that.

The CHAIRMAN (reading):

> But beets would grow on unimproved land just as well, which would be worth only $150 an acre. Of course, that is way out.
>
> Mr. RAKER. On this $250 land would you have a water right?
>
> Mr. BODKIN. Of course; and this cheaper land would, too; but I have other improvements and other things on my land, and it is closer to town. I am saying that sugar beets would grow away out from town on unimproved ground which could be had for $150 an acre.
>
> Mr. HINDS. By improvements, you mean buildings?
>
> Mr. BODKIN. Yes.
>
> Mr. HINDS. You mean buildings, and not improvements of the ground itself, as by fertilization?
>
> Mr. BODKIN. Yes; improvements and a desirable place to live; that is what I refer to.
>
> Mr. RAKER. The $250 land is land that is fenced and has been plowed and has sufficient houses and grounds and all sufficient farm buildings on it to run a place that would make it convenient.
>
> Mr. BODKIN. And close to the dump and elevators, and close to town, with mail and telephone and everything.
>
> Mr. RAKER. That is what I included; and with the water rights; and the water right paid goes with that land?
>
> Mr. BODKIN. Yes.

You have heard that testimony. Do you conclude from that testimony that Mr. Bodkin's land has water rights, or not?

Mr. GIBSON. I say that he has water rights; but if he has to hire water——

The CHAIRMAN (interposing). Of course, if he has to hire it he hasn't got it.

Mr. GIBSON. He did hire it.

The CHAIRMAN. Oh, no.

Mr. GIBSON. Yes; you go on and read his testimony and you will find he did hire water. I will read it for you:

> Mr. RAKER. That is labor?
>
> Mr. BODKIN. Yes. The next is three cultivatings, at 50 cents per acre each, $1.50 for the three; second ditching, 50 cents per acre; second irrigation, for the labor, $1; cultivating after that, 50 cents per acre; ditching after that, 50 cents per acre; third irrigation, $1 per acre. Price of the water for this third irrigation, $3.33 per acre. That is, for the labor for the third irrigation, $1; and the price I paid for the water for the third irrigation is $3.33 per acre.

Now, I say that land in Colorado to be worth $250 an acre has got to have a water right so you never have to hire any water.

The CHAIRMAN. Could not this be true, that what he meant was he charged up in his expense account, like you gentlemen all do, what it was worth if he did have to buy it?

Mr. GIBSON. What did he want to charge it up for if he didn't have to hire it?

The CHAIRMAN. What do you charge the land up for if you do not have to buy it?

Mr. GIBSON. If you have got a good right it is not worth $3.33.

Mr. MALBY. Your idea is if he allows himself $20 an acre for rent of the land he ought not to charge for the water in addition?

Mr. GIBSON. I do not charge up rent for my land in my statement.

The CHAIRMAN. Did you charge anything for irrigation in the statement you gave us?

Mr. GIBSON. Yes, sir.

The CHAIRMAN. And yet you own an irrigation right?

Mr. GIBSON. Yes.

The CHAIRMAN. Is not that exactly what Mr. Bodkin did?

Mr. GIBSON. No, sir.

The CHAIRMAN. What is the difference?

Mr. GIBSON. I do not charge up for irrigation.

The CHAIRMAN. I thought you said you did.

Mr. GIBSON. Just one minute.

The CHAIRMAN. Do you charge for irrigation or not?

Mr. GIBSON. I charge for the assessment.

The CHAIRMAN. You charge the water rate which you pay?

Mr. GIBSON. I charge for the assessment on the ditch.

The CHAIRMAN. You charge what you pay for maintaining the irrigation system which you pay as a landlord?

Mr. GIBSON. Yes, sir.

The CHAIRMAN. And what is your criticism as to what Bodkin charges?

Mr. GIBSON. He charges up $20 an acre for rent. If he rented his land outright to some one he would have to pay the same water tax on it just the same.

The CHAIRMAN. Now, as a matter of fact, do you know whether his land has water rights or not?

Mr. GIBSON. I know that it has a water right.

The CHAIRMAN. Then, the real mistake Bodkin made is charging a higher price for his land, and putting in the irrigation charges just as if he had to hire them; is that the point?

Mr. GIBSON. Yes, sir; that is the point. I want to show his land is not worth it, because the land adjoining him, nearer town, was sold for $150 an acre, with just as good a water right.

The CHAIRMAN. How long ago?

Mr. GIBSON. Last year.

The CHAIRMAN. Do you suppose there are any lands near yours that would sell for less than $225?

Mr. GIBSON. Yes, sir; I have 500 acres worth less than that.

The CHAIRMAN. That is hardly proof that Bodkin's land is not worth $250.

Mr. GIBSON. I am going to show what land adjoining him sold for.

The CHAIRMAN. I am trying to apply the same standard to you that you apply to him, to see whether your criticism is just or not.

Mr. GIBSON. Just across the road which corners with him was sold for $105 an acre, with just as good water rights. The water came out of the same ditch and out of the same lake.

The CHAIRMAN. Values, particularly when people are valuing their own property, are nearly always questions of opinion, and there is a good deal of room for differences of opinion.

Mr. GIBSON. Oh, yes. I would naturally consider, if some one offered him that, I would think that two fools met.

Mr. MALBY. Unless he took it?

Mr. GIBSON. Unless he took it; yes, sir.

The CHAIRMAN. Would you think that if some one were to take your land at the valuation you put on it?

Mr. GIBSON. I did not put a valuation on it.

The CHAIRMAN. I thought you valued it at $225 an acre.

Mr. GIBSON. Not myself. I said something like that. I will show you the difference between my water right and his. I have two water rights in the oldest ditches in that country, and I do not have to hire water at $3.33 to put water on the land. The assessment of mine you will find is 53 cents an acre.

Mr. RAKER. What do you mean by "assessment"?

Mr. GIBSON. Assessment for the maintenance of the ditch for the year. There will usually be more or less expense attached to it during the year.

Mr. RAKER. This is a company ditch you speak of?

Mr. GIBSON. They are all company ditches. The farmers go into a company, and each man will have shares of stock in the ditch.

Mr. RAKER. Does that apply to Bodkin as well as yourself?

Mr. GIBSON. Yes, sir. On one of my places I am under the same ditch he is.

The CHAIRMAN. Do you know a man named F. M. Downer?

Mr. GIBSON. I know Mr. Downer.

The CHAIRMAN. He is a good friend of yours?

Mr. GIBSON. I rather think he is.

The CHAIRMAN. A close friend?

Mr. GIBSON. Well, I would say, yes.

The CHAIRMAN. You are close business and political associates?

Mr. GIBSON. He is in Denver and I am in Longmont, but we are friends.

The CHAIRMAN. Mr. Downer was the man instrumental in occasioning the turning over of the Longmont factory to the Great Western Sugar Co.?

Mr. GIBSON. I was one of the ones that helped to get up the acreage for them.

The CHAIRMAN. You were instrumental in that, too?

Mr. GIBSON. I was; yes, sir. In the first place, before there was any factory in northern Colorado I went to Rocky Ford and looked over the sugar factory in Rocky Ford, as one of a committee from all up and down the line, and we tried to get a factory at Longmont and were not successful.

The CHAIRMAN. Have you got a man working for you named Harliss?

Mr. GIBSON. Yes, sir; Tom Harliss. He has been with me six years.

The CHAIRMAN. What is he?

Mr. GIBSON. A farmer.

The CHAIRMAN. Is he one of your bosses?

Mr. GIBSON. I hardly think so.

The CHAIRMAN. He rents land from you and grows beets on the land he rents from you?

Mr. GIBSON. Yes, sir.

The CHAIRMAN. That is your relation with him?

Mr. GIBSON. Yes, sir.

The CHAIRMAN. Do you know anything about his employing Russian labor?

Mr. GIBSON. We both employ them.

The CHAIRMAN. Did he have any trouble with his Russian labor last year?

Mr. GIBSON. He did not, but they had some trouble with themselves.

The CHAIRMAN. And he turned them off and sent them back to Denver?

Mr. GIBSON. No, sir.

The CHAIRMAN. What became of them? What was the trouble?

Mr. GIBSON. The man and his wife had trouble among themselves and separated. That was the trouble and that was the reason they did not stay with me.

The CHAIRMAN. They were with you, then?

Mr. GIBSON. On my place.

The CHAIRMAN. But in the employ of this man Harliss, were they not?

Mr. GIBSON. Yes; they were there on the place.

The CHAIRMAN. They were on the part of your land which he rented?

Mr. GIBSON. Yes, sir.

The CHAIRMAN. And you say he did not dismiss them in violation of the contract?

Mr. GIBSON. No, sir; they quit and separated.

The CHAIRMAN. And their places were supplied with Mexican labor?

Mr. GIBSON. Yes, sir. This same family, when they got into trouble, the wife went to Denver and sued for maintenance, I think you would call it.

The CHAIRMAN. Alimony?

Mr. GIBSON. Alimony; and she sued as a poor person, and they had their trial in Boulder, and I was subpœnaed to come there, and also the cashier of the bank, and the cashier's testimony showed that they brought to Longmont $550 as poor people.

The CHAIRMAN. That was doing pretty well for ordinary laborers.

Mr. GIBSON. Yes, sir; first-rate to come from the slums.

The CHAIRMAN. What sort of houses do these people live in?

Mr. GIBSON. I have got a photograph of one of them which I will show you. I want you to understand that this $20 an acre they get they are also furnished a house and water, and a place for a garden, and a place for chickens, and a place for a cow. [Exhibiting photograph to the committee.]

The CHAIRMAN. Mr. Gibson, how many banks are there in Longmont?

Mr. GIBSON. Three.

The CHAIRMAN. Are you interested in any one of them?

Mr. GIBSON. Yes, sir.

The CHAIRMAN. Which one?

Mr. GIBSON. I am interested in the Emerson & Buckingham Banking & Trust Co.

The CHAIRMAN. Are you a director in this bank?

Mr. GIBSON. No, sir.

The CHAIRMAN. You are one of the stockholders?

Mr. GIBSON. I am.

The CHAIRMAN. Does the sugar company do business with this bank?

Mr. GIBSON. That I can not tell you, sir. I do not know. I have always done business over across the street with the Farmers' National Bank and all the checks I have ever gotten from them have been at the Farmers' National Bank.

The CHAIRMAN. In other words, when the sugar company paid you any money they paid you with a check on the Farmers' National Bank?

Mr. GIBSON. Yes, sir.

The CHAIRMAN. You do not know whether they have an account with the other banks also or not?

Mr. GIBSON. I do not know.

The CHAIRMAN. You have no interest in the Farmers' National Bank?

Mr. GIBSON. No, sir.

The CHAIRMAN. And you are not a director, although a stockholder, in the other bank?

Mr. GIBSON. That is correct.

The CHAIRMAN. Is there any other matter you wish to bring to the attention of the committee?

Mr. GIBSON. I think I told you that the land across the road sold for $125 an acre, which I consider just as good land as his, with just as good improvements and all. I want to say that this little town—I want you to get this straight—which is called Meade is not a town. It is nothing but a burg, what I would call a loading station.

The CHAIRMAN. Has it a church and schoolhouse?

Mr. GIBSON. It has a church and schoolhouse; yes, sir.

The CHAIRMAN. And a few little stores?

Mr. GIBSON. I think there are two stores.

The CHAIRMAN. It is a little village, then, rather than a town?

Mr. GIBSON. Yes, sir. The majority of the business houses are vacant. It has gone down.

The CHAIRMAN. Is there a railroad station there?

Mr. GIBSON. Yes, sir. There was no town there until the sugar company built a road through that section of the country for the delivering of beets for the farmers that raised beets through that country, and they put these loading stations along every, perhaps, 4 miles, so the people won't have to haul more than 2 miles to the dump; and I think all land in that country has increased in value I will say $75, and it is due entirely to this road going through our country.

The CHAIRMAN. Is there anything else, Mr. Gibson?

Mr. GIBSON. Yes; I want to say that 60 of the beet raisers who raised beets for the sugar factory this past year are help that came to our country to work in the beet fields when we first commenced to raise beets, and if you want them I will give you the names.

The CHAIRMAN. It will not be necessary to read the names.

Mr. GIBSON. What I have here was gotten for me by the commercial association, and I want to show them I have done what they asked me to do. The exact number is 63.

Mr. FORDNEY. Sixty-three farmers located at that station?

Mr. GIBSON. Yes, sir; and they furnish beets to Longmont.

Mr. FORDNEY. Is that where Mr. Bodkin loads his beets?

Mr. GIBSON. No, sir; Mr. Bodkin loads at Meade, but they go to Longmont, as I understand it.

The CHAIRMAN. You need not put the names in the record.

Mr. GIBSON. The number is 63.

The CHAIRMAN. That is a list which the real estate exchange got up for you to show how many farmers there were now raising beets who formerly came there as laborers?

Mr. GIBSON. Yes, sir; I want to say that one of the names that appears here is a man who worked for me; he and his family. I think it was the second year I raised beets, and that was when I raised them for the Loveland factory, before the Longmont factory was built. That man told me not over three months ago that he had bought 160 acres of land and paid for it, 10 miles from our place, in one piece, and he had 35 acres that joined up to the town of Berthoud, that he had not quite paid for. The name of the man I speak of is Jacob Klein.

Mr. FORDNEY. Were they foreigners?

Mr. GIBSON. Yes, sir; they are what you call Russians.

The CHAIRMAN. Do you know Mr. Dakin?

Mr. GIBSON. Yes, sir; I know Mr. Dakin.

The CHAIRMAN. Do you know him very well?

Mr. GIBSON. Yes; I know him quite well.

The CHAIRMAN. Is he a lawyer of character and standing in his community?

Mr. GIBSON. He is; yes, sir.

The CHAIRMAN. A nice man and gentleman?

Mr. GIBSON. I think that Mr. Dakin is a nice fellow. There was nothing ever against him that I know of.

The CHAIRMAN. He has a fairly good practice for a town of that size?

Mr. GIBSON. I hardly think so. I do not think he is what I would call a successful lawyer. Perhaps you gentlemen would not call him a successful lawyer. I hardly think you would want him to attend to your business. I know I would not want him to attend to mine.

Mr. FORDNEY. A sort of justice-of-the-peace lawyer?

Mr. GIBSON. No, sir; not hardly; but a nice fellow.

The CHAIRMAN. Is he a reputable gentleman and citizen, whether you regard him as a successful lawyer or not?

Mr. GIBSON. Oh, yes, sir; he is.

The CHAIRMAN. Now, is there anything else you desire to say?

Mr. GIBSON. I want to say that practically all the small beet raisers that raise 10 acres or less take care of their own beets.

The CHAIRMAN. The small farmers?

Mr. GIBSON. Yes, sir; the small farmers take care of their beets with their own families.

The CHAIRMAN. And this foreign labor we have been speaking of is required on the larger farms—above 10 acres?

Mr. GIBSON. Yes, sir. I would also like to contradict Mr. Bodkin's testimony in regard to the sugar company owning the papers in Colorado and the politics of Colorado. That would be impossible.

The CHAIRMAN. Did he say he owned the papers?

Mr. GIBSON. If I understood it correctly, that was stated in Mr. Bodkin's testimony.

The CHAIRMAN. Not exactly, as I recall it. I think "controlled" is a better word.

Mr. GIBSON. Then, maybe it was "controlled."

Mr. FORDNEY. He said the farmers could not get anything into the papers stating their side of the question.

Mr. GIBSON. I would say that is absolutely false, and as far as their controlling the politics of the State, I think that is not true. I will admit that politics in Colorado are not as nice and as pleasant as what perhaps you would like to have your politics. I was going to say, unfortunately for Colorado, we are Democratic.

The CHAIRMAN. I can understand some of your testimony now.

Mr. GIBSON. Because, you see, we have not very many United States Senators from Colorado, for which I am very sorry.

The CHAIRMAN. No; we have but one, and he is a Republican Senator.

Mr. GIBSON. And the other one ought to be.

The CHAIRMAN. Are the sugar people deeply concerned in politics in Colorado?

Mr. GIBSON. I never heard of them entering politics in my life; I never did.

The CHAIRMAN. You sympathize, though, with the protective policies of the Republican Party?

Mr. GIBSON. I certainly do, sir.

The CHAIRMAN. I gathered as much. I ask you that, as long as you have brought the matter up yourself.

Mr. GIBSON. I am glad you asked me, because I am only too glad to tell you.

The CHAIRMAN. Now, as long as you have brought up this question, I will ask you if you are a sort of politician out there, Mr. Gibson?

Mr. GIBSON. No, sir; I am not a politician.

The CHAIRMAN. Are you not a sort of political lieutenant out there?

Mr. GIBSON. No; I deny the charge absolutely.

The CHAIRMAN. You know a man, I believe you said, by the name of Downer?

Mr. GIBSON. Yes, sir; a director of the mint.

The CHAIRMAN. He is a sort of boss out there in politics?

Mr. GIBSON. No, sir; he is not.

The CHAIRMAN. Is he not a very influential man in politics out there?

Mr. GIBSON. Not in our country. He does not live there at all.

The CHAIRMAN. He lives in Denver and pulls the strings from there; and are you not recognized as his political lieutenant in Boulder County?

Mr. GIBSON. No, sir; I deny that absolutely. They all know I am a Republican, and I express myself so, and I take that much interest in politics that I go to the primaries and aim to get as good people as possible.

The CHAIRMAN. You always take an active interest in politics?

Mr. GIBSON. No; I do not say I really take an active interest in it.

The CHAIRMAN. And you would not like to be classed, then, as one of the active political leaders in the Republican Party of Boulder County?

Mr. GIBSON. No; I would not.

The CHAIRMAN. And that would not be a fair statement of your position?

Mr. GIBSON. I have not been elected as a delegate to the convention, I do not think, for——

The CHAIRMAN (interposing). Are you on the executive committee, or anything of that sort?

Mr. GIBSON (continuing answer). For four years.

The CHAIRMAN. Have you any personal active connection with the party in your county?

Mr. GIBSON. No, sir; I have not. I never looked at Mr. Bodkin's testimony about that, and I don't know just what there is in it. If he testified to anything about my being connected with politics——

The CHAIRMAN (interposing). There was no testimony on that subject, and I was just asking the question to find out. Have you about concluded your schedule?

Mr. GIBSON. I have, as far as I can think of at the present time.

Mr. FORDNEY. Mr. Chairman, there was considerable discussion last evening between yourself and the witness about the real definition of the word used by Mr. Bodkin as to what "slums" meant, and the record will show that the witness stated that good laboring people came from the slums in the cities. Now, I do not think the witness intended to make any such statement, or to imply that the honest, hard-working laboring men inhabited or lived in the slums of the cities.

The CHAIRMAN. He denied saying that.

Mr. FORDNEY. But he was made to say that.

The CHAIRMAN. No; I do not think so.

Mr. FORDNEY. I want to say to you, Mr. Gibson, there is a vast difference between the locality in a town where honest, hard-working people live and those who live in the slums, and in order to define that I went to the dictionary last night, and here is what the dictionary says about the word "slums":

> Slums: A low, filthy quarter of a city or of a town; a street or place where debauched and criminal persons live or resort.

Now, that is not the kind of people you employ on your farms cultivating beets, is it?

Mr. GIBSON. No, sir.

Mr. FORDNEY. That is what Mr. Bodkin said.

Mr. GIBSON. So far as that goes, I was going to ask this morning what he would mean by "slums" himself, so I could know what the term "slums" means. Now, this same man who worked for us in the spring worked in the iron works in Denver all winter and came there in the spring.

Mr. FORDNEY. Then, as to that question, Mr. Gibson, you take issue with Mr. Bodkin that the people who work in the beet fields of Colorado do not come from the slums?

Mr. GIBSON. No, sir; they do not.

Mr. FORDNEY. They are not criminals and debauched persons; they are honest, hard-working laboring people?

Mr. GIBSON. Yes, sir. I would say of the people who work in the beet fields in and around Longmont that one-third live in and around Longmont in these same shacks we have on the ranch, and get their rent free, and live there all winter.

The CHAIRMAN. Gunny shacks?

Mr. GIBSON. They are made just the same as the houses. They live in the houses.

The CHAIRMAN. Are they gunny shacks?

Mr. GIBSON. No; they are made of boards.

The CHAIRMAN. And not of tar paper and gunny sacks?

Mr. GIBSON. Yes; they put tar paper on them.

The CHAIRMAN. Gunny sacks don't go into them?

Mr. GIBSON. I do not know anything about that. I do not know what they have in the house.

Mr. FORDNEY. Mr. Gibson, I am familiar with the class of labor employed in the beet fields in the State of Michigan, and on leaving this room last night, and thinking this matter over, I discovered a lot of ladies here in the hall on their knees scrubbing these halls, and in my opinion that is more degraded work than work in the beet fields. What have you to say about that?

Mr. GIBSON. I would say so.

Mr. RAKER. You do not call that degraded work, do you, working for an honest living?

Mr. GIBSON. If you call working in the beet fields, out in the sunshine, degraded.

Mr. RAKER. Is not this work just as good and honest as any other work people can do on earth?

Mr. GIBSON. I say, if it is degraded.

The CHAIRMAN. Of course, no honest work is degrading. There is no question about that.

Mr. GIBSON. No, sir.

Mr. FORDNEY. Mr. Gibson, you take exception to the statement made by Mr. Bodkin and others, if there were any others who made that statement, that the politics of the State of Colorado are controlled by the Great Western Sugar Co., as stated by Mr. Bodkin?

Mr. GIBSON. Yes.

Mr. FORDNEY. He stated also that the agricultural department of the State was under the control of the sugar company and that they would not give a test to the farmers of the sugar contents of the beets, for fear the sugar company would use its influence in the legislature and stop the appropriation for the agricultural department; is that true?

Mr. GIBSON. I would not say it was.

Mr. FORDNEY. He also made that statement as to the University of the State of Colorado. You have said you do not believe that is correct?

Mr. GIBSON. I do not believe that is correct.

Mr. FORDNEY. He said he could not get a test either through the agricultural department, the State university, or from any individual chemist in the State—or he had been unable to get it—because they all said they did not want to offend the sugar company. Do you think that condition exists in your State?

Mr. GIBSON. No; I do not think that condition exists.

Mr. FORDNEY. Has that been your experience?

Mr. GIBSON. I never had any experience in having any tests made, if that is what you want to know.

Mr. FORDNEY. You stated yesterday the experience you had had in tests made by some gentlemen you had employed from Perry.

Mr. GIBSON. No, sir; that was another gentleman who testified yesterday.

Mr. MALBY. Mr. Gibson, I was not here yesterday to hear your testimony, and possibly this has all been gone over. I got the impression in some way that Mr. Bodkin and the others who appeared before the committee were members of some kind of an organization. I simply want to ascertain whether they do belong to a farmers' association or farmers' organization.

Mr. GIBSON. I understand there is an organization known as the Farmers' Union. I do not belong to it.

Mr. MALBY. You do understand there is a farmers' organization there of some kind?

Mr. GIBSON. I do.

Mr. MALBY. Organized for purposes of looking after their interests and bettering their condition, if they can?

Mr. GIBSON. I presume that is it. I do not know.

Mr. MALBY. Is there any considerable number of farmers belonging to that organization?

Mr. GIBSON. I do not know. I do not think there are a great many. There are a few. I do not think that a majority of the farmers belong to the union. I do not think so.

Mr. MALBY. Do you know of anyone outside of that organization who is complaining about present conditions?

Mr. GIBSON. I never heard of one.

Mr. MALBY. Or is it confined somewhat to that organization?

Mr. GIBSON. Yes. Of course, I have always been against the Sugar Company in regard to siloing beets, as far as that is concerned.

Mr. MALBY. All I wanted to know is whether there was an outcry against the manufacturers from those who are not members of the organization, or whether it is confined chiefly to the organization itself?

Mr. GIBSON. Not to my knowledge.

Mr. RAKER. Did I understand, Mr. Gibson, from your testimony that you have lived in that community a good many years?

Mr. GIBSON. Since 1886.

Mr. RAKER. How far from Longmont?

Mr. GIBSON. My farm is just a mile from the corner.

Mr. RAKER. Is it your intention to state that since your residence there and within the last 10 years you have heard no complaints by the farmers who raise sugar beets?

Mr. GIBSON. No; I do not mean that.

Mr. RAKER. In regard to the treatment received from the Great Western Sugar Co.?

Mr. GIBSON. I object myself as to siloing the beets, sure. I object to that.

Mr. RAKER. Has there not been objection, and have not you heard of it?

Mr. GIBSON. Sure; whenever it comes to siloing beets or when we are short of cars we object to the treatment we get, when we have to wait to unload.

Mr. RAKER. And have you not objected to the price? Have you not heard that complaint from the farmers?

Mr. GIBSON. I rather think that is true.

Mr. RAKER. Is not that complaint quite general among the farmers, about the price they are getting for their beets, and have they not combined into an organization for the purpose of trying to get a better price for their beets?

Mr. GIBSON. Now, you mean?

Mr. RAKER. At any time.

Mr. GIBSON. No; most assuredly not. When I get $6.31 a ton for my beets I ought not to object, ought I?

Mr. RAKER. I am asking you what the farmers are doing?

Mr. GIBSON. I can not tell you what all the farmers are doing.

Mr. RAKER. You have heard no complaint among the farmers?

Mr. GIBSON. No, sir. I raised beets the first time for $4.50 and sent them to Loveland, and they have increased the price all along.

Mr. RAKER. In addition to that, has there not been quite a general complaint of the sugar factory by the farmers, that the farmer was making but a small percentage or a small amount per ton, and the company was making seven or eight dollars?

Mr. GIBSON. Not to my knowledge; no, sir.

Mr. RAKER. You have not heard that complaint at all?

Mr. GIBSON. No, sir.

Mr. MALBY. Do you understand that at the present time there is quite general satisfaction over the price for beets?

Mr. GIBSON. Why, yes, sir.

Mr. MALBY. And is there any complaint at the present time that the factories are not correctly analyzing their beets?

Mr. GIBSON. I haven't heard a complaint made by anybody in our neighborhood at all.

Mr. MALBY. I thought those were the two chief propositions presented by Messrs. Combs, Dakan, and Bodkin. One was as to the farmers complaining about the price; and the other, divided into two parts, was, first, the analysis of sugar by the sugar factories, and secondly, that there was no established authority in Colorado by which the sugar-beet farmer might have his beets analyzed. Have you heard any complaint recently about any one of these propositions?

Mr. GIBSON. No, sir. I brought with me my sheet, which the sugar company furnishes to the beet farmers who deliver beets, showing the percentage of sugar in my beets, and I will be glad to have the committee examine same if so desired. I think the beets made on one place of mine tested 21.2 per cent sugar.

Mr. MALBY. The factory gave you that test?

Mr. GIBSON. Yes, sir; and that is the highest test I have had.

The CHAIRMAN. We already have in the record similar test sheets or records, and I do not see any reason for encumbering the record with another. Well, gentlemen, if there are no other questions we will excuse Mr. Gibson, with the thanks of the committee for his attendance.

TESTIMONY OF JOHN E. LAW.

Witness is duly sworn by the chairman.

The CHAIRMAN. What is your full name?

Mr. LAW. John E. Law.

The CHAIRMAN. Where is your residence?

Mr. LAW. Windsor, Colo.

The CHAIRMAN. How far is that from Longmont?

Mr. LAW. About 30 miles.

The CHAIRMAN. How far from Fort Morgan?

Mr. LAW. About 60 to 70 miles.

The CHAIRMAN. What is your business?

Mr. LAW. Farming; that is, my interests are all in farming. But my farming is done by tenants.

The CHAIRMAN. What other business have you besides farming?

Mr. LAW. No other at this time.

The CHAIRMAN. Are you interested in any bank?

Mr. LAW. I am not at this time, and haven't been for two years.

The CHAIRMAN. What bank were you interested in?

Mr. LAW. The First National Bank of Windsor, Colo.

The CHAIRMAN. Is that the only bank there?

Mr. LAW. No, sir; there is the Farmers' National Bank of Windsor, Colo.

The CHAIRMAN. The First National Bank and the Farmers' National Bank are located at Windsor, Colo.?

Mr. LAW. Yes, sir.

The CHAIRMAN. You have no interest at all at this time in the First National Bank of Windsor, Colo.?

Mr. LAW. No, sir.

The CHAIRMAN. Nor in the Farmers' National Bank of Windsor?

Mr. LAW. No, sir.

The CHAIRMAN. You have no interest at present, do you mean, except as a farmer?

Mr. LAW. No business interests except as a farmer and in the lines relating to farming.

The CHAIRMAN. Is Windsor, Colo., in the beet-growing section of northern Colorado?

Mr. LAW. Yes, sir.

The CHAIRMAN. What factory does that Windsor section supply?

Mr. LAW. The Windsor factory, belonging to the Great Western Sugar Co.

The CHAIRMAN. Do you own any stock in the Great Western Sugar Co.?

Mr. LAW. I do not.

The CHAIRMAN. You have no interest in that company, either directly or indirectly?

Mr. LAW. Not as a sugar company; only as a market for the beets that are grown on my farm.

The CHAIRMAN. I mean that you have no other interest except to sell them beets that you grow?

Mr. LAW. No other interest at all.

The CHAIRMAN. Is there any other sugar factory in that territory, or is that the only customer you have for the beets that you grow?

Mr. LAW. That is the only market we have for our beets, unless we simply feed them to the stock.

The CHAIRMAN. That is what I mean; that is the only factory in that territory where you may sell them for use for the purpose of extracting sugar?

Mr. LAW. Yes, sir. I would like, if I may, to describe the location a little more in detail, and perhaps I can do so without being questioned.

The CHAIRMAN. All right; suppose you do, making your description as brief as possible.

Mr. LAW. Windsor is practically in the middle of the Cache La Poudre Valley, through which valley one of the streams comes down from the mountains. It is practically the same distance, or, perhaps, not a difference of over 1 or 2 miles, between the distance from Windsor to Greeley in a southeasterly direction. Windsor and Eaton in a northeasterly direction, Windsor and Fort Collins in a northwesterly direction, and Windsor and Loveland in a southwesterly direction, while Longmont is directly south. It is about 14 miles from Windsor to Greeley, Eaton, Fort Collins, and Loveland, and about 30 miles to Longmont. The first sugar factory to be located in our vicinity was built at Loveland, if I am not mistaken, in 1900 or 1901. A few beets were grown on one of my farms both in 1901 and 1902—or, at least, I think in 1901 and I know in 1902—and shipped to the Loveland factory over the Colorado Southern Railroad. In 1903 a factory was built in Windsor. In order to secure the factory in Windsor, many of the business men of Windsor, as well as many of the farmers in the surrounding territory, contracted to grow a certain number of acres of beets for, if I am not mistaken, three years in succession. Many of us subscribed for what we then considered a large acreage——

The CHAIRMAN. Yes, we understand; in order to secure the erection of the factory. That is, to plant and grow sugar beets?

Mr. LAW. Yes, sir. The business men, some of them not being landowners, secured others to take their contracts, while others owning land grew their own beets, so that the contracts were fulfilled to the satisfaction of the sugar company, so far as I know. They grew beets for the Windsor sugar factory in 1903, 1904, 1905, and 1906, reaching the maximum production in the season of 1906.

The growing of sugar beets has a wide range. While the average of that factory district since 1904, and including 1911, has been a trifle over 12 tons per acre, many farmers produced much less than 12 tons per acre for their crop. We were receiving $5 per ton for the first few years, and when the proposition came up to the farmers of siloing a portion of their beets many objected to it on the ground that it would be additional expense and trouble. I recall that there was a meeting of the beet growers called for Fort Collins to discuss the question of siloing beets. At this meeting there was a diversity of opinion among us beet growers, some saying positively they would not grow beets if they must silo them. Others did not take so unfavorable a view of the proposition, but all felt that any additional expense for growing sugar beets with the price at no more than $5 per ton was a questionable matter, so far as our profits were concerned. The action of the farmers was not uniform and the silo clause was put in.

The CHAIRMAN. You finally got that question settled satisfactorily, at any rate?

Mr. LAW. Satisfactorily in a measure.

The CHAIRMAN. It is settled now, anyhow, is it?

Mr. LAW. It was settled so that we siloed beets for two seasons. For the past two seasons we have not been required to silo beets.

The CHAIRMAN. That is not a matter of special interest here, so I better ask you questions in order to get along. Do you come here at the request of any commercial or other organization or body?

Mr. LAW. Mr. Frazer, chairman of the Windsor Commercial Club, asked me if I would come here and testify.

The CHAIRMAN. You come as the representative of the Windsor Commercial Club, at their request or in their interest, and at their expense?

Mr. LAW. I come to represent the beet growers in our immediate vicinity.

The CHAIRMAN. And at their expense?

Mr. LAW. Yes, sir.

The CHAIRMAN. Is there any particular reason why they wanted you to come, and is there any particular information that they wanted you to give the committee as the representative of its commercial body?

Mr. LAW. We felt that the facts in regard to growing sugar beets in our district had not been presented to the committee.

The CHAIRMAN. And you wanted them presented?

Mr. LAW. We did.

The CHAIRMAN. On what particular point did you want to present views that either have not been presented or, if presented, have not been properly presented to the committee? We do not want to cover too much ground, but want to know precisely what you want to give us the benefit of. You have heard the testimony of these other gentlemen who testified from your State and near your neighborhood about the cost of growing beets and the profit resulting therefrom, both from the standpoint of the landlord and the tenant farmer. Do you agree substantially with their testimony?

Mr. LAW. I can say yes, that I agree substantially with their testimony.

The CHAIRMAN. Although your figures would vary a little in each individual case, for the people of each locality, would they not?

Mr. LAW. They will; and I would like to state the action in our district in regard to that matter.

The CHAIRMAN. All right; do it briefly.

Mr. LAW. Two years ago there was a feeling among the farmers, when we were receiving $5 per ton for our beets——

Mr. MALBY (interrupting). Was that a flat price?

Mr. LAW. Yes, sir; $5 per ton. As I started to say, at that time there was a feeling among the beet growers that beet growing was not satisfactory. The 1909 crop had been one of our low crops; the tonnage of the district for that year being but little more than 9 tons the acre. The tonnage from the farms in which I was personally interested was only about 9 tons per acre. The feeling among the farmers was that it was not profitable to grow beets at those prices. A meeting of the beet growers was called, I think in February, to get some uniform action in regard to whether we would grow beets at $5 per ton at all or not. A committee was appointed, one member of which was myself, to make up an estimate of the cost of growing beets and return our report to this meeting. The estimate brought in by that committee was, if I am not mistaken, $47.50 per acre for growing and delivering to the dump a 12-ton average yield of beets. That report made to the meeting resulted in some one moving that we demand $6 flat per ton from the sugar company. The question was being discussed when another extreme farmer offered an amendment that the demand be made for $7 per ton. That was put and carried. That action left the conservative farmers in an unsatisfactory position. While we all felt that we needed an advance, at the same time we felt that it was absurd to ask so great an advance as that.

The CHAIRMAN. In other words, you felt that you wouldn't get anything if you planted yourself on such extreme ground?

Mr. LAW. We did.

The CHAIRMAN. What was the result? That you finally got on some middle ground?

Mr. LAW. That year a graduated scale of prices was offered in our contracts, and we grew beets for the season of 1910 and for the past season, 1911, on the graduated scale, if I am not mistaken.

The CHAIRMAN. Did that result in a better and more satisfactory price?

Mr. LAW. It did.

The CHAIRMAN. Did it placate and satisfy the farmers?

Mr. LAW. It did, practically.

The CHAIRMAN. Have you that graduated scale with you, or has it been put in the record?

Mr. LAW. It is the same graduated scale we have been receiving, which meant for the crop of 1910 of beets from the farms in which I was personally interested instead of $5 per ton an average of about $5.57 per ton.

The CHAIRMAN. The yield was better, too, wasn't it?

Mr. LAW. I mention that as an indication of what it was in the district.

The CHAIRMAN. I ask if the yield was not better that year as well?

Mr. LAW. The yield in 1910 was a better average yield than the yield of 1909.

The CHAIRMAN. The increased yield and the increased price went a good long ways toward making the sugar-beet farmers better satisfied?

Mr. LAW. It did. While in 1911 the six crops in which I was directly interested varied in price for the different crops from $5.25 and a fraction per ton to $6.12 and a fraction cent per ton, the total tonnage averaged $5.64 and a fraction cent per ton. This is the experience for the beets produced by six different farmers on acreage ranging from 5 acres for one to about 50 acres for the farmer growing the largest acreage of beets.

Mr. MALBY. What year was that?

Mr. LAW. 1911.

The CHAIRMAN. All right, Mr. Law; go ahead.

Mr. LAW. I was just stating the average price received for beets from the six different crops that I was personally interested in.

Mr. RAKER. I do not really understand the witness's testimony. As I understood from the other testimony, the sugar-beet farmers received a flat pay for 12 per cent beets and then for every 1 per cent above that percentage they got 25 cents more. From your testimony, Mr. Law, it would appear that there must be a graduated scale of prices.

Mr. LAW. We receive $5 per ton for beets testing not less than 12 per cent and under 15 per cent sugar. For beets testing not less than 15 per cent and under 15½ per cent sugar we receive $5.25, and it advances in price as you pass above that percentage sugar content.

The CHAIRMAN. Twenty-five cents for each one-half per cent sugar content?

Mr. LAW. Yes, sir. For instance, beets testing not less than 18 per cent and under 18½ per cent sugar content we receive $6 per ton for.

The CHAIRMAN. What was that point you made about the average price under that system; it was what?

Mr. LAW. The average price for the district I was told was $5.50 and something. The average price for my six different tenants on land in which I was personally interested was $5.64 and a fraction.

The CHAIRMAN. Which was a little bit better than the general average for the neighborhood?

Mr. LAW. Yes, sir.

The CHAIRMAN. Is there anything else along that line that you wish to submit to the committee?

Mr. LAW. I do not think of anything.

The CHAIRMAN. Is there any particular matter that any witness before us heretofore has testified to that you of your own knowledge wish to present in a different light or not?

Mr. LAW. There was not. I was simply to present the facts as to the sugar beet growing industry in our neighborhood.

The CHAIRMAN. And you think that you have covered that field?

Mr. LAW. I have not covered the whole field. I want to say this in regard to the beet help, if I am to go on talking without being questioned.

The CHAIRMAN. Well, suppose you do, right along that line.

Mr. LAW. In 1903, the first year of the Windsor factory operating in our neighborhood, among the first lot of beet help that came into my neighborhood was the help to supply the farms in which I was personally interested. There were three or four families of German people that were brought, as I understood, from the Arkansas Valley, where they had worked in the beet-growing district there.

The CHAIRMAN. You say "they were brought;" who brought them?

Mr. LAW. The sugar company secured them for the people who were going to raise beets.

The CHAIRMAN. All right. They were to do the handwork?

Mr. LAW. They were to do the handwork. Two or three families that worked on my farm, however, for the two or three years now just past have been tenant farmers. One of them has this year, as tenant, the farm that I then called my home farm; one of the best farms I own.

The CHAIRMAN. Can you tell me whether or not the bulk of the handwork in your section is done by foreigners who come from the great cities?

Mr. LAW. I can not tell you as to their having lived in cities. I know this, that the most of the hand work in our neighborhood is performed by the Germans or German-Russians. My information is that some of them come from other sugar districts of the United States, having been in this country for 15 or 20 years. If I am not mistaken, some come directly from Germany.

The CHAIRMAN. Or from Russia?

Mr. LAW. Or from Russia. At least, they come from the old country.

The CHAIRMAN. Are the most of them Germans or Russians?

Mr. LAW. I can not make the distinction. They are sometimes called Russians and sometimes called Germans.

The CHAIRMAN. What country do they come from?

Mr. LAW. I have been told that the reason for their being called Russians is that they come to America directly from Russia, but that they formerly went from Germany to Russia, and so are Russian-Germans.

The CHAIRMAN. Don't you know the difference out there in your country between a man of Russian nationality and a man of German nationality?

Mr. LAW. I can not say that I do.

Mr. RAKER. What language do they speak?

Mr. LAW. The German language.

The CHAIRMAN. There is a considerable difference between a German and a Russian?

Mr. LAW. Perhaps so.

Mr. MALBY. There may not be when in the beet fields of Colorado, but would be in the State of New York.

Mr. FORDNEY. But the position that the witness takes is that they were born Germans and went from their native country to Russia, and immigrated to this country from Russia.

Mr. LAW. Yes, sir.

The CHAIRMAN. Do you know how many were Russians and how many were Germans, except as you have explained?

Mr. LAW. No, sir.

The CHAIRMAN. Do they constitute the help that perform the handwork?

Mr. LAW. They are the majority of the workers that do the handwork. We have had quite a few Japs in our neighborhood.

The CHAIRMAN. Have you any Mexicans?

Mr. LAW. A few.

The CHAIRMAN. Outside of these Germans or Russians, whichever they are, and the Japs, and the Mexicans that come up from New Mexico, have you anybody else—any other labor of foreign nationality?

Mr. LAW. I would say no, with the qualification that there may be here and there an individual case.

The CHAIRMAN. I understand—maybe isolated cases of some foreigner of other nationality—but these are the principal foreigners?

Mr. LAW. Yes, sir.

The CHAIRMAN. They do the bulk of the handwork on this sugar-beet crop?

Mr. LAW. Yes, sir.

The CHAIRMAN. When you speak of Mexicans do you speak of them as coming up from New Mexico or from old Mexico?

Mr. LAW. From New Mexico.

The CHAIRMAN. They are Mexicans all the same?

Mr. LAW. They are termed "Mexicans" with us.

The CHAIRMAN. Well, they are people of the Mexican race?

Mr. LAW. Yes, sir.

The CHAIRMAN. No matter whether they become citizens of the United States up there or not, they are really of the Mexican race, just like the people of old Mexico?

Mr. LAW. They have come directly to Colorado from New Mexico.

The CHAIRMAN. But originally came from old Mexico?

Mr. LAW. I don't know.

The CHAIRMAN. At any rate, they are of that race? You know what is meant by a Mexican?

Mr. LAW. I do, and they are of the Mexican race.

The CHAIRMAN. Are they citizens of the United States at all or not?

Mr. LAW. I couldn't answer that question.

The CHAIRMAN. You don't know?

Mr. LAW. No, sir.

Mr. MALBY. Do they live there in the community?

Mr. LAW. There have been but few Mexicans working in our district.

Mr. MALBY. The few that you have, are they transitory—that is, do they come and go back again, or do they remain there?

Mr. LAW. The few I have known were transitory.

The CHAIRMAN. They go back home when the beet season is over?

Mr. LAW. So far as I know.

The CHAIRMAN. Anyhow, they go somewhere?

Mr. LAW. They go away from Windsor.

The CHAIRMAN. What sort of houses do these people live in? Do they have a quarter of their own at Longmont, for instance, or at Windsor, where you live?

Mr. LAW. I live at Windsor.

The CHAIRMAN. Do they have a separate quarter for them at Windsor?

Mr. LAW. The landowner is expected to furnish the building that the family that works the beets, that does the handwork on the beets, can live in comparatively comfortably during the working season.

The CHAIRMAN. Is there a separate quarter for them at Longmont? [A pause without reply.] Answer the question one way or other.

Mr. LAW. I am not talking about Longmont.

The CHAIRMAN. Is there one at Windsor, or do you know?

Mr. LAW. I know in a general way. The same practice is common in all factory districts.

The CHAIRMAN. Do they have a separate quarter for these people?

Mr. LAW. On the farms?

The CHAIRMAN. No; no: in the little towns?

Mr. Law. Oh, the most of the German people occupy one portion of Windsor during the winter season.

The Chairman. Is that a separate quarter from the balance of the town, where the American citizens live?

Mr. Law. It is only a separate quarter as they congregate in one portion of the town, many of them buying lots and building their own houses, which they move into from the field as soon as the beet work is completed, so that their children may go to school with greater convenience.

The Chairman. That is exactly right. You would answer that question in the affirmative. You know what is meant by the Jewish quarter in a great city, or the Italian quarter, or the French quarter?

Mr. Law. In a qualified way they have a separate quarter; the Germans of Windsor have.

The Chairman. I do not mean that you segregate them, but that they themselves get together in a little quarter in the little towns?

Mr. Law. In Windsor they have two church buildings and hold their regular church services.

The Chairman. Are those houses that they live in at Windsor or at Longmont—have you any conditions there such as have been described by other witnesses, or what are those houses made of?

Mr. Law. They are usually built of lumber. The cheaper ones are frame of dimension lumber and boards, sometimes covered with tar paper.

The Chairman. And also covered with gunny sacks?

Mr. Law. Not unless it is a temporary house.

The Chairman. Are there such houses in those towns?

Mr. Law. Not gunny-sack houses.

The Chairman. Are there some such houses?

Mr. Law. Not that I know of; no.

The Chairman. But they do have tar-paper houses?

Mr. Law. There are cheaper frame houses built and covered with various grades of tar paper in order to make the building practically close, so far as moisture and wind are concerned.

Mr. Fordney. To make them warm for winter weather?

Mr. Law. Yes, sir; and a little fire in one of those rooms warms it right up.

The Chairman. Is that the character of the houses they have there?

Mr. Law. That is the character of the cheaper houses.

The Chairman. Well, what I want to get at is this: Are the most of their houses of that sort or not? I don't know myself—never have been there—and you have been there and know. Just tell us about that.

Mr. Law. Those cheaper houses are the ones that are built on the farms for the accommodation of the summer workers. Many of those Germans have bought lots in Windsor and built their own houses, and they have either bought lots and built houses or bought houses already built; and they will run from those cheaper houses on the farms to their fairly comfortable residences in the fall.

The Chairman. What I am trying to get at, and you must know about it, is whether the most of them are fairly comfortable residences or the most of them just the cheaper huts?

Mr. Law. The most of them are fairly comfortable residences, but of course in a modest way; that is, in the sense of being inexpensive.

The Chairman. Are they those tar-paper houses that you spoke of—the most of them of that construction?

Mr. Law. More or less tar paper is used in the cheaper houses.

The Chairman. I am just trying to find out whether that covers the most of them or not—these tar-paper houses. That is, I want to know whether the rule is the more comfortable residence or whether the rule is the tar-paper house. Now, just tell us which it is, if you know?

Mr. Law. I don't know that I could give you that, in the way of the proportions, but should say that the Germans, as a rule, that have worked in the district for a few years have comfortable houses.

The Chairman. That is not an answer to the question I asked you. I mean which is the existing rule of the houses as they are? You know where those quarters are; you live there?

Mr. Law. I do.

The Chairman. I want you to tell the committee about that matter. You want to tell the committee all that you know, I presume. I want to know whether the majority of the houses in this foreign quarter are the one type of house or the other; that is to say, the cheap houses or the more comfortable. That is a fair question and I think you ought to be able to answer it. If you can not answer it, just tell us.

Mr. Law. Please ask the question again, for I do not know that I just get the point.

The Chairman. Please state whether the majority of the houses in those quarters in these little towns in the sugar-beet section are of the one description that you have given to the committee, to wit, fairly comfortable residences, although not expensive, or of the other description that you have given to the committee, to wit, very cheap houses with tar paper to keep the cold out, and really almost a hull, as I understand. Now, which is the rule?

Mr. Law. The majority of them are fairly comfortable residences.

Mr. Malby. The chairman may have a little different impression about a tar-paper house from what I have of it. Tar-paper houses may be very expensive and very, very comfortable houses. I have one of my own which is fairly comfortable, and there is considerable tar paper about it.

The Chairman. Is that tar paper put inside of the wall?

Mr. Malby. No; you nail your boards on to the studding and then you put a roll of tar paper over the boards, and it makes your house perfectly air tight; the wind can't get through, and then you put on another sheeting of boards, and then put on more paper, and it makes a very comfortable house, and may be a very expensive one.

Mr. Law. From the standpoint of the German families, their work and condition where they have come from and where they have lived, the majority of them have very comfortable residences in the town of Windsor.

The Chairman. But nowhere like the average American citizen's residence, either in comfort or expensiveness?

Mr. LAW. They are very much like the westerner's house, the man who goes West without capital and builds a cheap house for his residence until he can do better.

The CHAIRMAN. Like the temporary residence that we build when poor?

Mr. LAW. Temporary in the sense of being until he can do better.

The CHAIRMAN. I guess, then, I understand the house matter.

Mr. LAW. Don't misunderstand with reference to the tar paper. Many of us use tar paper in all our buildings.

The CHAIRMAN. I caught that from Mr. Malby's explanation.

Mr. RAKER. The distinction that I wish to draw is that when tar paper is used as Judge Malby describes it a full wall of sheeting is put in, and then tar paper put on, and then rustic or weather boarding is put outside, which makes up three thicknesses. But a great many put up framing 18 inches or 2 feet apart and do nothing else but put tar paper on. Now, what kind of houses are these at Windsor that these Germans live in?

Mr. LAW. None of those last-described houses are used.

Mr. RAKER. Well, I just wanted to know.

The CHAIRMAN. Is there anything else that you want to add to your description of conditions out in Colorado for the benefit of the committee?

Mr. LAW. I do not think of anything just now.

Mr. RAKER. Do you intend to convey the idea that a tar-paper house is made more expensive and different from the ordinary house, where it is lined on the inside with sheathing and then weatherboarded on the outside; that they put the additional tar paper between the walls?

Mr. LAW. The better houses——

Mr. RAKER (interrupting). No; I mean the houses you described that these people occupied. That is not the way they build them, is it?

Mr. LAW. The houses occupied by the hand labor on the farms are for temporary summer residence, and are usually built with these sheathing boards, with sufficient framing of dimension stuff to support these sheathing boards continuously around. The tar paper is then put around on these boards with strips of batten stuff covering the cracks, which makes a close wall.

Mr. RAKER. And nothing else?

Mr. LAW. That is the common tar-paper house, as you may call it, although the bulk of the house is made of lumber that costs us $30 per thousand feet.

The CHAIRMAN. I will ask you one or two other questions along the line suggested to you by me awhile ago. You were at one time connected with the First National Bank of Windsor, Colo.?

Mr. LAW. I was.

The CHAIRMAN. And were so connected up to a couple of years ago?

Mr. LAW. Yes, sir.

The CHAIRMAN. Were you a director, president, vice president, cashier—or what office did you hold in that bank?

Mr. LAW. I served for a few years as president of the bank.

The CHAIRMAN. You were president of that bank?

Mr. LAW. Yes, sir.

The CHAIRMAN. You had considerable financial interest in the bank?

Mr. LAW. I had; comparatively.

The CHAIRMAN. I mean relatively to the total capital stock?

Mr. LAW. Yes.

The CHAIRMAN. Was the sugar company your principal customer during that time?

Mr. LAW. I would say no.

The CHAIRMAN. Was it your largest customer?

Mr. LAW. I would say no, in the sense of a customer that was profitable to the bank.

The CHAIRMAN. The sugar company was about your largest depositor, wasn't it?

Mr. LAW. The sugar company had larger deposits in the bank at certain times than, possibly, any other depositor; but the sugar company's deposits were usually made immediately, we may say, before their checks were drawn in payment for beets.

The CHAIRMAN. So they did not stay very long?

Mr. LAW. No. The bank officers, in discussing the matter, many times felt that the sugar company's account was of no particular value to the bank.

The CHAIRMAN. Do the sugar companies in these communities where they have their factories exercise any considerable influence in matters financial—that is, the management, control and policy of banks, and such things as that—in your judgment? You are the very man, I think, that can tell us. The intimation has been made to this committee, for instance—and I express no opinion as to its truth or untruth, because I have none definitely formed—that in this territory where these large sugar factories are located the whole industrial life is so interwoven with the business of the community as to form one huge clique, and that all interests pull together. Is that a fair statement of the facts of the situation, or not?

Mr. LAW. Your question is too complicated for me to answer with yes or no.

The CHAIRMAN. Then, answer it in your own way.

Mr. LAW. The benefit to the banks in Windsor district of the sugar company is the incidental benefit accompanying the sugar industry, in the way of the prosperity of the farmers who grow beets for the factory, and so on.

The CHAIRMAN. And for that reason you have a very close feeling to the interests of the sugar companies?

Mr. LAW. We regard the sugar companies as we do any other interest that is desirable.

The CHAIRMAN. If it is the biggest interest and the most profitable interest, as has been testified to, the question I have asked you might be answered with some firmness in the affirmative. If it is the biggest and the most profitable industry you regard them with a rather kindly feeling; isn't that true?

Mr. LAW. It is natural that we would have a kindly feeling toward them, as we would toward any other large interest that was helping our community.

The CHAIRMAN. I suppose, as a farmer, you would like to see the farmer get as much as he can for his beets?

Mr. LAW. I certainly should.

The CHAIRMAN. And instead of getting $5 or $5.67 per ton you would like $7, if you could get it?

Mr. LAW. We certainly would not object to $7 per ton.

The CHAIRMAN. You would do a little more than not object; you would really be positively pleased to get it, wouldn't you?

Mr. LAW. I certainly should.

The CHAIRMAN. And you think that the most of the other farmers who grow beets, or who own land upon which beets may be produced, feel the same way about it?

Mr. LAW. I have no doubt about it.

The CHAIRMAN. I imagined so. That is human nature. And I can say that in my section of the country, Georgia, where we grow cotton, that is the feeling, and I reckoned they had about the same desires out in Colorado. You agree to that, do you?

Mr. LAW. Yes, sir.

The CHAIRMAN. Isn't this the view of the situation somewhat influencing the judgment of your associates and neighbors: That if you get into a row with the beet-sugar factories as to whether or not you receive a fair division of profits; that is, as to whether they are giving you as much as they can afford for your beets and still make a reasonable and generous return on their capital invested, that while you sugar-beet growers and the factories are fussing over that question possibly the tariff might be lowered and in that way everybody, from the standpoint of the people interested in production and manufacture, be injured? Now, isn't that the truth about the situation out there in Colorado, and isn't that the motive that influences this organization you represent in sending a representative here to appear before this committee?

Mr. LAW. Your question is another that I can not answer with a simple "yes" or "no."

The CHAIRMAN. Then answer it in your own way.

Mr. LAW. Answering for myself personally what I conceive to be your question I will say that it is not a matter with me whether the sugar company is giving me one-half of their profits or any other percentage of the profits of the industry. If the sugar companies pay me a price that justifies me in growing beets instead of growing potatoes or grain on my farm, I will grow beets and still have the potatoes. If they do not pay me and other farmers a price that will justify our growing beets as compared with other crops we may grow, then we will not grow beets.

The CHAIRMAN. You are all citizens of the United States. Suppose the sugar companies' profit is made up in large measure because of the tax imposed by law and therefore comes from the consumers. That is, that all who use sugar have to pay their proportionate part of that profit to the sugar companies. And further, suppose it should develop that even at the present prices, profitable as they are, saying they are paying the farmers $6 per ton for their beets, to illustrate, yet the sugar companies capitalize the tariff to such an extent that they are making 100 per cent or more. Would you then feel that they could and ought to give the farmer more of this profit than they are giving to him rather than keep so much for themselves, or would you feel that you have nothing whatever to do with that matter and therefore are not interested in it and no right to ask it?

Mr. LAW. I have only that interest which every other citizen has. I am not in a position where I must decide that question.

The CHAIRMAN. Who is?

Mr. LAW. Our Congress.

The CHAIRMAN. Oh, you mean about the imposition of a tariff. But suppose the tariff is to remain the same, or even to be raised, and suppose on account of this tariff, by paying present prices in your section your local sugar factory, with the tariff capitalized in fixing the price for its product, can make 100 per cent or 200 per cent, would you then think you should be entitled to more for your beets or not?

Mr. LAW. If I knew the sugar company was making as big a per cent profit as 100 per cent or 200 per cent after paying me $6 per ton for my beets I would certainly feel that they might pay me more.

The CHAIRMAN. And that they ought to pay you more, would you you not? I am not making the statement myself, but merely trying to find out your point of view. And that they ought to pay you more for your beets for the reason that they could not conduct their industry at all unless you farmers furnish them beets, and therefore would not be able to capitalize the tariff unless you farmers went in with them? You really are two partners in the sugar enterprise; joint contributors to it. Does that idea appeal to you?

Mr. LAW. That is a supposed case, and I will leave that matter to be determined when I come up against the practical working of it.

The CHAIRMAN. You feel like at present you are getting enough for your sugar beets?

Mr. LAW. I feel that at present I am getting enough for beets to justify me in growing beets as part of the crop on my farms, in rotation with other crops, because at the present price it will compare well with our crops, with other farm profits, and there are certain elements of certainty about the beet crop that we do not have with potatoes and grain.

The CHAIRMAN. Let me pursue that investigation one question further and then I will leave it as far as I am concerned. I will give you an actual case in my own experience which will compare with this situation, I believe, because it interests every community.

Take the farmer who raises cotton in the South. While now, although at 10 cents per pound, he might be satisfied it was profitable for him to plant his lands in cotton and raise cotton as against wheat, corn, or any other agricultural product, and would do it and be satisfied from the standpoint at which you have expressed yourself as being satisfied, yet I apprehend it is true—certain it is in our section, and I want to see if the same human nature subsists in Colorado—that some farmers when they get 10 cents want 12 cents and 15 cents or 20 cents, or just as much as he can get for his product, and always wants more unless there is a powerful motive that impels him to be satisfied with less. And I will say that I have never seen in our section a motive powerful enough to make our farmers want to accept less. Isn't that the same situation in Colorado? In other words, is human nature the same in Colorado that it is in Georgia, or have you a different sort of human nature out there?

Mr. Law. In so far is I have met people from the South I have found they have much in common as to the influences that control us.

The Chairman. I was just wondering why you people were so well satisfied with $5.50 per ton for beets, and whether or not the reason you were expressing yourselves that way was not occasioned by the fear that if you got into a row that you sugar-beet growers and sugar-factory owners—and, if you will excuse the analogy, like two dogs in a fight over a bone, that while you were scrapping over the bone you might both lose that bone you already have? You do not think that anything like that is true, or is it true? Be frank with me and tell me what you think about it. Is that the motive operating to make the farmers of Colorado say they are satisfied, or more or less satisfied?

Mr. Law. We are not so wonderfully satisfied with growing beets, except in comparison with our other crops. If the price were materially reduced we would grow other crops instead of beets. Yet at the present price we are——

The Chairman (interrupting). It is your best crop?

Mr. Law. I do not say it is our best crop. At the present price we will consider the growing of beets a profitable industry for us to continue as a part of our farm crops, to grow in rotation with other crops.

The Chairman. After all, you have studiously failed to answer my question. I do not say purposely because that might be offensive, but you have not answered my question. It is not human nature for anybody who has anything to sell to be satisfied as long as he has hope of getting anything more, and therefore isn't it because you fear an agitation of this question and a division of the two interests—the sugar-beet factories and the sugar-beet growers—might hurt the tariff and bring down the price instead of holding it up that you are satisfied to let it alone?

Mr. Law. We are unquestionably interested in whether there will be a change in the tariff that will affect prices.

The Chairman. Has that anything to do with your attitude of satisfaction with what you are getting now, or not?

Mr. Law. It has not had to do with it except in its bearing on what is ahead of us.

The Chairman. Well, your exception is the case, I think. What do you mean by the exception you refer to?

Mr. Law. I mean that if, as I have stated before, there is any material reduction in the price of beets that we farmers must grow other crops instead of sugar beets, and therefore give up the industry of growing sugar beets.

The Chairman. You fear that that might be the result if you are not satisfied to let well enough alone; that that has something to do with making you think present conditions are good enough?

Mr. Law. We must feel that any material changes in those influences that affect the price of sugar must affect the price that can be paid for beets to produce that sugar.

The Chairman. Well, after all, to put it plainly, and I am going to do it one more time, and I know you are a man of enough intelligence to understand my question and answer it, and I want you to do it. Is it your opinion that this is in the mind of the beet growers of Colorado? Now, if we go to scrapping with the sugar companies about whether or not we are getting enough—as some of the witnesses appear to think, that that will be the result of it—we will be injured in our case as to production of sugar before the American public, and therefore the most sensible attitude for us to assume is that of being content with what we have. Is that true or not? Give me yes or no to that question.

Mr. LAW. May I answer that in my own way?

The CHAIRMAN. No; I will ask you to answer it yes or no. If that is not true I will not ask you anything further.

Mr. LAW. It is true, but it needs some explanation.

Mr. FORDNEY. It is true but needs what?

Mr. LAW. It is true but needs some qualification.

The CHAIRMAN. All right, qualify it now.

Mr. LAW. It is true simply in the sense that a scrap between any two conflicting interests, whether it be sugar-beet interests or any other interests, will naturally produce——

The CHAIRMAN (interrupting). That is true of any line of industry. The same motive would operate with any sort of tariff proposition, I think. Isn't that so?

Mr. LAW. Yes, sir.

Mr. HINDS. I have listened with great interest to this line of examination and would like to ask the witness if it is not true of the ordinary prosperous farmer and business man, that he strives for a fair profit but does not exert himself specially to get the very highest prices. Does he not strive for a fair profit?

Mr. LAW. He does.

Mr. HINDS. In other words, I saw a remark once attributed to one of the Rothschilds. They asked him how he made so much money dealing in securities. He said, "By never buying at the bottom of the market and never selling at the top." Isn't that true of the ordinary farmer and business man, that he aims for a fair profit, but doesn't take the risks incident to trying for the very highest margin, for then he may lose all?

Mr. LAW. That is certainly the case with the prudent farmer.

Mr. HINDS. That is true of the prudent farmer or business man?

Mr. LAW. Yes, sir.

Mr. HINDS. Isn't that about the same way that you regard this price of beets? You regard that you now have a fair thing and you are contented with that?

Mr. LAW. Under present conditions we regard that we have a fair thing in the sense that the price justifies us to grow beets in comparison with our other crops.

Mr. RAKER. Irrespective of how much the other man makes?

Mr. LAW. Yes, sir.

Mr. FORDNEY. Mr. Law, do you know this Mr. Bodkin, whose name has been mentioned here, who came from Colorado to testify?

Mr. LAW. I do not.

Mr. FORDNEY. Have you read his testimony given before this committee?

Mr. LAW. I have read some of it.

Mr. FORDNEY. Was it because of his statements being circulated in your district that you came here? Was that the real cause of your coming here more than anything else, or did it have anything to do with bringing you here? Or the testimony given by him here and circulated in your district, was that what influenced your commercial club in sending some one here? Or do you know?

Mr. LAW. I must believe it did, for after I read the report of his testimony in the paper myself I felt that his statement did not present the conditions of beet growing in the Windsor district, as I was familiar with it.

Mr. FORDNEY. And therefore you wanted to come here and contradict some of the statements that he made?

Mr. LAW. Therefore, as an individual interested in beet growing, I was desirous that the facts as I knew them in regard to beet growing should be presented to the committee.

Mr. FORDNEY. Mr. Law, in reference to your profit and whether or not you are satisfied with the price you obtain for beets, you are fully aware that the factory to which you sell your beets must make a profit or it can not pay you a good price for your beets? Isn't that right? They can not pay you a big price for your beets and lose money and continue in business?

Mr. LAW. They can not, or only to a limited extent.

Mr. FORDNEY. So that when you get a fair price and feel satisfied you are not particularly interested in what their profits are?

Mr. LAW. That is not my business.

Mr. FORDNEY. Your business is to get a good profit for your crop, and when you get a good profit you are satisfied?

Mr. LAW. I am.

Mr. FORDNEY. And that is so with reference to your neighbors and all other people raising beets there, is it?

Mr. LAW. In a general way; yes, sir.

Mr. FORDNEY. Mr. Law, you have stated that you received for your beets $5.64; was that right?

Mr. LAW. That was as I figured the crop this last season.

Mr. FORDNEY. And they ran about 15 per cent sugar, did they?

Mr. LAW. They ran from less than 15 per cent to a little better than 18 per cent sugar.

Mr. FORDNEY. Well, for an average throughout the State of Colorado, is 15 per cent fair, or do you know?

Mr. LAW. I only know in the general statement.

Mr. FORDNEY. What is your belief or understanding about it?

Mr. LAW. I have been told by the field men of the Windsor factory that the average for the Windsor district the past season was something better than $5.50 per ton for the beets, which is——

Mr. FORDNEY (interrupting). I think you gave that is $5.57?

Mr. LAW. It would mean 16½ per cent sugar, if I read the table correctly.

Mr. FORDNEY. That would bring it up above where I am, but I have made some figures that I wish to call your attention to. It has been stated here, and I believe we have an abundance of evidence on that point, that the cost of producing sugar from beets is about 3¾ cents per pound throughout the United States. It costs more in some places and a little less in others. Now, if for 15 per cent beets you receive $5 per ton, you get about $2.40 per 100 pounds for the sugar content of your beets, or close to 2½ cents per pound. Then the difference between that $2.40 for 15 per cent beets and the proportionate amount for your 16½ per cent beets, or whatever you had, would bring it up to fit your individual case. But taking $2.40 from $3.75 would leave $1.35 for the cost of production in the factory and incidental expenses. Do you feel that you are getting a fair share of that cost of production of refined sugar, or sale price, when you get $5.50 per ton for your beets?

Mr. Law. I have not gone into the details of that myself.

Mr. Fordney. Do you raise any other crop on your farm that does not fluctuate in price except beets? That is to say, when you plant your crop there is no other crop that you plant that you know what you are going to get for it except beets, is there?

Mr. Law. There are less elements of certainty with all other crops than with a crop of beets.

Mr. Fordney. When you plant your crop of beets you know you are going to get not less than $5 per ton for it?

Mr. Law. We do when we make our contract.

Mr. Fordney. Do you get a greater price per acre from that crop than from any other crop that you raise?

Mr. Law. No, sir.

Mr. Fordney. What other crop do you raise that you get better return per acre on the same cost?

Mr. Law. On the basis of the figures that I have gotten for the Windsor factory district, I would say that, approximately, the average for the Windsor factory district for the time it has been in operation has been $60 per acre gross return for the farmers for beets. While in some instances the tonnage for a small acreage has gone as high as 28 tons per acre, which would mean over $100, this is the average. On the other hand, for instance, one farm that got a higher price for beets, which farm I was interested in—$6.12 and a fraction cents per ton—only realized 8 tons to the acre this past season. This is the sugar-beet situation.

I will say that I have good reason to believe that the average potato crop in our section in a series of years will not be above $50 per acre, represented in dollars; yet there is a possibility of getting $300 per acre from a crop of potatoes. Again, while the average grain crop in our district is presumably, from my general knowledge of the situation of farming, not more than $18 per acre, yet the possibilities of the grain crop are $60 per acre.

Mr. Fordney. But your beet crop, aside from potatoes, is perhaps better on an average?

Mr. Law. The beet crop has these two elements of certainty or advantage that other crops we produce do not have: First, there is the price they will bring when produced, which is certain. Secondly, we are subject to hailstorms in that section, and they will sometimes completely destroy a grain crop or a potato crop, and yet the beet crop will recover from such a disaster as none of our other crops do, and possibly after a severe hailstorm you can make a crop that will bring up the expenses of farming for the season. This is an advantage.

Mr. Fordney. In conclusion let me ask you, and I want to be clear about this: If it were not for what you saw in the papers or heard of Mr. Bodkin's attack upon the sugar-beet industry, would you have been here?

Mr. LAW. I probably would not have been here.

Mr. FORDNEY. That is all. I thank you.

Mr. RAKER. What about the alfalfa crop?

Mr. LAW. The alfalfa crop has been disappointing for us, the past three years especially. That is for two reasons apparent to my mind—first, climatic conditions peculiar to the two seasons, when we have suffered from drought, and, secondly, because of grasshoppers, which we have had for three years back as we have not had for a series of years just previous to that time.

Mr. RAKER. Do not grasshoppers hurt beets?

Mr. LAW. They do to some extent.

Mr. RAKER. But you drive them off from beets and can not get them off from alfalfa; is that it?

Mr. LAW. We can protect our beets better than we can our alfalfa. We usually have a few acres of beets and a larger acreage of alfalfa.

Mr. RAKER. The gross amount received per acre from alfalfa—what has it been in your territory?

Mr. LAW. It varies greatly. From my own experience, I should say that three tons per acre of alfalfa hay is a fairly good crop from a field of 20 or 40 acres of alfalfa.

Mr. RAKER. Per acre?

Mr. LAW. Yes; in three cuttings.

Mr. RAKER. Three tons per acre from three cuttings?

Mr. LAW. Three tons per acre in three cuttings; yes. I am speaking of the average field of alfalfa. A good growth, with a good stand, may make five or six tons per acre in the three cuttings, but that would be the exception.

Mr. RAKER. Then that is not a good country for alfalfa?

Mr. LAW. Well, those are the facts and you can draw your own conclusion.

Mr. RAKER. I would like to have a general statement on that subject, because I thought it being a dry country, and the climate being good, and the soil being good, with water, it would be an ideal country for raising alfalfa. Do I understand from you that this country in and about Longmont and Windsor is not good alfalfa country?

Mr. LAW. That depends on what you call——

Mr. RAKER (interposing). You can answer that question directly, can't you?

Mr. LAW. It will produce, as I say, from two to six tons of alfalfa hay per acre.

Mr. RAKER. Well, is it considered a good alfalfa country or a poor alfalfa country?

Mr. LAW. My impression is that it is considered a good alfalfa country.

Mr. RAKER. Will it on an average yield a crop worth $60 to $80 per acre, considering seed?

Mr. LAW. No, sir.

Mr. RAKER. You don't raise any seed?

Mr. LAW. There has been some seed grown.

Mr. RAKER. Not successfully?

Mr. LAW. Yes, sir; but not generally.

Mr. RAKER. Well, if you can raise seed successfully it ought to run from $50 to $100 an acre gross, ought it not?

Mr. LAW. Three years ago I had some seed on my own farm. My recollection is that I had thrashed 18 bushels of alfalfa seed from 3 acres.

Mr. RAKER. Still you do not answer as to the conditions in that country where these sugar-beet factories are. Do you know?

Mr. LAW. What is the question?

Mr. RAKER. Is that locality described by you, referring to these various towns with the whole locality within a radius of 50 miles, considered among the farmers and the people generally to be a territory where alfalfa hay can be raised successfully?

Mr. LAW. Yes, sir.

Mr. RAKER. Now, as to alfalfa seed, is that the same? May it be raised successfully, as a successful crop as it is ordinarily considered?

Mr. LAW. We can grow alfalfa seed successfully in the sense of producing good seed.

Mr. RAKER. Is there any crop known to the farmer that is more profitable and more sure and that gives a better return than a country where you can raise successfully alfalfa for hay or alfalfa seed that you know of?

Mr. LAW. The potato crop and the beet crop with us give larger returns than our alfalfa crop.

Mr. RAKER. Per acre?

Mr. LAW. Yes, sir; per acre.

Mr. RAKER. It is more certain?

Mr. LAW. What is that?

Mr. RAKER. The beet and potato crops are more certain than the alfalfa crop generally.

Mr. LAW. No, sir; not more certain than the alfalfa crop, but when produced will mean more dollars per acre than the alfalfa hay crop, which is the common alfalfa crop produced. The few that have attempted to grow alfalfa seed have not found it so profitable, but they have only grown for seed in isolated years.

Mr. RAKER. Isn't it a fact, Mr. Law, that the business men in and about your town took up and discussed among themselves and with you the advisability of keeping conditions just as they are in Windsor and your part of the State of Colorado?

Mr. LAW. We have not discussed that question particularly.

Mr. RAKER. Wasn't it discussed before you came on at all?

Mr. LAW. It was not discussed specially with me.

Mr. RAKER. Well, was it discussed generally if not specially?

Mr. LAW. I can not say what others did.

Mr. RAKER. Well, it was understood, sorter tacitly understood, that you people would like to represent to the committee and to the country generally that you would like to keep conditions in statu quo, just as they are now, so that there would not be any stir or anything said in regard to the matter that might bring a change in any way. Isn't that the real purpose of your coming here?

Mr. LAW. I can answer that question "yes."

Mr. RAKER. That is all.

Mr. MALBY. Mr. Law, the farmers of your locality raise a general crop, I take it; some potatoes, some alfalfa, some grain, and some sugar beets. Is that the situation?

Mr. LAW. Yes, sir.

Mr. MALBY. And you have found by experience that the raising of sugar beets is a profitable crop in your locality?

Mr. LAW. We have.

Mr. MALBY. And the farmers round about that community have had that general experience, have they?

Mr. LAW. They have.

Mr. MALBY. Something has been said by our chairman with reference to the sugar manufacturer, that if he made 100 per cent or 200 per cent you farmers might want a little more for your sugar beets. I take it that he did not know of any man in the sugar business who made that much money. I want to know of you if you know of any sugar manufacturing company that is making 100 per cent or 200 per cent profit?

Mr. LAW. I do not.

Mr. MALBY. Do you suspect anybody with making that sum of money?

Mr. LAW. I do not.

Mr. MALBY. Have you any reason to suppose they make any such sum of money?

Mr. LAW. From all the information I have I think not. I have no reason to think so.

Mr. MALBY. Isn't it a fact that for some time after the beet-sugar industry was established in your part of the country it was generally understood it was pretty hard sledding for the companies and the beet growers both?

Mr. LAW. I know that it was considered pretty hard sledding, as you term it, for the beet growers.

Mr. MALBY. Well, did you understand that the beet-sugar manufacturers were getting rich while you were having the hard sledding?

Mr. LAW. Not from them nor from any knowledge that I had of their business.

Mr. MALBY. There were three statements, I think, made by some other gentlemen from your State and to which I desire to call your attention and see whether those conditions exist in your locality. The first question I think you have answered, that yourself and other farmers feel that you are getting a fair price for your beets. That is correct, is it?

Mr. LAW. It is.

Mr. MALBY. The second proposition was that he did not know, but suspected that the beet-sugar manufacturers were not correctly analyzing the sugar in the beets. Did you have any reason to entertain such suspicion?

Mr. LAW. I haven't such suspicion myself, personally. I have heard the criticism made, but have had no reason myself to believe that it was well founded.

Mr. MALBY. Well, was the criticism made by some one who would be apt to know, or was it just simply an idle remark about the town?

Mr. LAW. All the criticism that I have heard has not been made by anyone, to the best of my knowledge, that really would know.

Mr. MALBY. Or would have any right to know, in your judgment?

Mr. LAW. The criticism that I have heard has been general talk by farmers.

Mr. MALBY. And not by anyone who had had any analysis made of his beets?

Mr. LAW. No, sir.

Mr. MALBY. Or had analyzed them himself?

Mr. LAW. No, sir.

Mr. MALBY. Or that really had any capacity himself to make an analysis?

Mr. LAW. I do not recall hearing anyone question the analysis that was prepared to determine that matter himself.

Mr. MALBY. Or to in anywise make good his expression of suspicion?

Mr. LAW. I think not.

Mr. MALBY. Have you knowledge of the fact that the State agricultural department, or your State agricultural school, or other public institutions have had applications made to them for analyses of the sugar content of beets and denied such applications?

Mr. LAW. I know in a general way of such. Last week at a farmers' institute, held in Greeley, President Lory, of the State agricultural college, made an explanation to the institute of the reasons why the agricultural college could not make analyses for individual farmers. The details of his explanation I can not give you, but his talk left me satisfied that the agricultural college was not refusing to do anything reasonable or consistent for the beet grower.

Mr. RAKER. In other words, the college was not instituted and was not intending to help the great State of Colorado generally in the way of assisting the farmers raising beets by way of furnishing them analyses of their beets.

Mr. LAW. That was not the idea of his talk at all.

Mr. MALBY. I am not asking that kind of a question. My search here is for information. I want to know if you have an agricultural department or an agricultural college that refuses, upon proper application, to advise the beet growers as to any interest which concerns them? My own individual opinion about the matter is that they ought to do it if practicable. Do you know of any application which has been properly made, consistently made, by anybody to have his beets analyzed and it has been turned down without just cause or provocation? If so, I would like to know it.

Mr. LAW. I do not, and I wish to say this: In President Lory's explanation it left the impression on my mind that if the beet growers' association desired analyses made that they could do it, but that if individual beet growers asked for analyses they could not make them, because if they made an analyses for one man they must, to be consistent, make it for another, and it would be impossible for them to comply with all the possible requests for analyses of beets.

Mr. MALBY. So that your impression of what he said was that it would entail labor which the college could not under present conditions and equipment undertake to make general analyses for everybody who might apply. Is that your impression about it or not?

Mr. LAW. It is.

Mr. MALBY. Do the same conditions exist in your agricultural department—and I am not now speaking of your college, but your State department of agriculture, and you have a department of agriculture in your State, have you not?

Mr. LAW. I am not entirely clear as to what you refer to.

Mr. MALBY. Have you a State agricultural department; a department of your State government which is called the department of agriculture?

Mr. LAW. Well, now, I am not familiar with the State departments. Our agricultural college, I suppose, includes all the public interests of the State of that kind.

Mr. MALBY. You don't know whether you have any other department of agriculture, outside the college, or not?

Mr. LAW. No, sir.

Mr. MALBY. You have a farmers organization in your locality?

Mr. LAW. There is a local organization of the farmers' union at Windsor.

Mr. MALBY. Is that affiliated with other local organizations throughout the State?

Mr. LAW. I suppose it is affiliated with other farmers' unions.

Mr. MALBY. You do not belong to it?

Mr. LAW. I am not personally a member of the farmers' union.

Mr. MALBY. Is it the opinion, generally, in your locality that it is desirable from a farmer's standpoint that the sugar industry be continued or promoted, or not?

Mr. LAW. I believe so; yes.

Mr. MALBY. That is, under present conditions?

Mr. LAW. Yes, sir.

Mr. MALBY. That is all.

Mr. RAKER. There is just one idea in my mind that I would like to know about, and possibly I can get it from this witness. Mr. Law, you are a farmer and own farms?

Mr. LAW. Yes, sir.

Mr. RAKER. Estimating your land to be worth so much per acre, you raise a certain crop upon this land, and, to illustrate, we will say of sugar beets, valuing your land at a certain amount, providing a certain amount required to raise your crop, then leaving you a net income of the amount you stated, or a reasonable income, you are satisfied with that, aren't you? So long as you get a reasonable income from your product you raise on your land, particularly sugar beets?

Mr. LAW. Yes, sir.

Mr. RAKER. If you sell your product to a third party and, we will say, for instance, to the Great Western Sugar Co., so far as you are concerned, it is wholly immaterial what they may make or what they may charge for the product they produce from the beets they buy from you that you raise on your farm? Now, taking the premises I started with, is that right?

Mr. LAW. Yes, sir.

Mr. RAKER. Whatever the law might be that would permit them to sell this product that they make from the beets they buy from you, and the amount that the people of the country generally have to pay for their product by virtue of the law, you are entirely indifferent upon that question?

Mr. LAW. I may say that so far as my relation to their business transactions withe country are concerned; yes.

Mr. RAKER. Then, it means this: That so long as you get a reasonable return for your product, estimating the value of your land—which product you sell to a third party—if the law is such that he may raise the price as high as he wants to and then charge the general consumer all over the country that price, you are not interested in that question at all, as I understand you? That is, as to controlling what he should charge for his product made from what he buys from you, if he may do that by virtue of the laws as they exist, that is all right with you?

Mr. LAW. I have no interest in that other than what every other citizen of the country has.

Mr. RAKER. Well, in this particular matter, relating to beet sugar, you are entirely indifferent and believe that to be none of your business?

Mr. LAW. That is not my business.

Mr. RAKER. You will let the sugar-beet factories attend to that for themselves?

Mr. LAW. That is certainly their business.

Mr. RAKER. That is all.

The CHAIRMAN. Mr. Law, we will excuse you with the thanks of the committee for your attendance.

RESOLUTIONS AS TO DEATH OF REPRESENTATIVE EDMUND H. MADISON.

The CHAIRMAN. At the beginning of the present session a subcommittee, of which I believe Mr. Hinds was chairman, was appointed to present some resolutions to the full committee to be spread upon the minutes relative to the death of our colleague and friend, Judge Madison, who was a member of this committee. Mr. Hinds, are you ready to present the resolutions?

Mr. HINDS. I am, and they are as follows:

Resolved, That the Select Committee on the Investigation of the American Sugar Refining Co. feels it appropriate to spread on its records an expression appreciative of the distinguished services of the late Representative Edmund H. Madison, of Kansas, as a member of this committee.

His clear and comprehensive intellect, unfailing tact and courtesy, great industry, and conscientious regard for duty, have made his loss to the committee serious from the standpoint of public service, and grievous in the relations of personal association.

Resolved, That the clerk of the committee be directed to spread these resolutions on the records, and transmit a copy to the family of Mr. Madison.

Mr. HINDS. I move the adoption of the resolutions.

Mr. RAKER. I second the motion.

The CHAIRMAN. Gentlemen of the committee, you have heard the resolutions read. The motion is that the resolutions be adopted, spread upon the minutes, and a copy sent to the family of the deceased member.

The resolutions were adopted.

At 1 o'clock p. m. the committee took a recess until 2.30 o'clock p. m.

AFTER RECESS.

The committee met pursuant to the taking of a recess at 2 o'clock p. m.

TESTIMONY OF MR. WILLIAM STANLEY.

The witness was duly sworn by the chairman.

The CHAIRMAN. Where do you live, Mr. Stanley?

Mr. STANLEY. I live 4 miles north of Greeley, Colo.

The CHAIRMAN. You live in the sugar-beet belt?

Mr. STANLEY. Yes, sir.

The CHAIRMAN. What business are you engaged in?

Mr. STANLEY. Farming.

The CHAIRMAN. Anything else except farming?

Mr. STANLEY. No, sir.

The CHAIRMAN. Have you any interest of any kind, directly or remote, in the sugar-beet factories, or any of them?

Mr. STANLEY. No, sir.

The CHAIRMAN. What organization, if any, do you represent here?

Mr. STANLEY. I represent the Greeley Commercial Club.

The CHAIRMAN. What is that club?

Mr. STANLEY. It is a bunch of farmers.

The CHAIRMAN. Farmers?

Mr. STANLEY. And produce men of our city of Greeley.

The CHAIRMAN. How large a town is Greeley?

Mr. STANLEY. About 14,000, I should judge.

The CHAIRMAN. And the commercial club is a business men's organization of that city?

Mr. STANLEY. A business men's organization of that city and country.

The CHAIRMAN. Some of the farmers belong to it, too?

Mr. STANLEY. Yes, sir.

The CHAIRMAN. Many of them?

Mr. STANLEY. I know of a few in our neighborhood who do.

The CHAIRMAN. How many?

Mr. STANLEY. I know of four or five.

The CHAIRMAN. How many members has the club altogether?

Mr. STANLEY. Probably 150.

The CHAIRMAN. And out of that 150 there are only four or five who are farmers?

Mr. STANLEY. Yes, sir.

The CHAIRMAN. The others, I suppose, are business men of various avocations and pursuits?

Mr. STANLEY. Yes, sir.

The CHAIRMAN. Do any of the sugar people belong to it?

Mr. STANLEY. I do not know that they do.

The CHAIRMAN. Is there a sugar factory at Greeley?

Mr. STANLEY. Yes, sir.

The CHAIRMAN. Do not the people who run the sugar factory belong to this business men's organization?

Mr. STANLEY. I do not know whether they do or not.

The CHAIRMAN. Did you discuss your coming on here with any of the sugar men?

Mr. STANLEY. No, sir; not in regard to farming. I have just talked with them.

The CHAIRMAN. I say, you talked it over with the sugar people, did you not?

Mr. STANLEY. No, sir.

The CHAIRMAN. With none of them?

Mr. STANLEY. No, sir.

The CHAIRMAN. Neither the sugar factory at Greeley nor any of its officers had any idea you were coming here?

Mr. STANLEY. No, sir.

The CHAIRMAN. You had no conference or talk with any of them about it?

Mr. STANLEY. No, sir; not in regard to farming.

The CHAIRMAN. I do not mean in regard to farming, but with regard to your coming here.

Mr. STANLEY. Yes, sir.

The CHAIRMAN. You had a talk with the sugar-factory people themselves?

Mr. STANLEY. Yes, sir.

The CHAIRMAN. And with other business men?

Mr. STANLEY. Yes, sir.

The CHAIRMAN. What was the nature of your talk with the sugar-factory people?

Mr. STANLEY. I went to the sugar factory at Eaton, Colo., 4 miles north of me, and got my statement for the past 10 years of what I had done in regard to raising beets.

The CHAIRMAN. And you told them why you wanted it?

Mr. STANLEY. Yes, sir.

The CHAIRMAN. Did you have any conversation with them as to what the condition was in the industry itself?

Mr. STANLEY. No, sir.

The CHAIRMAN. Did they make any suggestions about misrepresentations which had been made which you were to deny, or anything like that?

Mr. STANLEY. No, sir.

The CHAIRMAN. None at all?

Mr. STANLEY. No, sir.

The CHAIRMAN. Did you confer with anybody on those subjects?

Mr. STANLEY. No, sir.

The CHAIRMAN. You did not make any investigation yourself at all?

Mr. STANLEY. No, sir.

The CHAIRMAN. You relied on your knowledge with reference to those matters?

Mr. STANLEY. Yes, sir.

The CHAIRMAN. What was the occasion of the commercial club desiring you to come on here to testify before this committee?

Mr. STANLEY. They told me to come down here and state as a farmer what I am doing in regard to raising beets, potatoes, and other things, and told me particularly just to tell the truth and nothing else but the truth.

The CHAIRMAN. I did not mean to imply that they wanted you to tell anything but the truth, and I just want to know exactly what interests you represent here.

Mr. STANLEY. That is just the interest I represent.

The CHAIRMAN. You are a beet farmer?

Mr. STANLEY. Yes, sir.

The CHAIRMAN. You own the land and cultivate it yourself?

Mr. STANLEY. Yes, sir; by hired help.

The CHAIRMAN. I understand that. I mean you are a proprietor?

Mr. STANLEY. Yes, sir.

The CHAIRMAN. How much land did you have in beets last year?

Mr. STANLEY. Yast year I had 32 acres in beets.

The CHAIRMAN. How much did they net you per acre, without going into the details?

Mr. STANLEY. I have not got it down just in that way. I have got it for the 10 years I have raised beets.

The CHAIRMAN. Well, give me the figures in that way. What did it cost on an average, and what did you get? How many acres did you plant on an average?

Mr. STANLEY. I planted 277 acres in 10 years, and I got $21,772 and my expense was $10,557.

The CHAIRMAN. Your profits, then, were how much?

Mr. STANLEY. $11,557.

The CHAIRMAN. Have you figured that out to an acre basis?

Mr. STANLEY. No; I did not.

The CHAIRMAN. I want to get it on an acre basis—instead of saying you farmed so many acres for 10 years—if I can, just for the purpose of comparison, because the other witnesses have used that standard.

Mr. STANLEY. My expense per acre was $45.

The CHAIRMAN. That is what it cost you. Does that include rent for the land?

Mr. STANLEY. No, sir; handwork, plowing, harrowing, cultivating, irrigating, fertilizing, seed, and taxes, and delivery.

The CHAIRMAN. You do include your taxes?

Mr. STANLEY. Taxes and water assessment as a tax.

The CHAIRMAN. I thought you said you included irrigation? Have you included irrigation besides the water tax?

Mr. STANLEY. No; the irrigation goes with the land.

The CHAIRMAN. In other words, the only charge you put in for water was the water rights?

Mr. STANLEY. The water tax by the board.

The CHAIRMAN. That made a total of about $45 per acre, on an average, did it?

Mr. STANLEY. Yes, sir.

The CHAIRMAN. What were your total average proceeds per acre?

Mr. STANLEY. It averages up something over $90.

The CHAIRMAN. So that your profits would be about $45 per acre, allowing nothing for the rental of the land. What is your land worth?

Mr. STANLEY. $250 an acre.

The CHAIRMAN. $250 an acre? Have you any beet land in that part of Colorado worth that much per acre?

Mr. STANLEY. I have got 110 acres that are worth $250 an acre.

The CHAIRMAN. How far are you from a city?

Mr. STANLEY. I am 4 miles from Greeley and from Denver 52 miles, and Cheyenne about 52 miles. Denver is south and Cheyenne is north.

The CHAIRMAN. Is there any town closer to you than Greeley?

Mr. STANLEY. No, sir; Eaton is 4 miles north of me.

The CHAIRMAN. You are 4 miles from Eaton and 4 miles from Greeley, and yet your land is worth $250 an acre?

Mr. STANLEY. Yes, sir.

The CHAIRMAN. It is well-irrigated land?

Mr. STANLEY. Yes, sir.

The CHAIRMAN. And well-improved land?

Mr. STANLEY. No, sir.

The CHAIRMAN. It is unimproved land, and worth that much?

Mr. STANLEY. Not well improved. This land is located at Lawson. We have a dumping station at this particular point, between Greeley and Eaton.

The CHAIRMAN. Is there a village around this dumping station?

Mr. STANLEY. It is just a loading point for produce, having five spud warehouses—I guess you call them potatoes—and one grain elevator, a blacksmith shop, and one store; probably 50 inhabitants or maybe 100.

The CHAIRMAN. About 100 people live in that little settlement?

Mr. STANLEY. Yes, sir.

The CHAIRMAN. Do you know a man named Bodkin?

Mr. STANLEY. No, sir.

The CHAIRMAN. You do not know anything about his land?

Mr. STANLEY. No, sir.

The CHAIRMAN. But you think your own land is worth $250 per acre?

Mr. STANLEY. Yes, sir.

The CHAIRMAN. How much land have you in all?

Mr. STANLEY. I have 110 acres at Lawson.

The CHAIRMAN. And that is the land you speak of?

Mr. STANLEY. Yes, sir.

The CHAIRMAN. And that is the land for which you gave us the figures just now?

Mr. STANLEY. Yes, sir.

The CHAIRMAN. You have heard the testimony of these other gentlemen from Colorado, have you?

Mr. STANLEY. Yes.

The CHAIRMAN. Does your experience in the main correspond with theirs? I mean, not as to every detail but substantially, do you agree with what they say about the situation out there?

Mr. STANLEY. I do not know. I can not recall just what they said.

The CHAIRMAN. You heard them testify, and this is about a business you have spent most of your life in.

Mr. STANLEY. Yes; I expect they told the truth about it.

The CHAIRMAN. In other words, your experience would lead you to agree substantially with what they said?

Mr. STANLEY. Yes; it would.

The CHAIRMAN. What was the occasion for your being sent here to appear before this committee? Was there any evidence that anyone else had given that caused this commercial club of which you are a member and all the other business men to send you here?

Mr. Stanley. I did not say I belonged to the club. I do not belong to it.

The Chairman. You do not belong to this association?

Mr. Stanley. No, sir.

The Chairman. I thought you did.

Mr. Stanley. No; they just picked me out as a farmer to tell what I have done in regard to the beets.

The Chairman. The farmers did not pick you out, but they picked you out?

Mr. Stanley. Yes, sir.

The Chairman. What was the occasion for their sending somebody down here, do you know?

Mr. Stanley. No, sir; not definitely.

The Chairman. Do you know indefinitely?

Mr. Stanley. Well, probably it was something that Mr. Bodkin said.

The Chairman. In other words, on account of Mr. Bodkin's evidence. Why do you say that? Did they state to you that was the reason they wanted you to come here?

Mr. Stanley. No; I heard it discussed at a farmers' union meeting last week.

The Chairman. You say you heard it discussed at a farmers' union meting?

Mr. Stanley. No, sir; in a meeting in Greeley last week.

The Chairman. Not a farmers' union meeting.

Mr. Stanley. No.

The Chairman. A growers' meeting?

Mr. Stanley. Yes, sir.

The Chairman. Do the men who attended that meeting belong to the farmers' union or not?

Mr. Stanley. Some of them do.

The Chairman. Is the farmers' union pretty strong in your section?

Mr. Stanley. It is getting pretty strong.

The Chairman. Do you belong to it yourself?

Mr. Stanley. Yes, sir.

The Chairman. Do you know Mr. Combs, who seems to be an organizer for it?

Mr. Stanley. No, sir; I do not.

The Chairman. Do you know Mr. Dakin, a lawyer at Longmont?

Mr. Stanley. No, sir.

The Chairman. Do you know Mr. Bodkin?

Mr. Stanley. No, sir.

The Chairman. Now, leaving out your opinion as to the views they entertain, is there any fact either one of those gentlemen stated before this committee with which you wish to take issue?

Mr. Stanley. Their account of the labor. I do not know what Mr. Bodkin said, but I was sent here to discuss the labor question—what I have got in the way of labor and what I have had for the last 10 years.

The Chairman. Who has done your work?

Mr. Stanley. Germans.

The Chairman. Germans or Russians?

Mr. STANLEY. Germans. They would not consider me at all if I called them Russians.

The CHAIRMAN. What part of Germany do they come from?

Mr. STANLEY. They claim they just came through Russia.

The CHAIRMAN. But they came from Russia last?

Mr. STANLEY. Yes; but they claim they are Germans.

The CHAIRMAN. Their claim is they are from Germany, but they came to this country from Russia—is that a correct statement of it?

Mr. STANLEY. Yes.

The CHAIRMAN. Now, these farmers do the handwork, do they?

Mr. STANLEY. Yes, sir.

The CHAIRMAN. Where do they live?

Mr. STANLEY. In Greeley.

The CHAIRMAN. Greeley is a town, I believe you told me, of 14,000?

Mr. STANLEY. Yes, sir; or more.

The CHAIRMAN. Do any of them come from larger cities than Greeley?

Mr. STANLEY. They did 10 years ago, but not lately.

The CHAIRMAN. Have they a separate quarter of their own in Greeley?

Mr. STANLEY. Yes, sir.

The CHAIRMAN. Is it rather poorer and less attractive than the quarters of the city occupied by American citizens?

Mr. STANLEY. No; they live to the west of Greeley, near the Greeley sugar factory, at a little German settlement, so as to be close to the factory when the field work is through

The CHAIRMAN. What character of houses do they live in?

Mr. STANLEY. Pretty good houses.

The CHAIRMAN. Are their houses up to the American standard?

Mr. STANLEY. Up to the standard of the American people in their standing.

The CHAIRMAN. American people do not engage in this hand work in the beet fields much, do they?

Mr. STANLEY. Yes.

The CHAIRMAN. To any considerable extent in your section?

Mr. STANLEY. Yes, sir; they are getting to. I had them last year.

The CHAIRMAN. In what proportion?

Mr. STANLEY. Oh, not very large; that is, in proportion to the whole country, but I have had the work done by them in two years out of the 10 years I have raised beets.

The CHAIRMAN. Have you had all your work done by them or part of it?

Mr. STANLEY. I have had all of it done by American labor two years in the 10 years I have raised beets.

The CHAIRMAN. And the other eight years it was all done by this foreign help?

Mr. STANLEY. Yes.

The CHAIRMAN. You pay the American help the same price you do these foreigners?

Mr. STANLEY. Yes, sir.

The CHAIRMAN. There is no difference in the scale of prices paid to them?

Mr. STANLEY. No, sir.

The CHAIRMAN. Now, do you know whether the condition of the labor you refer to as to your own land is general in your neighborhood? Is it the same?

Mr. STANLEY. Yes; the conditions of the labor in my neighborhood are the same.

The CHAIRMAN. Do you know what it is throughout Colorado, generally?

Mr. STANLEY. Well, it is German help.

The CHAIRMAN. Have you been through the beet fields of Colorado pretty thoroughly.

Mr. STANLEY. Yes.

The CHAIRMAN. You know where Mr. Bodkin lives?

Mr. STANLEY. No, sir.

The CHAIRMAN. You do not know where he lives?

Mr. STANLEY. I know where Longmont is.

The CHAIRMAN. How about Mr. Combs? Do you know anything about the Fort Morgan neighborhood?

Mr. STANLEY. I have just been there several times.

The CHAIRMAN. Did you investigate conditions in the beet fields and the labor in the beet fields?

Mr. STANLEY. No, sir.

The CHAIRMAN. Did you do that anywhere except at your home?

Mr. STANLEY. No, sir.

The CHAIRMAN. Outside of the labor question is there any further matter you want to enlighten the committee upon?

Mr. STANLEY. No.

The CHAIRMAN. There is no other statement made by these witnesses you care to say anything about?

Mr. STANLEY. No.

Mr. FORDNEY. Mr. Stanley, you stated that in the 10 years you have planted 227 acres of beets.

Mr. STANLEY. Yes, sir.

Mr. FORDNEY. And your net profit was $11,557?

Mr. STANLEY. Yes, sir.

Mr. FORDNEY. If your net profit was $11,557, and you had 227 acres planted in the 10 years, it gives you a net profit of $50.91 per acre. Now, as I understand it, you took particular exception to the statement made by these gentlemen who were before the committee about the class of labor used in your country?

Mr. STANLEY. Yes, sir.

Mr. FORDNEY. Did you notice what they said about the influence of the sugar companies on politics of the State? Do you agree with them on that or not?

Mr. STANLEY. I do not know anything about that, sir.

TESTIMONY OF MR. FRED F. EVERETT.

The witness was duly sworn by the chairman.

The CHAIRMAN. What is your residence, Mr. Everett?

Mr. EVERETT. Scotts Bluff, Nebr.

The CHAIRMAN. What is your avocation or business?

Mr. EVERETT. Farming.

The CHAIRMAN. Have you any other business except farming?

Mr. EVERETT. No; I could not say I am in any other business.

The CHAIRMAN. Have you any side lines?

Mr. EVERETT. If running a milk route is a side line, I have.

The CHAIRMAN. I presume that is a branch of agriculture.

Mr. EVERETT. I have always done that.

The CHAIRMAN. You are not interested in any manufacturing enterprise?

Mr. EVERETT. No, sir.

The CHAIRMAN. Nor in any bank or anything like that?

Mr. EVERETT. No, sir.

The CHAIRMAN. You are simply engaged in farming in its various branches?

Mr. EVERETT. That is all.

The CHAIRMAN. Do you represent any particular class of people in giving this testimony or information you are about to give the committee?

Mr. EVERETT. I do not know that I do, aside from the farmers.

The CHAIRMAN. Have you got an organization of the farmers?

Mr. EVERETT. We have an organization. I do not know but what I should say I represent the commercial club and the farmers.

The CHAIRMAN. The Commercial Club of Scotts Bluff?

Mr. EVERETT. Yes, sir.

The CHAIRMAN. How large a place is Scotts Bluff?

Mr. EVERETT. About 2,500.

The CHAIRMAN. And the commercial club, I suppose, is composed of practically all the business men in the town?

Mr. EVERETT. A majority of them. Some of them would not come into the club.

The CHAIRMAN. Do any sugar men belong to the club?

Mr. EVERETT. I think some of the employees of the sugar company belong to the club.

The CHAIRMAN. I mean any of the managers or officers.

Mr. EVERETT. I think they do.

The CHAIRMAN. You said that besides representing this commercial club you also represented the farmers?

Mr. EVERETT. I do.

The CHAIRMAN. As an organization?

Mr. EVERETT. No, sir.

The CHAIRMAN. How were you elected to represent the farmers?

Mr. EVERETT. I have been in communication with the farmers.

The CHAIRMAN. What I mean is, why do you say you represent them?

Mr. EVERETT. Because the farmers—a good many of them—belong to the commercial club, and I am a farmer.

The CHAIRMAN. How many?

Mr. EVERETT. I think there are 25 or 30, probably.

The CHAIRMAN. Out of how large an organization?

Mr. EVERETT. Out of probably 100. May I explain that?

The CHAIRMAN. Certainly.

Mr. EVERETT. The commercial club is in town, and you can not reach out and get people 10 miles from town into the commercial club of the town. We have gone out from town into the country and worked with the farmers. Our interests and the farmers' are all together, and I think we can fairly say we represent the farmers and the town.

The CHAIRMAN. The organization represents the people who belong to it?

Mr. EVERETT. Yes.

The CHAIRMAN. You represent the farmers, then, so far as the farmers are members of this organization?

Mr. EVERETT. I was put onto the farmers' committee.

The CHAIRMAN. And, of course, as far as any other farmers are concerned—and there must be many of them outside of the organization—you do not speak for them by authority?

Mr. EVERETT. Not by authority.

The CHAIRMAN. Although you may represent what you think is their view and their interest; is that a proper way of stating it?

Mr. EVERETT. Yes, sir.

The CHAIRMAN. Of course this organization, I suppose, paid your expenses to come and make this representation to the committee?

Mr. EVERETT. They furnished me a part of the money.

The CHAIRMAN. Was there any particular occasion why they thought it was necessary to adopt that course?

Mr. EVERETT. I do not know the occasion. I did not know anything about coming until last Saturday noon, except I was told Sunday noon I might be wanted to come.

The CHAIRMAN. Who told you that?

Mr. EVERETT. The president of the commercial club.

The CHAIRMAN. Is he an officer of the sugar company?

Mr. EVERETT. No, sir.

The CHAIRMAN. Did he tell you why he wanted you to come?

Mr. EVERETT. My understanding was there was an investigation here of the conditions of the beet-sugar industry as it is carried on by the farmers and their interest in it; whether it was for their interest or not.

The CHAIRMAN. And your community wanted to present to the committee the situation as it exists there?

Mr. EVERETT. Yes, sir.

The CHAIRMAN. Was there any statement made to you that any testimony had been given before the committee which did not fairly present that situation?

Mr. EVERETT. I suppose it was this same thing. I have heard of that. I heard of it and I had the testimony to read.

The CHAIRMAN. Who furnished you with that testimony?

Mr. EVERETT. I read the testimony as I came through.

The CHAIRMAN. Who furnished you with that testimony?

Mr. EVERETT. Mr. Morrell, the president of the club, or Mr. McCleary. They are officers of the association.

The CHAIRMAN. And neither of them is a sugar man?

Mr. EVERETT. No, sir.

The CHAIRMAN. And none of the officers of the association is a sugar man?

Mr. EVERETT. No, sir.

The CHAIRMAN. Although some of the sugar people do belong to the club?

Mr. EVERETT. Yes. I will say that I think on the board of governors there is one of the officers of the sugar company or one of their clerks.

The CHAIRMAN. One of their employees, at any rate?

Mr. EVERETT. Yes; he is on the board of governors, but only one out of nine.

The CHAIRMAN. Did he have any talk with you about this matter?

Mr. EVERETT. No, sir.

The CHAIRMAN. They gave you the testimony of these three witnesses, Messrs. Bodkin, Combs, and Dakin?

Mr. EVERETT. Yes; I had the pamphlet.

The CHAIRMAN. Those officers furnished you with that testimony?

Mr. EVERETT. Yes, sir.

The CHAIRMAN. And you were to look into that on the way here and see what the testimony was?

Mr. EVERETT. Yes.

The CHAIRMAN. Now, to get down to the nub of the matter; in what respect, if any, do you differ from any of the statements made by those gentlemen?

Mr. EVERETT. Well, their conditions and our conditions may not be the same.

The CHAIRMAN. That is true, and is a fair statement on your part to make. Wherein, then, do the statements they have made about conditions in their own localities differ from the conditions in your locality, which you want to direct our attention to?

Mr. EVERETT. To start with, the rent that they charge for land is different from ours.

The CHAIRMAN. What is your average beet land worth?

Mr. EVERETT. It rents for $10 an acre, cash rent, or a crop rental——

The CHAIRMAN (interposing). Let us reduce it to a cash basis for the purpose of this estimate.

Mr. EVERETT. The crop rental may be a higher rent, and might produce more than any man would dare pay cash.

The CHAIRMAN. I understand that.

Mr. EVERETT. That is the reason I say that the crop rental may be a higher rent.

The CHAIRMAN. But the average cash rent is $10 an acre for good beet land?

Mr. EVERETT. $10 an acre has been quite a good rental for the last two years, and prior to that time six or eight dollars an acre rented a great deal of land.

The CHAIRMAN. You would say now $10 is a fair average?

Mr. EVERETT. I think $10 is a fair rental.

The CHAIRMAN. And the other witnesses figured the rental of some of their land at $20?

Mr. EVERETT. Yes.

The CHAIRMAN. This land you speak of has irrigation rights?

Mr. EVERETT. Yes, sir.

The CHAIRMAN. Does the rental include that?

Mr. EVERETT. Yes, sir.

The CHAIRMAN. Does the renter pay the irrigation taxes?

Mr. EVERETT. The man who rents the ground ordinarily pays for the water; that is, the man who furnishes the ground furnishes the water in connection with the ground.

The CHAIRMAN. And the $10 pays for the water as well as for the rent of the ground?

Mr. EVERETT. Yes, sir.

The CHAIRMAN. And the tenant pays neither the tax on the land nor the water tax?

Mr. EVERETT. No, sir.

The CHAIRMAN. What would you say is the value of this beet land, on an average, which you say rents for $10 in the way you have just described?

Mr. EVERETT. From about $100 to $125.

The CHAIRMAN. And if the land was worth twice that amount a rental of $20 would be about on the same scale?

Mr. EVERETT. It would be mighty close to it.

The CHAIRMAN. Have you ever actually raised beets yourself?

Mr. EVERETT. We raised 72 acres this year.

The CHAIRMAN. Have you reduced that to an acreage basis, and can you tell us what it costs you to raise an acre of beets and what you get for them?

Mr. EVERETT. We figure about $40 an acre as cost of production.

The CHAIRMAN. What do you get out of that on an average in an average year?

Mr. EVERETT. My beets this year brought $72.80 per acre, not including the beet tops.

The CHAIRMAN. And the beet tops are worth how much?

Mr. EVERETT. They are worth a ton of alfalfa hay.

The CHAIRMAN. What is that worth?

Mr. EVERETT. Mine sells for $8 a ton at the place, in the stack.

Mr. FORDNEY. How many tons per acre?

Mr. EVERETT. $8 a ton for the hay, and an acre of beet tops is equal to a ton of alfalfa hay as feed.

Mr. FORDNEY. So you figure the tops as worth $8 per acre?

Mr. EVERETT. We do not sell them at that.

The CHAIRMAN. You use them yourself?

Mr. EVERETT. They do sell at $4 to a man who is buying them to produce meat. I use them, and you could not buy my beet tops, because I have use for them.

Mr. FORDNEY. Mr. Chairman, if I am right in my figures, $72.80 are his gross receipts, and the cost is $40, which leaves him $32.80 besides $8 for the tops per acre, making a net profit of $40.80.

The CHAIRMAN. And if you deduct $10 for land rent, you would have $30.80 as profit.

Mr. EVERETT. That is true; but where we use our own land there are very few who figure the rent. There is another thing that no one has taken the view of it which I do, and I do not find it in any other place, where you charge up all your work to expense in the cost of producing and expect to pay that and say nothing about it. For instance, I raise these beets with a hired hand, doing the work with my own team. I pay so much, and the balance of it I am selling to myself or getting paid for.

The CHAIRMAN. That is correct. You figure that in your calculations?

Mr. EVERETT. I did not figure that as a profit to me.

The CHAIRMAN. But did you not include the expense of your teams, etc., in this $45?

Mr. EVERETT. It is figured in there, but I am getting that back myself.

The CHAIRMAN. I understand that, but you are paying yourself for an actual expense you have undergone?

Mr. EVERETT. Yes; it is an expense, but after all——

The CHAIRMAN (interposing). There is some profit in that?

Mr. EVERETT. In the corn-raising belt we never figure things that way.

The CHAIRMAN. Is the beet crop the most profitable crop you have?

Mr. EVERETT. It is the safest crop we have, and under certain conditions it is.

The CHAIRMAN. Why; because it is the hardiest crop?

Mr. EVERETT. It is a hardy crop and not subject to hailstorms.

The CHAIRMAN. Are you worried with hail at Scotts Bluff?

Mr. EVERETT. You are worried with hail wherever they irrigate along the Rocky Mountains. I have not found a place yet where they are not.

The CHAIRMAN. Is there any advantage to the farmer in having a fairly certain and stable price which he receives for his products, like he does for his beets; in other words, he makes his contract ahead and knows what he is going to get for his beets when he plants them?

Mr. EVERETT. It seems to me that is an advantage.

The CHAIRMAN. And that is something that makes the beet crop desirable?

Mr. EVERETT. Yes.

The CHAIRMAN. And you think this crop on the whole, considering its certainty both as to price and production, is probably the best crop you have?

Mr. EVERETT. It is the crop in connection with other crops which makes our country what it is. For instance, you may take alfalfa. Alfalfa is a good crop, a paying crop, but in my judgment the greatest value of alfalfa is to put your land in shape to raise the other crops, like potatoes and beets.

The CHAIRMAN. It all works together?

Mr. EVERETT. Yes, sir; it is a rotation of crops.

The CHAIRMAN. Now, what did you allow for handwork in your calculation?

Mr. EVERETT. $20.

The CHAIRMAN. That is pretty near the universal price, is it not?

Mr. EVERETT. I suppose that is the price everywhere.

The CHAIRMAN. Who does that hand labor?

Mr. EVERETT. We had Germans this year, and Japs, and some Americans.

The CHAIRMAN. Do the foreigners do the greater part of it?

Mr. EVERETT. The foreigners do the greater part of it, although since we have been raising beets there, I know of several Americans who have come in there and have done the handwork for a year or two, and then gone to raising beets for themselves.

The CHAIRMAN. But as a general proposition, the bulk of that labor is performed by the foreigners?

Mr. EVERETT. Yes, sir.

The CHAIRMAN. Where do you get that labor?

Mr. EVERETT. A good many of them live right there.

The CHAIRMAN. What proportion?

Mr. EVERETT. Probably half.

The CHAIRMAN. Where does the other half come from?

Mr. EVERETT. They come from the different cities. Lincoln has a great German population, and they come out from there—or a Russian population. You can call them either Russians or Germans.

The CHAIRMAN. I notice there seems to be some confusion about that.

Mr. EVERETT. They are German-Russians.

The CHAIRMAN. They belong to the German Province of Russia; is that true, or do you know?

Mr. EVERETT. I can not say from my knowledge; but that is what we suppose. He is the Polander.

The CHAIRMAN. The Polack?

Mr. EVERETT. Yes. We have some of them. This year we had the Mexicans—quite a lot of Mexicans.

The CHAIRMAN. Did you have any Indians?

Mr. EVERETT. I believe they had one Indian there. I guess if you get a Mexican you get a part Indian.

The CHAIRMAN. What about the Hindus? Do you have any of them?

Mr. EVERETT. None that I know of, except on the railroad work.

The CHAIRMAN. They have not come into the beet fields yet?

Mr. EVERETT. I do not think so.

The CHAIRMAN. Where do these foreigners come from?

Mr. EVERETT. From the different cities; perhaps Lincoln, perhaps Denver. When we were first going into the beet raising, the bulk of them came from Lincoln.

The CHAIRMAN. How much do these people make a day? Is there any way of averaging that?

Mr. EVERETT. I do not exactly know. It is a pretty hard thing to average, because they are men, women, and children from 10 years old up, working in the fields.

The CHAIRMAN. Is it pretty hard work?

Mr. EVERETT. It is hard work.

The CHAIRMAN. In your judgment, are they pretty liberally paid for that work?

Mr. EVERETT. I would think they are. I think if they were not, they would not do it.

The CHAIRMAN. Have you ever seen the quarters these people live in in the cities?

Mr. EVERETT. I have, in Lincoln. I have been through where I supopse they live in a part of West Lincoln.

The CHAIRMAN. Do you bring these laborers out from Lincoln and Denver and different places under contract to do this work?

Mr. EVERETT. They are under contract. They make a contract to do the work.

The CHAIRMAN. Before they ever leave Lincoln?

Mr. EVERETT. I do not know.

The CHAIRMAN. Who does that?

Mr. EVERETT. The beet-sugar company, I think, furnishes their agents to get them out.

The CHAIRMAN. You say you have seen the quarters where these people live in Lincoln?

Mr. EVERETT. I have seen the quarters I supposed they lived in. I have always understood it was the Russian quarter.

The CHAIRMAN. Is that quarter a squalid quarter or not?

Mr. EVERETT. Not particularly. Of course it is not the best section of Lincoln.

The CHAIRMAN. It is one of the poorer ones, I suppose?

Mr. EVERETT. I think so.

The CHAIRMAN. How is it to-day at Scotts Bluff and the places where this other half live?

Mr. EVERETT. Some of them have very good houses, according to how much money they have accumulated.

The CHAIRMAN. They are about like American citizens in that respect?

Mr. EVERETT. Yes; and some of them become American citizens.

The CHAIRMAN. What percentage of them are naturalized?

Mr. EVERETT. I do not know; but I do know there are quite a number of voters among the Germans who are beet tenders.

The CHAIRMAN. Do any considerable percentage of them speak English?

Mr. EVERETT. The bulk of them.

The CHAIRMAN. You would say the majority of them can speak English?

Mr. EVERETT. They would have to, or we could not use them. At least some member of the family would have to speak English.

The CHAIRMAN. But how about the rank and file of the laborers, do they speak English?

Mr. EVERETT. Yes; I think you can well say that. Of course, once in awhile you will get an old man who comes over here who can not catch on to our language.

The CHAIRMAN. The younger ones catch on quite rapidly?

Mr. EVERETT. Yes, sir; and they are a pretty intelligent bunch of people. Now, speaking of our own help, because that is the most accurate of anything——

The CHAIRMAN. Yes; that is right.

Mr. EVERETT. Last spring we hired two families for 72 acres. Our contract called for 80 acres, but we only had 72. One family consisted of a young man and his father and mother, and I think one or two younger children. We got pretty well along into the season and this young man got married. Directly he bought out one of the neighbors there, his whole beet crop, and went in there and turned his contract over to another man. Now, that man came from Russia or Europe, wherever they came from, less than three years ago, and he is now farming for himself.

The CHAIRMAN. He rents the land and is farming for himself?

Mr. EVERETT. Yes. He bought another man out, a German who had some 50 acres of beets and an 80-acre farm, and he is doing business for himself. That is the tendency of a great share of this help.

The CHAIRMAN. Of a considerable portion of it, you think?

Mr. EVERETT. I think so.

The CHAIRMAN. Is the proportion of them who do that sort of work and progress that rapidly large or small?

Mr. EVERETT. The proportion of those who progress that rapidly is not very large, because that man is above the average.

The CHAIRMAN. I should have thought so.

Mr. EVERETT. I think he is away above the average, but there are lots of them. Two years ago there was a man came up there from

Colorado to take a contract, and he had not anything, and he moved into the German part of town, and he had been working around, and they had a little German row up there one night and things got pretty hot, and the police pulled nine of them and fined them $5 apiece. As soon as he got out of that he made an arrangement with a party there who had a farm, and rented the farm, and they staked him—he gives them good rent—they furnished him the teams, and he went to farming for himself.

Last year he paid partly out, and this year he is practically paid out—in two years. It was a good thing for him and a good thing for the other party.

Mr. FORDNEY. Mr. Everett, your reason for coming here was to answer what you understood had been said by Mr. Bodkin, and Mr. Combs, and Mr. Dakin, which, in your opinion, was detrimental to the industry, or different from your opinion as to the character of labor and the treatment the farmers received from the factories, and so on. In other words, the general trend of his statement is the reason for your being here, is it not?

Mr. EVERETT. I think, probably, my idea of it was this: If this is a board examining into the beet-sugar industry as it affects the different places, it is nothing more than right that our conditions should be presented here. That is my idea of it.

Mr. FORDNEY. You are satisfied with the treatment you are getting from the factories and the profit you are getting out of your crop?

Mr. EVERETT. We are satisfied it pays us to do business with them.

Mr. FORDNEY. Are your farmers generally satisfied?

Mr. EVERETT. I can perhaps express that better by the statement that the first year of the factory they raised about 6,000 acres of beets; the past year they raised 10,000 acres of beets, and I believe they will raise from 12,000 to 15,000 acres the coming year. The sentiment of the people looks that way to me.

Mr. FORDNEY. You think the industry betters conditions, gives you a good staple crop, and adds to the value of your land?

Mr. EVERETT. It certainly does. Another thing: We are, you might say, a poor people. Eleven years ago we had no railroads in there. We were 60 miles from the railroad. There has been irrigation there for a good many years, and our condition perhaps is different from what it is in Colorado, where they have had the railroads and the irrigation and their beet factories for 10 or 12 years and running way back of that. And the beet contract, whenever it is made and your beets are put in, it is an item of credit. If I need the money, and I have got 70 acres of beets in the ground, I can go to the bank and get it.

The CHAIRMAN. Can you go to the sugar company and get it?

Mr. EVERETT. No, sir.

The CHAIRMAN. They do not lend you any money in your country?

Mr. EVERETT. No, sir; they do not. I will go back a little and state that the first raising of beets was for the Ames factory, in 1905. The Ames factory would furnish the money.

The CHAIRMAN. Where was that located?

Mr. EVERETT. At Ames, Nebr. That is the same factory we now have at Scottsbluff.

The CHAIRMAN. How far is Ames from Scottsbluff?

Mr. EVERETT. About 300 or 350 miles; way up toward Omaha.

The CHAIRMAN. Did you raise beets and ship them up there?

Mr. EVERETT. Yes, sir.

The CHAIRMAN. Did you pay the freight on them?

Mr. EVERETT. They paid the freight.

The CHAIRMAN. But they gave you a lower price?

Mr. EVERETT. Five dollars flat—the same as we are getting to-day; but they raised beets one year and busted, and we all lost a little money. I do not suppose we got over $4.50.

The CHAIRMAN. They did not keep their contracts?

Mr. EVERETT. They went broke.

Mr. FORDNEY. And then the factory was moved to your territory?

Mr. EVERETT. The factory was sold to the Great Western Sugar Co. and moved to our territory.

Mr. FORDNEY. And that is the factory you are now raising beets for?

Mr. EVERETT. Yes, sir.

Mr. FORDNEY. How far is that factory from your land?

Mr. EVERETT. About three-quarters of a mile from the site of the factory to my farm.

Mr. FORDNEY. The Ames factory could not afford to pay the freight that long distance and failed, and tore down their factory and brought it to where the beets are being raised now?

Mr. EVERETT. That was the effect of it. The factory stood idle some three or four years.

Mr. FORDNEY. Do you believe that the beet crop adds value to your land?

Mr. EVERETT. It certainly does.

Mr. FORDNEY. In what proportion do you believe that crop has added to the value of your farm land?

Mr. EVERETT. Well, it has nearly added one-half.

Mr. FORDNEY. You think the increased value is perhaps one-half on account of the beet crop you raise?

Mr. EVERETT. I do.

Mr. FORDNEY. Generally, you are satisfied to be let alone just as you are?

Mr. EVERETT. We are.

Mr. FORDNEY. You do not want any legislation, if that legislation is likely to lower the price of beets to the farmer?

Mr. EVERETT. No, sir; we would not want to have it lowered.

Mr. FORDNEY. But you would not object to having it raised?

Mr. EVERETT. We never object to that.

Mr. RAKER. I understand you to say that by virtue of the raising of the beets the value of the land has increased twofold?

Mr. EVERETT. Very nearly.

Mr. RAKER. Was the railroad in there when you commenced to raise beets?

Mr. EVERETT. The railroad went in there 12 years ago this spring.

Mr. RAKER. When did you commence to raise beets?

Mr. EVERETT. In 1905 I first raised beets there.

Mr. RAKER. And the price of land generally jumped up twice what it was before?

Mr. EVERETT. Not at that time. Land has gradually risen from the time the railroad went in.

Mr. RAKER. You do not mean to convey the idea to this committee and to the public that by the mere fact of starting to raise sugar beets, and that alone, the value of your land increased one-half?

Mr. Everett. I do not know as I would put it exactly that way; at the same time the factory coming in there has. Not simply the raising beets there to start with, but the factory coming in there with its varied lines, stock feeding of every description, and the building up that it does, the people it brings in there, has greatly increased the value of the land.

Mr. Raker. The railroad gives the farmers an opportunity to get their crops to market and bring in things they need, and, of course, that enhanced the value of the land, because the people get more interested in growing agricultural crops; is not that right?

Mr. Everett. Yes. May I answer that a little more fully? You say the railroad enhanced it. It did, but I went in there after the railroad came. I bought land 2 miles from Scottsbluff, one quarter for $2,000, another quarter for $3,900. The railroad was in there and the transportation was just as good then as it is to-day. That land has gradually increased until it is worth $135 or $140 an acre. Now this increase came rapidly after the factory came and after we commenced raising beets. The beet raising has had a great deal to do with the value of the land.

Mr. Raker. You had a product which you could depend upon?

Mr. Everett. Yes, sir; a product that you had a contract on, and when you start in you know what you are going to get out of it.

Mr. Raker. Do you raise alfalfa in this community?

Mr. Everett. Yes, sir.

Mr. Raker. Right side by side with the beets?

Mr. Everett. Yes, sir.

Mr. Raker. You put in an alfalfa crop and have it for two or three years and then put in grain and potatoes and rotate like that, do you?

Mr. Everett. We run from alfalfa to beets or potatoes, but not from alfalfa to grain.

Mr. Raker. You do not try that?

Mr. Everett. No; we usually think it is better to go direct to the root crop.

Mr. Raker. From alfalfa?

Mr. Everett. Yes; from alfalfa.

Mr. Raker. Has it not been demonstrated in your country that by the raising of alfalfa for two or three years and plowing up the land and putting it into grain you get from one-third to one-half more grain on the same land than before you put in any alfalfa?

Mr. Everett. It is too dangerous a proposition to break up alfalfa to put it into grain.

Mr. Raker. Why?

Mr. Everett. Because you would perhaps be like I was this year I had 60 acres of barley and it thrashed only 300 bushels.

Mr. Raker. Why?

Mr. Everett. Hailstorms.

Mr. Raker. You have hailstorms in your country which destroy your grain?

Mr. Everett. Whenever you have a hailstorm on small grain when it is about ready to cut, it is gone.

Mr. Raker. Then that country is not susceptible of successfully raising grain, either oats or wheat or barley or buckwheat, for that reason?

Mr. Everett. That is the danger period in raising small grain.

Mr. RAKER. If there is a danger period in the year and it comes along in rotation each year, it makes the raising of that crop dangerous, and therefore it can not be raised successfully; is that about the condition?

Mr. EVERETT. You would not take the chance of breaking up alfalfa for small grain, because alfalfa is safer. You have got three chances on alfalfa and one on small grain.

Mr. RAKER. Still, I would like to have an answer to my other question.

Mr. EVERETT. Yes.

Mr. RAKER. Alfalfa is as successful to the farmer as beets, and more so on an average?

Mr. EVERETT. No, sir.

Mr. RAKER. How much do you get a ton for alfalfa?

Mr. EVERETT. $8 in the stack at my place. About $6.50 where they are out a little distance.

Mr. RAKER. And from 4 to 6 tons to the acre?

Mr. EVERETT. About 3. You will find men who will tell you they have got 8 tons to the acre, but I do not get that on an average.

Mr. FORDNEY. About 3 tons is a good, fair average?

Mr. EVERETT. Yes, sir; some will get more and some will get less. I never figure on more than 3 tons to the acre when I figure out what my crop will be.

Mr. FORDNEY. You say there is less danger attending your beet crop than any other crop, unless it might be alfalfa?

Mr. EVERETT. And potatoes.

Mr. FORDNEY. Your hailstorms destroy your potatoes sometimes, do they not?

Mr. EVERETT. It destroys it or hurts it if the hailstorm catches it at the right time.

Mr. FORDNEY. And it is not so apt to destroy beets or damage them so much as the grain crops?

Mr. EVERETT. No, sir.

Mr. RAKER. I understood from the testimony of Mr. Palmer and Mr. Oxnard—I may have misunderstood it—that the hailstorm was one of the dangerous things in raising sugar beets, and that there was no crop as susceptible of destruction by hailstorm as the beet crop, because of the fact that all the sugar matter came from the beet leaf, and when the hailstorm came it broke the leaf off, and therefore it practically destroyed your crop; and therefore, if your country is susceptible to hailstorms in the summer, they would do more damage to the beets than any other crop. Is there anything in that?

Mr. EVERETT. I hardly think so, from the fact that this year I have got contracts that show the amount raised by beet raisers who were hailed out of part of their crop. Now, I do not know as to the sugar factories; it may not be so good for them. They may not have the sugar in them, but the crop comes on and it is all right for the farmers.

Mr. FORDNEY. After a hailstorm the leaves come on again?

Mr. EVERETT. Yes, sir. I have seen crops hailed on until you could not see the rows and in a week's time they would shoot up and go right ahead.

Mr. FORDNEY. The factory guarantees you $5 a ton?

Mr. EVERETT. Yes, sir.

Mr. FORDNEY. With increased pay with increase in the sugar contents of the beets?

Mr. EVERETT. Ours is a flat rate.

Mr. FORDNEY. You get $5 a ton straight?

Mr. EVERETT. We get $5 a ton, with 50 cents for siloing, and this year there was a bonus of 25 cents if we produced 100,000 tons, which we did, and for next year there is a bonus on 135,000 tons, I think.

Mr. FORDNEY. How much of a bonus?

Mr. EVERETT. Fifty cents per ton, which would be $5.50 if we raise 130,000 tons.

The CHAIRMAN. Now, are there any other gentlemen who came from Colorado, sugar-beet growers, whom we have not heard from?

Mr. PETRIKIN. I am the secretary of the Great Western Sugar Co., and there are a few things that I would like the opportunity of presenting.

The CHAIRMAN. I do not know that the committee cares to hear further from the Great Western Sugar Co. It has already had full opportunity to present its views, and I believe has done so. What is there in particular you wish to present?

Mr. PETRIKIN. Well, things like the University of Colorado refusing to make analyses, and the agricultural college refusing to make analyses, as charged by Mr. Bodkin. I have information from both of these institutions in reference to it, and am in a position to inform the committee of the true situation.

The CHAIRMAN. That at the very best would only be hearsay.

Mr. PETRIKIN. No, sir; they are letters bearing the signature of the heads of both schools.

The CHAIRMAN. Certainly; I am not disputing that fact, but that is hearsay evidence.

Mr. PETRIKIN. Not wishing to take issue with your views in the matter, I would like to ask if the testimony of Mr. Bodkin was not also entirely hearsay, and hearsay of the extremest kind? I have here the statement of the gentlemen concerned bearing their own signature, and merely lacking affidavit to bring it within the meaning of direct testimony, I take it.

The CHAIRMAN. No; it is not my recollection that Mr. Bodkin's testimony was hearsay.

Mr. PETRIKIN. Mr. Bodkin testified that he had been informed by a man named J. O. V. Wise.

The CHAIRMAN. My recollection is that he said he knew it independent of what he had been told.

Mr. PETRIKIN. If you will pardon me, I think by reference to Mr. Bodkin's testimony you will find that he said the other man told him. I do not want to bore the committee, but of course you gentlemen are seeking after the facts of matters, and I feel that I am here now prepared to give them to you on certain subjects.

The CHAIRMAN. I do not now recall the precise language that Mr. Bodkin used on that subject, but thought he was detailing his experience.

Mr. PETRIKIN. No; he said J. O. V. Wise told him that.

The CHAIRMAN. Didn't he say he had had the same experience himself?

Mr. PETRIKIN. No; when you asked him whether he knew it or not, he stated that he did not know whether the sun was coming up in the morning, but he believed it would.

The CHAIRMAN. Didn't he say he had had the same experience himself?

Mr. PETRIKIN. No, sir; I think not.

The CHAIRMAN. We will look it up in the record. I think we will find that he so stated.

Mr. PETRIKIN. Let me present you gentlemen with some photographs which may be of interest.

The CHAIRMAN. All right; we will be glad to take them and examine them. We do not want to deny anybody a hearing, but we had the officers of your company, the Great Western Sugar Co., before us, and we can not let the different parties spar for conclusion of the evidence.

Mr. PETRIKIN. For instance, here is a very important thing in reference to the testimony in regard to differential in freight rates on granulated sugar, it having been stated that we received 65 cents. Now, I have here a sworn statement showing just what we did receive.

Mr. FORDNEY. I always desire to agree with the chairman, and do not wish to unnecessarily prolong these hearings, but it seems to me this gentleman has, like the others we have been hearing, traveled a long ways to controvert certain hearsay and other statements made here before us, and I believe we ought to hear him briefly. That statement he has just referred to, it seems to me, would be extremely interesting.

The CHAIRMAN. Well, we will put that statement in the record. But we do not want to indefinitely continue these hearings; we wish to bring them to a close. We have given a general hearing to all parties interested. We do not want you people on different sides to be sparring for the conclusion of the evidence. Every time a man comes here and advances a view and it is published, then people all over the country differing with him, some of whom have already been heard, wish to be heard to dispute it, and although it may have been disputed. I do not see any use of that.

Mr. FORDNEY. Mr. Chairman, as I said, I do not want to disagree with you, for I really want to agree with you, but——

The CHAIRMAN. I understand that, Mr. Fordney, and believe you have shown that disposition along this line all the way through.

Mr. FORDNEY. For instance, the Federal Sugar Co. sent their man back here a second and maybe a third time, and at great length he went into the matter of answering certain statements. Now, this gentleman has come a long ways, and I hope it may be the pleasure of the committee to hear him at least briefly.

The CHAIRMAN. Very well; we will hear him briefly.

TESTIMONY OF MR. W. L. PETRIKIN.

Witness is duly sworn by the chairman.

The CHAIRMAN. Now, what is it that you wish to present to us, Mr. Petrikin?

Mr. PETRIKIN. I wish to present, first, a statemnt, made under oath, by W. L. Baker, manager sales department, the Great Western Sugar Co., showing freight rates on granulated sugar in carload lots. This is with refrence to the testimony to the effect that we received 65 cents differential in freight rates, and proves just what we do receive.

Freight rates on granulated sugar (carloads).

	To Missouri River.	To Iowa. Mississippi River points.	To Iowa. Interior Iowa.	To Minnesota.	To Chicago.	To St. Louis.	To Texas.	To Colorado.
Rate from— New York		29		30	22½			
New Orleans	33		34½			18½	46	
San Francisco								55
(Basing rate: Lowest rate is shown whether from New York, New Orleans, or San Francisco). Rate from Colorado (Great Western Sugar Co. factories)	25	30	30	30	25	25	49	10
Average freight differences	[2] 8	[3] 1¾		....	[4] 2½	[4] 6½	[4] 3	[3] 45
Number bags shipped from Great Western Sugar Co. factories	544,212	242,264		198,475	965,789	150,075	143,270	205,687
	$43,536.96	$4,239.62		....	$24,144.73	$9,754.88	$4,298.10	$92,559.15

	To east of Chicago. Buffalo.	Pittsburgh.	Cleveland.	Columbus.	Cincinnati.	Akron.	Toledo.	Sandusky.	Evansville.	Terre Haute.	Detroit.	Indianapolis.	Other points.
Rate from— New York	[1] 15	[1] 15	[1] 16½	[1] 17½	[1] 18[illegible]	[1] 17½	[1] 17½	[1] 17½		[1] 28½	[1] 17½	[1] 21½	[1] 18
New Orleans									[1] 18½				
San Francisco													
(Basing rate: Lowest rate is shown whether from New York, New Orleans, or San Francisco). Rate from Colorado (Great Western Sugar Co. factories)	[2] 43	[2] [illegible]	[2] [illegible]	[2] 40	[2] [illegible]	[2] 40	[2] 38	[2] 39½	[2] 35	[2] 36½	[2] 38	[2] 36½	[2] 40
Average freight differences	[4] 21												
Number bags shipped from Great Western Sugar Co. factories	211,183												
	$44,348.43												

[1] Average rate, 18 cents. [2] Average rate, 39 cents. [3] Freight protection. [4] Freight absorption.

Net freight protection on 2,462,480 bags, based on existing freight rates. Total production for 1907-8 was 2,660,955 bags, but 198,475 bags would have received no protection nor had to absorb any freight. $57,789.57 on 2,462,480 bags, at $0.028 per bag.

I hereby state that I have full knowledge of the facts testified to, and that from my own knowledge and belief I believe them to be truthful.

Respectfully, yours,

W. L. Baker, *Manager Sales Department.*

State of Colorado, *City and County of Denver, ss:*

I, Earl F. Shepard, a notary public within and for the county and State aforesaid, do hereby certify that W. L. Baker, who is personally known to me, being duly sworn, deposes and says that the foregoing facts and figures shown on above statement are true to his best knowledge and belief.

Given under my hand and notarial seal this 23d day of December, A. D. 1911.

[seal.]

Earl F. Shepard, *Notary Public.*

My commission expires November 24, 1913.

And then here is a detailed statement of some farming operations conducted by the Great Western Sugar Co., Secor Farm, showing the cost in detail:

Report of company farming operations for year ending Feb. 28, 1912 (Secord farm).

[The Great Western Sugar Co., Longmont factory.]

Beet crop (185.8 acres).	Amount.	Cost per acre.	
Extra water	....	......	$6.66
Fertilizing	$993.37	$5.346	......
Plowing	440.14	2.369	2.50
Harrowing and leveling	318.51	1.714	1.30
Seed, 3,957 pounds, at 10 cents	395.70	2.130	1.70
Planting	103.32	.556	.50
Thinning, first and second hoeing	1,858.00	10.000	......
Cultivating	321.85	1.732	2.60
Furrowing out and irrigating	232.70	1.252	5.70
Plowing out	311.69	1.678	2.50
Pulling, topping, etc	1,858.00	10.000	20.00
Hauling	1,141.51	6.144	6.37
Miscellaneous expenses	40.00	.215	......
Superintendence	459.30	2.472	......
Land rental	1,858.00	10.000	20.00
Maintenance:			
Tools, implements	107.58	.579	......
Buildings and fences	100.70	.542	......
Ditches, etc	97.36	.524	......
Harness and wagons	16.80	.091	......
Miscellaneous expense	95.13	.512	......
Total	10,749.66	57.856	69.83
Add for hauling 3.54 tons, at 50 cents	....	......	1.77
			71.60
Difference	....	13.74	......
Credits:			
3,028.1335 tons beets, at $5.55	16,450.23	88.54	......
173 acres beet tops, at $2	346.00	1.86	......
Total credits	16,796.23	90.40	......
Net profits	6,046.57	32.54	......

Here is another statement showing operations of same farm for a period of six years:

Condensed report of beet-farming operations on the Secor farm.

[The Great Western Sugar Co., Longmont Factory.]

	1906	1907	1908	1909	1910	1911
Number of acres	314	374	325	325	158	185.8
Yield per acre ....tons	17.42	14.96	11.53	13.71	16.45	16.29
Total cost	$19,110.66	$21,268.92	$17,844.87	$15,206.43	$8,879.96	$8,891.66
Cost per acre	60.86	56.86	54.91	46.79	56.20	47.86
Total revenue	29,346.60	29,053.56	19,410.90	23,128.82	14,734.15	16,796.23
Revenue per acre	93.46	77.68	59.73	71.17	93.25	90.40
Cost per ton	3.49	3.80	4.75	3.41	3.42	2.94
Revenue per ton	5.36	5.19	5.17	5.19	5.67	5.55
Profit	*1.87*	*1.39*	*$0.42*	*1.78*	*2.25*	*2.61*
Total profit	*10,235.94*	*7,784.64*	*1,566.03*	*7,922.39*	*5,854.19*	*7,904.57*
Profit per acre	*32.59*	*20.82*	*4.82*	*24.38*	*37.05*	*42.54*
Land rental per acre not included in above amounts	10.00	10.00	10.00	10.00	10.00	10.00

Profit shown in italics.

Each year from 90 to 175 acres were manured at an expense of $15 per acre, cost of which is included in total cost.

Irrigated in 1911, 3 times; cultivated in 1911, 5 times; ditched in 1911, 1 time.

And, in connection with these two statements of the operations at the Secor Farm of the the Great Western Sugar Co., I just want to correct one impression given by one of the witnesses, where he testified that his tonnage was 20 tons per acre and that it was the maximum yield, and that it was way above the average, and that unless you got the average in any line of business you wouldn't be a success, but that he was a success and was satisfied, and so on——

The CHAIRMAN (interrupting). Who was that?

Mr. PETRIKIN. Mr. Combs.

The CHAIRMAN. What page of the record?

Mr. PETRIKIN. At the bottom of page 3231.

The CHAIRMAN. All right. What is your statement on that point?

Mr. PETRIKIN. He says:

> Now, I will say, in all fairness to everybody concerned, that so far as I am concerned, I raised an average of 20 tons of beets to the acre this year on the beets harvested, which shows me a good profit. My yield was the maximum.

Now, I want to say that the witness Combs actually raised 12.49 tons on the measured acreage, an average of 14.6 per cent sugar, which brought him $5 per ton.

The CHAIRMAN. That is, this witness Combs?

Mr. PETRIKIN. Yes, sir.

The CHAIRMAN. He dealt with your company?

Mr. PETRIKIN. Yes, sir. At this station where he delivered his beets the average for the station was 13.7 tons of 16 per cent sugar, which brought $5.50 per ton. The total average of the Fort Morgan district was 12.9 tons beets per acre at 16.2 per cent sugar, or an average of $5.75 per ton, which showed he was below the average of the whole district.

The CHAIRMAN. Those figures come within your own knowledge, of course?

Mr. PETRIKIN. Yes, sir; they do.

The CHAIRMAN. You are the manager of that plant?

Mr. PETRIKIN. No, sir; I am the secretary of the Great Western Sugar Co., and have access to the records.

The CHAIRMAN. The records might be wrong, might they not?

Mr. PETRIKIN. They might, just as any records might contain some error, but as far as I know they are correct.

Mr. FORDNEY. Oh, well, they are just like all the records that have been admitted here, and we take it they are correct.

Mr. MALBY. Yes; if the information is a correct transcript of the company's records, they are all right.

Mr. PETRIKIN. Here is another matter I want to explain, in reference to the average crop in a large territory. Here is a statement in reference to 3,094 growers of sugar beets. While the average tonnage for all these growers was 12 tons per acre or a little above, 66.16 per cent of the 3,094 growers raised 10 tons per acre or more; 7 per cent of them raised over 18 tons per acre. This average is not fair, quite, and the reason for it is this, that we have a number of sugar-beet growers who have poor land or poor water arrangements for their land, and they do not get results raising beets. We would rather not take their beets, and because it does cut down the average and they are not a good thing for the industry, we would rather not encourage them to try to raise beets. But they do so, and we take them, and where they have only a small tonnage and they do their own work it is all profit to them, they say, and they persist in raising beets and we do not desire to turn them down, and therefore buy their beets.

Statement of yield per acre per grower, with percentage on total number of growers.—Six northern Colorado factories.

[The Great Western Sugar Co.]

Total per acre.	Number of growers.	Percentage on total growers.	Total per acre.	Number of growers.	Percentage on total growers.
Under 4 tons	60	2.53	20-22 tons	41	1.73
4-6 tons	136	5.75	22-24 tons	13	.55
6-8 tons	211	8.91	24-26 tons	2	.08
8-10 tons	329	13.89	26-28 tons	3	.13
10-12 tons	419	17.69	28-30 tons	2	.08
12-14 tons	440	18.58	30-32 tons	1	.04
14-16 tons	371	15.68			
16-18 tons	227	9.59		2,368	100.00
18-20 tons	113	4.77			

The CHAIRMAN. Is that all now?

Mr. PETRIKIN. I would like a little time to read you some things I know to be facts about the money received by hand labor; how much they get. Would you like to have it, or do you want to pass it?

The CHAIRMAN. I think that is pretty well covered. I don't think there is any real controversy on that subject.

Mr. MALBY. Is the evidence along about the same line and showing the prices paid?

Mr. PETRIKIN. Yes, sir.

Mr. RAKER. Let me see that statement.

Mr. PETRIKIN. I will be glad to have it go in if you are willing.

Mr. RAKER. This statement contains generally the facts that you were just going to read?

Mr. PETRIKIN. It shows the earnings of foreign labor; what they earn per day.

Mr. RAKER. Have you that information in tabulated form?

Mr. PETRIKIN. Yes, sir; and I can submit the statement.

The CHAIRMAN. I do not object, but hardly see the necessity for it.

Mr. PETRIKIN. And you do not want to admit the correspondence with the agricultural college and the University of Colorado about analyses?

The CHAIRMAN. You can put it in the record. If this other witness, Bodkin, based his statement on what somebody told him, then this ought to go in.

Mr. PETRIKIN. Here is the complete correspondence.

The CHAIRMAN. It is too large a mass to put all this in. Just state it.

Mr. PETRIKIN. Well, here is a letter from President Lory, of the State board of agriculture, saying he had referred the matter to one of his professors, and the professor replies, and to justify his position copies of all letters are here attached.

Mr. FORDNEY. Which explains why the test was not made?

Mr. PETRIKIN. Yes, sir.

The CHAIRMAN. Just state in a general way what the letters show without putting that great mass of correspondence into the record.

Mr. PETRIKIN. Here is a letter from John B. Ekeley, professor of chemistry, University of Colorado:

UNIVERSITY OF COLORADO,
DEPARTMENT OF CHEMISTRY,
Boulder, Colo., January 2, 1912.

President JAMES H. BAKER,
University of Colorado, Boulder, Colo.

DEAR SIR: In reply to your request I am stating the exact facts concerning the matter of a beet analysis for Mr. J. O. V. Wise.

About Thanksgiving Day, 1910, Mr. J. O. V. Wise called me up by telephone and asked if I would make a sugar analysis of a beet for him. I told him I would. Upon his arrival with the beet he said that it was a question between a farmers' association which he represented and the sugar company as to the sugar content of the beet. He also wished to know whether arrangements could be made to have control tests of beets made at the university. I replied that in that case I wished to consult with the university authorities before making the analyses, since they might not wish me, as professor of chemistry, to be drawn into a possible controversy between the farmers' association and the sugar company. I immediately went to the university office, where it happened that the regents of the university were meeting, though Mr. Ralph Talbot and President Baker were the only ones who had arrived that morning. I stated the case, asking whether I should make the analyses, calling attention to the fact that I might be drawn into a controversy between the farmers' association and the sugar company. Mr. Talbot and President Baker said to make the test. Regarding the making of arrangements for testing beets at the university, I was instructed to tell Mr. Wise to present his proposed plan and it would be acted upon.

I made the analysis of the beet for Mr. Wise. He seemed dissatisfied with the result, and the next day I repeated the analysis, carrying out every step in his presence. I told Mr. Wise to present his scheme for making beet tests at the university, but I have heard nothing from him since concerning the matter.

Regarding the testimony before the congressional committee given by Mr. Bodkin, whom I do not know, I will say that I was astonished when I read it, since it is false that the professor of chemistry at the University of Colorado must have the permission of the sugar company to make beet tests. Furthermore, the professor of chemistry at the University of Colorado has never refused to make tests on sugar beets.

Yours, very truly,

JOHN B. EKELEY,
Professor of Chemistry, University of Colorado.

Mr. PETRIKIN. Here is a letter from the secretary of the Bureau of Child and Animal Industry of Colorado, in reference to the condition of these children working in the beet fields.

The CHAIRMAN. I do not think we want that. There is no dispute on that point that I know of.

Mr. PETRIKIN. Here is another letter that I think important. It is from the former superintendent of our factory at Sterling, Colo., in regard to the employment of Mr. Keyes, the man who furnished the figures, according to Mr. Combs, as to cost of production. This letter shows that he was employed at our factory merely as an assistant storekeeper——

The CHAIRMAN. Well, you may just put that one letter, not the whole correspondence you have pinned together, in the record. I take it that letter will explain the point.

SCOTTSBLUFF, NEBR., *December 18, 1911.*

Mr. C. S. MOREY,
President the Great Western Sugar Co., Denver, Colo.

DEAR SIR: My attention has been called to the testimony of Mr. Combs, given before the special committee on the investigation of the American Sugar Refinery Co. et al., in part of which he quotes Mr. C. H. Keyes as having been connected with the Sterling factory in the capacity of superintendent. As you know, I was superintendent of the Sterling factory from the spring of 1907 until the spring of 1911. On account of the testimony given, quoting Mr. Keyes, it might interest you to know that Mr. Keyes was employed at the Sterling factory for a period of three or four weeks during January of 1908, as I recollect it, as assistant to the storekeeper at 22½ cents per hour. During his employment I am satisfied that it would be impossible for him to have acquired or obtained an intelligent idea of the operation of the factory, or any comprehensive notion of the cost of the manufacture of sugar. I am satisfied, from my acquaintance with Mr. Keyes, which has extended over a period of the past six years, that he is not qualified to give expert testimony upon the cost of the manufacture of sugar. He has had no experience in the manufacturing end of the business other than what he had in the sirup factory at Brighton, Colo., which attempted to make sugar and made an utter failure. Mr. Keyes made application to me for a position after the failure of the Brighton plant, but, owing to his inexperience, I could only give him a position as storekeeper helper, in which position he did not have access to any records of factory operation. Mr. Keyes quit of his own accord.

Trusting that the foregoing information will be of interest to you, I am,

Very truly, yours,

F. H. ROBERTS.

DENVER, COLO., *December 20, 1911.*

Mr. F. H. ROBERTS, *Scottsbluff, Nebr.*

DEAR SIR: Replying to above, I appreciate same very much, but in order to have any weight before the investigating committee in Washington it should be sworn to. Our manager at Sterling factory will make sworn statement that our records show Mr. C. H. Keyes was on our pay roll as assistant storekeeper in the factory from January 1 to January 19, 1908, at a rate of 22½ cents per hour. So far, we have not been able to find that Mr. Keyes was ever employed at any of our other factories.

Respectfully, yours,

——— ———.

STATE OF NEBRASKA, *County of Scotts Bluff, ss:*

F. H. ROBERTS, being duly sworn, deposes and says that statements made in the foregoing letter are true to his best knowledge and belief, and that affiant is personally known to me.

F. H. ROBERTS.

Subscribed and sworn to before me this 26th day of December, 1911.

[SEAL.]

S. STARK,
Notary Public.

My commission expires July 26, 1916.

Mr. PETRIKIN. Here is something that I have been personally connected with ever since I have been with the Great Western Sugar Co., and I would like to advise you on it; that is, in reference to the pulp, molasses, and meal-mill operations and the cattle-feeding operations. I want to deny, and most emphatically, that we have at any time refused to sell pulp to the farmers. The farmers have always used 76.95 per cent of the pulp. We have sold this stuff at a price from $2.50 to $5.50 per ton less than we could ship it away and get ready sale for it; and we have done that for no selfish reason. We have done it to improve the beet crop. Our molasses we have always sold there to the farmers. Mr. Dakan positively stated that we would not sell it. He also stated that the cattle-feeding operations were owned by subsidiary companies. That is not so. They are owned by the Great Western Sugar Co., and the profit or loss, as the case may be, is put in with our cost.

In reference to selling molasses, or refusing to sell molasses as he claimed, that is untrue. He said we had 10 alfalfa mills. That is untrue. We have one mill at Sterling which is capable of producing a marketable product; we have one at Brush which is only in a position to produce stuff for our stock. We have only refused to sell to one local manufacturer once, and that was after making sale to him at the local feeding price and for the purpose of local feeders, which was considerably below what we could ship at. He wanted us to route it to a manufacturer in the East to whom we were then supplying the product at a higher price.

Mr. MALBY. He wanted it for shipment?

Mr. PETRIKIN. Yes, sir; instead of for home consumption. We are perfectly willing at any time to supply same to the people in our own territory.

The CHAIRMAN. Does that statement cover all now?

Mr. PETRIKIN. I think, in the main, that is all, or as near as I can give it in the very hurried manner in which I have attempted to give it. You know, when rushed this way it is extremely hard to cover all points, and especially to cover them clearly.

I would like to ask you if you got clearly the requirements of our contract in reference to specifying that the beets shall be of a certain purity?

The CHAIRMAN. I think so. We have your contracts in the record.

Mr. PETRIKIN. In speaking of it it was intimated that they must be 80 per cent pure in the beet. That is not the meaning of it.

The CHAIRMAN. That is it in effect, I take it. You may make a brief explanation of that.

Mr. PETRIKIN. Eighty per cent purity means that 80 per cent of the solids in the juice after it is taken out of the beet shall be sugar.

The CHAIRMAN. That is what the 80 per cent expression in the contract means?

Mr. PETRIKIN. Yes, sir; it hasn't anything to do with the total weight of the beet.

Mr. FORDNEY. Is that the purity of the sugar contained in the beets, 80 per cent in your territory?

Mr. PETRIKIN. They vary so much.

Mr. FORDNEY. What is the average purity?

Mr. PETRIKIN. I think the contract specifies that we need not take beets containing less than 12 per cent sugar, or less than 80 per cent purity. I have explained what 80 per cent purity is. I would like to submit for your information——

Mr. FORDNEY (interrupting). Before you get away from that I would like to ask, have you refused beets on any contract because the purity was below 80 per cent?

Mr. PETRIKIN. No, sir. And I would like to take a few minutes to explain that matter. We have never refused any beets that I know of. We had beets last year and this year, but more especially last year, that had been hailed out during the period of growing season, and so late that they could not grow a new set of leaves; and those beets ran down to 7 per cent and 8 per cent. But they were raised in a territory where the people had worked conscientiously and hard and had put their money into beets; so, considering the circumstances and without saying anything to them or even letting them know about it, so far as I know, we took those beets in under the clause that we should not take any beets less than 12 per cent. Now, that desire on our part to be most liberal and to encourage and assist those who have honestly and conscientiously labored to raise beets, gives us trouble another year. When we see a man neglecting his beets and we tell him to go to work on them or they will be below the test, he will say to us, "It doesn't make any difference what the test is, you will take them anyhow." We have paid these people thousands of dollars rather than let them lose their work.

Mr. RAKER. You don't take any beets under the contract requirements that were grown not under contract?

Mr. PETRIKIN. Yes, sir; we do.

Mr. RAKER. Your policy is not to take them?

Mr. PETRIKIN. We have no policy of that kind.

Mr. RAKER. It has been stated here that you did not take beets except under contract?

Mr. PETRIKIN. I know; but we have taken them.

Mr. RAKER. The general policy is not to use beets unless grown under contract?

Mr. PETRIKIN. No; it is not our general policy not to use beets not grown under contract, but it is our policy to contract for all that we expect to use.

Mr. FORDNEY. Have you refused to take any beets that you did not contract for?

Mr. PETRIKIN. Not to my knowledge.

The CHAIRMAN. Now, have you anything else?

Mr. PETRIKIN. I think I have here a copy of the 1912 contract. I will say that it is the same as the 1911 contract, with the exception that there is 25 cents per ton more to be paid clear through, and instead of paying 50 cents per ton for siloing beets we are to pay 75 cents per ton.

The CHAIRMAN. All right, that is explained now.

Mr. PETRIKIN. There is one other thing that I would like to correct. First, Judge Raker, I would like to give you a little information, if you would like to have it, in reference to alfalfa.

Mr. RAKER. All right.

Mr. PETRIKIN. Here is a comprehensive statement of our experience, and I will be glad to have it go in the record, if you are willing. The average crop of alfalfa in northern Colorado, for a period of years, was 3½ tons per acre; cost per acre about $10.50; cost per ton $3 in the stack. Siloing price per ton is $6, and that is high. The profit per ton is $3; profit per acre $10.50, not including land rentals, water assessment, or taxes.

The CHAIRMAN. Now, is that all?

Mr. PETRIKIN. If you will bear with me just a moment longer I would like to correct one other thing testified to by Mr. Combs. I think, on page 3252, as to sugar content in his beets as being a certain amount, and I will give you what he claimed and what the records show the actual fact to be, as follows:

Sugar content claimed by Witness Combs (p. 3252) in his beets, and actual facts, season 1908–9.

Witness' claim.	Facts.	Witness' claim.	Facts.
Per cent.	*Per cent.*	*Per cent.*	*Per cent.*
17.18	14.15	17.57	13.34
16.81	15.25	16.56	13.18
17.34	14.28	16.67	13.63
18.56	13.64		
17.62	14.37	[1] 17.37	[1] 14.21
17.64	14.80		

[1] Average.

The CHAIRMAN. His actual average was 14.31 per cent, instead of 17.3 per cent as claimed by him?

Mr. PETRIKIN. Yes, sir. In looking that over it was a little hard to tell. There are 10 factories and he gave only 9. He eliminated 1 factory. I want to see that the Billings factory that year showed a sugar content in beets of 16.04 per cent, which would make the actual total average for the year 14.34 per cent. Now, these are true geometrical averages that each factory developed divided by 10.

The CHAIRMAN. Where did you get those figures?

Mr. PETRIKIN. From our records.

The CHAIRMAN. Where did Mr. Combs get his figures that he presented before this committee?

Mr. PETRIKIN. I don't know.

The CHAIRMAN. Are you familiar enough with the record to say where he claimed to have got them?

Mr. PETRIKIN. Yes, sir; he said he got them from Mr. Keyes.

The CHAIRMAN. And you say those figures are incorrect and that the ones you give are correct?

Mr. PETRIKIN. Yes, sir. And in Mr. Garrett's letter they are verified. You have them from each factory, and they are there verified.

The CHAIRMAN. All right.

Mr. PETRIKIN. I would like to explain one other thing. The witness, Mr. Dakan, testified that the sugar company would have a meeting on December 7——

The CHAIRMAN (interrupting). Who so testified?

Mr. PETRIKIN. Mr. Dakan, on December 8, page 3312 of the record, right where Mr. Dakan had his long talk, at the middle of the page. The witness testified that the sugar company would have a meeting on December 7 and decide on the 1912 contract. I want to say that the sugar company did have a meeting, gentlemen of the committee, of the managers and agricultural superintendents, and announced what the 1912 contract would be; but the increase in price to be paid for beets for this year was decided on in October, when Mr. Horace Havemeyer was in Colorado. What I want to state that for is this—that since these witnesses have returned to Colorado they have made claims in order to further their own interests and that of their organization—and as to their organization we think it might be a good thing and we have nothing to say against it at all—that it was because of their coming here and their testimony that an increased price is to be paid in 1912. That is not true at all.

The CHAIRMAN. You mean the Farmers' Union?

Mr. PETRIKIN. Yes, sir. Since their return they have been making capital out of the fact that the publicity given this matter in Washington was the cause for the change in the contract. I want to tell you sincerely that that had nothing to do with it.

Mr. MALBY. It was decided upon before?

Mr. PETRIKIN. Yes, sir; decided in October.

The CHAIRMAN. When was it actually published?

Mr. PETRIKIN. Published the same day they gave the testimony.

The CHAIRMAN. But it was really all decided upon before that?

Mr. PETRIKIN. Yes, sir; all talked over in October and decided upon at that time.

The CHAIRMAN. But only made public on the day that they testified?

Mr. PETRIKIN. Yes, sir.

Mr. RAKER. The testimony did have the effect of making it public?

Mr. PETRIKIN. No, sir.

Mr. RAKER. In other words, it was made public after the testimony was given here?

Mr. PETRIKIN. Yes; the very next day, but before anybody in Colorado knew anything about the testimony.

The CHAIRMAN. Is that all?

Mr. PETRIKIN. I could go for a long time into the details of cost and manufacture, etc., if you would take the time to hear me. I came here with a lot of data that I thought might be both interesting and valuable in your consideration of this subject, especially in view of what has been loosely stated by some witnesses.

The CHAIRMAN. I think your statement is already quite full on these matters.

Mr. PETRIKIN. Well, I thank you for giving me the time that you have this afternoon, and if there is anything further I shall be very glad to furnish it upon request.

The CHAIRMAN. You have shown these things according to your books?

Mr. PETRIKIN. Yes, sir; everything given you here is correct as shown on our books.

The CHAIRMAN. Does the statement you have given cover the supplemental matters you wished to give us?

Mr. PETRIKIN. Yes, sir; I presume so. I could have spent a good deal more of your time, but I have gone over the memoranda as well as I could in a hurried manner.

The CHAIRMAN. Well, we are very much obliged to you.

Mr. PETRIKIN. To give you an idea of about how correct their testimony was, I will call your attention to the fact that they said one factory was not operated because it was not profitable, when as a matter of fact we did operate it because it was profitable, and we wouldn't build a plant unless it was profitable.

TESTIMONY OF MR. IRA CURLEY.

Witness was duly sworn by the chairman.

The CHAIRMAN. Please give the reporter your full name.

Mr. CURLEY. Ira Curley.

The CHAIRMAN. Where do you live?

Mr. CURLEY. Ingle, Mich., in the Upper Peninsula of Michigan.

The CHAIRMAN. What business are you engaged in?

Mr. CURLEY. I have a diversified business, starting in with lumbering and farming.

The CHAIRMAN. Anything else?

Mr. CURLEY. I run a little store in connection with it.

The CHAIRMAN. Merchandising?

Mr. CURLEY. Yes, sir.

The CHAIRMAN. Are you a sugar manufacturer?

Mr. CURLEY. No, sir; but I have a little stock in the sugar company there.

The CHAIRMAN. You say you have?

Mr. CURLEY. Yes, sir.

The CHAIRMAN. Which one?

Mr. CURLEY. The Menominee River Sugar Co.

The CHAIRMAN. Is that the Michigan Sugar Co. or an independent sugar company?

Mr. CURLEY. It is an independent.

The CHAIRMAN. Do you own any considerable amount of stock?

Mr. CURLEY. Only $5,000.

The CHAIRMAN. Are you one of the directors?

Mr. CURLEY. No, sir.

The CHAIRMAN. Could you tell us, as briefly and succinctly as you can, what you think you could give the committee some light on?

Mr. CURLEY. Why, I had but very little preparation; I had only less than an hour in which to prepare to come here.

Mr. FORDNEY. What is the real object of your coming here?

Mr. CURLEY. For the general benefit of our country and community as affects the sugar industry.

Mr. FORDNEY. Is there any specific reason? How did you happen to think of it?

Mr. CURLEY. I was asked to come here.

Mr. FORDNEY. Who asked you to come?

Mr. CURLEY. I don't know whether it was from here or not. Mr. McCormick called me over the phone.

Mr. FORDNEY. Mr. B. W. McCormick?

Mr. CURLEY. Yes, sir; he is superintendent of the company in which I am a stockholder.

Mr. FORDNEY. He is the gentleman who asked you to come and testify?

Mr. CURLEY. Yes, sir.

The CHAIRMAN. What points did you want to enlighten us about?

Mr. CURLEY. I am sure I don't know.

Mr. FORDNEY. Did you want to tell us about what beets you raise?

Mr. CURLEY. Yes. I started in in a moderate way. It was a new thing. They formed our company and got it to going, and I have raised beets for it for the last nine years on lands I have cleared. Our country is a new country, just developing in the beet-industry way, and we have now got so we are raising beets very successfully.

Mr. FORDNEY. How many acres of beets do you raise, on an average?

Mr. CURLEY. I raise about 15 acres.

Mr. FORDNEY. For nine years you have raised on an average of 15 acres of beets per year?

Mr. CURLEY. Yes, sir.

Mr. FORDNEY. What is the average tonnage that you raised during those nine years, or do you know?

Mr. CURLEY. Why, I know very close to it. I haven't got my figures. I told Mr. McCormick that I didn't recall exactly, but could give an idea. He could have gotten from his books exactly what my production of beets was for the past nine years.

Mr. FORDNEY. Well, give them as close as you can.

Mr. CURLEY. I had a very fair crop. They run about from 10 to 16 and 17 tons per acre. As I say, I did not know what was required of me when I was requested to come here, and I did not prepare to give exact figures.

Mr. FORDNEY. You know in a general way about what your average crop is per year?

Mr. CURLEY. Yes, sir.

Mr. FORDNEY. Give your average price received and average tonnage, if you have it.

Mr. CURLEY. I haven't a record of that.

Mr. FORDNEY. What is the average price per acre?

Mr. CURLEY. This year it was $6 per ton. We received a flat rate on the start.

Mr. FORDNEY. This year you got $6 per ton for your beets?

Mr. CURLEY. Yes, sir; $6 per ton.

Mr. FORDNEY. How many tons did you raise per acre this year?

Mr. CURLEY. 15.1431.

Mr. FORDNEY. That is 14¾ tons to the acre?

Mr. CURLEY. Yes, sir.

Mr. FORDNEY. And you got $6 for them?

Mr. CURLEY. Yes, sir.

Mr. FORDNEY. That would be $94.50 per acre gross receipts?

Mr. CURLEY. Yes, sir.

Mr. FORDNEY. What did it cost you to raise that crop?

Mr. CURLEY. I raised this year my crop at an entire expense of $438.81.

The CHAIRMAN. How many acres does that expense cover?

Mr. CURLEY. Fifteen acres.

The CHAIRMAN. That means a cost of $438.81 for 15 acres of beets?

Mr. CURLEY. Yes, sir.

Mr. FORDNEY. That is about $32 per acre. What were your gross receipts?

Mr. CURLEY. $1,382.02.

Mr. FORDNEY. And net profit of what?

Mr. CURLEY. $943.21.

Mr. FORDNEY. On 15 acres?

Mr. CURLEY. Yes, sir.

Mr. FORDNEY. Your crop is a little better than we have been hearing about from Colorado?

Mr. CURLEY. It is better than some, and not so good as some up our way. There were a good deal better crops than I had.

Mr. FORDNEY. You have very good soil?

Mr. CURLEY. Yes, sir; very good soil and nicely adapted to the sugar-beet culture.

The CHAIRMAN. That figures out $62.88 per acre?

Mr. CURLEY. Yes, sir.

Mr. FORDNEY. Are you satisfied with the price you get for beets?

Mr. CURLEY. Very much so.

The CHAIRMAN. You could stand a small reduction in the price of sugar, couldn't you, in behalf of the poor consumer?

Mr. CURLEY. Well, not much.

Mr. FORDNEY. You would be satisfied with that profit in the lumber business?

Mr. CURLEY. Yes, sir; that is what has held up the lumber business.

Mr. RAKER. What do you figure as the market value of your land?

Mr. CURLEY. Lots of this uncleared land can be bought for $8 per acre.

Mr. Raker. I mean that you have improved?

Mr. Curley. Well, land that will grow these beets I consider worth from $100 to $150 per acre. But it can be bought for a good deal less than that.

Mr. Raker. $50 or $60 per acre?

Mr. Curley. Yes, sir.

The Chairman. It will pay for itself every year and then you have a reasonable profit?

Mr. Curley. Well, of course it takes some work to produce that sugar.

Mr. Raker. As a matter of fact Michigan is about the best State, as to climate and soil, for producing sugar beets that we have?

Mr. Curley. I don't think there is any question about that.

Mr. Fordney. You will never get a Michigander to deny that proposition. They sell sunshine out in California, in Judge Raker's State, and of course we can not beat that in Michigan.

Mr. Curley. I call that a pretty good yield. We had quite a time of it, we men raising sugar beets. We didn't have much cleared land at the start. I got a Frenchman interested and he wouldn't agree to take but 1 acre at the start, and his receipts for that acre were 21 tons 800 pounds. He then said, "I am going to plant next year"—well, I don't know how many acres.

Mr. McCormick. If permitted, I will say that I asked Mr. Curley to come here and state the situation from his standpoint as a beet grower. He is a man who went to that country 30 years ago, when it was a wilderness, and has witnessed and taken part in the vast improvement the country has undergone, and I thought maybe the committee would be glad to know what the sugar-beet industry has done and is doing toward the development of that country. We have a new country and it is not every crop that thrives there.

Mr. Malby. Is there much doing in the beet industry in your part of Michigan?

Mr. Curley. Everybody has got into it that can get into it.

Mr. Malby. Is there one factory or more there?

Mr. Curley. Just one factory.

Mr. Fordney. I would like to say for the benefit of the committee that I have personally tramped over the territory where Mr. Curley lives, doing so when it was an unbroken forest except for railroad right of way, being all a wilderness. I was at the time estimating timber.

Mr. Curley. Senator Stephenson was telling us a while ago about being up there and being familiar with that territory. When I got there 30 years ago there was not a rod of road from Menominee, except the old State road.

Mr. Malby. How much is the capacity of the factory that is there now?

Mr. Curley. It is a 1,000-ton factory.

Mr. Malby. Are there plenty of beets now grown to supply that factory?

Mr. Curley. Yes, sir; we had plenty to run it this year. Mr. McCormick can enlighten you on that.

Mr. Malby. Is it running yet?

Mr. Curley. No, sir; it has just finished.

Mr. Malby. How many days' run did you have this year?

Mr. CURLEY. Seventy thousand tons—70 or 80 days.

Mr. MALBY. How many acres of land have you under cultivation?

Mr. CURLEY. Seven thousand acres actually grown in beets by measured acreage.

Mr. MALBY. It has been of general benefit to the community—this sugar factory—has it not?

Mr. CURLEY. Why, it certainly has. There is no question about that. I am also interested in a little bank there, and we make small loans through the bank to carry the farmers through, and if you were to see the sugar-beet checks coming in and the increase in deposits you would think the sugar-beet industry was a good thing generally. It is something wonderful.

Mr. MALBY. This is a fair question, perhaps: Which of two investments of $5,000, in a sugar factory or in a farm, would give you the greater return in money?

Mr. CURLEY. I think the farm would, without doubt. I know for sure you are not getting a very big rake-off from the factory. We ran that factory for two years on wind.

Mr. MALBY. You ran it two years on wind?

Mr. CURLEY. Yes, sir.

Mr. RAKER. Why is it that all of the people from these cities are not going out to this valuable and productive farm land?

Mr. CURLEY. Why, now, that is rather a remarkable thing. I think that is a question that baffles the greatest men on earth, to think that men will live in cities, and live as they do, while there is so much good farm land to be had cheap, with its healthy and happy farm life they could enjoy by going out in the country. It is a matter of association or being where they can get together thick, I guess—get where they can see the red lights. I just can not account for it at all.

Mr. RAKER. When you use the words "see the red lights," do you do so in the same connection that my friend Fordney used the word "slums" awhile ago?

Mr. CURLEY. Oh, no. I do not know anything much about your slums. I mean that men seem to want to get out for recreation where they can have some fun, and see the bright lights. The boys want to get into the towns and meet the girls, and the girls want to get there to meet the boys, and you may know, probably, that sometimes these meetings are very pleasant.

Mr. HINDS. I suppose they never meet one another in the farming regions?

Mr. CURLEY. Well, yes, they do; but you can keep a little better string on them in that way.

Mr. FORDNEY. What class of labor do you have in the beet fields in your part of the country?

Mr. CURLEY. I have my neighborhood boys and girls.

Mr. FORDNEY. You have a little town connected with the sawmill?

Mr. CURLEY. Yes, sir.

Mr. FORDNEY. You employ the citizens of that country?

Mr. CURLEY. Yes, sir.

Mr. FORDNEY. Do you have any imported labor?

Mr. CURLEY. No, sir.

The CHAIRMAN. Do the community people do the handwork?
Mr. CURLEY. Oh, yes, sir; and very glad to do it.
Mr. FORDNEY. You have an unlimited territory of very good soil?
Mr. CURLEY. Yes, sir.
Mr. FORDNEY. And there is wild land there yet?
Mr. CURLEY. Yes, sir.
Mr. FORDNEY. The timber is cut off, leaving the land laying there waiting for somebody to come along and grow beets and potatoes? potatoes?
Mr. CURLEY. Yes, sir.
Mr. HINDS. Is that land subject to homestead regulations?
Mr. CURLEY. No, sir; there are no homesteads there any more, to speak of. The first farmers were homesteaders, but they were not a very energetic class of farmers, and never cleared a great deal of land. They took the timber and made themselves a little home, with a few exceptions; some have elegant homes, that went out to get one. But as a rule, they took off the timber, sold out, and went off to get on the prairie land. A great many of them have come back, too; the most of them have come back that went west.
Another thing, gentlemen, that I would like to call your attention to is that I think we have the finest alfalfa belt in America right in our sugar-beet country. I have taken into consideration the cost and know about the alfalfa fields, and we generally make the most with a crop of alfalfa after a crop of sugar beets.
Mr. FORDNEY. How much farm have you?
Mr. CURLEY. I have about 325 acres in tillable shape, and then I have some range-pasture land, about 3,000 acres.
Mr. FORDNEY. You raise alfalfa successfully?
Mr. CURLEY. Yes, sir; oh, fine.
Mr. FORDNEY. How many tons per acre of alfalfa per year do you get off your land?
Mr. CURLEY. Between 5 and 6 tons from three cuttings.
Mr. RAKER. That is nothing less than marvelous, is it, when out in Colorado, where it is susceptible of alfalfa raising by irrigation, you can only get 3 tons per acre, while in Michigan you can get 5 or 6 tons per acre?
Mr. CURLEY. Well, that is what struck me. I had heard so much about the alfalfa business that I made a little trip out through the West to rest up and see how they did it, but when I came back home and saw my field I didn't want to go to Colorado or Washington or Oregon or Idaho. I was entirely satisfied, and had no ambition to leave the old farm that I had started in on. We produce the goods, and there are men here in the Capitol that know about it. Then as to the oat crop after beets, I raised for two years in succession 100 bushels of oats to the acre.
Mr. RAKER. That is something like California, where they raise 100 to 125 bushels of oats to the acre.
Mr. CURLEY. I don't doubt it.
Mr. HINDS. Do you raise any wheat?
Mr. CURLEY. No, sir.
Mr. HINDS. Do some of your neighbors raise wheat?
Mr. CURLEY. Oh, yes.
Mr. HINDS. How much wheat do they get following the beet crop?

Mr. CURLEY. Well, now, I couldn't tell you about that, because I don't know of an individual that raised wheat in my vicinity after beets, but they have run up as high as 42 bushels to the acre.

Mr. HINDS. Forty-two bushels of wheat to the acre?

Mr. CURLEY. Yes, sir. But the average is about 24 bushels per acre.

Mr. HINDS. That is, following a beet crop or on ordinary land?

Mr. CURLEY. No, sir; outside of the beet crop.

Mr. HINDS. That is a surprising yield, is it not?

Mr. CURLEY. Yes, sir.

Mr. HINDS. That is not irrigated land?

Mr. CURLEY. Oh, no; that land is just as God left it.

Mr. MALBY. What is the nature of the soil?

Mr. CURLEY. It is a sandy loam.

Mr. MALBY. Dark?

Mr. CURLEY. Some of it is dark and others just light—or not light, but a nice brown.

Mr. FORDNEY. A reddish clay soil?

Mr. CURLEY. There is not enough clay to be sticky at all.

Mr. MALBY. Is there enough clay in it to make it productive?

Mr. CURLEY. Oh, yes; it is productive, all right.

Mr. MALBY. A light colored sandy soil isn't a very productive soil, is it?

Mr. CURLEY. No; but don't understand me that this is sand. It is a nice loamy soil that won't pack. It is almost invariably loose.

Mr. MALBY. Is it easy to cultivate?

Mr. CURLEY. Easily cultivated. It doesn't bake.

Mr. HINDS. Do you fertilize at all?

Mr. CURLEY. Oh, yes.

Mr. HINDS. This 48 bushels of wheat per acre would be on land that was fertilized?

Mr. CURLEY. No; not after a beet crop. I don't fertilize after a beet crop. I fertilize before a beet crop, when I can, and then sow my grain. I keep a good many horses and a good deal of stock, and I cater to grass, oats, and corn.

Mr. MALBY. Is your fertilizer manure?

Mr. CURLEY. Yes, sir.

Mr. MALBY. Exclusively manure?

Mr. CURLEY. Oh, yes. I never bought fertilizer. I tried a bag or two that Mr. McCormick sent up—patent fertilizer—but didn't think so much of it; never thought it cut any figure with me. I would rather take manure and let the patent fertilizers go.

The CHAIRMAN. If that is all, we will excuse Mr. Curley with the thanks of the committee for his attendance.

Mr. CURLEY. I am very much obliged for favoring me with an opportunity of testifying.

And at 4.45 o'clock p. m. the committee adjourned until to-morrow, Saturday morning, January 13. 1912, at 10.30 o'clock.

AMERICAN SUGAR REFINING CO. AND OTHERS.

Special Committee on the Investigation
of the American Sugar Refining Co. and Others,
House of Representatives,
Washington, D. C., Saturday, January 13, 1912.

The committee met at 10.30 o'clock a. m., Hon. Thomas W. Hardwick (chairman) presiding.

TESTIMONY OF MR. WALLACE P. WILLETT—Resumed.

The Chairman. Mr. Willett, before taking up the consular reports, are there any other matters you want to refer to?

Mr. Willett. One or two. In the hearings of my testimony not yet received from the printer I gave a statement by Mr. Prinsen-Geerligs from his book giving cost of production of sugar on some estates in Java as $1.49 per hundred pounds. From the same book, a translation of page 143, Java Handbook, volume 4, by Prinsen-Geerligs, Amsterdam, March 1, 1911, reads as follows:

> The yearly reports of the different companies gives for the cost price of sugar on the different estates a number of ciphers, which vary in accordance with the assortment of sugar, the distances from the seaport, the interest which has to be paid on the capital, the production, etc. That it is very difficult to state a positive cost price. In general, we can say that the ciphers of Mr. Jacob are still of value, so that the cost price of sugar No. 11 to 13 Dutch standard and 96° test, including all expenses except interest on the capital, can be accepted as being F. 5.50 per pikol or 88 F. per ton.

These figures equal $1.58 per 100 pounds.

The estimate on page 145 of this book, of about F. 5 ($1.49 per 100 pounds) was based on operations in only one district of Java.

In other words, the cost of production of sugars of No. 11 to 13 Dutch standard in the island of Java is given in Mr. Geerligs's book as $1.58 per hundred pounds.

The Chairman. What is that No. 11 to No. 13?

Mr. Willett. That is 96° sugar.

The Chairman. In other words, that is what we call raw sugar?

Mr. Willett. Yes; 96° sugar.

The Chairman. At one place he figures it at a little less than $1.50 and at another place a little more than $1.50.

Mr. Willett. At one place $1.49, and on the whole island 9 cents higher.

Mr. Malby. Mr. Willett, where can we find a reliable, authoritative statement with reference to the manufacture and raising of sugar in Java, as to the character of labor employed and what they are paid, if we should desire to go into such matters?

The Chairman. Mr. Geerligs's book gives that, does it not?

Mr. WILLETT. I have not translated it far enough to see whether it does or not. As to the labor question, I do not know of anybody in this country who could give you that. I could obtain it for the committee from Java from our correspondent there. We have a very careful correspondent in Java, and it may be, Mr. Malby, I have that information already in my office from his letters. I will look it up and see.

Mr. MALBY. If you have it, I would really like to have you file it.

Mr. WILLETT. If I have the information I will file it.

Mr. MALBY. I am somewhat interested, because apparently that price is somewhat less than anywhere else in the world, and there must be some cause for it; that is to say, to my mind it could not be simply the soil alone or the quantity produced; it must be in the actual money cost of the production, and for that reason I would like to know just what those conditions are.

Mr. WILLETT. At one time we made a comparative statement of the cost of sugars in Cuba and the cost of sugars in Java and published it in our paper.

The CHAIRMAN. Have you that paper here?

Mr. WILLETT. No, sir.

The CHAIRMAN. How much difference did it show; do you remember?

Mr. WILLETT. My recollection is we stated in that paper that Cuban estates varied from 1½ to 2 cents a pound in their cost, and, taking the whole island together, the cost of producing 96° test sugars in Cuba could be placed at $1.85 per hundred pounds.

The CHAIRMAN. They are pretty close together, then?

Mr. WILLETT. In making that comparison with Java we took such figures as we had at hand, and I think we stated that those figures represented a sterling cost which was slightly below the cost in Cuba. Exactly what that difference was I do not recall, but it could not have exceeded a quarter of a cent a pound. It could not have exceeded these figures of Mr. Geerligs of 1½ cents a pound.

Mr. MALBY. Did you have in that connection the amount of sugar cane or sugar per acre which is produced in each place?

Mr. WILLETT. No, sir; we simply took the statements of different parties as to the cost of those sugars in Java.

Mr. MALBY. What I really had in mind was to find out whether Java was really a country of greater productivity than other countries per acre.

Mr. WILLETT. I may have that information in my office. I will look it up.

Mr. MALBY. All of those conditions would be important, if briefly stated. I do not want a long statement of it, but if I could get something which went to show how much they produced per acre, and whether they have to have annual plantings or 10-year plantings, and what they paid their labor in the fields and in the mills, and anything which goes to make up the cost.

Mr. WILLETT. If I can ascertain that I will be pleased to do so.

I call the attention of the committee to the table on page 3551, which gives the effect of reciprocity with Cuba, showing that Cuba during six years before reciprocity received within 0.044 cents per 100 pounds of the world's price as made at Hamburg, while during the eight years of reciprocity, from 1904 to 1911, inclusive, Cuba has averaged 24 cents per 100 pounds below Hamburg parity.

Mr. MALBY. In other words, the consumer has got some benefit from Cuban reciprocity?

Mr. WILLETT. But not in every instance.

Mr. MALBY. What is the average?

Mr. WILLETT. The other tables show that at one time in one of these years, 1910 or 1911, Cuba sold at 99 cents per hundred pounds below Hamburg parity, giving away their entire 20 per cent advantage of 34 cents per 100 pounds and 56 cents per 100 pounds besides. That does not appear in the table.

Mr. MALBY. As I understand, this is a table of averages.

Mr. WILLETT. Yes, sir.

Mr. FORDNEY. Did the consumer get that, or did the refiners get a portion of it?

Mr. WILLETT. An analysis of the tables I have given you shows that.

The CHAIRMAN. The tables showing the differential between raw and refined sugar will show that?

Mr. WILLETT. Table No. 6-A, page 3549, shows that, the table entitled "Effect of reduction of 20 per cent reciprocity with Cuba under Dingley law." That table shows who got the reduction.

The CHAIRMAN. How much the refiner got and how much the consumer got is shown in that table?

Mr. WILLETT. Yes, sir. The summing up of the table says that the net gain of refiners by Cuban reciprocity was 0.063; the total amount of duty taken off was 0.361; leaving for division between Cuba and United States consumers, 0.298. The refiner took 0.063 and the consumer and Cuba got 0.298.

In order to obtain the correct division of the $0.298 per 100 pounds gained by Cuba and United States consumers separately, the following analysis must be made.

Then follows the table to which I called your attention.

The average difference between centrifugal sugars of 96° polariscope in New York and raw beet sugar 88° analysis f. o. b. Hamburg, reduced to the parity of 96° centrifugals in New York, for six years under Dingley bill preceding reciprocity, compared with eight years of reciprocity, is shown in the table.

These tables show that during the six years of the Dingley law preceding reciprocity, Cuba sold her crop within $0.044 per 100 pounds of the world's price as fixed by the Hamburg market notwithstanding it included countervailing duty of $0.27, was assessed by the United States, while during the eight years of reciprocity Cuba has sold her crop at an average per year of 24 cents per 100 pounds below the world's price.

The reciprocity duty allowance to Cuba is $0.337 per 100 pounds, of which amount Cuba received $0.097 per 100 pounds. Our first analysis shows that refiners received of the $0.337 allowance, $0.063; total, $0.16; leaving the gain to consumers by reciprocity $0.177 per 100 pounds.

The CHAIRMAN. That was divided between the three, the consumer getting the largest amount, about one-half, and the balance being divided between Cuba and the refiners?

Mr. WILLETT. Yes; the consumer received $0.177 out of the $0.337. That confirms the first table, that Cuba and the consumer received together $0.298.

Mr. MALBY. I think it was Mr. Lowry who suggested the Cuban planters might possibly combine, and, if so, they would be able to exact the full amount of the duty paid.

Mr. WILLETT. They are not able to do so for several reasons.

Mr. MALBY. And therefore no one would get any benefit.

Mr. WILLETT. The Cuban planter is not in a position to do that at the present time.

The CHAIRMAN. Why not?

Mr. WILLETT. And the chances are he never will be. To do that he would have to keep his sugars into the summer months, and they deteriorate, which, together with the cost of storage, would cause him to lose as much as he would selling at the lower prices at the height of the season. They are limited as to their warehouse facilities. There has also been difficulty as to finances for such a large amount of sugar.

The CHAIRMAN. So that even if they overcame the last two obstacles the first one, in your opinion, is a natural loss and insurmountable?

Mr. WILLETT. Yes, sir.

Mr. FORDNEY. Mr. Chairman, I would like at this point to state that in Willett & Gray's Journal of January 11, 1912, is this quotation:

> The difference in parity between European beet sugars and Cuban centrifugals during February was 0.47 cent in 1911; 0.66 cent in 1910, and during May, 1910, it was as much as 0.93 cent, while Cuba to-day is 0.79 cent below the parity of beets, with an abundant prospect of supplies for the United States, and an expected shortage in Europe.

What about that statement, Mr Willett?

Mr. WILLETT. It is a fact that Cuba is giving away its reciprocity advantage, and so much besides, if I have the figures correctly.

Mr. FORDNEY. According to that they have not only lost the difference in duty, but they have also lost 45.3 besides.

Mr. WILLETT. That is along the same line I mentioned just now, that one time during those years they were selling at 99 cents a hundred below the parity of Hamburg.

The CHAIRMAN. But that is an exception to the general rule, is it not?

Mr. WILLETT. No; that is according to the rule during the height of the Cuban crop.

The CHAIRMAN. Because of the coming onto the market of their crop?

Mr. WILLETT. Yes, sir.

Mr. MALBY. How long do they continue taking that low price?

Mr. WILLETT. Along in August and September, when Cuba has no more sugars to sell, or a very small amount to sell, then the Cuban price rises to the parity of the Hamburg f. o. b. price.

The CHAIRMAN. What good does that do the Cuban planter?

Mr. WILLETT. None.

The CHAIRMAN. Therefore, does he get anything from this reciprocity?

Mr. WILLETT. I doubt if he gets very much out of the reciprocity.

The CHAIRMAN. Well, do we get anything?

Mr. WILLETT. Oh, yes.

The CHAIRMAN. All he does not get the consumer gets?

Mr. WILLETT. Yes, sir.

The CHAIRMAN. Except the small amount the refiner gets?

Mr. WILLETT. Except the small amount the refiner may take. Before I forget it, in any new tariff bill to be passed that important thing should be recognized and studied out because while Cuba is taking 99 cents less than the world's price the beet-sugar men of this country are losing that much protection; their protection is that much reduced during that period.

Mr. MALBY. How long do these reduced prices on Cuban sugars continue?

Mr. WILLETT. They can not continue very long.

Mr. MALBY. Well, I do not care for the length of time, but does it apply to that period of time when they market a majority of their sugars?

Mr. WILLETT. It applies to the period of time when they are making their earliest production in the island of Cuba and want to sell it rapidly for various reasons, the first of which is they have borrowed money and they want to replace it, and the commission merchant of Cuba is urging them to sell their sugars to meet those obligations.

Mr. MALBY. That may be so, but that does not answer my question. My question is to ascertain whether those reductions in price apply during the period of time when they are actually marketing a majority of their sugars, or does it apply to only a portion of that time?

Mr. WILLETT. It applies to a time when they are marketing about one-fourth of their crop.

Mr. MALBY. Then for one-fourth of their crop they get less than the amount of the difference?

Mr. WILLETT. They get less than the amount of the difference by a large amount on the other three-quarters.

Mr. MALBY. Will you say that on three-fourths of the crop they get the full amount?

Mr. WILLETT. They never get the full amount except when they have no sugar to sell.

Mr. MALBY. I think this is important, and I do not quite understand you. I do not mean what portion of their crop is marketed at the very greatest loss, but what portion of their crop is marketed so that they do not realize anything by reason of the reciprocity?

Mr. WILLETT. A very infinitesimal part, probably not exceeding 100,000 tons.

Mr. MALBY. And it is gradated from nothing up to what?

Mr. WILLETT. From nothing up to 99 cents a hundred.

Mr. MALBY. Do you know what the average would be?

Mr. WILLETT. The average is given in the table, 24 cents for 1911.

Mr. MALBY. Their benefit would not be 24 cents?

Mr. WILLETT. Their loss is 24 cents. Their benefit is the difference between 24 cents and 34 cents.

Mr. MALBY. For instance they are allowed 33.7; what do they get?

Mr. WILLETT. Out of the 33.7 they lose 24, and they get 9 cents a hundred. Now, that was for 1911. Now, take the year 1910, when their average was 53.4 below Hamburg parity. They lost the entire reciprocity of 33.7 and more.

The CHAIRMAN. What was the cause of that?

Mr. WILLETT. A large crop and wanting to get the money.

Mr. FORDNEY. How is it now? They have got a short Cuban crop this year.

Mr. WILLETT. No; they have got a big Cuban crop now coming on.

Mr. MALBY. Mr. Willett, during the time that the Cuban crop is being marketed below their differential it is equally true that the Louisiana crop and the Hawaiian crop and the beet-sugar crops, or whatever crops are then being marketed, suffer exactly in a like proportion, do they not?

Mr. WILLETT. The Louisiana crop is out of the way by that time.

Mr. MALBY. But whatever crops are then being marketed have to sell at the Cuban price, do they not?

Mr. WILLETT. Yes, sir.

Mr. FORDNEY. Mr. Willett, I just want to make this clear. As the difference is 79 cents below European prices to-day, the real protection that the Cuban has on his sugar instead of being 1.345 is 89½ right now; in other words, deducting 79 from 1.685 leaves 89½?

Mr. WILLETT. I would not reason in that way.

The CHAIRMAN. You would not reason in that way?

Mr. WILLETT. No, sir.

Mr. FORDNEY. That is all the consumer pays, because their price is 79 cents right now below European prices, and that is at a time, too, when their crop is on the market, and when our domestic cane and beet crop is on the market, and that would have some influence.

Mr. WILLETT. You involve two things in your question. While that 79 cents is lost to the Cuban, yet bear in mind that the Cuban is getting over 1 cent a pound more for his sugars than it costs him to produce, consequently that amount must go in as a part of the protection to the beet-sugar industry.

Mr. FORDNEY. Well, it comes at a time when both the beet and domestic cane sugar is on the market. The Cuban crop and the Louisiana crop and the beet-sugar crop all come on the market about the same time.

Mr. WILLETT. The Cuban and the beet-sugar crop do, but the Louisiana crop has been pretty well placed before the Cuban crop comes in.

Mr. FORDNEY. But it is here on the market.

Mr. WILLETT. It is virtually gone. The Louisiana crop has virtually been sold at the present moment.

Mr. FORDNEY. Do they not grind about the same time Cuba does?

Mr. WILLETT. No, sir; they are through grinding before this cold weather comes on. If there is any cane in the field now it would not be worth grinding, in such weather as this.

Mr. MALBY. Has not Cuba been grinding for some time?

Mr. WILLETT. Cuba begins to grind about the middle of December, but there are less than 50 estates in Cuba grinding before the 1st of January out of 172.

Mr. MALBY. When does the Louisiana crop mature?

Mr. WILLETT. They begin grinding on the 15th of September and continue through October and November and December.

Mr. RAKER. This year were they not pretty near through along about the 1st of December?

Mr. WILLETT. Pretty nearly through.

Mr. RAKER. And what was left until the 1st of December was injured by frost?

Mr. WILLETT. Yes, sir.

Mr. MALBY. Was their sugar put on the market immediately?

Mr. WILLETT. Yes, sir; it was already contracted to the American Sugar Refining Co., 75 per cent of it, and sold in advance.

Mr. FORDNEY. Mr. Willett, is it true that the difference between Cuban sugar and the European sugars on our market was as marked before Cuban reciprocity became a law as it has been since that time?

Mr. WILLETT. Oh, no. Previous to reciprocity things were equalized.

Mr. FORDNEY. And previous to that time we had no beet sugar in this country?

Mr. WILLETT. No, sir.

Mr. FORDNEY. The two things together, and the making of sugar for supplying the United States has much to do with the price on our market, does it not?

Mr. WILLETT. It has everything to do with the price at the period between crops. I put in a statement the other day showing when every crop of the world matures and is made. That is what I constantly want to keep before the committee, that the vital point in getting low prices to the consumer is to increase your domestic and insular production to a point you will not have to go abroad for sugars.

Mr. HINDS. The Cuban sugar crop is on the market now, or coming on?

Mr. WILLETT. It is on the market for deliveries next month. A few arrivals will come in this month; but very few.

Mr. HINDS. How much below the world's price are they getting?

Mr. WILLETT. Seventy-nine cents below, Mr. Fordney says.

Mr. FORDNEY. Cuban sugars are selling on the New York market, quotations of yesterday, 79 cents per 100 pounds below Hamburg parity.

Mr. HINDS. I mean, how do their sugars stand in our market duty paid?

Mr. WILLETT. That is duty paid.

Mr. HINDS. And that much less than the Hamburg price?

Mr. WILLETT. Yes, sir.

Mr. HINDS. That is an abnormal situation, is it not?

Mr. WILLETT. It occurs every year at this period; perhaps not to the same extent.

Mr. HINDS. And it is that much less than the Hamburg price plus the duty?

Mr. WILLETT. Yes.

Mr. HINDS. Then Cuba is not getting the full 1.68; they are not getting even the full 1.34 difference which our law gives them.

Mr. WILLETT. No, sir.

Mr. HINDS. I questioned Mr. Lowrie when he was on the stand, and he thought it would only be a matter of a little time when Cuba would get the benefit of the full tariff rate as compared with Java, for instance.

Mr. WILLETT. Did he mean this year or a series of years?

Mr. HINDS. He thought some time in the future that would happen.

Mr. WILLETT. No; it will never happen, because in 1910 we were within 74,000 tons of equaling our supply to the consumption in the United States that year, and we had to call on foreign countries at full duty rates for only 74,000 tons of sugar. This year we have had to call on foreign countries for about 200,000 or 224,000 tons of foreign sugars at full duty rates, because of the shortness of last year's Cuban crop. This coming year Cuba will increase her crop that much, so that we will not have to call on foreign countries for any sugars, unless European countries are short and take our Cuban sugar supply away from us to meet a shortage over there. Now, it is fair to suppose that from 1912 onward the crops of Cuba, Porto Rico, Hawaii, and our domestic beet and cane crops will constantly increase, and increase probably to an amount in excess of the increase in the United States consumption, so that instead of having a deficiency of 72,000 to 200,000 tons to get from foreign countries, we will eventually have a surplus of from 72,000 to 200,000 tons to send to foreign countries. When that condition comes, as it will some day, in my opinion, then the competition for the United States market will begin between Cuba, Porto Rico, Hawaii, the Philippines, and the domestic cane and beet sugars, which will prove a great advantage to the consumers in this country. Now, the vital point in all this is to increase that production up to that point, and then you will solve the question.

Mr. HINDS. That is, you think low prices primarily come from having a large store of the commodity on the market and in the country?

Mr. WILLETT. That is shown conclusively in Russia. As I explained the other day, the Russian Government provides there shall never be a scarcity in Russia of sugar. When there is a scarcity in Russia of sugar, they lower their duties from over $5 a ton to $2.89 to bring in foreign sugars and bring the price back to level; and whenever the price of granulated sugar, crystal sugars, in Russia, exceeds 24 cents a hundred pounds above the price at Kief or Odessa, which the Government has fixed on the 1st of September, then a certain amount of what is called a reserve, kept back for contingencies by the Government, is immediately put on the market and immediately drops that price down below the Kief price.

Mr. HINDS. So that Cuba is the key to the situation with us, and Hawaii and the Philippines and Porto Rico have to go along with Cuba, do they?

Mr. WILLETT. At the present time.

Mr. HINDS. And probably will have to as long as Cuba keeps up its preeminence?

Mr. WILLETT. It all lies between those countries.

Mr. MALBY. How much did you say we were getting from Cuba this year?

Mr. WILLETT. We will get this year, estimated, 1,800,000 tons, as against 1,567,000 tons last year; between two and three hundred thousand tons more this year, if no one takes it away from us to cover any possible deficiency in their supplies, so that next August and September you will not see that same rise in prices.

Mr. FORDNEY. Mr. Willett, you say that last year we imported but 2 per cent of the sugar consumed in the United States, or 72,000 tons?

Mr. WILLETT. In 1910.

Mr. FORDNEY. Only 2 per cent of our consumption came from countries paying full duty of 1.685, and our supply practically and the price the consumer will pay for sugar in this country depends largely upon Cuba, Porto Rico, the Philippines, Hawaii, and our insular possessions.

Mr. WILLETT. Yes, sir.

Mr. FORDNEY. Now, when the supply of sugar from the sources mentioned gets above our consumption, the price of sugar is going to go down in our market?

Mr. WILLETT. By competition between those different interests?

Mr. FORDNEY. Yes, sir.

Mr. WILLETT. That is correct.

The CHAIRMAN. Of course, one element we can never overlook in fixing the price for the consumer, and that is the amount of duty we levy, because the amount of duty that is levied on sugar is always added to the price, is it not?

Mr. WILLETT. Yes; added to the cost price.

The CHAIRMAN. So that is an important element itself in determining the price to the consumer?

Mr. WILLETT. Yes.

Mr. HINDS. Is that true of all sugars? Have you not just shown that sugars coming from Java and Hamburg come in less than the Cuban defferential?

Mr. WILLETT. No. There was a time, if my recollection is correct, when we were selling granulated sugar in this country, this year, 1911, at a price below the parity of Hamburg for raw sugar.

Mr. MALBY. You do not mean to say, Mr. Willett, that the price is always enhanced by the amount of the tariff, do you?

Mr. WILLETT. It is enhanced by the amount of the tariff above or below what the price would be based on production, consumption, and all the other elements.

Mr. MALBY. For instance, to-day Cuba is not getting the full benefit of the tariff. The Cuban planter is not getting the benefit of the differential, but is selling for much less than that.

Mr. WILLETT. That is correct.

The CHAIRMAN. And but for the tariff the Cuban planter could sell it that much cheaper to the consumer?

Mr. WILLETT. Yes.

Mr. MALBY. That is speculative.

The CHAIRMAN. That is simply common sense.

Mr. FORDNEY. Mr. Willett, I want to read you this paragraph in the Tariff Board's report, found on page 5 of the first volume, as follows:

> On the other hand, the findings show that the duties which run to such high ad valorem equivalents are prohibitory since the goods are not imported, but the prices of domestic fabrics are not raised by the full amount of the duty. On a set of 1-yard samples of 16 English fabrics which are completely excluded by the present tariff rate it was found that the total foreign value was $41.84; the duties which would have been assessed had these fabrics been imported was $76.90; the foreign value plus the amount of the duty, $118.74, or a nominal duty of 183 per cent. In fact, however, practically identical fabrics of domestic make sold at the same time at $69.75, showing an enhanced price over the market value of but 67 per cent ad valorem, whereas if the full duty were applied they would cost laid down in our market in May $118.74.

Assuming this statement to be correct, how do you reconcile it with your statement that the tariff is always added to the price in the case of sugar?

Mr. WILLETT. I could not answer that at the moment. Will you place your question before me and let me consider it for a few days when I get home?

Mr. FORDNEY. I will be delighted to do that, Mr. Willett.

Mr. WILLETT. I will take your figures and analyze them alongside of what I know about sugar, and see how it applies to sugar, if that is what you would like to have me do.

Mr. FORDNEY. I thank you.

Mr. RAKER. Mr. Willett, I have received a number of letters from various chambers of commerce in California, and I have been wondering as to the object of them. This letter, Mr. Willett, sets out a number of facts, first:

Whereas persistent effort has been made and is being made by eastern cane-sugar refining companies to influence Congress in order to secure a reduction in the present tariff on sugar, if not its entire abrogation.

Now, what do you know about that?

Mr. WILLETT. The evidence is before the committee that Mr. Lowry, representing the Wholesale Grocers' Association, is doing that, and Mr. Spreckels is working in the same way.

Mr. RAKER. Well, how about the rest of them?

The CHAIRMAN. I do not see how Mr. Willett could have any more knowledge on that question than the committee has. We know what they are doing and what they testify to. Does that come within your knowledge as an expert, Mr. Willett?

Mr. WILLETT. I think it is in the evidence already. You will find it in my evidence where I was asked as to the effect of the reduction of the tariff. If you want to know the position of the American Sugar Refining Co. in that matter, they are entirely indifferent. They own both cane and beets. They do not come within the category of that statement, because they have both cane and beet holdings. That applies to cane and cane only. The American Sugar Refining Co. is excluded from the position occupied by the Federal.

Mr. RAKER. The reason I asked the question is this: Being in the sugar business and keeping statistics on these matters, I thought perhaps you would know whether or not these people are taking up this question for that purpose.

Mr. WILLETT. Will you repeat the question, please?

Mr. RAKER (reading):

Whereas persistent effort has been and is being made by eastern cane sugar refining companies to influence Congress in order to secure a reduction in the present tariff on sugar, if not its entire abrogation.

Mr. WILLETT. The answer to that is that certain companies are doing that; certain companies, but not all.

Mr. RAKER (reading):

Whereas this movement is prompted by self-interest on the part of said cane sugar refiners, because of the growth of the beet-sugar industry in the United States is admitted to be an increasing menace to their refinery investments, and they expect that a material reduction in the existing tariff will check the further development of the beet-sugar business and cripple some of the establishments that have come into existence under protective conditions.

Mr. WILLETT. That is not their object. Their object is to reduce the cost of their raw material so that the expenses of refining will not be as large, and they think they can make more money thereby. In doing that, however, they indirectly will cripple the other interests mentioned.

Mr. RAKER (reading):

Whereas it is of the highest importance, and it is entirely possible, that our Nation should become self-supplying in the article of sugar, and can be, because our annual consumption has reached approximately 3,920,000 tons, drawn from the following sources of supply: Domestic beet sugar, 560,000 tons; domestic cane sugar, Porto Rico, 336,000 tons; domestic cane sugar, Louisiana, 336,000 tons; domestic cane sugar, Hawaii, 560,000 tons; making a total of 1,792,000 tons; balance imported cane sugar, almost entirely from Cuba and Java, 2,128,000 tons.

Is that about right?

Mr. WILLETT. That is about right.

Mr. RAKER (reading):

Porto Rico, Louisiana, and Hawaii have nearly reached their limit of cane-sugar production, therefore the hope of increase in domestic product lies in the extension of the beet-sugar industry.

That is the matter I wanted particularly to ask you about, if you know, from your experience.

Mr. WILLETT. I think Hawaii has. I think Porto Rico has nearly, but not Cuba.

Mr. RAKER. This did not include Cuba.

Mr. WILLETT. Then I will answer yes.

Mr. RAKER. The letter I read from is as follows:

SANTA ANA CHAMBER OF COMMERCE,
Santa Ana, Cal., January 3, 1912.

Hon. JOHN E. RAKER,
Representative from California, Washington, D. C.

DEAR SIR: The board of directors of the Santa Ana Chamber of Commerce of the city of Santa Ana adopted the following resolution:

Whereas persistent effort has been and is being made by eastern cane-sugar refining companies to influence Congress in order to secure a reduction in the present tariff on sugar, if not its entire abrogation;

Whereas this movement is prompted by self-interest on the part of said cane-sugar refiners, because of the growth of the beet-sugar industry in the United States is admitted to be an increasing menace to their refinery investments, and they expect that a material reduction in the existing tariff will check the further development of the beet-sugar business and cripple some of the establishments that have come into existence under protective conditions;

Whereas it is of the highest importance and it is entirely possible that our Nation should become self-supplying in the article of sugar, and can be, because:

Our annual consumption has reached approximately 3,920,000 tons, drawn from the following sources of supply:

	Tons.
Domestic beet sugar	560,000
Domestic cane sugar, Porto Rico	336,000
Domestic cane sugar, Louisiana	336,000
Domestic cane sugar, Hawaii	560,000
	1,792,000
Balance, imported cane sugar, almost entirely from Cuba and Java	2,128,000
Total	3,920,000

"Porto Rico, Louisiana, and Hawaii have nearly reached their limit of cane-sugar production, therefore the hope of increase in domestic product lies in the extension of the beet-sugar industry;

"The United States Agricultural Department estimates that we possess 247,000,000 acres adapted to sugar-beet cultivation. To produce the present product of 560,000 tons of beet sugar requires the use of only 300,000 acres; to produce the 2,128,000 tons now imported would require only a little over 1,000,000 acres;

"Our importers send millions of dollars annually to purchase foreign raw sugar, and expend in our country at the rate of only one-half cent per pound for refining, but the use of 1,000,000 acres in sugar-beet culture, with the employment of resident farm labor, the investment of millions of American capital in factories, and the disbursement of moneys therefrom for beets, labor, and supplies, will be of incalculable benefit to our country;

"The outturn of beet sugar has grown from 45,000 tons in 1897 to 560,000 tons in 1911, and with proper governmental encouragement we should ultimately become exporters rather than importers of sugar; and

"Whereas California is producing nearly one-third of the total output of beet sugar and possesses ideal conditions of soil and climate to induce the greater development of this industry that has become established within her borders: Therefore be it

"*Resolved*, That this organization can not look with favor on such congressional action to retard the expansion of this promising business as will result from the reduction of the present rate of duty on sugar, and these resolutions are sent to our Senators and to the Representatives of this State to register the protests of their constituents against such action if contemplated, and to ask them to stand for, and to vote for, what we regard as of vital interest to our State and Nation."

I hereby certify that I am the secretary of the Santa Ana Chamber of Commerce, and that the foregoing resolution was adopted at a meeting of the said Santa Ana Chamber of Commerce on the 3d day of January, 1912, and that a majority of the members were present and voted therefor.

Very truly, yours,

J. A. WILLSON,
Secretary of the Santa Ana Chamber of Commerce.

Mr. FORDNEY. Mr. Willett, in connection with the question I asked you in reference to the tariff being added to the price, is it not true that it is only when the duty is not entirely prohibitive that the whole duty is added to the price? If the duty is entirely prohibitive, in that case the domestic producer adds just as much as local conditions, competition, local supply, and demand will permit him to add?

Mr. WILLETT. Suppose under those conditions your supplies were short of your consumptive demands, would not the price rise to the level of those prohibitive duties?

Mr. FORDNEY. Let me illustrate my question with sugar, because I know that is the thing you know best. Suppose, for instance, instead of a duty of 2 cents a pound we had a duty of 20 cents a pound, is it your judgment 20 cents a pound would be added to the cost of sugar to the American consumer?

Mr. WILLETT. It would not, with the single exception that there was only half a crop and we were obliged to buy sugars from other countries on the basis of that 20 cents, then it would rise to that price. If we had to buy it, we would have to pay the duties.

Mr. FORDNEY. To the extent we import?

Mr. WILLETT. Yes.

Mr. FORDNEY. Last year we imported 74,000 tons of full duty paid sugar, and would that affect the domestic price that much?

Mr. WILLETT. It would affect the price to the consumer to that extent, of course.

Mr. FORDNEY. If the duty had been 20 cents, would the price of sugar have been 25 cents last year?

Mr. WILLETT. At 20 cents people would go without sugar.

Mr. FORDNEY. That is exactly the point. If the duty is fixed high enough so that happens, then the pocketbook of the consumer holds the price down to some extent, does it not? For instance, if the duty on silk cloth is made $10 a yard—I am using extreme figures to reduce the proposition to an absurdity—then people simply would not buy silk cloth, would they?

Mr. WILLETT. That is correct.

Mr. FORDNEY. Is not that a correct statement of the situation as applied to sugar or anything else?

Mr. WILLETT. The consumer of sugar never does pay that high rate of duty which exists against foreign sugars except at such times when he can not get sugar in any other way. As long as he can get sugar on the Cuban basis he is not going to buy on a prohibitive basis, which might be 1 cent or might be more.

Mr. FORDNEY. Suppose, while the Cuban rate remained 1.348, at the same time we had a 50-cent rate on all other foreign sugars, do you think that 74,000 tons of sugar we brought in last year would have come in at all?

Mr. WILLETT. Not a pound of it.

Mr. FORDNEY. The consumption would have been reduced that much?

Mr. WILLETT. Certainly.

Mr. HINDS. Mr. Willett, in other words, if I go to the Waldorf-Astoria Hotel to-morrow, living costs me $10 a day. It does not follow, though, that it costs me $3,650 a year to live.

Mr. WILLETT. Not at all; it is only during the time you are at the hotel.

Mr. HINDS. When I stay at home it does not cost me so much.

Mr. WILLETT. During the time you are at the hotel you are paying that price, and during the time we are without sugar we are paying the high duty. Perhaps that answers Mr. Fordney's question.

Mr. FORDNEY. No. Mr. Willett, I want to ask you this question: Of the 3,500,000 tons of sugar we consume annually here, about one-half is imported, duty-paying sugar, which practically comes from Cuba. Of the 500,000,000 pounds of wool consumed by American citizens 40 per cent is imported, and the balance is the domestic crop. The two being an article or commodity used by the common people, I think they form a fair comparison. What would affect one would affect the other, the importations being somewhat alike. We import 40 per cent of the wool consumed in this country, which pays a duty, and the balance is the domestic crop, while we import 50 per cent of our sugar, which pays a duty, and what would be true of one would be true of the other, would it not?

Mr. WILLETT. I should say so.

Mr. MALBY. There is only one suggestion I have to make, and I will call your attention to it. When we are considering the effect of the reduction of a duty on an article, whether it be sugar or wool or anything else, as affecting the price to the consumer, we must always have in mind what the conditions would be with reference to our domestic product if the duty were removed. It must always be conceded, I think, that where we have a domestic product not equal to the supply of the market, but of considerable quantity, like sugar or wool, the domestic product does have an effect on the price to the consumer, because if the domestic product were entirely removed the world's supply would be reduced by that quantity, and if everything operated as it does in the case of sugar, as we have seen, the price would go up, so that in the consideration of a policy with reference to the reduction of the tariff, we should always have in mind what the effect is going to be on the world's supply, including our own contribution to the world's supply. If the reduction of the tariff upon a given article is going to wipe out or materially reduce our own local production, that should be taken into consideration, because it reduces the world's supply by that amount, which in the ordinary course of trade would be apt to affect the price in an upward direction. So that in dealing with this question and all others of the tariff, we should do nothing with the tariff by way of reduction which would imperil the local production, because when you imperil the local production you decrease the quantity going into the world's supply, and take a good, broad chance that the article will advance, so that really in the changed conditions the consumer gets no benefit and, on the contrary, you lose the benefit of the local production which you have theretofore enjoyed.

Therefore when we assemble ourselves and say "If it were not for the tariff we would get sugar 1¾ cents per pound less," I sincerely doubt it, because of the fact that if our expectations were realized and it was reduced 1¾ cents per pound I venture the suggestion there would be no sugar produced in the United States; and if no sugar were produced in the United States, which production now amounts to 850,000 tons, the price of sugar would not be reduced 1¾ cents, but by reason of that quantity being taken from the world's supply the chances are more than equal the price to the consumer under those conditions would be the full amount of the duty now paid. Now, those are matters which I want to submit to you, and ask you whether or not they are entitled to very careful consideration at all times when we are dealing with this subject.

Mr. WILLETT. I think, Judge Malby, you are absolutely correct in every statement you have made, in the event of the entire duty being taken off of sugar.

Mr. MALBY. Do you agree with me in the event of any duty being taken off which would interfere with the local production, whether it is much or little?

Mr. WILLETT. All duty taken off would have that effect, but you could reduce your duty a certain amount without interfering.

Mr. MALBY. I agree with you about that. I mean, if it does interfere.

Mr. WILLETT. You do not want to reduce your tariff to a point where it will interfere with the domestic production, and in considering what your reduction will be you have got to take into account such circumstances as these which apply to Cuba in selling her sugars below reciprocity.

Mr. MALBY. Then you and I agree exactly. I do not care how much you reduce it so long as you do not interfere with local production, because my unbiased opinion is that when you go so far as to interfere with the local production you have no guaranty which is worth the paper it is written on that under those conditions the price to the consumer will be any lower than it is to-day.

Mr. RAKER. What would be the result if Cuba had free sugar, if we admitted Cuban sugar free? Would that be of benefit to the United States?

Mr. WILLETT. It would be a splendid thing for the consumers of the United States provided you kept a high wall against all other sugars.

Mr. RAKER. How would that affect the consumer and the beet and cane industry in the United States?

Mr. WILLETT. For the first year or two it would affect the consumer very favorably, but it would be a very short time before Cuba would run ahead, with its lower cost of production, below the cost of producing cane and beet sugar in the United States, and those industries would begin to decrease instead of increase, and would be wiped out.

Mr. MALBY. Now, that is my honest opinion, and that is the way I look at it.

Mr. WILLETT. That would only come to pass when the production reached the consumption point.

The CHAIRMAN. Mr. Willett, here is another very important view of the proposition advanced by Mr. Malby, which I think he has not presented to your mind, and I want to see whether you think it is of importance or not. If you and I were to agree with his statement of the question, as I am somewhat inclined to do, yet you would have to figure how much that possible production was of the world's supply; that would be one side of your ledger, would it not? In other words, if we produced 800,000 tons of sugar, and even if the effect of having free sugar would be to wipe it out, that would be so much reduction, as Mr. Malby suggests, of the world's supply, and consequently would affect the world's price?

Mr. WILLETT. Unless replaced by 800,000 tons increase in the Cuban supply or the supply of some other place.

The CHAIRMAN. In other words, it would have a tendency to decrease the world's supply, and if conditions elsewhere remained the same, it would have a tendency somewhat to enhance the world's price, would it not?

Mr. WILLETT. All these matters are based on the United States being entirely clear of the world's supply, and getting our supply from Cuba.

The CHAIRMAN. But to my mind the difficulty about that proposition is—and I want to get your judgment about it, leaving out any tariff views you may have—whether or not we can afford to keep alive an industry that produces 800,000 tons of sugar, if it can not produce it at anything like what we can buy it for elsewhere, either now or in the near future. In other words, putting the question to you in this way, if it costs 4 cents a pound, or nearly that, to produce both beet and cane sugar in the United States, and if cane sugar can be produced in other parts of the world and the production can be increased in those parts of the world, and will, if the market is opened up for them, at 1½ cents instead of 4 cents, why should the consumer continue for ever to hurt himself with these high prices unless our people can come up to the standard the balance of the world sets?

Mr. WILLETT. If you maintain the duty unchanged as it stands to-day you will accomplish the result which I spoke of more quickly than you will by reducing the duty.

The CHAIRMAN. Accomplish what result?

Mr. WILLETT. The production of our sugar supply by our domestic industry and our insular possessions.

The CHAIRMAN. How are you going to accomplish the result I am speaking about more quickly, to get sugar cheaper to the American consumer?

Mr. WILLETT. I think you will get it cheaper by maintaining a protective tariff.

The CHAIRMAN. And if we do that the manufacturers will take advantage of the protective tariff wall.

Mr. WILLETT. Yes.

The CHAIRMAN. Hawaii did it.

Mr. WILLETT. Yes.

The CHAIRMAN. Porto Rico did it.

Mr. WILLETT. Yes, sir.

The CHAIRMAN. Just as Louisiana and the beet people do it.

Mr. WILLETT. Yes, sir.

The CHAIRMAN. To the extent you keep the protective wall around this country on sugar you give every fellow within that wall an opportunity to levy that much more price on his own domestic customer?

Mr. WILLETT. Certainly.

The CHAIRMAN. How is it to the interest of the people who consume sugar to do that?

Mr. WILLETT. That is what I say. That might not be to the interest of the consumer for a year or two.

The CHAIRMAN. Why?

Mr. WILLETT. For the simple reason that free sugar in Cuba might, probably would, mean less domestic cane and beet sugar within a few years thereafter.

The CHAIRMAN. What proportion of the world's sugar do we produce?

Mr. WILLETT (continuing). It would not then be any detriment to the consumer. The detriment then would be in transferring the profits of the sugar industry to the island of Cuba instead of to the farmers and others of the United States.

The CHAIRMAN. I am looking at it now from the standpoint of the consumer, leaving out these other people for the moment.

Mr. WILLETT. Naturally the consumer would benefit for a time.

The CHAIRMAN. What percentage of the total sugar production of the world, roughly, is represented by the American sugar production?

Mr. WILLETT. By American you mean everything?

The CHAIRMAN. No; we will leave out our insular possessions, just continental United States.

Mr. WILLETT. Eight hundred thousand tons.

The CHAIRMAN. Out of how many tons for the whole world?

Mr. WILLETT. Out of 15,000,000 tons.

The CHAIRMAN. Therefore it would not be any very considerable percentage of the entire production if we wiped out the whole business?

Mr. WILLETT. It would not.

The CHAIRMAN. The world's supply would be almost as large as it is now.

Mr. WILLETT. But to get possession of that world's supply, in the event of the 800,000 tons being wiped out, you would have to pay the world's prices?

The CHAIRMAN. Undoubtedly, and of course it might be increased by that percentage.

Mr. WILLETT. It would, because the speculators of Europe would immediately take advantage of that condition and would raise prices on us several cents a pound.

Mr. MALBY. There is only one other suggestion I have to make in connection with what the chairman has asked you, and we are getting now to the crux of the whole proposition, assuming the United States Congress should say: "We have husbanded this industry as long as we are going to; we will not take into consideration the scheme to increase the production of the United States and its insular possessions, which might be very seriously affected, as well as the home market; we will not any longer encourage the Hawaiian or the Porto Rican or the Filipino or the cane growers of Louisiana and Texas or the beet-sugar men of the United States; we will change our policy and we will have free sugar." Now, just what is going to happen? From the evidence which we have received here, without desiring to state a definite conclusion, the testimony would tend to show that the sugar industry of the United States would be a thing of the past; that whatever profit has come to our country and its people on that account would be lost; what effect it would have upon the Hawaiian planter who now produces 400,000 tons of sugar, whereas before he did not produce half that amount; what would happen to the industry in Porto Rico which has doubled their output under similar conditions; what might happen to the industry in the Philippines which has increased at least twice, if not quadrupled, during the same period of time and under the same conditions, I do not know, but that it would affect the quantity produced goes without saying.

Mr. WILLETT. Yes; if their cost of production is higher than other parts of the world.

Mr. MALBY. If we look for our supply from Cuba, from Java, from European beet-sugar countries, just what is our condition going to be? Is the price going to be as low as it is now, by the amount of the duty, or not? I think not. That is the first question to be inquired about.

Mr. WILLETT. The country that can produce sugar the cheapest will get the trade.

Mr. MALBY. Yes; that goes without saying. But is the price going to be reduced by the amount of the tariff? I think not, for this reason, the world's supply, in my judgment, would be materially decreased. Our own supply would be wiped out in the first place, and we have seen during the past summer that a very much less quantity than we produce in continental America has reduced the price of sugar 2 cents a pound. Instead of our getting the benefit of the tariff, the price would certainly go up somewhat. It would go up a great deal unless the other countries, rather than our own country and our insular possessions, greatly increased their present output of sugar.

Mr. WILLETT. That is the point.

Mr. MALBY. What assurance have we, in the name of common sense, that they would do that?

Mr. WILLETT. In other words, could they do it? Could Germany double her crop; could France double her crop; and could Java double her crop?

Mr. MALBY. Have we such assurance they would do that, in your judgment, that it would be a wise policy for us to take any such chances, or indeed take any chances which would materially reduce the quantity of sugar produced in the United States at the present time from all sources, or reduce the quantity of sugar which we receive from our insular possessions, in any appreciable manner?

Mr. WILLETT. Well, I never can get away from the convictions I have repeated here over and over again, that in changing the tariff, if we do change it, it should not be changed so as to stop the production of our domestic and insular possessions below the point of our consumption.

The CHAIRMAN. Can you think of any way to relieve the consumer except by reducing the tariff?

Mr. WILLETT. There is a way.

The CHAIRMAN. Would you tell us about that?

Mr. WILLETT. I have not studied it out, but it would be by changing your entire policy. You would not have any tariff. You would change to internal revenue.

The CHAIRMAN. Now, explain that to us, because I am interested in that question.

Mr. WILLETT. I can not talk on the subject now, because I have not studied it sufficiently.

The CHAIRMAN. Could you not at least outline it to us?

Mr. WILLETT. I have that in these reports.

The CHAIRMAN. When you come to the reports you will talk about that?

Mr. WILLETT. They gave me the idea which I suggest.

The CHAIRMAN. Now just elaborate on that as much as you can, without going too much into detail. Just give us your general ideas about it.

Mr. WILLETT. In the first place, I would put a duty on all foreign sugars, outside of domestic cane and beet and sugars from our insular possessions, so high that not a pound would ever come into this country, $5 a hundred, if necessary. I would trust to the increased production of sugars in our country and in our insular possessions to prevent the price rising to anything like the tariff wall. I would trust to the competition between those countries, which would result in a few years to keep the price down to the consumer.

The CHAIRMAN. Would you be afraid of combination among those people?

Mr. WILLETT. Not a bit; but at the same time I would prevent it by legislation, if necessary. If there was any necessity for it, it can be prevented by legislation. Now, having fixed your tariff wall so high that no sugar can come in from abroad, then fix your internal-revenue tax at 40 cents a hundred, the same as Great Britain's duty of 40 cents. Every consumer in Great Britain pays 40 cents a hundred tax in the way of customs duty. No individual in Great Britain gets his sugar without paying something on it.

The CHAIRMAN. In other words, that is the revenue we would get, and we would get it through an internal-revenue tax?

Mr. WILLETT. We would get 40 cents a hundred on all the sugars produced in Porto Rico, Hawaii, and the Philippine Islands, and all sugars produced in the United States, cane and beet.

The CHAIRMAN. That would be where we would get our revenue?

Mr. WILLETT. We would get our revenue there, and also on Cuban sugars. Now, I have not worked the plan out to see whether 40 cents should be charged to Cuban sugars or whether Cuban sugars should be assessed a certain duty, the same as Denmark does. Denmark has a duty of $1.20, and also they assess 41 cents after it passes through the refinery. How that should be adjusted I have not worked out at all. The simple idea I give you is getting 40 cents revenue on every 100 pounds of sugar which the consumer uses in the United States. That would figure out more than your present revenue—over $53,000,000. Now, as production and consumption increased, your revenue would increase on that basis, whereas on your present tariff basis, as your domestic production increases and your consumption increases, your revenue decreases.

The CHAIRMAN. Where would the consumer come in? How would he get sugar any cheaper? Has he got to wait until production is stimulated to the amount of our consumption, and, if we judge by past history, will that time ever come?

Mr. WILLETT. That must be regulated by the Government just as the Russian Government does.

The CHAIRMAN. In other words, we would have to regulate the price at which the sugar was sold to the consumer the same as Russia does?

Mr. WILLETT. Russia establishes the price. When the price rises above a certain amount, sugars can come in. If the duty is $5 a hundred against foreign sugars and there is a scarcity of sugar in the United States, or the price rises above a certain limit, then your Secretary of the Treasury or the President and his Cabinet shall have discretion to reduce the duty for a limited period of time to bring in sugars to equalize the market. That is the way in Russia. It makes an entire change in your method, but it will come some day.

Mr. MALBY. Mr. Willett, we are talking somewhat informally about this matter, and I am not trying to talk in any partisan sense, but to get your judgment about these matters.

Mr. WILLETT. As to a reduction of tariff?

Mr. MALBY. Yes. This Government is not wholly without experience as to the effect of a total reduction of our tariff, under very advantageous circumstances. For instance, during the McKinley law, when we admitted sugar free, in order to see to it that our domestic industry did not perish we gave a bounty, and in that manner kept it alive.

Mr. WILLETT. Not at all. It had no such influence. At the time the bounty was put on we had six factories in the country, and at the time the bounty was taken off there were only five in operation. That is increasing the business in an Irish way. In other words, bounties do not go in this country.

Mr. MALBY. I do not think they go anywhere. They have been abolished substantially everywhere. What I wanted to call your attention to in particular was this: It is true our own supply was very small, and at that time we were getting our supply very largely from abroad?

Mr. WILLETT. Our domestic production was almost nothing.

Mr. MALBY. Well, say it was nothing. Therefore we would naturally expect that our own home supply being practically nothing, and our market being in the control of foreign countries, under those circumstances we would have gotten the full amount of the reduction of the tariff; but my recollection of the matter is that we did not, even when we did not have any domestic supply.

Mr. WILLETT. That leads me to say that circumstances and conditions and the amount of production in those days as compared with these days requires a different outlook on the tariff from what it did in those days.

Mr. MALBY. Well, we did not get it at that time. I do not know for what reason. We reduced the tariff, took it off, and the consumer did not get the benefit.

Mr. WILLETT. As a matter of fact, we are marching on toward an internal-revenue tax, like all other countries of Europe. If this proposition can be worked out I would like to see two bills introduced in Congress at this session, one along present lines and the other along other lines.

The CHAIRMAN. I do not see how the consumer would benefit unless the production greatly increased.

Mr. WILLETT. The consumer would have to trust to Congress to prevent a combination or a rise in prices; otherwise you could not put your tariff wall as high as I suggest. You could do that by putting your tariff wall low or by Government protection.

The CHAIRMAN. For instance, here is a situation we are confronted with: It is admitted, so far as sugar conditions in continental United States are concerned, counting both its refining and its beet-sugar interests, that the American Sugar Refining Co. controls a very large amount—probably more than 50 per cent—of the industry. Is that a condition to invite trusting those people to that extent? Does not the overpowering size of this one concern make it easy for them to cooperate?

Mr. WILLETT. Is there any evidence before the committee that the American Sugar Refining Co. have taken advantage of their position to enhance the price of sugars in the United States? Mr. Wiley testified they had not.

The CHAIRMAN. Of course, we would not like to express an opinion as to what has been proven. I am just asking whether there is not danger they might do that.

Mr. WILLETT. If there was any danger about it, it would have been under the former management and not under the present management.

The CHAIRMAN. How would we control that, unless we fixed the price by law?

Mr. WILLETT. Study the way other nations control it. You can control it the same as they do.

The CHAIRMAN. How do they control it, by fixing the price?

Mr. WILLETT. Russia controls it in the way I have described, by fixing a maximum price. Whenever the price of granulated rises 24 cents a hundred pounds above the price which the Government had fixed on the 1st of September that it should not exceed, at least, then, as I say, the Government takes measures to let in foreign sugars, or if they did not let in foreign sugars, they would put the reserve on the market.

Mr. HINDS. Is not that action of Russia a part of her system of paternalism?

Mr. WILLETT. Entirely so. It is all paternalism in the sugar industry in Russia.

Mr. HINDS. And while it may be admitted that paternalism in this instance works well, yet on the whole the paternalism of Russia is a curse to the country, is it not?

Mr. WILLETT. It is a great disadvantage to the consumers of sugar throughout the world. For instance, in 1910, when European sugars rose to 19 shillings, there were 700,000 tons of sugar bottled up in Russia by the Government, which could not possibly come out. If that sugar had come on the market, the price would never have risen above 12 or 13 shillings.

Mr. HINDS. It is possible that even the worst system of government ever devised on earth could have some good things in it. We may admit that this paternalism regulating the price of sugar works well, and yet, generally, the paternalism of Russia, applied to the various relations of her people, works badly, does it not? It is a bad principle, is it not?

Mr. WILLETT. From my experience of late years, it does not seem to me that would be required at all. The Government would never find it necessary to do that sort of thing. I think the people interested in the sugar industry of their own accord would see to it that such a measure was not likely to be called into action or needed to be called into action.

Mr. MALBY. Mr. Willett, I have in mind a case in this country which I think verifies absolutely your theory. I recall the fact to be that not so many years ago everybody seemed to recognize the absolute necessity of having a very high tariff on iron and steel in order that that industry might be firmly established in the United States. We have continued a policy of protecting that industry until to-day, notwithstanding the fact, strange as it may seem, that we pay at least twice as much to our employees in every single department of that industry, from the time the miner sticks his pick into the mine up to the time the manufacturer turns out the finished article; notwithstanding the fact twice the wages are paid, we find that the king of that industry testifies under oath before a special committee of Congress that the time has arrived, in his judgment, when steel does not require any further protection on the part of this country.

In other words, the industry has planted itself so firmly, and with its wonderful development of ways and means of manufacture and of economy in manufacture, that to-day we are able, single handed and alone, to compete with the world. It seems to me if that can be accomplished with reference to that industry, your theory of accomplishing it by taking into consideration a uniform tax on sugar from our insular possessions, and excluding the world, would in a very short period of time, when we are so near there already, accomplish the same result. And, on the contrary, our local competition among the Hawaiian planters, the Porto Ricans, Filipinos, and our own producers would do with sugar exactly as it has done with steel, the price would fall so low the question of a tariff would have nothing to do with regulating the price to the consumer. It is a great question, and I may be entirely mistaken, but it seems to me as though that is exactly where it would lead.

Mr. WILLETT. In my judgment the time will never arrive when you can remove the duty on sugar entirely.

Mr. MALBY. I do not know that I should ever want to. It is a source of great revenue, to begin with.

Mr. WILLETT. The time will never come when we will want to throw the United States open to the whole world.

Mr. MALBY. People are very loath to take to a new form of revenue. In producing revenue I think it is a good thing for all the people to contribute something. We have got to have the revenue, and to unload an internal tax or an external tax from one hand is simply to put it upon the other, and one class of our people would have to pay the tax of the other class.

Mr. WILLETT. In making such a change you must not lose sight of the fact that your tariff must be extremely high so that no foreign sugars can come in under any conditions. Some of these foreign countries charge over $8 foreign tax in order to promote their domestic industries.

Mr. MALBY. Perhaps we may get to this a little later, and I may be anticipating what you are going to say, but is it not a fact that since Germany has put on a tax sufficiently high to keep out all importations, the actual cost of production has been very much lowered?

Mr. WILLETT. I think Germany reached its lowest cost of production years ago. The industry has been a long time in existence and the cost of production in Germany has not varied much in the last 20 years.

Mr. MALBY. When did Germany put on a tariff so as to keep everybody out?

Mr. WILLETT. I could not answer that question.

Mr. MALBY. Was it more than 20 years ago?

Mr. WILLETT. Yes; along about the beginning of the industry, undoubtedly. Germany has always, from the beginning, protected her domestic industry. Of course, in the early years, when she was producing very much less sugar than her consumption required, her import taxes would naturally not be as high as to-day.

Mr. MALBY. In other words, the question resolves itself into this, whether Germany and other countries have decreased the cost of production under a policy of putting on a tariff which was so high that no country could get in.

Mr. WILLETT. The cost of production has been so extremely low for the last 20 years there has been very little opportunity for Germany to reduce it lower.

Mr. MALBY. So has the tariff been extremely high.

Mr. WILLETT. Do you think the tariff has anything to do with the cost of production?

Mr. MALBY. Not just at present; but did it not have in the beginning? Did it not have the effect of stimulating the home industry, and did it not cause the price of sugar to go down instead of going up?

Mr. WILLETT. Germany's cost of production was brought about in the early years by the increased percentage of sugars which she has been able to produce from her beet roots. Originally she produced only about 7 per cent, as against 17 per cent now, and that would reduce the cost of production.

Mr. MALBY. Undoubtedly that greatly assisted in doing so, but the question still remains as to whether or not she has progressed with that industry by reason of the fact she isolated herself from the whole world so no one could get in.

Mr. WILLETT. Decidedly.

Mr. RAKER. Under this theory you have been talking about, Mr. Willett, in regard to making a change, how would we prevent combination and restriction of production to keep the price at a point fixed by the refiners?

Mr. WILLETT. A combination between Hawaii, Porto Rico, Cuba—domestic cane and beets?

Mr. RAKER. Yes.

Mr. WILLETT. It is too big a proposition for a combination to entertain, it seems to me.

Mr. RAKER. How would you prevent a restriction being put upon production? Would they not take that subject up as they have done in the past and restrict the production of sugar?

Mr. WILLETT. There would be no occasion to do that until the production exceeded the consumption of the United States, would there?

Mr. RAKER. Evidently not.

Mr. WILLETT. And the moment the production increased the consumption of the United States from 200,000 to 500,000 tons, we immediately become an export nation, do we not?

Mr. RAKER. We ought to.

Mr. WILLETT. And there is the United Kingdom open to us and other foreign countries. Suppose we had had two or three hundred thousand tons more sugar this last fall than we required, could we not have sent them into Europe and obtained the high prices for them? Of course.

Among these consular reports is one which indicates that the refiners in China might have exported refined sugars to the United States largely were it not for some combination made by thePacific coast refiners to prevent them from so doing. Now the prices of sugar in Hongkong plus the duty on refined sugars in the United States do not show that there would be any profit by any such movement, and that as a matter of fact very few sugars come to the Pacific coast except at the port of Vancouver, British Columbia. So the statement made is not provable.

The CHAIRMAN. In your judgment, is it untrue?

Mr. WILLETT. Untrue, yes. How can you bring in sugar costing plus the duty more than you can buy it for in San Francisco?

The CHAIRMAN. You could not, if that is true.

Mr. WILLETT. That is a fact.

The CHAIRMAN. We have had some evidence in the record from some witnesses that at various times certain quantities of Asiatic sugars had been imported from China and sold at a considerable profit, in relatively small quantities, on the Pacific coast. If that is true, why would it not be to the interests of the American refiners to keep them from doing that?

Mr. WILLETT. I think I have already put into the record the amount of sugars from every country imported into San Francisco for a series of years, which shows a very small amount coming from China.

The CHAIRMAN. And yet several witnesses, who are on various sides of this controversy, have said that at different times a considerable amount, although relatively a small amount, has come from China.

Mr. WILLETT. It principally went into British Columbia, where there is a refinery which has a monopoly of that section of Canada, and these sugars were imported especially to offset the high prices which that particular refinery was charging for its sugars.

The CHAIRMAN. Now, that was this consul's idea—that they were about to do that same thing at San Francisco and they were interfered with by men he thought were representatives of the American Sugar Refining Co. or some of its allies?

Mr. WILLETT. I do not think there is anything in it at all.

Mr. HINDS. Mr. Willett, do you not think, considering the very low price of labor and low cost of doing business in the Orient, it might be possible for Hongkong to absorb a good part of that tariff difference and still make a profit?

Mr. WILLETT. Just the opposite.

Mr. HINDS. You think the expenses are higher in Hongkong?

Mr. WILLETT. Well, I will put it in this way: The Hongkong refiners make only about 200,000 tons of sugar a year, and they have a market for that sugar at prices which added to our 1.90 duty would not permit them to come into this country.

Mr. HINDS. They can do better by keeping it at home?

Mr. WILLETT. Yes, sir.

Mr. HINDS. But as a mere matter of what they might be able to do, by building new refineries with that cheap labor might it not be that they could absorb the difference and come in on the Pacific coast at a profit to themselves?

Mr. WILLETT. No; they could not, because they have been getting their supplies from the Philippine Islands largely, and our recent bill takes that supply away from them and that comes to the United States. They would have to pay more for their supplies of sugar from Formosa and other places, and since they have lost the Philippine sugars their supplies are going to cost them more.

The CHAIRMAN. Now, Mr. Willett, we will take up these reports, and if you can do so, give us a general idea of your method of analysis.

Mr. WILLETT. First, I reduced each consular report to a summary of its contents into United States currency and terms; second, reduced all the above for each country into a summary of the conditions and prices of sugar in each country in United States currency and terms.

Each of the above analyses can be printed in connection with the full consular report of each country, or the consular reports can be placed on file and the above two summaries printed, giving the sum and substance of each of the consular reports in good form for American readers. I have indicated pages in consular reports for comparisons in some instances.

The CHAIRMAN. Mr. Willett, what country or countries of any considerable size have you found where the consumer, after he pays taxes of all kinds, buys granulated sugar at the retail stores at a smaller price than the United States consumers?

Mr. WILLETT. It is dearer in every country with possibly three or four exceptions.

The CHAIRMAN. What countries are the exceptions?

Mr. WILLETT. The exceptions are the United Kingdom, Switzerland, and Germany at the present time. On the other hand, Italy is an exception the other way, paying about 12 cents a pound for sugar.

The CHAIRMAN. Now, suppose you take up the reports from the countries which present any unusual conditions, and the balance we will have printed without any explanation.

Mr. WILLETT. I can state the conditions in China in a very few words, and China is a very peculiar country. A Chinese retailer buying sugars down the coast where he gets his supplies from never knows what his sugars are going to cost him in his store ready to sell to the retail trade until he gets the goods in and has paid the taxes, because they generally come by boat up the coast and through canals, and whenever they pass a post or a station the authorities there assess a tax on it, and he never knows what that tax is until he gets his goods. There may be a half dozen of those taxes between the place where he has bought the sugar and the place he is going to sell it.

Mr. MALBY. Does the tax vary from time to time?

Mr. WILLETT. Yes, sir; various collectors collect the local tax and the boat goes along and pays it just like passing a tollgate.

Mr. FORDNEY. Mr. Willett, you stated that in Germany at the present time granulated sugar was furnished to the consumer at a less price than is paid here.

Mr. WILLETT. The refiner's price is less than paid here, and the consumer pays more, about the same difference, between the refiner's price as is paid here.

Mr. FORDNEY. I am unable to turn to it quickly, but I had it before me the other evening, that the consumer in 1910 paid 9.4 cents for refined sugar in Germany.

Mr. WILLETT. At Aix la Chappelle on July 6, 1911, the consul reports that the wholesale price of powdered sugar was 4.76 cents per pound, and the retail price was 5.01 cents, and that the wholesale price for granulated was 4.79, and the retail price 5.72 per pound; while the corresponding price in New York for granulated was 5.10 at wholesale. At Brunswick, in Germany, the wholesale price in 1911 averaged 4.42; in 1906, 3.88; in 1901, 6.23; in 1896, 4.64; in 1891, 5.61; in 1886, 5.56.

Mr. HINDS. Mr. Willett, what would be the price of sugar to the consumer in Germany if you deducted their internal revenue taxes?

Mr. WILLETT. Their internal revenue tax is 1.51.

Mr. HINDS. Mr. Willett, may I ask you a question? I do not know but what it is out of your line as a sugar expert, but do you think there are any families in the United States that reckon the use of sugar down so fine as the German families?

Mr. WILLETT. Never.

Mr. HINDS. Why don't we?

Mr. WILLETT. All our people are on a higher plan as regards a method of living.

Mr. HINDS. Have larger incomes and do not have to reckon so fine?

Mr. WILLETT. No, sir.

Mr. FORDNEY. Mr. Willett, what is the comparative per capita consumption of sugar in Germany and the United States? Have you got that information, or do you know about what it is?

Mr. WILLETT. I have it, but I have not got it before me. It is in the record. It is lower, of course, than it is in the United States. There are only two countries as high as the United States—the United Kingdom and Denmark. Denmark has run ahead of the United States. From 25 pounds she ran up to 86 pounds per capita.

Now, I am going to take up Canada, because Canada is a neighbor of ours, and we are perhaps interested in one particular feature of Canada.

In Canada the four cane refineries divide the territory and sell only through wholesalers, whom they employ as agents, giving them 5 per cent commission.

Mr. MALBY. They divide the whole territory?

Mr. WILLETT. Yes; the whole territory of Canada is divided into sections.

A wholesale grocers' guild at Quebec and Toronto and a maratime association guild at Halifax fix the prices for themselves and for the retailers as well. The refiners' prices follow New York prices closely. We cable them every day New York prices.

Mr. MALBY. Do they follow them by virtue of an agreement between themselves?

Mr. WILLETT. Yes; undoubtedly. They are all working together in harmony. So the refiner's price is the list price, less 5 per cent to wholesalers. Wholesaler's price is refinery price, less 1 per cent to retailer, and the retailers are requested to add at least 25 cents per hundred pounds to cost. The consumers pay about the same prices as in the United States. Refiners, wholesalers, and retailers all make some money. The average difference between raws and refined is

$1.25 against 89 cents at New York. Duties: The general duties are 83½ cents per hundred pounds on 96° raws, and $1.25 per hundred pounds on 100° test refined, and there is a preferential duty of 52.5 cents per hundred pounds on 96° test raws.

Mr. MALBY. A preferential duty to whom?

Mr. WILLETT. With Great Britain and her colonies.

Mr. MALBY. Her possessions?

Mr. WILLETT. Her possessions. There is a dumping duty which keeps the United States sugar out of Canada.

The CHAIRMAN. How much is that duty?

Mr. WILLETT. That dumping duty really applies only against the United States.

The CHAIRMAN. You mean it is a tax of so much in addition to the regular duties?

Mr. WILLETT. Yes, sir; in addition to those I have mentioned.

The CHAIRMAN. Why do they call it a dumping duty?

Mr. WILLETT. That is what they call it in Canada. It prevents refined bought in New York at export prices from going into Canada at the general tariff rate of $1.25 per hundred pounds, as it would constantly do but for the dumping tax, which tax is the difference between the export price in New York and the refiners' duty-paid list price in New York. November 1, say, if list price, duty paid, is $6.468 per hundred pounds, and the export price is $4.70 per hundred pounds, the difference is $1.768, and that would be the dumping tax. But if that difference ever amounts to more than 15 per cent ad valorem, the dumping tax in actual operation at present is limited to an increase of 15 per cent. If it ever amounts to more than 15 per cent, then 15 per cent is substituted for the $1.76. At the present time the local duty-paid price in New York is $6.46, and 15 per cent of that would be 97 cents a hundred. The tax to-day in Canada would be 97 cents a hundred pounds, and then the general duty of $1.25 per hundred pounds added to that would make a total duty into Canada of $2.22 a hundred pounds, which is prohibitive.

On this basis the cost of American granulated delivered in Montreal, duty paid, would be: Export price in New York, $4.70 per hundred pounds; freight, 10 cents per hundred pounds; duty and dumping tax, $2.22 per hundred pounds; a total of $7.02 per hundred pounds; against a price of $5.90 per hundred pounds, less 5 per cent, in Montreal for Canadian granulated on the same date.

In addition to that they have what they call equalizing sugar freight rates for the Province of Quebec; that is to say, a refiner in Montreal, if the actual rate to a point is 44 cents by railroad, will charge the buyer of his sugars only 40 cents freight, losing the difference of 4 cents. In other cases, to another point, the freight is 6 cents and the buyer is charged 8 cents; at another point the freight is 34 cents and the buyer is charged only 25 cents, equalizing freight rates for the purpose of preventing competition between two wholesale dealers in a certain town.

Mr. RAKER. Who establishes the freight rates—the Government of Canada?

Mr. WILLETT. No, sir; the refiners of Canada.

The CHAIRMAN. And the sellers of sugars are the people who equalize those rates?

Mr. WILLETT. They issue these books every summer and winter, which they give their salesmen when they go out, and the object of that is explained in these papers. I can explain it in a few words like this, for instance: Suppose Michigan was selling sugars at Detroit at a certain price and suppose New York wanted to compete; New York could not compete, because the rate of freight would be put on greater for New York than for the Michigan factories, and that gives Michigan that factory to sell in; but under this arrangement the Halifax people can sell sugar right down to within 5 miles of Montreal at the same prices that the Montreal refiner can sell sugars there at, but not less. They are all regulated so that no one district can interfere with any other district.

Mr. FORDNEY. Mr. Willett, in addition to that, in order to encourage the production of domestic beet sugar, Canada permits the sugar factory to import two pounds of foreign sugar for one made and reduces the duty 50 cents a hundred pounds, or something like that. Have you any information on that subject?

Mr. WILLETT. Oh, yes; it is all in these reports. The three beet-sugar factories in Canada are located at Wallaceburg, Berlin, and Raymond. These factories produce granulated refined sugar direct from the beet root, and their factory prices are 10 cents to 20 cents per hundred pounds below the cane granulated prices. The Canadian Government privileges the beet factories to import at preferential rates twice the amount of sugar they produce from domestic beets. This enables them to run the year around.

Mr. FORDNEY. What is the preferential; do you know, Mr. Willett?

Mr. WILLETT. Fifty-four and one-half cents a hundred pounds against the regular rate of $1.25 per hundred pounds.

Mr. RAKER. That is a sort of bonus to those people?

Mr. WILLETT. Yes; it is a sort of bounty.

Now, for instance, within a few days they have purchased a cargo of Java sugars which are now landing at Philadelphia at a cost in Philadelphia of $3.41 per hundred pounds for 96° test basis. As these Java sugars test from 97½ to 98° polarization must add 0.0625, and to place them on a 98° basis costs $3.4725. The freight to Wallaceburg is 13 cents per hundred pounds. The Canadian preferential duty on 98° test, 0.545, making the total cost at factory $4.1475 per hundred pounds, and the price of cane granulated at the factory was $5.65, less 5 per cent, or $5.37, and raws cost at factory $4.15, difference covering cost of refining and profit, $1.22 per hundred pounds.

And not only that, but under a new clause in their tariff they allow the cane-sugar refiners to import on the same preferential basis a specified amount.

Mr. RAKER. Do they give them a preferential, too?

Mr. WILLETT. Yes; on the same basis as the beet men, but a less amount, not one-half, but 20 per cent of their production. All sugars that go into Canada from Great Britain or British possessions come in under a preferential duty.

Mr. FORDNEY. Of 25 per cent?

Mr. WILLETT. On page 16 of this summary you will find the Canadian duties. Above No. 16 Dutch standard, all refined, per hundred pounds, they start from 88° test and pay 72 cents preferential against $1.08 general that runs up by degrees to 100 test. On the 100° test the preferential is 84 cents and the general is $1.25. Not above No. 16 Dutch standard there is a preferential and a general running from 75° up to 100°, and from 31.5 cents up to 56.5 as against a general tariff from 52 cents to 89.5, and then there is the beet-factory special, per hundred pounds, from 31.5 cents to 56.5 cents.

The beet-sugar production started in Canada with 7,478 tons in 1903 and has now reached 9,000 tons. They have not made a great success of it in Canada. Two of the original four factories were moved to the United States and one has been built since. There are only three factories now established in Canada.

Mr. RAKER. Do they import any of that sugar from Michigan?

Mr. WILLETT. What sugar?

Mr. RAKER. Does the dumping tax against the United States apply on the sugar which the beet factories import?

Mr. WILLETT. Oh, yes.

I might say that the beet-sugar factory at Wallaceburg is managed by people who are independent and who have cut loose from these arrangements of the cane-sugar refiners in Montreal and Toronto. They are a free lance and sell where they please and put the prices where they please.

Mr. RAKER. Is there any quantity of beets raised in Canada shipped to the United States?

Mr. WILLETT. Oh, yes.

Mr. RAKER. Any considerable quantity?

Mr. WILLETT. I do not think there is very much.

Mr. RAKER. You have not gone into that?

Mr. WILLETT. No; I know they do, but I do not know the amount.

I wish to give a comparison of grade refined made by Henry Tate & Son, of London and Liverpool, with the grades made by New York refiners.

English cubes better than American cubes, but not as good as American cut-loaf. Mineral-water crystals are a semicoarse granulated, without bluing. Crushed is a semisoft sugar, about what our confectioner's A would be when dried. Caster is extrafine granulated, used in casters for sprinkling on pies or desserts. Icings and pulverized are standard powdered. Coffee crystals are large, brilliant crystals, made larger than manufactured here. Crystals are large, brilliant grain sugars, made in several sizes. In the United States there is a large grain sugar called confectioner's granulated, which might compare favorably with some grades of English crystals. Yellows—the four grades of English yellows—are hard to compare with softs here. Tate's thirds are about our No. 4 or No. 5; Tate's 4 about our No. 8 or No. 9; Primrose about our No. 12; Canary about our No. 14, only much brighter in color.

I wish to submit one of the price lists of Henry Tate & Sons, as follows:

(Stamped:) American Consulate, Bradford, England, July 1, 1911.

[Agents and wholesale dealers only—London, June 29, 1911.]

Price List—Henry Tate & Sons (Ltd.), Sugar Refiners, London and Liverpool.

CONDITIONS OF SALE.

Payment.—Cash (in London or Liverpool) within 14 days, less 2½ per cent discount, or before delivery, if required. Interest allowed for unexpired time on cash payments. If 14 days are exceeded, interest will be added from date of invoice to day of payment. Discount will be forfeited unless payment be made within 21 days.

All sugar, whether paid for or not, is covered from risk of damage by fire whilst lying at the refineries or warehouses in London or Liverpool or at any depot, but in no case exceeding the market value of the goods immediately before the fire.

Every care is taken to keep sufficient sugar at the various depots to supply all requirements, but immediate delivery is not guaranteed, and no responsibility will be admitted for delay in consequence of strikes or stress of weather, fog, ice, or other causes beyond sellers' control.

Depots are not intended for use as warehouses.

Buyers must take delivery at once.

Any free depot may be withdrawn without notice, and a charge made for conveyance.

Telegrams, "Tateson, London," "Tateson, Liverpool."

[All quotations subject to March fluctuations.]

London sugars.

	Price in London, less 2½ per cent discount.	Alterations.
Cubes:		
No. 1 .... 1-cwt. cases	19/3	4.29–4.18.
H. T. S. .... do	18/9	
No. 2 .... do	18/9	4.08–3.98.
Afternoon Tea .... do	20/-	
(Any of the above in 28-pound boxes at 6d. per hundredweight extra.)		
Granulated, fine	17/9	3.86–3.77.
In cotton-lined bags 1½d. per hundredweight extra.		
Granulated, fine, 4 and 7 pound linen bags	19/6	
Granulated, fine, 2-pound linen bags	19/9	
Granulated, in 14-pound jute bags	18/9	
Granulated, in 28-pound jute bags	18/6	
Granulated, standard	17/4½	3.78–3.69.
Granulated, standard, 4 and 7 pound linen bags	19/1½	
Granulated, standard, 2-pound linen bags	19/4½	
Caster, A .... in cotton-lined bags	18/-	
Caster, B .... do	17/10½	
Mineral water crystals, No. 1	17/6	
Mineral water crystals, No. 2 (Ex. London only)	17/-	
Crushed, No. 1	17/4½	
Crushed, No. 2	.....	
Nibs (1-hundredweight bags)	17/9	
Carriage paid to station on 3 hundredweights and over:		
Caster, finest—		
In cotton-lined bags	19/6	
14-pound jute bags	20/6	
28-pound jute bags	20/3	
4 and 7 pound linen bags	21/3	
2-pound linen bags	21/6	
Icing (1-hundredweight drums [1])	19/6	
Pulverized	19/6	
1-hundredweight bags 3d. per hundredweight extra.		

[1] Drums charged for, but will be credited on return.

FORWARD DELIVERY.

No. 1 cubes, at 19/4½; No. 2 cubes, at 18/10½—August.
No. 1 cubes, at 19/1½; No. 2 cubes, at 18/7½—September.

SUGAR IN CARTONS AND TINS.

[In 1-hundredweight cases.]

Carriage paid on three hundredweights and over where C. and D. rates apply in England and the principal towns in Scotland and chief seaports in Ireland:

Cubes, afternoon tea, 1, 2, and 7 pound cartons	23/3
Cubes, No. 1—1, 2, 4, and 7 pound cartons	22/6
Caster, 1 and 2 pound cartons	22/6
Coffee crystals, 2-pound cartons	24/9
Granulated, fine, 2 and 4 pound cartons	21/9

Carriage paid on three hundredweights and over to stations in England and Wales, principal towns in Scotland, and chief seaports in Ireland:

Caster, icing or pulverized—

4-pound tins	27/–
7-pound tins	26/–
14-pound tins	24/6
28-pound tins	23/9

Liverpool sugars.

	Price in Liverpool less 2½ per cent discount.	Alterations.
Crystals:		
Ones	17/9	
Small ones	17/7½	
Twos	17/6	
Bright	17/6	
Granulated:		
Standard	17/3	3.848-3.752
H. T. S	17/4½	3.76 -3.69
Coarse	17/9	
Fine	17/9	
Superfine[1]	18/–	
Caster[1]	18/1½	
Caster C[2]	18/7½	
Caster A[2]	18/7½	
Caster B[2]	18/9	
Icing, in 2-hundredweight bags[2]	19/1½	
Icing, in 1-hundredweight drums[3]	18/10½	
Icing, in 28-pound tins	21/3	
Icing, in 14-pound tins	22/1½	
Icing, in 7-pound tins	23/7½	
Pulverized, in 2-hundredweight bags[2]	19/–	
Pulverized, in 1½-hundredweight drums[3]	18/9	
Yellows:		
Thirds	16/–	
Fourths	15/3	
Primrose	14/6	
Canary	14/–	
Caster, in 4 and 7 pound linen bags, in 1-hundredweight cases	19/10½	
Granulated, fine, in 4 and 7 pound linen bags, in 1-hundredweight cases	19/6	
Mineral-water sugars:		
Crystals, A	17/9	
Crystals, B	17/7½	
Crystals C	17/6	
Granulated	17/6	

[1] In cotton-lined bags. [2] Paper-lined bags. [3] Drums charged for, but will be credited on return.

1-hundredweight bags 3d. per hundredweight extra.

London sugars.

LIST OF DEPOTS FOR CUBES.

	Cubes.	Extra charge, if any, per hundredweight.
England:		
*Ashford	1, 2, and H. T. S.	Nil.
*Aylesbury	do	Nil.
Birmingham	do	Nil.
*Bishop's Stortford	do	Nil.
Blackburn	do	3d.
*Boston	do	Nil.
Bradford	do	Nil.
Brentford	do	Nil.
Brighton	do	Nil.
*Bristol	do	Nil.
Burnley	do	3d.
*Cambridge	do	Nil.
*Canterbury	do	Nil.
Carlisle	do	3d.
*Chatham	do	Nil.
*Colchester	do	Nil.
Coventry	do	Nil.
*Cowes, Isle of Wight	do	Nil.
*Croydon	do	Nil.
Derby	do	Nil.
Dewsbury	do	Nil.
Douglas, Isle of Man	do	4d.
*Dover	do	Nil.
Dudley Port	do	Nil.
Emscote	do	Nil.
Etruria	do	3d.
*Falmouth	do	Nil.
*Faversham	do	Nil.
*Folkestone	do	Nil.
Gloucester	do	Nil.
*Goole	do	Nil.
Gravesend	do	Nil.
*Grimsby	do	Nil.
Halifax	do	Nil.
*Hemel Hempstead	do	Nil.
Huddersfield	do	Nil.
*Hull	do	Nil.
*Ipswich	do	Nil.
Lancaster	do	4½d.
Leeds	do	Nil.
Leicester	do	Nil.
Liverpool	do	Nil.
*Lincoln	do	4½d.
*Lowestoft	do	Nil.
*Lynn	do	1½d.
*Maidstone	do	Nil.
Manchester	do	Nil.
*Margate	do	Nil.
*Middlesbrough	do	Nil.
*Newcastle-on-Tyne	do	Nil.
*Newport, Isle of Wight	do	Nil.
*Northampton	do	Nil.
*Norwich	do	Nil.
England—Continued:		
Nottingham	1, 2, and H. T. S.	Nil.
*Oxford	do	Nil.
*Plymouth	do	Nil.
*Poole	do	Nil.
*Portsmouth	do	Nil.
Preston	do	Nil.
*Ramsgate	do	Nil.
*Reading	do	Nil.
*Ryde, Isle of Wight	do	2d.
*Sandwich	do	Nil.
*Scarborough	do	Nil.
Sheffield	do	Nil.
*Sittingbourne	do	Nil.
*Southampton	do	Nil.
Southend-on-Sea	do	Nil.
Stockport	do	Nil.
*Stockton	do	Nil.
*Sunderland	do	Nil.
*Tonbridge	do	1½d.
*Torquay, ex quay only, 25 cases or 25 bags.	do	4½d.
*Torquay, ex quay only, 5-ton lots.	do	3d.
Wakefield	do	Nil.
Walsall	do	1½d.
*West Hartlepool	do	Nil.
*Weymouth	do	3d.
Whitehaven	do	3d.
*Whitstable	do	Nil.
Wigan	do	3d.
Wolverhampton	do	Nil.
*Yarmouth	do	Nil.
*York	do	Nil.
Wales:		
Barry	do	Nil.
Cardiff	do	Nil.
Llanelly	do	Nil.
Newport, Monmouth	do	1½d.
Swansea	do	Nil.
Scotland:		
Aberdeen	do	Nil.
Dundee	do	Nil.
Glasgow	do	Nil.
Leith	do	Nil.
Ireland:		
Belfast	do	1½d.
Cork	do	3d.
Dublin, ex store	do	1½d.
Dublin, ex quay (25 cases).	do	Nil.
Limerick	do	6d.
Londonderry	do	3d.
Waterford	do	3d.

*Caster, granulated, and mineral-water crystals delivered from these depots.

Liverpool sugars.

LIST OF DEPOTS FOR ALL QUALITIES.

	Extra charge per hundred-weight.
England:	
Apperley Bridge	3d.
Ashton-under-Lyne	Nil.
Atherton	1½d.
Bacup	2d.
Barnsley	3d.
Barrow, 2-ton lots	Nil.
Barrow, lesser lots	1d.
Bingley	2d.
Birkenhead	Nil.
Birmingham	2d.
Blackburn	Nil.
Blackpool	2d.
Bolton	Nil.
Botany Bay	Nil.
Bradford	2d.
Brighouse	2d.
Bristol	2d.
Burnley	1½d.
Bury	1½d.
Carlisle	2d.
Chester	1½d.
Chesterfield	3d.
Church	1½d.
Derby	3d.
Dewsbury	2d.
Dudley Port	2d.
Elland	2d.
Etruria	1½d.
Potteries group—	
Burslem	
Cobridge	
Fenton	
Hanley	
Longport	1½d.
Longton	
Newcastle-under-Lyme	
Stoke	
Tunstall	
Halifax	2d.
Hebden Bridge	2d.
Heywood	1½d.
Huddersfield	2d.
Hyde	1d.
Kendal	4d.
Lancaster	Nil.
Leeds	2d.
Leicester	3d.
Leigh	Nil.
Macclesfield	3d.
Manchester	Nil.
Nelson	2d.
Nottingham	3d.
Oldham	2d.
Penrith	4½d.
Prescot	Nil.
Preston	Nil.
Rochdale	1½d.
Sheffield	2d.
England—Continued.	
Shipley	2d.
Shewsbury	2d.
Skipton	2d.
Southport	Nil.
Sowerby Bridge	2d.
Stalybridge	Nil.
Stockbridge (for Keighley)	2d.
Stockport	Nil.
St. Helens	Nil.
Todmorden	2d.
Tottington	3d.
Tyldesley	1d.
Ulverston (steamer)	1½d.
Ulverston (rail)	4d.
Wakefield	3d.
Walsall (rail)	3d.
Walsall (canal)	2d.
Warrington	Nil.
Whitehaven	2d.
Wigan	Nil.
Wolverhampton	2d.
Workington	3d.
Wales:	
Brymbo	3d.
Carnarvon and Menai Straits	1½d.
Cardiff	Nil.
Conway	1½d.
Haverfordwest	3d.
Llanelly	Nil.
Milford Haven	3d.
Mold	3d.
Newport (Mon.)	Nil.
Pembroke Dock	3d.
Port Talbot	Nil.
Swansea	Nil.
Wrexham	2d.
Isle of Man:	
Castletown [1]	
Douglas [1]	
Peel [1]	Nil.
Port St. Mary [1]	
Ramsey [1]	
Douglas I. of M. S. P. Co.	Nil.
Ramsey (1 ton), I. of M. S. P. Co.	
Ramsey (4 cwt. and under 1 ton)	1½d.
Scotland:	
Aberdeen	3d.
Annan	1½d.
Ayr, direct steamer, 2-ton lots	1½d.
Ayr, via Belfast and Ayr S. S. (5 cwt. and over)	3d.
Dumfries	1½d.
Dundee	3d.
Glasgow	Nil.
Inverness [2]	3d.
Kirkcaldy	4d.
Kirkcudbright	1½d.
Leith	3d.

[1] Manx Steam Trading Co.

[2] Shore dues buyer's account.

Special rates per rail when required.

This shows that on this date, June 29, 1911, cubes No. 1 were 4.18 net to anybody in any part of England, regardless of freight. There is no freight on cube sugars. Henry Tate & Sons have 67 stations, or depots, they call them, throughout the United Kingdom, Scotland, Wales, Ireland, and the Isle of Man, at which they deliver their cube sugars free of all expense at the same prices they charge in London, and the same is true of granulated from Liverpool. They do not manufacture granulated in London.

The CHAIRMAN. That is entirely different from our system.

Mr. WILLETT. Entirely different. It is just as if the New York price was the same in Chicago, Kansas City, or anywhere else. Of course, England is a smaller country. That is one feature of England, and another feature is that England has sugar organizations all over the country which make the prices for the retail grocers' association. As I say, that applies to cube sugars. On other grades—there are 20 or 30 grades of sugar—freight is added in some instances and in some instances it is not.

The CHAIRMAN. Why do they make that distinction between cubes and other sugars?

Mr. WILLETT. I think it is because other sugars come in from foreign countries, from Germany and elsewhere.

The CHAIRMAN. Are the cube sugars made in England?

Mr. WILLETT. Yes, sir; they are made in London.

The CHAIRMAN. You mean they are refined there from raw sugars shipped from other countries?

Mr. WILLETT. Yes, sir; the granulated sugars are sold at London at the f. o. b. Hamburg price plus the freight to Liverpool and to destination, and run below the London prices about a quarter of a cent a pound.

Now, the next and only other feature I will call your attention to about Great Britain is that there are organizations in every district of Great Britain, Wales, and Scotland which regulate all the prices of sugars to the retailers.

The CHAIRMAN. Wholesale organizations?

Mr. WILLETT. They are retail organizations and wholesale, too. This paper called the Grocer and Oil Trade Review, of July 15, 1911, was among the reports, and gives an account of the annual meeting of the Federation of Grocers' Associations.

The CHAIRMAN. That is an English trade journal?

Mr. WILLETT. Yes; and gives the number of its different committees regulating prices on almost everything you can conceive of in the grocery line—canned goods, proprietary articles, and everything else. They are just now discussing a rather singular thing, that all sugars sold are sold with the paper package included in the weight, and the Government proposes to make statutory regulations that they shall be sold by the net weight, and this association says: "Looked at from the retailer's point of view, the inspector's proposal (that is, the Government's proposal) for new legislation to provide for the sale of all goods, with certain exceptions, by net weight are neither practicable nor desirable."

The CHAIRMAN. They want to charge for the weight of the paper?

Mr. WILLETT. Yes; and they are opposed to a change.

The CHAIRMAN. Do we do that in America?

Mr. WILLETT. No; we sell net weight in America, but selling by gross weight is a very common occurrence among the various countries.

The CHAIRMAN. In this country do we not charge the gross weight in selling to the consumer? Don't they put the sack on the scales and then weigh out the sugar in 1-pound or 2-pound or 5-pound packages?

Mr. WILLETT. Oh, no; they put the sugar into the scales and then do it up in a paper, but in England they do it up in a paper and weigh it.

The CHAIRMAN. That is not materially different from our own practice, after all.

Mr. WILLETT. No. This association is also discussing objectionable forms of advertisements, like house-to-house canvassing, and also the subject of stocking bonuses.

Mr. RAKER. In this country they sell the gross weight. In other words, they take a sack and put it on the scales and fill it with sugar, and the sack and sugar weighs so many pounds.

Mr. WILLETT. No; I beg your pardon. The scales are regulated so the amount of sugar which goes in the scales is, say, 100 pounds.

This paper also gives an account of the meeting of the management committee of the Birmingham and Midland Counties Association, and they say:

> In accordance with the instructions of the committee, arrangements have been made with the whole of the company shops to advance the price of sugar throughout Birmingham and district and the outlying places in the Black country, with the exception of Great Bridge and Bilston. The prices now ruling were: Pieces, 1¾d. per pound; granulated and crystals, 2d. per pound; lump and castor, 2¼d. per pound. He was glad to say that according to correspondence which had come to hand that morning there was a possibility that Great Bridge and Bilston would come into line before the end of the week.

They were holding out from accepting the prices fixed by the association.

The CHAIRMAN. Your report will show how much cheaper the people of Great Britain get sugar than the people of the United States?

Mr. WILLETT. Yes, sir.

The CHAIRMAN. In detail?

Mr. WILLETT. Yes. It is very little; 1.04 is the total difference they can possibly get. That is the difference in the tariff of the two countries. As a matter of fact, I think during 1911 they have not got anything like the difference which they ought to get.

The CHAIRMAN. Considering the tariff difference, they ought to get sugar a little over a cent a pound cheaper.

Mr. WILLETT. The internal-revenue system which I refer to would give the United States sugars at much less cost than Great Britain.

The CHAIRMAN. Does the United Kingdom have an internal-revenue system?

Mr. WILLETT. No; they have a duty of 40 cents a hundred.

The CHAIRMAN. As against our duty of what?

Mr. WILLETT. 1.04. I mean the difference is 1.04 between their duty and ours. I am comparing refined sugars which go into consumption there with refined sugars which go into consumption here.

The CHAIRMAN. You would not call the duty on refined here 1.34?

Mr. WILLETT. 1.44 I called the duty here and their duty is .40, making a difference of 1.04.

The CHAIRMAN. And there ought to be that difference in the price?

Mr. WILLETT. There ought to be, but during this last year there has not been that difference.

The CHAIRMAN. But ordinarily is there that difference?

Mr. WILLETT. From my recollection I would not say so.

The CHAIRMAN. The report will show?

Mr. WILLETT. Yes; the report will show that.

One of the members of the committee asked about Sweden. Sweden is one of the countries frequently referred to, but there is nothing about Sweden that compares with conditions in Denmark. Some one thought the conditions did compare.

The point about Sweden is that she has now brought her production up to her consumption, and is forced this coming year to either curtail her production or else get some means of exporting; and, by agreement with the Brussels convention, she has agreed not to export any sugar. So she is in a corner. She can not export, if she produces more sugar than she wants, to convention countries. Since this report came in they are putting up a new refinery. There are only two refineries there. They are just getting in the position the United States would be in if we were producing just a little more sugar than we required for our consumption. Then would come the problem which is up in Sweden to-day, as to what to do with that surplus. We could export, of course, because we are not bound by the Brussels convention.

The CHAIRMAN. Of course, after all, the world's supply and demand and the world's price is what regulates that.

Mr. WILLETT. But they can not export.

The CHAIRMAN. But we are not parties to the Brussels convention.

Mr. WILLETT. No. The production in Sweden is limited by a tariff of $1.82 a hundred on refined. The Brussels convention provides that if a country wants to export any of its sugars it must not have a tariff exceeding 52 cents a hundred—its excise tax. The production now is 110,000 to 140,000 tons, and there are countervailing duties on sugar from bounty countries, and the whole sugar production in Sweden is controlled by an industrial combination which sets the price by prices abroad and keeps the price just low enough to make imports unprofitable. Price lists issued July 7, just after the rise in German and English markets on the 1st of July, read: Cubes, $7.41 per hundred pounds wholesale, retail $8.18 per hundred pounds; granulated, $6.93 wholesale, $7.65 retail; against New York granulated, $5.10 wholesale, and New York cubes, $5.35. Retail prices are fixed by retail dealers' associations. Great complaint against the sugar trust.

Mr. FORDNEY. Mr. Willett, has this overproduction in Sweden changed the price to the consumer any?

Mr. WILLETT. It only takes place this present year. Last year they imported; they did not have enough by 1,100 tons. We did not have enough by 72,000 tons. It is a new condition in Sweden, so you can not tell.

The sugar industry is almost entirely in the hands of a trust, with paid-up capital of $36,180,000, which owns all Swedish refineries except one. All beet-sugar beets are grown in southern Sweden. Prices practically the same all over the country. The Government excise tax is $1.85 per 100 pounds, and also the customhouse duty is $1.85 per 100 pounds to $1.03 per 100 pounds, according to Dutch standard color. Sweden is a country which has not adopted the polariscope at all. There are two or three other countries which do not use the polariscope.

According to our own private information, this coming year the production in Sweden will exceed the consumption by 40,000 tons and as a consequence the factories' association estimates the coming crop at 121,600 tons against 171,000 tons last year. This reduction is largely due to the forced reductions in sowings, due to oversupply resulting from the large crop of last year. Based on present estimated stocks and average consumption, an oversupply of about 40,000 tons is indicated at the close of this campaign.

In regard to Spain, here is an item which may interest you. Since the Spanish War no sugars have gone from Cuba into Spain, with slight exceptions, and they have a tariff on imports of $6.94 at Valencia, $7 at Tenerife, and $7.44 at Seville, which is and was intended to be absolutely prohibitive. The direct tax paid by manufacturers to the Spanish treasury during the last three years amounted to about $2.85 per hundred pounds. Other consuls vary in their statement of this tax. There is a Spanish sugar corporation which deducts $0.177 per 100 pounds on sales above 10 tons from list prices of 10 tons or below. The independents undersell in some instances. Valencia says the Government compels refiners to open in all principal cities a regulating retail store, which fixes prices under Government sanction. The only difference in price allowed is the difference in freight to different points. Freight from factory to Madrid is 32 cents per 100 pounds, which is added to factory's price of $8.43 per 100 pounds for granulated and $10.64 per 100 pounds for loaf, making cost, wholesale, at Madrid, $8.75 for granulated and $10.96 for loaf, selling in Madrid at retail at 9.78 cents per pound for granulated and 12¼ cents per pound for loaf. Spain's crop of sugar beets in 1907 was 978,000 tons and in 1910 666,000 tons. The production of sugar and consumption, etc., from 1906 to 1909 is given in table on page 10. In 1910 there were 51 sugar refineries in Spain in operation. These factories apparently produced refined direct from the sugar beets, as no raw sugars appear to be marketed. In 1910 the per capita consumption was 13.02 pounds.

Mr. FORDNEY. What is the price of granulated sugar to the consumer?

Mr. WILLETT. Factories' price is $8.43 per 100 pounds, and of course the price to the consumer is more than that.

It is generally held by farmers' associations that beets can not be profitably raised in any part of Spain for less than $5.80 to $6.10 per ton of 2,000 pounds, while the relatively higher rates in Spain for coal, taxation, and freight are said to contribute to the abnormally high cost of sugar. The high cost of sugar and low wage scale prevents sugar from entering into the ordinary food of the laborers and small farmers, and is regarded by them as an inaccessible luxury. One consul says: "Wholesale prices refined at $8 to $8.20 per 100 pounds is considered excessively high, owing to the caprices of the ring of producers, who are exuberantly protected against competition from abroad by the customs tariff." Consumers suffer, recollecting that the average price of the best cane sugar, far superior to the present article, imported from Habana, used to cost no more than $6.54 to $8.20 per 100 pounds. The law of 1907 limiting the free manufacture of sugar by prohibiting the establishment of new refineries within a radius of 50 kilometers of any other refinery in operation has been repealed at the instance of beet-root growers, who complained that the restriction converted the industry into a complete monopoly and left them at the mercy of the sugar manufacturers' association, both as to the quantity of beets to be cultivated and the prices to be obtained for the crop. There was a consolidation of the sugar refineries, which was formed about 11 years ago, and consumption has fallen off heavily during that time.

Mr. MALBY. And there has been a constant rise in price?

Mr. WILLETT. Yes; and an enormous profit made by these refiners.

Mr. RAKER. Why do they not increase their production?

Mr. WILLETT. The reports say that the production is regulated. Now, in consequence of that complaint on the part of the consumers that they are paying so much more for sugar than they were when they got their sugars from Cuba, they are now agitating a reciprocity treaty with Cuba. My impression is they passed that through the Spanish Cortes quite recently.

Mr. Chairman, I want to thank you and the members of the committee for your many courtesies to me, and to say to you that I have given my testimony strictly from the standpoint of an expert, regardless of any personal views I may have. Furthermore, while the question has not been asked me or suggested by anyone, I want to make the statement that I do not own, and have not for a long time, a share of stock in any cane or beet factory or a sugar-producing factory in any country of the world. I have not a dollar's worth of interest in any sugar corporation and neither has my family, with the exception of 10 shares of American Sugar Refining Co. common and 5 shares of the Federal.

AUSTRIA-HUNGARY—BOHEMIA.

[Book 1, page 4, Budapest, July 11, 1911.]

Current prices of raw 88° analysis, $2.17 per 100 pounds.
Current prices of refined per 100 pounds wholesale:

Granulated	$7.50
Powdered	7.68
Cube	7.77
Loaves, 17.6 to 22 pounds	7.59
Loaves, 6.6 to 11 pounds	7.66

Retail prices vary from $0.097 to $0.194 per pound above wholesale. The custom in large towns of Hungary is to sell at retail with just enough advance over wholesale to cover cost of handling without profit. The State requires sugar to be sold to manufacturers at $5.91 per 100 pounds for same sugar selling wholesale at $7.50 per 100 pounds. Outports pay factory prices plus freight.

	Per 100 pounds.
Debreezen pays for granulated	$7.50
Plus 25 cents per 100 pounds freight	.25
	7.75
New York granulated	5.15
New York cubes	5.40

All refiners in Hungary are combined to maintain prices and avoid the competition of former years and have appointed the Hungarian General Credit Bank the sole agents for the sale of their product to retailers. The result of this combination is shown in change of prices and conditions.

In 1885 with raw sugar at $4.66 per 100 pounds, refined sold at $6.77 per 100 pounds. In 1900 raw had dropped to $2.72 per 100 pounds and refined advanced to $7.94.

[Per 100 pounds.]

Year.	Raw, 88°.	Refined loaf.	Difference.
1885	$4.66	$6.77	$2.11
1890	2.77	5.84	3.07
1895	2.31	5.30	2.99
1900	2.40	7.75	5.35
1905	2.41	7.57	5.16
1910	2.72	7.94	5.22

These prices are for loaf sugar.

[Book 1, page 7, Carlsbad, Bohemia, July 5, 1911.]

Prices, wholesale, governed by the Sugar Trust.

Granulated, wholesale, $7.50 per 100 pounds; cubes, wholesale, $7.70 per 100 pounds.

Retail prices fixed by shopkeepers in different parts of city, usually about 1 cent per pound above wholesale.

Factories deduct 2 per cent from list prices, cash 14 days, on lots of 22 pounds or over.

State excise tax is stated at $0.022 per pound ($3.50 per 100 pounds).

Aussig prices per 100 pounds f. o. b. for raw sugar 88° test.

1885	$4.71
1890	2.81
1895	2.35
1900	2.48
1905	2.41
1908	2.19

Prague prices per 100 pounds, refined.

	High.	Low.
1896	$6.58	$5.39
1898	6.65	6.63
1900	7.73	7.73
1902	7.73	7.73
1904	7.18	5.78
1906	6.10	5.58
1908	7.07	6.58

[Book 1, page 9, Eger, Bohemia, July 9, 1911.]

Wholesale, granulated, $6.12 per 100 pounds; wholesale, cubes, $7.37 per 100 pounds.

Retail prices are $1.22 per 100 pounds higher, which includes freight, etc., from factory to store and also a very small profit.

[Book 1, page 10, Prague, Bohemia, July 2, 1911.]

Forms of sugar:

(1) Cones, of about 13, 15, 22, and 26 pounds weight. Cones, also broken up.

(2) Small blocks one-half inch thick, seven-eighths inch square, used for tea and coffee, in paper boxes of 11 pounds each.

(3) Granulated in sacks of 220 pounds.

(4) Powdered in sacks of 55, 110, and 220 pounds.

Wholesale prices, cubes, $7.40 per 100 pounds; retail, 7.50 cents per pound. Wholesale prices, granulated, $6.41 per 100 pounds; retail, 6.80 cents per pound.

In Austria there is an internal-revenue tax amounting to $3.50 per 100 pounds for consumption.

When Bohemian sugar is exported the tax is remitted.

Wholesale prices are less 2 per cent discount cash in 10 days.

All Bohemian sugar is beet-root sugar.

[Book 1, page 12, Reichenburg, Austria, July 1, 1911.]

Wholesale, cubes, $7.36 per 100 pounds; retail, 7.386 cents per pound. Wholesale, granulated, $7.27 per 100 pounds; retail, 7.386 cents per pound.

Consul says no error in retail prices, as retailers claim to sell without profit. State tax of $3.50 per 100 pounds included in above prices.

[Book 1, page 14, Vienna, July 3, 1911.]

No taxes on exports.

Internal tax on consumption, $3.50 per 100 pounds.

Wholesale, cubes, $7.61 per 100 pounds; wholesale, granulated, $6.57 per 100 pounds.

Retail prices practically the same as wholesale. Use sugar to sell tea, coffee, etc.

No bounties in Austria.

[Book 1, page 1, Fiume, Aug. 5, 1911.]

No refiners in this district. No trade in raw sugar.

Government excise tax per 100 pounds ($3.498)	$3.50
Customs duty per 100 pounds on refined imports	.527
	4.027

Add these duties to wholesale quotations of raw or refined and add $0.092 to $0.18 for retail prices.

Refined quoted December, 1910	$2.65	per 100 pounds.
Add excise tax	3.50	
Refined, wholesale price	6.157	per 100 pounds.
For retail price add	.092	to 18 cents per 100 pounds.
	6.249 to $6.857	

Retail price December, 1910, 6.77 cents to 6.86 cents per pound.

Prices since 1901 have varied only about 1 cent to 2 cents per pound.

AUSTRIAN-HUNGARIAN CUSTOMS TARIFF.

New general tariff: Rates as modified by treaties with Germany, Russia, Italy, Belgium, Switzerland, and the United States:

Raws under 98° test, regular rate $2.40 per 100 pounds, but modified by treaties with above-mentioned countries to $0.481 per 100 pounds. Refined and all sugar testing over 98°, regular rate $2.40 per 100 pounds, but modified by treaties with above-mentioned countries to $0.527 per 100 pounds.

In addition to customs duties a consumption tax is levied at the rate of $3.50 per 100 pounds on beet sugar and cane sugar of even conditions.

Date.	Place.	Cubes, wholesale, per 100 pounds.	Cubes, retail, per pound.	New York refined, cubes.	Granulated, wholesale, per 100 pounds.	Granulated, retail, per pound.	New York granulated, net, refined.
1911.			Cents.			Cents.	
July 11.	Budapest	$7.77	0.0787-0.0796	5.292	$7.50	0.076-0.086	5.047
July 5.	Carlsbad	7.70	.087	5.145	7.50	.085	4.900
July 9.	Eger	7.37	.085	5.243	6.12	.072	5.047
July 2.	Prague	7.40	.075	5.145	6.41	.068	4.90
July 1.	Reichenburg	7.36	.07386	5.145	7.27	.0738	4.90
July 3.	Vienna	7.61	.0765	5.145	6.57	.0660	4.90
Aug. 5.	Fiume			5.782	6.15-6.67	.0625-.0675	5.537

Consuls at Reichenburg and Vienna call attention to retail prices as being about same as wholesale prices.

SUMMARY.

I gather from these consular reports that—

1. Beet sugar only is produced.

2. That 88° analysis is the basis of price for raw sugar, and the value declines by percentage of test, i. e., if 88° analysis is worth 2.17 cents per pound, 78° analysis is

worth 10 per cent less, or 1.95 cents per pound. (The trade allowance per degree is about 2.7 cents per 100 pounds. For 10° 27 cents, making 78° value 1.90 cents.—W. P. W.)

3. That the price of raws for export is the Hamburg f. o. b. quotation less freight from Aussig to Hamburg, or from other shipping station to Hamburg.

4. That inasmuch as all raw and refined sugar produced in Austria-Hungary and Bohemia and sold for export is based upon the Hamburg f. o. b. quotations, which are more accessible, steadier, and reliable than interior quotations, it is best to accept these as the value of both raws and refined for export. The interior quotations at Prague and Budapest can be used to advantage in estimating the difference between the cost of raw sugars to refiners and the wholesale price of refined for consumption, which difference covers the cost of refining and the refiners' profit.

1910—107 pounds raw cost	$2.72–$2.91	$7.94
Tax	3.50	
Refiners' cost of refining and profit on cubes, $0.53 per 100 pounds		6.41
		1.53

5. That the grades of refined manufactured and sold for consumption and export are principally loaves, cubes, granulated, and powdered, and also cone sugars.

6. The "cone" sugar is hot granulated poured into the cone-shaped molds, cooled and hardened, which when inverted are in the shape of "pyramids," so called in the United States.

7. That loaf (crushed sugar) is the cone broken up.

8. That granulated consists principally of so-called "first marks" granulated, which are not suitable for table use in the United States, but may be used by some manufacturers, and are valued at about 0.25 cent per pound below the price of American standard granulated.

9. That "first marks" granulated, as described in the London Sugar Exchange, means that the seller of such has the option of delivering any one or more of 27 marks or manufactures. When any special "first marks" are named in the sales, the price is about ¾d. to 1½d. higher to United Kingdom per 112 pounds.

10. That "cube" sugars are the ordinary cubes of the United States and other countries.

11. That the principal consumption is of loaf (or crushed), although that of granulated is on the increase, and is most largely exported.

12. That all the refiners in Hungary are united in a Sugar Trust (or Zucker-Kartell).

13. That all sugars for consumption are sold through one agent of this trust, the Hungarian General Credit Bank, and that the wholesale prices are fixed at Budapest for Hungary and at Prague for Bohemia.

14. That the price on July 2, 1911, of loaf sugar refined at Prague was 7.20 cents per pound, including the Government tax of 3½ cents per pound.

15. That the price of granulated "first marks" on the same date and place was 6.410 cents per pound, including the Government tax of 3½ cents per pound (retailing at 6.80 cents per pound).

16. That on July 6, 1911, the price of granulated at Hamburg was 3 cents per pound free on board without tax; plus tax, 1.51, makes 4.51.

17. That on July 2, 1911, the price of 88° analysis raw sugar at Prague was 5.89 cents per pound, including tax of 3½ cents (2.39 cents net), and retailed at 7 cents per pound, and at Hamburg 2.56 cents per pound, plus consumption tax of Germany, $1.51 per 100 pounds, makes $4.07 wholesale.

18. That during the past 25 years the Government tax has made changes. In 1889–90 and in 1894–95 the consumption tax was 2.003 cents per pound, and in 1899–1900 and up to the present time the consumption tax has been 3½ cents per pound.

19. That there is no bounty.

20. That there is no city tax on sugar imported into Prague.

21. That discounts of 2 per cent for cash are made on wholesale prices, if same are paid within 30 days.

22. That no raw sugar is used in Reichenburg, Bohemia, a city of 37,000 people, and loaf sugar is mostly used, the wholesale price of which on July 1, 1911, was 7.27 cents per pound and retailed at 7.36 cents per pound, with a tax of 3½ cents per pound included.

23. That throughout Austria-Hungary and Bohemia the retail-shop people make their own prices and generally claim to sell with little or no profit. An exception is at Carlsbad where the retailers add 10 points to the wholesale price.

24. That sugar is packed in various forms, boxes, bags, cartons, etc., and in various sizes, but no barrels are mentioned.

25. That a crown is $0.203 and that a kronen is the same, $0.203.

26. That in selling sugar for consumption from a center of production, the freight to destination is added to the price at the center of production, the same as in the United States.

27. That the yearly average quotation of raws of 88° analysis f. o. b. Aussig was in—

1885, 4.71 cents per pound against 3.00 cents f. o. b. Hamburg.
1890, 2.21 cents per pound against 2.67 cents f. o. b. Hamburg.
1895, 2.35 cents per pound against 2.13 cents f. o. b. Hamburg.
1900, 2.48 cents per pound against 2.24 cents f. o. b. Hamburg.
1905, 2.41 cents per pound against 2.48 cents f. o. b. Hamburg.
1908, 2.19 cents per pound against 2.22 cents f. o. b. Hamburg.

28. The Hungary State law provides sales of sugar to manufacturers at special reduction in price. In July, 1911, price to manufacturers 5.91 cents against price to other consumers 7.50 cents for same grade sugar.

29. There is a reciprocal duty or tax on transfers of sugar from Austria into Hungary or from Hungary into Austria of $0.294 per 100 pounds on raws and $0.322 per 100 pounds on refined.

30. French Fabricants Book gives a copy of the law confirmed January 2, 1908, in Austria and January 1, 1908, in Hungary, as follows:

"In order to assure to the industry of each of these two parts of the monarchy their natural market, a tax interchanging has been reestablished on the sugars transferred from the one into the other of these two countries. This tax on transfers is 3.50 and 3.30 crowns per 100 kilos ($0.294 to $0.322 per 100 pounds) of refined and of raws, respectively. These surtaxes on importations into the countries are well within the stipulations by the Brussels convention."

(Tax equals in United States currency $0.321 per 100 pounds on refined and $0.308 per 100 pounds on raws, according to the Fabricants Book. A German book says 3.20 crowns per 100 kilos on raw, which would be $0.294 per 100 pounds, as above, instead of $0.308.)

Brazil.

[Book 1, page 16, Pernambuco, September 9, 1911.]

1. Pernambuco is the chief market for receipts and exports of the sugar of Brazil.

2. Average production 65 tons per hectare (2.47 acres), averaging 10 Baumé (system of testing) and giving 17.4 per cent of the weight of the juice (higher in November and December); 17.4 per cent gives 17.1 per cent of available sugar.

3. Cost of producing a tons of cane is $1.32 to $1.65 per ton and cost of working is 66½ cents.

4. There are about 60 sugar mills near Pernambuco (10 open kettle to 1 sugar mill).

5. Sugar is made by American process (Louisiana).

6. (The largest factory is American built and another is now being planned by Americans.)

7. Cane bought from small planters is paid for on basis of price of sugar.

8. 1$000=1 milrei. 100 milreis=3¼ cents. 0$100=100 milreis.

9. There are 8 grades of sugar mentioned in consular report, none of which come to the United States, and nearly all of them are above No. 16 Dutch standard. (The grades which come to the United States are crystals—centrifugals—of No. 16 Dutch standard and lower. Muscovados of 84° to 88° test. These Brazil crystals in New York on November 17 were sold at 5.12 cents per pound, including duty of 1.685 cents, netting in Brazil about 3.20 to 3.25 cents f. o. b. at the shipping port, and at the same time sugars of 84° test were sold at 4.01 cents, including a duty of 1.265 cents. Few low-grade sugars have come here recently, but are sold to the United Kingdom every year to some extent.—W. P. W.)

New York granulated, 6.75; New York cubes, 6.95.

10. Prices of sugar given in the consulate general's report dated Rio de Janeiro, July, 1911, are as follows for crystals (centrifugals) from 1897 to 1911.

	Cents per pound
1897	7.22– 8.45
1898	8.18– 8.77
1899	11.36–11.81
1900	6.81– 7.55
1901	3.93– 4.54
1902	6.95– 8.45
1903	5.91– 7.22
1904	5.91– 6.36
1905	4.23– 4.84
1906	3.23– 3.63
1907	7.22– 7.54
1908	7.54– 8.45
1909	4.39– 5.00
1910	3.78– 4.39
1911	3.33– 3.93

[Para, November 25, 1911.]

Largest producers of sugar are States of Pernambuco, Bahia, Alagoas, Rio de Janiero. A quality like Demerara crystals is made for export.

For local consumption three qualities are manufactured. The type most used is "Uzina," clear and white. Prices of "Uzina," superior, 5.90 cents per pound; "Uzina," good, 5.60 cents per pound.

Very little difference in price at retail. People buy just enough for one meal or the day. The amount is never weighed, but guessed at. First-class stores sell crystals at 8.18 cents per pound for 2-pound lots. Wholesalers' profit is 8 to 10 per cent.

Prices: 1907, 7.80 cents per pound for "Uzina" quality; 1908, 8.18 cents; 1909, 5.20 cents; 1910, 4.46 cents; 1911, 4.46 cents per pound.

There is a rumor that the Sugar Trust is to be reorganized, and prices are rising in consequence during the last 10 days.

[Buenos Aires, August 4, 1911.]

No local taxes and no bounties, but in Province of Tucuman there is a provincial tax of $0.00639 per 2.2046 pounds ($0.0029 per 100 pounds), except for cut sugar, the sugar here is very different from the refined in the United States. There is no native granulated. Three samples sent Government of the only sugar refined at the only refinery in Argentina, at Rosario.

Argentina production: 1875, 1,570 tons; 1887, 24,750 tons; 1896, 163,000 tons; 1909, 117,209 tons; 1908, 161,688 tons; 1910, 148,854 tons.

Small changes in native refined quotations since 1896, when lump sugar was $6.37 per 100 pounds wholesale, and in 1910 was $6.79 per 100 pounds, the highest of any year. In 1903 the price dropped to $5.17 per 100 pounds, the lowest of any year.

Retail prices for lump sugar was $0.0964 per pound in 1907, 1908, 1909, and 1910, and from $0.0964 to $0.106 per pound in 1911.

Statistics are given of importation and exports and production for series of years and cultivation of cane.

New York, granulated, 5.65; New York, cubes, 5.90.

HAGEMEYER TRADING CO.,
New York, November 22, 1911.

HENRY FORSTER HITCH, Esq.,
Alstead Center, N. H.

DEAR PATER: Messrs. Willett & Gray have a consular report on Pernambuco sugars which they are working, in which there are some rather extraordinary statements, but among other things they give price, on September 11, of sugars at Pernambuco per kilo. The list is as follows:

Fine-grained white crystal, 2.40 to 2.50; white crystal, 2.30 to 2.40 (test 100 per cent, if dry; price low, I think).

Yellow crystal, 1.90 to 2.00 (test 92° to 97°; price low).

Muscavinhos, 1.70 to 1.90 (test 89° to 92°; price high).

Somenos, 1.80 to 1.90 (test 86° to 90°; price high).

Mascavo, 1.50 to 1.60 (test 84°; price high).

Medium, 1.45, and low, 1.30 to 1.35 (test 80° to 82°; price high).

Do these prices strike you as more or less correct, and what would you say the tests of the various qualities mentioned would be?

Affectionately, your son, A. D. H.

(I think the first three too low, at least comparing with opening price, as you know one firm gave 3$200, and that was delivered at station. That for 15 kilos, which is over 212 per kilo, and besides they have to be in 60-kilo bags, which would make it dearer. Whatever the prices now, the above prices are too low for September 11; in fact, all prices would be nominal at that date, as there would be no new sugar and probably all old crop was exhausted, and September 11 was about the time that one firm bought at 20 reis over Williams for delivery, which, as I have said, is over above quotations. I don't think consular reports can be very accurate.—H. F. H.)

COLOMBIA.

[Book 1, page 76, Bogota, June 27, 1911.]

Requires no explanation.

COSTA RICA.

[Book 1, page 78, Port Limon, July 19, 1911.]

1. Prices of best home-made sugar, 5 cents per pound wholesale; 7 cents per pound retail. Common, used by poorer classes, 4 cents per pound wholesale to 4½ cents retail. Practically no imports. Duty on raws, 0.264 cent per pound; on refined, 0.71 cent per pound.

2. San Jose, Costa Rica, September 12, 1911. Annual production of centrifugal sugar about 3,500 tons. No refined produced or sold. The grades used are centrifugals and common crude of lowest grade.

3. Wholesale price of centrifugal white sugar is $6.51 per 100 pounds; No. 2, $5.58 per 100 pounds; No. 3, $4.65 per 100 pounds (10 per cent discount 30 days and 2 per cent more for cash). The lowest grade of raw sugar is worth $2.32½ per 100 pounds, cash.

4. The retail price is quite uniform throughout the city.

	Per 100 pounds.
White centrifugal, 7½ cents per pound	$7.50
No. 2 centrifugal, 6½ cents per pound	6.50
No. 3 centrifugal, 5¾ cents per pound	5.80
Lowest grade raw, 3½ cents per pound	3.50

5. Very little change in prices for five years past. No exports of sugar.

July 19: New York granulated, 5.15; New York cubes, 5.40.

CUBA.

[Book 1, page 81, Habana, July 20, 1911.]

1. Poorer classes use centrifugal sugar.
2. Few statistics in Cuba. (Plenty in United States on Cuba.)
3. Average net price of 96 test centrifugals last 10 years 2.241 cents per pound, and last 3 years about 2.15 cents per pound.
4. Semirefined (made by sprinkling water from an ordinary watering pot by hand into the centrifugal machine when in motion, thus washing the sirup off the crystal, making it white and above No. 16 Dutch standard) prices:

	Cents per pound.
1907	3.16
1908	3.23
1909	3.05
1910	3.35
1911 to date	3.03

5. Cuban refined (there is one small refinery on the island at Cardenas which makes granulated) prices:

	Cents per pound.
1907	3.88
1908	4.62
1909	4.72
1910	5.40
1911 to date	4.00

6. No special taxes on sales.
7. (Cuban import duty on raw sugar is $1 per 100 kilos, on refined $0.75 per 100 kilos.) (Raw, $0.4536 per 100 pounds; refined, $0.4252 per 100 pounds.)

8. Retail price for Cuba sugar:

	Cents per pound.
1906	4.50
1908	5.50
1909	5.30
1910	5.30
1911 to date	4.50

9. American refined is imported in small quantities, for which no prices are given.

Cuban refined sugar, which was selling in early summer at wholesale at 4 cents per pound, rose to 7 cents per pound in September and October, and in November was about 6 cent per pound at wholesale and 8½ cents per pound at retail at same time. Loaf sugar, 12 cents per pound.

New York granulated, 6.65; New York cubes, 6.85.

November 1: Cuban refined, wholesale, $7 per 100 pounds; Cuban refined, retail, 8½ cents per pound; loaf, 12 cents per pound.

Twenty per cent reduction of duties to United States; $0.337 on raws; $0.380 on refined.

Dominican Republic.

[San Domingo, October 26, 1911.

Centrifugal sugar mostly produced here for use.

Refined comes from the United States.

Raw sugar, wholesale, per 100 pounds, $3.50, against $2.80 in 1910; retail, 4.40 cents per pound now, against 3 cents per pound in 1910. Centrifugals, wholesale, $4.75, against $3.25 per 100 pounds in 1910; retail, 5 cents per pound, against 4 cents per pound in 1910. Refined sugar, per pound, retail, 7 cents per pound, against 6 cents in 1910.

New York granulated, 6.75; New York cubes, 6.95.

There is no wholesale market in refined. No local taxes. No back year prices except 1905, about the same as 1910.

Mexico.

[Book 6, page 49, Ciudad Juarez, July 18, 1911.]

Mostly refined sold here, in cut loaf and granulated.

Cut loaf, wholesale, $4.42 per 100 pounds, and retail, 5 cents per pound. Granulated, wholesale, $4.31 per 100 pounds, and retail, 4¾ cents per pound.

New York granulated, 5.45; New York cubes, 5.70.

Taxes are 4 per cent at retail, 1 per cent at wholesale.

No national bounties. In five years prices have risen about 1½ cents per pound.

[Chihauhau, July 3, 1911.]

Cone sugar mostly, broken in pieces (crushed). Cut or loaf next used. Difference merely in form. Raw sugar in cone shape also sold. A small amount of American loaf and granulated is used.

	Wholesale (per 100 pounds).	Retail (cents per pound).
Pilon cane	$4.28	4.97-5
Loaf	4.50	5.65-5¾
Granulated:		
Mexican	4.58	5.65-5¾
American	....	9.03-9

New York granulated, 5.00; New York cubes, 5.25.

(Factory or jobbers.) Taxes are 1½ per cent mercantile on amount of business and a surtax of 20 per cent of amount paid to State government is collected for the Federal Government.

Sale contracts must be stamped of 1½ per cent, which is paid by purchasers. Wholesalers also pay 1½ per cent on volume of their sales and surtax of 20 per cent. Retailers also pay the same taxes in addition to both the above. The local taxes, amounting to 4½ per cent, as follows: Jobbers' State tax, 1½ per cent; jobbers' Federal tax, 0.3 per cent; wholesalers' State tax, 1½ per cent; wholesalers' Federal tax, 0.3 per cent; and wholesalers' invoice stamp, ½ per cent; a total of 4½ per cent up to retailers.

[Book 6, page 43, Zacatecas, July 27, 1911.]

Refined, wholesale, 6½ cents per pound, and retail, 8 cents per pound.

Raw, wholesale, 5½ cents per pound, and retail, 6½ cents per pound.

Refined: 1885–1890, 10½ cents per pound wholesale and 12½ cents per pound retail; 1890–1895, 9½ cents per pound wholesale and 11½ cents per pound retail; 1895–1900, 8¾ cents per pound wholesale and 10½ cents per pound retail; 1900–1905, 7½ cents per pound wholesale and 8½ cents per pound retail.

[Book 6, page 50, Ciudad Porfirio Diaz, July 22, 1911.]

First grade refined white, 10 cents per pound wholesale and 12 cents per pound retail; second grade (native sugar), 7 cents per pound wholesale and 12 cents per pound retail; unrefined brown sugar, 6 cents per pound wholesale and 9 cents per pound retail.

No change in prices for five years. No sugar ever imported here.

[Book 6, page 52, Frontera, July 17, 1911.]

All grades granulated sold here.

First grade, 3½ cents per pound wholesale and 5 cents per pound retail; second grade, 3¼ cents per pound wholesale and 4 cents per pound retail; third grade, 3 cents per pound wholesale and 3½ cents per pound retail.

From San Juan Bautista: First grade, 3 cents per pound wholesale and 6 cents per pound retail; second grade, 2¾ cents per pound wholesale and 5½ cents per pound retail; third grade, 2¼ cents per pound wholesale and 5¼ cents per pound retail.

1910 production, 4,114,447 pounds of tabasco. Sells at wholesale in coarse hemp bags of 211 pounds. No local taxes or other charges and no bounties granted to sugar growers.

[Book 6, page 55, Guadalajara, July 6, 1911.]

Lump sugar, $4 to $4.07 per 100 pounds wholesale and 5 cents to 5¾ cents per pound retail.

Granulated, $3.63 to $4.07 per 100 pounds wholesale and 5 cents to 5¾ cents per pound retail.

Some manufacturers make better quality than others.

[Book 6, page 56, Manzanillo, and Colia, July 7, 1911.]

Retail prices 4 to 6 cents per pound. Cheaper in Colima on account of nearness to factories.

No special or local taxes

Wholesale cut loaf, $4.07 per 100 pounds.

[Book 6, page 57, Hermosillo, July 6, 1911.]

Only kind sold here is half refined loaf sugar, made in State of Sinaloa. They have a sugar trust there called Union de Sinaloa, which tries to keep prices just low enough so that sugar can not be imported from the United States or other countries. Some does come from the United States on account of better white, but sells at about the same price—wholesale, 4.24 cents per pound; retail, 5 cents.

Loaf: Refiners' price, $4.32 per 100 pounds to jobbers; jobbers' price, $5.11 per 100 pounds to retailers; retailers' price, 5⅝ to 6 cents per pound.

[Book 6, page 59, Mazatlan, Sinaloa, July 12, 1911.]

Refined, 4.32 cents per pound wholesale and 4 55 cents per pound retail. All local make.

Prices: November 1, 5.50 cents per pound wholesale and 6½ cents per pound retail; July 1, 4.75 cents wholesale and 5 cents per pound retail.

[Book 6, page 61, Matamoras, July 7, 1911.]

All sugar here made in Mexico from sugar cane.

Wholesale prices $3.90 per 100 pounds and 4½ cents per pound retail.

No sugar imported, owing to high duty. Very little change in prices for five years. Production increasing. Soil well adapted to cane culture.

[Monterey, July 27, 1911.]

Granulated, wholesale, $4.08 per 100 pounds, and retail, 4.55 cents to 4½ cents per pound. Cut loaf, $4.55 per 100 pounds, and retail, 5 cents per pound.

[Book 6, page 64, Nogales, July 7, 1911.]

Cubes, wholesale, 6.10 cents per pound; retail, 6¾ to 6¾ cents per pound.

(Pages 65 and 66 for description of sugar.)

Annual production of Panocha, 440,000 pounds. State tax, eight-tenths of 1 per cent. Some granulated comes from Nogales, Ariz., costing 8½ cents per pound, plus a duty of $1.13 per 100 pounds to the consumer of Mexico.

Wholesale price of refined, 1904, was 6 cents per pound; 1885, 6¾ to 7½ cents per pound.

Prices here controlled by the sugar union.

July 11: Refined now reduced to $5.42 per 100 pounds wholesale. This refined tests 86°.

[Book 6, page 69, San Luis Potosi, July 7, 1911.]

Refined, wholesale, $4.06 per 100 pounds, and retail, $4.54 per 100 pounds, or 4½ cents per pound.

Raw, wholesale, $2.95 per 100 pounds. Retail, $3.30 per 100 pounds, or 3½ cents per pound.

Refined wholesales in sacks of 50 kilos and retails in bulk.

(For cost of production see trade report of June 16, 1911. No. 140, page 1190.)

Nov. 1: No change in prices at retail, as dealers had laid in large supplies.

[Book 6, page 70, Tampico, September 19, 1911.]

Granulated, wholesale, $3.86 per 100 pounds, and retail, 4 cents per pound. Dominoes from United States sell at retail at 10 cents per pound.

New York granulated, 6.80; New York cubes, 7.00.

[Book 6, page 72, Vera Cruz, June 27, 1911.]

A sugar producing and refining district.

Loaves, $3.20 to $4.20 per 100 pounds wholesale and 5 to 5½ cents per pound retail.

[Book 6, page 74, Tapachula Chiapas, October 21, 1911.]

Wholesale cubes or loaf, $4.20 per 100 pounds; retail, 5½ cents per pound to 7½ cents. Wholesale granulated, $4 per 100 pounds; retail, 4½ cents per pound to 5 cents.

New York granulated, 6.80; New York cubes, 7.00.

[Mexico City, November 15, 1911.]

November 1: Granulated, No. 1, $4.50 per 100 pounds wholesale; No. 2, $4.25 per 100 pounds wholesale. Cubes, No. 1, $5.50 per 100 pounds wholesale; No. 2, $5.25 per 100 pounds wholesale.

New York granulated, 6.25; New York cubes, 6.45.

Retail prices same as on August 8. No local quotations until January, when the Mexican crop is due.

[Saltello, November 9, 1911.]

November 1: Prices, granulated, 4.50 cents, against 4.10 cents on August 14, wholesale; retail, 5½ cents on November 1, against 5½ cents on August 1. Cubes, wholesale, 5 cents on November 1, against 4.75 cents on August 14. Retail, on November 1, 5¾ cents, against 5.45 cents on August 14.

Summary.

Date.	Places.	Cut loaf, wholesale, per 100 pounds.	Cut loaf, retail, per pound.	Granulated, wholesale, per 100 pounds.	Granulated, retail, per pound.
			Cents.		*Cents.*
July 27	Zacatecas	$4.42	5	$4.31	4⅜
3	Chihuahua	4.50	5⅝	4.58	[1] 5⅝ [1] 9
18	Ciudad Juares	6.50	8		
12	Ciudad Porfirio Diaz	10.00	12	7.00	9
17	Frontera (native)	3.50	5	[2] 3.25	4
17	Bautista (native)	3.00	6	[2] 2.62½	5½
6	Guadalajara	4.00–4.07	5½–5	3.63–4.07	5–5⅝
7	Manzanillo	4.07	6	([2])	4
6	Hermosillo (refiners and jobbers)	4.32–5.11	5⅝–6		
12	Mazatlan (native)	4.32	4.55–4½		
Nov. 1	Mazatlan	5.50	6¼		
July 7	Matamoras (native)	3.90	4½		
27	Nogales [3]	6.10	6⅜–6⅝		
7	San Luis Potosi	4.06	4½	([4])	
Sept. 19	Tampico			3.86	4
June 27	Vera Cruz	3.20–4.20	5–5½		
Oct. 2	Tapachula	4.20	6½–7½	4.00	4½–5
Nov. 1	Hermosillo	4.24	5		
1	Mexico City	5.25–5.50	6–6½	4.25–4.50	4¾–5½
1	Saltillo	5.00	5.66	4.50	5½

[1] Taxes for American.
[2] Native.
[3] State tax, 0.3 per cent. American, 8.50 cents plus duty $1.13 per 100 pounds. Retail, 10 cents per pound.
[4] Raw, 2.95 wholesale; 3½ cents per pound retail.

Nearly all sugar used in Mexico is native refined of inferior color. Variation in prices are because of State, Federal, and stamp taxes in many parts. These taxes at Chihuahua are 1½ per cent on amount of business plus surtax of 20 per cent, stamp tax 1½ per cent, say, amounting to 4½ per cent altogether, plus an additional tax on the retailer of 1½ to 20 per cent.

Mexico has a Sugar Trust which keeps prices just low enough to prevent imports. Very poor people use very little sugar and that little is simply boiled cane juice of very dark color. They buy 1 cent's worth at a time.

SWEDEN.

[Book 1, p. 108, Gothenburg, July 12, 1911.]

Demand almost supplied by domestic production. Production, 110,000 to 140,000 tons of beet sugar. Import about 1,100 tons (less than 1 per cent of consumption). Most of the production is in the district of southern Sweden.

Consumption per capita steadily rising for 100 years.

	Pounds per capita.
1861–1870	10.74
1871–1880	16.82
1881–1890	23.30
1890–1895	35.45
1895–1900	40.74
1909	52.14

Production is protected by a tariff of $1.82 per 100 pounds on refined. Also on unrefined if No. 18 Dutch standard or over. Raws under No. 18 Dutch standard, $1.21 per 100 pounds duty. Countervailing duties on sugar from bounty countries. Sugar production in Sweden is controlled by an industrial combination, which sets the price by prices abroad and keep price just low enough to make imports unprofitable. Price list issued July 7, just after the rise in German and English markets on the 1st of July. (Read full report, pp. 108, 109, 110.)

	Wholesale (per 100 pounds).	Retail (per pound).
		Cents.
Cubes	$7.41	8.18
Granulated	6.93	7.65

New York granulated, 5.10; New York cubes, 5.35.

Retail prices fixed by retail dealers' association. Great complaint against Sugar Trust.

Sweden exports no sugar and is under agreement to Brussels convention not to export; therefore is obliged to reduce its sowings, which it is doing now to reduce the crop 40,000 tons.

No polariscope tests for duties.

[Stockholm, August 24, 1911.]

The sugar industry is almost entirely in the hands of a trust with paid-up capital of $36,180,000, and which owns all Swedish refineries except one.

All beet-sugar beets grown in southern Sweden.

August 27: Lump, wholesale, $7.70 per 100 pounds; retail, 8.45 cents per pound. Granulated, wholesale, $7.30 per 100 pounds; retail, 8.05 cents per pound.

August 27: New York, granulated, 5.95; New York, cubes, 6.20.

Prices practically the same all over the country.

Government excise tax is $1.85 per 100 pounds, and also the customhouse duty is $1.85 per 100 pounds to $1.03 per 100 pounds, according to Dutch standard color.

Retail prices given for 1886 to 1910 varying less than 1 cent per pound.

Scarcely any sugar imported since Sugar Trust has controlled.

DENMARK.

[Book 1, Copenhagen, July 8, 1911.]

(A country from which much may be learned for use in the United States.)

1. The beet-sugar industry is carried on by two large companies, owning and operating seven factories on near-by islands. (One company has six factories and the other one factory.)

2. Production in Denmark in 1909, 62,434 tons; in 1908, 95,116 tons, and in 1910–11, 109,000 tons. (Otto Licht.)

3. Consumption in 1909, 103,862 tons, of which 42,501 tons were imported. Consumption per capita, 86.42 pounds. (According to Otto Licht, 77.75 pounds.)

4. Importations have remained unchanged since the sugar factories were started in 1874. Imports in 1909–10 were 33,553 tons. Germany exported to Denmark 24,038 tons in 1909–10 and in 1910–11, 7,115 tons. (No data from Denmark in regard to imports in 1910–11.)

5. Consumption is four times larger than in 1874 (25,765 tons in 1874). Per capita consumption in 1874 was about 29 pounds.

6. Exports not mentioned. (Given by Otto Licht as, in 1909–10, 5,216 tons; in 1908–9, 3,083 tons.)

7. Present prices: Wholesale, best white granulated (cane and beet), $4.40 to $4.49 per 100 pounds; second best white granulated (cane and beet), $3.90 to $4.40 per 100 pounds. (Equal to $3.29 and $3.20, respectively, in bond. New York, July 8, 1911, duty-paid price of best white granulated, $5.10 per 100 pounds; second best white granulated, $4.85. In bond price, $3.20 per 100 pounds.) Raw prices at Copenhagen (part cane and part beet), 88° test to 93° test, $3.50 to $3.60 per 100 pounds. Raw (cane), 83.6° test to 94° test, $3.30 to $4 per 100 pounds. (New York price of part beet and part cane, $3.868 with an in-bond price of $2.50, and raw (cane), $3.926 per 100 pounds, with an in-bond price of $2.565.) Peruvian, Barbados, etc. (cane), 83° test to 96° test at $3.10 to $3.40 per 100 pounds.

Retail prices vary considerably, usually 30 to 80 cents per 100 pounds, or more.

Wholesale prices: White granulated in 1900, $4.70 to $5.20 per 100 pounds; in 1905, $4.50 to $6 per 100 pounds; and in 1910, $4.30 to $5.60 per 100 pounds. Second-grade granulated (all cane), in 1900, $4.20 to $4.70 per 100 pounds; in 1905, $4 to $5 per 100 pounds; and in 1910, $3.90 to $5 per 100 pounds. (Granulated at New York, average price, duty paid for 1900 was $5.320; in 1905, $4.278; and in 1910, $4.188. Without duty, $3.420 in 1900; $2.378 in 1905; and $2.288 in 1910.)

8. Import duties are on refined sugar, polariscopic test above 98°, $1.21 per 100 pounds; refined sugar above 86° test and not above 98° test, $0.79 per 100 pounds; raw for refining, no test stated, $0.72 per 100 pounds, and other sugars of 88° test and less, $0.49 per 100 pounds. July 8: New York granulated, $5.10; New York cubes, $5.35.

9. The law of May 27, 1908, places an internal tax on the home production of beet sugar and the refining of sugar. Tax on the production of beet sugar polarizing above 98°, $0.49 per 100 pounds (less than one-half cent per pound) and is not specially

refined. The tax or duty on sugar for refining for each 2,205 pounds of sugar sent to the refineries and not polarizing above 96° is $0.63 per 100 pounds.

	Per 100 pounds.
Above 96 test up to 96.5 test	$0.6213
Above 96.5 up to 97 test	.6394
Above 97 up to 97.5 test	.6576
Above 97.5 up to 98 test	.6757
Above 98 test	.6939

The duty adds $0.01815 per 100 pounds for each one-half degree.

[St. Croix, Danish West Indies, July 21, 1911.]

Prices of crystals, 96° test (centrifugals), wholesale, 2.35 cents per pound, or $2.35 per 100 pounds; retail, 4 cents per pound, or $4 per 100 pounds. Muscovados of 89° test, wholesale, at 2.12 cents per pound, or $2.12 per 100 pounds; retail, 3 cents per pound, or $3 per 100 pounds. Imported sugar (white), wholesale, 5.75 cents per pound to 6.25 cents per pound; retail, at 6 cents to 6½ cents per pound.

[St. Thomas, Danish West Indies, July 31, 1911.]

Prices of 96° test crystals (centrifugals), wholesale, 2.85 cents to 3 cents per pound; retail, 3½ cents per pound. 89° test Muscovados (wholesale), at 2.80 cents to 2.60 cents per pound; retail, at 3 cents per pound. Imported white sugar (wholesale), 5 cents per pound, and retail, 5½ cents to 6 cents per pound.

(Nov. 3, 1911: Crop 1911 is 10,920 tons; exported to United States, 7,950 tons; Canada, 1,500 tons; Scotland, 900 tons; Denmark, 145 tons; local, 425 tons.)

Duty on refined sugar of 98° test is $1.21 per 100 pounds. Duty on raws for refining is $0.72 per 100 pounds; internal tax on home production above 98° is $0.49; total, $1.21 per 100 pounds.

Duty on refined, 98° test or over, is $1.21 per 100 pounds; internal tax on home production is $0.49; protection to home industry, $0.72 per 100 pounds.

Denmark home production is not sufficient for consumption by a certain amount each year, which has not varied much in the past 25 years.

For this extra supply required above consumption consumers must pay $0.72 per 100 pounds more than for cost of the home product of refined if it is imported from the world markets, or if the refiner pays duty on raws imported for refining of $0.72 per 100 pounds and, in addition, the tax of $0.49 per 100 pounds he must get from the consumer the $0.72 per 100 pounds as well as the $0.49 tax.

The internal tax of $0.49 per 100 pounds is on the home production, which evidently includes imported raws which pass through the refineries.

Denmark shows in several ways a counterpart of the conditions in the United States and will merit a more careful study than I can give it now. Denmark in 25 years increased its home production of beet sugar largely, under an apparent protection of $0.72 per 100 pounds, and with an excise tax of less than one-half cent per pound the consumption has risen equally as much in tons, as well as in per capita, until now the latter is much the same as the United States, Denmark being 86.42 pounds and the United States 81.6 pounds.

Best granulated produced from cane and beet mixed was $4.49 per 100 pounds in Copenhagen July 8, 1911; deducting duty of $1.21 per 100 pounds, theoretical reduction, leaves $3.28 per 100 pounds. Cane granulated in New York on July 8, 1911, was $4.98 per 100 pounds, duty paid; deducting theoretical duty of $1.90 leaves $3.08 per 100 pounds; less actual duty, $1.44, leaves $3.54 per 100 pounds.

Denmark has made great progress in production and consumption under a duty of $1.21 per 100 pounds on refined above 98° test, and a duty on raws (presumably 96° test) of $0.6213 per 100 pounds, and an internal tax on home production of $0.49 per 100 pounds.

Only a small part of Denmark appears to be suitable for beet culture, as it is all carried on on a few small islands, and none on the mainland.

The question of labor in Denmark versus the United States would be of interest as related to the remarkable growth of an industry in a small country.

The influence of the entire Denmark sugar industry, home and foreign, is in the control of only two companies.

Denmark does not adhere to the Brussels convention. It is a study by itself, different from European countries generally and not much different in several ways from the United States.

Denmark's methods applied to the United States would mean—

1. A duty of $1.21 per 100 pounds on imported sugar above 98° test, for direct consumption.
2. A duty of $0.72 per 100 pounds on imported raw sugar for refining.
3. A government tax on the domestic cane and beet production, Porto Rican, Hawaiian, and Philippine Islands production, brought into the United States, of $0.49 per 100 pounds (about one-half cent per pound).
4. An adjustment of Cuban reciprocity.

A duty on 107 pounds raws to make 100 pounds refined, at $0.72 per 100 pounds for raws, equals	$0.77
Internal tax	.49
Per 100 pounds refined	1.26
Present United States duty on 107 pounds Cuban raws (96 test) to make 100 pounds refined, at $1.348 per 100 pounds	1.45
Difference—saving to consumer per 100 pounds	.19

If duty on Cuba 96 test sugar is fixed at $0.72 per 100 pounds and 20 per cent reciprocity continued, the duty on sugar from other countries would be $0.90 per 100 pounds ($0.90 less 20 per cent, 18=$0.72).

The revenue to the United States Government from a duty of $0.72 on imported foreign raws and a consumption tax of $0.49 on home production based on the 1910 consumption would amount to $18,000,000 on 1,637,780 tons produced in the United States (beet, cane, etc.), Hawaii, Porto Rico, and Philippines, and $46,000,000 on 1,712,575 tons imported from Cuba and other foreign countries, a total of $64,000,000.

FRANCE.

[Book 2, p. 2, Bordeaux, July 24, 1911.]

One franc equals 19.3 cents; 100 kilos equals 220.46 pounds.

Raws, 100° test; consumption tax, $2.19; tax on refining, $0.175; inspection tax, $0.007; total taxes, $2.372 per 100 pounds. The grades quoted are lump (loaf), cubes (cut) granulated for refined and No. 3 crystals 98° standard for raws. Loaf sugar standard for refined. No. 3 crystals (raws) 98° test go to refiners in the north of France or to warehouses in Paris at 3.26 cents (cost, July 18, 1911). Government tax on 98° is 2.15 cents, making total cost to refiners 5.41 cents.

If No. 3 crystals are exported in natural state, the customs authorities grant an exportation certificate of 2.15 cents per 100 pounds. The net export price of No. 3 crystals of 98° test is 3.26 cents.

(There is in France another grade of crystals called No. 3 white crystals "extra," which go into direct consumption. There are few, if any, raw-beet sugars of 88° analysis and 94° polariscope made in France for export.)

No. 3 crystals (raw 98°) delivered to refiners cost 5.41 cents. July 18 the Paris quotation for refined, as stated at Bordeaux, was 6.08 cents. The difference covering cost of refining 98° white raws and the profit was 0.67 cent.

	Cents.
July 18, cost of refined (loaf standard) at refinery in Paris	6.08
Government tax on refining added to invoice (2 francs per 100 kilos)	.175
Government tax for inspection 0.08 francs per 100 kilos	.007
Refined delivered at refinery, Paris	6.262
July 18, refined wholesale price at Bordeaux	6.60
Transportation and charges, Paris to Bordeaux	.338

Refiners either buy raws 98° test at 5.41 cents tax of 2.15 cents paid, and not pay 2.19 cents on the refined product, or else buy the raws at 3.26 cents without tax and pay 2.19 cents on the refined product. In the first instance there would be taxes of 2.15 cents and 0.175 cent and 0.007 cent, a total of $2.332 taxes per 100 pounds on refined. In the last case the taxes would be 2.19 cents plus 0.175 and 0.007 cent, or $2.372 on refined.

SUMMARY.

Comparison on cost of refining in France and the United States. French refiners pay for 103 pounds 98° test raws at 5.41 cents per pound to make 100 pounds of granulated, equals 5.67 cents. They sell refined per 100° test at 6.08 cents and have left to cover cost of refining and profit, 0.41 cent, excluding loss in weight.

If the United States refiners buy 96° test raws at 5.28 cents per pound (the United States market difference of value between 98° and 96° test is 0.125 cent per pound), 0.0625 in bond, he pays for 107 pounds to make 100 pounds refined, 5.65 cents. He sells the refined at same price as Paris, say 6.08 cents, and thus the United States refiner would have to cover cost of refining and profit, excluding loss in weight, 0.43 cent).

If the American refiner buys 96° test raws at 5.28 cents he adds for difference between raws and refined, 0.88 cent, and sells refined at 6.16 cents.

The French refiner buys 98° test raws at 5.41 cents and adds for difference between raws and refined, 0.67 cent, and sells refined at 6.262 cents.

The French refiners obtain $0.102 per 100 pounds more than the United States refiner. Where the difference between raws and refined goes higher or lower in either country the figures change accordingly, but I take it that a difference of 67 cents as against 88 cents in the United States is a minimum comparison. The United States refiner loses 7 pounds in working at 5.28 cents, or 0.369 cent per hundred pounds. The French refiner loses 3 pounds in working at 5.41 cents, or 0.162 cent per 100 pounds. The United States refiners' excess loss in working 96 test is 0.207 cent per 100 pounds. The United States difference between raws and refined is 0.877 cent; in France, 0.67 cent. The difference between raw and refined in the United States and France in the United States, 0.21 cent per 100 pounds, is the difference between the loss of 7 pounds and 3 pounds in working, or 0.207 cent.

		Cents.
New York quotation, cubes, on July 18, 1911		5.50
Less 2 per cent		.11
Net		5.39
Centrifugals, 96° test, c. f., sellers, July 18, 1911		3.00
French charge tax, 96° test, per 100 pounds		2.09
		5.09
107 pounds (96° test, at 5.09 cents), cost of raws to refiners if pay French tax		5.44
United States cost of refining, excluding loss in weight		.43
Per pound		5.87
	Cents.	
French tax on refining	0.175	
French tax, inspection	.007	
		.182
United States cost of 100 pounds refined on French basis		6.052
New York quotation for granulated July 18, 1911		5.047
Higher cost on French basis to consumers, per pound		1.005
New York quotation for granulated July 18, 1911		5.15
Less 2 per cent		.103
Net		5.047

Centrifugals, 96° test, 4.36 cents. Difference, 0.243 cents.
5.44 cents.

Loaf sugar, July 18, 1911.

[Cents per pound.]

Cities.	Wholesale.	Retail.	Difference.
Bordeaux	6.60	7.25	0.65 cents.
Cognac (Sept. 1)	7.02	7.28	
Grenoble	6.20	7.00	
Havre	No price.	6.57	
Lyons	6.29	6.84	
Marseille	6.31	6.58	
Nice	6.34	7.00	
Nantes	No price.	5.89	
Paris (June 10)	5.85	6.36	New York, 5.92, granulated: 0.155; Paris, granulated, 6.36.
Roubaix	5.91	6.80	
Rheim	6.08	6.56–6.99	
Rouen (July 10)	6.25	6.57	
St. Etienne (July 20)	6.21	6.35	
St. Pierre	6.00	6.25	
Algiers	8.42	8.55	Subject to certain taxes in Algiers (p. 57).
Guadeloupe	4.80	5.00	
Tahiti	8.33	No price.	Native refined white sugar. (Crystals No. 3 sent to France.)

Wholesale price of 98° test raws from manufacturers delivered at refineries, 3.26 cents per pound without tax; 2.15 cents per pound equals tax. Cost with tax, 5.41 cents per pound.

[Book 2, page 3, Bordeaux.]

Refined follows raw with slight fluctuations (same as United States), being at retail 7 francs ($0.6125 per 100 pounds) above wholesale.

Basis for refined is loaf sugar. July 18, 1911, loaf sugar at Paris was $6.08; tax on refining, 0.175 cent; inspection tax, 0.007 cent; raw sugar 98° test, 0.338. Difference between raws 98° and refined 100°, 6.600 cents.

No. 3 raw crystals 98° test (basis of raws), without tax, per 100 pounds:

1880	$5.09 –$6.67
1885	3.33 – 4.56
1890	2.72 – 3.42
1895	2.191– 2.95
1900	2.28 – 2.60
1905	2.02 – 3.95
1910	2.54 – 4.12

By months, 1911: Raws, January, $2.70 per 100 pounds; February, $2.51; March, $2.97; April, $3.09; May, $3.06; June, $3.10; July (18), $3.26.

[Book 2, p. 4, Cognac, July 15, 1911.]

La Rochelle is the typical city of this district. Four forms of sugar sold here. Cut loaf (cubes) sells at $7.28 per 100 pounds at retail. Broken sugar (the small irregular pieces after cutting the loaves into cubes) retails at $6.81 per 100 pounds. Crystallized (No. 3 extra) retails at $6.36. Light brown (Cassonade), $5.91 per 100 pounds retail (this is a low grade granulated). Wholesale prices are $0.175 to $0.263 per 100 pounds less.

Sugar is sold in 1 pound 1¾ ounces, 2 pounds 3½ ounces, 11 pounds ¼ ounce, 55 pounds 2 ounces, 110.23-pound packages, and in loaves (pyramids) 22 pounds ¾ ounce, to 26 pounds 7 ounces and in sacks 220.46 pounds. There may be either cane or beet sugar. Prices vary from 1 to 2 cents for granulated in the poorer quarter of the city.

No local taxes here.

[Book 2, p. 5, Grenoble, June 29, 1911.]

Buying and selling regulated at Paris for this city and Province. The little difference in prices throughout France turns upon the difference in cost of transportation, according to distance from distributing center.

(Present prices Paris refiners' prices, page 6.)

Loaf, $5.70 per 100 pounds, including Government tax, $2.19. Add 0.182 per 100 pounds for refining tax equals $5.882 per 100 pounds at Paris. To this add 0.318 as cost of transportation to Grenoble equals $6.20 per 100 pounds. Six dollars and thirty cents per 100 pounds is charged by wholesalers; 0.10 per 100 pounds is profit to wholesalers. Seven dollars is charged by retailers, leaving a profit of 0.70 per 100 pounds to retailers.

No. 3 (98° test) at Paris, per 100 pounds, wholesale $5.33
Grenoble 5.65

Freight .... .32

Retail prices of cut loaf (cubes) quite uniform at about 7 cents per pound. The profit shared by the wholesaler and retailer is very small, about 1 cent on 3 pounds. One house says, "only carried because of other articles." Some retailers decline to sell sugar unless some other article is bought with it.

[Book 2, page 8, Havre, June 29, 1911.]

Havre is not a sugar market, but only a port of transit for Paris, which is the one and dominating market of the country. All sales at Havre are on account of Paris and on the basis of the preceding day's Paris quotations. All prices quoted at Havre are Paris prices. These prices on June 29 were: Wholesale, cane crude, $4.56 per 100 pounds; light brown, $5.08; and light brown crystals, $5.51; white crystals, $5.61; retail, lump cubes, Say refineries, 6.57 cents per pound; in cardboard boxes, Lebanos, 6.13 cents per pound; French beet-root sugar in 100 pound cases, 3.09 cents, plus tax of 2.19 cents equals 5.28 cents per pound.

Sugar "in powder" (raws): Custom duties, from French colonies, $2.19 per 100 pounds of 100 per cent not less than 65° from French colonies, which on refining will produce 98° or less, $2.65 per 100 pounds; on refining will produce more than 98°, $2.99 per 100 pounds. (Meaning raws of 98° polariscope pay $2.65 with 0.022 per pound reduction.)

Home protection against colony sugar 98° test, 0.46 cent per 100 pounds; against foreign sugar 98° test, 0.80 cent per 100 pounds.

[Book 2, page 10, Lyons, July 1, 1911.]

Wholesale price of raw sugar No. 3 crystallized is regulated here by the Sugar Bourse of Paris, which fixes prices every day. Tax, 2.19 cents on 100° test, 2.15 cents on 98° test, 2.13 cents on 97° test, 2.11 cents on 96° test. June 29, 1911, No. 3 at Paris, 3.116 cents; State tax (97°), 2.136 cents, indicates 97 test. Freight (by water), 0.105 cent; commission, 0.050 cent; total, 5.406 cents. Freight (by rail), 0.108 cent more equals cost at Lyons, 5.514 cents. (Cost of cut loaf, cubes, on page 12.) "Say" refined sells at $0.108 per 100 pounds more than the Lebanos sugar, due to old refining system in use in Say refinery, which causes more waste than new methods.

Cost of "Say" sugar at Paris (raws), $3.111 per 100 pounds; cost of refining, including State tax, $2.844; refining tax and operating tax, $0.181; freight by rail, $0.154; cut loaf in 11.02-pound boxes, $6.290 per 100 pounds; cost of Lebaudy refined, $6.16, or $0.13 less per 100 pounds.

Above in light pasteboard boxes of 112 pounds.

If loaf is cut and in 2.2-pound boxes, it costs $0.129 more per 100 pounds (⅛ cent per pound). Granulated is 6.16 cents in addition to transportation charges of 0.15 cent, equal to 6.31 cents per pound in cotton bags of 110.23 and 220.46 pounds. Wholesalers sell to retail grocers at $0.435 to $0.875 profit per 100 pounds. Grocers sell to consumers in loaves at 6.848 cents per pound; granulated, 7 cents per pound; cut loaf in small cubes, 7 cents per pound; powdered, 7 cents per pound; and broken cut loaf pieces, 6.14 cents. Grocery stores sell sugar as a leader at small profits and sometimes at a loss.

Sugar for export does not pay the State tax of $4.71 ($2.136 per 100 pounds for 97° test raws per 220 pounds).

Average wholesale prices at Lyons at 5-year intervals were:

Kinds.	1886	1891	1896	1901	1906	1911
	Cents.	*Cents.*	*Cents.*	*Cents.*	*Cents.*	*Cents.*
Raw, 97° test	7.64	8.82	8.11	8.14	4.79	5.53
Cut cubes:						
Wholesale	9.05	10.46	9.24	9.60	5.44	6.40
Retail	11.30	10.90	10.40	10.40	6.12	6.58
Granulated:						
Wholesale			8.85	9.41	5.36	6.41
Retail			10.40	10.40	6.22	6.53

Taxes reduced in 1891.

No local taxes now. There was a heavy State tax (war tax) in 1870-71, following the Franco-Prussian War.

[Book, Marseille, July 7, 1911, and July 19, 1911.]

Wholesale prices June 30, 1911.

No. 3 (standard for raws), $3.118 per 100 pounds, plus tax 2.19 cents equals 5.308 cents per 100 pounds (p. 22). Raws 88°, 2.856 cents per 100 pounds plus tax 2.19 cents, equals 5.046 cents per pound.

NOTE.—Lyons adds 2.136 cents for State tax.

Wholesale refined cubes, 6.13 cents.

Crystallized No. 3 extra (granulated), 5.50 cents.

Refined tax on both grades, 0.175 cent.

Operating tax on both grades, 0.007 cent.

Wholesale price cubes, 6.315 cents; No. 3 extra, 5.682 cents.

Retail price cubes, 6.55 cents; No. 3 extra, 6.15 cents.

Average prices at five-year periods for 25 years (wholesale).

Raw No. 3 (standard).	1911	1906	1901	1896	1891	1886
98 test:	*Cents.*	*Cents.*	*Cents.*	*Cents.*	*Cents.*	*Cents.*
Cost	2.94	2.25	2.28	2.67	3.22	3.12
Tax	2.19	2.19	5.25	5.25	5.25	4.38
	5.13	4.44	7.53	7.92	8.47	7.50
Refined cubes cost	6.09	5.45	9.44			
Refining tax	.179	.179	.087			
Operating tax	.007	.007	.003			
	6.276	5.636	9.53	9.23	9.85	8.80
Crystallized No. 3	5.66	4.72	8.05	8.01	8.58	7.52
Average retail prices:						
Cubes	6.62	5.95	9.80	9.52	10.16	9.09
Extra crystallized No. 3	6.21	5.44	8.30	8.30	8.84	7.71
Government consumption tax	2.19	2.19	5.25	5.25	5.25	4.38

Tax reduced in 1901.

[Book 2, p. 26.]

Both raw and refined sold here. Raws nearly all from French colonies and are subject to same duties as native beet-root sugar. Three qualities are sold.

No. 1, white crystallized: This sugar is resold now at about $3.10 per 100 pounds following the official type crystal No. 3 of Paris market for white sugar the standard of raw sugar in France and about 98 per cent raw. Three dollars and ten cents makes it equal to about 3 cents on 96 test (3.02 cents) not including duty of 2.19 cents per 100 pounds and 100° test.

No. 2, brown, crystallized is about $3 per 100 pounds for 98° French yield, equal to $2.84 per 100 pounds for 96 test not including duty of 25 francs $2.19 per 100 pounds ($0.022 off for each degree.)

No. 3, sirups sugar, French standard, 70° equals parity of 85° America 4½ cents duty included. (The retail prices refer to raws above mentioned, page 25.)

Retail prices would include all duties and taxes.

Actual market prices for refined sugar: Loaf (cones) 5.89 cents per pound; cubes, 6.06 cents to 6.21 cents.

Sold in paper boxes of various sizes. No local tax on sugar.

[Book 2, p. 27, France, Nantes.]

Owing to difference in values of French and foreign sugars it was possible to import this year into France foreign raw sugar from nonbounty-paying countries, but American raw or refined could not, under present French legislation, enter into France.

Last year French sugar industries protested against the importation into England of American refined sugar as contrary to the spirit of the Brussels convention. The Brussels convention has many adversaries in France.

French legislation has already provided a raising of duties in order to preserve the national industry against imports from present nonbounty-paying countries who, after the breaking up of the convention should again resume paying bounties on production.

[Nice, Sept. 9, 1911.]

The fall in prices in 1904 was due to reduction of taxes and failure of several large speculators. (See table, p. 32.)

[Book 2, p. 34, Nice, July 5, 1911.]

No raw sugar used, but about 6,500 tons of refined consumed annually, of which 3,500 tons come from Marseille, and is mostly cane sugar; 2,500 tons come from Paris, chiefly beet, and the rest from other French refineries.

Sold in bags, 110 to 220 pounds; loaf, 11 to 22 pounds.

Wholesale prices of bag sugar are 6.12 cents to 6.21 cents per pound, and retail about 6½ cents per pound in large and 7 cents in small quantities.

Wholesale prices of lump sugar sold in pasteboard boxes, 2.2 to 11 pounds each, or wooden boxes of 132 pounds, at $6.34 to $6.38, and retails at a little over 7 cents per pound. In different localities retail prices vary 1 cent over or 1 cent under prices quoted for Nice, according to freight and rentals. No local taxes in this consular district, but Government taxes of $2.45 per 100 pounds, which is included in the above prices. In other cities the tax is given.

Table showing prices of sugar at Paris and Nice during the last 24 years.

Years.	Market price for unrefined at Paris (per 100 pounds).		Wholesale price refined at Paris (per 100 pounds).		Wholesale price refined at Nice (per 100 pounds).		Retail price refined at Nice (per pound).	
	Highest.	Lowest.	Highest.	Lowest.	Highest.	Lowest.	Highest.	Lowest.
1887	$4.52	$2.88	$10.50	$8.11	$10.70	$9.29	$0.113	$0.104
1888	4.19	3.26	10.10	9.43	10.80	10.20	.113	.108
1889	6.11	2.88	11.70	9.52	12.40	10.25	.113	.108
1890	3.57	2.88	9.88	9.34	10.60	10.00	.113	.108
1891	3.84	3.12	9.57	9.57	10.70	10.29	.113	.108
1892	3.77	3.25	......	......	......	......	.113	.108
1893	4.79	3.24	11.10	9.61	11.80	10.40	.117	.108
1894	3.59	2.30	11.00	8.93	10.70	9.66	.113	.104
1895	3.10	2.26	9.34	8.79	10.00	9.52	.108	.997
1896	3.49	2.35	9.47	8.79	10.20	9.52	.108	.997
1897	2.93	2.30	9.25	8.43	9.97	9.16	.108	.997
1898	2.93	2.64	9.66	9.28	10.30	9.93	.108	.104
1899	3.65	2.49	9.70	9.38	10.40	10.10	.108	.104
1900	3.45	2.44	9.84	9.11	10.50	9.84	.108	.104
1901	2.75	2.40	9.25	8.66	9.97	9.38	.108	.997
1902	2.35	2.89	8.75	8.39	9.47	9.11	.997	.952
1903	2.38	2.19	8.66	5.11	9.38	5.89	.997	.635
1904	3.86	2.13	......	4.98	......	5.71	......	.589
1905	4.09	2.13	6.98	5.17	7.71	5.89	.816	.635
1906	2.64	2.14	5.53	5.08	6.25	5.80	.680	.635
1907	2.64	2.28	5.44	5.03	6.16	5.76	.680	.635
1908	2.98	2.49	5.71	5.33	6.44	6.12	.680	.635
1909	3.28	2.69	6.07	5.44	6.80	6.16	.725	.635
1910	4.25	2.59	6.98	5.86	7.71	6.53	.771	.680

[Book 2, p. 36, Paris, June 30, 1911.]

1. Consumption comes from (1) French beet industry, (2) imports from French colonies, and to a small extent from foreign countries.

2. Production of campaign, 1908–9, on 14,700,722 acres of land was 5,949,301 tons beets, or 723,082 tons raw sugar. Estimated on basis of refined product; metric ton is 2,204.6 pounds.)

Production, 1909–10:

Imports, 1909, 101,728 tons of raw sugar, of which 99,576 tons from French colonies (Martinique, Mayotti, Reunion, Guadaloupe) and 2,152 tons foreign countries.

Also, in 1909, imports of 841 tons refined from Egypt, Belgium, and Great Britain.

3. The total sugar supply of France from all sources for an average year was 825,790 tons, against which was exported and reexported 83,736 tons of native imported raws and 142,430 tons of refined, leaving the approximate consumption of France 599,322 tons (2,240 pounds).

4. Import duties: Sugar in powder (semirefined crystals No. 3) from French colonies, $2.19 per 100 pounds per 100° (minimum being 65°); $0 0222 per 100 pounds per degree, less duty from 100° polariscope test.

Sugar from foreign countries which will produce in refining 98° or less, $2.66 per 100 pounds; which will produce in refining over 98°, $2.88.

5. There are no local taxes on sugar brought into Paris and no bounties paid since Brussels convention.

6. Present internal-revenue tax in France fixed by law of January 22, 1903, as follows: "On raw or refined, $2.19 per 100 pounds."

7. Sugar for general consumption is classified in two groups: (1) Refined white, which is sold in loaves or cut into cubes for use in coffee or tea; (2) what is known as white No. 3 extra, in crystals, which is the standard household sugar for the majority of the population.

Wholesale prices June 10, 1911, compare with same date in 1910 and 1909, as follows:

	1911	1910	1909	New York (net).		
				1911	1910	1909
	Cents.	Cents.	Cents.	Cents.	Cents.	Cents.
Refined white (with duty):						
Loaves and cubes	5.85	6.63	5.40	5.145	5.346	4.851
Granulated				4.90	5.099	4.603
White No. 3 raw in crystals, without tax	3.08	3.90	2.72			

Retail prices at Paris on June 3, 1911.

The following grades and designations are sold. The retail prices of each on June 29, 1911, as follows:

	Paris retail price.	New York refiners' price.
1. Refined white:	Cents.	Cents.
In loaves	6.36	
Small cubes	6.36	5.145
Flat blocks	6.82	
Powdered	6.36	4.998
Fine powdered	6.82	
White No. 3 crystals	5.91	[1] 4.655
2. Cassanades [2]	6.36	
Light-brown granulated		[3] 4.90
Cassanades gray granulated	5.91	

[1] German granulated. [2] Consul writes this is granulated sugar. [3] Cane granulated.

Brown and crystallized sugars are sold at wholesale in 110-pound bags and at retail in bulk of any quantity desired.

Cubes are sold in pasteboard boxes 2.2 to 22 pounds.

Loaf is sold in cases of 2.2 pounds.

For Paris quotations for granulated for a series of years see Nice.

[Book 2, p. 41, Rheims, July 1, 1911.]

Wholesale prices of raw sugar, $5.24 per 100 pounds.

Wholesale prices of refined sugar, $6.08 per 100 pounds.

Retail price of raw sugar, tax paid, $5.64 per 100 pounds.

Retail price of refined sugar cut in lumps, $6.12, $6.56, and $6.99 per 100 pounds. Quite frequently sold at or below cost in order to attract customers.

Lump is in paper boxes of 2.2 and 11 pounds and in cases of 22, 65, and 110 pounds.

Raw sugar is delivered in linen (cloth) bags of 220.46 pounds. Loaf sugar comes in conically shaped pieces weighing about 24.2 pounds. Granulated and powdered is packed in linen bags of 220.46 pounds or in paper boxes holding 2.20 and 11.02 pounds.

No local taxes imposed on sugar, and no bounty given by Government.

[Book 2, p. 42, Roubaix, July 24, 1911.]

No local taxes, but there is a Government tax of 0.175 cent per 100 pounds (called elsewhere refiners' tax), which is paid at the sugar factory or mill at the time of purchase, but applies only on refined sugar. (Refiners pay Government tax direct.)

Wholesale prices of raw sugar: July, 1911, 3.32 cents. Futures, August, 3.37 cents; September, 3.33 cents; October–December, 2.97 cents; October–January, 1912, 2.98 cents; and January–April, 1912, 3.07 cents.

Present prices of refined sugar at wholesale are 6.21 cents per 100 pounds, including duties of $2.36 per 100 pounds; say, Government, $2.19; State tax, $0.175; refiners' ax, $0.007; total, $2.382.

Raw sugar, wholesale price, 5.69 cents per 100 pounds, including duty of 2.19 cents r 100 pounds.

Prices of refined sugar.

[Book 2, p. 42.]

	Wholesale.	Retail.
	Cents.	*Cents.*
In boxes, 11 pounds	6.15	
In boxes, 2.2 pounds	6.25	6.80
In cases, 110-132 pounds	6.16	
In cases, 55-66 pounds	6.21	
In cases, 22 pounds	6.25	
Loaf sugar	5.91	6.80
Broken (large and in sacks)	5.68	6.35
Broken (medium and in sacks)	5.68	
Broken (small and in sacks)	5.68	
Powdered	5.64	6.80
Granulated	5.47	6.35
Granulated powder	5.53	6.80

[Book 2, p. 44, Rouen, July 3, 1911.]

Wholesale prices of July 1, 1911, are (January 1 to May 1 prices were about $0.17 per 100 pounds lower): Raw sugar, one grade only, $3.10 per 100 pounds without tax.

Refined sugar, wholesale, powdered, pure in sacks, 220.4 pounds, 6.33 cents per pound and 7 cents retail in 1-pound bags. Powdered in paper boxes, 2.2 pounds, 6.55 cents wholesale. Crystallized (coarse crystals) sacks, 220.4 pounds, 5.85 cents wholesale and 6.13 cents retail. Cut sugar in paper boxes, 11 pounds, each 6.55 cents wholesale and 6.57 retail. Cut sugar in 2.2-pound paper boxes, 6.66 cents wholesale. Irregular sugars, odds and ends of cut loaf, 6.07 cents wholesale and 6.13 cents retail. The gross weight of sack and sugar is paid for. Net weight when in boxes. Above prices include following charges: Refining tax (droit de rafinage), 0.175 cent per 100 pounds; State tax (droit de exescice), 0.007 cent, and transportation charges to Rouen, 0.109 cent, a total of 0.291 cent per 100 pounds.

Wholesale prices of raw and refined sugar from 1901 to 1910, inclusive, at St. Etienne.

	White, No. 3, 98° raws.	Refined loaf.	Retail refined.
1901	$2.59	$8.88	$9.97
1902	1.86	8.36	9.52
1903	2.20	8.18	9.07
1904	2.40	4.78	5.90
1905	3.03	6.02	6.80
1906	2.30	4.95	5.44
1907	2.36	5.03	5.44
1908	2.80	5.49	5.90
1909	2.72	5.46	5.90
1910	3.84	6.60	7.26

The roux cuite, 88°, is used in manufacture of confectionery.

Prices of refined and raws at retail during 10 years, 1901-1910, averaged 7.25 cents per pound for refined and 4.54 cents per pound for raws.

No local taxes; conditions such that sugars may be purchased as cheap in smallest hamlet as in the largest grocery store in the city.

WHOLESALE AND RETAIL PRICES OF SUGAR AT ROUEN, FRANCE.

Wholesale prices extending back to 1898 are given herewith; those of years previous to this date could not be obtained. Retail prices follow closely these prices, as there are few grocers who attempt to make any profit on sugar, selling it practically at cost.

Wholesale prices.

RAW SUGAR.

Year.	Per 100 kilos.	Per 220.4 pounds.	Per pound.
	Francs.		*Cents.*
1898	76.33	$14.73	6.68
1899	78.33	15.12	6.86
1900	80.33	15.50	7.03
1901	78.33	15.12	6.86
1902	69.33	13.38	6.07
1903	48.33	9.33	4.23
1904	58.83	11.35	5.15
1905	45.33	8.75	3.97
1906	45.33	8.75	3.97
1907	47.33	9.13	4.14
1908	47.83	9.23	4.19
1909	53.83	10.39	4.71
1910	55.33	10.68	4.85

REFINED SUGAR (CRYSTALLIZED).

Year.	Per 100 kilos.	Per 220.4 pounds.	Per pound.
1898	99.33	$19.17	8.69
1899	101.33	19.56	8.87
1900	96.33	18.59	8.43
1901	87.33	16.85	7.64
1902	91.33	17.63	8.00
1903	54.33	10.48	4.75
1904	64.95	12.53	5.68
1905	54.33	10.48	4.75
1906	55.33	10.68	4.85
1907	58.45	11.28	5.12
1908	59.58	11.50	5.22
1909	69.70	13.45	6.10
1910	64.08	12.37	5.61

CUT SUGAR.

Year.	Per 100 kilos.	Per 220.4 pounds.	Per pound.
1898	113.33	21.87	9.92
1899	112.33	21.68	9.84
1900	109.33	21.10	9.58
1901	103.33	19.94	9.05
1902	101.33	19.56	8.88
1903	64.33	12.41	5.63
1904	72.83	14.06	6.38
1905	64.33	12.41	5.63
1906	66.83	12.90	5.85
1907	69.93	13.50	6.12
1908	69.93	13.50	6.12
1909	79.58	15.36	6.97
1910	75.58	14.59	6.62

IRREGULAR SUGAR (ODDS AND ENDS FROM CUT SUGAR).

Year.	Per 100 kilos.	Per 220.4 pounds.	Per pound.
1898	109.33	21.10	9.58
1899	109.33	21.10	9.58
1900	105.33	20.33	9.22
1901	98.33	18.98	8.61
1902	98.33	18.98	8.61
1903	63.33	12.22	5.54
1904	70.33	13.57	6.16
1905	61.33	11.84	5.37
1906	61.33	11.84	5.37
1907	66.43	12.82	5.82
1908	68.33	13.19	5.98
1909	78.33	15.12	6.86
1910	73.33	14.15	6.42

At retail, refined (cut and loaf), 6.35 cents per pound; raws, 5.94 cents per pound.
Packages for raws, 220 pound bags.
Refined retails in small bags same as in the United States.

[Book 2, St. Pierre, St. Pierre Island, July 29, 1911.]

Consul is informed that sugar imported here from France comes within certain bounties allowed by the French Government, and for that reason is actually cheaper here than in France. No information in regard to these bounties can be obtained in St. Pierre.

(Brussels convention allowed France to give certain privileges to the colonies.)

Prices vary with different merchants. Average prices now are: Wholesale—Loaf, 6 cents per pound; best granulated, 5½ cents per pound; unrefined or yellow granulated, 4.80 cents per pound. Retail—Loaf, 6.25 cents; best granulated, 6 cents; unrefined or yellow, 5.40 cents.

The general tariff of France applies to sugar imported into this colony from any other country than France, and since there is no duty on French sugar, the entire supply here is imported from France.

There are no local taxes.

[St. Pierre, Sept. 6, 1911. (Supplementary)].

In 1900, prices practically same as now, i. e., best granulated 5½ cents per pound wholesale, and 6 cents retail. Unrefined, 4.80 cents wholesale and 5.40 cents retail.

All sugar here comes from France and price here depends on price there. Before the French law providing certain bounties on exported sugar became effective in 1895, sugar was imported in considerable quantities from the United States.

[Book 2, p. 58, Algeria, Sept. 18, 1911.]

Wholesale and retail prices last 11 years.

Year.	Raw sugar.		Refined sugar.	
	Wholesale.	Retail.	Wholesale.	Retail.
1901	10.24	10.67	11.20	11.54
1902	9.71	10.60	10.59	11.02
1903	8.67	9.10	9.53	9.98
1904	9.10	9.53	9.88	10.30
1905	6.91	7.35	8.31	8.75
1906	7.61	8.05	8.49	8.92
1907	8.05	8.49	8.49	8.92
1908	7.78	8.22	8.25	9.01
1909	7.61	8.06	8.66	9.07
1910	9.01	9.45	9.88	10.32
1911	8.32	8.75	9.45	9.62

Quotations in cents per pound.

[Book 2, Algiers, Sept. 18, 1911.]

Refined and raw sugars are carefully separated in the import tariff of Algiers. Refined grades are: Best sugar made in north of France, valued at 8.48 cents per pound and 8.92 cents per pound wholesale, and at retail 9.358 cents per pound. Cane sugar from Marseille 7.84 cents per pound wholesale to 8.28 cents retail.

First grade 2.2-pound packages to 11 pounds, and second grade 55 to 110 pounds.

Only the crystallized sold in sacks at 0.0872 cent to 0.174 cent per pound less.

Sugars pay two separate taxes on entering Algiers.

Sugars "in powder," consul says, which the presumed rendering is of 98° at least net of refined sugar, pays $0.875 per 100 pounds of 100°; over 98°, $1.57 per 100 pounds, and $0.435 per 100 pounds added to 0.875 equals $1,310 per 100 pounds of 100°.

Refined sugar from foreign countries other than that used for making candies, $1.57 per 100 pounds duty. Crystallized, $1.67 per 100 pounds duty. There is a tax (not stated) for the schools, divided by the number of population, added to the above taxes, meaning also there are the following taxes on raw sugar made from the waste in factories: In powder, $1.39 per 100 pounds net weight; refined in every form, $1.39 per 100 pounds net weight; sugar for candies, $1.39 per 100 pounds net weight.

[Book 2, Guadeloupe, June 27, 1911.]

Only one quality made in the colony, called "sugar d'usine les jet," meaning refined white sugar (semirefined washed), which all goes to France except what is kept for local consumption, say 900 tons yearly. The 1909 production was 26,000 tons; the

1910 production was 44,000 tons; the 1909 export was (to France) 25,000 tons, the 1910 export was (to France) 43,000 tons.

Prices now are 4.80 cents per pound wholesale and 5 cents per pound retail which rises to 6 cents per pound under freight and charges to the interior. All selling in bags 200 pounds net, 202 pounds gross. Sales at 30 days sight at 20 per cent discount.

No local taxes. No national bounties.

Prices for each 5 years for 25 years have varied from $3 to $6 per 100 pounds.

[Book 2, Tahiti, Society Islands, Aug. 17, 1911.]

A leading industry, but not enough produced to supply the local market and very little exported. Grade is practically No. 1 Demerara yellow.

No taxes on home production.

Imported sugars are lump and granulated, mostly from France, paying duty $0.812 per 100 pounds. Balance comes from America at duty $3.09 per 100 pounds. This is charged on all sugars except from France. (Protection on French refined, $2.27 per 100 pounds.)

French and American lump sugar and granulated bring the same prices, which five years ago were 0.07½ cent per pound, and is now 0.06½ cent per pound. Imports in 1910 were valued at $6,297, of which United States gave $1,663 worth.

Anam prices for last six years (home production).

	Wholesale.	Retail.
	Cents.	*Cents.*
1906	0.04¾	0.05
1907	.04½	.05⅛
1908	.04⅞	$.05\frac{3}{10}$
1909	.05⅛	.05½
1910	.05¼	.05¾
1911	.05⅜	.06

[Translation.]

JANUARY 8, 1912.

Messrs. WILLETT & GRAY,
New York, N. Y.

DEAR SIRS: We have your letter of December 15, and are pleased to give you herewith some information on "de taxes de distance," which will enable you to advise properly those interested.

The "de taxes de distance" are allowances accorded to sugars from French colonies imported into France and, under certain conditions, to domestic sugar.

That allowed to sugars imported from French colonies has for its object the compensating of the colonies for the distance traveled compared with domestic sugars. This is allowed in accordance with amount of freight paid by the colonies, but it can not exceed 2.25 francs for Atlantic colonies and 2.50 francs for other colonies.

This allowance is for 100 kilos of sugar based on refined.

The allowance accorded to domestic sugars is destined to facilitate the supplies of refiners distant from centers of production. It is allowed:

First. Raw sugars made in factories of the metropolis shipped from French ports on the North Sea or English Channel, destined to French ports on the Atlantic and the Mediterranean, to be worked in the refineries of these ports for exportation and to be subject to the "coasting trade laws" (régime de cabotage).

Second. Raw sugars produced by factories in the metropolis, shipped by railroad to the refineries of Atlantic ports and the Mediterranean, to be worked for export, subject to the condition that the factory is at least 250 kilometers from the port where the refinery is located.

Third. Raw sugars produced by factories in the metropolis, shipped by railroad or canals to refineries in the interior for exportation, under the conditions that the factory and refinery be 300 kilometers apart.

For domestic sugars the allowance is established per 100 kilos, actual weight, on the amount of freight, without exceeding the rate of 2 francs per 100 kilos.

These "de taxes" are allowed in form of drawback certificates (bons de droits), and when settled serve to balance the obligations of "temporary admission," as these sugars are entered and placed under the laws of temporary admission.

Trusting that this will be of service to you and assuring you of the fact that we are always pleased to be of service.

Yours, very truly,

GERMANY.

[Book 3, p. 1, from Consular Reports, July 6, 1911.]

At Aix la Chapelle prices are, for powdered, at wholesale, 4.76 cents per pound; retail, 5.01 cents. For granulated, 4.79 cents per pound wholesale and 5.72 cents per pound retail.

Powdered is packed in linen bags of 220.4 pounds each, while granulated is in boxes of 25, 55, 110 pounds, and packages. New York, wholesale, granulated, 5.10; cubes, 5.35, of 5½ pounds.

[Book 3, p. 4, at Brunswick, July 7, 1911.]

Tax equals $1.66 per 110 pounds or $1.51 per 100 pounds.

	1911	1906	1901	1896	1891	1886
Granulated price:	*Cents.*	*Cents.*	*Cents.*	*Cents.*	*Cents.*	*Cents.*
Wholesale	4.42	3.88	6.23	4.64	5.61	5.56
Retail	4.96	4.75	7.34	5.39	6.91	6.47
Loaf and cut:						
Wholesale	4.64	4.26	6.39	5.12	6.15	5.72
Retail	5.61	5.61	7.77	6.04	7.77	6.91

No sugar exchange at Brunswick. Newspaper quotations are those of Magdeburg, which is the central sugar market of Germany.

[Book 3, p. 8, at Berlin, July 5, 1911.]

Raw sugar in original state not consumed, but when denatured and made unfit for food it pays no tax. Raw quotations here are for Hamburg f. o. b. on basis of 88° yield for first product and basis of 75° for after products. Sugar yield first product 87.90° to 95.60°, and for after products 71.40° to 90.30° (in refined). No raw sugar is handled in Berlin. See page 5 for Hamburg f. o. b. quotations for 1910. Refined quotations depend upon Magdeburg Sugar Exchange. See page 6 for prices on June 30, 1911. Retail prices vary. Department stores sell at less than smaller ones. See page 6 for prices and description of packages. No local taxes in Berlin, but a consumption tax of 14 marks ($3.33) per 100 kilos, which equals 1.51 cents per pound, on all sugar intended for consumption.

[Book 3, p. 7.]

Gives prices of refined in Magdeburg for 5 years with taxes.

The high prices of 1901–3 were owing to the selling regulations of the sugar kartel which existed from June, 1901, to September 1, 1903.

[Book 3, p. 9, at Bremen, July 5, 1911.]

Prices governed by Brunswick and Magdeburg. No demand for cane sugar.

Raw sugar not handled.

See page 9 for prices and description of packages.

[Book 3, p. 10, at Breslau, July 10, 1911.]

Raw sugar prices are Hamburg f. o. b. quotations. The Brussels Convention went into effect September 1, 1903, in England, Germany, France, Austria-Hungary, Holland, Belgium, and Italy. It abolished bounties and allowed only the imposition of the regular internal tax plus 2.40 marks ($0.57) per 50 kilos (110 pounds).

If a convention country exports sugar to Germany, the latter country can collect only the internal tax of 7 marks ($1.51) plus 2.40 marks, in all, 9.40 marks ($2.04 per 100 pounds). On the date when convention went into effect Germany reduced the tax to 7 marks from 10 marks.

April 1, 1903, the saccharine law took effect, requiring the purchase of the saccharine on prescription for artificial sweetening, reducing the annual consumption of sugar by more than 100 million pounds. The tax reduction has increased consumption among the masses and is strongly and steadily increasing. Sales include Silesian cube sugar.

See page 11 for prices and description of packages.

[Book 3, p. 13, at Cassel, July 1, 1911.]

See page 13 for prices and description of packages.

[Book 3, p. 14, at Chemnitz, Saxony.]

The grades are cut, cubes, crushed, powdered.

Three-fourths of the consumption is powdered.

Retail dealers purchase directly from factories or their agents, so wholesale prices are identical with refiners' prices. For prices see page 14.

Sugar delivered at Chemnitz adds $0.065 per 100 pounds for cost of sacks and freight.

Improved methods have increased the yield of refined sugar during past 25 years.

There are no local taxes in Saxony.

[Book 3, p. 17, at Coburg, July 22, 1911.]

Sales only of fine white sugar, lump and cones.

See pages 17–18 for prices.

[Book 3, p. 18, at Cologne, July 7 and 14, 1911.]

Cologne has a chamber of commerce.

All information refused by factories and chamber of commerce, showing feeling that exists in giving information for use in the United States.

See pages 18, 19, and 20 for dealers' prices.

[Book 3, p. 21, at Dresden, Aug. 22, 1911.]

Retailers make small profit.

See page 22 for prices.

[Book 3, p. 23, at Erfurt, July 1, 1911.]

Nearest sugar factories are at two not very distant cities.

Retail customers who belong to a rebate savings association receive from merchants a discount from the retail prices of 4 per cent cash or trading stamps.

For prices see pages 23 and 24.

Sugars used include raw, white granulated, loaf, cones, and pulverized.

Cones and "blued" are preferred for preserving and canning.

No local taxes on production or sale.

Conditions do not differ much from Magdeburg owing to nearness of factories.

[Book 3, p. 27, at Frankfort on the Main.]

Two grades, refined 99° loaf, lump and ground, and a coarser white sugar.

Retailers sometimes buy direct from refiners.

No local taxes.

Sugar is used as a leader.

Sugar comes from Frankenthal, Hildesheim, Magdeburg, and by water from Pomerania and Silesia.

No sugar factories near.

For prices see page 30.

[Book 3, p. 32, at Hamburg, July 17, 1911.]

No local taxes.

Retail prices are not affected by any conditions other than such as apply throughout the German Empire.

See page 33 for prices at Cologne and Magdeburg, 1885–1909, at wholesale.

There is an association of retail grocers in Hamburg for the purpose of purchasing supplies and regulating the retail prices.

See page 34 for retail prices from 1904 to 1911.

[Book 3, p. 35, at Hanover, 1911.]

Sugar sold by factories at Hildesheim and Brunswick delivered to the car and freight prices are extra. Grocers (retailers) have an association which buys in carload lots and ahead of wants when prices are low.

See page 35 for prices.

[Book 3, p. 39, Kehl, Baden, July 13, 1911.]

Magdeburg and Hamburg exchanges make prices for raw sugar.

Basis for sale of all refined sugar is the large loaf. Other grades are blocks, granulated, ground, powdered, pearl, and crystal.

See pages 39 and 40 for prices and terms.

[Book 3, p. 41, at Leipzig, July 5, 1911.]

No raw sugar handled.

Refined prices governed by Hamburg.

Small difference between wholesale and retail granulated, and loaves are sold also.

A local tax of $1.51 per 100 pounds is collected by the Government from the sugar manufacturers.

For prices see page 41.

[Book 3, pp. 42-47, at Magdeburg, July 10, 1911.]

No local or other taxes except consumption tax of $1.51 per 100 pounds is levied on all refined sugar, but is intended only for that used for inland consumption. If the sugar is exported, the amount already paid is refunded to the refineries. All national bounties are abolished.

See pages 42, 43, 44, 45, 46, and 47 for prices from 1884 to 1905.

[Book 3, p. 49, Manheim, June 30, 1911.]

The largest sugar factory in Germany is at Frankenthal, Pfalz.

Prices are quoted to the trade by this factory. Crystals, 4.45 cents per pound; loaf, 4.67 cents per pound.

Sugar is imported from Cuba, Java, Jamaica, Trinidad, and Egypt.

The duty is $2.027 per 100 pounds.

As a rule laborers buy loaf sugar, so the amount given to each member of the family can be accurately measured.

For prices see page 49.

[Book 3, p. 50, Nuremberg, July 10, 1911.]

No raw sugar sold, only German sugar sold. In loaves, cubes, and powdered.

For prices see pages 50-51.

[Book 3, p. 53, Plauen, July 11, 1911.]

Sugar sold here comes from Magdeburg and is beet.

No sugar factories and no sugar grown in the Vogtland.

Kinds are cones, granulated, and cubes.

People buy by the German pound, which is 1.1023 English pounds.

See page 53 for prices.

[Book 3, p. 55, Serau, July 7, 1911.]

Beet sugar of Silesia used exclusively.

Three kinds, white granulated, loaf, and cubes. Granulated the most largely used. Powdered used by confectioners.

For prices see page 55.

[Book 3, p. 57, Stettin, July 6, 1911.]

Quite difficult to obtain information, owing to reluctance of local interests, official and commercial, to impart the same. There is a Stettin Chamber of Commerce. Wholesale prices are determined by that of Hamburg and Madgeburg markets. Consumption tax was 10 marks per 50 kilos until October 1, 1903, when reduced to 7 marks because the annulment of export bounty of marks 125 per 50 kilos in Prussia on October 1, 1903, and German manufacturers could not continue to pay 10 marks tax in view of the loss of the bounty. Market conditions since 1903 are greatly influenced by Brussels convention. Sugar merchants in Stettin doubt its renewal in 1913. There was one export of sugar to the United States in 1910 on December 20, of 50,000 sacks of raw 88 test beet to B. H. Howell, Son & Co., of New York, by the steamer *Rubonia*, valued at 9.15 marks f. o. b. Stettin.

One of the largest refineries of Germany is located here. This factory, although reluctant, finally gave figures for 1885-1910, which may be found on page 60 of the report.

The consumption tax is 7 marks per 50 kilos equal to 1.51 cents per pound.

No duty on exports. Import duty is marks 2.40 per 50 kilos.

[Book 3, p. 62, Wiesbaden, July 1, 1911.]

Loaf sugar is basis of value.

Raw sugar not traded in.

For prices, wholesale and retail, see page 62.

[Book 3, p. 63, Stuttgart, July 3, 1911.]

Sugar is refined in Stuttgart and Heilbrom.
The raw sugar is produced from beets grown in Wistemburg and sells f. o. b. Hamburg at $2.27 per 110 pounds.
No cane sugar is refined or sold.
For prices see page 63.

[Book 3, p. 64, Samoa (German), Aug. 11, 1911.]

Ninety per cent of sugar brought into Apia Samoa is produced in Fiji and comes by Auckland and Sydney, the remaining 10 per cent is from Queensland.
Only refined is imported, consisting of three grades. No. 1 crystallized, No. 2 white, and No. 3 brown. Wholesale prices No. 1 in 56-pound bags $2.75, retail 10 cents per pound. No. 2, wholesale. $2.50 and retail 8 cents per pound. No 3, wholesale, $2.25 and retail 6 cents per pound. Cubes in 24-pound bags $2.16 and retail at 12½ cents per pound.
No taxes.
Custom duty 12½ per cent ad valorem.
Until 1900 over 50 per cent was imported from San Francisco in barrels, but this was given up on account of lower freight rates from British colonies.

[Book 3, Summary, November, 1911.]

The consuls' reports from 24 places show that:
1. Magdeburg Sugar Exchange makes the market for refined at Brunswick every day, and Magdeburg and Brunswick make the market for all Germany.
2. The largest sugar factory in Germany is at Frankenthal, and its prices given to the wholesale trade on June 20 were $4.67 per pound for loaf; June 20, 1911, New York granulated $5 per 100 pounds; $5.25 for cubes.
3. The Magdeburg prices on the same day were 4.64 cents per pound. Prices elsewhere vary by amount of freight.
4. No raw-beet sugars are used for consumption in Germany.
5. Granulated and cubes (loaf) are most largely used, loaf sugar being the basis of value.
6. The poorest class use the cubes so as to measure the pieces given each member of the family.
7. Retail stores at Magdeburg and the suburbs fail to show differences of more than one-fifth to two-fifths cents per pound.
8. Usually sold at retail in paper bags of 1.1023 pounds (German pound).
9. Retail grocers in Germany combine and purchase by carloads from refiners.
10. Department stores undersell others, making sugar a leader.
11. The forced use by law of saccharine has reduced use of sugar largely.
12. Reduction of tax in 1903 has largely increased consumption.
13. Retail dealers (Chemnitz) purchase direct from refiners, so wholesale prices are refiners' prices. See page 14 for prices; also Frankfort prices on page 27.
14. Information difficult to obtain (Cologne, p. 18) on account of feeling existing against giving such information for use in the United States.
15. Retailers make small profits. (Dresden, p. 21.)
16. Retail customers in the association receive 4 per cent rebate. (Erfert, p. 23.)
17. No local taxes or others besides the consumption tax.
18. Hamburg has a retail grocers' association to regulate retail prices and buy supplies. (Retail prices on p. 34.)
19. Sugar sold at factories is delivered to cars and freight is extra to place of consumption.
20. Magdeburg and Hamburg make prices for raw sugars (Kehl, p. 39), meaning Magdeburg makes prices for sales from raw sugar makers to the German refineries. (There are 350 raw-sugar factories and 43 refineries in Germany, and there are other factories which make refined direct from the beet juice.) W. P. W.
21. Some cane sugar imported at Mannheim.
22. A German pound is 1.1023 pounds, English.
23. One export of raw sugar to the United States was made in 1910 (December).
24. One of the largest refineries is at Stettin. (Prices, pp. 59–60.)
25. Import duty is 2.40 marks per 50 kilos, or 0.518 cent per pound. (P. 57.)
26. Prices for raws at Magdeburg are basis of sales of raws to refiners.
Prices of refined at Magdeburg are basis of sales to consumers.
Prices of raws and refined at Hamburg are basis for exports.
27. The refiners make lists of prices.

28. Prices at Magdeburg were, on July 10:
New York prices, granulated, $5 per 100 pounds; cubes, $5.35 per 100 pounds.
Crystals, $0.054 per pound retail; no price for wholesale.
Granulated, $0.049 per pound retail; no price for wholesale.
Fine powdered, $0.044 per pound retail; $0.0438 per pound wholesale.
Loaf, $0.056 per pound retail; $0.0464 per pound wholesale.
Lump, $0.055 per pound retail; $0.0441 per pound wholesale.
Raw, 88° test, $0.0248 per pound.
July 8, 1911. Raws, 88° f. o. b. Hamburg, 11s. 8½d.=$0.0255 per pound.
There is always a market in Hamburg for the world trade.
There is not always a market in Magdeburg for the local trade.

29. Prices at Frankenthal factory on June 26, 1911, were: Crystals, $0.045 per pound, loaf sugar $0.0467 per pound, against $0.0445 per pound at Madgeburg on July 1st.

30. Prices at Stettin were controlled by Hamburg and Magdeburg.

31. The price of refined at Magdeburg, Frankenthal, and Stettin fairly represents the refiners' prices for all Germany

32. No information of production, consumption, exports, etc., is given in these reports.

33. The Stettin consul says:

"To estimate the prices for granulated sugar, the German tax of $1.51 per 100 pounds and the cost of granulation $0 538 per 100 pounds must be added to price of raw 88° test and for refined sugar $0.215 per 100 pounds more must be added."

Cost of semirefining granulated from 88° raws is $0.538 per 100 pounds.

Cost of full refining granulated from 88° raws is $0.753 per 100 pounds.

Great Britain.

ENGLAND.

[Book 4, p. 2, Birmingham June 30, 1911.]

English sugar refiners use raw beet or cane sugar and do not guarantee their product as either beet or cane, but sell simply as refined granulated, or lump, or powdered sugar. Just now refiners are using raw beet sugar as cheaper than cane.

The refined sugars of Messrs. Henry Tate & Sons (Ltd.) govern the wholesale prices of all sugars in the United Kingdom, whether refined in the United Kingdom or on the continent of Europe. When this firm raises or lowers their prices other refiners follow.

The lump sugar used in Birmingham is refined in London and the granulated in Liverpool. There is no charge for freight from London on cubes, but there is a freight of $0.107 per 100 pounds on granulated from Liverpool.

Tate's standard sugars are offered to-day to Birmingham purchasers as follows:

No. 1 cubes, per 100 pounds	$4.17
Less 2½ per cent at London	.104
Wholesale cost	4.066

(Should be $4.18 net, as Tate's price is given elsewhere as $4.18 net.)

Cost at Birmingham, $4.066 per 100 pounds. Retail, 5 cents per pound.

June 30, 1911, at New York lump sugar was quoted at 5.80 cents per pound subject to a discount of 2 per cent.

Tate's granulated (fine), per 100 pounds	$3.848
Less 2½ per cent at Liverpool	.096
Plus freight to Birmingham	3.752
Freight	.107
Wholesale per 100 pounds at Birmingham from London	3.859

Retails at 4.50 cents per pound. (Same standard—Liverpool—costs $3.79.)

Continental lump (standard T. T. D.), per 100 pounds at Liverpool	$3.25
Duty	.399
Per 100 pounds net cash	3.649
Freight to Birmingham	.107
Wholesale	3.756

Retails in cheap shops to poorer classes at 4 cents per pound.

Continental granulated (Z. R.), per 100 pounds	$2.78
Duty	.399
Per 100 pounds net cash at Liverpool	3.179
Freight to Birmingham	.107
Cost at Birmingham	3.276

Retails in cheap stores to poorer classes at 3.50 cents per pound.

Pages 5 to 7 give retail methods in full.

The lowest price at which any sugar is sold at retail is 3 cents per pound, for a soft brown sugar of very poor quality.

[Book 4, p. 11.]

Wholesale prices vary each normal year from 1¼ cents to 1¾ cents per pound.

Prices generally vary (advance) considerably in the period between old and new crops. (Same as in the United States. W.)

Tates Cubes No. 1 is a high grade.

Tates Cubes No. 2 is a lower grade of lump or cube sugar and sells in Birmingham at 2.14 cents per pound less than the No. 1. (Tates No. 2 should be used for comparison with American sugars. W.)

Tates list prices are subject to 2½ per cent discount and plus $0.107 freight to Birmingham on granulated, and $0.027 per 100 pounds for cartage. London refiners establish depots, and make no charge for deliveries at that point. Bradford is one such, but from Liverpool a delivery charge is made of $0.055 per 100 pounds to Bradford.

London and Liverpool wholesalers have advantage of freight over Birmingham buyers.

Duties.—Prior to 1901 there was no tax or duty on sugar, but from 1901 to 1908 there was a duty of $0.90 per 100 pounds, 100° test, on sugar of 98° test, but since 1908 the duty has been $0.399 per 100 pounds.

	Per 100 pounds.
The refiner in London (June 30) buys raw beet sugar 88° analysis in Hamburg at a free on board price of 11 s.	$2.378
Transportation charges to London	.214
	2.592
Duty on 88° analysis	.338
Cost to London refiner	2.930
London list price for standard granulated, net	3.69
Difference between raw and refined	.760
Difference between raw and refined at New York on June 30, 1911	.920

[Book 4, pp. 13 to 15.]

Gives fluctuations of raw beet sugar 88° analysis f. o. b. Hamburg 1885 to 1910 to which the London and Liverpool refiners must add $0.219 per 100 pounds for freight and charges.

To these prices the Birmingham consul says $0.437 per 100 pounds should be added to bring the prices to those of the refined granulated and also the duty of $0.399 per 100 pounds.

For example·

[Book 4, p. 21, Birmingham, July 17, 1911.]

The speculative beet market shows considerable activity, enormous commitments having been entered into. Fabricants buying back at higher prices than they sold it for is significant.

Wholesalers sell to retailers at $0.107 per 100 pounds above wholesale price of granulated of foreign origin, and for $0.053 per 100 pounds more for English and one month's credit is given.

Where the grocer (retailer) can buy granulated at $3.50 to $3.80 per 100 pounds he charges the customer 4 cents per pound. When his costs over $4.80 he charges 4.94 cents to 5 cents per pound.

Some retail dealers whose specialty is tea give sugar away to encourage trade.

[Book 4, p. 22, Bradford, June 30, 1911.]

Messrs. Henry & Sons (Ltd.) price list, London, June 29, 1911, names 67 towns (depots) in England, 4 in Wales, 4 in Scotland, and 1 in Ireland at which their cube sugars will be delivered without charge.

They name 17 depots in England, 5 in Wales, 7 in Isle of Man, 1 in Scotland, where all grades of their sugars will be delivered free of freight and charges.

Rates of freight, mostly at $0.107 per 100 pounds, are given for nearly every point outside of depots in England, Scotland, and Wales.

They quote prices of cubes as far forward as August and September delivery. August 1½d. higher than prompt, or $3.27 per 100 pounds, and September 1½d. lower than prompt, or $3.27 per 100 pounds.

Their list prices give many grades of hard and soft refined sugar, although not as many of the latter as American refiners make. Their selling terms are cash in London or Liverpool within 14 days less 2½ per cent discount.

If not paid in 14 days, interest is added from date of invoice to date of payment, and the 2½ per cent discount will be forfeited unless payment is made within 21 days.

Tate's prices June 29 were:

At London and all depots in England, Scotland, Ireland, and Wales, cubes No. 1, hundredweight cases, $4.18 net per 100 pounds; cubes No. 2, hundredweight cases, $3.98 per 100 pounds; fine granulated, $3.77 net per 100 pounds; and standard granulated, $3.69 net.

All their cubes are made at their London refinery and all crystals and softs at their Liverpool refinery. Granulated is made at both refineries, and prices are the same for fine granulated and 1½d. less at Liverpool for standard granulated.

[Book 4, p. 22, Bradford, June 30.]

Foreign granulated wholesales at $3.40 to $3.50 per 100 pounds and retails at 4 cents to 5 cents per pound.

English cubes, wholesale, $4.09 to $4 20 per 100 pounds. Foreign cubes, wholesale, $3.97 per 100 pounds.

All cubes retail at 4½ cents to 5 cents per pound.

Seventy-five per cent of sugar consumed in Bradford is foreign granulated. Retail demand is for 1, 2, and 7 pound quantities, weighed out and wrapped ready to deliver to customers.

[Book 4, p. 26, Bristol, Aug. 1, 1911]

The port of Bristol being without sugar refineries, draws its supplies from Germany, Russia, France, Holland, and Belgium, and through Bristol a large district around is supplied.

Crystallized raw sugars from Trinidad, Jamaica, Surinam, St. Lucia, Demerara, Peru, and Mexico are all sold under the trade term of "Demeraras."

All these pay duties on their polarization. Some pay the highest duty of $0.399 per 100 pounds. These sugars come to Bristol by way of London and Liverpool, paying freight from there. The wholesale price for Demeraras is $3.36 to $3.90 per 100 pounds plus freight (not stated).

Refined cubes are largely purchased from Tate, London, and present prices (Aug. 1) are $4.45 ($4.34 net) to $4.72 per 100 pounds. Freight paid to Bristol. Cubes from the Continent vary in price from $3.47 to $3.80 per 100 pounds f. o. b. Hamburg and plus duty, $0.399 per 100 pounds, say, $3.80 f. o. b. plus freight, etc., $0.214, and plus duty, $0.399, and which equals $4.413 per 100 pounds, cost of continental cubes at Bristol.

"First marks" granulated from the Continent have chief sale at cost of $3.15 to $3.36 per 100 pounds f. o. b., plus duty $0. 399 equals $3.55 to $3.76 per 100 pounds cost at Bristol.

Finer qualities of English granulated cost $4.50 ($4.39 net) to $4.67 ($4.55 net) per 100 pounds freight and duty paid.

As to retail prices all towns, large or small, have associations of grocers and retail prices are fixed from time to time, grocers undertaking not to sell below the minimum prices fixed. Sometimes somebody cuts prices. One large company may have 500 to 600 shops in various towns and some one cuts and all the others follow.

Retail prices in shop of high rent and delivery wagons sell No. 2 cubes at 4 cents to 6 cents per pound. No. 2 granulated at 4 cents to 6 cents per pound, and Demeraras at 5 cents to 6 cents per pound.

English refiners pack in cartons but grocers prefer to sell by the pound so as not to make it a proprietary article. There is a duty on imports of $0. 399 per 100 pounds maximum.

Russian granulated has a small bounty about $0.214 per 100 pounds, and did not join the Brussels convention for abolishing sugar bounties and, in consequence, their exports to England are restricted to a certain quantity, which they are not allowed to exceed.

Wholesale prices for past years have varied only because of short crops and from atmospheric conditions. This year there has been a great time of dryness on the continent of Europe and the best plants have suffered so much that the market has bounded up 44 cents to 65 cents per 100 pounds on refined in this country. And, then, last year there was a great speculation in continental sugars by one man who worked the market up several shillings, and when he had made his pile and got out holders had to realize and down came the market here and great was the loss to many holders.

Note the fine position of the United States during that 1910 speculation when prices soared in Europe and our supplies were had at 54 cents per 100 pounds below the European parity simply because our free and partially free from duty supplies were within 77,000 tons of our entire requirements. Had we been as short of local supplies last year as we were this year prices in the United States would have soared with Europe.

These occurrences in Europe point the way for the United States to be independent of their short crops and speculative prices by promoting our domestic cane and beet industries to an amount somewhat in excess of our yearly requirements. Whenever these supplies become larger than our requirements, a competition among the free of duty and the partially free of duty sugar will become a feature of the sugar business of the United States, through which competition our consumers will benefit.

As a sugar expert I see that the vital point of the whole sugar situation here lies in the direction of increased domestic production.

Russia's production exceeds her consumption and limited exports and, as a result, consumers there are entirely independent of short crops and high prices elsewhere.

[Book 4, p. 32.]

Retailers in the United Kingdom do not change their prices with every variation in the wholesale prices, but frequently hold prices down to the wholesale cost for a time. (New York granulated, $5; New York cubes, $5.25.)

[Book 4, p. 33, Stoke on Trent, June 30, 1911.]

Population, 235,000 people. Burselm, Tate's, wholesale, standard granulated, $3.79 per 100 pounds, and retail 4 cents to 5 cents per pound.

Fine granulated, wholesale, $3.80 per 100 pounds, and retail 4 cents to 5 cents per pound. Lump (cubes), $4.02 to $4.23 per 100 pounds wholesale and 5 cents per pound retail.

Liverpool packs granulated in 4 and 7 pound bags.

Other manufacturers: Standard granulated, $3.67 per 100 pounds wholesale and 4.05 cents per pound retail; fine granulated, $3.80 per 100 pounds wholesale and 5.06 cents per pound retail; Demerara crystals, $3.90 per 100 pounds wholesale and 5.06 cents per pound retail.

Margin between wholesale and retail prices is very small.

Wholesale prices here may be ascertained by adding freight to Liverpool refinery prices and to Hamburg f. o. b. prices.

Freight from Liverpool refiners, except Tate, is $0.116 per 100 pounds by canal and $0.135 by rail. Tate's freight charge and depot charge is $0.053 per 100 pounds from Liverpool.

Continental sugar is bought from Manchester and Liverpool merchants who buy f. o. b. Hamburg and a freight charge of $2.21 per 100 pounds from Hamburg to Liverpool; to Stoke and delivery to store of buyer is included in price. (Must include duty also of $0.399 per 100 pounds and seems too high then. W.)

[Book 4, p. 39. Huddersfield, June 29.]

Population, 107,825 people; principal city for manufacture of woolens and worsted or men's wear.

Prices for sugar are 3 per cent lower than London, 11 per cent lower for coal, 2 per cent lower for meat, 10 per cent lower for rent, as well as lower for all other commodities.

June 30, 1911.	Prices.	
	Wholesale (per 100 pounds).	Retail (per pound).
		Cents.
Lump	$4.20	5.0
Tate's cubes No. 2	3.98	5.0
Standard granulated	3.66	4.20

[Book 4, pp. 42 and 43.]

Gives prices for 1886 to 1911 by five-year periods, running from 4 to 6 cents per pound retail.

No local charges or conditions affecting sugar.

[Book 4, p. 45, Leeds, July 1, 1911.]

Tate's cubes No. 1, $4.23 per 100 pounds, wholesale, and retail, 5 cents per pound; Tate's cubes No. 2, $4.12 per 100 pounds, wholesale, and retail, 5 cents per pound; German granulated, $3.58 per 100 pounds, wholesale, and retail, 4 cents per pound.

One family paid yesterday 5¼ cents per pound for granulated and for lump sugar 5.80 cents per pound.

Another American family bought yesterday cane granulated at 4 cents per pound and lump at 5 cents per pound.

The consul says a retail dealer gave me best granulated lump at 5 cents per pound.

Manchester merchants keep large stocks in store here at the canal and deliver to stores.

The strike at Hull advanced prices, $0.16 per 100 pounds to some dealers.

(Book 4, p. 48, gives prices for five years.)

[Book 4, p. 50, Liverpool, June 30, 1911.]

1. Raw 88° analysis, $2.67, with 3 cents per pound per degree above and below.
2. Refiners refine these sugars in bond and pay on f. o. b. Hamburg terms basis 88°.
3. Cost of freight to quay in Liverpool 15 cents per 112 pounds in bond, including 2½ per cent discount.
4. Cane raw is sold on 96° polarization, and often "telquel" valuation $2.92 ex quay less 2½ per cent.
5. Real raw sugar is retailed in Liverpool at $0.045 per pound refined, wholesale.
6. American fine pure cane granulated of Franklin quality $3.52 per 100 pounds, less 2½ per cent ex store Liverpool, $3.44 net.
7. A. Z. R. (Austrian) star fine granulated similar to above American but reputed by local trade to be rather better in quality and certainly preferred in Liverpool, $3.52 less 2½ per cent; $3.44 net per 100 pounds.
8. "Meyer castor" similar to A. Z. R. rather finer grain is $3.62 less 2½ per cent; $3.54 net per 100 pounds.
9. Above prices are for sugars in store but the wholesale trade in this country buy and sell chiefly on f. o. b. Hamburg terms-prices per hundredweight (112 pounds), discount two months at 5 per cent per annum, cash against bill of lading, ship lost or not lost and payment against bill of lading before the goods arrive.
10. June 20, prices for A. Z. R. and R. P. N. fine, $3.295 f. o. b. Hamburg, and for Meyer castor $3.265 f. o. b. Hamburg.
11. First marks granulated stated by the local trade to be not quite as good quality as American standard granulated is $3.16 f. o. b. Hamburg. These sugars landed in Liverpool 66 cents per hundredweight over the f. o. b. Hamburg price, including duty and 2½ per cent discount.
12. June 29, 1911, the published prices of sugar manufactured in Liverpool and sold to shop dealers who in turn sell retail to customers.

Tates standard granulated, 3.75 cents; first quality cubes, 4.18 cents.

June 29, 1911, New York standard granulated, 5 cents; New York standard cubes, 5.25 cents.

13. Fairrie & Co., granulated A, 3.76 cents; cubes, 4.02 cents.

Retail in Liverpool June 30, 1911.

14. Granulated, pure cane per pound, 4 cents; granulated (Dutch), 4 cents; loaf sugar, double refined, 4½ cents.

15. Retail sometimes sells at cost and even below for a "draw." Near-by suburban towns increase prices one-half cent to 1 cent per pound over wholesale.

16. Retailers sell in paper bags, including weight of bag. Export duty. No bounties—beet.

17. Sugar which has passed a refining in Great Britain or Ireland and on which proper import duties have been paid, upon being exported or deposited in any bonded warehouse for use as ship stores or removal to the Isle of Man, a drawback equal to the duty on sugar is of the like polarization.

(United States refiners tried hard to get similar terms on exported sugar.)

18. English duties.

19. Retail prices in Liverpool at five-year intervals from 1886 to 1906, on page 55 of book 4.

[Book 4, p. 56, London, July 1, 1911]

20. The request made of consuls by Mr. Knox for specified information.

21. All the grades and prices of raws and refined sold in London, some 60 kinds, are quoted at wholesale and 20 quoted at retail. Wholesale terms less 2½ per cent, 14 days; less 1 per cent, 28 days; net, 28 days.

[Book 4, p. 58]

22. Cubes at wholesale (Dutch), $3.89 to $3.95 per 100 pounds.

23. Cubes at wholesale (German or Austrian), $3.78 to $3.84.

24. Cubes at wholesale (English fine to finest, but not Tates No. 1), $4.02 to $4.07 per 100 pounds net.

25. Granulated at wholesale (German medium), $3.36 to $3.42 per 100 pounds.

26. Granulated at wholesale (German fine), $3.58 to $3.79.

27 Granulated at wholesale (Lyles medium), $3.48 to $3.56.

28. Granulated at wholesale (Lyles fine), $3.70 to $3.78.

29. Granulated at wholesale (Tates standard), $3.69.

30. Granulated at wholesale (Tates fine), $3.77 per 100 pounds.

Sales at wholesale are in quantities of three 112-pound bags or in five cases of 112 pounds each. For the less amount 12 cents per 112 pounds is added.

Retail prices in London:

31. Granulated, 4 cents per pound; granulated (finest), 5 cents per pound.

32. Loaf (good), 5 cents per pound; Tates No. 1 best, 5 cents to 6 cents per pound; Tates No. 2, 4½ cents to 5 cents per pound; after-tea cubes, 5 cents per pound; sparkling lump, 5 cents per pound.

[Book 4, p. 60]

Retailers sell as they please.

[Book 4, p. 61.]

Some make "special line" of sugar without profit, sold at retail in paper bags, 1, 6, and 7 pounds, put up in advance. Very unusual to weigh out sugar in presence of customer.

[Book 4, p. 62.]

No bounty paid on home-grown sugar, but one is being considered by the Government in view of efforts to produce beet sugar in various parts of the United Kingdom.

[Book 4, p. 63, July 18, 1911]

London wholesale prices at five-year intervals, 1886 to 1906:

	1886	1891	1896	1901	1906
Granulated (per 100 pounds):					
British	$4.17	$4.00	$4.07	$3.85	$4.12
German	3.45	3.66	2.88	2.33	2.94
Retail (per pound):					
Loaf	.05¼	.05	.04½	.05	.05-.06
Finest castor	.05½	.05	.04¾	.05	.06
Loaf, first double	....	.05	.04½	.04½	....

[Book 4, pp. 64 to 66.]

Lowest prices from 1886 to 1910, inclusive, were in 1887, when Tate's cubes or Lebaudy loaves reached $3.17 per 100 pounds, and in 1910, $3.75 to $5.13 per 100 pounds. Beet root 88° lowest was in 1902.

[Book 4, p. 65.]

Duties into United Kingdom were abolished on May 1, 1874, and not reimposed until April 19, 1901, when the rate varied from $0.43 to $0.90 per 100 pounds as to polarization.

On May 18, 1908, the duty was reduced to $0.178 to $0.40 per 100 pounds, according to degrees of polarization.

[Book 4, p. 66.]

It is to be observed that the retail prices of sugar since the duty of 1901, and since the present rate has applied, have not been affected by such impost.

[Book 4, p. 67.]

Retail prices have not varied in 25 years more than one-half to 1 cent per pound in normal years of normal European crops.

[Book 4, p. 68, Manchester, July 4, 1911.]

Tate's cubes No. 1, $4.17 per 100 pounds net; No. 2, $3.98 per 100 pounds net; granulated, $3.75 per 100 pounds net.

Retail prices in different stores were found to vary from 3 to 4 cents per pound for ordinary granulated. Sold at very small profit and sometimes at a loss. Some large grocery stores with many local branches sell as low as 2 cents per pound to their regular customers, but with the proviso that they take other groceries at the time of purchasing. The sugar serves as a bonus to the purchaser.

No special conditions affecting prices except labor disputes, which affect supplies and unsettle the market both for present needs and future delivery, raising prices.

Manchester fluctuations depend entirely upon the London and Liverpool market quotations.

New York granulated, 5 00; New York cubes, 5.25.

[Book 4, p. 72, Newcastle on Tyne, July 1, 1911]

Fine granulated sugar brought from Hamburg at $2.99 to $3.11 per 100 pounds f. o. b.; freight is $1.08 per 100 pounds; duty, $0.399; together $4 47 to $4.59 per 100 pounds, and is retailed at 4½ to 5 cents per pound. Ordinary granulated retails at 4 to 4½ cents per pound.

July 15, 1911, Tate's cubes No. 1, $4.29 net per 100 pounds. Retail price not given. No. 2 cubes, $4.19 net per 100 pounds, and retail price not given. Fine granulated, $3.98 net per 100 pounds. No retail price given. Standard granulated, $3.92 per 100 pounds net. Retail price probably 4 to 5 cents per pound.

[Book 4, p. 76, Nottingham, July 1. 1911]

English tubes, $4.14 per 100 pounds wholesale; retail, 5 cents per pound. English granulated, $3.70 per 100 pounds net wholesale price, and retail, 4½ cents per pound. Foreign granulated, $3.50 per 100 pounds net wholesale price, and 4 cents per pound retail price.

[Book 4, p. 77, Plymouth, July 2, 1911.]

Plymouth imports about 10,750 tons refined per year of two kinds, cubes and granulated.

Foreign cubes, 112-pound boxes, wholesale, $3.82 per 100 pounds, retail 4 to 5 cents per pound. Foreign granulated, 224-pound bags, $3.32 per 100 pounds wholesale; retail, 4 to 4½ cents per pound.

[Book 4, p. 78, Sheffield, July 1, 1911.]

First marks German granulated, wholesale, $3.44 per 100 pounds; retail, 4 to 5 cents per pound. Castor sugar, wholesale, $3.57 per 100 pounds, and retail, 4 to 5 cents per pound. Lump sugar, wholesale, $3.89 to $4.16 per 100 pounds wholesale, and 4½ to 5½ cents per pound retail.

The stone (14 pounds) and its subdivision, one-fourth stone, one-half stone, and the pound, are the units of measurement at retail.

No local charges affecting prices.

[Book 4, p. 82.]

Prices at five-year intervals at Sheffield show small variations from year to year.

[Book 4, p. 87, Southampton, June 30, 1911 (a depot).]

Tate's cubes No. 1, $4.18 net per 100 pounds; retail, 5½ cents per pound. Tate's fine granulated, $3.84 net per 100 pounds; retail, 5 cents per pound. Lyle's fine granulated, $3.91 per 100 pounds wholesale and 5 cents per pound retail. Lyle's castor (wholesale), $3.96 net per 100 pounds, and retail 8 cents per pound. Tate's icing sugar, $4.12 net per 100 pounds, and retail 9 cents per pound. Bright demeraras, $3.57 net per 100 pounds, and retail 4 cents per pound.

[Book 4, p. 88.]

Prices at five-year intervals, January 1 of each year (per 100 pounds):

Jan. 1, 1890	$4.00–$4.34
Jan. 1, 1895	2.36– 3.45
Jan. 1, 1900	2.42– 3.42

[Book 4, p. 89, Hull, June 30, 1911.]

Wholesale price foreign granulated, $3.47 to $3.63 per 100 pounds; retail, 3½ to 4 cents per pound. Wholesale price foreign cubes, $3.91 per 100 pounds; retail, 4 to 6 cents per pound. Tate's No. 1 cubes, 5 cents per pound.

The prices quoted are slightly above the usual prices, probably owing to the shortness of the Cuban crop.

London wholesale and retail prices control the market.

IRELAND.

[Book 4, p. 92, Belfast, July 31, 1911.]

New York granulated, $5.65; New York cubes, $5.90

Raw sugar (Demerara?) costs $3.92 per 100 pounds f. o. b. shipping port. Importer sells to retailer at $4.30 and retailers sell at 5.14 cents per pound.

Imported refined granulated, $3.69 wholesale; retail 4 cents per pound. Importers to retailers, $3.71 per 100 pounds; retail 4 cents per pound. Retail rates uniform throughout the city. Import duty is $0.40 per 100 pounds. Harbor dues, 16 cents per ton ($0.071 per 100 pounds). No other local taxes. No former years obtainable.

[Book 4, p. 93, Cork, July 3, 1911.]

Austrian refined supplied from London is mostly used here.

Price, wholesale, cubes $4 per 100 pounds; retail, 4½ cents per pound. Price, wholesale, granulated, $3.50 per 100 pounds; retail, 4 cents per pound.

Prices include import duty of $0.0399 per 100 pounds and freight from London 3 cents per 100 pounds on cubes.

Crystals and granulated sell in 224-pound bags; cubes in cases of 112 pounds each.

Retailed in paper bags at uniform prices.

Over 80 per cent is crystal grain; 10 per cent is granulated; 7½ per cent is cube or loaf sugar.

[Book 4, p. 96, Dublin, July 3, 1911.]

J. K. cubes, $3.91 per 100 pounds wholesale; retail, 4.05 cents per pound. Granulated, $3.66 per 100 pounds wholesale; retail, 4.05 cents per pound. Tate's cubes No. 2, $3.95 per 100 pounds wholesale, and 4.05 cents per pound retail.

Stone (14 pounds) is basis of sales at retail.

Castor sugars (like Austrian fine granulated) in 7-pound linen bags.

Wholesale and retail prices in some cases are about the same.

As a rule the wholesale price affects the retail price but little, the trade being peculiar, and sugar used as an advertisement.

SCOTLAND.

[Book 4, p. 101, Dunfermline, June 30, 1911.]

New York granulated, 5.00; New York cubes, 5.25.

Refined sugar, wholesale, $3.47 per 100 pounds; retail, 4.05 cents per pound. Government duty, $0.399 per 100 pounds on refined. In 1901 refined was $3.58 per 100 pounds wholesale; retail, 4.05 cents per pound. In 1901 raw sugar was $2.80 per 100 pounds wholesale, and retail 3.47 cents per pound. Duty in 1901 was $0.90 per 100 pounds, included in above prices. In 1906 refined was $3.42 per 100 pounds, wholesale, retail, 4.05 cents per pound. In 1906, raw sugar was $3.03 per 100 pounds wholesale; retail, 3.47 cents per pound. Duty $0.90 per 100 pounds, included in price. Difference between raw and refined, 1901, 78 cents per 100 pounds; in 1906, 39 cents per 100 pounds.

[Book 4, p. 103, Dundee, July 3, 1911.]

Tate's granulated, $3.71 per 100 pounds wholesale; retail, 4.13 cents per pound. Tate's No. 1 loaf, $4.02 per 100 pounds wholesale; 4.57 cents per pound retail. Tate's fine granulated, $3.99 per 100 pounds whlesale; retail, 4.57 cents per pound. Continental granulated, $3.40 per 100 pounds wholesale; 3½ cents per pound retail. Dutch granulated, $3.68 per 100 pounds wholesale; retail, 4 cents per pound. Dutch loaf, $3.82 per 100 pounds wholesale; retail, 4 cents per pound.

At one time a considerable retail trade was done in 7-pound bags, but as this added somewhat to the cost and the retailers were obliged to sell at the refiners' prices, the trade in this class has almost disappeared.

No local or other charges affecting prices. No prices for past years obtainable.

[Book 4, p. 108, Edinburgh, June 30 and September 14, 1911.]

Tate's cubes for five-year periods given.

Wholesale prices, Dutch cubes, for five-year periods given.

Wholesale prices, Dutch granulated, for five-year periods given.

Retail prices not obtainable.

Sugar is neither manufactured nor refined in this part of Scotland. Only refined used.

Wholesale, granulated sells in 224-pound bags; cubes in 112-pound bags.

Retailers sell by the pound weighed out, except a few 7-pound bags by Scotch refiners.

June 30, 1911, prices: S. & T. granulated, $3.52 per 100 pounds wholesale, and 4½ cents per pound retail. P. P. 2 granulated, $3.70 per 100 pounds wholesale, and 5 cents per pound retail. S. & T. cubes, $3.96 per 100 pounds wholesale, and 5 cents per pound retail.

No local charges.

[Book 4, p. 112, Glasgow, Scotland, July 13, 1911.]

New York granulated, 5.15; New York cubes, 5.40.

British cubes, $4.28 per 100 pounds wholesale; retail, 5 to 5½ cents per pound. Foreign cubes, $4.09 per 100 pounds wholesale; retail, 5 to 5½ cents per pound. British granulated, $3.84 per 100 pounds wholesale; retail, 4½ to 5 cents per pound. Foreign granulated, $3.84 per 100 pounds wholesale; retail, 4½ to 5 cents per pound.

There are several stores, such as Lipton's, which are selling some classes of sugar at 3 cents per pound. They have branches in practically every town in Great Britain and can sell at low prices on account of their enormous turnover.

During the summer season in coast towns higher prices are charged summer residents.

Sugar is refined in this district (but no particulars given W.).

Large quantities sold during fruit season for jams, jellies, and preserves to the poorer classes.

WALES.

[Book 4, p. 116, Cardiff, June 30, 1911]

No raw sugar used.

Z. H. German granulated and "First marks" represent the classes consumed.

Cones in 224-pound bags, and occasionally in casks, and are retailed in paper bags by weight, bags included in weight.

Sugar is so cheap and competition so great that it is not regarded as a profit bringer to the retailer. The standard retail price for granulated is 4 cents per pound, but if a buyer takes tea at 30 cents per pound he is given sugar at 2 cents per pound of a quality inferior to "Z. H."

In the coal mining district buyers use large crystals, which sell at 5 cents per pound retail.

Tates and German cubes sell at retail at 6 cents per pound for No. 1 and 5 cents for No. 2. German granulated "Z. H." and "First marks," $3.45 per 100 pounds wholesale, and 4 cents per pound retail. German cubes, $3.93 per 100 pounds net and 5 cents per pound retail. Tates cubes, No. 1, $4.30 per 100 pounds wholesale, and 5 cents per pound retail; No. 2, $4.12 per 100 pounds wholesale, and 5 cents per pound retail. "First marks" granulated, 1886, wholesale $3.95 per 100 pounds, retail 5 cents per pound; 1891, wholesale $3.89, and retail 5 cents per pound; 1896, wholesale $3.12 and retail 4 cents per pound; 1901, wholesale $2.64, and retail 3 cents to 4 cents per pound;

1906, wholesale $4.55, and retail 5 cents per pound; 1911, wholesale $3.40 per 100 pounds net, and retail 4 cents per pound.

German cubes, 1886, wholesale $4.50 per 100 pounds, and retail 5 cents per pound; 1891, wholesale $4.57, and retail 5 cents per pound: 1896, wholesale $3.33, and retail 4 cents per pound; 1901, wholesale $3.19, and retail 4 cents per pound: 1906, wholesale $3.73, and retail 4 cents to 5 cents per pound; 1911, wholesale $3.93 per 100 pounds, and retail 5 cents per pound.

No. 1 English cubes, 1886, wholesale, $5.10 per 100 pounds, and retail 6 cents per pound; 1891, wholesale, $5.05, and retail 6 cents per pound; 1896, wholesale, $3.90, and retail 5 cents per pound; 1901, wholesale, $3.58, and retail 5 cents per pound; 1906, wholesale, $3.93 per 100 pounds, and retail 5 cents per pound; 1911, wholesale, $4.30 per 100 pounds, and retail 6 cents per pound.

1886 to 1901. No duty.

1906. Duty $0.89 per 100 pounds.

1911. Duty $0.399 per 100 pounds.

First marks granulated, 1911, less 1½ per cent for cash.

All others net cash.

New York granulated, $5; New York cubes, $5.25.

[Book 4, p. 116, Swansea, July 5, 1911.]

Wholesale prices governed by London.

Raw sugar, $2.92 less 2½ per cent, or $2.87 net per 100 pounds. Granulated (foreign), $3.27 less 2½ per cent, or $3.19 net per 100 pounds; retail, 4 cents per pound. Lump (foreign), $3.25 to $3.37 less 2½ per cent or $3.17 to $3.29 net per 100 pounds; retail, 4 cents to 5 cents per pound. Demerara, $3.20 to $3.37 less 2½ per cent or $3.12 to $3.29 net per 100 pounds; retail, 5 cents per pound.

SUMMARY OF ENGLAND, IRELAND, SCOTLAND, AND WALES.

1. The most remarkable and notable feature of the consular reports of Great Britain is the fact that the wholesale prices of English refined are exactly the same throughout the whole length and breadth of England, Scotland, Ireland, and Wales, except in some instances where a small charge of 1½ to 5 cents per 100 pounds is made for delivery.

2. This results from the London and Liverpool refiners, Tate & Lyle, establishing depots or warehouses in 67 cities of England, 4 in Wales, 4 in Scotland, and 1 in Ireland, where they keep a constant supply, and deliver from these depots at the London prices free of freight or charges for all London manufacturers, and they have 17 depots in Enlgand, 5 in Wales, 7 in the Isle of Man, 1 in Scotland, where they deliver at Liverpool prices free of freight or charges. At all other points a very small charge is made of 2 to 7 cents per 100 pounds for delivery. For example, Tate's No. 1 cubes were delivered in any part of England, Scotland, Ireland, and Wales, with four exceptions, at list price then (June 29, 1911) of $4.18 per 100 pounds wholesale, and were retailed everywhere at 4½ to 5½ cents per pound.

3. The refined sugars of Henry Tate & Sons (Ltd.), having refineries at London and Liverpool, govern the wholesale prices of all sugars in the United Kingdom, whether refined in the United Kingdom or on the continent of Europe. When this firm raises or lowers the prices other refiners follow.

4. Their No. 1 cubes are called a proprietary article and sell at 20 cents per 100 pounds above their No. 2 cubes, which compare with cubes of other countries. Price June 29 for No. 2 cubes, $3.98 per 100 pounds. Their fine granulated on the same date was $3.77 per 100 pounds, and standard granulated, $3.69 per 100 pounds, all net cash.

5. Lyle's sugars are scarcely mentioned by the consuls and few quotations given.

Continental refined is largely used, and sells at lower prices than the English, but within one-fourth cent per pound for the best grades at wholesale and generally at the same price for retail for granulated, except the lowest grades, which sell down to 3 cents per pound sometimes.

7. The English refiners use raw beet or cane sugar, as is cheapest, and do not guarantee their product, but sell simply as refined granulated, or lumps, or powdered. Just now (July 1, 1911) they are using raw beet sugar as cheaper than cane.

8. June 30. The refiner in London buys raw beet sugar 88° analysis (94° test) in Hamburg at a -

	Per 100 pounds.
Free-on-board price of	$2.378
Freight and charges to London	.214
	2.592
Duty on 88° analysis (94° pol.)	.338
Raws cost London refiner	2.930
Refiners' list price standard granulated, net	3.69
Difference between raw and refined	.760
Difference between raw and refined in New York	.920

Birmingham consul says $0.437 per 100 pounds must be added to cost of raws to bring the prices up to those of refined.

9. Wholesalers sell to retailers at $0.107 per 100 pounds advance on granulated of foreign origin and $0.053 per 100 pounds advance on English, and one month's credit.

10. When the retailer can buy granulated at $3.50 to $3.80 per 100 pounds he charges 4 cents per pound. When his cost is over $4.80 he charges 5 cents per pound. Some retail dealers whose specialty is tea give away sugar in Birmingham to encourage trade.

11. Tate & Sons name prices June 29 for delivery in August and September; August. 3.27 cents per 100 pounds higher and September. 3.27 cents per 100 pounds lower than June 29 prices.

12. Their list prices give many grades of hard and soft refined though not as many as American refiners. Their selling terms are cash in London or Liverpool within 14 days, less 2½ per cent discount. If not paid in 14 days, interest is added from date of invoice to day of payment, and the 2½ per cent will be forfeited unless payment is made within 21 days. Tate's cubes are made only at London, but granulated at both London and Liverpool.

13. At Bradford 75 per cent of all sugar consumed is foreign granulated.

14. The port of Bristol draws its supplies from Germany, Russia, France, Holland, and Belgium, and through Bristol a large district is supplied. Crystallized raw sugar comes here by way of London from Trinidad, Jamaica, Surinam, St. Lucia, Demerara, Peru, and Mexico, and all are sold under the trade term of "Demeraras."

15. All towns, large or small, have associations of grocers who fix retail prices from time to time, grocers undertaking not to sell under the minimum price fixed. Sometimes somebody cuts prices.

One large company (like Liptons) with 500 or 600 shops in various towns, when one of them cuts others follow. One consul says Lipton will sell sugar at 2 cents per pound to a buyer of tea at 30 cents per pound.

16. Duty on foreign refined sugar is $0.399 per 100 pounds, 100° test.

17. Russia gives a small bounty, about $0.214 per 100 pounds, and did not join the Brussels convention for abolishing sugar bounties, and hence their exports to England are restricted to a certain quantity.

18. The Bristol consul says wholesale prices for past years have varied only because of short crops from atmospheric conditions. This year there has been a great spell of dryness on the Continent of Europe and prices have bounded up. Last year there was a great speculative movement in continental sugars by one man who worked the market up several shillings, and when he had made his pile and got out, holders had to realize, and down came the market and great was the loss of many holders.

19. The Huddersfield consul says that this is the principal center of woolen manufacture and prices of sugar are 3 per cent lower than London. Coal is 11 per cent lower, meat 2 per cent lower, and rents 10 per cent lower.

20. At Leeds the Manchester merchants keep large stocks of foreign refined. The strike at Hull advanced prices.

21. Refiners refine in bond. Freight from Hamburg to quay in Liverpool is 15 cents per 100 pounds, including 2½ per cent discount on f. o. b. price Hamburg.

22. The wholesale trade buy and sell chiefly on f. o. b. Hamburg terms per hundredweight discount 2 months at 5 per cent per annum, cash against bill of lading, ship lost or not lost, and payment against bill of lading before the goods arrive.

23. Drawback on export equal to duty paid on sugar of like polarization. (United States refiners tried hard to get this on their exports.)

24. A bounty on home-grown sugar is being considered by Government.

25. Duties were abolished May 1, 1874, and not reimposed until April, 1901, when rate was $0.43 to $0.90 per 100 pounds as to polarization. May 18, 1908, duties were reduced to present basis. Retail prices were not affected by change of duties.

26. Glasgow sells large quantities of sugar during the fruit season.

27. In the coal-mining districts of Cardiff, Scotland buyers use large crystals at 5 cents per pound. (Probably because they can portion it out in lumps to the family.) This is about all that can be gathered from the consuls' reports.

ENGLAND.

Date.	Place.	Cubes No. 1 net, wholesale, per 100 pounds.	Cubes No. 1 retail, cents per pound.	Cubes No. 2 net, wholesale, per 100 pounds.	Cubes No. 2, retail, cents per pound.	Fine granulated net, wholesale, per 100 pounds.	Fine granulated, retail, cents per pound.	Standard granulated net, wholesale, per 100 pounds.	Standard granulated, retail, cents per pound.
June 29	London:								
	Tates	$4.18	....	$3.98	....	$3.77	....	$3.69	....
	Lyles	....	....	....	....	....	....	3.75	....
30	Birmingham:								
	Tates	4.18	4½	3.98	....	....	4½	3.79	4½
	Low grade	....	....	3.75	4	....	....	3.285	3½
29	Bradford:								
	Tates	4.18	4½–5½	3.98	4½	3.77	4–5	3.79	4–5
	Foreign	....	....	3.97	4½	....	....	3.69	4–5
Aug. 1	Bristol:								
	Tates	4.70	6	4.45	5	4.29–4.55	5	....	....
	Continental	....	....	4.41	5	....	....	3.55–3.76	4
June 30	Burselm (Stoke on Trent):								
	Tates	4.23	6	4.02	5	[1] 3.80	5	3.80	4½
	Others	....	....	....	....	3.80	5	3.67	4
29	Huddersfield:								
	Tates	4.20	5	3.98	5	....	....	....	....
	Others	....	....	....	....	....	....	3.66	4.2
July 1	Leeds:								
	Tates	4.18–4.23	5	4.12	5	....	....	....	....
	German	....	....	....	....	....	....	3.58	4
June 30	Liverpool:								
	Tates	4.18	4½	....	....	....	....	3.75	4
	Farrie & Co.	....	....	4.02	4½	....	....	3.76	4
	Franklin Am.	....	....	....	....	....	....	3.44	4
	A. Z. R. Austrian	....	....	....	....	....	....	3.44	4
	Castor [2]	....	....	....	....	3.54	4	....	....
July 1	London:								
	Tates	4.18	5–6	3.98	5	3.77	5	3.09	4
	Lyles	4.07	5	4.02	5	3.70–3.78	4½	3.48–3.56	4
	Dutch	....	....	3.89–3.95	5	....	....	....	....
	German-Austrian	....	....	4.02–4.07	5	3.58–3.79	4½	3.36–3.42	4
4	Manchester: Tates	4.18	(3)	3.98	(3)	3.75	(3)	(3)	3, 4, 2
1	Newcastle: Tates	4.18	(4)	3.98	....	3.77	....	3.69	....
15	....do	4.29	....	4.19	....	3.98	....	3.92	....
1	Nottingham:								
	Not tates	4.14	5	....	....	....	....	3.70	4½
	Foreign	....	....	....	....	....	....	3.50	4
2	Plymouth:								
	Tates	4.18	....	....	....	....	....	....	....
	Foreign	....	....	3.82	4–5	....	....	[5] 3.32	4–4½
1	Sheffield, England:								
	Tates	4.16	5–5½	3.89	4½	....	....	....	....
	First marks, German	....	....	....	....	....	....	3.44	4–5
June 30	Southampton:								
	Tates No. 1	4.18	5½	....	....	3.84	5	(6)	(6)
	Lyle's	....	....	....	....	3.91	5	....	....
	Lyle's castor	....	....	....	....	3.96	8	....	....
30	Hull:								
	Tates No. 1	4.18	5	....	....	....	....	....	....
	Foreign	....	....	3.91	4	....	....	3.47–3.63	3½–4

[1] Liverpool, $3.67 per 100 pounds, freight, $0.12 per 100 pounds. Total, $3.79 per 100 pounds.
[2] Castor like A. Z. R., but finer.
[3] Irregular.
[4] Not given.
[5] Imports direct.
[6] Freight from Liverpool.
W=Wholesale in dollars per 100 pounds. R=Retail in cents per pound.

IRELAND.

Date.	Place.	Cubes No. 1 net, wholesale, per 100 pounds.	Cubes No. 1 retail, cents per pound.	Cubes No. 2 net, wholesale, per 100 pounds.	Cubes No. 2, retail, cents per pound.	Fine granulated net, wholesale, per 100 pounds.	Fine granulated, retail, cents per pound.	Standard granulated net, wholesale, per 100 pounds.	Standard granulated, retail, cents per pound.
July 3	Belfast: Tates	[1] $4.21	[1] 3						(2)
	Importers' cost, foreign							$3.69	4
	Importers sell retailers, foreign							3.71	4
3	Cork, freight 5½ cents:								
	Tates	4.23½							
	Foreign, Austrian			$4.00	4½			3.50	4
3	Dublin:								
	Tates	4.18-0.21		3.95	4-4½				
	J. K			3.91	4-4½			3.66	4-4½
	SCOTLAND.								
June 30	Dunfermline: Foreign							$3.47	6.405
July 3	Dundee:								
	Tates	$4.18	4½	$3.91	4½	$3.99	4½	3.71	4½
	Continental in stock	4.02						3.40	3½
	Dutch			3.82	4			3.68	4
June 30	Edinburgh:								
	S. & T.			3.96	5			3.52	5
	P. P. Q.							3.70	5
July 13	Glasgow:								
	Tates	4.28	5.5½					3.84	4½-5
	Foreign			4.09	5.5½			3.84	4½-5
	WALES.								
June 30	Cardiff:								
	Tates	$4.30	6	$4.12	5				
	German			3.93	5				
	Z. H. and first Marks							$3.45	4
July 5	Swansea:								
	Tates	4.18	5						
	Foreign				4-5		4	3.19	4

[1] Freight.

[2] Duty plus harbor dues.

Imports here from Hamburg.

BRITISH WEST INDIES.

[Book 5, p. 109, Barbados, July 13, 1911.]

Crop available for export, 240,000 tons per year, exported 39,899 tons in 1910.

This is a sugar-producing country.

Export prices for year 1911 for dark muscovados, $1.70 to $1.85 per 100 pounds, and average $1.77 per 100 pounds, and retails at 2½ cents per pound.

Centrifugals, lighter color and dryer, export prices $1.85 to $2.05 per 100 pounds, average $2 per 100 pounds, and retails at 3 cents per pound.

Dark crystals; export prices, $2.25 to $2.35; average $2.29 per 100 pounds, and retails at 3½ cents per pound.

Retailers pay 10 to 15 cents per 100 pounds above export prices.

A grocery muscovado cooled in oscillation (centrifugals) sells at $2.50 per 100 pounds wholesale, and 3 to 3½ cents per pound retail.

A small and so-called white crystal is made and sells at wholesale at $4 per 100 pounds and retails at 5 cents per pound.

Prices are uniform at Bridgetown.

All refined is imported from the United States, costing retailers 5 cents per pound, and retailing at 6 cents per pound to customers.

Customs duty 48 cents per 100 pounds. No taxes and no bounties.

[Book 5, p. 110.]

Muscovados export prices 1905, $15.50 to $3.10 per 100 pounds; 1906, $1.35 to $1.50; 1907, $1.40 to $1.65; 1908, $1.70 to $2.30; 1909, $1.70 to $1.80; 1910, $2.15 to $2.45, all per 100 pounds.

Export prices: Centrifugals (dark crystals), 1905, $2.10 to $3.50; 1906, $1.85 to $1.90; 1907, $2 to $2.30; 1908, $2.25 to $2.80; 1909, $2 28; 1910, $2.80 to $2.90.

Export prices. Centrifugals, 1909, $1.80 to $1.90, and 1910, $2.50 per 100 pounds.

Centrifugals produced during only last three years.

July 13: New York granulated, $5.15; New York cubes, $5.40.

[Book 5, p. 111, Bermuda, July 7, 1911.]

Hamilton produces no sugar.

United States fine granulated, wholesale, in 100-pound bags or barrels, $3.92 per 100 pounds, plus duty 10 per cent (39 cents)=$4.31. Retails at 5 cents per pound.

European in 224-pound bags $3.70 per 100 pounds, plus duty 10 per cent (37 cents) =$4.07. Retails at 5 cents per pound.

Barbados centrifugals, muscovados in barrels, $3.05 per 100 pounds.

Customs duties 10 per cent ad valorem, including package.

No local tax or bounties.

[Book 5, p. 112, Kingston, Jamaica, July 17, 1911.]

Jamaica exports 19,960 tons in 1910.

American granulated in barrels, wholesale, $4.62 per 100 pounds, duty paid (duty 48 cents per 100 pounds).

Jamaica made white vacuum pan in barrels, 4½ cents per pound.

Jamaica made yellow vacuum pan in bags, 3 cents per pound.

Jamaica made good muscovado in bags, 3 cents per pound.

Jamaica made common muscovado in bags, 2½ cents per pound.

New York granulated, $5.15; New York cubes, $5.40.

[Book 5, p. 114, Port Antonio, Jamaica, July 12, 1911.]

Imported granulated, wholesale, $5.35 per 100 pounds, and retail 6 cents per pound.

Cubes, wholesale, $5.84 per 100 pounds, and retail 8 cents per pound.

Duties, 48 cents per 100 pounds.

Sugar sold in bags with charge of 12 cents for bag.

Sugar sold in barrels with charge, 24 cents per barrel.

Sugar industry improving in last two years.

[Book 5, p. 116, Nassau, N. P., July 12, 1911.]

Refined, wholesale, 6¼ to 6¾ cents per pound; retail, 7 cents per pound.

Unrefined (beet, granulated), 5¼ to 5¾ cents per pound; retail, 6 cents per pound.

All merchants jealous of each other and refuse information.

[Book 5, p. 117, Turks Island, July 14, 1911.]

Larger grocers or dealers buy direct from dealer or plantation in Jamaica and St. Domingo in lots of 5 to 10 bags or barrels. (Barrels from Jamaica, bags from San Domingo.)

Home dealers sell to small grocers at slight advance on cost here. Original cost is 3 to 3½ cents per pound. Import duty, 48 cents per 100 pounds. No other taxes.

1910: Imports, 115,607 pounds brown; 55,441 pounds refined.

Refined from United States cost 2½ to 2¾ cents plus duty of 48 cents per 100 pounds and sells at 6 cents per pound, the same as brown sugar.

No changes in prices for many years.

[Book 5, p. 119, Caracas, W. I., Oct. 10, 1911.]

Sugar comes mostly from Venezuela.

Wholesale, $3 to $3.20 per 100 pounds; retail, 3½ to 4 cents per pound.

Refined comes from United States largely and price has risen lately. Wholesale has been $6 to $7 per 100 pounds; retail, 7 to 8 cents per pound.

1891. Refined, wholesale, $5 to $7 per 100 pounds; retail, 6 to 8 cents per pound.

1896. Refined, wholesale, $5.20 to $6.50 per 100 pounds; retail, 6 to 7 cents per pound.

1901. Refined, wholesale, $5 to $6 per 100 pounds; retail, 6 to 7 cents per pound.

1906. Refined, wholesale, $5 to $6 per 100 pounds; retail, 6 to 7 cents per pound.
New York, granulated, $6.80; New York, cubes, $7.

Approximate prices: Consul does not give duty, but probably 48 cents per 100 pounds.

[Book 5, Trinidad, Nov. 1, 1911.]

Exports, 46,247 tons in 1910.

Consumption is local production mostly and consists of three grades.

White crystals, wholesale, at $5 per 100 pounds; retail, 6 cents per pound. Yellow crystals, wholesale, $4 per 100 pounds; retail, 5 cents per pound. Brown crystals, wholesale, $3 to $3.50 per 100 pounds; retail, 4 cents per pound. Retailers sell by pound or pennyworth.

Granulated and cubes, imported from America, and retail at 8 and 9 cents per pound, giving 1 to 2 cents per pound profit.

Cubes, wholesale, $7 per 100 pounds; retail, 9 cents per pound.

Granulated, wholesale, $6 per 100 pounds; retail, 8 cents per pound.

No bounties or taxes on consumption.

A small emigration tax, so-called, on sugar exported.

Average price last 10 years, 4 to 6 cents per pound.

1910. Production, 51,950 tons; exports, 46,248 tons; (to United Kingdom, 22,600 tons; Canada, 19,155 tons; and United States, 1,200 tons).

Importations, 400 tons.

[Book 5, p. 90, Georgetown, Guiana, Sept. 16, 1911.]

Sugar made here is vacuum-pan "Demerara crystals" (raw centrifugals).

All sold on 96° test basis. Wholesale: Dark, $3.60 to $4 per 100 pounds; yellow, $4.60 to $4.70 per 100 pounds;

Small amount of granulated imported for higher classes, and which retails at 6 cents per pound.

Yellow crystals retail at 5 to 5½ cents per pound; dark crystals retail at 4 to 4½ cents per pound.

Higher prices now than for a number of years, owing to shortage in the markets of the world.

No taxes, charges, or bounties to affect prices.

British West Indies—Summary.

Date.	Place.	Wholesale, cut loaf (per 100 pounds).	Retail, cut loaf (cents per pound).	Wholesale, granulated (per 100 pounds).	Retail, granulated (cents per pound).
July 13	Barbados			$5.00	6
7	Hamilton, Bermuda			[1] 4.31	5
17	Kingston, Jamaica			[2] 4.07	5
12	Port Antonio, Jamaica	$5.84	8	5.35	6
12	Nassau, N. P	6.50-6.75	7	5.25-5.75	6
19	Turks Island			[3] [4] 3-3.50	{ 6 4

[1] United States.
[2] British.
[3] Price doubtful.
[4] Jamaica.

Customs duties stated as 10 per cent ad valorem as Bermuda, 48 cents per 100 pounds at Barbados, Jamaica, and Turks Island, and presumably at Nassau.

Barbados produces Muscovados, and during last three years has produced centrifugals.

Jamaica produces white vacuum-pan sugar and Muscovados, and industry is improving. Their home-made sugars sell retail at 2½ to 4½ cents per pound, as to quality, and for export in 1910 at $2.15 to $2.45 per 100 pounds for Muscovados and $2.80 to $2.90 for centrifugals.

INDIA.

[Book 5, p. 92, Calcutta, Aug. 17, 1911.]

New York granulated, $5.75; New York cubes, $6.

First white, $3.76 per 100 pounds wholesale; retail, 4.02 to 4.43 cents. Granulated, $3.55 per 100 pounds wholesale; retail, 3.87 to 4.21 cents. Java white, $3.30 per 100 pounds wholesale; retail, 3.65 to 4.02 cents.

Market reports interesting.

[Book 5, p. 94.]

Review of Trade of India, 1910–11, page 95.
Imports about 740,000 tons per annum (read 97 to p. 101).
The crop in all India is probably about 2,900,000 tons, to which palm sugar must be added.

India supply of foreign cane and beet sugar.

	1909-10	1910-11
	Hundredweight.	*Hundredweight.*
CANE SUGAR:		
From Mauritius	2,435,560	2,923,983
From China	22,096	129,363
From Java	7,816,015	8,758,715
From Straits Settlements	3,113	962
From other countries	1,114	1,164
Total	10,276,897	11,814,187
BEET SUGAR:		
From Austria-Hungary	782,773	714,093
From Germany	51,538	8,206
From Belgium	1,474	1,139
From France	306	444
From other countries	23,096	1,076
Total	859,187	724,958
Total sugar	11,136,084	12,539,145

India is the largest single producer of cane sugar in the world, her share being 34 per cent.
(Read statement, pp. 94 to 101.)

[Book 5, p. 102, Madras, India, Aug. 16, 1911.]

Wholesale, first quality white crystals, $3.87 per 100 pounds; retail, 6 cents per pound. Wholesale, second quality granulated, $4.09 per 100 pounds; retail, 5½ cents per pound.
Page 103 explains inconsistency in prices.
Refined sugar used here is produced in India and also imported from Java and Europe.
Indian granulated, wholesale, $2.90 per 100 pounds; retail, 3 cents per pound.
Java granulated, wholesale, $3.18 per 100 pounds; 3½ cents per pound retail.
1886–1901 prices on page 104.
The use of raw sugar (jaggery) is limited entirely to native classes.
Wholesalers pay $1.95 per hundredweight for jaggery and sell to retailers at $2.27 per hundredweight and it retails at 2.56 cents per pound.
No native bounties in Madras, but there are octroi (local) taxes on sugar sent into Hyderabad State of $1.42½ per 500 pounds, and into Bangalero District of $0.15 per 500 pounds.
Customs duties on imports from foreign countries 10 per cent ad valorem.

[Book 5, p. 105, Rangoon and Burma, Aug. 28, 1911.]

New York granulated, $6.05; New York cubes, $6.30.
Refined sugar to-day wholesale:
Java superior white crystallized $3.22 per 100 pounds wholesale, and retail 3.88 cents per pound.
Raw sugar is not imported into Burma. A small amount of lump sugar from Great Britain is used, only by Europeans.
English loaf sugar retails at 10 cents per pound.
(India calls Java sugar (white crystals) refined sugar, but Java has no sugar refineries such as are in the United States and other countries.)

Summary of India.

		Wholesale cut loaf (per 100 pounds).	Retail cut loaf (cents per pound)	Wholesale granulated (per 100 pounds).	Retail granulated (cents per pound).
1911.					
Aug. 17	Calcutta	$3.76	4.02	$3.55	3.87–4.21
16	Madras	3.87	6.00	4.09	5½
	Indian brands			2.90	3
	Java brands			3.18	3.30
28	Rangoon		[1] .10.00	[2] 3.22	3.88

[1] English, used by Europeans. [2] Java.

India is the largest single producer of sugar (cane sugar) in the world, her share being 34 per cent of entire production and probably reaches 2,900,000 tons, to which must be added the palm-sugar production.

India imports foreign sugars to extent of about 740,000 tons per annum from Java and Europe, mostly refined.

The use of raw sugar (jaggery) is limited to native classes. This grade wholesales at $1.73 per 100 pounds and retails at 2.03 cents per pound.

Customs duties 10 per cent ad valorem.

No local taxes but a small tax on sugar sent into certain States of India.

No bounties paid.

NOTE.—Java white sugars are called refined in India.

AUSTRALIA.

[Book 5, p. 79, Melbourne, Sept. 2, 1911.]

Grocery Association of Victoria fixes the retail prices of sugar, adding about 7½ per cent to the wholesale.

[Book 5, p. 5.]

Crystals (granulated), $5.13 per 100 pounds (grade mostly used); 6 cents per pound retail.

Australia taxes, customs duties, cane, $1.30 per 100 pounds; beet, $2.17 per 100 pounds: excise duty, $0.866 per 100 pounds.

[Book 5, p. 82.]

Bounty to growers of cane of 10 per cent of quantity grown by white labor, $1.96 per ton.

[Book 5, Newcastle, New South Wales, Australia, Sept. 22, 1911.]

Local charges, excise tax, $19.46 per ton, $0.866 per 100 pounds; freight from Sydney, $1.94 per ton, $0.086 per 100 pounds.

Bounty to local growers, $1.46 per ton of cane giving 10 per cent of sugar produced solely by white labor. Bounty rises and falls from 10 per cent.

1909–10 production, 147,470 tons, the proportion produced by black labor was less than 10½ per cent.

Wholesale granulated, $5.10 per 100 pounds; retail, 6 cents per pound. Wholesale, cubes, $6.15 per 100 pounds; retail, 8 cents per pound.

(Other grades and prices on page 85, book 5.)

[Book 5, p. 79, Sydney, Sept. 26, 1911.]

A strike in the sugar mills has just been settled by substantial concessions to the men.

Sugar industry is confined to New South Wales and Queensland.

1910, Queensland had 128,178 acres under cane cultivation; New South Wales had 5,903 acres under cane cultivation.

Queensland crop, 1,163,494 tons cane; New South Wales crop, 131,081 tons cane.

Imports, 2,159 tons from Mauritius, Java, and Fiji.

Australia gives a bounty of $1.46 per ton of cane of 10 per cent quantity grown by white labor, provided the rate of wages and conditions of employment of such labor are fair and reasonable and in accordance with the act.

Excise tax, 97 cents per hundredweight, $0.866 per 100 pounds.

Amount paid in sugar bounties and expenses therewith in 1909–10 was $1,981,806.

Bounty is $1.46 per ton, $0.651 per 100 pounds.
Australian sugar production is controlled by one great company.
The Victorian Wholesale Grocers Association regulates retail prices.
Prices now at Sydney:

	Wholesale (per 100 pounds).	Retail (per pound).
		Cents.
Boxes	$5.31	5½
No. 1	5.10	
No. 2	5.00	
No. 3	4.60	

Melbourne retails at 6 cents per pound.

Summary.

Date.	Place.	Wholesale, per 100 pounds of cut loaf.	Retail, per pound of cut loaf.	Wholesale, per 100 pounds of granulated.	Retail, per pound of granulated.
			Cents.		Cents.
Sept. 9	Melbourne			$5.13	6
22	New Castle	$6.15	8	5.10	6
26	Sydney			5.10	5½

The Grocers Association of Victoria fixes retail prices, adding about 7½ per cent to the wholesale.

Custom duties, $1.30 per 100 pounds on cane sugar; $2.17 per 100 pounds on beet sugar; excise tax, $0.866 per 100 pounds.

Bounty of $1.46 per ton of cane, giving 10 per cent of sugar produced solely by white labor. Bounty rises or falls from 10 per cent as to outturn, and provided the rate of wages and condition of employment of such labor are fair and reasonable and in accordance with the act.

All production is controlled by one great company and confined to New South Wales and Queensland.

1909–10 production 147,470 tons, less than 10½ per cent of which was produced by black labor.

Queensland produced 1,163,494 tons of cane; New South Wales produced 131,081 tons of cane.

Imports 2,159 tons from Mauritius, Java, and Fiji.

September 26, 1911: A strike at the sugar mills just settled by concessions to the men.

BRITISH HONDURAS.

[Book 5, p. 86, Belize, July 28, 1911.]

New York granulated, 5.65; New York cubes, 5.90.

Produces 2,000,000 pounds of brown sugar annually, with one manufacturer of refined granulated of fairly good quality but limited production. Now shut down.

Imports best grade of granulated and cubes.

Import duty of 3 cents per pound on refined; 1½ cents per pound on raws.

No bounty.

	1885	1890	1895	1900	1905	1910
Imported refined:	Cents.	Cents.	Cents.	Cents.	Cents.	Cents.
Wholesale	12	11	8	8	8	8
Retail	15	15	10	9	9	9

November 1, 1911: United States refined, 6½ cents per pound wholesale, and 8 cents per pound retail. European loaf, 10 cents per pound wholesale, and 11 cents per pound retail.

Large advance in October.

CANADA.

[Book 5, p. 2, Fernie, British Columbia, July 6, 1911.]

New York granulated, $5.10; New York cubes, $5.35.

No records previous to fire of August 1, 1908.

No raw sugar sold.

Wholesale cutloaf in 50-pound boxes, $6.40; barrels, $6 per 100 pounds. Granulated, 100 pound-bags, $5.70 per 100 pounds wholesale. Retail, cutloaf, 12½ cents per pound; 2-pound cartons, 25 cents. Granulated, 10 cents per pound; 20-pound bags, 6½ cents per pound.

[Book 5, p. 5, Victoria, British Columbia, July 17, 1911.]

No raw sugar sold. Refined bought at Vancouver refineries. Wholesale, granulated, in 100-pound sacks, $5.25 per 100 pounds. Granulated, in 20-pound sacks, $5.40 per 100 pounds; retail, 6¼ cents per pound. In 1896 prices were the same.

[Book 5, p. 7, Vancouver, British Columbia, July 18, 1911.]

New York granulated, $5.15; New York cubes, $5.40.

The British Columbia Sugar Refining Co., built in 1899, controls local market. Owns plantations in Fiji Islands for raws. Also imports raws from East and West Indies, Java, and Australia. Very arbitrary in its business relations.

Wholesale cubes, $6.85 per 100 pounds; retail, 10 cents per pound, 25 pounds for $2. Granulated, $5.35 for 100 pounds; retail, 7 cents per pound, 18 pounds for $1 to $1.15. Practically no price cutting at retail.

Vancouver and its suburbs spreads over a large area and the suburban retail stores charge 15 to 20 per cent more than the down-town stores. In 1889, before the refinery was here, granulated was sold at wholesale at $7.25 per 100 pounds. Later at $12 per 100 pounds, and retailing at 6 to 9 pounds for $1. 1893–1911, the wholesale rate has fluctuated from $4.50 to $6 per 100 pounds, and the retail from 5 to 7½ cents per pound.

[Book 5, p. 13, Halifax, Nova Scotia, July 25, 1911.]

Grade.	Wholesalers to retailers (per 100 pounds).	Refiners to wholesalers (per 100 pounds).
Cut loaf	$5.55	$5.22
Granulated	5.05	4.95

Retail, cut loaf, 8 to 10 cents per pound; granulated, 5½ cents per pound.

Wholesales in barrels, boxes, and bags; retails in barrels, boxes, bags, and paper packages, assorted quantities.

Prices governed by prices reigning in the New York market. In touch by wire. Twenty cents per 100 pounds advance within 5 days past.

Impossible to obtain prices for last 25 years.

[Book 5, p. 14, Sydney, Nova Scotia, July 6, 1911.]

Grade.	Wholesale (per 100 pounds).	Retail (per pound).
		Cents.
Cut loaf	$5.30	None.
Granulated	4.70	6

Ninety-five per cent of sales are standard granulated.

Year.	Wholesale (per 100 pounds).	Retail (per pound).
		Cents.
1906	$4.64	6
1907	4.74	6
1908	5.14	6
1909	4.52	5
1910	5.32	6

It is believed that a "sugar guild," located at Montreal, controls territory prices, etc. (See p. 15 in book 5.)

No American sugar sold, but some Scottish sugars. No taxes except regular Canadian duties and dumping taxes.

[Book 5, p. 17, Cornwell, Ontario, July 5, 1911.]

Granulated (Redpath, Montreal), wholesale, $4.75 per 100 pounds; retail 5 cents per pound, 18 pounds for $1. One hundred-pound bags, $5. Inferior grade of granulated, made in Nova Scotia sells at $4.45 per 100 pounds.

[Book 5, p. 18, Kingston, Ontario, July 3, 1911.]

Only granulated sold.

[Book 5, p. 20.]

Gives Montreal quotations only and says for Kingston add 5 cents per 100 pounds and deduct 5 per cent, say, wholesale $4.30 per 100 pounds at Montreal. Add 5 cents equals $4.35. From this deduct 5 per cent, which is 21 cents, and Kingston granulated is then $4.14 to wholesalers. Wholesalers sell retailers at $4.40, and retailers sell at 5 cents per pound.

Whenever the wholesale price is below an even quotation the retailers advance prices to the even figure. Retailed at same prices at all stores.

New York granulated, $5.45; New York cubes, $5.70.

[Book 5, p. 21, Niagara Falls, Ontario, July 27, 1911.]

Only one wholesale dealer who buys at Montreal, Quebec, and Halifax.

Granulated, wholesale, $5.15 per 100 pounds, and retail. 5½ cents per pound regular. 1901, granulated, wholesale, $4.65 per 100 pounds, and retail, 5 cents per pound. 1906, granulated, wholesale, $4.35 per 100 pounds, and retail, 4½ cents per pound.

[Book 5, p. 22, Orillia, Ontario, July 10, 1911.]

No wholesale dealer here. Granulated retails at 5½ cents per pound.

No special taxes or bounties.

[Book 5, p. 23, Ottawa, Ontario, July 12, 1911.]

Granulated, 5 cents per pound retail, and $4.50 per 100 pounds wholesale. Loaf, wholesale, $7.50 per 100 pounds and 8 cents per pound retail.

Gives Montreal prices from 1900 to 1911 and says if 5 cents per 100 pounds is added, it represents Ottawa prices.

[Book 5, p. 25, Owen Sound, Ontario, July 13, 1911.]

Granulated, $4.91 to $4.96 per 100 pounds wholesale, and retail 6 cents per pound. 17 pounds for $1 and 100 pounds for $5. Sugar is now cheaper than ever before in past years.

[Book 5, p. 26, Sarnia, Ontario, July 8, 1911.]

Two kinds of refineries in Canada, cane and beet, same as in the United States. Cane sells 20 to 25 cents per 100 pounds higher than beet. Cane granulated, wholesale, $4.80 per 100 pounds. Retails 18 pounds for $1, either cane or beet.

Four cane refineries in Canada, two at Montreal, one at Halifax, and one in Vancouver. Three beet factories, one at Wallaceburg, one at Berlin, both under same management, and one at Raymond, Alberta. Cane refiners import raws and sell refined only to wholesalers Beet factories sell anyone. Prices in Canada are standard and fixed at Montreal as far west as this point and farther. Retailers make 25 to 50 cents per 100 pounds. Prices here and in Michigan are alike.

For last five years prices tallied with United States prices. Inclosed interesting letter from a large beet-sugar refinery. (See p. 28, book 4.)

[Book 5, p. 29, Sault Ste. Marie, Ontario, July 5, 1911.]

Granulated, cane, wholesale, $4.82 per 100 pounds, and retails at 5.35 cents per pound. Granulated, beet, wholesale, $4.62 per 100 pounds, and retails at 5.15 cents per pound Gives Montreal prices 1896 to 1911. Freight from Montreal during navigation, 34 cents per 100 pounds. All-rail, 42 cents per 100 pounds.

[Book 5, page 31, Toronto, Ontario, July 11, 1911.]

Granulated, wholesale, $4.80 per 100 pounds, in barrels, and $4.70 per 100 pounds in sacks. Retail, 5 cents to 6 cents per pound, 18 to 20 pounds for $1.

Large stores sell cheapest, 5 to 5½ cents per pound; smaller stores charge 5½ to 6 cents, and some at 5 cents per pound.

Loaf sugar retails at 7 cents per pound.

Wholesale price table, 1899 to 1901 (page 31) and given herewith:

	Per 100 pounds.		Per 100 pounds.
1899	$4.55	1906	$4.25
1900	4.90	1907	4.55
1901	4.65	1908	4.85
1902	3.70	1909	4.65
1903	4.10	1910	5.25
1904	4.45	1911	4.80
1905	5.05		

[Book 5, page 33, Sherbrooke, Ontario, July 10, 1911.]

July 1, New York granulated, $5; New York cubes, $5.25.

Granulated, wholesale, $4.65 and retail 4.90 cents per pound.

Refined, per bag of 100 pounds:

Grade No. 1.	Wholesale (per 100 pounds).	Retail (per 100 pounds).	Grade No. 1.	Wholesale (per 100 pounds).	Retail (per 100 pounds).
July 1—			July 1—		
1911	$4.65	$4.90	1907	$4.50	$4.75
1910	5.20	5.45	1906	4.25	4.50
1909	4.60	4.85	1905	5.75	6.00
1908	4.85	5.10	1904	4.30	4.55

[Book 5, p. 34, Windsor, Ontario, Sept. 12, 1911.]

Cut loaf, wholesale, $7 per hundredweight; retail, 10 cents per pound. Granulated, $6 per hundredweight; retail 7, cents per pound. (In bulk or bags of 1 to 10 pounds.)

(Page 34 gives prices at Montreal 1889 to 1911 by months.)

[Book 5, p. 36, Fort Erie, Ontario, Aug. 11, 1911.]

Granulated, wholesale, $5 to $5.50 per 100 pounds; retail, 6 cents per pound, 17 pounds for $1.

Wholesale prices generally a little less than in the United States and retail prices about the same as the United States.

Consumers generally buy $1 worth at a time.

[Book 5, p. 37, Montreal, Quebec, Aug. 12, 1911.]

New York, granulated, $5.75; New York cubes, $6.

In Montreal there are two cane-sugar refineries, the Canada Sugar Refining Co. (Ltd.), and the St. Lawrence Sugar Refining Co. (Ltd.). Capacity of each, 300 to 400 tons daily. Their raw supplies of 96° test centrifugals and Muscovados come mainly from British West Indies.

Product is sold to wholesalers at list prices, which also control the sales of wholesalers.

Refineries' list prices: Granulated in bags, $5.15 per 100 pounds, $5.20 in barrels; $5.20 in 20-pound bags, and $5.25 in barrels Retail 5½ to 6 cents per pound. Lump loaf, wholesale, $5.85 in 100-pound boxes; $5.95 in 50-pound boxes; and $6.25 in 25-pound boxes. Retails at 6 to 8 cents per pound.

(See page 39 quoting granulated in barrels.)

No local charges or special conditions affecting prices. No beet factories in the Province of Quebec. They are located in Ontario and the west. Beet industry is protected by the tariff and by bounties. The tariff gives the beet industry free entry of all machinery connected with the manufacture of beet sugar and the iron for construction of factories. The beet manufacturers are allowed to import at the British preferential rate, twice the amount they manufacture; that is, if a factory turns out 1,000 tons it can import 2,000 tons of the same sugar from other countries (?).

[Book 5, p. 41, St. Johns, Quebec, July 5, 1911.]

Little if any sugar sold at wholesale and is bought from wholesalers of Montreal. This sugar is refined in Canada.

The retailers pay $4.75 per 100 pounds for beet granulated and sell it at 5½ cents per pound in 10 to 20 pound bags.

Another grade of granulated but darker, commonly called Austrian or Russian sugar is largely used. Montreal wholesalers sell this to retailers at $4.40 per 100 pounds and it retails at 5 cents per pound.

A third variety, imported from Barbados, a light brown soft sugar, is also generally used. This is bought from the Montreal wholesalers at $4.40 per 100 pounds and retails at 5 cents per pound.

Present prices are practically the same as the last ten years; 1885–1890 prices were 2 to 3 cents per pound higher and at times the best grades retailed at 10 cents per pound.

[Book 5, p. 42, Rimouski, Quebec, July 20, 1911.]

Storekeepers purchase in small quantities from wholesale houses in Montreal and Quebec and prices there are practically the same as prices here. Up to 15 years ago about 60 per cent of the sugar sold here was Nos. 1, 2, and 3 yellow refined, the balance being granulated and raw sugar from Barbados in barrels, but now there is more granulated sold than any other grade. Raw sugar is used in the springtime to adulterate maple sugar, a considerable quantity of which is made in this district. Some families use maple sugar the year round.

Granulated, at wholesale $4.60 per 100 pounds; retail, 6 cents per pound.

Gives prices from 1897 to 1911, but may be Montreal or Quebec prices (not stated).

Maple sugar, 10 to 12 cents per pound.

[Book 5, pp. 45 and 46, Quebec, Aug. 5, 1911.]

Granulated, wholesale, $5.15 to $5.25 per 100 pounds; retail, 6 cents per pound. Lump, wholesale, $6.05 per 100 pounds; retail, 6½ cents per pound. Raw (Barbados), $3 to $3.25 per 100 pounds wholesale, and 5 cents per pound retail.

The refined is manufactured in Montreal, Quebec, and Halifax, Nova Scotia. The raw sugar is from Barbados, Jamaica. Retail prices regular.

[Book 5, p. 47, Prince Edward Island, Canada, July 8, 1911.]

Raw Muscovados, $3.60 per 100 pounds wholesale, and 4 to 4½ cents per pound retail.
Cut loaf (boxes), $5.50 per 100 pounds wholesale, and 6 to 6½ cents per pound retail.
Cut loaf (½ barrels), $5.50 per 100 pounds wholesale, and 6 to 6½ cents per pound retail.
Cut loaf (barrels), $5.40 per 100 pounds wholesale, and 6 to 6½ cents per pound retail.
Granulated (20-pound bags), $5.10 per 100 pounds wholesale, and 5½ to 6 cents per pound retail.

Retail prices firmly held.

Extra standard granulated used almost exclusively. Delivered at Charlottetown during November of each year, wholesales per 100 pounds, as follows: 1886, $6.13; 1891, $4.38; 1896, $4.13; 1901, $4.30; 1906, $4.40. Retails at 1 cent higher for 10 pounds or less, and for 10 pounds or over one-half cent per pound higher.

[Book 5, p. 49, Winnipeg, Manitoba.]

Kinds used are standard granulated, yellow extra ground, powdered and loaf and Barbados, a West Indian dark-brown sugar. The principal refiners are four in number, located at Halifax, Wallaceburg (Ontario), Raymond (Alberta), and Vancouver. Halifax and Vancouver handle cane sugar exclusively. Wallaceburg and Raymond, beet and cane sugar. A special concession is allowed the Wallaceburg factory by Government allowing it for every pound of ground beets used in its factory to import 2 pounds of foreign material free of charge ordinarily collected under the revenue act. It is asserted that the larger part of this foreign material is imported from Germany. This tariff is the only thing in the line of an octroi tax, national bounties, etc., existent and is mentioned in the second paragraph of the department circular.

[Book 5, p. 50.]

Granulated is the chief sugar sold. Wholesales at $5.25 to $5.30 per 100 pounds in bags and barrels, respectively.

Three-fourths of a cent to 1 cent per pound difference between wholesale and retail prices.

Loaf, $6.35 in 100-pound boxes at retail. No wholesale prices given. No past prices obtainable.

[Book 5, p. 51, Dawson, Yukon Territory, Canada, July 15, 1911.]

New York granulated, $5.15; New York cubes, $5.40.

Granulated, wholesale, 9¾ cents per pound; retail, 10 cents per pound.

No variation in prices by different dealers.

No bounties, taxes, or other charges affecting prices.

[Book 5, p. 52, Hamilton, Canada, July 1, 1911.]

Standard granulated, $4.70 per 100 pounds wholesale; retail, 6 cents per pound.

Acadia granulated, $4.60 per 100 pounds wholesale; retail, 17 pounds for $1.

Quotations here are based on refinery list prices ruling in Montreal on the first of each month. Retal prices are uniform, and reported to be fixed by the guild.

Average prices of granulated are as follows:

	Wholesale.	Retail.
1891	$7.11 per 100 pounds	$1 for 18 pounds.
1896	$4.55 per 100 pounds	$1 for 20 pounds.
1901	$4.82 per 100 pounds	$1 for 18 pounds.
1906	$4.30 per 100 pounds	$1 for 20 pounds.
Seven months of 1911	$4.57 per 100 pounds	$1 for 17 pounds.

[Book 5, p. 54, St. John, New Brunswick, July 11, 1911.]

[Price per 100 pounds.]

	Refiners' price, less 5 per cent 14 days.	Jobbers' price, less 1 per cent 10 days.	Retail.
Standard granulated (bags or barrels)	$4.70	$4.80	$5.05
Lump (loaf)	5.40	5.50	5.75
In 1906, prices:			
Granulated	4.20	4.30	5.55
Lumps	5.00	5.10	5.35

Great regularity with all dealers.

Summary of prices, July, 1911.

		Cut loaf.		Granulated.	
		Wholesale (per 100 pounds).	Retail (cents per pound).	Wholesale (per 100 pounds).	Retail (cents per pound).
British Columbia:					
Fernie	July 6	$6-$6.40	12½ cents	$5.70	10 cents; 20 pounds at 6¼ cents.
Victoria	July 17	None	None	$5.25-$5.40	6½ cents.
Vancouver	July 18	$6.85	10 cents; 25 pounds, $2.	$5.35	7 cents; 18 pounds, $1 to $1.15.
Nova Scotia:					
Halifax	July 25	$5.22-$5.55	8 to 10 cents.	$4.95 to $5.05	5½ cents.
Sydney	July 6	$5.30	None	$4.70	6 cents.
Ontario:					
Cornwell	July 5	None	do	$4.75	5½ cents; 18 pounds for $1.
Kingston	July 3	None used	do	$4.40	5 cents.
Niagara Falls	July 27	None	do	$5.15	5½ cents.
Orillia	July 10	do	do	None	5½ cents.

Summary of prices, July, 1911—Continued.

		Cut loaf.		Granulated.	
		Wholesale (per 100 pounds).	Retail (cents per pound).	Wholesale (per 100 pounds).	Retail (cents per pound).
Ontario—Continued.					
Ottawa	July 12	$7.50	8 cents	$4.50	5 cents.
Owen Sound	July 13	None	None	$4.91-$4.96	6 cents; 17 pounds, $1.
Sarnia	July 8	...do	...do	$4.80, cane	18 pounds, $1.
				$4.60, beet	Do.
Sault Ste. Marie	July 5	...do	...do	$4.82, cane	5.35 cents.
				$4.62, beet	5.15 cents.
Toronto	July 11	Not given	7 cents	$4.80	5 to 6 cents; 18-20 pounds, $1.
Sherbrooke	July 10	None	None	$4.65	5 cents, or $4.90 per 100 pounds.
Windsor	Sept. 12	$7	10 cents	$6	7 cents.
Fort Erie	Aug. 11	None	None	$5-$5.50	6 cents; 17 pounds, $1.
Quebec:					
Montreal	Aug. 12	$5.85-$6.25	6 to 8 cents	$5.15-$5.20	5½ cents.
St. John	July 5	None	None	$4.75	Do.
Rimouski	July 20	...do	...do	$4.60	6 cents.
Quebec	Aug. 5	$6.05	6½ cents	$5.15-$5.25	Do.
Prince Edward Island		$5.50	6 to 6½ cents	$5.10	5¼ to 6 cents.
Winnipeg	July 14	$6.35	6¼ to 6¾ cents	$5.25-$5.30	6 to 6½ cents.
Dawson	July 15	None	None	$9.50	10 cents.
Hamilton	July 1	...do	...do	$4.70-$4.60	6 cents.
St. John, New Brunswick.	July 11	$5.40-$5.50	5¾ cents	$4.70-$4.80	5.05 cents.
Moncton	July 1	$5.40	10 cents	$5.15	5½ cents.
St. Stephen	Aug. 30	None	None	$5.55	5.80 cents.

Supplementary prices, Nov. 1, 1911.

Place.	Date.	Granulated.		Cut loaf.		Refiners' list, New York (cents per pound).
		Wholesale (per 100 pounds).	Retail.	Wholesale (per 100 pounds).	Retail.	
Victoria	Nov. 1	$6.55	$6.90 per 100 pounds.	$7.65	Not given	6.468
	Sept. 1	6.15				6.125
Fernie	Nov. 1	7.00	8 cents per pound			6.468
Moncton	...do	6.05	6½ to 7 cents per pound.	6.50	9 cents per pound.	6.468
Hamilton	..do	5.96	15 pounds, $1			6.468
(Acadia)		5.91	...do			
Sarnia	Nov. 1	6.00	14 pounds, $1			6.468
Montreal	...do	[1] 5.90	6½ cents per pound	([2])	8 to 12 cents	6.468
(Not changed since Sept 8; refiners' prices given July 1.)	July 31	5.20				5.537
	Aug. 9	5.30				5.537
	Aug 24	5.40				5.831
	Aug. 29	5.50				6.027
	Aug 31	5.60				6.125
	Sept. 5	5.70				6.125
	Sept. 8	5.90				6.468
	...do	5.85				
	Nov. 7	5.90				6.615
Niagara Falls:						
(Montreal)	Nov. 1	6.11	7 cents per pound; 15 pounds, $1.			6.468
Acadia		6.01	...do			
St. Johns, Quebec	Nov. 1	6.02	7 cents per pound			6.468
Winnipeg	..do	6.40 to 6.35	...do			6.468
Owen Sound	...do	6.01	7 cents per pound; 4 pounds, 25 cents.	([3])		

[1] Less 5 per cent.
[2] Not quoted.
[3] Compared with July wholesale price is 10 cents higher; retail, 1 cent higher.

Supplementary prices, Nov. 1, 1911—Continued.

Place.	Date.	Granulated. Wholesale (per 100 pounds).	Granulated. Retail.	Cut loaf. Wholesale (per 100 pounds).	Cut loaf. Retail.	Refiners' list, New York (cents per pound).
Sherbrooke	Nov. 1	$5.85	$6.25 per 100 pounds.			
Halifax	...do	R. 6.15 W. 7.25	7 cents per pound.	$6.65	10 cents per pound.	6.468
St. Stephen	...do	6.05	14 pounds, $1			6.468
	Aug. 30	5.55	0.058 per pound			
New Brunswick	Nov. 1	6.00	6½ cents per pound.	6.90	9 cents per pound.	
Cornwell	...do	[1] 6.10	7 cents per pound; 14¼ pounds, $1.	6.60	10 cents per pound; 3 pounds, 25 cents.	6.468
Orillia	...do	6.00	6¾ cents per pound			6.468
Windsor	...do	6.00	7 cents per pound.	7.00	8 cents per pound.	6.468
Quebec	...do	6.00	6.63 cents per pound.	7.00	9.03 cents per pound.	6.468
Ottawa	...do	5.95	7 cents per pound.	7.00	10 cents per pound.	6.468
Vancouver	...do	6.55	18 pounds, $1.25	7.55	12½ cents per pound.	6.468
Kingston	...do	6.00	7 cents per pound.			
St. Johns, Newfoundland [2]	...do	8.37	9 cents per pound.	9.82	12 cents per pound.	

[1] Less 1 per cent.

[2] Separate Government from Canada.

A much condensed summary.—(1) Four cane refineries divide the territory and sell only through wholesalers, whom they employ as agents, giving them 5 per cent commission.

(2) Three beet-sugar factories are independent and sell to anyone.

(3) A wholesale grocers' guild at Quebec and Toronto and a maritime association guild at Halifax fix prices for themselves and for retailers

(4) Refiners' prices follow New York closely in normal years.

(5) Refiners' price is the list price less 5 per cent to wholesalers. Wholesalers' price is refinery list price less 1 per cent to retailers. Retailers are requested to add at least 25 cents per 100 pounds, to cost.

(6) Consumers pay about the same prices as in the United States. Refiners, wholesalers, and retailers all make some money.

(7) Average difference between raws and refined is $1.25 against 89 cents at New York.

(8) Cost of refining is higher than New York, as refiners are small as compared with some in New York.

(9) Duties: General, $0.83½ per 100 pounds on 96° raws; $1.25 per 100 pounds on 100° test refined. Preferential, $0.52½ per 100 pounds on 96° test raws.

(10) A dumping duty keeps United States sugar out of Canada.

(11) Beet factories have special duty on raws of $0.52½ per 100 pounds for 96° test and import raws from Java or Europe, during the off season for domestic beets.

(12) The most important sugar guilds are at Montreal and Toronto, but every Province has its own guild.

(13) Refiners have an equalizing freight rate which differs from the actual and is so arranged that cost of sugar plus freight to certain points will prevent competition between refiners at that point.

(14) The dumping tax really applies only against the United States and prevents refined bought in New York at export prices from going into Canada at the general tariff rate of $1.25 per 100 pounds, as it would constantly do but for the dumping tax, which tax is the difference between the export price in New York and the refiners' duty, paid list price in New York, November 1, say, if list price duty paid is $6.468 per 100 pounds, and export price is $4.70 per 100 pounds, the dumping tax is apparently $1.768 per 100 pounds; but this amounting to more than 15 per cent ad valorem, the dumping tax, in actual application at present, is 15 per cent of $6.468, the local duty paid price in New York say, $0.970 per 100 pounds dumping tax, to which must be added $1.250 per 100 pounds general duty, making a total duty of $2.220 per 100 pounds, which is prohibitive.

On this basis the cost of American granulated delivered in Montreal duty paid, would be, export price in New York, $4.70 per 100 pounds; freight, 10 cent per 10[illegible] pounds; duty and dumping tax, $2.22 per 100 pounds; total, $7.02 per 100 pounds net cash, against price of $5.90 per 100 pounds, less 5 per cent in Montreal for Canadian granulated on same date, say November 1.

Beet-sugar industry.—Three beet-sugar factories, located at Wallaceburg, Ontario; Berlin, Ontario; Raymond, Alberta.

These factories produce granulated refined sugar direct from the beet roots and their factory prices are 10 to 20 cents per 100 pounds below the cane granulated prices.

The Wallaceburg factory after the domestic beet season closes continues refining raw beet sugar imported from Europe and cane from Java and any other country.

The Canadian Government privileges the beet factories to import at the preferential rates twice the amount of sugar they produce from domestic beets.

The Wallaceburg factory has just received (Dec. 15) a cargo of raw beet sugar from Germany for which they paid 18s. 3d. per hundredweight. This was purchased several months ago but is only now arriving for use.

Within a few days they have purchased a cargo of Java sugars which is now landing at Philadelphia at a cost in Philadelphia of $3.41 per 100 pounds for 96° test basis.

Cost, $3.41 per 100 pounds; as these Java sugars test from 97½° to 98° polarization must add $0.0625; place them on 98° test basis plus cost, $3.4725; freight as engaged to Wallaceburg, $0.13 per 100 pounds; total, $3.6025; Canadian preferential duty on 98° test, $0.545; total cost at factory, $4.1475 per 100 pounds.

Price of cane granulated at factory, $5.65 (Montreal basis), less 5 per cent, $0.28; granulated, net at factory, $5.37; raws cost at factory, $4.15. Difference covering cost of refining and profit $1.22 per 100 pounds.

Canadian duties.

Above No. 16 Dutch standard, all refined (per 100 pounds).			Not above No. 16 Dutch standard (per 100 pounds).		Beet factories, special (per 100 pounds).
Test.	Preferential.	General.	Preferential.	General	
°	°		*Cents.*	*Cents.*	*Cents.*
75	....	....	31[illegible]	52	31[illegible]
76	....	....	32[illegible]	53½	32[illegible]
77	....	....	33[illegible]	55	33[illegible]
78	....	....	34[illegible]	56½	34[illegible]
79	....	....	35[illegible]	58	35[illegible]
80	....	....	36[illegible]	59½	36[illegible]
81	....	....	37[illegible]	61	37[illegible]
82	....	....	38[illegible]	62½	38[illegible]
83	....	....	39[illegible]	64	39[illegible]
84	....	....	40[illegible]	65½	40[illegible]
85	....	....	41[illegible]	67	41[illegible]
86	....	....	42[illegible]	68½	42[illegible]
87	....	....	43[illegible]	70	43[illegible]
88	72	1.08	44[illegible]	71½	44[illegible]
89	73	1.095	45[illegible]	73	45[illegible]
90	74	1.11	46[illegible]	74½	46[illegible]
91	75	1.125	47[illegible]	76	47[illegible]
92	76	1.14	48[illegible]	77½	48[illegible]
93	77	1.155	49[illegible]	79	49[illegible]
94	78	1.17	50[illegible]	80½	50[illegible]
95	79	1.185	51[illegible]	82	51[illegible]
96	80	1.20	52[illegible]	83½	52[illegible]
97	81	1.215	53[illegible]	85	53[illegible]
98	82	1.23	54[illegible]	86½	54[illegible]
99	83	1.245	55[illegible]	88	55[illegible]
100	84	1.25	56[illegible]	89½	56[illegible]

Beet sugar production in Canada started 1902–3 with four factories. Two of the original four factories were moved to the United States, and one built since. Now established, three factories.

Crop:	Tons.
1902-3	7,478
1903-4	6,710
1904-5	8,034
1905-6	11,419
1906-7	11,367
1907-8	7,943
1908-9	6,964
1909-10	8,802
1910-11	9,000
Total	77,717

Summary of prices.—Table of prices from 25 consuls, given for granulated sugar, do not vary much when the different dates are considered and with British Columbia left out. The retail prices particularly are quite regular. They do not go below 5 cents per pound, and when they rise above 5½ cents, it appears to be generally because of the later date of the consuls' letters when a general advance was taking place.

There is no cutting of prices in Canada to draw trade. In fact, all prices in most Provinces of Canada made by wholesalers and retailers are directed and controlled by sugar guilds with headquarters at Montreal, Halifax, and Toronto, and with grocers' associations in every Province. All refiners' prices in Canada are regulated by daily wire advices of prices in New York. When New York advances, Montreal and Canada follow. When New York declines, Montreal and Canada follow suit. This applies under normal conditions such as the year 1910 but in an abnormal year like 1911, when New York was advancing rapidly, Montreal followed at some distance behind, and when in September, 1911, New York quotation for granulated was at $7.35 per 100 pounds net, Montreal's highest price was $5.90 less 5 per cent or $5.61 net per 100 pounds, but, on the other hand, New York has since declined 1¾ cents per pound to $5.635 per 100 pounds, and Montreal has declined but 10 cents per 100 pounds to $5.80 less 5 per cent, or, say, $5.51 net per 100 pounds. In other words, Montreal on the upward trend kept from 55 cents to $1.40 per 100 pounds under the parity of New York, and held nearly its full advance until New York came back to its level.

British Columbia consumers do not get sugar as cheaply as other Provinces for the reason, as stated by consul, that the refiners located at Vancouver (the British Columbia Sugar Refining Co.), who also receive the New York quotations, control the local market, owning plantations in the Fiji Islands for raw sugar growing and draw other supplies from East and West Indies, Java, and Australia, and they are somewhat arbitrary in their business relations. Still, it seems that before this refinery was built in 1889 that British Columbia was paying $7.25 up to $12 per 100 pounds even at wholesale.

It is a notable fact that the refiners and the wholesalers and also the retailers all have an advantage from the Canadian tariff, while the consumer does not, but pays about the same prices as are current in the United States under our higher tariff.

The consul at Sarnia (p. 26, book 5) says retail prices are the same here as in Michigan. From 1893 to 1911 wholesale prices have fluctuated from $4.50 to $6 per 100 pounds, and retail from 5 to 7½ cents per pound. As already mentioned, the refiners fix their prices by the New York quotations, and sell to the wholesaler at list prices, less 5 per cent, payable in 14 days, which per cent is considered a commission to them for acting as selling agents for the Guild. Wholesalers sell to retailers at refiners' list prices, less 1 per cent. Regarding the sugar guild, the consul at St. Stephen writes on August 30, 1911, as to the Halifax Guild: "Prices are fixed by the Maritime Grocers' Association, which includes most of the jobbers in the maritime Provinces of Canada. The price in each locality differs with the difference in freight from the refinery in Halifax, Nova Scotia."

The jobber sells for 10 cents per 100 pounds above the price quoted ($5.55), and any sale to a consumer must be 25 cents per 100 pounds above this. At the end of the quarter, if the rules have been adhered to, the jobber gets a rebate of 5 per cent on his purchases for the quarter. Very little sugar other than granulated goes into consumption in Canada. The refiners make about as many grades of hards and softs as the refiners in the United States do. (These varieties are shown on p. 38, book 5.) Fifteen or twenty years ago 60 per cent of the consumption of Canada was of soft yellow refined sugar, but now 95 per cent is of granulated.

There are three cane sugar refineries in Canada, two of which are in Montreal and one in Halifax. The Canadian Sugar Refinery (Ltd.) and the St. Lawrence Sugar Refining Co. (Ltd.), both at Montreal, each having capacity of 300 to 400 tons daily.

There are also the two cane refineries at Halifax under the same management (the Acadia Sugar Refining Co.), which make a granulated sugar of less value than made in the Montreal refineries.

There is also the cane refinery at Vancouver already mentioned, making four cane refineries in all the Provinces of Canada. There are three beet-sugar factories in the Provinces of Canada, i. e., one at Wallaceburg, and one at Berlin, both under the same management and which refine both cane and raw beet (cane during the off season for domestic beet), and another one at Raymond, Alberta, which refines beet.

The cane refiners sell only through the wholesaler, while the beet factories sell to anyone and everybody.

To enlarge somewhat the consular information, I may add from my information and knowledge of the Canadian business and from records in our office, several conditions affecting the sugar trade in Canada:

First. Regarding the Wholesale Grocers' Sugar Guild, already mentioned, to facilitate the acts of this guild the cane refiners of Montreal and of Halifax divided their territory for selling refined. The two Montreal refiners do not sell in Halifax or east of the Province of Quebec. Halifax refiners can not sell in Montreal, but can go west of Montreal. The Vancouver, British Columbia, refinery sells only so far toward the east and Montreal and Halifax only so far toward the west. They meet at Winnipeg. Halifax, which manufactures a granulated inferior to Montreal, is allowed to sell under Montreal prices, but where the Halifax trade has a monopoly of the lower Provinces the refiners keep the trade of consumers and get full prices.

Second. Regarding wholesalers and jobbers' prices to retailers, the guild fixes an "equalized freight rate" for refiners to charge which is not the actual freight rate to destination and the difference between the "equalized rate" and the actual rate to destination is either borne by the refiner, if the actual rate is more than the "equalized," or is for the benefit of the refiner if the actual is less than the "equalized" rate

In many cases the equalized freight rate is greater than the actual rate, so the refiners get no actual benefit out of the freight and many make a sacrifice.

Tariff.

The consular report makes no special reference to the Canadian tariff, which is somewhat complicated and has an important bearing on the sugar trade of Canada.

Canada has a general tariff, an intermediate tariff, a preferential tariff, and a "dumping" duty, the latter evidently made especially to prevent exports from the United States into Canada of refined sugar while sugar refined in the United Kingdom is specially excepted from this dumping duty.

This dumping duty which specially interests the United States, as without it refined sugars of the United States might go into Canada freely under our drawback system, which reads as follows: From Canada customs tariff, chapter 2, page 406—.

"In the case of articles exported to Canada of a class or kind made or produced in Canada, if the export or actual selling price to an importer in Canada is less than the fair market value of the same article when sold for home consumption in the usual and ordinary course in the country whence exported to Canada at the time of its exportation to Canada, there shall in addition to the duties otherwise established be levied, collected, and paid on such articles on its importation into Canada a special duty (or dumping duty) equal to the difference between said selling price of the article for export and the said fair market value thereof for home consumption, and such special duty (dumping duty) shall be levied, collected, and paid on such article, although it is not otherwise dutiable (Limitation: Provided that the special duty shall not exceed 15 per cent ad valorem in any case); provided also the sugar refined in the United Kingdom shall be exempt from such special tax."

In actual practice the dumping tax applies as follows:

Without such dumping duty granulated to-day (January 5) could go into Canada at a cost in New York of $3.75 per 100 pounds plus freight to Montreal of $0.10 per 100 pounds and the general tariff duty of $1.25 per 100 pounds; a total cost in Montreal of $5.10 per 100 pounds. To-day (January 5) refiners' list price of granulated in Montreal is $5.55, from which must be deducted 5 per cent, $0.28, making wholesale cost $5.27 for Montreal sugar against cost of importation from New York of $5.10, without the dumping tax, or $5.93 with the dumping tax. This explains the reason why the United States can not export refined sugar to Canada at our in-bond prices.

The refined which came from Hongkong paid the same duties as if from the United States, but they came into Vancouver, B. C., to compete with the refinery there which is charging higher prices than elsewhere in Canada.

	Preferential.	Intermediate.	General.
All sugar above No. 16 Dutch standard and all refined of whatever kinds or grades or standards, testing not more than 88° by the polariscope per 100 pounds	*Cents.* 72	*Cents.* 98	$1.08
Each additional degree over 88° test, per 100 pounds	1	1½	.01½
Provides fractions of one-half a degree or less shall not be subject to duty and that fractions of more than one-half shall be dutiable as a degree.			

Refined sugar shall be entitled to entry under the preferential tariff upon evidence satisfactory to minister of customs that such refined sugar has been manufactured wholly of raw sugar produced in the British colonies and possessions and not otherwise.

Item 135.—Sugar No. 1, not above No. 16 Dutch standard in color, sugar drainings, molasses, etc., testing over 56 and not more than 75° polariscope per 100 pounds. Preferential tariff, 31½ cents; intermediate, 45 cents; and the general tariff, 52 cents, and for each additional degree over 75° 1 cent; preferential, 1½ cents; intermediate and 1½ cents general tariff, respectively, must be added, provided that all raw sugar, including sugar specified in this item the product of any British colony or possession, shall be entitled to entry under the British preferential tariff when imported direct into Canada from any British colony or possession.

Item 135 A.—Raw sugar as described in tariff item 135, when imported to be refined in Canada by Canadian sugar refineries to the extent of twice the quantity of sugar refined during the calendar years 1906, 1907, and 1908 by such refiners from sugar produced in Canada from Canadian beet root, under regulation by the minister of customs, per 100 pounds testing not more than 75°, 31½ cents, and per 100 pounds for each additional degree over 75° 1 cent, provided that sugar under this item shall not be subject to special duty.

Item 135 B.—Raw sugar as described in tariff item 135, when imported to be refined in Canada by any sugar refining company not engaged in refining sugar from the product of Canadian beet root, to the extent of one-fifth of the weight of sugar refined from the raw sugar by such refinery in Canada during the calendar year in which such raw sugar is imported under regulations by the minister of customs per 100 pounds, testing not more than 75° by polariscope, 31½ cents per 100 pounds, and 1 cent per 100 pounds for each additional degree over 75°.

Preferential tariff applies to goods the product or manufacture of British colonies when imported direct from any British colony.

Intermediate tariff shall apply to goods the product or manufacture of any British or foreign country to which the benefits of such intermediate tariff shall have been extended in the manner hereafter provided when imported direct from such foreign country or from a British country.

Articles the produce or manufacture of any foreign country which treats imports from Canada less favorably than those from other countries may be subject to a surtax of one-third of the duty in general tariff. Act began November 30, 1906.

The intermediate tariff applies to treaties with other countries. (An advance in market value after purchase of goods not subject to special duty.)

For five months ending August, 1911:

The following sugars above No. 16 Dutch standard and all refined were entered for consumption into Canada.

From—	General tariff.	Preferential tariff.
	Pounds.	*Pounds.*
Great Britain	123,047	9,630,848
United States	97,550	
Hongkong	1,236,836	
Chinese Empire	1,248	
Other countries	14,777	324,067
Total	1,473,458	9,954,873
5 months (1910) comparison	2,346,991	10,642,311
Decrease	873,533	687,487

The refined sugars from Great Britain under general tariff paid $1.08 per 100 pounds and under preferential tariff paid 72 cents per 100 pounds, all consisting exclusively of sugar refined in "bonded" refineries in Great Britain from raw sugar from British colonies and paying no export duty out of Great Britain.

The refined sugar from the United States were fancy brands, such as crystal dominos, which a few people in Canada will have at any cost. These paid the general duty of $1.08 per 100 pounds and the dumping duty of the difference in the value in the United States for home consumption, say $7.50 per 100 pounds, and the price at which it was sold for export, say $5.70 (less United States drawback of $1.80 per 100 pounds).

The entire duty on such sugar being ——— per 100 pounds.

United States granulated sugar if sent into Canada would pay general tariff duty of ——— per 100 pounds plus dumping tax of ——— per 100 pounds, the difference between New York refiners' price to consumers and price for export.

The consular reports give no prices paid for raw sugar by the Canadian refiners. For five months ending August 31, 1911, the sugar entered for consumption and for refining was as follows: The intermediate tariff applies only to treaties and none exist for Canada. (Great Britain has a treaty with Japan with special duty on refined sugar but excludes Canada.)

[Not above No. 16 Dutch standard.]

Countries.	General tariff.	Preferential tariff.	Raw sugar for rfining by beet factories.
	Pounds.	*Pounds.*	
Great Britain			
United States	103,521		
British Guiana		47,737,539	
British East Africa			
British West Indies	1,028,541	115,858,753	
British Oceania			[1] 2,212,343
Dutch East Indies	13,014,740		5,062,271
Germany			19,868,312
San Domingo	24,380,283		
Other countries	8,025,848		8,997,851
Total 1911	46,552,933	163,596,292	36,140,777
5 months 1910	18,827,271	148,034,510	36,264,124
Comparison	[2] 27,725,762	[2] 15,561,782	[3] 123,347

	Above No. 16 Dutch standard.	Not above No. 16 Dutch standard.
	Pounds.	*Pounds.*
General tariff	1,473,458	46,552,933
Preferential tariff	9,954,825	163,596,292
For beet refiners		36,140,777
	11,428,285	246,290,002

[1] Belgium [2] Increase. [3] Decrease.

The duties paid under general tariff were $1.25 per 100 pounds on refined 100° test. Duty on raws 96°, not above No. 16 Dutch standard, 83½ cents per 100 pounds.

Preferential duty on raws of 96°, not above No. 16 Dutch standard, 63 cents per 100 pounds.

Beet refiners' duty on raws 96°, not above No. 16 Dutch standard, 52½ cents per 100 pounds.

Comparative statement of prices of granulated sugar in Montreal, Halifax, and New York from July 1, 1911, to Dec. 31, 1911.

[Quotations in dollars per 100 pounds.]

	Montreal.			Halifax.		New York refiner's net.
	Refiner's list.	Refiner's net.	Wholesaler's net.	Refiner's list.	Refiner's net.	
July 1	4.65	4.4175	4.6035	4.60	4.37	4.90
4	4.65	4.4175	4.6035	4.60	4.37	4.90
11	4.75	4.5125	4.7025	4.70	4.465	4.998
18	4.75	4.5125	4.7025	4.70	4.465	5.047
25	4.95	4.7025	4.9005	4.90	4.655	5.248
Aug. 1	5.15	4.8925	5.0985	5.10	4.845	5.537
9	5.25	4.9875	5.1975	5.20	4.94	5.537
15	5.25	4.9875	5.1975	5.20	4.94	5.635
22	5.25	4.9875	5.1975	5.20	4.94	5.635
29	5.35	5.0825	5.2965	5.30	5.035	6.027
Sept. 6	5.65	5.3475	5.5935	5.60	5.32	6.272
12	5.85	5.5575	5.7915	5.80	5.51	6.615
19	5.85	5.5575	5.7915	5.80	5.51	6.615
26	5.85	5.5575	5.7915	5.80	5.51	6.615
Oct. 3	5.85	5.5575	5.7915	5.80	5.51	6.615
10	5.85	5.5575	5.7915	5.80	5.51	6.615
17	5.85	5.5575	5.7915	5.80	5.51	6.615
24	5.85	5.5575	5.7915	5.80	5.51	6.566
31	5.86	5.5575	5.7915	5.80	5.51	6.468
Nov. 7	5.85	5.5575	5.7915	5.80	5.51	6.272
15	5.85	5.5575	5.7915	5.80	5.51	6.076
22	5.85	5.5575	5.7915	5.80	5.51	5.978
29	5.85	5.5575	5.7915	5.80	5.51	5.880
Dec. 6	5.75	5.4625	5.6925	5.70	5.415	5.635
13	5.75	5.4625	5.6925	5.70	5.415	5.635
20	5.65	5.3675	5.5940	5.60	5.32	5.635
27	5.65	5.3675	5.5940	5.00	5.32	5.635

Halifax.—Quotations are fixed by Montreal basis, and the quotations given are for delivery wherever Halifax competes with Montreal. At other points Halifax prices rise above the Montreal parity. Halifax is allowed to sell at points near by Montreal at 10 cents per 100 pounds less than Montreal net prices. Wholesalers sell to retailers at refiner's list prices less 1 per cent.

Wallaceburg is a free-lance in the sugar trade. Wallaceburg sells, delivered in Montreal, at 15 cents per 100 pounds less than Montreal refiner's net price. Wallaceburg sells at other points at variable prices, depending on whether they sell to wholesalers or direct to retailers.

New York.—Arbuckle list price, 7.50 cents, or 7.35 cents net, from September 19 to September 25.

Compiled from Willett & Gray's Statisticals.

STRAITS SETTLEMENT.

[Book 5, p. 106, Singapore, Straits Settlement, Aug. 26, 1911.]

Bulk of sugar is Java, imported by Chinese merchants. European refined sugar is insignificant.

	Wholesale per 100 pounds.	Retail per pound.
Bags:		
First-grade white refined	$2.98	$0.032
Second-grade white refined	2.92	
Third light brown	2.81	
Baskets, fourth-grade dark brown	2.56	.028

The Penary consul writes, until recently considerable trade in Austrian crystals.

Lump sugar from England, 4-pound tins, retails at 25 cents per tin. Bulk of sugar comes from Java and retails at 6¼ cents per pound. First-grade Java sells at $2.65 per

100 pounds; second-grade Java sells at $2.57 per 100 pounds; third-grade Java sells at $2.52 per 100 pounds; Penary sells at $2.62 per 100 pounds.

Formerly land under sugar cultivation is now in rubber and sugar is not likely to be grown here again in the future.

[Book 5, p. 107.]

No duties or bounties.

Great Britain and accordingly Straits Settlement is a party to the convention refusing entrance of subsidized sugar. There is an export duty, however, on sugar and sugar cane sent from the Federated Malay States. Sugar cane is grown largely by the natives, who chew the cane to extract the juice. (This beats Philippine process.)

(Page 108 gives imports, 1909.)

AFRICA.

[Book 5, p. 57, Natal, Durban, Aug. 17, 1911.]

No tax and a protection duty. Up to 10 years ago Natal produced only raw sugar. First refinery opened in 1901.

1. Largest town and center of sugar growing industry. Has two refineries. Prices fixed here for other sections plus freight. Sudden rise of three-quarters of a cent per pound in the last three weeks owing to drought in beet-growing countries and speculation.

2. Customs duty of 85 cents per 100 pounds, and preferential railway freight at 42½ cents per 100 pounds.

3. Mosambique sugar comes in free of duty since 1909 in return for labor from Mosambique (Portugal) for the gold mines of the Transvaal.

4. Wholesale prices white refined, 1911. $4.26 per 100 pounds; retail, 6.06 cents per pound. Other grades cheaper. (Other years, p. 58.)

[Book 5, p. 63, Johannesburg. Aug. 21, 1911.]

Natal producers control entire South African market, having no taxes to pay and railway concession of less than one-half charged on imported sugar. Thus dictate price and keep out imported sugar. Crop begins in May and runs six or seven months. The amount of imports depends entirely upon large or short crops. Cane sugar comes from Australia and Mauritius (crop marketed from December to April). Prices lowest ever known for year ending June 30, 1911. Past six weeks 61 cents per 100 pounds advance governed by London quotations. No. 1 refined, wholesale, $5.65 per 100 pounds; retail, 6 cents per pound. Cube sugar from England and Germany wholesales at $8.14 to $8.36 per 100 pounds. England has 3 per cent preference in duty.

Imported sugar pays 85 cents per 100 pounds plus $1.10 freight from Durban to Johannesburg against no duty on Natal sugar and 53⅞ cents per 100 pounds freight. No local taxes.

Interesting story of early mining days when sugar was 12 cents per pound (p. 67).

In 1891 wholesale price $7.90 and retail, 12 cents per pound.

In 1901 wholesale, $6.90 and retail, 8 cents.

[Book 5, p. 71, Lourenco Marques, Sept. 15, 1911. (Portugal East Africa.)]

The sugar industry develops rapidly by modern machinery. Entire Transvaal free of duty under treaty. Imports some sugar. Portuguese Government derives excise duty on sugar consumed in Mosambique and an export duty on all exported sugar up to a limited amount per annum. Mozambique sugar into Portugal has a colonial preference of one-half the customs duty on the first 6,000 tons. Sugar produced in district of Beira, Inhampanc, and Zambezia when imported into Lourenco pays a duty of 20 Reis, or 2 cents. White foreign sugar pays 80 Reis, or 8 cents. Tates cubes, 112-pound packages, at wholesale, $7.50 per 100 pounds. Retail, 12 cents per pound.

Mozambique whites, $7.60 per 100 pounds wholesale and 8½ cents per pound retail.

[Book 5, p. 96, Port Elizabeth, Cape of Good Hope, Aug. 31, 1911.]

Wholesale beet, refined, granulated, 4.67 cents per pound and 6 cents per pound landed.

Wholesale to retail 25 cents per 100 pounds higher. (Charges less 5 per cent for cash and retails at 6 cents per pound.)

(See page 75.)

Freight from Port Elizabeth to Kimberly (485 miles), Natal sugar, 56 cents per 100 pounds; other sugar, $1.03. Effect of bounty on Natal sugar. Prices 25 years, page 77.

[Book 5, Sierra Leone, Africa, Oct. 24, 1911. Freetown.]

Cubes and lump, $6.75 per 100 pounds wholesale and 8 cents per pound retail.

Granulated, $6.50 per 100 pounds wholesale and 8 cents per pound retail.

Import duty, $1.62 per 100 pounds on refined; $0. 54 on unrefined.

Prices of unrefined, $6.33 per 100 pounds wholesale and 7 cents per pounds retail.

No local taxes. No back prices. Purchases not delivered but taken away by buyers.

SUMMARY.

1911	Wholesale per 100 pounds cut loaf.	Retail per pound cut loaf.	Wholesale per pound granulated.	Retail per pound granulated.
		Cents.		*Cents.*
Aug. 17, Durban			$4.26	6.06
Aug. 21, Johannesburg	$8.14-$8.36	12	5.65	6.00
Sept. 15, Lourenço Marquez (Tates)	7.50	12		
Aug. 31, Port Elizabeth			4.67	6.00
Oct. 8, Seirra Leone	6.75	8	6.50	8.00
Sept. 15, Lourenço Marquez (Mozambique)	7.60	8½		

Import duty at Sierra Leone is $1.62 per 100 pounds on refined, $0.54 per 100 pounds on unrefined.

Durban has two refineries. Prices fixed at Durban for other sections plus freight. Customs duty on imported sugars $0.85 per 100 pounds and preferential railway freight of $0.42½ per 100 pounds. Mozambique sugar comes in free of duty by treaty.

Natal producers control entire South African market having no taxes to pay and railway concessions less than one-half charged on imported sugar. Freight from Johannesburg to Durban $1.10 per 100 pounds on imported sugar against 53¾ cents per 100 pounds on Natal sugar.

Freight to Port Elizabeth 485 miles from Durban 56 cents per 100 pounds on Natal sugar and $1.03 on imported.

Everything done to keep out imported sugar from Africa and to promote the domestic Natal industry.

The Portuguese Government levies excise tax on sugar consumed in Mozambique and an export duty on all exports up to a certain limit per annum. Mozambique sugar into portugal has a colonial preference of one-half the customs duties on the first 6,000 tons.

Sugar industry is developing very rapidly in Mozambique with new modern machinery, etc.

CHINA.

[Book 1, p. 30, summary of 10 consular reports, including Amoy, Canton, Chungking, Foochow, Harbin, Hongkong, Mukden, Tsingtau, Swatow, and Tientsin.]

1. The sugar conditions in most of these districts are quite similar.

2. Hongkong supplies most of the real refined sugar; China supplies native so-called refined, which is really semirefined or "washed sugar" and Java supplies the raw white sugars. Philippine Islands sugar goes to Hongkong now to a much less extent than before the United States last tariff bill, and the three refineries at Hongkong receive supplies now from Java and the Dutch East Indies.

3. At open ports sugars pay an import duty on entry and are subject to a tax on being sent inland, and are also subject to several other local taxes at each "likin" or station they pass through, so that a buyer never knows just what his sugar will cost him delivered until he receives it and pays these so-called "squeezes" (graft). Prices do not vary much throughout China at the outports, or places where first received from Hongkong or other manufacturers, hence Hongkong and a few other places are a good example of Chinese prices.

4. Hongkong is a "free port," as no duties are assessed on importations of the raw or refined sugar. There are 3 refineries there which can refine about 500,000 tons sugar per year. (They do not seem to do so much, as the total imports in 1910 are given as 254,677 tons; 1909, 339,634 tons; 1908, 250,469 tons.) Less than four-fifths of the imports go into refineries. Exports are given as nearly the same. In 1910 four-fifths of imports would be only 203,741 tons, and one-fifth goes into the Chinese markets or into industries. (One-fifth equals 50,936 tons.)

5. The rise of the sugar production in Formosa the last three or four years has interferred with the Hongkong trade of refiners. Hongkong claims that by its situation and buying facilities it could have shipped to the Pacific coast of the United States.

6. The three refineries work in harmony. One issued a price list this season which we give and also the retail prices of a native dealer.

Hongkong prices.

	Per pound wholesale.	Per pound retail.
	Cents.	*Cents.*
Powdered (5-pound tins)	5.20	6.30
Cubes (6-pound tins)	4.83	5.30
Cubes (3-pound tins)	4.90	5.60
Cubes, casks (200 pounds)	3.93	4.62
Cubes, casks (112 pounds)	4.03	4.75
Crystals (granulated)	2.91	3.78
Soft sugars:		
No. 1	2.84	3.36
No. 2	2.80	3.30
No. 3	2.75	3.15
No. 4	2.62	3.00
No. 5	2.49	2.90

New York refiners' prices on same date.

	Cents per pound.		Cents per pound.
Powdered (in barrels and bags)	5.733	Soft sugars—Continued.	
Cubes (in 250-pound barrels)	5.88	No. 7	5.194
Granulated (in barrels and bags)	5.635	No. 8	5.145
Soft sugars:		No. 9	5.096
No. 1	5.488	No. 10	5.047
No. 2	5.439	No. 11	4.998
No. 3	5.39	No. 12	4.949
No. 4	5.341	No. 13	4.90
No. 5	5.292	No. 14	4.90
No. 6	5.243	No. 15	4.90

7. Low-grade raws from Mauritius and Javas are sold by native dealers at 1.75 to 2.20 cents per pound.

8. The theoretical profits of retailers at Hongkong and elsewhere in China, as shown by the reports, are 10 per cent above cost, but actually are much more, for special reasons.

9. Hongkong refiners' export prices are uncertain but understood to be about 10 per cent lower than list prices.

10. The consul at Hongkong says the export prices are of interest in determining the relation of the Hongkong refineries to dominant interests in the United States as regards the trade of the Pacific coast. (The receipts of raw and refined sugar from China at San Francisco were in 1902, 90 tons; in 1903, none; 1904, none; 1905, none; 1906, 69 tons of refined; 1907, 189 tons (mostly raws); 1908, 294 tons (mostly raws); 1909, 367 tons (mostly raws); 1910, 282 tons (mostly raws); 1911, to date, 1,732 tons (mostly refined.) W. P. W.

(Prices have been so low in the United States during recent years that no foreign refined can afford to pay the duty.) W. P. W.

Hongkong being a free port (no duties) supplies of refined, as well as raws, can be had from all over the world at short notice, so that jobbers' prices, of necessity, follow the world prices.

11. *At Amoy.*—The imports of 1910 were valued at $11,969 for white sugar and at $43,334 for refined. The sugars used are native, Javas, and some from Hongkong. Foreigners use the Hongkong sugar and Chinese the others. There is an import duty up to No. 10 Dutch standard of 9.2 cents per 100 pounds; No. 11 Dutch standard and above (raws and refined), 11.6 cents per 100 pounds. Price of best native sugar is 1.80 cents per pound, of poorest grade 1.40 cents per pound.

Price of semirefined sugar No. 1, 2.77 cents; No. 3, 2.26 cents. Foreign sugar (refined) No. 1, 2.81 cents; No. 3, 2.65 cents.

Retail prices.

	Cents per pound.
Native sugar	1.04 to 1.59
Native semirefined	2.94 to 2.43
Foreign refined	3.05 to 3.82

As these foreign refined quotations are below the Hongkong quotations for cubes, they are probably the lower grades of granulated and soft sugar.

12. *At Canton* (population about 1,000,000 people, but a distributing center for 50,000,000 people).—No statistics are published. Has small imports of foreign sugar. In 1909, 2,050,000 pounds brown and 31,948;000 pounds white sugar. Best native white sugar (semirefined) sells at 3.24 cents per pound wholesale and 3.72 cents per pound retail. Cheapest native brown sugar 1.66 cents per pound wholesale, 1.91 cents per pound retail. Java sugar, No. 24 Dutch standard (white), sells at 3.14 cents per pound wholesale and 3.61 cents per pound retail.

13. *At Chungking* (August 21, 1911).—Report covers a province of 50,000,000 people. No foreign sugar imported. Three kinds of sugar are manufactured, two of raw and one of refined. The latter adulterated with pea flour (soy peas). The best brown sugar wholesales at 1.73 cents per pound and retails at 1.90 cents per pound. The lowest browns wholesale at 1.58 cents per pound and retail at 1.74 cents per pound. The best white (semirefined) wholesales at 3.07 cents per pound and retails at 3.18 cents per pound. The lowest white wholesales at 2.85 cents per pound and retails at 3 cents per pound. The sugar is universally grown throughout the Province. A small local tax is collected at place of manufacture of .18 cent per pound. Prices five years ago were from 5 per cent to 20 per cent lower than now.

14. *At Foochow* (August 19, 1911).—Hongkong refiners are large importers of refined. Native sugar comes to a shipping port, Hsing, about halfway to Amoy. Competition is active. Best white sugar (native) is 3.46 cents per pound; poorest brown 2.60 cents per pound wholesale and retails at 10 per cent to 20 per cent higher. There is an internal revenue tax at several stations between shipping point and Foochow, and each one passed collects toll, and $50 to $100 may have to be paid before the goods reach Foochow. After the buyer at Hsing pays these bills he arranges his prices according to the cost of shipment. Foreign sugars do not come under these charges, being imported through the customhouse and paying 5 per cent ad valorem duty. If shipped out of port they are subject to an inland transit duty of $2\frac{1}{2}$ per cent more. Foreign sugar is sold with 4 per cent tare and 3 per cent off for cash, or 1 per cent for 60 days. Java sugars, No. 24 Dutch standard, wholesale at 3.70 cents. Best Manilas at 3.60 cents per pound; retail at 10 per cent and 20 per cent higher. In 1891 Javas (white) No. 24 Dutch standard sold at 5.31 cents per pound. In 1901 at 3.51 cents, in 1906 at 2.82 cents. Refined in 1896 was 3.95 cents, in 1901 3.51 cents, and in 1906 3.09 cents per pound.

15. *At Harbin* (September 11, 1911).—The sugar business is divided between the Chinese and Russian trade. The Chinese sell Japanese and Hongkong sugars. Prices for best brown sugar were 4.20 cents per pound wholesale, 4.50 cents retail. Lowest grade brown, 3.70 cents wholesale to 4 cents retail. Japanese best, 4.10 cents wholesale to 4.30 cents retail, and a brown Chinese sugar, imported from Canton, sells at 3 cents wholesale to 3.30 cents retail. There is a small local tax at one place near the European settlement. The Russians sell two kinds of sugar, cubes and granulated, part of which is made in Russia and part in Poland, at a factory near Harbin. These are both beet sugars. Lately the local granulated has driven out the Russian.

Prices in cents per pound.

	At Harbin (Sept. 11).		At New York (same date).	
	Wholesale.	Retail.	Wholesale.	Retail.
Russian cubes	4.70	5.00	6.86	$7\frac{1}{2}$–8
Granulated	3.50	4.00	6.66	6.90
Poland cubes	3.80	4.60	....	....
Granulated	3.20	4.00	....	....

Cubes are sold in boxes of $162\frac{1}{3}$ pounds, barrels $216\frac{2}{3}$ pounds, while granulated is sold in bags of $234\frac{1}{10}$ pounds.

16. *At Mukden, China* (September 2, 1911) —There are here three grades of white sugar, of which prices at wholesale are $3\frac{1}{8}$ cents, $2\frac{7}{8}$ cents, $2\frac{1}{4}$ cents per pound, and three grades of brown sugar, at $2\frac{3}{4}$ cents, $2\frac{5}{8}$ cents, and 2 cents per pound. Whites in bags of 10 pounds and 133 pounds each have the largest sale, and browns in bags of 133 pounds. There is a duty of $1\frac{1}{8}$ mills per pound on white sugar and $\frac{8}{10}$ mills per pound on the brown at ports which are open to receive shipments, plus slight wharfage dues, and to this there is added a tax of one-half of the amount of the duty if the sugar is sent into the interior. Other taxes of 3 per cent maximum are levied, making whole-

sale prices at the interior about 15 per cent higher than at the seaboard. Chinese retailers charge 20 per cent over wholesale prices plus duties, taxes, etc. The white sugar used is chiefly supplied by Hongkong refiners, while most of the brown sugar comes from South China. Prices have been very steady for five years.

17. *At Tsingtau, China* (August 12, 1911).—Hongkong brands are almost exclusively used. Some wholesale quotations of white powdered at $3 93 per 133 pounds, equal to 2.95 cents per pound down to 2.50 cents per pound. Since the middle of June prices have soared, advancing 32 cents per 100 pounds (about ¼ cents per pound). Hongkong refiners refused orders and sold ahead to November. All sugars sold in tin boxes, gunny bags, tea mats, bags and bulk. No local taxes except import duty of $0.088 per 100 pounds on brown sugar; $0.113 per 100 pounds on white sugar. Hongkong granulated is retailed at foreign shops at 5.70 cents per pound, or 100 pounds for $4.57. Cubes retail in 6-pound tins at 7 cents per pound. Chinese shops retail granulated at 4 cents and cubes at 6½ cents. Powdered or confectionary sugar is retailed at 11 cents per pound, or 10 pounds can be bought at 9½ cents per pound. Prices have fluctuated about 5 per cent in five years.

18. *At Swatow, China* (August 14, 1911).—Center of ancient sugar industry of China and is still important. The exports in 1910 were 42,312 tons of brown and 14,701 tons of white sugar. There are four grades of white sugar (refined). No. 1 sells at 3.89 cents per pound, No. 2 at 3.63 cents per pound, and No. 3 at 3.53¼ cents per pound, and No. 4 at 3 cents to 3.06 cents per pound. The retail price is about 20 per cent above the wholesale. Grades Nos. 1, 2, and 3 are known as refined sugar. No. 4 is a medium raw sugar (brown) and is worth about 2.43 cents to 3 cents per pound.

1910. Two thousand five hundred and four tons white sugar imported; 1,000 tons refined imported (mostly from Hongkong) and retailed at 4.23 cents to 4.86 cents per pound in 10-pound cloth bags. The wholesale price is 3.38 cents per pound.

19. *At Tientsin, China* (October 6, 1911).—Raw sugars are mostly Chinese and Javas. The former from Swatow, Amoy, and Canton. Although called raw sugar, they have been subjected to some process of refining called "washing." Refined sugar mostly comes from Hongkong. Japanese making strong effort to get the market and the imports are increasing. One Persian sells so-called "American Cuba sugar" in 100-pound cans. Wholesale prices of refined white sugar are 4.01 cents per pound, and yellow sugar 3.70 cents per pound. Retail prices of refined white are 5 cents per pound, and yellow 4 cents per pound. Hongkong cubes retail at 7.50 cents per pound. American cubes (so called) retail at 9 cents per pound.

[Book 1, at Chefoo, China, Aug. 9, 1911.]

The raw sugar is grown in south of China, exported to Hongkong and refined, and then imported into China.

It is subject only to a small ad valorem duty and escapes the native customs tax which it would have to pay if shipped from South China direct to other provinces of the Empire.

Hongkong prices: Refined, $4 to $5 per 100 pounds; retail prices, about 10 cents per pound

Chinese sugar will go about three times as far as American.

[Book 1, at Nanking, China, Aug. 3, 1911.]

Sugar is handled by retail trade only from Hongkong refiners.

White granulated, 4.30 cents per pound; light brown, 4 cents per pound; cubes, 8 cents per pound; and pulverized (icing), 10 cents per pound.

Freight from Shanghai is $65 per ton by rail and $57 per ton by river.

No local charges.

[Book 1, Newchwang, China, Aug. 4, 1911.]

Sugar used here is imported from the Philippines, Formosa, and Japan proper by way of Hongkong.

No local taxes beyond a 5 per cent ad valorem duty which foreign and native sugar share alike.

Present prices: Pure granulated, wholesale, $4 per 100 pounds; retail, 4.40 cents per pound. White granulated, wholesale, $4 per 100 pounds; retail, 4.40 cents per pound.

ABYSSINIA.

[Book 1, p. —, Adis Ababa, Aug 14, 1911.]

1. Produces no sugar.
2. Imports granulated from Austria, cut sugar (cubes and dominos) from France, cones (loaf and crushed) from France and Italy. These are mostly made from beets.

3. Prices: Granulated, wholesale, 8½ cents per pound; retail, 14 cents per pound. cut sugar, wholesale, 9 cents per pound; retail, 14 cents per pound; cones, wholesale, 11 cents per pound; retail, 14 cents per pound.

4. The import duty is 10 per cent on local valuation. The price at interior points rises to 20 cents per pound.

5. Importations for consumption in 1909 were about 58,253 pounds (about 26 long tons).

6. There are no local charges or other conditions affecting prices.

Greece.

[Book 6, p. 1, Athens, July 4, 1911.]

Lump sugar only. From Austria (2 grades), import duty and tax stated by Patras.

[Page 3, Patras, July 18, 1911.]

A1 white, $0.118 per pound, wholesale, and $0.123 per pound retail.
Small squares (loaf), $0.118 wholesale and $0.123 retail.
A loose white (granulated), $0.117 per pound wholesale and $0.123 retail.
B loose white (granulated), $0.116 per pound wholesale and $0.12 per pound retail.
No variation in prices. Sold in bulk at retail.
Import duty, $0.075 per pound on all sugar.
Octroi tax, $0.004 per pound on all sugar.
No manufacture. No back prices.

[Athens, Nov. 1, 1911.]

Prices: A1 white, 12.30 cents per pound wholesale and 13.30 cents per pound retail.
Small squares (loaf), 12.30 cents per pound wholesale and 13.30 cents per pound retail.
A loose white (Austrian moist), wholesale, 12.10 cents per pound; retail, 12.50 cents per pound.
B loose white (Austrian moist), wholesale, 12.10 cents per pound; retail, 12.50 cents per pound.

Egypt.

[Supplementary, Alexandria, Aug. 15 1911.]

The Societe Generale et de la Raffinerie d'Egypte is practically the only sugar refinery in Egypt.

Prices: Loaf, $3.75 per 100 pounds, wholesale; retail, 5¼ to 6 cents per pound. Granulated, $3.22 per 100 pounds, wholesale, and 4½ to 5½ cents per pound retail.

Large retail stores use delivery wagons.

Ceylon—Columbo.

[Book 5, p. 87, Sept. 2, 1911.]

Australian, Mauritius, and Fiji sugar imported but less than 3,300 hundredweight for 11 months.

Price of these varies from $2.75 to $3.25 per hundredweight and retailed at 5 to 6½ cents per pound; now 6 cents per pound.

Cuba sugar sells 1½ cents more than granulated.

Natives sell in palm-leaf packages and keep accounts on palm leaves.

Importations from Austria, Java, and Hongkong for past 12 months, 330,000 hundredweight; Java, 170,000 hundredweight; Hongkong, 130,000 hundredweight; Austria, 30,000 hundredweight; Hongkong preferred, Austria second, and Java last.

All 224-pound bags.

Retailers sell at same prices for same grades.

China sugar is bought in China at $4 and sold at 4.87 cents per pound retail.

Austria sugar is bought in Austria at $3.24 per 100 pounds and sold at 4.38 cents per pound retail.

Java sugar is bought in Java at $3.12 per 100 pounds, wholesale, and sold at 4.54 cents per pound retail.

Retailers sell at 6 cents now.

TURKEY.

[Book 7, p. 71, Constantinople, July 12, 1911.]

Prices early part of June:

1. Trieste· Beet fine granulated, $0.0351 per pound wholesale to $0.395 per pound retail; Russian crystals, $0.0295 per pound wholesale (raw, hard sugar), $0.0324 per pound retail; Trieste squares, $0.038 per pound wholesale to $0.0505 per pound retail; Tate's No. 1 cubes, $0.048 per pound wholesale to $0.072 per pound retail.

Prices fluctuate much. For instance, fine granulated sold at $0.046 per pound and at $0.0418 per pound. The large stores make deliveries in all the suburbs at same as town prices. The smaller stores charge extra. Above prices include duty, shipping fees, and deliverage. Duties are 11 per cent ad valorem at customhouse and 2 per cent port fees. No other charges. No change in prices in the last two years and very little in former years. No statistics available. One class of dealers who contract with the sugar companies for one entire year's output at a certain fixed price are thus being independent of the rise and fall of the market. Majority of sugar comes from Trieste. When a ship leaves Trieste a telegram is sent to the merchants of Constantinople naming quantity. The merchants get together, compare notes on the amount of sugar on hand, and then the price is arranged. If there is much on hand, the price will be lower; if scarcity, the price will rise. Dutch and French sugar no longer can compete with Austrian.

[P. 74, Beirut, July 25, 1911.]

Sugar comes from France, Austria, Russia, and Egypt in the order named.

Only refined sugars used.

Prices to-day are:

	Wholesale, per 100 pounds.	Retail, per pound.
French	$4.65	$0.0497
Austrian	4.01	.0417
Russian	3.04	.0357
Egyptian	3.69	.0401

Retail prices the same in all localities in small packages.

The only tax levied is the custom duty of 11 per cent ad valorem.

Prices fluctuate by London Exchange quotations.

[P. 77, Jerusalem, Syria, Sept. 26, 1911.]

Book 7, page 77, gives prices at Jerusalem and Jaffa since 1887. Some considerable variations shown, with 1910 and 1911 the highest with one exception, 1888 (6 cents per pound), when all the world was high.

(No summary needed.)

ZANZIBAR.

[Book 7, p. 81, Aug. 31, 1911.]

Sugar imported enters for domestic use. No manufacturers demanding it.

Only one grade brought in—crystalized sugar from Germany, Russia, Austria, Mauritius, and Java.

Wholesale prices, 4 cents per pound; duty paid of 7½ per cent; $0.044 per pound on three months' credit.

Retail price, $0.0455 per pound.

Retail trade entirely in hands of the Indian merchant. No delivery wagons. Buyers take the goods with them.

Customhouse duty, 7½ per cent.

No local taxes or bounties.

No figures for past years.

(No summary required.)

SERVIA.

[Book 7, p. 30, Belgrade, June 30, 1911.]

The entire consumption of Servia is supplied by the one beet-sugar factory in the country, situated near Belgrade, whose output is just equal to the total consumption of the country.

Importations are made impossible by an import duty of $2.62 per 100 pounds, so that the factory has a practical monopoly of the trade.

The following are the factory prices in not less than 10-ton lots:

	Wholesale, per 100 pounds.	Retail, per 100 pounds.
Cubes in boxes	$7.87½	$8.87½
Granulated, in bags	7.61	8.87½
Powdered, in bags	7.61	8.87½

These prices include excise tax of $2.62 per 100 pounds on all consumed in the country. None ever exported.

Granulated is not retailed, but used mostly by manufacturers (confectioners). Cubes and powdered generally used for consumption. No prices obtainable for past years.

VENEZUELA.

[Book 7, p. 78, Porto Cabello, June 27, 1911.]

Two grades, both local Venezuela sugar, of what is called refined.

Maracaibo sells wholesale at $6.54 per 100 pounds.

Juan Diaz sells wholesale at $7 per 100 pounds.

Retail prices, both grades, 7½ cents per pound.

Sugar business pays same tax as other business, and depends on amount of business; also a local or municipal tax of $0.70 per 100 pounds which is brought into the State from another State.

Brown sugar from sugar cane is sold in its natural state and is most used.

Sugar is higher than five years ago.

Consul sends samples and sorts.

[Book 7, p. 79, La Guaira, Venezuela, June 27, 1911.]

Venezuela sugar is of recent development in grain sugar.

Wholesale, $6.46 per 100 pounds in large lots; $6.50 per 100 pounds in small lots; $6.95 per single 100-pound sack.

Retails at $0.0965 per pound.

Guatire sugar sells wholesale at $6.17 per 100 pounds and retails at 9 and 9½ cents per pound.

Maracaibo sugar, $7.52 per 100 pounds at wholesale, and duty too high for importations, 55 per cent plus 1 per cent on what?

HONDURAS.

[Book 6, p. 4, Celba, Honduras, Aug. 2, 1911.]

New York refined, cubes, and granulated control the market.

Wholesale, $0.092 per pound, and retail, 10 cents per pound.

Crude sugar sold, all for domestic use, in molds: 5.60 cents per pound wholesale; 6¼ cents per pound retail. No change in five years. Small tax on crude sugar. Import duty, national tax, customhouse fees amount to 3½ cents per pound.

[P. 6, Puerto Cortes, Aug. 7, 1911.]

Supplies come from Guatemala, United States, and Germany, which sends beet sugar, and the consumption of which is decreasing.

Guatemala sugars are from brown to white (semirefined) and come in free of duty under treaty. It sells at wholesale at $3.80 to $5.20 per 100 pounds at the dock, and inland at $5.80 to $6.60 per 100 pounds, and retails at 7½ cents per pound.

United States refined comes in barrels and bags of cubes and granulated, and pays duty of 2 cents per pound; municipal tax of 0.40 cent per pound, and customhouse fees of 1.60 cents per pound; a total of 4 cents per pound.

Wholesales at $8 to $8.80 per 100 pounds, and retails at 7 cents per pound.

German sells at the same price as American. Native crude used by the natives makes fine sirup and would doubtless find ready market in the United States. A large amount of sugar cane is grown in Honduras for rum making to be sold to the Government, which controls the liquor monopoly.

[P. 8, Tegucigalpa, Honduras, July 27, 1911.]

Almost all sugar used in this district is imported from Salvador and Nicaragua. Inferior quality of refined and only one grade.

Wholesale, $5.60 to $6.40 per 100 pounds.

Say cost at Amapala, $3.25 per 100 pounds (retail 5 cents per pound).

Freight, road tax, sanitary tax, 52 cents to San Lorenzo.

Dispatch agent fees, 6 cents.

Freight to Tegucigalpa, 80 cents.

Municipal tax, 40 cents.

Charges, $1.28.

Wholesale cost, $5.03 per 100 pounds. retail at 6 cents per pound and sometimes less.

NICARAGUA.

[Book 6, p. 95, Corinto, July 26, 1911.]

All domestic manufacture used here.

No refineries.

White sugar, wholesale, $4.15 per 100 pounds, and retail, 4.60 cents per pound; second grade, wholesale, $3.38 per 100 pounds, and 3.80 cents per pound retail.

Considerable raw sugar is shipped to Vancouver.

No local taxes and no bounties.

[P. 96, Boma Kongo.]

All cubes, English and Belgium, cost 7 cents per pound.

All retail, no wholesale. Sells retail at 8.75 cents.

NORWAY.

[P. 98, Bergen, July 5, 1911.]

No sugar refineries here. No raw sugar is imported. No local taxes or charges affecting prices.

Loaf cubes, $6.27 per 100 pounds wholesale and 6.82 cents per pound retail.

Granulated (English), $5.90 wholesale and 6.09 cents per pound retail.

Granulated (German), $5.78 per 100 pounds wholesale, and 6.09 cents per pound retail.

[P. 100, Christiania, June 30, 1911.]

Imports to Norway, 45,000 tons, mostly from Germany.

Prices as quoted by board of trade to-day. Wholesale loaf, 6½ cents per pound, including import duty of 2.14 cents per pound, retail, 7½ cents per pound.

Granulated, 6 cents per pound wholesale and 7 cents per pound retail (all beet sugars).

Cane cubes, 8½ cents per pound wholesale and 9½ cents per pound retail.

PARAGUAY.

[Book 6, p. 119, Ascuncion, Aug. 22, 1911.]

New York, granulated $5.75; New York, cubes $6.

Sugar imported. Based on July Montevideo quotation, first class, "Say" French cut, $6.36 per 100 pounds, "Say" lump sifted, $4.13 per 100 pounds; German lump, $3.70 per 100 pounds; Austrian granulated, $3.60 per 100 pounds.

Importers pay duty and customhouse fees, amounting to 42½ per cent ad valorem, the valuation being fixed by tariff act, $0.053 per 100 pounds for refined in general, and at $0.065 per 100 pounds for special cut sugar. Imported sugar is also subjected to an internal-revenue tax of $0.00034 to $0.00038 per 100 pounds.

The value of the pesos is subject to great fluctuations. Retail prices are neither uniform or stable. Each dealer fixes his prices to suit his business. Imported sugar now retails at 9½ cents per pound, and domestic at 8½ cents per pound.

There is but one sugar factory in Paraguay.

Production of Paraguay sugar factory in 1911 will be 540 tons. Three years ago it was 1,280 tons, or about one-half its capacity.

The industry is badly handicapped by lack of production of sugar cane, which is cultivated only in small patches.

[Book 6, p. 120.]

When the industry was started the factory offered planters $2.40 per ton of cane, which was not sufficient to stimulate production, and the price was raised to $3 per ton and is now $3.40 per ton, but the production is still far below requirements for local trade. To-day 22 pesos is equal to $1.65 United States currency. In a week it may be $1.97 United States currency, but the price of sugar will still be $1.65 for 10 kilos, 7½ cents per pound.

(Peso, 7½ cents to 8½ cents, varies constantly.)

Morocco.

[Book 6, p. 75, Tangiers.]

For five centuries or more no sugar produced.

Supplies come from France, Austria, Germany, Belgium, and Holland.

Only two grades imported.

First. Double refined in loaves or blocks of 5 pounds.

Second. Refined cubes in 110-pound cases.

Third. A small amount of granulated.

French bring most. No local or other taxes except customhouse duties, 12½ per cent ad valorem.

Retail prices very regular.

Wholesale prices are based on f. o. b. Marseilles for French, f. o. b. Trieste for Austrian, f. o. b. Hamburg for German, f. o. b. Antwerp for Belgium, f. o. b. Amsterdam for Dutch.

Retail price now is 5 cents per pound and varies with fluctuation of the currency as well as with prices in export countries.

Portugal.

[Book 6, p. 122, Lisbon, July 24, 1911.]

The wholesale prices of raw sugar most extensively used in Portugal are as follows:

Pernambuco sugar, $2.73 per 100 pounds, Mozambique, $3.33; Austrian, $3.33; Madeira, $9.80 (out of market).

Say the difference between in bond and duties and local taxes paid is $0.64 per 100 pounds, the customhouse duty being $0.55 per 100 pounds, there is a duty allowance on colonial sugars of 27½ per cent less than the $0.64 duty. The corresponding difference on refined is $0.74 per 100 pounds; wholesale prices, cut loaf, $12.27 per 100 pounds, and retail, 13¾ cents to 13¼ cents.

Granulated, $10.27 wholesale and 10¾ cents to 11¼ cents per pound retail.

Consul was probably in error, and when corrected, then price would be, cut loaf, $8, wholesale, against 8½ cents to 9 cents per pound retail.

Granulated, $7.40 per 100 pound, wholesale, against 7¾ cents to 8¼ cents per pound, retail.

Sales at retail in paper bags, except loaf, which comes in pasteboard boxes.

Roumania.

[Book 7, p. 1, Bucharest, July 14, 1911.]

Factory price, loaf and cubes, $5.69 to $5.95 per 100 pounds; granulated, $5.25 to $5.52.

There are four or five refineries and all vary a little in grades.

Retail prices vary from 50 cents to 55 cents per 100 pounds above the refiners.

Loaf, 6¼ cents to 6½ cents, and granulated, 5¾ cents to 6 cents.

Import duty, $3.06 per 100 pounds until March, 1918. (French book says $2.45 per 100 pounds.) Export duty, $0.789 per 100 pounds on exports.

Bounty to sugar manufacturers, $0.965 per 100 pounds. Bounty ceases in March, 1914.

No statistics for 25 years.

Prices are fixed by the Trieste Bourse for Black Sea ports and by Prague for towns on the Danube or in the interior.

Duties and taxes on loaf sugar are (agrees with French book):

Duty (per 100 pounds)	$2.45
Excise tax	1.75
Local tax	.50
Total	4.70
Duty	2.45
Excise tax	1.75
Protection	.70

Prices at Varna on the Black Sea:

Cubes in cases, $7.87 per 100 pounds wholesale; retail, $8.80 to $8.75.

Granulated in bags, $7.70 wholesale; retail, $8.34 to $8⅜.

PANAMA.

[Book 6, p. 112, July 17, 1911.]

	Tons.
Consumption:	
1909	1,800
1910	1,403
United States supplied	420
England supplied	133
Germany supplied	165
Spanish America	685
	1,403

(All refined sugar.)

Refined is loaf and granulated. An inferior quality, used mostly by natives. Comes from Central and South America (San Salvador and Ecuador) and costs in Panama, freight and duty included, 3 cents to 3¼ cents per pound and retails at 3½ cents to 3¾ cents per pound.

Import duty 12½ per cent ad valorem. No local taxes.

American granulated retails at 5 cents per pound and American cubes at 7½ cents.

As a rule sugar is a trifle cheaper in San Francisco than in New York for import here. Granulated, present price, f. o. b., San Francisco or New York, 3½ cents to 3¾ cents per pound. Price in Panama per 100-pound sack, $4.25 to $4.50, and 5 cents per pound at retail.

Cut loaf and cubes f. o. b. New York, $3.75 per 100 pounds; in Panama, $6.50 per barrel; retail, 7½ cents per pound.

The Panama Railroad retails American sugar (National Sugar Refinery Co., brand) to employees: Yellow sugar, 3½ cents per pound; granulated, 4 cents per pound in 20-pound sacks; cubes, 10 cents per pound in 2-pound boxes; 9 cents per pound in 5-pound boxes; 1901 (impossible to go very far back), $4.80 per 100 pounds; 1896, $4.25 per 100 pounds.

JAPAN.

[Book 6, p. 30, Yokohama, Sept. 23, 1911.]

Sugar at wholesale is sold in double mat bags of 133 pounds each. Sugar retails in paper bags of 1.3 to 6.6 pounds; small wooden boxes also used in retailing.

Formosa furnished increased supplies under tariff changes, and refiners in Japan are very active and prices declined.

	Wholesale (per 100 pounds).	Retail (per pound).
Page 33:		
Prices to-day, cubes	$10.21	$0.11
Sept. 23, refined, highest	9.40	.11
Granulated, lowest	9.16	.09½-.10½
Page 32:		
1907, average refined	6.15	.066
1908, average refined	6.84	.073
1909, average refined	7.02	.073
1910, average refined	7.04	.075
1911, average refined, July	7.02	.075

Retail prices fixed by Sugar Retailers' Guild in Yokohama, of which every retailer is a member (compulsory by law). (Custom of buying, p. 34.)

The national business taxes are:

	Wholesale dealer.	Retail dealer.
On $5,000 sales	$6.00	$15.00
On rental value of stores per cent	9	9
On employees and assistants each	$1.00	$1.00

Local taxes in Yokohama, 40 per cent of the national tax.

Bounties: The Government of Formosa has for 10 years been granting bounties to cane-sugar growers, this year amounting to $900,000. The bounty ceases at end of fiscal year 1912.

Production of Formosa, 1911-12, established at 500,000,000 pounds.

Consumption tax: Latest revision, April, 1910, now in force is imposed on sugar (molasses and sirup), taking deliveries of from factories, customhouse, or bonded warehouse for consumption in the Empire of Japan, as follows:

[Book 6, p. 35.]

	Per 100 pounds.
First-class, sugar below No. 11 Dutch standard in color:	
A. Black (raw), in casks	$0.75
B. Black, other	1.12
Second-class, sugar below No. 15 Dutch standard	1.87
Third-class, sugar below No. 18 Dutch standard	2.62
Fourth-class, sugar below No. 21 Dutch standard	3.00
Fifth-class, sugar below No. 22 Dutch standard	3.37
Sixth-class, rock candy, Cuba, loaf or lump, and the like	3.75

[Book 6, p. 36, Tokyo prices, Sept. 23, 1911.]

	Wholesale, per 100 pounds.	Retail, per pound.
Japan refined No. 1	$7.27-$7.50	$0.11¼-$0.09¾
Japan refined No. 2	6.90- 6.97	.08¼- .07¼
Japan refined No. 3	6.64	.06¾- .06
Brown sugar No. 1	6.00	.06¼- .06
Brown sugar No. 2	5.14- 5.20	.06 - .0660

Tokyo has a wholesale dealers' guild, but prices practically controlled by the Sugar Refineries' Union, which represents several sugar refiners as sole agents.

In each of the 15 administrative districts in the city of Tokyo there is a retail sugar dealers' guild. All prices are uniform as controlled by these guilds and are publicly announced.

[Book 6, p. 38, Kobe, Sept. 26, 1911.]

Formosan raw sugar, value 3½ cents per pound (Nov., 1910-Nov., 1911).

1910-11, 122,397 tons Java sugar imported at cost of $2.25 to $3 per 100 pounds, most of which was used by the refiners' companies.

The Japan Co. (Ltd) (at Osaka) sold their standard refined sugar during this year at $6.39 to $7.89 per 100 pounds, and their S. K. standard crystals one-fourth cent more.

Retail prices for this refiners' sugars: Cubes, 12½ cents; granulated, 9½ cents per pound.

Summary of prices.

Place.	Date, 1911.	Cubes, wholesale, per 100 pounds.	Cubes, retail, cents per pound.	Granulated, wholesale, per 100 pounds.	Granulated, retail, cents per pound.
Yokohama	Sept. 23	$10.21	11	$9.40	11
Tokyo	Sept. 23	....	....	$7.27–7.50	9¼
Kobe	Sept. 26	9.89	10½	6.39	9½

JAVA.

[Supplementary, Batavia, Java, Oct. 30, 1911.]

Wholesale Java raw sugar No. 12 to 14 Dutch standard, generally known as American assortment, during month of October, $0.022 to $0.0226 per pound; closing at $0.031 per pound. No. 16 Dutch standard and above during October, $0.0251 to $0.0262 per pound, closing at $0.0325 to $0.0336 per pound.

Superior grade white, but not refined, in October, at $0.031 to $0.034, closing at $0.0355 per pound, all with upward tendency.

Retail prices for Java sugars a fraction higher than above wholesale prices.

Refined sugars, generally imported from Holland, retail now at $0.055 per pound, sold in tins of 2 pounds, 5 pounds, and 10 pounds.

No local or other taxes.

No export duty or bounty.

No import duties on sugar.

Year.	Nos. 12-14 Dutch standard.		Nos. 16 and above.		Superior.	
	Wholesale, per 100 pounds.	Retail, cents, per pound.	Wholesale, per 100 pounds.	Retail, cents per pound.	Wholesale, per 100 pounds.	Retail, cents per pound.
1906	$1.74	0.0274	$2.10	0.0314	$2.25	0.0225
1907	1.81	.0281	1.89	.0289	2.20	.0320
1908	2.00	.03	2.06	.0308	2.32	.0332
1909	2.00	.03	2.13	.0313	2.42	.0342
1910	2.19	.0319	2.30	.0330	2.67	.0430

No record for 25 years or other Java data.

Java white sugar (consular report):

Price, year 1910, per 100 pounds, "Superior" sugar (white)	$2.67
Freight and insurance to United States	.25
	2.92
Duty above No. 16 Dutch standard	1.90
Cost landed at New York, duty paid	4.82
Average price granulated, 1910	4.97
Javas cheaper—difference	.15
Above No. 16 Dutch standard, duty	1.90
Test 99°, duty	1.79
Without No. 16 Dutch standard limit (less duty)	.11
Above difference	.15
Without No. 16 Dutch standard limit (Javas cheaper)	.26

Siam.

[Book 7, p. 68, Bankok, Aug. 29, 1911.]

The sugar sold is manufactured or refined sugar from Hongkong, China, Singapore, and Java.

Local production insignificant.

The import duty is 3 per cent ad valorem.

There are no local taxes, bounties, or other conditions affecting prices.

Very little difference in retail prices in city.

No record for 25 years, but it is understood prices have not varied much.

Present prices according to quality are: Best Hongkong sugar, wholesale, $4.50 per 100 pounds; retail, 5 cents per pound. Best Singapore sugar, wholesale, $3.18 per 100 pounds; retail, 3½ cents per pound. Castor sugar, retail, 10 cents per pound.

Loaf or cube sugar.

(No summary required.)

Luxemburg.

[Book 6, p. 40, July 2, 1911.]

New York granulated. $5 per 100 pounds; New York cubes, $5.25 per 100 pounds.

Two hundred and sixty-two thousand inhabitants.

No sugar refineries.

All refined sugar imported from Germany, because Luxemburg belongs to the German custom union.

Zollverein: All large German factories have agents here to sell to wholesalers.

Wholesale prices of refined are the same in all 10 districts.

Calculation: Raw beet sugar 88° analysis M 15 per 50 kilos, 100 kilos, 30 marks; add cost refining, freight, commission, etc., 100 kilos, 7 marks; add German consumption tax, 100 kilos, 14 marks; makes price of refined sugar, 100 kilos, 51 marks

Importers' price to wholesalers of cut loaf in boxes will be, 100 kilos 51 marks; plus additional charges in 50-kilo boxes, 2 marks; total, 53 marks.

In 25-kilo boxes, 53.50 marks.

Wholesaler's price to retailers at a profit per 100 kilos, 2 to 3 marks.

Retailers sell at profit of 1 to 6 pfennigs per kilo. Many retailers sell at little profit and sometimes at a loss to retain customers. Small dealers rather prefer not to sell sugar at all.

Italy.

[Book 6, p. 10, Catania, Sicily, July 12, 1911.]

Customs duty, $8.67 per 100 pounds, to $7.70 and below as to grade; revenue tax, $6.23 per 100 pounds.

No sugar manufactured in Sicily. Comes from sugar works in northern Italy. Mostly beet sugar. Some from potatoes.

Raws, first product, 95–96° test; raws, second product, 90–92° test. Refined crystallized loaf, 99.6° to 99.7° test. Centrifugals, 99.7° to 99.8°; Pili cones, loaf, 99.8° to 99.9°; extra, about 100°.

Wholesale granulated, $11.73 per 100 pounds, and retail, 14½ cents per pound.

Wholesale, cut loaf, $12.70 per 100 pounds, and retail, 15½ cents per pound.

New York granulated, $5.15 per 100 pounds, cubes, $5.40 per 100 pounds.

Special weight made by law.

Government excise tax, $6.23 per 100 pounds for 94° test or over; $5.88 per 100 pounds on 63° to 94° test. Less than 63° test used for alcohol; Government tax none on alcohol.

[Book 6, p. 12, Florence, July 8, 1911.]

Best loaf, $13.74 per 100 pounds wholsale, and 14½ cents per pound retail with local tax of $1.15 per 100 pounds. Common granulated, $12.84 per 100 pounds wholesale, with local tax of $1.15 per 100 pounds. Outside the gates: Loaf $11 86 to $11 92 per 100 pounds with no local tax. Octroi tax, $1.15 per 100 pounds.

[Book 6, p. 13, Genoa, Italy, July 9, 1911.]

New York granulated, $5.10 per 100 pounds; cubes, $5.35 per 100 pounds.

Price regulated by the Trieste market

Imports only cane sugar.

Duty of $8.67 per 100 pounds on 94° test or over; $7.70 duty per 100 pounds on less polariscope test.

Italy has 37 sugar factories, four now idle; 6 sugar refineries. Annual production, 165,289 tons raws, yielding about 155,000 tons refined. Last year, 6,545 tons imported.

Granulated, $11.94 to $12.08 per 100 pounds wholesale; 14 cents per pound retail. Loaf, $12.88 to $13.01 per 100 pounds wholesale; 15¼ cents per pound retail. Add Octroi tax of $1.31 per 100 pounds.

Sugar industry in Italy started in 1888. Wholesale prices for selling include local taxes of all classes.

	Price per pound.	
	Lowest.	Highest.
	Cents.	*Cents.*
1886-1890	10.53	10.95
1891-1895	11.23	11.40
1896-1900	10.53	11.40
1901-1905	10.25	11.23
1906-1910	11.58	11.58

Parliament fixed tax on manufactures.

	Per 100 pounds.
Cost to refinery	$2.36 to $2.44
Manufacturers' tax (goes up each year; see p. 13)	6.23
	8.59
Octroi tax	1.13
	9.72

Italy exports no sugar and can not under Brussels convention terms.

No export bounty. (See Brussels convention, art. 6.)

Only first-grade raw sugar 94° and over are made on account of better protection.

Manufacture is given a protective duty of $8.67 per 100 pounds.

Brussels convention, article 6, provides that limitation of surtax to 52 cents per 100 pounds will not apply as long as Italy exports no sugar.

Sugar in Lombardy.

[Book 6, p. 16, Milan, July 10, 1911.]

	Per 100 pounds.
Wholesale, raws, 94° and over	$11.36
Wholesale, refined	11.55
Retail, raws	Not sold.
Retail, refined	$11.77

New York granulated, $5.10; cubes, $5.35.

No difference in prices in Lombardy. Lump sold in boxes, other grades in bags. No local duty in Milan, but there is in other towns.

Customs duties can not be allowed, as fixed by Brussels convention.

[Book 6, p. 17, Naples, July 3, 1911.]

Granulated, wholesale, $13.42 per 100 pounds, including taxes, same as elsewhere; import duty, $8.67 per 100 pounds; granulated, retail, 14¾ cents per pound; loaf, retail, same price.

Nearly all sugar sold in Italy is local beet product.

The Trieste means Austria-Hungary. First class means over 94° test.

Definitions for Italy: Exbrafend quadretto (lump cubes), Exbrafend commune (lump), Semolato (granulated).

Wholesale price per 100 pounds of cubes, $14.14; retail, 15.42 to 15¼ cents per pound.

Lump or granulated $13.54 wholesale and 14¾ cents per pound retail.

No special taxes or conditions except municipal tax, $0.0131 per pound.

[Book 6, p. 20, Rome, Italy, July 3, 1911.]

Only refined sugar used in Rome.

Italian sugar manufacturers watch the nearest foreign market, and fix prices so that they can undersell foreign sugars plus the Italian duty. Roman market regulated by prices in the Trieste (Austria-Hungary) market (the nearest market).

Italian custom duty on first class is $8.67 per 100 pounds; second class pays duty of $7.70 per 100 pounds.

Italy has a countervailing duty against bounty countries. There is a tax on refining of \$6.23 per 100 pounds on all sugar manufactured in Italy. There is no bounty.

The advantage of the Italian manufacturer is in the difference between the internal tax of \$6.23 per 100 pounds and the custom duty of \$8.67 per 100 pounds, a difference of \$2.34 per 100 pounds.

July 3, 1911: Prices—Wholesale without octroi tax, small cubes, \$12.78 per 100 pounds; with octroi tax of \$1.31, a total of \$14.09 wholesale. Retails at 15.33 to 15½ cents per pound.

Best granulated wholesale, without tax, \$12.08 per 100 pounds. With tax of \$1.31, the wholesale cost, including octroi tax, is \$13.39 per 100 pounds. The retail price is 14 cents per pound.

[Book 6, p. 25, Piedmont, Turin, July 14, 1911.]

Retailers receive little or no profit on sugar, so as to draw buyers for other articles. The domestic market competes successfully with all foreign sugar, on account of customs tariff of \$8.67 per 100 pounds. Notwithstanding they pay a national tax of 71.15 francs per quintal, importations for three years have been only \$200,000 to \$400,000, all from Austria and Switzerland for consumption along the Italian frontier at distance from the sugar factories. Under present conditions Italy can only consume of foreign sugars under some striking failure of crops which necessitates imports. Local tax, \$0.739 per 100 pounds.

[Book 6, p. 27, Venice, July 11, 1911.]

New York granulated, \$5.15 per 100 pounds; cubes, \$5.40 per 100 pounds.

Granulated, wholesale, \$12.20 per 100 pounds and 15½ cents per pound retail. Lump sugar, wholesale, \$12.88 per 100 pounds and 17¼ to 17½ cents per pound retail.

Local tax, \$1.08 per 100 pounds.

Prices at five-year intervals 1891–1911 do not vary materially from those given for Rome.

Summary for Italy, December, 1911.

Province.	Date.	Cut loaf, wholesale (per 100 pounds).	Cut loaf, retail (cents per pound).	Granulated, wholesale (per 100 pounds).	Granulated, retail (cents per pound).
Cantania	July 12	\$12.70	15½	\$11.73	14½
Florence City	July 8	13.74	14½	12.84	(1)
Outside gates	..do	11.86–11.92			(2)
Genoa	July 6	12.88–13.11	15¼	11.94–12.08	14
Milan	July 10	11.36	11¾	11.26	[3] 11¾
Naples	July 3	(4)	14¾	13.42	[5] 14¾
Palermo	July 17	14.14	15¼	13.54	[6] 14¾
Rome	July 3	(7)	15½	(8)	(9)
Turin, Piedmont	July 14	12.82	18¼	12.47	[10] 13¾
Venice	July 11	12.88	17½	12.20	[11] 15½

[1] Not given; local tax, \$1.15.
[2] Local tax, none.
[3] No local tax.
[4] Not quoted.
[5] Including local tax of \$2 per 100 pounds.
[6] Including local tax of \$1.31 per 100 pounds.
[7] \$12.78 without local tax, \$14.09 with tax.
[8] \$12.08 without local tax, \$13.39 with tax.
[9] Local tax \$1.31 per 100 pounds; 14 cents tax inclusive.
[10] Local tax \$0.739 per 100 pounds; retailers receive about no profit.
[11] Local tax \$1.08 per 100 pounds.

Rome.

	1886	1893	1896	1901	1906	1911(July 3)
Cut loaf	\$11.59–\$13.05	\$13.65–\$14.48	\$12.95–\$16.04	\$12.43–\$13.22	\$12.34–\$12.43	\$12.78
Granulated	11.06– 12.16	12.60– 13.30	12.16– 14.74	11.73– 12.43	11.55– 11.64	12.08

Without local taxes which vary from \$0.738 to \$2 per 100 pounds.

Annual production: Raws, 165,289 tons yielding in refined about 155,000 tons.

Imports last year, 6,545 tons, which are sold on frontier, long distance from any factory.

Customs duty on imports, $8.67 per 100 pounds on 96 test or above. Government excise tax, $6.23 per 100 pounds on 94 test or above.

Customs duty on import, $7.70 per 100 pounds on 63 to 94 test; Government excise tax, $5.88 per 100 pounds on 63 to 94 test.

No excise tax on less than 63 test, which grade is used for alcohol.

The protection to refiners is the difference between the customs duty of $8.67 per 100 pounds and the excise tax of $6.23 per 100 pounds or $2.44 per 100 pounds protection.

Cost of raws:	Per 100 pounds.
First product 96 test (p. 15)	$2.36–$2.44
107 pounds 96 test to make 100 pounds refined of 100 test, at $2.36	2.53
Manufacturers tax (excise), 1911	6.23
Cost without local taxes	8.76
Granulated without local taxes (at Genoa)	12.00
Difference to cover cost of refining and profit	3.24

Consumers have, in addition to the $12 refiners' price, bounty to pay, the local taxes at different cities from $0.74 per 100 pounds to $2 per 100 pounds, except at Milan and "outside city gates," where no local taxes are collected.

The refiner watches the Trieste, Austria-Hungary, marks closely, and keeps his price just enough below cost of import and duty to retain the trade of Italy entirely.

There are 37 raw beet-sugar factories in Italy, and 6 sugar refineries; all in northern Italy. The sugar industry began in 1888. Italy exports no sugar and is within the Brussels convention.

Italy has a countervailing duty against bounty countries. Italy has no bounty.

Italy is relieved of abiding by the Brussels convention limit of 5 francs per 100 kilos (52 cents per 100 pounds) so long as she does not export sugar, which explains why Italy can have a protection of $2.44 per 100 pounds instead of only 52 cents per 100 pounds as other convention countries which export sugar.

(Spain and Sweden have the same privilege.)

NETHERLANDS.

Duty, $4.89 to $3.26 per 100 pounds; excise tax, $0.49 per 100 pounds.

[Book 6, p. 79, Scheveningen, July 7, 1911.]

Granulated, 100°, wholesale $8.08 per 100 pounds and retail 8.16 cents per pound; small lots, 8.70 to 8.75 cents per pound. New York granulated, $5.10; cubes, $5.35.

Adulterated sugar, $6.16 per 100 pounds wholesale and 6.75 to 8.75 cents per pound retail. Cane sugar must be imported and pay duty and therefore costs $7.52 per 100 pounds. Import duty, $4.89 per 100 pounds on 100° test and declining; $4.40 per 100 pounds on 90° test by degrees; minimum, $3.26 per 100 pounds (reduces 0.049 per degree).

Factories produce granulated standard and fine, loaf and lump. Colors of adulterated sugar vary from brown to white. Dealers give discount from 3 to 12 per cent. Barrels, cases, and paper bags used for packing. Barrels charged to purchasers, but cases and bags not.

[Book 6, p. 81.]

Prices, November 1 of each year, 1898 to 1901; 1½ per cent off for cash 30 days. Sugar sold by manufacturers through agent and subagents in different provinces to wholesale and retail dealers.

Cooperative societies divide a yearly percentage or dividend. Very little profit in handling sugar by dealers. The local agent receives a commission of $0.108 per 100 pounds. The subagents receive from local agents a commission of $0.023 to $0.046 per 100 pounds on sales to wholesalers and $0.046 per 100 pounds on sales to retailers. Refiners charge $0.453 per 100 pounds for refining. In Amsterdam a company receives the sugar from foreign countries and forwards it, charging $0.027 per 100 pounds. Adulterated sugar is preferred because it is a product from cane while other is from beets.

Cost of refining, $0.453 per 100 pounds.

NETHERLANDS.

[Book 6, p. 84, Zeeland, July 7, 1811.]

No sugar making in this district.

Grocers here buy from Amsterdam agents.

In June and July contracts are made for November delivery.

Forty-five to fifty-five cents duty per kilo, including 29 cents duty per kilo Government dues.

[Book 6, p. 85, Rotterdam, July 6, 1911.]

No sugar bounties, but an excise tax of 27 florins per 100 kilos. ($0. 49 per 100 pounds; 1 florin is $0. 402.)

Import duties are the same as the excise tax on each grade.

The following countries not members of the Brussels Convention grant bounties on sugar exported and pay a countervailing duty in addition to the Dutch import duty, equal to the amount of the export bounty granted:

	Per 100 pounds.
Argentine Republic:	
On refined	$1. 74
On raw	1. 32
Crystallized	. 92
Brazil:	
On raw	3. 15
On refined	3. 06
Canada, on refined	. 318
Chile:	
Refined lump or ground	1. 17
White granulated or ground	. 945
Granulated (first product)	. 563
Impure sugar	. 522
Costa Rica, white sugar	1. 78
Denmark:	
Raw	. 159
Refined	. 304
Spain, raw and refined	1. 92
Australia:	
Raw	. 818
Refined	. 49
Japan, raw and refined	. 222
Mexico, raw and refined	. 263
Nicaragua:	
Raw	2. 57
Refined	3. 01
South African Union:	
Raw	. 177
Refined	. 34
Mozambique:	
Raw	1. 17
Refined	1. 13
Roumania:	
Raw	1. 70
Refined	1. 74

[Book 6, p. 87.]

Prices in Netherlands and in Rotterdam are always practically the same. July 6, 1911. Prices, granulated, $2.90 per 100 pounds; wholesale in bond without discount, $3.41 with tax. Raw beet, 88° analysis, $2.49 per 100 pounds wholesale, in bond without discount. Raw cane, 96° test, $2.67 per 100 pounds wholesale, in bond without discount. Plus duty, $4.89, equals $7.56 per 100 pounds.

No local charges or taxes in any Netherlands cities.

In Rotterdam, a place of 430,000 souls, the price is the same in all parts of the city. No one buys more than 5 or 10 pounds at a time. This is on account of dampness of the Dutch climate.

Retail prices now, lump, 5¼ cents per pound; white refined sugar (granulated), 4½ cents per pound; New York granulated, $5.10; cubes, $5.35. Excise tax, 27 florins per 100 kilos ($0.49 per 100 pounds).

Page 91 for 5-year intervals, 1886 to 1911.

Little variation in 25 years.

[Book 6, p. 92, Amsterdam, July 13, 1911.]

Most of the refined comes from France and raw from London. The principal market for Java product. Price, July 1, 1911. Raw beet, 88° analysis, $2.41 per 100 pounds wholesale in bond. Inferiority on each degree lowers price $0.0272 per 100 pounds. Refined beet sugar, 100° test, $3.05 per 100 pounds. Any inferiority in grade lowers the price at the rate of $0.051 per 100 pounds. The wholesale prices do not include excise tax. If intended for consumption in Holland an excise tax of $0.49 per 100 pounds must be added.

Retail prices, July 1: Loaf, 5⅝ cents; white refined (granulated), 4½ cents per pound.

Spain.

SUMMARY.

[Book 7, p. 1.]

Sugar is regarded as material for direct special taxation for internal revenue, and the tariff on imports of $6.94 at Valencia, $7 at Teneriffe, and $7.44 at Seville per 100 pounds is and was intended to be absolutely prohibitive.

[Book 7, p. 6.]

The direct tax paid by manufacturers to the Spanish Treasury during the last three years amounted to about $2.85 per 100 pounds. Other consuls vary in their statement of this tax. Barcelona says $2.85 per 100 pounds. Bilboa says sugar refineries are taxed 35 per cent to 40 per cent of their production. Jerez de la Frontera says 10 cents to 13 cents per kilo of 2.2 pounds ($4.54 to $5.96 per 100 pounds), and by agreement sugar is exempt from local taxes.

[Book 7, p. 4.]

Palma de Mallorca says 45 per cent on all the sugar manufacturers sell, and a local port charge of 30 cents a ton in this city.

[Book 7, p. 5.]

Malaga says the Government tax on refined, irrespective of grade, amounts to $3.06 per 100 pounds, assessed on shipment as made from refiners' stores.

[Book 7, p. 7.]

Valencia says $2.85 per 100 pounds, to be increased from August 1 to $3.06 per 100 pounds; also a local tax of about 2¾ cents per pound on all product containing added sugar.

[Book 7, p. 8.]

Madrid says no local tax, but Government tax of $2.85 per 100 pounds is imposed at the factory. (Taking reports altogether, the excise tax appears to be $2.85 per 100 pounds, paid by refiners as delivered from refineries. W. P. W.)

[Book 7, p. 9.]

Barcelona mentions a Spanish sugar corporation and independents; the former deduct $0.177 per 100 pounds on sales above 10 tons from list prices of 10 tons or below. The independents undersell in instances.

[Book 7, p. 10.]

Valencia says Government compels refiners to open in all principal cities a regulating retail store, which fixes prices under Government sanction.

The only difference in price allowed is the difference in freight to different points. Freight from factory to Madrid is 32 cents per 100 pounds, which is added to factories' price of $8.43 per 100 pounds for granulated and $10.64 per 100 pounds for loaf, making cost, wholesale at Madrid, $8.75 for granulated and $10.96 for loaf, selling in Madrid at retail at 9¾ cents per pound for granulated and 12¼ cents per pound for loaf.

[Book 7, p. 11.]

Spain's crop of sugar beets in 1907 was 978,000 tons, and in 1910, 666,000 tons. The production of sugar and consumption, etc., from 1906 to 1909 was as follows: (See table, p. 10.)

In 1910 there were 51 sugar refineries in Spain in operation. These factories apparently produce refined direct from the sugar beet, as no raw sugars appear to be marketed (p. 12.)

In 1910 the per capita consumption was 13.02 pounds.

[Book 7, p. 12.]

It is generally held by farmers' associations that beets can not be profitably raised in any part of Spain for less than $5.80 to $6.10 per ton of 2,000 pounds, while the relatively higher rates in Spain for coal, taxation, and freight are said to contribute to the abnormally high cost of sugar.

[Book 7, p. 14.]

The high cost of sugar and low wage scale prevents sugar from entering into the ordinary food of the laborers and small farmers, and is regarded by them as an inaccessible luxury.

One consul says, "Wholesale prices refined at $8 to $8.20 per 100 pounds is considered excessively high, owing to the caprices of the ring of producers who are exuberantly protected against competition from abroad by the customs tariff" (p. 15).

Consumers suffer recollecting that the average price of the best cane sugar (far superior to the present article) imported from Habana used to cost no more than $6.54 to $8.20 per 100 pounds.

[Book 7, p. 16.]

The law of 1907 limiting the free manufacture of sugar by prohibiting the establishment of new refineries within a radius of 50 kilometers of any other refinery in operation has been repealed at the instance of beet root growers, who complained that the restriction converted the industry into a complete monopoly and left them at the mercy of the Sugar Manufacturers' Association both as to the quantity of beets to be cultivated and the prices to be obtained for the crop.

Barcelona says, "Retail prices vary much; some stores that laid in large supplies at low prices are now retailing at less than the present prices. (This seems to contradict Valencia, p. 10. W.) Retail prices from 1900 to 1909 varied not more than 1¾ cents per pound, being that much higher now than in 1900. Retailers under nominal get not over ½ cent per pound profit."

[Book 7, p. 19.]

In January last prices were 20 per cent lower. Mostly lump and loaf sugar used for home consumption. Granulated for making wines and brandy. No raw sugar used. Better class buy 25 to 50 pound packages.

[Book 7, p. 20.]

Majority buy from day to day and from ¼ pound to an ounce at a time. The consolidation of sugar refineries was formed about 11 years ago.

[Book 7, p. 21.]

Consumption has fallen off heavily during the past 10 years.

Canary Islands produce about 15,000 tons sugar per year and is protected by customs duties of $7 per 100 pounds, but import some sugar from Hamburg. Qualities of refined in Spain much inferior to America (p. 23).

Relative average prices of refined for past three years as submitted to Spanish Cortez recently per 100 pounds. Spain, $8.92; Brussels, $2.97; London, $2.99; Amsterdam, $3.15; Paris, $3 70; New York, $3.86 (probably without duties, except Spain. W.)

[In cents per pound]

1911	Cut loaf wholesale.	Cut loaf retail.	Granulated wholesale.	Granulated retail.
July 6:				
Barcelona—				
Trust	8.54	9.18	8.10	8.18
Independents	8.54	9.82	8.50	8.54
Bilboa	8.95	9.50	8.20	9.00
July 19, Jerez de la Frontera	8.28	[1] 9.50 [2] 12.00		
July 11, Malaga	9.22	9.75	9.82	9.99
July 15, Palma de Mallorca	8.91	9.00 10.25	[3] 7.60	8.50
July 27, Seville	8.11 10.19	8¾-12¼	7.90-9.67	8½-11¼
July 8, Tarragona			8.00-20	
July 21, Teneriffe	12.00	15.00	8.50	12.00
July 21, Madrid factory	[4] 10.64	12¼	[4] 8.43	9⅞
Freight added	10.96		10.64	
Average price in Spain with duties	8.50-10.96	9-12¼	9.60-8.50	8¼-11¼
Teneriffe	12.00	15.00	8.50	12.00
Average price in Spain without duty	5.65-8.11	6.15-9.40	4¾-5.65	5.27-8.40

[1] Beet. [2] Cane. [3] Raw. [4] Plus freight.

[Book 7, p. 33, Barcelona, July 6, 1911.]

New York granulated, $5.10; New York cubes, $5.35.

Prices for beet refined: Cut loaf $8.54 per 100 pounds wholesale; granulated $8.10 per 100 pounds wholesale.

[Book 7, p. 9]

Above prices are the list prices of the Spanish Sugar Corporation (Sugar Trust). The independent factories quote as follows: Cut loaf, wholesale, $8.54 per 100 pounds and granulated, wholesale, $8.50 per 100 pounds.

Retail department stores sell granulated at 8.18 cents and cut loaf at 9.18 cents per pound. Grocery stores sell granulated at 8.54 cents and cut loaf at 9.82 cents per pound.

The Sugar Trust deducts $0.177 per 100 pounds in quantities of 10 tons or over.

Retail prices vary much. Some stores that laid in large supplies at lower prices are now retailing at less than present prices. Granulated sells at wholesale in sacks of 132 pounds. Refined for making Anisette and other liquors is sold in boxes of 55 to 110 pounds each. No local taxes. The only charges being the Government bounty (tax) on the production of $2.85 per 100 pounds. Impossible to give prices for 25 years back. Prices from 1900 to 1909 varied not exceeding 1.75 cents per pound, being that much higher now than in 1900, a small advance in nearly every year.

[Book 7, p. 18.]

Retailers under normal conditions get not over ½ cent per pound profit.

[Book 7, p. 31, Bilbao, July 6, 1911.]

Prices, lump sugar $8.95 per 100 pounds, wholesale, and 9½ cents per pound, retail.
Granulated, $8.20 per 100 pounds ,wholesale, and 9 cents per pound, retail.
In January last prices were 20 per cent lower.

[Book 7, p. 9.]

Custom duty on sugar imported into Spain is $4.53 per 100 pounds (a mistake). Sugar refineries are taxed from 35 to 40 per cent of their production by Government. No local taxes.

[Book 7, p. 31, Jerez de la Frontera, July 19, 1911.]

New York granulated, $5.15; New York cubes, $5.40.

All sugar used comes from mills at Grenada which make beet sugar or from mills at Malaga which makes both beet and cane sugar.

[Book 7, p. 19.]

No raw sugar sold here but mostly loaf or lump beet sugar. Granulated used for wines and brandy.

Loaf (beet), $8.28 per 100 pounds, wholesale, and 9½ cents per pound, retail.
Loaf (cane), 11.90 cents per pound retail.
Loaf Malaga, 12.70 cents per pound retail.
Small variations in price in retail stores. No local taxes.

[Book 7, p. 3.]

Government tax is 10 cents to 13 cents per kilo (2.2 pounds), $4.54 per 100 pounds and $5.96 per 100 pounds and, by agreement, sugar is exempt from local charges.

Wholesale prices since 1886 by 5-year periods show an increasing trend nearly every year and are now about 1½ cents higher than 1886.

[Book 7, p. 39, retail prices.]

Beet lump, 1891, $0.087; 1896, $0.099; 1901, $0.103; 1906, $0.095; 1911, $0.099.
Cane lump, 1891, $0.111; 1896, $0.119; 1901, $0.119; 1906, $0.111; 1911, $0.119.

[Book 7, p. 40, Malaga, July 11, 1911.]

Cane granulated, wholesale per 100 pounds $7.82, retail per pound 8.99 cents.
Grenada cut loaf, wholesale $9.22 and retail 9.75 cents per pound.
No raws sold. Better classes buy in 25 and 50 pound packages.

[Book 7, p. 20.]

Majority buy from day to day from one-fourth pound to an ounce.

[Book 7, p. 5.]

The Government tax on refined, irrespective of grade, amounts to $3.06 per 100 pounds. This tax is assessed as shipments are made from refiners' stores. Retailers' prices have increased in 25 years, but no advance to speak of since 1896.

Consumption has fallen off heavily in the past 10 years. A consolidation of sugar refineries was formed about 11 years ago.

[Book 7, p. 42, Palma de Mallorca, July 15, 1911.]

New York granulated, $5.15; New York cubes, $5.40.

Cut loaf, wholesale, per 100 pounds, $8.91; retail, 9 to 10⅛ cents per pound. Raw sugar, wholesale, per 100 pounds, $7.60, and retail, 8½ cents per pound.

The local charges are 45 per cent. to be paid by the manufacturers on all the sugar they sell, being a Government tax to allow the manufacture of sugar. Also a small tax of 30 cents per ton, which has to be paid in this city as port charges. Prices have not varied greatly since 1895.

[Book 7, p. 44, Seville, July 26, 1911.]

New York granulated, $5.35; New York cubes, $5.60.

	Wholesale.		Retail.	
	Beet, per 100 pounds.	Cane, per 100 pounds.	Beet, per pound.	Cane, per pound.
			Cents.	*Cents.*
Refined white	$7.90	$9.67	8¼	11
Cut loaf	8.11	10.19	8⅜	12⅜

Retail prices regular throughout city. Few delivery teams employed. Import duty on foreign sugar, $7.44 per 100 pounds, which is prohibitively high.

	1886–1890	1891–1895	1896–1900	1901–1905	1906–1910
Cut loaf:	*Cents.*	*Cents.*	*Cents.*	*Cents.*	*Cents.*
Wholesale	11.13	11.30	11.13	11	10.10–11
Retail	12.00	12.00	12.00	12	10⅜–12

[Book 7, p. 46, Tarragona, July 8, 1911.]

This Province neither produces, nor imports sugar. Draws its supplies from Barcelona in the shape of Spanish-grown refined white sugar. Wholesale price of this sugar is $8 to $8.20 per 100 pounds, which is considered excessively high, owing to the caprice of the ring of producers who are exuberantly protected against competition from abroad by the customs tariff.

Consumers suffer, recollecting that the average price of the best cane sugar (far superior to the present article) imported from Habana used to cost no more than $6.54 to $8.20 per 100 pounds.

No record of prices for 25 years.

[Book 7, p. 47, Teneriffe, Canary Islands.]

Cubes per 100 pounds wholesale, $12, and 15 cents per pound retail. Granulated, per 100 pounds wholesale, $8.50, and 12 cents per pound retail.

Customhouse duty, $7 per 100 pounds.

Importations chiefly from Hamburg. The high duty is imposed to protect the home industry, which amounts to about 15,000 tons annually. All sugars of lower quality than American granulated.

[Book 7, p. 48, Valencia, July 9, 1911.]

Sugar here for 25 years has scarcely been influenced by world markets. It is regarded as material for direct to special taxation for internal revenue, and the tariff on imports of $6.94 per 100 pounds is and was intended to be absolutely prohibitive.

[Book 7, p. 7.]

The direct tax paid by manufacturers to the Spanish treasury during the last three years amounted to about $2.85 per 100 pounds. (Other consuls say $3.06, 45 per cent, $4.54, $5.96.)

This tax is to be increased from August 1 to $3.06 per 100 pounds.

[Book 7, p. 16.]

The law of 1907 limiting the free manufacture of sugar by prohibiting the establishment of new refineries within a radius of 50 kilometers of any other refinery in operation has been repealed at the instance of beet growers, who complained that the restriction converted the industry into a complete monopoly and left them at the mercy of the sugar manufacturers' combination, both as to the quantity of beets to be cultivated and the prices obtainable for the crop.

[Book 7, p. 48.]

In 1910 there were 51 refineries in operation (p. 12); 1907, crop of sugar but 978,000 tons; 1910, declined to 666,000 tons.

Sugar production.

	Production.	Consumption.	Stock carried over.	Wholesale prices (firsts), per 100 pounds.
	Tons.	*Tons.*	*Tons.*	
1906	97,223	105,974	73,271	$8.25
1907	111,065	102,571	84,523	8.82
1908	122,399	96,471	106,397	9.65
1909	120,126	94,286	114,828	9.85

Retailers acted about three-fourths cent to 1 cent per pound above wholesale prices.

[Book 7, p. 10.]

Government compels refiners to open in all principal cities of Spain a regulating retail store, which fixes prices under Government sanction. Only difference in prices allowed is the difference in freight. Prices have fallen during last three months nearly 1½ cents per pound, and are still by far the high quoted in leading markets of Europe and America. In 1910 the per capita consumption was 13.02 pounds. Relative average prices of refined sugar for past three years from sugar statistics submitted to the Spanish Cortez in a recent discussion: Spain, $8.92; Brussels, $2.97; London, $2.99; Amsterdam, $3.15; Paris, $3.70; New York, $3 86 per 100 pounds. (Probably without duties.)

[Book 7, p. 50]

It is generally held by farmers' associations that sugar beets can not be profitably raised in any part of this country for less than $6.40 to $6.75 per ton of 2,204 pounds ($5.80 to $6.12 per ton of 2,000 pounds), while the relatively higher rates in Spain for coal, taxation, and freight are said to contribute to the abnormally high cost of sugar owing to the high price of sugar and the low wage scale ruling in Spain. Sugar does not enter into the ordinary food of laborers and small farmers and is generally regarded by them as an inaccessible luxury (pp. 13–14).

No local taxes on sugar itself, but all products containing added sugar pay local tax at rate of about 2¾ cents per 100 pounds.

(See table, p. 48, in book on Spain.)

[Book 7, p. 54, Madrid, July 25, 1911.]

New York granulated, $5.35; New York cubes, $5.60.

Granulated, wholesale, $8.43, and 9.82 to 9¾ cents retail. Loaf, wholesale, $10.64 per 100 pounds, and 12.18 to 12¼ cents retail.

[Book 7, p. 9.]

Freight from factory to Madrid is 32 cents per 100 pounds plus drayage.

[Book 7, p. 8.]

No local tax, but Government tax of $2.86 per 100 pounds is imposed at the factory. Retail dealers' prices have remained practically the same for past five years.

GIBRALTAR.

[Book 5, p. 88, July 8, 1911.]

New York granulated, 5.10; New York cubes, 5.35.

Granulated and cubes and crushed of German make. Some Austrian and Russian occasionally.

A free port, and no duty on sugar; 35,000 to 40,000 bags, 112 pounds each, of granulated, and 4,000 bags, 112 pounds each, of cubes, imported annually.

Wholesale to-day, granulated, 224-pound bags, $8.25 ($3.68 per 100 pounds). Cubes, 112-pound boxes, $4.38 ($3.91 per 100 pounds). Retail, granulated, 4 cents per pound, and cubes, 4½ cents per pound, retailed in paper bags 1 to 28 pounds.

No local taxes or charges.

A difference of 1 cent per pound has rarely occurred in 25 years.

SWITZERLAND.

[Book 7, p. 55, Basel, July 11, 1911.]

Nothing sold but 98° refined sugar in different forms. Loaf and cube are standard. The Great Cooperative Society fixes prices.

	1885	1890	1895	1900	1905	1910
98° test refined loaf and cubes:						
Wholesale	5.44	3.55	2.80	2.67	3.29	3.25
Retail	6.56	5.79	5.09	4.72	5.21	5.52

[Book 7, p. 57, Berne, July 7, 1911.]

Cut loaf, wholesale, $4.34 to $4.82 per 100 pounds; retail, 4.91 to 5.26 cents per pound. Granulated, wholesale, $3.73 per 100 pounds; retail, 4.34 cents per pound.

The sugar sold her is largely German and Austrian beet sugar. Cane and raw sugar not sold. Call granulated unrefined sugar.

[Book 7, p. 59, Geneva, July 12, 1911.]

New York granulated, $5.15; cubes, $5.40 per 100 pounds.

Sugar has ceased to be an article of profit to wholesale and retail dealers, and is frequently sold at a loss. It ranks as an advertisement.

Granulated, wholesale, $3.97 per 100 pounds; retail, 4.38 cents per pound. Lump sugar, wholesale, $4.78 per 100 pounds; retail, 5.26 cents per pound.

No local taxes except custom duties.

Sugar bought in Paris costs in Geneva for freight, $0.218 per 100 pounds; custom duty, $0.79; total, $1.008.

Customhouse duty on raws and pounded refined, $0.438 per 100 pounds.

Selling price in Geneva: Lump, wholesale, $4.91 per 100 pounds; retail, 5.26 cents per pound. Granulated, wholesale, $4.20 per 100 pounds; retail, 4.90 cents per pound.

[Book 7, p. 63, St. Gall, July 19, 1911.]

New York granulated, $5.15 per 100 pounds; cubes, $5.40 per 100 pounds.

Wholesale price (as to quality) $3.50 to $4.20 per 100 pounds. Retail lump, 5½ cents per pound; retail granulated, 4½ cents per pound.

The one sugar refinery in Switzerland, at Aarberg, produces annually about 3,000 tons. No sugar exported, but considerable imported. Customhouse duty ranges from $0.436 per 100 pounds on broken and best white to $0.79 per 100 pounds on lump.

All sugar imported comes from Austria, Germany, and France, Austria supplying two-thirds of same.

Cut loaf, 1900, $5.20; 1905, $5.25; 1910, $5.61 per 100 pounds.

[Book 7, p. 66, Zurich, July 14, 1911.]

Samples sent to United States Government department of the qualities of sugar sold here.

Most sugar comes from Austria and Germany.

No quotations given.

Summary.

Customs duties, $0.436 to $0.79 per 100 pounds. No Government tax.

Production is by one sugar refinery of 3,000 tons per year capacity. Importations not stated in tons, but in dollars. Customhouse duty ranges from $0.436 per 100 pounds on low refined to $0.79 per 100 pounds on lump and cut loaf. Sugar comes from Austria mostly, but also from Germany and France. All 98° in different forms. No raw sugar sold. The Government corporation society fixes prices of sugar in Geneva. Has ceased to be an article of profit to wholesale and retail dealers and is frequently sold at a loss.

No local taxes except customhouse duties.

Prices in Switzerland, 1911: New York granulated, $5.15; cubes, $5.40. July 11, Basel, loaf, $4.34 to $4.52 per 100 pounds wholesale, and 4.91 cents per pound retail; granulated, $3.97 wholesale, and $4.34 cents retail. July 12, at Geneva, $4.78 wholesale, and 5.26 cents per pound retail for cut loaf; granulated, $3.97 wholesale, and 4.38 cents per pound retail. July 19, at St. Gall, cut loaf, $4.20 wholesale to 5.50 cents retail; granulated, $3.50 per 100 pounds wholesale to 4.50 cents per pound retail. July 14, at Zurich, prices sent with samples.

	1885	1890	1895	1900	1905	1910
98° test refined loaf and cubes:						
Wholesale	$5.44	$3.55	$2.80	$2.67	$3.29	$3.25
Retail	6.56	5.79	5.09	4.72	5.21	5.52

Freight from Paris to Geneva is $0.218 per 100 pounds; customhouse duty, $0.79; cost from Paris to Geneva, $1.008.

RUSSIA.

(From consular reports.)

[Book 7, p. 4, Batum, July 14, 1911.]

No sugar refineries in the Caucausus.

[Book 7, p. 5, Riga, July 17, 1911.]

Sugar not produced in this consular district. City is supplied from mills at Kiev and Warsau.

[In cents per pound.]

	Wholesale prices.	Retail prices.
Granulated in bags	6.90	7.20
Lump in barrels and sacks	8.13	8.60
Loaf in barrels and sacks	7.70	8.60

Retail prices here do not vary much in the stores but sometimes sell at cost or below to draw trade. Sold in bulk. No local taxes or charges, but imports pay port dues of ½ copeck per 36 pounds. (0.005 cent per pound.)

Russian excise laws govering production empower the minister of finance:

1. To fix annually the amount of sugar to be produced for consumption and for reserve.

2. To impose a supertax of roubles 1.75 per pud (36 pounds) ($2.49 per 100 pounds) on the amount produced over and above what the mills are annually authorized to offer for consumption and to be held in reserve.

3. When domestic prices have a downward tendency, to facilitate the export of sugar by refunding the excise tax of 1.75 roubles per pud and when prices rise to place the sugar reserve on the market.

4. Or to withhold the refunding on exports of the excise tax (2.49 per 100 pounds), and the supertax of $2.49 per 100 pounds (together 4.98 cents per pound) when high foreign prices favor the export of Russian sugars. These things have the effect of keeping the wholesale prices of sugar in Russia in a stable condition.

[Book 7, p. 8, St. Petersburg, July 11, 1911.]

Raw sugar, $6.70 per 100 pounds wholesale to 6.84 cents to 6.875 cents per pound retail. Refined loaves, $7.70 wholesale, 7.78 cents to 7.875 cents per pound retail. Granulated, $6.62 wholesale to 6.84 cents to 6.875 cents per pound retail.

A loaf is 18 to 24 inches high and the base is about 12 inches in diameter, tapering to a rounded cone at the top. It may contain 10 to 28 pounds. This is broken up by means of saw knives into lumps and these are cut by means of sugar tongs to the size wanted.

Granulated is bought by the barrel at wholesale and retailed in paper bags.

The excise tax is 1.75 roubles per pud (about 90 cents per pud) or $2.49 per 100 pounds.

[Book 7, p. 9, Odessa, July 9, 1911.]

As regards output, the sugar trade of Russia centers within this consular district. Prices, however, are governed wholly by Government decree.

Read all page 9 from Russia yearbook for 1911.

Grades.	Wholesale per 100 pounds.	Retail per pound.
		Cents.
Loaf	$6.84–$7.11	7[illegible]–7[illegible]
Cubes	7.28– 7.51	7[illegible]–7[illegible]
Crystals (granulated)	6.14	6[illegible]–6[illegible]

Retailers weigh a heavy paper package with sugar and keep the sugar where it will absorb moisture to increase the profit.

Sugar shipped to Persia is sent in boxes so that two of them can be slung over backs of horses for a load.

Prices for 25 years have varied but little. See page 13 for 1885 to 1910.

[Book 7, p 12, Moscow, June 21, 1911.]

A large American company wrote this office for sugar information, including prices paid by consumers without any reductions for tariff or taxes. Prices on June 10, 1911: Loaf, $6.92 to $6.98 per 100 pounds refiners to wholesalers, and wholesalers to retailers get small profit, and the retailers also make a small profit. Consumers pay 7.72 cents to 8 cents per pound, as to quality.

June 14 (Russian date, June 1). By agreement of the Russian refineries (sugar combination) and the minister of finance and trade, 10 per cent of the refined sugar ready for market was ordered to be taken out (about 90,000 tons). The rise in prices resulting from this action was: For granulated up to $7.11 per 100 pounds, and loaf up to $7.47 per 100 pounds, with other grades in the same ratio.

Prices in Moscow are dictated at Kiev. There are two sugar refineries in Moscow. A third was absorbed by the two after a struggling existence. Moscow refineries pay freight on raws from near Kiev, and the Government adjusted transportation so these factories can refine on same basis as Kiev refiners.

The Russian Government took over a refinery on the Volga and is now running it without profit just to uphold the Government prestige and to support the workmen engaged in sugar refining. Read pages 17 to 18. There is a general accepted decision to lessen the Government product during the next two years.

July 14, 1911. Prices: Loaves, wholesale per 100 pounds, $7.70; granulated, $6.48 wholesale. Wholesalers get 0.28 cent or just over one-fourth cent per pound profit. Retailers get about one-eighth to one-fourth cent per pound profit.

SUMMARY.

1. The Russian Council and minister of finance fix annually in September the amount of sugar to be produced for consumption and the excess amount to be produced as a "reserve" for certain exigencies.

2. This amount of production pays an excise tax of 1.75 roubles per pud ($2.49 per 100 pounds.)

3. If the factories produce sugar in excess of the allowances as above, then such excess pays another tax of the same amount, called a supertax, making a double tax of 1.75 roubles per pud or $4.98 per 100 pounds on such excess.

4. When sugars are exported the minister of finance has authority to refund the excise tax of 1.75 roubles per pud, or the excise tax plus the supertax, or together $4.98

per 100 pounds if the export sugars have paid the double tax. He also has authority to withhold from refineries any portion or all of the excise tax or the double tax, or exportations. He uses his discretion to allow the full refund when domestic prices have a downward tendency and he wishes to facilitate exports to improve the domestic market prices, and he uses his discretion to withhold part or all of the excise tax from the refinery when high foreign prices favor free exports with the excises included.

These discretions in the hands of the minister of finance have the effect of keeping the wholesale prices of sugar in Russia in a stable condition. The Russian Government claims that it grants no bounties but other nations, including the United States, find a bounty benefit in these export refunds and the United States countervails against Russian sugars to the extent of \$0.713 per 100 pounds on refined of 99° test or over and \$0.627 per 100 pounds on 88° to 99° beet sugar.

5. For example of application. July 10, 1910, the council of ministers fixed the quantity of sugar for issue on the home market during the year September 1, 1910, to September 1, 1911, at 1,130,000 tons. The inviolable reserve for the same time was fixed at 128,000 tons, together 1,258,000 tons, paying \$2.49 per 100 pounds excise tax (any excess of production above 1,258,000 pays \$4.98 per 100 pounds). The maximum prices, including excise charges for September 1, 1910 to January 1, 1911, was fixed at \$5.84 per 100 pounds for white crystals, and from January 1, 1911, to September 1, 1911, at \$5.98 per 100 pounds. In addition to the excise tax there is a small fee for excise license of \$0.0071 per 100 pounds.

If in St. Petersburg, Moscow, Odessa, Kief, Warsau, or Kharkof the sale prices of sugar shall exceed by \$0.276 per 100 pounds the prices fixed annually by the council of ministers, the council, upon representation of the minister of finance is empowered to—1. Temporarily discontinue the refund of duty on exports of sugar abroad and temporarily to discontinue the double duty on exports of the surplus sugars of production. 2. And also to temporarily reduce the import duty on refined sugar should the prices of such sugar in any of the above towns exceed by \$1.42 per 100 pounds the price fixed for raw sugar.

In carrying out this provision, the minister of finance, on August 6, 1910, authorized the admission from abroad of white crystallized sugar on payment of duties at the reduced rate of \$2.85 per 100 pounds (regular duty is \$8.56 per 100 pounds refined) to the extent of 6,450 tons through St. Petersburg and 806 tons through the Riga customs and 806 tons through the Libau customs. (The excise tax being \$2.49 and this tax \$2.85, the protection is 36 cents per 100 pounds.)

No local charges do or can exist or be made as such would raise prices above the limit of prices including taxes.

Another feature of Russia is shown in the fact that on June 14, 1911, by agreement between the Russian refiners (sugar combination) and the minister of finance and trade, 10 per cent of the refined sugar of all grades now ready for the market was ordered to be taken out (that is, withheld from sale. W.). This amounted to 90,000 tons, withheld from the market in order to raise the prices in Russia. (Which it did to some extent. W.)

No cane sugar is produced in Russia, only beet sugar.

[Book 7, p. 17, another restriction.]

By agreement with refiners the difference in prices between granulated sugar and loaf, or "head-mouthed" sugar (which is dissolved in the mouth with the tea. W.), must not exceed \$1.14 to \$1.28 per 100 pounds, otherwise the Government has the right to admit foreign sugar free of duty or such quantities as will effect a lowering of market prices to the limit of differences agreed upon. This law passed in 1910 to exist two years.

Everything is done for the sugar refineries by the Government to regulate overproduction and to maintain prices. The Government adjusted the transportation tariff in favor of the large refineries and thereby compelling the small refiners to work in concert with the big refineries This is because many of the raw sugar mills are putting in small refineries and converting the raw material into the refined article instead of selling it to the big refineries.

The masses in Russia use loaf sugar with their tea, not sweetened in the cup or glass, but by biting off minute particles of sugar from the lump and sweetening the tea in the mouth while drinking it The sugar therefore must be very hard, and its process of refining is "hygroscopic and well crystallized."

Very favorable conditions exist for carrying sugars by the banks in Russia, so that manufacturers do not have to force their sugars for sale in order to pay the excise tax, which comes due on the 1st of June, September, and December.

Another proviso.

Prices of granulated futures have been fixed at ¼ cent to ½ cent per pound lower than Government limit, but little business results just now, owing to the abundance of sugar now, and the prospective large production. There are some 576,000 tons to pass over into the next campaign.

Another feature. After the 1st of September, 1911, these surpluses of former crop of both the inviolable and free reserves will all be converted into free sugar, which will inundate the market. Accepted rules for reduced production have been accepted to apply as follows:

1911-12, 885,000 tons, of which 44,252 tons are reserve.

1912-13, 1,859,940 tons, of which 46,498 tons are reserve. (Probably error, 859,940 tons.)

Another feature. Whenever the disparity of prices between loaf and granulated sugar reaches $1.42 per 100 pounds, the Government liberates the reserve sugars and curtails the proportionate amount for export distinctly granted by the certificates for export to the refineries according to their manufacture. These proportional allotments and issuance of certificates are made each year in September, which is the beginning of the sugar campaign in Russia.

These certificates are known in the trade as "X" certificates, and have a market value of about $0.27 per 100 pounds to $2 per 100 pounds. Just now they are worth $1.14 per 100 pounds.

Granulated sugar to-day, July 14, 1911, is calculated as follows for export values:

Price at Kief refineries, per 100 pounds	$5.84
Freight to Odessa	.19
Per 100 pounds	6.03
Refund of duties paid	2.49
Total price	3.54
Value of "X" certificate	1.14
Actual price for export at Odessa, per 100 pounds	2.40

The same price applies to any port in Russia, varying only by distance of transportation.

There is no explanation of details of the issuance of the "X" certificates in the Consular Report, but such explanation is given in Willett & Gray's statistical of December 21, 1911.

Duty on refined is $8.56 per 100 pounds.

In Willett & Gray's statistical of December 21, 1911, is given the cost of Russian refined for export as follows in United States currency:

Cost at refinery, per 100 pounds	$5.66
Freight to shipping port	.19
	5.85
Refund of duty paid	2.49
	3.36
Value of export certificate	.84
	2.52
Cost of permit for export to convention countries at market value	.79
Cost f. o. b. shipping port per 100 pounds	3.31

About the same time Russian crystals were offered in New York, but not bought, at $3.65 per 100 pounds f. o. b. shipping port in Russia, giving exporters apparent profit of $0.34 per 100 pounds, and costing in New York $6.50 per 100 pounds, including countervailing duty of $0.713 per 100 pounds, or $5.68 per 100 pounds with $1.90 per 100 pounds duty only. On same date in New York granulated was quoted at $5.635 per 100 pounds.

"X" CERTIFICATES.

The amount of sugar to be made by each factory in Russia for home consumption, or export, at manufacturers' option, during the campaign is fixed by the Government on September 1 of each year and pays an excise tax of $2.49 per 100 pounds at stated intervals—September 1, January 1, and June 1 of each year.

The Government also fixes the amount to be made by each factory to be kept as a "reserve" for contingencies, which reserve can not be used for any purpose until the end of the campaign, except by special permission.

Any factory can make as much more sugar than the above requirements as it wishes, up to its recognized capacity, but can only sell such surplus into consumption by paying the Government double the excise tax of $2.49 per 100 pounds, say, $4.98 per 100 pounds, but can export it after payment of one excise tax of $2.49 per 100 pounds.

A factory which exports a portion of its manufacture for home consumption or export, and which has already paid the excise tax of $2.49 per 100 pounds, receives from the Government an "excise certificate," stating the amount exported, and this certificate permits the holder to sell an equal amount of the "surplus" into consumption, without paying another excise tax to which it is liable without such certificate. These "X" certificates are transferable and have a market value. They also entitle the holder to sell into consumption an equal amount of the home consumption or export manufacture contingent without paying any tax on it, but this can only be done toward the close of the campaign at special periods to be named by the Government.

A factory which does not export at all, but sells all its home consumption and export manufacture into consumption, and wants to sell also its supplies into consumption without paying double tax, buys these certificates from a factory which exports mainly and thus avoids paying the double tax of $4.98 per 100 pounds upon its surplus contingent and pays only the single tax of $2.49 per 100 pounds. If home trade is brisk the price of these certificates rises in proportion, but can never rise above the excise tax of $2.49 per 100 pounds. The factory buying "X" certificates saves the difference between the double tax of $4.98 per 100 pounds and the single tax of $2.49 per 100 pounds plus the cost of the "X" certificate.

Sugars for export can therefore be sold as much cheaper than for home consumption by the amount of the excise tax, plus the value of the excise certificate, that is, although the consumption tax of $2.49 per 100 pounds has to be paid, the Government at stated periods, June 1, September 1, and January 1, and the sugars for export have paid the tax, yet as an equal amount of sugar is allowed later on to go into consumption without the payment of any tax by the holder of the excise certificate, it amounts to the same result as if the export sugar paid no tax and the equal amount sold into consumption free of tax paid the tax by the "X" certificate.

The value of the "X" certificate therefore on the market fixes the amount of the countervailing duties to be assessed by the United States and other countries, which value varies from day to day, but the United States has fixed its countervailing duty at $0.713 per 100 pounds, which is, just now, $0.077 per 100 pounds below the value of excise certificates.

Russia.

The 200,000 tons which Russia is allowed to export to convention countries is quite another matter from the preceding.

Each factory receives a permit to export its proportion of the 200,000 tons in accordance with its size and annual output.

The factories turn these permits into a "pool" and the pool sells them to anyone wishing to export, and exports to convention countries can not be made without these permits.

The permits have a fluctuating value fixed by the pool. The money received by the sale of these permits is finally distributed among the members of the "pool" in proportion to their export contingent to convention countries, regardless of what disposition they may have made of their own sugar manufacture.

Russian prices by Willett & Gray's records.

[June–August prices from Willett & Gray Dec. 7, 1911, p. 494; others from Willett & Gray's weekly Russian letter.]

1911	Kief.	St. Petersburg.	Odessa.	Hamburg f. o. b.	Hamburg parity New York.	New York granulated.
June	4.90–5.16	....	....	2.69–2.80	4.72–4.80	4.80 –4.90
July	5.06–5.16	....	....	2.80–3.40	4.83–5.45	4.90 –5.341
August	5.22–5.16	....	....	3.40–4.90	5.45–6.02	5.537–6.125
Sept. 5	4.85–4.90	....	....	4.36	6.39	6.37
12	5.11	....	....	4.36	6.39	6.615
Oct. 3	....	5.42	....	4.42	6.45	6.615
17	5.06	....	....	4.50	6.53	6.615
31	5.06	....	....	4.25	6.28	6.615
Nov. 14	4.95	....	....	4.17	6.20	6.076
21	4.90	....	5.27	4.06	6.10	5.978
28	4.90	....	5.27	4.06	6.10	5.88

AMERICAN SUGAR REFINING CO. AND OTHERS.

SPECIAL COMMITTEE ON THE INVESTIGATION
OF THE AMERICAN SUGAR REFINING CO. AND OTHERS,
HOUSE OF REPRESENTATIVES,
Washington, D. C., Monday, January 15, 1912.

The committee met at 10.30 o'clock a. m., Hon. Thomas W. Hardwick (chairman) presiding.

TESTIMONY OF MR. W. T. NEWLAND.

The witness was duly sworn by the chairman.

Mr. RAKER. State your name.

Mr. NEWLAND. W. T. Newland.

Mr. RAKER. Where do you live, Mr. Newland.

Mr. NEWLAND. Huntington Beach, Cal., Orange County.

Mr. RAKER. How long have you lived there, Mr. Newland?

Mr. NEWLAND. About 14 years.

Mr. RAKER. What is your business now?

Mr. NEWLAND. Raising sugar beets.

Mr. RAKER. How long have you been in the business of raising sugar beets?

Mr. NEWLAND. About 10 years. This will be the eleventh crop.

Mr. RAKER. At what place?

Mr. NEWLAND. At Huntington Beach.

Mr. RAKER. Did you have any experience in raising sugar beets before you entered the business at Huntington Beach?

Mr. NEWLAND. I did not.

Mr. RAKER. Are you fairly well acquainted with the method and mode of raising sugar beets?

Mr. NEWLAND. Yes, sir.

Mr. RAKER. You are acquainted with the rest of the beet-sugar farmers in your locality?

Mr. NEWLAND. Well, yes; in my locality, but not altogether in the county.

Mr. RAKER. About how many are there engaged in this business in and about Huntington Beach?

Mr. NEWLAND. Oh, somewhere in the neighborhood of 60 or 70, right around in the neighborhood of Huntington Beach.

Mr. RAKER. You have a factory close by, have you?

Mr. NEWLAND. Yes, sir.

Mr. RAKER. Is that the Huntington Beach factory?

Mr. NEWLAND. It is the Holly Sugar Co.

Mr. RAKER. How long has that factory been established?

Mr. NEWLAND. It started a little over a year ago.

Mr. RAKER. Where did you send your beets before that factory was established?

Mr. NEWLAND. Some to Las Alamitos, some to Oxnard, and some to Chino.

Mr. RAKER. By freight?

Mr. NEWLAND. Yes, sir; by freight.

Mr. RAKER. Are you acquainted in and around Anaheim, in that beet-sugar district?

Mr. NEWLAND. Yes, sir.

Mr. RAKER. How long have they been raising sugar beets there?

Mr. NEWLAND. About 18 or 19 years, with a lapse in between. They did not grow any at all about a year ago.

Mr. RAKER. Where do they dispose of their beets?

Mr. NEWLAND. Chino.

Mr. RAKER. How far is Chino from Anaheim?

Mr. NEWLAND. Offhand I would judge about 16 or 17 miles.

Mr. RAKER. Huntington Beach is about 15 miles from Anaheim?

Mr. NEWLAND. About 11.

Mr. RAKER. Have you any knowledge of the beet-sugar culture in and about Oxnard?

Mr. NEWLAND. No, sir; not personally.

Mr. RAKER. Have you any knowledge about beet-sugar culture around Chino?

Mr. NEWLAND. No, sir.

Mr. RAKER. Your experience, then, is confined in and about Huntington Beach and whatever knowledge you may have in regard to Anaheim?

Mr. NEWLAND. My knowledge is confined to Anaheim, and also Las Alamitos, Compton, Downey, and Norwalk.

Mr. RAKER. About what is the average market value of the land you have been raising beets on for the last 10 years?

Mr. NEWLAND. Do you mean the average price?

Mr. RAKER. Yes; the average market price.

Mr. NEWLAND. Well, 10 years ago, when we started to raise beets, it was worth about $100 an acre, and as we have opened up the beet business and got it subdued, as beet land, the market value has raised until it is worth from three to five hundred dollars an acre.

Mr. RAKER. Does that correspond in about the same way with the rest of the land?

Mr. NEWLAND. That is, all good beet land is worth from three to five hundred dollars an acre, and some even higher than that.

Mr. RAKER. What is the price of the other land there, such as for walnuts and cabbage and the other products they raise in and about that country?

Mr. NEWLAND. Walnut land without the trees on it?

Mr. RAKER. Give it to me in both ways.

Mr. NEWLAND. I would say from four to twelve or fifteen hundred dollars an acre; some even higher than that, with good bearing orchards.

Mr. FORDNEY. With the trees on the land?

Mr. NEWLAND. Yes, sir.

Mr. RAKER. The orange groves there are worth about how much an acre?

Mr. NEWLAND. I am not versed in the orange business very well.

Mr. RAKER. I just want to get a general idea of it.

Mr. NEWLAND. Judging from what my neighbors tell me, a good bearing grove in a good locality outside of the frost belt will sell sometimes from three to four thousand dollars an acre.

Mr. RAKER. Now, this land you raise beets on is of the same character as the cabbage land and the nut land, the walnut lands and the orange lands?

Mr. NEWLAND. No, sir.

Mr. RAKER. That land is down farther in the peat land?

Mr. NEWLAND. Yes, sir. As to the cabbage land, we grow good cabbage. It is quite a cabbage country.

Mr. RAKER. That cabbage land averages about what?

Mr. NEWLAND. Cabbage land and celery land is pretty near all the same in our country, and worth anywhere from three to seven hundred dollars an acre.

Mr. RAKER. Now, that general body of land in and around Anaheim and Fullerton and Orange and Huntington Beach, is within a radius there of 10 or 15 miles, is it not?

Mr. NEWLAND. Yes, sir.

Mr. RAKER. They used to use that land for grain, and do yet to some extent. About what is that worth?

Mr. NEWLAND. You have reference now to grain land?

Mr. RAKER. Well, to-day it may be used for grain land and to-morrow it will be in something else.

Mr. NEWLAND. It is either used for grain or beans; and when it goes into fruit that means developed water, and that makes high-priced land, where it is fruit land.

Mr. RAKER. Grape land is worth about the same?

Mr. NEWLAND. Grape land is not so valuable as walnut or orange land.

Mr. RAKER. That is, the grape land with the grapes planted?

Mr. NEWLAND. It is not so valuable; no, sir.

Mr. RAKER. But the land itself?

Mr. NEWLAND. The land itself is; yes.

Mr. RAKER. Now just explain to the committee your method of handling beets and the cost from the planting of the seed to the harvesting of the beets.

Mr. NEWLAND. The cost varies, you know, according to the tonnage.

Mr. RAKER. Give us your method of cultivation, first, to see whether it corresponds with others we have heard from other places.

Mr. NEWLANDS. Different lands require a different amount of work. Hard land, which is hard to plow and hard to subdue, costs more to take care of than if it was sandy land or silt land. To plow beet land, plow it at the proper depth, it will cost anywhere from $4 to $6.50 an acre, with us.

Mr. FORDNEY. What would be a fair average?

Mr. NEWLAND. If you do not have to plow a second time, about $5.

Mr. RAKER. Can you give us each item in detail from the planting of the seed until you have got the beets pulled and topped and delivered at the railroad station?

Mr. NEWLAND. Your harrowing will cost you, four times, about $2 an acre; your dragging, after you get ready to plant, will cost you 50 cents. I would call that the average. Your planting, then, will cost you about six bits an acre. Your seed will cost you about $2.25.

Your cultivating, four times, will cost you about $2; your thinning will cost you about $5 an acre. Your hoeing will cost you about $3 an acre, and your plowing out your beds will cost you about $2.75 or $3.

Mr. RAKER. What is about the average?

Mr. NEWLAND. About $3, as near as I can come at it. Your topping is something that varies according to the tonnage.

Mr. FORDNEY. What would be a fair average?

Mr. NEWLAND. Your topping will cost you about $10 an acre, average. Your hauling will cost you probably 60 cents a ton; but that varies, according to whether you have got 2 miles to haul, or 4 miles, or just a little way to haul. That is hard to get at.

Mr. RAKER What is the average?

Mr. NEWLAND. Sixty cents a ton within 1 mile, and every mile farther costs you more money.

Mr. RAKER. What is the average yield per acre?

Mr. NEWLAND. Six thousand acres this last year averaged a little over 10 tons.

Mr. RAKER. That would be $6 an acre for hauling?

Mr. NEWLAND. Yes, sir; and when you get them hauled you are through, as far as the farmer is concerned.

Mr. RAKER. Have you given us about all you can think of as to the cost from the seeding to the delivery?

Mr. NEWLAND. I think I have not missed anything.

Mr. RAKER. What is the yield per acre? Does it average 10 tons?

Mr. NEWLAND. I quoted you 6,000 acres averaging about 10 tons.

Mr. RAKER. Now, let us get down to your place.

Mr. NEWLAND. My tonnage last year was 15½ tons on 350 acres.

Mr. FORDNEY. What did you get per ton for them?

Mr. NEWLAND. I got $5.57.

Mr. RAKER. How much did you get gross?

Mr. NEWLAND. Well, it is 15½ tons at $5.57 a ton.

Mr. FORDNEY. I make that $86.335 per acre.

Mr. RAKER. That is about the average, you think, Mr. Newland?

Mr. NEWLAND. The average in our immediate section. The heavy land averages somewhere about 15 or 16 tons. The sandy land runs less.

Mr. RAKER. That figures a profit of $46.83, counting 15½ tons to the acre.

Mr. NEWLAND. About $43, gentlemen, they paid me after all expenses were paid, to say nothing about wear and tear on wagons, and so on, and taxes and everything of that kind. It does not net you quite $40.

Mr. FORDNEY. From that amount do you deduct anything for money invested in the land or rent per acre?

Mr. NEWLAND. No, sir.

Mr. FORDNEY. That has been given to us by various beet growers. What would your land rent for per acre?

Mr. NEWLAND. From $20 to $30 an acre.

Mr. FORDNEY. Would $25 an acre be a fair average rent?

Mr. NEWLAND. Yes, sir; from $25 to $30 is about the average rent for beet land where you have got a close haul. If the haul is farther, the rent is cheaper.

Mr. RAKER. What is your rate of interest?

Mr. NEWLAND. Seven per cent.

Mr. RAKER. That is about the average?

Mr. NEWLAND. Yes, sir; from 6 to 8 per cent. Seven per cent is the average.

Mr. RAKER. You have not said anything about water.

Mr. NEWLAND. No; I omitted the water. Now, your water will cost you for one time about $5 an acre. If you have to water twice, it will cost you in the neighborhood of $10, provided you have got your own plant and everything. If you have to buy water, which we do not have to do, it would be more.

Mr. RAKER. I understand that in estimating the value of the land you have estimated the land with the water rights belonging to it?

Mr. NEWLAND. Yes, sir; either by wells or springs or ditches, and so on, and you have to lift your water with a pumping plant or run it by gravity.

Mr. RAKER. A man who owns land without a water right, of course, he would estimate his land at less than what you have given here?

Mr. NEWLAND. Oh, yes.

Mr. RAKER. You estimate the water would cost about $10 an acre?

Mr. NEWLAND. Yes, sir; watering twice.

Mr. RAKER. But you figure the $10 in the full value of your land; and the amount the land would rent for, $25 on an average, would include the water which belongs to the land?

Mr. NEWLAND. He would have to distribute the water, which would cost him about $5 an acre.

Mr. RAKER. In estimating the cost of handling the crop, you charge $10 for distributing the water?

Mr. NEWLAND. Yes, sir.

Mr. FORDNEY. Is that water charge included in your $25 per acre rent?

Mr. NEWLAND. No, sir.

Mr. FORDNEY. You get $25 per acre besides the water, even where you furnish the water yourself?

Mr. NEWLAND. We furnish the water, but he has to do the distributing.

Mr. RAKER. Which would cost him about $10 an acre?

Mr. NEWLAND. That is for watering twice. As a rule, we only have to irrigate once, but sometimes we have to irrigate it twice.

Mr. RAKER. That would be about the same, irrespective of what kind of crop it was in that neighborhood?

Mr. NEWLAND. Yes, sir.

Mr. RAKER. Oranges or walnut trees or cabbage or beans?

Mr. NEWLAND. As a rule, we do not have to water cabbage at all. Oranges are not in my line of business. They water them at all times of the year.

Mr. RAKER. How much do you get for your beets; what is the scale?

Mr. NEWLAND. They are paid on a percentage basis. Eleven per cent beets this year will be $4 a ton; 12 per cent beets, $4.25; 13 per cent beets, $4.50; 14 per cent beets, $4.75; 15 per cent beets, $5; 16 per cent beets, $5.30; 17 per cent beets, $5.60; 18 per cent beets, $5.90; 19 per cent beets, $6.20; 20 per cent beets, $6.50; 21

per cent beets, $6.80: 22 per cent beets, $7.10; 23 per cent beets, $7.40; 24 per cent beets, $7.70; 25 per cent beets, $8.

Mr. FORDNEY. Where is the dividing line between the 25-cent increase and the 30-cent increase?

Mr. NEWLAND. At 16 per cent.

Mr. FORDNEY. The price for 16 per cent beets is $5.30?

Mr. NEWLAND. Yes, sir.

Mr. FORDNEY. And 30 cents for every 1 per cent above that?

Mr. NEWLAND. Yes, sir.

Mr. FORDNEY. And above 11 per cent beets, 25 cents for each additional per cent?

Mr. NEWLAND. Yes, sir.

Mr. RAKER. What is about the average of saccharine matter in the beets in your community?

Mr. NEWLAND. About 18 per cent; 17 to 19. We sometimes get as high as 21 and 22, but the average is about 18 or 19. That is hard to get at. One year will vary from another. I am giving you last year's figures.

Mr. RAKER. That would make the price of your beets per ton on an average about $6?

Mr. NEWLAND. Yes, sir: mine did not average $6 last year. I irrigated a little too late. My beets averaged me $5.57 last year.

Mr. FORDNEY. Mr. Raker, the other day when Mr. Riley was on the stand he was asked for a copy of his contracts and he has sent them to the committee, and I would like to put them into the record at this point.

MEMORANDUM OF AGREEMENT BETWEEN ——— ———, GROWER, AND AMERICAN BEET SUGAR COMPANY.

1. The grower agrees to plant, cultivate, irrigate, harvest, and deliver during the season of 1912, in compliance with the directions of the company, as may be given from time to time, —— acres of sugar beets, on the following-described lands, to wit: —— quarter, section ——, township ——, range ——, —— County, Colorado.

2. Seed will be furnished by the company at 10 cents per pound; not less than 20 pounds per acre shall be planted, and none other shall be used.

3. The grower agrees that all beets grown by him will be delivered to the company, in the factory sheds, or aboard cars, and as ordered by the company, properly topped at the base of the bottom leaf, subject to proper deductions for tare, free from dirt, stones, trash, or foreign substances liable to interfere with the work of the factory, and that he will protect the beets from sun and frost after removal from the ground. The company has the option of rejecting any diseased, frozen, or wilted beets, beets of less than 12 per cent sugar or less than 80 per cent purity, or beets that are not suitable for the manufacture of sugar.

4. Beets delivered and accepted will be paid for by the company at the rate of $5.50 per ton for beets testing 12 per cent to 16 per cent of sugar, and $6 per ton for beets testing 16 per cent or above.

Payment the 15th of each month for beets delivered during the previous month.

5. The company will pay 50 cents per ton additional for beets siloed and delivered; siloed beets shall not be delivered except upon call of the company.

6. The company will pay the freight on all beets delivered by railroad, but cars must be loaded to their capacity. Extra charges for cars loaded less than capacity will be charged to the grower.

7. The company will give to the grower, at the factory, without charge, beet pulp not exceeding 20 per cent of the weight of the beets delivered by him under this contract, providing the grower gives written notice to the company previous to July 1st of the quantity desired; the pulp to be taken by the grower during the time of slicing, as the company may direct.

8. Any advances made to the grower by the company in the way of seed, cash, labor, or otherwise, shall be considered as part payment for the crop of beets and be a first

lien thereon. The grower agrees not to assign this contract without written consent of the company.

9. No agent of the company is authorized to change the provisions of this contract.

(Signature of grower) —— ——.

American Beet Sugar Company,
By —— ——.

Date: —— ——.

(On back:) Acres ——. No. ——. American Beet Sugar Company. —— factory. Memorandum of agreement with —— ——. P. O. ——. R. F. D. No. ——. Box No. ——. Ship —— lbs. seed to ——. Canal ——.

MEMORANDUM OF AGREEMENT BETWEEN —— ——, GROWER, AND AMERICAN BEET SUGAR COMPANY.

1. The grower agrees to plant, cultivate, irrigate, harvest, and deliver during the season of 1912, in compliance with the directions of the company, as may be given from time to time, —— acres of sugar beets, on the following-described lands, to wit: —— quarter, section ——, township ——, range ——, —— County, Colorado.

2. Seed will be furnished by the company at 10 cents per pound; not less than 20 pounds per acre shall be planted, and none other shall be used.

3. The grower agrees that all beets grown by him will be delivered to the company, in the factory sheds, or aboard cars, and as ordered by the company, properly topped at the base of the bottom leaf, subject to proper deductions for tare, free from dirt, stones, trash, or foreign substances, liable to interfere with the work of the factory, and that he will protect the beets from sun and frost after removal from the ground. The company has the option of rejecting any diseased, frozen, or wilted beets, beets of less than 12 per cent sugar or less than 80 per cent purity, or beets that are not suitable for the manufacture of sugar.

4. Beets delivered and accepted will be paid for by the company at the rate of $5.00 per ton for beets testing 12 per cent sugar, and 33⅓ cents additional for each per cent above 12 per cent, fractions in proportion.

Payment the 15th of each month for beets delivered during the previous month.

5. The company will pay 50 cents per ton additional for beets siloed and delivered; siloed beets shall not be delivered except upon call of the company.

6. The company will pay the freight on all beets delivered by railroad, but cars must be loaded to their capacity. Extra charges for cars loaded less than capacity will be charged to the grower.

7. The company will give to the grower, at the factory, without charge, beet pulp not exceeding 20 per cent of the weight of the beets delivered by him under this contract, providing the grower gives written notice to the company previous to July 1st of the quantity desired; the pulp to be taken by the grower during the time of slicing, as the company may direct.

8. Any advances made to the grower by the company in the way of seed, cash, labor, or otherwise, shall be considered as part payment for the crop of beets and be a first lien thereon. The grower agrees not to assign this contract without written consent of the company.

9. No agent of the company is authorized to change the provisions of this contract.

(Signature of grower) —— ——.

American Beet Sugar Company, Date —— ——
By —— ——.

(On back:) Acres ——. No. ——. American Beet Sugar Company. —— factory. Memorandum of agreement with —— ——. P. O. ——. R. F. D. No. ——. Box No. ——. Ship —— lbs. seed to ——. Canal ——.

SCHEDULE OF PRICES.

For beets testing—	Per ton.
25 per cent sugar	$9.33⅓
24 per cent sugar	9.00
23 per cent sugar	8.66⅔
22 per cent sugar	8.33⅓
21 per cent sugar	8.00
20 per cent sugar	7.66⅔
19 per cent sugar	7.33⅓
18 per cent sugar	7.00
17 per cent sugar	6.66⅔
16 per cent sugar	6.33⅓
15 per cent sugar	6.00
14 per cent sugar	5.66⅔
13 per cent sugar	5.33⅓
12 per cent sugar	5.00

33⅓ cents per ton additional for each per cent above 25 per cent, fractions in proportion.

Mr. Raker. Mr. Newland, is this a copy of the contract you use [handing a paper to witness]?

Mr. Newland. Yes, sir.

Mr. Raker. I will put this in the record.

THE HOLLY SUGAR COMPANY.

CONTRACT FOR SUGAR BEETS.

This agreement, entered into this 13th day of Nov., 1911, between the Holly Sugar Company, a corporation, party of the first part, and W. T. Newland, of Huntington Beach, County of Orange and State of California, party of the second part,

Witnesseth, That for and in consideration of the covenants hereinafter contained it is mutally agreed as follows:

That the party of the second part shall and will in a farmer-like manner, and in conformity with the directions of the party of the first part, during the cropping season beginning November first, 1911, and ending when the crop is harvested at the close of the factory season of 1912, plant, cultivate, harvest, and deliver to the factory of the party of the first part near Huntington Beach in Orange County, California, 350 acres of sugar beets, the land upon which said beets are to be grown being described as follows: East ½ of section twelve (12) and southwest ¼ of section one (1), township six (6), range eleven (11) west.

The seed to be used in growing said beets shall be furnished by the party of the first part for the price of twelve (12) cents per pound, which the party of the second part agrees to pay, and which shall be deducted from the price of beets first delivered under this contract.

In harvesting beets they are to be properly trimmed below the base of the bottom leaf, and delivered free from stones, trash, or other foreign substances, and subject to the usual deductions for tare. After removal from the ground the party of the second part shall protect them from the sun.

The railroad freight charges for delivering beets, if the cars are loaded to capacity, will be paid by the party of the first part. Any extra charges because of cars not so loaded must be paid by the party of the second part.

All sound beets shall be bought and paid for by the party of the first part at the following rates:

Beets testing fifteen per cent sugar, five ($5.00) dollars per ton with an addition of thirty (30) cents per ton for each one (1) per cent of sugar above fifteen (15) per cent, and a deduction of twenty-five (25) cents per ton for each one (1) per cent below fifteen (15) per cent, down to and including eleven (11) per cent; fractions in proportion.

Beets testing under eleven (11) per cent will be accepted as if testing eleven (11) per cent if weighing less than five (5) pounds. The party of the first part reserves the right to reject beets testing under eleven (11) per cent and weighing over five (5) pounds.

Payments to be made on the fifteenth (15) of each month for beets delivered during the previous month.

In case said factory is damaged by fire or otherwise in such a way that it would be impossible to use or replace it in time to work the crop of beets the party of the first part shall have the option either of maintaining this contract or of paying the party of the second part for said crop of beets fifteen (15) dollars per acre for every acre actually planted with beet seed by the party of the second part at the time of the disaster, and allowing him to keep the crop thereon. In case said damage occurs before seeds are planted, then this contract becomes void and there shall be no claims whatever against the party of the first part.

The party of the second part may at his own expense have a representative to check the work done in the tareroom at the factory, such representative to be experienced in the line of work to be performed, and satisfactory to the party of the first part; wages not to exceed that paid by party of the first part for the same class of work.

The party of the second part agrees not to assign this contract without written consent of the party of the first part.

No agent of the party of the first part is authorized to change the provisions of this contract.

This agreement shall be in duplicate, each of which shall be signed by both of the parties above named.

THE HOLLY SUGAR COMPANY,
By A. JOHNSON.
W. T. NEWLAND,
Grower.

(On back:) 1911-1912. No. ——; acres, ——. Contract for sugar beets. The Holly Sugar Company with —— ——. Post office, ——. Dated ——. Land ——. Sec. ——, twp. ——, R. ——. Rental ——. Due to —— ——, owner of land. P. O. address, ——. Receiving station, ——.

SCHEDULE OF PRICES PAID FOR BEETS UNDER THIS CONTRACT.

	Per ton.
25 per cent	$8.00
24 per cent	7.70
23 per cent	7.40
22 per cent	7.10
21 per cent	6.80
20 per cent	6.50
19 per cent	6.20
18 per cent	5.90
17 per cent	5.60
16 per cent	5.30
15 per cent	5.00
14 per cent	4.75
13 per cent	4.50
12 per cent	4.25
11 per cent and under	4.00

Fractions of 1 per cent in proportion.

Mr. RAKER. Mr. Newland, what is the best crop the farmers have in your community?

Mr. NEWLAND. For the quality of the land we have got in there next to the beets, beets.

Mr. RAKER. It is more profitable than any other product you have?

Mr. NEWLAND. Yes, sir; because they stand the alkali better.

Mr. RAKER. Is it not a fact that this peat land is more valuable for celery?

Mr. NEWLAND. Certain small acreages of it; yes, sir.

Mr. RAKER. Are you using one patch of land for celery and across the road another patch for beets, and across in another field some other products?

Mr. NEWLAND. Alkali land is not good for celery, but it is good for beets.

Mr. RAKER. Do you rotate with your beet crops?

Mr. NEWLAND. I have some land that has been in beets, this is the eleventh crop, right straight along.

Mr. RAKER. Do you find any difference in the second and third crops?

Mr. NEWLAND. It takes a little more water, that is all.

Mr. RAKER. That is about the only difference you find?

Mr. NEWLAND. That is the only difference I have found so far.

Mr. RAKER. Then, so far as your experience is concerned, the statement that the beet crop has to be rotated at least every two years does not hold good so far as your land is concerned?

Mr. NEWLAND. Not with heavy land, but with the lighter land you have to rotate.

Mr. RAKER. Is there not another condition which has a great deal to do with it, and that is the water?

Mr. NEWLAND. Well, yes; water has something to do with it, but our alkali soils are pretty strong, and after we get beets started to growing on it it takes quite a while to wear it out; in other words, after we tame it down so that it makes ideal beet land, and it is not much good for anything else; that is, take it as a whole. There may be one little spot that will be good, but take the whole thing in general, you get an even beet crop over it where you do not get an even crop of anything else.

Mr. RAKER. Now, taking the other crops raised in that part of California within 15 or 20 or 30 miles, is there any crop that yields as much to the farmer as the beet crop?

Mr. NEWLAND. I do not know of any crop that yields as much year after year to the farmers on good land that is not in the fruit belt as the beet crop.

Mr. RAKER. How about the fruit belt?

Mr. NEWLAND. The fruit belt and the beet belt is altogether different. It is a different kind of land.

Mr. RAKER. What strikes me as being so peculiar is that when I drive through the beet fields at Anaheim, and then I come right out across the road to a great orchard of walnut, and another field of celery, and another one of cabbage, and then a grove of oranges and lemons, and I do not quite understand the distinction between the beet land and the other land. I wish you would explain that.

Mr. NEWLAND. All right, sir. Pretty nearly all heavy sediment land which has been overflowed at some time is good beet land; it is heavy soil; it is rich soil. The upper land is the fruit land. As you begin to go up, the sediment runs down deeper and there is more sand in it, and that is your fruit belt. There is a difference between the fruit belt and the beet belt and the cabbage belt. If you had been farming there for 30 years you would understand it. Of course, it is hard for me to sit here, being a farmer, and explain it to you people who do not know the conditions, because it took us 30 years to learn those conditions and we do not know them all yet.

Mr. RAKER. Well, I know something about farming. How do you know just exactly what each tract of land is best adapted to?

Mr. NEWLAND. We have to demonstrate sometimes for 10 years.

Mr. RAKER. Have the farmers in your neighborhood any complaint in relation to this factory or the other factories you have dealt with—the Chino or the Anaheim factory—as to the price you are getting for your beets?

Mr. NEWLAND. No, sir; I have no objection to make against any of them.

Mr. RAKER. Well, how about the rest of the farmers?

Mr. NEWLAND. Well, you take a farmer who is a farmer and understands the business, who owns his land and is not paying rent, as far as I know he has got no objection. You take a man who rents a poor piece of land and is a poor farmer, he objects to pretty near anything that comes along.

Mr. RAKER. Have you any number of that kind of farmers?

Mr. NEWLAND. No, sir; only a very few.

Mr. RAKER. Then I would take it from your statement that the general conditions as they exist now are very satisfactory to the beet growers?

Mr. NEWLAND. Yes, sir; very satisfactory. We, as beet growers, are proud of the factories we have got there and the men who run them.

Mr. RAKER. And you are able to make a very good income off of the land?

Mr. NEWLAND. Yes, sir.

Mr. RAKER. You do not have any idea as to the amount of money per ton that the beet-sugar company makes out of the beets delivered by you people?

Mr. NEWLAND. No, sir; that is not our business at all, not a bit. I do not know anything about that part of it.

Mr. RAKER. The farmers have never made an investigation of that question?

Mr. NEWLAND. No, sir; we just organized here recently and we have not made any investigation at all.

Mr. RAKER. For what purpose did you organize?

Mr. NEWLAND. Well, first, above all, the price of labor and everything else has gone up on an average until it is a little below the even keel, and we know that one man doesn't carry much strength, but a good many do, and we demanded a dollar a ton raise and finally got a raise of 6 bits a ton for this coming year.

Mr. RAKER. Let me see if I understand that. In 1911 you got for your 16 per cent beets $5.30?

Mr. NEWLAND. Yes.

Mr. RAKER. Now you are getting a 6-bit raise?

Mr. NEWLAND. Six bits on the ton, all the way through.

Mr. RAKER. Commencing with 11 per cent, a raise of 75 cents according to the amount of saccharine matter?

Mr. NEWLAND. A 75 cents a ton raise right straight through.

Mr. RAKER. That is for the season of 1912?

Mr. NEWLAND. Yes, sir.

Mr. RAKER. Did you have a committee to meet the sugar-factory people before you got this raise?

Mr. NEWLAND. Yes, sir. We had the factory people to meet the committee.

Mr. RAKER. Oh; that is better. That is the way it ought to be.

Mr. NEWLAND. That is the way it was, gentlemen.

Mr. RAKER. What was your object in having this raise?

Mr. NEWLAND. On account of the cost of labor and feed in the beet districts, where we used to grow all our own feed and everything of that kind, when you come to consider there is about 35,000 acres in beets, we now have to go on the outside. Feed has raised in price from $25 a ton to $42 a ton and hay from $8 and $10 to $20, and everything else along the line, and we figured we could not continue in the beet business if we did not go up the line, too. So as farmers we organized together, representing about 35,000 acres, and demanded $1 a ton raise, and we got six bits finally before we got through. That is what it was for.

Mr. RAKER. Before we pass the question of cost of raising beets per acre, is there not some other revenue the farmer gets outside of what you have named?

Mr. NEWLAND. Yes; he gets a little from his tops.

Mr. RAKER. About what? It has been testified here from five to ten dollars. How is it in your community?

Mr. NEWLAND. The most I ever got was $2.50 from a man who has bought my tops for the last five years. Next year he pays me $3 for them, and that is the rule in our section of the country.

Mr. FORDNEY. $3 an acre?

Mr. NEWLAND. $2.50 this last year, for good tops, of course. Some fields have good beets, but not good feed tops.

Mr. RAKER. You are raising a little right along on the tops as well as the beets?

Mr. NEWLAND. Well, cattle products are raising, and his market is up and he can afford to pay more.

Mr. RAKER. Has there been any objection raised on account of the beet factories there, either of them, selling the farmer the offal of the manufacturing plant, pulp and such as that?

Mr. NEWLAND. No.

Mr. RAKER. Or the sirup?

Mr. NEWLAND. No; no objection, so far as I know; and I have bought both pulp and sirup.

Mr. RAKER. Are there any meal plants in your neighborhood?

Mr. NEWLAND. No, sir.

Mr. RAKER. None of it being used for that purpose?

Mr. NEWLAND. No, sir; not that I know of.

Mr. RAKER. Then I would take it from your statement, Mr. Newland, that the beet farmers in your country are very well satisfied and have no complaint to make.

Mr. NEWLAND. No, sir; no complaint to make.

Mr. RAKER. Well, what do you think about the consumer of sugar?

Mr. NEWLAND. Well, I do not know. We consume a lot of it ourselves.

Mr. RAKER. But comparing the farmers to the rest of the people at Anaheim and Santa Ana and Riverside, they are about 30 to 1, or more than that?

Mr. NEWLAND. That is not a part of my business. I know when it is 5 cents a pound and I know when it is 7 cents a pound and I know when it is 9 cents a pound. I buy it and pay the price and there is no use of kicking, because I don't regulate that part of it.

Mr. RAKER. You do not mean to say that so long as you get a price for your beet crop that will justify you in raising the beets, and get a fair remuneration for the same in comparison with the value of your land, it is quite immaterial to you as to what the sugar manufacturer gets for his sugar?

Mr. NEWLAND. I am not running his end of the business, understand. He runs that and I run mine, and I do not know anything about the rise of sugar at all. I know it went up; that is all.

Mr. RAKER. I did not ask you anything about the rise in the price of sugar. What I am getting at is, so long as you, as a farmer raising beets, get a reasonable, living price for your product the price of sugar charged by the manufacturer is an immaterial matter so far as you are concerned?

Mr. NEWLAND. Yes, sir.

Mr. RAKER. Do you think there would be any objection to arranging it so the consumer would get sugar a little cheaper?

Mr. NEWLAND. No; I do not suppose anybody would kick on that part of it, because we all use sugar.

Mr. RAKER. That would not affect the beet-sugar people any, would it?

Mr. NEWLAND. Well, now, I don't know. If I knew what beet sugar would stand from the time it struck the mill until it was sugar at the other end, then I would be able to tell you.

Mr. RAKER. Suppose it should appear that while you get $5 and make a small amount on your beets, the sugar man makes per ton all the way from $5 to $8. Do you think that would be right?

Mr. NEWLAND. Well, no; hardly. But then I do not know anything about that part. That is something I do not know anything about. I would not think that would be right; but nevertheless if he is working, he must earn a percentage on his money which he has wrapped up in that factory, because it deteriorates, and if he is paying me from $4 to $8 a ton or an average of $6 a ton, and $7 a ton would put him out of business, then I certainly would take the factory's side that sugar was as cheap as they could produce it.

Mr. RAKER. But you would want to know that fact before you objected to a change in the price of sugar to the consumer, would you not?

Mr. NEWLAND. Yes, sir.

Mr. RAKER. Mr. Newland, how did you happen to come to Washington?

Mr. NEWLAND. We knew that both parties declared for a reduction of tariff, and we are beet raisers, and if we were to get raw sugar in here, it would probably affect the factory, and if it affected the factory it would put our business out of existence; and as an organization our president wired here to our Representative, Mr. Stephens, and he made the arrangements for the association to send one man. The association saw fit to send two, and let you gentlemen know just exactly where we as farmers stand as beet growers; that is what we were sent here for by the association.

Mr. RAKER. Did you discuss this matter to any extent with the sugar factory before you came?

Mr. NEWLAND. I saw Mr. Johnson, who is manager of our factory, Sunday morning, and that is the only discussion I had, and that was about a minute and a half before the train started, because I did not know anything about it until Saturday noon, and Sunday morning I was on the road here.

Mr. RAKER. In other words, your position as a beet grower is you would like to have things left, so far as you are concerned, just as they are?

Mr. NEWLANDS. Yes, sir.

Mr. RAKER. Because you are getting along nicely and you would have the other fellow take care of himself?

Mr. NEWLAND. That is the idea, exactly. We are here from the farmers' standpoint to represent the farmers' side of the question.

Mr. RAKER. You are also here to keep things in nice shape for the manufacturer, too, are you not?

Mr. NEWLAND. The manufacturer did not order me to do that, but if legislation would put him out of business it puts the farmer out of business also, because the beets are no good without a factory, and for the last 10 years it is a business which certainly has forged ahead in our section of the country.

Mr. RAKER. Have you much land there that is capable of raising beets?

Mr. NEWLAND. About 500 acres.

Mr. RAKER. In that community?

Mr. NEWLAND. Yes, sir; of my own.

Mr. RAKER. How much land have you in that section of California which is susceptible of raising sugar beets successfully?

Mr. NEWLANDS. I do not know. I want to be honest with you people. I do not believe there is a man in southern California to-day who does know, because we have seen land that is good beet land now which a year or two ago we did not think was good for anything, and there is lots of that kind of land in southern California. But I will say it runs into the thousands of acres, which will come in in the next few years. But to tell you how many acres, I could not do that.

Mr. RAKER. I mean just an estimate.

Mr. NEWLAND. I could not tell you. There will be lots of it, that is one thing certain, but when you come to the number of acres, that is further than I can go.

Mr. RAKER. And your idea is that the statement you have given us here would be about what would apply to all of the other farmers in your locality?

Mr. NEWLAND. Yes, sir; as near as I can get at it.

Mr. RAKER. Can you tell us anything about the kind and character of labor that is used by the beet farmers?

Mr. NEWLAND. Yes; we have a little of all kinds—the Jap, the Hindu, the Mexican, and the white man.

Mr. RAKER. What proportion of Japs have you?

Mr. NEWLAND. At the present time about one-fourth or one-fifth; something of that kind.

Mr. RAKER. And the Hindu?

Mr. NEWLAND. One-twentieth, just a few of them scattered around.

Mr. RAKER. And the Mexicans?

Mr. NEWLAND. The Mexicans would comprise—there are but a few white men, and the Mexicans will comprise about four-fifths of the labor in the beet fields in southern California. They do the hoeing and thinning and topping.

Mr. RAKER. The white man is pretty scarce, so far as the work is concerned?

Mr. NEWLAND. The white man is the man who does the plowing, and harrowing, and planting, and cultivating, and so on.

Mr. RAKER. And the men who do the other work are those you have named?

Mr. NEWLAND. Yes, sir.

Mr. RAKER. Where do these Mexicans come from?

Mr. NEWLAND. Some from California, but the best part of them come from Mexico.

Mr. RAKER. New or old Mexico?

Mr. NEWLAND. Old Mexico.

Mr. RAKER. How do you get them?

Mr. NEWLAND. They come in the field; that is all I can tell you. They come and apply for a job. In the first place, I am speaking now particularly of my own place.

Mr. RAKER. Let us get at the general condition in your community, and not your own individual case.

Mr. NEWLAND. It will apply all over that country. A Mexican who comes from old Mexico comes out there and gets one year's work, and the next year he has half a dozen coming back with him, and if they work for me on a contract one year, then the next year he comes back for another contract and will bring more of his brethren to help him.

Mr. RAKER. Do I understand that the Mexicans come from old Mexico up to these beet fields during the time of the planting and thinning and topping?

Mr. NEWLAND. Yes, sir.

Mr. RAKER. They are there for three or four months?

Mr. NEWLAND. There are but few of them who go back. They just keep coming. Of course, 11 years ago when we started in we had only about 25 or 30 in our immediate neighborbood thinning beets, and last year we had about 2,000. He comes up there and it is a pretty good country to live in and he stays there, and his relations follow him there and stay. When the work is finished, I do not know where he goes. That is the condition in our country.

Mr. RAKER. You do not know what becomes of him when the work is finished?

Mr. NEWLAND. No, sir. I know what becomes of those who stay. Any man raising beets to any extent will have a few little houses, and they live right there from the time you commence to thin until you get your beets harvested, and then he stays the balance of the winter. If he can get little jobs around at different places, he will work.

Mr. RAKER. When you speak of winter, you do not mean winter like we have here in Washington?

Mr. NEWLAND. No, sir; and I want to get away from here as quick as I can.

Mr. RAKER. What wages do you pay the Mexicans?

Mr. NEWLAND. About $2 a day, and he boards himself; that is, in topping time. In the thinning, he generally takes that by contract.

Mr. RAKER. And the boys and girls and women all work?

Mr. NEWLAND. No, sir; the boys, but no women. I never saw but one woman in a beet field myself, and she was a Mexican woman.

Mr. RAKER. Are any of them citizens of the United States?

Mr. NEWLAND. I do not know. I would judge not.

Mr. RAKER. As to the Hindus, where do you get them?

Mr. NEWLAND. They come from the northern part of the State. We do not get them at all; they just come there.

Mr. RAKER. What price do you pay them?

Mr. NEWLAND. About the same price.

Mr. RAKER. Do the women work in the fields?

Mr. NEWLAND. The Hindu women?

Mr. RAKER. Yes.

Mr. NEWLAND. I never saw one in my life. I never saw a Hindu woman to know it.

Mr. RAKER. On the railroads and other places the men and women work together and you can not tell which is which, so far as their clothing is concerned.

Mr. NEWLAND. That may be; I do not know.

Mr. RAKER. The Japs are permanently located there, are they?

Mr. NEWLAND. Yes, sir; that is, they are all renters. Of course he may rent one piece of land this year and another piece next year, or he may lease the land for three or four years. They are not landlords.

Mr. RAKER. What proportion of those Japs come from old Mexico?

Mr. NEWLAND. I do not know. I could not say. I do not know that any of them come from old Mexico.

Mr. RAKER. Have you any Chinese?

Mr. NEWLAND. No Chinese.

Mr. RAKER. What price is paid the Jap as compared with the others?

Mr. NEWLAND. The same thing all the way through. It does not make any difference who comes into the beet fields, if he is not worth so much he has to go.

Mr. RAKER. Do you furnish them a house to live in and water, and such things as that?

Mr. NEWLAND. Yes, sir.

Mr. RAKER. Do the rest of the farmers generally do that?

Mr. NEWLAND. Any man who is farming on a large scale; yes, sir.

Mr. RAKER. Are the Japs themselves renting any land and going into the beet business?

Mr. NEWLAND. Yes, sir. They have been in it for the last six or seven years, but not very extensively.

Mr. RAKER. Then the statement, if it was ever made, that the labor employed by the beet growers are American citizens or Americans with families, is not a fact so far as it would apply to beet growing in your part of California?

Mr. NEWLAND. No, sir; it is not.

Mr. RAKER. The statement should be made the other way, that at least 90 per cent are foreigners, such as Japs, Hindus, and Mexicans, arranged in a percentage about as you have given it?

Mr. NEWLANDS. Yes, sir. We could not grow beets unless we did have that kind of labor or else had more white labor in there.

Mr. RAKER. You do not mean to say, Mr. Newland, that white men could not do this work, do you?

Mr. NEWLAND. No, sir; I do not mean to say he could not do it.

Mr. RAKER. Is it not a fact that there are a great many white men around these towns in southern California that could be doing this kind of work?

Mr. NEWLAND. That could be.

Mr. RAKER. Yes.

Mr. NEWLAND. I do not know. The next question is, "Would he?" It is pretty hard to say.

Mr. RAKER. Is there not another very important fact in relation to your business because of the kind and character of men you employ, that when the beet grower or any other man interested in any other business begins to employ the Japs and Hindus, it is pretty hard to get an American to go in the same field and do the same kind of work?

Mr. NEWLAND. No, sir; not in our beet section. The trouble is they are not there. The men we have got in the towns in southern California are men who will not work.

Mr. RAKER. Of course, you do not apply that to northern California?

Mr. NEWLAND. I said southern California.

Mr. FORDNEY. Do the Japs and Hindus and Mexicans you have do other farm labor as well as work in the beet fields?

Mr. NEWLAND. Well, no; not very much. He shucks a little corn or something of that kind, when he can get a day's work. He has about four months he does not get but a very few days' work.

Mr. RAKER. At $2 a day and boarding himself it would average him about $1.25 or $1 a day?

Mr. NEWLAND. Yes, sir; along there.

Mr. RAKER. You figure—at least we do in other places—from $1 to 75 cents a day as the cheapest board you can get, with the high cost of all things that go to make up a living.

Mr. NEWLAND. Of course, that is not a part of my business, and I do not know what it costs him to live. I know it costs him considerable, because I have the bills to pay to the storekeeper every once in a while.

Mr. RAKER. Well, they do not live like the Americans live, do they?

Mr. NEWLAND. In what way do you mean? In what he eats?

Mr. RAKER. Yes; what he eats.

Mr. NEWLAND. No, sir; he does not.

Mr. RAKER. And his clothing is not like the American's? He is not as prolific in the use of clothing as the Americans?

Mr. NEWLAND. When he goes out and gets $1.50 a day, he generally has pretty good clothes on except when he is in the beet field.

Mr. RAKER. But, generally speaking, he wears much inferior clothing to the American?

Mr. NEWLAND. The Hindu is the worst. The Japs are pretty proud little fellows and wear pretty good clothes.

Mr. RAKER. The Mexican next and the Japs third?

Mr. NEWLAND. The Hindu first for cheapness, second the Mexican, and the Jap a little higher.

Mr. RAKER. But all under the American standard?

Mr. NEWLAND. Yes, sir.

Mr. RAKER. And they do not participate in any public functions or contribute to anything that goes on in the community such as the schools, the church, or sociable affairs, and Fourth of Julys, or anything of that sort?

Mr. NEWLAND. Yes, sir; in church matters the Mexican as well as the Jap.

Mr. RAKER. In the way of the equipment of their homes, inside, that is much inferior to the American homes?

Mr. NEWLAND. Yes, sir.

Mr. RAKER. Then the labor employed by the beet-sugar people is quite below the standard of the American workingman.

Mr. NEWLAND. Yes, sir.

Mr. RAKER. And, as a matter of fact, the beet-sugar industry—that is, so far as the raising of beets is concerned—is not conducive to the building up of the American citizenship of this country?

Mr. NEWLAND. As it stands to-day?

Mr. RAKER. Yes.

Mr. NEWLAND. Correct.

Mr. FORDNEY. Mr. Newland, I do not know that you understood my question fully a few minutes ago. Do the Japs and Mexicans and Hindus work in your cabbage fields in California? Do they do any other farm labor except little odd jobs?

Mr. NEWLAND. Yes, sir; they work in the celery fields and cabbage fields and in the orange orchards; not so many Mexicans as Japs.

Mr. FORDNEY. Do they do the heft of that class of common labor on your farms, outside of what the farmer does himself?

Mr. NEWLAND. Yes; you can say they do the dirty work on the farms.

Mr. FORDNEY. In all kinds of farm labor?

Mr. NEWLAND. Yes; the drudgery work. That is what they do.

Mr. FORDNEY. Are they employed in the factories, the beet-sugar factories and other factories?

Mr. NEWLAND. Not in the factories. They are employed in the limekilns, where they can not get a white man to stay.

Mr. FORDNEY. But in the factory the white man is employed?

Mr. NEWLAND. Yes, sir.

Mr. FORDNEY. Where it takes some skill and a higher class of labor, and so on?

Mr. NEWLAND. Yes, sir.

Mr. FORDNEY. Judge Raker asked you if it did not cost the Jap and the Hindu from 75 cents to $1 a day to board himself. Will he work for you for $1 a day and board?

Mr. NEWLAND. The Hindu would not board with me no way it could be fixed. You could not cook for him. Our class of cooking would neither suit the Jap nor the Mexican, consequently he boards himself.

Mr. FORDNEY. He lives a little cheaper in cooking his way than he would to board with you and accept your kind of cooking?

Mr. NEWLAND. Well, probably, but in some things he is very extravagant in his own cooking.

Mr. FORDNEY. Are they generally prosperous? Do they save their money?

Mr. NEWLAND. The men who work for me save their money right up to the handle, and of course you have some that do not. The Jap saves his money up very close.

Mr. FORDNEY. You have stated that since you began raising beets the price of hay has gone up, the price of barley, and all kinds of feed for your stock.

Mr. NEWLAND. Yes, sir.

Mr. FORDNEY. Am I correct in saying that your cost of living has gone up on account of the fact that 35 acres of land in that valley is now planted to beets and is eliminated from the production of other crops?

Mr. NEWLAND. Yes, sir.

Mr. FORDNEY. Consequently it has lessened the territory for the production of other crops and advanced the price of those crops?

Mr. NEWLAND. As to the prices of living everywhere I would not say, but it has advanced in our surrounding country because we have to ship the supplies from other places, principally out of the Joaquin Valley and out of Imperial County. Our foodstuffs have to come from there, because we do not raise them, and that would raise the price. The railroads have to have something out of it, and the farther away you get them the more they cost you.

Mr. FORDNEY. The fact is the raising of beets in your country diverts the land to a different use from what it was used for before the beet factories came there?

Mr. NEWLAND. Yes, sir.

Mr. FORDNEY. And consequently lessened the supply of other crops, and the consequence is that the supply and demand has advanced the prices?

Mr. NEWLAND. Yes, sir.

Mr. FORDNEY. Therefore you feel you are entitled to a higher price per ton for your beets under those conditions than you were before?

Mr. NEWLAND. Yes, sir.

Mr. FORDNEY. And you are now going to get it?

Mr. NEWLAND. We think so; yes, sir.

Mr. FORDNEY. Did I not understand you to say the factories had agreed to give you 75 cents per ton above this year's prices?

Mr. NEWLAND. Yes, sir.

Mr. FORDNEY. That is a nice advance, and on 10 tons per acre will give you an increase of $7.50 per acre for your crop?

Mr. NEWLAND. Yes, sir; $7.50 per acre.

Mr. FORDNEY. About what do you pay for granulated sugar, do you know?

Mr. NEWLAND. Well, of course, sugar has been up this summer and then down. I do not know anything about that part of it. It started in at 5½ cents along in March, and went on up the line until it got ready to come down again, 6½ and 8½.

Mr. FORDNEY. It was at the highest price at a time when your domestic crop was not on the market, was it not, in July, August, and September?

Mr. NEWLAND. I do not know whether it was on the market or not, but the factories were making sugar. I do not know anything about their markets.

Mr. FORDNEY. In California you make sugar as early as July?

Mr. NEWLAND. Yes, sir.

Mr. FORDNEY. When do you plant your crop there, Mr. Newland?

Mr. NEWLAND. Some is planted before January, but we will say January, February, March, and I have known them to be planted along in May, but February and March is the proper time in our section of the country, as near as we can demonstrate it, up to the 20th of March is the proper time to plant a beet crop.

Mr. FORDNEY. And you harvest them when?

Mr. NEWLAND. We commence just after the 4th of July. Last year they did not open until about the 15th, but usually about the 4th or 5th of July.

Mr. FORDNEY. Do you believe that the sugar-beet industry has added value to farm lands in your part of the country, and is a good thing?

Mr. NEWLAND. It has doubled the prices.

Mr. FORDNEY. You would be opposed to any legislation that would affect that industry and would compel the farmer to raise the beets for a less price than he is raising them for now?

Mr. NEWLAND. I would.

Mr. FORDNEY. I do not want to go into the tariff question, but at the present time, Mr. Newland, the principal supply of sugar coming to this country, outside of our domestic crop and the crop produced in our insular possessions of Porto Rico, Hawaii, and the Philippines, comes from Cuba. I say the principal part of our supply. I believe it to be correct that last year only 72,000 tons of full duty-paying sugar came to this country. Cuba has an advantage over Europe and all other duty-paying countries of 20 per cent. If the duty were reduced or removed altogether, so that the beet manufacturer of this country would have to produce his sugar and sell it for a cent or a cent and a half a pound below what he is selling it at to-day, if that came out of the farmer, you would be opposed to it, would you?

Mr. NEWLAND. I would.

Mr. RAKER. What would you say if it came out of the consumer? Let it go?

Mr. NEWLAND. Now, I am not figuring on the consumer's side at the present time. I have to consume a whole lot of it myself, and I have to buy it and pay for it. Now, I believe in protecting the American farmer; and, by the way, I am a Democrat, too.

Now, listen to me, because I want you to hear this, it is the only thing I know of we are protected in, because we export a million sacks of grain and we are not protected in that. I used to be in the grain business, when I used to raise 50,000 sacks of grain, and there is no protection on it, because my grain had to leave the country. But I am in the sugar business now, gentlemen, and we import sugar, and as long as the tariff is not removed I am protected. I am a farmer, and that is the way I figure that part of it.

Mr. FORDNEY. In other words, Mr. Newland, you are absolutely satisfied with present conditions if they will only let you alone?

Mr. NEWLAND. Yes. If there is any sugar trust, the beet people of the United States will soon put him out of existence, if you will let us go into the business and encourage local factories going up. If there ever was a sugar trust, he will have to go out of existence.

Mr. FORDNEY. Mr. Newland, the Secretary of Agriculture reports that in 1910 we had 420,000 acres of land in the United States planted to beets, and by an exhaustive investigation by the Agricultural Department it was found there were 274,000,000 acres of land in the United States adapted to the raising of beets. Do you believe if we had sufficient protection against foreign sugars the production of beet sugar would rapidly increase in this country?

Mr. NEWLAND. I do.

Mr. FORDNEY. Do you believe it would be a good thing to produce our sugar at home, and keep that money at home, instead of sending it abroad?

Mr. NEWLAND. Now you are giving it just exactly right. I do.

Mr. RAKER. Right in that connection, Mr. Newland, if your land has doubled in value by virtue of the sugar factory, and the farmer is better satisfied with the raising of beets than any other thing he can raise in southern California, why has he not been busy in the last 10 years improving that industry as it ought to be?

Mr. FORDNEY. Do you want him to answer that, or me?

Mr. RAKER. Either one of you.

Mr. NEWLAND. I would like to answer it, if there is no objection. I am only a common farmer, and I only went to school about three months in my life.

Mr. RAKER. Well, as far as this proposition of a common farmer is concerned, I think he is about the brightest man we have to-day.

Mr. NEWLAND. There never was a country that went out of the rough and went into beet culture as fast as southern California on the face of the earth. I do not care where you go. You take that 35,000 acres of land. A few years ago it was a swamp and a wilderness, with brush and everything else in it, and to-day you have got 35,000 acres a man can travel over, and it will make any man feel good, and you would know that somebody had been at work encouraging it.

Mr. FORDNEY. Mr. Newland, when you plant your beet crop, you know what you are going to get per ton for your crop, do you not?

Mr. NEWLAND. No; we know we will get paid on a schedule according to the saccharine matter.

Mr. FORDNEY. Then it devolves upon you to produce the tonnage and the quality of sugar in the beet?

Mr. NEWLAND. Yes, sir.

Mr. FORDNEY. If intense cultivation gives you a better crop and better sugar content, you know your labor is going to be rewarded?

Mr. NEWLAND. Yes, sir; that is right.

Mr. FORDNEY. Do you produce any other crop on your farm that does not fluctuate in price except beets? That is to say, is there any other crop you plant that when you plant it you know about what you are going to get for it? Do they not fluctuate up and down, all other crops except beets?

Mr. NEWLAND. Yes; all other crops except beets. You can figure exactly on your beets, but no other crop can you figure on except beets.

Mr. FORDNEY. In other words, you can calculate more nearly accurately the price you are going to get for your beets than for any other crop you raise?

Mr. NEWLAND. Yes. sir.

Mr. FORDNEY. Which makes it a very substantial crop?

Mr. NEWLAND. Yes, sir.

Mr. RAKER. During the months of September and October the Holly factory was in full operation?

Mr. NEWLAND. Yes, sir.

Mr. RAKER. Do you know about when it commenced grinding this year?

Mr. NEWLAND. I think the 3d day of August.

Mr. RAKER. If they commenced on the 3d, on the 4th they should have had sugar ready for shipment?

Mr. NEWLAND. It takes about three days, I think.

Mr. RAKER. But in that immediate locality, or in that entire country, the price of sugar went up just the same as every other place, from 5 to about 9 cents along in October?

Mr. NEWLAND. Yes, sir.

Mr. RAKER. And your people did not sell at any different price from the rest?

Mr. NEWLAND. I do not know anything about their selling.

Mr. RAKER. The price of sugar to the consumer in the market was about the same?

Mr. NEWLAND. Yes, sir.

Mr. RAKER. The price went up in your section as well as all over the United States?

Mr. NEWLAND. Yes, sir.

Mr. FORDNEY. Mr. Newland, do the proprietors or the manager of the factory try to make conditions agreeable and advantageous for the farmer in furnishing him seed and labor, if he asks them to furnish him labor, and cars for the shipment of his beets? Do they try to aid you in those respects?

Mr. NEWLAND. Yes, sir; in every particular, and furnish money to the poorer classes of people who haven't got money. They will take more risks in order to get a beet crop cultivated and taken care of then any other one thing I ever saw.

Mr. FORDNEY. They will lend you money, will they, on your crop?

Mr. NEWLAND. Yes, sir; they do lend money on crops.

Mr. FORDNEY. What I mean to say is, if you are raising a crop of beets they will lend you money on it?

Mr. NEWLAND. They have lent me as high as $6,000, so that will make it plain. However, for the last year or two I did not have to ask them.

Mr. FORDNEY. What rate of interest do you pay them?

Mr. NEWLAND. Seven per cent.

Mr. FORDNEY. Then the conditions, so far as the treatment of the people by the proprietors is concerned, is very satisfactory, is it?

Mr. NEWLAND. It could not be better from the farmer's standpoint. Taking the magnitude of the business into consideration and the farmers as a whole, it could not be better.

Mr. FORDNEY. What do they charge you for seed?

Mr. NEWLAND. They charge us 12½ cents a pound. I think you will find that in the contract.

Mr. RAKER. Mr. Newland, did you take any stock in the Anaheim factory?

Mr. NEWLAND. No, sir; I have no stock in any factory.

Mr. RAKER. Were you spoken to about it?

Mr. NEWLAND. No, sir.

Mr. RAKER. Did you see any of the promoters when they went around in regard to it?

Mr. NEWLAND. No; not the Anaheim factory.

Mr. RAKER. You do not know what per cent they guaranteed the farmers and business men if they took stock in the factory?

Mr. NEWLAND. Not Anaheim, no, sir. I am closer to Santa Ana.

Mr. RAKER. If the sugar refiners did not have their hands on the beet-sugar industry and the beet-sugar industry was entirely independent, it would be a great thing, would it not, if such a thing does exist?

Mr. NEWLAND. Now, I do not know anything about the sugar end of it. I do not know anything about that at all. As long as you will keep on the line of agriculture and what it takes to raise a crop of beets, in my weak way I will endeavor to make it as plain as I can, but inside of the sugar factory I do not know anything about it, gentlemen. It is not my business.

Mr. RAKER. You have stated to Mr. Fordney that the beet-sugar industry has enhanced the value of real estate twofold.

Mr. NEWLAND. Yes, sir.

Mr. RAKER. And that it was one of the best businesses there was, and if they were left alone they would be doing a fine business?

Mr. NEWLAND. Yes, sir.

Mr. RAKER. Now, if it should turn out that the refining factories were interested largely in the beet-sugar industry for the purpose of controlling not only the refining business, but the producing of sugar from beets, it would have some effect upon whether they should be left alone or not?

Mr. NEWLAND. Yes; I would think so. Of course, I do not know anything about their earnings—what it takes to put them out of business—I do not know anything about that part of it. I know if they are struck hard enough it comes back to me. If they take a dollar a ton off, I will quit the business. I could not stay in it. I know that, but I do not know anything about their end of it.

Mr. RAKER. What was the lowest price you ever got for your beets when you first started in?

Mr. NEWLAND. I think $3 a ton when I first started in.

Mr. RAKER. Do you know about what was the percentage of saccharine matter?

Mr. NEWLAND. I have had them run as low as 9 per cent, but $3 was the lowest they would pay. We figured we could not raise them for less than $3, if they went as low as 6 per cent. After it struck 11 per cent, you will see there is no reduction.

Mr. RAKER. Mr. Newland, you are intensely interested in the citizenship of this country?

Mr. NEWLAND. Yes, sir.

Mr. RAKER. You would not believe it right to encourage any industry that would bring in a foreign population, not citizens of this country, required to run that business as against the American citizenship?

Mr. NEWLAND. Well, if you have got enough American citizens to carry on the business, all right, but if you have not got the labor, we must have it if we are going to produce the beets.

Mr. RAKER. If higher wages were paid for the planting and ploughing and thinning of beets, and the topping, American labor could do it, could it not?

Mr. NEWLAND. It could.

Mr. RAKER. It is a good, healthy, wholesome, honorable employment, is it not?

Mr. NEWLAND. What; the beet business?

Mr. RAKER. All that is connected with the raising of beets.

Mr. NEWLAND. I think so.

Mr. RAKER. There is not a disagreeable piece of work about it?

Mr. NEWLAND. Oh, yes.

Mr. RAKER. I mean, if a man wants to work, there is no difference in raising beets or raising turnips or radishes, or anything else you have to handle? You simply have to get down and work and attend to them.

Mr. NEWLAND. The only difference is your radish and turnip business is not on the same magnitude like the beet business, but you stand there in that dust for a hundred days and I think you would call it pretty disagreeable. You stand there with a shovel, shoveling maybe 7 or 8 tons as hard as you can shovel them in the dust there,

I think you would call it disagreeable work. I know I do. I do it sometimes myself, but it is disagreeable. It is not pleasant work.

Mr. FORDNEY. It is very hard work?

Mr. NEWLAND. Yes; it is very hard work.

Mr. RAKER. Well, all work on the farm is hard work.

Mr. NEWLAND. That depends. If you work hard at it, yes; if you do not work hard at it, none of it is very hard.

Mr. RAKER. You do not mean to tell this committee that American labor could not be obtained for this work if the effort was made, do you?

Mr. NEWLAND. Under present conditions in my section of the country I do not know where you would get them. I do not know what you would do when you have to employ, like I do, 50 or 60 men. I do not know how you would cook for them and do for them for that short period of the year.

Mr. RAKER. Do you think it is for the best interests of your part of the country to continue bringing in this kind and character of labor as against the American labor?

Mr. NEWLAND. Yes; unless you people here in the East send us something that is better. We will take them when you send them, but as it stands right now I do not see any way out of it, if the beet business is to be encouraged.

Mr. RAKER. Let us take an assumed condition: Is it not a fact that that kind and character of labor competing with the American people is a disadvantage, even if it adds a little more to the perquisites of the man who handles the business, in the long run?

Mr. NEWLAND. Well, no. I do not think so. If I understand you right, you say that the American labor would not work along with the Mexican labor, we will say. Now, I have at least half a dozen school boys in the high school who come out there and work with them. It does not look to me like it is bad for them. These boys are only there a month or two, until they have to go to school again. The young man, when he gets through high school, goes to college, or he leaves the country, and I can not get him in the beet field because his labor is not to be had. I think I made that plain to you before, but I will try to do so again. The labor is not there. If we had plenty of labor that would go into the beet fields we would be all right, but we haven't got it in southern California.

Mr. RAKER. Your idea is, then, that it is justifiable to bring in the Hindus and the Japs and the Mexicans from foreign countries to do this kind of work, because it will add a little more to the revenue of the man who employes them?

Mr. NEWLAND. No; I did not say add more revenue. If you wanted 100 men, or I will say 50 men, and you were in business and you could not hire white labor, or we will say American labor, what would you do? If you had to have those 50 men, if you should run across the Hindus, and the work had to be done in a certain length of time, you would put him in; or if the Mexican came to you and spoke for the job you would put him in. I am putting myself in the condition I would be in if I was home. When he comes along and I need him I put him to work. If he is a white man and wants to work, I put him to work, everything that comes along until I have got enough help. We are not prejudiced against the American labor, but if you have got a job of work you have got to hunt somebody to do it or have somebody hunt you.

Mr. RAKER. You spoke about the beet industry being advantageous to the country.

Mr. NEWLAND. It is.

Mr. RAKER. Is it not advantageous to the country to increase the efficiency of American labor?

Mr. NEWLAND. It would be if we had a sufficient amount of labor there, sure.

Mr. RAKER. And to offer inducements to get families in that part of the country that will become American citizens instead of others who can not become American citizens because of their nonassimilation with the American race; is not that the condition?

Mr. NEWLAND. That is the condition, if we could get them. Now, you show us where we can get that labor.

Mr. RAKER. Ought we not to make the same effort to get that kind and class of citizenship that we make to raise a few dollars for the man in a particular business? Is it not more important for this Government to give some consideration to advancing that kind of manhood and improving our citizenship?

Mr. NEWLAND. Sure; if we can find him. Let us hunt him up. I am with you. Send me 50, commencing in March, and there will not be a Mexican on the ranch; but if you can not get him, I have got to have the Mexicans.

Mr. FORDNEY. Now, Mr. Newland, if you were unable to employ or find such labor as this foreign labor you speak of, the Hindus, Japs, and so on, and were unable to produce the beets at home, we would have to send money abroad to buy foreign sugar produced in some other country by that very class of labor. Which would be the better of the two, to send that money abroad to employ the Hindu in some foreign country, or give him employment in our country and raise the crop here, where he spends his money among us; which of the two would be the most meritorious, in your opinion?

Mr. NEWLAND. I will answer that this way: If I could not get the labor I could not raise the beets; then it naturally would have to go to some foreign country.

Mr. RAKER. Is it not the disposition of the man who has a farm, no matter what he is raising, to get the cheapest labor he can that will do the work?

Mr. NEWLAND. Sometimes the dearest labor is the cheapest, my dear fellow; but if you can not get dear labor you are bound to take cheap labor, and that is the condition we are in.

Mr. RAKER. Have you gone out to the cities to seek American labor for these places?

Mr. NEWLAND. Many and many is the time I have gone to Los Angeles to the labor bureaus to send me down a man, and maybe he would not stay long enough to pull off his coat before he would be going back. I would offer to pay him his price, and maybe he would stay about half an hour and then he would say—I will not use the language, because it is not becoming—but he would not do the work, and you have got to go out and get some labor that will do it. There is no man who is following the railroad or hoboing it all over the United States, and that is the class of people the employment agencies have, who will make you a hand on the farm. Even if you give him

$40 a day, he would not make you a hand, but he might stay for one day and get his $40, and then would be gone.

Mr. RAKER. It is a sad state of affairs, is it not?

Mr. NEWLAND. That is the way it is, I can not say whether it is sad or not.

Mr. RAKER. Do you not believe that this cheap foreign coolie labor has brought about this condition in California?

Mr. NEWLAND. I can not say. I do not think so.

Mr. RAKER. You are not able to say whether it has or not?

Mr. NEWLAND. No, sir.

Mr. RAKER. You stated, and other witnesses have stated, in regard to the value of the land having doubled by virtue of this industry: have the taxes doubled on you also?

Mr. NEWLAND. Yes, sir. My taxes 11 years ago, my land was valued at $20 an acre, and to-day it is valued at $100 an acre, and I pay $6 an acre taxes on every foot of land I own.

Mr. FORDNEY. What did you pay 11 years ago per acre?

Mr. NEWLAND. I paid about 65 cents an acre.

Mr. FORDNEY. Quite a substantial advance.

Mr. NEWLAND. Yes.

STATEMENT OF MR. STEPHEN STRONG.

The witness was duly sworn by the acting chairman.

Mr. RAKER. Where do you live, Mr. Strong?

Mr. STRONG. I live 17 miles out from Los Angeles, at Norwalk.

Mr. RAKER. Is there any factory near there?

Mr. STRONG. Not nearer than Anaheim, 12 miles.

Mr. RAKER. How long have you lived there?

Mr. STRONG. About 37 years.

Mr. RAKER. And your business?

Mr. STRONG. I am a farmer.

Mr. RAKER. What kind of farming?

Mr. STRONG. Raising sugar beets.

Mr. RAKER. How long have you been raising sugar beets?

Mr. STRONG. Well, off and on, for the last 12 or 15 years.

Mr. RAKER. Where have you been disposing of your beets?

Mr. STRONG. I have always sold to the American, the Oxnard company, at Chino.

Mr. RAKER. This last year?

Mr. STRONG. Yes, sir.

Mr. RAKER. You ship them from your place to Oxnard?

Mr. STRONG. Yes, sir.

Mr. RAKER. That is how far?

Mr. STRONG. I can not say whether they ship them to Oxnard or to Chino.

Mr. RAKER. From your place to Chino is how far?

Mr. STRONG. About 40 miles.

Mr. RAKER. And from Norwalk to Oxnard is about how far?

Mr. STRONG. I think it is about 60 miles, if I am not mistaken.

Mr. RAKER. How did you happen to come on to Washington to testify before this committee, Mr. Strong?

Mr. STRONG. I was elected to come by the association.

Mr. RAKER. What association?

Mr. STRONG. The Southern California Beet Growers' Association.

Mr. RAKER. What is the nature of that association?

Mr. STRONG. It is an association of the beet growers of southern California which includes Ventura, San Bernardino—the five southern counties—Santa Barbara, Orange, and Los Angeles.

Mr. RAKER. What is the occupation of the men who belong to the association?

Mr. STRONG. They are all beet farmers.

Mr. RAKER. Any bankers?

Mr. STRONG. Some of them have some banking interests, but they are not really bankers.

Mr. RAKER. The association is practically a farmers' organization?

Mr. STRONG. Yes, sir.

Mr. RAKER. Their business being beet raising?

Mr. STRONG. Yes, sir.

Mr. RAKER. Did you discuss the subject with the organization before you came here?

Mr. STRONG. Yes, sir.

Mr. RAKER. Did your organization discuss it to any extent with the beet-sugar manufacturers?

Mr. STRONG. I do not think they have. I never have talked with any of them. In fact, I am not acquainted with any of the factory men outside of the superintendent of the Chino factory.

Mr. RAKER. This association sent you on at their expense?

Mr. STRONG. Yes, sir.

Mr. RAKER. What did they expect you to accomplish? What was the grievance which they desired you to present?

Mr. STRONG. There was a hint, I suppose, there would be a reduction in the tariff on raw sugar or something to that effect, and they wanted to put the farmers' end of the case before the committee; what the cost was, and so on, of farming sugar beets.

Mr. RAKER. What do you mean by "the farmers' end"?

Mr. STRONG. Well, the cost of production.

Mr. RAKER. To the end that the tariff on the importation of raw sugar may be left just as it is?

Mr. STRONG. Yes.

Mr. RAKER. Am I to understand from that that the farmers are satisfied with present conditions?

Mr. STRONG. Yes, sir.

Mr. RAKER. As to the tariff on the importation of sugar, and desire no change?

Mr. STRONG. They desire no change whatever.

Mr. RAKER. Now, why do they desire no change?

Mr. STRONG. Well, they feel if there was a reduction in raw sugar it would make a reduction in the price of sugar beets, which would virtually put them out of business.

Mr. RAKER. They have discussed that subject?

Mr. STRONG. Yes, sir.

Mr. RAKER. And that is the question upon which they want to be heard?

Mr. STRONG. Yes, sir.

Mr. RAKER. How many acres of beets have you been raising, on an average?

Mr. STRONG. About 200 acres.

Mr. RAKER. Will you give us the average cost per acre to raise and to handle an acre of beets from seeding to delivery at the railroad dumping ground?

Mr. STRONG. I can tell you exactly what it cost me last year.

Mr. RAKER. You have a statement of that in detail, have you?

Mr. STRONG. As the committee will understand, I am not running this myself, but my boys do; and this is just as I take it from the books. The plowing was $5 an acre, harrowing, four times, $2; pulverizing once, 50 cents; packing the ground—you see, we have a machine that runs over the ground to settle the top of the ground—that was 50 cents an acre. Planting was 75 cents; seed, $2.25: rolling the beets after they were up, once before and once after thinning, 50 cents an acre; cultivating—we cultivated four times last year—75 cents for each cultivating, $3; the thinning, I pay $4 an acre for thinning, and hoeing, we had to go over it three times, and that cost me $3.50 an acre. Now, we only irrigated of this ground about 20 acres, and that cost us $5 an acre, but that does not count on the whole tract, but just what we irrigated.

Mr. FORDNEY. How many acres have you?

Mr. STRONG. Two hundred.

Mr. FORDNEY. And you irrigated only 20 acres?

Mr. STRONG. Yes, sir.

Mr. FORDNEY. You only irrigated one-tenth of it, and that would be 50 cents an acre for the 200 acres; is not that right?

Mr. STRONG. Yes, sir. That brings it up to harvesting. Now, the harvesting, plowing the beets out ready for the toppers, was $3 an acre; the hauling was about 50 cents a ton.

Mr. FORDNEY. How many tons per acre did you raise?

Mr. STRONG. We averaged 15 tons.

Mr. FORDNEY. That makes $7.50 an acre, then, for hauling?

Mr. STRONG. Yes, sir; and the topping was 60 cents a ton, or $9 an acre. That is all.

Mr. RAKER. How much do you figure that altogether?

Mr. FORDNEY. Forty-two dollars per acre, I have it. You say you got 15 tons per acre?

Mr. STRONG. Yes, sir.

Mr. FORDNEY. What price did you get for them per ton?

Mr. STRONG. Here are some of the statements I got from the factory, and you can see about the average run.

Mr. RAKER. About what was the average?

Mr. STRONG. I think they will average around 18 to 18½ per cent, and that would be $5.40.

Mr. RAKER. That would make $39 profit?

Mr. STRONG. Yes, sir.

Mr. RAKER. In figuring up the cost of the raising of beets per acre, as you have given it, does that include the team hire and men hire?

Mr. STRONG. That counts the actual expense.

Mr. RAKER. That is the gross expense of cultivating and raising and putting the beets on the market at the railroad station an acre of beets?

Mr. STRONG. Yes, sir; 15-ton beets.

Mr. RAKER. About what is the average price of this land of yours?

Mr. STRONG. Well, my land will sell for $500 to $550 an acre readily, I think, while it is not for sale.

Mr. RAKER. It is not for sale at that price?

Mr. STRONG. No, sir.

Mr. RAKER. But that would be about the market price if it had to go to sale?

Mr. STRONG. Yes, sir.

Mr. RAKER. Well, what do you figure it worth?

Mr. STRONG. I do not know. It is my home.

Mr. RAKER. And you do not want to sell it?

Mr. STRONG. No, sir; it is not for sale.

Mr. RAKER. Is that about the average price for the land in this immediate vicinity of yours?

Mr. STRONG. Yes, sir.

Mr. RAKER. And the interest rate is about 7 per cent?

Mr. STRONG. Yes. Anything like a good loan you get for 6 per cent for two or three years.

Mr. RAKER. What is the ordinary rental price for such land as this?

Mr. STRONG. Well, that varies. My land, where I have irrigating plants—two large plants there on my place—I have been offered $25 an acre cash rent for it. You will understand that considerable of the land is not under irrigation, and that of course is cheaper. It runs from $15 to $20.

Mr. RAKER. You have a water right belonging to this land?

Mr. STRONG. My own cistern; yes, sir.

Mr. RAKER. And the man who would rent it would get the use of the water for the land?

Mr. STRONG. Yes, sir.

Mr. RAKER. Where there is no water right attaching to the land, about what is the price of the land per acre?

Mr. STRONG. Well, it would run from $350 to $450 per acre.

Mr. RAKER. And then they have to pay for the use of the water?

Mr. STRONG. Yes.

Mr. RAKER. What other kinds of produce do they raise in this locality where you live besides sugar beets?

Mr. STRONG. There is some alfalfa grown. Outside of the sugar business it is principally dairying.

Mr. RAKER. You are on the Southern Pacific between Los Angeles and Santa Ana and Anaheim?

Mr. STRONG. Yes, sir.

Mr. RAKER. Is the raising of sugar beets the most profitable business for the farmers?

Mr. STRONG. Yes, sir.

Mr. RAKER. Even where they have to ship them as far as you have to ship?

Mr. STRONG. Yes, sir; we do not have to pay that. We get the same rate as they do everywhere else; at least, I suppose that is the way of it. I have never seen any of the other contracts.

Mr. RAKER. What kind and character of labor do you employ in the beet fields?

Mr. STRONG. I use Mexican labor altogether.

Mr. RAKER. What do you mean by Mexican labor? Mexicans from old Mexico?

Mr. STRONG. Yes, sir.

Mr. RAKER. Are they transients? That is, do they come up and work a season and then go back home after the beet season is over?

Mr. STRONG. No, sir; very few of them go back.

Mr. RAKER. They stay around the locality there?

Mr. STRONG. Yes, sir.

Mr. RAKER. None of them citizens?

Mr. STRONG. No; not that I know of.

Mr. RAKER. Do they come there with their families?

Mr. STRONG. No. Some of them have families, but there is only one family on my place.

Mr. RAKER. As a general thing do a number of them return to old Mexico for a while and then come back again?

Mr. STRONG. No, sir; they do not.

Mr. RAKER. Well, what do they do with their money?

Mr. STRONG. They are pretty good livers when they have got the money, and dress well. Of course we do not have quite so many saloons in the lower end as in the northern end, and therefore they do not have a chance to spend their money that way.

Mr. RAKER. Of course they could get busy in Los Angeles?

Mr. STRONG. Yes.

Mr. RAKER. About what do you pay per day for the labor?

Mr. STRONG. I let my thinning and hoeing out by contract.

Mr. RAKER. How much per acre do you pay?

Mr. STRONG. I pay $4 an acre for thinning and about $3.50 for hoeing.

Mr. RAKER. Have you any idea about what they average per day in working on those contracts?

Mr. STRONG. They averaged a little over $2 a day last year.

Mr. RAKER. About how many hours do they work?

Mr. STRONG. They work about 10 hours.

Mr. RAKER. And live right on the farm?

Mr. STRONG. Yes, sir.

Mr. RAKER. Is that about the general condition with the other farmers in your neighborhood raising sugar beets?

Mr. STRONG. Yes, sir; I think our contracts are about the same.

Mr. RAKER. About how many sugar-beet factories are there in this locality where you live?

Mr. STRONG. Well, I could not say as to that.

Mr. RAKER. About how many acres of land devoted to beet culture?

Mr. STRONG. Something like 2,000 acres that goes over the two dumps at Norwalk.

Mr. RAKER. Are there any dumps near-by Norwalk?

Mr. STRONG. There are only two beet dumps there, and then a mile and a half, at Studebaker, there is one dump there, so that makes three dumps within a mile and a half of my place.

Mr. RAKER. Well, take a radius of 10 or 15 miles, how many dumps are there, in the neighborhood there, that do not send their sugar beets to Anaheim, and have been sending them away before the Anaheim factory was put up?

Mr. STRONG. Before the Anaheim factory was put up there were not more than about four dumps that belonged to the American in the country there.

Mr. RAKER. And about how many are there now?

Mr. STRONG. I could not tell you. They are on all the lines except the Santa Fe and the electric lines.

Mr. RAKER. Can you give us an idea of the whole acreage in sugar beets?

Mr. STRONG. About 90,000 acres in the southern end of the State, but south of Oxnard I could not say.

Mr. RAKER. In other words you are unable to give us the acreage, even approximately?

Mr. STRONG. No, sir.

Mr. RAKER. What do you figure on getting net per acre on raising sugar beets?

Mr. STRONG. Well, I figure on from $30 to $40 to $45. We had a splendid year last year. This year, of course, it is problematical, because we have not had any rain as yet.

Mr. RAKER. Is there any other crop in that country which yields so well to the farmer as the beet crop?

Mr. STRONG. No, sir.

Mr. RAKER. About how much above the average crop will the beet crop go?

Mr. STRONG. Well, it will very near double it.

Mr. RAKER. Has the raising of beets any bad effect on the land?

Mr. STRONG. No, sir; from my experience it has a good effect on the land.

Mr. RAKER. In what way?

Mr. STRONG. Well, you get a deeper cultivation and a better cultivation. Your land is thoroughly cultivated, and while I have never rotated crops very much, what I have rotated has always proved very satisfactory.

Mr. RAKER. Do you raise beets for a series of years upon the same land?

Mt. STRONG. Yes, sir.

Mr. RAKER. Do you find any bad effects by virtue of that mode of cultivation?

Mr. STRONG. No, sir. For several years it seemed to get better. Of course, you will understand that our land is alluvial soil—it is all made land—and it seems as if you are turning up new soil all the time, and it seems to produce just the same all the time, if not a little better.

Mr. RAKER. How has the tax question been affected by the raise in the value of your land within the last 11 years?

Mr. STRONG. Well, taxes have gone up about 70 per cent.

Mr. RAKER. About what do they assess you on this $550 an acre land?

Mr. STRONG. I think my assessment last year was close to $200 an acre or $150 an acre, something like that. I do not just remember the exact amount it was.

Mr. RAKER. The rate was about what?

Mr. STRONG. I think our rate last year for the State, roads, and everything, was about $2.

Mr. FORDNEY. Two dollars per acre?

Mr. STRONG. No; $2 per hundred.

Mr. FORDNEY. How much per acre, Mr. Strong?

Mr. STRONG. I think we were assessed at about $150; I am not sure. I could not state. I do not remember now just what it was.

Mr. FORDNEY. What I mean is, Mr. Strong, the total tax paid by you; how much would it amount to per acre on the amount of land you own?

Mr. STRONG. My taxes last year were something like $600.

Mr. FORDNEY. On how many acres?

Mr. STRONG. One hundred and forty acres.

Mr. FORDNEY. About $4.50 to $5 an acre.

Mr. RAKER. How are the farmers in your vicinity around Anaheim and Orange and Fullerton and Norwalk and other places getting along generally with their business who do not raise sugar beets?

Mr. STRONG. All those who have land adapted to sugar beets are raising sugar beets. Other men who have not lands adapted to sugar beets are in the dairying business. Some of them raise cabbage and sweet potatoes and things like that.

Mr. RAKER. And they have orange groves and walnut groves, and raise celery?

Mr. STRONG. Yes.

Mr. RAKER. How are they getting along?

Mr. STRONG. Well, I do not think there is any celery grown in there. They are getting along all right.

Mr. RAKER. Prospering?

Mr. STRONG. Prospering; yes, sir.

Mr. RAKER. Making a good income off of their land in proportion to its value?

Mr. STRONG. I suppose they are, I do not know.

Mr. RAKER. And the sugar-beet man is just about doubling what they are doing?

Mr. STRONG. Well, I do not know as to that.

Mr. RAKER. You have said that you get about as much again from a sugar-beet crop as you would from any other crop.

Mr. STRONG. Any crop you can raise in that immediate vicinity. That is not walnut land and it is not orange land.

Mr. FORDNEY. Your orange land is your upland, is it?

Mr. STRONG. Yes, sir; the higher land.

Mr. RAKER. It seems to me I noticed through that section beet fields and orange groves and celery and walnut groves one right after the other.

Mr. STRONG. You did; but that is not saying the land is all beet land.

Mr. RAKER. If the sugar-beet man is doing as much again as the other man, he could stand a little reduction, could he not?

Mr. STRONG. What in?

Mr. RAKER. In the price he is getting for his beets.

Mr. STRONG. Yes. If he had a guarantee his beets would always be the same price and the crop would always be the same, it would be a different thing, but they are not always the same.

Mr. RAKER. Why not?

Mr. STRONG. Well, it is for the want of rain.

Mr. RAKER. That applies to the other farmers just as well, does it not?

Mr. STRONG. No, sir.

Mr. RAKER. You have been doing first rate in the sugar-beet business and you have not paid any attention to what the manufacturer is doing, have you?

Mr. STRONG. No, sir.

Mr. RAKER. You do not know anything about his profit?

Mr. STRONG. No, sir.

Mr. RAKER. Your sugar-beet factories were working last year about the first week in August?

Mr. STRONG. We started to hauling beets on the 18th of July.

Mr. RAKER. And that would apply to that whole southern territory?

Mr. STRONG. No; there were some factories that did not start until after that.

Mr. RAKER. Well, between July and the middle of August?

Mr. STRONG. Yes, sir.

Mr. RAKER. But the high price of sugar was prevalent through your part of the country as elsewhere?

Mr. STRONG. Yes.

Mr. RAKER. And the price went up as high as 8 or 9 cents, did it not?

Mr. STRONG. I do not know; I bought some at 8, or somewhere along there.

Mr. RAKER. And that did not make any difference in their output, and they were paying the same price for beets as the year before?

Mr. STRONG. Yes, sir; they had contracts a year ahead.

Mr. RAKER. Then the coming on of the beet sugars did not have any tendency, so far as even the location where the beets were grown—and where within a radius of 100 miles there were some 8 or 10 factories, are there not?

Mr. STRONG. Yes; six or eight factories.

Mr. RAKER. That had no effect upon the prices at which the consumer bought sugar?

Mr. STRONG. No, sir.

Mr. FORDNEY. When the factories you delivered your beets to began to grind, what did the factories sell their sugar for, do you know?

Mr. STRONG. I do not know.

Mr. FORDNEY. When you speak of paying 8 cents a pound for sugar, that is the price at which you purchased it at retail, was it?

Mr. STRONG. It was not exactly retail. I generally buy 300 or 400 pounds at a time.

Mr. FORDNEY. But you bought it from the grocery store?

Mr. STRONG. Yes, sir.

Mr. FORDNEY. You did not buy from the factory?

Mr. STRONG. Oh, no.

Mr. FORDNEY. You do not know what they did sell their sugar for?

Mr. STRONG. No, sir.

Mr. FORDNEY. Are the conditions generally satisfactory to the farmers in your territory who are raising beets?

Mr. STRONG. Yes. Of course, farmers are a peculiar lot of men. There are always some men who are not satisfied under any conditions, but, taking it generally, they are satisfied.

Mr. FORDNEY. The conditions are generally satisfactory as between the farmer and the factory?

Mr. STRONG. Yes, sir.

Mr. RAKER. Mr. Strong, the position your people take is that the beet-sugar farmers are doing well?

Mr. STRONG. Yes, sir.

Mr. RAKER. Getting a good, fair living price for their beets and making twice as much money out of the beet culture as they can out of any other product thay can raise in that country off the same land?

Mr. STRONG. Yes, sir.

Mr. RAKER. And what the sugar manufacturers are doing you are unable to say?

Mr. STRONG. I do not know anything about that at all.

Mr. RAKER. And as to the condition of the consumer, you do not know?

Mr. STRONG. No, sir.

Mr. RAKER. In other words, so long as you people are getting what you think is right, you are not considering the other fellow?

Mr. STRONG. No. The farmers, if you will let them alone, they will settle their own difficulties with the factories.

Mr. RAKER. But you are not considering the consumer?

Mr. STRONG. No, sir.

Mr. FORDNEY. Mr. Strong, is it not a fact that unless the factory is making a reasonable profit out of their product you can not expect them to pay you good prices for your beets; is that right?

Mr. STRONG. Yes, sir; that is right. You have got to guarantee them some interest on the money they have got invested.

Mr. FORDNEY. In your State the factory is the market for your beets, and you have no other market for them, have you?

Mr. STRONG. No, sir.

Mr. FORDNEY. Therefore, you do not want to see anything done that would injure that industry, for fear it would interfere with your raising of beets?

Mr. STRONG. Yes, sir; that is right, and I might state right here that in that country the beet-sugar business is only in its infancy now. There are thousands of acres being developed every year, as more factories come in and require more land.

Mr. FORDNEY. Conditions are getting better for you all the time?

Mr. STRONG. Yes, sir. Land which a few years ago would produce nothing is now producing a good income.

Mr. RAKER. Is not this the real condition, that about 90 per cent of the land in southern California a few years ago was a desert waste which the people thought was practically worthless, and to-day it is worth from $100 to $1,500 an acre?

Mr. STRONG. No; the land I allude to is alkali land that you can produce no other crop on; but by changing the mode of cultivation we are able to grow beets.

Mr. RAKER. As to the condition of the land generally in southern California in the last 15 years, the price has jumped by leaps and bounds?

Mr. STRONG. Yes, sir; all over the State.

Mr. RAKER. And particularly in southern California, on account of diversified agriculture?

Mr. STRONG. Yes, sir.

Mr. FORDNEY. But the land you are now planting to beets is better adapted to the raising of beets than any other crop, as I understand you to say?

Mr. STRONG. Yes, sir; better than anything we have ever found.

Thereupon the committee took a recess until 2.15 o'clock p. m.

AFTER RECESS.

The committee met, pursuant to the taking of a recess, at 2.15 o'clock p. m.

TESTIMONY OF MR. CHARLES H. ALLEN.

The witness was duly sworn by the acting chairman.

Mr. Raker. Give us your place of residence, Mr. Allen.

Mr. Allen. Paulding, Ohio.

Mr. Raker. What is your age?

Mr. Allen. Fifty.

Mr. Raker. What is your business?

Mr. Allen. Banker and farmer.

Mr. Raker. What is the character of your farming?

Mr. Allen. Well, I own several different farms there.

Mr. Raker. You are engaged in general farming?

Mr. Allen. General farming; and what we call general farming is more grain farming than anything else, because we are not much on cattle or anything of that sort.

Mr. Raker. What sort of grain farming?

Mr. Allen. Corn, oats, and wheat; more corn and oats than anything else. We do not have many cattle there.

Mr. Raker. Or sheep?

Mr. Allen. No; our land won't stand trampling.

Mr. Raker. Are you interested in the beet-sugar business in any way?

Mr. Allen. No, sir; I have no interest at all in any sugar factory in any manner, shape, or form.

Mr. Raker. Do you know anything about the sugar-beet business?

Mr. Allen. In what respect do you mean?

Mr. Raker. In regard to the growing of them.

Mr. Allen. Yes, sir; I think so.

Mr. Raker. By what method did you acquire it?

Mr. Allen. By observation and by experience.

Mr. Raker. You have had experience in the raising of sugar beets, have you?

Mr. Allen. Yes, sir.

Mr. Raker. Where?

Mr. Allen. At Paulding.

Mr. Fordney. He misunderstood you. He thought you asked him if he had an interest in a sugar factory.

Mr. Raker. No; I mean in the raising of beets.

Mr. Allen. I am interested in the raising of beets.

Mr. Raker. You raise beets on your farm?

Mr. Allen. Yes, sir.

Mr. Raker. About how many acres of land is devoted to beets in and about the town where you reside?

Mr. Allen. The factory at our place has had about 10,000 acres under cultivation this year.

Mr. Raker. What is the name of that factory?

Mr. Allen. The German-American Sugar Co.; but that is not the only factory getting beets from our section, the Continental Beet Sugar Co. and the Mount Clemens Sugar Co. also get beets from there.

Mr. RAKER. How long have you been engaged in the raising of beets?

Mr. ALLEN. Some four or five years.

Mr. RAKER. How long has the industry been in operation there?

Mr. ALLEN. About that length of time. I think I was one of the first ones to do anything in the raising of beets.

Mr. RAKER. Then it is a new industry so far as your part of the territory is concerned?

Mr. ALLEN. To a certain extent. I became greatly interested in the raising of beets sometime along about 1900. I made some experiments and had some of our farmer friends make some experiments on beets. I became convinced at that time our country was peculiarly fitted for the raising of sugar beets; but nothing was ever done toward that until about five years ago, when the Continental Sugar Co. sent a man through our section of the country, more particularly into Defiance County, and a lot of farmers there, knowing I had had some interest in developing the beets there, or making experiments, sent him to me, and from that time on the business has increased a great deal.

Mr. RAKER. Until to-day you have about 10,000 acres?

Mr. ALLEN. That is only the one factory. This year the number of acres of beets under cultivation will be nearly 40,000 acres.

Mr. RAKER. What counties does that include?

Mr. ALLEN. That includes northeastern Indiana, where there is a new factory being built at Decatur; it includes all of northwestern Ohio, and that means Paulding, Williams, Van Wert, Mercer, Putnam, Fulton, Sandusky, Hancock—and they are even raising some of the beets as far south as Columbus. It is entirely confined to northwestern Ohio.

Mr. RAKER. And the western part of Indiana?

Mr. ALLEN. The northeastern portion of Indiana and the southern portion of Michigan.

Mr. RAKER. How many factories are there in this territory you have described, leaving out Michigan entirely?

Mr. ALLEN. One year ago the 1st of October, we inaugurated or started a factory at Paulding, a million-dollar factory. It cuts 1,000 tons of beets a day. Since that time, they are erecting a factory at Ottawa, in the adjoining county, and one at Decatur, Ind., which will be a 1,000-ton factory. They are building a factory at Findlay, Ohio, which is in Hancock County, and they are building a factory at Toledo, Ohio, which will cut from 1,000 to 1,200 tons a day. In other words, there is about $5,000,000 invested in factories there in one year, including the factory we have put up. There is another factory in the State, the Fremont factory, belonging to the Continental Sugar Co.

Mr. RAKER. About the same capacity?

Mr. ALLEN. No; that is about a 350 to 400 ton factory, as I understand it.

Mr. RAKER. Per day?

Mr. ALLEN. Yes. Now, a lot of the beets in northwestern Ohio formerly and do yet go to the Blissfield, Mich., factory, just across the line, just north of Toledo.

Mr. RAKER. You are also interested in banking there, are you, Mr. Allen?

Mr. ALLEN. Yes, sir.

Mr. RAKER. And have money invested in some of these factories?

Mr. ALLEN. I have no money at all invested in them, nor have any of my immediate friends; what I mean by that, my farmer friends or any of the people there, neither has my family any interest in any factory at all.

Mr. RAKER. Are you interested with them in money matters?

Mr. ALLEN. Not a cent. I never even loaned them a dollar.

Mr. RAKER. At what place are you interested in the banking business?

Mr. ALLEN. At Paulding, Ohio, and Oakwood, Ohio.

Mr. RAKER. How did you happen to be a witness here, Mr. Allen?

Mr. ALLEN. I was called here by this committee on telegram from the committee.

Mr. RAKER. And to represent the interests or to present the interests of the farmers as to the conditions, method, and mode of raising and handling and disposing of sugar beets?

Mr. ALLEN. Indeed, I have not asked to find out yet. I just told Mr. Hardwick when I came in I was here at his request.

Mr. RAKER. But the raising of sugar beets is the subject you do know something about?

Mr. ALLEN. Well, I think I do, at least.

Mr. RAKER. Do you use any irrigating in this part of the country you speak of?

Mr. ALLEN. No; no irrigating.

Mr. RAKER. That feature of the expense is eliminated?

Mr. ALLEN. Yes, sir. I am sorry we did not have it this year.

Mr. RAKER. About how many acres during the last year did you handle?

Mr. ALLEN. About 100 acres.

Mr. RAKER. Has that been about the amount you have raised during the last five years?

Mr. ALLEN. That is just the amount I have had one year.

Mr. RAKER. Within a distance of 20 miles, about how many acres are under cultivation?

Mr. ALLEN. I could not tell that. In a radius of 20 miles from what little I know about it I would say there was about 4,000 acres that were wagon-hauled beets this year. They obtain beets as far south as Darke County, that is across our county, across Van Wert County and Mercer County.

Mr. RAKER. Those are sent in by train?

Mr. ALLEN. Yes, sir. I think they had altogether this year between 90,000 and 100,000 tons at the factory.

Mr. RAKER. When do they commence to run the factory?

Mr. ALLEN. Along about the 15th of September, but this year they did not get started until the 15th of October, or very close to that. I do not know the exact date.

Mr. RAKER. About what is the market value of this land of yours per acre?

Mr. ALLEN. At the present time?

Mr. RAKER. Well, last year, say.

Mr. ALLEN. Well, it runs from $100 to $125, and $150 or $175 up to $225. In fact, I have one farm I want $225 for.

Mr. RAKER. That, of course, means——

Mr. ALLEN (interposing). It just simply means the differenec between the improvements upon it and the tiling that is on it. Our land is all the same.

Mr. RAKER. Instead of irrigating in your country your people are busily engaged in tiling your land to drain it?

Mr. ALLEN. Yes, sir.

Mr. RAKER. And that makes it valuable and adds just that much value to it, according to the amount and character and condition of your tiling which will drain the land?

Mr. ALLEN. Yes, sir; there is no question about that.

Mr. RAKER. Is your land a fair sample of the rest of the land in that country?

Mr. ALLEN. I think so.

Mr. RAKER. And the amount of produce raised on that land in the shape of sugar beets is about the same?

Mr. ALLEN. I think so; yes. Some of them will raise more and some of them will raise less.

Mr. RAKER. The expense you have been compelled to go to to raise an acre of beets, would it correspond or compare favorably with others in the neighborhood?

Mr. ALLEN. Well, that depends. The cost of raising sugar beets in our neighborhood depends to a great extent on how the farmer handles them. For instance, a great number of our people have been used to plowing shallow, say 3 inches deep. That work can be done for $1.50 an acre. Now, to get the best results out of sugar beets, we must change that, and we must plow deeper, and that costs considerably more money. We have been working for the last two or three years most faithfully to find some instrument that will turn up this soil 15 or 16 inches deep. We have not succeeded in doing that until this year. We have a very tough clay loam. We have found the only machine at the present time that will do that work, the Spaulding tilling machine, and they told me when I had them down there before a lot of farmers, that our soil was the hardest to plow that they had found in 38 different States. To demonstrate to the farmers what can be done in the raising of sugar beets by deep plowing I have plowed this season 40 acres with that deep plowing and I have got a seed bed of 16 inches, but that will cost me from $5 to $6 an acre.

Mr. RAKER. Would it cost practically the same in any other part of that country?

Mr. ALLEN. Certainly; in all that section of country.

Mr. FORDNEY. Will it cost you that much next year?

Mr. ALLEN. No; not on that 40 acres. I won't have to plow it at all.

Mr. FORDNEY. The first plowing is the expensive plowing?

Mr. ALLEN. I would not have to plow that land that way for four years. Next year I would not have to plow it at all. I won't have to do a thing but put it into oats.

Mr. RAKER. What is the best agricultural crop you folks can raise or have been able to raise in your part of the country, say, within the last five years?

Mr. ALLEN. The best crop we have ever had up to the time of sugar beets was corn. We are great corn raisers, but we have made more money in sugar beets than corn, not only because we get more money out of the land out of sugar beets, but because we get more in the succeeding crop. For instance, I can give you my own experience. I had beets on a piece of land, 70 acres, two years in succession, but I do not advocate that way of doing it. In other words, we must rotate. You must rotate in any crop; but I put two crops of beets on that land and the succeeding year I put it in oats; and my returns on 70 acres of oats was 4,945 bushels; just across the fence my neighbor had 50 bushels of oats to the acre.

Mr. FORDNEY. What did yours amount to per acre, Mr. Allen?

Mr. ALLEN. Seventy bushels; and I have friends there, for instance, a man by the name of Ed. Dellott told me he had 88 bushels of oats to the acre after sugar beets. That is so well known there that if any of our farmers mention what yield they are getting of oats, they will say: "Oh, well, you did that on beet land." They never think of anything else.

Mr. RAKER. Now, is there any other crop you raise there where you prepare the land as well and cultivate it as well in the summer as you do with sugar beets?

Mr. ALLEN. No, sir.

Mr. RAKER. While this may not be directly relevant, just to get a comparison I will ask you if it is not a fact that the deep cultivation and cultivating it during the summer when your crops are growing, by getting the weeds out, that adds materially to the quantity and quality of the crop you will obtain next year, irrespective of what the crop might be?

Mr. ALLEN. That unquestionably has some effect upon it, but I have found this one thing true: For instance, this last year I had some oats out on some land, and part of it was in sugar beets and part of it was in corn. There they lay right side by side. There was a storm came through that section of the country and it flattened every bit of oats on that corn land just as flat as a pancake. The others stood up, and I have made investigation and asked the different farmers if they had had the same kind of results, and they advised me they had, and I attribute that more especially to the roots being left in the ground when the sugar beet is ripe and rottening, so the oats get more potash from that soil, and that gives a stronger straw. Those are just simply observations that have come my way.

Mr. RAKER. Have you given any thought to the average cost per acre of raising beets on your land within the last five years, handling them from the time of seeding until they are put on the dump or on the train?

Mr. ALLEN. We figure between $30 and $35 an acre it costs us. I do not put anything on the train, because I haul right to the factory. I am only a mile away.

Mr. RAKER. Could you give us an itemized account of what makes up this $30 or $35 an acre?

Mr. ALLEN. I could not do that.

Mr. RAKER. I want to get that itemized statement to compare it with California and Utah and California.

Mr. ALLEN. I can not give all those separate items except that the blocking and thinning and hoeing and lifting of the beets is done by contract, and that is $18 an acre.

Mr. RAKER. It is $2 cheaper than it is in the West?

Mr. ALLEN. It depends altogether on the width of the rows. For instance, I told my hunky, as we call those fellows, the labor obtained from the city—in fact, I have one on the place all the time. I told him next year I wished him to block these beets not over 8 inches apart. They have been blocking them 14 and 16 inches. I decided I wanted them 8 inches apart, and I will pay him more money. I shall pay him $20 an acre to do that.

Mr. RAKER. How far apart are the rows?

Mr. ALLEN. About 20 inches.

Mr. RAKER. Of course, that will make a little more work.

Mr. ALLEN. Yes, sir; and I pay him extra for it. I am perfectly willing to do that.

Mr. RAKER. You think you can grow them more successfully and get better results by having them 8 or 9 inches apart than having them 14 or 16 inches apart?

Mr. ALLEN. Well, he objected to that on the ground that I would have small beets. I said: "Yes; I know that. I want small beets. I do not want beets weighing 4 or 5 pounds; I want them weighing 2 or 3 pounds." The larger the leaves are on sugar beets the more sugar you get, because the sugar is practically taken from the air. There is no fertilizing element in sugar; it does not take anything from the ground.

Mr. RAKER. And in the country where there are a great many hailstorms to knock off the leaves it will affect the beets very materially?

Mr. ALLEN. No, sir; I do not know of anything less affected by hailstorms than beets. They will kill our corn, but the beets simply put on more leaves and go right on. The fact of the matter is, this year I did not have hailstorms, but I had a leaf blight. It was the second year on another piece of beets I had, and those leaves all died off but other leaves came on, but I did not have as large a crop as I would have had if I could have saved those leaves.

Mr. RAKER. About what is the average amount of beets produced per acre in your community?

Mr. ALLEN. Last year they ran 15 tons to the acre.

Mr. RAKER. What is the average percentage of saccharine matter in the beets?

Mr. ALLEN. I have forgotten exactly what that ran. I think it ran somewhere near 14 or 15 per cent last year. We had a very good season last year.

Mr. RAKER. I suppose the lowest was about 9 per cent?

Mr. ALLEN. They had some this year that were very low.

Mr. RAKER. What is the highest percentage?

Mr. ALLEN. We have had some as high as 19 or 20. It very seldom goes above that with us. In fact, our farmers have not learned yet how to raise beets.

Mr. RAKER. What is the price you obtained for your beets delivered?

Mr. ALLEN. They pay $4.50 a ton for beets of 12 per cent sugar in the juice and 33⅓ cents for every 1 per cent above that, but they guarantee we will get $5 a ton for our beets.

Mr. RAKER. Irrespective of the percentage?

Mr. ALLEN. Yes, sir; and they are paying that this year.

Mr. RAKER. What is the principal thing in raising sugar beets to get the sugar matter in them?

Mr. ALLEN. Knowledge as to how to do it, the hoeing and cultivating of it. A beet, in order to make a success of it, must be cultivated quite a good many times, and you must hold the sugar in it. That is what the Germans say, and that is what our hunkies say. In other words, the reason we cultivate is for two things; one is to keep down the weeds, and the other is to fix the soil so the water will not escape from it and go into the air. That is true of any kind of a crop, but especially must be true of a beet crop, because beets are so much water; from 80 to 85 per cent of the beet is water. The important thing is the cultivation of the beets and the size of the leaves. You must have a large leaf surface, because that takes a lot of the carbonic acid gas.

Mr. RAKER. That is practically true in raising corn and potatoes and all other products of that kind?

Mr. ALLEN. Yes, sir; anything that has a green leaf.

Mr. RAKER. The same is true of your orchards?

Mr. ALLEN. Yes, sir; unquestionably. The leaves pump the water out of the ground.

Mr. RAKER. Your net profit per acre would be about $47.50?

Mr. ALLEN. Some of our farmers last year made all the way from $20 to $75 an acre net profit.

Mr. RAKER. Off of their beet land?

Mr. ALLEN. Yes, sir; This year they have not made so much. I have had many men come in and say to me: "I made $22 an acre this year. I am satisfied, but I made $63 last year." I have a friend next to me who said he made $1,100 this year as a profit, and I said: "Well, are you satisfied?" He said: "Yes; I have signed up for 40 acres next year." I had one man come in to me, an old German farmer, who has been raising beets as long as anybody there, and he said he had 18 tons to the acre. That is the highest yield we have had this year.

Mr. FORDNEY. How many acres did the man have who made $1,100 profit?

Mr. ALLEN. I think about 30 acres.

Mr. RAKER. Well, that is pretty hard to beat.

Mr. ALLEN. It can not be beaten with any other crop. I will tell you the other side of the story. The farm I have close to town there, a mile from the factory, we had some beets 12 and 14 tons to the acre, and right across the line was a man getting 4 or 5 tons to the acre. Now, that is not because of the land; it is simply because of the man. I do not say that because I have done it, because the man on my farm attended to all of that work. The other man did not plough his land right, in the first place, and when he seeded that land he left lots of the seed on top of the ground, and he did not get any yield. He could not get any yield. It is a great deal in the farmer. You can not expect a poor farmer to make any money raising sugar beets.

Mr. MALBY. Or anything else?

Mr. ALLEN. No, sir; nor anything else; but especially sugar beets, because they take labor.

Mr. MALBY. It is a crop which requires attention?

Mr. ALLEN. Yes, sir; it requires great attention. If there is anything I know of that has made good farmers in our section of the country, it is the raising of sugar beets.

Mr. RAKER. The offal in the way of leaves, what do you get for them?

Mr. ALLEN. They are not sold there.

Mr. RAKER. What do you do with them?

Mr. ALLEN. They feed them to the cows and hogs.

Mr. RAKER. That is, the farmers use them themselves?

Mr. ALLEN. Yes, sir.

Mr. RAKER. What are they worth?

Mr. ALLEN. We do not know. We do not figure on it being worth anything at all.

Mr. RAKER. What is hay worth per ton?

Mr. ALLEN. Timothy hay about $20.

Mr. RAKER. It has been claimed that 1 acre of beet tops is equal to a ton of hay.

Mr. ALLEN. Well, we did not get any this year.

Mr. RAKER. You did not get any tops?

Mr. ALLEN. No.

Mr. RAKER. What did you do with them?

Mr. ALLEN. They rotted in the field before we got to them. We had a very bad season this fall. We had a heavy freeze in November that froze the tops and they rotted afterwards. We had warm weather all during December, and those tops rotted so they had to pull the beets out with their hooks. We could not get them out any other way. They had to take their hooks and hook them out.

Mr. RAKER. Whatever they would be worth would add just that much more to the farmer's profit?

Mr. ALLEN. Yes; if you have the hogs and cattle to use them.

Mr. RAKER. Well, pretty nearly every farmer has a little stock.

Mr. ALLEN. Very small. A great number of our farmers have not anything but a milch cow. They sell all their corn and sell everything off. It is a ruinous way of doing, but our land has been so rich they have not seen the necessity of building it up.

Mr. RAKER. Did you state the rate of interest in your community?

Mr. ALLEN. Six per cent.

Mr. RAKER. Does this beet land, worth from $100 to $150 an acre, correspond with the land they use for corn?

Mr. ALLEN. Yes, sir; the same land exactly. We rotate our crops in this way: We put our beets in, then we will put in oats after that, then we will put in clover, then after clover we will put in corn. Then we will cut the corn stubble down fine and put in beets again and keep that rotation up.

Mr. RAKER. Where do you get your seed to plant?

Mr. ALLEN. From the factory.

Mr. RAKER. In regard to labor, what is the kind and character of your labor?

Mr. ALLEN. The hand labor that is there?

Mr. RAKER. Yes.

Mr. ALLEN. That labor is brought in; this last year from South Bend, some from Detroit, some from Toledo, some from Cleveland, and some from Youngstown. There were three special trains of that labor brought in there.

Mr. RAKER. Of what nationality?

Mr. ALLEN. This year I think they were mostly Bohemians. One year we had mostly Hungarians.

Mr. RAKER. Who attends to getting this labor?

Mr. ALLEN. The factories do.

Mr. RAKER. They bring them in for you?

Mr. ALLEN. The factory does this: They go and make contracts with these people in the cities and bring them out there to the farmers. Then when they begin work they have little houses on wheels which they take out into these fields.

Mr. RAKER. That is, the factory has those houses?

Mr. ALLEN. The factory owns those houses. After they have blocked and thinned these beets and hoed them through once, then they go to the farmer and take his note for the amount they have paid those people up to $9 an acre, and that is taken out of the first beets that go into the factory.

Mr. RAKER. Does the farmer contract individually with these laborers?

Mr. ALLEN. They are beginning to, to quite a great extent. I did this year.

Mr. RAKER. But originally they contracted with the sugar factory?

Mr. ALLEN. Yes. In fact, we could not raise beets if we did not have the labor.

Mr. RAKER. And you have to pay so much for each particular kind of work?

Mr. ALLEN. No; we pay so much an acre for all that work. We pay $18 an acre for all that work.

Mr. RAKER. Are they men and women and boys?

Mr. ALLEN. Men, women, and children.

Mr. RAKER. How young are the children?

Mr. ALLEN. Well, I have seen them in the fields all the way from three months up. Of course the ones three months didn't do anything. The whole families work.

Mr. RAKER. What I mean is, how old are the youngsters who are pulling the beets?

Mr. ALLEN. I could not tell you that. It would be mere guesswork. I have not seen very many young children in the fields working.

Mr. RAKER. The majority of them are single men, are they?

Mr. ALLEN. I could not say.

Mr. RAKER. Pretty well equalized?

Mr. ALLEN. I should think so.

Mr. RAKER. When they get through with this work they then return to the large cities?

Mr. ALLEN. Those that do not stay there. Quite a number have stayed there and have rented land and are raising beets.

Mr. RAKER. You do not know how or where they live when they get into the large cities, do you?

Mr. ALLEN. No, sir.

Mr. RAKER. You have paid no attention to that?

Mr. ALLEN. As far as that is concerned, no.

Mr. RAKER. You have never investigated the subject at all?

Mr. ALLEN. No.

Mr. RAKER. Very few of them are citizens; they are practically all foreigners, are they not?

Mr. ALLEN. I think they are all citizens of these towns they live in. They are workers in the factories in the towns; in the steel mills, more particularly.

Mr. RAKER. How can they leave the mills and come out to the fields?

Mr. ALLEN. I could not tell you that. Quite a number of foreigners I know live in the city of Detroit, and from their names they must be foreigners.

Mr. RAKER. Do any of these people who work in the fields participate with the electorate of your community?

Mr. ALLEN. Not with us. There are some who stay there. I know quite a number of families who stay there entirely and do not pretend to go away. They have rented land there and do not want to go back to the city, and they have sent over to Europe for their relatives and friends. I remember one man, a man by the name of Vergott, who sent over for his father.

Mr. RAKER. Do you know anything about the condition of the sugar factory as to what their profits are per ton or per acre as compared with the farmer?

Mr. ALLEN. Only by hearsay, that is all.

Mr. RAKER. Well, what is it?

Mr. ALLEN. I was told this year that the factory last year lost $2,500 on their sugar. This year, if there is a factory in Michigan or Ohio that comes out even, I think they will be doing well. That is my own observation of it, and that is because they have lost so many beets.

Mr. RAKER. Then in this particular instance the farmers are getting all the cream and the factories are taking the skimmed milk?

Mr. ALLEN. In this particular instance that was the case, and it was explained to me in this way: In the crystallization of sugars, sometimes there appears an inverted sugar—I do not know what the name of it is; it was explained to me, but I can not explain it to anybody else. Last year there was an immense amount of that invert sugar in our section of the country. The way it was explained to me, they could not detect it using the polariscope. In paying for the beets they can not detect it, but afterwards they find out when they go to make their sugar, and that is a loss to them. That was the explanation given to me. I do not know how true it is.

Mr. RAKER. How large a rate of interest upon the money invested in your land, supposing it to be worth $150 an acre, do you get?

Mr. ALLEN. It just depends on how we are using it and what we are putting in, and we figure also upon the increase in the value of the land from year to year. We ought to have 10 per cent.

Mr. RAKER. Not what you ought to have, but what you get?

Mr. ALLEN. Well, that is what I think we are getting.

Mr. RAKER. You get about 10 per cent?

Mr. ALLEN. Yes, sir; if I can not make 10 per cent I will quit it.

Mr. RAKER. Did you not get considerably more than that at the rate of about $47 per acre?

Mr. ALLEN. Yes; on beets I did; but you can not put all your land in sugar beets.

Mr. RAKER. Taking the land that was in beets, it would be much more than that?

Mr. ALLEN. Yes, sir. It did that well last year, but this year it won't do so well.

Mr. RAKER. How was it in 1910?

Mr. ALLEN. It did not do so well. I can not judge the two, for this reason: The first year I put those beets out I did not have my land thoroughly tilled—I did not have it tilled right—consequently, I had to go to work and retill that land in order to get a good crop of beets or anything else.

Mr. RAKER. You till your land for other crops in that country?

Mr. ALLEN. For everything; yes, sir. I would not have got a good crop of corn if the land had not been tilled.

Mr. RAKER. Is there any complaint among the farmers raising sugar beets as to the price they are getting for the beets?

Mr. ALLEN. Unquestionably. There always is complaint. You can not get a thousand or two thousand farmers together and not find a complaint.

Mr. RAKER. What is the feeling of a majority of them?

Mr. ALLEN. Well, I will explain that. Last year there was no complaint. The fact of the matter is, I had man after man come into our office and take me in the back room and say: "Here, Charlie, I wish you would use your influence with that factory to allow me to put in 10 or 20 acres of beets." They were more than satisfied. This year it is another story, and that other story is told, not because of anything that the sugar company has done, but simply because of weather conditions which nobody could govern. We have had a very poor year this year, not only for beets, but for corn. Of course whenever anything like that comes up you will always find people complaining, it makes no difference where you are.

Mr. RAKER. Is there any complaint as to the analyses of the beets that the farmer sells to the factory or his returns?

Mr. ALLEN. Yes, sir; I have heard complaint about that.

Mr. RAKER. Has there been any effort by the Farmers' Association to make a personal investigation with their own chemists?

Mr. ALLEN. I think not; no, sir. There was not any complaint last year.

Mr. RAKER. Does your contract provide that the farmers may put a chemist in the factory to see what is actually done?

Mr. ALLEN. I do not think so.

Mr. RAKER. Have you a copy of your contract with you?

Mr. ALLEN. No, sir; I have not. I could have brought it along if I had thought of it; but I was in a great hurry to get here, and I had so much to do, I did not think of bringing any papers.

Mr. RAKER. Is there anything you would like to tell the committee which I have not asked you about?

Mr. ALLEN. Yes, sir.

Mr. RAKER. I would be glad for you to present any matter to the committee you may desire.

Mr. ALLEN. I do not think there is anything the farmers in our region can do that will produce better results, not only to them, but to the benefit of the people living in the cities in lowering the cost of living, than our sugar beets.

Mr. RAKER. Just explain that a little more in detail. What do you mean by lowering the cost of living to the people in the cities?

Mr. ALLEN. I will explain that in this way: There has been a great deal of talk for quite a number of years about the cost of living. There is no question but it has gone up, and there have been a great many different reasons given for it. For instance, I have heard such reasons as the large amount of gold mined and put into circulation. I have heard also it is the middleman who is getting the large profit—that is, the groceryman—and different things like that. I have heard different kinds of reasons given for the high cost of living, but I think if we look at it in the right line, if we look at it according to the reasons given by such men as Prof. Hopkins, of Illinois, and read the articles of the Hon. James J. Hill, of the Great Northern, and President Brown, of the New York Central, we will see that the great cause of the high cost of living is because we are not raising the amount of products per acre we should raise upon our land. That is one reason. If we are going to reduce the cost of living, or even if we aré going to keep it at its present point, there must be a change in our farming. We must make two blades of grass grow where one grew before. There is no question of that; otherwise our children and our children's children are going to suffer.

Mr. RAKER. Have you any ways or means in your own mind by which you can get these people from these large cities, or smaller towns, or medium-sized towns, into the farming regions and districts to grow these beets?

Mr. ALLEN. The only way I know of is through these factories. There are quite a number of our citizens that do that work, quite a number of them, but the number we have is so small in comparison to the number we need that we must go out some place and get those laborers. This year there will be 5,000 of those laborers brought into our section to work on the farms.

Mr. RAKER. Are they pretty good citizens in the way of their behavior, and so forth?

Mr. ALLEN. Very good, sir. I have one man on my place at the present time who worked for us two years ago, from South Bend, Ind., and this last year in the spring he wrote to us and wanted to come back, and we are very glad to have him.

Mr. RAKER. How are they as to law and order? Have they a pretty good record in that way?

Mr. ALLEN. Yes, sir; very good.

Mr. RAKER. Are they any tax or expense upon the county?

Mr. ALLEN. I have never heard of a thing of that sort. We do not sell liquor in our county, and that is one thing that helps us to a great extent.

Mr. RAKER. The more sugar beets you raise the less liquor they drink?

Mr. ALLEN. I do not know about that, but that has not got anything to do with the sugar business at all. We are a dry county, and that makes quite a difference with us. Of course, some of them ship the liquor in, but the Americans do that, too. They are no different in that respect. I have found these laborers on an average just about as I find the American laborers. I have some on my land who are very good, and on another part of my land some who are very poor.

Mr. RAKER. The main question is, are they becoming a part and parcel of your country and assimilating with our institutions and our people?

Mr. ALLEN. Indeed they are, sir. The third and fourth generation they will be just the same as any of the Americans.

Mr. RAKER. Of course, that is one of the main conditions that should be considered.

Mr. ALLEN. Yes, sir.

Mr. RAKER. Have you taken into consideration the consumer of sugar at all?

Mr. ALLEN. I think I have.

Mr. RAKER. Have you thought of his position?

Mr. ALLEN. I have.

Mr. RAKER. What do you think about the way things stand now?

Mr. ALLEN. Well, I will tell you. I think if we in America could raise all our sugar, which we can do absolutely just the same as we can raise our corn, the consumer will be a great deal better off. It is somewhat funny, but it is a fact, I believe, that the sugar factories of the United States—the independent factories, I mean—do not want a high price for sugar. Now, that is strange, but I will explain why: Simply because the lower the price of sugar, the more it is going to be used. There is going to be an immense amount of it used every year. There has been an increase in the average amount used year after year, a tremendous increase in the last 20 years, and that is what the sugar factories want. They want to take care of that increase and get a smaller price. When you put the price up like it is at the present time, it lessens the amount of sugar consumed.

Mr. RAKER. While that is a very nice way to look at it, have you thought about the condition that existed last year? For instance, along in July and August and September and October, when the sugar people were making sugar, instead of our market going down, it kept going up right along.

Mr. ALLEN. That was not home sugar. When the beet sugar came in, then the price dropped down.

Mr. RAKER. Did you find that to be the case in your locality?

Mr. ALLEN. Certainly we did.

Mr. RAKER. You heard the witness from California testify that they went right along just the same getting 7, 8, and 9 per cent for their sugar?

Mr. ALLEN. I did not hear that. I know that sugar dropped in the central part of the United States quite materially; and I will tell you what you will find. You will find before the 1st of May, at least before the 1st of May, sugar will begin to climb, in my estimation.

Mr. RAKER. Why?

Mr. ALLEN. Because the beet sugar will all be used up. It will take but a very short time for all the sugar raised by the beet people to be used up, because we raise but a very small amount of sugar in the United States compared with what we use, and after that is gone it will be in the hands of the trust and the sugar refiners of the East.

Mr. RAKER. Now, assuming that the sugar-refining interests in the East and Southeast and Middle Northwest, wherever they are located, are largely interested in the sugar-beet industry; that is, in the manufacturing of sugar from beets, and they keep the prices practically the same all over the country, irrespective of the supply and demand, would it not look as though they were not figuring for the benefit of the farmer or the consumer, but looking entirely after their own interests?

Mr. ALLEN. Well, it is human nature to look after your own interests, so far as that is concerned. That would be the case in everything. But the sugar factories of the West and of the Middle West are not, as I understand it, controlled by the sugar trust. For instance, there is a large number of independents, and the fact of the matter is that the factories being built now in our section of the country, outside of the Findlay factory, which was built under peculiar circumstances, are all independent factories, every one of them. The factory at Paulding is independent, the factories at Decatur, Ottawa, and Toledo, are all independent, every one of them.

Mr. RAKER. And all separate institutions?

Mr. ALLEN. Yes, sir; all separate institutions.

Mr. RAKER. And managed by different men?

Mr. ALLEN. Yes, sir. The factory at Paulding is the German-American Co. of Bay City. That company was organized quite a number of years ago by a lot of German-American farmers up around Bay City. They ran it for several years on a capital of $350,000, and ran the factory into debt year after year, until finally they went into Bay City and asked several of the capitalists of Bay City if they would not buy them out. They made an investigation, and said: "Yes, we will."

Mr. RAKER. If the entire beet industry was in that condition all over the country, from an economical standpoint, and from the standpoint of the consumer, and possibly from the standpoint of the men who manufacture the sugar, it would be a very ideal condition, would it not?

Mr. ALLEN. If the factories were owned by the farmers in the field, it would be a very good idea, I think; but I do not think they can handle it as well as men who have the capital and know how to do it.

Mr. RAKER. I mean to have separate factories owned by separate men in one county or one community, and in the adjoining county let another set of men put their money into a factory, and then you would get good results, would you not?

Mr. ALLEN. I think so.

Mr. RAKER. But suppose you had a large refining institution that handled a great deal of the refining, say 90 per cent of it, and they dipped in here and there in the beet-sugar business with from 35 to 60 per cent of that interest, it would look as though they would be getting themselves into a position to handle it pretty well, would it not?

Mr. ALLEN. Most assuredly it would; that is, you mean they could handle the prices and do as they please?

Mr. RAKER. Yes.

Mr. ALLEN. Unquestionably; there is no question about anything of that sort. If they controlled it and had all these factories under their control, they could do that.

Mr. RAKER. Has not that been the impression of the American people for the last 10 years?

Mr. ALLEN. Unquestionably it is, and it is a bad impression, I think. It is not correct.

Mr. RAKER. If the records show they really do control 90 per cent of the sugar produced in the United States, it would be a very bad situation, would it?

Mr. ALLEN. As I understand it, there are probably 30 factories con trolled by that kind of a control, and the other factories, some 40 factories, as I understand it, are independent.

Mr. RAKER. Your view of the situation is, notwithstanding what the cost might be to the consumer of the completed product, they ought to be willing to pay more for it for the benefit of helping the few struggling sugar-beet factories; is that the view you take?

Mr. ALLEN. My view is this: If we can develop the sugar business of the United States as it should be developed, we should not borrow one dollar of sugar in Europe or in the West Indian Islands, and we should raise our own sugar just the same as we raise our own corn, and we should not be under the domination of the sugar factories on the refiners on the coast. That is exactly my position.

The CHAIRMAN. Let me ask you one question right there. You would entertain that view regardless of the price at which they furnish the sugar to the consumer?

Mr. ALLEN. I say if we will put the right number of factories in there, if we get factories enough to supply our own demand, and if we will educate the farmers so they will grow 18 per cent beets and get 20 tons to the acre, we can lessen the cost of sugar to the consumer very materially over what it is now in spite of the low cost of labor in Europe, which we are competing with now.

The CHAIRMAN. If we can do that, why keep up this tariff wall?

Mr. ALLEN. I say we can not do it now.

The CHAIRMAN. You want this protection a little longer while you are getting ready to do that?

Mr. ALLEN. All the beet grower would ask is that we be protected against the difference in the price of labor in the fields in this country and what it is in Europe, for instance. That is all, and we do not ask a thing more.

The CHAIRMAN. Could you hold out any hope to us that a. any time in the near future or in the remote future, if we do that for you, you will be able to give us sugar anything like as cheap as we could buy it but for this protection?

Mr. ALLEN. This is the opinion I have, and I have formed this opinion from my studies of the sugar situation. If you will give us, say, 15 years, we will be in a position to do that, and you can take your tariff off of sugar, and we will not care a continental. The fact of the matter is if you will give us 15 years you won't have any tariff on sugar, because we will furnish the sugar in this country.

The CHAIRMAN. And the tariff will not do us any good as a revenue measure?

Mr. ALLEN. No, sir. That is my position, because this business is growing by leaps and bounds, and the only thing that has kept it down for the last 10 years is simply this continual agitation of taking the tariff off of sugar. For instance, I was in Toledo just the other day, and I was in a meeting of parties trying to get some men to put some money in this factory in Toledo. The very first question they asked was how about the tariff. We do not want to go in it on account of the tariff. We are up against the tariff agitation all the time. I have a friend in Mississippi, in fact my own brother, and he has a lot of friends who were already to build a factory in Mississippi and this agitation about the sugar tariff just simply stopped it.

The CHAIRMAN. Is that condition peculiar to the sugar industry?

Mr. ALLEN. Certainly.

The CHAIRMAN. Is not that a trouble, if you call it a trouble, inherent to all classes of business that reap a benefit from protective duties; and every time people talk about lowering or raising the duties, does it not necessarily affect every business interest in this country, sugar, or steel, or cotton, or anything else?

Mr. ALLEN. Unquestionably; but you were asking me what chance we would have of ever having any relief, as you claimed, and I was explaining to you that if you gave us 15 years without any agitation——

The CHAIRMAN (interposing). Is not that absolutely impossible?

Mr. ALLEN. I do not know.

The CHAIRMAN. Have you ever heard of a period of 15 years when there was not any tariff agitation?

Mr. ALLEN. We want to be treated in the United States and ought to be treated just the same as Germany and Russia and France are treating their people. They are using every means they can and doing everything they can to increase the yield of sugar. They are doing everything to increase the yield of sugar beets, not because of the sugar so much, but because it has revolutionized the agriculture of those countries.

The CHAIRMAN. What about Great Britain's policy?

Mr. ALLEN. Great Britain is starting to establish the same thing.

The CHAIRMAN. Protection on West Indian sugar, for instance?

Mr. ALLEN. I do not know what their protection is.

The CHAIRMAN. Have they got any protection?

Mr. ALLEN. They are a tempting at the present time to establish some factories in England.

The CHAIRMAN. Are they trying to do that with the help of tariff laws?

Mr. ALLEN. That I can not tell you anything about.

The CHAIRMAN. Well, that is a very important feature. You seem to have made a wide investigation of the sugar industry. Do you not know, as a matter of fact, that the proposition is not seriously advanced in Great Britain at present—as far as you know—that there should be any tax on sugar produced in the West Indian colonies, for instance?

Mr. ALLEN. I do not know what their ideas are.

The CHAIRMAN. So they have not adopted that policy in England.

Mr. ALLEN. That is probably true; I do not know. But I am speaking more particularly of Germany, and Germany has increased her agricultural production wonderfully in the last 25 or 30 years.

Mr. MALBY. Outside of beets?

Mr. ALLEN. Yes, sir.

The CHAIRMAN. In what period of time, you say?

Mr. ALLEN. I do not quite know the number of years back, but say the last 50 or 100 years.

The CHAIRMAN. Are you familiar with the German situation?

Mr. ALLEN. Not very much, only as I have read about it in these different papers and magazines and in the speeches of Prof. Hopkins.

The CHAIRMAN. You have no personal knowledge of it?

Mr. ALLEN. No, sir; I have not been over there.

The CHAIRMAN. For instance, do you know how long it took Germany to reach a production equal to her home consumption?

Mr. ALLEN. I do not. I am not posted on that subject. They protect their sugar, though, do they not?

The CHAIRMAN. Yes.

Mr. ALLEN. Russia protects her sugar, does she not?

The CHAIRMAN. Russia protects it and fixes a maximum price, too. They also protect the consumer. Would you advocate that for America?

Mr. ALLEN. Well, I do not know whether that could be done or not. I do not know how that is.

The CHAIRMAN. I just wanted to know whether or not you had any knowledge as to how much the German consumer suffered while they were protecting this industry.

Mr. ALLEN. All I was figuring on was the increase in agricultural production in Germany.

The CHAIRMAN. Have you figured on anything else except sugar?

Mr. ALLEN. On all the other products, on account of the protection.

The CHAIRMAN. Your information on that subject comes entirely from magazine articles?

Mr. ALLEN. No; I have read quite a number of articles of Prof. Hopkins, of Illinois, and I have got most of that information from the sugar experiment stations.

The CHAIRMAN. Have you ever been over there? I am not asking this to discredit your testimony at all, but simply to find out.

Mr. ALLEN. No; I have never been over there myself. I have never made any personal examination.

The CHAIRMAN. Have you ever made an examination of the question of how the price of refined sugar varies to the consumer thereof as the protection is increased or maintained?

Mr. ALLEN. No; I have never made such an examination.

The CHAIRMAN. Now, let me ask you this question, because I want to see what is exactly and candidly your point of view: Suppose it were demonstrated in Germany, for instance, that beet sugar can be produced at 2 cents a pound, and in this country it can not be produced under 4 cents, we will say, would you think, unless the American producer could at some time hope to put the article down to somewhere near the foreign price, we should continue carrying this burden indefinitely on the consumer?

Mr. ALLEN. I think the American producer can do that.

The CHAIRMAN. I am very glad to hear you say that.

Mr. ALLEN. I do, most assuredly.

The CHAIRMAN. I was not here when you were examined originally; you are not a sugar manufacturer, are you?

Mr. ALLEN. No, sir; I have no interest at all in any sugar factory.

The CHAIRMAN. You are a beet grower?

Mr. ALLEN. Yes, sir.

The CHAIRMAN. I think some of the beet growers have given us the impression, if they have not made the precise statement, that they could produce sugar that cheaply, provided the factories gave the farmer a little less for his beets.

Mr. ALLEN. Well, I think we could do that if our farmers were educated to raise sugar beets as they ought to raise them.

The CHAIRMAN. You think after awhile the farmers could stand a reduction?

Mr. ALLEN. Yes, sir; I believe you could take the tariff off of sugar in time.

The CHAIRMAN. In 15 years?

Mr. ALLEN. In 10 or 15 years; but the farmer has to be educated.

The CHAIRMAN. Educated how to cultivate the land?

Mr. ALLEN. How to handle the land, how to plough, how to raise the crops. That is exactly my idea.

The CHAIRMAN. I tried my best to get all the beet-sugar factory men to fix a time in the future when we could hope to relieve the consumer and they would not state any definite time. They said we would have to appeal to the farmers.

Mr. ALLEN. Mr. Hardwick, that is a very hard matter to state, for this reason: The increased use of sugar every year is very immense in this country. It will take ten times as many factories to keep up with the increased use.

The CHAIRMAN. I think more than that. Have you compared the total production of all the beet-sugar factories in the country with the capacity of the American Sugar Refining Co.'s largest plant, the Havemeyers & Elder plant?

Mr. ALLEN. They are refiners.

The CHAIRMAN. I say, have you compared the two?

Mr. ALLEN. We do not begin to make as near as much sugar as they do.

The CHAIRMAN. You do not manufacture as much sugar as that one plant?

Mr. ALLEN. No; but give us time and we will do it.

The CHAIRMAN. I am afraid it will take too many thousand years.

Mr. ALLEN. Not a bit of it.

Mr. FORDNEY. Especially if you do not have any tariff agitation?

Mr. ALLEN. Yes, sir.

The CHAIRMAN. You do not suppose, with a democratic form of government, we will ever have a period of time when there will be no tariff agitation?

Mr. ALLEN. I am very much afraid that is the case.

Mr. RAKER. Mr. Allen, the witnesses are always referring to the conditions in Germany. Their conditions as to raising beets are quite ideal, are they?

Mr. ALLEN. Indeed, I do not know. At least I know they have used that land over there for, say, 2,000 years, and they have land that is not equal to our land in productivity; but they raise a larger number of beets to the acre and more sugar to the acre than we do. That is what I am trying to get at. If we raised in proportion the same amount of sugar to the acre that they do over there, I believe in spite of their low-priced labor we could beat them entirely and take the tariff off. It takes Americans to do things, and I think American ingenuity and American work would change those things. As an illustration, I will give you this one idea: It costs us $18 acre, as I told you, to do this hand work. In that hand labor there is the lifting and the topping of the beets, in the latter part of the season, and they charge $9 an acre for that. Now, American ingenuity is going to stop that. In fact, we think we have got something in our section of the country at the present time—an instrument—that will reduce the price of that labor, and instead of being $9 an acre it will not be over $2 an acre.

Mr. FORDNEY. And you will do it by machinery?

Mr. ALLEN. Yes, sir. Then if American ingenuity can develop a beet that will have only one germ to a seed, we will wipe out the rest of it, and that is what will be done; but there will be no chance of going on with this development at all, and people will not put their money into a sugar factory, just as I explained to you about these two instances that have come before me, when there is this eternal agitation and a fear their money is going to be lost if put into these factories.

Mr. RAKER. The farmer would not lose anything?

Mr. ALLEN. The farmer would lose the entire thing. He would not be able to raise any beets.

Mr. RAKER. But he has his land and can put it in corn and still get a fair rate of interest on the amount invested in his land?

Mr. ALLEN. Unquestionably that is true, but the increased value of the property in our county in one year on account of that sugar factory there has been $5,000,000.

Mr. RAKER. You think the sugar factory did it alone?

Mr. ALLEN. I do, most assuredly. I will give you an instance of it. I have a friend by the name of David Meek, and several years ago he offered his land for $110 an acre, and came very near selling it. The other day he was in our office, and I said: "Dave, I have been telling the fellows over the county that you have handled all your land in beets; that is, in rotation, and that they could not find a cleaner or a more productive farm than you have got." I said: "Am I right about that?" He said: "Yes; you are right, excepting one thing. There are 5 acres I have not put in beets yet." I said: "What do you value your land at?" He said: "I would not sell it to-day for $200 an acre." That is a direct result of sugar development and nothing else in the world.

Mr. RAKER. You think the cost of production in Germany and the cost here is a very material thing to consider, so far as the sugar-beet farmers are concerned?

Mr. ALLEN. As close an investigation as I can make of it, the cost of our labor is $18 an acre, and over there it is $6.40 for the same work. According to the investigation I have made among these hunkies, as we call them, they get from 20 to 50 cents a day over there, while they will make from $2 to $3 a day here. They come and deposit in the bank with us.

Mr. RAKER. So you catch them going and coming?

Mr. ALLEN. I catch their deposits until they want to send them to Europe to bring over their families or go back themselves. I have known the men to come over here and make eight or nine hundred dollars and then go out and rent a farm.

Mr. FORDNEY. The chairman a few minutes ago, in speaking of tariff agitation, said it affected your values whether the agitation was for a lower tariff or a higher tariff. As a matter of fact, the agitation affects values in a different direction, does it not?

Mr. ALLEN. Certainly.

Mr. FORDNEY. Agitation for a lower tariff generally lowers values, does it not?

Mr. ALLEN. Either lowers values or stops the people from putting money into a factory.

Mr. FORDNEY. The increase in the tariff rates in the Dingley tariff law of 1897 did not depreciate the value of any property in your neighborhood, did it?

Mr. ALLEN. No, sir; not that I know of.

Mr. FORDNEY. Now, Mr. Allen, the chairman made quite a strong point of this question which he asked you, that no matter what the result to the consumer might be as to the high cost of sugar, you would advocate the production of beets at home. Now, the fact of the matter is that you think it would be but a short time before we could produce all our sugar at home, and could produce it at a lower price, and we could afford to pay a higher price for a while?

Mr. ALLEN. I think so; yes, sir. My investigation has been this way, that the cost of sugar has lessened in value over a term of years, while other products have gone up in value.

Mr. FORDNEY. I think you stated that last fall, in August and September, at the time abnormally high prices were prevailing for refined sugar in New York, when your domestic crop came on the market the price dropped immediately?

Mr. ALLEN. There is no question of that. It dropped to us at retail there.

Mr. FORDNEY. Do you think the domestic crop had anything to do with that reduction in price?

Mr. ALLEN. I do, most assuredly; and I think the price will go up when the domestic product is gone.

Mr. FORDNEY. Tinkering with our tariff laws always causes unsettled conditions?

Mr. ALLEN. Unquestionably.

Mr. FORDNEY. And causes capital to become timid in investment, does it not?

Mr. ALLEN. Most assuredly.

Mr. FORDNEY. Mr. Allen, the question was asked you about how long it would take to reduce the price or the cost of refined sugar and beet sugar in this country to a point where we could stand free trade, and you said 15 years. You mean 15 years if they will give us some settled policy and stop any tariff agitation?

Mr. ALLEN. Yes, sir.

Mr. FORDNEY. We have in the record a statement made by the Michigan Sugar Co. that in the past six years that company has reduced the cost of production 68.2 cents per hundred pounds. I state that to you as bearing out your contention.

Mr. ALLEN. I did not know that.

Mr. FORDNEY. I state it for this reason: When Cuban reciprocity was agitated in 1901, 1902, and 1903 the sugar-beet men took that position at that time, that if let alone until we became more skilled in the industry and utilized the by-products, which at that time were being thrown away, we could produce sugar at a less price. The statement of the Michigan Sugar Co. bears out the statements presented at that time.

Is there any question in your mind but that we have reached the highest state of cultivation and perfection in the manufacture of beet sugar?

Mr. ALLEN. We have just begun, so far as our section of the country is concerned.

Mr. FORDNEY. It is my recollection, in Germany, when this industry first started they produced 9 tons of beets to the acre, with 9 per cent sugar. I had in my hands last evening a report from the Agricultural Department showing that the production of beets last year was 10.99 tons per acre in Germany in 1910, and the percentage of sugar averaged 17.63 per cent. In your opinion, is there any reason why we should not attain as high a standard of cultivation in this country as they have in Germany?

Mr. ALLEN. I think we ought to obtain a higher one, simply for this reason: Our land is newer, and there is more fertility in the soil to produce the beets; but we must teach the farmers how to do it; that is the main thing and that is what takes time.

Mr. RAKER. And we must teach our farmers by getting Japs and Hindus?

Mr. ALLEN. No, sir, not by a good deal; but by getting more sugar factories in our country. Do you know of a concern that goes out to buy anything from the farmer and tries to teach him how to raise the crop? It is the only thing I know of that does it, unless it is the onion raiser. They keep men on purpose to teach the farmers how to raise sugar beets, how to farm. In fact, I consider that factory at Paulding of more benefit to our community of farmers than I do our experiment station, and when I say that I want to say I have been very closely connected with the experiment station.

Mr. RAKER. We have farmers' institutes from the university that travel all over the country, and we are demonstrating the proper way of engaging in agriculture in all its various phases, and also trying to educate our boys and girls at our high schools in such a course.

Mr. ALLEN. We have that in our State.

Mr. RAKER. We are trying to get the boys and girls from the streets and put them into school and make good citizens, so they can go on the farm.

Mr. ALLEN. We will go you one better than that.

Mr. RAKER. I hope you can.

Mr. ALLEN. We have a college of agriculture in our State using every means they possibly can to teach the young fellows how to farm. In addition to that we have a law in our State compelling the teaching of agriculture in the public schools. In addition to that, we have an extension school in our State—and, by the way, I was the founder of that extension school—in which the professors of the college of agriculture go out into the different cities and different towns of our State and stay for a week and teach and instruct not only the children but the older people how to do things. In addition to all that, we have taken the exhibit that is made up by the college of agriculture, put it on a car, and we are showing that in the winter time all over the State, for the purpose of teaching the farmers.

Mr. RAKER. What I wanted to know is: Do we not miss the mark all the time when we simply educate the Americans to domineer and boss some other fellow, instead of having the man who goes right out in the field and hoes the beets, tops them, and tends to them, and is able to take it all along the line until it gets into the factory. We ought to educate our boys and girls to do that work and not have Japs and Hindus and Mexicans to do the little, hard work. In other words, we should teach them to work with their hands as well as their brains.

Mr. ALLEN. In other words, you want to put our boys and girls out into the fields and have them do a horse's work?

Mr. RAKER. No, sir.

Mr. ALLEN. I do not want that.

Mr. RAKER. No; I want them to do the good, honest labor like our fathers used to do.

Mr. ALLEN. What I want to teach them is to do their work but put more brains with it.

Mr. RAKER. You do not want to establish an aristocratic class in this country composed of a few who will boss all the rest who do the manual labor?

Mr. ALLEN. I do not think that would be the case.

Mr. RAKER. Is not that what the result would be?

Mr. ALLEN. The main thing about farming in this country to-day is not to do the work with your hands but to do it with your brains, with machinery.

Mr. RAKER. That is the trouble with this country.

Mr. ALLEN. I think not. I think that is the improvement in this country.

Mr. RAKER. The farmer wants to get some piece of machinery and then sit in the shade with a canopy over him and do his farming.

Mr. ALLEN. That is exactly what we want. If you want to do the work the other way, you want to go back to when we used to use the scythe to cut our grain. How much would you pay for your wheat if that was the case?

Mr. RAKER. No; we do not want to return to those conditions.

Mr. ALLEN. That is the same thing exactly. I want to see inventions made in this country by which we can take, for instance, sugar beets and raise them out of the ground and top them and also put them in the ground with machinery, so we won't have to use that hand labor. The sooner we can do that the less the sugar is going to cost us.

Mr. RAKER. You know that on the farm there is a certain amount of farm work which the human hand must do.

Mr. ALLEN. Yes, sir.

Mr. RAKER. Now, the more you improve the machinery and the appliances the better brain you give the brain who has to do that work, and you ought not to establish a class simply to sit up and boss the other fellow, but should teach them to get down and do the manual labor.

Mr. ALLEN. Unquestionably that is true.

Mr. RAKER. By virtue of educating our boys and our girls in the idea they should not do any manual work and permitting the foreigners to do all, the Japs, the Hindus, and the Mexicans, are we not doing something that will do them more harm than the few dollars we may lose by handling our sugar beets as we are now?

Mr. ALLEN. There is no labor as good as educated labor.

Mr. RAKER. I agree with you on that.

Mr. ALLEN. For instance, if I could go to work and get college professors, doctors, and lawyers, or even Members of Congress, down in my beet fields, I believe I could get better results than I can with hunky labor.

Mr. RAKER. Well, here is one who can hoe right beside you and pull as many beets as the other fellow.

Mr. ALLEN. But you won't.

Mr. RAKER. You bet I do.

Mr. ALLEN. But you won't as long as you can use your brain to do other work or get something else to do. That is common sense. You won't do it, and I won't do it, and that is one of the great troubles.

Mr. RAKER. I want to convey this idea to you, because I think it is the proper one. It was only by virtue of being able to pull the weeds out on the farm and to work independently that I was able to come to Congress.

Mr. ALLEN. That might possibly all be true.

Mr. RAKER. And if it had been that one man could sit on the fence in the shade and keep me working on one tract of land so I could not have gone to school or become a citizen here and participated in Governmental affairs, I would be there yet doing just like the other fellows. We want a citizenship where any man may have the opportunity and have the education and so we will not have a class of any kind.

Mr. ALLEN. There is no question about that.

Mr. RAKER. And any business that will establish classes is a detriment to this country and ought to be wiped out. If that injures some particular men in that particular business, let them suffer for the time being. The manhood is above the dollar.

Mr. ALLEN. Unquestionably that is true. There is no question about that.

Mr. RAKER. And are we not going too far in the sugar business?

Mr. ALLEN. I do not think so.

Mr. RAKER. That is exactly what I am trying to get at.

Mr. ALLEN. There has been a great deal of talk about keeping the boys on the farm, and that was one of the things discussed at the convention at Kansas City this year. It was not expected to come up, but it came up all through that convention, in spite of everything that could be done.

The CHAIRMAN. What convention?

Mr. ALLEN. The conservation congress. That matter was not expected to come up. You can not keep the boy on the farm if you are going to make a horse out of him.

Mr. RAKER. But, my dear sir, if you will give the boy on the farm the piano, if you will give him the automobile and show him a good time, and if you will give him some consideration and have him invite his company out to see him on the farm, instead of attending altogether to your stallion or your bull or something else, you will keep your boy on the farm and he will become an important part of this development.

Mr. ALLEN. Undoubtedly, and you will attain that by education. But you do not want to educate him to get down on his hands and knees and weed a beet patch.

Mr. RAKER. Will it hurt him to get down on his knees and weed a beet patch?

Mr. ALLEN. Our boys don't do that, because they are using their brains in doing the other things.

Mr. RAKER. You can not build up the American manhood unless you get down to the ground and build up.

Mr. ALLEN. Unquestionably that is true, and that is what our boys are doing. That is why we want to send them to college and that is what they are doing.

Mr. FORDNEY. Mr. Allen, I saw last summer a farmer cultivating corn with a two-horse cultivator with a canopy over him reading a newspaper.

Mr. ALLEN. I can go you one better by telling of a farmer with an overcoat on him to keep from getting cold.

Mr. GARRETT. Mr. Allen, this discussion seems to have taken a tariff range, at least it seems so to me since I came in, and I want to ask you this question: Could you stand any cut in the present rate?

Mr. ALLEN. Well, if it cuts the price of beets, no; and I will tell you why. Because the minute you cut the price of beets in our county, that means our farmers will go back to raising corn. We are going to raise there whatever it is that pays the best. That is human nature everywhere. If they can raise corn better than beets and make more money, that is what they are going to do, unquestionably. Now, if we can find some other product in our section of the country that will make more money for the farmers than beets, that is the thing I am going to look for. I have no interest in the sugar factory. All my interest is simply to help the farmer. All my interest is with the farmer, simply because I am a business man and a farmer, and the better off they are the better off I am.

Mr. GARRETT. Now, I was asking the question of you as a practical man, whether or not the beet interests can stand any cut in the present rate. You answer: "If it cuts the price of beets, no." That is your answer, as I understand it?

Mr. ALLEN. Yes, sir.

Mr. GARRETT. Of course, that is not very definite to me. What is your idea about a cut in the price of beets?

Mr. ALLEN. What I mean is this: There is competition between beets and corn with us. We are great raisers of corn, and if you get the price of beets to such a point that it makes more for our farmers to raise corn, they are going to raise corn. That is all there is to it. In fact, when we first started that sugar factory there the Continental Sugar Co. fought us tooth and nail. They are the trust. I have no axe to grind for the trust, not a bit. I am glad enough to get them out of business. They said we could not put a sugar factory in our section of the country simply because the competition with corn was too much. Now, we demonstrated the fact that that was not true. Now, what it will be in the future, I do not know. It depends upon the price of the corn, and it depends upon the price of any other product. For instance, we are investigating the raising of beans. If we can raise beans and make more money than in raising sugar beets, that is what they are going to do.

Mr. GARRETT. Undoubtedly; that is common sense.

Mr. ALLEN. We are going to raise the thing that is best for our section of the country.

Mr. GARRETT. They are going to raise that out of which they can make the most money, but I have been impressed throughout these hearings—and, by the way, I think it will be noticed, Mr. Chairman, I have not asked many questions touching the tariff phase of this matter, because I have really thought that a matter this committee had nothing to do with—but I have been impressed with this idea, that the beet crop in the sections in which it can be raised is the most valuable crop, viewing it from various angles, that can be raised, including its value to the lands themselves on which the beets are raised, and I have wondered why it should be insisted so strongly a tariff ought to be maintained to enable them to raise the very best crop they can raise.

Mr. ALLEN. I think we make considerable money raising beets, but our main advantage—this is simply the experience I have found in the last five years, and also from what I have observed—the greatest advantage in raising beets is not in the amount of tons per acre nor the price we get; it is the increased value of the product coming afterwards which makes our land that much more valuable.

Mr. GARRETT. Precisely that.

Mr. ALLEN. In other words, we can raise more product to the acre after that to feed our citizens.

Mr. GARRETT. Precisely.

Mr. ALLEN. That is my idea.

Mr. GARRETT. That is the impression I have gotten throughout these hearings.

Mr. ALLEN. It is unquestionably so in our section.

Mr. GARRETT. And in all the sections where they can grow beets. Now, that being true, and it being such a valuable crop for that reason, leaving out every other consideration, why would it not pay them to raise beets without a tariff?

Mr. ALLEN. You convince the farmers to accept a lower price for beets, will you? Just try it once. It is a question of competition with other products, and we have got to meet that competition.

Mr. GARRETT. And most of those products are not protected.

Mr. ALLEN. Certainly not; and I will tell you that you won't need any protection on this crop if you will leave it alone until our farmers know how to grow it right. You can not take a farmer who does not know anything, I mean a poor farmer, and have him make any money out of beets. He can not do it to save his neck. He will lose money year after year, although he may once in a while make a little money.

Mr. GARRETT. Leaving out the revenue phases of the tariff, and upon the idea that it is hothoused now, it is your idea, at least it is the logic of your position, that it is better to maintain this condition by law than by throwing the farmer upon his own resources and risking his judgment and discretion to engage in the growing of this most valuable crop that can be grown in the sections where the climate suits the growing of beets?

Mr. ALLEN. Unquestionably I do, until the farmer is educated so he can raise them right.

Mr. RAKER. Then having experiment stations in all other lines, it would be to the interest of the Government to have experiment stations of its own at each one of these locations where there is a sugar factory, so that the farmers would get education as well as get the results of what is actually in their beets, through the Government agency?

Mr. ALLEN. Unquestionably that is true.

Mr. RAKER. And if it is a fact that the crop is the most valuable one, and I am not going to say it is not, the Government could do no better service?

Mr. ALLEN. I think not. I will say this: In our State we passed a law two years ago allowing any county in our State to put in an experiment station, and our county was the first county in the State to do that, and the superintendent of our factory told me this summer that in 10 years we would be an authority upon sugar beets in the United States.

Mr. RAKER. You can not get ahead of California on that question.

Mr. ALLEN. Well, we are going to try. We can do that much. We are going to rush you along, any way. The conditions are a great deal different in California. We can not raise a sugar beet with the same amount of sugar in it that they can out there, because, for instance, there is a difference in climate.

Mr. RAKER. We have more sweetness in our climate.

Mr. ALLEN. You have more sunshine; that is one thing that causes the sweetness. We have a good deal of sunshine in our section, but our trouble is in having the cold nights in the fall to ripen the sugar beets. The sugar beet is a hothouse plant. There is no question of that. In other words, it has been developed by selection over a large term of years. The original beet was nothing but a little thing about as big as your finger, and it has been developed, and if you let it run back, in a few years it would go to nothing. It is a question of continual selection all the time year after year that keeps our beets up to the point they are.

Mr. FORDNEY. Mr. Allen, Mr. Garrett spoke to you a few minutes ago, and in asking about the beet crop and why you needed more protection, you stated that you raised it by the side of many other crops on which you had no protection. I want to correct the gentleman. I do not think there is an article produced upon your farm that has not adequate protection. For instance, potatoes have 25 cents a bushel protection, wheat has 25 cents per bushel protection; your oats have 15 cents per bushel protection; your hay has $4 per ton protection; milk has 2 cents a quart, butter so much per pound, eggs, 5 cents per dozen, and everything raised on your farm is on the protected list. I can not think of an article at all raised on the farms in this country that is not protected, except cotton. Do you know whether that is true or not, Mr. Allen?

Mr. ALLEN. I knew part of it was so.

Mr. FORDNEY. Now then, as to the class of labor: Is it not true that your small beet growers, the man who raises three or four acres of beets, he and his family tends that crop without any contract labor at all?

Mr. ALLEN. Yes, sir.

Mr. FORDNEY. And your contract labor is employed where you have a crop too large for a man and the help in his immediate vicinity to handle?

Mr. ALLEN. Yes, sir; one of my friends, a farmer there named Arnold, was in the other day, and he said he attended to all of his work, and his profits this year—he included his labor—were $90 an acre.

Mr. FORDNEY. So that Americans can raise the crop if you can get the American labor, but greater advantages are offered to the average American laboring man somewhere else, and that takes him away from the farm; and in order to get the contract work on your farm done, you must get some of that class of labor?

Mr. RAKER. You could pay $3 a day, could you not?

Mr. ALLEN. I have told the farmers on the agricultural trains and in the institute that the reasons we got this hunky labor, or the labor from the cities, were two; one was the lack of it in the country. We have a very hard time in our section of the country to get labor on the farm; in fact, so hard is it that our secretary of agriculture, Mr. Saunders, is using every endeavor he can to form a department to obtain labor for the farmers. In addition to that, the American farmer will not get down on his hands and knees and weed beets, for the same reason he will not go down South and raise cotton; he is not going to bend his back to do it, and I don't blame him. I wouldn't do it when I can get it done by somebody else.

TESTIMONY OF MR. WILLIAM L. BASS.

The witness was duly sworn by the chairman.

The CHAIRMAN. Mr. Bass, give us your full name.

Mr. BASS. William Louis Bass.

The CHAIRMAN. Your residence?

Mr. BASS. My family is in New York. My business as a rule is in the West Indies.

The CHAIRMAN. Are you interested to any extent in the sugar industry?

Mr. BASS. Yes, sir.

The CHAIRMAN. What is your interest? Are you a planter or manufacturer, or what interest have you in the sugar business?

Mr. BASS. I am a professional sugar maker, sir; a sugar producer.

The CHAIRMAN. How long have you been engaged in that business?

Mr. BASS. Twenty-eight years.

The CHAIRMAN. As a sugar planter?

Mr. BASS. Twenty-five years; owning my own plantation, 23 years.

The CHAIRMAN. You are in the business of producing sugar from cane?

Mr. BASS. Professionally.

The CHAIRMAN. And have you been in that business professionally for 28 years?

Mr. BASS. Yes, sir.

The CHAIRMAN. Where is your sugar plantation?

Mr. BASS. To be exact, I have just sold it, on the 8th day of November; but my interests are still involved.

The CHAIRMAN. They have not paid you all the money yet?

Mr. BASS. That is right.

The CHAIRMAN. Where is this plantation on which you spent so many years?

Mr. BASS. S. P. de Macoris, Dominican Republic.

The CHAIRMAN. What we call Santo Domingo?

Mr. BASS. Yes, sir.

The CHAIRMAN. What is its extent, without trying to be exact about it?

Mr. BASS. The largest plantation in that country.

The CHAIRMAN. About how many acres, in round numbers?

Mr. BASS. My sale, which has just taken place—sold nearly 30,000 acres.

The CHAIRMAN. You plant sugar cane? You do not have any beet interests?

Mr. BASS. No, sir.

The CHAIRMAN. Did you refine your sugar after you produced it?

Mr. BASS. I was prevented from so doing.

The CHAIRMAN. You were prevented from doing what?

Mr. BASS. Prevented from producing what you would call refined sugar.

The CHAIRMAN. By what?

Mr. BASS. By the tariff as it stands to-day in the United States.

The CHAIRMAN. You say you were prevented by the tariff laws of the United States from refining your own sugar?

Mr. BASS. Yes, sir.

The CHAIRMAN. What particular part of the tariff laws operated in that way?

Mr. BASS. The color restrictions.

The CHAIRMAN. What is commonly called the Dutch standard?

Mr. BASS. Yes, sir.

The CHAIRMAN. In what way did that operate to prevent you from refining your own sugar?

Mr. BASS. To answer that I would like to explain to the committee, as I have seen from the questions asked here by the members of the committee they did not thoroughly understand the difference between different kinds of sugar, and I would like to explain that.

The CHAIRMAN. We would be very glad to hear it.

Mr. BASS. For that purpose you will permit me to go back to the very beginning of sugar manufacturing. I said I was a professional sugar producer. By that I mean I go where nature is most bountiful, and my aim is to make sugar for the least amount of money in the world.

The CHAIRMAN. You try to make it as cheap as you can?

Mr. BASS. Yes, sir; I am before the committee to tell them the cheapest you can make sugar, not the dearest. You folks have more or less of an idea what sugar cane is. When sugar cane starts to grow it has very little juice in it; by and by it has a little juice and a little sugar in it; by and by it reaches its maturity. It reaches maturity anywhere from 10 months to 22 months. I have just had cane 24 feet long, 24 months old, over a thousand acres of it. Now, sugar cane has no sugar in it. It has a juice which, taken at the proper moment, you can crystallize and get tangible commercial sugar from. If the cane is too green you will not get much crystallizable sugar. If the cane has passed a certain agé, its capacity for the liquor to crystallize into sugar begins to decrease very rapidly, finally it evaporates, and the stalk itself is left without a remnant of any sign of sugar in it.

Mr. FORDNEY. How long has the stalk got to remain before the sugar departs from it, after it is ripe?

Mr. BASS. We can hold sugar cane 30 months and still have it all right commercially; that is, we accept it from the farmers as good cane 30 months old.

I first want to describe what is called the Muscovado system of manufacture.

Mr. FORDNEY. How long can the cane stand after it ripens or after it has been cut?

Mr. BASS. I said 30 months old from the time it is planted. You plant the seed and it will last 30 months.

The CHAIRMAN. If you cut it you have to take the juice right away?

Mr. BASS. Please do not anticipate the story.

Mr. FORDNEY. But that question has been asked you.

Mr. BASS. I beg you will excuse me from being embarrassed with it just now. I thought I explained that when I said from the time you planted cane the cane can stand 30 months and still I will take it from the farmer as perfectly good cane, without deducting or penalizing him.

Now, in the olden times, when they had crude machinery out at the front, as we call it; that is, out in the West Indies, where there was not much government or law or anything else, you could only take kettles and very crude machinery. At first they could only get a very little extraction, and although they had slaves, they did not know much about what is called clarifying the juice. Now, the clarifying of the juice is the modern part that has come into the manufacture of sugar; that is, it takes the juice and by properly treating it or neutralizing it, you get the maximum amount of crystals out of the juice in the cane, regardless of what stage of ripeness the cane is in. Now, the Muscovado system took the juice right from the mills and immediately put it in a series of open kettles in the air. There was no effort made to clear this stuff or to neutralize any acidity or anything else. The liquor was then boiled from kettle to kettle, and finally when it got to a certain consistency it was taken and drained off, and then it was put into vats, long wooden troughs, we will say. Now, the purpose of putting it in the long troughs was to cool it; that is, a big trough will hold 10 different batches. It has a first layer, second layer, and third layer, and then finally they let it stand a couple of days while it is cooling off and crystallizing. Then it is afterwards taken and put in hogsheads, and these hogsheads are left to drain naturally. Now, after not having cleared first in what we call the defecation department or clarification department, it had all the impurities which tended to keep it from crystallizing.

Next the application of heat also tended to kill these properties for crystallizing, and that created more molasses. Second, as the molasses simply drained off of the stuff without any mechanical assistance, the separation of the liquor from the crystal was very imperfect; in fact, the sugar sort of made itself. When the cane was ripe it so happened that this process produced nevertheless a great deal of sugar; but if the cane was young or if the cane was a product of new land, where it had what we call gum, or if the cane was overripe you could pass it through this process and get very little, if any, crystals. It would pretty nearly all turn into molasses. In the course of time Englishmen came into the West Indies and Dr. Shier taught the people how to take this first juice and by the addition of a little lime and settling and the application of heat one could take a muddy mass of liquor and gradually it would be just like clarified wine. Lime is the thing used to arrest the acidity. In handling the cane it gets crunched, broken, and any time it is bruised it immediately begins to acidify. This acidification tends to interfere with the capacity for getting crystals out of the juice.

Now, in order to arrest this acidity—we do not know how much the acidity is changing, so you have to experiment as you go along—it is customary to put this liquor into different kettles, and then you apply so much lime. We do this either under the guidance of a chemist or without the guidance of a chemist. We apply the lime to the point of killing the acidity, and then afterwards, when it is boiled, it immediately takes on what we call color, and begins to give color to the molasses. If we did not put in enough lime the acidity would continue on through and prevent the crystallization taking place later. If you put in too much lime that lime in the course of concentration becomes precipitated up against your heating surface and kills the efficiency of your evaporating apparatus. The art of clarification, therefore, is to know how to apply in different instances with an exact nicety just the amount of lime, and the instructions in my particular factory have always been to put "just a little under." Now, that is in regard to the liming. Next comes the concentration. In the Muscavado system the juice is concentrated until it thickens up under the atmospheric pressure. That afterwards was improved to some extent by using steam coils and things, but nevertheless it was under atmospheric pressure.

As time wore on in Europe they devised what is called the vacuum pan. The vacuum pan is simply a large kettle with a heating surface and covered so that on its inner surface while it is boiling you can maintain a vacuum. It was found that the lower the temperature applied to concentrating this liquor the greater would be the proportion of crystals acquired from a given quantity of juice. It was found that the higher the vacuum you could maintain on the surface of any liquor while it was boiling, the lower would be the temperature required to take out the water. Under the circumstances, in order to get the maximum quantity of crystals out of whatever juice you are handling, it is necessary to have the greatest amount of vacuum possible. Now, this liquor in the vacuum has to stand the application of heat; that is, to the liquor of the same pan you are applying heat on one side and on the other side you are applying vacuum. If there is the least bit too much lime, your heating surfaces become foul and you have to put an excess of steam on. In putting the excess of steam you immediately lessen the vacuum, and in so doing in turn you lessen the capacity for the liquor to crystallize later on.

Now, in order to economize fuel, because the only fuel we have there, or the principal fuel, is the refuse from the cane itself after it is squeezed, we put two of these vacuum pans together, which is called a double effect, three of them put together called a triple effect, and four of them a quadruple effect. Then we have our deposit tanks, and then we have one pan on which is maintained a maximum of vacuum, and that is called the strike pan or the crystallizing pan. I forgot to mention that when you have a series of vacuum pans taken up the first pan will carry low, say, 7 inches, vacuum, and the second 15 inches, and the others 25 to 28; that is, the vacuum pans are compounded, which I won't bother the committee about, but I want you to follow me through this compounding in connection with the application of lime. Now, when it gets to the crystallizing pan, naturally if you fill a pan and then keep boiling off a lot of liquor until it has a certain mass of crystals, it gets lower and lower, so they keep injecting and injecting in order to keep the heating surface covered up, so none of it is exposed. Once you charge the strike pan with liquor, if you have a heavy liquor injected, it immediately becomes many, many little crystals, and that is starting the primary grain, as it is called. If the liquor injected into this charge already starting to crystallize is of heavy consistency, it starts to make up a great many more crystals of its own and has not a tendency to boil on to the primary crystals. If you inject a light liquor into this mass of crystals, this liquor boiling down to its thickness, it will boil on and form almost rock candy. In fact, some samples of sugar, which no doubt the committee has seen, what you would call rock candy in the trade, is just simply that process.

I have tried to make it clear why it is and how it is we get the different sizes of grain. Now, this batch of stuff called the massequite is then discharged, and we have the crystals and its attending liquor with a lot of color, together. The next thing is to separate this. If our primary clarification has been good; if our concentrating apparatus has used lots of vacuum and very little steam; if our strike pan has had good vacuum and very little steam, and if the cane was what you would call in prime condition when it started, from that time it is a question whether we might at once separate the liquor from the crystals, or whether we have to deposit it to one side and let the liquor dry like paint on the crystals. The one process of immediately separating the molasses from the crystal is called hot purging; the other process of putting it in sugar wagons and letting it stand around from 24 to 48 hours is called cold purging; and its object in all West Indian sugar estates is to keep the color on the crystals in order to avoid being penalized by the Dutch standard when we ship to the United States.

The CHAIRMAN. Now, that brings us to the question of the Dutch standard, does it not?

Mr. BASS. Yes; if you understand it as well as I would like to have you understand it. I have tried to explain to you briefly why there are different-sized crystals, and I have explained what is hot purging and cold purging. I have exlpained the difference between the Muscovado sugar, which is a natural draining, and the centrifugal or forced draining. This is an illustration of the centrifugals [exhibiting drawing to the committee]. If the batch is dropped immediately from the crystallizing pan into the tank of the centrifugal and immediately separated out, you are liable to get very high sugar, 99° at the least.

The CHAIRMAN. In what way does the Dutch standard in our tariff law affect you when you try to bring that sugar into the United States? Have you some samples of that plantation sugar?

Mr. BASS. Yes, sir; I have, large grain and small grain of the same degree of polarization. This is called 96 small, and this is called 94 large, and this is called 96 medium, and this is 95 small [exhibiting sampels to the committee].

The CHAIRMAN. This is what we call unrefined sugar?

Mr. BASS. Yes, sir.

The CHAIRMAN. Have you any samples of the sugar which you say is about white?

Mr. BASS. No, sir.

The CHAIRMAN. Did you see this Louisiana plantation sugar we had here?

Mr. BASS. No, sir; I did not see that.

The CHAIRMAN. It is white, but it is a little coarser than the granulated.

Mr. BASS. These samples I have brought here in perfect good faith, and the difference of color is caused by the difference in the size of the crystals.

The CHAIRMAN. The small is a good deal lighter in color, I notice.

Mr. BASS. Yes, sir. For instance, the crystals of sugar repel all impurities to the surface. If you take a lump of marble and put it in brown paint, it will look brown, but when you take that lump of marble and break it up into small pieces you will find it takes on a lighter color; and so it is with sugar. I have already shown Congressmen and Senators that you could take these crystals of sugar and break them up and they will assume a much lighter color, until finally they are almost white.

The CHAIRMAN. What duty would this 96° sugar pay to come into the United States?

Mr. BASS. 1.685.

The CHAIRMAN. And the others according to the tariff schedule for their respective degrees?

Mr. BASS. Each one of those. No matter what the color of the one is, or the color of the other, they both pay the same. I tried to get samples of the lighter sugars, but I had a letter from the refiners saying they could not very well send me a sample of them because "we are not interested in the color, Mr. Bass. We do not buy according to color." If I can, I would like to submit that letter to the committee.

The CHAIRMAN. Yes; you can do that at your leisure.

Mr. BASS. I would like to show you what is called "account sales of sugar." An account sale of sugar shows what happens to the sugar when it is sent from the West Indies into the United States. This shows exactly what happens. I am an American who goes abroad and buys the land, takes out American machinery, makes the sugar, and sends it to the United States. You will see I do not pay the import duty when I ship the sugar. I borrow that here in New York; that is, I consign my sugar to agents, who sell it to the refiners on 10 days.

Mr. MALBY. What does that paper purport to be?

Mr. BASS. A printed copy of an account sales, and I would like to describe exactly what this means.

The CHAIRMEN. You can do that and at the conclusion of your remarks give it to the reporter.

Mr. BASS. The sugar sold for 10 days cash. This was sold March 14, 1901. It was sold on a basis of 4.96, one-sixteenth up and one-tenth down to 94°. Note that for every degree up they only offer me 6¼ cents a hundred pounds.

The CHAIRMAN. Over 96° test?

Mr. BASS. Yes, sir; and for everything under 96° they take 10 cents a hundred off, while I only save on the part of the Government 3½ cents.

Mr. FORDNEY. When you say 3½ cents, is that the duty paid?

Mr. BASS. Yes, sir; I sold it in all good faith and to the customhouse I paid 1.687, which means it was over 96° test, but when the refiners took it they only gave me 95.9° and 95.8°.

The CHAIRMAN. They said it was not quite 96°?

Mr. BASS. Yes, sir. Under those circumstances at 4 cents the gross sales were $30,367.30. Then come a bunch of charges which we have to meet; one is called marine insurance, freight, customhouse expenses, lighterage, wharfage, insurance, duties—the duties were $12,849.95—and then come cooperage and weighing, mending, interest on duty, brokerage, commissions, and guaranty. The total expenses deducted from that account sale, $16,047.50.

Mr. FORDNEY. Your duty was 40 per cent of your total receipts?

Mr. BASS. The net receipts for putting it right in New York because I paid the duty and everything, practically at the refiner's wharf; I received $14,319.80, and I paid duty $12,849.95.

Mr. FORDNEY. You stated a minute ago it brought you $30,000.

Mr. BASS. No, sir; I mean the difference between the gross sales and what I got.

Mr. FORDNEY. The amount of your gross sales was $30,000, and your duty was $12,000, and that is 40 per cent.

Mr. BASS. No, sir.

Mr. FORDNEY. Is not $12,000 40 per cent of $30,000?

Mr. BASS. No, sir; not when you add your duty twice.

Mr. FORDNEY. The duty is not added twice.

Mr. BASS. The sugar to me was worth $14,000.

Mr. FORDNEY. That is not the point. What rate of duty did you pay on the gross sales of sugar when you delivered it in NewYork?

Mr. BASS. Had I sold that sugar——

Mr. FORDNEY (interposing). You did sell it for $30,000 and paid $12,000 duty. I want to know if that is not 40 per cent of your gross receipts?

Mr. BASS. Of my gross receipts?

Mr. FORDNEY. You said you sold it for $30,000.

Mr. BASS. I would not dispute that. My gross receipts were so much and my net receipts were so much.

Mr. FORDNEY. We are not talking about your net receipts, but what it brought on the New York market. You say it brought $30,000?

Mr. BASS. Yes, sir.

Mr. FORDNEY. And you say you paid $12,000 duty, that is 40 per cent?

Mr. BASS. If you say so, it is, then.

The CHAIRMAN. While you got $30,000, so far as the calculation went, counting in the duty, yet you actually got $14,000 for the sugar down in Santo Domingo and you paid $12,000 worth of duty; is that the point?

Mr. BASS. Yes, sir.

Mr. FORDNEY. What made up the balance to $30,000?

Mr. BASS. That is what we call marketing charges.

The CHAIRMAN. Mr. Fordney, they paid the duty for him.

Mr. BASS. Now, let me tell the story so you may get it right. I have what are called agents in New York. They are men who attend to the northern end of my business, just like I have a manager on the plantation. My manager in the South puts the commodity on the steamer—whether it is a chartered steamer or a regular liner is indifferent. That steamer goes to New York, and when it gets to New York these agents take charge of it. Sometimes they sell before arrival, and sometimes they sell before the sugar is even made. I have never encouraged selling before I make the sugar, but I do not mind selling it after I have it on board the vessel. When the sugar gets there it is offered under two conditions: One is what is called cost and freight, and the other is duty paid. If the refiners are good natured and they want the sugar, they will offer to buy it cost and freight, in which instance, if you have it on a chartered vessel, you offer to deliver it to any of three ports, Philadelphia, Boston, or New York. If they say we will take it cost and freight, that is a simple calculation, and is made and tabulated, and they know to the one ten-thousandth of a cent exactly what that means in different ports all over the world.

They simply say, we will give you on the basis of so much, cost and freight. If you add the duty to it, it will come out, in this instance, 4 cents. If they had taken it and wanted to divert it to Philadelphia, and the sale had taken place before the sugar arrived or while it was in transit, they would have said: "We will give you so much cost and freight," in which instance I or my agents would not have paid the import duty. As it was, this sugar lands in New York and was immediately subject to the payment of the duty. Therefore my agent himself either pays the duty or gives the bond. In doing that they borrow the money from the bank and pay the customhouse the money immediately. It is then sold to the refiners, and the refiners, 10 days after settlement and acknowledgment of the good receipt of that sugar, send you a check for it. In the meantime that sugar has practically gone through the refiner's hands, is out on the market and sold, and the refiners get their money before they pay me.

The CHAIRMAN. So the duty on the sugar is advanced?

Mr. BASS. Yes, by my agent. When the refiners pay my agent the money, they in turn pay back the bank, in proof of which I have been charged on this statement "interest on duty." In business—I do not know how it is in the legislative branches—we consider that the country to which the goods go pays the duty, and as I stand here to-day—because I have my ax to grind, gentlemen—it is indifferent to me how much the duty is. I do not care whether the duty is 1 cent, 2 cents, or 3 cents, provided you will fix it so that I, as an outside producer, can get around the refiners and get the consumers to bid against the refiners.

Mr. FORDNEY. In other words, if you can get your sugar onto the American market, you do not care what the duty is?

Mr. BASS. No, sir; I do not.

The CHAIRMAN. According to this account sales, did you really send to this country $14,000 worth of sugar?

Mr. BASS. It was only worth that because that was all the insurance I could carry. It is all I could value it at.

Mr. FORDNEY. What did that give you per pound for your sugar?

Mr. BASS. We figure if this is taken as an average, that the duty of 1.685 plus marketing charges gives us 2 cents a pound.

The CHAIRMAN. You got 2 cents a pound for your sugar?

Mr. BASS. The duty and the marketing charges amount to 2 cents, and 2 cents from 4 cents leaves 2 cents a pound for my sugar.

The CHAIRMAN. Your sugar, then, sold f. o. b. Santo Domingo for 2 cents?

Mr. BASS. No, sir; ex steamer *Cherokee*, alongside wharf in Williamsburg, for 2 cents. After everything was deducted I still had 2 cents left. It was immaterial whether my agents sold it in England, Canada, or the United States; I got my 2 cents.

Mr. FORDNEY. You got 2 cents f. o. b. Santo Domingo, did you not?

Mr. BASS. It does not make any difference where I got it from.

Mr. FORDNEY. It makes a lot of difference. You say you get 2 cents, and by the time you get it to the American market it is sold for 4 cents.

Mr. BASS. I deliver it for 2 cents to the United States.

Mr. FORDNEY. Now, let us get that clear. You did not sell it for 2 cents, because you say you advanced the duty yourself?

Mr. BASS. Yes, sir.

Mr. FORDNEY. Then you sold it duty paid and got more than 2 cents for it?

Mr. BASS. Yes, sir.

Mr. FORDNEY. But you get 2 cents net f. o. b. Santo Domingo?

Mr. BASS. Yes, sir.

Mr. FORDNEY. It costs 2 cents, then, to get it on the market, to pay the duty, the taxes, insurance, etc.?

Mr. BASS. In our particular part of the world those different charges amount to about 33 cents a hundred.

The CHAIRMAN. The duty of 1.68 and your cost, 0.33, would amount to about 2 cents a pound.

Mr. BASS. Yes; and 2-cent sugar with us is "easy street." We can make plenty of money out of that. We will get to that by and by.

The CHAIRMAN. Even if it is this 99° sugar which you would like to put on the market in competition with the refiners?

Mr. BASS. It is all the same. There will have to be absolutely nothing done to it except purged hot; that is, the paint separated from the crystals immediately instead of allowing it to cool off for 24 or 48 hours. If I purge hot it would be 99° sugar, showing that there is no necessity for any additional machinery.

Mr. FORDNEY. It would not pay you to make 99° sugar out of it?

Mr. BASS. Yes, sir; it would pay me.

Mr. FORDNEY. How would you make anything out of it?

Mr. BASS. Because, instead of them being charged a duty on a difference of three degrees, which is the difference between 96° and 99°, or three times 3½ cents, or 10½ cents, in those days the difference ran from 1.68 to 1.95 by the clause which says——

Mr. FORDNEY (interposing). But on your 99° sugar the rate you would have paid then is identically the same as it is now.

Mr. BASS. Two years ago you took off 5 cents. It was then 1.95, and it is now 1.90.

Mr. FORDNEY. What do you pay on 99° sugar now?

Mr. BASS. It would be impossible for me to make 99° sugar without being penalized 1.90.

Mr. FORDNEY. It would be 1.79, wouldn't it?

Mr. BASS. No, sir; 1.90.

Mr. FORDNEY. The duty on 96° sugar is 1.685, with 3 cents added for every 1 per cent on every 100 pounds.

Mr. BASS. You will excuse me, sir.

Mr. FORDNEY. Is not that right?

Mr. BASS. No, sir.

Mr. FORDNEY. Is not that the law? I beg to differ from you.

Mr. BASS. You will not differ from me when you read your own tariff law.

Mr. FORDNEY. I have read it, and I helped to make it. Is it not 3½ cents per 100 pounds on each degree above 96° sugar?

Mr. BASS. No, sir; that is conditional. It is providing it is not lighter than 16 Dutch standard in color, and then that clause applies, but that is a condition it is impossible to attain. There is the trickery. That is the joker.

Mr. FORDNEY. Trick, or no trick, that is the law to-day, and that was the law when you imported that sugar in 1901.

Mr. BASS. Yes, sir.

Mr. FORDNEY. That is exactly what I asked you, and you said it was not. I asked you if the law is not identical now with what it was when you imported that sugar, and you said "No."

Mr. BASS. I made a mistake. I still maintain though, it is not the same; there is 5 cents difference.

Mr. FORDNEY. On 99° sugar?

Mr. BASS. Yes, sir; on 99° sugar.

Mr. FORDNEY. The difference does not begin until you get up to 100 per cent.

Mr. BASS. I beg your pardon, sir.

Mr. FORDNEY. I think that is right.

Mr. BASS. Would you mind reading this? It is your own tariff law.

Mr. FORDNEY. You read it.

Mr. BASS. The sentence starts off—

Sugars not above 16 Dutch standard in color.

In other words, provided they are dark like that sample, this part of the tariff law begins to operate. And then, in another part of the tariff law, it says:

And on sugar above 16 Dutch standard——

Mr. FORDNEY (interposing). Are you reading the tariff law?

Mr. BASS. Yes.

Sugars not above No. 16 Dutch standard in color.

Mr. FORDNEY. Who copied that from the tariff law?

Mr. BASS. I will give you the book itself.

Mr. FORDNEY. If you say it is correct, and you copied it, very well.

Mr. BASS. Yes; I am responsible for everything here.

Sugars not above No. 16 Dutch standard in color, tank bottom, sirup of cane juice, melada, concentrated melada, concrete and concentrated molasses, testing by the polariscope not above 75°, 0.95 of 1 cent per pound, and for every additional degree shown by the polariscopic test, 0.035 of 1 cent per pound additional, and fractions of a degree in proportion.

Mr. FORDNEY. You imported that sugar which you gave us a sample of in 1901?

Mr. BASS. Yes, sir.

Mr. FORDNEY. What difference is there between that law and the law of 1909?

Mr. BASS. None, because this is the tariff of 1897 I am reading.

Mr. FORDNEY. Is that the tariff of to-day?

Mr. BASS. This is identical with the tariff of to-day less 5 cents on refined sugar.

Mr. FORDNEY. Is there any difference between the tariff on 99° sugar to-day and in 1901?

Mr. BASS. Yes, sir.

Mr. FORDNEY. What is it?

Mr. BASS. Five cents a hundred pounds.

Mr. FORDNEY. That is pure sugar.

Mr. BASS. I beg your pardon, sir. Then it says: "And on sugar above No. 16 Dutch standard in color"—which means another kind of sugar entirely, because I can not give you this sugar 99° unless I have exceeded the color restrictions. Therefore it arbitrarily jumps me in the category of refined sugar. It puts on two conditions—on sugar above 16 Dutch standard and on all sugars which have gone through a process of refining. There are two conditions under which sugar has to pay above 1.90 cents per pound. Now, you see, you have put an impractical condition there. I can not possibly make 99° sugar without coming in contact with the first condition and being penalized.

Mr. MALBY. What is the specific thing about the law you complain about as applied to the sugar which you offer to put on the market or which renders it impossible for you to put your product on the market?

Mr. BASS. I have a substitute for the present law, but I can not lay my hands on it right now. It is to leave out the color restriction.

Mr. MALBY. The Dutch standard test?

Mr. BASS. Just leave out that color restriction and collect the duties on sugar according to whatever the purity happens to be.

The CHAIRMAN. In other words, eliminate from our tariff law all reference to the Dutch standard and let them pay duty according to whatever scale we determine on, if we have any duty at all?

Mr. BASS. The refiners buy according to the purity. They never even look at the sugars.

Account sales of sugar ex-S. S. "Cherokee," 3—14, from Macoris 3.5-01, consigned to ——— ———, and sold by order and for account of Estate Consuelo.

1901.			
Mch. 14	Sold cash 10 days—		
W. L. Bass	1,200 bags 1st sugar, test 95.9.		
Consuelo	1,200 " " " " 95.8.		
	Weighing 384,860, 3,840, 381,020, @ $3.99	$15,202.70	
	384,860, 3,840, 381,020, @ $3.98	15,164.60	
			$30,367.30
	CHARGES.		
	Marine insurance, $25,344, @ 1 per cent	253.44	
	Freight, $3.85 per 2,240 lbs. on 768,332 lbs	1,320.57	
	Customhouse expenses	5.00	
	Lighterage, 12c. per bag	288.00	
	Wharfage, $120; insurance, $69.84	189.84	
	Duties, 761,632, 96.06184, $1.68716	12,849.95	
	Coop'ge, weigh'g, $76.97; tare, $12; test, $2	90.97	
	Mending	48.00	
	Interest on duty, 3-18, 25	14.79	
	Brok'ge, ½ per cent	75.92	
	Comms. and guar., 3 per cent	911.02	
			16,047.50
	Net pcds. due Mch. 25th		14,319.80
	E. & O. E.		

Sold @ 4c. basis 96, 1-16 up, 1-10 down to 94.

Thereupon the committee adjourned until 10 o'clock a. m., Tuesday, January 16, 1912.

AMERICAN SUGAR REFINING CO. AND OTHERS.

SPECIAL COMMITTEE ON THE INVESTIGATION
OF THE AMERICAN SUGAR REFINING CO. AND OTHERS,
HOUSE OF REPRESENTATIVES,
Washington, D. C., Tuesday, January 16, 1912.

The committee met at 10 o'clock a. m., Hon. Thomas W. Hardwick (chairman) presiding.

The CHAIRMAN. Gentlemen, on behalf of the committee the chair desires to make an announcement for the benefit of witnesses and parties in attendance on the hearings. It is the purpose of the committee to close this hearing without much delay. The committee has determined we will not hear any further evidence on the tariff question, except a short explanation of the Dutch standard by the witness we now have on the stand, and his testimony will be confined strictly to the Dutch standard and its application to the present situation in the United States. I want to state publicly we do this because under the resolution creating this committee the committee has determined that while it is true in that resolution it has no authority to report recommendations about the tariff, and while incidentally, connected with other questions, we have heard considerable evidence that bears more or less directly on that subject, yet the direct investigation of that matter belongs to the Ways and Means Committee of the House of Representatives.

TESTIMONY OF MR. WILLIAM L. BASS—Resumed.

The CHAIRMAN. Mr. Bass, we want you to explain to us as briefly as you can, because the committee is trying to close this matter, what the Dutch standard is. how it operates against the producers in the West Indies, and also whether it operates against the consumer of the United States. There was one expression you used here that members of the committee thought ought to be explained. You said you had been kept from selling your product in this country by the tariff laws of the United States. Did you not make some statement to that effect?

Mr. BASS. Yes, sir.

The CHAIRMAN. Did you mean you had been kept from selling your product in this country by the Dutch standard in the tariff laws?

Mr. BASS. Yes, sir.

The CHAIRMAN. That was the sole thing, independent of the duty?

Mr. BASS. I said afterwards that as a producer I do not care what the duty is, and given an opportunity I can make it all clear to you.

The CHAIRMAN. Without going too much into details, I would be glad if you would come right down to that point.

Mr. BASS. I want to take an exception to what you have just said.

The CHAIRMAN. There will be no exceptions taken, Mr. Bass.

Mr. BASS. This is about what the Sugar Trust has just been doing lately. They have just acquired a law in their favor from the Dominican Republic that I wish to submit to you. [Handing paper to the chairman.]

The CHAIRMAN. Just explain it briefly.

Mr. BASS. It is a concession from the Dominican Government guaranteeing all sorts of favors and privileges necessary to export cane from Santo Domingo over to Porto Rico.

[Official Gazette, Santo Domingo, July 8, 1911.]

The National Congress, in the name of the Republic, having declared its urgency, has voted the following law:

ARTICLE 1. Agricultural enterprises are:

All establishments which are or contemplate being destined to the cultivation of lands.

ART. 2. Any natural or judicial individuals who are proprietors of an enterprise of this nature, will enjoy the following exonerations:

(a) The right to plant, cultivate, prepare, manufacture, refine, distill, store, utilize, purchase, sell, transport, and export all products in their natural state, such as wood, timber for construction and furniture, railroad sleepers, sugar cane, nuts, fibers, coffee, cotton, chocolate bean, tobacco, resins, and whatever else can be obtained from them through the medium of manufacture, such as sugar, molasses, turpentine, and similar products.

(b) The right to construct, maintain, use, and operate any kind of factory, establishments, or installations to work up, preserve, dry, manufacture, refine, distill, or prepare for private use, or for the market, any articles from the soil produced in the Republic, as well as to construct works, edifices, machinery, and tools necessary for the operating of the aforesaid establishments or plants and for depositing and handling its products, including pipe lines, conveyors, syphons, tanks, and other apparatus to handle, store, ship, and convey water or other products of said enterprises.

(c) The right to construct ways and to construct and extend, and maintain, use, and operate with any kind of motive power, private railroads of any nature and dimensions to be used exclusively for the transporting the products of or other properties annexed to the enterprises, and to construct bridges, switches, and necessary stations as well as all other works appropriate and convenient to connect with all other railroads.

(d) The right to construct, maintain, use, and operate bridges and wharfs, providing these do not impede or hinder the free navigation where so established, in navigable or unnavigable rivers for the private use of such enterprises, of any nature or size, with corresponding bridges and approaches, fills, edifices, deposits, store houses, tanks, machinery, and convenient works.

(e) The right to dredge, deepen, broaden, and to better by any means whatever the ports or rivers where the wharfs are constructed that belong to the enterprises, in accordance with this law.

(f) The right to construct ships, tugboats, and lighters of foreign nationality for the exportation of the products of these enterprises and the importation of such effects as are necessary from abroad, considering jointly each tugboat with its string of lighters in tow, on each voyage as one single outfit.

(g) The right to take and distribute by pumps, gravity, or other means, the water of the sea or any port or river or public water whatever, the quantity which is necessary and convenient to irrigate the lands possessed, rented, or occupied by these enterprises, and utilize it for any railroad, factory, or other works connected with the same and for any agricultural or industrial purpose whatever, and to construct, maintain, and use in the localities judged most convenient, wells, dams, deposits, canals, ditches, pipes, aqueducts, pumps, and all other class of irrigation and distribution equipment, deemed necessary to collect, raise, carry, distribute, and use said waters.

(h) The right to construct, maintain, use, and operate for the exclusive use of these enterprises, radio-telegraphy for the reception and transmission of radio-telegrams from and to any point or distance, as well as private telephone and telegraph lines within the lands possessed, rented, or occupied by those enterprises.

(i) The right to establish, maintain, use, and operate stations and machinery for the production of the electricity, lines with posts for its transmission to any spot or to wharfs or lands possessed, rented, or occupied by these enterprises, or any of the railroad lines used by the enterprise, and to use and to dispose of the electric force for any ends of the referred to enterprise.

ART. 3. The exonerations accorded in article 2 are subject to the following restrictions:

(1) In what relates to the exportation by these enterprises of cotton, fiber, tobacco, resins, sugar canes, fuel, and railroad sleepers referred to in paragraph (*a*), these are to be free of taxes for a period of no less than 8 years, beginning from the date of the publication of this law and after this period they may be prohibited or taxed by Congress; and what refers to the rest of the products mentioned in this referred-to paragraph (*a*), these are to be subject to the laws which at present are in force, and not subject to any increase for a term of no less than 25 years from the date of the publication of this law the taxes which are now imposed upon them.

NOTE.—In case that during the period accorded in this article local interests should require burdening in some form the articles referred to in paragraph (*a*) of article 2 any tax which is imposed, be it municipal or national or municipal and national, is not to exceed either singly or jointly the 2 per cent of the ad valorem values of products exported, as quoted in the domestic market of the country.

2*a*. Those referred to in paragraph (*b*) will not have any more limitations than are warranted by the law which guarantees the rights of third parties; and regarding what relates to the products whose exportation, depositing, or handling are subject at present to special laws these will continue subject to such special laws.

3*a*. Those referred to under paragraphs (*c*) and (*d*) are to remain subordinate to the regulations issued by the executive power, and all plans of such work will require the executive power's approval.

4*a*. That which refers to paragraph (*e*) may not be utilized without prior authorization in each instance from the executive power.

5*a*. That which refers to paragraph (*f*) referring to shipments such enterprises will be subject to the payment of port charges when they bring directly freight for the establishing of same in the proportion of 50 per cent of the established rates or which may be established for other vessels in general, and in that which relates to the exportation when it deals with an article exported by these enterprises, the value of which does not exceed $5 a ton, there is to be paid 1 per cent ad valorem and 50 per cent of the export tax of the established rate, or which may be established when it exceeds such $5 per ton valuation.

6*a*. Those pertaining to paragraph (*g*) which refers to the utilization of water the enterprises should present to the executive power when the matter deals with sea water a statement of the volume of water required with indications of the rivers and lakes from which such water is to be drawn in order that, if the executive power determines that it will not injure the neighboring properties or neighbors it will authorize same, limiting the quantity of water which the enterprise may dispose of for such ends, which it may continue to use, while there continues the necessity which originally prompted the request and the corresponding authorization.

No dam may be constructed in public waters and no hydraulic works may be under taken on territory of the public domain without the authorization of the executive power and without his approval of the plans and estimates which must be submitted of the work contemplated.

7*a*. The exonerations accorded in paragraph (*h*) are subject to such restraints as not to be used for public service the radio-telegraph stations and telephone and telegraph lines which may be constructed and to the obligation to place these at the disposal of the Government when the latter requires to use them in some urgent moment.

8*a*. Those accorded in paragraph (*i*) are limited in that the electric force produced by the enterprises is not to be used otherwise than for private ends, unless the executive power gives special permission to make more extensive use of same.

ART. 4. The stamped paper which must be used by the enterprises to satisfy the import duties on machinery, as well as any taxes of exportation and port charges, as well as the charges for clearance of vessels of same is to be 50 per cent of the amount which the law of stamped paper indicates to be used in general in such instances.

ART. 5. Each person, society, or corporation, national or foreign, desiring to establish agricultural enterprises in the Republic in accordance with this law, should, in order to obtain the authorization to so establish, present to the executive power:

(*a*) Name, civil state, domicile, title of the partners, if there are any, the place where it is contemplated to establish the enterprise, class of cultivation to which it is to be dedicated, the amount of personal or business capital and the locality of the principal office of the undertaking.

In case it is a corporation or society organized under the laws of a foreign state, it must indicate the locality which it selects for its domicile in the Republic as well as the name and residence of a person of legal age duly authorized to represent it.

(*b*) Authentic title which justifies the possession of lands or the renting of the same or the right to utilize it for a term of no less than 10 years, and upon a quantity which must not be less than 50 hectareas if it is for the cultivation of nuts, coffee, chocolate, tobacco, fruits, vegetables, and 100 hectareas if for cotton, fibers, sugar canes, rice, and similar objects.

ART. 6. Once the permit to which the preceding article refers has been accorded, interested ones may immediately begin work, a step which gives them the right to begin to enjoy all the exemptions guaranteed by this law subject to the limitations stated.

ART. 7. The exonerations recorded by this law cease:

1. If the work has not been started within a year counting from the date when the executive power authorized its undertaking.

2. If there has not been cultivated within the period of 2 years, from the date when the authority is given, the minimum area of land referred to a particular class of cultivation.

3. By the secession or abondonment of the work during two consecutive years.

ART. 8. In case these enterprises find it necessary to construct cart roads or railroad lines, be it to unite portions cultivated which are separated by the property of some third party, or be it to facilitate a connection of any of these areas with lands or waterways necessary to transport its products, the construction of such lines as well as wharfs and storehouses deemed necessary for deposits are to be considered of public utility, and faculty is accorded to these enterprises to apply for the legal expropriation of the land necessary to carry out any of the said referred-to works.

ART. 9. The agricultural enterprises must not bring in for their installation immigrants who are not of the white race, and all immigration which comes for these enterprises, must be subject to the laws which exist at present and any regulations which may be established.

Except when it is demonstrated that the crops or harvest of any year may suffer by the lack of help, then the executive power may authorize immigrants of any other race from the neighboring islands or locality, and solely for the crops of that particular year.

ART. 10. The exoneration which this law accords does not include that of internal revenue or excise which may be imposed in accordance to the law upon establishments created by these enterprises in the same form as on any other similar establishments. (This refers to distillation.)

ART. 11. The agricultural enterprises which exist at present in the Republic may enjoy the exonerations of this law if within the period of one year from the date of its publication they place themselves within its scope, complying with all its details and obtaining from the executive power the necessary authorization to enter in upon the enjoyment of such exonerations.

ART. 12. This law annuls all prior legislation which may conflict with it.

Passed by the Dominican Senate April 27, 1911.
Passed by the Dominican House May 11, 1911.
Signed by President R. Caceres June 26, 1911.
Published in the Official Gazette July 8, 1911.
Translated December 9, 1911.—Bass.

The CHAIRMAN. Who do you say is back of this law?

Mr. BASS. The American Sugar Refining Co. indirectly and the Romana people directly.

Mr. FORDNEY. Does the Dutch standard control that?

Mr. BASS. No, sir; this gets around it. This is cane, not sugar.

The CHAIRMAN. Then explain how this new law operates.

Mr. BASS. In your tariff you will find that the import duty on cane is 20 per cent.

The CHAIRMAN. Sugar cane?

Mr. BASS. Yes, sir; into the United States. Now, I am here to explain to you that the value of cane in the Dominican Republic varies from $1 to $1.25 per ton. When I speak of a ton I mean a ton of 2,000 pounds. Now, with the cane at $1 exported, certified to by the American consul, when the lighters leave the country and go to Porto Rico they only have to pay 25 cents import duty.

Mr. FORDNEY. Into where?

Mr. BASS. Into Porto Rico. The natural place to take that is from the southeastern end of the island of Santo Domingo to the southwestern end of the island of Porto Rico, where they have their Guanica factory established. That same cane ex railroad cars to my factory where I must make the sugar is only worth from $1 to $1.25. All my business is based on that price for the cane.

Mr. FORDNEY. Is that cane changed in any way from its natural condition as it comes from the field before it is exported?

Mr. BASS. No, sir. These people plan to take that cane and instead of dumping it into the factory they propose to dump it into lighters. The law provides that every tugboat with its string of lighters will be considered one embarkation, to be charged only 50 per cent of the charges charged to other people. They are guaranteed that for eight years there will be no increase in any taxes whatever in the country. They are also guaranteed that the present or future combined national and municipal taxes shall not exceed 2 per cent of the value of the exportable product.

Mr. FORDNEY. You can take advantage of that law the same as any other cane raiser?

Mr. BASS. No, sir; I have no factory in Porto Rico. I have a factory in Santo Domingo.

Mr. FORDNEY. Have other people in Santo Domingo a factory in Porto Rico?

Mr. BASS. No, sir.

Mr. FORDNEY. Then you have the same advantage any other planter there has, have you not?

Mr. BASS. Where do you mean when you say "there"?

Mr. FORDNEY. I have just said San Domingo.

Mr. BASS. Yes; we are all pretty well alarmed.

Mr. FORDNEY. What advantage can any other planter get out of that law which you can not get?

Mr. BASS. My neighbors can not get any advantage.

The CHAIRMAN. You say it is a disadvantage to all of you?

Mr. BASS. Yes, sir. As I told you, a ton of cane ready to go to my factory is worth $1.25; a ton ready to go to the lighters for Porto Rico is worth $3.50; consequently, when there is a shortage of labor, they can pay $3.50 to get a ton, while we can only pay $1.25. There is a natural shortage of labor in the country. Under those conditions, there is only one argument they use in that country, and that is fire. I have pictured it in my illustrations. That is my part of the story in Santo Domingo. I think you folks are interested in Porto Rico, and I think this cane should not go to Porto Rico.

The CHAIRMAN. If I understand your description of it, the effect of that law would be, or its tendency would be, to transfer the industry of grinding the cane from the Dominican Republic to Porto Rico?

Mr. BASS. Yes, sir.

The CHAIRMAN. What effect would that have upon the producer or the consumer in the United States, any?

Mr. BASS. No, sir.

The CHAIRMAN. Why?

Mr. BASS. Because the game is not being carried on in the interest of the consumer. This cane first goes into the Porto Rico factory, and the Porto Rico factory is so dominated by the New York refiners that their administration deems it proper not to make high-grade sugar, and all that sugar goes to the refiner in New York, making a source of primary production which is thrown into the hands of the refiners, with which they can whip down other American production.

Mr. FORDNEY. Tell what relation the Dutch standard has to that sort of contract or arrangement. It was agreed here your testimony should be confined to the Dutch standard and nothing else.

Mr. MALBY. Do our tariff laws affect raw sugar manufactured in any of our insular possessions from cane which comes from any foreign country?

Mr. BASS. That is a funny question. It did not come right. I did not get that right.

Mr. MALBY. It is a very plain question.

The stenographer read the pending question.

Mr. BASS. No, sir; there is no tariff on that sugar coming from Porto Rico to the United States. There is only the import duty to be paid on the cane introduced into the country.

Mr. MALBY. That is to say, Porto Rico is privileged to import any quantity of cane it pleases?

Mr. BASS. Yes, sir; paying 20 per cent duty on the cane, and that 20 per cent——

Mr. MALBY (interposing). And then sending the raw sugar to the United States free?

Mr. BASS. Yes, sir; and any other kind of sugar. Now the same thing can be done between Cuba and Key West, Fla., or the same can be done across the Rio Grande River.

Mr. FORDNEY. Anywhere in the United States. Your Cuban cane can come into our market by paying that same rate of duty and be manufactured in this country.

Mr. BASS. Yes, sir; but there has never been an opportunity so convenient as the one between Santo Domingo and Porto Rico.

Mr. FORDNEY. On account of the proximity of the two islands?

Mr. BASS. Yes, sir; the cane will not deteriorate to any extent whatever.

Mr. MALBY. Could they import it under like regulations into the United States?

Mr. BASS. They could; yes, sir. It could go from Cuba to Florida, the same as from San Domingo to Porto Rico.

The CHAIRMAN. Or from Cuba to New Orleans?

Mr. BASS. That is a little too far.

The CHAIRMAN. But water hauls are pretty cheap.

Mr. BASS. Then it begins to deteriorate. There is a deterioration of the cane which makes it not feasible.

The CHAIRMAN. It takes too long for the cane to be transported?

Mr. BASS. Yes, sir.

Mr. HINDS. Why is that cane worth $3 in Porto Rico and only worth $1.25 in San Domingo?

Mr. BASS. Just one matter, and then I will answer that question. I have just received word from San Domingo that those people had bought——

Mr. FORDNEY. Who are "those people"?

Mr. BASS. The people who are interested in getting this particular law passed.

Mr. FORDNEY. Who are they?

Mr. BASS. It is a farm called the Romana Central Sugar Co.

Mr. FORDNEY. Of Santo Domingo?

Mr. BASS. Of New York City. These people went over the ground very throroughly a year and a half ago, and they did not like the local atmosphere of the country, so they sent some prominent lawyers down there, and after a while they finally got the Government to enact this law.

Mr. MALBY. Is this the law now?

Mr. BASS. Yes; it came out on the 8th of July. I have just learned, the letter reaching my hands to-day, that they have bought 175 times 200 acres. I have to use that expression because this letter is in Spanish.

Mr. FORDNEY. They have bought that much land in Santo Domingo?

Mr. BASS. Yes, sir.

Mr. FORDNEY. This New York firm which was instrumental in having the Dominican Republic adopt or enact such a law has now purchased 175 times 200 acres of land there?

Mr. BASS. Yes, sir. You will see that this law accords to them the privilege of reaching any port on the coast through private land for private ends, as if it were for public transportation. That is the vicious part of this law, sir.

Mr. FORDNEY. You have not answered my question. What has the Dutch standard to do with this contract or this law?

Mr. BASS. I have not answered that because another member of the committee had asked me another question.

Mr. FORDNEY. I asked you that question some time ago, and I will ask you to please answer it.

Mr. BASS. I think I made it clear yesterday that my sugar was sold on the basis of 96 per cent purity. That is an arbitrary standard adopted by the refiners. I also made it clear that on anything under that the refiners penalized me more than the United States Government exempts the duty on it. I also made it clear that the refiners offer very little for the excess purity in every 100 pounds of sugar over and above what the American Government charges. Now, my factory makes from 800 to 900 bags of sugar in 24 hours, each bag weighing 320 pounds. If by the least bit of negligence on the part of my operatives the polarization or the purity of my sugar will drop from 96 to 94, there is a difference of 2°. That 2° exempts me from 7 cents per hundred pounds import duty.

Mr. FORDNEY. Seven cents per 100 pounds, or $1.40 a ton?

Mr. BASS. Yes, sir; the United States Government exempts me from 7 cents import duty. The refiners, however, have penalized me 20 cents a hundred pounds on every bag.

Mr. FORDNEY. Why do they penalize you that 20 cents?

Mr. BASS. Arbitrarily.

Mr. FORDNEY. The law, then, has nothing to do with it at all?

Mr. BASS. No, sir.

Mr. FORDNEY. The Dutch standard has nothing to do with that 20 cents, so then leave that out.

Mr. BASS. I am coming to that.

Mr. FORDNEY. If the Dutch standard has nothing to do with it, then leave it out.

Mr. BASS. It has something to do with it.

Mr. FORDNEY. We want to confine your testimony to the Dutch standard and that is why I wanted to stop you right there.

Mr. BASS. I am penalized, then, sixty-odd cents on 800 bags, or something over $500 a day.

Mr. FORDNEY. How much per pound?

Mr. BASS. One tenth of a cent per pound for each degree.

Mr. FORDNEY. Then you think the bringing of cane from Santo Domingo into Porto Rico is not to evade the tariff of 1.685, but to evade this one-tenth of a cent per pound you have just mentioned?

Mr. BASS. No, sir; I do not think that.

Mr. FORDNEY. That is all the Dutch standard has to do with it, this one tenth of a cent.

Mr. BASS. No, sir. If you will let me continue my Dutch-standard explanation I will explain that.

Mr. FORDNEY. But I want to understand you as you go along. I do not want to interrupt you unnecessarily.

Mr. BASS. In my manufacturing of sugar, when the sugar goes down a little bit from this 96° standard, if the sugar is purged—what we term hot—or the molasses is separated from the crystals immediately, the first thing you know I am making 97° or 98° sugar, and they are a little too light; say it is a 97° sugar; and the molasses runs off too soon and the color is too light. I do not know that that has taken place, because it goes into the bags hurriedly; it is shipped on vessels and reaches New York. When it strikes the customhouse they say, "Hold on; that is lighter than the 16 Dutch standard; that pays specifically 1.90." There is no question about looking as to the purity. It does not get as far as examining the purity.

The CHAIRMAN. The color determines it in advance?

Mr. BASS. Yes, sir; and it pays $1.90. Now, the purity of that sugar may be only 97, as has been the case. The increased duty then which I have to pay should be 3½ cents more than for the 96 standard. The refiners have offered me one-sixteenth of a cent more, which is 6¼ cents a hundred pounds, but the American Government has charged me at once the difference between $1.71 and $1.90, arbitrarily.

The CHAIRMAN. That is, 19 cents?

Mr. BASS. Yes, sir. The refiners only give me 3½ cents for the extra degree.

The CHAIRMAN. They give you that much more?

Mr. BASS. And the American Government has charged me 19 cents.

Mr. FORDNEY. To ascertain your loss in that case, the 3½ should be deducted from the 19 cents?

Mr. BASS. No, sir; in that case it is 22½ cents.

Mr. FORDNEY. You do not deduct the difference between what the sugar companies give you and what you pay the Government? You add it; is that what you mean?

Mr. BASS. Let me make that clear. I want you to understand this.

Mr. FORDNEY. I am trying to understand you. You say you pay 19 cents more?

Mr. BASS. You will best understand it if you will let me explain it.

Mr. FORDNEY. I want to ask you this: You have said now that the difference in the duty is 19 cents.

Mr. BASS. The difference between the import duty on 96° sugar and $1.90 would be 21 cents, but we are not talking about 96° sugar now. I am telling you that my people on the plantation have made 97° sugar.

Mr. FORDNEY. Which should pay $1.71?

Mr. BASS. Yes, sir.

Mr. FORDNEY. And you say that they charge you $1.90 on that sugar, and the difference between $1.90 and $1.71 is 19 cents?

Mr. BASS. Yes; the Government charges me $1.90 instead of $1.71, and the refiners, to compensate for that, have given me 3½ cents more money.

Mr. FORDNEY. That is what I say. That should be deducted from the 19 cents, should it not?

Mr. BASS. Yes, sir. I lose net on the transaction the difference between 19 cents and 3½ cents.

The CHAIRMAN. Does the consumer get any benefit from that?

Mr. BASS. No, sir.

Mr. HINDS. Does the refiner get any benefit from that?

Mr. BASS. Yes, sir; for this reason: I will ask you to multiply that 16 cents per 100 pounds by the amount of sugar in the bags, 320 pounds, and it is nearly 50 cents. I am making 800 bags a day, which means $400 which I am penalized, and the way I get that news is by a cablegram.

Mr. FORDNEY. I can get that clear if you will tell me how much that amounts to per net ton. It is just 20 times that amount?

Mr. BASS. Yes, sir.

The CHAIRMAN. That would make $3.20 a ton.

Mr. BASS. I got word by cable, "Look out for color." That is all I receive. Then I immediately go back to the factory, and then I have got to delay the purging; that is, after the crystals of sugar are made, they must be cooled off, and then the paint adheres a little more to the crystals, so when we separate it in the wringers the color remains, and we are not penalized.

Mr. FORDNEY. You have explained the difference in the color. That $3.20 per ton is your loss is it, on account of the 16 Dutch standard law?

Mr. BASS. I have more than that.

Mr. FORDNEY. Well, what is it, please?

Mr. BASS. That is the beginning of my troubles in hard times.

Mr. FORDNEY. Is the law different in hard times and good times?

Mr. BASS. Yes, sir; different in its application and its reaching, very different.

Mr. HINDS. What do you define as "hard times?"

Mr. BASS. Low prices all over the world. When sugar gets to $3.25, as it was in 1902, and you deduct $2, you will find we full-duty paid sugar importers were making sugar abroad for $1.25 a hundred. Place me in a condition where I only get $1.25 for my sugar, the man whom I obliged to have sell it for me will penalize me if I try to go around and avoid him, to start in with, 15½ cents more; I also have the cost of extra packages to try to reach a local market; I also have to use a little more sugar, because there is a loss in the manufacture, when I try to make higher grade sugars, and those three things together so circumstance me in hard times and so keep me down and depress the tropical sugar production in which I at least have been interested—and it applies also to Cuba and Porto Rico, but not so much to-day, because they do not feel it now—that when big prices come along, I am not circumstanced so as to turn around and make higher grade sugars and meet the American market and sell in competition with the refiners.

Mr. FORDNEY. Now let me ask you this question: You have shown that your loss was $3.25, which is one-sixth of a cent per pound.

Mr. BASS. Three dollars is nothing when the price of sugar is high; but when the price of sugar is low it is a great deal.

Mr. FORDNEY. The law is the same no matter what the price of sugar is; that is a matter between the man you sell to and yourselves.

Mr. MALBY. I think what he means is this, whether times are good or bad his fixed charges of all kinds are substantially the same, and when times are poor and prices are low his returns are not so large.

Mr. FORDNEY. He can stand a loss in good times much better than he can in hard times, and that is natural with any man in any business, but what I am trying to find out is the application of the Dutch standard to this law you have spoken of by which somebody brings sugar cane from Santo Domingo into Porto Rico and there manufactures it and brings the sugar here.

Mr. BASS. Mr. Fordney, I did not present that law with a view to mixing it up with the Dutch standard.

Mr. FORDNEY. And I am trying to eliminate it. We have agreed here that nothing but the Dutch standard shall be testified to by you, and I want to eliminate everything else. You have said that this law has been brought about to get around the Dutch standard.

Mr. BASS. No; I did not say to get around the Dutch standard.

Mr. FORDNEY. I understood you to say that.

Mr. BASS. You must have misunderstood me. I slipped this law in before the committee so as not to have it shut out from the hearing.

Mr. FORDNEY. I do not want to shut out anything that has reference to the Dutch standard.

Mr. BASS. It looked to me as if information interesting to the beet-sugar people of this country might be closed out from the hearing, and I introduced that.

The CHAIRMAN. You have no right to do that, Mr. Bass.

Mr. BASS. He is trying to mix the two things together.

Mr. FORDNEY. Do you believe this law for the importation of sugar cane from Santo Domingo into Porto Rico has been brought about to overcome this loss which you have sustained of 33.7 cents per ton on sugar?

Mr. BASS. It is to avoid the big import duty on sugar.

Mr. FORDNEY. Then the Dutch standard has nothing to do with it?

Mr. BASS. No, sir.

Mr. FORDNEY. Then, Mr. Chairman, it should be eliminated from the record.

The CHAIRMAN. If you want it stricken out, I will order that done. Mr. Bass, just confine yourself strictly to what we ask you about.

Mr. FORDNEY. Mr. Chairman, that is the law in Santo Domingo, and there is a process now in progress in Cuba for grinding the cane juice, pulp and all, together, and bringing it into this country in a pulp. I have some of that pulp in my possession. Whether it is going to be successful or not I do not know, but it is to get around the tariff law on sugar and bring that cane pulp into this country and convert it into sugar at a less cost than the duty now on Cuban sugar.

The CHAIRMAN. If you want it done, the Chair will order the testimony stricken from the record, but I do not think it does any particular harm.

Mr. FORDNEY. I do not think it does, either, but I want it distinctly understood that the gentleman's testimony is to be confined strictly to the Dutch standard.

The CHAIRMAN. Mr. Bass, that is the ruling of the committee, and you will try to do that.

Mr. BASS. I have tried to do so, sir.

Now, when we are manufacturing tropical cane sugar, we can not, practically, adulterate. This I wish to say because when the last agitation was on Senator Smoot in the Senate—it was contended that if the color restriction were removed we would adulterate the sugar, have it a light sugar, high in impurities, deceive the American Government, deceive the American consuming public. Such a thing is practically impossible, and the sugar which Senator Smoot presented to the Senate was not an unrefined sugar.

Mr. MALBY. It was not what?

Mr. BASS. It was not an unrefined sugar. It was a sugar which had been made in one country, taken to another, refined, and presented to the Senate.

The CHAIRMAN. Mr. Bass, I want to invite your attention to this practical suggestion, and it seems to me about all you could say about the Dutch standard. A number of experts have testified before this committee and have stated that the Dutch standard is unscientific, archaic, and ought not to be left in any tariff law, but but that they see no hope to get any considerable relief to the American consumer of sugar by a reduction in price from the elimination of the Dutch standard, if such a thing should be done, for the reason they do not think it is a commercial success to refine sugars which the Dutch standard operates against; and that there was not a sufficient supply of that sugar to come on our market from anywhere they know of to materially help the situation from the standpoint of the consumer. Can you give us any light on that question?

Mr. BASS. Yes, sir. It is so practical and so feasible to make high-grade tropical sugar that in all the dealings of the United States State Department with foreign countries it has been very careful to put a handicap on all treaties, fearing the possibility that some sugar of high grade would get in that was not refined. Every tariff law you will notice took particular pains to keep the color restrictions in, and in the 1897 tariff law it was put in twice—once at the beginning and once afterwards. That was because the refiners began to realize that we, in the Tropics, could make very high-grade sugar without the necessity of refining. The art of refining was developed there—probably greater in Cuba than it was in the United States. In 1876 refined sugar was made in Cuba, and at that time the refiners of the United States were in danger as a refining industry, and I contend that the art of refining to-day is not necessary if the Dutch standard is removed or the color restriction is removed and duty paid only in proportion to purity. The entire island of Cuba will immediately proceed to make hot purged sugars—that is, it will be 97°, 98°, or 99°, whatever comes along. When those sugars come here, if the refiners want them they will bid for them, and if they do not want them the consuming public will take them.

Mr. FORDNEY. Do you think you could put your high-grade sugars of dark color onto our markets and find a market for them anywhere except to the refiners?

Mr. BASS. No, sir. You said "dark sugars." I said sugars without a color restriction in it.

Mr. FORDNEY. I said your high-grade sugars of dark color.

Mr. BASS. No; not of dark color. It is no longer a high-grade sugar unless it is light in color. It becomes lighter in color as you remove the impurities.

Mr. FORDNEY. But you have said you could make a high-grade sugar.

Mr. BASS. Then it will not have a dark color. It will be very white, sir.

Mr. FORDNEY. Then you make a refined sugar, practically?

Mr. BASS. No, sir; I do not refine the sugar.

The CHAIRMAN. Will it be above 16 Dutch standard?

Mr. BASS. Yes, sir; 99½ per cent pure.

The CHAIRMAN. How about the color?

Mr. BASS. If your color restriction is in, we are up around the 20 at present.

The CHAIRMAN. But suppose the Dutch standard is eliminated, what would be its color?

Mr. BASS. Pretty near white.

The CHAIRMAN. Then what good will the elimination of the Dutch standard do you?

Mr. BASS. We can make white sugar and pay the full duty, or will pay higher duties, and if the refiners want it they will bid for it, and if they don't want it we will put it on the market. Now we must make such a dark sugar that the consuming public will not take it.

Mr. FORDNEY. What prevents you now from bringing that sugar in here?

Mr. BASS. The molasses which we are obliged to keep on the sugar.

Mr. HINDS. You mean the high-grade sugar in color may be a low-grade sugar in polariscopic test?

Mr. BASS. No, sir; that is what Senator Smoot wanted to say, and he did not get it right. He had imported white refined sugar and he called it an unrefined sugar.

Mr. FORDNEY. Mr. Bass, I am willing you should continue any explanation you care to give us on the 16 Dutch standard, but no further. I will ask the chairman, when you divert from the 16 Dutch standard and its effects, then to eliminate from the record your testimony. I am going to insist upon that, because that has been agreed to by the committee this morning.

The CHAIRMAN. Please do that, Mr. Bass.

Mr. BASS. I will put it in another way. The tropical producer does not care how high or how low the duty is provided there is no penalty on the color.

Mr. FORDNEY. Is there any other penalty except through the Dutch standard?

Mr. BASS. No, sir; that is all the penalty.

Mr. FORDNEY. What effect has the polariscope upon it?

Mr. BASS. The refiners buy by the polariscope. If the Government will collect its duties by the polariscope, everything is lovely, sir; but that is the thing you seem to be afraid to do.

Mr. FORDNEY. Me? Do not say I am afraid to do it.

Mr. BASS. I say the United States Government seems to be afraid to take off that color restriction.

Mr. FORDNEY. Does the Government protest against taking off the Dutch standard?

Mr. BASS. The Government does not, but all its legislative acts tend to that end, and have for the last four tariff bills.

Mr. HINDS. Suppose you have a bag of this sugar which you want to put on the market, this sugar which our market will take——

Mr. BASS (interposing). It is the same as Mr. Oxnard makes in Louisiana.

Mr. HINDS. Suppose you have a bag of that sugar, how high will it rank under the Dutch standard test?

Mr. BASS. When the system of Dutch standards only had 20 samples it would rank over 19. I believe they have now a Dutch standard which runs up to 25.

Mr. HINDS. So that sugar which would go onto our market and which our consumers would take, would have a pretty high duty on it because of the Dutch standard?

Mr. BASS. Yes, sir. It will be 99½°, and we would have to pay so many more times 3½ cents, we will say, if 3½ cents is continued to be made the deducting unit.

Mr. HINDS. How would that bag of 100 pounds of sugar, or whatever your standard bag is, pay in cash at present? How much duty would you pay to the customhouse with the present Dutch standard?

Mr. HINDS. Yes.

Mr. BASS. $1.90 per hundred pounds.

Mr. HINDS. Now, if the Dutch standard were removed, how much would you pay?

Mr. BASS. $1.80.

Mr. HINDS. A difference of 10 cents, then?

Mr. BASS. From $1.82½ I deduct 1½ cents, and that gives me $1.81.

Mr. HINDS. So it is a difference of 10 cents a hundred pounds, or one-tenth of a cent a pound?

Mr. BASS. Yes, sir; but I am selling 99½° sugar.

Mr. HINDS. That is the kind you are going to sell to the American consumer?

Mr. BASS. Yes, sir; that is the kind I want to be privileged to ship here, pay a little more duty than at present, and if the refiners do not want it, I can find an American market, and the American consumer will bid against the refiner for it.

Mr. HINDS. What I was trying to get at was how much benefit the consumer would get from eliminating the Dutch standard, and according to that it would be one-tenth of a cent a pound.

Mr. BASS. If the refiners to-day, having control of the market, both buying and selling, if they do not abuse the American public, then they would only get one-tenth of a cent a pound; but if the fact that they can buy high-grade white sugars from the West Indies competing against the refiners will prevent the refiners from abusing them, then the consumer can get the sugar cheaper, sir.

Mr. FORDNEY. You think the refiner has control of the United States market and controls the price they pay for sugar and the price they sell it for?

Mr. BASS. I may not be able to convince you, sir, but I thoroughly believe it.

Mr. FORDNEY. I have not said anything to the contrary.

Mr. BASS. I mean I not only believe it myself, but I have lived under its domination, and I know it, sir. You have cut me short here, otherwise I would convince you. My contention is that it has been a misfortune to the American producers of beets, as well as the cane producers of Louisiana, that the legislators have not understood what this Dutch standard has meant in the interest of the refiners for the last 15 years. It has been the misfortune of those people.

Mr. MALBY. I think what the witness means to say to the committee is that under the present law, in order to take advantage of the tariff imposed by the Dutch standard, he must of necessity import his sugars into the United States of a degree of darkness in color which is unmerchantable when offered for sale for consumption; that if he increases it to a point of colorization where it would be acceptable to the American people to purchase it, he has to pay such an additional amount upon it as a tariff that it becomes at once such an expense as to destroy more than the profit which he could gain by such sale.

The CHAIRMAN. Is that right or not, Mr. Bass?

Mr. BASS. Yes, sir.

Mr. MALBY. In other words, if the Dutch standard were eliminated he would not be obliged to sell his dark sugars in the market and thereby have to deal exclusively with the refiner; but if the Dutch standard were removed, he could import his sugar, which would be a merchantable commodity, which the people would buy, and he would go right by the refiner to the consumer himself; is that about the situation?

Mr. BASS. Yes, sir. For instance, the beet-sugar industry in this country does not require the existence of the refiners, so, Mr. Congressman, we planters in the cane business also do not require the existence of refineries. We did 20 or 30 years ago, but not to-day. We know how to handle the machinery and make everything just as good as the beet people do, but the refiners seem to be imposed upon us, and no sugar that comes into this country gets a chance to get to the public until the refiners have gotten them first.

Mr. FORDNEY. Your duty would be 1.80 instead of 1.90 per 100 pounds if the 16 Dutch standard was eliminated from the law?

Mr. BASS. For 99½° sugar; yes, sir.

Mr. HINDS. This sugar you bring in and sell to the refiner, this dark sugar, how much duty do you pay on that?

Mr. BASS. 1.685.

Mr. HINDS. Now, suppose you should be allowed to wash that sugar?

Mr. BASS. We do not need to wash it, sir.

Mr. HINDS. Well, let the darkness drain out of it, or whatever you do; suppose you should do that; it would be no better sugar for sweetening, I suppose?

Mr. BASS. Yes, sir; because as you remove the color you remove that which is not sweet, and what is left is all sweetness.

Mr. HINDS. Would that increase the polariscopic test of it?

Mr. BASS. Yes, sir; every time you take impurities away it gets better and better by the polariscope, and you have to pay a higher and higher duty.

Mr. HINDS. How much more duty would you pay?

Mr. BASS. Three degrees more; the Government will charge 10½ cents more duty.

Mr. HINDS. And you said you pay now 1.68?

Mr. BASS. 1.68 for the dark sugars. When I turn it into 99½° it would be white sugar; then I would have to pay at least 10 cents more—10 or 11 cents more—import duty.

Mr. FORDNEY. It would save you 10 cents per 100 pounds on your sugar if the Dutch standard were eliminated from our laws, would it not, when you import your 99½° sugars?

Mr. BASS. My benefit would not come in that 10 cents. My benefit would come in having somebody bidding for the sugar.

Mr. FORDNEY. It would save you that much in the tariff you pay upon it, would it not? That is what you have said.

Mr. BASS. No, sir; I expect to pay more duty.

Mr. FORDNEY. You have said, and I want to get this clear, that if the 16 Dutch standard on 99½° sugar were removed, instead of paying 1.90 per 100 pounds on it you would pay 1.80 per 100 pounds; therefore you would save 10 cents per 100 pounds in the tariff.

Mr. BASS. Yes, sir; you call it the tariff. I call it the penalizing conditions of the present, because nobody ever gets that duty. It is something that does not exist.

Mr. FORDNEY. We do not claim here that our tariff law is penalizing the people of this country. It may penalize you as an importer, and that is what we wanted it for; that is what it was made for, to protect the industry at home.

The CHAIRMAN. In other words, the Dutch standard benefits nobody on earth except the refiner, neither the consumer nor anyone else, except the refiner?

Mr. BASS. Not in the understanding of those who understand its operations.

Mr. FORDNEY. Does not that depend upon the price at which the refiners sell that article to the consumer?

Mr. BASS. No, sir; absolutely not.

Mr. FORDNEY. If he gets it for 10 cents less, he can sell it for 10 cents less.

Mr. BASS. But he does not do that.

Mr. FORDNEY. But can he not do that?

Mr. BASS It is possible if he were working for charity; yes, sir.

Mr. FORDNEY. He does not give anything away, but if the law is changed he has saved 10 cents per hundred pounds.

Mr. BASS. He won't save that, because he is going to give me more money. To-day he beats me out of the parity.

Mr. FORDNEY. The consumer then pays it to benefit you?

Mr. BASS. I have not said so.

Mr. FORDNEY. If you get the 10 cents and the consumer pays it, it must benefit you.

Mr. BASS. I will tell you who gets it, sir.

Mr. FORDNEY. You have said you get it. You said you are going to get 10 cents more for your sugar.

Mr. BASS. No; I said I was going to avoid a 10-cent penalty.

Mr. FORDNEY. Well, you get it if you avoid it.

Mr. BASS. No, sir.

Mr. FORDNEY. If you pay it you are penalized, and if you do not pay it you are not penalized. Now, what difference is there between getting it and being penalized?

Mr. BASS. I have avoided a condition which prevents me from being penalized, and in doing that I am prevented from falling into the hands of the refiner.

Mr. FORDNEY. I submit the witness is not fair when he says he will get the 10 cents per hundred pounds and not be penalized that much.

The CHAIRMAN. I think we understand that, and we will draw our own conclusions.

Mr. BASS. I am beaten out of the parity, what you folks know as the Hamburg parity. For instance, my sugar comes from Santo Domingo, and it should net me in New York the equivalent of bringing sugar from somewhere else. I can not get that because I can not get anybody to bid against them. Only the refiners take my sugar, and that puts them in a condition where they can play all sorts of different interests against me. For instance, you will read in Willett & Gray: "The refiners are not in the market for San Domingo sugars to-day."

Mr. FORDNEY. Mr. Bass, Mr. Willett has testified and Dr. Wiley, Chief Chemist of the Department of Agriculture, has testified that the American people have become educated to the use of refined white sugar. Now, you are going to educate them to use your sugar which is not absolutely white; is that right?

Mr. BASS. No, sir; I am going to educate them to use the same sugar that Mr. Oxnard is handing them out in Louisiana, and I do not think he is poisoning them; is he?

Mr. HINDS. Mr. Oxnard is making a refined sugar in Louisiana.

Mr. BASS. Is he using bone black?

Mr. HINDS. No.

Mr. BASS. Then I do not think he has correctly used the word "refining." We consider when we take the juice from cane and keep on making and making and making, and put that out on the market, that is primary production. If at any time we stop and melt up what we have got, and filter and use bone black, that is refining, sir. But what is primary production is not refining, and it can not be considered as refining.

Mr. HINDS. Mr. Oxnard has said that he has to use very expensive machinery in Louisiana.

Mr. BASS. Just give us a chance to indulge in that expensive machinery.

Mr. FORDNEY. Mr. Oxnard has not testified he is putting his sugar on the market to the consumer; he is preparing to do that.

Mr. BASS. If I am mistaken I will cut Oxnard out, and I will say the Gramercy factory. I know that because I was there. There was a place called the Gramercy factory in Louisiana which made a high-grade, beautiful sugar.

Mr. FORDNEY. Was it refined sugar?

Mr. BASS. No, sir; it was primary-made sugar without any refining. They knew how to make sugar. Immediately the refiners bought up that place and installed a bone-black plant. This was the place where a bone-black plant was put in, on the sugar estate of Gramercy, and to give it a high-toned name they called it the Gramercy Refinery. They not only refined the sugars there, but took their neighbors' sugars

The truth was the Gramercy people could make sugar in competition with the refiners without any bone black.

Mr. FORDNEY. When was that?

Mr. BASS. Some time after 1900, whatever the date was when they put the machinery in the Gramercy place.

Mr. FORDNEY. That is when they were wiping out competition, so said?

Mr. BASS. I do not know what you call it, but they stopped the example of showing people how to make white sugar.

Mr. FORDNEY. That is not the condition to-day, so we have not any of that sugar.

Mr. BASS. Of course, they do not do that now.

Mr. HINDS. We have been given to understand here in some of the testimony that primary sugar was made in Louisiana by simply letting it drain. How do you make your primary sugar in Santo Domingo?

Mr. BASS. First, permit the remark that Louisiana has always been very far behind. The highest grade of sugar manufacture was in Cuba, where we have had to make sugar under adverse conditions, and use all skill, mechanical, chemical, and everything we could. We make sugar at once, as I say, without any bone black, simply hot purging.

Mr. HINDS. Now, what is hot purging?

Mr. BASS. That means when you have got your liquor so thick it is full of crystals of molasses, and the next thing is to separate the molasses from the crystals. That separation is called purging.

Mr. HINDS. You mean the liquor that is boiling in your boilers?

Mr. BASS. It has already been boiled. You have got it up to a thick consistency of crystals and molasses, and the next thing is to get the crystals away from the molasses. That particular act is called purging the sugars.

Mr. HINDS. What do you do that with?

Mr. BASS. With a centrifugal machine, a picture of which I showed you yesterday. That revolves around very rapidly, and the gauze is on the side and the centrifugal force pushes this up against the side, and the liquor runs through while the crystals remain on the inside. Then, if it is free purging, you do not have to do anything much to it, but if the primary canes have been full of gum or immature juice, or there has been what is called false grain gotten in there, it refuses to purge. The molasses does not go away very easily in that case. All we have to do is to put a little water in it.

Mr. HINDS. Is that the sugar we see referred to as Cuban centrifugals?

Mr. BASS. Cuban centrifugal means this same sugar I am talking about now, with the molasses very poorly taken away from it. For instance, the high skilled and the highest priced labor in Cuba to-day is employed in the art of taking the molasses and adding it into the pan so they make sugar just 96, and keep loading and carrying as much molasses to the New York market as it will stand. Those are the highest paid men on the island of Cuba to-day, people who know how to take the molasses and inject it into the pan. Those are called soft sugars. Certain places supply hard sugars and others soft sugars.

There is another thing about the 16 Dutch standard, and that is the second sugars. After we have rung off the first sirup it is still rich in matter which we can crystallize, so we take that and handle it a second time and from that we make second sugars. They will polarize anywhere from 88 to 92. Those are called second-grade sugars. Now, the refiner's logical function is to go out and buy those low sugars and make them high sugars and hand them to the American public. But instead of that if a cargo comes to New York and has second-grade sugars in it, they say "We do not want that cargo. Can you give us a cargo of all first sugars?" and they are discouraging the production of all second-grade sugars, and that is what caused the island of Cuba to import a great many high-grade chemists to try and handle all the sugars first. Then the sugar plantation makes what is called all first, but in making all first they run a chance of making 94 or 95 sugars, because they are carrying the seconds in with the first sugars. There are some sugar States that take the high-grade 97 sugars and they let them run down together in a bin and mechanically combine them and ship that to New York and get away with unloading the seconds on to the Americans with the first. The firsts then do not polarize 97. They are 95 or 96, but they have unloaded the second sugars in the same bag with the first.

TESTIMONY OF MR. ROBERT PATTERSON RITHET.

The witness was duly sworn by the chairman.

The CHAIRMAN. Mr. Rithet, will you give the committee your full name?

Mr. RITHET. Robert Patterson Rithet.

The CHAIRMAN. Your residence?

Mr. RITHET. San Francisco.

The CHAIRMAN. Your occupation?

Mr. RITHET. Merchant and president of the California & Hawaiian Sugar Refining Co.

The CHAIRMAN. How long have you been president of that company?

Mr. RITHET. Since it was started in 1897.

The CHAIRMAN Are you a large stockholder or a considerable stockholder in the company, besides being its president?

Mr. RITHET. I owned stock when it was started, but it was reconstructed some years ago, and the Sugar Factors Co., of Honolulu, own the control of the stock.

The CHAIRMAN. However, you are still its president?

Mr. RITHET. I am still its president, and there is some stock in my name.

The CHAIRMAN. Who are the principal owners of the company?

Mr. RITHET. The Sugar Factors Co., of Honolulu.

The CHAIRMAN. Is that a corporation?

Mr. RITHET. Yes.

The CHAIRMAN. The Sugar Factors Co., of Honolulu, owns this concern called the California & Hawaiian Sugar Refining Co.?

Mr. RITHET. And Col. Spaulding is an individual stockholder.

The CHAIRMAN. Who is Col. Spaulding?

Mr. RITHET. He is a Hawaiian sugar planter.

The CHAIRMAN. Who owns a majority of the stock?

Mr. RITHET. The Sugar Factors Co., of Honolulu.

The CHAIRMAN. Which is a corporation of the Hawaiian Islands?

Mr. RITHET. Yes.

The CHAIRMAN. And Col. Spaulding is a minority stockholder?

Mr. RITHET. Yes, sir.

The CHAIRMAN. Are there any other minority stockholders?

Mr. RITHET. I think those are all.

The CHAIRMAN. Those are the two stockholders?

Mr. RITHET. Yes, sir.

The CHAIRMAN. In what proportion do they own it?

Mr. RITHET. I think 50,000 shares is the capital of the company, $5,000,000, and Col. Spaulding of that owns about 5,800 shares.

The CHAIRMAN. Is he a large sugar planter?

Mr. RITHET. Well, he is not now. He used to be a large sugar planter.

The CHAIRMAN. Is he a stockholder in the Sugar Factors Co.?

Mr. RITHET. Yes, sir.

The CHAIRMAN. So that he owns an interest besides his interest as a stockholder in the refinery?

Mr. RITHET. Yes, sir.

The CHAIRMAN. Where does this company get its supply of raw sugar?

Mr. RITHET. From the Sugar Factors Co. and the allied plantations in the Hawaiian Islands.

The CHAIRMAN. Entirely?

Mr. RITHET. Well, not entirely. We have to buy some duty-paid sugar for certain trades; that is, the canning trade, which is entitled to a drawback on imports, and we can only use in that trade duty-paid sugar.

The CHAIRMAN. The bulk of your sugar, however, comes from the Hawaiian Islands, and from this Sugar Factors Co. and their allied plantations?

Mr. RITHET. Yes, sir; that is it.

The CHAIRMAN. Is Mr. John D. Spreckels interested in that company in any way?

Mr. RITHET. He is not; in no way whatever.

The CHAIRMAN. Have you any relations of any sort with the American Sugar Refining Co., and when I say "you" I mean your corporation?

Mr. RITHET. No; none whatever.

The CHAIRMAN. Do they own any interest, direct or indirect, in your corporation or its stock?

Mr. RITHET. No.

The CHAIRMAN. Have you any trade agreements with them of any kind whatever?

Mr. RITHET. None whatever.

The CHAIRMAN. Is there any apportionment of territory between you and them?

Mr. RITHET. None.

The CHAIRMAN. Do you agree with them as to what territory you shall sell your sugar in or they shall ship theirs in?

Mr. RITHET. No; we get all the business we can, and I suppose they do the same.

The CHAIRMAN. You do not consult with them about that?

Mr. RITHET. No, sir; not at all.

The CHAIRMAN. In what territory do you market your sugars?

Mr. RITHET. The Pacific coast territory and the Missouri River points.

The CHAIRMAN. You get as far east as the Missouri River points?

Mr. RITHET. Yes.

The CHAIRMAN. And cover all the intervening territory, to some extent; at least, as far as your production will permit?

Mr. RITHET. Yes, sir; I think there are 11 States in what we call Pacific coast territory.

The CHAIRMAN. Can you name them?

Mr. RITHET. California, Oregon, Washington, Idaho, Michigan, Montana, Wyoming, Utah, Nevada, and Colorado. Missouri is in another district. We call that the Missouri district, and the other district is the Pacific Coast district.

The CHAIRMAN. Do you get to Missouri?

Mr. RITHET. Yes, sir.

The CHAIRMAN. Any farther east than Missouri?

Mr. RITHET. Well, very rarely.

Mr. RAKER. Do you ship to Minnesota?

Mr. RITHET. I do not think so; not very much. We may ship there occasionally.

The CHAIRMAN. Mr. Rithet, were you president of the California & Hawaiian Sugar Co. in 1903?

Mr. RITHET. I was.

The CHAIRMAN. Do you remember making a contract with John D. Spreckels and William H. Hannam, directors of the Western Sugar Refining Co., in that year?

Mr. RITHET. No, sir; I do not. I remember having a contract with D. Y. Campbell, our lawyer.

The CHAIRMAN. A contract with D. Y. Campbell?

Mr. RITHET. Yes, sir.

The CHAIRMAN. I do not care to go into your contract with your own lawyers, but there has been some testimony given by Mr. John D. Spreckels, and I want to ask you if this is substantially true:

> In April, 1903, John D. Spreckels and William H. Hannam, both of whom were directors of the Western Sugar Refining Co., caused their company to enter into an agreement with the California & Hawaiian Sugar Refining Co., whereby it was provided that the California & Hawaiian Sugar Refining Co. should for three years from April, 1903, refrain from importing raw sugar and from manufacturing refined sugar from imported raw sugar, and from selling, shipping, or distributing throughout the several States and Territories of the United States any refined sugar, and permit Western Sugar Refining Co. to market or refine sugar manufactured by it from sugar beets, and to receive, use, and pay for all raw sugar thereafter to arrive from the Hawaiian Islands for California & Hawaiian Sugar Refining Co., for which it had contracted with certain planters, and Western Sugar Refining Co. was to pay California & Hawaiian Sugar Refining Co. for its refined sugars sold by it upon an agreed basis, and in addition to pay it $200,000 each year of the agreement.

Is that true?

Mr. RITHET. That is substantially correct; yes, sir. The names are not. I do not remember Hannam.

The CHAIRMAN. Did you hear of Spreckels in this transaction?

Mr. RITHET. Yes, sir; the transaction was really with the Western Sugar Refining Co.

The CHAIRMAN. And Spreckels represented the Western in this negotiation?

Mr. RITHET. Yes; and I represented the other company.

The CHAIRMAN. Is that a fair statement of what you did agree to?

Mr. RITHET. I think so.

The CHAIRMAN. You do not desire to correct that at all?

Mr. RITHET. No; except this, the way it is put there it would look as if the stipulations were easy to make, but they were not. It was not easily made, and it was not easily got.

The CHAIRMAN. You mean there was a good deal of difficulty about getting the contract made?

Mr. RITHET. Yes.

The CHAIRMAN. But you finally did get it made, after a good deal of difficulty, and it was substantially as I have outlined?

Mr. RITHET. Yes, sir; substantially so.

The CHAIRMAN. Now, let us continue:

From April, 1903, to April, 1906, after entering into this agreement, California & Hawaiian Sugar Refining Co. closed its factory and kept it closed and refrained from purchasing any raw sugar or sugar beets and manufacturing any raw sugar or sugar beets into refined sugar, and from selling, shipping, or distributing any refined sugar whatsoever.

Mr. RITHET. We did not operate at all during those years. It was under a lease, as I understood it.

The CHAIRMAN. That is substantially the contract, as I have outlined it to you?

Mr. RITHET. Yes, sir.

The CHAIRMAN. Now, Mr. Rithet, is there anything further you care to call the committee's attention to other than what has been covered by the questions I have asked?

Mr. RITHET. No; I do not know of anything, unless you want some information as to the working out of the arrangement and as to the fact we have been entirely independent ever since we started. We started as an independent institution and we have been independent ever since, except during that period, and we did that because we had reasons of necessity for doing it.

The CHAIRMAN. Would you mind telling the committee what those reasons were?

Mr. RITHET. I will be very glad to. We had been fighting, I think, for five years or more.

The CHAIRMAN. Fighting whom?

Mr. RITHET. The Western Sugar Refining Co.; that is, the company of John D. Spreckels.

The CHAIRMAN. And that is the company in which the American Sugar Refining Co. was also interested?

Mr. RITHET. Yes, sir; but it was called the Western Sugar Refining Co. We had been endeavoring to build up a trade and hold it. We had succeeded in doing that fairly well, and we had reserved for our purposes about 50,000 tons of sugar a year. Before starting the refinery, I might tell you, we were induced to do so because we were told by Mr. Spreckels, sr., who was then in control, that he would not make a contract with us. We had had a contract previous to that time for 15 or 20 years.

The CHAIRMAN. A contract of what kind?

Mr. RITHET. A contract for our raws. The object of our starting up was to find a market for our raws in the Pacific territory, which we claimed, being the nearest to us in the United States, we were entitled to; and they had been making a contract until, I think, it was in 1897. Then Mr. Spreckels said he would not give us a contract any longer.

The CHAIRMAN. How did he control the supply of raws?

Mr. RITHET. He did not control the supply of raws. He bought them.

The CHAIRMAN. And he would not let you have any of them?

Mr. RITHET. He would not give us a contract. He would not buy our raws.

The CHAIRMAN. He was running a refinery?

Mr. RITHET. Yes, sir.

The CHAIRMAN. And it was the only refinery there?

Mr. RITHET. Yes, sir.

The CHAIRMAN. And then you started this company?

Mr. RITHET. Yes, sir; to protect ourselves.

The CHAIRMAN. Why did you make this agreement about closing down your factory?

Mr. RITHET. We were short of working capital, and I wanted to have a little time to look over the situation and see what I could do, and I agreed to lease the property for three years.

The CHAIRMAN. Now, after you did establish this refinery, the California & Hawaiian Co., was the competition pretty fierce between you and the Western?

Mr. RITHET. Yes; and it is now.

The CHAIRMAN. Was it what you commonly call in trade parlance "cutthroat competition?"

Mr. RITHET. I think it was as near as you could get to it.

The CHAIRMAN. And that is what induced you to make this agreement with the Western?

Mr. RITHET. We had been in beets, too, and had lost money on beets, and while we never lost very much on the refining, we did lose money on the beets.

The CHAIRMAN. And the competition had kept you from making profitable returns?

Mr. RITHET. Yes; and it was getting more difficult all the time, and we thought we might play a little bit of the game, too.

The CHAIRMAN. So you leased out to your competitor?

Mr. RITHET. Yes; we had contracts with our own people for the raw sugar, and we compelled them to take those contracts.

The CHAIRMAN. In other words, you said: "Now take over our contracts and pay us $200,000 a year and we will not refine any sugar"?

Mr. RITHET. Yes; and they had to purchase their raw sugar from those who were associated with me in the refining, which was an important matter to us, because it shut out the others a little, and then they were easier subjects to work on when we wanted to reconstruct again; and we did reconstruct and we got through all right.

The CHAIRMAN. Have you a copy of that contract?

Mr. RITHET. Yes, sir.

The CHAIRMAN. Where is it?

Mr. RITHET. I do not know.

The CHAIRMAN. Did you not keep a copy for your company?

Mr. RITHET. I do not know. I will have to refer that to our lawyer. He got all that.

The CHAIRMAN. Do you know the facts about what has become of that contract?

Mr. RITHET. I do not.

The CHAIRMAN. Did you sign the contract?

Mr. RITHET. I think I did.

The CHAIRMAN. Did you not retain a copy of so important a document?

Mr. RITHET. I do not know. My copy probably was destroyed in the fire.

The CHAIRMAN. You remember signing the contract?

Mr. RITHET. That is my belief; yes, sir.

The CHAIRMAN. Now, do you have any recollection at all as to whether you retained a copy of it or not? Was not the contract executed in duplicate?

Mr. RITHET. I think if the copy was retained, it was probably retained by Mr. Campbell.

The CHAIRMAN. Was Mr. Campbell present at the negotiations?

Mr. RITHET. Well, no.

The CHAIRMAN. Was he present when the contract was signed?

Mr. RITHET. No; if a contract was made it was drawn by him and it was signed at his request, but we are quite at sea as to whether it was signed or not. I believe it was.

The CHAIRMAN. But if you kept a copy of it, you say it went to your lawyer with your other papers?

Mr. RITHET. Or else it was in our safe.

The CHAIRMAN. And in either event you think it was destroyed by the fire?

Mr. RITHET. I know it must have been destroyed.

The CHAIRMAN. Have you ever made any search for it?

Mr. RITHET. Yes, sir.

The CHAIRMAN. And you can not find it?

Mr. RITHET. I can not find any sign of it at all.

The CHAIRMAN. I have stated substantially what its contents were?

Mr. RITHET. Yes, sir.

Mr. MALBY. How many shares of stock are there in your company?

Mr. RITHET. Fifty thousand.

Mr. MALBY. And Col. Spaulding owns 5,800?

Mr. RITHET. Yes, sir.

Mr. MALBY. And the par value of the shares is $100 a share?

Mr. RITHET. Yes, sir.

Mr. HINDS. How did you happen to go back into the business after you once made this contract?

Mr. RITHET. That was part of the play I told you about. We were taking a rest for three years to get in shape to get back in again and fight.

Mr. HINDS. And you raised the money?

Mr. RITHET. Yes; we got new stockholders and we declined to renew the contract, absolutely, when the lease expired.

Mr. HINDS. And with this new financing and new encouragement, you have been able to hold your own?

Mr. RITHET. Oh, yes. We are as big as any of them now, but we have no affiliation and no association whatever with anybody.

The CHAIRMAN. Do you happen to know whether the Western is now owned by the American Co. or not?

Mr. RITHET. I saw only a newspaper report to that effect.

The CHAIRMAN. You do not know anything about that?

Mr. RITHET. No; I do not know about that.

Mr. RAKER. I understand, Mr. Rithet, the Hawaiian Sugar Factors Co. reduces the raw sugar in Hawaii?

Mr. RITHET. They do.

Mr. RAKER. And that company, the Sugar Factors Co., own all of the stock of the California & Hawaiian Refining Co. except 5,800 shares?

Mr. RITHET. Yes, sir.

Mr. RAKER. Do you not own a little of it?

Mr. RITHET. It is in my name, just to qualify me as a director.

Mr. RAKER. Who else is qualified as a director besides yourself?

Mr. RITHET. Warren D. Clark, Frank B. Anderson, Wallace M. Alexander, W. H. Huntington, August Hamburg, D. Y. Campbell, and myself.

Mr. RAKER. And this stock is simply held by them as trustees for the purpose of qualifying as directors?

Mr. RITHET. Yes, sir.

Mr. RAKER. The Sugar Factors Co. has a contract with the American Sugar Refining Co., which has heretofore been entered in the record?

Mr. RITHET. Yes, sir.

Mr. RAKER. That contract, as entered in the record, is correct, is it?

Mr. RITHET. I believe so. We have a stipulation of so much reserve for the Pacific coast in the American Sugar Refining Co.'s contract, and we do not have to get any authority from the American Sugar Refining Co. for our supplies.

Mr. RAKER. The point I was getting at is, you have contracted, or this Sugar Factors Co. has contracted all their sugar in the Hawaiian Islands except 50,000 tons——

Mr. RITHET (interposing). More than that; 150,000 tons now.

Mr. RAKER. All their sugar in the Hawaiian Islands except 150,000 tons, which you reserve exclusively for your factory?

Mr. RITHET. Yes, sir.

Mr. RAKER. Now, the Sugar Factors Co. do not sell to anyone else on the Pacific coast?

Mr. RITHET. No.

Mr. RAKER. Does the Western Sugar Refining Co. handle any of that sugar on the Pacific coast?

Mr. RITHET. We have sold to them once or twice, but not lately.

Mr. RAKER. Why do they not sell to the Western Sugar Refining Co.?

Mr. RITHET. Well, we are human.

Mr. RAKER. What is the object of that?

Mr. RITHET. They think, and perhaps it is a narrow-minded view to take, but they do take that view on the islands, that they might be assisting a competitor.

Mr. RAKER. If they sold it to the Western Sugar Refining Co.?

Mr. RITHET. Yes, sir; that is the only reason I know of.

Mr. RAKER. Can you give any distinction, so far as the real facts are concerned, between selling directly to the American Sugar Refining Co. all of the sugar except what you reserve and selling it to a company in which they own half of the stock? Can you draw any distinction at all?

Mr. RITHET. One is for the New York market and the other is for the Pacific coast market.

Mr. RAKER. I understand that; but what is the purpose of it? There must be something back of it?

Mr. RITHET. Just to prevent them from competing too strongly on the coast, that is all. I do not see anything else. The New York market and the San Francisco market are separate markets altogether.

Mr. RAKER. Is it not for the purpose of taking the extra quantity or supply of sugar that would land on the Pacific coast and bringing it East, so that the price on the Pacific coast is kept up by the present arrangement?

Mr. RITHET. No; I do not think the price has anything whatever to do with it.

Mr. RAKER. As a matter of fact, if it were not for this agreement between the Sugar Factors Co. and the American Sugar Refining Co., would not this sugar come to San Francisco naturally, because of its location, because of the freight rate, and a factory being there which could refine; and would not that great territory you speak of get sugar much cheaper than they now do owing to this contract with the American Sugar Refining Co.; and therefore this contract does keep up the price of sugar on the western coast.

Mr. RITHET. All the time I have been in the sugar business, for the last 25 or 30 years, the prices on the Pacific coast and New York have been regulated by the world's prices. I do not think it would affect the deliveries or the prices one particle if we were not to ship to New York. We have always shipped to New York, even before this company was in existence. We shipped to New York and marketed our supply in New York, because it is a larger market. The Pacific market is not sufficient to absorb the products of the islands now. They have grown so much they could not take it. And then we have the beets to be taken care of. They are marketed principally in the local market, and consequently we are shut out.

Mr. RAKER. That is just what I am trying to get at. Your prices and the prices of the Western Sugar Refining Co. are practically the same on the coast.

Mr. RITHET. Well, I will tell you about that. Of necessity, they must be the same.

Mr. RAKER. I do not know anything about the necessity, of course, and I just want the facts.

Mr. RITHET. Will you let me explain that?

Mr. RAKER. I will be pleased to have you explain it. I just want the facts.

Mr. RITHET. There are only two of us there. Now, there is a very limited market, and each one of us has our own customers. If we are 10 cents under the Western to-day, we will get all the business, and we can not take care of it. If the Western is 10 cents under us, they would get all the business, and I do not think they could take care of it for very long. We have fought that out, and I have never been able to make a scheme that would fit a position of that kind without going back to the old idea. For instance, we are selling to-day at 5.10 or 5.20 or 5.60; they will sell at 5.10 or 5.20 or 5.60, just as we are selling. If they move, we move; or if we move, they move, but we have to move together.

Mr. RAKER. Then, as a matter of fact, there is a tacit or gentlemen's understanding——

Mr. RITHET (interposing). None whatever, sir.

Mr. RAKER. Just one moment; I had not finished my question. In your business relations you work so that the price will be the same?

Mr. RITHET. No; we do not. We are compelled to work according to the conditions of the business.

Mr. RAKER. I understand that.

Mr. RITHET. You are making us out to do that by arrangement.

Mr. RAKER. Oh, no.

Mr. RITHET. And we do not do that, because we are as far apart as the poles.

Mr. RAKER. I do not want to assume that, and I am not assuming that.

Mr. RITHET. Well, don't, please.

Mr. RAKER. But it comes about in some way, by virtue of publishing reports or telegrams, or something else, and you know the price of sugar at the other place, and you both sell at the same price to avoid any rush upon either one of the businesses.

Mr. RITHET. No; it is not that. It is simply because we can not do otherwise.

Mr. RAKER. I can not understand how you can both keep at just exactly the same price.

Mr. RITHET. We don't. Sometimes we are up and sometimes they are up. If we go up, they follow; and if they go down, we have to follow. There are only two of us in the business. The prices have been kept pretty well, anyway, and I have never had to complain that they were too high or too low, either. We would have been nearly crowded out of business if it had not been we had quite strong support.

Mr. RAKER. During the high prices of sugar you both sold at the same price?

Mr. RITHET. We made no money at all last year. We did not get the benefit of the prices at all on the Pacific coast.

Mr. RAKER. But you sold at practically the same price?

Mr. RITHET. We can not help it.

Mr. RAKER. And the reason you did not get any benefit out of the raise was because you had sold in advance?

Mr. RITHET. Yes.

Mr. RAKER. And you think by virtue of this arrangement with the Hawaiian people and the American Sugar Refining Co. being able to place that quantity of sugar so as not to overstock the market, it keeps an even price for the beet-sugar people as well as yourselves in the West?

Mr. RITHET. No; we have no idea of that kind at all. We are marketing our own product, and we are marketing it in the way it will accomplish the best results for ourselves; that is to say, we find it cheaper for us to make a contract with a responsible firm like the American Sugar Refining Co. I may tell you that when the first contract of that kind was made I was on the committee, and I made the first contract with B. H. Howell Sons & Co. in New York for our product to be shipped to the Atlantic coast here. That contract was for three years, and it was carried out all right, but B. H. Howell Sons & Co. had come forward when the next contract was before us and had to say they could not handle it.

Mr. RAKER. Did I understand you correctly in saying that if it was not for this arrangement between the Hawaiian Factors Co. and the American Sugar Refining Co. this great quantity of sugar would come to the port of San Francisco, primarily speaking?

Mr. RITHET. No.

Mr. RAKER. And you would get more sugar than could be consumed?

Mr. RITHET. We would if we shipped all our stock there.

Mr. RAKER. You would get more sugar there?

Mr. RITHET. And would have to pay the railroad freight on it, but now we do not do that. It is a matter of economy in handling the product; that is all it is. It is no combination and no understanding.

Mr. RAKER. I am not assuming that, Mr. Rithet.

Mr. RITHET. I know; but you have asked your questions a little that way, and so I was a little careful.

Mr. RAKER. This contract does prevent that sugar coming into San Francisco.

Mr. RITHET. I do not think that is the proper way to put it. We can not market it there, and we can in New York, consequently we send it to New York.

Mr. RAKER. I will put the question in this way: The contract is that that sugar is to be delivered in New York?

Mr. RITHET. Yes, sir.

Mr. RAKER. And not delivered in San Francisco?

Mr. RITHET. Yes.

Mr. RAKER. Now, if it was not delivered in New York, leaving out the freight rate for a moment, the consequence would be there would be more sugar thrown on the local market than San Francisco could use, and that would also cover the western territory?

Mr. RITHET. Yes.

Mr. RAKER. And consequently would bring down the price of beet sugar as well as refined sugar which is shipped there?

Mr. RITHET. We never suppose anything in the sugar business. We have to take it just as we find it. We have to know what the effect is going to be, and we have got to figure that out. We are not philanthropists. We have to go where the best market is for our product, and we do not consider whether it is going to effect the beet or any other product. We just go there because it is the best market. There is no other market we could go to and do as well.

Mr. RAKER. Would not the Hawaiian people get more for their product if it was delivered at the port of San Francisco instead of shipping it to New York?

Mr. RITHET. It would depend upon what they could sell it there for.

Mr. RAKER. Ordinarily, they would have to send it by freight from San Francisco around to New York, and taking the freight from the price they get in New York, if they get the same price at San Francisco as at New York, it would give them more net for their sugar, would in not?

Mr. RITHET. You could not market it there. We have to consider that question. We can not take a theory. If we sent it to San Francisco we would not have a market there for it. Theoretically you probably are all right, but we as sugar men would not want to do that kind ot thing unless it was going to pay.

The CHAIRMAN. If you marketed more than the San Francisco territory would absorb, then the price would naturally go down.

Mr. RITHET. It would have to be sent to New York by a much more expensive route, because once in San Francisco it would probably have to go by rail to New York, and sometimes we do take more there than we can market, and that is when we get into the Missouri River territory. We market all we can at Missouri River points in competition with the Eastern refiners. I think you will find that out. I wish you were in the business, and then you would find that out.

The CHAIRMAN. There was another refinery in San Francisco which closed down some two years ago, was there not?

Mr. RITHET. The American; yes, sir.

The CHAIRMAN. That refinery was established there for the purpose of refining sugar to supply the Western States?

Mr. RITHET. It was the same crowd. The original founders had died, and I had come in as a younger element and took up the fight. That is all there was to that.

Mr. MALBY. I understand you to say you ship such quantity of sugar to San Francisco as seems in the judgment of your company to be sufficient for that market, and that the balance you find a market for where you can?

Mr. RITHET. Yes, sir.

Mr. MALBY. Of course, when you have supplied the California market, that is all there is of it, I take it?

Mr. RITHET. When we have supplied the California market, in order to make the production as much as possible, up to the capacity of our refinery, we then refine what we can market in the Missouri River territory.

Mr. MALBY. When I speak of California I mean the States contiguous to it, as well as California.

Mr. RITHET. We do that for the purpose of reducing the cost.

Mr. MALBY. My idea is when you have supplied that market, that is all there is to it. There is no use clogging the market by putting on more than the market will absorb.

Mr. RITHET. That is right.

Mr. MALBY. And hence one of the reasons you sell in the New York market is because the Pacific coast market will not take any more?

Mr. RITHET. Yes, sir; you are quite right.

Mr. MALBY. And there is another reason, perhaps, which occurs to me, and that is, if you landed all your sugar in California there would be the question of freight rates to be considered in getting out the surplus.

Mr. RITHET. That is it. We have that to do now.

Mr. MALBY. You actually do send your raw sugars to New York by Tehuantepec?

Mr. RITHET. Yes; by Tehuantepec.

Mr. MALBY. How much does it cost you to ship your raw sugars that way?

Mr. RITHET. I think about $9 a ton.

Mr. MALBY. And what would be the overland rate?

Mr. RITHET. To the Missouri River it is 55 cents, and that would be about $12 a ton.

Mr. MALBY. If you had to send it to New York, what would be the freight?

Mr. RITHET. I do not know what it would be to New York. It would not be very much more, about 55 cents or 50 cents on raw sugar.

Mr. MALBY. Is there in fact any combination between you and the American Sugar Refining Co. or other companies by which you do not put more sugar on the San Francisco market? To my mind the reason you do not do that is because a man conducts his business along those lines which he regards as the most profitable, perhaps.

Mr. RITHET. That is exactly what the sugar men do.

Mr. MALBY. And a man will not attempt to sell 100,000 tons of sugar in San Francisco if there is no market for it?

Mr. RITHET. No, sir; that is the point, exactly.

Mr. MALBY. And that would perhaps be an answer to the suggestion as to why you send it to New York?

Mr. RITHET. Yes, sir.

Mr. MALBY. Not that there is a combination, but trade conditions lead you to believe as a business proposition that is the thing to do?

Mr. RITHET. Yes; that is exactly it.

Mr. MALBY. I think Mr. Claus Spreckels testified he endeavored to secure some sugar from your company or from the Sugar Factors Co. and that he offered you a better price than the American Sugar Refining Co. was offering and that you would not take it.

Mr. RITHET. That is a mistake; that is a misstatement.

Mr. MALBY. Were you present at the time?

Mr. RITHET. I think I was the man he complained of. I was not on the committee, but I was there in an advisory position with the committee from the islands. I suppose when you talk about Mr. Claus Spreckels you mean Gus Spreckels.

Mr. MALBY. C. A. Spreckels.

Mr. RITHET. Yes.

Mr. MALBY. He testified as follows:

> Mr. SPRECKELS. At the time I was negotiating with them, they had no contract.
> Mr. MALBY. When was that?
> Mr. SPRECKELS. About five years ago.
> Mr. MALBY. And they had no contract at that time?
> Mr. SPRECKELS. No, sir. The committee of the Factors Co., which was appointed to come on to New York and negotiate with the refiners in New York for the purchase of their product, came to me and I offered to buy it, and was unable to get one pound.
> Mr. MALBY. To whom did they sell it at that time?
> Mr. SPRECKELS. Sold it to the American Sugar Refining Co.
> Mr. MALBY. Did you offer the same price?
> Mr. SPRECKELS. I offered to give them a better price.
> Mr. MALBY. A better price than the American Sugar Refining Co. offered?
> Mr. SPRECKELS. Yes, sir; I said I would better any price they might offer.
> Mr. MALBY. Was the declination to sell based upon any question about your financial standing, or simply because they did not want to sell to you?
> Mr. SPRECKELS. No, sir; I volunteered the statement that, in order that there might be no question about the financial standing, I would give any bond from any bank they might designate, and that they would be paid accordingly.
> Mr. MALBY. Was that an offer to purchase the entire output?
> Mr. SPRECKELS. Or that part of it which they should control.
> Mr. MALBY. Was it conditioned that you should receive it all?
> Mr. SPRECKELS. No, sir; I was ready to take all or any part of it. Their objection was we could not handle it all. I said, "We will take any part of it, but, for your information, we can handle it all and I will handle it all."

Did you have any such negotiation or consultation with Mr. C. A. Spreckels?

Mr. RITHET. I fancy there is some mistake about that in some way. At the time he refers to there the contract was in existence, but it was about to expire in the following year, and we generally renewed the contract a year previous, because we have to ship in March and begin in February and January. We always made our contract a little in advance of the expiration of the previous contract. I was here at that time, and I had some conversation with Mr. C. A. Spreckels.

Mr. MALBY. That would not be wholly inconsistent with Mr. Spreckles's statement.

Mr. RITHET. I was just coming to that. He said we had no contract.

The CHAIRMAN. Well, if the contract was about to expire, it amounts to about the same thing.

Mr. RITHET. I had some conversation with him about that, although, as I said, I was not on the committee, but I was here in an advisory position.

The CHAIRMAN. You were with the committee there at the time he speaks of?

Mr. RITHET. No: at that interview it was alone with me.

The CHAIRMAN. Alone with you?

Mr. RITHET. Yes. I do not know how many conversations he had with the committee, but he called me into his office and I had a conversation with him, and he wanted to get a chance to bid on the contract. I said: "What will you give, Mr. Spreckels? What will I say to the committee you will pay for the sugar?" He said: "Oh, you go and see the American and come back and see me." I said: "We do not do that kind of business; and I am not going to do anything of the kind;" and we did not go near Mr. Spreckels again, and I consider we were perfectly justified, when he refused to give us a bid in the first instance, and we went over to the American and got terms which were satisfactory.

Mr. MALBY. Then he made no bid whatever to you?

Mr. RITHET. No.

Mr. MALBY. At that time or any other time?

Mr. RITHET. Never.

Mr. MALBY. Did he make a bid to your committee that you know of?

Mr. RITHET. Not that I know of.

Mr. MALBY. Did your committee report back to you that any price had been named by Mr. Spreckels?

Mr. RITHET. No, sir.

The CHAIRMAN. Did he offer to raise any price the American offered?

Mr. RITHET. I do not know what he would have done in that way, but we do not do business in that way. I would not go to a concern like the American Sugar Refining Co. and say: "Now, we want our price for this," and name the terms we would take, and then get them to say they would agree to that and then go to another buyer. I would not do that.

The CHAIRMAN. Would you not ask different people to bid against each other?

Mr. RITHET. Yes; but I would not ask Mr. Gus Spreckels, if you want my opinion.

The CHAIRMAN. Why not?

Mr. RITHET. Because he is a difficult man to handle.

Mr. HINDS. Did he have the capacity to take your product?

Mr. RITHET. I do not think he did at that time. I am sure he did not. I think we would have had a fight on every shipment we delivered to him if we had gone to him, and we do not want that. We sugar men are peaceable men.

Mr. FORDNEY. Mr. Rithet, you say there are two refining companies on the Pacific coast—your own firm and some other firm?

Mr. RITHET. Yes, sir; the Western Sugar Refining Co.

Mr. FORDNEY. What proportion of the sugar consumed in the 11 States you have mentioned do you produce?

Mr. RITHET. I think our capacity is about the same as their capacity now.

Mr. FORDNEY. You are about equal?

Mr. RITHET. Yes. Your point is very well taken, Mr. Fordney. Mr. Knapp brought that out, but it was given confidentially, and I could not tell you what the proportions were sold in the profitable part of the territory of the Pacific coast, and what was sacrificed, as we call it, on the Missouri River, but Mr. Knapp had it in that way, and I think he was convinced, at least I imagine so, when he saw that, that there was absolutely no evidence of combination in any way, because I infer we did rather more of the profitable business than they did, and they had been there for a great many years and had the prestige of their association with their father in the business and his influence, and I think we did pretty well to catch up.

Mr. FORDNEY. Mr. Rithet, if you produced the same proportion of that sugar, you could bother the other man, or the other man could bother you, and one must watch the other as to the price asked for the sugar?

Mr. RITHET. Absolutely.

Mr. FORDNEY. You could not sell for more than the other man asked?

Mr. RITHET. No, sir.

Mr. FORDNEY. If you were the smaller dealer and offered sugar below his price, you could bother him or make him come down to your price?

Mr. RITHET. Absolutely; but we have to keep our customers, Mr. Fordney, and customers are very valuable in a market where there are only two sellers, as perhaps you know.

Mr. FORDNEY. I understand that. You can market no more sugar than can be consumed in that particular territory, and it would be futile to bring more raw sugars to San Francisco?

Mr. RITHET. Yes, sir.

Mr. FORDNEY. Because if you did bring more to that territory than was consumed there, your freight East is double what it would be to the Missouri River points?

Mr. RITHET. Direct from the point of shipment, yes.

Mr. FORDNEY. How long did your company operate before you entered into this lease?

Mr. RITHET. From 1897 until 1903.

Mr. FORDNEY. 1903, at the time you entered into the lease?

Mr. RITHET. Yes, sir.

Mr. FORDNEY. You say you entered into the lease for various reasons; first, you were short of capital?

Mr. RITHET. Yes, sir.

Mr. FORDNEY. And wanted time to better your financial condition?

Mr. RITHET. Yes; to reconstruct.

Mr. FORDNEY. And you continued during the time of that lease to manufacture beet sugar?

Mr. RITHET. No, sir; when the lease was made, it was in March, and we had already planted part of that year's crop of beets, and I arranged with the Western that we would run our beet plant, but that we would dissolve our selling organization, and they would sell out beet sugar, and we were to pay them a quarter of a cent a pound, which we did.

Mr. FORDNEY. For selling those sugars?

Mr. RITHET. Yes, sir.

Mr. FORDNEY. During the time that lease was in existence, three years, they paid you $200,000 per year for the lease?

Mr. RITHET. Yes.

Mr. FORDNEY. They paid that in quarterly payments. I think that was mentioned here.

Mr. RITHET. Yes, sir; they did.

Mr. FORDNEY. And you did recuperate and prepare to go into the business again at the end of that lease?

Mr. RITHET. We did.

Mr. FORDNEY. But in the meantime you succeeded in getting a very satisfactory contract with Mr. Spreckels to take your raw sugars?

Mr. RITHET. Yes, sir.

Mr. FORDNEY. I presume that was one of the reasons for making the lease?

Mr. RITHET. We got everything covered that we had any liability on. We were liable for the raws, and we made him take them over.

Mr. FORDNEY. Have you any further explanation along the line I have just asked you which you would like to make?

Mr. RITHET. No; I think I have covered the ground fairly well. Of course, we were in a hole a little, as I thought; and as a prudent measure I thought it best to take time and recover my breath, as it were, and we did that, and since we have got started again we have absolutely refused to make such an arrangement.

Mr. FORDNEY. The San Francisco market could not take and does not take all of the Hawaiian raws?

Mr. RITHET. Oh, no.

Mr. FORDNEY. A large amount must go to the Atlantic coast?

Mr. RITHET. They produce now 600,000 tons, practically.

Mr. FORDNEY. And you aim to bring sufficient raws to the Pacific coast for the market on that coast?

Mr. RITHET. Yes, sir; exactly.

Mr. HINDS. Mr. Rithet, it is quite a difficult matter to find a customer, even in New York, who can take your whole product, is it not?

Mr. RITHET. Yes, sir; I think the American Sugar Refining Co. are about the only people who could.

Mr. HINDS. Arbuckles could not?

Mr. RITHET. Arbuckles said they could not.

Mr. HINDS. I believe they so testified in a hearing three years ago?

Mr. RITHET. Yes, sir.

Mr. FORDNEY. It is human nature in every line of business, is it not, to get the highest price obtainable, at least up to a reasonable profit?

Mr. RITHET. Yes, sir.

Mr. FORDNEY. And that is what you practice in the sugar business?

Mr. RITHET. Exactly.

The CHAIRMAN. Mr. Rithet, is it true or not that when the beet crop comes on the market it affects the price of sugar?

Mr. RITHET. It has no effect on it whatever. The price is regulated by the world's price in Europe, and you can not get away from it; and the price is regulated by supply and demand, barring occasionally a few rich men who speculate in sugar and who jump the price up beyond what it ought to be very often; but we have nothing to do with that whatever.

Mr. FORDNEY. During this last season we claim our domestic crop in Michigan did have some effect upon the price of sugar——

Mr. RITHET. I beg Michigan's pardon.

Mr. FORDNEY (continuing). As quoted on New York markets—European raws, in other words. There was a time when our refined sugar was being sold for less money than European raws were quoted at in New York.

Mr. RITHET. That is true. It is a very strange thing, and I am sorry we did not get the benefit of it. We had a very bad year last year, and it was altogether on account of the speculative people who took charge of the market entirely.

Mr. HINDS. Mr. Rithet, the testimony has been that beet sugar generally sells 10 or 20 points under cane sugar?

Mr. RITHET. Yes.

Mr. HINDS. But that is not true on the Pacific coast?

Mr. RITHET. Oh, yes; it is.

Mr. HINDS. The Pacific beet sugar sells cheaper than the cane?

Mr. RITHET. Yes.

Mr. HINDS. Does not that bring down the price a little for you?

Mr. RITHET. No; we buy some beet sugar, too.

The CHAIRMAN. But the merchant sells it all to his consumer at the same price; is not that true?

Mr. RITHET. I do not know. We do not sell it that way. We have to brand our cane sugar and our beet sugar differently, altogether.

The CHAIRMAN. You mean the refiners do?

Mr. RITHET. Yes.

The CHAIRMAN. Do you know how that affects the consumer; whether if I buy a dollar's worth of sugar I get the same amount, whether it is beet or cane sugar?

Mr. RITHET. Go for the retailers or the wholesalers; they are the parties who are getting the benefit of it.

Mr. HINDS. Somewhere that 10 or 20 points difference between beet and cane sugar on the Pacific coast is absorbed before it gets to the consumer.

Mr. RITHET. It does not go to the refiner.

Mr. HINDS. The consumer does not get the benefit of that, does he?

Mr. RITHET. I really do not know. I do not buy enough to know, and I do not know whether they sell beet sugar for any less than cane or not. I could not answer that question, but I fancy the difference goes into the hands of the jobbers, if you want my opinion.

The CHAIRMAN. Have you a table showing the range of prices?

Mr. RITHET. I have charts here which I would be glad to leave with you.

The CHAIRMAN. You may file them as a part of your remarks. What do the charts show?

Mr. RITHET. The range of prices since 1906.

The CHAIRMAN. San Francisco prices?

Mr. RITHET. San Francisco and New York prices.

The CHAIRMAN. Refined and raw sugar?

Mr. RITHET. Yes, sir.

The CHAIRMAN. The charts cover that period of time for those two markets on those two grades of sugar?

Mr. RITHET. Yes, sir; showing the New York market price of the day for raws and refined and the market price for refined at San Francisco, and the price at which we sold our sugars from day to day, when we did not get the list price.

The CHAIRMAN. Gentlemen, the committee has about concluded its investigation of this subject, and so far as we are now advised there will be no further hearings. Mr. Fordney will present certain information which will be printed as a part of to-day's record.

Mr. FORDNEY. The information will show the prices received by the farmers for beets in France and Germany. I will also submit a table showing the advantages or disadvantages of the rates received by sugar manufacturers in the West; also the difference in the purity of the sugar in the beets as between this country and Germany.

The papers referred to are as follows:

WASHINGTON, D. C., *January 17, 1912.*

Hon. J. W. FORDNEY,
House of Representatives, Washington, D. C.

DEAR SIR: Agreeable to the verbal request of Hon. Thomas W. Hardwick, chairman of the Special Committee on the Investigation of the American Sugar Refining Co. and Others, I hand you herewith the following documents relative to the freight protection enjoyed by sugar manufacturers in different sections of the United States:

1. A letter from the secretary of the Michigan Sugar Co., showing that their average freight protection is 5.82 cents per 100 pounds.
2. A letter from C. S. Morey, of the Great Western Sugar Co., with accompanying tables, showing that the average freight protection enjoyed by the Great Western Sugar Co. is 2.3 cents per 100 pounds.
3. A letter and tables from Thomas R. Cutler, vice president and general manager of the Utah-Idaho Sugar Co., showing that instead of having a protection, they have an actual net average freight handicap of 2.85 cents per 100 pounds.
4. A letter from Henry H. Rolapp, president of the Amalgamated Sugar Co., Ogden, Utah, stating that they do not have any freight protection, but that they have a net average freight handicap which is nearer 5 cents than 3 cents per 100 pounds.
5. A letter from F. B. Case, general manager of the Southern California Sugar Co., located in Santa Ana, Cal., showing that they do not have a freight protection, but that they have a net average freight handicap equal to — cents per 100 pounds.

Yours, respectfully,

F. R. HATHAWAY.

WASHINGTON, D. C., *January 17, 1912.*

Hon. J. W. FORDNEY,
House of Representatives, Washington, D. C.

DEAR SIR: As per your verbal request, I beg leave to state that a thorough examination of the books of the Michigan Sugar Co. shows that the amount of freight protection enjoyed by that company in marketing its entire crop of sugar manufactured during the season of 1909–10 was 5.82 cents per 100 pounds of sugar.

Yours, respectfully,

F. R. HATHAWAY,
Secretary Michigan Sugar Co.

THE GREAT WESTERN SUGAR CO.,
Denver, Colo., December 27, 1911.

Mr. F. R. HATHAWAY,
Secretary Michigan Sugar Co., Detroit, Mich.

DEAR SIR: I beg to acknowledge receipt of yours 18th. In reply to same, I have had our auditor figure up what rate of protection we received on our total production for the year 1907–8, to which I am having affidavit made, and will deliver to Mr. Hamlin, who will be here to-morrow. This copy is sent for your information. The original, with affidavit attached, Mr. Hamlin can present to the committee when he is called to the stand.

Thanking you for calling our attention to this important matter.

Yours, very truly,

C. S. MOREY, *President.*

Freight rates on granulated sugar (carloads).

	To Missouri River.	To Iowa.		To Minnesota.	To Chicago.	To St. Louis.	To Texas.	To Colorado.	To east of Chicago.												
		Mississippi River points.	Interior Iowa.						Buffalo.	Pittsburgh.	Cleveland.	Columbus.	Cincinnati.	Akron.	Toledo.	Sandusky.	Evansville.	Terre Haute.	Detroit.	Indianapolis.	Other points.
Rate from—																					
New York		29		30	22½				[1] 15	[1] 15	[1] 16½	[1] 17½	[1] 18½	[1] 17½	[1] 17½	[1] 17½		[1] 23½	[1] 17½	[1] 21½	[1] 18
New Orleans	33		34½			18½	46										[1] 18½				
San Francisco								55													
(Basing rate: Lowest rate is shown whether from New York, New Orleans, or San Francisco.)																					
Rate from Colorado (Great Western Sugar Co. factories)	25	30	30	30	25	25	49	10	[2] 43	[2] 43	[2] 40	[2] 40	[2] 40	[2] 40	[2] 38	[2] 39½	[2] 35	[2] 36½	[2] 38	[2] 36½	[2] 40
Average freight differences	[3] 8	[3] 1⅞		....	[4] 2½	[4] 6½	[4] 3	[3] 45	[4] 21												
Number of bags shipped from Great Western Sugar Co. factories	544,212	242,264		198,475	965,789	150,075	143,270	205,687	211,183												
	$45,536.96	$4,239.62		....	$24,144.73	$9,754.88	$4,298.10	$92,559.15	$44,348.43												

[1] Average rate, 18 cents. [2] Average rate, 39 cents. [3] Freight protection. [4] Freight absorption.

Net freight protection on 2,462,480 bags, based on existing freight rates. Total production for 1907–8 was 2,660,955 bags, but 198,475 bags would have received no protection nor had to absorb any freight. $67,789.57, or 2,462,480 bags at $0.028 per bag.

UTAH-IDAHO SUGAR CO.,
Salt Lake City, Utah, December 29, 1911.

Mr. F. R. HATHAWAY,
Michigan Sugar Co., Detroit, Mich.

DEAR SIR: Referring to your favor of the 18th instant, I append a statement on the lines that you spoke of which shows an actual deficiency over protection of $23,842.97, taking as a basis the central points of large consumption in each State. If we were to work this out to the individual shipment, I believe the deficit would show considerably over 3 cents per bag. In other words, instead of having an advantage of 65 cents, as Mr. Lowry claims in his testimony, we have a deficiency of over 3 cents per bag.

I have taken the fiscal year 1910–11, from the 1st day of March, 1910, to the 28th of February, 1911, which is an average year, so far as the sugar company's business is concerned:

	Number of bags sold.	Protection.
		Cents.
Utah	113,747	43
Nevada	2,456	46
Idaho	47,558	72
Montana	2,100	56
Wyoming	1,310	20

Making a total freight protection of $86,175.53.

I have taken our distribution in the following States, in which our shipments show a freight deficit:

	Number of bags sold.	Freight deficit.
		Cents.
Illinois	15,434	27½
Iowa	258,941	15½
Nebraska	99,400	18
North Dakota	3,000	21½
South Dakota	26,400	16½
Kansas	99,680	12
Missouri	50,770	18
Minnesota	57,000	20
Wisconsin	600	35
Oklahoma	55,750	18

Making a total freight deficit of $110,018.40, or a surplus of deficiency over protection of $23,842.97, which divided amongst the total number of bags sold, namely, 835,846, shows a deficit of .0285 cents per bag.

Yours, very truly,

THOMAS R. CUTLER,
Vice President and General Manager.

OFFICE OF AMALGAMATED SUGAR CO.,
Ogden, Utah, December 29, 1911.

Mr. H. R. HATHAWAY,
Care of Michigan Sugar Co., Detroit, Mich.

MY DEAR MR. HATHAWAY: Further answering yours of December 18, regarding Mr. Lowry's testimony before the Hardwick committee, desire to say that I have made diligent search, but it would be of so little value to you to get what few figures I have that I have given up the attempt.

I find, however, that Mr. Geoghegan has sent a letter to Mr. Cutler, a copy of which I inclose, and to a certain extent that covers our condition, except that we are still worse off than the Utah-Idaho, because we have been able to sell but very little sugar in the State of Idaho, where the 72-cent protection is given that company, for the reason that they have factories at various places throughout the State and patriotism seems to induce the merchants to want to patronize a firm with factories in their own State. So that I should imagine that our freight deficit will be nearer 5 cents than 3 cents.

I am very pleased to have you take this matter up in your characteristic forceful way and hope you will just overwhelm Mr. Lowry with figures, because he knows he was incorrect in his statement. I am sending a copy of this letter to Mr. Hamlin.

Wishing you the compliments of the season, I remain,

Yours, very truly, HENRY H. ROLOFF.

GEOGHEGAN BROKERAGE CO.,
Salt Lake City, Utah, December 28, 1911.

Mr. THOS. R. CUTLER,
Salt Lake City.

DEAR SIR: Referring to letter of Mr. Hathaway, under date of December 18, drawing attention to evidence given by Mr. Lowry before the Hardwick committee on December 9, in which Mr. Lowry claims that the average advantage which the domestic beet-sugar factory has in the way of freight is 25 cents per 100 pounds, note that he goes on to state that this is probably too low, especially as far as the western factories are concerned; that their protection is larger than that—65 cents and so on. Now I have taken the fiscal year 1910–11—that is the period from the 1st of March, 1910, to the 28th of February, 1911—which is an average year so far as the sugar company's business is concerned, and find that during that time our distribution was as follows:

	Number bags sold.	Protection.
		Cents.
Utah	113,747	43
Nevada	2,456	46
Idaho	47,558	72
Montana	2,100	50
Wyoming	1,310	20

Making a total freight protection of $86,175.53. I have taken our distribution in the following States, in which our shipments show a freight deficit:

	Number bags sold.	Freight deficit.
		Cents.
Illinois	15,434	27½
Iowa	258,941	15½
Nebraska	99,400	18
North Dakota	3,080	21½
South Dakota	26,409	16½
Kansas	99,680	12
Missouri	50,770	18
Minnesota	57,900	20
Wisconsin	600	35
Oklahoma	55,750	18

Making a total freight deficit of $110,018.40, or a surplus of deficiency over protection of $23,842.97, which, divided amongst the total number of bags sold, namely, 835,846, shows a deficit of 0.0285 cent per bag.

In arriving at these conclusions, I take as a basis the central points of large consumption in each State. As a matter of fact, if we were to work this out to the individual shipment, I believe the deficit would show considerably over 3 cents per bag. In other words, instead of having an advantage of 65 cents, as Mr. Lowry claims in his testimony, we have a deficiency of over 3 cents per bag.

Yours, very truly, JOS. GEOGHEGAN.

WASHINGTON, D. C., *January 18, 1912.*

Hon. JOSEPH W. FORDNEY,
House of Representatives, Washington, D. C.

DEAR SIR: We desire very much to have presented to the committee, in order that we may go into the record, a statement of the freight rates condition as existing in California.

We manufacture in the State a larger amount of sugar than is consumed. We therefore are compelled to ship our surplus product to some nonproducing consuming section. Distances in California are great, and we have no low freight rates on sugar. Our lowest rate is 10 cents a hundred in a market in which we sell about one-sixth of our output. The balance, or five-sixths, goes to a market where our freight rate will average 60 cents a hundred. It may be stated that we enjoy no benefits from our 10-cent rate, because while we ship to one jobbing point against the 17½-cent basing rate from San Francisco, a larger amount is shipped into San Francisco at the same or higher rate to the basing point. We must, therefore, be satisfied to ship five-sixths of our sugar to a 60-cent freight rate market and sell the other sixth at the basing point. In the 60-cent market we meet the New Orleans and New York rate, so that we may have a benefit of about 25 cents to be deducted from our 60 cents; therefore our sugar is marketed at a freight cost of from 30 to 35 cents. This applies to the beet-sugar factories of California and to the refineries of California, in so far as they market their surplus on the Missouri River.

We would like, therefore, to have it appear that we bear the 25 to 30 cent rate without any compensating advantages.

Very truly, yours,

F. B. Case,
Manager, Southern California Sugar Co., Santa Ana, Cal.

Department of Commerce and Labor,
Office of the Secretary,
Washington, January 13, 1912.

Sir: In compliance with your recent verbal request, made to the Chief of the Bureau of Statistics of this department, I hand you inclosed herewith two tables, taken from official sources, showing the quantities of sugar beets worked up in German factories and the average factory prices paid for these beets in the open market during the seasons 1904–5 to 1910–11, also similar table for France showing the weight of sugar beets worked up in French factories and the average prices paid for these beets during the sugar seasons 1902–3 to 1909–10, the latest year for which official French figures are available.

Respectfully,

Benj. S. Cable,
Acting Secretary.

Hon. J. W. Fordney,
House of Representatives, Washington, D. C.

Factory prices of sugar beets in France: 1902–3 to 1909–10.

[Data taken from the Official Bulletins de Statistique published by the French Ministry of Finance.]

Departments.	Weight of the beets worked up		Average price.	
	Metric tons.	Short tons.	Per metric ton.	Per short ton.
			Francs.	*Dollars.*
Aisne	1,475,392	1,626,339	23.70	4.15
Ardennes	91,921	101,324	24.03	4.21
Nord	1,051,694	1,159,293	25.75	4.51
Oise	694,603	765,668	23.37	4.09
Pas-de-Calais	747,496	823,972	25.30	4.43
Seine-et-Marne	414,303	456,690	23.25	4.07
Seine-et-Oise	156,129	172,103	22.26	3.90
Somme	1,013,410	1,117,092	25.08	4.39
All other	601,896	663,476	23.70	4.15
Total:				
1909–10	6,246,845	6,885,960	24.37	4.27
1908–9	5,949,301	6,557,974	23.90	4.18
1907–8	5,505,660	6,068,944	22.71	3.98
1906–7	5,475,284	6,035,571	21.78	3.81
1905–6	8,415,808	9,276,829	24.61	4.31
1904–5	4,669,454	5,147,186	22.33	3.91
1903–4	6,505,049	7,170,581	22.39	3.92
1902–3	6,266,946	6,908,117	23.01	4.03

Factory prices of sugar beets in Germany, 1905–1911.

[Data taken from the official quarterlies of the German imperial statistical office.]

Provinces.	Weight of beets worked up.		Average price.[1]	
	Metric tons worked.	Short tons worked.	Per metric ton.	Per short ton.
			Marks.	*Marks.*
East and west Prussia	888,390	979,272	22.80	4.92
Brandenburg	661,137	728,771	25.00	5.40
Pomerania	861,188	949,286	24.40	5.26
Posen	1,974,977	2,177,017	24.00	5.18
Silesia	2,379,565	2,622,994	23.40	5.05
Province of Saxony	3,911,004	4,311,100	22.30	4.81
Schleswig-Holstein and Hanover	1,221,118	1,346,038	22.30	4.81
Westphalia	112,812	124,353	22.50	4.86
Hessen-Nassau	64,563	71,168	20.10	4.34
Rhineland	547,821	603,863	20.50	4.43
Total Prussia	12,622,575	13,913,864	22.70	4.90
Other States:				
Bavaria	205,576	226,606	22.60	4.75
Saxony	157,599	173,721	24.30	5.25
Wurttemberg	105,953	116,792	22.00	4.75
Baden and Alsace-Lorraine	83,927	92,513	21.20	4.58
Hessia	207,368	228,582	20.70	4.47
Mecklenburg	612,814	675,505	22.50	4.86
Thuringia	209,872	231,342	22.40	4.84
Brunswick	833,156	918,388	23.30	5.03
Anhalt	710,141	782,788	21.40	4.62
Total German Customs Union:				
1910–11	15,748,981	17,360,102	22.50	4.86
1909–10	12,892,068	14,211,055	21.90	4.73
1908–9	11,809,182	13,017,379	21.30	4.60
1907–8	13,482,750	14,862,170	19.60	4.23
1906–7	14,186,536	15,637,960	18.70	4.04
1905–6	15,733,478	17,343,170	20.00	4.32
1904–5	10,071,212	11,101,598	20.10	4.34

[1] Refers only to beets bought in the open market.

Per cent extraction in terms of raw sugar for all beet-working factories in Germany for the seasons 1904–5 to 1910–11.

[From official reports of the German imperial statistical office.]

Season.	Per cent.	Season.	Per cent.
1904–5	14.92	1908–9	16.77
1905–6	14.71	1909–10	15.11
1906–7	14.97	1910–11	15.96
1907–8	14.96		

Average daily wages of employees in French beet-sugar factories.

[From the official Bulletins de Statistique of the French finance department.]

Years.	Men.		Women.		Children.	
	Francs.	United States currency.	Francs.	United States currency.	Francs.	United States currency.
1902–3	3.97	$0.766	2.18	$0.421	1.71	$0.330
1903–4	3.98	.768	2.15	.415	1.69	.326
1904–5	4.03	.778	2.13	.411	1.67	.322
1905–6	4.07	.786	2.18	.421	1.73	.334
1906–7	4.14	.799	2.26	.436	1.75	.338
1907–8	4.20	.811	2.26	.436	1.75	.338
1908–9	4.22	.814	2.32	.448	1.70	.328
1909–10	4.32	.834	2.39	.461	1.75	.338

THOMAS W. HARDWICK,
Chairman Special Committee on the Investigation of the American Sugar Refining Co. and Others.

GENTLEMEN: Arriving too late to appear before your honorable committee, your chairman has given me permission to hand in a written report from the Billings, Mont. beet-sugar district.

Name, I. D. O'Donnell, Billings, Yellowstone County, Mont.

Have been farming in Yellowstone County, Mont., for 29 years, and have grown sugar beets 6 years, or since factory started at Billings. Grew 120 acres first year and increased each year up to 230 acres in 1911. Sugar beets in this district are all grown under irrigation. The district seems to be naturally adapted to the growing of sugar beets. There was grown in 1906 about 4,000 acres and gradually increased to 16,000, acres in 1911, and now expect to contract for 20,000 acres for 1912.

In 1911 the sugar company paid the farmers $1,200,000 for sugar beets, or an average price of $6 per ton.

This irrigation district could support at least six factories. They employed some over 2,000 handworkers in the fields and about that many more to do the other labor. The total cost of the factory represents $1,500,000, and they employ 350 men during the beet campaign and 125 men the year round. Then field men work continuously with the farmers, teaching them good farming, especially in rotation with growing of sugar beets.

In connection with the factory there are being fed 8,000 cattle and 20,000 sheep, which are being fed the beet pulp and sirup in connection with alfalfa. It makes a market for a class of stock that can hardly be fed or fattened with other feeds, such as aged cows and sheep.

The growing of sugar beets makes a market for other farm products, as for every acre of sugar beets it takes fully an acre of other crops to feed the stock and laborers.

The growing of sugar beets, owing to the thorough cultivation of the soil, leaves the ground in such shape that the following crops do fully 50 per cent better, and as a rotation crop there is none better.

It builds up all kinds of business, encourages good roads, good horses, and the best kind of farming and stock feeding, as the tops are a splendid forage. There is more profit in growing sugar beets than any crop one can raise. But the farmer is entitled to more, as there is much greater cost. It costs fully four times as much to grow beets as hay or grain. And it is the only crop in which we have an assured market. By having a contract and stipulated price, the farmer knows just what he is doing. In other crops he does not know until he goes to market if he is to receive a living price or not.

In the Billings district it has solved the labor problem.

The German-Russian who do the hand labor, do the other extra labor on the farm, such as haying, harvesting, and thrashing, which work comes just at a time when they are not employed in the beet fields. These Russians are splendid workers, are sober, industrious, and thrifty. A great many of them are now citizens and the rest are becoming such as fast as the law allows, or they are in the State five years. These people send their children to the public schools, have their churches, keep the Sabbath, and in every way we consider them a desirable addition to our community.

They soon accumulate funds and buy their own outfits, then rent land and then purchase. A great many who came the first year, 1906, now own their own farms.

The farmer has the best of it, as the factory can not run without beets, while the farmer could live without the factory. In fact, the factory must see the beet grower do well, or they will stop growing beets.

We have a well organized Beet Growers' Association, but have never been called on to take action, as the prices and terms have always been satisfactory. In fact, the entire management of the sugar company seems to have been and is to be fair with the grower.

The Huntley irrigation project built by the Government and opened to settlement in 40-acre units in 1911, had water on 12,000 acres, of which 3,600 acres was in sugar beets, and they were the most successful crop they raised. In fact the Huntley project is reported to be the most successful project in the West, due to being in a sugar-factory district.

Nearly every irrigated valley in Montana is striving for a factory, since seeing the splendid results of the Billings district.

The Billings district has shown by far the greatest gain in population, assessed valuations, and value of crops raised than any other section in Montana, mostly due to the growing of sugar beets.

After thoroughly looking over the field from the farmers' standpoint as a practical farmer and studying the market situation in its various phases, I know of no single industry that so appeals to the farmer, that so blends itself with diversified farming, and that adds wealth to the community, as the growing of sugar beets, and I hope your honorable committee will see fit to encourage it.

Yours, truly, I. D. O'DONNELL.

DISTRICT OF COLUMBIA, ss:

Subscribed and sworn to before me this 18th day of January, 1912.

[SEAL.] J. M. MCKEE,
Notary Public.

SUPPLEMENTAL TESTIMONY OF W. P. WILLET.

Mr. FORDNEY. Mr. Willet, assuming that this paragraph in the Tariff Board's report, found on page 5 of the first volume of that board's report, is correct, which is as follows:

> On the other hand, the findings show that the duties which run to such high ad valorem equivalents are prohibitory, since the goods are not imported, but that the prices of domestic fabrics are not raised by the full amount of duty. On a set of 1-yard samples of 16 English fabrics, which are completely excluded by the present tariff rates, it was found that the total foreign value was $41.84; the duties which would have been assessed had these fabrics been imported, $76.90; the foreign value plus the amount of the duty, $118.74; or a nominal duty of 183 per cent. In fact, however, practically, identical fabrics of domestic make sold at the same time at $69.75, showing an enhanced price over the foreign market value of but 67 per cent.

Assuming this statement to be correct, how do you reconcile this statement with your statement that the tariff is always added to the price in the case of sugar?

Mr. WILLETT. Upon inquiry of woolen goods manufactures I find that the particular class of English fabrics referred to are not imported. These goods are said to be made probably out of a special wool unknown in the United States.

Similar woolens, in outward appearance, are manufactured out of domestic wool to a very large extent and sold here at very competitive prices. Consumers are satisfied to accept these American woolens at the prices sold at rather than pay the excessive duty on the British fabric. But if a customer insisted upon having the British fabric he would have to pay the full duty upon it. If a person goes to a tailor and orders a suit of clothes from English fabrics the full duty is included in the cost, and this is constantly done in New York, where buyers insist upon having the foreign goods.

The only exception to this statement that the consumer pays the full duty on a suit of clothes might be that the importers of the British fabric overestimated the demand for such goods and over-imported them, in which case, in order to find a market for their surplus imports, they might sell at less than cost price plus duty, to compete with some similar but not the same goods made in the United States.

I am told that the American Woolen Co., of Massachusetts, has 35 woolen mills and controls 60 per cent of the manufacture, but that no one suggests that they are a monopoly in restraint of trade, because of the active competition of the other 40 per cent manufacturers, including their largest competitor, the Cleveland Worsted Co., of Ohio. I am told that competition is carried to such extremes that when the American Co. sends its agents to the trade and books orders largely at 92½ cents per yard, the Cleveland Co. follows with offers to supply the goods at 90 cents per yard, forcing the American Co. to reduce its contracts to 90 cents or lose its customers.

At present these concerns are selling at, say, 92½ cents per yard for staple goods, delivering immediately to the clothing manufacturers, but bill to date from June 10, 1912, with 10 per cent discount 30 days. The mills have a surplus stock, and the competition to sell is extremely fierce, and a reduction of the tariff on their goods to near the selling prices would not influence the business. On the other hand, if the manufacturers combined they could force prices up to near the present duty without allowing the foreign fabrics to come in.

The statement in the question that the "prices of domestic fabrics are not raised by the full amount of duty" is correct as to similar manufacturers in this special instance, but, in the instance cited of a very considerable demand by well-to-do customers for suits of clothes from foreign fabrics the full duty on such fabrics is fully paid by the customer, except as influenced by an oversupply or deficient demand.

Now, as to sugar: I have here 2-pound boxes of Lebaudy Bros. & Co. refined sugars, packed in France and imported here, paying the full duty of $1.90 per 100 pounds. I paid 24 cents for the 2 pounds, which price includes the full duty. There is a certain select trade for these sugars in this country, and the consumer insists on having them and pays the full duty, although he can buy just as good sugar made here at 10 cents per pound or less. If there were an oversupply of these sugars which the importers desired to sell they might accept prices in competition with the American prices, in which special cases the consumer would not pay the duty.

Thus the answer to Mr. Fordney's question is that the consumer pays the exact duty on all importations of sugar paying a duty, unless prices are influenced up or down from the amount of duty paid parity by the market conditions of supply and demand.

In the case of raw sugars from Cuba the tables submitted show that quite frequently supply and demand affect the amount of duty paid by consumer.

Take the Table No. 8, page 3554, for instance, which divides a period of nearly 20 years; it would seem that during the period of time the consumer had gone from paying the full duty at the outset to paying in 1910 only $0.845 of the duty of $1.432 on 107 pounds raws (100 pounds granulated) and that the Cuban product paid or remitted $0.587 of the duty.

As a matter of fact, the Cuban planter did sell his crop in 1910 at $0.534 below what he could have secured had he held for the full amount of the cost of importing under the former tariff.

He sold his crop in 1910 at $0.197 less than the duty assessed by the United States against his sugar.

The consumer in 1910 paid $1.151 per 100 pounds of the $1.348 duty on Cuban sugar. By Table No. 6B, page 3551, similar comparisons can be made for each year, showing that the consumer has not paid full duty in any year of reciprocity while in the years preceding reciprocity the consumer naturally paid the full duty.

The effect of giving reciprocity to Cuba appears to have been to change the old statement that "the consumer pays the full duty" on sugar except in such cases as the consumer insists upon a certain specified sugar that he can not get without paying the full duty assessed upon it and which as a matter of fact is imported to a very small extent.

As exists in the woolen fabric trade may not, at the time when the production of domestic and insular and Cuban sugars exceed the requirements for consumption, a fierce competition between these interests reduce the price of sugar to the consumer far below the full tariff protection if it remains unchanged?

In all these analyses I reach the same conclusion—that to decrease the price of sugar to the consumer increase the domestic production as rapidly as possible.

RESOLUTIONS OF FARMERS' UNION OF LARIMER COUNTY, COLO.

LOVELAND, COLO., *January 11, 1912*.

THOMAS W. HARDWICK,
Chairman Congressional Committee, Washington, D. C.

Whereas many garbled reports of the testimony of James Bodkin before the congressional committee at Washington have been printed in some of the newspapers of the State, and a number chambers of commerce have adopted resolutions condemning that testimony, and declaring that it misrepresents the beet industry of Colorado: Now, therefore,

Be it resolved by the County Farmers' Union of Larimer County, That the attention of such newspapers and chambers of commerce be respectfully called to the congressional records of his testimony and challenge them to prove by pamphlets 38-39-40 the false and garbled statements attributed to Mr. Bodkin. Many false statements have been circulated with the evident intention of misrepresenting the position of the farmers' union which are not borne out by the testimony given before the congressional committee, and which can only reflect upon the authors of such false statements and those who willfully circulate them.

Be it further resolved, That a copy of these resolutions be forwarded to the congressional committee, to the several chambers of commerce in Larimer, Boulder, and Weld Counties, and to the several newspapers of Larimer County, with the request to publish them.

J. Y. MUNSON,
P. H. BOOTHROYD, Jr.,
CHAS. WETZLER,
Committee.

Unanimously adopted by the Larimer County Union of the F. E. & C. U. of A. in convention at Loveland, Colo., January 8, 1912.

Lightning Source UK Ltd.
Milton Keynes UK
UKHW032003020219
336576UK00009BA/202/P

9 780260 745958